# TASC™ | STRATEGIES, PRACTICE, & REVIEW

## Test Assessing Secondary Completion™

New York

**ACKNOWLEDGEMENTS**

Special thanks to the team that made this book possible:
Arthur Ahn, Mikhail Alexeeff, Gina Allison, Kim Bowers, Erik Bowman, Julie Choi, Margaret Crane, Alisha Crowley, Lola Disparte, Boris Dvorkin, Paula Fleming, Tom Flesher, Joanna Graham, Allison Harm, Gar Hong, Kevin Jacobson, Wyatt Kent, Jennifer Land, Heather Maigur, Terrence McGovern, Eli Meyer, Kathy Osmus, Anthony Parr, Rachel Pearsall, Neha Rao, Rachel Reina, Teresa Rupp, Scott Safir, Glen Stohr, Alexandra Strelka, Caren Van Slyke, Lee Weiss, and many others who have shaped this book over the years.



Published by Kaplan Publishing, a division of Kaplan, Inc.
395 Hudson Street
New York, NY 10014



Printed in the United States of America

10 9 8 7 6 5 4 3 2 1

ISBN: 978-1-61865-765-7

Kaplan Publishing books are available at special quantity discounts to use for sales promotions, employee premiums, or educational purposes. For more information or to purchase books, please call the Simon & Schuster special sales department at 866-506-1949.

# CONTENTS

The material in this book is based on the best information available from the testmaker at the time of writing. However, the Test Assessing Secondary Completion™ was still in the process of development at the time of this writing. Thus, CTB/McGraw-Hill may have instituted changes or refinements to the TASC since this book was published. Visit www.tasctest.com for the most up-to-date information about the TASC contents and registration process. If there are any important changes or corrections to the Kaplan test preparation materials in this book, we will post that information online at kaptest.com/publishing.

Moreover, this book is designed to help students prepare for the 2014 version of the TASC. CTB/McGraw-Hill plans to introduce changes to the test in 2015 and 2016. Visit www.tasctest.com to learn more.

# KAPLAN'S TASC™ BOOK AND ONLINE CENTER

## WELCOME

Congratulations on your decision to pursue high school equivalency, and thank you for choosing Kaplan for your TASC preparation! This book and the included online resources will be all you need to prepare for the TASC. To help you create a study plan, let's start by walking you through everything you need to know to take advantage of your book and your Online Center.

## YOUR BOOK AND ONLINE CENTER

This book contains a complete study program, including:

- Detailed instruction covering the essential concepts of Reading, Writing, Mathematics, Social Studies, and Science
- Effective methods and strategies for every question type
- A pretest featuring questions from all sections of the TASC, designed to help you diagnose your strengths and weaknesses
- Over a thousand practice questions, plus answer explanations for each
- A timed, full-length practice test

Your online center includes videos explaining how to understand concepts in Reading, Writing, Mathematics, Social Studies, and Science.

### GETTING STARTED

**How to Study**

Step 1: Register your Online Center.

Step 2: Take the pretests.

Step 3: Fill out the study planners.

Step 4: Create a study plan.

Step 5: Learn and review, practice and review, assess and review.

Step 6: Take the practice tests.

Step 7: Confirm your readiness to take the TASC.

### Step 1: Register your Online Center.

To take full advantage of your Kaplan study resources, visit kaptest.com/booksonline. Click on the word "TASC" and answer the questions that appear.

After creating your username and password, log in to your syllabus at kaptest.com. There you will be able to access videos that reinforce concepts covered in this book. Each chapter has a preview video you'll want to watch before reading that chapter.

### Step 2: Take the pretests.

Begin by learning what strengths you're already bringing to the TASC and what subject areas you need to work on most. To do so, take the diagnostic pretests beginning on page 1. These pretests are not designed to simulate the TASC, but rather to assess the essential skills you'll need to master the TASC.

When you've completed the pretests, check your responses against the answers and explanations that begin on page 53. Be sure to review the explanations for each question: By doing so, you'll learn a great deal about why the right answer was right and you'll start building your TASC skills.

### Step 3: Fill out the study planners.

Once you've compared your answers to the correct answers, use that information to fill out the study planners on pages 65 through 69. These study planners will give you a rough estimate of which subjects are your strongest and which need the most work.

If you can, it is wisest to study and review *all* of the topics tested by the TASC. However, if you are pressed for time, the study planners will help you prioritize those topics that present you with the greatest challenges.

### Step 4: Create a study plan.

Before you begin your studies, make a plan—and then stick to it.

To begin with, **make a study schedule**. Make a list of all your commitments: jobs, family, sports, holidays, trips, and anything else that takes chunks of your time. Figure out how you can fit a few hours of TASC study into that schedule each week. The amount of time you have to spend might vary, but try to spend at least six hours a week studying. The amount of time you study in one session can also vary. In the beginning, study for as long as you can hold your focus; if that is only 15 minutes, that's fine. Continue to add time onto each study session until you can build up the stamina to study for two hours straight. You might want to do three study sessions, of two hours each, every week. If you want to take the TASC soon, you might need more time each week.

**Be realistic** in your planning; if you are overly ambitious in creating your study schedule, you may find it difficult to follow through. Also be sure to take at least one day off from studying each week so that you don't exhaust yourself. Most importantly, once you've made your study schedule, **stick to it.** Treat it like a job and discipline yourself accordingly. Imagine yourself "clocking in" at the beginning of a study session and "clocking out" at the end of it.

Think about how you'll cover all five tests between now and the time you would like to take the TASC. If your state allows you to take the TASC subject tests on different days, you may choose to study (for example) Reading and Writing first, and then take the Reading test and the Writing test, before you move on to Mathematics or another subject. If you plan to—or if your state requires you to—take the five subject tests all at once, you will have to **allot the months you have to study** among the five subjects.

It's normal to be stressed about taking the TASC. Throughout your studies, **manage your stress** so that it doesn't get in the way of your learning. To do so, keep yourself on a regular sleep schedule, eat right, exercise, and continue to spend time with friends and/or family. If you're studying and find yourself becoming very stressed and anxious, step away for a moment. Take a walk, work out, cook a meal, work on your car, play sports, do breathing exercises, meditate—do something healthy to release your stress and then return to your studies. Don't fuel your studies by loading up on caffeine or sugar: you won't be able to focus well.

### Step 5: Learn and review, practice and review, assess and review.

Once you have your study schedule in place, begin work on the concepts presented in this book. You'll do this in three stages:

> **Learn and Review:** Each lesson presents you with information you need to learn to master the TASC. Carefully read and absorb each lesson, paying particular attention to the bolded words and to the "Key Ideas" presented in the left margin of the lesson page. "When you are finished, review any concepts that gave you trouble before moving on to the practice questions."
>
> **Practice and Review:** Each lesson ends with practice questions that will ask you to apply the concepts you just learned. Do the practice questions without worrying about how much time you're taking, but don't stop there! After you do a practice set, review each question's explanation (found in the back of the book). Ask yourself what you did right on that question and what you could have done better. This review will help you learn more about what you need to work on.
>
> **Assess and Review:** At the end of each chapter, there will be another set of practice problems that test you on all of the concepts presented throughout the chapter. Reviewing your answers and studying the explanations will provide you with a good assessment of which topics you are comfortable with and which topics you should spend more time on.

Another key component of review is periodically revisiting concepts you haven't studied in a while. For example, you might begin by studying reading and then move on to math. If you do, pause every week or so while studying math to review what you learned about reading, so your reading skills don't get rusty.

### Step 6: Take the practice tests.

Once you have studied all the concepts the TASC assesses, take the practice tests that begin on page 587. These tests are designed to mimic the TASC as much as possible. Time yourself, just as you will be timed on the real TASC.

Score your practice tests using the practice test answers and explanations in the back of the book, and fill out the practice test scoring charts that follow those explanations.

### Step 7: Confirm your readiness to take the TASC.

As of the time of this printing, the makers of the TASC exam have not released scoring information. If scoring information becomes available, we will post it in your online center.

You may decide that you need to study some subjects more before taking the real TASC. If you are ready to test, contact your state's department of education, or visit that agency's website, to learn how to register for the exam.

As you approach Test Day, do a review of all the concepts in this book in the week or two before you take the real TASC. Then, the day before the test, don't study. You need to be rested to do well.

## Good Luck!

All of us at Kaplan wish you the very best of luck on the TASC. If you absorb the concepts presented in this book and do well in your practice, walk into the test feeling confident. As you take the test, be sure to keep breathing deeply and don't let stress get in the way. You can do it!

# TASC EXAM OVERVIEW

TASC stands for "Test Assessing Secondary Completion." The TASC is an exam that measures whether you have achieved a level of academic accomplishment equivalent to having graduated from high school. Your state may require you to take the TASC if you are seeking a high school equivalency degree.

You may have heard people refer to getting a high school equivalency degree as "getting a GED." However, this way of referring to the degree is inaccurate. The GED® is an exam that has long been used in most states to determine whether a person should be granted a high school equivalency degree by the state. The degree itself is not "a GED." Recently, some states have decided to stop using the GED® test or to offer another testing option in addition to the GED® test for people who are seeking a high school equivalency degree. TASC is one such alternative to the GED® test. As of December 2013, New York, Indiana, and West Virginia have chosen to use the TASC instead of the GED® exam. Other states may be considering using the TASC instead of the GED® exam as well. Individuals seeking a high school equivalency degree in Nevada, Wyoming, and New Jersey will take one of the TASC test, the GED® test, or another exam called the HiSET®. Contact your state's department of education to find out which exam you should study for.

There are two ways to take the TASC: using paper and pencil or on a computer. Which format you will take may depend on your state. Contact your state's department of education to find out whether you will test on paper or on a computer. It may be that you have a choice, or your state may require you to test in a specific format.

The TASC will be available in Spanish. If you would like to take the Spanish version of the test, contact your state's department of education to find out if and where you can test in Spanish. The timing guidelines for the Spanish version of the test allow an additional five minutes for each section.

The TASC is composed of five subtests in the following subjects:*

**Language Arts—Reading:** The Reading Test assesses your ability to understand and reason about fiction and nonfiction passages. You will have 75 minutes to answer approximately 50 multiple-choice items.

**Language Arts—Writing:** The Writing Test assesses your language skills and has two parts. A multiple-choice component assesses your ability to use correct grammar and to edit text for clarity. On that portion of the Writing test, you will have around 55 minutes to answer approximately 50 multiple-choice questions. On the second part of the Writing test, you will have approximately 50 minutes to write one essay in response to a passage or passages.

**Mathematics:** The Mathematics Test assesses your ability to reason with numbers and apply mathematical formulas to solve problems. The test will be split into two sections. You will have 50 minutes to answer questions with a calculator and 55 minutes to answer questions without a calculator. Those two sections will be separated by a 15 minute break. Most of the questions will be multiple-choice format. Some answers will require you to use a bubble grid (see page 268).

**Science:** The Science Test assesses your ability to reason with scientific information as well as your familiarity with high-school level concepts in life science, physical science, and Earth and space science. Most Science Test questions will be based on a short passage or graphic, but some may require you to remember a basic science concept. You will have 85 minutes to answer approximately 47 multiple-choice items on the Science Test.

**Social Studies:** The Social Studies Test assesses your ability to reason with social studies information as well as your familiarity with high-school level concepts in U.S. history, civics and government, economics, world history, and geography. Most Social Studies Test questions will be based on a short passage or graphic, but some may require you to remember a concept from social studies. You will have 75 minutes to answer approximately 47 multiple-choice items on the Social Studies Test.

***Note:** The information given here was the latest information available as of January 2014. For updates, visit www.tasctest.com.

## When to Take the TASC

When should you plan to take the TASC? The best answer is: When you're ready. You may have to do a significant amount of studying before being ready to test, especially if you have been away from school for some years. That said, it can be helpful for you to set a goal—a date by which you would like to have the TASC completed. Having a date in mind can motivate you to stick to your study schedule and manage your studies. It can also help you stay focused on your ultimate goal of earning your high school equivalency degree.

You may decide that you would like to take the TASC before the end of 2014. There are a couple of reasons to do so. First, with a fixed time frame, you may find that you are more motivated and put more energy into your studies. Second, the TASC will change somewhat in 2015. Over the course of those two years, the paper and pencil version of the test will be phased out in favor of all computer-based testing. In addition, the TASC may begin to test higher-difficulty topics and to use additional question formats made possible by the computer. (For example, some questions on future computer versions of the TASC may ask you to use the computer's mouse to drag dots or numbers to specific spots on the screen.) Now, there are good reasons for those higher-difficulty topics and computer-based testing: They are an opportunity for you to demonstrate not only a higher level of academic achievement but also computer literacy. However, you may prefer to test before those changes are introduced if you will not have a computer on which to practice for the future version of the TASC.

## Registering for the Exam

How you will register for the exam depends partly on your state. Contact your state's department of education or visit www.tasctest.com to learn more.

Your state may allow you to take different subject tests on different days, or to split the TASC between two days.

The TASC is available in large print, audio, and Braille formats for those who have a disability. In other cases of disability, extended time may be granted. If you have a disability that would require one of these formats you can learn more at www.tasctest.com—and plan ahead: Allow at least 30 business days for your request to be processed.

If you do not pass one of the TASC subtests, you may retake that subtest twice within a year at no additional charge. If you need to take a subtest a fourth time, contact your state department of education to find out about retesting options.

## Scoring Information

There are two scoring levels on the TASC exam:

**High school equivalency:** To receive a high school equivalency degree from your state, you must pass all TASC subtests at this level.

**Career and college readiness:** This is a higher scoring level that will be used to indicate that a test-taker is ready to apply to college or another postsecondary program, or that a test-taker is prepared to train for a more advanced career. If your goal is to enroll in postsecondary training (such as college), you should try to score at this level.

As of January 2014, TASC has not yet released information regarding the numerical scores that will correspond with those two scoring levels.

## Taking the Paper-based TASC

Through the end of 2014 (and possibly longer), you can take the TASC in a paper-based format. You will be given an answer sheet to fill in: This will be a page with circles, or bubbles, for the answer choices for each question, that you will fill in as you take the test. For the multiple-choice questions in each section, you will fill in the bubble corresponding to the answer choice you think is correct, using a no. 2 or HB pencil. (Remember to take pencils with you!) On the Mathematics Test, you will encounter several questions that require you to bubble a numerical answer into a grid. In the second half of the Writing Test, you will write your essay by hand. You will be allowed to use scratch paper for calculations and to organize your thoughts for the essay. On part of the Mathematics Test and for Science Test questions requiring calculations, you will be permitted to use a calculator. See page 227 through 229 for more information about handheld calculators for the paper TASC.

## Taking the Computer-based TASC

Depending on where you live, you may take the TASC on a computer. This means that to succeed on the test, you will need to familiarize yourself with basic computer skills. If you do not have a computer at home and are not familiar with computers, try to find a computer you can use to practice using a mouse, typing on a keyboard, and navigating through items on a computer screen. Many public libraries or community centers may have computers you can use. Your state department of education may know of other resources.

If you are taking the computer-based version of the TASC, you must still test at a testing center established by your state. You *cannot* test at home. Unfortunately, there may be unscrupulous people who will try to sell you an “online” version of the TASC for you to take at home over the Internet. *This is not a real TASC exam, so don’t be taken in.*

When you take the computer version of the TASC, you will use the following functions of the computer-based test.

## Navigating through questions

You will use the mouse to choose answers to questions, and also to move from one question to the next. The bottom of your screen will look something like this:

Click "Go Back" to return to a previous question. Click "Go On" to move to the next question. If you would like to move from question 8 to question 3, you can simply click on the box marked "3" on the progress bar that runs across the bottom of the screen. If you get stuck on a question or are unsure of your answer, you can click "Mark for Later Review." When you do, that question will be highlighted in the progress bar so that you can easily find it later.

## Tools to use as you are answering questions

Use the **online highlighter**. If you wish to highlight a portion of a passage or question, click on the highlighter icon at the top-left corner of the screen:

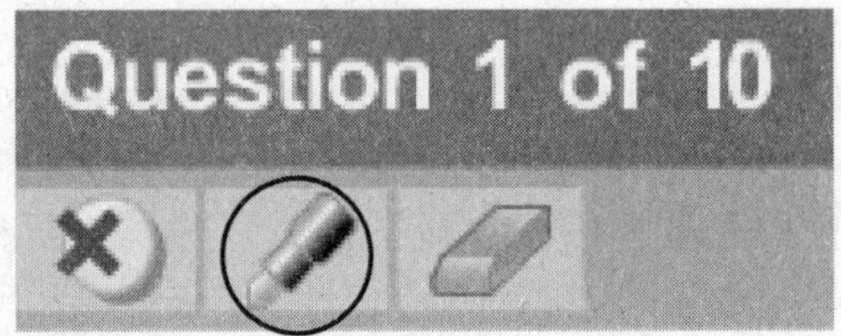


To use the highlighter, click at the top-left corner of the portion of the passage you would like to highlight and then drag the mouse down and to the right. Release the mouse button when you reach the end of the portion you'd like to highlight. Use the eraser icon to erase any highlighting you would like to remove.

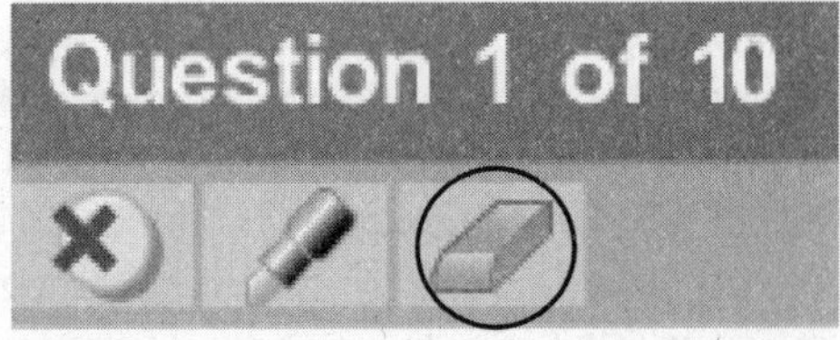


As you're working on a question, use the **Option Eliminator** to cross out any answer choices that you are sure are incorrect. This will help you focus on the remaining choices. To use the Option Eliminator, click on the icon which is a circle with the red *X*:

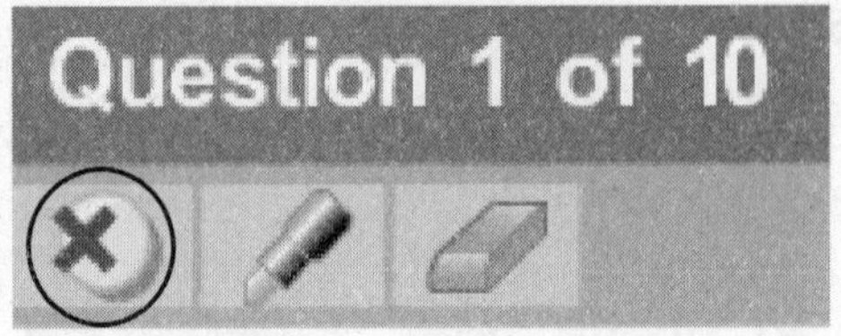

Then click on the answer choices you believe are incorrect:

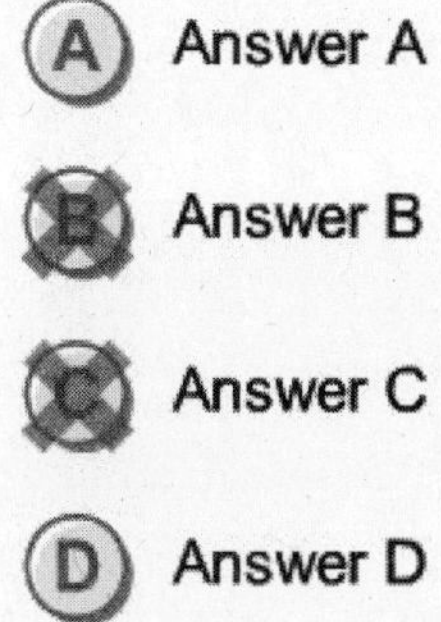


You can use option eliminator even if you plan to come back to the question later. The red *X*'s will still be in place when you return to the question.

If you are taking the computer version of the TASC, you will be able to use an online version of the **Texas Instruments TI-30XS MultiView™ scientific calculator** for most of the Mathematics Test and for portions of the Science Test. You can access the online calculator by clicking on the word "Calculator" when it appears on the screen.

On the Writing Test, you will use the **keyboard** to type your essay into a text box. You will have some basic word-processing tools such as cut, copy, and paste. You will not have any spelling- or grammar-checking functions.

### Managing your time

At the top-right corner of the screen, you will see a button that says "Show Timer." If you click on this button, a **timer** will appear just above that button. The timer shows how much time you have remaining. You may want to leave the timer up for the entire test, or only check it periodically if you find it distracting. When the timer is showing, the button below it will say "Hide Timer." Click it to remove the timer from the screen.

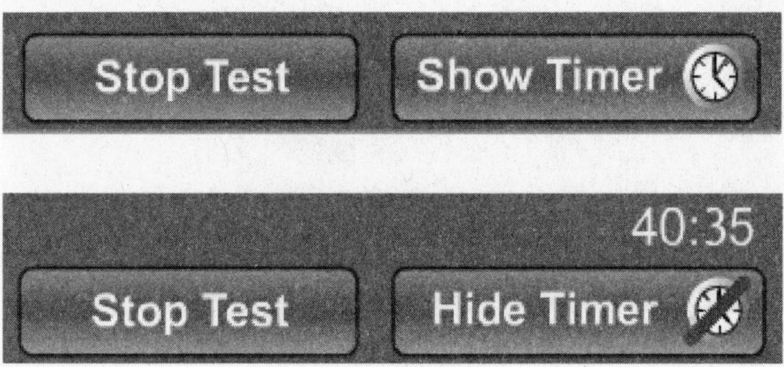

# PRETESTS

The pretests are intended to help you decide what you need to study in order to pass the actual TASC exam. After you take the pretests, you will check your answers and then use the Pretest Study Planners to determine your course of study.

The pretests are designed to assess your skills in an efficient manner. Thus, they are shorter than the actual TASC exam. To see what the actual TASC exam will be like, flip through the *Practice Tests* beginning on page 587.

**STEP 1:** Take the following pretests that correspond to the five TASC test areas.

**Language Arts: Reading, pages 2–9**

20 questions

**Language Arts: Writing, pages 10–17**

Part I: Language Skills, 18 questions

Part II: Essay

**Mathematics, pages 18–28**

Part I: Quantitative Reasoning—18 Questions

Part II: Algebraic Reasoning and Geometry—22 Questions

**Social Studies, pages 29–40**

Part I: Social Studies Skills—10 Questions

Part II: Social Studies Content—26 Questions

**Science, pages 41–52**

Part I: Science Skills—10 Questions

Part II: Science Content—25 Questions

Most of the questions are in multiple-choice format. The essay requires writing an extended response. For the **multiple-choice questions**, you may fill in the circles next to the correct answers in this book, or you can write your answers on a separate piece of paper.

**STEP 2: Check your answers** with the *Pretest Answers and Explanations* that begin on page 53.

**STEP 3: Fill in** the *Pretest Study Planners*, starting on page 65. These charts will allow you to target your problem areas so that you can study in the most efficient manner.

**STEP 4: Use the study planners** on pages 65 through 69 to map out your work.

# LANGUAGE ARTS: READING PRETEST

**Directions:** You may fill in the circles next to the correct answers or write your answers on a separate piece of paper.

Questions 1 through 5 refer to the following passage about introverts.

**Excerpted from "Don't Call Introverted Children 'Shy'"**

1 Imagine a 2-year-old who greets you with a huge smile, offering a toy. Now here's another child who regards you gravely and hides behind his parent's leg. How do you feel about these two children? If you're like most people, you think of the first child as social and the second as reserved or . . . "shy." . . . But this misses what's really going on with standoffish kids. Many were born with a careful, sensitive temperament that predisposes them to look before they leap. And this can pay off handsomely as they grow, in the form of strong academics, enhanced creativity, and even a unique brand of leadership and empathy.

2 One way to see this temperament more clearly is to consider how these children react to stimuli. When these children are at 4 months, if you pop a balloon over their heads, they holler and pump their arms more than other babies do. At age 2, they proceed carefully when they see a . . . toy robot for the first time. When they're school age, they play matching games with more deliberation than their peers. . . . Notice that none of these things—popping balloons, toy robots, matching games—has anything to do with people. In other words, these kids are not antisocial. They're simply sensitive to their environments. . . . [Children with this type of temperament are highly likely to grow up to be introverted, but s]hyness and introversion are not the same thing. Shy people fear negative judgment, while introverts simply prefer less stimulation. . . .

3 Children with an alert, sensitive temperament also pay close attention to social cues and moral principles. By age 6, they cheat and break rules less than other kids do—even when they believe they won't be caught. At 7, they're more likely than their peers to be described by parents and caregivers as empathetic or conscientious. As adults, introverted leaders have even been found to deliver better outcomes than extroverts when managing employees, according to a recent study by management professor Adam Grant of the Wharton School of the University of Pennsylvania, because they encourage others' ideas instead of trying to put their own stamp on things. And they're less likely to take dangerous risks. . . .

4 But we wouldn't want to live in a world composed entirely of cautious introverts. . . . The two types [introverts and extroverts] need each other. Many successful ventures are the result of effective partnerships between introverts and extroverts. The famously charismatic Steve Jobs teamed up with powerhouse introverts at crucial points in his career at Apple, cofounding the company with the shy Steve Wozniak and bequeathing it to its current CEO, the quiet Tim Cook. . . .

5 The ideal scenario is when those two toddlers—the one who hands you the toy with the smile and the other who checks you out so carefully—grow up to run the world together.

1. Which one of the following best expresses the main idea of the passage?
   - A. Companies should include both introverted and extroverted workers on teams.
   - B. There are advantages to being sensitive and introverted.
   - C. Children who are sensitive are more deliberate when playing a game.
   - D. Introverts simply prefer less stimulation than others do.

2. According to the passage, children with sensitive temperaments are more likely to be which of the following?
   - A. empathetic
   - B. risk-taking
   - C. antisocial
   - D. noisy

3. According to the passage, the partnership between Steve Jobs and Steve Wozniak is an example of which of the following?
   - A. the negative consequences of a mixture of different personality types in the workplace
   - B. a successful collaboration between two introverts
   - C. a successful collaboration between an introvert and an extrovert
   - D. a combination of people who should "run the world"

4. Which one of the following is the best summary of the second paragraph?
   - A. Some children respond more dramatically than others to unfamiliar or startling events.
   - B. Observing how children respond to stimuli is the best way to study different kinds of social behavior.
   - C. Children who are perceived as "shy" are actually more sensitive than other children to stimuli in their environments.
   - D. If sensitivity in a child is not corrected by around age 2, that child will grow up to be an oversensitive adult.

5. Based on the passage, which one of the following activities would an introvert most likely prefer?
   - A. enjoying a quiet dinner with a handful of friends
   - B. going alone to a club to enjoy loud dance music
   - C. accompanying one friend to a crowded street festival
   - D. participating solo in a sport called "extreme ice-slope surfing"

Questions 6 through 10 refer to the following information about forklifts and the related diagram.

**Excerpt from "Forklift Safety Guide"**

1 Driving a forklift differs from driving a car. In a car or truck, the front wheels steer the vehicle. A forklift has the steering wheels in the rear. The rear end of the forklift swings in a circle around the front wheels, which support most of the load. The operator must check that there is room for the rear end to swing when making turns. This clearance can be maintained in your workplace by permanently marking aisles with painted lines or arranging storage racks in a way that creates obvious aisles for travel. However, these marked aisles will only be effective if you keep them clear of stored materials.

2 A forklift is not as responsive as a car when the steering wheel is turned. Rear-wheel steering makes it difficult to stop a forklift quickly or swerve and still maintain control. It is important, then, not to drive a forklift fast or around corners quickly.

3 Driving with the load downhill can result in loss of the load and control of the forklift. If you drive a forklift on an incline, you must keep the load on the uphill side. Otherwise, you may have no weight on the wheels that steer, and you can lose control! The load could also fall off or cause the forklift to tip.

4 Often a large forklift load obstructs the driver's view in one direction. It may be necessary to travel long distances with the load to the rear (in reverse for most forklifts). Use extra caution when traveling in reverse.

Adapted with permission from the State of Washington, Department of Labor and Industries.

6. According to the passage, which one of the following is an effect of rear-wheel steering on a forklift?
   - A. The front wheels carry most of the load.
   - B. The driver may have some difficulty in controlling the forklift.
   - C. There is a danger that the forklift will tip over.
   - D. The forklift driver may have little visibility.

7. Which one of the following identifies a pair of things or ideas between which the author draws a contrast?
   - A. driving a forklift and driving a car
   - B. the turning radius of a forklift and the turning radius of a car
   - C. a warehouse with clearly marked aisles and a highway with clearly marked lanes
   - D. driving a forklift in reverse and walking backward

8. Together, the passage and the graphic support which one of the following conclusions?
   - A. A forklift should never carry a load taller than the forklift itself.
   - B. A forklift should travel backward only when traveling downhill.
   - C. A forklift cannot drive uphill unless it is carrying a load.
   - D. A forklift that is traveling downhill with a heavy load should travel backward.

9. Which of the following best describes the author's purpose?
   - A. to inform drivers of cars about the differences between driving a car and driving a forklift
   - B. to warn the general public about the dangers of forklifts
   - C. to explain safe practices to forklift drivers
   - D. to describe the difference between skilled and unskilled forklift drivers

10. Which of the following best describes the organization of the passage?
    - A. The author lists potential dangers inherent in forklift driving and explains how to avoid them.
    - B. The author states that forklift driving is dangerous and gives examples of forklift accidents to support that idea.
    - C. The author lists the features of forklifts and describes their benefits.
    - D. The author explains the pros and cons of forklift driving to present a balanced picture of the value of forklifts.

Questions 11 through 15 refer to the following selections about genetically modified organism (GMO) foods.

## World Food Prize Goes to Three Biotech Scientists

1 The World Food Prize Foundation took the bold step of awarding this year's prize to three pioneers of plant biotechnology whose work brought the world genetically modified crops.

2 Van Montagu and Chilton independently developed the technology in the 1980s to stably transfer foreign genes into plants, a discovery that set up a race to develop tools to genetically engineer plants. It allowed other scientists to incorporate genetic traits that allow plants to better withstand drought and extreme heat and to fight off pests and disease. Fraley was the first to successfully transfer immunity to specific bacteria into a plant. Fraley genetically engineered the first herbicide-resistant soybean in 1996.

3 Genetically enhanced crops are grown on more than 420 million acres in nearly 30 countries by over 17 million farmers worldwide, the foundation said. More than 90 percent of the users are small, resource-poor farmers in developing countries.

4 Many U.S. farmers credited genetic modifications in corn with saving last year's crop from all but total devastation, as half of the nation endured the worst drought in 60 years. Modern corn plants are more stable and can withstand a wider variety of climate conditions because of genetically improved leaves, roots, and reproductive capability.

5 Fraley said biotechnology will enable the farming industry to meet the needs of a growing global population. "We know we need from a demand perspective to double food production around the world in the next 30 years," he said.

Adapted from David Pitt, "World Food Prize goes to 3 biotech scientists," Associated Press, June 19, 2013

## Dangers of GMO Foods

1 The rise in autoimmune diseases, infertility, gastrointestinal problems, and chronic diseases may be associated with the introduction of GMO (genetically modified organism) foods. In a position paper by the American Academy of Environmental Medicine, the authors ask all physicians to consider the role of GMO foods in the nation's health crisis and advise their patients to avoid all GMO foods whenever possible. The Academy also recommends a moratorium on GMO seeds and calls for immediate independent safety testing and the labeling of all food items containing genetically modified products.

2 As the reliance on GMO seeds expands worldwide, concerns about food supply and safety continue to escalate. Genetically engineered seeds are identical in structure, and if a problem affects one particular crop, a major crop failure can result. For example, following the recent failure of three GMO corn crops in three South African provinces, the Africa Centre for Biosecurity has called for an investigation and immediate ban of all GMO food. Corn is a primary source of food for southern African nations.

3 Most GMO seeds are genetically engineered to be herbicide tolerant and resistant to insect infestation and disease. Environmentalists worry that the characteristics of GMO crops may encourage farmers to increase their use of herbicides and pesticides, which will raise human consumption of dangerous toxins. GMO crops also manufacture their own pesticides, which puts further poisons into humans and soil and may cause unforeseen changes in the environment.

Adapted from Susan Brassard, "Dangers of GMO Foods," Livestrong.com, September 2, 2010

11. The author of Passage 1 most likely notes that the majority of GMO crops are cultivated by "small, resource-poor farmers in developing countries" in order to
   - A. highlight how GMO foods can be harmful to struggling farmers.
   - B. suggest that GMO foods can be beneficial to struggling farmers.
   - C. illustrate how GMO foods can be more expensive for consumers.
   - D. explain why GMO crops often fail.

12. Passage 2 is primarily concerned with
   - A. the uses and misuses of GMO foods.
   - B. the origin and development of GMO foods.
   - C. the unexpected benefits of GMO foods.
   - D. the safety and reliability of GMO foods.

13. What can be inferred from the first paragraph of Passage 2?
   - A. American physicians, as a group, are completely unaware of the potential dangers of GMOs.
   - B. The labels of some foods containing GMO ingredients do not indicate that the products contain genetically modified components.
   - C. GMO foods have been proven to cause certain chronic conditions.
   - D. Independent safety testing has been completed for most GMO foods.

14. The two passages primarily disagree about whether or not
   - A. GMO foods can help support a growing world population.
   - B. GMO foods are better able to withstand drought and insect infestation than natural foods.
   - C. GMO foods are largely a positive development for global food production.
   - D. Scientists who study GMO foods are worthy of recognition.

15. Passage 2 cites the example of a major crop failure in South Africa to illustrate the dangers of planting with GMO seeds. Which paragraph in Passage 1 offers a counterexample that weakens this position?
   - A. Paragraph 1
   - B. Paragraph 2
   - C. Paragraph 4
   - D. Paragraph 5

Questions 16 through 20 refer to the following.

**Excerpted from *Black Beauty***

1 The first place that I can well remember was a large, pleasant meadow with a pond of clear water in it. Some shady trees leaned over it, and rushes and water lilies grew at the deep end. Over the hedge on one side we looked into a plowed field, and on the other we looked over a gate at our master's house, which stood by the roadside. . .

2 One day, when there was a good deal of kicking, my mother whinnied to me to come to her, and then she said:

3 "I wish you to pay attention to what I am going to say to you. The colts who live here are very good colts, but they are cart-horse colts, and of course they have not learned manners. You have been well-bred and well-born; your father has a great name in these parts, and your grandfather won the cup two years at the Newmarket races; your grandmother had the sweetest temper of any horse I ever knew, and I think you have never seen me kick or bite. I hope you will grow up gentle and good, and never learn bad ways; do your work with a good will, lift your feet up well when you trot, and never bite or kick even in play."

4 I have never forgotten my mother's advice; I knew she was a wise old horse, and our master thought a great deal of her. Her name was Duchess, but he often called her Pet.

5 Our master was a good, kind man. He gave us good food, good lodging, and kind words; he spoke as kindly to us as he did to his little children. We were all fond of him, and my mother loved him very much. When she saw him at the gate she would neigh with joy, and trot up to him. . . . All the horses would come to him, but I think we were his favorites. My mother always took him to the town on a market day in a light gig.

6 There was a plowboy, Dick, who sometimes came into our field to pluck blackberries from the hedge. When he had eaten all he wanted, he would have what he called fun with the colts, throwing stones and sticks at them to make them gallop. We did not much mind him, for we could gallop off, but sometimes a stone would hit and hurt us.

7 One day he was at this game, and did not know that the master was in the next field, but he was there, watching what was going on; over the hedge he jumped in a snap, and catching Dick by the arm, he gave him such a box on the ear as made him roar with the pain and surprise. As soon as we saw the master, we trotted up nearer to see what went on.

From *Black Beauty*, by Anna Sewell. Used by permission of Random House, Inc.

16. Who is the narrator in this passage?

- A. a servant
- B. a hired plowboy
- C. a young horse
- D. a child

17. What is the setting of the story?

- A. a town
- B. a racetrack
- C. a forest
- D. a farm

18. The narrator's account of his youth can best be described as

- A. melancholy.
- B. contented.
- C. regretful.
- D. humorous.

19. The narrator would most likely describe the master in the story as

- A. affectionate and protective.
- B. arrogant and abusive.
- C. playful and light-hearted.
- D. bold and aggressive.

20. The mother's speech in paragraph three most likely serves to

- A. correct the narrator for playing too roughly.
- B. assure the narrator he will grow up to win races like his grandfather.
- C. reprimand the narrator for insulting the master.
- D. accuse the narrator of stealing blackberries.

**Answers and explanations for the *Reading* Pretest start on page 53.**

# Language Arts: Writing Pretest
# Part I: Language Skills

**Directions:** You may fill in the circles next to the correct answers or write your answers on a separate piece of paper.

Questions 1 through 6 refer to the following paragraphs.

To: Parents and Guardians
From: Sonia Vasquez, School Nurse

**(A)**

(1) A student in your child's class have been diagnosed with strep throat. (2) Strep throat is a highly contagious disease and a common illness in children. (3) Unlike most sore throats, which are caused by viruses, strep throat is caused by bacteria and is treatable with antibiotics. (4) The time between exposure to the disease and the appearance of symptoms is usually one to three days. (5) To safeguard your child's health, please take the following precautions. (6) Watch your child for strep symptoms. (7) Such as sore throat, fever, swollen glands, and headache. (8) If your child developed any of these symptoms, take him or her to the doctor. (9) If a throat culture is positive, treatment can be started. (10) It is extremely important to take all the prescribed medicine until it is gone.

**(B)**

(11) Children should get immediate treatment for several reasons. (12) For one, treatment reduces spread of the disease. (13) In addition antibiotics may prevent rheumatic fever. (14) Treatment also prevents other rare but possibly dangerous complications.

**(C)**

(15) Your child may return to school after taking medicine for 24 hours and the fever must be gone. (16) Please call us with any questions or concerns you have.

1. Sentence 1: **A student in your child's class have been diagnosed with strep throat.**

   Which correction should be made to sentence 1?

   - A. replace your with you're
   - B. change child's to children
   - C. insert a comma after class
   - D. change have to has

2. Sentences 6 and 7: **Watch your child for strep symptoms. Such as** sore throat, fever, swollen glands, and headache.

   Which is the best way to write the underlined portion of these sentences?

   - A. symptoms. Such as
   - B. symptoms, the best known are
   - C. symptoms, such as
   - D. symptoms examples are

3. Sentence 8: **If your child developed any of these symptoms, take him or her to the doctor.**

   Which correction should be made to sentence 8?

   - A. replace your with you're
   - B. change developed to develops
   - C. remove the comma
   - D. replace him or her with them

4. Which revision would improve the effectiveness of the passage?

   Begin a new paragraph with

   - A. sentence 3
   - B. sentence 4
   - C. sentence 5
   - D. sentence 6

5. Sentence 13: **In addition antibiotics may prevent rheumatic fever.**

   Which correction should be made to sentence 13?

   - A. insert a comma after addition
   - B. insert a comma after antibiotics
   - C. change may prevent to are preventing
   - D. change rheumatic fever to Rheumatic Fever

6. Sentence 15: **Your child may return to school after taking medicine for 24 hours and the fever must be gone.**

   The most effective revision of sentence 15 would begin with which group of words?

   - A. After the fever is gone and your child has taken
   - B. Having taken medicine for 24 hours and the fever
   - C. Your child, once having taken medicine for 24 hours, may
   - D. The fever being gone and the medicine being finished,

Questions 7 through 12 refer to the following paragraphs.

### Compulsive Gambling

**(A)**

(1) Most of us can bet on a football game, or buy a lottery ticket with little damage to our finances. (2) In contrast, compulsive gamblers cannot stop even when their behavior had threatened to ruin their lives.

**(B)**

(3) Gambling frequently occupies the thoughts of compulsive gamblers. (4) For instance, they may be reliving past gambling experiences or coming up with schemes to get more money for gambling. (5) Although they may have tried several times to stop gambling, their efforts met with failure. (6) When trying to stop gambling, they feel irritable and restless. (7) They need to gamble with more and more money in order to enjoy it, losing money increases their desire to gamble. (8) They may even commit fraud forgery, or theft to get the funds to continue their habit. (9) Many of them have lost jobs, important relationships, or career opportunities because of their involvement with gambling.

**(C)**

(10) Compulsive gambling is like any other addiction. (11) As gamblers lose control over gambling, they lose control over their lives as well. (12) They may become anxious and depressed or they may fail to live up to their obligations, causing others to stop trusting them.

7. Sentence 1: **Most of us can bet on a football game, or buy a lottery ticket with little damage to our finances.**

   Which correction should be made to sentence 1?

   - A. insert a comma after us
   - B. change bet to be betting
   - C. remove the comma
   - D. insert a comma after ticket

8. Sentence 2: **In contrast, compulsive gamblers cannot stop even when their behavior had threatened to ruin their lives.**

   Which is the best way to write the underlined portion of this sentence?

   - A. had threatened
   - B. will threaten
   - C. threatens
   - D. having threatened

9. Which sentence would be most effective if inserted at the beginning of paragraph B?

- A. Compulsive gamblers have a lot of problems.
- B. Some people engage in compulsive gambling.
- C. Gamblers escape from negative emotions.
- D. Compulsive gamblers display a number of consistent traits.

10. Sentence 7: **They need to gamble with more and more money in order to enjoy it, losing money increases their desire to gamble.**

Which is the best way to write the underlined portion of this sentence?

- A. it. Losing
- B. it but losing
- C. it, now that losing
- D. it and losing

11. Sentence 8: **They may even commit fraud forgery, or theft to get the funds to continue their habit.**

Which correction should be made to sentence 8?

- A. insert a comma after fraud
- B. insert a comma after theft
- C. replace their with there
- D. replace their with they're

12. Sentence 12: **They may become anxious and depressed or they may fail to live up to their obligations, causing others to stop trusting them.**

Which is the best way to write the underlined portion of this sentence?

- A. depressed, or they
- B. depressed, they
- C. depressed. And they
- D. depressed and they

Questions 13 through 18 refer to the following paragraphs.

**Choosing a Pet**

**(A)**

(1) People often make impulse buys at Pet Stores just because they see an adorable puppy or kitten. (2) Unhappily, these poor creatures are likely to end up at animal shelters when the owners find he can't care for them. (3) To avoid this outcome, choose your pet wisely. (4) Remember that your pet will become a member of your family and a daily responsibility.

**(B)**

(5) There's several factors to consider when selecting a pet. (6) First of all, do you have the time to care for a pet? (7) While some pets require little care, puppies and kittens need to be housebroken and to train them. (8) If the animal needs exercise, is your home large enough? (9) Would you enjoy taking your pet outdoors for exercise? (10) Do you think people should get a lot of exercise? (11) Can you afford the costs of food, vaccinations, and health check-ups? (12) Does your building allow pets? (13) Finally, if you must leave home for a few days, can you find someone to care for your pet?

**(C)**

(14) Once you choose a pet that is appropriate for your lifestyle, bring the animal to a veterinarian for examination. (15) You should be able to return the pet if he or she was unhealthy.

13. Sentence 1: **People often make impulse buys at Pet Stores just because they see an adorable puppy or kitten.**

    Which correction should be made to sentence 1?

    - A. change buys to bys
    - B. change Pet Stores to pet stores
    - C. insert a comma before because
    - D. insert a comma before or

14. Sentence 2: **Unhappily, these poor creatures are likely to end up at animal shelters when the owners find he can't care for them.**

    Which correction should be made to sentence 2?

    - A. remove the comma
    - B. change animal shelters to Animal Shelters
    - C. insert a comma after shelters
    - D. replace he with they

15. Sentence 5: **There's several factors to consider when selecting a pet.**

    Which correction should be made to sentence 5?

    - A. change There's to There are
    - B. insert a comma after factors
    - C. replace to with too
    - D. insert a comma after consider

16. Sentence 7: **While some pets require little care, puppies and kittens need to be housebroken and to train them.**

    Which is the best way to write the underlined portion of the sentence?

    - A. be housebroken and to train them
    - B. housebreaking and training
    - C. be housebroken and trained
    - D. be housebroken and training

17. Which revision should be made to the placement of sentence 10?

    - A. move sentence 10 to the beginning of paragraph B
    - B. move sentence 10 to follow sentence 6
    - C. move sentence 10 to the beginning of paragraph C
    - D. remove sentence 10

18. Sentence 15: **You should be able to return the pet if the animal was unhealthy.**

    Which correction should be made to sentence 15?

    - A. change You to One
    - B. insert a comma after pet
    - C. replace if with and
    - D. change was to is

**Answers and explanations for *Language Arts: Writing, Part I* start on page 55.**

# Language Arts: Writing Pretest
## Part II: Essay

**Directions:** Read both the selection and the writing prompt and answer the questions that follow.

Questions 1–10 are based on the process of writing a response to a reading selection.
**Note: Do not start writing your response until you are asked to do so at question 9.**

**Essay Prompt**

The following passage is from Helen Keller's autobiography. Keller was the first deaf and blind person to earn a college degree. She went on to become a leading author, lecturer, and political activist for the rights of the disabled and for peace and human rights.

Before working with her teacher, Helen did not understand what language was. Write an essay explaining how Helen's teacher helped her to come to understand what language was. Include several specific details from the passage to support your explanation.

**Excerpted from *The Story of My Life***

The morning after my teacher came she led me into her room and gave me a doll. The little blind children at the Perkins Institution had sent it and Laura Bridgman had dressed it; but I did not know this until afterward. When I had played with it a little while, Miss Sullivan slowly spelled into my hand the word "d-o-l-l." I was at once interested in this finger play and tried to imitate it. When I finally succeeded in making the letters correctly I was flushed with childish pleasure and pride. Running downstairs to my mother I held up my hand and made the letters for doll. I did not know that I was spelling a word or even that words existed; I was simply making my fingers go in monkey-like imitation. In the days that followed I learned to spell in this uncomprehending way a great many words, among them pin, hat, cup and a few verbs like sit, stand and walk. But my teacher had been with me several weeks before I understood that everything has a name.

One day, while I was playing with my new doll, Miss Sullivan put my big rag doll into my lap also, spelled "d-o-l-l" and tried to make me understand that "d–o–l–l" applied to both. Earlier in the day we had had a tussle over the words "m-u-g" and "w-a-t-e-r." Miss Sullivan had tried to impress it upon me that "m-u-g" is mug and that "w-a-t-e-r" is water, but I persisted in confounding the two. In despair she had dropped the subject for the time, only to renew it at the first opportunity. I became impatient at her repeated attempts and, seizing the new doll, I dashed it upon the floor. I was keenly delighted when I felt the fragments of the broken doll at my feet.

Neither sorrow nor regret followed my passionate outburst. I had not loved the doll. In the still, dark world in which I lived there was no strong sentiment of tenderness. I felt my teacher sweep the fragments to one side of the hearth, and I had a sense of satisfaction that the cause of my discomfort was removed. She brought me my hat, and I knew I was going out into the warm sunshine. This thought, if a wordless sensation may be called a thought, made me hop and skip with pleasure.

We walked down the path to the well-house, attracted by the fragrance of the honeysuckle with which it was covered. Someone was drawing water and my teacher placed my hand under the spout. As the cool stream gushed over one hand she spelled into the other the word water, first slowly, then rapidly. I stood still, my whole attention fixed upon the motions of her fingers. Suddenly I felt a misty consciousness as of something forgotten—a thrill of returning thought; and somehow the mystery of language was revealed to me. I knew then that "w-a-t-e r" meant the wonderful cool something that was flowing over my hand. That living word wakened my soul, gave it light, hope, joy, set it free! There were barriers still, it is true, but barriers that could in time be swept away.

I left the well-house eager to learn. Everything had a name, and each name gave birth to a new thought. As we returned to the house every object which I touched seemed to quiver with life. That was because I saw everything with the strange, new sight that had come to me. On entering the door I remembered the doll I had broken. I felt my way to the hearth and picked up the pieces. I tried vainly to put them together. Then my eyes filled with tears; for I realized what I had done, and for the first time I felt repentance and sorrow.

From *The Story of My Life* by Helen Keller

### Unpack the Writing Prompt

1. What is the topic of the writing prompt?

______________________________________________

2. What does the prompt ask you to do?

______________________________________________

3. What does the prompt tell you that you need to include in the response?

______________________________________________

4. Are you being asked to argue for your opinion or to explain something from the passage?

______________________________________________

### Develop Your Topic Sentence and Supporting Details

5. Write a sentence that introduces the topic of your essay. This will be the first sentence of your essay.

______________________________________________

6. What are three details from the passage you will use to develop your explanation?

______________________________________________

______________________________________________

______________________________________________

7. Write a concluding sentence that summarizes your explanation.

______________________________________________

### Plan, Draft, Revise, and Edit Your Response

8. On a piece of paper, make a plan for your response.
9. On a computer or on a piece of paper, write a response to the prompt that includes an introduction, a body, and a conclusion.
10. On the computer or on the paper, make revisions to improve your response and edit to correct errors in grammar, usage, spelling, capitalization, and punctuation.

**The *Writing, Part II: Essay* evaluation guide begins on page 56.**

# MATHEMATICS PRETEST

## PART I: QUANTITATIVE REASONING—18 QUESTIONS

**Directions:** You may fill in the circles next to the correct answers or write your answers on a separate piece of paper. You MAY use a calculator.

Questions 1–2 refer to the following information and graph.

Video Warehouse has divided the surrounding community into four advertising zones. The graph shows the total number of customers from each zone for a three-week period.

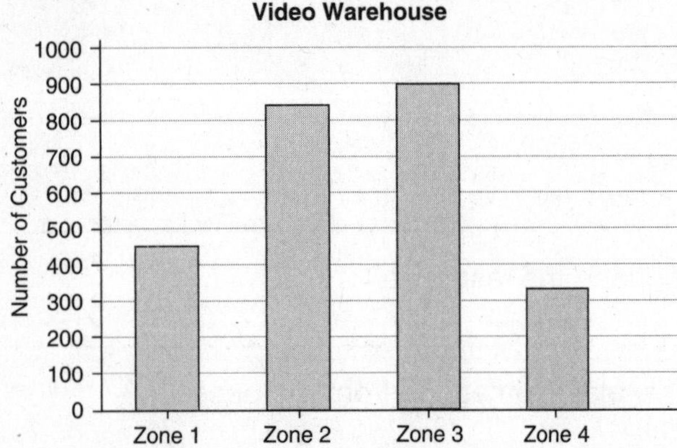


1. During the three weeks, how many customers came from Zones 3 and 4?
   - A. between 900 and 1,000
   - B. between 1,000 and 1,100
   - C. between 1,100 and 1,200
   - D. between 1,200 and 1,300

2. Approximately what is the ratio of customers from Zone 1 to customers from Zone 3?
   - A. 3:5
   - B. 3:2
   - C. 2:1
   - D. 1:2

3. A potter uses $\frac{3}{5}$ of a pound of clay to make a bowl. How many bowls could the potter make from 10 pounds of clay?
   - A. 6
   - B. 8
   - C. 16
   - D. 17

4. Janelle has recently been hired for the job of library assistant. The following graph shows what percent of her time will be spent on each of five tasks each day.

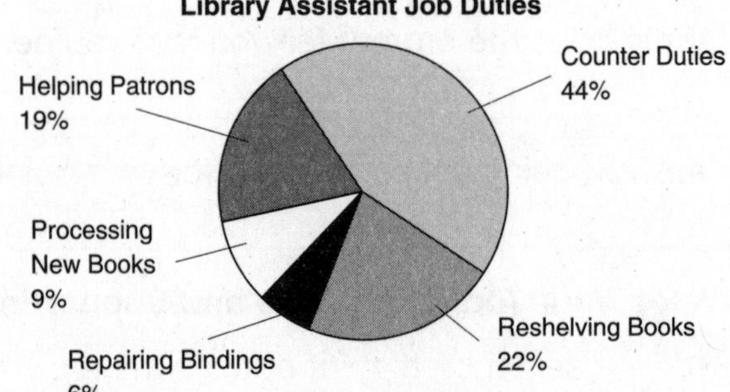


The number of hours that Janelle will spend working at the counter is about how many times the number of hours that she will spend processing new books and repairing bindings?

   - A. 2
   - B. 3
   - C. 4
   - D. 6

5. Fifteen percent of the workers at Nationwide Industries earn minimum wage. If 24 workers earn minimum wage, how many total workers are there at Nationwide Industries?

   - A. 4
   - B. 36
   - C. 160
   - D. 360

6. An accountant is going to pay the following four bills:

| Bill | Amount |
|---|---|
| W | \$27.10 |
| X | \$261.00 |
| Y | \$2.80 |
| Z | \$27.20 |

   The accountant will pay the bills in order from smallest to largest. In what order will he pay them?

   - A. W, X, Z, Y
   - B. X, W, Z, Y
   - C. Y, X, W, Z
   - D. Y, W, Z, X

7. A jar holds 16 ounces of honey. A cook is going to make two recipes. One of the recipes calls for 2.5 ounces of honey, and the other calls for 4.25 ounces of honey. After the cook has made those two recipes, how many ounces of honey will be left in the jar?

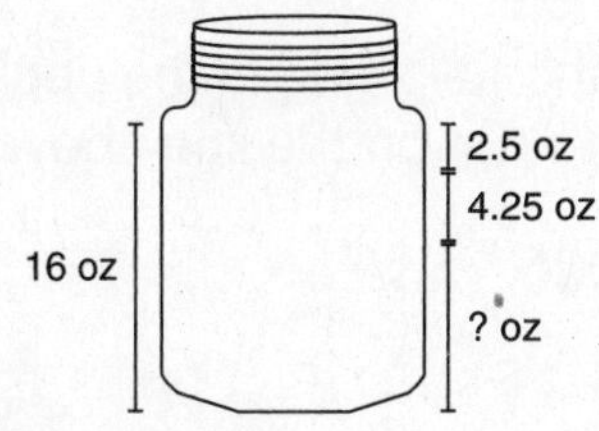


   - A. 6.75
   - B. 9.25
   - C. 10.00
   - D. 11.75

8. All numbers that are evenly divisible by both 6 and 14 are also divisible by which of the following numbers?

   - A. 8
   - B. 12
   - C. 21
   - D. 28

9. Alice, Kathy, and Sheila work as medical assistants at Valley Clinic. Alice has worked 8 years longer than Kathy. Kathy has worked half as long as Sheila. If Sheila has worked at the company for 10 years, how many years has Alice worked there?

   - A. 5
   - B. 8
   - C. 10
   - D. 13

Question 10 is based on the spinner below.

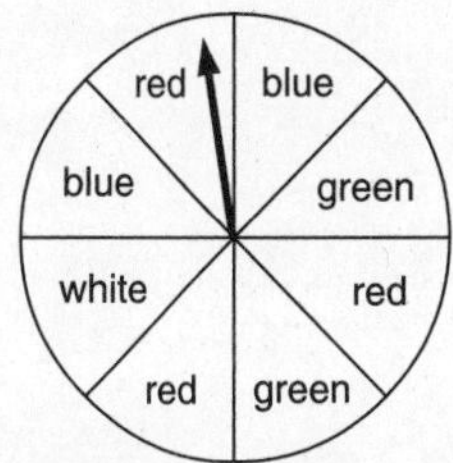


10. The spinner shown in the drawing is divided into eight equal sections. If you spin the spinner one time, what is the probability of not getting blue?

   - A. $\frac{1}{8}$
   - B. $\frac{1}{4}$
   - C. $\frac{3}{4}$
   - D. $\frac{7}{8}$

11. A computer monitor is regularly priced at \$320. During a two-day sale, the price was decreased to \$240. Which of the following is the percentage decrease of the monitor's price during the sale?

- A. 25%
- B. 33%
- C. 75%
- D. 80%

12. For a 10-day period, a bank kept track of the number of new accounts opened each day. The results are shown in the table below. What is the median number of accounts opened per day during this 10-day period?

| Day | Accounts | Day | Accounts |
|---|---|---|---|
| May 7 | 6 | May 14 | 4 |
| May 8 | 2 | May 15 | 8 |
| May 9 | 7 | May 16 | 6 |
| May 10 | 5 | May 17 | 4 |
| May 11 | 4 | May 18 | 7 |

- A. 5
- B. 5.3
- C. 5.5
- D. 6

13. Jim is a salesperson, and his employers expect him to sell at least \$12,000 in merchandise per month. In April, Jim sold \$2,500 in the first week of the month and twice that much in the second week. How much must he sell in the rest of April combined in order to sell the minimum expected of him?

- A. \$4,500
- B. \$5,500
- C. \$9,500
- D. \$12,000

14. Angela likes to use two walking sticks when she goes hiking, but the two walking sticks she has been given recently are different lengths. One is $3\frac{4}{5}$ feet long, and the other is $3\frac{1}{2}$ feet long.

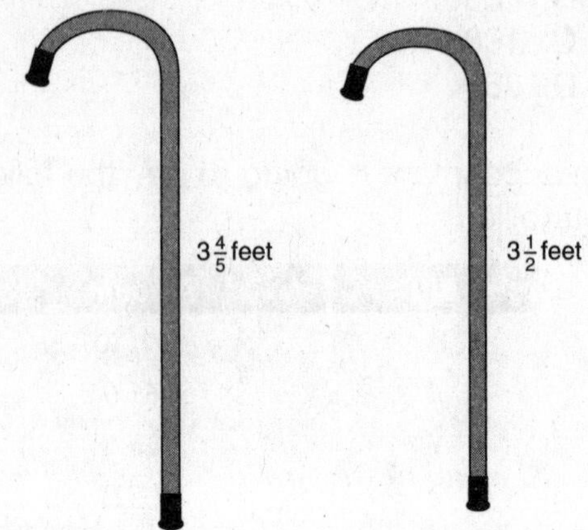


Angela wants to cut the longer stick to match the shorter one. How much should she cut from the longer stick so that the two walking sticks will be the same length?

- A. $\frac{3}{4}$ feet
- B. $\frac{3}{5}$ feet
- C. $\frac{3}{10}$ feet
- D. $\frac{1}{4}$ feet

Question 15 is based on the following number line.

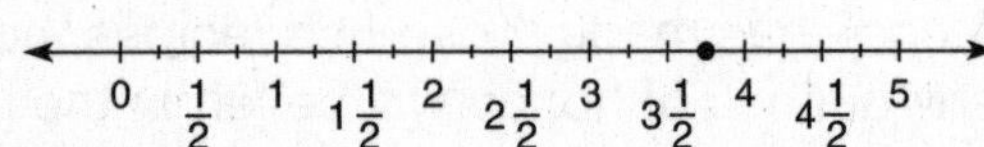


15. Which of the following is the decimal point value of the dot on the line above?

- A. 3.25
- B. 3.50
- C. 3.75
- D. 4.00

Question 16 is based on the following information and graph.

Marjorie has a class of 35 students, and she tracked their performance on a recent math exam. The graph below represents how their scores were distributed along the range of possible scores, from F to A.

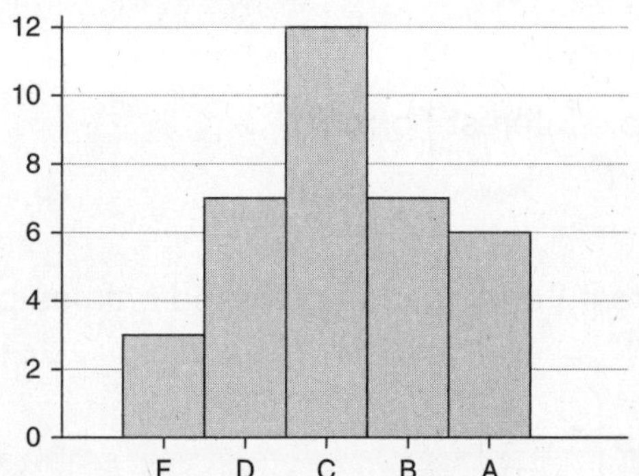


Based on the graph, which of the following is a true statement?

- A. None of Marjorie's students received an F on the exam.
- B. Most of Marjorie's students received either an A or a B on the exam.
- C. If Marjorie gave the same exam again to another group of students, most of those students would receive a C.
- D. More students received either an A or a B than received either a D or an F.

---

17. Jason deposits $5,000 in a bank account that will pay him 4% simple interest annually. If Jason deposits no more than the initial $5,000, how much money will be in the account at the end of five years? (The formula for simple interest is $I = prt$ or *interest* = *principal* × *rate* × *time*. Use a decimal to express the interest when using that formula.)

- A. $200
- B. $1,000
- C. $5,000
- D. $6,000

18. A local library shows movies on Thursday evenings. The library administrator has chosen the next six movies he will show, but he has not decided in which order to show them. How many possible orderings of the six movies are there?

- A. 21
- B. 36
- C. 720
- D. 1,012

**Answers and explanations for *Mathematics, Part I* start on page 57.**

# Mathematics Pretest

## Part II: Algebraic Reasoning and Geometry—22 Questions

The next two pages display formulas that you will be given when you take the TASC. You can refer to these pages on Part II of this pretest.

**Volume**

Cylinder: $V = \pi r^2 h$

Pyramid: $V = \frac{1}{3}Bh$

Cone: $V = \frac{1}{3}\pi r^2 h$

Sphere: $V = \frac{4}{3}\pi r^3$

**Coordinate Geometry**

Midpoint formula:

$$\left(\frac{x_1 + x_2}{2}, \frac{y_1 + y_2}{2}\right)$$

Distance formula:

$$d = \sqrt{(x_2 - x_1)^2 + (y_2 - y_1)^2}$$

Slope: $m = \frac{y_2 - y_1}{x_2 - x_1}, x_2 \neq x_1$

**Special Factoring**

$a^2 - b^2 = (a - b)(a + b)$

$a^2 + 2ab + b^2 = (a + b)^2$

$a^2 - 2ab + b^2 = (a - b)^2$

$a^3 + b^3 = (a + b)(a^2 - ab + b^2)$

$a^3 - b^3 = (a - b)(a^2 + ab + b^2)$

**Quadratic Formula**

For $ax^2 + bx + c = 0$

$$x = \frac{-b \pm \sqrt{b^2 - 4ac}}{2a}$$

**Interest**

Simple Interest Formula:
$I = prt$

Interest Formula (compounded $n$ times per year):

$$A = p\left(1 + \frac{r}{n}\right)^{nt}$$

$A$ = Amount after $t$ years.

$p$ = principal

$r$ = annual interest rate

$t$ = time in years

$I$ = Interest

**Trigonometric Identities**

Pythagorean Theorem: $a^2 + b^2 = c^2$

$$\sin\theta = \frac{opp}{hyp}$$

$$\cos\theta = \frac{adj}{hyp}$$

$$\tan\theta = \frac{opp}{adj}$$

$$\sin^2\theta + \cos^2\theta = 1$$

$$Density = \frac{Mass}{Volume}$$

**Central Angle**

$m\angle AOB = m\overset{\frown}{AB}$

**Inscribed Angle**

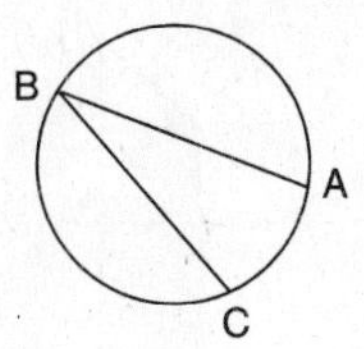


$m\angle ABC = \frac{1}{2} m\overset{\frown}{AC}$

**Intersecting Chords Theorem**

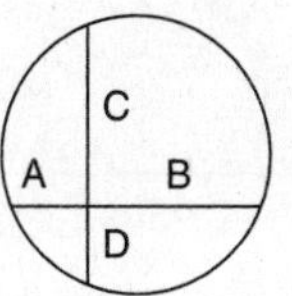


$A \cdot B = C \cdot D$

**Probability**

Permutations: ${}_nP_r = \frac{n!}{(n-r)!}$

Combinations: ${}_nC_r = \frac{n!}{(n-r)!r!}$

Multiplication rule (independent events): $P(A \text{ and } B) = P(A) \cdot P(B)$

Multiplication rule (general): $P(A \text{ and } B) = P(A) \cdot P(B|A)$

Addition rule: $P(A \text{ or } B) = P(A) + P(B) - P(A \text{ and } B)$

Conditional Probability: $P(B|A) = \frac{p(A \text{ and } B)}{p(A)}$

Arithmetic Sequence: $a_n = a_1 + (n-1)d$ where $a_n$ is the $n$th term, $a_1$ is the first term, and $d$ is the common difference.

Geometric Sequence: $a_n = a_1 r^{(n-1)}$ where $a_n$ is the $n$th term, $a_1$ is the first term, and $r$ is the common ratio.

**Directions:** You may fill in the circles next to the correct answers or write your answers on a separate piece of paper. Refer to the formula sheet on page 22 as needed. You MAY use your calculator.

1. Which point on the number line below represents the value $-\frac{16}{6}$?

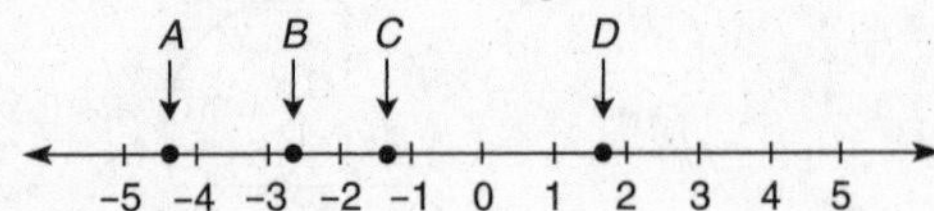


A. Point $A$
B. Point $B$
C. Point $C$
D. Point $D$

2. Evaluate the expression $2x - (4y - 3) + 5xz$, when $x = -3$, $y = 2$, and $z = -1$.

A. 45
B. 16
C. 4
D. −10

3. On April 1 of this year, the high temperature in Northville was 46 degrees Fahrenheit. Then a sudden snowstorm arose, and the temperature dropped sharply to a low of −8 degrees Fahrenheit. What was the magnitude of the change in temperature on that day?

A. 54
B. 46
C. 36
D. −36

Question 4 refers to the following drawing.

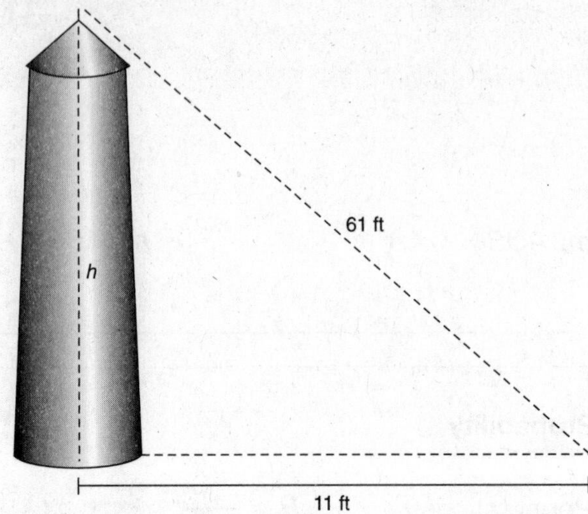


4. A tower casts a shadow 11 feet long. The distance from the top of the tower to the end of the shadow is 61 feet. How many feet tall is the tower?

A. 50
B. 60
C. 61
D. 72

Question 5 is based on the following information.

Designer Furnishings sells premade cabinets and cupboards, as shown below.

| Model | Dimensions (in inches) |
|---|---|
| 411R | 32 by 22 by 10 |
| 412R | 28 by 36 by 15 |
| 413S | 24 by 72 by 18 |
| 414S | 25 by 24 by 6 |

5. Each face of cabinet 413S is in the shape of a rectangle. What is the volume of Model 413S in cubic feet?

- A. 18
- B. 31
- C. 36
- D. 108

---

6. Together, Levy and Matthew earn $4,680 per month. Levy earns $520 more per month than Matthew earns. How much does Levy earn per month?

- A. $2,080
- B. $2,340
- C. $2,600
- D. $4,160

7. The design for a new cone-shaped closed container is shown below. What is the surface area of this container, in square inches? You can select the correct formula from the formula sheet on page 22.

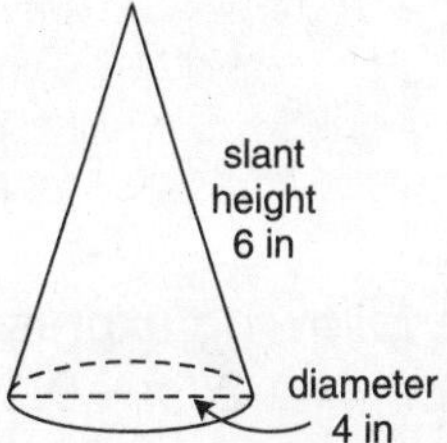


- A. $4\pi$
- B. $12\pi$
- C. $16\pi$
- D. $28\pi$

8. Simplify this polynomial:
$3x^3 + x + 2x^3 - 4x^2 + 14y - 2(y + x)$.

- A. $3x^3 - 3x^2 + 14(-2y + 2x)$
- B. $5x^3 - 3x^2 + 14y - 2y - 2x$
- C. $3x^3 - x + 4x^2 + 12y$
- D. $5x^3 - 4x^2 - x + 12y$

9. A rectangle is drawn on a coordinate grid. Three of its four vertices are located at points (–1, – 2), (–1, 4), and (2, – 2) What is the location of the fourth vertex?

- A. (–2, –4)
- B. (–1, –4)
- C. (1, 4)
- D. (2, 4)

10. Which of the following expressions is equal to the expression $4x - 2(3x - 9)$?

- A. $18 - 2x$
- B. $-10x - 18$
- C. $-2x - 18$
- D. $10x - 18$

11. In the equation $3x^2 - 10x = 8$, which of the following values for $x$ will make the equation true?

- A. –4
- B. –3
- C. 3
- D. 4

12. Solve for $x$: $12(x - 2) < 24$

- A. $x < 0$
- B. $x > 0$
- C. $x < 12$
- D. $x < 4$

13. Scientists estimate that Earth is 4,540,000,000 years old. What is that number expressed in scientific notation?

- A. $4.54 \times 10^7$
- B. $4.54 \times 10^9$
- C. $454 \times 10^{10}$
- D. $2(127 \times 10^7)$

14. Joe just purchased an oddly shaped piece of property, depicted in the figure below.

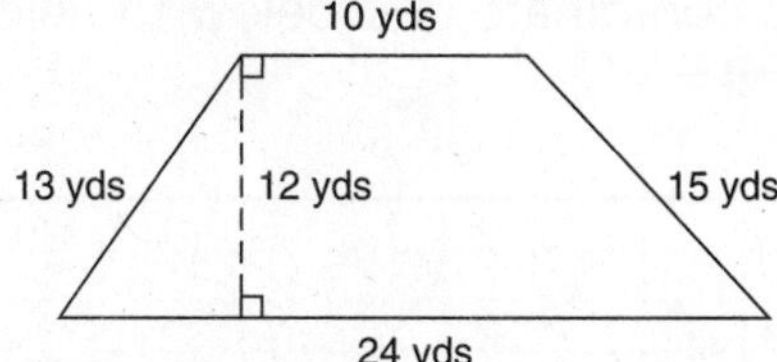


What is the area, in square yards, of Joe's new property?

- A. 120
- B. 134
- C. 140
- D. 204

15. The XYZ Company sells hats and will monogram them if customers choose. The price for each monogram varies depending on how many hats a customer would like to have monogrammed. The monogram prices for several order sizes are shown below:

| Number of hats to be monogrammed ($n$) | Price per monogram ($p$) |
|---|---|
| 1 | \$5 |
| 2 | \$4.50 |
| 3 | \$4.00 |
| 4 | \$3.50 |
| 5 | \$3.00 |
| 6 | \$2.50 |

Which of the following best expresses the relationship of price per monogram (for all nonnegative values of $p$) to number of hats monogrammed shown in the table above?

- A. $p = \$5.00 - (n - 1)\$0.50$
- B. $p = \$5.00 - n(\$0.50)$
- C. $p = (n - 1)\$5.00$
- D. $p = \$0.50(10n)$

16. A parallelogram has two obtuse angles and two acute angles. If the measure of one of the obtuse angles is 110°, what is the measure, in degrees, of one of the acute angles?

- A. 10°
- B. 70°
- C. 110°
- D. 240°

Question 17 refers to the following graph.

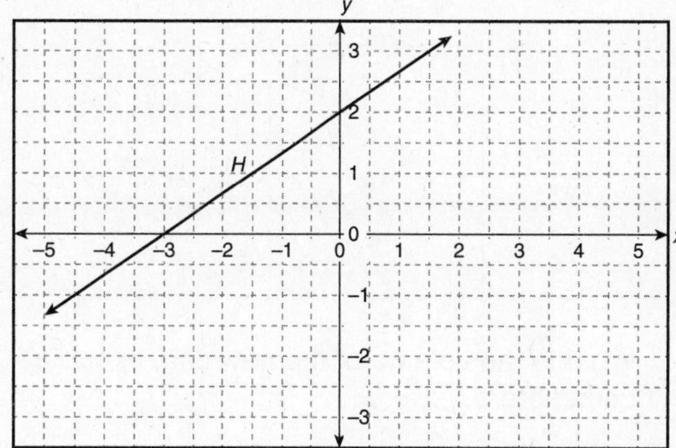


17. Line $H$ is the graph of which of the following equations?

- A. $y = \frac{1}{3}x + 2$
- B. $y + 2 = \frac{2}{3}x$
- C. $y = \frac{2}{3}x + 2$
- D. $y = 3(x - 2) + 2$

18. A fountain's pool is enclosed by a circular plastic tank. The distance from the center of the pool to the wall of the tank is 10 feet. How long is the wall of the tank in feet?

- A. $20\pi$
- B. $\frac{20}{\pi}$
- C. $25\pi$
- D. $100\pi$

19. Line $W$ passes through the following points on the coordinate grid: (0, − 9) and (4, −1). What is the slope of line $W$?

- A. −2
- B. $-\frac{1}{2}$
- C. $\frac{1}{2}$
- D. 2

20. Beansey's Baked Beans, Inc., has developed a new can for its baked beans, shown below:

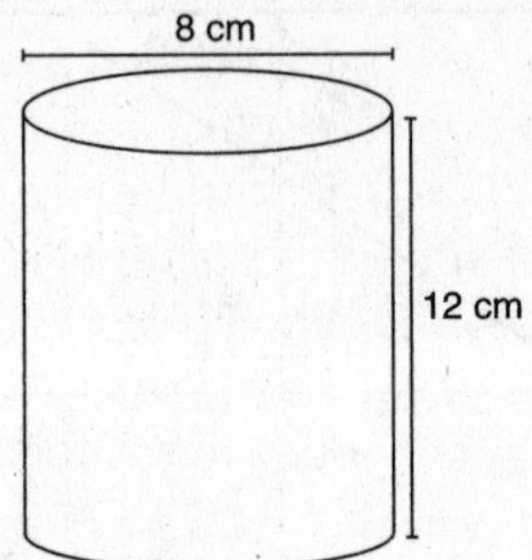


What is the volume of the new can, in cubic centimeters?

- A. $48\pi$
- B. $96\pi$
- C. $192\pi$
- D. $768\pi$

21. Tina is considering renting a commercial space for her business. The space is shown below.

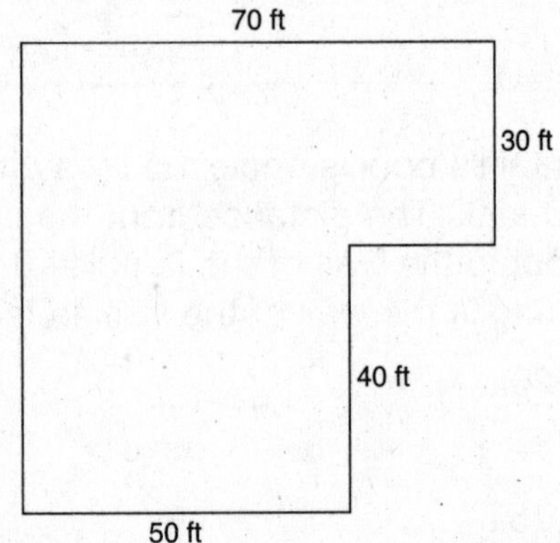


What is the area of the commercial space, in square feet?

- A. 290
- B. 2,100
- C. 2,800
- D. 4,100

22. In the system of equations $3x - 3y = -9$ and $2x + y = 9$, solve for both $x$ and $y$. You may use the coordinate grid below to help your work.

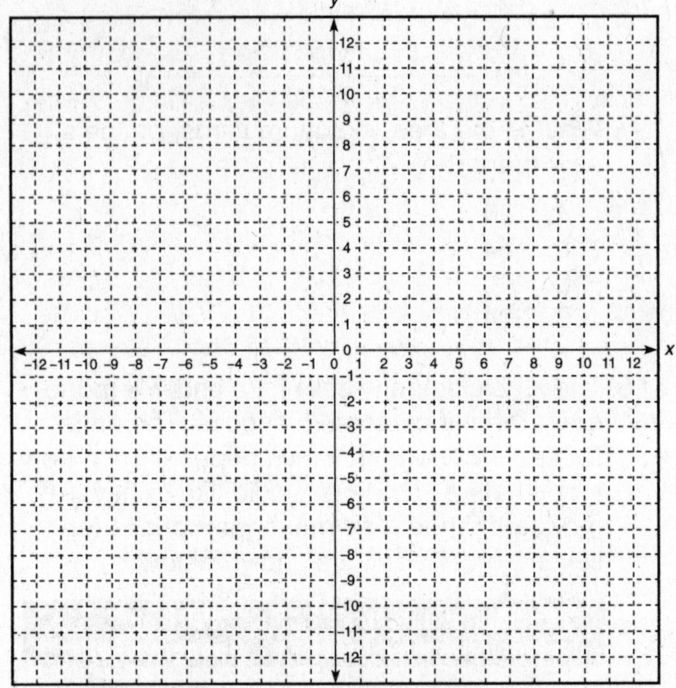


What is the solution set for $x$ and $y$?

- A. (2, − 5)
- B. (0, 3)
- C. (0, 9)
- D. (2, 5)

**Answers and explanations for *Mathematics, Part II* start on page 57.**

# SOCIAL STUDIES PRETEST

## PART I: SOCIAL STUDIES SKILLS—10 QUESTIONS

**Directions:** You may fill in the circles next to the correct answers or write your answers on a separate piece of paper.

Question 1 refers to the following passage.

With the passage of the Fifteenth Amendment in 1870, all African Americans were given the right to vote throughout the United States. However, many Southern states quickly enacted legislative barriers to disenfranchise these new voters. Provisions such as poll taxes, literacy tests, and the grandfather clause prevented many African Americans from exercising their rights. For nearly one hundred years, these restrictions persisted in many Southern states. The civil rights movement, which gained national momentum in the 1950s, sought to address this unequal treatment in voting rights laws. Finally, in 1965, the Voting Rights Act provided for federal oversight of states that had previously raised unfair barriers to African American voting and outlawed discriminatory measures such as poll taxes and literacy tests. Voter participation among African Americans dramatically increased in the following years.

1. Which of the following describes the author's main idea?

   - A. The Voting Rights Act of 1965 ended discrimination in all areas of American society.
   - B. The main effect of the Voting Rights Act of 1965 was to empower individual states to end discriminatory measures against African American voting.
   - C. The Voting Rights Act of 1965 gave the federal government oversight of state elections to end barriers against African American voting.
   - D. The Fifteenth Amendment did not end racism in Southern states.

Question 2 refers to the following passage.

To address the nation's financial insolvency after the Revolutionary War, George Washington turned to his Secretary of the Treasury, Alexander Hamilton. Hamilton proposed creating a national bank, which would help to pay back the nation's debt and stabilize the nation's currency. Immediately, Hamilton faced stiff opposition from those who believed in a **strict construction** of the Constitution; they believed that Congress and the president could only exercise powers specifically written in the Constitution. Because the Constitution did not give the power to create a national bank, Hamilton's actions would be unconstitutional. In response, Hamilton offered a justification for the constitutionality of his bank based on a **loose construction** of the Constitution, meaning that Congress could use the Necessary and Proper Clause of the Constitution to stretch its power beyond what was specified in the words of the document. In Washington's first great test of presidential leadership, he sided with Hamilton and the idea of a national bank.

2. What is meant by the term "construction" in the passage?

   - A. building
   - B. creation
   - C. interpretation
   - D. structure

Questions 3 and 4 refer to the following passage.

In an attempt to make consumers more aware of the nutritional value of the foods they purchase, the Food and Drug Administration (FDA) is attempting to impose strict new regulations on all food retailers. These regulations would require that the caloric information of each food product be clearly posted on the premises, typically through signs that would be expensive to create and maintain. While these regulations would place a financial burden on all food retailers—an expense that would necessarily be passed on to consumers—the regulations would be particularly devastating to smaller restaurants, grocery stores, and convenience stores that offer fresh food items. To relieve this burden on smaller businesses, Congress has proposed the Common Sense Nutritional Disclosure Act, which would exempt smaller food establishments that primarily sell prepackaged foods from having to post on-site information. Also, under this legislation, restaurants that take most of their orders remotely can post caloric information online.

3. What is the author's point of view regarding the FDA's new food regulations?
   - A. The FDA's new regulations would place a financial hardship on small food retailers.
   - B. The FDA's new regulations would help consumers choose foods of a higher nutritional value.
   - C. The FDA's new regulations would have a more severe financial impact on chain restaurants than on smaller food retailers.
   - D. The FDA's new regulations would give food retailers more diverse options for displaying caloric information.

4. Which one of the following words points to the author's viewpoint regarding the FDA's strict new regulations?
   - A. "aware"
   - B. "strict"
   - C. "devastating"
   - D. "remotely"

Questions 5 and 6 refer to the following paragraph.

It is known that a significant quantity of oil exists within the Arctic National Wildlife Refuge (ANWR) of Alaska. Shockingly, there are many who would have us ignore this incredible resource housed right within our national borders. One commonly cited reason against drilling for oil in the ANWR is that the drilling process would endanger the existence of the porcupine caribou, whose calving grounds encompass much of the region. But science has shown us that as many as 99 percent of all the species that once existed on Earth are now extinct, and the vast majority of these extinctions were not caused by humans. Clearly, then, extinctions are a sad but natural aspect of life on Earth, and we have no reason not to drill in the ANWR.

5. Which of the following statements is a correct evaluation of the argument?
   - A. The argument is valid, because it relies on scientific evidence that has been shown to be true.
   - B. The argument is valid, because extracting oil would bolster the national economy.
   - C. The argument is invalid, because it confuses correlation with causation.
   - D. The argument is invalid, because it attempts to refute one reason against doing something while ignoring other possible reasons.

6. Which of the following considerations, if true, best illustrates why the author's evidence is inadequate?
   - A. Some people depend on the porcupine caribou for food.
   - B. People who call themselves "scientists" may make claims that are long held to be true yet are eventually shown to be false.
   - C. There is not enough oil in the ANWR to have a measurable impact on global oil prices.
   - D. Extracting oil from the ANWR would reduce the foreign trade deficit.

Questions 7 and 8 are based on the following information and map.

After World War II, Germany was split into two nations: democratic West Germany and communist East Germany. West Germany was under the control of the victorious Allies, who formed an alliance called the North Atlantic Treaty Organization (NATO). In 1955, NATO decided to allow West Germany to join NATO and to rearm. In response, the U.S.S.R. (that is, the Soviet Union) and a number of communist Eastern European countries formed what they called a "Treaty of Friendship, Co-operation, and Mutual Assistance," commonly referred to as the Warsaw Pact. In the Warsaw Pact, the communist countries agreed to band together if one of them was attacked, and the smaller communist countries agreed to put their military forces under the command of the Soviet Union.

Source: Central Intelligence Agency

7. Some historians believe that, in forming the Warsaw Pact, the Soviet Union wanted to create a buffer between itself and NATO countries. How does the map support that view?
   - A. The map indicates that many of the World War II Allies joined the Warsaw Pact, but not until the 1960s.
   - B. The map shows that most of the Warsaw Pact countries lay between the Soviet Union and Western countries, including France, West Germany, and Great Britain.
   - C. The map shows that the Warsaw Pact involved the building of a wall between the Soviet Union and Western Europe.
   - D. The map indicates that the Soviet Union was made up of smaller republics on its western border.

8. The map could be used to dispute which one of the following claims?
   - A. In forming the Warsaw Pact, the Soviet Union greatly increased its access to oceanic coastline.
   - B. In forming the Warsaw Pact, the Soviet Union wished to increase its trade with Africa.
   - C. The Warsaw Pact benefitted Bulgaria and Romania no less than the Soviet Union.
   - D. The Warsaw Pact initially included Albania.

Question 9 refers to the following table and map.

| Average Yearly Rainfall in New England | |
|---|---|
| **State** | **Avg. Rainfall/Year** |
| Connecticut | 47 inches |
| Maine | 41 inches |
| Massachusetts | 45 inches |
| New Hampshire | 42 inches |
| Rhode Island | 44 inches |
| Vermont | 39 inches |

Source: netstate.com

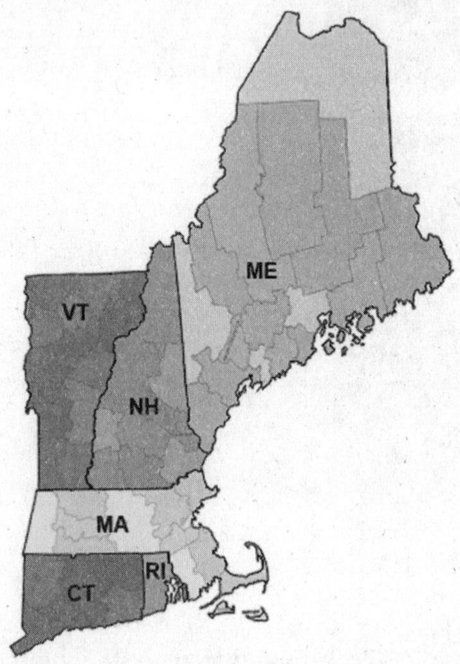


9. What is the average (arithmetic mean) yearly rainfall, in inches, of the three northernmost states in New England?

   - A. $40\frac{2}{3}$
   - B. 41
   - C. 42
   - D. $43\frac{1}{3}$

Question 10 refers to the following graph.

The graph below shows the percent of people who voted in presidential elections from 1996 to 2012.

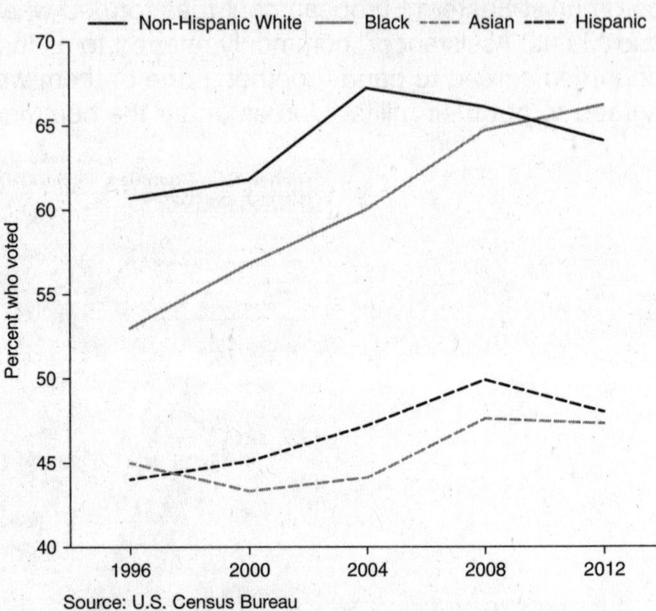


10. Over the period illustrated by the line graph, the rate at which eligible black voters participated in presidential elections

    - A. fluctuated up and down, but ended higher than it began.
    - B. steadily increased, surpassing that of white voters in the 2012 elections.
    - C. increased sharply in the middle of the time period shown on the graph before dropping back closer to its original level.
    - D. was consistently lower than the rates of most other races and ethnic groups.

**Answers and explanations for *Social Studies, Part I* start on page 60.**

# Social Studies Pretest

## Part II: Social Studies Content—25 Questions

**Directions:** You may fill in the circles next to the correct answers or write your answers on a separate piece of paper.

Question 1 and 2 refer to the following map.

**Colonial Triangular Trade**

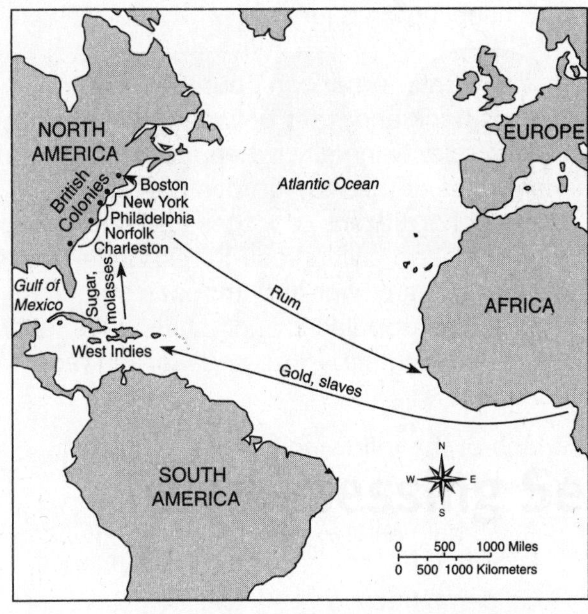


1. Based on this map, what were the three sides of the triangle in the triangular trade?
   - A. Europe to the West Indies; the West Indies to Africa; Africa to the British colonies
   - B. the West Indies to the British colonies; the British colonies to Africa; Africa to the West Indies
   - C. the West Indies to England; England to the British colonies; the British colonies to Africa
   - D. South America to Africa; Africa to the West Indies; the West Indies to the British colonies

2. Which statement is a conclusion based on the map rather than a supporting detail from the map?
   - A. Cargo ships never had to sail empty on any leg of a profitable triangular journey.
   - B. The journey of Africans from Africa to the Americas was called the Middle Passage.
   - C. Slaves sometimes were transported on cargo ships from the West Indies to the British colonies.
   - D. Rum was shipped from one of the ports on the east coast of North America.

---

Question 3 refers to the following information.

Several types of U.S. banking institutions and some of their main services are described below.

**Federal Reserve Banks** control the nation's monetary policy and maintain stability of the banking and financial systems.

**Commercial banks** accept deposits, make loans, and provide related services to corporations and other businesses.

**Retail banks** provide savings and checking accounts, mortgages, personal loans, and debit and credit cards to consumers.

**Community development banks** serve residents and spur economic development in low- to moderate-income areas.

**Credit unions** provide their members with checking and savings accounts, mortgages, and other services at a lower interest rate than other financial institutions.

3. At which type of financial institution would the ABC Printing Company be most likely to take out a loan to finance the purchase of a new printing press?
   - A. Federal Reserve Bank
   - B. commercial bank
   - C. retail bank
   - D. community development bank

Questions 4 and 5 refer to the following passage.

Somerville has had a long history of corruption. From the 1960s to the 1980s, its mayor, councilors, and tax assessors were involved in a complex network of bribery and favors. The "strong-mayor" system of government is responsible for this corruption; in the history of Massachusetts, all but a single instance of municipal corruption occurred under a strong-mayor government. Because that tainted system is still in place to this day in Somerville, the current mayor must be viewed with strong suspicion.

4. Which of the following words or phrases is based on the author's opinion, not fact?

   - A. long history
   - B. tainted system
   - C. bribery
   - D. mayors, councilors, and tax assessors

5. Is the author's conclusion properly supported by evidence?

   - A. Yes, because the corruption in Somerville spreads beyond the office of the mayor.
   - B. Yes, because 20 years of corruption can accurately be called a "long history."
   - C. No, because there is no mention of criminal investigation or charges.
   - D. No, because no indication is given that the current mayor will behave as past mayors did.

6. Most Americans believe it is their duty as citizens to take part in our system of government.

   Which of the following actions represents participation in government?

   - A. pursuing higher education
   - B. displaying the American flag
   - C. volunteering at a hospital
   - D. serving on a jury

7. In many Latin American countries, control passes back and forth between military and civilian rule. Generally, when a civilian government rules, it tries to improve conditions for the nation's citizens, but these attempts lead to turmoil and civil unrest. In response, the military takes power and imposes strict controls on the populace. Such shifts have taken place in Argentina, Peru, and Chile in recent decades.

   Which of the following is highly valued by those who favor military rule?

   - A. social welfare
   - B. freedom
   - C. democracy
   - D. law and order

Questions 8 and 9 refer to the following chart.

**Presidential Powers in Several Nations**

| Constitutional Power | U.S.A. | South Africa | France | Mexico |
|---|---|---|---|---|
| Control armed forces | ✔ | ✔ | ✔ | ✔ |
| Approve legislation | ✔ | ✔ | ✔ | ✔ |
| Appoint executive branch officials | ✔ | ✔ | ✔ | ✔ |
| Appoint judges | ✔ | ✔ | ✔ | ✔ |
| Appoint prime minister | | | ✔ | |
| Dissolve legislature | | | ✔ | |

8. Which of the following is a difference between the powers of the U.S. and French presidents?
   - A. The U.S. president controls the armed forces, and the French president does not.
   - B. The U.S. president approves legislation, and the French president does not.
   - C. The French president has the power to dissolve the legislature, while the U.S. president does not.
   - D. The French president has the power to appoint judges, while the U.S. president does not.

9. Which of the following statements is a conclusion based on the chart rather than a detail?
   - A. The president of South Africa cannot dissolve the legislature.
   - B. Of all the presidents shown, the French president has the greatest variety of powers.
   - C. The president of Mexico has the power to appoint judges.
   - D. The U.S. president has the power to approve legislation.

Question 10 refers to the following paragraph.

After the Civil War, southern states passed Jim Crow laws, which kept whites and blacks apart in public places like restaurants, buses, and restrooms. In an 1896 case, *Plessy v. Ferguson*, the U.S. Supreme Court upheld a Louisiana law requiring separate railroad cars for white and black passengers. The Court ruled that it was constitutional to have "separate but equal" facilities for whites and blacks and other minorities. The Court reasoned that "legislation is powerless to eradicate racial instincts or to abolish distinctions." One justice dissented, saying that the decision was "inconsistent with the personal liberty of citizens, white and black."

10. Which of the following statements is an opinion rather than a fact?
    - A. In the late 1800s, many southern states passed Jim Crow laws to keep whites and blacks separate in public places.
    - B. In Louisiana, a law required separate railroad cars for white and black passengers.
    - C. *Plessy v. Ferguson* was an 1896 Supreme Court case that challenged the Louisiana law related to segregated railroad cars.
    - D. The U.S. Supreme Court ruling in *Plessy v. Ferguson* was wrong because it infringed on freedoms guaranteed in the Constitution.

Questions 11 and 12 refer to the following paragraph and chart.

When the U.S. government cannot cover its expenses, it borrows money by selling bonds. It pays back the principal and interest on the bonds over a period of many years. The national debt is the total amount the U.S. government owes at any particular point in time. In 2010, this was about $13.2 trillion.

One way of measuring the national debt is by computing the per capita national debt. The per capita national debt is the total national debt divided by the population of the United States. The graph below shows the per capita national debt every five years from 1990 to 2010.

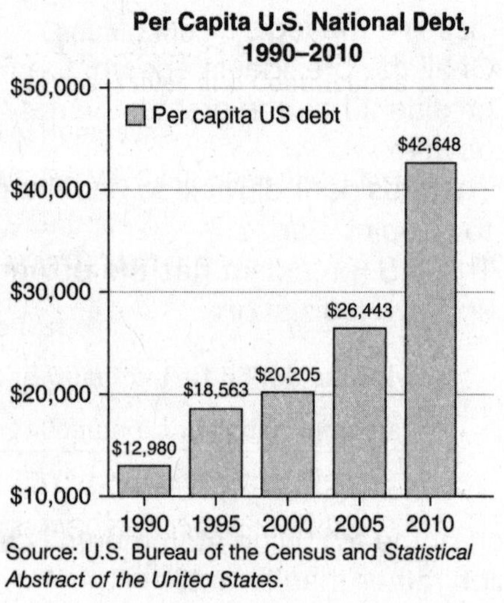

Source: U.S. Bureau of the Census and *Statistical Abstract of the United States.*

11. Which of the following conclusions is supported by the data in the paragraph and the graph?
   - A. The nation's debt increased at a faster rate than did the U.S. population during the period shown on the graph.
   - B. Every person in the United States owed an average of $20,000 to the government in the year 2000.
   - C. In 1990, the U.S. government owed every American about $13,000.
   - D. The U.S. government sold about $5.7 trillion worth of bonds in 2000.

12. Which action would enable the U.S. government to reduce its debt?
   - A. Postpone payment of that debt.
   - B. Pay interest to foreign investors.
   - C. Pay interest to U.S. investors.
   - D. Raise taxes and cut spending.

Question 13 refers to the following paragraph.

The ninth-century BCE collapse of the Mayan empire is often attributed to a massive drought. But new geological and archaeological evidence from the Yucatan peninsula in Mexico shows that the Maya engaged in massive deforestation, clearing land for crops and burning the wood to bake bricks for their cities and temples. Modern weather models show that the destruction of native vegetation could have contributed to as much as 60 percent of the dry weather that is believed to have ended this civilization.

13. According to the theory presented in the paragraph, what was the effect of Mayan deforestation of the Yucatan peninsula?
   - A. The Mayans needed more land to grow crops.
   - B. Scientists discovered new evidence in the geological record.
   - C. A drought was significantly worsened due to lack of native vegetation.
   - D. Baking bricks required an enormous amount of wood.

Question 14 refers to the following map.

**Great Britain during the Industrial Revolution, 1830**

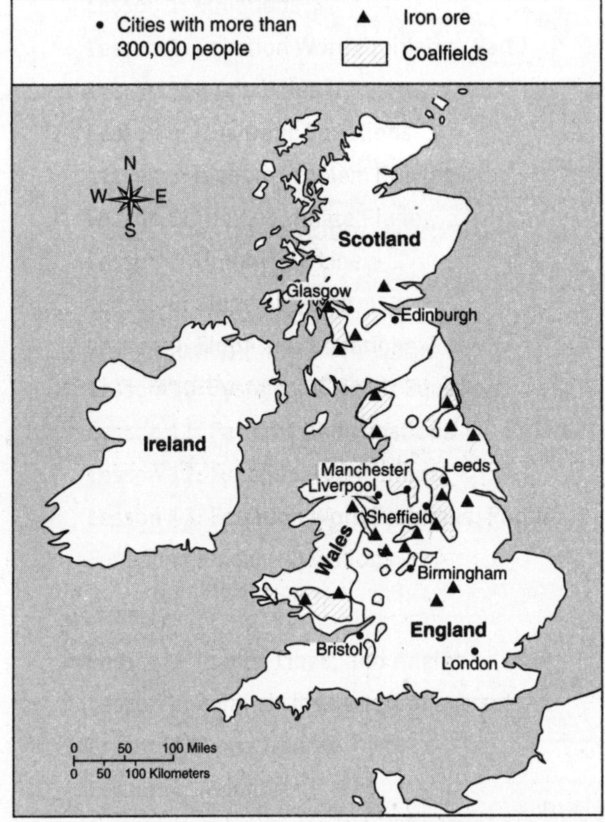


14. Which of the following is a conclusion based on the map rather than a supporting detail from the map?
    - A. The Industrial Revolution took place in Great Britain around the year 1830.
    - B. More than 300,000 people lived in Sheffield around 1830.
    - C. Many cities had large populations because nearby coal and iron ore deposits meant jobs.
    - D. There was a large area with coal deposits in southern Wales around 1830.

15. When a nation follows a policy of appeasement, it makes concessions to an aggressor in order to preserve the peace.

    Which of the following is an example of appeasement?
    - A. Italy's support of Spanish Nationalists in the Spanish Civil War in the late 1930s
    - B. Great Britain's acceptance of Germany's takeover of Austria and Czechoslovakia in the late 1930s
    - C. Germany's 1939 invasion of Poland, which started World War II
    - D. Japan's alliance with Germany and Italy in 1940, which created the Rome-Berlin-Tokyo Axis

16. The Global Positioning System can pinpoint any location on Earth. Twenty-four GPS satellites orbit Earth, transmitting signals that can be picked up by anyone with a GPS receiver anywhere on the planet. A basic handheld GPS receiver gives its location in terms of degrees of latitude and longitude on the global grid.

    Michael bought a basic handheld GPS receiver because he thought it would help him find his way around Los Angeles. Which of the following best explains why his GPS receiver was not very useful for this purpose?
    - A. GPS satellites do not orbit over Los Angeles.
    - B. The latitude and longitude grid does not extend over urban areas.
    - C. Knowing only latitude and longitude does not help a person get around a city.
    - D. Not all of the streets in Los Angeles run in a straight line.

Questions 17 through 19 refer to the following poster.

Source: Library of Congress. World War I Posters Collection. Artist Dan Sayre Groesbeck.

17. The person who designed this poster used irony to make a point. Behind this irony was an assumption with which the designer expected viewers to agree.

    Which of the following statements summarizes this assumption?

    - A. People will give to the war effort because they are doing well economically.
    - B. Financing the war requires selling bonds and raising taxes.
    - C. During wartime, people have little money to spend on their sons.
    - D. People value the lives of their children more than they value money.

18. During which war was this poster part of a government advertising campaign?

    - A. the Civil War
    - B. World War I
    - C. World War II
    - D. the Vietnam War

19. If the government were running a similar advertising campaign today, which medium would probably reach the most people?

    - A. posters
    - B. leaflets and brochures
    - C. print ads in financial newspapers
    - D. television ads on primetime

---

Question 20 refers to the following table.

**The Five Most Populous American Colonies, 1750**

| Colony | Population (estimate) |
|---|---|
| Massachusetts | 188,000 |
| Pennsylvania | 119,700 |
| Connecticut | 111,300 |
| Maryland | 141,000 |
| Virginia | 231,000 |

Source: U.S. Bureau of the Census

20. Which of the following statements is supported by the data in the chart?

    - A. The population of all of the American colonies was less than 700,000.
    - B. Virginia had more than twice as many people as Maryland.
    - C. Most of the population of Massachusetts was of English origin.
    - D. The population of the colony of New York was smaller than that of Connecticut.

Questions 21 through 23 refer to the following paragraph and flowchart.

The U.S. Civil Service system is designed to ensure that people are appointed to government positions because of their skills and abilities rather than because of their political affiliation. Over 90 percent of federal jobs are covered by civil service rules. The typical steps in applying for a civil service job are shown below.

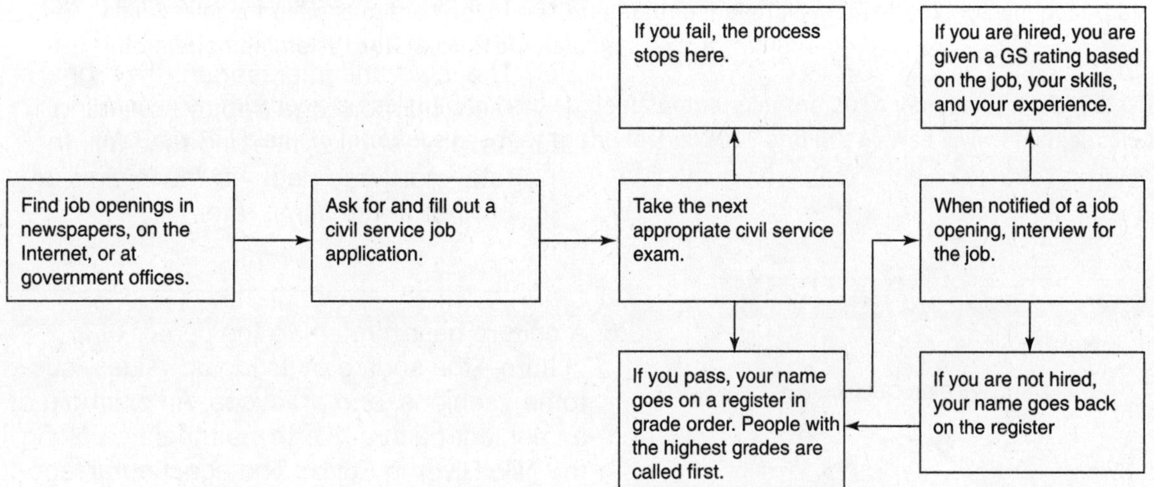


21. Which of the following is the best title for the flowchart?
    - A. A History of the Civil Service
    - B. The Qualifications of Civil Service Workers
    - C. Applying for Civil Service Jobs
    - D. Interviewing for a Civil Service Job

22. What does a civil servant's GS rating probably affect most?
    - A. salary
    - B. length of service
    - C. job security
    - D. education level

23. On which of the following values does the structure of the Civil Service system primarily rest?
    - A. patriotism
    - B. equal opportunity
    - C. freedom of speech
    - D. respect for seniority

Questions 24 and 25 refer to the following graphs.

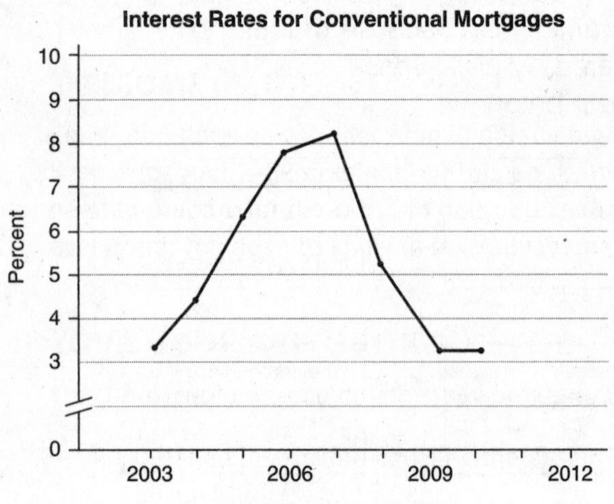


Source: U.S. Bureau of the Census

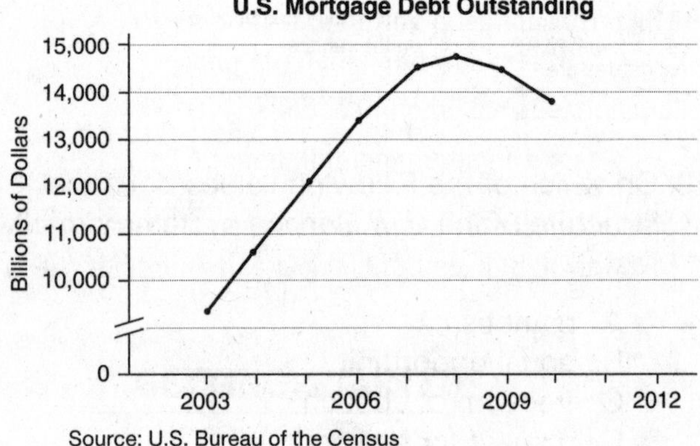


Source: U.S. Bureau of the Census

24. In 2005, what were the approximate interest rate and approximate total mortgage debt outstanding for a conventional mortgage?
   - A. 8 percent and $13,000 billion
   - B. 4 percent and $11,000 billion
   - C. 6 percent and $12,000 billion
   - D. 6 percent and $9,000 billion

25. Based on the graphs, how do mortgage interest rates and total mortgage debt outstanding compare?
   - A. Interest rates rise in direct proportion to decreases in total mortgage debt outstanding.
   - B. The higher the interest rate, the lower the total mortgage debt outstanding.
   - C. The lower the interest rate, the higher the total mortgage debt outstanding.
   - D. As interest rates rise and then fall, the total mortgage debt will move similarly but not at the same rate.

26. A culture hearth refers to the center of a culture—the source of its ideas, values, customs, fashions, and practices. An example of an ancient culture hearth was the area along the Nile River in Egypt. The agricultural, economic, social, artistic, and religious ideas and practices that grew up there spread through trade to other areas of the ancient world.

   Which of the following is an example of a modern culture hearth with worldwide influence?
   - A. Pyongyang, capital of North Korea, which has a 95 percent literacy rate
   - B. Ottawa, capital of Canada, with a population of about one million
   - C. New Zealand, which exports wool and textiles
   - D. Hollywood, California, which produces movies and television shows enjoyed around the world

**Answers and explanations for *Social Studies, Part II* start on page 60.**

# SCIENCE PRETEST
## PART I: SCIENCE SKILLS—10 QUESTIONS

**Directions:** You may fill in the circles next to the correct answers or write your answers on a separate piece of paper.

Questions 1 and 2 refer to the following passage.

For many years, scientists believed that all living things depended on sunlight for their energy. For example, human beings derive energy from food. Our food comes either from plants that require sunlight or from animals, which eat plants that require sunlight.

However, in the 1970s scientists discovered hot springs, called *hydrothermal vents*, in the ocean floor. These vents are miles below the surface of the ocean, far beyond the reach of sunlight. Yet these vents are surrounded by fascinating life forms, including giant red tube worms, eyeless shrimp, hairy-looking crabs, and communities of bacteria that grow like carpets on the ocean floor.

Those bacteria feed on minerals, like sulfur, that flow upward through the vents. The bacteria use a process called *chemosynthesis* to turn the minerals into nutrition. The bacteria, in turn, are eaten by many of the animals that live near the vents. Thus, those animals take in a source of energy that does not derive from sunlight.

1. Which of the following would be a good title for this passage?
   - A. "The Advantages and Disadvantages of Life Near Hydrothermal Vents"
   - B. "Hydrothermal Vents: A Potential Fuel Source for Our Energy-Hungry Economy"
   - C. "Hydrothermal Vents Suggest That Not All Life Is Solar-Powered"
   - D. "Major 20th-Century Advances in Oceanography"

2. Which of the following is a detail that supports the main idea of the passage?
   - A. Many scientists believe that all living creatures depend on sunlight for their energy.
   - B. Hydrothermal vents were not discovered until the 1970s.
   - C. The hairy-looking crabs are covered in structures that enable them to catch tiny particles of food.
   - D. No sunlight penetrates to the world of hydrothermal ocean vents.

Questions 3 and 4 refer to the following passage.

In a *radioactive* element like uranium, atoms give off some of their particles. In the 19th century, chemist Marie Curie discovered that the radioactivity of a compound depends on the amount of a radioactive element it contains.

Then Curie noticed something strange. Pitchblende, a compound that contains radioactive uranium, gives off more radiation than pure uranium. Curie wondered why that would be the case. She guessed that pitchblende might contain another element that was even more radioactive than uranium.

To find out, Curie and her husband isolated the elements that make up pitchblende. After isolating each element, they measured its radioactivity. As a result of this process, the Curies discovered that pitchblende contains a highly radioactive element, which no one had identified before. They named their discovery *polonium*.

3. Which of the following restates Marie Curie's hypothesis about pitchblende?
   - A. Pitchblende contains uranium.
   - B. Uranium interacts with the nonradioactive elements in pitchblende to increase its radioactivity.
   - C. Polonium was discovered by the Curies as a result of their experiment.
   - D. Pitchblende contains an element that is more radioactive than uranium.

4. Which of the following is a reasonable conclusion based on Curie's experiment?
   - A. Pitchblende is more radioactive than pure uranium because it contains polonium.
   - B. Polonium is only one of many reasons why pitchblende is more radioactive than pure uranium.
   - C. Marie Curie would become famous.
   - D. The Curies were not the first physicists to isolate polonium.

Questions 5 and 6 refer to the following passage.

The **ozone layer** is a part of the upper atmosphere with high concentrations of ozone, a form of oxygen. The ozone layer absorbs between 97 percent and 99 percent of the sun's medium-frequency **ultraviolet light**, which can cause skin damage and even skin cancers. For this reason, depletion of the ozone layer is potentially a global health risk. The ozone layer has been decreasing in thickness for decades due to atmospheric pollution. In particular, **chlorofluorocarbons** (CFCs), used in aerosol sprays and refrigerators, were so harmful to the ozone layer that a global ban was implemented in 1994, and production had almost entirely ceased by 2004. However, this ban was not effective; the hole in the ozone layer that appeared over Antarctica reached its largest recorded size in 2006.

5. Which evidence from the passage supports the conclusion that CFCs remain in the atmosphere for some time after their use?
   - A. The ozone layer started thinning decades ago.
   - B. The hole in the ozone layer reached its largest size after CFCs were banned from production and use.
   - C. CFCs are used both in aerosols and as refrigerants.
   - D. CFCs absorb medium-frequency ultraviolet light.

6. Which of the following additional pieces of evidence would best counter the author's opinion that the ban on CFCs was not effective?
   - A. The ozone hole is not literally a hole but rather an area in which the ozone layer is depleted by more than 50 percent.
   - B. While the ozone layer continues to thin, it is thinning at a rate much lower than it has in the past.
   - C. Skin cancer rates near the equator, far from Antarctica, have not changed significantly since 1994.
   - D. The CFC ban contains a few extremely narrow exceptions for uses where no suitable replacement exists, such as in fire-suppression systems on airplanes.

Questions 7 and 8 refer to the following text.

**Adenosine triphosphate** (ATP) is one of the most important chemicals for the function of the cells of all known living organisms. It stores and transports energy within and between cells. When a cell needs to use this energy, a chemical reaction releases it. Adenosine triphosphate and water can combine to remove either a **phosphate** ($P_i$) or **pyrophosphate** ($PP_i$) from the ATP, leaving **adenosine diphosphate** (ADP) or **adenosine monophosphate** (AMP) respectively.

| Equation | Energy released (in kilocalories per mole) |
|---|---|
| $ATP + H_2O \rightarrow ADP + P_i$ | 7.3 |
| $ATP + H_2O \rightarrow AMP + PP_i$ | 10.9 |

7. Which answer choice describes the process in the equation $ATP + H_2O \rightarrow AMP + PP_i$?
   - A. Adenosine triphosphate is transported from one part of a cell to another.
   - B. Adenosine triphosphate is broken down into adenosine monophosphate and a pyrophosphate, releasing energy.
   - C. Adenosine monophosphate is broken down into water and a pyrophosphate, releasing energy.
   - D. Adenosine monophosphate stores energy, which is transported to another cell.

8. Which of the following chemicals plays a role most similar to that of ATP?
   - A. Lactase, which breaks down the lactose sugar found in milk for easier digestion
   - B. DNA, which is found in the nucleus of every cell and contains instructions for the cell to manufacture proteins
   - C. Hemoglobin, which allows red blood cells to carry oxygen
   - D. Glycogen, which stores sugars that can be broken off in differing amounts when the body needs energy

Question 9 refers to the following information and table.

| | P | P |
|---|---|---|
| w | Pw | Pw |
| w | Pw | Pw |

| | P | w |
|---|---|---|
| P | PP | Pw |
| w | Pw | ww |

9. An equal number of seeds are produced from each of two pairs of flowers. One pair is a purebred pink plant with dominant pink genes (P) and a purebred white plant with recessive white genes (w). The other pair is made up of two hybrid plants, which are pink. The Punnett squares above show all possible combinations of alleles for the two pairs. If a seed is selected at random from the offspring of those two pairs, what is the probability that the selected seed will grow to be white?

   A. $\frac{1}{8}$

   B. $\frac{1}{4}$

   C. $\frac{3}{4}$

   D. $\frac{7}{8}$

Question 10 refers to the following graph.

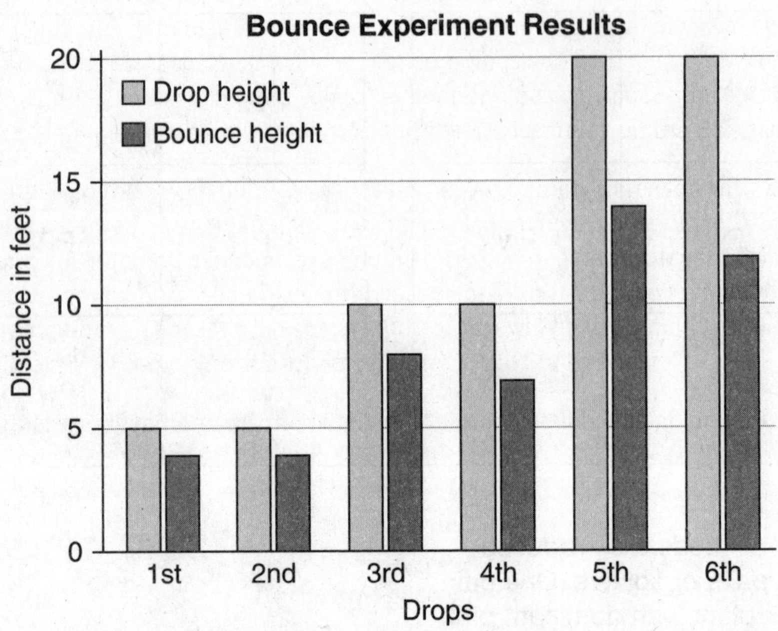


10. A ball was dropped onto a surface from different heights, and the height of the first bounce of each drop was recorded. The graph above illustrates the initial heights and bounce heights of the six trials in the experiment. What was the average (arithmetic mean) difference between the drop height and the first bounce height, in feet?

- A. $2\frac{1}{2}$
- B. $3\frac{1}{2}$
- C. 8
- D. 21

**Answers and explanations for *Science, Part I* start on page 62.**

# Science Pretest

## Part II: Science Content—25 Questions

**Directions:** You may fill in the circles next to the correct answers or write your answers on a separate piece of paper.

Question 1 refers to the following paragraph and diagram.

A neuron is the basic functional unit of the nervous system. Neurons transmit information throughout the body.

**A Neuron**

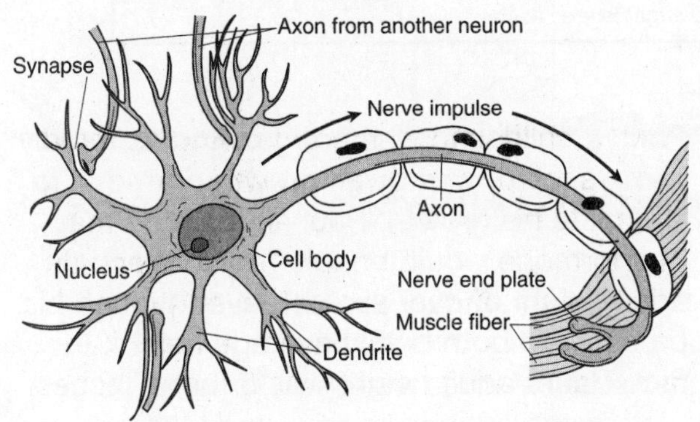


1. Which of the following is implied by the paragraph and the diagram?
   - A. Neurons are part of the endocrine system.
   - B. Oxygen is carried throughout the body by neurons.
   - C. Neurons transmit instructions regarding movement to muscles.
   - D. Nerve impulses travel from the axon to the cell body.

2. A comet is a small body made of ice and dust that orbits the sun in an elliptical, or oval, path. As the comet approaches the sun, its core heats up, releasing gas and dust. The gas and dust stream away from the comet in a tail that may be millions of miles long. Some scientists believe that comets formed when the solar system was born.

   Based on the paragraph, which of the following statements is an opinion rather than a fact?
   - A. Comets are small bodies of ice and dust.
   - B. The orbit of a comet has an elliptical shape.
   - C. Comets release gas and dust as they approach the sun.
   - D. Comets formed when the solar system was born.

3. In a photochemical reaction, light starts the reaction. Light can start a chemical reaction by exciting atoms and molecules, making them unstable and more likely to react with other atoms and molecules.

   Which of the following is an example of a photochemical reaction?
   - A. polymerization, in which long-chain organic compounds are formed from repeating units called monomers
   - B. fractional distillation, in which various petroleum products are separated out of crude oil
   - C. neutralization, in which an acid and a base react to form a salt and water
   - D. photosynthesis, in which green plants use the energy from sunlight to make carbohydrates from water and carbon dioxide

Questions 4 through 6 refer to the following chart.

**Some Glands of the Endocrine System**

| Endocrine Gland | Hormone | Function |
|---|---|---|
| Pituitary gland | Growth hormone | Promotes bone and muscle growth |
| Ovary | Estrogen | Stimulates development of female secondary sexual characteristics |
| Testis | Testosterone | Stimulates development of male secondary sexual characteristics |
| Adrenal gland | Adrenaline | Increases heart activity, breathing rate, and blood flow to muscles for "fight or flight" |
| Thyroid | Thyroxine | Regulates metabolism and growth |
| Pancreas | Insulin | Regulates blood sugar levels |

4. What is the function of the hormone thyroxine?
   - A. It controls female secondary sexual characteristics.
   - B. It controls male secondary sexual characteristics.
   - C. It speeds up the pulse and breathing rate for "fight or flight."
   - D. It helps control metabolism and growth.

5. People who have one form of the disease diabetes mellitus do not produce enough insulin. Based on the chart, what is the general effect of this disease?
   - A. stunted growth
   - B. excess growth
   - C. overproduction of estrogen
   - D. uncontrolled blood sugar levels

6. Paul, a child who was not growing as rapidly as he should, was given growth hormone to stimulate his growth. Paul anticipated that the hormone would enable him to reach an adult height of over six feet, even though his parents are both below average height. In fact, Paul's adult height was 5 feet 7 inches.

   What was wrong with Paul's thinking?
   - A. Growth hormone is only one of several factors that determine a person's adult height.
   - B. Growth hormone, when administered as a drug, does not affect a person's height.
   - C. In order to grow to over six feet tall, Paul would have had to take insulin, too.
   - D. In order to grow to over six feet tall, Paul would have had to take testosterone, too.

7. An emulsion is a mixture of two liquids whose particles are evenly scattered in one another without dissolving. Emulsions are unstable. After a time, the liquids separate.

   Which of the following is an emulsion?
   - A. tea with sugar
   - B. salt water
   - C. oil and vinegar salad dressing
   - D. food coloring and water

8. Earth science includes the study of Earth's atmosphere—the layer of gases that surrounds Earth—and Earth's hydrosphere—the oceans, rivers, lakes, and groundwater.

   Which of the following scientists would be most likely to apply knowledge from a study of both the atmosphere and hydrosphere to his or her work?

   - A. a geologist who studies volcanoes and mountain formation
   - B. an astronomer who studies the planets of the solar system
   - C. a meteorologist who studies weather patterns and predicts weather
   - D. an ecologist who studies the distribution of populations of organisms

Question 9 refers to the following chart.

**Organisms in a Food Chain**

| Role | Description |
|---|---|
| Producer | A green plant, which produces its own food using energy from sunlight |
| Herbivore | An animal that gets nutrients by eating plants |
| Carnivore | An animal that gets nutrients by eating other animals |
| Omnivore | An animal that gets nutrients by eating both plants and animals |
| Decomposer | An organism that gets nutrients from feeding on dead organisms and returns nutrients to the soil in the process |

9. Earthworms break down large pieces of dead organic material in the soil. What role do earthworms play in the food chain?

   - A. They are producers.
   - B. They are herbivores.
   - C. They are carnivores.
   - D. They are decomposers.

Question 10 refers to the following graph.

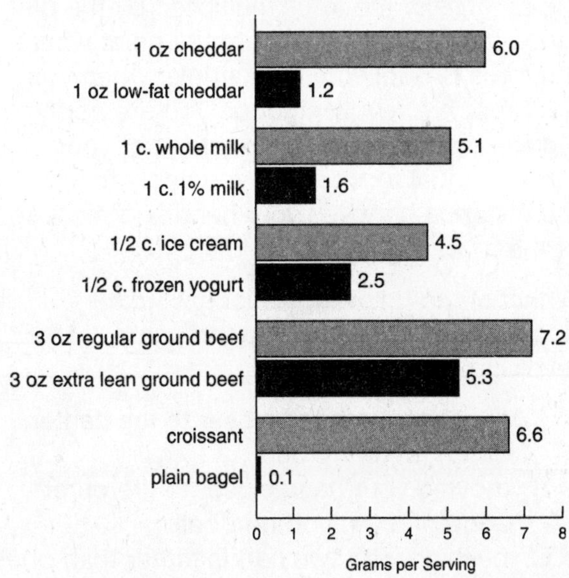


10. Suppose a child's diet usually includes two servings of cheese, four servings of milk, one serving of ice cream or frozen yogurt, one serving of ground beef, and a croissant or bagel every day.

    If the child's parent wanted to decrease the amount of saturated fat in the child's diet, which of the following actions would be most effective?

    - A. switch from regular to low-fat cheddar
    - B. switch from whole milk to 1 percent milk
    - C. switch from frozen yogurt to ice cream
    - D. switch from regular to extra lean ground beef

11. Torque is the ability of a force to produce rotation. The torque of any force is equal to the amount of the force multiplied by the distance from the pivot point to the point where the force is applied. For example, when you go through a revolving door, you are applying force as you push. The torque of your force is equal to the force you apply times the distance between your hand and the axis of the revolving door.

    Which of the following actions would decrease torque as you go through a revolving door?

    - A. moving your hand closer to the center of the revolving door
    - B. moving your hand closer to the outer edge of the revolving door
    - C. pushing with two hands rather than one hand
    - D. leaning toward the door as you push to increase your force

Question 12 refers to the following graph.

**U.S.Consumption of Energy by Source, 1997 (in common unit of metric tons oil equivalent [TOE])**

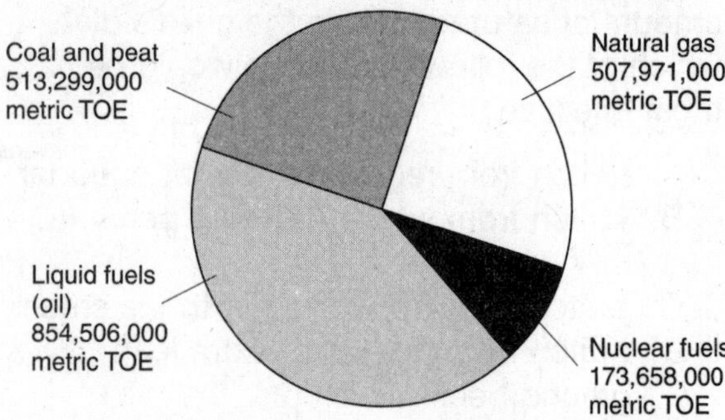


Source: World Resource Institute

12. Of the four energy sources shown, which two are the most similar in the proportion of energy they supply in the United States?

    - A. coal/peat and natural gas
    - B. natural gas and nuclear fuels
    - C. nuclear fuels and liquid fuels
    - D. liquid fuels and natural gas

Question 13 refers to the following paragraph and map.

In 1620, the eastern half of the United States was covered by virgin forest—forest that had never been cut down. Many parts of this region today are covered by second-growth forest—the ecosystem that eventually grows back after farmland is abandoned.

**Virgin Forest of the United States 1620–1990**

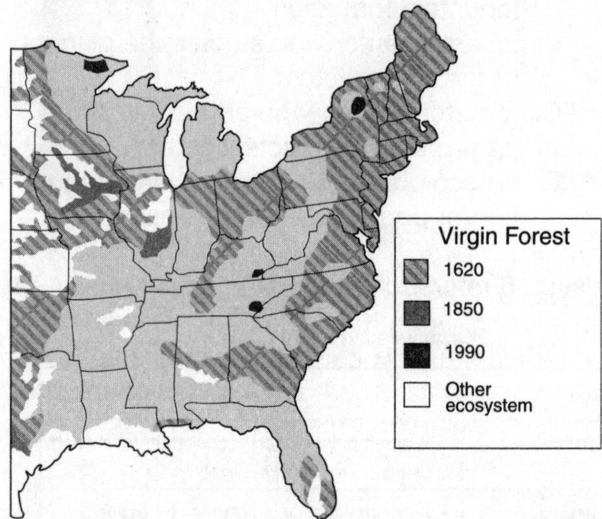


Source: *National Geographic*

13. Which of the following conclusions is supported by the paragraph and the map?

    - A. The western half of the United States had far less forest cover in 1620 than did the eastern half.
    - B. As European Americans moved from the East Coast westward between 1620 and 1850, they cut down forests to build farms.
    - C. A number of relatively large areas of virgin forest remain in the eastern half of the United States today.
    - D. Today's second-growth forests in the eastern United States have fewer species of plants and animals than the virgin forest did.

Questions 14 and 15 refer to the following information and diagram.

The seasons occur because the axis of Earth is tilted. At different times of year, different parts of Earth get more hours of higher-intensity sunlight. As the diagram shows, summer begins in the Southern Hemisphere on December 21, when that hemisphere is tilted toward the sun.

**Why Earth Has Seasons**

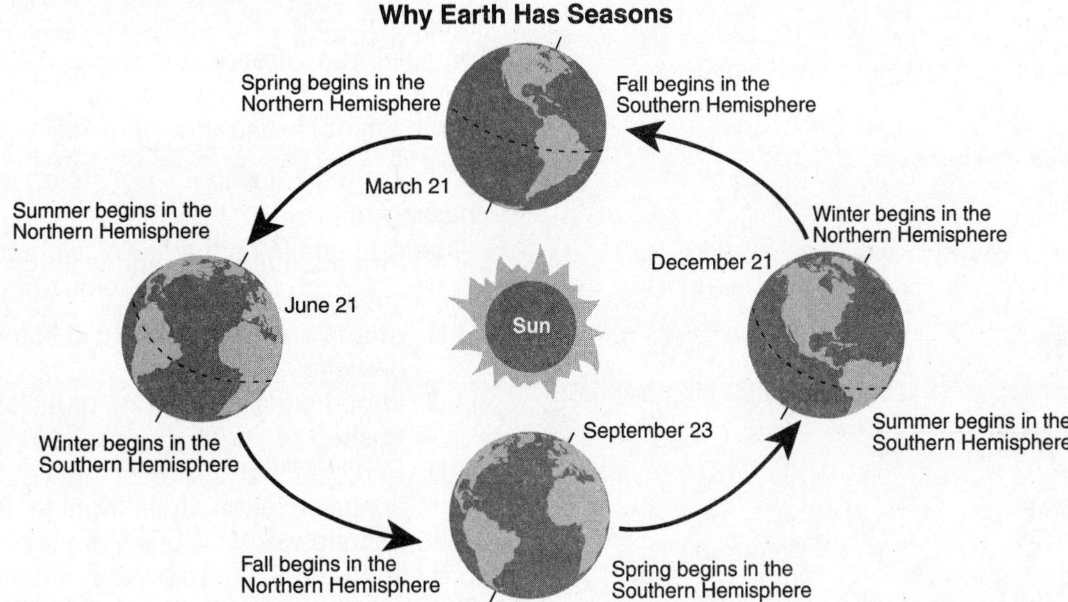


14. Which portion of Earth is tilted toward the sun on June 21?
    - A. the Southern Hemisphere
    - B. the Northern Hemisphere
    - C. the axis
    - D. the equator

15. Which of the following statements is supported by the information in the diagram?
    - A. Earth rotates once around its axis each and every day.
    - B. When it is summer in the Northern Hemisphere, it is summer in the Southern Hemisphere.
    - C. On March 21, the Northern Hemisphere is tilted toward the sun.
    - D. On the first day of spring and fall, neither the Northern Hemisphere nor the Southern Hemisphere is tilted toward the sun.

16. Ecologists use a tool called a quadrat when doing field studies of plant distribution. A quadrat is an open, four-sided structure about a meter square. It is placed on the ground, whether in a meadow, on a hillside, or at the beach. The ecologist then counts the plants of different species inside the quadrat. By using a quadrat, an ecologist can get a more accurate understanding of species distribution than by doing a random count.

    Which of the following statements is a conclusion based on the given facts?
    - A. A quadrat is a tool used by ecologists.
    - B. A quadrat is a frame about a meter square.
    - C. To use a quadrat, the ecologist places it on the ground.
    - D. A quadrat makes plant distribution estimates more reliable.

17. According to Charles's Law, when the pressure of a gas remains constant, the volume of a quantity of gas varies directly with the temperature. In other words, as the temperature of a gas rises, the volume of the gas increases.

Which of the following graphs illustrates Charles's Law?

A.

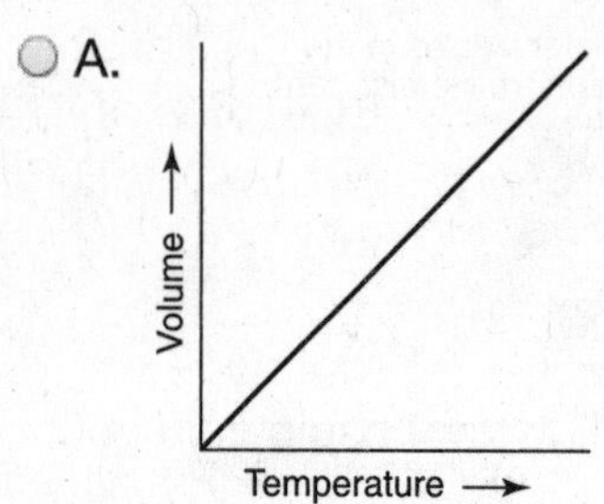


B.

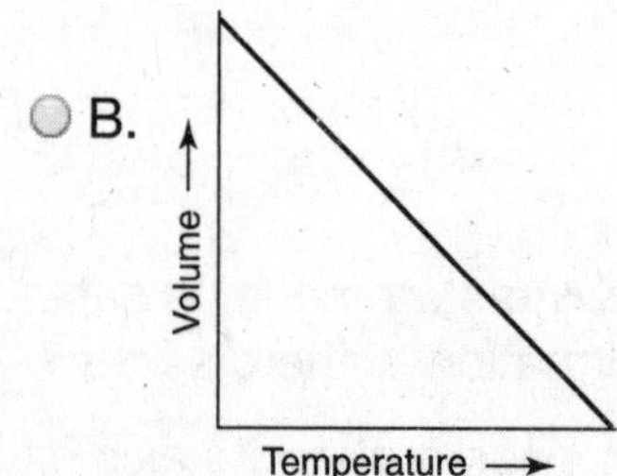


C.

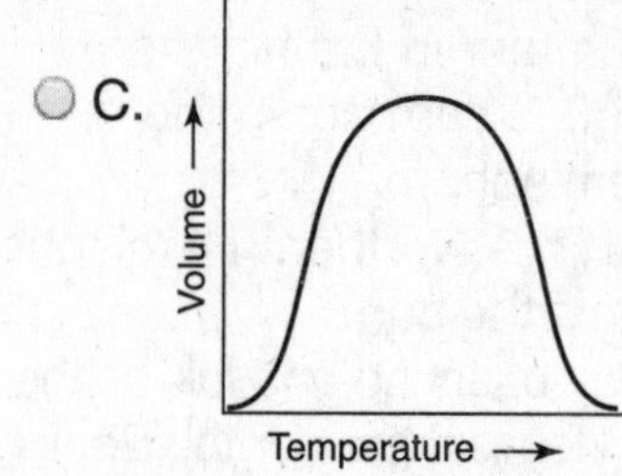


D.

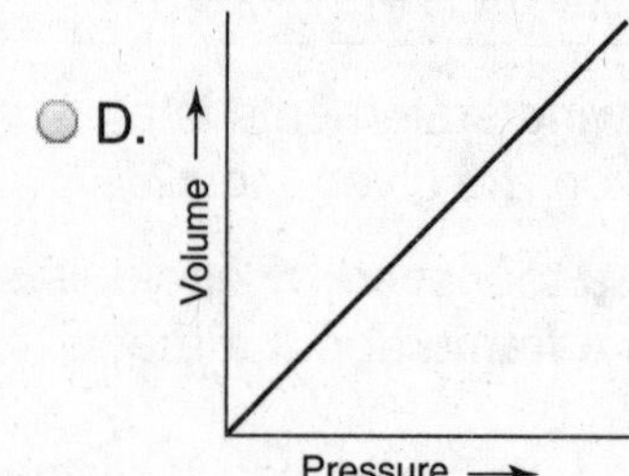


18. At the beginning of the twentieth century, only three subatomic particles were known: protons, neutrons, and electrons. In the last half of the century, dozens of new particles were discovered using new technology. Machines called particle accelerators push particles to tremendous speeds. When two particles collide at high speed, they annihilate each other and new particles are formed.

Which of the following is not stated in the passage?

- A. Protons, neutrons, and electrons are subatomic particles.
- B. Atoms are composed of subatomic particles.
- C. In particle accelerators, particles are pushed to very high speeds.
- D. Particles that collide at high speed annihilate each other, forming new particles.

19. Density is the amount of matter, or mass, in a given volume of a substance. To find the density of an object, you divide its mass by its volume. A student wanted to find the density of a 3-cm cube of lead. First, she used a scale to find the mass of the cube. Next, she calculated the volume by multiplying 3 cm × 3 cm × 3 cm. Finally, she divided the volume by the mass to find the density of the lead cube.

Why was the density the student calculated inaccurate?

- A. A scale cannot be used for finding mass.
- B. Multiplying three sides of the cube will not give the cube's volume.
- C. The student should have found the volume first.
- D. The student should have divided the mass by the volume.

Questions 20 and 21 refer to the following information and diagram.

When the U.S. Mint had to design a new dollar coin to replace the old Susan B. Anthony dollar, it faced a problem. It wanted to design an appealing, distinctive golden-color coin that vending machines would recognize as an Anthony dollar, which looks like a quarter. Vending machines identify coins by their weight, size, and electromagnetic signature. They test a coin by passing an electric current through it and measuring the resulting magnetic field. Thus the new Sacagawea dollar coin had to be similar to the Anthony dollar in size, weight, and electromagnetic signature.

Size and weight were easy to imitate, but the electromagnetic signature was not. The Anthony dollar had a copper core covered by a silver-colored copper-nickel alloy. All the golden alloy sample coins had three times as much electrical conductivity as the Anthony dollar. Vending machines did not recognize them. Finally, metallurgists came up with the idea of adding manganese, which has low conductivity, to zinc and copper. The result was a coin consisting of 77 percent copper, 12 percent zinc, 7 percent manganese, and 4 percent nickel. The pure copper core was covered with a golden alloy of manganese, zinc, copper, and nickel. This golden coin has electromagnetic properties similar to those of the Anthony dollar, so it is recognized by U.S. vending machines.

20. It can be inferred from the passage above that an alloy is

- A. a magnetic material.
- B. a material that stops electricity.
- C. a mixture of metals.
- D. the core of a coin.

21. The U.S. Mint could have solved its technical problems with the Sacagawea dollar by making it out of the same metals as the Anthony dollar. Why did the people at the Mint decide against this?

- A. The metals in the Anthony alloy were too rare and expensive to use in the new coin.
- B. Like nickels, dimes, and quarters, the Anthony dollar was silver-colored and therefore not distinctive.
- C. The electromagnetic signature of the Anthony coin was not recognized by vending machines.
- D. The size and weight of the Anthony coin made it impractical for use in vending machines.

Question 22 refers to the following chart.

**Types of Plants**

| Type | Characteristics |
|---|---|
| Annual | Completes life cycle in one growing season |
| Biennial | Completes life cycle in two growing seasons; flowers during second year |
| Perennial | Lives for years and flowers each year |
| Tender | Sensitive to cold (can be annual, biennial, or perennial) |
| Hardy | Can withstand frosts (can be annual, biennial, or perennial) |

22. Marion has little interest in or time for gardening, yet she would like to have flowers in her front yard. Which of the following types of plants would probably give her the most flowers for the least effort?

- A. annuals
- B. biennials
- C. tender plants
- D. hardy perennials

Question 23 refers to the following information and diagram.

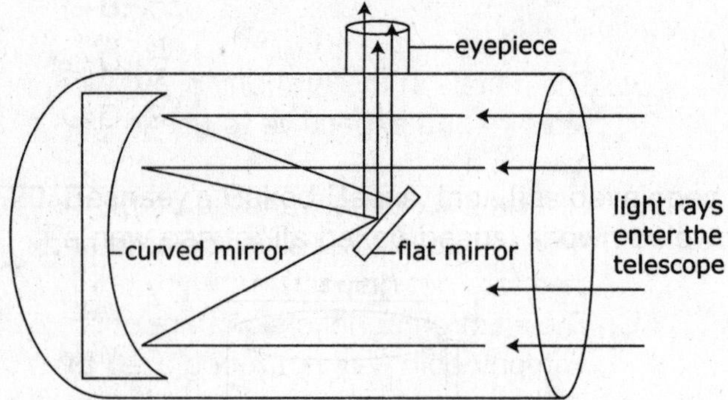


23. If the flat mirror were removed from this telescope, what would happen as a result?
    - A. Light rays would not enter the telescope.
    - B. Light rays would not reflect off the curved mirror.
    - C. A viewer could not see anything through the telescope.
    - D. A viewer could see only objects that were in focus.

24. The discovery of a new drug was once largely the result of trial and error, laboratory experiments, and clinical trials. Although these methods are still used, computer science is being applied to the drug discovery process to refine it and speed it up. For example, computers can analyze genetic material to locate genes that may hold promise in the development of new drugs. Computers can analyze data generated by lab experiments. Computer simulations can even help predict how a particular drug will work under specific circumstances.

    What is the main reason that computers are now being used in the drug discovery process?
    - A. They enable scientists to abandon trial-and-error methods.
    - B. They help scientists analyze large amounts of data in a systematic way.
    - C. They have made laboratory experiments unnecessary.
    - D. They have made clinical trials unnecessary.

25. People planning to visit tropical countries may need to be vaccinated against disease. For example, two to four weeks before a trip, travelers should be vaccinated against typhoid fever. The vaccine is 50 to 80 percent effective. Additional precautions against typhoid fever include avoiding food and water that may be dirty.

    If a traveler is vaccinated against typhoid fever two to four weeks before a brief trip to the tropics, which of the following best explains why he or she should take extra precautions against contracting the disease?
    - A. The typhoid fever vaccination is effective for only a few months.
    - B. The typhoid fever vaccination is only 50 to 80 percent effective.
    - C. The typhoid fever vaccination can cause soreness, fever, and headache.
    - D. Typhoid fever spreads only through air and water.

**Answers and explanations for *Science, Part II* start on page 62.**

Congratulations! You have completed the pretests. Your next step is to check your answers with the Pretest Answers and Explanations that begin on the next page and fill in the study planners that appear on pages 65–69.

# PRETEST ANSWERS AND EXPLANATIONS

## Reading, page 2

1. **B. There are advantages to being sensitive and introverted.** The main idea of a passage is the idea that is most important to the author. The author wrote this passage to convey the idea that being introverted can be beneficial. Choices (C) and (D) both contain ideas the author expresses, but neither of those are the main idea of the entire passage. Choice (A) might be a reasonable inference based on the fourth paragraph but is not the author's main point.

2. **A. empathetic** The third passage states that children with sensitive temperaments "are more likely than their peers to be described by parents and caregivers as empathetic or conscientious." Choice (B) is contradicted by the author's statements that sensitive children tend to grow up to be introverts, and that introverts are less likely than others "to take dangerous risks." The author says explicitly that sensitive children "are not antisocial," so choice (C) is incorrect. Choice (D) is not supported by the passage.

3. **C. a successful collaboration between an introvert and an extrovert** The author mentions the partnership between Jobs and Wozniak in order to support her point that "[m]any successful ventures are the result of effective partnerships between introverts and extroverts."

4. **C. Children who are perceived as "shy" are actually more sensitive than other children to stimuli in their environments.** The author's purpose in the second paragraph is to help her readers understand the temperaments of the so-called "shy" children introduced in the first paragraph.

5. **A. enjoying a quiet dinner with a handful of friends** The author explains that introverts are not antisocial, so an introvert will not necessarily prefer to be alone. However, introverts are more sensitive to stimuli in their environment, so an introvert would not be likely to prefer (B) loud dance music or (C) a crowded street festival. Moreover, the author says that introverts are "less likely to take dangerous risks," and you can infer that (D) "ice slope surfing" is a dangerous sport.

6. **B. The driver may have some difficulty in controlling the forklift.** Paragraphs one and two discuss rear-wheel steering in forklifts. According to the second paragraph, rear-wheel steering is the reason why forklifts are not as responsive as cars and can be difficult to control.

7. **A. driving a forklift and driving a car** The first and second paragraphs discuss the differences between driving a car and driving a forklift.

8. **D. A forklift that is traveling downhill with a heavy load should travel backward.** The third paragraph explains that, when driving a forklift with a load on an incline, "you must keep the load on the uphill side." The graphic reinforces this by showing a forklift with the load on the uphill side. The arrow above the graphic points in two directions, and this suggests that the forklift should keep its load on the uphill side and travel backwards even when going downhill.

9. **C. to explain safe practices to forklift drivers** The author is primarily concerned with helping drivers of forklifts understand and use safe practices. The author's primary focus is on safety, not on convincing people that forklifts are dangerous, as choice (B) suggests, or describing different kinds of forklift drivers, as choice (D) suggests. The differences between driving a car and driving a forklift (mentioned in choice (A)) are discussed in the passage. However, the author's purpose in discussing those differences is to help forklift drivers understand how to operate forklifts safely.

10. **A. The author lists potential dangers inherent in forklift driving and explains how to avoid them.** Each paragraph discusses a different potential danger of forklift driving. 1st paragraph: the forklift's wide swing when turning; 2nd paragraph: the difficulty of controlling a forklift; 3rd paragraph: the dangers of driving on an incline with the load facing downhill; 4th paragraph: large loads that obstruct the driver's view. Each paragraph also discusses how best to deal with those dangers.

11. **B. suggest that GMO foods can be beneficial to struggling farmers.** This detail supports the overall purpose of the passage—to highlight the benefits of GMO foods for world food production. The fact that "small, resource-poor farmers" would choose to produce GMO crops implies that these are more reliable and potentially more lucrative than natural crops.

12. **D. the safety and reliability of GMO foods.** Passage 2 primarily discusses how GMO foods can pose a threat to human health and how GMO crops can be especially susceptible to massive failures.

13. **B. The labels of some foods containing GMO ingredients do not indicate that the products contain genetically-modified components.** The last sentence of the first paragraph states that the American Academy of Environmental Medicine called for "the labeling of all food items containing genetically-modified products." Therefore, at least some GMO foods do not yet have this labeling.

14. **C. GMO foods are largely a positive development for global food production.** The authors of the two passages disagree primarily about whether GMO foods are beneficial or dangerous.

15. **C. Paragraph 4** In Passage 1, Paragraph 4 details how GMO corn crops survived a devastating drought that natural corn crops

would not have been able to withstand. This addresses the issue of reliability raised by the example of the South African corn in Passage 2.

16. **C. a young horse** The context clues in the passage indicate that the speaker is actually a horse. In paragraph 2, we learn that the speaker's mother "whinnied," and in paragraph 4, she is specifically referred to as a horse. In paragraph 5, the speaker mentions that he and his mother are the master's favorites among all of the horses.

17. **D. a farm** The description of the setting in paragraph 1 indicates that the story takes place in a rural location. In paragraph 6, the speaker's reference to an event that occurred in his "field" also supports this setting.

18. **B. contented.** The overall tone of the speaker's account is positive. The passage describes the pleasant setting of his childhood, the respect he had for his mother, and the kind treatment he received from his master. Even the one negative memory, the occasional teasing by the plowboy, serves to show how the speaker was cared for by his master.

19. **A. affectionate and protective.** Paragraph 5 describes the master's gentle way of treating his horses. Paragraph 7 recounts how the master punished the young boy who was harming the horses.

20. **A. correct the speaker for playing too roughly.** The mother's speech is introduced in paragraph 2 after the phrase "when there was a good deal of kicking." Towards to end of the speech in paragraph 3, the mother implores the speaker to "grow up gentle and good" and "never to bite or kick even in play."

## Writing

### PART I: LANGUAGE SKILLS, page 10

1. **D. change have to has** The third-person singular subject student requires the verb form has.
2. **C. symptoms, such as** This links a fragment to an independent clause to form a complete sentence.
3. **B. change developed to develops** The verb should be in the present tense because the action is occurring in the present. Moreover, the present tense is consistent with the majority of verbs in the passage.
4. **C. sentence 5.** Sentences 1–4 explain basic facts about strep throat. Sentences 5–10 explain what parents should do if their child has strep throat.
5. **A. insert a comma after addition** Generally, an introductory phrase is followed by a comma.
6. **A. After the fever is gone and your child has taken** Combining the detail about taking medicine and the second independent clause about the fever into an introductory subordinate clause results in a smooth, effective sentence.
7. **C. remove the comma** No comma is needed between two verbs in a compound predicate (*bet on a football game or buy a lottery ticket*).
8. **C. threatens** The action is always true, so the present tense is correct. Moreover, the present tense is consistent with the majority of verbs in the passage.
9. **D. Compulsive gamblers display a number of consistent traits.** This is the only topic sentence that sums up the main point and is neither too specific nor too general.
10. **A. it. Losing** Choice (A), which forms two complete sentences, is the only choice given that properly corrects the comma splice here. Choice (D) is incorrect because a comma must precede *and* in a compound sentence.
11. **A. insert a comma after fraud** Commas are required between items in a series.
12. **A. depressed, or they** A comma should precede a coordinating conjunction that joins independent clauses.
13. **B. change Pet Stores to pet stores** This term is not capitalized because it is not the name of a store; it is just a type of a store.
14. **D. replace he with they** The antecedent *owners* is plural, so *they* is the correct pronoun to use.
15. **A. change There's to There are** The verb agrees with the subject, *several factors*, which is plural.
16. **C. be housebroken and trained** Only option (C) has both verbs in parallel structure and creates a correct sentence.
17. **D. remove sentence 10** The sentence about exercise and people is not relevant to pets, the topic of the article.
18. **D. change was to is** The statement is always true, so the present tense is correct. Moreover, the present tense is consistent with the majority of verbs in the passage.

**PART II, ESSAY, page 16**

Your responses to items 1 through 4 may vary but should be similar to the following.

1. Helen Keller's coming to understand what language is
2. Explain how her teacher helped her understand what language is
3. Several specific details from the passage
4. Explain something from the passage; no opinion called for

Your responses to items 5 through 7 may vary. The following are sample responses.

5. This essay will explain how Helen Keller's teacher helped her understand what language is.
6. Helen's teacher taught her to spell words for *doll*, *mug*, and *water*. Helen's teacher ran water over one of Helen's hands while repeatedly spelling "w-a-t-e-r" into the other hand. Helen wrote that "suddenly" she understood something.
7. Although Helen did not initially understand that language relates to things in the world, Helen's teacher patiently taught words to Helen until Helen had a flash of insight about what language is.
8. Responses to item 8 might vary quite a bit. You may have written a rough outline or a map of ideas you wished to include in your essay.
9. **Drafting Checklist** Check off each task that you performed. Give yourself a score of 0–5 based on how many checks you made.

   _______ I wrote a first sentence that clearly introduced my explanation.

   _______ I developed several paragraphs responding to the prompt.

   _______ In my response, I cited specific details from the text to support my central idea.

   _______ In my response, I provided additional relevant information based on my own knowledge and perspectives.

   _______ I wrote a conclusion that summarized my explanation.

10. **Revising and Editing Checklist** Give yourself a score of 0–6 based on how many checks you made.

   _______ My piece was well organized, or I improved its organization so that one idea relates to another.

   _______ I made sure that my sentences were complete, clear, and correct.

   _______ Each of my paragraphs has a central idea and supporting details from the text.

   _______ My piece has a clear beginning, middle, and ending.

   _______ I corrected subject-verb agreement, pronoun agreement, and verb tense errors.

   _______ I have corrected punctuation, capitalization, and spelling.

## Mathematics

### Part I: Quantitative Reasoning, page 18

1. **D. between 1,200 and 1,300** The graph shows that roughly 900 customers came from Zone 3 during this period and that somewhere between 300 and 400 customers came from Zone 4 during the same period. Thus, adding them together will result in a number between 1,200 and 1,300.

2. **D. 1:2** The bar for Zone 1 is a little less than halfway between 400 and 500; round to 450. The best estimate for the bar for Zone 3 is 900. Make sure you write the ratio in the order stated in the problem. Zone 1: Zone 3 = 450:900, which simplifies to 1:2.

3. **C. 16** Divide 10 by $\frac{3}{5}$. The answer is 16 with a remainder. Since the question asks for how many bowls the potter can complete, ignore the remainder.

4. **B. 3** The graph doesn't give the actual number of hours Janelle will work, but it does show how her time spent at one activity compares to another. If she works 100 hours, she will spend 44 hours working at the counter, 9 hours processing new books, and 6 hours repairing bindings. Compare 44 to 15. The number 44 is about 3 times as great as 15.

5. **C. 160** To solve, set up a ratio. 15 percent = $\frac{15}{100}$ . Set that equal to the ratio of employees who make minimum wage to the total number of employees, and use a variable to represent the total number of employees. $\frac{15}{100} = \frac{24}{x}$. Cross multiply: 24 × 100 = 2400. Divide: 2400 ÷ 15 = 160.

6. **D. Y, W, Z, X** Compare the numbers and list in order from smallest to largest: $2.80, $27.10, $27.20, $261.00.

7. **B. 9.25** Add together the amounts of honey the cook will use in the two recipes: 2.5 + 4.25 = 6.75. Subtract that amount from the total amount of honey in the jar. 16 – 6.75 = 9.25.

8. **C. 21** One way to solve the problem is to find a number that is evenly divisible by 6 and 14, and then try dividing that number by each of the answer choices. Go through the multiples of 14 until you find one that is divisible by 6: 14, 28, 42. The number 42 is divisible by both 14 and 6. Then review the answer choices. 42 cannot be evenly divided by 8, 12, 28, or 35. It can be evenly divided by 21.

9. **D. 13** Work backward through the facts. Sheila has worked 10 years. Kathy has worked half as long as Sheila, which equals 5 years. Alice has worked 8 years longer than Kathy. 5 + 8 = 13 years.

10. **C. $\frac{3}{4}$** Two sections, which equal $\frac{2}{8}$ or $\frac{1}{4}$, are marked "blue." Thus, the chance of not getting blue is $1 - \frac{1}{4} = \frac{3}{4}$.

11. **A. 25%** To find percent of change, divide the amount of change by the original price. Then multiply by 100 to change the result from a decimal to a percent: $\frac{\$320 - \$240}{\$320} \times 100 = \frac{\$80}{\$320} \times 100 = 0.25 \times 100 = 25\%$.

12. **C. 5.5** The median is the middle number of a group of numbers. Arrange the numbers of accounts in order: 2, 4, 4, 4, 5, 6, 6, 7, 7, 8. The middle numbers are 5 and 6. When there are two numbers in the middle, find the mean of those two numbers: $\frac{5+6}{2} = 5.5$ .

13. **A. $4,500** Add together the amounts that Jim has sold so far in April: $2,500 + $5,000 = $7,500. Then subtract that amount from the minimum his employers expect him to sell: $12,000 – $7,500 = $4,500.

14. **C. $\frac{3}{10}$ feet** Subtract the length of the shorter stick from the length of the longer one: $3\frac{4}{5} - 3\frac{1}{2}$ . To solve, find a common denominator: $3\frac{8}{10} - 3\frac{5}{10} = \frac{3}{10}$ .

15. **C. 3.75** The number line is divided into increments, each of which equals one-fourth, or .25. The dot is three increments to the right of the number 3, so its value is 3.75.

16. **D. More students received either an A or a B than received either a D or an F.** Based on the graph, 6 students received an A and 7 students a B. 7 + 6 = 13. Also, 7 students received a D, and 3 received an F. 7 + 3 = 10. Since 13 is greater than 10, the A-and-B group is larger than the D-and-F group. Choice (A) is not supported because some students did fail the exam. Choice (B) suggests that most—more than half—of Marjorie's students received an A or B. However, the A-and-B group (13 students) is smaller than the total number of students who got a C (12 students), a D (7 students), or an F (3 students). Choice (C) is unsupported because the graph has no information about how any other group of students would perform.

17. **D. $6,000** Use the formula provided to find the interest Jason's deposit would earn over the five years. As directed, express the percent interest as a decimal, 0.04. $5000 × 5 (years) × 0.04 = $1000. Then, to find out how much is in the account at the end of the five years, add that interest to Jason's original deposit: $5,000 + $1,000 = $6,000.

18. **C. 720** To find out how many possible orderings, or sequences, of six items are possible, multiply. There are six possibilities for the first movie. Then after the first movie has been chosen, there are five possibilities for the second movie, then four for the third movie, and so on: 6 × 5 × 4 × 3 × 2 × 1 = 720.

### Part II: Algebraic Reasoning and Geometry, page 22

1. **B. Point B** Convert the improper fraction to a mixed fraction: $-\frac{16}{6} = -2\frac{4}{6} = -2\frac{2}{3}$ , which is the value of Point B.

2. **C. 4** Substitute and simplify:
$= 2x - (4y - 3) + 5xz$
$= 2(-3) - (4[2] - 3) + 5(-3)(-1)$
$= -6 - (8 - 3) + 15$
$= -6 - 5 + 15$
$= -11 + 15$
$= 4$

3. **A. 54** To find the magnitude of the change in temperature, subtract the lowest temperature from the highest temperature: $46 - (-8) = 46 + 8 = 54$.

4. **B. 60** The tower, its shadow, and the distance between them form a right triangle. Use the Pythagorean relationship to find the missing distance:

$61^2 = 11^2 + h^2$
$3721 = 121 + h^2$
$3600 = h^2$
$60 = h$

5. **A. 18** To find the volume of a rectangular prism, multiply *base* × *width* × *height*. Here, however, the question asks for the volume in feet, while the measurements are given in inches. Therefore, start by converting the inches of model 413S to feet: 24 in × 72 in × 18 in = 2 ft × 6 ft × 1.5 ft = 18 ft$^3$.

6. **C. $2,600** The question stem gives us two equations. First, we know that $M + L = 4{,}680$. Also, since Levy earns $520 more than Matthew earns, that can be expressed as $L = M + 520$, or, put another way, $M = L - 520$. Since the question asks for a solution for Levy, substitute the value of M from the second equation in the first equation:

$(L - 520) + L = 4{,}680$

$2L - 520 = 4{,}680$

$2L = 5{,}200$

$L = 2{,}600$

7. **C. 16$\pi$** The formula for the surface area of a cone is: $SA = \pi rs + \pi r^2$. In that formula, $SA$ means *surface area*, $r$ represents the *radius*, and $s$ is the *slant height*, or the distance from the bottom of one side of the cone to the point. The diagram indicates that the diameter of the base is 4, so its radius is 2. The slant height is 6. Substitute and simplify:

$SA = \pi(2)(6) + \pi(2)^2$

$SA = 12\pi + 4\pi = 16\pi$

8. **D. $5x^3 - 4x^2 - x + 12y$** Start by removing the parentheses:
$3x^3 + x + 2x^2 - 4x^2 + 14y - 2(y + x) =$
$3x^3 + x + 2x^3 - 4x^2 + 14y - 2y - 2x.$
Then, identify like terms that can be combined:
$3x^3$ and $2x^3$, which add to $5x^3$.
$-4x^2$ cannot be combined with any other term.
$x$ and $-2x$ add to $-x$.
$14y$ and $-2y$ add to $12y$.
Combine into a new expression:
$5x^3 - 4x^2 - x + 12y$.

9. **D. (2, 4)** On scratch paper, draw the three points given in the question stem:

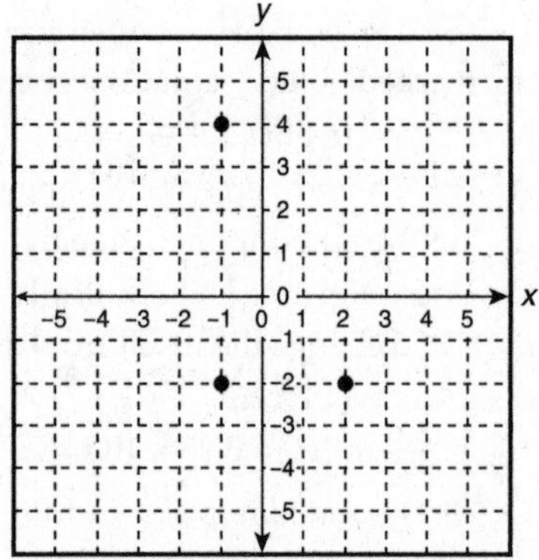


The fourth corner of the rectangle will be at (2, 4).

10. **A. 18 – 2x** Simplify: $4x - 2(3x - 9) = 4x - 6x + 18 = -2x + 18$. That can also be expressed as $18 - 2x$.

11. **D. 4** The simplest way to solve this problem is to try the values of $x$ given in the answer choices in the equation. Starting with (A), where $x$ equals $-4$: $3(4)^2 - 10(-4) = 3(16) + 40 = 88$. That's a great deal more than 8. That result suggests that (B), where $x$ equals $-3$, would also be likely to yield a result that's far too large. Try (C) or (D) to see what result a positive number yields. In (C), $x$ equals 3: $3(3)^2 - 10(3) = 3(9) - 30 = -3$. That's a little too small, so the answer must be (D), $x$ equals 4. Try it to confirm: $3(4)^2 - 10(4) = 3(16) - 40 = 8$. (D) is correct.

12. **D. $x < 4$** Simplify the expression:

$12(x - 2) < 24$

$12x - 24 < 24$

$12x < 48$

$x < 4$

13. **B. $4.54 \times 10^9$** Writing a number in scientific notation involves expressing it as the product of two terms: one term is a number and the other is 10 raised to some power. To find how large the power of ten should be, imagine counting spaces to the left of the decimal point. Choice (B) reflects the correct number and the correct power of 10, or places to the left of the decimal point.

14. **D. 204** The shape of Joe's new property is a trapezoid, and the formula for the area of a trapezoid is $A = \frac{1}{2}h(b_1 + b_2)$. In that formula, $A$ is area, and $h$ means the height, which is 12 yards here. The variables $b_1$ and $b_2$ are the two bases, which here are 10 yards and 24 yards. Plug those values into the formula: $A = \frac{1}{2}(12)(10 + 24) = (6)(34) = 204$. (You can tell that Joe's property is a trapezoid because the two bases are parallel; the right angles indicated at the two ends of the *height* line indicate this.)

15. **A. $p$ = $5.00 – ($n$ – 1) $0.50** If a customer requests only one monogram, the fee is $5.00. However, if a customer requests 2, the price per monogram drops by $0.50 (which you can think of as 1 × $0.50). If a customer requests 3 monograms, the price per monogram drops another $0.50, or 2 × $0.50 in total. Thus, the price per monogram is $5.00 minus a multiple of $0.50. The multiple is one less than the number of hats ordered.

16. **B. 70°** In any four-sided figure, all four interior angles add up to 360°. In a parallelogram, the two obtuse angles are equal to one another, and the two acute angles are equal to one another. Here, you know that the two obtuse angles add up to 220°. 360° – 220° = 140°. Since there are two acute angles, divide that number by two.

**17. C. $y = \frac{2}{3}x + 2$** The answer choices are in slope-intercept form, so begin by finding the *y*-intercept, which is 2. Then find the slope, which represents $\frac{rise}{run}$. Find two points on line H, and count the difference between the *y*-coordinates for those two points in order to find the *rise*. Then count the difference between the *x*-coordinates for those two points to find the *run*. For each vertical increase of two (*rise*), the line moves three numbers on the horizontal axis (*run*). Thus, the slope is $\frac{2}{3}$, and the equation is $y = \frac{2}{3}x + 2$.

**18. A. 20π** The question asks for the circumference of the pool. The question stem gives the distance from the middle of the pool to the edge—that's the radius of the circle, which is half the diameter. Thus, the diameter of the circle is 20 ft. Plug that into the formula for the circumference of a circle: $C = d\pi$. $C = 20\pi$.

**19. D. 2** The slope of a line can be expressed as $\frac{rise}{run}$. To find the slope using two points, subtract one *y*-coordinate from another to find the *rise*, and subtract one *x*-coordinate from another to find the *run*. It does not matter which point you subtract from the other, as long as you are consistent about which point you are subtracting when finding both rise and run. $\frac{-1-(-9)}{4-0} = \frac{8}{4} = 2$.

**20. C. 192π** The formula for the volume of a cylinder is $V = \pi r^2 h$. In that formula, *V* is volume, *r* is the radius of the base, and *h* is height. In this case, you know that the diameter of the base of the can is 8, so the radius is 4. Plug in the values: $V = \pi \times (4\text{ cm})^2 \times (12\text{ cm}) = \pi \times 16\text{ cm}^2 \times 12\text{ cm} = 192\pi\text{ cm}^3$

**21. D. 4,100** To find the area of a compound figure like this one, split it up into simpler shapes. Here, the space can be split into two rectangles:

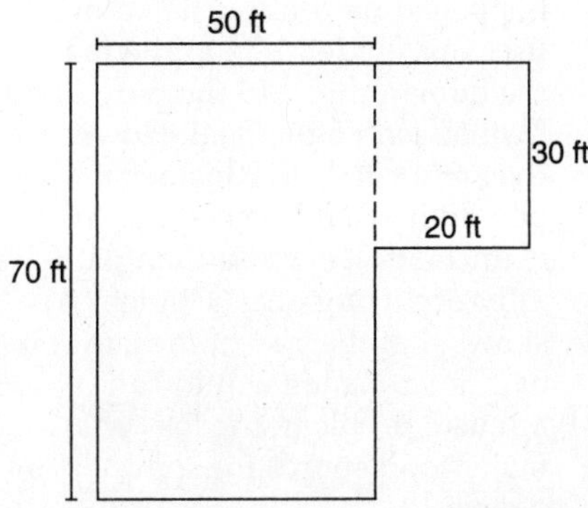


Find the area of the two rectangles and add those two areas together: $(70 \times 50) + (30 \times 20) = 3{,}500 + 600 = 4{,}100$.

**22. D. (2, 5)** There are two ways to solve this problem. First, you could graph both lines. After doing so, your scratchwork should have looked like this:

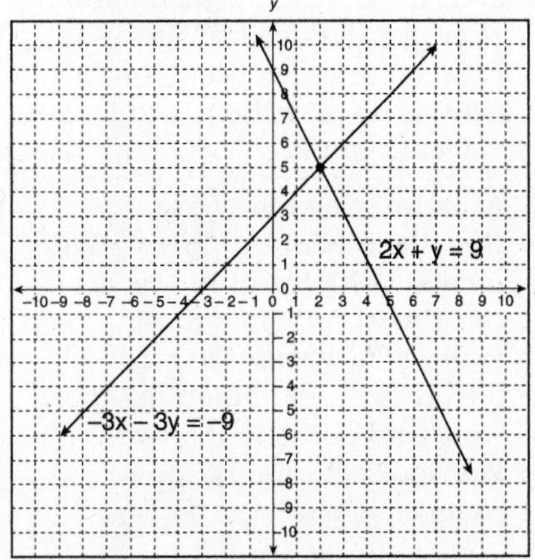


Based on that sketch, the two lines intersect at (2, 5), which means that those coordinates are the solution to the system of equations.

Alternatively, you could also have plugged each answer choice into both equations in order to find the answer choice that works in both equations. For example, to test choice (A) in this way:

Plug (2, –5) into the first equation: $-3x - 3y = -9$.

$-3(2) - 3(-5) \stackrel{?}{=} -9$

$-6 + 15 = -9$. So choice (A) works fine in the first equation. Now try the second: $2x + y = 9$

$2(2) + (-5) \stackrel{?}{=} 9$

$4 - 5 \neq 9$. Answer choice (A) does *not* work in the second equation. Therefore, it is incorrect. Try the other answer choices in a similar way. Only (D) will work in both equations.

## Social Studies

### Part I: Social Studies Skills, page 29

1. **C. The Voting Rights Act of 1965 gave the Federal Government oversight of state elections to end barriers against African American voting.** The passage described the historical events that led to the Voting Rights Act, and how this legislation ended the voting discrimination that certain states enacted after the passage of the Fifteenth Amendment.

2. **C. interpretation** According to the passage, the terms "strict construction" and "loose construction" refer to different ways in which people interpret the range of powers that the Constitution grants to the federal government.

3. **A. The FDA's new regulations would place a financial hardship on small food retailers.** According to the passage, smaller food retailers would feel more of the burden than larger establishments, and the Common Sense Nutritional Disclosure Act seeks to relieve this burden.

4. **C. "devastating"** This word highlights the author's point of view that the FDA's new regulations would be especially harmful to smaller food retailers.

5. **D. The argument is invalid, because it attempts to refute one reason against doing something while ignoring all the others.** The paragraph states that possible danger to the porcupine caribou is "one commonly cited" reason against drilling in the Arctic National Wildlife Refuge. This implies that there are other reasons as well. Thus, the author's conclusion that "we have no reason not to drill in the ANWR" is unsupported, since the author has attempted to refute only one of the possibly many reasons against drilling in the refuge.

6. **A. Some people depend on the porcupine caribou for food.** The primary evidence in this argument is that almost all of the species that have ever lived on Earth have gone extinct, and the vast majority of these extinctions happened naturally. The author uses this evidence to argue that the human threat to the porcupine caribou isn't a big deal. However, the author fails to consider the possibility that human-caused extinctions are worse than naturally-occurring ones. Choice (A) shows that the loss of the caribou by human hands would cause a severe problem: the loss of a major food source for some people.

7. **B. The map shows that most of the Warsaw Pact countries lay between the Soviet Union and Western countries, including France, West Germany, and Great Britain.** The passage states that the World War II Allies, which included France and Great Britain, formed NATO. It also states that West Germany was allowed to join NATO. And the map makes clear that the smaller Warsaw Pact countries lay geographically between those nations and the Soviet Union.

8. **A. In forming the Warsaw Pact, the Soviet Union greatly increased its access to oceanic coastlines.** Although most of the Warsaw Pact countries touched the ocean, most of their borders were land borders, and two of the Warsaw Pact countries were completely landlocked.

9. **A. $40\frac{2}{3}$** The three northernmost states are Maine (ME), New Hampshire (NH) and Vermont (VT). To find the average, sum the rainfall of each state and divide by 3. $\frac{41+42+39}{3} = 40\frac{2}{3}$ .

10. **B. steadily increased, surpassing that of white voters in the 2012 elections.** The solid gray line corresponds to the rate at which black voters participated in presidential elections. It increases consistently from year to year, and shows the highest rate of all groups in the 2012 election.

### Part II: Social Studies Content, page 33

1. **B. the West Indies to the British colonies; the British colonies to Africa; Africa to the West Indies** According to the map, the West Indies exported sugar and molasses to the British colonies in North America. The British colonies exported rum to Africa. Finally, Africa exported slaves and gold to the West Indies. The trade routes formed a triangle.

2. **A. Cargo ships never had to sail empty on any leg of a profitable triangular journey.** This is a general conclusion that is supported by the details of the map, which show goods traveling along each leg of the triangular trade route. Therefore, a very profitable journey must have meant a ship carried cargo on each leg of the route. The remaining options state details that may or may not be confirmed by the map.

3. **B. Commercial bank** According to the descriptions, commercial banks provide services to businesses and other corporations. None of the other descriptions describe financial institutions making loans to companies. They focus either on national financial systems or on individual borrowers.

4. **B. tainted system** "Tainted" is a loaded word that indicates the author's belief that a "strong-mayor" system is inherently corrupt.

5. **D. No, because no indication is given that the current mayor will behave as past mayors did.** A strong-mayor system may enable—but does not guarantee—corruption. Past corruption is not by itself enough reason to have a strong suspicion toward the current government.

6. **D. serving on a jury** Serving on a jury, like voting, is a civic duty of each citizen. It is a way to participate in the judicial branch of government. Note that although choice (B), displaying the American flag, is a patriotic act, it does not involve participating in government

in any way and so is not a way of participating in the political system.

7. **D. law and order** The hallmark of military rule is strict control over the citizenry; in other words, law and order.

8. **C. The French president has the power to dissolve the legislature, while the U.S. president does not.** The checkmark in the last row under "France" indicates that the French president can dissolve the legislature. The U.S. president does not have this power.

9. **B. Of all the presidents shown, the French president has the greatest variety of powers.** This statement is a conclusion, a generalization based on the details in the chart. Choices (A), (C), and (D) are specific details from the chart.

10. **D. The U.S. Supreme Court ruling in *Plessy v. Ferguson* was wrong because it infringed on freedoms guaranteed in the Constitution.** This statement is a rephrasing of the dissenting justice's opinion, or belief, about the case. The other statements are all facts from the paragraph.

11. **A. The nation's debt increased at a faster rate than did the U.S. population during the period shown on the graph.** You can tell this is true because the per capita debt figure increased steadily from 1990 to 2010. This would happen only if the debt increased faster than the population of the United States.

12. **D. Raise taxes and cut spending.** You can conclude from the text that to cut the national debt, the U.S. government would have to increase income (raise taxes) and lower costs (cut spending).

13. **C. A drought was significantly worsened due to lack of native vegetation.** According to the passage, the deforestation caused a significant portion of the drought that led to the Mayan collapse. Choices (A) and (D) are both causes, not effects, of the deforestation.

14. **C. Many cities had large populations because nearby coal and iron ore deposits meant jobs.** Coal and iron ore were among the most important raw materials of the Industrial Revolution. By examining the relationship of the location of the cities to that of the coalfields and iron ore deposits, you can conclude that Great Britain's most populous cities (with the exception of London) were large partly because of their proximity to the important raw materials of the Industrial Revolution. The remaining statements are details from the map.

15. **B. Great Britain's acceptance of Germany's takeover of Austria and Czechoslovakia in the late 1930s** Of all the options, this is the only one that has the element of concession without opposition that is the hallmark of appeasement.

16. **C. Knowing only latitude and longitude does not help a person get around a city.** Being able to pinpoint precise location in terms of latitude and longitude is not of much value in a city unless this information is translated into streets and highways. A basic receiver such as the one described in the paragraph does not do that; however, other more sophisticated models, such as those built into vehicle dashboards or cellular phones, do just that.

17. **D. People value the lives of their children more than they value money.** This is the underlying assumption of the poster: that Americans have been willing to send their sons into battle where they risk their lives, but haven't been donating money to the war cause with equal willingness. The poster thus plays upon their sense of guilt.

18. **B. World War I** The poster is dated 1917, so the war is World War I.

19. **D. television ads on prime time** Today the government could probably reach the most people with TV ads rather than print ads, because so many people watch TV.

20. **D. The population of the colony of New York was smaller than that of Connecticut.** Since the chart shows the five colonies with the largest populations in 1750, it follows that any colony not listed has a population smaller than that of Connecticut, which ranked fifth. The other options are not supported by the data in the table.

21. **C. Applying for Civil Service Jobs.** This title best describes what the flowchart shows—the steps in applying for a civil service job.

22. **A. salary** The GS rating of a job, based on the job description and the candidate's skills and experience, is directly related to the salary level of the position. The other options would not be affected by the GS rating.

23. **B. equal opportunity** Since Civil Service jobs are open to all who apply and are awarded on merit, they are designed to provide equal opportunity for employment, regardless of gender, race, ethnicity, party affiliation, or other factors.

24. **C. 6 percent and $12,000 billion** Locate 2005 on each graph. (Note that each tic mark on the horizontal axis indicates a year, even if it is not labeled.) The first graph shows the mortgage interest rate was about 6 percent in 2005. The second graph shows the total outstanding mortgage debt was about $12,000 billion in 2005.

25. **D. As interest rates rise and then fall, the total mortgage debt will move similarly but not at the same rate.** Look at the general trend shown by each graph. Note that as interest rates rise and fall, the mortgage debts rise similarly but fall at a different rate.

26. **D. Hollywood, California, which produces movies and television shows enjoyed around the world** The movies and TV shows that originate in Hollywood are distributed worldwide, helping to spread American popular culture to other nations.

## Science

### Part I: Science Skills, page 41

1. **C. "Hydrothermal Vents Suggest That Not All Life Is Solar-Powered"** The author's main point is that some of the life forms around hydrothermal vents derive energy from a source other than the sun. Choice (C) captures that idea. Choices (A) and (B) mischaracterize the subject matter of the passage, and choice (D) is far too broad.

2. **D. No sunlight penetrates to the world of hydrothermal ocean vents.** Only choice (D) supports the idea that some life forms derive energy from a source other than the sun. Choice (A) distorts the meaning of the first line of the passage. Choice (B) is true but does not serve to support this idea. Choice (C) is not stated in the passage.

3. **D. Pitchblende contains an element that is more radioactive than uranium.** A hypothesis is a guess made by a scientist before the scientist conducts an experiment. Before Marie Curie and her husband conducted their experiment with pitchblende, she guessed that pitchblende was more radioactive than pure uranium because pitchblende contained a radioactive element other than uranium. Curie already knew choice (A) to be true, so it was not a hypothesis she intended to test. Choice (B) is not stated in the passage. Choice (C) describes the outcome of the Curies' experiment—not their initial hypothesis.

4. **A. Pitchblende is more radioactive than pure uranium because it contains polonium.** As a result of their experiment, the Curies discovered that pitchblende contained polonium, a highly radioactive element. This suggests that Marie Curie's initial hypothesis was correct. Choice (B) is not supported by the passage. Choice (C) is unsupported by the passage.

5. **B. The hole in the ozone reached its largest size after CFCs were banned from production and use.** According to the passage, the hole in the ozone layer reached its largest size after CFCs were discontinued. The presence of CFCs that stayed in the atmosphere for years after use is a likely explanation for this phenomenon.

6. **B. While the ozone layer continues to thin, it is thinning at a rate much lower than it has in the past.** If the rate of ozone depletion has slowed significantly, it is likely that the CFC ban was at least partially effective.

7. **B. Adenosine triphosphate is broken down into adenosine monophosphate and a pyrophosphate, releasing energy.** The text describes this relation between ATP (adenosine triphosphate), AMP (adenosine monophosphate), and $PP_i$ (pyrophosphate).

8. **D. Glycogen, which stores sugars that can be broken off in differing amounts when the body needs energy** Both glycogen and ATP store energy, and both can release different amounts of energy depending on the needs of the cell or organism.

9. **A.** $\frac{1}{8}$ Because white is a recessive trait, a plant must have two white genes (ww) in order to be white. Of the 8 possible outcomes illustrated in the Punnett squares, only one has this pair of genes.

10. **B.** $3\frac{1}{2}$ The difference between the drop height and the first bounce height for the first drop was 1 foot. For the second, it was also 1 foot, and for the third, 2 feet. Find these differences for all the drops. The average of a set of items is the sum of the items divided by the number of items in the set. Thus, to find the average here, add all the differences and divide by the number of drops:

$$\frac{1+1+2+3+6+8}{6} = \frac{21}{6} = 3\tfrac{1}{2}$$

### Part II: Science Content, page 45

1. **C. Neurons transmit instructions regarding movement to muscles.** Since neurons transmit information and the function of muscles is to move, it follows that neurons transmit instructions regarding movement to muscles. The paragraph and the diagrams show that all the other options contain incorrect information.

2. **D. Comets formed when the solar system was born.** Opinions are usually signaled by words like "believe," "think," or "feel." In this case, the last sentence of the paragraph states that scientists believe that comets formed when the solar system was born, showing that this is an opinion.

3. **D. photosynthesis, in which green plants use the energy from sunlight to make carbohydrates from water and carbon dioxide** The key element in a photochemical reaction is light. Of the options listed, only photosynthesis involves light.

4. **D. It helps control metabolism and growth.** First locate thyroxine in the "Hormone" column, then move along the row to the "Function" column to find the answer.

5. **D. uncontrolled blood sugar levels** The chart shows that insulin regulates blood sugar levels, so problems with insulin production will cause problems with blood sugar levels.

6. **A. Growth hormone is only one of several factors that determine a person's adult height.** Growth hormone alone does not determine height. A person's genetic make-up—the height of his parents and other family members—contributes, as do nutrition and the action of other hormones. Paul's expectations were therefore unrealistic.

7. **C. oil and vinegar salad dressing** This is an example of an emulsion—two liquids

mixed together but not dissolving. If you let oil and vinegar dressing stand, the oil will rise to the top. The other options are all solutions, which do not separate over time.

8. **C. a meteorologist who studies weather patterns and predicts weather** Knowledge gained from a study of the atmosphere and hydrosphere is closely related to the study of weather, which is influenced by both.

9. **D. They are decomposers.** Since earthworms are feeding on dead organic matter, which comes from dead organisms, they must be decomposers.

10. **B. switch from whole milk to 1 percent milk** The switch from whole milk to low-fat milk reduces fat intake by 3.5 grams/serving. While the difference in saturated fat per serving is greater in cheddar cheese than in milk, since the child drinks 4 servings of milk daily, this would be a reduction of 14 grams per day. The reduction from switching cheeses comes to 9.6 grams, since the child eats two servings of cheese per day.

11. **A. moving your hand closer to the center of the revolving door** Moving your hand closer to the center of the door decreases distance to the pivot point. Since the force remains the same in this case, when you multiply distance times force you will come up with a lower number, which indicates decreased torque.

12. **A. coal/peat and natural gas** Look on the circle graph for energy sources occupying wedges of approximately the same size. The only two that are about the same size are coal/peat and natural gas, indicating they provide about the same proportion of energy consumed in the United States.

13. **B. As European Americans moved from the East Coast westward between 1620 and 1850, they cut down forests to build farms.** The map shows and the paragraph implies that the virgin forests of the eastern United States were almost all cut down between 1620 and 1850. The paragraph further implies that the forests were cut down for farmland, which has since been abandoned. Based on this information, choice (B) is the only conclusion that is supported by the map and the paragraph. The map and the paragraph either lack support for or contradict the other options.

14. **B. the Northern Hemisphere** First locate June 21 on the diagram and then examine the tilt of Earth. Note that at that time of year, the Northern Hemisphere tilts toward the sun, and it is summer there.

15. **D. On the first day of spring and fall, neither the Northern Hemisphere nor the Southern Hemisphere is tilted toward the sun.** According to the diagram, on March 21 and September 23 Earth's axis is tilted neither toward nor away from the sun, so neither hemisphere is tilted toward the sun. The remaining choices are not supported by the diagram.

16. **D. A quadrat makes plant distribution estimates more reliable.** This option is a conclusion, or a general statement, that is supported by all the details in the paragraph. The other options are specific details paraphrased from the paragraph.

17. **A.**

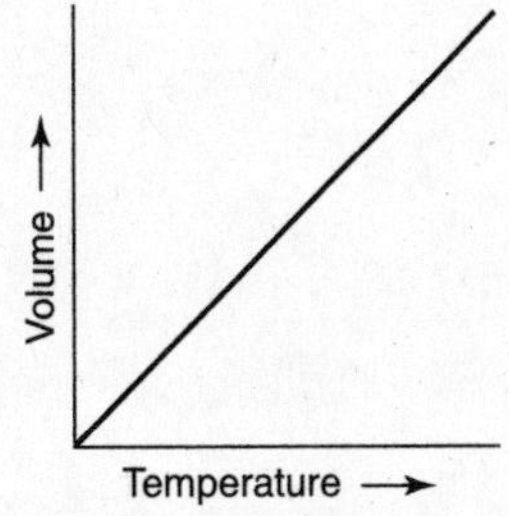


Charles's Law involves the relationship of a gas's volume and temperature. Since volume increases with increases in temperature, the first graph must be correct. Note that you can eliminate choice (D) immediately because it involves changes in pressure, and Charles's Law assumes that pressure remains constant.

18. **B. Atoms are composed of subatomic particles.** This is an assumption made by the writer of the paragraph. He or she does not explain this but assumes it is common knowledge. All the other options are statements made or strongly implied in the passage.

19. **D. The student should have divided the mass by the volume.** The paragraph states that density is calculated by dividing mass by volume. The student did the reverse, which is incorrect. All of the other steps the student followed were correct.

20. **C. a mixture of metals.** According to the passage, the Anthony dollar was made of a copper-nickel alloy, and the final Sacagawea dollar, of a manganese, zinc, copper, and nickel alloy. From these examples, you can infer that an alloy is a mixture of metals.

21. **B. Like nickels, dimes, and quarters, the Anthony dollar was silver-colored and therefore not distinctive.** The Mint wanted to replace the Anthony dollar with a distinctive coin—a coin that looked different from the coins already in circulation. Making the new coin out of the same metals as the silver-colored Anthony dollar would not accomplish this.

22. **D. hardy perennials** Hardy plants withstand frost, so they are more likely to survive than tender plants. Perennials come up and flower for many years. Therefore hardy perennials are likely to provide the most flowers with the least effort on the gardener's part.

23. C. **A viewer could not see anything through the telescope.** The function of the flat mirror is to redirect the light rays toward the eyepiece so the viewer can see the object in the telescope's sights. If the flat mirror were removed, the reflection of the object would no longer be visible through the eyepiece.

24. B. **They help scientists analyze large amounts of data in a systematic way.** The ability of a computer to process lots of data, far more systematically and quickly than a human being can, has helped speed up and refine the drug discovery process although the older methods of running laboratory experiments and clinical trials are still also important.

25. B. **The typhoid fever vaccine is only 50 to 80 percent effective.** Because getting vaccinated against typhoid fever does not completely eliminate the traveler's chance of getting the disease, it makes sense that he or she should take extra precautions against contracting this food and water-borne disease.

## KAPLAN TASC TEST STUDY PLANNERS

If you have not already done so, take the pretests starting on page 1. Then check your answers against the Pretest Answers and Explanations starting on page 53. Use your results to fill in the charts that follow so that you can target the areas that need the most work.

### LANGUAGE ARTS: READING, 20 QUESTIONS

Circle the question numbers that you answered correctly in the second column. Write the number correct in the third column. If you do not have time to review all of the Reading sections, target your study to the content areas in which you missed several questions.

| Content Area | Question Numbers | Number Correct Out of Total |
|---|---|---|
| **Interpreting Informational Text**<br>Pages 71–95 | 1, 2, 3, 4, 5, 6, 7, 12, 13 | ____ out of 9 |
| **Analyzing Informational Text**<br>Pages 96–111 | 8, 9, 10, 11, 14, 15 | ____ out of 6 |
| **Reading Literature**<br>Pages 112–127 | 16, 17, 18, 19, 20 | ____ out of 5 |

## Language Arts: Writing

### Part I: Language Skills, 18 questions

Circle the question numbers that you answered correctly in the second column. Write the number correct in the third column. If you do not have time to review all of the Writing sections, target your study to the content areas in which you missed several questions.

| Content Area | Question Numbers | Number Correct Out of Total |
|---|---|---|
| **Writing Effective Sentences** and **Connecting Ideas**<br>Pages 130–147 and 148–159 | 2, 6, 9, 10, 12, 17 | _____ out of 6 |
| **Polishing Your Writing**<br>Pages 186–195 | 4, 16 | _____ out of 2 |
| **Using Grammar Correctly**<br>Pages 196–211 | 1, 3, 8, 14, 15, 18 | _____ out of 6 |
| **Using Writing Mechanics**<br>Pages 215–225 | 5, 7, 11, 13 | _____ out of 4 |

## Language Arts: Writing

### Part II: Essay

Circle the question numbers that you answered correctly in the second column. Write the number correct in the third column. If you do not have time to review all of the Writing sections, target your study to the content areas in which you missed several questions.

| Content Area | Question Numbers | Number Correct Out of Total |
|---|---|---|
| **Unpack the Writing Prompt**<br>Pages 160–161 | 1, 2, 3, 4 | _____ out of 4 |
| **Read the Passage(s) with the Prompt in Mind, Develop a Thesis Statement,** and **Collect Supporting Evidence**<br>Pages 162–167 | 5, 6, 7 | _____ out of 3 |
| **Plan Your Response**<br>Pages 168–171 | 8 | My score is _____ based on the Planning Checklist, page 55. |
| **Draft Your Response**<br>Pages 172–177 | 9 | My score is _____ based on the Drafting Checklist, page 56. |
| **Revise and Edit Your Response**<br>Pages 178–181 | 10 | My score is _____ based on the Revising and Editing Checklist, page 56. |

## MATHEMATICS

### Part I: Quantitative Reasoning, 18 Questions

Circle the question numbers that you answered correctly in the second column. Write the number correct in the third column. If you do not have time to review all of the Mathematics sections, target your study to the content areas in which you missed several questions.

| Content Area | Question Numbers | Number Correct Out of Total |
|---|---|---|
| **Number and Quantity I: Problem Solving** Pages 232–257 | 6, 8, 9, 13 | _____ out of 4 |
| **Number and Quantity II: Decimals and Fractions** Pages 258–281 | 3, 7, 14, 15 | _____ out of 4 |
| **Number and Quantity III: Ratio, Proportion, and Percent** Pages 282–301 | 2, 5, 11, 17 | _____ out of 4 |
| **Statistics and Probability** Pages 302–333 | 1, 4, 10, 12, 16, 18 | _____ out of 6 |

### Part II: Algebraic Reasoning and Geometric Measurement, 22 Questions

Circle the question numbers that you answered correctly in the second column. Write the number correct in the third column. If you do not have time to review all of the Mathematics sections, target your study to the content areas in which you missed several questions.

| Content Area | Question Numbers | Number Correct Out of Total |
|---|---|---|
| **Algebraic Expressions** Pages 334–367 | 1, 2, 3, 8, 10, 13 | _____ out of 6 |
| **Functions** Pages 368–399 | 6, 9, 11, 12, 15, 17, 19, 22 | _____ out of 8 |
| **Geometry** Pages 400–435 | 4, 5, 7, 14, 16, 18, 20, 21 | _____ out of 8 |

## Part I: Social Studies Skills, 10 Questions

Circle the question numbers that you answered correctly in the second column. Write the number correct in the third column. If you do not have time to review all of the Social Studies sections, target your study to the content areas in which you missed several questions.

| Content Area | Question Numbers | Number Correct Out of Total |
|---|---|---|
| **Determine Central Idea and Draw Conclusions, Interpret Words and Ideas**<br>Pages 438–441 | 1, 2 | _____ out of 2 |
| **Analyze and Evaluate Author's Purpose, Reasoning, and Evidence**<br>Pages 442–445 | 3, 4, 5, 6 | _____ out of 4 |
| **Analyze Relationships Between Materials and Interpret Data and Statistics**<br>Pages 446–451 | 7, 8, 9, 10 | _____ out of 4 |

## Part II: Social Studies Content, 26 Questions

Circle the question numbers that you answered correctly in the second column. Write the number correct in the third column. If you do not have time to review all of the Social Studies sections, target your study to the content areas in which you missed several questions.

| Content Area | Question Numbers | Number Correct Out of Total |
|---|---|---|
| **U.S. History**<br>Pages 456–469 | 1, 2, 10, 17, 18, 19, 20 | _____ out of 7 |
| **Civics and Government**<br>Pages 470–483 | 4 ,5, 6, 21, 22, 23 | _____ out of 6 |
| **Economics**<br>Pages 484–495 | 3, 11, 12, 24, 25 | _____ out of 5 |
| **World History**<br>Pages 496–509 | 7, 8, 9, 13, 14, 15 | _____ out of 6 |
| **Geography**<br>Pages 510–519 | 13, 16, 25 | _____ out of 3 |

## Science

### Part I: Science Skills, 10 Questions

Circle the question numbers that you answered correctly in the second column. Write the number correct in the third column. If you do not have time to review all of the Science sections, target your study to the content areas in which you missed several questions.

| Content Area | Question Numbers | Number Correct Out of Total |
|---|---|---|
| **Comprehend Scientific Presentations** Pages 522–523 | 1, 2 | ____ out of 2 |
| **Use the Scientific Method** Pages 524–525 | 3, 4 | ____ out of 2 |
| **Reason with, Express, and Apply Scientific Information** Pages 526–529 | 5, 6, 7, 8 | ____ out of 4 |
| **Use Statistics and Probability** Pages 530–531 | 9, 10 | ____ out of 2 |

### Part II: Science Content, 25 Questions

Circle the question numbers that you answered correctly in the second column. Write the number correct in the third column. If you do not have time to review all of the Science sections, target your study to the content areas in which you missed several questions.

| Content Area | Question Numbers | Number Correct Out of Total |
|---|---|---|
| **Life Science** Pages 536–555 | 1, 4, 5, 6, 9, 10, 16, 22, 24, 25 | ____ out of 10 |
| **Earth and Space Science** Pages 556–569 | 2, 8, 12, 13, 14, 15 | ____ out of 6 |
| **Physical Science** Pages 570–585 | 3, 7, 11, 17, 18, 19, 20, 21, 23 | ____ out of 9 |

ABOUT THE TEST

# Language Arts: Reading

UNIT 1

The TASC™ Reading Test assesses your ability to understand and analyze written passages. You will read a passage and then answer several questions about it. You will have 75 minutes* to answer approximately 50 questions, which will be based on 7 or 8 passages. On the 2014 TASC, all Reading questions will be multiple choice.

Seventy percent of the Reading Test will cover nonfiction and informational text. Questions in this portion target skills such as:

- Identifying an author's main point
- Describing the structure of a passage
- Analyzing an author's argument
- Restating or applying ideas from the passage
- Understanding words in the context of an informational passage

Pages 72–111 of this unit cover these skills.

Thirty percent of the Reading Test will cover fiction. Questions in this portion target skills such as:

- Understanding plot, character, and theme
- Describing the structure of a story
- Understanding figurative language
- Understanding words in the context of a fictional passage

Pages 112–127 of this unit cover these skills.

* Note: The information given here was the latest information available as of January 2014. It is possible that timing restrictions may change between this printing and your test date. For updates, visit www.tasctest.com.

LESSON 1

# Main Ideas and Details

## The Main Idea

A writer has a message, or **main idea**, to get across. Sometimes the main idea is stated directly; often you have to figure it out yourself. You can find the main idea by asking, "What is the *most important* point the writer is making?" Most of the information in a passage will point to and explain the main idea.

As you read this passage, ask yourself what *main* point the writer is making. The answer will be the main idea.

> When I am reading a poem, I rarely feel alone in the room. The poet and I are together. It's as if the poet wrote a secret diary years ago. I am unlocking it as I sit alone and read.
>
> At times I don't understand what a poem means. I just like the way it sounds or the strange images that it provokes. The world is so peculiar in a poem. At the same time, it is so enticing. Sometimes I understand exactly, as if the poet is whispering to me, as if we shared the same experience.
>
> I must be fully concentrated on reading, or I cannot enter the world of a poem. There are too many daily tasks to attend to—tasks that are very far removed from the magic and imagination involved in a poem.
>
> On a cold, snowy day, I cuddle up inside my apartment and read and read. Then, I'm free to ride through the imagination of all those who came before me.

► Which of the following statements expresses the main idea?

(1) The writer has a love of poetry.
(2) The writer cuddles up on cold days to read.

You are correct if you chose **(1)**. While the passage mentions that the writer reads on cold days, the main point of all the information is how much the writer enjoys reading poetry.

Each paragraph has a main idea. To find the main idea of a passage with more than one paragraph, put together the ideas from all the paragraphs.

## Supporting Details

A writer explains the main idea of a passage with supporting details. **Supporting details** include facts, examples, descriptions, and specific pieces of information. When you read, you need to identify details that support the main idea.

► Which detail helps you understand the writer's main point?

(1) At times, the writer does not understand a poem.
(2) The writer feels poetry is filled with magic and imagination.

You are correct if you chose **(2)**. That detail helps you see that the main idea is the writer's love of poetry. The fact that the writer doesn't always understand a poem is true, but it alone does not support the main idea.

### KEY IDEAS

- The most important point of a passage is called the main idea.
- Sometimes a main idea is stated, but often you must figure it out.
- Supporting details point to and explain the main idea.

### TASC TEST TIP

*Be sure you don't confuse a supporting detail of a passage with the main idea. If you are asked for the main idea, choose the most important, general point.*

# PRACTICE 1

**Questions 1 through 5 refer to the following passage from a diary.**

**EXCERPTED FROM *ARIADNE'S THREAD***

1 I feel I have never had a home. All my life moving from place to place. The only thing that remained the same, that was stable, was Oklahoma. Even the landscape never changed. The towns there never grew up into cities. The people were the same each year, wearing the same clothing, saying the same things.

2 The search for a homeland is part of the Chickasaw migration legend. It was ordained by the deities and began in the past when the people lived in the land of the "setting sun." During the days they would walk over the land, searching for their home. The priests carried a pole. They carried it in their hands by day and planted it each night. During the night it moved about and by morning it would be pointing the direction they were to travel. For a while it commanded the people to journey east, toward the morning sun. They crossed the Mississippi River eventually, and on the other side, the pole finally ceased to move during the night. The land was settled, crops were planted. It became known as the Old Fields. But one morning the pole leaned westward. The people gathered together and began the long journey back. They abandoned their village but did not feel sorrow because the pole had commanded it.

3 And I am still moving, looking for a home. I don't know if I will ever escape my tradition, my past. It goes with me everywhere, like a shadow.

By Linda Hogan from *Ariadne's Thread,* edited by Lyn Lifshin, New York: Harper & Row, 1982.

**1.** How does the author describe herself?

She feels as if she is

A. searching for a place to call home
B. doomed to stay in Oklahoma
C. tired of the sameness in her life
D. being shadowed by failure

**2.** Who do the Chickasaw believe are responsible for making them move?

A. the priests
B. white people
C. themselves
D. the gods

**3.** Why did the Chickasaw not feel sad when they left their homes in the east?

A. They knew they were headed to a better place to live.
B. They had been forced to move east to begin with.
C. They were returning to their ancient homeland.
D. It was simply part of their beliefs to follow the pole.

**4.** Which of the following best summarizes the main idea?

The writer

A. has always lived in Oklahoma and plans to stay there
B. feels trapped by tradition and wants to move far away
C. understands that her tendency to search is part of her Chickasaw heritage
D. believes that people in Oklahoma are all the same

**5.** How does the statement "I don't know if I will ever escape my tradition" (paragraph 3) support the main idea?

It shows that the writer

A. is trying to escape by moving around
B. lives in a more modern time
C. believes in the power of Indian legends
D. accepts that she is Chickasaw

**Review your work using the explanations that start on page 667.**

## STUDY ADVICE

Remember that practice has three levels: Learn and Review, Practice and Review, Assess and Review. For each lesson, absorb the concepts on the left page. Then practice using the page on the right, and carefully review the explanations in the back of the book. Finally, use the question sets at the end of each chapter to assess your progress. Don't forget to review the explanations for those question sets, too.

LESSON 2

# Rephrasing and Summary

**KEY IDEAS**

- To rephrase an idea, put it in your own words.
- To summarize, choose the most important details that explain the main idea of a piece.

## Rephrasing Ideas

**Rephrasing** an idea means putting it into your own words. For example, a friend may tell you that a movie wasn't worth the eight dollars she spent to see it. You might then tell a co-worker that your friend said the movie was no good.

As you read the passage below, rephrase in your mind what you are reading.

> In Canton, Ohio, we take our desserts seriously. There are two local candy stores that receive over 90 percent of the city's candy business: Heggy's and Baldwin's. Those who prefer Heggy's won't befriend anyone who buys their sweets at Baldwin's.
>
> My family has always patronized Heggy's. At the Heggy's factory, Gerty wraps by hand each large chocolate candy in clear cellophane wrap. She's in the back of the store with her hairnet, seated at a table filled with hundreds of chocolates. My favorite chocolates at Heggy's are the dark chocolate creams, peanut clusters, and caramels.
>
> Heggy's aficionados point out that their candy of choice is a larger size and therefore superior. The rivalry runs deep . . . at Easter, Hanukkah, Christmas, Thanksgiving, and all occasions. Baldwin's loyal followers claim its sweets are sweeter. It's a feud over the best chocolate in town.

▶ How do the people of Canton feel about chocolate candy?
(1) They consider it a serious health issue.
(2) They feel it's important enough to take a stand on.

**TASC TEST TIP**

*As you read a TASC passage, check your understanding by pausing occasionally to see if you can rephrase and summarize what you are reading.*

You are correct if you chose **(2)**. The phrase "take our desserts seriously" means that the candy is important to people.

On the Reading Test, the correct answer will not always use the exact words from the passage. You will have to recognize that an idea has been rephrased.

## Summarizing

If you want to tell a friend about a movie you liked, you might **summarize** what happens in the movie. You certainly will not give all the details—that would take too long. A summary includes only the most important facts and ideas.

▶ Which of the following statements best summarizes the difference in opinion over the candy?
(1) Some people prefer Heggy's candy because it's bigger, while others prefer Baldwin's because it's sweeter.
(2) People argue whether to buy Heggy's or Baldwin's candy for different holidays.

You are correct if you chose **(1)**. The last paragraph sums up the difference in people's opinions. Statement (2) merely states a detail in the last paragraph.

# PRACTICE 2

**Questions 1 through 3 refer to the following business letter.**

**EXCERPTED FROM *THE ENCYCLOPEDIA OF BUSINESS LETTERS***

Dear Richard,

1 Attached is a copy of my June 8th letter to Customer Service. After having my car serviced on June 30th, the list of problems has grown. These matters need your immediate attention.

2 Although I did finally receive my copy of the warranty after waiting two months, it is not bumper-to-bumper as Mr. Schecht promised. It also requires service at your facility unless the warranty administrator waives that requirement. I purchased the car from you at a premium price with the expectation that I would have a bumper-to-bumper warranty that I could use at any dealer. I never would have bought this car from you if I knew about these limitations. I expect two things: A written waiver from the warranty administrator that allows me to have warranty service performed at any dealer, and a wrap-around warranty, provided at your cost, that turns this limited warranty into the promised "bumper-to-bumper" warranty.

3 I expect an itemized list of registration costs, and the exact amount of credit I received from the Department of Motor Vehicles for the canceled plates voucher I gave to Mr. Schecht. If there is a refund due, I expect it within 15 days.

4 I expect a proper bill of sale that itemizes and describes the payments for the alarm system and the extended warranty, and includes all the items on the original bill of sale.

5 Your mechanic was unable to locate a cause for the burning smell. The smell persists. I expect your written assurance that if and when the cause for this smell becomes known, you will repair the problem at your cost.

6 The mechanic did *not* repair the left front marker light, although he promised he would. Enclosed is a copy of your invoice for this repair, which wasn't made, as well as an invoice from another dealer who actually made the repair. I expect reimbursement for $22.90.

cc: Joe Smith, Department of Consumer Affairs



**1.** The problems that the writer mentions in the first paragraph and outlines in his letter include which of the following?

A. receiving repairs the writer did not ask for
B. rude treatment
C. lack of proper paperwork
D. the premium price paid for the car

**2.** What does the customer want done about the burning smell?

A. the mechanic to find the cause of the smell
B. the car to be repaired free of charge if the cause of the problem is discovered
C. a refund of the money that was paid to have the problem fixed
D. reimbursement for having the problem fixed by another dealer

**3.** Which of the following statements best summarizes this letter?

A. A letter to customer service was never responded to and is being attached.
B. Mechanics have been unable to fix one problem and did not fix a second.
C. The service and warranty on the customer's car have been unacceptable.
D. Some dealers and garages are better than others.

**Review your work using the explanations that start on page 667.**

LESSON 3

# Application of Ideas

When you **apply ideas**, you use information you already know in a new but similar situation. For example, suppose you know that a friend loves country music. When you need to buy a gift for that friend, you walk past the jazz and rock sections in the music store and head straight for the country. You're applying what you've learned about your friend to help you choose a gift.

To apply ideas when reading, look for elements in the new situation that are similar to elements in the passage you have read. Read this selection and then see if you can apply some of the ideas in it.

> When the delivery truck pulled up to my house the day before my mother's birthday, I knew her gift had finally arrived. I was excited. Not only had I ordered a beautiful art book for her, but I'd also ordered a mystery novel for myself and a book each for my nephew and niece. I couldn't resist buying them while I was choosing my mother's gift from an online bookstore. The carton looked bigger than I expected, but perhaps it had a lot of filler to keep the books from becoming damaged.
>
> I lugged the huge box into the kitchen so I could open it and begin wrapping my mother's gift. I tugged at the industrial staples and then tore open the carton. To my surprise, it was filled with many copies of the same book. To make matters worse, it was a book I had not ordered. *Who Moved My Cheese?* What kind of book was that? And who would order *one* copy of that book, let alone 11? I certainly didn't want these books. I knew my family wouldn't want them either. They wanted *The Art of Diego Rivera*, *Harry Potter*, and Dr. Seuss. So much for buying online. I'm sticking to in-store buying.

► Which of the following situations is most like the situation that happened to the writer?

(1) buying groceries only to discover you brought someone else's bag home
(2) buying 11 boxes of the same pasta at the store

Option **(1)** is correct. It shares the elements of intending to buy something and getting the wrong thing by mistake. The second option is wrong because the writer did not intentionally buy 11 copies of the book. Now try this question.

► If the writer attended an auction, she would be most likely to

(1) decide which item to bid on and how much she would bid
(2) get involved in the excitement and bid on many things

You are correct if you chose **(2)**. The writer states that she couldn't resist buying additional items when she was shopping online. Therefore, she seems the type to get caught up in buying things. If she had carefully chosen which book to buy her mother and had ordered only that one, then option (1) would be correct.

## KEY IDEAS

- Applying ideas means using information in a new but similar situation.
- To apply ideas, ask yourself, "How is this new situation just like the situation in the passage?"

## TASC TEST TIP

*As you work through questions on the TASC Reading Test, refer back to the passage to confirm whether your answers make sense.*

# PRACTICE 3

Questions 1 through 4 refer to the following excerpt.

**EXCERPTED FROM *MAKING THE MOST OF YOUR MONEY***

1 Once you stop using credit cards, three things will happen.

2 You will buy less—and whatever you do buy will probably be a less expensive model or make. Studies have found that people spend more when they pay with plastic, because it doesn't feel like real money. When it is real money, you're more sensible.

3 Your total debt will shrink rapidly. You are paying *off* back bills, you are not adding new ones, and you have extra money because you're buying less. That surplus cash will reduce your debt faster than you could imagine.

4 You will grow incredibly smug. You're the first on your block to get out of debt. Others will follow, but you'll be the first.

5 I'm not against credit cards. They're easy to use. They're handy. If your card has a low annual fee and a 25-day, interest-free grace period for paying your bills, you're getting monthly loans for practically nothing. What I'm against is buying more on your credit cards than you can pay for at the end of the month.

6 Once you've fought your way out of debt you can start using credit cards again—but only for the convenience of not carrying cash. Your days of debt are done. A big expense may sometimes drive you over the limit. A stereo. A llama. A hot-air balloon. Whenever you limp home, back in debt, recite your mantra: "From now on, I'm not going to put down a charge card for anything." Stick with it until you're free again.

From *Making the Most of Your Money* by Jane Bryant Quinn, New York: Simon & Schuster, 1991.

**1.** According to the writer, becoming debt-free is a behavior most similar to

A. overcoming a bad habit
B. learning a new trick
C. forgetting a friend's birthday
D. setting a good example

**2.** If you have five credit cards with high interest rates and no grace periods, how can you become debt free?

A. pay your debt off slowly so that you have extra cash for necessities
B. never use the credit cards
C. use them only when it is not convenient to carry cash
D. cut up four of the credit cards right away

**3.** Which of the following situations is most like the process of becoming debt free?

A. driving a car
B. wearing a patch to give up smoking
C. losing weight by avoiding all-you-can-eat buffets
D. running a marathon race

**4.** Earlier in the book, the author made the statement "It's so simple that I'm almost embarrassed to mention it. Don't borrow any more."

Based on this information and the information in this passage, with which of the following statements would the author most likely agree?

A. "Money is the root of all evil."
B. "You can never have enough money."
C. "Live within your means."
D. "You deserve only the best."

**Review your work using the explanations that start on page 667.**

**STUDY ADVICE**

Mastering new skills, such as applying ideas from a Reading passage, takes practice. The more you work on these skills, the stronger they will become.

Interpreting Informational Text

LESSON 4

# Cause and Effect

When one event or idea influences another, there is a cause-and-effect relationship. For example, if you forget to fill your car with gas, the car will stall. The lack of gas is the **cause,** or the reason. The stalled car is the **effect**.

**KEY IDEAS**

- To determine the cause of an event, answer the question "Why did this happen?"
- To determine an effect, ask yourself, "What was the result?"

As you read this passage, look for cause-and-effect relationships.

He is deceptively sweet upon waking up, and lets out a large yawn, showing his thin pink puppy tongue, and simultaneously letting out a high-pitched squeaking sound. Not two minutes later, he's eaten my favorite magazine and stuffed his entire head in the kitchen wastebasket to find a leftover turkey bone. The pup searches under the bed, on top of the dresser, and beside the nightstand for anything to chew. He's on a rampage in the morning—it's just his puppy nature.

To calm him down, we head to the park for one hour of exercise with the other neighborhood dogs. Afterwards, he plays with his stuffed animal squeaky toy, sleeps for an hour, then finds his favorite bone. He lies down like an angel, chewing with contentment.

► What causes the puppy's owners to take him to the park?
(1) They like to see the other neighborhood dogs.
(2) The puppy is acting too wild and energetic.

You are correct if you chose **(2)**. The first paragraph describes wild behavior, and the second paragraph says, "To calm him down, we head to the park . . ."

**ON THE TASC TEST**

*In a Reading Test passage, a writer might discuss one cause and all its effects, one effect and all its causes, or a chain of events in which each effect becomes the cause of another event.*

► Why is the puppy so wild and energetic?
(1) It is just the way a puppy is.
(2) He has a behavioral problem.

You are correct if you chose **(1)**. The writer doesn't indicate that the puppy's behavior is a problem. In fact, she clearly states that it's just the puppy's nature.

► What effect does the activity in the park have on the puppy?
(1) It calms him and tires him out.
(2) It teaches him to obey his owner.

You are correct if you chose **(1)**. When they get back from the park, the puppy plays quietly, sleeps for an hour, and then lies down to chew.

► Why does a walk in the park have a calming effect on the puppy?
(1) because the puppy enjoys seeing the other dogs
(2) because the puppy gets plenty of exercise

You are correct if you chose **(2)**. The exercise brings on the effect—calm behavior. This cause is not directly stated. You have to apply what you know about exercise and its effects in order to understand the relationship.

# PRACTICE 4

**Questions 1 through 5 refer to the following excerpt from an essay.**

**EXCERPTED FROM "THE DEPRESSION"**

1 Some events are so important that their influence cuts across class lines, affects all races and ethnic groups, and leaves no region untouched. The depression of the 1930s was such an event. No one who lived through those years in the United States could ever completely forget the bread lines, the millions of unemployed, or the forlorn and discouraged men and women who saw their mortgages foreclosed, their dreams shattered, their children hungry and afraid.

2 The depression was precipitated by the stock market crash in October 1929, but the actual cause of the collapse was an unhealthy economy. While the ability of the manufacturing industry to produce consumer goods had increased rapidly, mass purchasing power had remained relatively static. Most laborers, farmers, and white-collar workers, therefore, could not afford to buy the automobiles and refrigerators turned out by factories in the 1920s, because their incomes were too low. At the same time, the federal government increased the problem through economic policies that tended to encourage the very rich to over-save.

3 Herbert Hoover, a sensitive and humane engineer, had the misfortune of being President when the depression began. Even though he broke with the past and used the power of the federal government to stem the tide of depression, especially through loans to businesses and banks, his efforts proved to be too little and too late.

From "The Depression" from *Generations: Your Family in Modern American History*, 2nd ed., edited by James Watts and Allen F. Davis, New York: Alfred A. Knopf, 1974, 1978.

**1.** According to the authors, why was the depression of the 1930s so important?

A. It could have been prevented.
B. It was a time of economic hardship.
C. It affected nearly everyone.
D. It was unforgettable.

**2.** According to the passage, which of the following was an effect of the depression?

A. Many people lost the mortgages on their homes.
B. The stock market collapsed in October 1929.
C. Herbert Hoover was elected president.
D. The rich began to save too much of their money.

**3.** According to the passage, which of the following was one cause of the depression?

A. a static stock market
B. low worker incomes
C. not enough productivity
D. laborers refusing to buy products

**4.** In the early part of the depression, what effect did government policies have on the economy?

A. Banks and businesses began to need loans.
B. They had little effect.
C. Some of the poorer people were helped.
D. The very rich were helped.

**5.** One person who lived during the depression stated, "I can remember one time, the only thing in the house to eat was mustard. . . . And we can't stand mustard till today."

This account supports which of the following ideas from the passage?

A. Workers should have been paid more.
B. The depression touched everyone.
C. Herbert Hoover could have done more to help the economy.
D. The depression left people emotionally scarred.

**Review your work using the explanations that start on page 667.**

LESSON 5

# Comparison and Contrast

You are probably familiar with comparing and contrasting whenever you go shopping. If you are looking at two cars or even two bottles of aspirin, you want to know if the price of the two is the same or different.

Writers **compare** to point out what is similar and **contrast** to point out what is different about ideas or things.

As you read this passage, look for things being compared and contrasted.

> In December, it seems everyone is hurrying to bake holiday treats, decorate, and buy gifts. Some holiday shoppers trek through store after store, while others prefer catalog or online shopping. Just two of the holidays that keep everyone so busy this time of year are Christmas and Hanukkah.
>
> These holidays are, of course, times of celebration. People plan parties and family get-togethers. Both involve gift giving. Both also coincide with the winter solstice in the Northern Hemisphere, a time when many ancient cultures rejoiced.
>
> Christmas is a celebration of the birth of Jesus, though celebrating Christmas on December 25 did not become common until the fourth century.
>
> Hanukkah, the Jewish Festival of Lights, celebrates the belief that a flask of oil sufficient for only one day miraculously burned for eight days in a temple in the second century B.C.E. That's why on Hanukkah an additional candle is lit each evening until, on the eighth night of the holiday, eight candles are burning.

**KEY IDEAS**

- To compare ideas or things, find out how they are alike.
- To contrast ideas or things, find out how they differ.
- A writer might compare two things, contrast two things, or compare and contrast in one passage.

► What is the writer comparing and contrasting?

(1) methods of shopping
(2) Christmas and Hanukkah

You are correct if you chose **(2)**. The similarities and differences between the two holidays are the focus of the discussion. Two methods of shopping are merely mentioned.

**ON THE TASC TEST**

*In a Reading Test passage, a writer may (1) compare in one paragraph and contrast in the next or (2) go back and forth, discussing similarities and differences on different points.*

► What is one basis on which the writer compares the two?

(1) time of year celebrated
(2) kinds of meals served

You are correct if you chose **(1)**. The similarities discussed in this passage include the time of the winter solstice in the Northern Hemisphere, close to when each holiday is celebrated.

► What is one basis on which the writer contrasts the two?

(1) gift giving
(2) their histories

The correct answer is **(2)**. The two holidays have very different histories. Both holidays involve gift giving, so that is not a point of contrast.

# PRACTICE 5

**Questions 1 through 5 refer to the following excerpt from a diary.**

### EXCERPTED FROM *DIARIES OF THE WESTWARD JOURNEY*

1 Mr. West from Peoria, Ill. had another man, his wife, a son Clay about 20 years of age and his daughter, America, eighteen. Unfortunately Mr. West had gone to the extreme of providing himself with such a heavy wagon and load that they were deemed objectionable as fellow argonauts. After disposing of some of their supplies they were allowed to join us. They had four fine oxen. This wagon often got stalled in bad roads much to the annoyance of all, but as he was a wagon maker and his companion a blacksmith by trade and both were accommodating there were always ready hands to "pry the wheel out of mire."

2 A mule team from Washington, D.C. was very insufficiently provisioned . . . [by] Southern gentlemen "unused to work. . . ." They deserted the train at Salt Lake as they could not proceed with their equipment and it was easier to embrace Mormonism than to brave the "American Desert."

3 Much in contrast to these men were four batchelors Messers Wilson, Goodall, Fifield and Martin, who had a wagon drawn by four oxen and two milch cows following behind. The latter gave milk all the way to the sink of the Humboldt where they died, having acted as draught animals for several weeks after the oxen had perished. Many a cup of milk was given to the children of the train and the mothers tried in every way possible to express their gratitude.

By Catherine Haun from *Women's Diaries of the Westward Journey,* edited by Lillian Schlissel, New York: Schocken Books, 1982.

1. What did Mr. West do that allowed his group to join the wagon train?
   A. make wagons for the others
   B. bring four fine oxen
   C. offer milk to the children
   D. leave some of his possessions behind

2. What purpose did the cows serve?
   A. They led the oxen through rough terrain.
   B. They carried children when wagons were full.
   C. They provided milk and pulled wagons.
   D. They provided food and replaced the mules.

3. Which of the following is contrasted in this excerpt?
   A. the provisions of each group of travelers
   B. the stability of each of the wagons
   C. the number of people in each group
   D. the ability of each group to feed the children

4. Suppose the writer were comparing a woman with five children who could sew and cook to one man with an old ox. Which of the following would be her most likely response?

   The writer would

   A. be happy to have people who could cook and sew
   B. prefer to add fewer people to the group of travelers
   C. feel sorry for the man and welcome him
   D. offer the man one of her own animals

5. Based on the information in this excerpt, how is this trip similar for all the travelers?
   A. They must cooperate and work together.
   B. They will be rewarded for their efforts.
   C. They have similar backgrounds and relate to each other.
   D. They have all been forced to go on the journey.

**Review your work using the explanations that start on page 667.**

**STUDY ADVICE**

Practice looking for examples of these concepts in daily life. You can pick out cause/effect and comparison/contrast relationships in TV news stories, articles, and magazines. That will help you to become a stronger reader for your TASC test.

LESSON 6

# Conclusions and Generalizations

## Conclusions

A detective draws a **conclusion** when he looks at different pieces of evidence and figures out who committed a crime. A doctor draws a conclusion when she looks at different symptoms and figures out what illness a patient has. You, as a reader, can draw a conclusion when you take pieces of information and put them together to figure out something that the writer has not directly stated.

**KEY IDEAS**

- A conclusion is an idea figured out from different pieces of information.
- You can use your knowledge of the real world to help you draw conclusions when you read.

See what conclusions you can draw from this notice sent by an employer.

> Thank you for sending your resume in response to our newspaper advertisement. We consider our company—and especially our employees—to be the best. And we want to keep it that way. For that reason, we carefully review each resume that is sent to us. We want to ensure that our company and the new employee we hire are a perfect match.
>
> This process, of course, takes some time. We want to assure you that your resume is part of this process and will be reviewed. If we feel we have an opening that matches your qualifications, we will contact you. If you have not heard from us within ten business days of the postmark of this notice, be assured that we will keep your resume on file for one year and review it when future openings arise.

► If a job applicant has not heard from this company three weeks after reading this notice, what can she conclude?

(1) The review process is taking longer than expected.
(2) She did not get the job that she applied for.

**TASC TEST TIP**

*Be sure to read an entire passage before answering the questions about it. That way, you'll take all the information into account and won't jump to conclusions.*

Option **(2)** is correct. The notice says that the review process takes some time. It also says that the company will contact the applicant if it feels she matches the opening. Finally, if she doesn't hear from the company within ten business days, her resume will go on file. You can conclude that the review process takes about ten business days, and if she hasn't been contacted in that time, she didn't get the job.

► What kind of notice can you conclude this is?

(1) a personal note sent to this individual applicant
(2) a form notice sent to all applicants

Again, you're correct if you chose **(2)**. The way the notice is worded, with no personal details, lets you conclude this. You can also use your knowledge of the real world and business form letters to conclude that this, too, is a form letter.

► What conclusion can you draw about the company's attitude?

(1) It cares about its employees and their job satisfaction.
(2) It cares only about profits and employee productivity.

You are correct if you chose **(1)**. The fact that the company states not only that it considers its employees to be the best but also that it takes the time to communicate sincerely with potential employees lets you conclude that.

# PRACTICE 6.1

**Questions 1 through 5 refer to the following excerpt from an autobiography.**

**EXCERPTED FROM *THE STORY OF MY LIFE***

1 Once there were eleven tadpoles in a glass globe set in a window full of plants. I remember the eagerness with which I made discoveries about them. It was great fun to plunge my hand into the bowl and feel the tadpoles frisk about, and to let them slip and slide between my fingers. One day a more ambitious fellow leaped beyond the edge of the bowl and fell on the floor, where I found him to all appearance more dead than alive. The only sign of life was a slight wriggling of his tail. But no sooner had he returned to his element than he darted to the bottom, swimming round and round in joyous activity. He had made his leap, he had seen the great world, and was content to stay in his pretty glass house under the big fuchsia tree until he attained the dignity of froghood. Then he went to live in the leafy pool at the end of the garden, where he made the summer nights musical with his quaint love-song.

2 Thus I learned from life itself. At the beginning I was only a little mass of possibilities. It was my teacher who unfolded and developed them. When she came, everything about me breathed of love and joy and was full of meaning. She has never since let pass an opportunity to point out the beauty that is in everything, nor has she ceased trying in thought and action and example to make my life sweet and useful.

3 It was my teacher's genius, her quick sympathy, her loving tact which made the first years of my education so beautiful.

From *The Story of My Life* by Helen Keller.

**1.** What can you conclude about the writer's view of learning?

A. It is rewarding and one of life's joys.
B. It is better with a strict teacher.
C. It happens very slowly, if at all.
D. It happens most often when you are alone.

**2.** What conclusion can you draw about the writer's character?

The writer is

A. self-centered and demanding
B. confused and searching
C. fearful and shy
D. insightful and grateful

**3.** If Helen's teacher was trying to teach her addition, what method would the teacher most likely use?

A. make Helen stand and recite addition facts for one hour every day
B. assign an abundance of addition homework
C. show Helen how addition is used in everyday life
D. ask a well-known mathematician to teach the subject

**4.** How are the thoughts in this personal account organized?

A. as a comparison with a frog followed by a contrast
B. as a problem followed by its solution
C. in chronological order, or time sequence
D. as an anecdote followed by a generalization based on the anecdote

**5.** Later in her story, Helen compares a child's mind to a shallow brook "which ripples and dances merrily over the stony course of its education. . . ." Based on this information and the excerpt above, what is similar about the tadpole and a child?

A. They learn from others.
B. They are eager to grow into adulthood.
C. Youth can make them do dangerous things.
D. Their development is not entirely smooth.

**Review your work using the explanations that start on page 668.**

## Generalizations

A **generalization** is a broad statement about a group of people, objects, or things, or about a type of event. Usually, it takes something that is true in one specific case and extends it to every possible case. For example, "My hometown celebrated Independence Day with fireworks last summer," is a fact about a specific Fourth of July in a specific town; a generalization could be "Every Independence Day, my hometown celebrates with fireworks."

▶ Identify one statement with *F* for a fact and the other with *G* for generalization.

(1) Every clerk in the store focuses on customer service more than any other aspect of the job.

(2) Tina, the manager of the women's shoe department, helps customers select just the right pair of shoes.

If you identified option **(2)** as being a fact and option **(1)** as being a generalization, you were correct. One hint that **(1)** is the generalization is the word "every." Words like *all, never,* and *always* show up in sentences that make broad, sweeping statements. The sentence about Tina, on the other hand, gives specific information about a specific person and so is not a generalization.

### KEY IDEAS

- A generalization is a broad statement about a group or class.
- When assessing a generalization, evaluate the writer's evidence.
- An important factor in thoughtful reading is distinguishing between faulty and valid generalizations.

Generalizations can be valid and true when properly made. A writer can support a generalization with an example (like Tina, above) and information that shows why the example represents the whole group. Often, a generalization is too broad to apply to every member of a group, and a good writer will acknowledge that there are exceptions.

"Dogs are typically more attached to their owners than cats are, due in part to their evolution as pack animals. My dog will jump up to meet me as soon as I get home from work, while my cat will continue napping serenely until hunger motivates him to do otherwise."

▶ What example is given to support the generalization that "Dogs are typically more attached to their owners than cats"?

(1) Dogs evolved as pack animals.

(2) The author's dog jumps up to meet her, while her cat ignores her.

### TASC TEST TIP

*If you see a generalization, look for supporting evidence that may be introduced by phrases such as "for example," "such as," or "for instance."*

The example of the author's dog's attachment to her, **(2)**, illustrates and supports the generalization that most dogs show greater attachment to their owners. The specific example helps to show that the statement is based on experience.

Writers sometimes make the mistake of drawing **faulty generalizations** based on too little information. Imagine a person who bites into an apple, finds a worm, and concludes that all apples have worms in them. Since a generalization is a broad statement, a **valid generalization** requires broad knowledge to justify it. A generalization about American cities is more likely to be faulty if the writer bases on it only one city but more likely to be valid if the writer supports it with knowledge of 20 cities. With a larger sample, the writer is also better able to know whether to qualify a generalization as something that is true in most, but not all, cases.

▶ Identify one statement with *FG* for a faulty generalization and the other with *VG* for a valid generalization.

(1) Every breed of dog has four legs, so almost all dogs have four legs.

(2) Some dogs bark at kids, so all dogs must dislike or fear children.

You are correct if you chose **(1)** as the valid generalization: the writer shows awareness of many different types of dogs. Option **(2)** is a faulty generalization; dogs may bark at children for reasons other than fear or dislike.

# PRACTICE 6.2

**Questions 1 through 3 are based on the following newspaper editorial.**

### OPINION: DOUBTS ABOUT GLOBAL WARMING

1 Shady Hollow was hit yesterday with record cold temperatures. And yet, despite this deep freeze, we'll continue to be subjected to the doctrine of global warming.

2 There is plenty to be said for fuel economy—anyone who lived through the energy crisis of the 1970s learned that lesson the hard way—but it's time we dispense with the terror campaign of doomsday climatology and recognize it for the pseudoscience that it is. Whenever Shady Hollow gets a big hit of winter weather, common sense tells us that the idea of "warming" seems fishy, yet climatologists insist on playing the same tune. More and more, this tune is taken up by policy-makers and government bodies, who steer our administrations accordingly. It must be the case that ivory towers have good weather stripping and excellent heating systems; as for the man on the street, he's finding his street a chilly one these days.

3 The simple fact is that it is logically impossible to reconcile a record cold temperature with the idea that it's getting warmer. A record cold temperature, and this may be worth spelling out, means exactly this: it has never been colder on this date in recorded history. If "warming" means what it sounds like it means—that temperatures are rising, not falling—then there is a real problem here, because that is quite simply not what is happening.

4 It may take years to get out from under the orthodoxy of the accepted opinion on climate change, but the facts themselves will not go away. Sooner or later, we'll be forced to acknowledge that we're still bundling up, and when that happens, we can stop building policy discussions around fictions.

**1.** What is a generalization that is made in paragraph 3?

A. Shady Hollow has the coldest temperatures in the region.
B. Global warming can only be valid if it predicts high temperatures.
C. On the whole, temperatures are not rising.
D. If children are taught a simpler theory, then a more complex theory should be set aside.

**2.** What evidence does the author give to support his generalization about global warming?

A. Shady Hollow was hit with a record cold temperature yesterday.
B. Ivory towers have good weather stripping.
C. It may take years to change opinions on climate change.
D. There is plenty to be said for fuel economy.

**3.** Which of the following pieces of information would put the author in a better position to make a generalization about climate change?

A. an account of the energy crisis of the 1970s
B. minutes of policy discussions from the 1970s through today
C. interviews with the "man on the street" from the 1990s through today
D. worldwide data tables of temperatures from the 1980s through today

**Review your work using the explanations that start on page 668.**

LESSON 7

# Word Choice

Writers make careful decisions to select words that will impact their audience. One choice that writers make is to select words that have a **connotation** associated with a particular image or feeling. Think of the different connotations of *dog*, *mutt*, and *man's best friend*. The word *dog* has a neutral connotation; it just describes the animal. To some, the word *mutt* would have a negative connotation, while the phrase *man's best friend* would have a positive connotation.

► Assign a *P* (positive) or an *N* (negative) to the following words to indicate the connotation that might be associated with them:
(1) shack
(2) villa

You are correct if you assigned an *N* to (1) and a *P* to (2). The word *shack* probably brings to mind a small, poorly built or run-down building. On the other hand, the word *villa* might be associated with a house in the countryside or a vacation destination.

Writers use **figurative language** to make their descriptions clearer and more vivid. They use **similes**, which use the words *like* or *as* to compare two things; for example, "Her new coat fit like a glove." This indicates that the coat fit perfectly. Another type of figurative language is a **metaphor**, which implies a comparison between two things. One familiar metaphor is "Life is a journey"; this compares two dissimilar things in order to describe life. A third figure of speech is **personification**, by which a writer assigns human characteristics to something that is not human. For example, a writer may describe a storm as "slashing at the windows and knocking on the door."

> If you look very carefully, you can find the island of Ascension on a map about midway between Angola, in Africa, and Brazil, in South America. This South Atlantic island has a population of about 1,000 people and is home to an important GPS ground antenna and a British air force base. Its volcanic terrain greets visitors with a forbidding aspect; place names like "Comfortless Cove" indicate how rocky and uninviting Ascension Island may appear. Even so, with its dry subtropical weather, excellent sport fishing, and unique wildlife, this barren outpost attracts about 1,000 tourists each year.

► What does the personification in the third sentence suggest about Ascension Island?
(1) Tourists are forbidden to visit the island.
(2) The island doesn't look like a good place to visit.

You are correct if you chose **(2)**. The writer refers to the island as if it were a person with an unfriendly appearance. Since the last sentence states that tourists do visit the island, you know that they are not forbidden to do so.

### KEY IDEAS

- Writers choose words carefully to make an impact on the reader.
- They deliberately choose words with positive, negative, or neutral connotations.
- Writers also use figurative language such as similes, metaphors, and personification to enhance descriptions.

### TASC TEST TIP

*Read closely to see how a writer's word choice affects how you picture something or feel about it. You may have to answer questions that require an awareness of the impact of both words' connotations and figurative language.*

# PRACTICE 7

<u>Questions 1 through 5</u> **refer to the following product description.**

### A COOL NEW BLANKET

1 Many people rely on electric blankets to keep warm on winter nights without turning on expensive central heating. In summer, though, there's no alternative to noisy fans and energy-hogging air conditioners if you want to stay cool . . . until now. The Starlight company recently introduced its newest product: an electric blanket that keeps you cool even on sweltering summer nights.

2 The CoolForter blanket works like an electric blanket, but it feels like a dream. The blanket contains a full tenth of a mile of flexible hose, fully insulated between layers of soft cotton. A small, quiet compressor refrigerates the safely enclosed cooling chemical and circulates it continuously through the coils. The CoolForter coddles you in refreshing comfort, and you never have to worry about waking up shivering. That's because your sleeping temperature is precisely controlled by the built-in thermostat, which can be adjusted to your exact temperature preference.

3 Your CoolForter blanket also matches your decorating preferences: the replaceable cover comes in a wide variety of bland colors to suit any décor. If you decide to redecorate, choose from a selection of fun and gaudy prints to liven up your room.

4 Best of all, the CoolForter saves you money every time you use it. Consuming an average of just 80 watts, the twin-size blanket is like a regular household lightbulb, costing just pennies per day to run. It's an investment in comfort that will pay for itself many times over the lifetime of its generous ten-year warranty and beyond.

**STUDY ADVICE**

To practice spotting figurative language, similes, metaphors, and personification, pay particular attention to advertisements. Think about how an ad's wording conveys a strong positive connotation about the product being advertised (or a negative connotation about the competitor's product).

**1.** In paragraph 2, what is compared to a dream?

A. an electric blanket
B. the flexible hose used in the CoolForter blanket
C. the cotton insulating layers
D. the CoolForter blanket

**2.** What could be a reason that the writer used the word "coddles" in paragraph 2?

A. to show that the blanket keeps its user warm
B. to show that the blanket is a pleasant indulgence
C. to show that the blanket keeps its user cool
D. to show that the user can wrap herself up in the blanket

**3.** What word could the writer have used instead of "chemical" in paragraph 2 that would have a less negative connotation?

A. fluid
B. antifreeze
C. contaminant
D. water

**4.** Which word in paragraph 3 means "neutral" and has a negative connotation?

A. decorating
B. replaceable
C. bland
D. gaudy

**5.** Why is "like a regular household lightbulb" from paragraph 4 an effective use of a comparison using figurative language?

A. It reminds the consumer that, while a lightbulb generates heat, the CoolForter blanket keeps its user cool.
B. It makes the CoolForter blanket seem ordinary.
C. It emphasizes the difference in cost between running a regular lightbulb and operating a compact fluorescent lightbulb.
D. It allows the consumer to compare the CoolForter's energy usage to that of a familiar item.

**Review your work using the explanations that start on page 668.**

LESSON 8

# Writer's Tone and Point of View

## Tone

A writer usually has a certain attitude toward the subject he or she is writing about. This attitude is the **tone** of the piece. The tone is not directly stated. You have to sense it by the writer's choice of words and manner of expression.

As you read this drama review, ask yourself, "What tone of voice would the author have if she were reading this aloud to me?"

> Watching actor Brian Dennehy as Willy Loman in the stage production of *Death of a Salesman* was transforming. I know intellectually that live theater is better than movies. Movie actors reshoot scenes until they are perfect. An actor on stage has one chance to get it right. It is immediate. The actors are breathing human beings in the same room with you. Theater provides the opportunity for strong emotions to surface, right there, in the moment. Seeing a play often envelops me in energy.
>
> But I've never gone so far as to cry at a theater performance until now. I cried because Dennehy's Loman reminded me of my father, of the brevity of our lives, of how easy it is to waste our lives. This was not an intellectual response. I suddenly heard what this man on stage was saying—his life wasn't worth living, though he had tried hard, had a devoted wife and two sons. It didn't matter that this play was written in the 1940s. Mr. Dennehy stood on stage and roared at us about our lives now. It was hard-hitting, emotional drama.

► Which of the following best describes the tone of this piece?
(1) positive and somewhat awed
(2) cool and objective

The correct response is **(1)**. The writer states positive opinions. She also chooses short, clipped expressions—"It is immediate" and "right there, in the moment"—that by themselves create a sense of drama and awe. If the tone were cool and objective, you would not sense the writer's emotional attitude toward the play.

## Point of View

The **point of view** of a piece is "where the author is coming from"—that is, the writer's background and experiences that may affect her opinions. For example, when you read an editorial in a newspaper, you can usually tell whether the writer has a liberal or a conservative point of view.

► What point of view does the writer of the review above have?
(1) that of a person who prefers sitting at home watching TV
(2) that of an enthusiastic theatergoer

You are correct if you chose **(2)**. You can conclude that the writer goes to the theater ("Seeing a play often envelops me") and enjoys it ("theater is better than movies"). Knowing this helps you evaluate the merits of the review.

### KEY IDEAS

- The writer's attitude toward a subject is conveyed by the tone of the writing.
- To determine tone, look at word choice and manner of expression. How would the writer sound reading the piece?
- The writer's point of view is the position he or she is writing from.

### ON THE TASC TEST

*Some kinds of tone you might see in Reading Test passages are formal or informal, positive or negative, objective, sarcastic, arrogant, concerned, affectionate, or nostalgic.*

# PRACTICE 8

<u>Questions 1 through 5</u> **refer to the following review.**

## EXCERPTED FROM "TALKING BACK TO THE TUBE"

1 CBS delivered a television low mark called *Big Brother.* Focusing on ten fame-seeking, people-pleasing, hair-teasing losers willing to submit to surveillance by a nation of snoops for three months, it was so bad that it wasn't even good. Forget about camp reversals that transform trash into the perversely fascinating, forget about the Cheese Factor, which allows a pop-cultural product to be moldy and musty and stinky and still taste good. *Big Brother* was so bad that even Jean-Paul Sartre would have yawned, and the dude wrote hundreds of pages about useless passion in *Being and Nothingness.*

2 But something good did come of *Big Brother,* something wicked and warped and witty, something created by people with way too much time on their hands and way too much venom in their bite. While the reality series was channeling banality through the cable cords and over the airwaves six nights a week, a small crew of writers were deconstructing and eviscerating the tedium on the Internet. They were taking hours and hours of prime-time dross and turning it into decadent, amoral, sharp, electronic gold.

3 Internet sass.

4 You gotta love it, if only because it keeps razor-tongued fanatics and uncensored savants off the streets and out of trouble.

5 Not only was there a site devoted entirely to the ridiculing of CBS, *Big Brother,* its ten cast members, their families, host Julie Chen, and the gaseous *Big Brother* house pug, but a number of other general interest sites, notably Salon.com, spent the summer providing wry daily updates on the non-goings-on of the non-people in the non-house. They, too, took the non-pulse of a DOA television series and gave it a semblance of life on the Internet.



**1.** Who are referred to as "razor-tongued fanatics and uncensored savants" (paragraph 4)?

A. the television writers
B. the television cast of *Big Brother*
C. the Internet writers
D. the Internet audience

**2.** Which of the following best summarizes the reviewer's point about *Big Brother*?

A. The Internet reviews were much more interesting than the TV show.
B. The TV show was so bad that it was funny.
C. Internet writers are better than TV writers.
D. The main problem was with the ten people on the TV show.

**3.** What opinion is supported by the statement "even Jean-Paul Sartre would have yawned, and the dude wrote hundreds of pages about useless passion" (paragraph 1)?

A. The show was boring.
B. The show should have been longer.
C. The show needed more passion.
D. The show was incomprehensible.

**4.** Which of the following best describes the tone of this review?

A. apologetic
B. nostalgic for earlier shows
C. informal and hip
D. objective

**5.** From whose point of view is this piece likely written?

A. a television script writer
B. a person who hates watching TV
C. someone knowledgeable about the media
D. a disgruntled fan

**Review your work using the explanations that start on page 668.**

LESSON 9

# Text Structure

Writers make choices about how to organize informational and nonfiction materials based on their purpose. You have already seen two text structures: cause and effect, which shows how one thing made another happen, and comparison and contrast, which illustrates similarities and differences.

There are other **text structures** often used for informational text:

- **Example**—introduces an unfamiliar topic and then follows with common examples to aid understanding.
- **Pros and Cons**—explains a situation by first presenting its benefits and then portraying its deficiencies in order to present both sides.
- **Chronological Order** or **Process**—presents details in the order in which they occur; also referred to as a **sequence** of events.
- **Elaboration**—makes a statement and indicates that additional information or an explanation will follow.

These text structures use different types of **transitions** to guide the reader from one idea to the next. Many of these are familiar to you.

**KEY IDEAS**

- Writers may use different text structures depending on what they are writing about.
- One of the main tools writers use to create different text structures is transition words, which create relationships between ideas.

| Text Structure | Purpose | Sample Transitions |
|---|---|---|
| **Example** | Organizes illustrations that support a concept | for example, for instance, such as, to illustrate |
| **Pros and Cons** | Shows benefits and drawbacks | on the one hand, on the other hand |
| **Chronological Order or Process** | Describes events and procedures | before, after, next, following, meanwhile, until |
| **Elaboration** | Expands with additional details | additionally, furthermore, moreover |

**TASC TEST TIP**

*You will need to be aware of different types of text structure to answer questions, but you will not need to identify any structures by their names.*

Practice using an understanding of text structure by reading the paragraph and answering the question below.

> Today, there are millions of workers who are not employees in the traditional sense; they are called "contract workers." These are self-employed individuals who have contracts with different businesses. For example, a graphic artist may have several different clients and design a newsletter for one and a website for another. Contract workers pay for their own equipment, supplies, and benefits—such as health insurance.

► What is a detail from the passage that explains the concept of "contract workers"?

(1) They are not employees in the traditional sense.
(2) They may have contracts with several businesses.

Choice **(2)** illustrates the concept of contract workers by explaining that they have several different clients rather than one employer. Choice (1) does not help to explain contract work; it just explains what contract workers are not.

# PRACTICE 9

<u>Questions 1 and 2</u> **refer to this scientific experiment.**

### COWPOX, SMALLPOX, AND IMMUNITY

In 1796, British physician Edward Jenner conducted an experiment intended to help develop a viable treatment for the deadly smallpox disease. Some time before, he had noticed that dairymaids in his village commonly became infected with cowpox. Cowpox is an illness that is very similar to smallpox, but it is not deadly. The dairymaids who caught cowpox later turned out to be immune to smallpox. This led Jenner to experiment with whether he could make a test subject immune to smallpox by first infecting that person with cowpox. His test subject was a young boy named James. First, Jenner made small cuts on James's skin and inserted liquid from the cowpox sores of a local dairymaid. After being exposed to the disease, James caught cowpox and later recovered. After the boy's recovery from cowpox, Jenner exposed James to smallpox and found that the boy was immune. Today, scientists and medical professionals know that the cowpox and smallpox viruses are so similar that the body's immune system cannot tell them apart.

**1.** What step in the process came before James's recovery from cowpox?

A. his immunity to smallpox
B. exposure to the cowpox disease
C. scientists' discovery that cowpox and smallpox are similar
D. Jenner exposing James to smallpox

**2.** Which of the following phrases from the passage helps to understand the order of the steps in the process?

A. "cannot tell them apart"
B. "Jenner made small cuts"
C. "After being exposed to the disease"
D. "make a test subject immune"

<u>Question 3</u> **refers to this discussion of gardening.**

### THE UPS AND DOWNS OF GARDENING

Planting and maintaining a backyard garden can have many benefits, but it also brings challenges. On the one hand, successful gardeners often express deep feelings of accomplishment and satisfaction in their gardens. Gardening can involve good exercise and fresh air, and spending time outdoors can be a healthy escape from everyday responsibilities and concerns. A flower garden provides a beautiful view that often attracts delightful visitors, including butterflies and hummingbirds. A vegetable garden provides nutritious food and can add up to significant savings on your grocery bill. An herb garden can supply alternatives to unhealthy ingredients such as salt and oil.

On the other hand, planting and maintaining a garden can be very expensive and time-consuming, and a garden may fail despite your best efforts. Proper soil and fertilizers must be bought, and plants or seeds must be chosen. It is also important to consider the watering and feeding of the garden to ensure proper growth. A number of factors beyond your immediate control may affect the success of your garden. If the season's weather is extreme in any way—too dry, too rainy, too hot, or too cold—it can damage tender plants and undo your hard work, wasting your investment of time and money. Similarly, invasive pests and diseases can be devastating to your home garden and can be difficult and expensive to control.

**3.** Which of the following is one of the writer's arguments against planting and maintaining a backyard garden?

A. Time outdoors often alleviates stress.
B. A number of factors can damage a garden.
C. Having too many daily chores is stressful.
D. Rain is bad for a garden.

**Review your work using the explanations that start on page 668.**

**STUDY ADVICE**

Congratulations—you're almost done with the first chapter of this book! The last few pages of each chapter will give you additional practice items to reinforce what you've learned in that chapter. Before you begin the first of these on the next page, you may want to review anything that seemed challenging in the lessons so far.

## Interpreting Informational Text Practice Questions

**Questions 1 through 4 refer to the following excerpt from an autobiography.**

### EXCERPTED FROM *THE LIAR'S CLUB*

1 That fall my school career didn't go much better. I got suspended from my second-grade class twice, first for biting a kid named Phyllis who wasn't, to my mind, getting her scissors out fast enough to comply with the teacher, then again for breaking my plastic ruler over the head of a boy named Sammy Joe Tyler, whom I adored. A pale blue knot rose through the blond stubble of his crew cut. Both times I got sent to the principal, a handsome ex-football coach named Frank Doleman who let Lecia and me call him Uncle Frank. (Lecia and I had impressed Uncle Frank by both learning to read pretty much without instruction before we were three. Mother took us each down to his office in turn, and we each dutifully read the front page of the day's paper out loud to him, so he could be sure it wasn't just some story we'd memorized.)

2 He let me stay in his office playing chess all afternoon with whoever wandered in. He loved pitting me against particularly lunkheaded fifth- and sixth-grade boys who'd been sent down for paddlings they never got. He'd try to use my whipping them at chess to make them nervous about how dumb they were. "Now this little bitty old second-grader here took you clean in six plays. Don't you reckon you need to be listening to Miss Vilimez instead of cutting up?" When Mrs. Hess led me solemnly down the hall to Frank Doleman's office, I would pretend to cry, but thought instead about Brer Rabbit as he was being thrown into the briar patch where he'd been born and raised, and screaming *Please don't throw me in that briar patch!*

From *The Liar's Club* by Mary Karr, New York: Penguin Books, 1995.

1. If the writer had attended an elementary school dance, which of the following might she have done?

   A. made fun of everyone as they danced
   B. sat and played chess with the boys
   C. been too shy to dance with anyone
   D. hit a boy in the arm to get his attention

2. What is meant by the statement "I . . . thought instead about Brer Rabbit as he was being thrown into the briar patch where he'd been born and raised and screaming *Please don't throw me in that briar patch!*" (paragraph 2)?

   A. She was so upset that she wanted to scream.
   B. She was just pretending she didn't want to go to the principal's office.
   C. She hoped the teacher would let her back in class if she pleaded with her.
   D. She was afraid of what would happen in the principal's office.

3. What type of principal was Frank Doleman?

   A. strict
   B. ineffective
   C. unusual
   D. mean

4. Later in the autobiography, the narrator describes herself as "small-boned and skinny, but more than able to make up for that."

   Based on this description and the excerpt, which of the following best describes the narrator?

   A. confident
   B. serious
   C. friendly
   D. hopeful

**<u>Questions 5 through 9</u> refer to this article about soda.**

### TURNING BACK A SUGARY TIDE

1 The popular soft drinks known as soda, pop, or both trace their origins all the way back to 1767, when English chemist Joseph Priestley invented a method for carbonating water. Over the last two and a half centuries, soda has risen to prominence primarily as a sweet beverage for social occasions. By the mid-1990s, soda had become the beverage of choice for adolescents. This increase in consumption has not been without negative consequences. Since the early 1980s, obesity rates for young Americans have risen steadily, as has the incidence of juvenile diabetes, heart disease, and myriad other ailments related to poor diet.

2 To counteract the harmful effects of overindulging in soda, federal, state, and local governments have taken steps in recent years. First Lady Michelle Obama promotes healthier diet choices and campaigns against childhood obesity. Several states now require that restaurants post calorie information next to all menu items, including beverages. In a controversial move, New York City mayor Michael Bloomberg proposed banning the sale of sodas over 16 ounces in city eateries. Additionally, many school districts around the country have banned the sale of soda in school vending machines.

3 These efforts appear to be paying off: latest statistics indicate that the percentage of teens who consume soda daily has fallen from 75 percent in the 1990s to 62 percent in 2009. However, most teens who abandon soda as a daily beverage replace it with other high-sugar choices, such as juice or energy and sport drinks. While many of these products have slightly less sugar than soda, the net impact of regular consumption is likely to be just as damaging in the long term. Regulating the sale of soda is a step in the right direction, but more can be done to educate young people about the dangers of a diet overflowing with sugary beverages.

5. Which of the following best describes the tone of this article?
   A. playful but informative
   B. pessimistic and sarcastic
   C. concerned but hopeful
   D. neutral and inquisitive

6. Which of the following best describes the author's point of view on reducing soda consumption?
   A. The sale of soda should be outlawed due to the beverage's negative impact on health.
   B. Consuming diet soda is healthier than consuming regular soda.
   C. A young person's decision to consume soda is a personal choice that must be respected.
   D. Young people will choose healthier beverages if they are better educated about the dangers of consumption of sugared beverages.

7. According to paragraph 3, what will likely be the "net impact" of regularly consuming juice, energy, and sport drinks instead of soda?
   A. Teenagers who consume these beverages instead of soda will avoid the health hazards associated with soda.
   B. Soda manufacturers will likely go out of business since fewer consumers will be purchasing their products.
   C. Young people who drink these beverages regularly will eventually suffer from the same ailments as those who drink soda regularly.
   D. Many of the teenagers who drink juice, energy, and sport drinks will choose healthier food options to supplement their diets.

8. According to the passage, the author most likely regards the steps to curb soda consumption described in paragraph 2 as
   A. disruptive but essential
   B. effective to some extent
   C. invasive and extreme
   D. well-intentioned but unenforceable

9. In the beginning of paragraph 3, the words "These efforts" refer to which of the following?
   A. Creating soda from carbonated water
   B. Recommending energy and sport drinks instead of soda
   C. Reducing excessive consumption of soda
   D. Increasing educational programs about the effects of soda

**Questions 10 through 12 refer to the following business document.**

**EXCERPTED FROM *INDEPENDENT CONSULTANT'S BROCHURE AND LETTER HANDBOOK* BY HERMAN HOLTZ**

1 The National Association of Temporary Services (NATS), which represents the nation's temporary help employers, testified today before the House Ways and Means Committee on the employer mandate and related provisions of the President's Health Security Act (H.R. 3600).

2 Edward A. Lenz, NATS senior vice president, legal and government affairs, said that the temporary help industry supports the principle of universal coverage, but has serious concerns that the cost of mandates could weaken the ability of the temporary help industry to act as a "jobs bridge" to regular, full-time employment.

3 According to Lenz, the temporary help industry has recently "assumed a new and vital role—by helping to ease the burden on individuals during the current restructuring of the American work force. Temporary work offers displaced workers a critical safety net of income, benefits, and skills training and often provides a bridge back to regular, full-time employment."

4 In addition, the Association is concerned that the mandates, as currently structured, would "also impose enormous administrative burdens" due to annual temporary employee turnover in the range of 400 to 600 percent. If employer mandates are adopted, Lenz urged Congress to create a mechanism that relates premium payments to hours worked, such as a simple payroll tax.



10. Which of the following states one of the main concerns of NATS?

A. NATS won't be able to offer skills training to temporary employees if the government mandates coverage.
B. There will be an increase in turnover of temporary employees if the government mandates coverage.
C. The cost of mandated coverage will lessen the ability of NATS to hire and supply temporary workers.
D. Restructuring the work force is a burden to all Americans.

11. According to the press release, why have businesses supplying temporary help become even more necessary?

A. Many workers are losing their jobs and need temporary jobs until they find permanent work again.
B. There is not enough work for everyone to have a full-time permanent job.
C. The job turnover rate has gone as high as 400 to 600 percent.
D. More and more workers do not want permanent full-time work.

12. What is the overall purpose of this piece?

A. to stimulate debate over universal health insurance coverage
B. to impress both the Congress and the president
C. to describe various alternatives to mandated coverage
D. to raise awareness of an issue

**Questions 13 through 16 refer to the following excerpt from a historical feminist speech.**

### EXCERPTED FROM *A TREASURY OF THE WORLD'S GREAT SPEECHES*

1 We have met here today to discuss our rights and wrongs, civil and political, and not, as some have supposed, to go into the detail of social life alone. We do not propose to petition the legislature to make our husbands just, generous, and courteous, to seat every man at the head of a cradle, and to clothe every woman in male attire. None of these points, however important they may be considered by leading men, will be touched in this convention. As to their costume, the gentlemen need feel no fear of our imitating that, for we think it in violation of every principle of taste, beauty, and dignity; notwithstanding all the contempt cast upon our loose, flowing garments, we still admire the graceful folds, and consider our costume far more artistic than theirs. Many of the nobler sex seem to agree with us in this opinion, for the bishops, priests, judges, barristers, and lord mayors of the first nation on the globe, and the Pope of Rome, with his cardinals, too, all wear the loose flowing robes, thus tacitly acknowledging that the male attire is neither dignified nor imposing. No, we shall not molest you in your philosophical experiments with stocks, pants, high-heeled boots, and Russian belts. Yours be the glory to discover, by personal experience, how long the kneepan can resist the terrible strapping down which you impose, in how short time the well-developed muscles of the throat can be reduced to mere threads by the constant pressure of the stock, how high the heel of a boot must be to make a short man tall, and how tight the Russian belt may be drawn and yet have wind enough left to sustain life.

2 But we are assembled to protest against a form of government existing without the consent of the governed—to declare our right to be free. . . .

From a speech at a woman's-rights convention by Elizabeth Cady Stanton, as reprinted in *A Treasury of the World's Great Speeches*, edited by Houston Peterson, New York: Simon & Schuster, 1954, 1965.

**STUDY ADVICE**

Don't forget to review the answers and explanations, and compare them to your own work. Doing so will give you valuable information about what kinds of mistakes you're prone to. Then you can practice to avoid those mistakes!

13. Which of the following best rephrases the lines "Yours be the glory to discover . . . how long the kneepad can resist the terrible strapping down which you impose" (paragraph 1)?
    A. Men do not understand how uncomfortable women's clothes are.
    B. Women will not resort to wearing pants or other restrictive men's clothing.
    C. Men will only understand women when women dress like them.
    D. Men and women will be equal only when they both wear belts and collars.

14. What is a "stock" (paragraph 1)?
    A. a man's jacket
    B. a wooden frame holding a prisoner
    C. a loose shirt
    D. a cloth worn around the neck

15. If the speaker attended a fancy tea party, which of the following would she be most likely to do?
    A. be on her best behavior
    B. speak up about current events
    C. treat the hostess like royalty
    D. comment on everyone's clothing

16. Later in the speech, Stanton states that "over the horns of bigotry and prejudice will be our way." Based on this and the excerpt, you can conclude that Stanton is giving this speech for what reason?
    A. Women are fighting for the right to vote.
    B. Women are tired of being made to wear dresses.
    C. Husbands need to be made just and generous.
    D. Many people mistakenly judge others by their appearance.

**Review your work using the explanations that start on page 668.**

LESSON 1

# Purpose of Text

When you read TASC Reading Test passages, it is important that you comprehend not only what the author is writing about but also the **purpose**—the reason *why* he or she is writing this passage. Authors of nonfiction passages have one or more of the following purposes:

- **Narrate**—Narrative passages typically recount events chronologically, that is, in the order in which they happened. Examples include a person's life story and hour-by-hour developments in a news story.
- **Inform**—The author seeks to present facts and data to explain a subject, situation, or idea. Examples include news articles, financial summaries, and scientific findings.
- **Persuade**—The author seeks to change readers' minds, and the passage includes the author's opinions, recommendations, or conclusions. Examples are political speeches, newspaper editorials, and entertainment reviews.
- **Entertain**—Authors writing to entertain are trying to amuse or interest their readers. Examples include a humorous memoir or articles about celebrities.

Read the paragraph and answer questions about the writer's purpose.

> According to market research, video games sales—including digital downloads and apps—in the United States topped $15 billion in 2010. The most popular game genres were Action (21.7% of sales), Sports Games (16.3%), and Shooter (15.9%). Family Entertainment games accounted for only 9.1 percent of sales.

▶ What is the writer's purpose for this paragraph?
(1) to present facts about video game sales
(2) to convince readers that Family Entertainment games' sales should be increased

▶ Imagine there is an additional sentence at the end of the paragraph. "Because popular games in the Action and Shooter genres may contain extremely graphic violence, parents must be educated about how to monitor their children's purchases and game play." What would be the purpose of the revised paragraph about video games?
(1) to entertain readers with an amusing fact about video games
(2) to persuade parents to become more involved in their children's use of video games

In the first question, choice **(1)** is correct because the writer gives facts and not persuasive information. In the second question, once the information about violence has been added, choice **(2)** is correct because the statement offers a recommendation to persuade, not entertain, parents.

**KEY IDEAS**

- Writers have different reasons, or purposes, for writing.
- The main purposes for writing are to narrate a story, to inform, to persuade, and to entertain.

**TASC TEST TIP**

*As you are reading passages on the test, ask yourself, "Why did the author write this story, article, or speech?" That will help you to understand the purpose.*

# PRACTICE 1

After an explosion damaged critical systems on the spacecraft of the Apollo 13 mission, the three astronauts aboard were forced to make the journey back to Earth inside the Lunar Module (LM), the small vessel originally designed to land on the Moon's surface. Using the LM as a "lifeboat" provided the astronauts with enough oxygen and water for the return trip, but it also introduced a new problem: there was no way to recycle used air. To solve the problem, engineers back on Earth cataloged all of the spare parts and detachable pieces inside the Apollo modules. From these, they prototyped various devices the astronauts might use to make filters to use inside the LM. The Earth-based engineers talked the astronauts through the process of constructing and installing the makeshift filters. The engineers' quick thinking and creativity provided the astronauts with a way to maintain breathable air throughout their journey back to Earth.

**1.** The purpose of the paragraph above is to

A. explain how the Lunar Module worked
B. tell how creative engineers saved astronauts
C. inform about the space program's value
D. convince that engineers are essential workers

Our state should cut all sales taxes on the purchase of new automobiles to encourage buying new cars. Older cars do not run as cleanly as new vehicles and, thus, contribute to air pollution. Additionally, older cars are less safe to operate. One study estimates that last year, as many as 500 deaths or serious injuries from accidents in our state could have been prevented by the sorts of safety features that are standard on newer-model cars.

**2.** The writer most likely includes the fact about preventable deaths or serious injuries in automobile accidents because it

A. is the conclusion the writer is trying to prove
B. supports the writer's main recommendation
C. may shock readers into becoming safer drivers
D. will encourage legislators to cut sales taxes

**Questions 3 and 4 are based on this passage.**

**SILK: NOW AND THEN**

Modern consumers do not appreciate the historical importance of the fabric silk. Silk fabric is valued for its smooth texture and shimmering appearance. It is also highly absorbent, making silk clothing comfortable in both high and low temperatures. Today, silk fabrics remain somewhat more expensive than cotton cloth and synthetic textiles, but many would be surprised to learn that silk was arguably the most important product in Asia and Europe for nearly 1,000 years.

Originally, sericulture—the technology of making silk cloth from silkworm cocoons—was known only in China. Around 2,000 years ago, nomads from Central Asia would travel to China to trade horses and other goods for silk cloth. As these nomads ventured West, silk became known to people in the Middle East and Europe. Over time, traders established routes over 4,000 miles long from China to Europe that became known as the Silk Road. Throughout the ancient and medieval world, silk was the preferred fabric for the robes of royalty and the very wealthy.

**3.** This purpose of this passage is to

A. criticize ancient peoples for overvaluing silk
B. explain how silk fabrics are made
C. entertain readers who enjoy historical travel
D. inform about the historical importance of silk

**4.** How does the information in the second paragraph support the purpose of the passage?

A. It illustrates why silk remains an expensive product today.
B. It refutes the notion that silk is a valuable product in the modern world.
C. It provides examples of silk's historical importance in trade and culture.
D. It compares the value of silk to that of other products from Asia.

**Review your work using the explanations that start on page 669.**

# Analyzing Informational Text

## LESSON 2

# Effectiveness of Argument

You may think of an argument as being a quarrel between people. However, in reading and writing, an **argument** consists of the following:

- A **conclusion** (that is, main point) about something
- The **evidence**, which is support that is given for the conclusion
- The author's **assumptions**, or ideas the author takes for granted, behind the argument

Writers should provide supporting evidence for their argument; otherwise, they are just making an unsupported claim. You may need to read carefully to **infer** their assumptions.

Read the argument below and answer the questions that follow.

> In the past few years, the majority of state governments have passed laws making it illegal to send text messages while driving. These laws are clearly a good decision for which legislators should be praised. Drivers are 23 times more likely to have accidents while texting than they are while driving undistracted. It is common sense that the government has a responsibility to protect its citizens from the recklessness of a careless few.

1. What is the writer's argument about anti-texting laws?
   (1) Such laws are a good idea because drivers are prone to accidents while texting.
   (2) The majority of state governments have passed laws making it illegal to text while driving.

2. What evidence is given in support of the author's argument?
   (1) Drivers are 23 times more prone to accidents while texting.
   (2) Members of state legislatures should be praised.

3. Which of the following is likely one of the author's unstated assumptions?
   (1) Drivers must police themselves to avoid dangerous situations.
   (2) A state government should pass laws to ensure citizens' safety.

The answer to Question 1 is **(1)**. The author's opinion is that anti-texting laws are "good" and "should be praised." The rest of the argument supports that opinion. The answer to Question 2 is **(1)**. A statistic such as "23 times more likely" is typical of the factual evidence you can expect to see on the TASC. The answer to Question 3 is **(2)**. We know that the assumption that governments should protect citizens is a premise of the author because he praises legislators for passing these laws to make roads and highways safer.

### KEY IDEAS

- An argument is a statement that takes a position.
- An argument consists of a conclusion about the issue and supporting evidence.
- Critically reading an argument involves understanding the stated or implied assumptions behind the claim.

### TASC TEST TIP

*On some passages, writers may use terms such as "for these reasons," "it follows that," or "therefore" to indicate their conclusion. In other cases, you may have to carefully analyze the passage to find the argument.*

# PRACTICE 2

**Questions 1 through 4 refer to this passage about the minimum wage.**

### MAKING MINIMUM WAGE WORK FOR WORKERS

1 The minimum wage is the lowest salary that a company can legally pay its employees. The federal minimum wage is the lowest allowed in the nation, but many states have set minimum wages higher than the national number.

2 Several states have taken the sensible step of automatically raising their minimum wage to adjust for inflation and consumer price increases. This policy ensures that low-paid workers are paid a stable, livable income over the long term. Raising the federal minimum wage, however, requires direct action by lawmakers. As a result, over the past 40 years, the federal minimum wage has not kept pace with the rate of inflation. Nowadays, full-time minimum-wage workers earn so little money that many have fallen below the poverty line. In the case of the minimum wage, the federal government should follow the lead of the states. Congress needs to establish automatic wage increases triggered by increases in inflation and changes to the consumer price index. That is the only way to ensure sustainable earnings for hard-working citizens.

**1.** Which of the following is the main point of the passage?

A. States' minimum wages differ from the federal minimum wage.
B. The federal government should automatically raise the minimum wage to match price increases.
C. The federal minimum wage ensures a comfortable living for people earning it.
D. State minimum wages are the result of political games played with people's livelihoods.

**2.** What is the writer's argument about states that automatically raise their minimum wages?

A. Those states' wages have not kept pace with the rate of inflation.
B. People earning more than minimum wage in those states are wealthy.
C. Those states have many workers in poverty.
D. Those states have systems superior to the federal system of manual increases.

**3.** What evidence is given to support the author's argument?

A. Some states have minimum wages lower than the federal minimum wage.
B. The federal government should adjust its minimum wage automatically.
C. Over the past 40 years, the federal minimum wage has not kept pace with inflation.
D. As a result of inflation, $1 in 1972 was worth more than $5 is worth today.

**4.** Which of the following is most likely to be one of the author's assumptions?

A. Employees under the age of 18 might be paid less than the minimum wage.
B. Ensuring sustainable incomes for hardworking citizens is a responsibility of lawmakers.
C. Employees earning the federal minimum wage cannot support themselves and their families.
D. The past 40 years have experienced significantly higher inflation than was expected.

**Review your work using the explanations that start on page 669.**

**STUDY ADVICE**

On page 96, you learned to ask yourself *why* an author wrote a passage, and you learned that sometimes authors want to persuade their readers about something. The questions on this page are about *how* an author goes about persuading her readers.

LESSON 3

# Validity of Arguments

Just because a writer makes an argument does not mean you have to accept it as **valid**, or convincing. You need to analyze the supporting evidence. Below are some types of **support for arguments** and ways that you can question their legitimacy.

### KEY IDEAS

- An argument may or may not be valid.
- For the argument to be valid, it needs to be supported by relevant and provable evidence.
- Critical thinking requires questioning both the method of argument and the source of supporting evidence.

| Type of Support | Description | Questions to Ask |
|---|---|---|
| **Facts** | Objective facts that can be tested or measured | Is the information complete, or is it partial or selectively chosen? |
| **Data or Statistics** | Numerical data that have been gathered or sampled | Do the numbers accurately represent the subject? How were they gathered? |
| **Examples or Anecdotes** | Stories to demonstrate the "truth" | Are the stories true? Are they relevant? |
| **Authority** | Testimonials from a recognized authority | Does the person really know the issue, or is he or she a spokesperson or celebrity? |
| **Causality** | Assertions that one thing caused another | Is this really a cause, or is it just a related factor? |

In addition to analyzing the evidence, you need to be aware that sometimes writers use **emotional appeals** based on fear, pity, or getting you to "jump on the bandwagon" of the argument's popularity.

### TASC TEST TIP

*When you are reading a writer's argument, don't evaluate it based on what you already believe. Think critically about whether or not the writer adequately and validly supports the argument.*

Gasoline prices spiked suddenly in the Weston metropolitan area last week when the local oil refinery went offline due to a facility-wide computer malfunction. Shortly thereafter, the average number of miles driven daily by Weston residents fell by a whopping 55 percent. Clearly, the higher gas prices were responsible for the decline in miles driven.

► What is the argument in the paragraph?

(1) Higher gas prices were responsible for the decline in miles driven.
(2) The spike in gas prices was due to a computer malfunction at the local refinery.

► Which of the following undermines the writer's argument?

(1) Oil refineries have stopped production in the past.
(2) Last week, a blizzard struck the Weston area, causing a state of emergency that required all nonemergency vehicles to stay off the roads.

For the first question, choice **(1)** is correct. The writer concludes that high gas prices caused the decline in driving and uses the background about the refinery shutdown as support. For the second question, choice **(2)** is correct. The writer's argument is faulty because she assumes that the high price of gasoline was the only cause of the reduction in driving. Choice **(2)** supplies another reasonable explanation for the reduced driving, thereby weakening the argument.

# PRACTICE 3

**<u>Questions 1 through 4</u> refer to this passage about voting technology.**

### DIGITAL VOTING: A BETTER WAY TO COUNT

1 The large-scale adoption in 1996 of direct-recording electronic (DRE) voting marked the beginning of an era of superior voting technology. For as long as elections have been held, voting systems have been flawed in various ways. In mid-18th century America, voters called out their selections publicly. This assured an accurate count but meant voting could not be private. Paper ballots, on the other hand, were anonymous but could be easily forged or miscounted.

2 The next innovation was the mechanical-lever voting machine, introduced in the late 19th century. The use of this voting system peaked in the 1960s. Over the next several decades, the mechanical-lever machines were replaced by two early electronic voting systems: bubble sheets recorded by optical scanner and punch cards processed electronically. All of these systems were prone to glitches, such as the notorious "hanging chads" and unreadable ballots in Florida after the 2000 U.S. presidential election.

3 Now, many jurisdictions use all-electronic DRE systems. Every step of the voting process is electronic: the ballot appears on a screen, the voter indicates his or her selection via buttons or touch-screen technology, and results are stored on a memory card. In DRE voting, there is always a record of a voter's choices, and there is no chance of voters filling in the wrong bubble or of poorly punched cards that cause votes to go uncounted. For all of these reasons, DRE is clearly the most secure and accurate voting system available.

**1.** The main point of the passage is that

A. unlike optical-scanning and punch-card voting systems, DRE voting is completely electronic
B. punch-card voting systems caused a problem in the 2000 presidential election
C. DRE systems offer more security and accuracy than other voting systems
D. elections in America have changed greatly over the years

**2.** Which of the following is evidence to support the writer's argument?

A. When technology changes, voting systems change along with it.
B. DRE voting avoids problems associated with other voting systems.
C. Several voting systems have become obsolete because they violated voters' privacy
D. No modern-day election would ever be conducted using a public voice vote.

**3.** What evidence is given to support the writer's argument?

A. Each voter's choices are recorded in the DRE voting system.
B. Mechanical-lever voting machines were replaced by other mechanical voting devices.
C. Punch-card voting involves electronic processing.
D. In the mid-18th century, public votes were popular.

**4.** Which of the following is an example of faulty reasoning that weakens the argument?

A. The writer claims that punch-card systems contributed to problems in the 2000 presidential election without providing any support for the claim.
B. The writer suggests that DRE voting was responsible for the demise of older voting systems, overlooking the possibility that there might have been another cause.
C. The writer fails to consider that even if DRE voting addresses all the flaws of previous systems, it may introduce other flaws of its own.
D. The author fails to provide evidence that voters in 18th-century America were wary of elections.

**Review your work using the explanations that start on page 670.**

LESSON 4

# Text Related by Theme or Topic

On the TASC Reading Test, you may need to read related **paired passages** and answer questions based on your understanding of both of them. The two texts will be related by **topic** (what the passages address) or **theme** (the writer's message about a topic). You will need to understand each passage on its own and be able to **synthesize** (blend) information to draw a conclusion.

Below are two paragraphs about the same topic. One is a news story, and the other is an opinion piece. Read both selections and answer the questions based on your understanding and analysis of both texts.

**News Story**

Candy, greasy meals, and high-calorie sodas may be banned in U.S. elementary and high schools. According to news reports, new standards proposed by the Department of Agriculture would replace such items as fried potato chips with baked chips and sugary sodas with lower-calories sport drinks. These regulations are a result of a child nutrition law, passed by the U.S. Congress to combat childhood obesity.

**Response Letter**

*The paper announced that the government will be mandating "healthier food" in school cafeterias. Doesn't the government have anything better to do than to "babysit" our schools? Shouldn't the schools be focused on improving education, not monitoring behavior? Where is the research to show that school meals account for childhood obesity? This is just one more government intrusion into our personal lives.*

▶ What is the topic of both of these selections?
(1) greasy food in school cafeterias
(2) new guidelines for healthy school meals

▶ What information is given in the news story?
(1) The government is "babysitting" our schools.
(2) Certain unhealthy foods may be banned from public schools.

▶ Which relevant argument is made in the response letter?
(1) The new regulations are a good way to help combat childhood obesity.
(2) The new regulations are a poor idea because monitoring student behavior is not a school's responsibility.

The correct choice in the first question is **(2)** because the news story reports on the regulations while the response letter criticizes them. In the second question, choice **(2)** is correct because it summarizes the factual information in the news story. The correct choice in the third question is **(2)** because the writer of the response letter clearly states her opposition to the new regulations.

### KEY IDEAS

- The TASC Reading Test may present two selections on a related topic or theme.
- Some questions will require comprehension and analysis of each piece on its own.
- Other questions will require a synthesis of information from the two sources.

### TASC TEST TIP

*When you are presented with two selections, identify the main point of both passages. Doing so will help you to spot what the authors agree or disagree about.*

# PRACTICE 4

Questions 1 through 4 refer to the paired passages below.

**Passage 1**

The online piracy of digital files is a major problem for the music industry. From 2004 to 2009, 30 billion songs were downloaded illegally, representing a loss of billions of dollars of revenue. Recent legislation, along with the shutdown of certain major file-sharing websites, has begun to stem the tide of piracy. The organization representing the music and recording industry, however, reports that the annual harm to the economy from piracy may be as high as $12.5 billion dollars a year. More must be done.

**Passage 2**

Online piracy is harmful to the music industry, but not only for the reasons the industry claims. The financial harm caused by piracy is often exaggerated. The recording industry's estimates are based on the prices of songs and the number of songs downloaded; in reality, a person who illegally downloaded 10,000 songs would download only a fraction of that number if forced to pay for each file. As a result, the actual loss of revenue caused by piracy is certainly much lower than the industry estimates. However, a fear of piracy has made investors cautious about signing new, experimental artists. That in itself is a cause for concern and a reason more needs to be done to halt illegal downloading.

---

**1.** The topic of both passages is

A. ways in which industries can exaggerate financial harm
B. examples of recent legislation to protect an industry
C. online piracy of music files
D. the signing of new, experimental musicians

**2.** The main argument of Passage 1 is that

A. new, experimental artists are necessary for the music industry to succeed
B. additional action to combat online piracy is warranted because piracy causes financial losses to the music industry
C. the shutdown of major file-sharing websites was a positive development because they contributed to $12.5 billion per year in damages
D. from 2004 to 2009, 30 billion songs were downloaded illegally

**3.** Which claim in Passage 2 supports the conclusion drawn in Passage 1?

A. Fear of piracy makes it difficult for new, experimental acts to get signed.
B. Recent legislation has begun to reduce the amount of online music piracy.
C. A person who downloads music illegally would likely download fewer songs if he or she had to pay for them.
D. Financial harm from illegal music downloads is often exaggerated.

**4.** With which of the following statements would the writers of both passages agree?

A. Online piracy of digital files has a harmful effect on the music industry.
B. Online piracy of digital files causes serious damage to the economy.
C. The main reason to combat online piracy is to ensure that new, experimental artists can find investors.
D. Music is important for a healthy society to function properly.

**Review your work using the explanations that start on page 670.**

Analyzing Informational Text

LESSON 5

# Texts with Opposing Arguments

You have learned about writers' arguments and have seen how the Reading Test may require you to work with two related texts. In some cases, you may read two selections that have **opposing arguments** about the same topic. Read the selections below and think about the authors' claims, the **assumptions** or the thinking behind their positions, and the supporting evidence for each.

**KEY IDEAS**

- The TASC Reading Test may present opposing arguments on the same topic.
- Some arguments will reach different conclusions because they use different types of evidence.
- Other opposing pairs of arguments may use the same evidence but have different underlying assumptions.

**Argument**

Coal, the source of half the energy in the United States, has been the dirtiest of all fossil fuels because it creates harmful emissions when burned. Help is on the way with the development of new "clean coal" technologies that reduce coal's environmental impact. These new technologies purify exhaust gases as coal burns (wet scrubbers) and prevent the formation of harmful emissions in the first place (low-NOx burners). There is even gasification, which avoids burning coal altogether.

**Opposing Argument**

"Clean coal" amounts to just an advertising slogan. Don't be fooled by claims about new technologies making coal a clean-burning fuel. The hazards to our environment start well before that. Coal mining wastes huge amounts of water—70 to 260 million gallons daily. Today's mining companies now use mountaintop removal, instead of traditional mining, to extract coal. Forty-nine states have issued fish intake advisories due to high mercury concentration in water, much of it due to run-off from coal mining.

**TASC TEST TIP**

*When you read two selections with opposing viewpoints, carefully analyze each writer's arguments. Don't let your opinions on the topic influence how you answer the questions.*

► What is the topic of both of these selections?

(1) preventing air pollution from coal
(2) the usefulness of "clean coal" technologies

You were right to pick choice **(2)**. The Argument suggests that "clean coal" will reduce coal's environmental impact, while the Opposing Argument contends that coal will continue to harm the environment.

► What type of evidence is provided in the Argument?

(1) statistics demonstrating the effectiveness of "clean coal" technologies
(2) facts about new "clean coal" technologies

Here, choice **(2)** is correct. The Argument lists and briefly describes the new technologies.

► How does the Opposing Argument confront the underlying assumption of the Argument?

(1) It points out environmental damage caused by coal before it is burned, when "clean coal" technologies are not used.
(2) It cites studies showing that "clean coal" technologies are less effective than their advocates claim they are.

Choice **(1)** is correct. Impacts from mining, water waste, and mercury run-off are among the other harms cited in the Opposing Argument.

# PRACTICE 5

**Questions 1 through 4 refer to the Argument and Opposing Argument below.**

**ARGUMENT: Rating Systems for Movies Are Beneficial**

In 1968, the Motion Picture Association of America (MPAA) replaced the complicated, morals-based Hays Code with the current, user-friendly MPAA rating system. This system is designed specifically to help parents decide whether a movie is appropriate for their child. Every parent in America knows what G, PG, PG-13, and R mean and can use these ratings to quickly judge suitability. Moreover, ratings now include descriptions that give even more information that parents can use to assess content and make wise movie-viewing decisions for their children. MPAA ratings take the guesswork out of at least one aspect of parenting!

**OPPOSING ARGUMENT: Movie Rating Systems Are a Joke**

A movie's MPAA rating—G, PG, PG-13, or R—is a familiar tag that parents, in particular, use to make fundamental decisions about family entertainment. Sadly, the rating system is more a marketing tool for the industry than a useful guide for parents. Consider that, in the early 1980s, unknowing parents exposed their children to alarming gore and violence under the PG rating, prompting the creation of the PG-13 rating. The result is that now, a movie that includes violence, drug use, gore, and sexual content can be marketed as a family-friendly PG-13 experience. Parents are better off finding an unbiased source of realistic reviews than trusting the MPAA rating system.

---

1. The topic of both passages is

   A. violence in movies
   B. good and bad parenting decisions
   C. the MPAA movie rating system
   D. motion picture marketing strategies

2. Which of the following is the main point of the Argument?

   A. The MPAA rating system replaced the Hays Code.
   B. The MPAA rating system is a useful tool for parents.
   C. Parents should consult a variety of sources before deciding which movies to allow their children to watch.
   D. The G, PG, PG-13, and R ratings are familiar and easy to understand.

### STUDY ADVICE

How long are your study sessions? Start by studying for as long as you can easily focus on the material—which might be 15 minutes or an hour. Gradually train yourself to focus on the material for longer stretches, until your study sessions are two to three hours each. After all, you will need to maintain your focus on Test Day.

3. The writer of the Opposing Argument would agree with which of the following statements?

   A. Parents overreacted to movie content in the 1980s.
   B. The PG-13 rating introduced a helpful distinction to the system.
   C. Violence and drug use are examples of family-friendly movie content.
   D. The MPAA rating system should not be trusted.

4. Which of the following conclusions could be drawn about the writer of the Argument?

   A. She largely approves of the MPAA rating system as a guideline for parents.
   B. She allows her children to watch movies rated PG but not those rated PG-13.
   C. She is wary of how the MPAA rating system judges violent content in movies.
   D. She believes that the Hays Code was detrimental to the movie industry.

**Review your work using the explanations that start on page 670.**

Analyzing Informational Text

LESSON 6

# Texts with Related Graphic Information

When you read nonfiction and informational text in a textbook, magazine, or website, it is often accompanied by a **graphic**—an illustration, photograph, or diagram—that helps you to understand the information. On the TASC Reading Test, you may need to combine information from text and graphics to draw conclusions and to make observations about how the graphic supports the information in the text. Practice with the text and graphic below.

### KEY IDEAS

- The TASC Reading Test may present some selections with accompanying graphics.
- Read the passage carefully and analyze the graphic.
- Evaluate whether each question is based on the text, the graphic, or a combination of the two.

### TASC TEST TIP

*When you see that a graphic accompanies a selection, ask yourself, "Is this graphic providing supporting material, or is it providing additional information?" If you understand that, you will be better able to answer the test questions.*

**"Mayfield" No More? The Changing American Household**

Although *Leave It to Beaver* was a fictional television show, many advertisements, politicians, and movies still echo its portrayal of the typical American household of the 1950s: a married couple with children. A closer look at government statistics shows that it might be time to retool that image; today, fewer than half of American households are husband-wife households. In fact, more than a quarter of American households are now occupied by one person living alone—a significant group for marketers to target, as those who live alone are entirely responsible for all household purchases.

**Percent Distribution of Households by Type**

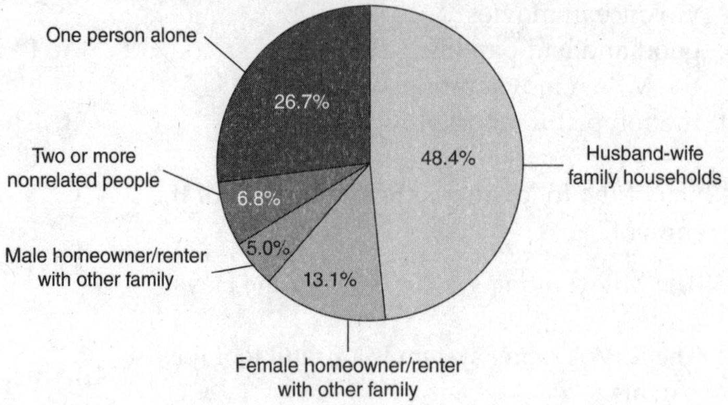

Source: U.S. Census Bureau

▶ What is the topic of the story and the graphic?

(1) the composition of American households
(2) advertising on *Leave It to Beaver*

If you answered **(1)**, you were correct. The story outlines the current makeup of American households, and the graphic supplies factual detail.

▶ How does the pie chart support the information in the story?

(1) It provides statistics comparing American households in the 1950s with American households today.
(2) It confirms the story's point about current household composition and provides additional details not discussed in the story.

Choice **(2)** is correct. The pie chart supplies statistics about husband-wife households (48.4%) and single-resident households (26.7%) that match the article's assertions and show the proportion of Americans living with other family and with roommates to whom they are not related.

# PRACTICE 6

<u>Questions 1 through 3</u> **refer to the following passage and the two figures below.**

**Gerrymandering: An Electoral Advantage**

1 The term *gerrymander* is used to describe the process by which electoral districts are given curious shapes in order to favor the interests of the party in power of a state legislature. Through this process, the governing political party tailors the electoral map to group unfavorable neighborhoods into a few districts likely to vote for the opposition while configuring the majority of districts to favor the party in power.

2 Figures 2(a) and 2(b) show how a governing political party can benefit from gerrymandering. In both figures, there are 40 gray squares and 60 white squares, and the area is divided into four equal-sized districts. In Figure 2(a), the white-square party will win only two seats out of four, but in Figure 2(b), the white-square party will take three of the four districts, as most of the gray votes are consolidated into one oddly shaped and geographically separated district. In fact, Illinois's 4th Congressional District is similar in shape to the gray district in Figure 2(b).

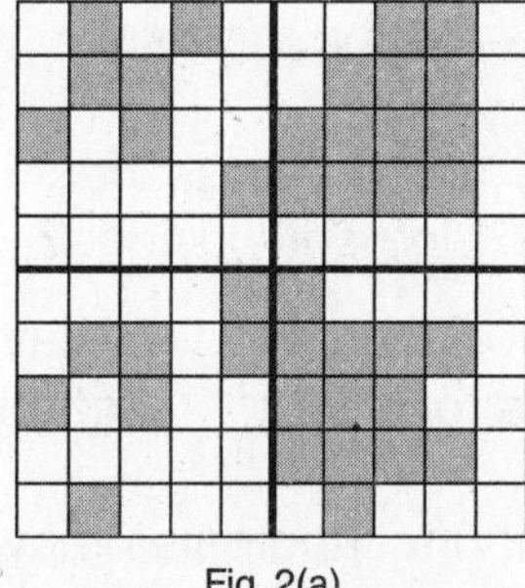

Fig. 2(a)

Geographically Uniform Districts.

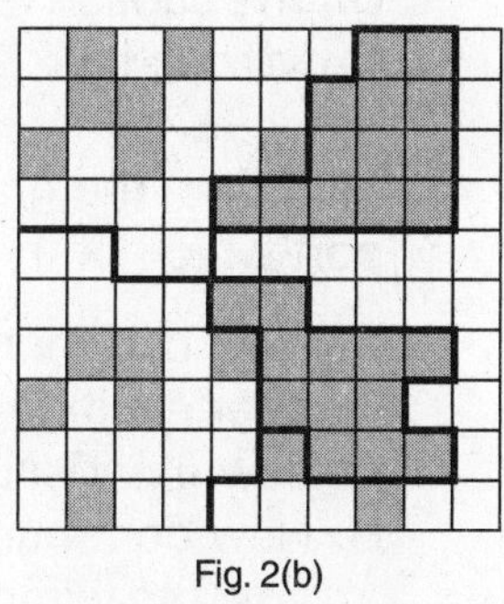

Fig. 2(b)

Gerrymandered Districts.

1. Which of the following is the main point of the passage and figures?
   A. Illinois's 4th Congressional District has now been in existence for over 200 years.
   B. Curiosity is the most important ingredient in the democratic process.
   C. Gerrymandered congressional districts are a major threat to the democratic system.
   D. Governing parties can use their power to shape electoral districts to their advantage.

2. Which of the following conclusions can be drawn from the passage and the figures?
   A. Gerrymandering is more common in Illinois than in other American states.
   B. Through gerrymandering, a governing party can be elected to a greater number of seats than its voter support might otherwise allow.
   C. Through gerrymandering, impartial committees draw boundaries to keep elections fair.
   D. Gerrymandering convinces citizens who would ordinarily be unfavorable to a party to change their votes.

3. In what way do the figures support the passage?
   A. They illustrate the advantages a party can obtain through gerrymandering.
   B. They predict victory for the gray party in the upcoming election.
   C. They are more relevant to Chicago than to rural Illinois.
   D. They show that voter turnout will continue to decline if governing parties continue to gerrymander districts.

**Review your work using the explanations that start on page 670.**

**STUDY ADVICE**

On the next few pages, you'll do some Analyzing Text practice questions. If you get most of them correct, pat yourself on the back! If you get several wrong, work through the lessons and practice problems again. As our founder Stanley H. Kaplan said, "Repetition breeds familiarity. Familiarity breeds confidence. Confidence breeds success."

# Analyzing Informational Text Practice Questions

**Questions 1 through 4 refer to the following passage about communication technology and the accompanying cartoon.**

### SOCIAL NETWORKING AT WHAT COST?

1 Sit in any restaurant or coffee shop long enough, and you're bound to witness a familiar scene: a couple, a family, or a group of friends gathered to enjoy a meal, but instead of conversing, each person at the table sits staring at his or her cell phone. In this age of social media, the question arises: does technology enhance or limit our ability to make strong emotional connections with other people?

2 Social networks have broadened with the expansion of communication technology. We connect easily with new acquaintances, old friends, potential clients, and complete strangers. For loved ones who are separated by distance, technology provides an important lifeline. Soldiers, deployed for long tours of duty, meet their newborn children over video chat. Grandparents, limited by ill health, watch their grandchildren grow through pictures and videos posted to social media sites.

3 With all the benefits of social media, however, come considerable costs. Each new connection we make (and old acquaintance we maintain) demands time, energy, and emotional investment. This often comes at the expense of time we could give to the most important people in our lives. Moreover, much of what we share through social media is superficial or entertaining. Only when technology is used to enhance our deepest, most valuable connections can it be considered real progress for humankind.

*"A bunch of friends are coming over to stare at their phones."*



1. What is the purpose of the passage and the graphic?

   A. to discuss different forms of social media
   B. to suggest a new form of communication technology
   C. to examine ways in which modern families use technology to communicate
   D. to discuss whether communication technology helps or hurts relationships

2. What is the topic of the passage and the graphic?

   A. maintaining long-distance relationships
   B. how technology affects interpersonal connections
   C. the limits of social media
   D. the expense of new technologies

3. Which of the following details in the graphic supports the author's point of view in the passage?

   A. The caption reveals that the woman is expecting friends to visit.
   B. The woman in the cartoon is speaking on the phone with a computer nearby.
   C. The woman in the cartoon is alone.
   D. The caption reveals that the woman's friends will use their phones during their visit.

4. Together, the graphic and the passage support which of the following conclusions?

   A. New communication technologies may offer exciting ways for people to establish new friendships.
   B. New communication technologies may adversely impact important human relationships.
   C. New communication technologies may offer positive solutions for friends who are separated by distance.
   D. New communication technologies may help people to complete several tasks at once.

**<u>Questions 5 through 8</u> refer to this passage about the giant squid.**

### THE GIANT SQUID: MORE THAN COLOSSAL?

1 The giant squid is the world's longest cephalopod. Based on measurements of over 100 full specimens (including adult and adolescent individuals) recovered from the stomachs of sperm whales and other predators, scientists have determined that the giant squid can reach a length of 13 meters.

2 Some have argued that the honor of longest cephalopod should instead go to the colossal squid, a distant relative of the giant squid, but this belief is incorrect. It is true that the colossal squid may outweigh its giant cousin. However, of the few specimens of the colossal squid (all of them juveniles) described in the scientific literature, the longest measured ten meters. Therefore, the giant squid wins the length contest.

3 No other cephalopod is even close in length to either of these animals. For example, the giant Pacific octopus, the world's longest octopus species, has a maximum arm span of only about six meters. The giant squid's status as the world's longest cephalopod remains uncontested.

5. The main point of the passage is that

    A. the colossal squid weighs more than the giant squid
    B. the giant squid is the world's longest cephalopod
    C. the giant Pacific octopus is the world's longest octopus species
    D. the giant squid can reach a length of 13 meters

6. Which of the following best summarizes the writer's argument in paragraph 2?

    A. The colossal squid is the world's longest cephalopod.
    B. The colossal squid is a distant relative of the giant squid.
    C. The giant Pacific octopus is not as long as the giant squid.
    D. The giant squid is longer than the colossal squid.

7. What evidence is given to support the writer's argument in paragraph 2?

    A. The colossal squid can weigh more than the giant squid.
    B. The giant squid is the world's longest cephalopod.
    C. The length of the longest known colossal squid specimen is ten meters.
    D. The giant Pacific octopus has a maximum arm span of only about six meters.

8. Which of the following is an example of faulty reasoning that weakens the writer's argument?

    A. The longest known colossal squid is ten meters long, so there is no colossal squid longer than the longest giant squid.
    B. The giant Pacific octopus is the world's longest species of octopus, but it is not as long as the giant squid.
    C. Many specimens of the giant squid have been measured.
    D. Because sperm whales prey on giant squid, they must also prey on colossal squid.

**Questions 9 through 15 refer to these two passages about mercury.**

### Passage 1

The use of mercury amalgam for dental fillings has already been banned in several European nations, and it should also be banned in the United States. The mercury contained in amalgam fillings slowly leaches into the mouth and is swallowed. It is then absorbed by the small intestine and accumulates in various body tissues, including the brain, kidney, and liver. This accumulated mercury causes a variety of health problems. In 2001, a study reported that patients with a higher number of amalgam fillings also had higher occurrences of cancer, respiratory disease, and diseases of the nervous system.

In addition to its health impact, the mercury released from dental amalgam has a number of damaging environmental consequences. Mercury waste produced by dental offices is sometimes directly disposed of into sewage water or landfills. Mercury can leach from landfills into groundwater and get into rivers and lakes. It has been estimated, for example, that dental amalgam is the source of 4 percent of the mercury found in the water of Lake Superior.

Due to the alarming health and environmental consequences of mercury amalgam, dental fillings should be made from resin composites instead. These composites are already becoming popular due to their cosmetic appeal, so banning mercury amalgam will create no consumer backlash. There are demonstrable advantages (and no disadvantages) to banning mercury dental amalgam in the United States.

### Passage 2

In recent years, uneducated consumers have expressed a growing fear of the mercury commonly found in dental fillings. The environmental impact of mercury is serious, and the release of mercury into the environment must be better controlled. However, the health risks associated with mercury amalgam fillings are minimal.

It is well-known that people who have mercury amalgam fillings absorb small amounts of mercury. However, most of this mercury is excreted in the urine. To date, no convincing scientific study has demonstrated that mercury absorbed from dental fillings causes any serious health problems. Because mercury amalgam fillings tend to last longer than resin composite fillings, amalgam is preferable for use whenever there is no cosmetic need for a tooth-colored filling.

However, the disposal of mercury amalgam in dental offices absolutely must be regulated. The Environmental Protection Agency estimates that 40 to 50 percent of the mercury in the wastewater processed at public treatment plants comes from dental amalgam. This is inexcusable, especially because devices that remove mercury from wastewater are inexpensive and easy for dental offices to use. While mercury amalgam should remain available because it is more durable than composites, every dental office must have a device to remove mercury from wastewater.

9. The topic of both passages is
   A. groundwater contamination
   B. mercury dental amalgam
   C. resin composite fillings
   D. dental health risks

10. What is the main argument of Passage 1?
   A. Mercury amalgam fillings are not unhealthy, but their disposal should be regulated for environmental reasons.
   B. Resin composite should replace mercury amalgam for dental fillings because it tends to last longer.
   C. Mercury amalgam fillings should be banned because they are unhealthy and bad for the environment.
   D. Mercury dental amalgam leaches mercury into a patient's mouth and can damage the liver.

11. Which statement best describes the supporting evidence in paragraph 3 of Passage 2?
   A. It appears convincing at first glance, but no source is cited.
   B. It is a seemingly convincing statistic, but the source is untrustworthy.
   C. It is an unconvincing statistic from an untrustworthy source.
   D. It is a convincing statistic from a reliable source.

12. In paragraph 3, the author of Passage 1 states that "These composites are already becoming popular due to their cosmetic appeal, so banning mercury amalgam will create no consumer backlash." Which of the following is an assumption the author of Passage 1 makes about consumers?
   A. Consumers have no other reason, such as cost or durability, to prefer mercury amalgam to composite fillings.
   B. Consumers will be happy with whatever material they are offered for dental fillings.
   C. Consumers are not generally vocal about their preferences.
   D. Consumers never discuss the choice of filling material with their dentists.

13. The writer of Passage 2 would be most likely to agree with which of the following statements?
   A. Mercury amalgam fillings should be banned because they are unhealthy.
   B. Resin composite fillings look better than mercury amalgam fillings when each is used on visible tooth surfaces.
   C. Mercury contamination of public wastewater is an unimportant issue.
   D. Resin composite fillings are preferable to mercury amalgam in all cases.

14. Which of the passages has weaker supporting evidence and why?
   A. Passage 1, because it cites no sources for the study or the statistic it cites
   B. Passage 1, because it argues that mercury should be banned in dental fillings
   C. Passage 2, because it cites the Environmental Protection Agency as the source of a statistic it cites
   D. Passage 2, because it argues that mercury used by dental offices should be better regulated

15. Which of the statements in Passage 1 is an example of faulty reasoning?
   A. Resin composites are already gaining in popularity.
   B. The use of mercury dental amalgam has already been banned in several European nations.
   C. The mercury released from dental amalgam has damaging environmental consequences.
   D. Mercury that accumulates in body tissues causes a variety of health problems.

**Review your work using the explanations that start on page 671.**

LESSON 1

# Plot Elements

**Plot** refers to the events in a story. Generally, the events are told in order—what happened first, next, and so on. Understanding the order of events, the sequence, can help you see which events caused or affected others.

A story usually contains at least one **conflict**, or problem. The conflict may be between characters, within a character, or between a character and nature. Conflict creates tension. When it is resolved, the tension ends.

The following excerpt is about a brother and sister whose mother has a tumor. As you read it, look for the order of events and the conflict.

> Robert didn't phone until evening. His voice was fatigued and thin. "I've moved her to the university hospital," he said. "They can't deal with it at home."
>
> Kate waited, saying nothing. She concentrated on the toes of her shoes. They needed shining. *You never take care of anything,* her mother would say.
>
> "She has a tumor in her head." He said it firmly, as though Kate might challenge him.
>
> "I'll take a plane tomorrow morning," Kate answered, "I'll be there by noon."
>
> Robert exhaled. "Look," he said, "don't even come back here unless you can keep your mouth shut and do it my way."
>
> "Get to the point."
>
> "The point is they believe she has a malignancy and we're not going to tell her. I almost didn't tell you." His voice faltered. "They're going to operate but if they find what they're expecting, they don't think they can stop it."
>
> For a moment there was no sound except an oceanic vibration of distance on the wire. Even that sound grew still. Robert breathed. Kate could almost see him, in a booth at the hospital, staring straight ahead at the plastic instructions screwed to the narrow rectangular body of the telephone. It seemed to her that she was hurtling toward him.

From "Souvenir" by Jayne Anne Phillips, from *Black Tickets,* NY: Delacorte Press, 1979. Reprinted with permission of Jayne Anne Phillips.

► When did Robert decide not to tell his mother about the tumor?

(1) before talking to Kate
(2) after discussing the issue with Kate

**(1)** is correct. Robert has already decided what to do when he calls Kate.

► Which of the following identifies a conflict in this excerpt?

(1) Kate tells Robert she will fly there tomorrow.
(2) Robert tells Kate that she must do as he says.

**(2)** is correct. Robert challenges Kate. That creates tension.

### KEY IDEAS

- The plot is the series of events in a story. Understanding the order of the events helps you see how they are related.
- The conflict is a problem between characters, between a character and nature, or within a character.

### TASC TEST TIP

*To understand the events and conflict in a story, pay attention to the dialogue. Remember that every time the speaker changes, a new paragraph begins.*

# PRACTICE 1

<u>Questions 1 through 4</u> **refer to the following excerpt from a short story.**

**EXCERPTED FROM "THE PIECE OF STRING"**

1 The countryman looked at the Mayor in astonishment, already terrified by this suspicion resting on him without his knowing why.

2 "Me? Me? I picked up the pocket-book?"

3 "Yes, you, yourself."

4 "On my word of honor, I never heard of it."

5 "But you were seen."

6 "I was seen, me? Who says he saw me?"

7 "Monsieur Malandain, the harness-maker."

8 The old man remembered, understood, and flushed with anger.

9 "Ah, he saw me, the clodhopper, he saw me pick up this string, here, Mayor." And rummaging in his pocket he drew out the little piece of string.

10 But the Mayor, incredulous, shook his head.

11 "You will not make me believe, Maître Hauchecorne, that Monsieur Malandain, who is a man we can believe, mistook this cord for a pocketbook."

12 The peasant, furious, lifted his hand, spat at one side to attest his honor, repeating:

"It is nevertheless God's own truth, the sacred
13 truth. I repeat it on my soul and my salvation."

14 The Mayor resumed:

15 "After picking up the object, you stood like a stilt, looking a long while in the mud to see if any piece of money had fallen out."

16 The old fellow choked with indignation and fear. . . .

17 He was confronted with Monsieur Malandain, who repeated and maintained his affirmation. They abused each other for an hour. At his own request, Maître Hauchecorne was searched. Nothing was found on him.

18 Finally the Mayor, very much perplexed, discharged him with the warning that he would consult the Public Prosecutor and ask for further orders.



**1.** What was the peasant doing when he "lifted his hand, spat at one side to attest his honor" (paragraph 12)?

A. thinking of striking the Mayor
B. swearing that he was telling the truth
C. pleading to the Mayor for mercy
D. performing a peasant ritual

**2.** How did the peasant react when confronted with Malandain, the harness-maker?

He

A. became choked with fear and indignation
B. tried to explain what had actually happened
C. became respectful and subdued
D. confronted him and then asked to be searched

**3.** Which of the following statements best describes the conflict in this excerpt?

A. A town mayor is abusing his authority.
B. A peasant leads a harsh life and is often at odds with others.
C. A peasant is accused of taking a pocketbook.
D. Someone has lost a pocketbook with a great deal of money in it.

**4.** What is the most likely reason the harnessmaker is believed?

A. A string can't be mistaken for a pocketbook.
B. The peasant was looking in the mud for money.
C. The harness-maker is higher in social status than the peasant.
D. Other people saw the peasant pick up a pocketbook.

**Review your work using the explanations that start on page 671.**

LESSON 2

# Inferences

To understand a story, you can't just rely on what is directly stated. You also need to "read between the lines," or make **inferences**. An inference is based on information you are given *plus* what you have learned about the real world—the way things happen and the way people act.

As you read this excerpt from a story, look for suggested meanings behind people's actions and words.

> "Last night?" The old blue eyes looked blank, then brightened. "Ah no, I must have taken one of my Seconals. Otherwise I'd have heard it surely. 'Auntie,' my niece always says—'what if there should be a fire, and you there sleeping away?' Do what she says, I do sometimes, only to hear every pin drop till morning." She shook her head, entering the elevator. "Going up?"
>
> "N-no," said Mrs. Hazlitt. "I—have to wait here for a minute." She sat down on the bench, the token bench that she had never seen anybody sitting on, and watched the car door close on the little figure still shaking its head, borne upward like a fairy godmother, willing but unable to oblige. The car's hum stopped, then its light glowed on again. Someone else was coming down. . . .
>
> The car door opened. "Wssht!" said Miss Finan, scuttling out again. "I've just remembered. Not last night, but two weeks ago. And once before that. A scream, you said?"
>
> Mrs. Hazlitt stood up. Almost unable to speak, for the tears that suddenly wrenched her throat, she described it.

From "The Scream on Fifty-Seventh Street" by Hortense Calisher, from *Tales for the Mirror,* reprinted in *Women and Fiction,* edited by Susan Cahill, New York: New American Library, 1975.

► What happened before the beginning of this excerpt?

(1) Mrs. Hazlitt heard a scream the night before and asked Miss Finan if she heard it too.

(2) Mrs. Hazlitt asked Miss Finan about her health and whether she is sleeping well.

The correct answer is **(1).** You can infer it from details such as "Last night?" and "Not last night, but two weeks ago. And once before that. A scream, you said?"

► What is the most likely reason that "tears suddenly wrenched" Mrs. Hazlitt's throat?

(1) She was upset at Miss Finan's inability to remember.

(2) She was relieved that Miss Finan had heard a scream too.

You are correct if you chose **(2).** Mrs. Hazlitt is so relieved that someone else heard the scream that she has to fight back tears.

**KEY IDEAS**

- To understand a story, you must make inferences.
- Making inferences means that you look closely at the details in the story, think about your knowledge of the real world, and then ask yourself, "What does this information point to?"

**TASC TEST TIP**

*Do not leave a question unanswered. If you read a tough question, do your best to think about it, look back at the passage for information you may need, and then choose the best answer.*

# PRACTICE 2

**Questions 1 through 4 refer to the following excerpt from a short story.**

### EXCERPTED FROM "THE STORY OF AN HOUR"

1 She knew that she would weep again when she saw the kind, tender hands folded in death; the face that had never looked save with love upon her, fixed and gray and dead. But she saw beyond that bitter moment a long procession of years to come that would belong to her absolutely. And she opened and spread her arms out to them in welcome.

2 There would be no one to live for during those coming years; she would live for herself. There would be no powerful will bending her in that blind persistence with which men and women believe they have a right to impose a private will upon a fellow creature. A kind intention or a cruel intention made the act seem no less a crime as she looked upon it in that brief moment of illumination.

3 And yet she had loved him—sometimes. Often she had not. What did it matter! What could love, the unsolved mystery, count for in face of this possession of self-assertion, which she suddenly recognized as the strongest impulse of her being!

4 "Free! Body and soul free!" she kept whispering . . .

5 Some one was opening the front door with a latchkey. It was [her husband] Brently Mallard who entered, a little travel-stained, composedly carrying his grip-sack and umbrella. He had been far from the scene of accident, and did not even know there had been one. He stood amazed at [his wife] Josephine's piercing cry; at Richards' quick motion to screen him from the view of his wife.

6 But Richards was too late.

7 When the doctors came they said she had died of heart disease—of joy that kills.

From "The Story of an Hour" by Kate Chopin.

**1.** How did Brently Mallard generally feel toward his wife?

He

A. had always loved her
B. kept her at arm's length
C. liked to play practical jokes on her
D. had cruel intentions toward her

**2.** Which detail best expresses Josephine's vision of her future?

A. that bitter moment
B. she'd weep again
C. spread her arms out in welcome
D. blind persistence

**3.** What was the doctors' meaning when they said that Josephine died of "joy that kills" (paragraph 7)?

They thought that

A. she was overcome and thrilled to see her husband
B. she was excited about her upcoming life of freedom
C. her heart was worn out from giving so much love
D. her heart was weakened from the strain of living

**4.** Why did Josephine die?

A. She was overcome with relief.
B. She was shocked that she would not be free.
C. She was confused by feelings of love and hate.
D. She thought there would be no one to live for.

**Review your work using the explanations that start on page 672.**

## STUDY ADVICE

As you're getting settled into your study schedule, remember to build in rewards and breaks. Celebrate a job well done with a fun outing. Commemorate your successes in practice with a study partner or with your cheering section (family or friends). You need these moments to build confidence, which is a necessary component of success.

LESSON 3

# Character

**Characters** are the people who inhabit a story. The personalities and motivations of characters are often stated directly by the **narrator**—the person telling the story. Sometimes you can also infer characters' personalities or motivations by what they do, what they think, and what they say.

As you read this excerpt, look for details that describe each character.

> Axel Olsen was going to paint Helga Crane. Not only was he going to paint her, but he was to accompany her and her aunt on their shopping expedition. Aunt Katrina was frankly elated. Uncle Poul was also visibly pleased. Evidently they were not above kow-towing to a lion. Helga's own feelings were mixed; she was amused, grateful, and vexed. It had all been decided and arranged without her, and, also, she was a little afraid of Olsen. His stupendous arrogance awed her.
>
> The day was an exciting, not easily to be forgotten one. Definitely, too, it conveyed to Helga her exact status in her new environment. A decoration. A curio. A peacock. Their progress through the shops was an event; an event for Copenhagen as well as for Helga Crane. Her dark, alien appearance was to most people an astonishment. Some stared surreptitiously, some openly, and some stopped dead in front of her in order more fully to profit by their stares. "*Den Sorte*" dropped freely, audibly, from many lips.
>
> The time came when she grew used to the stares of the population. And the time came when the population of Copenhagen grew used to her outlandish presence and ceased to stare. But at the end of that first day it was with thankfulness that she returned to the sheltering walls of the house on Maria Kirkplads.

From "Quicksand" by Nella Larsen, in *The Norton Anthology of African American Literature,* edited by Henry Louis Gates, Jr., and Nellie Y. McKay, New York: W.W. Norton, 1997.

► Which of the following describes Helga?
(1) attractive, down-to-earth, embarking on a new life
(2) self-centered, smug, enjoys being watched

Choice **(1)** is correct. An artist is painting her, suggesting she is attractive. Yet she prefers not to be the center of attention (see the end of the last paragraph).

► Which of the following would Olsen most likely do at a party?
(1) snub the hostess if the wine was below his expectations
(2) offer to drive anyone home who needed a ride

Choice **(1)** is correct. Apply what you know about people with "stupendous arrogance" (see the end of the first paragraph) to answer this question.

### KEY IDEAS

- Characters are the people in the story.
- You can understand a character by noting what the narrator tells you directly as well as by inferring from the character's appearance, actions, words, and thoughts.

### ON THE TASC TEST

*A common kind of question asks you to choose how a character would act in a different situation, based on what you know about the character's personality.*

# PRACTICE 3

**Questions 1 through 3 refer to the following excerpt from a story.**

### EXCERPTED FROM "HIZAKURIGE"

1 "I shall never forget it," the witch went on. "When you were ill you gave your sickness to me. Our only child, who had to carry on our name, grew weak and thin because there was no rice to fill his empty stomach. Every day the bill collectors were knocking at the door and the rent remained unpaid. Yet I did not complain—not even when I slipped in the dogs' dirt in the lane."

2 "Don't talk of it," said Yaji. "You'll break my heart."

3 "And then, when through my labors I had saved enough money to buy a kimono, I had to pawn it for your sake and never saw it again. Never again did it come back to me from the pawnbroker's."

4 "At the same time you must remember what a pleasant place you are in now," said Yaji, "while I have to worry along down here."

5 "What? What is there pleasant about it? It is true that by the help of your friends you erected a stone over my grave, but you never go near it, and you never contribute to the temple to get the priests to say prayers for my soul. I am nothing to you. The stone over my grave has been taken away and put into the wall, where all the dogs come and make water against it. Not a drop of water is ever placed on my grave. Truly in death we suffer all sorts of troubles."

6 "True, true," said Yaji.

7 "But while you thus treat me with neglect," the witch went on, "lying in my grave I think of nobody but you and long for the time when you will join me in the underworld. Shall I come to meet you?"

8 "No, no, don't do that," said Yaji. "It's really too far for you."

9 "Well then, I have one request to make."

10 "Yes, yes. What is it?"

11 "Give this witch plenty of money."

12 "Of course, of course."

13 "How sad the parting!" cried the witch. "I have yet much to tell you, countless questions to ask you, but the messenger of Hell recalls me!"

14 Then, recovering from her trance, the witch twanged her bow.

From "Hizakurige" by Jippensha Ikku in *The Longwood Introduction to Fiction,* Boston: Allyn and Bacon, 1992.

**1.** Why does Yaji say, "No, no, don't do that . . . It's really too far for you" (paragraph 8)?

A. He is trying to be more considerate than he had been in the past.
B. He is frightened about seeing the ghost of his wife.
C. He has no real interest in seeing his wife again.
D. His wife can't really travel to him anyway.

**2.** Which of the following is the best description of the witch?

A. caring
B. straightforward
C. untrustworthy
D. thoughtful

**3.** Earlier in the story the witch, speaking as Yaji's wife, says, "Ah, what agony I went through when I was married to you—time and again suffering the pangs of hunger and shivering with cold in the winter."

Based on this information and the excerpt, what kind of husband did Yaji seem to be?

A. angry
B. kind-hearted
C. responsible
D. neglectful

**Review your work using the explanations that start on page 672.**

LESSON 4

# Theme

Every story has a subject. The subject might be about fighting a war or growing up in poverty. But there is more to a story than its subject. As a reader, look for what the author is trying to say about the subject. That is the **theme**—the message the author wants the reader to understand. In fiction, the theme is often a statement about life. For example, the theme might be that fighting in a war changes a person's life forever.

The theme may be directly stated. If it is not, you can infer the theme from the characters' thoughts and actions and from the things that happen in the story.

As you read the following excerpt, ask yourself what message about the people and their lives the author is trying to tell you.

> While the boys were getting the Doctor's horse, he went to the window to examine the house plants. "What do you do to your geraniums to keep them blooming all winter, Mary? I never pass this house that from the road I don't see your windows full of flowers."
>
> She snapped off a dark red one, and a ruffled new green leaf, and put them in his buttonhole. "There, that looks better. You look too solemn for a young man, Ed. Why don't you git married? I'm worried about you. . . ."
>
> Sometimes the Doctor heard the gossipers in the drugstore wondering why Rosicky didn't get on faster. He was industrious, and so were his boys, but they were rather free and easy, weren't pushers, and they didn't always show good judgment. They were comfortable, they were out of debt, but they didn't get much ahead. Maybe, Doctor Burleigh reflected, people as generous and warmhearted and affectionate as the Rosickys never got ahead much; maybe you couldn't enjoy your life and put it into the bank, too.

From "Neighbor Rosicky" by Willa Cather, from *Obscure Destinies*.

### KEY IDEAS

- The subject of a story is what the story is about.
- The theme of a story is different from the subject. The theme goes beyond the subject and expresses a point of view about life.

### TASC TEST TIP

*Read the whole passage carefully but not too slowly before you begin to answer the questions. If you read a question that really stumps you, skip it and go on. You can come back to it.*

► Which of the following statements is the theme of the story?

(1) A good life is measured in terms of love, not money.
(2) People should not gossip about others.

You are correct if you chose **(1).** Doctor Burleigh's thoughts at the end of the excerpt help you understand that this is the author's main message.

► Which of the following details supports the theme?

(1) Mary Rosicky lovingly "worries" about the doctor.
(2) The Rosickys keep out of debt.

Again, you are correct if you chose **(1).** The flowers Mary grows, the fact that she snaps off one to give the doctor, and her expressed concern for him all show her warmth and happiness. They help support the theme that the doctor reflects on.

# PRACTICE 4

**Questions 1 through 5 refer to the following excerpt from a short story.**

**EXCERPTED FROM *GONE FISHIN'***

1 Early morning is the best time. You're fully rested but not awake enough to remember how hard it all is. Morning is like being a child again, and morning before the sun is out is like those magic times that you hid under the bed and in between the clothes hanging in your mother's closet. Times when any kind of miracle could come about just as normal as a spider making her web.

2 I remember waking up in the dark once when I was very small. I jumped right out of bed and went up next to the screen door on the back porch to see what kind of fantastic thing was going on outside. At first I couldn't see anything but there was a clopping sound, nickering, and a deep voice that made me feel calm and wondering. Slowly, coming out from the darkness, I saw a gray shimmering next to a tall black pillar. The shimmer turned into a big horse and the pillar became my father holding out an apple and cooing in his bass voice, "Ho! Yeah, boy," even though the horse was tame and eating from his hand.

3 I drifted into sleep thinking that we were poor and didn't own a horse. When I woke up it was light and there was no horse to be seen. I asked my father about it but he told me that I was dreaming—where were poor people like us going to find big gray stallions?

4 But there were horse chips behind the barn and hoofprints too.

5 I decided that it was a magic horse and man that I'd seen. From that day on I believed that magic hides in the early morning. If you get up early enough you might find something so beautiful that it would be all right if you just died right then because nothing else in life could ever be better.

From *Gone Fishin'* by Walter Mosley, Baltimore: Black Classic Press, 1997.

**1.** In the story, the boy __________ after hearing his father's explanation.

A. feels confused
B. finds a new explanation
C. no longer trusts his father
D. tries to convince his father

**2.** Which of the following is the best description of the boy?

A. hard-hearted
B. imaginative
C. skeptical
D. chatty

**3.** What is the most likely reason the boy decides he saw a magic horse and man?

A. He wants to reconcile what he saw with what his father told him.
B. He enjoys magic and likes to make up stories.
C. He wants to prove his father was mistaken.
D. This kind of miracle can happen.

**4.** Which of the following would the father probably enjoy most?

A. daydreaming about the future
B. having enough money to pay some bills
C. keeping his son's hopes up about getting a new bicycle for his birthday
D. sharing ghost stories around a campfire

**5.** Which of the following statements fits the theme of this story?

A. False hopes will not get you anywhere.
B. Dreams really can come true.
C. Adults cannot see what children see.
D. Morning and youth are full of possibility.

**Review your work using the explanations that start on page 672.**

**STUDY ADVICE**

Remember, you'll be able to work on more questions at the end of this chapter. So, if you are struggling with a topic and don't feel you have more time to spend on it right now, flag it for later! Keeping a good list of what you should come back to is important in organizing your study plan.

Reading Literature

LESSON 5

# Style and Point of View

## Style

A writer has many choices when deciding how to write a story. A writer may use long, complex sentences; short, clipped sentences; or anything in between. A writer may use flowery or formal language, slang, or spoken dialect. One writer may use vivid images or symbols, while another writes a plain, spare story. The individual characteristics that a writer chooses—sentence structure, choice of words, use of images, and other devices—are all part of the writer's **style.**

As you read this excerpt, look for the characteristics that this particular author chose. Ask yourself what effect they have on your understanding of the writing.

> The only part of the night I recall without feeling anger or sadness is loading the horses. Andy and I hardly had the fencing up before Brett came along with the first ten or twelve. . . . A couple of roans and an Appaloosa stood out in that first bunch in the starlight, and a bay with a roached mane. Then Ed brought up a second bunch, about fifteen mostly dark but a palomino and two paints in there, I remember. Andy and I shooed them up the ramp, which clattered and thundered under their hooves. It was a cool night, still. I could feel the horses on my skin, their body heat swirling around us. I could . . . hear their nostrils fluttering. I felt hard muscle ripple under my hand when I clapped a hip to steer them around. I felt their tails slap my back, and caught a glint in their bared eyes.

From "Stolen Horses" by Barry Lopez, from *Writers Harvest 3,* edited by Tobias Wolff, copyright © 2000 by Share Our Strength. Used by permission of Dell Publishing, a division of Random House, Inc.

► What is the effect of the author's description of the horses?
(1) It creates a depth of feeling for the horses' vitality.
(2) It provides insight into what the characters are doing.

You are correct if you chose **(1).** The vivid, descriptive details allow you to imagine the horses and sense their vitality and strength.

## Point of View

Another choice a writer makes is which **point of view** to write from. Will the narrator be outside the story, watching and revealing the characters' actions and perhaps even their thoughts and feelings? If so, the writer will use *third person* point of view. Or will the narrator be a character in the story, able to report only what he or she thinks? In that case, the writer will use *first person* point of view.

► Which of the following indicates that the narrator is a character and so we can know only his thoughts?
(1) "The only part of the night I recall . . ."
(2) "Then Ed brought up a second bunch . . ."

**(1)** is correct. The narrator tells his own thoughts. A clue is the word *I.*

### KEY IDEAS

- The style of a piece of writing is determined by the choices a writer makes in words, sentence structure, images, and other devices.
- A story is written from a narrator's point of view. The narrator may be an "outsider" or a character who can reveal only what he or she sees and thinks.

### ON THE TASC TEST

*You will not have to identify and use terms such as third person and first person, but you should be able to understand and appreciate the effect of the writers' choices.*

# PRACTICE 5

<u>Questions 1 through 4</u> **refer to the following excerpt from a short story called "Coach."**

### EXCERPTED FROM *AN AMATEUR'S GUIDE TO THE NIGHT*

1 "This apartment your mom found is like an office or something. A studio for her to go to and get away every now and then. . . ."

2 "She wants to get away from us," Daphne said.

3 "Definitely not. She gave me a list, is how this whole thing started. She's got stuff she wants to do, and you with your school problems and me with the team—we're too much for her, see? She could spend her entire day on us, if you think about it, and never have one second for herself. If you think about it fairly, Daphne, you'll agree." . . .

4 She made a sigh and marched over to a trash can to deposit her slumping cone. Then she washed up at the children's drinking fountain and rejoined Coach, who had finished his Brown Cow but had kept the plastic spoon in the mouth.

5 "What was on this list of Mom's?" Daphne asked.

6 "Adult stuff," Coach said.

7 "Just give me an example."

8 Coach removed the plastic spoon and cracked it in half.

9 "Your mother's list is for five years. In that time, she wants to be speaking French regularly. She wants to follow up on her printmaking."

10 "This is adult stuff?" Daphne said.

11 Coach raised a hand to Bobby Stark. Stark had three malt cups in a cardboard carrier and he was moving toward the parking lot.

12 "Hey, those all for you?" Coach called out.

13 "I got a month to get fat, Coach. You'll have five months to beat it off me," the boy called back.

14 The people at some of the tables around Coach's lit up with grins. Bobby Stark's parents were grinning.

15 "Every hit of that junk takes a second off your time in the forty—just remember that!" Coach shouted.

16 Stark wagged his head ruefully, his cheeks blushing. He pretended to hide the malts behind his arm.



**1.** What is Bobby Stark's attitude?

A. He worries about his weight problem.
B. He takes things in stride.
C. He is looking forward to the sports season.
D. He feels unfairly criticized by the coach.

**2.** Because of the narrator's point of view, what does the reader know?

A. only Bobby Stark's actions
B. thoughts and feelings of the characters
C. the actions and speech of the characters
D. only Daphne's thoughts and feelings

**3.** Through their dialogue, what kind of relationship can you conclude the characters have with each other?

A. informal
B. tense
C. suspicious
D. deteriorating

**4.** Later in the story, Coach has this discussion with his wife, Sherry: "'It's like my apartment,' Sherry said. 'A place apart.' Coach cut her off. 'Don't go on about how much you love your apartment.'"

Based on this information and the excerpt, which of the following best describes Coach in his discussion with Daphne?

A. brutally frank
B. angry and hostile
C. loving and warm
D. not entirely honest about his feelings

**Review your work using the explanations that start on page 672.**

LESSON 6

# Figurative Language

KEY IDEAS

- Fiction writers and poets use figurative language—words that do not have their literal meaning—to compare different things.
- Some comparisons are introduced by like or as; others are not. Some comparisons give human characteristics to nonhuman things.

**Figurative language** refers to words that are being used to mean something other than their actual, literal meaning. Writers and poets use figurative language to help paint a mental picture in the reader's mind. Instead of saying, "His voice was soothing and pleasing," for example, a writer might say, "His voice was like velvet."

Figurative language often compares two different things. Sometimes the comparison is signaled by the words *like* or *as,* but not always. A writer might also say, "His voice was velvet." Another favorite technique of writers and poets is to give a human characteristic to something nonhuman, such as, "The wind sighed."

As you read this poem, look for figurative language and what it might mean.

**The School Children**

The children go forward with their little satchels.
And all morning the mothers have labored
to gather the late apples, red and gold,
like words of another language.

And on the other shore
are those who wait behind great desks
to receive these offerings.

How orderly they are—the nails
on which the children hang
their overcoats of blue or yellow wool.

And the teachers shall instruct them in silence
and the mothers shall scour the orchards for a way out,
drawing to themselves the gray limbs of the fruit trees
bearing so little ammunition.

From "The House on Marshland" from *The First Four Books* by Louise Gluck. Copyright 1968, 1971, 1972, 1973, 1974, 1975, 1976, 1977, 1978, 1980, 1985, 1995.

TASC TEST TIP

*You are not penalized for wrong answers on the TASC Test, so do not leave any answers blank. If you return to a skipped multiple-choice question and still cannot determine the answer, narrow the choices to the two most reasonable and then select the one that makes the most sense.*

► What is suggested by comparing apples to "words of another language" in the fourth line?
(1) a sense of strangeness, not a part of one's world
(2) useless things that have no meaning

You are correct if you chose **(1).** A language different from your own can seem strange and removed. The mothers feel removed from the world of teachers and schoolchildren.

► What does the word *shore* in the fifth line refer to?
(1) the other side of an ocean
(2) the world of the classroom

You are correct if you chose **(2).** The mothers in the poem think of school as far away from them.

# PRACTICE 6

<u>Questions 1 through 5</u> **refer to the following poem.**

**EXCERPTED FROM "DÉJEUNER SUR L'HERBE" ("LUNCH ON THE GRASS")**

1 It's pleasant to board the ferry in the sunscape
As the late light slants into afternoon;
The faint wind ruffles the river, rimmed with foam.
We move through the aisles of bamboo
Towards the cool water-lilies.

2 The young dandies drop ice into the drinks,
While the girls slice the succulent lotus root.
Above us, a patch of cloud spreads, darkening
Like a water-stain on silk.

3 *Write this down quickly, before the rain!*

4 Don't sit there! The cushions were soaked by the shower.
Already the girls have drenched their crimson skirts.
Beauties, their powder streaked with mascara, lament their ruined faces.

5 The wind batters our boat, the mooring-line
Has rubbed a wound in the willow bark.
The edges of the curtains are embroidered by the river foam.

6 Like a knife in a melon, Autumn slices Summer.

7 *It will be cold, going back.*



**1.** What is compared to "a water-stain on silk" (Stanza 2)?

A. foam on the edge of the river
B. rain clouds approaching
C. lotus root juice on a tablecloth
D. ice cubes dropping into cold drinks

**2.** What is meant by the statement "lament their ruined faces" (Stanza 4)?

A. They could no longer smile.
B. They were growing old.
C. The rain caused their makeup to run.
D. The wind was chapping their faces.

**3.** Why is "The edges of the curtains are embroidered by the river foam" (Stanza 5) an effective use of figurative language?

It helps the reader see that

A. the people forgot to close the windows and curtains
B. the wind is so strong that it is blowing spray from the river into the boat
C. the curtains are beautifully edged with lace
D. the river is rising quickly

**4.** According to the speaker, how was the change from summer to autumn (Stanza 6)?

A. quick and easy
B. halting and uncertain
C. slow and predictable
D. pleasant and smooth

**5.** Which of the following words best describe the tone of this poem?

A. gentle and calm
B. humorous and playful
C. wry and observant
D. dry and formal

**Review your work using the explanations that start on page 672.**

**STUDY ADVICE**

The TASC Reading Test will include some passages from plays or poems. Use the same skills you've been learning to understand plays and poems: Look for the author's point of view, tone, and use of figurative language.

# READING LITERATURE PRACTICE QUESTIONS

**Questions 1 through 3 refer to the following excerpt from a story.**

**EXCERPTED FROM *SHILOH & OTHER STORIES***

1 Leroy Moffitt's wife, Norma Jean, is working on her pectorals. She lifts three-pound dumbbells to warm up, then progresses to a twenty-pound barbell. Standing with her legs apart, she reminds Leroy of Wonder Woman.

2 "I'd give anything if I could just get these muscles to where they're real hard," says Norma Jean. "Feel this arm. It's not as hard as the other one."

3 "That's cause you're right-handed," says Leroy, dodging as she swings the barbell in an arc.

4 "Do you think so?"

5 "Sure."

6 Leroy is a truckdriver. He injured his leg in a highway accident four months ago, and his physical therapy, which involves weights and a pulley, prompted Norma Jean to try building herself up. Now she is attending a body-building class. Leroy has been collecting temporary disability since his tractor-trailer jackknifed in Missouri, badly twisting his left leg in its socket. He has a steel pin in his hip. He will probably not be able to drive his rig again. It sits in the backyard, like a gigantic bird that has flown home to roost. Leroy has been home in Kentucky for three months, and his leg is almost healed, but the accident frightened him and he does not want to drive any more long hauls. He is not sure what to do next. In the meantime, he makes things from craft kits. He started by building a miniature log cabin from notched Popsicle sticks. He varnished it and placed it on the TV set, where it remains. It reminds him of a rustic Nativity scene. Then he tried string art (sailing ships on black velvet), a macramé owl kit, a snap-together B-17 Flying Fortress, and a lamp made out of a model truck, with a light fixture screwed in the top of the cab. At first the kits were diversions, something to kill time, but now he is thinking about building a full-scale log house from a kit. It would be considerably cheaper than building a regular house, and besides, Leroy has grown to appreciate how things are put together. He has begun to realize that in all the years he was on the road he never took time to examine anything. He was always flying past scenery.



1. Which of the following best describes Leroy's wife, Norma Jean?

   A. shy
   B. loving
   C. self-concerned
   D. grumpy

2. By comparing Leroy's truck to a bird that has flown home to roost, the author suggests that Leroy ________.

   A. comes and goes as he pleases
   B. always preferred to be at home "nesting"
   C. won't be driving his truck for a while
   D. is a bit "flighty" and unpredictable

3. Why might Leroy be continually making things from craft kits?

   Because he

   A. is impatient with his leg healing
   B. has always enjoyed working with his hands
   C. grew tired of bodybuilding
   D. doesn't want to face what to do next

**Questions 4 through 7 refer to this excerpt from a story.**

### EXCERPTED FROM *WINTER'S TALES*

1 A small sailor-boy, named Simon, stood on the wet, swinging deck, held on to a shroud, and looked up towards the drifting clouds, and to the upper top-gallant yard of the main-mast.

2 A bird, that had sought refuge upon the mast, had got her feet entangled in some loose tackle-yarn of the halliard, and, high up there, struggled to get free. The boy on the deck could see her wings flapping and her head turning from side to side.

3 Through his own experience of life he had come to the conviction that in this world everyone must look after himself, and expect no help from others. But the mute, deadly fight kept him fascinated for more than an hour. He wondered what kind of bird it would be. These last days a number of birds had come to settle in the barque's rigging: swallows, quails, and a pair of peregrine falcons; he believed that this bird was a peregrine falcon. He remembered how, many years ago, in his own country and near his home, he had once seen a peregrine falcon quite close, sitting on a stone and flying straight up from it. Perhaps this was the same bird. He thought: "That bird is like me. Then she was there, and now she is here."

4 At that a fellow-feeling rose in him, a sense of common tragedy; he stood looking at the bird with his heart in his mouth. There were none of the sailors about to make fun of him; he began to think out how he might go up by the shrouds to help the falcon out. He brushed his hair back and pulled up his sleeves, gave the deck round him a great glance, and climbed up. He had to stop a couple of times in the swaying rigging.

5 It was indeed, he found when he got to the top of the mast, a peregrine falcon. As his head was on a level with hers, she gave up her struggle, and looked at him with a pair of angry, desperate yellow eyes.

6 He had to take hold of her with one hand while he got his knife out, and cut off the tackle-yarn. He was scared as he looked down, but at the same time he felt that he had been ordered up by nobody, but that this was his own venture, and this gave him a proud, steadying sensation, as if the sea and the sky, the ship, the bird and himself were all one.

From *Winter's Tales* by Isak Dinesen, Random House, Inc ©1942.

4. What can you infer about the boy's decision to climb the rig?

   A. It took some courage.
   B. It was a familiar task.
   C. It felt like a chore.
   D. He was ordered to do it.

5. Which of the following best describes both the boy and the bird at the beginning of the excerpt?

   A. confident
   B. alone
   C. scared
   D. wary

6. Which ideas are most clearly contrasted in this excerpt?

   A. love and hate
   B. youth and experience
   C. fear and fearlessness
   D. loneliness and sense of belonging

7. The word ____________ best describes the mood created by the author in this excerpt.

   A. mournful
   B. nostalgic
   C. peaceful
   D. triumphant

**Questions 8 through 11 refer to this excerpt from a story.**

## EXCERPTED FROM "THE LEGEND OF SLEEPY HOLLOW"

1 "Who are you?" He received no reply. He repeated his demand in a still more agitated voice. Still there was no answer. Once more he cudgelled the sides of the inflexible Gunpowder, and, shutting his eyes, broke forth with involuntary fervor into a psalm-tune. Just then the shadowy object of alarm put itself in motion, and, with a scramble and a bound, stood at once in the middle of the road. Though the night was dark and dismal, yet the form of the unknown might now in some degree be ascertained. He appeared to be a horseman of large dimensions, and mounted on a black horse of powerful frame. He made no offer of molestation or sociability, but kept aloof on one side of the road, jogging along on the blind side of old Gunpowder, who had now got over his fright and waywardness.

2 Ichabod, who had no relish for this strange midnight companion, and bethought himself of the adventure of Brom Bones with the Galloping Hessian, now quickened his steed, in hopes of leaving him behind. The stranger, however, quickened his horse to an equal pace. Ichabod pulled up, and fell into a walk, thinking to lag behind—the other did the same. His heart began to sink within him; he endeavored to resume his psalm-tune, but his parched tongue clove to the roof of his mouth, and he could not utter a stave. There was something in the moody and dogged silence of this pertinacious companion, that was mysterious and appalling. It was soon fearfully accounted for. On mounting a rising ground, which brought the figure of his fellow-traveller in relief against the sky, gigantic in height, and muffled in a cloak, Ichabod was horror-struck, on perceiving that he was headless!—but his horror was still more increased, on observing that the head, which should have rested on his shoulders, was carried before him on the pommel of the saddle: his terror rose to desperation; he rained a shower of kicks and blows upon Gunpowder, hoping, by a sudden movement, to give his companion the slip—but the spectre started full jump with him.

3 Away then they dashed, through thick and thin; stones flying, and sparks flashing at every bound. Ichabod's flimsy garments fluttered in the air, as he stretched his long lank body away over his horse's head, in the eagerness of his flight.

From "The Legend of Sleepy Hollow" by Washington Irving.

8. What is meant by "he endeavored to resume his psalm-tune" (paragraph 2)?

   Ichabod Crane tried to

   A. remind himself to stay calm
   B. ride more steadily
   C. start singing again
   D. think of a realistic solution

9. What is the effect of the author's use of words such as "dashed," "stones flying," and "sparks flashing" (paragraph 3)?

   The words create a feeling of

   A. panic
   B. clumsiness
   C. playfulness
   D. magic

10. Which of the following best describes the mood of this excerpt?

   A. angry
   B. sorrowful
   C. suspenseful
   D. sentimental

11. Later in the story, the narrator implies that the horseman had a pumpkin on the pommel of his saddle. Given this additional information, Ichabod can best be described as __________ given his actions in the excerpt.

   A. brave in the face of great danger
   B. too scared to think rationally
   C. moving too quickly
   D. quick thinking in his escape

**Questions 12 through 14 refer to this excerpt from a play.**

A man named John Wright has been murdered, and the County Attorney and Sheriff are trying to determine whether Wright's wife might have had a motive.

**EXCERPTED FROM *TRIFLES***

COUNTY ATTORNEY: Well, that's interesting, I'm sure. [*Seeing the birdcage.*] Has the bird flown?

MRS. HALE: [*Putting more quilt pieces over the box.*] We think the—cat got it.

COUNTY ATTORNEY: [*Preoccupied.*] Is there a cat?

[*MRS. HALE glances in a quick covert way at MRS. PETERS.*]

MRS. PETERS: Well, not now. They're superstitious, you know. They leave.

COUNTY ATTORNEY: [*To* SHERIFF PETERS, *continuing an interrupted conversation.*] No sign at all of anyone having come from the outside. Their own rope. Now let's go up again and go over it piece by piece. [*They start upstairs.*] It would have to have been someone who knew just the—

[MRS. PETERS *sits down. The two women sit there not looking at one another, but as if peering into something and at the same time holding back. When they talk now it is in the manner of feeling their way over strange ground, as if afraid of what they are saying, but as if they cannot help saying it.*]

MRS. HALE: She liked the bird. She was going to bury it in that pretty box.

MRS. PETERS: [*In a whisper.*] When I was a girl—my kitten—there was a boy took a hatchet, and before my eyes—and before I could get there—. [*Covers her face an instant.*] If they hadn't held me back I would have— [*Catches herself, looks upstairs where steps are heard, falters weakly.*]—hurt him.

MRS. HALE: [*With a slow look around her.*] I wonder how it would seem never to have had any children around. [*Pause.*] No, Wright wouldn't like the bird—a thing that sang. She used to sing. He killed that, too.

MRS. PETERS: [*Moving uneasily.*] We don't know who killed the bird.

MRS. HALE: I knew John Wright.

MRS. PETERS: It was an awful thing was done in this house that night, Mrs. Hale. Killing a man while he slept, slipping a rope around his neck that choked the life out of him.

MRS. HALE: His neck. Choked the life out of him. [*Her hand goes out and rests on the birdcage.*]

MRS. PETERS: [*With rising voice.*] We don't know who killed him. We don't know.

MRS. HALE: [*Her own feeling not interrupted.*] If there'd been years and years of nothing, then a bird to sing to you, it would be awful—still, after the bird was still.

Excerpted from *Trifles*, by Susan Glaspell, published by Penguin Putnam, Inc.

12. Who does Mrs. Hale think killed the bird?

    A. John Wright
    B. Mrs. Peters
    C. the cat
    D. Mrs. Wright

13. Based on the excerpt, which of the following best describes John Wright?

    A. a person who is loving and attentive
    B. someone who smothers all the joy in another person
    C. a person capable of murder
    D. someone devoted to law and order

14. Which of the following conclusions can you draw about Mrs. Peters and Mrs. Hale?

    A. Together they committed murder.
    B. Each one thinks the other one is the murderer.
    C. They are eager to tell the police all they know.
    D. They understand how someone could be driven to murder.

**Review your work using the explanations that start on page 673.**

ABOUT THE TEST

# Language Arts: Writing

UNIT 2

The TASC Writing Test assesses your language skills in two different ways. You will have 105 minutes to complete the Writing Test.

1. Expect to spend around 55 minutes answering approximately 50 multiple-choice items that assess language skills. These questions will target skills such as:
   - constructing sentences
   - using grammar correctly
   - using words correctly
   - organizing ideas into paragraphs
   - connecting ideas
2. You will have around 50 minutes to write one essay in response to a passage or pair of passages. You will read the passage or passages and then write an essay that either:
   - argues for one side of a debate and against the other side or
   - explains something from the passage(s)

If you are taking the paper version of the TASC, you will write your essay on paper. If you are testing on computer, you will type your essay into a box on the screen.

This unit is organized into skills needed to write effective sentences and paragraphs, skills required to write the essay, and skills needed to edit writing and correct mistakes in grammar and usage. Be aware that the skills you will practice in this unit in multiple-choice questions will also be useful to you as you edit your essay for the TASC Writing Test.

* Note: The information given here was the latest information available as of January 2014. It is possible that timing restrictions may change between this printing and your test date. For updates, visit www.tasctest.com.

LESSON 1

# Simple Sentences

A complete simple sentence has at least one subject and one verb. The **subject** is the person, place, or thing that the sentence is talking about. The subject performs an action or is described. The **verb** is the word that tells what action the subject is doing or links the subject to a modifier.

**Action verb:** Elaine took notes on the meeting.
subject verb

**Linking verb:** They were long.
subject verb modifier

If a sentence is missing either the subject or the verb, it is incomplete. An incomplete sentence is called a **fragment.**

**EXAMPLES**
**No subject:** Typed up her notes.
**Complete sentence:** Elaine typed up her notes.

**No verb:** The computer in the main office.
**Complete sentence:** The computer in the main office crashed several times.

A complete sentence must also express a complete thought. The reader should not be left asking questions.

**Incomplete thought:** When she lost her work. (What happened when she lost her work?)
**Complete thought:** Elaine was very frustrated when she lost her work.

**Incomplete thought:** The person in charge of computer support. (What about that person?)
**Complete thought:** Elaine called the person in charge of computer support.

**Incomplete thought:** By replacing the hard drive.
**Complete thought:** Elaine can fix the computer by replacing the hard drive.

Finally, a complete sentence should have correct end punctuation. A statement should end with a period, and so should a command. A question should end with a question mark. An exclamation should end with an exclamation point.

**Statement:** Elaine has lost several files this way.
**Command:** Turn off the computer.
**Question:** Will the computer ever be fixed?
**Exclamation:** What a mess we're in!

If you find a fragment in your writing, rewrite it to make it a complete sentence.

- If the sentence does not have a subject, add a subject.
- If the sentence does not have a verb, add a verb.
- If the thought is incomplete, add words or combine the incomplete thought with a complete sentence.

**KEY IDEAS**

- Make sure each sentence has a subject and verb and expresses a complete thought.
- If a sentence doesn't express a complete thought, you may need to add a subject, verb, or other words.
- Use correct end punctuation.

**TASC TEST TIP**

*Read each sentence in a TASC passage to yourself and pause at its end. That may help you "hear" whether the sentence is actually an incomplete thought or a sentence fragment.*

# PRACTICE 1

**A. Directions: Write *C* if the sentence is complete or *F* if the sentence is a fragment. Rewrite any fragments to make them complete.**

**EXAMPLE**

Talks all the time on the telephone. *F Dave talks all the time on the telephone.*

**1.** Drives his girlfriend crazy. ______

**2.** As soon as he comes home from work. ______

**3.** He calls everyone he knows. ______

**4.** Dave's sister and his best friend. ______

**B. Questions 5 through 7 refer to the following advertisement.**

**What Is Three-Way Calling?**

**(A)**

(1) Three-way calling is a unique service that enables you to conduct a conference call. (2) From the privacy of your own home. (3) You can talk to your sister in Florida and your mother in Nebraska at the same time. (4) It's even possible to seek a third person's advice when you're in the middle of a regular call. (5) For instance, if you're closing a deal, can bring your lawyer into the conversation.

**(B)**

(6) Why wait? (7) This useful and convenient service. (8) Can be yours for only pennies a month.

**5. Sentences 1 and 2:** Three-way calling is a unique service that enables you to conduct a conference call. From the privacy of your own home.

Which is the best way to write the underlined portion of these sentences?

A. call. And from
B. call. It from
C. call from
D. calling from

**6. Sentence 5:** For instance, if you're closing a deal, can bring your lawyer into the conversation.

Which correction should be made to sentence 5?

A. remove the comma after instance
B. change closing to close
C. insert you before can
D. replace lawyer with closing

**7. Sentences 7 and 8:** This useful and convenient service. Can be yours for only pennies a month.

Which is the best way to write the underlined portion of these sentences?

A. service is
B. service it can
C. service can
D. service. That can

**Review your work using the explanations that start on page 674.**

**STUDY ADVICE**

Remember that you will use grammar skills in two ways on the TASC Writing Test. You will answer multiple-choice questions about grammar, and you will also be expected to use correct grammar in your essay. Learn to recognize grammatical mistakes not only in others' writing but also in your own.

LESSON 2

# Compound and Complex Sentences

## Compound Sentences

The simple sentences described in Lesson 1 are also called **independent clauses.** An independent clause has a subject and a verb and expresses a complete thought. You can join two or more independent clauses in one **compound sentence.** To make a compound sentence, you should:

- Choose a logical **coordinating conjunction** to join the independent clauses. The most common coordinating conjunctions are *and, but, or, nor, for, so,* and *yet*.
- Insert a comma before the coordinating conjunction.

**KEY IDEAS**

- You can join two independent clauses into one compound sentence.
- Use a coordinating conjunction preceded by a comma.
- Choose a conjunction that correctly relates the two ideas.

**EXAMPLES**

**Two independent clauses:** Sam saw a design flaw. He wrote a memo.
**Joined correctly:** Sam saw a design flaw, so he wrote a memo.

**No coordinating conjunction:** Sam asked his boss, she told him to send it.
**Correct:** Sam asked his boss, and she told him to send it.

**No comma:** Sam's boss was busy so she asked Sam to write the memo.
**Correct:** Sam's boss was busy, so she asked Sam to write the memo.

Be sure the coordinating conjunction expresses the correct relationship between the ideas in the two independent clauses.

| Relationship between Ideas | Coordinating Conjunction |
|---|---|
| join two equally important ideas | and |
| contrast two ideas | but, yet |
| show a cause | for |
| show an effect | so |
| give a choice | or |
| give no choice | nor |

**TASC TEST TIP**

*Be sure that a coordinating conjunction separates two independent clauses before you choose the option that inserts a comma before the conjunction.*

**Incorrect conjunction:** Sam showed initiative, **yet** his boss praised him.
**Correct conjunction:** Sam showed initiative, **so** his boss praised him.

Be sure that you are actually joining two independent clauses and not just two subjects or two verbs.

**Incorrect:** The designers, and the builders got the memo.
**Correct (no comma):** The designers and the builders got the memo.

**Incorrect:** The designers needed the information, and appreciated the memo.
**Correct (two independent clauses):** The designers needed the information. They appreciated the memo.
**Correct (no comma):** The designers needed the information and appreciated the memo.

# PRACTICE 2.1

**A. Directions: Using the list on page 132, choose a coordinating conjunction for each sentence. On a separate sheet of paper, rewrite the sentence using the conjunction preceded by a comma.**

**EXAMPLE**

I didn't want to seem timid, ____*so*____ I didn't tell anyone about my experience.

1. It was late ________________________________ I was walking home from work.
2. My coworker, Judy, had offered to drive me ____________________ I had refused.
3. It was a warm night ________________________ I decided to get some fresh air.
4. It was really my choice. I could have taken a cab ____________________ I could have walked.
5. I heard a loud noise ________________ I ran the last block to my house. Later, I learned that it was only a car backfiring.

**B. Questions 6 through 8 refer to the following paragraph.**

**Air Couriers**

(1) If you want to travel abroad but don't have a lot of money, one option is to be an air courier. (2) An air courier carries shipping documents on an international flight, and gets a cheap ticket in return. (3) Companies use couriers because it often costs less to check freight as baggage than to ship it as cargo. (4) Air couriers fly on the major airlines, so sometimes they can't check any baggage of their own. (5) Couriers usually book their trips in advance but they get their tickets on the day of the flight.

6. **Sentence 2:** An air courier carries shipping documents on an international flight, and gets a cheap ticket in return.

   Which correction should be made to sentence 2?

   A. change carries to carry
   B. remove the comma
   C. replace and with but
   D. insert so after and

7. **Sentence 4:** Air couriers fly on the major airlines, so sometimes they can't check any baggage of their own.

   Which is the best way to write the underlined portion of this sentence?

   A. airlines, but
   B. airlines but
   C. airlines nor
   D. airlines, or

8. **Sentence 5:** Couriers usually book their trips in advance but they get their tickets on the day of the flight.

   Which correction should be made to sentence 5?

   A. replace usually with never
   B. insert a comma after advance
   C. insert a comma after but
   D. replace they with she

**Review your work using the explanations that start on page 674.**

## KEY IDEAS

- Join a subordinate and an independent clause to form a complex sentence.
- Use a subordinating conjunction that shows the correct relationship between ideas.
- Put a comma after the subordinate clause when it comes at the beginning of a sentence.

## ON THE TASC TEST

*You may need to select the correct subordinating conjunction to link two clauses. Choose the word or phrase that correctly conveys the relationship between the ideas.*

## Complex Sentences

A **complex sentence** is made up of an independent clause and a **subordinate clause.** A subordinate clause has a subject and verb, but it does not express a complete thought.

**EXAMPLES**

**Subordinate clause:** Because their pay was too low.
**Complex sentence:** Teachers went on strike because their pay was too low.
(independent clause: Teachers went on strike; subordinate clause: because their pay was too low.)

Every subordinate clause begins with a **subordinating conjunction** that shows the relationship between the subordinate clause and the independent clause. Below is a list of common subordinating conjunctions.

| Relationship between Clauses | Subordinating Conjunction |
|---|---|
| cause/reason | because |
| effect/result | in order that, so that |
| time | after, as, before, once, since, until, when, whenever, while |
| place | where, wherever |
| choice | if, whether |
| contradiction | although, even though, though |

Choose the subordinating conjunction that conveys the meaning you are trying to express.

**Incorrect meaning:** The strike continued for more than a month once it finally ended.
**Correct meaning:** The strike continued for more than a month before it finally ended.

When a subordinate clause comes at the beginning of a sentence, put a comma after it. If the subordinate clause comes at the end of a sentence, you generally don't need a comma before it.

**At beginning of sentence:** While teachers were on the picket line, kids stayed home.
**At end of sentence:** Kids stayed home while teachers were on the picket line.

However, when a subordinate clause at the end of a sentence begins with *although, though,* or *even though,* put a comma before the clause.

**At beginning of sentence:** Even though the public supported the teachers, the school board did not concede to the teachers' demands.
**At end of sentence:** The school board did not concede to teachers' demands, even though the public supported the teachers.

A subordinate clause cannot stand independently. By itself, a subordinate clause is a sentence fragment. Make sure that every subordinate clause is joined to an independent clause.

**Incorrect:** After the strike finished. The school year began.
**Corrected by joining independent and subordinate clauses:** After the strike finished, the school year began.

# PRACTICE 2.2

**A. Directions: Join the clauses to form complex sentences. Use the subordinating conjunctions in parentheses.**

**EXAMPLE**

(if) You buy a smoke detector. You can protect your family.

*If you buy a smoke detector, you can protect your family.*

**1.** Most fatal fires occur. (when) A family is asleep.

______________________________

**2.** (because) A smoke alarm wakes you up. It can allow you to escape.

______________________________

**3.** Try to replace the smoke detector's battery. (before) It goes dead.

______________________________

**4.** (although) Smoke detectors cost money. The expense is worth it.

______________________________

**B. Questions 5 through 7 refer to the following paragraph.**

**Phone Etiquette**

(1) When you are making business call, it's wise to keep a few key rules in mind. (2) First of all, be prepared. (3) Have paper and pencil ready so that you won't have to fumble for them. (4) Whenever you identify yourself, ask the person whether this is a good time to talk. (5) Get to the point quickly. (6) Before you hang up. (7) Thank the person for his or her time. (8) Finally, put the phone down gently. (9) Slamming down the receiver makes a poor impression.

**5. Sentence 1:** When you are making business call, it's wise to keep a few key rules in mind.

Which correction should be made to sentence 1?

A. change are making to is making
B. insert a after making
C. remove the comma
D. change it's to its

**6. Sentence 4:** Whenever you identify yourself, ask the person whether this is a good time to talk.

Which correction should be made to sentence 4?

A. replace Whenever with After
B. remove the comma
C. insert a comma after person
D. replace the person with them

**7. Sentences 6 and 7:** Before you hang _______ the person for his or her time.

Choose the option that correctly completes the sentence.

A. up and then Thank
B. up and thank
C. up thank
D. up, thank

**Review your work using the explanations that start on page 674.**

**STUDY ADVICE**

Don't underestimate the value of grammar: Good grammar helps others understand your writing. Being able to write clearly will help you on the TASC Writing Test, on job applications, in advancing your career, in school (if you plan to pursue postsecondary studies), and in your life as a citizen. Therefore, if anything so far is unclear, spend more time on it before moving on.

LESSON 3

# Run-Ons and Comma Splices

## Run-Ons

There are two errors people commonly make when they join independent clauses to form a sentence. The first type of error is called a **run-on.** In a run-on, two independent clauses are combined without proper punctuation.

**Run-On:** Banks offer many helpful services you should check them out.

You can correct a run-on in one of several ways:

- Break the run-on into two separate sentences.

  **Correct:** Banks offer many services. You should check them out.
- Make a compound sentence (add a coordinating conjunction and a comma).

  **Correct:** Banks offer many services, so you should check them out.
- Make a complex sentence (add a subordinating conjunction and, if necessary, a comma).

  **Correct:** Because banks offer many services, you should check them out.

A run-on can also consist of independent clauses strung together with *and.* Correct this kind of run-on by dividing it into one or more compound sentences or by combining ideas into one sentence.

**Run-On:** Banking is getting more and more convenient and you can check on your account using bank-by-phone services and it's possible to do your banking on the Internet.
**Correct:** Banking is getting more and more convenient. You can check on your account using bank-by-phone services, and it's possible to do your banking on the Internet.

**Run-On:** Friday I got paid and I went to the bank and I cashed my check.
**Correct:** Friday I got paid, went to the bank, and cashed my check.

## Comma Splices

The second type of error people sometimes make when joining independent clauses is called a **comma splice.** A comma splice occurs when two sentences are joined with just a comma. To correct a comma splice, add a coordinating conjunction after the comma:

**Comma splice:** You can check on your account using bank-by-phone services, it's possible to do your banking on the Internet.
**Correct:** You can check on your account using bank-by-phone services, and it's possible to do your banking on the Internet.

You can also correct a comma splice using the methods described above for correcting a run-on. You can also join two related ideas with a semicolon.

**Comma splice:** There are fewer bank tellers today, banks do offer other services.
**Corrected by creating a complex sentence:** Although there are fewer bank tellers today, banks do offer other services.

### KEY IDEAS

- A run-on sentence is two or more sentences that are connected without correct punctuation.
- In a comma splice, two sentences are joined with only a comma.
- To correct a run-on or comma splice, make a compound or complex sentence or separate the sentences.

### TASC TEST TIP

*When you read a run-on sentence or a comma splice, look for the place where you would pause if you read the sentence aloud. That is where you should make the correction.*

# PRACTICE 3

**A. Directions: Correct the following run-ons and comma splices using the methods explained on page 136.**

1. Jeff just got his driver's license, he's very excited.

_______________________________________________

2. He bought a car that has a lot of miles on it it wasn't very expensive.

_______________________________________________

3. He doesn't have a lot of free time, he'd like to take a car trip.

_______________________________________________

4. He needs to find out about car insurance and he needs to get a good map and he needs to join an auto club.

_______________________________________________

**B. Questions 5 through 7 refer to the following paragraph.**

**Photography Tips**

**(A)**

(1) It's not hard to take great pictures just keep these tips in mind. (2) For one thing, you need to get close to your subject, or you won't get a good shot. (3) Be patient, wait for the right moment to shoot. (4) Make sure the lighting is sufficient. (5) Even outdoors, you can use a flash to fill in shadows.

**(B)**

(6) Think about what you want to emphasize in your picture. (7) You don't have to use the autofocus option, most cameras allow you to select the focus point you prefer. (8) For example, many photographs of people focus on the eyes.

5. **Sentence 1:** It's not hard to take great pictures just keep these tips in mind.

   Which is the best way to write the underlined portion of the sentence?

   A. pictures if you just
   B. pictures if you just that
   C. pictures, if you just
   D. pictures that just

6. **Sentence 3:** Be patient, wait for the right moment to shoot.

   Which correction should be made to sentence 3?

   A. remove the comma
   B. insert and after the comma
   C. insert but then after the comma
   D. insert a comma after moment

7. **Sentence 7:** You don't have to use the autofocus option, most cameras allow you to select the focus point you prefer.

   Which correction should be made to sentence 7?

   A. delete the comma after option
   B. insert and after option
   C. insert because after the comma
   D. delete you after allow

**Review your work using the explanations that start on page 674.**

LESSON 4

# Subordinate Ideas

Writing is more effective when it flows smoothly. Therefore, try to eliminate short, choppy sentences whenever possible. You can do this by using **subordination** in a variety of ways.

You already know how to form a complex sentence with a subordinating clause. You also know how to create compound sentences. Either of these methods can be used to combine short sentences.

**EXAMPLES**

**Short and choppy:** Carla ran for the bus. She missed it.
**Complex sentence:** Although Carla ran for the bus, she missed it.
**Compound sentence:** Carla ran for the bus, but she missed it.

If two sentences have the same subject, you can combine them to form one sentence with a compound predicate. The **predicate** includes the verb plus anything else that is not part of the subject:

**Short and choppy:** Carla sat on the bench. She looked at her watch.
**With compound predicate:** Carla sat on the bench and looked at her watch.

Likewise, when two sentences have the same predicate, you can combine them to form one sentence with a compound subject. The resulting sentence will be less repetitive and wordy:

**Short, choppy, and repetitive:** Carla missed the bus. Dave missed the bus, too.
**With compound subject:** Carla and Dave missed the bus.

Finally, several short sentences that are related can be combined into one longer and more detailed sentence:

**Short and choppy:** Carla missed the bus. It was the 7:45 bus. She was on her way to work.
**More detailed sentence:** Carla missed the 7:45 bus on her way to work.

Sometimes, you can use two methods at the same time. For instance, in the sentence below, you can make a complex sentence with combined details:

**Short and choppy:** Carla found a pay phone near the bus stop. She called her boss. Then she called one of her coworkers.
**Complex sentence with combined details:** After Carla found a pay phone near the bus stop, she called her boss and one of her coworkers.

**Repetitive:** Her boss thanked her for calling. Her coworker thanked her for calling, and they both offered to pass along any messages.
**With compound subject and compound predicate:** Both her boss and her coworker thanked her for calling and offered to pass along any messages.

**KEY IDEAS**

- Use smooth, flowing sentences rather than short, choppy sentences.
- Form compound or complex sentences from short sentences.
- Combine two predicates to make a compound predicate or combine two subjects to make a compound subject.

**TASC TEST TIP**

*Read the passages on the test to yourself as if you could hear them in your mind. That "silent hearing" will help you notice sentences that are choppy or repetitive.*

# PRACTICE 4

**A. Directions: Write each set of short, choppy sentences as one longer, smooth sentence.**

**EXAMPLE**

If you are in a tornado, keep the windows closed. You should go to a safe place.

*If you are in a tornado, keep the windows closed and go to a safe place.*

**1.** Tornadoes can cause a lot of damage. Earthquakes are also capable of causing a lot of damage.

______________________________

**2.** Earthquakes are somewhat common in California. Many Californians do not seem to mind.

______________________________

**3.** On May 20, 2013, there was a tornado. It happened in Oklahoma. Twenty-four people were killed. Almost 400 people were injured.

______________________________

**4.** Tornadoes can occur anywhere in the United States. They can happen any time of year.

______________________________

**B. Questions 5 through 7 refer to the following warranty.**

**Limited Warranty**

(1) If there is any defect, Pantronics will repair this unit free of charge. (2) Audio components will be repaired. (3) Repairs will take place up to one year after the date of purchase. (4) The unit may be brought to the service center. (5) It can also be mailed. (6) A proof of purchase, such as a receipt, must be presented in order to receive service. (7) This warranty does not cover damage due to accidents. (8) It does not cover damage due to mishandling or faulty installation.

**5. Sentences 2 and 3:** Audio components will be ______________ to one year after date of purchase.

Which is the best way to fill in the blank?

A. repaired. Repairs will then take up
B. repaired and repairs will take place up
C. repaired, the repairs will take place up
D. repaired up

**6. Sentences 4 and 5:** The unit may be brought to the service center. It can also be mailed.

The most effective combination of sentences 4 and 5 would include which group of words?

A. brought or mailed to
B. once brought to the service center,
C. units that are mailed to the service center
D. bringing it to the service center, or mailing

**7. Sentences 7 and 8:** This warranty does not cover damage due to accidents. It does not cover damage due to mishandling or faulty installation.

The most effective combination of sentences 7 and 8 would include which group of words?

A. accidents, and it
B. accidents, and this warranty
C. accidents, and, in addition, it
D. accidents, mishandling, or faulty installation

**Review your work using the explanations that start on page 674.**

LESSON 5

# Modify Ideas

**Modifiers** are words and phrases used to add descriptive details. A modifier might be a word like *sweaty,* a verb phrase like *dragging the heavy box,* a prepositional phrase like *from the storage room,* or a clause like *that we packed this morning.* Modifiers make writing clearer, more specific, and more interesting.

### KEY IDEAS

- Modifiers make writing clearer and more interesting.
- Correct a dangling modifier by turning it into a subordinate clause or by making the word that is modified the subject of the sentence.
- Place a modifier as near as possible to the word or phrase it describes.

**EXAMPLES**

**Without modifiers:** Our friends Jack and Tina helped us while we were moving.
**With modifiers:** Our good friends Jack and Tina helped us while we were moving, watching our baby in their home.

**Without modifiers:** We realized the weather would not cooperate.
**With modifiers:** Sweating profusely at 9 A.M., we realized the weather would be uncooperatively hot.

Use modifiers carefully, or your meaning will be unclear. A **dangling modifier** is a word or phrase at the beginning of the sentence that has no clear subject to describe. To correct a dangling modifier, turn it into a subordinate clause, or make the word that the modifier describes into the subject of the sentence.

**Dangling modifier:** Driving the truck, one of the boxes fell out. (Who was driving the truck—one of the boxes?)
**Correct:** As we were driving the truck, one of the boxes fell out.
**Correct:** Driving the truck, we heard one of the boxes fall out.

**Dangling modifier:** Parking in a tow zone, a police officer gave us a ticket. (It sounds as if the police officer were parking in the tow zone.)
**Correct:** Because we parked in a tow zone, a police officer gave us a ticket.

**Dangling modifier:** Never having planned a move before, the real estate agent gave us some tips. (It sounds as if the real estate agent is the one who had never planned a move.)
**Correct:** Never having planned a move before, we asked the real estate agent for some tips.

### TASC TEST TIP

*When a modifying phrase is at the beginning of a sentence, use a comma to separate it from the rest of the sentence.*

**A misplaced modifier** is poorly placed in the sentence. It is not clear which word it modifies, or it modifies the wrong word in the sentence. To correct a misplaced modifier, put the modifier next to the word it describes.

**Misplaced modifier:** The moving van was just large enough that we rented.
**Correct:** The moving van that we rented was just large enough.

**Misplaced modifier:** We hoisted and lugged all our furniture up two flights of stairs panting heavily. (What was panting heavily—*we* or *the stairs*?)
**Correct:** Panting heavily, we hoisted and lugged all our furniture up two flights of stairs.

# PRACTICE 5

**A. Directions: Revise each sentence, correcting the misplaced or dangling modifier.**

**1.** Trent's sister encouraged him to become a nurse, who is a health professional.

______________________________________________

**2.** Waking up the patients to take their blood pressure, they get rather annoyed.

______________________________________________

**3.** He writes their temperature and blood pressure on their charts carefully.

______________________________________________

**4.** Talking with the patients, it is hard to make visitors leave at 9 P.M.

______________________________________________

**B. Questions 5 through 7 refer to the following passage about adoption.**

### Adoption

**(A)**

(1) Adoption is a legal procedure that gives a person the rights of a son or daughter who is not the birth child of the adopter. (2) This practice dates back to ancient Greece. (3) People without heirs used it to perpetuate their estates.

**(B)**

(4) Adoptions may be handled through an agency or by independent placement. (5) Going through an agency, a "home study" to decide whether prospective parents will be fit is required. (6) In an independent placement, there is no study. (7) Lawyers handle these adoptions when parents ask them to frequently.

**5. Sentence 1:** Adoption is a legal procedure that gives a person the rights of a son or daughter who is not the birth child of the adopter.

The most effective revision of sentence 1 would include which group of words?

A. a legal procedure, adoption that gives
B. a person who is not the birth child
C. the son or daughter of the adopter
D. the birth child, who is a son or daughter

**6. Sentence 5:** Going through an agency, a "home study" to decide whether prospective parents will be fit is required.

The most effective revision of sentence 5 would begin with which group of words?

A. For parents, going through an agency
B. Requiring a "home study"
C. An agency requires a "home study"
D. Deciding whether a parent is fit

**7. Sentence 7:** Lawyers handle these adoptions when parents ask them to frequently.

Which correction should be made to sentence 7?

A. insert a comma after adoptions
B. replace to with too
C. insert a comma after to
D. move frequently to follow Lawyers

**Review your work using the explanations that start on page 674.**

**STUDY ADVICE**

Keep in mind that people often do not correctly use modifiers when speaking. Learn the rules in this lesson and don't rely on your ear for modifiers.

LESSON 6

# Parallel Structure

When you write a sentence that lists two or more words, phrases, or clauses, the elements in the list must be in the same grammatical form. In other words, the sentence must have **parallel structure.** Writing that has parallel structure is clearer and easier to follow.

**KEY IDEAS**

- Listed items should be parallel in form and structure.
- Each phrase should have the same elements as other phrases in the series.
- Don't put words and clauses together in the same series.

### Examples

**Not parallel:** Jim wants to eat less, exercise more, and be getting more sleep.
**Parallel:** Jim wants to eat less, exercise more, and get more sleep.

**Not parallel:** Walking and to swim are good aerobic exercises.
**Parallel:** Walking and swimming are good aerobic exercises.

**Not parallel:** Try to lose weight slowly, sensibly, and be careful.
**Parallel:** Try to lose weight slowly, sensibly, and carefully.

To be sure that your sentences have parallel structure, follow the guidelines below.

Make sure that verbs in a list are in the same form and tense:

**Not parallel:** Jim went to the store, bought an exercise mat, and is doing exercises.
**Parallel:** Jim went to the store, bought an exercise mat, and did exercises.

Be sure that phrases in a list are parallel in form and wording. For example, if one phrase in a list begins with a preposition, the others should, too. If one phrase begins with the word *the*, the others should, too.

**Not parallel:** Avoid exercising on busy streets, near traffic jams, and polluted areas.
**Parallel:** Avoid exercising on busy streets, near traffic jams, and in polluted areas.

**Not parallel:** He left the gym shoes, sweatpants, and the shirt in the gym.
**Parallel:** He left the gym shoes, the sweatpants, and the shirt in the gym.

Each list must have single words, short phrases, or clauses. Don't put single words and clauses together in the same series:

**TASC TEST TIP**

*When you revise a sentence to use parallel structure, use the comma to separate each element as shown in these examples.*

**Not parallel:** The most effective fitness programs are low impact, informal, and you can do them at home.
**Parallel:** The most effective fitness programs are low impact, informal, and home based.

Finally, notice that a comma separates each item within a list of three or more: *low impact, informal, and home based.*

# PRACTICE 6

**A. Directions: Rewrite each sentence to make the structure parallel.**

**EXAMPLE**

Jenna works quickly, carefully, and is thorough.

*Jenna works quickly, carefully, and thoroughly.*

1. Jenna has worked in a factory, a store, and has a waitressed.

   ______________________________

2. She would like putting her kids in a better school and to get a better job.

   ______________________________

3. She thinks the kids' father is irresponsible, lazy, and doesn't care about them.

   ______________________________

4. He doesn't have the time, the energy, or money to give them what they deserve.

   ______________________________

**B. Questions 5 through 7 refer to the following memo.**

**TO: All Employees**

**(A)**

(1) A new alarm system has been installed. (2) It is designed to make our workplace safer, more comfortable, and pleasant. (3) However, we need everyone's cooperation.

**(B)**

(4) If you are the last one to leave, turn off all lights, computers, and check the coffee makers. (5) Then go to the alarm system located by the door. (6) Punch in the secret code, press ON, and be leaving immediately. (7) Lock the door behind you.

5. **Sentence 2:** It is designed to make our workplace safer, more comfortable, and pleasant.

   Which correction should be made to sentence 2?

   A. replace our with are
   B. remove the comma after safer
   C. insert more before pleasant
   D. no correction is necessary

6. **Sentence 4:** If you are the last one to leave, turn off all lights, ______________ coffee makers.

   Choose the option that correctly completes the sentence.

   A. and computers, and the
   B. computers, and check the
   C. computers, and checking the
   D. computers, and

7. **Sentence 6:** Punch in the secret code, press ON, and be leaving immediately.

   Which correction should be made to sentence 6?

   A. change punch to punching
   B. remove the comma after ON
   C. change be leaving to leave
   D. insert a comma after leaving

**Review your work using the explanations that start on page 675.**

**STUDY ADVICE**

Love reading novels or comic books? That's fantastic, because you're building your language skills every time you read. However, sometimes authors deliberately break the rules of grammar to create an artistic effect. So don't mimic your favorite writer on the TASC; rather, use the rules in this chapter when you write your essay.

# Writing Effective Sentences Practice Questions

**Questions 1 through 5 refer to the following paragraphs.**

**Conserving Household Energy**

**(A)**

(1) According to the Department of Energy, many families spend an average of 14 percent of their yearly income on heating and cooling costs. (2) Although you can't do much about high fuel prices, you can try some energy-saving measures.

**(B)**

(3) To reduce wintertime energy costs, keep the shades drawn at night. (4) Seal your windows, so that cold air can't get through the cracks. (5) You can use sealing material available at any hardware store. (6) If you have an air conditioner, cover it with thick plastic. (7) Keep your thermostat at 68°F during the day. (8) Keep it at 62°F at night.

**(C)**

(9) In the summer, use fans and natural breezes rather than air-conditioning whenever possible. (10) If you have windows that get direct sunlight. (11) Keep the shades down during the day. (12) Don't leave your air conditioner running when you're not at home, change the filter every summer. (13) With a clogged filter, the air conditioner's energy use can go up as much as 5 percent. (14) Put your air conditioner on a low setting. (15) Your home will not cool down when your air conditioner is on full blast any faster.

1. Sentence 4: **Seal your windows, so that cold air can't get through the cracks.**

   Which correction should be made to sentence 4?

   A. change seal to sealing
   B. remove the comma
   C. change can't to couldn't
   D. change through to out

2. Sentences 7 and 8: **Keep your thermostat at 68°F during the day. Keep it at 62°F at night.**

   The most effective combination of sentences 7 and 8 would include which group of words?

   A. keeping your thermostat at
   B. during the day and 62°F
   C. the day, keeping it at
   D. at night, it should be kept

3. Sentences 10 and 11: **If you have windows that get direct sunlight. Keep the shades down during the day.**

   Which is the best way to write the underlined portion of these sentences?

   A. sunlight and
   B. sunlight and to keep
   C. sunlight keep
   D. sunlight, keep

4. Sentence 12: **Don't leave your air conditioner running when you're not at home, change the filter every summer.**

   Which is the best way to write the underlined portion of the sentence?

   A. home and change
   B. home change
   C. home, so change
   D. home. Do change

5. Sentence 15: **Your home will not cool down when your air conditioner is on full blast any faster.**

   The most effective revision of sentence 15 would begin with which group of words?

   A. Your home will not cool down any faster
   B. Having the air conditioner on full blast, it
   C. When your home will not cool down,
   D. Air-conditioning your home on full blast,

**Questions 6 through 10 refer to the following letter of complaint.**

Cole Electronics
2514 Broadway
New York, NY 10057

Dear Manager:

**(A)**

(1) On August 2, I purchased a television at your store. (2) When I got the television home I discovered that the picture was fuzzy. (3) Returning to the store to see if the problem could be fixed easily. (4) I assumed that there would be no problem because I had just purchased the set.

**(B)**

(5) The customer service personnel said they had no time to handle my complaint. (6) They were extremely rude and unprofessional. (7) Finally, a salesman told me that I would have to send the TV to a service center in Detroit. (8) At that point, I demanded a refund. (9) Claiming that the TV had been used, it could not be returned.

**(C)**

(10) I am angry about the treatment I received and I am also very frustrated. (11) I would now like to receive a full refund or getting the TV repaired locally. (12) Please contact me to let me know what action will be taken. (13) My phone number is (212) 555-2719.

Sincerely,
Jeffrey Barnes

6. Sentence 2: **When I got the television home I discovered that the picture was fuzzy.**

   Which correction should be made to sentence 2?

   A. replace When with Since
   B. insert a comma after home
   C. insert a comma after discovered
   D. change was to be

7. Sentence 3: **Returning to the store to see if the problem could be fixed easily.**

   Which correction should be made to sentence 3?

   A. replace Returning with I returned
   B. add a comma after store
   C. change could to can
   D. change easily to easy

8. Sentence 9: **Claiming that the TV had been used, it could not be returned.**

   The most effective revision of sentence 9 would begin with which group of words?

   A. He claimed that because
   B. The TV was claimed to
   C. Returning the TV,
   D. Making a claim about the TV

9. Sentence 10: **I am angry about the treatment I received and I am also very frustrated.**

   The most effective revision of sentence 10 would include which group of words?

   A. angry and frustrated about the
   B. feeling angry about the treatment
   C. being the recipient of such treatment
   D. the manner in which I was treated

10. Sentence 11: **I would now like to receive a full __________ the TV repaired locally.**

    Choose the option that correctly completes the sentence.

    A. refund, getting
    B. refund, or getting
    C. refund or get
    D. refund to getting

**Questions 11 though 15 refer to the following paragraphs.**

### Workplace Friendships

**(A)**

(1) Should you make friends at work or keep your distance? (2) Most experts agree that it's not wise to get too chummy with your boss. Relationships with coworkers, however, are a more complex matter. (3) Although workplace friendships between peers can be beneficial, they can also cause problems.

**(B)**

(4) Workplace friendships have many positive aspects. (5) It's hard to work if you feel alone and in a productive way. (6) Having friends at work can make your day more pleasant, and give you energy. (7) Friends can serve as a sounding board for problems and help you succeed.

**(C)**

(8) However, like any other friendship, workplace friendships can turn sour. (9) Things get messy, when the friendship unravels in plain view of your boss and coworkers. (10) Discrimination and harassment suits have even been brought in some cases.

**(D)**

(11) Experts recommend keeping your social life with work friends out of the workplace. (12) For instance, don't exchange presents at work or talking about your evening out. (13) Avoid praising a friend publicly if it could make someone else resentful. (14) Keeping your work life separate from your social life may be hard but it's worth the effort.

11. Sentence 5: **It's hard to work if you feel alone and in a productive way.**

    The most effective revision of sentence 5 would include which group of words?

    A. work productively if you
    B. to work, it isn't easy if
    C. if you feel alone and productive
    D. work, feel alone, and be productive

12. Sentence 6: **Having friends at work can make your day more pleasant, and give you energy.**

    Which correction should be made to sentence 6?

    A. change Having to Have
    B. insert a comma after work
    C. remove the comma
    D. change give to giving

13. Sentence 9: **Things get messy, when the friendship unravels in plain view of your boss and coworkers.**

    Which correction should be made to sentence 9?

    A. change get to are getting
    B. remove the comma
    C. insert a comma after unravels
    D. insert a comma after boss

14. Sentence 12: **For instance, don't exchange presents at _________ about your evening out.**

    Choose the option that correctly completes the sentence.

    A. work or talk
    B. work, or talk
    C. work, or talking
    D. working or talking

15. Sentence 14: **Keeping your work life separate from your social life may be hard but it's worth the effort.**

    Which correction should be made to sentence 14?

    A. insert it after social life
    B. insert a comma after hard
    C. insert a comma after but
    D. replace it's with its

Questions 16 through 19 refer to the following paragraphs.

### Computer Virus Hoaxes

**(A)**

(1) If you use email, you've probably received at least one message warning you of a terrible virus that will ruin your computer. (2) Most of these messages are hoaxes. (3) Designed to scare you. (4) Though some messages about viruses are accurate, most are just inaccurate rumors.

**(B)**

(5) Virus hoax messages are similar to one another. (6) Frequently, they describe viruses that will destroy your hard drive or computer. (7) These hoaxes also claim that a respected authority, such as a government agency, has issued a warning about the virus. (8) You can check a claim like this. (9) Contacting the agency is a good way to check. (10) Finally, hoaxes urge you to send the message to everyone you know, this just creates panic.

**(C)**

(11) If you receive a virus warning, don't pass it on. (12) However, you don't have to worry about opening the email message itself. (13) Your computer can't get a virus that way. (14) Don't open any suspicious attachments, though, as you might infect your computer with a real virus. (15) By following these guidelines, you can keep your computer equipment safe, and avoid spreading hysteria.

16. Sentences 2 and 3: **Most of these messages are _________ to scare you.**

    Choose the option that correctly completes the sentence.

    A. hoaxes and they are designed
    B. hoaxes and they designed
    C. hoaxes, designing
    D. hoaxes designed

17. Sentences 8 and 9: **You can check a claim like this. Contacting the agency is a good way to check.**

    The most effective combination of sentences 8 and 9 would include which group of words?

    A. Checking a claim like this
    B. To check a claim like this, contact
    C. The agency in question can check
    D. A good way to check, contacting

18. Sentence 10: **Finally, hoaxes urge you to send the message to everyone you _________ just creates panic.**

    Choose the option that best completes the sentence.

    A. know and this
    B. know, this
    C. know. This
    D. know that this

19. Sentence 15: **By following these guidelines, you can keep your computer equipment safe, and avoid spreading hysteria.**

    Which correction should be made to sentence 15?

    A. change By following to To follow
    B. replace these with this
    C. remove the comma after guidelines
    D. remove the comma after safe

**Review your work using the explanations that start on page 675.**

**STUDY ADVICE**

Congratulations on completing another practice set! If you are struggling with a topic and don't feel you have more time to spend on it right this second, flag it for later. Keeping a list of what you should come back to will save time and guide your future studies.

LESSON 1

# Organize Ideas into Paragraphs

## KEY IDEAS

- Each paragraph should have one main idea.
- Each sentence in a paragraph should relate to the main idea.
- Join short paragraphs if they both relate to the same main idea.

## TASC TEST TIP

*If a paragraph is especially long, check to see if the main idea shifts at some point. If so, that is where the paragraph should be divided in two.*

### Effective Paragraphs

A **paragraph** is a group of sentences that relate to one main idea. If the sentences do not help develop the same main idea, the paragraph seems disorganized, and the writer's meaning is unclear.

**Incorrect:**

Houseplants make a home more beautiful, but many people find them difficult to take care of. I water my houseplants once a week. There are many different kinds of houseplants. If you are buying a houseplant as a gift, consider how much light the person's home gets.

In the example above, each sentence is about houseplants, but there is no main idea. In the paragraph below, however, each sentence supports one idea: *helping houseplants adjust to a new home.*

**Correct:**

Houseplants need help to adjust to a new environment. Your home is probably less bright and humid than a greenhouse or plant store. Therefore, when you get a new houseplant, keep it near a south-facing window at first. Move it away from the light over a period of four weeks. Use a humidifier to make the air in your home more humid. These actions will help avoid the loss of foliage that often occurs when plants change locales.

One paragraph should stop and a new one begin when the main idea shifts. In the example below, the first four sentences describe what road rage is, while the last four sentences tell how to react to road rage. The writer should have started a new paragraph with sentence 5.

**Incorrect:**

(1) Road rage is an episode of violent behavior that takes place when one driver's actions anger another driver. (2) Young males are the most likely to lose their cool on the road. (3) Most road rage incidents take place during rush hour, when people often get frustrated. (4) Warm weather is another factor in road rage. (5) If you're a victim of an aggressive driver, try to stay calm. (6) Don't react or make eye contact. (7) Try not to brake or swerve in retaliation. (8) These actions will only infuriate the other driver, and you might lose control of your car.

Sometimes the ideas in two paragraphs really belong in one paragraph:

**Incorrect:**

To make chicken broth, boil a pot of water. Take some chicken, onions, parsnips, carrots, and herbs, and wrap them up in cheesecloth.

Make sure it is real cotton cheesecloth, or you won't be able to eat the broth! Simmer the cheesecloth-wrapped vegetables and chicken in the water for several hours; then remove them. Add salt and pepper to taste.

# PRACTICE 1.1

**A. Directions: Read each group of sentences. If there is a main idea, underline it. If there is no main idea, write "No MI."**

____ 1. The pharmacist at the local drugstore is very helpful. She can always get the medicines we need. She arranges deliveries of our prescriptions when we're sick. When we don't have money, she lets us pay the next time. Many people have written to thank her.

____ 2. Keep your toolbox well equipped, and you'll always be able to make home repairs. Common home repairs include replacing lighting fixtures and fixing furniture. The community center offers a class on this subject. You can pay someone to do home repairs.

____ 3. Some people don't vote because they think their vote doesn't count. However, elections have been won by just a few hundred votes. If people don't vote, they are giving up their voice. Every vote counts, so let your voice be heard and vote!

____ 4. When you are traveling, it's a good idea to mark your luggage clearly. Put a luggage tag on every piece you intend to bring, including hand luggage like backpacks. To recognize your luggage quickly, put a brightly colored ribbon on it.

____ 5. Listening to music can benefit you in many ways. When you are feeling stressed, music can help soothe and relax you. When you need energy, rock 'n' roll or hip-hop can give you a boost. If you have a baby or small child, soft music can help lull the child to sleep.

**B. Questions 6 and 7 refer to the following paragraphs.**

**The Common Cold**

**(A)**

(1) How frequently you get colds depends on your age. (2) The average young adult gets two to four colds a year. (3) Adults over 60 have fewer than one cold a year, while children have six to ten colds annually. (4) Colds are caused by viruses. (5) Contrary to popular belief, being cold will not cause you to get a cold. (6) Vitamin C is thought to prevent colds, but there is no proof.

**(B)**

(7) Because there is no cure for the common cold, prevention is key. (8) Washing your hands is the best way to avoid getting a cold. (9) Encourage others who have colds to sneeze into a tissue and throw it away immediately.

**(C)**

(10) Refrain from touching your eyes and nose, and stay far from people who have colds.

**6.** Which revision would improve the effectiveness of the article?

Begin a new paragraph with

A. sentence 2
B. sentence 3
C. sentence 4
D. sentence 5

**7.** Which revision would improve the effectiveness of the article?

A. remove sentence 1
B. remove paragraph (B)
C. remove paragraph (C)
D. join paragraphs (B) and (C)

**Review your work using the explanations that start on page 675.**

KEY IDEAS

- A topic sentence states the main idea of a paragraph.
- Each sentence in a paragraph should provide details to support the main idea.
- An essay should have a main idea statement that states the main point of the entire essay.

## Topic Sentences in Paragraphs

Every paragraph should have a **topic sentence** that states the main idea. The other sentences in the paragraph are **supporting details.** These details tell more about the topic sentence. The topic sentence usually appears at the beginning of the paragraph, though it may appear elsewhere.

A topic sentence must do two things:

- Identify the topic, or subject, of the paragraph
- State the central point that the writer wants to make about the topic

In the paragraph below, the topic sentence is underlined. Notice how the topic sentence tells the subject of the paragraph *(graffiti in our neighborhood)* and states the central point about the topic *(graffiti is a serious problem in the neighborhood and should be addressed).*

**EXAMPLE**

> We need to do more to stop the problem of graffiti in our neighborhood. Recently, several bus stops and the exterior walls of many buildings have been defaced with unsightly graffiti. The neighborhood is fast becoming a much less desirable place to live. As a result, prospective renters feel frightened and look elsewhere.

A topic sentence should not be too specific or too general. If it is, readers won't know what the overall point is. A topic sentence like "The market is covered with gang symbols," would be too specific for the paragraph above. "There is graffiti in our neighborhood," would be too general.

TASC TEST TIP

*Be sure that every paragraph has a clear topic sentence.*

## Main Idea Statements in Essays

Just as every paragraph should have a topic sentence, every essay should have a **main idea statement**. Whereas a topic sentence states the main idea, or "point," of a single paragraph, a main idea statement expresses the central point of all the paragraphs in an essay. In the essay below, the main idea statement is underlined. Notice that while the main idea statement appears in the first paragraph, it is not the first sentence.

**EXAMPLE**

> While graffiti is indeed a serious problem facing our neighborhood, other issues also need to be addressed. Two of the most pressing neighborhood issues are the crime rate and the lack of decent housing.
>
> In recent months, crime has increased. For example, a number of muggings have occurred. As a result, residents are nervous about going out at night. The number of apartment break-ins has increased as well. We need a stronger police presence to combat the crime problem.
>
> In addition, much of the housing in this neighborhood is in poor condition. Every day, residents are put in danger by loose roof tiles, broken locks, and rundown fences. We must put pressure on landlords to resolve their tenants' complaints, perhaps by showing them that, in the long run, it is in their financial interest to do so.
>
> If we do not act immediately, our neighborhood will decline even more. Therefore, I recommend that we form a community task force to tackle these issues. We should ask our city councilwoman to be an advocate for us. With full participation of community members, we will be on our way to a safer, more livable neighborhood.

# PRACTICE 1.2

**A. Directions: Write topic sentences for each of the following paragraphs.**

**1.** ______________________________________________

Weather satellites send us information about weather around the world. Thanks to satellite TV, we have an ever-widening range of programs to choose from. Satellites even play a role in long-distance telephone communication.

**2.** ______________________________________________

First of all, stock prices are falling. Second, home sales have slowed to a crawl. Finally, many consumers have cut back on big purchases such as cars, home improvements, and vacations.

**3.** ______________________________________________

According to the new dress code, employees of the library may now wear "semi-casual" clothing. Khakis, blue jeans with no holes, and other slacks are acceptable for men and women. Skirts must be knee-length or longer. Sandals are acceptable in the summer. Employees are requested not to wear gym shoes.

**B. Questions 4 and 5 refer to the following paragraphs.**

**Repetitive Strain Injury**

**(A)**

(1) Repetitive strain injury is a problem. (2) The injury can affect factory workers, computer users, and meatpackers, among others. (3) Anyone who uses his or her hands all day may be affected, even if the work does not seem to require a lot of physical effort. (4) When fine hand movements are repeated for many hours a day, they eventually strain the forearms, wrists, and fingers.

**(B)**

(5) Maintaining a stiff and constrained posture, as is required for working at a computer, places a lot of stress on the body. (6) Likewise, holding muscles still for long periods causes fatigue and discomfort. (7) In addition, many jobs require workers to work at top speed all day long. (8) Consistently working quickly deprives the body of natural rest breaks, forcing workers to push themselves to the limit.

**4.** Which is the most effective revision of sentence 1?

A. Some workers get repetitive strain injury.
B. Just what, you may ask, is repetitive strain injury?
C. Workers suffer many injuries on the job, and repetitive strain injury is just one of them.
D. Repetitive strain injury is a painful condition resulting from repeated use of the hands.

**5.** Which sentence would be most effective if inserted at the beginning of paragraph (B)?

A. Repetitive movements cause muscle strain.
B. A number of factors contribute to repetitive strain injury.
C. Watch your posture as you work.
D. Repetitive strain injury is very common.

**Review your work using the explanations that start on page 675.**

## STUDY ADVICE

Remember that practice has three levels: Learn and Review, Practice and Review, Assess and Review. For each lesson, absorb the concepts on the left side of the page. Then practice using the page on the right, and carefully review the explanations in the back of the book. Afterwards, you'll be able to assess your comprehension by completing the practice set and reviewing the explanations. By following these steps, you'll learn a great deal about how the questions work and what you're doing well.

LESSON 2

# Use Logical Order and Relevant Ideas

**KEY IDEAS**

- The sentences in a paragraph should follow a logical order.
- Keep reasons and examples close to the point you are making with them.
- Eliminate any irrelevant details.

When you are writing a paragraph, it is important to put your sentences in a logical order. For instance, you may choose to sequence supporting details from most important to least important, from least important to most important, or in time order. All the sentences in the paragraph should follow the same order. If not, your readers may get confused. Look at the sample paragraphs below:

**Incorrect:**

To clear a clogged drain using a plunger, fill the sink with enough water to cover the plunger cup. Put petroleum jelly on the rim of the cup to form a tight seal. Before you begin, check to make sure that the plunger's suction cup is big enough to cover the drain. Block the sink overflow with rags. Plunge 15 or 20 times.

**Correct:**

To clear a clogged drain using a plunger, first check to make sure that the plunger's suction cup is big enough to cover the drain. Fill the sink with enough water to cover the plunger cup. Put petroleum jelly on the rim of the cup to form a tight seal. Block the sink overflow with rags. Plunge 15 or 20 times.

The reasons and examples you use to support your points should come immediately after you make each point. If they come later, they will be less effective.

**Incorrect:**

Don't make a habit of using chemicals to clear your drain. Always wear rubber gloves to protect your hands when using chemical drain cleaners. These powerful cleaners can damage the pipes.

**Correct:**

Don't make a habit of using chemicals to clear your drain. These powerful cleaners can damage the pipes. Always wear rubber gloves to protect your hands when using chemical drain cleaners.

**ON THE TASC TEST**

*Make sure that every supporting sentence is relevant to the topic sentence. Ask yourself, "Does this support the main idea of the paragraph?" If not, delete it or move it to where it belongs.*

Sometimes a sentence in a paragraph relates to the topic in a general way but does not support the topic sentence. This mistake is a type of **irrelevant detail**, as shown in the paragraph below:

In many cultures, blonde is considered a desirable hair color. Perhaps blonde hair is valued because few people are naturally blonde. The practice of bleaching one's hair blonde is very old, dating back to ancient Roman times, and it continues to be popular today. My sister dyed her hair last year. A number of hair-bleaching products are sold in drugstores and supermarkets.

The sentence "My sister dyed her hair last year," is an irrelevant detail. While it relates to the topic of bleaching one's hair, it does not support the idea that blonde is a popular hair color in many cultures. This sentence should be deleted.

## PRACTICE 2

**A. Directions: Cross out the irrelevant detail in each paragraph.**

1. Why do people blame themselves when things go terribly wrong? Some psychologists believe that by blaming themselves, people find a reason for the upsetting event. Getting very ill is one bad thing that could happen. Finding a reason is more comforting than believing that the event took place for no reason at all.

2. It's almost time for the back-to-school rush. This year, come to Wunnzie's to make sure that your child is outfitted with all the things that he or she needs. We have school supplies at rock-bottom prices. Adult students can also use school supplies. Check out our backpacks and lunch boxes in colors your kids will love. At Wunnzie's, we have everything your kids will ever need!

3. Tenants: On Friday, April 23, the boiler in this building will be fixed. This job will be extremely expensive! There will be no water from 8 A.M. to 5 P.M. Please plan in advance, and draw out water the night before to be used the next day. We apologize for the inconvenience.

**B. Questions 4 through 6 refer to the following cover letter.**

**(A)**

Dear Mr. Soros:

(1) Thank you very much for taking the time to speak with me about the carpentry position. (2) It was a pleasure to meet you and to learn about your organization. (3) I enjoyed meeting you and learning about your organization.

**(B)**

(4) As you will see from the enclosed resume, I recently completed a program in carpentry at Dade Community College. (5) I have also worked in the carpentry field. (6) In addition, I held a secretarial job.

**(C)**

(7) With my education and experience, I believe that I could make a valuable contribution to your company. (8) Thank you for considering me for this position. (9) I look forward to hearing from you soon. (10) I would be honored to take the job if it were offered to me.

Sincerely,

Sandra Barnes

4. Which revision would improve the effectiveness of paragraph (A)?

   A. remove sentence 1
   B. move sentence 1 to follow sentence 2
   C. move sentence 2 to the beginning of paragraph B
   D. remove sentence 3

5. Sentence 6: **In addition, I held a secretarial job.**

   Which revision should be made to the placement of sentence 6?

   A. move sentence 6 to follow sentence 4
   B. move sentence 6 to follow sentence 8
   C. move sentence 6 to follow sentence 10
   D. remove sentence 6

6. Sentence 10: **I would be honored to take the job if it were offered to me.**

   Which revision should be made to the placement of sentence 10?

   A. move sentence 10 to follow sentence 2
   B. move sentence 10 to follow sentence 4
   C. move sentence 10 to follow sentence 5
   D. move sentence 10 to follow sentence 8

**Review your work using the explanations that start on page 676.**

Connecting Ideas

## LESSON 3

# Relate Sentences and Paragraphs

Good writing flows smoothly and logically from one sentence to the next and from one paragraph to the next. To make your writing flow, use **transitions** to show how ideas are related. Here are some common transitions and their uses.

| Transitional Word or Phrase | Use it to . . . |
|---|---|
| for example, for instance | give an example |
| also, furthermore, in addition, in the same way, likewise, moreover, similarly | compare ideas or add to an idea |
| however, nevertheless, on the other hand, in contrast | contrast ideas |
| first, second, then, next, after that, later, at last, finally, in conclusion | show steps in a process or time order |
| because | show a cause |
| as a result, consequently | show a result |
| therefore, thus | draw a conclusion |

**KEY IDEAS**

- Use transitions to help your writing flow from sentence to sentence and from paragraph to paragraph.
- Choose the transition that expresses the correct relationship between ideas.

You can link two sentences using transitions in the following ways:

**EXAMPLES**

**Begin the second sentence with a transition followed by a comma:** Raquel has many hobbies. For example, she paints furniture and sews clothes.

**Put the transition within the second sentence and set it off with commas:** Raquel has many hobbies. She paints furniture, for example, and sews clothes.

**Combine the two sentences into one. Put a semicolon before the transition and a comma after it:** Raquel has many hobbies; for example, she paints furniture and sews clothes.

Transitions can also be used to link one paragraph to another, highlighting the relationship between the two paragraphs.

**EXAMPLE**

> Top performance in sports depends on "mental economy." Mental economy involves focusing the mind on the task at hand. When athletes think too much about what they're doing or worry about the outcome, they interfere with the communication between the brain and the muscles.
>
> In addition, athletes must strive for "physical economy." Although athletes put forth a tremendous amount of effort, they must take care to pace themselves in order to conserve energy for the end of the event.

**TASC TEST TIP**

*When you use a transition at the beginning of a sentence, be sure you put a comma after the transition.*

To decide which transition to use, see how the paragraph is organized and what you are trying to accomplish. For example, are you comparing two things? If so, you will want to use transitions that compare ideas. Similarly, when choosing transitions to introduce paragraphs, consider the organization of the entire essay.

# PRACTICE 3

**A. Directions: Rewrite each pair of sentences using a transition from the chart on page 154. Change the punctuation if necessary. Write your answers on a separate sheet of paper.**

**Example:** We have worked very hard this year. Sales are at an all-time high.
*We have worked very hard this year. As a result, sales are at an all-time high.*

1. Our marketing efforts need to be enhanced. We will soon begin another marketing initiative.
2. Sales representatives say their jobs are extremely demanding. The salary is attractive.
3. The marketing director has instructed sales representatives to try some new ideas. Sales representatives can give away free samples.
4. A new ad campaign will be launched in just a few weeks. We expect sales to increase.

**B. Questions 5 through 7 refer to the following paragraphs.**

**Library Cafés**

**(A)**

(1) Until very recently, eating was not something that most people associated with libraries. (2) A patron would likely be chased out for munching on a sandwich in a corner. (3) Times are changing, and these days patrons can even buy coffee and a croissant in some public libraries.

**(B)**

(4) Following the lead of successful bookstores, libraries across the country are installing cafés. (5) Some library cafés have menus that offer just as much variety as a regular restaurant. (6) In addition, one of them offers 20 varieties of coffee, hot cider, and muffins. (7) These refreshments make going to the library more pleasant and may therefore increase library patronage.

**(C)**

(8) To have a café may benefit a library financially. (9) The income from the café adds to library revenues. (10) Also, as more people enjoy coming to the library, they may be more likely to approve tax increases for it.

**STUDY ADVICE**

The way your ideas relate to each other may be obvious to you, but it won't be to your readers. It's your job to make it clear how sentence 2 relates to sentence 1, and how sentence 3 relates to sentence 2. As you write, think about how you can make it *really easy* for your readers to follow the flow of your ideas.

5. **Sentence 3:** Times are changing, and these days patrons can even buy coffee and a croissant in some public libraries.

   Which correction should be made to sentence 3?

   A. insert however after Times
   B. insert however, after the comma
   C. insert , however after these days
   D. insert , however after coffee

6. **Sentences 5 and 6:** Some library cafés have menus that offer just as much variety as those of a regular _________ one of them offers 20 varieties of coffee, hot cider, and muffins.

   Choose the best option that correctly completes the sentence.

   A. restaurant, in addition,
   B. restaurant. For example,
   C. restaurant. Nevertheless,
   D. restaurant. Thus,

7. **Sentence 8:** To have a café may benefit a library financially.

   Choose the best option that corrects the sentence.

   A. In addition, having a café
   B. On the other hand, having a café
   C. A café, by benefiting a library,
   D. Financially a café

**Review your work using the explanations that start on page 676.**

## Connecting Ideas Practice Questions

**Questions 1 through 5 refer to the following paragraphs.**

**The Effects of Lack of Sleep**

**(A)**

(1) Research shows that about 70 million North Americans have experienced the problem of sleep disruption. (2) Losing sleep is more than just an annoyance. (3) In some cases, it can have catastrophic results. (4) In the United States, sleepy drivers are responsible for at least 100,000 car crashes each year. (5) Most people need at least eight hours of shut-eye a night but get only six or seven. (6) Their fast-paced lives leave them little time for sleep. (7) Another factor is poor bedtime habits. (8) Family stresses may also cause sleep loss.

**(B)**

(9) A study of high school students showed that students with low grades went to bed 40 minutes later and got 25 minutes less sleep than students with high grades. (10) On the other hand, another study shows that when one gets fewer than six to eight hours of sleep, it is harder to learn new skills.

**(C)**

(11) If you have trouble sleeping, avoid caffeine and alcohol. (12) Get regular exercise during the day, when it won't make you too energized to sleep. (13) Exercise can also help you lose weight.

**(D)**

(14) Set times for going to bed and getting up each day, and stick to them. (15) Don't watch TV or use a computer late at night, since these stimulate visual response and interfere with sleep. (16) If you find you still can't sleep, get up and do something.

1. Which revision would improve the effectiveness of the article?

   Begin a new paragraph with

   A. sentence 3
   B. sentence 4
   C. sentence 5
   D. sentence 6

2. Which sentence would be most effective if inserted at the beginning of paragraph (B)?

   A. Some high school students get better grades than others.
   B. High-achieving students get more sleep.
   C. Lack of sleep interferes with mathematical ability.
   D. People need more sleep than they used to.

3. Sentences 9 and 10: **A study of high school students showed that students with low grades went to bed 40 minutes later and got 25 minutes less sleep than students with high __________ another study shows that when one gets fewer than six to eight hours of sleep, it is harder to learn new skills.**

   Choose the best option that correctly completes the sentence.

   A. grades. Similarly,
   B. grades, likewise,
   C. grades. As a result,
   D. grades. Therefore,

4. Sentence 13: **Exercise can also help you lose weight.**

   Which revision should be made regarding sentence 13?

   A. move sentence 13 to follow sentence 11
   B. move sentence 13 to follow sentence 14
   C. move sentence 13 to follow sentence 15
   D. remove sentence 13

5. Which revision would improve the effectiveness of the article?

   A. join paragraphs (B) and (C)
   B. move sentence 11 to the end of paragraph (B)
   C. remove sentence 14
   D. join paragraphs (C) and (D)

**Questions 6 through 10 refer to the following paragraphs.**

### Getting Out Those Troublesome Stains

**(A)**

(1) Have you ever ruined a nice piece of clothing by staining it? (2) If so, the following information on stain removal may interest you. (3) By learning a few simple rules and keeping some household cleaners on hand, you can preserve your clothing. (4) First of all, the faster you act, the better. (5) With time, the stain will set. (6) Be sure to blot the stain rather than scrubbing it. (7) Scrubbing can actually drive the stain into the fabric.

**(B)**

(8) Use hot water on a grease stain such as salad dressing and cold water on a water-based stain such as wine, pasta sauce, or blood. (9) If you don't know what the stain is or where it came from, use room-temperature water. (10) Otherwise you might set the stain.

**(C)**

(11) Sometimes other liquids are more effective than water. (12) Lemon juice, for example removes ink, rust, and iodine. (13) White vinegar takes out alcohol, coffee, deodorants, and glue. (14) Liquid shampoo can be used on oil, tar, and grease. (15) Not surprisingly, it works the same way on an oil stain as it does on oil in your hair. (16) Rubbing alcohol removes stains from grass and soft drinks.

**(D)**

(17) If you find that a stain is not going away or is getting worse, stop and take your clothes to a dry cleaner. (18) Professionals know best. (19) Home remedies may not work on every stain.

6. Which revision would improve the effectiveness of the article?

   Begin a new paragraph with

   A. sentence 3
   B. sentence 4
   C. sentence 5
   D. sentence 6

7. Which sentence would be most effective if inserted at the beginning of paragraph (B)?

   A. Hot and cold water have many uses.
   B. Choose the right water temperature for cleaning each stain.
   C. Hot water takes out tough stains.
   D. The second step is to determine the proper use of hot water.

8. Sentence 12: **Lemon __________ ink, rust, and iodine.**

   Choose the option that correctly completes the sentence.

   A. juice, for example removes
   B. juice, for example. Removes
   C. juice for example removes
   D. juice, for example, removes

9. Which revision would improve the effectiveness of paragraph (C)?

   A. move sentence 11 to follow sentence 12
   B. move sentence 12 to follow sentence 14
   C. remove sentence 14
   D. remove sentence 15

10. Sentence 19: **Home remedies may not work on every stain.**

    Which revision should be made to the placement of sentence 19?

    A. move sentence 19 to the beginning of paragraph (C)
    B. move sentence 19 to follow sentence 13
    C. move sentence 19 to the beginning of paragraph (D)
    D. move sentence 19 to follow sentence 17

**Questions 11 through 14 refer to the following memo.**

To: All Employees
From: Denise Ellis, Benefits Manager

**(A)**

(1) Starting on January 1, Allcity will no longer be our insurance carrier. (2) Instead, you will have a choice of two other insurance carriers: HealthPlan and Rainbow Insurance Company.

**(B)**

(3) HealthPlan is an HMO. (4) You will not have to pay any money to doctors in advance with this plan, but you must go to doctors listed with the insurance company. (5) HMOs are becoming increasingly popular. (6) With Rainbow Insurance, you may choose any doctor you wish. (7) However you must pay the health providers when you receive the service. (8) Afterwards, you submit the receipts to Rainbow Insurance. (9) Representatives of both companies will be here on December 2 to discuss the details of their plans. (10) Please sign up for an informational session on that day. (11) The sign-up sheet is on the door of the conference room, where the meetings will take place.

**(C)**

(12) At the meeting, you will receive a card on which you must indicate your choice of company. (13) Please mark your choice in the appropriate box and submit it to me by December 5.

**(D)**

(14) If you do not submit your card in time, you may not be insured for the month of January. (15) If you are not able to attend any of the informational sessions, please let me know right away. (16) Feel free to contact me at ext. 2453 with any questions you may have about this process.

11. Which revision would improve the effectiveness of paragraph (B)?

    A. remove sentence 3
    B. move sentence 5 to the beginning of paragraph (B)
    C. remove sentence 5
    D. remove sentence 10

12. Sentence 7: **However you must pay the health providers when you receive the service.**

    Which correction should be made to sentence 7?

    A. insert a comma after However
    B. Insert a comma after pay
    C. insert a comma after when
    D. change receive to receives

13. Which revision would improve the effectiveness of the memo?

    Begin a new paragraph with

    A. sentence 7
    B. sentence 8
    C. sentence 9
    D. sentence 10

14. Sentence 14: **If you do not submit your card on time, you may not be insured for the month of January.**

    Which revision should be made regarding sentence 14?

    A. move sentence 14 to the end of paragraph (C)
    B. move sentence 14 to follow sentence 15
    C. move sentence 14 to follow sentence 16
    D. remove sentence 14

**Questions 15 through 19 refer to the following paragraphs.**

### Repairing a Flat Bicycle Tire

**(A)**

(1) The first step in fixing a flat bicycle tire is to remove the wheel. (2) Next, release the brake. (3) Before you begin, let out any air in the tire. (4) If you are removing the back wheel, put the derailleur in high gear. (5) Then take off the axle nuts by unscrewing counterclockwise. (6) If your bike has safety washers, remove these also. (7) Then remove the wheel.

**(B)**

(8) Remove the tire, and mark the valve stem position on it. (9) If possible, remove the tire without using tools, because the inner tube punctures easily. (10) Use tire levers or the backs of forks and spoons if necessary. (11) When you find the leak, scrape the spot with sandpaper. (12) Remove the inner tube and inflate it, listening and feeling for air leaks. (13) Then apply cement to the tube, and let it dry completely before putting the patch on.

**(C)**

(14) First, inflate the tube and make sure the leak has been fixed. (15) Next, slip the inner tube back into the tire, and put the tire back on the rim. (16) Then inflate the tube to the correct pressure. (17) The pressure is right when there is enough air to steady the tire but not so much air that the tire cannot be squeezed between the brake pads.

**(D)**

(18) Put the bike back on its wheels, and then tighten the wheel nuts. (19) Moreover, readjust the tire pressure, and you're ready to ride!

15. Which revision would improve the effectiveness of paragraph (A)?

    A. move sentence 2 to follow sentence 3
    B. begin a new paragraph with sentence 5
    C. move sentence 5 to follow sentence 7
    D. remove sentence 6

16. Which revision would improve the effectiveness of paragraph (B)?

    A. move sentence 11 to follow sentence 8
    B. move sentence 11 to follow sentence 9
    C. move sentence 11 to follow sentence 12
    D. move sentence 11 to follow sentence 13

17. Which sentence would be most effective if inserted at the beginning of paragraph (C)?

    A. All you have to do now is take care of the tire pressure.
    B. Fixing a flat tire is a long process that requires a lot of patience.
    C. The next step is to put the tire and tube back onto the rim.
    D. Patching the leak properly is also very important.

18. Which sentence would be most effective if inserted at the beginning of paragraph (D)?

    A. The final step is to reinstall the wheel.
    B. Fixing a flat tire requires careful planning.
    C. Whether you are an experienced cyclist or just a beginner, you can fix a flat tire.
    D. Try not to use sharp tools to fix a flat tire.

19. Sentence 19: **Moreover, readjust the tire pressure, and you're ready to ride!**

    Which correction should be made to sentence 19?

    A. replace Moreover, with Then
    B. change readjust to readjusting
    C. remove the comma after pressure
    D. replace you're with your

**Review your work using the explanations that start on page 676.**

LESSON 1

# Unpack the Writing Prompt

On the TASC Writing Test, you will write an essay in response to a passage or pair of passages and a **prompt,** or assignment. You will want to spend roughly 50 minutes on this task. To master this portion of the exam, you need to employ **evidence-based writing.** This type of writing requires that you develop an argument or explanation by using evidence and details from the text(s). The passages may discuss topics from science, history, or any other field. However, you do not need to have any prior knowledge about the topics. All the information you need will be provided for you in the passage(s).

There are two types of essays on the TASC, but you will only have to write one. You do not know which type of essay you will be asked to write in advance, so practice both types before Test Day. The two types are:

- **Argument/Opinion Essay:** You will be given a passage or pair of passages that present two sides of a debate. You will be asked to argue for one side and against the other side, using logical reasoning and evidence from the passage(s) to support your position.
- **Informative/Explanatory Essay:** You will be given a passage and asked to explain an idea, process, point of view, or sequence of events from the passage. You should use several details from the passage(s) to develop your explanation.

Regardless of which type of essay you are assigned, your task will be largely the same: to write a few paragraphs (three or four) that clearly develop a line of thought. You will introduce your essay with a thesis statement; organize it into paragraphs, each of which develops one idea in support of that thesis statement; and conclude it with a summary of your explanation or argument.

Unpack the writing prompt to determine what your task is. What does it mean to "unpack" a prompt? When you unpack a suitcase, you take things out and think about what you are going to do with them—wash them, fold them, hang them up, or put them in a drawer. Similarly, with a writing prompt, you will take it apart in your mind and plan how you are going to accomplish the task.

Unpack the prompt by asking yourself these questions:

1. What is the writing assignment about?
2. Based on the prompt, how many passages will I be given, and what will they contain?
3. What does the prompt ask me to do?
4. Am I being asked to make an argument or to explain something?
5. What am I being asked to include in my response?

**KEY IDEAS**

- The essay will require reading one or two passages and writing a response to a prompt.
- To draft an acceptable response to the text, the first step is to "unpack" the prompt—to focus on the specific question you need to address.
- Your response must be evidence based, which means that it needs to be grounded in facts, details, and examples from the text.

**TASC TEST TIP**

*It is advisable to read the prompt before you read the passages. That will help you to focus on the argument and the supporting evidence in the passage or passages.*

Practice using the following prompt. (This prompt does not have passages associated with it, and you will not be writing an essay in response to it.)

Hydraulic fracturing is currently used in many parts of the United States to extract natural gas from deep in the ground. There is an ongoing debate about whether hydraulic fracturing (or "fracking") should be allowed. Read the two passages, weigh the arguments on both sides, and write an argumentative essay in which you argue for or against allowing hydraulic fracturing. Use details and evidence from both passages in your essay.

Make sure that you:

- Include your thesis statement early.
- Give reasons and evidence from the passages to support your thesis statement.
- Argue against the opposite side.
- Organize your ideas, and show how the ideas relate to each other.
- Use a businesslike style.
- Conclude with a short summary of your argument.

**1.** What is the writing assignment about? *Whether hydraulic fracturing should be allowed*

**2.** Based on the prompt, how many passages will I be given, and what will they contain? *Two passages, which present the two sides of the argument about hydraulic fracturing*

**3.** What does the prompt ask me to do? *Pick a side and argue for it. Should hydraulic fracturing be allowed and why?*

**4.** Am I being asked to make an argument or to explain something? *Make an argument*

**5.** What am I being asked to include in my response? *Introduction, details from the passages, logical reasons why my argument is right, argument against the opposing view, good organization, concluding statement*

---

**In response to the prompt below, answer the five questions listed at the bottom of page 160.**

Most people probably don't think about where the calendar came from, but it actually has a long and fascinating history. Read the passage describing the history of the Gregorian calendar (the one used by most people in the United States) and the development of other calendars used in other parts of the world. Write an essay explaining how the Gregorian calendar differs from other calendars and how those differences came about. Use details, facts, and definitions from the passage in your essay.

Make sure that you:

- Include your topic clearly.
- Give details, facts, and definitions from the passage to develop your explanation.
- Organize your ideas, and show how the ideas relate to each other.
- Use a businesslike style.
- Conclude with a short summary of your explanation.

**Review your work using the explanations that start on page 676.**

LESSON 2

# Read the Passage(s) with the Prompt in Mind

Before writing your essay, you will first analyze the passage or passages while keeping the prompt in mind. A TASC writing prompt asks you to explain a topic or make an argument. Thus, as you read, ask yourself some questions that will equip you to perform that task. Take brief notes about these questions as you read.

First, identify the topic of each passage. Then ask: Is the author neutral about the topic—that is, is she merely giving you the history of something, explaining how something works, or describing something? Or does the author have an opinion about the topic?

If the author has an opinion, is she arguing for a certain policy or method, or is she countering someone else's argument? What evidence does she use to support her argument?

If she does not have an opinion, why did she write the passage? Your answer to that might sound like one of these examples:

- "The author wrote the passage to explain the history of the civil rights movement."
- "The author wrote the passage to describe the two sides of a debate, but she herself doesn't take a side."
- "The author wrote the passage to introduce a new way of thinking about her topic."
- "The author wrote the passage to compare and contrast two new products."

Read the following short passage. Consider whether the author is neutral or whether she has an opinion.

> Secondhand smoke is the smoke that comes either from the lighted end of a cigarette, pipe, or cigar or from the exhalation of a smoker. Most people consider secondhand smoke to be less dangerous than the nicotine that a cigarette user intakes. However, the particles that come from the smoke of the lighted end of a cigarette, called side-stream smoke, contain higher concentrations of carcinogens, which are chemicals that cause cancer. These particles can be breathed in easily by people around smokers, especially in enclosed areas. Therefore, all restaurants should ban smoking inside.

1. What is the writer's topic?
   (1) Secondhand smoke and its effects
   (2) The most common carcinogens

2. What is the writer's opinion about the topic?
   (1) Sidestream smoke contains high concentrations of carcinogens.
   (2) Smoking should be banned inside restaurants.

In question 1, choice **(1)** is correct. The writer focuses on secondhand smoke throughout the passage. In question 2, choice **(2)** is correct. The writer uses the information about secondhand smoke as support for the claim that smoking should be banned inside restaurants.

### KEY IDEAS

- As you read a passage on the TASC Writing Test, keep the writing prompt in mind. Gather information that will allow you to complete the writing task.
- As you read, ask yourself, "What is the writer's topic? Does the writer have an opinion about that topic?"
- If the writer has an opinion, ask yourself what evidence she uses to support that opinion. If she does not have an opinion, ask yourself why she wrote the passage.

### TASC TEST TIP

*When you are reading the passages for the essay, ask yourself: What is the writer's conclusion?*

# PRACTICE 2

**Directions: For each passage, answer the questions about topic, opinion, and evidence.**

**Passage 1**

Some U.S. representatives advocate a bill requiring all young people to perform two years of military service by the age of 25. Proponents of the bill argue that this will not only prepare the U.S. military for any potential threat from other nations but will also build a greater spirit of patriotism among U.S. citizens. Citizens, they argue, will be able to appreciate the service of the military and acquire a deeper respect toward honoring their country. On the other side of the debate, opponents of the bill argue that requiring military service would lead people to feel resentful toward their government. They argue that, instead of requiring military service, the government should more heavily promote volunteer programs. Then young people could serve their countries by helping the poor or marginalized in their communities. At the present time, the bill's proponents and opponents continue to debate without reaching an agreement.

1. What is the writer's topic?

______________________________

______________________________

2. Does the writer have an opinion, or is she neutral?

______________________________

3. If the writer has an opinion, how does she support it? If she's neutral, what was her purpose in writing the passage?

______________________________

______________________________

______________________________

**Passage 2**

To best protect children from being subjected to portrayals of violence, we must reduce the amount of violence that is present in video games. Numerous studies done by various groups show a positive correlation between video game usage and violence.

Many people consider violence in video games a recent trend, but one of the earliest and most controversial video games was Death Race, released in 1976. In this game, the players controlled cars that ran over gremlins. The game was later pulled from stores due to public outcry. With the successful protest against Death Race as a model, we should be as proactive now to reduce or eliminate violence in video games.

4. What is the writer's topic?

______________________________

______________________________

5. Does the writer have an opinion, or is he neutral?

______________________________

6. If the writer has an opinion, how does he support it? If he's neutral, what was his purpose in writing the passage?

______________________________

______________________________

______________________________

**Review your work using the explanations that start on page 677.**

## STUDY ADVICE

Remember to build up your study time in increments. If writing tends to tire you out in the beginning, don't worry! You can spend an entire study session on the essay sample and then take a break. Over time, you can work up to longer study sessions.

LESSON 3

# Develop a Thesis Statement

You have been reading and analyzing writers' arguments. Now it is your turn to develop a response to what writers have to say. Once you have unpacked the prompt and read the reading passages, you will construct a **thesis statement** for your writing. The thesis statement either states your central claim (for an Argument/Opinion essay) or summarizes your explanation (for an Informative/Explanatory essay).

A thesis statement does the following:

- Makes your main point clear
- Provides the reader with a preview of what you will be discussing

### Thesis Statements in Argument/Opinion Essays

Compare the following two sentences, written in response to the prompt about hydraulic fracturing on page 161. Put a *T* next to the one sentence that fulfills the purpose of a thesis statement as described previously.

____ Hydraulic fracturing has some good points and bad points, though the bad points can threaten to outweigh the good points.

____ Hydraulic fracturing should not be allowed because of the threats it poses to the environment.

If you put a *T* next to the second sentence, you are correct. The first sentence does not clearly state its claim, and it does not preview what the rest of the essay will discuss. The second sentence states its claim very clearly and also tells the reader that the rest of the essay will discuss the environmental threats posed by hydraulic fracturing.

### Thesis Statements in Argument/Opinion Essays

Now compare the following two sentences, written in response to the prompt about calendars on page 161. Put a *T* next to the one that fulfills the purpose of a thesis statement.

____ The Gregorian calendar differs from other calendars in many ways for a variety of complex reasons.

____ The Gregorian calendar, unlike some calendars, is guided by the sun rather than the moon, has a Leap Day, and uses 12 months, because this arrangement suited religious and business needs in Europe several centuries ago.

You should have placed a *T* next to the second sentence. The first provides very little information about what the essay will explain. The second not only lists the main differences between the Gregorian calendar and other calendars but also previews the rest of the essay. Someone reading this essay now knows that the next few paragraphs will be about how religious and business needs influenced the Gregorian calendar.

**KEY IDEAS**

- A thesis statement makes a claim and indicates that the passage will support the claim with specific and relevant information.
- A thesis statement differs from an opinion, which is a feeling or belief about the topic of the passage.
- A thesis statement should introduce the topic that will be discussed in the essay.

**TASC TEST TIP**

*Although writers have different approaches, it is best to introduce your essay response with your thesis. This will let a reader know your position right away. Also, come back to your thesis statement as you write. This will keep you on track.*

# PRACTICE 3

**Directions: Read each paragraph and answer the questions that follow.**

Sit down to enjoy any television show today, and you'll find that almost every other commercial seems to be pushing a prescription drug. Although this form of direct-to-consumer (DTC) advertising of prescription medication has become commonplace in American programming, it remains a relatively new development in the medical world. In fact, the practice is currently legal in only two countries, the United States and New Zealand. Patient advocates and those who wish to maintain high standards of healthcare argue that DTC advertising should be eliminated altogether. Advertising prescription medications on television creates a popular demand for the drugs, and it may lead individuals to pressure their health-care providers for treatments that are inappropriate or even dangerous. At the same time, because prescription commercials must name all potential side effects of a certain medication, the ads may frighten other individuals away from using drugs that are both safe and effective for the general public. While such DTC advertisements serve to increase the profits of drug companies, they do little to ensure that the public is better educated about its health-care choices.

1. Is the writer neutral (giving a history, explaining something, etc.), or does he make an argument?

   ______________________________________________________________________

2. What is the writer's argument about prescription drug advertising on TV?

   ______________________________________________________________________

3. Write a thesis statement in which you take a stand for or against advertising prescription drugs on TV. State your position and preview how you will support it.

   ______________________________________________________________________

   ______________________________________________________________________

**HOW DID THE MOON FORM?**

There are several theories about how the Moon formed. Some scientists have suggested that the Moon was originally part of Earth and somehow broke off early in the history of the solar system. Others have suggested that the Moon was formed separately from Earth and then at some point was drawn into Earth's gravitational field, where it remains. Another possible answer involves rings. Earth (and other planets with a moon or moons) may have originally had rings like those of the planet Saturn. According to this idea, a moon begins to come together out of debris near the outer edges of a planet's rings. At those outer edges, the newly formed moon has a better chance of holding together without being broken up again by the planet's gravity. (Small objects orbiting close to a planet tend to be pulled toward the planet by gravity; they often ultimately crash into the planet.) The initial products of this process are small "moonlets" that spin outward from the planet. The moonlets collide and fuse with other moonlets as they travel. The process would be somewhat similar to that of a snowball rolling downhill, gathering more material as it rolls.

4. Is the writer neutral (giving a history, explaining something, etc.), or does she make an argument?

   ______________________________________________________________________

5. What does the author explain in this passage?

   ______________________________________________________________________

6. Write a thesis statement in response to this question: How do the various theories about the formation of the Moon differ? Make sure your thesis statement summarizes your explanation and previews the rest of the essay.

   ______________________________________________________________________

**Review your work using the sample answers on page 677.**

LESSON 4

# Collect Supporting Evidence

Once you have formulated your thesis statement, you need to use **evidence** and **details** from the passage or passages to support your claim. You should preview the **prompt** before you read the passage or passages. That benefit of this strategy is that you can:

- formulate your thesis statement while you are reading
- gather specific and relevant evidence and details to support your thesis

How can you gather evidence while you read? If you are taking the paper version of the test, you can underline portions of the passage, take notes in the margins of your test booklet, or take notes on scratch paper. If you are taking the computer version of the test, take notes on scratch paper. You may also have an online highlighter you can use to highlight portions of the passage.

**Thesis statement:** Family time is a thing of the past because too many distractions interfere with conversation and other interactions.

Practice gathering evidence with the passage below. Circle specific pieces of evidence that support the thesis statement above.

> I know it sounds corny, but I miss the way my family was together when I was growing up. Even though Mom and Dad worked, we usually had breakfast together. Now, I work the night shift and sleep in the morning, while my husband is too harried with getting the kids to eat and making their lunches to get a preview of their day.
>
> After school, our kids have part-time jobs, and everyone gets home at different times. Even though I have dinner ready before I leave at 8:00 p.m., someone is doing homework, someone is on the Internet, and someone is texting friends that he or she saw an hour before. I can't remember the last time we all ate together and had a conversation. Even when I try to organize a movie night, it seems that one of us has social or work obligations. We all love each other, but it is hard to have what we can call family time. Thank goodness for holidays and vacations when we can slow down and enjoy each other.

**Evidence statements** that support the thesis statement:

- Breakfast time is hectic and one parent is asleep.
- After school, people are working or engaged in distractions.
- Family members don't eat dinner together.
- Not everyone is available for common activities, like movie night.

### KEY IDEAS

- Formulate your thesis statement and collect supporting evidence or relevant details while you read.
- As you read, take notes about which details you can use to support your thesis statement.

### TASC TEST TIP

*When you cite the writer's evidence, use phrases such as "The passage stated . . ."; "In the text . . ."; and "One example from the text is . . ."*

# PRACTICE 4

**Directions: Read the prompt, the reading selection, and the writer's conclusion. List three pieces of supporting evidence from the passage that you could use in a response to the prompt. Add one piece of supporting evidence from your own experience or observations. <u>You will not be writing a response to this prompt</u>.**

**Drinking Age Prompt**

The writer of this passage has a position on keeping the minimum legal drinking age at 21. Take a position in response to the writer's argument, using relevant and specific information from the selection to support your response.

**The Case for Keeping the Minimum Drinking Age at 21**

We owe it to young adults, teens, and children to keep the minimum drinking age right where it is: at 21. The dangers of alcohol are often overlooked due to the fact that it is not a prohibited substance, but make no mistake: it is eminently dangerous, particularly to our youth.

In larger doses—consistent with binge drinking— alcohol wreaks havoc on the sensitive chemistry of the brain. The feast-and-famine pattern of drinking that is typical of teenage drinkers can lead to permanent damage to the prefrontal cortex, the part of the brain responsible for planning and decisions. Since this portion of the brain continues to develop later in life, younger brains are particularly vulnerable to the effects of alcohol. Even in moderate doses, it causes long-term damage to the heart, the liver, and the stomach.

Proponents of a lower drinking age maintain that the allure of the taboo of alcohol encourages abuse among youth. The United Kingdom, however, has a long history of social drinking, and the legal drinking age is 18 in bars and 16 in restaurants; despite this, alcohol-related deaths had doubled in the U.K. in the decade before 2008. Indeed, a 2008 BBC documentary ranked alcohol as the fifth most dangerous drug in the U.K., ahead of speed, LSD, ecstasy, and cannabis.

As a nation, we recognized the dangers that alcohol represented to our citizens and communities when we united to pass a constitutional amendment against it a century ago. That experiment was abandoned only due to challenges of enforcement, but Al Capone could never have built a crime empire on the dimes of 18- to 20-year-olds alone. We owe it to our youth—and the future of our nation—to protect their brains and their lives.

**Writer's Conclusion**

The conclusion is that despite some logical reasons for lowering the legal drinking age, it should remain at 21.

1. Three pieces of evidence used in the passage to support this conclusion are . . .
   a. The passage states that ______________________________
   b. Another fact from the passage is ______________________________
   c. In support of this position, the text further says that ______________________________
2. I (agree/disagree) with the position of this piece.
3. One piece of personal evidence I would use to support my position is ______________________________

**Review your work using the sample answers that start on page 677.**

LESSON 5

# Plan Your Response

You will want to spend about 50 minutes to complete the essay. You want to use that time wisely, and the best thing you can do is to take 10 minutes for **prewriting**, or planning, what you are going to write.

Successful test takers do this type of planning. It ensures that you understand the prompt, write a thesis statement, gather the relevant evidence, and have your ideas in place before you begin to write.

### KEY IDEAS

- Take ten minutes to unpack the prompt, read the passage(s), and plan your response.
- As you read the passages, develop your thesis statement and collect supporting evidence by taking notes.
- Plan your response by either outlining or mapping the key ideas that you will use in the response.

## Essay-Writing Strategy

This **Essay-Writing Strategy** will maximize your ability to use the 50 minutes efficiently and effectively. As you work through the rest of this unit, practice managing each stage of the strategy.

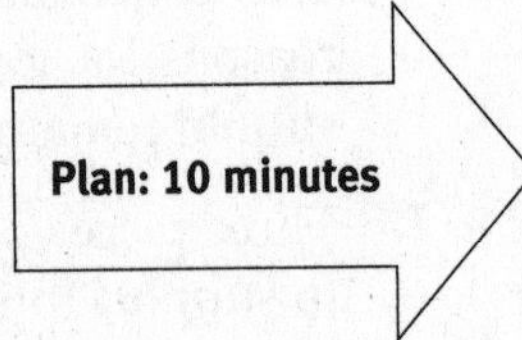


- Preview the writing prompt.
- Read the passage(s), making notes of key details on scratch paper.
- Use scratch paper to write your thesis statement and plan your response with either an outline or an idea map.

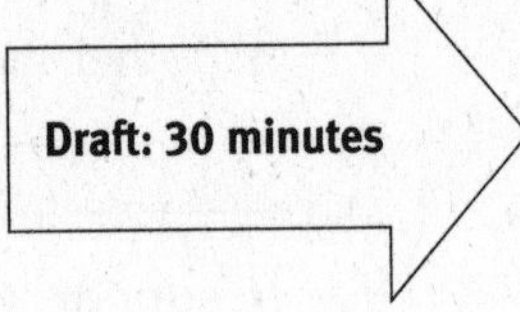


- Write a thesis statement as the introduction to your response.
- Use your plan, citing specific evidence from the text to support your ideas.
- Provide other relevant information based on your own knowledge and perspective.
- Write a closing that summarizes your position or restates the thesis statement in another way.

### TASC TEST TIP

*Follow through on all of the planning steps before you write. You will have plenty of time to execute your plan, and your score will be higher if you have thought your response through and mapped it out.*

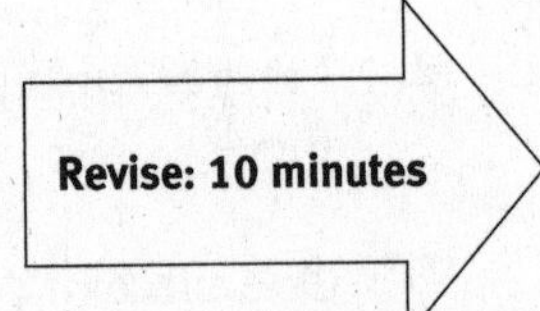


- Reread your thesis statement and review your response to make sure your response stayed focused on the prompt.
- Use the **Revision Questions** on page 178 to improve the response.
- Use the **Editing Questions** on page 180 to correct errors.

## Prewriting Strategies

Two of the most useful prewriting strategies for any kind of writing, including evidence-based writing, are outlining and mapping. Look at both methods of grouping ideas based on the same thesis statement.

> **Thesis statement:** *People need both close friends and acquaintances because they meet our social needs in different ways.*

An **outline** depicts each main topic by using a system of numbers and letters stressing a logical progression of ideas. Here is an outline based on the thesis statement above.

I. Benefits of close friends
   - a. Will always be there for you
   - b. Can always be yourself with them
   - c. Can have intimate conversations that are satisfying but confidential
   - d. Stand the test of time

II. Benefits of acquaintances
   - a. Add variety to your life
   - b. Expand your world

III. Acquaintances fulfill some special needs
   - a. Social needs—if you can't see closest friends every day
   - b. Networking needs—when you need to search for a job, find a new day care provider, etc.
   - c. Can make a party or other social event more interesting

An **idea map** uses a drawing to visually group ideas. To make a map, write your main idea in the center. Then draw lines from there to your main topics. From there, you attach the supporting ideas.

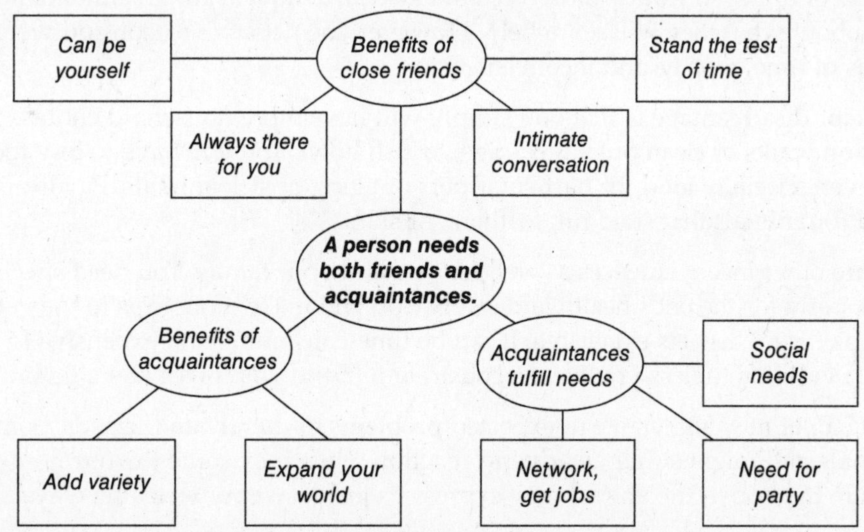


**STUDY ADVICE**

You won't write a good essay if you don't have a good plan for it. If this is something you struggle with, spend some time working on just the planning step. With practice you will get the hang of it!

# PRACTICE 5

**Directions: Follow these steps to plan a response.**

- Read the writing prompt to understand your task.
- Read the passage. Think about your thesis statement. Underline and take notes on key points that you will want to summarize or respond to.
- Write a thesis statement based on responding to the prompt and the passage.
- Make an outline and an idea map based on the selection.

**Family Pets Writing Prompt**

The writer of this passage explains the reasons a family should not own a pet. Read the selection and take a stand for or against the author's viewpoint.

Use details and evidence from the passage in your essay.

Make sure that you:

- Include your thesis statement early.
- Give reasons and evidence from the passages to support your thesis statement.
- Argue against the opposite side.
- Organize your ideas, and show how the ideas relate to each other.
- Use a businesslike style.
- Conclude with a short summary of your argument.

When you are trying to decide whether or not to buy a household pet, you need to weigh the pros and cons of doing so. Your children will make heartfelt pleas for an animal and will make wild claims about what they will do to help. However, the negative reasons outweigh the positive ones in terms of time, money, and inconvenience.

One major disadvantage is that you simply will have more household chores. You will need to take the pet on walks or clean out a box, cage, or fish bowl. You will have to buy food regularly, sometimes even specialty food for particular pets or aging or sick animals. Finally, ongoing cleanup is needed for animals that shed fur, feathers, or skin.

There are other inconveniences as well for you and your family. You need specialized knowledge to care properly for the pet's health and safety. You will make more trips to the vet than you do to the doctor's office. This gets expensive. It can be time-consuming and expensive to go away for a weekend or a vacation, unless you have a cousin or a friend who owes you a favor.

Owning a pet may also create unexpected problems for family and friends. Some people are allergic to animals and might suffer an adverse reaction when they come to your home. Also, if a new baby arrives in the house, the animal may express its jealousy in unwelcome ways.

I do have to recognize the positive side of having a pet. Animals can be great companions and return your love unconditionally. They can provide security (or at least a sense of security). Also, that walking I belittled at the outset can actually be good exercise. Finally, I have to admit that with all of the work involved, caring for an animal is still less work than caring for a child.

On balance, I think the wisest course of action for a family is to forgo the joys of pet ownership. The time and money saved can be put to different uses, which hopefully will give you satisfaction and companionship as well.

1. **Thesis Statement** According to the prompt, you are to take a position in agreement or disagreement with the writer of "Family Pets." Decide what you think and write your thesis statement below.

   I. I think that the writer's position on owning a family pet is ______________________________

   because ______________________________________________________________

   ______________________________________________________________

On Test Day, you may write an outline or make an idea map. Practice both approaches on this page.

2. **Outline** Write an outline, using this as a model. **Keep your outline; you will use it in Lesson 6.**

Also address related reasoning issues, either by stating and contradicting the **counterargument** (main argument against your position) *or* by addressing the writer's **faulty reasoning** (if any).

I. Thesis statement
II. Main supporting reason related to the text
III. Another supporting reason related to the text
IV. Another supporting reason related to the text
V. Related arguments
   A. Counterargument
      i. Argument against my position
      ii. My rejection of the counterargument, with example
   B. Writer's faulty reasoning (if any)
      i. Why the writer's reasoning is faulty
      ii. Supporting example

3. **Idea Map** Make a map of your response to the passage. Use facts and evidence from the passage as well as your own ideas. Draw it on a sheet of paper. **Keep your map; you will use it in Lesson 6.**

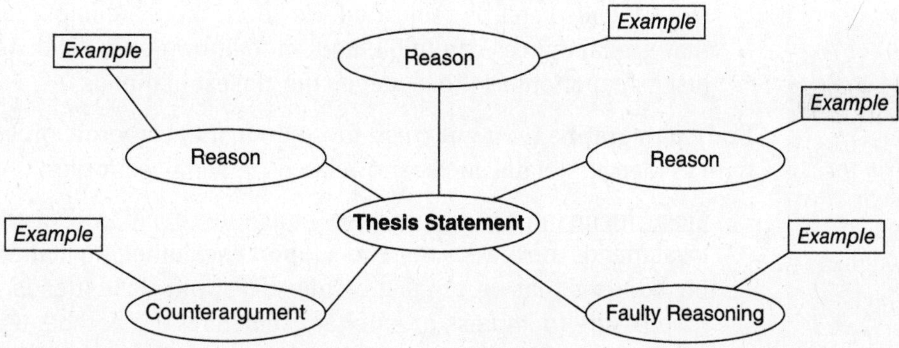


4. **Reflect** Which way worked better for you—outline or map? Practice both until you find the method that will work best for you on the test.

**Review your work using the sample responses on page 677.**

LESSON 6

# Draft Your Response

You have practiced the first part of the **Essay-Writing Strategy: Planning**. Once you have planned your writing, the next stage is to **draft** your response. You should take about 30 minutes to do the following:

- Use your thesis statement to **introduce** your argument or explanation and how you intend to support it.
- Use your plan to write the **body** of your response, **citing specific evidence and details from the text** to support your ideas.
- Provide **additional relevant information** based on your own knowledge and perspective.
- Consistently **check back** with your thesis statement to make sure that you are staying on track.
- Write a **closing** that summarizes your position or restates the thesis statement in another way.

Review the planning on page 169 for writing on the topic of close friends and acquaintances. See how that planning was used to draft the writing below. (Note that an underlined **topic sentence** introduces each paragraph.)

An **introduction** lays out your argument and how you will support it:

> People need both close friends and acquaintances because they meet our social needs in different ways. The special bond a person has with close friends can't be replicated. However, there are important needs that acquaintances can fulfill, and, in their own way, these needs are just as important as those met by the closest of friends.

**Body paragraphs** (you will need more than one) elaborate on your support with evidence, details, facts, and related personal examples.

> Close friendships certainly have numerous benefits. For one thing, loyal friends are always there to support each other, no matter what. A big bonus is that we can just be ourselves with close friends. There is no pressure to impress or entertain someone who accepts us for who we are. Some friendships last years, becoming deeper and more meaningful with time. For example, even though I am now 35, my best friend from high school and I are still in touch, sharing stories about our two-year-old boys.

A **closing paragraph** restates your main point to reinforce it.

> So while it is important to have close friends, it is really rewarding to have a wide circle of acquaintances as well. Even though the quality of the relationship may not be as deep, these people broaden our lives and networks to enrich our experiences and help us to grow.

### KEY IDEAS

- Use your thesis statement to begin your introductory paragraph and to keep you focused as you write.
- Write several body paragraphs based on the facts, details, and evidence in your outline or idea map.
- Wrap up the response with a concluding paragraph that reinforces your thesis.

### TASC TEST TIP

*One key to a good score on the TASC essay is to cite specific evidence from the reading passage(s). This is called an "evidence-based" writing activity because you are expected to base your response on evidence from the text.*

# PRACTICE 6.1

**Part A: Introduction**

**Directions: Practice writing an introduction based on the prompt and passage from page 171 and your planning from page 171. If you are taking the TASC on paper, complete this exercise on paper. If you are taking the computer version of the TASC, try to write your introduction on a computer if possible. Save the file as *Family Pets Introduction.***

**Family Pets Writing Prompt**

The writer of this passage explains the reasons a family should not own a pet. Read the selection and take a stand for or against the author's position. Use details and evidence from the passage in your essay.

Make sure that you:

- Include your thesis statement early.
- Give reasons and evidence from the passages to support your thesis statement.
- Argue against the opposite side.
- Organize your ideas, and show how the ideas relate to each other.
- Use a businesslike style.
- Conclude with a short summary of your argument.

- Begin with a topic sentence that summarizes your thesis statement from page 171.
- Support your topic sentence with either
    - a preview of the main points you will be covering based on your outline or idea map; or
    - an example, description, or personal story—tied to the thesis statement—that will interest the reader.

**Part B: Concluding Statement**

**Directions: Practice writing a concluding statement based on the prompt above and your planning from page 171. If you are taking the TASC on paper, complete this exercise on paper. If you are taking the computer version of the TASC, try to write your conclusion on a computer if possible. Save the file as *Family Pets Conclusion.***

- Restate your thesis statement from page 173 in different words. (Don't just repeat what your reader has already read.)
- Make a statement that answers the question "So what?" Give your reader a reason to care about your argument.
- Don't introduce new arguments but leave the reader with something to think about that wraps up the paper.

**Review your work using the sample responses on page 678.**

**STUDY ADVICE**

If you can, enlist a partner to help you with the essay portion of the TASC. This may be a friend or family member with good writing skills. Ask that person to read this chapter of your TASC book, so that he or she will understand what the TASC essay requires. Then ask that person to give you feedback about your practice essays.

# PRACTICE 6.2

**Directions: Plan and draft an essay in response to the prompt below and the passage on the facing page. If you will be taking the TASC on paper, practice writing your essay on paper. If you will be taking the TASC on a computer, try to practice writing your essay on a computer if possible.**

**Step 1—Plan:** Take 10 minutes to read the prompt and the passage. Under the prompt, make an outline *or* draw an idea map to organize the following:

- your thesis statement
- your main points and supporting evidence from the passage
- counterarguments and your response *or* faulty reasoning in the passage

**Step 2—Draft:** Take 30 minutes to draft your response, which will include the following:

- an introductory statement with your thesis statement as the topic sentence
- body paragraphs, with your reasons accompanied by supporting evidence from the text
  - use phrases such as "As the writer says . . . ," "The information in the passage states . . . ," "This is supported in the passage by . . ."
- a concluding statement wrapping up the piece

**Save your response, since you will be revising and editing it in Lesson 7.**

**Cell Phone Writing Prompt**

The writer of the passage on the next page discusses the "risks and unknowns" of cell phone use. Read the passage and write an essay in which you explain the known risks of cell phone use, as well as the gaps in our current scientific knowledge about these devices. Use details, facts, and definitions from the passage in your essay.

Make sure that you:

- Include your topic clearly.
- Give details, facts, and definitions from the passage to develop your explanation.
- Organize your ideas, and show how the ideas relate to each other.
- Use a businesslike style.
- Conclude with a short summary of your explanation.

**Cell Phones: Risky or Safe?**

The Federal Communications Commission has determined that there is not enough evidence to link cell phones to cancer. But a lack of evidence does not mean that such a risk does not exist. Moreover, cell phones carry other safety hazards. You should be aware of the risks and unknowns associated with mobile phones and take steps to protect yourself.

Cell phones emit types of radiation that can penetrate several inches into the brain. These types of radiation are not normally associated with cancer, and most scientific studies show that frequent cell phone users do not have an increased risk of tumors. But a few scientists claim to have found a connection between mobile phones and a type of brain cancer known as glioma. Even a small chance of brain cancer should make you very nervous.

Also, we may eventually discover that the cancer risk is greater than it currently appears. Mobile phones were very rare before the late 1990s. If the risk of phone-related disease increases sharply after 20 or 30 years of constant use, we might only find out after millions of people get sick. It's true that there is no increased illness observed among people who have worked at radio towers for 30 years or more, but cell phones are held much closer to the body than radio equipment is.

Finally, in addition to the possible cancer risk, cell phones come with a much more obvious safety issue. While being able to contact emergency services from anywhere is a major advantage of modern technology, being distracted by that technology can cause accidents. Calling or texting while driving or operating machinery is dangerous.

Be cautious with your cell phone. You may find that you need it to function in today's modern society, but your health and well-being are too important to risk through careless use of this technology. Do not assume that your phone is completely free of danger.

**Review your work using the** ***Essay Evaluation Guide for Informative/Explanatory Essays*** **on page 760.**

# PRACTICE 6.3

**Directions: Plan and draft an essay in response to the prompt and the paired passages on the facing page. If you will be taking the TASC on paper, practice writing your essay on paper. If you will be taking the TASC on a computer, try to practice writing your essay on a computer if possible.**

**Step 1—Plan:** Take 10 minutes to read the prompt below and the passages. Take notes as you read, or underline evidence that you will want to use. Make an outline *or* an idea map to organize:

- your thesis statement
- your main points and supporting evidence from the passages
- counterarguments and your response *or* faulty reasoning in either of the passages

**Step 2—Draft:** Take 30 minutes to draft your response with:

- an introductory statement with your thesis statement as the topic sentence
- body paragraphs, with your reasons accompanied by supporting evidence from the text
- a concluding statement wrapping up the piece

**Save your response, since you will be revising and editing it later.**

**Gettysburg Address Writing Prompt**

Abraham Lincoln's Gettysburg Address is renowned as one of the most significant speeches of all time. Delivered in the midst of a brutal civil war, this address places that war in the context of U.S. history—past, present, and future. However, it was not universally acclaimed at the time, as shown by the excerpt from the *Chicago Times* newspaper.

Read both of the passages closely. Take a stand on which passage does a better job of explaining the significance of the Battle of Gettysburg's casualties. There were a total of more than 45,000 casualties on both sides, Union and Confederacy.

Make sure that you:

- Include your thesis statement early.
- Give reasons and evidence from the passages to support your thesis statement.
- Argue against the opposite side.
- Organize your ideas, and show how the ideas relate to each other.
- Use a businesslike style.
- Conclude with a short summary of your argument.

**STUDY ADVICE**

Some people don't enjoy writing essays. However, it's important to practice before Test Day. Discipline yourself to write each essay when it's assigned in this book. The only way to get better at writing is to *write*.

## Abraham Lincoln's Gettysburg Address

Fourscore and seven years ago our fathers brought forth on this continent a new nation, conceived in liberty and dedicated to the proposition that all men are created equal. Now we are engaged in a great civil war, testing whether that nation or any nation so conceived and so dedicated can long endure. But in a larger sense, we cannot dedicate, we cannot consecrate, we cannot hallow this ground. The brave men, living and dead who struggled here have consecrated it far above our poor power to add or detract. The world will little note nor long remember what we say here, but it can never forget what they did here. It is for us the living rather to be dedicated here to the unfinished work which they who fought here have thus far so nobly advanced. It is rather for us to be here dedicated to the great task remaining before us—that from these honored dead we take increased devotion to that cause for which they gave the last full measure of devotion—that we here highly resolve that these dead shall not have died in vain, that this nation under God shall have a new birth of freedom, and that government of the people, by the people, for the people shall not perish from the earth.

**—Abraham Lincoln, November 19, 1863**

## Critical Review of the Gettysburg Address

. . . The President's exhibition . . . was an insult at least to the memories of a part of the dead, whom he was there professedly to honor—in its misstatement of the cause for which they died, it was a perversion of history so flagrant that the most extended charity cannot regard it as otherwise than willful. As a refutation. . . . we copy certain clauses in the Federal constitution:

"Representatives and direct taxes shall be apportioned among the several States which may be included in this Union, according to their respective numbers, which shall be determined by adding to the whole number of free persons, including those bound to service for a term of years, and excluding Indians not taxed, three-fifths of all other persons.

"The migration or importation of such persons as any of the States now existing shall think proper to admit shall not be prohibited by the Congress prior to the year 1808, but a tax or duty may be imposed on such importation, not exceeding ten dollars for each person. . . . No amendment to the constitution, made prior to 1808, shall affect the preceding clause.

"No person held to service or labor in one State under the laws thereof, escaping into another, shall, in consequence of any law or regulation therein, be discharged from such service or labor, but shall be delivered up on claim of the party to whom such service or labor may be due."

Do these provisions in the constitution dedicate the nation to "the proposition that all men are created equal"? Mr. Lincoln occupies his present position by virtue of this constitution, and is sworn to the maintenance and enforcement of these provisions. It was to uphold this constitution, and the Union created by it, that our officers and soldiers gave their lives at Gettysburg. How dared he, then, standing on their graves, misstate the cause for which they died, and libel the statesmen who founded the government?

**Excerpted from the *Chicago Times*, November 23, 1863**

**Review your work using the *Essay Evaluation Guide for Argument/Opinion Essays* on page 759.**

Writing the Essay

# LESSON 7

## Revise and Edit Your Response

### KEY IDEAS

- Take about ten minutes to revise and edit your response.
- Reread the response to improve the clarity of your arguments; sufficiency of evidence from the text; and organization of sentences, paragraphs, and the entire piece.
- If you are taking the computer version of the TASC, you can use the delete, copy, and paste functions to make revisions. Otherwise, use your pencil and neatly erase or strike out text you are changing.

### TASC TEST TIP

*Reviewing your essay allows you to double-check that you stayed on track the entire time.*

### Revising Your Work

Once you have completed your draft, you need to **revise**. You should take about five minutes to read over your response and make improvements. If you are taking the paper version of the TASC, use your pencil to erase or strike out portions you would like to change. If you are taking the computer version of the TASC, use the copy, delete, and paste functions on the computer. As you edit your essay, ask yourself:

- Does the introductory paragraph contain the **thesis statement** and lay out the main point of my response?
- Does each paragraph have **one main idea**, begin with a **topic sentence**, and support the thesis statement?
- Is there **specific and relevant supporting evidence from the text** for each main idea?
- Have I assessed the **validity** of the arguments in the passages?
- Is there a **clear flow of ideas** from one paragraph to the next, using transitional words, phrases, and ideas?
- Are there any **irrelevant ideas or sentences** that can be removed?
- Are there any **short, choppy sentences** that could be combined?
- Can I improve my **word choice** to be more specific or interesting?
- Is there a concluding paragraph that **restates and reinforces** the thesis?

Read the writing sample below and review the revisions that were made by hand to improve the draft. Think about why each change was made.

A job is much more pleasant when you like and admire your supervisor. A good supervisor must have excellent communication skills and must make it a priority to help workers get ahead.

*Communication is a key part of management.* ^ Supervisors need to give clear directions to spare the workers many hours of frustration. In addition, supervisors should be confident ^*and decisive.* ~~They should also be decisive.~~ Finally, supervisors should be as honest as possible. Once they make a decision, they should stick to it, so ^*that* everyone knows what the policy is. ^

Good bosses want to see their workers progress. Therefore, supervisors should give lots of encouragement and reward workers who display initiative and problem-solving abilities. ^*Also,* Supervisors should offer opportunities for workers to improve their skills ^*and education*.

# PRACTICE 7.1

**A. Directions: Read the response below, and revise the problems in sentence structure and organization. Try to complete your revisions in five minutes, but use more time if needed.**

Most of us are aware of the consequences of speeding, which range from receiving a speeding ticket to getting into an accident. A quick survey of any highway will show that many drivers exceed the speed limit. Why do people speed? One common reason is that people do not think they will suffer any consequences. If they have never been stopped by the police or crashed their car, they don't see any reason to worry.

People simply need to get somewhere in a hurry. They realize that they are speeding but they have such a need to arrive on time that they don't care. They've got ants in their pants. A final reason is lack of respect for other drivers, one driver who is speeding makes road conditions less safe for everyone. Drivers who act as though they are in the Indy 500 they have no regard for the safety of others.

We know that people speed because of impatience and they don't fear the consequences. Another reason is no respect. Let's figure out what will make them stop.

**B. Directions: Revise the response that you wrote on the topic below on page 175. Time yourself. Try to complete the revision in ten minutes. Save your work. You will use the response again.**

**Cell Phone Writing Prompt**

The writer of the passage on the next page makes an argument about the safety of cell phones. Read the passage and write an essay in which you explain what additional information would be necessary before we determine whether or not cell phones are safe. Use details, facts, and definitions from the passage in your essay.

Make sure that you:

- Include your topic clearly.
- Give details, facts, and definitions from the passage to develop your explanation.
- Organize your ideas, and show how the ideas relate to each other.
- Use a businesslike style.
- Conclude with a short summary of your explanation.

**C. Directions: After you check your answers to the exercises above, complete the strategy box below. If you need more practice with specific skills and concepts, study "Connecting Ideas" on pages 148–159 and "Polishing Your Writing" on pages 186–195.**

**MY TEST-TAKING STRATEGY**

I need to pay special attention to these areas of revising. (Check all that apply.)

- ❑ Writing introductory paragraphs
- ❑ Writing concluding paragraphs
- ❑ Writing topic sentences
- ❑ Adding support to body paragraphs
- ❑ Putting sentences in logical places
- ❑ Putting in paragraph breaks
- ❑ Remembering to use transitions
- ❑ Deleting irrelevant details
- ❑ Combining short, choppy sentences
- ❑ Making sure each sentence makes sense

**Review your work using the explanations that start on page 678.**

## Editing Your Work

Once you're satisfied with the organization and clarity of your essay, check for other errors in sentence structure, as well as errors in grammar, usage, and mechanics. To edit your response, take another five minutes to reread your response, and ask yourself these questions:

- Are all the sentences complete?
- Are there any run-ons or comma splices that should be corrected?
- Are all lists parallel in structure?
- Are nouns and pronouns used correctly?
- Are verb forms and tenses used correctly?
- Does the subject of each sentence match the verb?
- Is the punctuation correct?
- Is capitalization used correctly?
- Are all words correctly spelled?
- Are there any inappropriate word choices?

### KEY IDEAS

- Edit your work to make sure there are no errors in sentence structure, grammar, usage, or mechanics.
- An editing checklist can help you find errors as you practice for the Writing Test.

▶ Read the paragraph below, and notice how the errors were corrected.

A job is much more pleasant when you like and admire your supervisor. A good supervisor must have excellent communication skills, and must make it a priority to help workers get ahead. In addition, a supervisor should be a fair and moral person.

Clear communication is a key part of Management. Supervisors need to give clear directions. To spare the workers many hours of frustration. In addition, supervisors should be confident and decisive. Once they made a decision, they should stick to it so everyone knows what the policy is. Finally, supervisors should be as honest as possible.

Good bosses want to see their workers progress. Therefore, supervisors should ~~give lots of~~ encourage~~ment~~ and reward workers who display initiative, and problem-solving abilities. Also, supervisors should offer opportunities for workers to improve their skills, and education.

Top-notch supervisors ~~has~~ have a high level of moral character. They reward honesty and fire workers who have lied or cheated. Some bosses keep employees who lie if ~~his~~ their skills are valuable to the Company, but I feel that this is an example of poor management.

Knowing the qualities of a good supervisor is important for both bosses and workers. The next time you apply for a job, think about whether ~~you're~~ your prospective boss is a moral person and a clear communicator who wants you to succeed.

### ON THE TASC TEST

*Whether you take the paper or computer version of the TASC, there will be no "spell check" or "grammar check" tools available to you. Practice spotting spelling and grammar mistakes on your own. If you are practicing the TASC essay on a computer, turn off the "spell check" and "grammar check" features while you practice and turn them back on as you review your work.*

# PRACTICE 7.2

A. **Directions: Read the body of the writing sample. Correct errors in sentence structure, grammar, usage, mechanics, and word choice. Try to finish editing in five minutes, but use more time if needed.**

One common reason for speeding is that people don't think they will suffer any consequences. If they have never been stopped by the Police or crashed there car they don't see any reason too worry.

Another reason is that people simply are needing to get somewhere in a hurry. They realize that they are speeding, but they have such a need to arrive on time that they dont care. There impatience get the better of them.

A final reason is lack of respect for other drivers, one driver who is speeding make road conditions less safe for everyone. Drivers who act as though they are in the indy 500 got no regard for the safety of others.

B. **Directions: Edit the response that you wrote on the topic below, which you saw on page 175. Time yourself and try to complete the edit in five minutes.**

**Cell Phone Writing Prompt**

The writer of the passage on the next page makes an argument about the safety of cell phones. Read the passage and write an essay in which you explain what additional information would be necessary before we determine whether or not cell phones are safe. Use details, facts, and definitions from the passage in your essay.

C. **Directions: After you check your answers to the exercises above, complete the strategy box below. If you need more practice with specific skills and concepts, review the sections in the book that correspond to these skills.**

**MY TEST-TAKING STRATEGY**

I need to pay special attention to these areas of editing. (Check all that apply.)

| | |
|---|---|
| ❑ Making sure my sentences are complete | ❑ Matching subjects and verbs |
| ❑ Correcting run-ons and comma splices | ❑ Making sure punctuation is correct |
| ❑ Using parallel structure | ❑ Using capitalization correctly |
| ❑ Using nouns and pronouns correctly | ❑ Making sure words are spelled correctly |
| ❑ Using verb forms and tenses correctly | ❑ Choosing appropriate words |

**Review your work using the explanations that start on page 678.**

**STUDY ADVICE**

Often when you are writing, ideas might come into your head in an illogical order. That's okay. For one thing, taking the time to plan will help with that. But also be sure to practice rereading your writing and moving sentences around as necessary.

# WRITING THE ESSAY PRACTICE QUESTIONS

**Part A**

**Directions: Plan and draft an essay in response to the prompt below and the passage on the facing page.** If you will be taking the TASC on paper, practice writing your essay on paper. If you will be taking the TASC on a computer, try to practice writing your essay on a computer if possible.

**Step 1—Plan:** Take 10 minutes to read the prompt and the passage. Under the prompt, make an outline *or* draw an idea map to organize:

- your thesis statement
- your main points and supporting evidence from the passage
- counterarguments and your response *or* faulty reasoning in the passage

**Step 2—Draft:** Take 50 minutes to draft your response, which will include the following:

- an introduction, with your thesis statement as the topic sentence
- body paragraphs, with your reasons accompanied by supporting evidence from the text
    - use phrases such as "As the writer says . . . ," "The information in the passage states . . . ," "This is supported in the passage by . . ."
- a concluding statement wrapping up the piece

**Step 3—Revise and Edit:** Take 10 minutes to reread your response to:

- revise to improve organization, cohesion, and clarity of sentences, paragraphs, and the entire piece
- edit to correct errors in sentence structure, grammar, punctuation, capitalization, and spelling

**Social Networking on the Internet—Positive or Negative?**

The passage addresses the serious impact that the explosion of social networking has had on our lives. In recent years, social relations have developed online that allow us to connect with friends or create communities around common interests. Supporters feel that these networks create greater interaction and increased information. Critics say that this trend actually limits social interactions and creates short- and long-term risks for the users.

In your response, compare the arguments in the reading selection and take a position favoring either the benefits or the drawbacks of social networking. Use relevant and specific information to support your response.

Make sure that you:

- Include your thesis statement early.
- Give reasons and evidence from the passages to support your thesis statement.
- Argue against the opposite side.
- Organize your ideas, and show how the ideas relate to each other.
- Use a businesslike style.
- Conclude with a short summary of your argument.

**"Social Networking on the Internet—Positive or Negative?"**

In a hundred years, humanity will look back and try to pinpoint the moment in its history when it overcame the clumsy limits of flesh-and-blood existence. When it does, Internet social networking will stand out as an important change, not just in the ways in which we communicate with each other but also, and perhaps more importantly, in the ways in which we perceive ourselves.

At this primitive moment, our contacts on social networks are still people we have met in person, for the most part. And there was a time when this was natural: you have to choose your friends from the selection available to you. But the menu has changed. The great promise of Internet socialization is that congregation is no longer at the mercy of geography. If I join an online community of checkers enthusiasts whose members are scattered across four continents, our interactions will be little different than if we all lived in the United States. Our shared interest, rather than where our bodies happen to live, is what brings us together.

As our online friendships increasingly supplant our in-person friendships, our online personalities begin to replace our old selves, too. What happens when two-thirds of my acquaintances know me by an invented username rather than by my real name, or by an animated icon of a dancing stick-figure rather than by my face? The answer: I learn that I can essentially define myself for this group of people. I can be exactly who I want to be.

With time, we will all come to shift to interest-based interactions almost exclusively. If you've always felt alone because you've never been able to find anyone who shares your greatest passion—and that passion happens to be watching macramé competitions—then the Internet opens up a new world of like-minded individuals to you. You'll share experiences, pictures, and tips and live as you never could have 30 years ago, when you would have been forced to endure your isolation.

At the same time, we must ask ourselves: Is this something we want to encourage? One of the great protective mechanisms of the flesh-and-blood version of human communities is shame. As unfair as it may sound to ridicule our poor macramé enthusiast, social disapproval is an important tool for discouraging destructive behavior and extremism. When online communities offer a meeting place for outcasts, the shunning of these tendencies loses its force. It is no coincidence that online communities are the single most fertile recruiting ground for terrorism. And isn't accepting differences in others—rather than surrounding ourselves with homogeneous communities of like-minded friends—an important part of the human experience?

For children of the 20th century, there is something else very alarming in the idea of channeling so many of our interactions through the Internet. In the heyday of the Soviet Union, a video camera in every home was presented as the greatest tool a totalitarian state could wish for. If all my interactions pass through the Internet, won't the government be watching me? Regardless of whether it will or won't, it certainly seems now to have that option.

We also must wonder what will become of our most cherished traits as we transition to an existence of ones and zeroes. As biological beings, we have emotional needs tied to touch and warmth. None of my online friends can give me a hug!

Ultimately, the new possibilities that the online world opens up to us are irresistible and herald a new era of finely tuned communities with unprecedented potential. The challenge will lie in making the most of this new world without losing the vital elements of our nonelectronic human experience.

**Review your work using the *Essay Evaluation Guide for Argument/Opinion Essays* on page 759.**

**Part B**

**Directions: Develop an essay in response to the prompt below and the paired passages on the facing page. If you will be taking the TASC on paper, practice writing your essay on paper. If you will be taking the TASC on a computer, try to practice writing your essay on a computer if possible.**

**Step 1—Plan:** Take 10 minutes to read the prompt and the passages. Under the prompt, make an outline *or* draw an idea map to organize:

- Your thesis statement
- Your main points and supporting evidence from the passage
- Counterarguments and your response *or* faulty reasoning in the passage

**Step 2—Draft:** Take 30 minutes to draft your response, which will include the following:

- An introductory statement, with your thesis statement as the topic sentence
- Body paragraphs, with your reasons accompanied by supporting evidence from the text
  - Use phrases such as "As the writer says . . . ," "The information in the passage states . . . ," "This is supported in the passage by . . ."
- A concluding statement wrapping up the piece

**Step 3—Revise and Edit:** Take 10 minutes to reread your response and do the following:

- Revise to improve organization, cohesion, and clarity of sentences, paragraphs, and the entire piece.
- Edit to correct errors in sentence structure, grammar, punctuation, capitalization, and spelling.

**Health and Safety on the Job**

The first passage presents regulations of the U.S. Occupational Safety and Health Administration (OSHA). The second passage is a newspaper article about workers who successfully sued their employer, claiming that they were fired because they had reported injuries on the job.

Read both the OSHA regulations and the news report carefully. Take a position on whether or not you think that the court decision was correct based on the OSHA guidelines.

Use relevant and specific information from both passages to support your response.

Make sure that you:

- Include your thesis statement early.
- Give reasons and evidence from the passages to support your thesis statement.
- Argue against the opposite side.
- Organize your ideas, and show how the ideas relate to each other.
- Use a businesslike style.
- Conclude with a short summary of your argument.

**STUDY ADVICE**

If you aren't taking the TASC Writing Test for a while, be sure not to let your writing skills rust. Every couple of weeks, write an essay (you can rewrite one of the essays from this chapter if you like). Continue to practice using the method outlined in this chapter so that it will be second nature on Test Day.

## OSHA Standards and Worker Protection

OSHA standards are rules that describe the methods that employers must use to protect their employees from hazards. There are OSHA standards for Construction work, Agriculture, Maritime operations, and General Industry, which are the standards that apply to most worksites. These standards limit the amount of hazardous chemicals workers can be exposed to, require the use of certain safe practices and equipment, and require employers to monitor hazards and keep records of workplace injuries and illnesses. Examples of OSHA standards include requirements to: provide fall protection, prevent trenching cave ins, prevent some infectious diseases, assure that workers safely enter confined spaces, prevent exposure to harmful substances like asbestos, put guards on machines, provide respirators or other safety equipment, and provide training for certain dangerous jobs.

## You Cannot Be Punished or Discriminated Against for Using Your OSHA Rights

The OSHA Act protects workers who complain to their employer, OSHA or other government agencies about unsafe or unhealthful working conditions in the workplace or environmental problems. You cannot be transferred, denied a raise, have your hours reduced, be fired, or punished in any other way because you used any right given to you under the OSHA Act. Help is available from OSHA for whistleblowers.

If you have been punished or discriminated against for using your rights, you must file a complaint with OSHA within 30 days of the alleged reprisal for most complaints.

Source: U.S. Occupational Safety and Health Administration

## OSHA fines Norfolk Southern $802K for firing workers

The U.S. Occupational Safety and Health Administration announced Monday that it was fining a Norfolk Southern Corp. subsidiary more than $800,000 for firing three workers who had reported injuries on the job.

OSHA, a division of the U.S. Department of Labor, ordered Norfolk Southern Railway Co. to pay the former workers a total of $802,169 in damages. The agency also said the railroad company must clear the workers' disciplinary records and post workplace notices and offer training on whistleblower rights.

"OSHA's investigations have found that the company continues to retaliate against employees for reporting work-related injuries and has effectively created a chilling effect in the railroad industry," the Labor Department said in a news release.

Norfolk Southern spokesman Robin Chapman said the company would appeal the decisions on all three workers before an administrative law judge at the Labor Department.

Two of the three incidents occurred in 2010, according to the agency's release. An engineer in Louisville, Ky., and a conductor in Harrisburg, Pa., were fired after reporting injuries from falls in or near company bathrooms.

Norfolk Southern accused the employees of falsifying their injuries, the agency said. The company also accused the conductor of failing to promptly report the injury. "The day before the injury, the employee had been lauded for excellent performance, highlighted by no lost work time due to injuries in his 35-year career," according to the Labor Department release.

OSHA found that the company hearings for both workers were "flawed." In the case of the engineer, the hearing "was orchestrated to intentionally support the decision to terminate the employee," the release said.

In the third incident, an employee in Greenville, S.C., was fired after he reported being hit by a company truck. Norfolk Southern accused him of "improper performance of duties." The agency found he was treated "disparately in comparison to four other employees involved in the incident," none of whom had reported injuries.

"Firing workers for reporting an injury is not only illegal, it also endangers all workers," David Michaels, an assistant U.S. secretary of labor, said in a statement. "To prevent more injuries, railroad workers must be able to report an injury without fear of retaliation."



**Review your work using the *Essay Evaluation Guide for Argument/Opinion Essays* on page 759.**

Polishing Your Writing

LESSON 1

# Strengthen Sentences

## Revising Unclear and Incorrect Sentences

When you write your response, your first step is to get your ideas down. To do this, you follow a prewriting and drafting plan like the ones in the previous chapter. When you are finished drafting, go back and reread what you have written. As you read each sentence, ask yourself:

- Do the ideas in the sentence make sense? If not, how can I make the sentence clearer? Add some words? Drop or move a confusing word or phrase? Insert or delete punctuation? Change the words?
- Is the sentence structure correct? If not, how can I correct it?

Read the paragraph below and think about how you would revise the errors in clarity and sentence structure. Then compare it with the revised paragraph.

**Paragraph with unclear and incorrect sentences:**

Working outdoors has many advantages over working indoors. When you are outside you are in contact with nature. You can enjoy the sunshine on your face, hear the birds, and to smell the flowers. You don't have to consult the weather forecast on TV. In contrast, sitting in a climate-controlled cubicle, it is not known whether the sky is sunny or cloudy. Also, most outdoor jobs require you to use your body, that can be a huge advantage. Finally, if you work indoors, you might be sitting down at a desk, and typing all day long. After work, instead of relaxing. You'll probably have to go to the gym to work out.

**Paragraph with revised sentence structure:**

Working outdoors has many advantages over working indoors. When you are outside, you are in contact with nature. You can enjoy the sunshine on your face, hear the birds, and smell the flowers. You don't have to consult the weather forecast on TV. In contrast, when you sit in a climate-controlled cubicle, you don't know whether the sky is sunny or cloudy. Also, most outdoor jobs require you to use your body, and that can be a huge advantage. Finally, if you work indoors, you might be sitting down at a desk and typing all day long. After work, instead of relaxing, you'll probably have to go to the gym to work out.

Use these **revision marks** when you revise your sentences on paper:

- To delete a word or punctuation mark, cross it out.
- To add a word or punctuation mark, insert a caret ( ^ ) in the line where you want it to go, and then write it in above the line.
- To change a word, cross it out and write the new word above it.
- To move a word or phrase, circle it and draw an arrow to its new position.
- To capitalize a letter, draw three lines under it.

**KEY IDEAS**

- Read your work as a whole to make sure that it is clear and logical.
- Imagine that you are reading your work for the first time.
- Correct any sentences that have errors in structure or punctuation.

**TASC TEST TIP**

*To prepare for the essay, practice prewriting, drafting, and revising often. Frequent practice will help you feel more comfortable and confident as a writer.*

# PRACTICE 1

**A. Directions: Read and revise the sentences. Correct these problems by using revision marks.**

☑ fragments, run-ons, and comma splices
☑ incorrect coordination and subordination
☑ misplaced or dangling modifiers
☑ problems in parallel structure

**EXAMPLE:** It's fun to do a family tree⊙ you can learn a lot.

1. First, write down what you know about your family then interview relatives.
2. Videotaping or to record the interviews is a good idea.
3. Ask relatives to provide exact names, dates, and give other details.
4. Making copies of documents such as birth certificates and marriage licenses.
5. Interviewing older family members, they'll often tell you stories you never heard.
6. Record all the information you get and put it in a three-ring binder carefully.
7. Some people use their computers to do genealogy searches, they get very good results.
8. However, one must have the time, the patience, and know-how to use the Internet.
9. If you decide to learn more about your roots don't be surprised to find yourself at a huge family reunion.
10. The whole process of putting together a family tree and contacting long-lost family members.

**B. Directions: Read the paragraphs below. Use revision marks to correct problems with sentences.**

It was a beautiful day, the blue ocean sparkled in the sunlight. A perfect day for going to the beach. Looking across the sand, two little girls were building a sandcastle and made a moat next to it. Renelle spread out her towel she anchored it with her shoes and beach bag and began to read a magazine. Suddenly she heard a voice. "Are you going to get in the water, or are you just going to lie there?" Renelle looked up, and saw her friend Terry. She laughed softly and she got up and she greeted Terry. Putting on her sandals, the two of them walked across the burning sand to the water's edge.

Renelle loved going to the beach. Going to the beach relaxed her. Going to the beach helped her forget about her problems. It didn't cost money like most other forms of entertainment. Most of Renelle's friends also spent a lot of time at the beach so that was another incentive.

**Review your work using the explanations that start on page 678.**

LESSON 2

# Improve Organization

**KEY IDEAS**

- Revise your response so that the organization is clear to the reader.
- Make sure that paragraph breaks fall in the right places.
- Check for faulty transitions and irrelevant details.

**TASC TEST TIP**

*When you practice writing essays on paper, leave wide margins and space between the lines so that you can more easily revise your work. If you are taking the TASC on a computer, try to practice writing your essays on a computer.*

## Revising Problems in Organization

When you reread your response, you may also need to make changes in organization to make the response clearer to the reader. As you read, ask yourself:

- Is my main idea clear?
- Are there a clear introduction, body of support, and conclusion?
- Is the paragraphing correct? Does each paragraph relate to only one main idea? Should any paragraphs be split into two? Should any be combined?
- Does each paragraph have a topic sentence that tells the main idea? Are any of the other sentences in a place that doesn't make sense? Are there any irrelevant details that should be removed?
- Does the writing flow smoothly from sentence to sentence and from paragraph to paragraph? If not, where can I add transitions?

Read the sample paragraph below. Think about how you would correct the errors in organization. Then compare it with the revised paragraph.

**Paragraph with problems in organization:**

(1) Many people believe that changes in technology have improved our communication with others. (2) I believe that the opposite is true. (3) So-called technological improvements have led to a marked decline in the quality of interpersonal communication. (4) In the old days, when you called someone, the person was likely to pick up the phone to find out who was calling. (5) Nowadays, caller ID makes that unnecessary. (6) The person you call can simply decide not to pick up once she sees that you are the caller. (7) This encourages long games of "phone tag." (8) Television is another example—you can barely get a word out of someone who is glued to the tube.

**Paragraphs with revised organization:**

(1) Many people believe that changes in technology have improved our communication with others. (2) <u>However</u>, I believe that the opposite is true. (3) So-called technological improvements have led to a marked decline in the quality of interpersonal communication.

<u>(*) Phone use is one area in which communication has suffered.</u> (4) In the old days, when you called someone, the person was likely to pick up the phone to find out who was calling. (5) Nowadays, screening devices make that unnecessary. (6) The person you call can simply decide not to pick up once she sees that you are the caller. (7) This encourages long games of "phone tag."

# PRACTICE 2

In the revised paragraphs, the transition *however* was added to sentence 2. The piece was divided into two paragraphs—an introductory paragraph and a body paragraph about phone use. A topic sentence (marked with *) was added. Sentence 8 of the original, which was not related to telephones, was deleted.

Use these symbols to revise essay organization:

- To change whole sentences, use the same marks you used to change words.
- To start a new paragraph, use the paragraph symbol (¶).

---

**A. Directions: Using the revision marks, revise the paragraphs below. One revision has been made for you.**

We've all heard countless advertising campaigns warning us not to litter. Yet some people still think nothing of throwing a soda can out of their car window onto the highway or dropping a candy wrapper on the sidewalk. Most of us realize that we are upsetting a delicate ecological balance when we don't dispose of our trash properly. ¶ Why do people continue to litter? One reason people litter is that they just don't care about others. It doesn't bother them to leave their trash in front of someone else's apartment building, forcing another person to deal with the problem.

This inconsiderate attitude is also reflected in the refusal to recycle plastic, glass, and newspapers. People figure that they won't be around in the future when the landfills are used up, so who cares? Another possible reason for littering is low self-esteem. If people don't feel good about themselves, they won't be motivated to keep their environment looking attractive. Low self-esteem can cause many other problems, including depression and lack of self-confidence. People who have high self-esteem believe that it's important to keep their home, the planet Earth, clean and beautiful.

**B. Directions: Revise the response that you wrote to the Gettysburg Address writing prompt on page 176.**

Be sure to check for:

- ☑ clear main idea
- ☑ introduction, body, and conclusion
- ☑ correct paragraphing
- ☑ topic sentences
- ☑ logical placement of sentences
- ☑ irrelevant details that should be removed
- ☑ clear transitions

Save your work. You will use it in the next step of the writing process, editing.

**Review your work using the explanations that start on page 678.**

LESSON 3

# Word Choice

After you have written and revised your response, you will need to edit it. In the editing stage of the writing process, you check for correct grammar, usage, and word choice. You may already have made some organizational changes. The kinds of changes you make when you are editing will be smaller—more like fine-tuning.

**Word choice** is an important aspect of writing. There are several aspects of word choice to look at when you are editing: using precise words, avoiding wordiness, and avoiding slang.

People often use vague terms when they are speaking. They say things like, "It was a great party!" or "The weather is nice today." General words like *great* and *nice* are okay in conversation because the listener can ask questions such as, "What was so great about the party?" In writing, however, you should try to write specific words that create a clear picture for the reader.

**With vague words:** Tim took a long hike in the beautiful mountains.
**With precise words:** Tim took a 12-mile hike in the rocky, snowy mountains.

**With vague words:** He walked through a forest where the ground was covered with pine needles.
**With precise words:** He meandered through a forest where the ground was carpeted with pine needles.

It's also helpful to your reader if you write concisely and avoid wordiness. Being brief helps the reader focus on your message. If you notice that you have said the same thing twice, cut out the extra words.

**Too wordy:** Tim's dream and the thing he hopes for most of all is to make a home for himself and live in a cabin in the woods.
**More concise:** Tim's most cherished dream is to live in a cabin in the woods.

**Too wordy:** The only thing getting in the way of his having this dream come true is that his wife isn't so sure that it's such a fantastic idea.
**More concise:** The only obstacle to realizing his dream is his wife's resistance.

Finally, avoid using slang when writing your essay. Though people sometimes use informal language when speaking, essay writing calls for more formal language. Take care to express yourself appropriately.

**With slang:** Tim is going to hit the road at seven tonight.
**With more formal language:** Tim is going to leave town at seven tonight.

**With slang:** He needs a better map because he's totally clueless about directions.
**With more formal language:** He needs a better map because he has difficulty understanding directions.

**KEY IDEAS**

- Use precise words instead of vague ones.
- Express your ideas in as few words as possible.
- When writing a response, use formal language instead of slang.

**TASC TEST TIP**

*When you read your draft, focus on the specific words and ask yourself, "Can I make this clearer or more concise?" If so, revise accordingly to improve your score on the response.*

# PRACTICE 3

**A. Directions: Replace each of the underlined words or phrases with more appropriate language. Write your answers on a separate sheet of paper.**

1. Families International is a nonprofit organization that does not make any money.
2. We give aid to many children in the Third World every year.
3. These children must endure lousy living conditions.
4. Your donation, even if it is only five bucks, will help a child get food and clothing.
5. Please send your donation as soon and as quickly as possible to the following address.

**B. Directions: Edit the paragraphs below for correct grammar and usage, paying special attention to nouns and pronouns, subject-verb agreement, and regular and irregular verbs.**

If you ever order merchandise from a catalog, you should be aware of your rights. All companies, regardless of what state they are located in, is required to ship your order within 30 days unless they have advertise a different shipping time. If a company is unable to meet the shipping deadline, they must send you an "Option Notice." You can choose to wait longer or get a refund.

Some consumers complaining about receiving merchandise that they did not order. They were told that companies that engaged in this practice broken the law. If they send you a product you haven't order, it is yours to keep.

If you receive a package that been damaged, don't open it. Write "REFUSED" on the package, and return it to the seller. There's no need to add new postage as long as the package come by regular mail.

**C. Directions: Revise the response you wrote to the Gettysburg Address writing prompt on page 176.**

Be sure to check for:

☑ Correct use of nouns and pronouns
☑ Correct use of regular and irregular verbs
☑ Subject-verb agreement
☑ Word choice

**Review your work using the explanations that start on page 679.**

### STUDY ADVICE

How's your stress level about the TASC at this point? Remember to manage your stress just as you manage other aspects of the test. Stay on a regular sleep schedule, exercise, and eat right. Whenever you're feeling stressed, step away. Remember: You *can* do this. Just don't let stress get in your way.

# Polishing Your Writing Practice Questions

**Questions 1 through 5 refer to the following paragraphs.**

**Gardening for success**

**(A)**

(1) Flowers, herbs, and shrubs can beautify both small and large spaces in your home or yard. (2) If you want to be a successful gardener. (3) It's important that you follow some simple guidelines.

**(B)**

(4) First, determine whether you'll be gardening indoors or outdoors. (5) This might depend on what type of home you live in, or it might depend on the climate. (6) If you live in an apartment building and don't have access to a community garden, an indoor garden might be right for you. (7) An indoor garden is also an option if you live in a climate that is not good for the plants that you'd like to grow.

**(C)**

(8) Indoors, you'll need to place your plants near a window where they'll get some sunlight each day. (9) Choose your growing space carefully, whether indoors or outdoors. (10) Outdoors, find a spot that doesn't have a lot of rocks or clay. (11) Likewise, you should choose your plants carefully.

**(D)**

(12) Investigate various plants, find out how much sunlight and water they need and what temperature they prefer. (13) You might be surprised to find, for instance, that you shouldn't try to grow basil in a shady side yard or impatiens in full sun. (14) A little extra effort up front will help you avoid common gardening pitfalls and enjoy your garden more.

1. Sentences 2 and 3: **If you want to be a successful gardener. It's important that you follow some simple guidelines.**

   Which is the best way to write the underlined portion of these sentences?

   A. gardener, importantly
   B. gardener, but it's important that
   C. gardener, it's important that
   D. gardener. And it's important that

2. Sentence 7: **An indoor garden is also an option if you live in a climate that is not good for the plants that you'd like to grow.**

   Which revision would improve the effectiveness of sentence 7?

   A. replace not good with too extreme
   B. replace you live with one lives
   C. insert a comma after option
   D. replace also with additionally

3. Which revision would improve the effectiveness of paragraph (C)?

   A. move sentence 11 to the beginning of paragraph (C)
   B. move sentence 8 to follow sentence 9
   C. move sentence 8 to follow sentence 10
   D. move sentence 8 to follow sentence 11

4. Which revision would improve the effectiveness of the article?

   A. move sentence 12 to the end of paragraph (C)
   B. move sentence 3 to the beginning of paragraph (B)
   C. move sentence 7 to the beginning of paragraph (C)
   D. move sentence 11 to the beginning of paragraph (D)

5. Sentence 12: **Investigate various plants, find out how much sunlight and water they need and what temperature they prefer.**

   Which is the best way to write the underlined portion of the sentence?

   A. plants, but
   B. plants or
   C. plants to
   D. plants, and then

**Questions 6 through 10 refer to the following paragraphs.**

**Rowing Across the Atlantic**

**(A)**

(1) When I was a child, my grandmother often told me stories about her father. (2) He was born in Wales which had come to the United States when he was 2 years old. (3) His trip to this country was a mystery to me.

**(B)**

(4) "Dad always said he came over in a rowboat," Granny explained. (5) I tried to imagine a 2-year-old boy rowing across the ocean it seemed impossible that he could have done that. (6) Could he have crossed the really big Atlantic Ocean *in a rowboat*?

**(C)**

(7) I had many questions for Granny. (8) "Were his parents with him?" I asked. (9) "No, I think he came by himself," she explained, laughing. (10) Was she totally pulling my leg? (11) The stories always ended with Granny wiping tears from her eyes. (12) She had several grandchildren. (13) "Oh, how I wish you had known him," she cried.

6. Sentence 2: **He was born in Wales which had come to the United States when he was 2 years old.**

   Which correction should be made to sentence 2?

   A. change which had come to and had come
   B. change had come to coming
   C. change He was born to Having been born
   D. insert a comma after Wales

7. Sentence 5: **I tried to imagine a 2-year-old boy rowing across the ocean it seemed impossible that he could have done that.**

   Which is the best way to write the underlined portion of the sentence?

   A. ocean however it
   B. ocean, thus it
   C. ocean. Thus it
   D. ocean; it

8. Sentence 6: **Could he have crossed the really big Atlantic Ocean *in a rowboat*?**

   Which correction should be made to sentence 6?

   A. replace have crossed with had crossed
   B. change Could he to He could
   C. replace really big with vast
   D. remove have

9. Sentence 10: **Was she totally pulling my leg?**

   Which is the best way to write the underlined portion of the sentence?

   A. totally pulling the leg of mine
   B. kidding me
   C. totally joking
   D. for real

10. Sentence 12: **She had several grandchildren.**

    Which correction should be made to sentence 12?

    A. replace had with have
    B. remove the sentence
    C. remove several
    D. replace grandchildren with grandkids

**Questions 11 through 14 refer to the following paragraphs.**

**Southern Gothic Writer**

**(A)**

(1) Flannery O'Connor was a gifted Southern writer. (2) She wrote many short stories and two novels. (3) She is known for writing in a Southern gothic style and exploring topics of religion, ethics, and morality she also frequently explored the dark side of human nature.

**(B)**

(4) One of O'Connor's most popular stories, "A Good Man is Hard to Find" was written in 1953 and focuses on a man called The Misfit. (5) Many reckon this is her most shocking story. (6) It raises important questions of good and evil, morality and immorality, and Southern historical issues.

**(C)**

(7) When Flannery was just 26, she was diagnosed with lupus. (8) The disease that had killed her father. (9) To manage her health, she returned to her family's farm, Andalusia, in Milledgeville, Georgia. (10) There, she lived with her mother Regina and wrote many of her most important works. (11) She delighted in raising birds of all varieties, including peafowl.

**(D)**

(12) During her time at Andalusia, Flannery also maintained many fulfilling correspondences with friends, family, and other writers which is why she is believed to have had a special insight into human behavior that is displayed in her writing. (13) Although she was only expected to live for five years after her lupus diagnosis, she managed to survive for fourteen.

11. Sentence 3: **She is known for writing in a Southern gothic style and exploring topics of religion, ethics, and morality she also frequently explored the dark side of human nature.**

    Which correction should be made to sentence 3?

    A. place a comma after <u>morality</u>
    B. place a comma after <u>also</u>
    C. remove <u>she also</u>
    D. place a period after <u>morality</u> and begin a new sentence with <u>She</u>

12. Sentence 5: **Many reckon this is her most shocking story.**

    Which is the best way to rewrite this sentence?

    A. Many reckon this is her most shockingest story.
    B. Many consider this her most shocking story.
    C. Many think it ought to be a most shocking story.
    D. Many reckon this ought to be her most shocking story.

13. Sentences 7 and 8: **(7) When Flannery was just 26, she was diagnosed with lupus. (8) The disease that had killed her father.**

    Which is the best way to revise these two sentences?

    A. move sentence 8 to before sentence 7
    B. move sentence 8 to after the comma in sentence 7
    C. change <u>lupus. The</u> to <u>lupus, the</u>
    D. change <u>with lupus. The disease that</u> to <u>with the disease, lupus, that</u>

14. Sentence 12: **During her time at Andalusia, <u>Flannery also maintained many fulfilling correspondences with friends, family, and other writers which is why she is believed to have had a special insight into human behavior that is displayed in her writing</u>.**

    Which is the best way to rewrite the underlined portion of this sentence?

    A. Flannery maintained many fulfilling correspondences that gave her the insight into human behavior that is evident in her writing.
    B. Flannery also maintained many correspondences with friends, family, and other writers, which is why she had a special insight into human behavior that is displayed in her writing.
    C. Flannery also maintained many fulfilling correspondences with friends, family, and other writers which is why she is believed to have had a special insight into human behavior that is in her writing.
    D. Flannery maintained many correspondences with friends, family, and other writers which is why she is believed to have had a special insight into human behavior.

**Questions 15 through 19 refer to the following paragraphs.**

### Notification of Utility Repairs

**(A)**

(1) Universal Utilities will soon begin repairs of the underground lines in your neighborhood. (2) This will ensure you always continue to receive the exceptional service you have come to expect from us.

**(B)**

(3) We will begin by installing a new pipeline under your street. (4) Then next we will replace the smaller line that runs from the street to your home. (5) Lastly we will install a new meter at your home.

**(C)**

(6) This work will require our company's trucks to be in your neighborhood. (7) We apologize for any inconvenience this may cause during peak travel times and you may experience a temporary disruption in your utility service. (8) However we will adjust your bill accordingly if your service is interrupted.

**(D)**

(9) If you have any questions about the scheduled repairs. (10) Please contact our office. (11) We can be reached by telephone, or you may visit our website. (12) Thank you for allowing us to serve your utility needs.

15. Sentence 2: **This will ensure you always continue to receive the exceptional service you have come to expect from us.**

    Which correction should be made to sentence 2?

    A. remove always
    B. insert a comma after service
    C. change will ensure to is ensuring
    D. replace you with they

16. Sentence 4: **Then next we will replace the smaller line that runs from the street to your home.**

    Which correction should be made to sentence 4?

    A. change then to than
    B. remove next
    C. insert a comma after line
    D. change replace to have replaced

17. Sentence 7: **We apologize for any inconvenience this may cause during peak travel times and you may experience a temporary disruption in your utility service.**

    What is the best way to write the underlined portion of the sentence?

    A. times, you
    B. times but you
    C. times. You
    D. times, and so you

18. Sentence 8: **However we will adjust your bill accordingly if your service is interrupted.**

    Which correction should be made to sentence 8?

    A. change interrupted to interrupts
    B. change accordingly to according
    C. replace if with thus
    D. insert a comma after However

19. Sentences 9 and 10: **If you have any questions about the scheduled repairs. Please contact our office.**

    Which correction should be made to sentences 9 and 10?

    A. change If you have to Having
    B. change repairs. Please to repairs, please
    C. place sentence 10 before sentence 9
    D. insert a comma after questions

**Review your work using the explanations that start on page 679.**

# LESSON 1

## Noun and Pronoun Agreement

### Using Nouns and Pronouns

A **noun** names a person (such as *woman* or *Anne*), a place (such as *drugstore* or *Florida*), a thing (such as *car* or *Titanic*), or an idea (*truth* or *Buddhism*). A **proper noun** refers to a specific person, place, thing, or idea; a **common noun** is more general. For example, *Anne* is a proper noun; *woman* is a common noun.

A **pronoun** is a word that replaces a noun. The **antecedent** is the noun that is being replaced, as shown below:

**EXAMPLE**

Steven lost his address book. It held many important phone numbers.
antecedent (address book) — pronoun (It)

There are three types of pronouns: subject, object, and possessive.

**EXAMPLES**

A **subject pronoun** replaces the subject of a sentence.

Steven called home. He was very worried.
subject (Steven) — subject pronoun (He)

An **object pronoun** replaces the object of a verb or of a preposition.

Steven's wife called him. She asked him what the problem was.
object pronoun (object of a verb) (him)

She and Steven looked for it.
object pronoun (object of a preposition) (it)

A **possessive pronoun** replaces a possessive noun.
Steven needed Kelly's number. He called 411 to get her number.
possessive noun (Kelly's) — possessive pronoun (her)

Use this chart for help in remembering the three types of pronouns:

| Subject Pronoun: replaces subject | Object Pronoun: replaces object | Possessive Pronoun: shows ownership |
|---|---|---|
| I | me | my, mine |
| you | you | your, yours |
| he | him | his |
| she | her | her, hers |
| it | it | its |
| we | us | ours |
| they | them | their, theirs |

Avoid these mistakes with pronouns in compound subjects and objects:

**Incorrect pronoun in compound subject:** Linda and me went to the movies.
**Correct:** Linda and I went to the movies.

**Incorrect pronoun in compound object:** We saw Kareem and he at the theater.
**Correct:** We saw Kareem and him at the theater.

**KEY IDEAS**

- A noun names a person, place, thing, or idea.
- A pronoun takes the place of a noun.
- Use subject, object, and possessive pronouns in the proper places.

**TASC TEST TIP**

*To choose the option with the correct pronoun in a compound like "They went to the party with James and I," take out "James and" and ask yourself whether the sentence still sounds correct.*

# PRACTICE 1.1

**A. Directions: Write the correct pronoun to replace each underlined noun.**

1. Laurie and Paul just moved to California. ______________________

2. A neighbor told Laurie and Paul that saving water was important there. ______________

3. He said they should turn the water off when brushing their teeth. ______________

4. Laurie's sister suggested getting a special shower head that saves water. ______________

5. Laurie and Laurie's sister will go shopping for it on Sunday. ______________

**B. Questions 6 through 8 refer to the following letter.**

To Whom It May Concern:

**(A)**

(1) I am writing to recommend Bonetta Williams for the position of managerial assistant in your firm. (2) I believe that she is highly qualfied for the position, and I urge you to strongly consider her candidacy.

**(B)**

(3) Bonetta and me have worked together for three years. (4) As my secretary, she has proven to be responsible and efficient. (5) She always getting her work done on time and looks for ways to help others. (6) In addition, I find her extremely intelligent and likable. (7) I will be sorry to see her go.

**(C)**

(8) My supervisor, Walter Constantine, has also worked with Bonetta and would be happy to speak with you if necessary. (9) Please contact Walter or I if you need any further information.

Sincerely,

Carol Rhodes

**6. Sentence 3:** Bonetta and me have worked together for three years.

Which correction should be made to sentence 3?

A. replace me with I
B. replace Bonetta with She
C. insert a comma after me
D. change have worked to been working

**7. Sentence 5:** She always getting her work done on time and looks for ways to help others.

Which correction should be made to sentence 5?

A. replace She with Her
B. insert a comma after time
C. change looks to looking
D. change getting to gets

**8. Sentence 9:** Please contact Walter or I if you need any further information.

Which is the best way to write the underlined portion of the sentence?

A. Walter and I
B. Walter or me
C. him or I
D. he or me

**Review your work using the explanations that start on pag 680.**

## Pronoun-Antecedent Agreement

Pronouns should agree with their antecedents, or the nouns they refer to. For example, a pronoun and its antecedent must agree in number. If the antecedent is singular, the pronoun should be singular. If the antecedent is plural, the pronoun should be plural.

**KEY IDEAS**

- A pronoun should match its antecedent in person and number.
- Make sure it is clear which antecedent a pronoun refers to.
- If necessary, use a noun in place of a pronoun, or construct the sentence differently so that the antecedent is clear.

**EXAMPLES**

Andy's company is very progressive. It pays for his college classes.
singular antecedent — singular pronoun

Many employees want to learn more skills, so they take classes.
plural antecedent — plural pronoun

**Incorrect:** Any employee who is interested should submit their application.
**Correct:** Any employee who is interested should submit his or her application.
**Correct:** Employees who are interested should submit their applications.

Note that for collective nouns (such as *company, jury, family, team, committee, union*), you generally use the singular pronoun *it*.

**Incorrect:** The committee announced that they will hold weekly meetings.
**Correct:** The committee announced that it will hold weekly meetings.

**TASC TEST TIP**

*Take into account the whole passage when you are determining which pronoun is correct. A common error to watch for is when a paragraph begins with the third-person form* one *and then shifts to the second-person form* you.

A pronoun and its antecedent must agree in person. To agree, they both must be first person (referring to the speaker), second person (the person spoken to), or third person (the person or thing spoken about).

| First person | Second person | Third person |
|---|---|---|
| I, me, my mine | you, your, yours | he, him, his |
| we, us, our, ours | | she, her, hers |
| | | it, its |
| | | they, them, their, theirs |

The indefinite pronoun *one* is like a third-person personal pronoun. A common error in writing is an incorrect shift between the third-person *one* and the second-person *you*.

**Incorrect shift:** If one attends college classes, you can be reimbursed.
**Correct:** If one attends college classes, one can be reimbursed.
**Correct:** If one attends college classes, he or she can be reimbursed.
**Correct:** If you attend college classes, you can be reimbursed.

It must be clear which antecedent a pronoun refers to. If necessary, use a noun in place of the pronoun, or reconstruct the sentence.

**Unclear:** Carlos spoke to his boss, and he told him about the program.
**Clear (noun replaces pronoun):** Carlos spoke to his boss, and his boss told him about the program.
**Clear (different construction):** Carlos spoke to his boss, who told him about the program.

**Unclear:** Michelle helped Shania fill out the financial aid application that she had picked up.
**Correct (different construction):** After picking up a financial aid application for Shania, Michelle helped her fill it out.

# PRACTICE 1.2

**A. Directions: Correct any errors in pronoun use. If there are no errors, write *C*. You may also have to change some verbs.**

**EXAMPLE:** People who live in small towns know ~~one has~~ they have access to fewer amenities than big-city dwellers.

___ **1.** Sally is moving to a small town. Her mother is concerned about the health-care options they offer.

___ **2.** Sally tried to reassure her mother, but it was hard for her to believe her.

___ **3.** Sally asked a friend who lives in the town for information about it's health-care facilities.

___ **4.** The town has a freestanding clinic where a person can go when they are sick.

___ **5.** There is also a nearby hospital, and they have a very good reputation.

___ **6.** If one is concerned about health care, you should sign up for a good insurance plan.

**B. Questions 7 through 9 refer to the following paragraphs.**

**The Best Discipline**

**(A)**

(1) What should parents do when their children act up? (2) Parents often like the idea of punishment, but punishment may not be the most effective solution. (3) If the punishment results from the parent's anger, it won't work. (4) Instead, children will learn only that they shouldn't make one's parents angry.

**(B)**

(5) One parenting expert feels that they should be clear about their expectations from the outset so that children will not unknowingly violate rules. (6) They should respond to children's misbehavior in a calm and neutral fashion. (7) It's also important to choose a consequence related to the action. (8) If a child hits or bites in a play group, for example, it would be most appropriate not to allow the child to play with them for a short time. (9) He or she will begin to see the connection.

**7. Sentence 4:** Instead, children will learn only that they shouldn't make one's parents angry.

Which correction should be made to sentence 4?

A. remove the comma after Instead
B. change learn to have learned
C. replace they with you
D. replace one's with their

**8. Sentence 5:** One parenting expert feels that they should be clear about their expectations from the outset so that children will not unknowingly violate rules.

Which is the best way to write the underlined portion of this sentence?

A. he
B. we
C. one
D. parents

**9. Sentence 8:** If a child hits or bites in a play group, for example, it would be most appropriate not to allow the child to play with them for a short time.

Which correction should be made to sentence 8?

A. insert a comma after hits
B. replace the child with them
C. replace them with the group
D. change it to you

**Review your work using the explanations that start on page 680.**

LESSON 2

# Verb Forms and Tenses

KEY IDEAS

- Each verb has four forms: present, present participle, past, and past participle.
- Verb forms are used to create different tenses, which show time relationships.
- Use clues in the sentence and paragraph to help decide which tense to use.

## Regular Verbs

An important part of writing correctly is using the right verb forms. A **verb** is a word that indicates action or being. Each verb has a base form and four other forms. A **regular verb** follows a consistent pattern to create each verb form.

**Base form:** look

| Tense | Verb form | How to write it |
|---|---|---|
| Present | look/looks | with *I, you, we, they:* use the base form |
| | | with *he, she, it:* add *-s* to the base form |
| Present participle | looking | add *-ing* |
| Past | looked | add *-ed* (*-d* if verb ends with *e*) |
| Past participle | looked | add *-ed* (*-d* if verb ends with *e*) |

The forms are used to create different **verb tenses**, or times. The table below shows how verb tense and form are related. Notice that when you use certain tenses, you must also use a **helping verb**—often a form of *be* or *have*.

| Tense | Verb form | Use |
|---|---|---|
| **Present** | look/looks | a habitual action, general truth, or state of being: *I look at the newspaper every day.* |
| **Past** | looked | an action that has been completed: *I looked at it this morning.* |
| **Future** | will look | an action that has not yet happened: *I will look at it tonight, too.* |
| **Present progressive** | am/is/are looking | an action in progress: *I am looking at it right now.* |
| **Present perfect** | have/has looked | an action that began in the past and continues until now: *I have looked at it every day this week.* |
| **Past Perfect** | had looked | an action that was completed before a specific time in the past: *I had looked at it before it got wet.* |
| **Future Perfect** | will have looked | an action that will be completed by a specific time in the future: *I will have looked at it by the time I get home.* |

TASC TEST TIP

*Some passages on the TASC Writing Test may have a verb-tense question based on the tense of the entire passage. Make sure you select verb forms that are consistent with the tense of the passage.*

Sentences often contain clues that tell you which tense to use. For instance, time words and phrases like *yesterday* or *last week* show that the past should be used, *tonight* and *next month* indicate the future, and *by tonight, since 2000,* and *for seven years* indicate the perfect tenses.

Other verbs in the sentence can be clues: *I look at the newspaper whenever I get the chance.* Finally, verbs in other sentences also can be clues. The verbs in a paragraph or passage are generally in the same tense.

# PRACTICE 2.1

**A. Directions: Rewrite each verb in its correct tense. Use clues in each sentence for help in choosing the tense.**

**EXAMPLE:** Between 1892 and 1924, about 12 million immigrants *entered* (enter) the U.S. through Ellis Island in New York.

1. By the 1950s, Ellis Island ____________ (cease) to be an important immigration checkpoint.
2. The government ____________ (close) Ellis Island to immigration in 1954.
3. Now Ellis Island ____________ (function) as a national monument.
4. Since the island was reopened as a museum in 1990, many tourists ____________ (visit) it.
5. Soon, a genealogical center ____________ (open).
6. The island ____________ (look) different than it did originally because 24 acres of landfill have been added.
7. Now we ____________ (think) about taking a trip to Ellis Island next month.

**B. Questions 8 through 10 refer to the following advertisement.**

**Don't Miss Your Chance!**

**(A)**

(1) The Express Lane credit card has offered a fantastic deal right now, for a limited time only. (2) If you are signing up for Express Lane before April 9, you will receive a 20 percent discount on your first five purchases!

**(B)**

(3) The Express Lane card carries no monthly charge. (4) You'll pay a low $35 fee just once a year. (5) Become an Express Lane member now. (6) Your savings opportunities will be amazing you!

8. **Sentence 1:** The Express Lane credit card has offered a fantastic deal right now, for a limited time only.

   Which is the best way to write the underlined portion of the sentence?

   A. offered
   B. is offering
   C. offers
   D. will offer

9. **Sentence 2:** If you are signing up for Express Lane before April 9, you will receive a 20 percent discount on your first five purchases!

   Which correction should be made to sentence 2?

   A. change are signing to have signed
   B. change you will to one will
   C. change will receive to receive
   D. change are signing to sign

10. **Sentence 6:** Your savings opportunities will be amazing you!

    Which correction should be made to sentence 6?

    A. change Your to You're
    B. change Your to One's
    C. insert a comma after opportunities
    D. change will be amazing to will amaze

**Review your work using the explanations that start on page 680.**

**STUDY ADVICE**

Remembering the *names* of verb tenses (in the first column of the second table on page 200) isn't nearly as important as remembering how to use them. You may want to make flash cards out of the second and third columns of the tables on page 200. On one side of each card, put a time frame and an action word (such as "an action that has been completed; look"). On the other side, put the verb form that matches (in this case, "looked").

KEY IDEAS

- Irregular verb forms do not follow a single pattern.
- Some irregular verbs follow an *i, a, u* pattern.

## Irregular Verbs

Most verbs are regular verbs; their past and participle forms follow the same pattern. Some verbs, however, are **irregular verbs.** Although some irregular verbs follow a pattern, most do not.

A common error with irregular verbs is using the past participle in place of the past—for instance, *I been there* instead of *I was there.* Discover which irregular verb forms, if any, give you problems. Then learn the correct forms. Here are some tips for learning the forms of irregular verbs:

- If you find two verbs that rhyme in the present form (for example, *grow* and *throw*), check to see if they have the same forms in the past and past participles (*grew, grown; threw, thrown*). If so, learn them together.
- Learn which verbs follow the *i, a, u* pattern: *sing, sang, sung; drink, drank, drunk; sink, sank, sunk.* However, be aware that there are exceptions (*bring, brought, brought*).

Here is a list of common irregular verbs.

| Present Form | Past Form | Past Participle Form |
|---|---|---|
| am, are, is | was, were | been |
| become | became | become |
| begin | began | begun |
| blow | blew | blown |
| break | broke | broken |
| bring | brought | brought |
| buy | bought | bought |
| choose | chose | chosen |
| come | came | come |
| do | did | done |
| drink | drank | drunk |
| eat | ate | eaten |
| fall | fell | fallen |
| fly | flew | flown |
| freeze | froze | frozen |
| get | got | gotten |
| give | gave | given |
| go | went | gone |
| grow | grew | grown |
| have, has | had | had |
| know | knew | known |
| leave | left | left |
| lose | lost | lost |
| ride | rode | ridden |
| run | ran | run |
| see | saw | seen |
| shake | shook | shaken |
| show | showed | shown |
| speak | spoke | spoken |
| steal | stole | stolen |
| take | took | taken |
| throw | threw | thrown |
| wear | wore | worn |
| write | wrote | written |

TASC TEST TIP

*When you choose an answer that changes a verb, read the sentence again, with your choice in it. Doing so may help you "hear" whether the verb form is correct.*

# PRACTICE 2.2

**A. Directions: Write the correct form of the verb shown in parentheses.**

**EXAMPLE:** Since November, the school's heating system ___*has broken*___ (break) down several times.

**1.** Yesterday the technician ______________ (come) to resolve the problem once and for all.

**2.** School employees ______________ (show) him the boiler.

**3.** The technician said, "If you ______________ (speak) to me about this sooner, it would have been easier to fix."

**4.** He ______________ (take) parts out of the heating system and replaced them with new ones.

**5.** He said, "I've never ______________ (see) such a poorly installed system."

**B. Questions 6 through 8 refer to the following paragraphs.**

**TV Rating Systems**

**(A)**

(1) In 1996, television industry representatives announced that the industry had formed TV Parental Guidelines. (2) This rating system, designed to give parents advance warning about the content of TV shows, begun to appear on TV in 1997. (3) The ratings system was broke down into six different categories, ranging from "All Children" to "Mature Audiences Only."

**(B)**

(4) Six months later, after pressure from advocacy groups, the television industry agreed to include additional labels to advise viewers if a show they were about to view contained violence, sexual activity, coarse language, or sexually suggestive language. (5) These labels now given viewers more specific and therefore more helpful information about an upcoming show.

**6. Sentence 2:** This rating system, designed to give parents advance warning about the content of TV shows, begun to appear on TV in 1997.

Which correction should be made to sentence 2?

A. remove the comma after system
B. change give to be giving
C. change begun to had begun
D. change begun to began

**7. Sentence 3:** The ratings system was broke down into six different categories, ranging from "All Children" to "Mature Audiences Only."

Which is the best way to write the underlined portion of this sentence?

A. broke itself
B. broke
C. was broken
D. had broken

**8. Sentence 5:** These labels now given viewers more specific and therefore more helpful information about an upcoming show.

Which correction should be made to sentence 5?

A. change given to will give
B. change given to give
C. insert a comma after information
D. insert a comma after specific

**Review your work using the explanations that start on page 680.**

LESSON 3

# Subject-Verb Agreement

## Agreement with a Simple Subject

In the present tense, subjects and verbs must agree in number. To understand the basics of subject-verb agreement, study the chart below. Notice that present tense verbs take an *-s* ending when they are used with the pronoun subjects *he, she,* and *it* or their noun equivalents.

**KEY IDEAS**

- A verb must match its subject in number.
- Collective nouns are singular when they refer to a group as a single unit.
- Indefinite pronouns may be singular, plural, or both.

| Verb Forms for Singular Subjects | Verb Forms for Plural Subjects |
|---|---|
| *I* jump | *we* jump |
| *you* jump | *you* jump |
| *he, she, it* jumps | *they* jump |

To master subject-verb agreement for the Writing Test, be aware of these special nouns and pronouns:

**Collective nouns** are usually singular, even though they may seem plural. A collective noun names a group, such as *army, crew, crowd, staff, family, herd,* or *flock.* If the group is considered to be a single unit, it is singular.

**EXAMPLES**

The army is a good place to learn discipline.
The church choir sings each Sunday.

Some nouns that end in -*s* may look plural, but in fact they are not.

**EXAMPLE**

Politics is an interesting topic.

**TASC TEST TIP**

*To check for correct subject-verb agreement, ask yourself: Does the verb agree with its subject? Is the verb in the right form? Is the verb in the right tense for both the sentence and the passage?*

**Indefinite pronouns** do not refer to a specific person. Some indefinite pronouns are singular, some are plural, and some may be either.

| | |
|---|---|
| Singular | anyone, everyone, someone, no one, one, anybody, everybody, somebody, nobody, anything, everything, something, nothing, another, other, either, neither, each, much |
| Plural | many, several, few, both |
| Singular or plural | all, none, some, any, part, most |

**EXAMPLES**

**Singular:** These days, it seems as if almost everyone is joining a health club.
**Singular:** Most of the equipment is easy to use.
**Plural:** Most of the exercise classes are fun
**Plural:** A few are advanced classes for those already in great shape.

# PRACTICE 3.1

**A. Directions: Underline the correct verb form to complete each sentence.**

**EXAMPLE:** Every Monday, the National Orchestra (perform, performs) live on the radio.

**1.** The public (is, are) invited to listen free of charge.

**2.** Free tickets (becomes, become) available one hour before the performance.

**3.** The performance (is, are) usually held in Barnes Hall.

**4.** Many well-known musicians (has, have) played there.

**5.** Everyone (seem, seems) to enjoy these concerts very much.

**6.** The concert series (is, are) very popular.

**B. Questions 7 through 9 refer to the following article.**

**The Speed of Sound**

**(A)**

(1) Most of us has heard airplane noise that is so loud it sounds like an explosion. (2) That noise occurs when a plane start to fly faster than the speed of sound. (3) Listeners on the ground hear the noise, but it is not audible to passengers.

**(B)**

(4) The speed of sound is 1,088 feet per second at 32°F at sea level. (5) It is different at other temperatures and in other substances. (6) For example, sound travels faster in water than in air. (7) Sound takes about one second to move a mile under water, but five seconds to move a mile through air. (8) It travels through ice cold vapor at 4,708 feet per second and through ice cold water at 4,938 feet per second. (9) Surprisingly, some other materials conducts sound very well. (10) For instance, sound travels through glass at speeds up to 19,690 feet per second.

**STUDY ADVICE**

How long are your study sessions at this point? Remember to push yourself, little by little, until you can focus on the material for two to three hours at a time. It may take weeks or months to get there, but don't give up. Remember: You need to train yourself so that you can focus for a few hours on Test Day.

**7. Sentence 1:** Most of us has heard airplane noise that is so loud it sounds like an explosion.

Which is the best way to write the underlined portion of this sentence?

A. were hearing
B. have heard
C. having heard
D. hears

**8. Sentence 2:** That noise occurs when a plane start to fly faster than the speed of sound.

Which correction should be made to sentence 2?

A. change occurs to occur
B. change occurs to occurred
C. change start to starts
D. replace than with then

**9. Sentence 9:** Surprisingly, some other materials conducts sound very well.

Which correction should be made to sentence 9?

A. replace some with any
B. change conducts to conduct
C. change conducts to conducted
D. insert a comma after sound

**Review your work using the explanations that start on page 680.**

## Agreement with a Compound Subject

A compound subject is made up of two or more subjects joined by *and* or *or.* To make a verb agree with a compound subject, follow these guidelines:

When two or more subjects are joined by *and,* the compound subject is plural. Use the correct verb form for the plural.

**EXAMPLE:** Tricia and her sister are caring for their mother.

If two subjects are joined by *or,* the verb agrees with the subject closer to it:

**EXAMPLE:** A health aide or a nurse visits each day.

When subjects are joined by *either . . . or* or *neither . . . nor,* the verb agrees with the subject closer to it.

**EXAMPLE:** Neither the brother nor his sisters have medical training.

## Interrupting Words

Sometimes a word or group of words comes between the subject and the verb. In that case, locate the subject by asking yourself, What is this sentence really about? Mentally cross out the interruptor. Then make the verb agree with the subject.

**EXAMPLE:** The medicine ~~prescribed by the doctors~~ is on a high shelf.
subject interruptor verb

Interrupting phrases often begin with prepositions, such as *of, in, on, from, with, to,* and *for.*

**EXAMPLE:** A pile ~~of medical supplies~~ rests in the front hallway.

Interrupting phrases may be set off by commas. Watch especially for phrases beginning with words like *along with, as well as, besides,* and *in addition to.*

**EXAMPLES**

Dr. Silva~~, who is one of the surgeons,~~ consults with the family.
The sisters~~, along with the medical team,~~ keep the patient comfortable.

## Inverted Structure

Checking subject-verb agreement can be tricky when the sentence structure is **inverted**—that is, when the subject comes after the verb. Most questions and sentences that begin with *here* or *there* are inverted.

**EXAMPLES**

Does the pharmacy have enough medicine to fill the prescription?
Here are the hospital supplies that Tricia ordered.

**Incorrect:** What is Tricia and her family going to do?
**Correct:** What are Tricia and her family going to do?

**Incorrect:** Do Tricia want to send her mother to a hospital?
**Correct:** Does Tricia want to send her mother to a hospital?

**Incorrect:** There's the bandages. (Remember that *There's* is short for *There is.*)
**Correct:** There are the bandages.

### KEY IDEAS

- If a compound subject is joined by *and*, use a plural verb.
- If a compound subject is joined by *or, either . . . or,* or *neither . . . nor,* the verb should agree with the subject closer to it.
- When checking subject-verb agreement, ignore interrupting phrases and watch for inverted structure.

### TASC TEST TIP

*Read* there's *as* there is *and* here's *as* here is.

# PRACTICE 3.2

**A. Directions: If a sentence contains an interrupting phrase, cross out the interruptor. Then underline the correct verb to complete the sentence.**

**EXAMPLE:** Brushing and flossing ~~with regularity~~ (is, are) key to good dental health.

1. Many toothpastes on the market (carry, carries) a seal of approval from the American Dental Association.
2. Products carrying the seal (are, is) tested to guarantee that they are safe and effective.
3. Fluoride, an important ingredient in many toothpastes, (strengthens, strengthen) teeth and (attacks, attack) bacteria that cause tooth decay.
4. There (is, are) toothpastes that claim to have special benefits, like tartar control or whitening.
5. Some pharmacies and supermarkets (offers, offer) store-brand toothpaste at a low price.
6. Any toothpaste with fluoride and good flavor (is, are) fine to use, even if it's not a brand-name toothpaste.

**B. Questions 7 through 9 refer to the following paragraphs.**

**Unemployment Insurance**

**(A)**

(1) Unemployment insurance provides workers who have lost their jobs with partial replacement of their salary. (2) Each state administers its own program and have its own laws. (3) The amount received is determined by wage level and the length of employment. (4) When the unemployment rate rises above a certain level, states are required to extend the benefits. (5) The state and federal governments share the cost of the additional benefits.

**(B)**

(6) In most states, employer contributions pay for this program. (7) Unemployed workers who wish to draw benefits reports regularly to their public employment office to learn about job openings.

7. **Sentence 2:** Each state administers its own program and have its own laws.

   Which correction should be made to sentence 2?

   A. change administers to administering
   B. change administers to administer
   C. change have to has
   D. replace its with it's

8. **Sentence 3:** The amount received is determined by wage level and the length of employment.

   If you rewrote sentence 3 beginning with

   Wage level and the length of employment

   the next word(s) should be

   A. determine
   B. determines
   C. is determined
   D. was determined

9. **Sentence 7:** Unemployed workers who wish to draw benefits reports regularly to their public employment office to learn about job openings.

   Which correction should be made to sentence 7?

   A. change wish to wishes
   B. insert a comma after benefits
   C. change reports to report
   D. replace their with there

**Review your work using the explanations that start on page 680.**

# Using Grammar Correctly Practice Questions

**Questions 1 through 5 refer to the following paragraphs.**

**Unorthodox Tennis Stars**

**(A)**

(1) Venus and Serena Williams are not your typical tennis stars. (2) For one thing, they are African Americans in a game that few African Americans have become famous for playing; those who preceded them were Althea Gibson, Arthur Ashe, and Zina Garrison. (3) For another, Venus and Serena are sisters.

**(B)**

(4) Tennis players often receive hours of instruction from highly paid coaches, but it doesn't happen that way for Venus and Serena. (5) Instead, their father, the former owner of a security-services business, taught them how to play on public courts, after teaching himself through books and films. (6) The family lived in a rough neighborhood, and gang members watched over the girls while she practiced.

**(C)**

(7) The practice paid off. (8) Venus had won 63 tournaments by the time she turned 12, and she became a professional at 14. (9) In just a few years, she earns millions of dollars in endorsements and prizes. (10) Serena, turning professional a year after Venus, had a slower start. (11) However, some experts think she may now be better than her sister.

**(D)**

(12) The two sisters, who live in Palm Beach Gardens, Florida, is best friends. (13) Though they sometimes face each other on the court, there been no trace of sibling rivalry.

1. Sentence 4: **Tennis players often receive hours of instruction from highly paid coaches, but it doesn't happen that way for Venus and Serena.**

   Which correction should be made to sentence 4?

   A. change receive to receives
   B. remove the comma
   C. change doesn't to didn't
   D. insert a comma after Instruction

2. Sentence 6: **The family lived in a rough neighborhood, and gang members watched over the girls while she practiced.**

   Which is the best way to write the underlined portion of the sentence?

   A. they
   B. the girls
   C. each
   D. them

3. Sentence 9: **In just a few years, she earns millions of dollars in endorsements and prizes.**

   Which is the best way to write the underlined portion of the sentence?

   A. is earning
   B. earned
   C. earn
   D. will earn

4. Sentence 12: **The two sisters, who live in Palm Beach Gardens, Florida, is best friends.**

   Which correction should be made to sentence 12?

   A. remove the comma after sisters
   B. change live to lives
   C. remove the comma after Florida
   D. change is to are

5. Sentence 13: **Though they sometimes face each other on the court, there been no trace of sibling rivalry.**

   Which correction should be made to sentence 13?

   A. change face to faced
   B. remove the comma after court
   C. change been to was
   D. change been to is

**Questions 6 through 10 refer to the following paragraphs.**

**Getting the Best Service for Your Car**

**(A)**

(1) Have you had trouble finding a good mechanic? (2) By following these tips, you can improve your chances of getting quality service.

**(B)**

(3) Even before your car breaks down, look for a shop you like and trust. (4) Ask people where they will receive good service at a reasonable price. (5) Don't have picked a shop just because it's close to home, for another shop may have a better deal. (6) Be wary of ads that offer rock-bottom prices. (7) Specials like these often comes with restrictions attached.

**(C)**

(8) Be as specific as possible when you describe your car's problem to the mechanic. (9) If the technician must spend time trying to determine what's wrong, it will cost more. (10) You also need to request information about both estimates and guarantees before the repair work starts. (11) Ask for a price range rather than an exact estimate. (12) Find out how long the guarantee lasts and whether there's any time or mileage limits.

**(D)**

(13) If you don't understand a repair explanation, ask for clarification right away. (14) In addition, keep records of all repairs and billing in case of a dispute.

6. Sentence 4: **Ask people where they will receive good service at a reasonable price.**

   Which correction should be made to sentence 4?

   A. change Ask to To ask
   B. change will receive to have received
   C. change will receive to receiving
   D. change people to them

7. Sentence 5: **Don't have picked a shop just because it's close to home, for another shop may have a better deal.**

   Which correction should be made to sentence 5?

   A. change have picked to pick
   B. change have picked to be picking
   C. replace it's with its
   D. remove the comma

8. Sentence 7: **Specials like these often comes with restrictions attached.**

   Which correction should be made to sentence 7?

   A. replace these with this
   B. insert a comma after these
   C. change comes to came
   D. change comes to come

9. Sentence 9: **If the technician must spend time trying to determine what's wrong, it will cost more.**

   Which correction should be made to sentence 9?

   A. change must spend to spent
   B. change what's to what are
   C. remove the comma
   D. replace it with the repair job

10. Sentence 12: **Find out how long the guarantee lasts and whether there's any time or mileage limits.**

    Which is the best way to write the underlined portion of the sentence?

    A. there is
    B. there be
    C. there are
    D. there were

**Questions 11 through 15 refer to the following letter.**

**Taxpayer Notification**

**(A)**

(1) We have received your tax return and have noted some inconsistencies in it. (2) We are therefore proposing a number of changes to your return. (3) These changes and its effect on your refund are outlined below.

**(B)**

(4) First, the amount you claimed for self-employed income differs from our records. (5) If you wish to contest this change, please send photocopies of one's records. (6) Second, you have made an error in your calculations. (7) Please review our calculations, which is appended to this letter.

**(C)**

(8) These changes having been made to your return, there is an increase in the amount of taxes you owe. (9) Your refund has therefore been reduced accordingly.

**(D)**

(10) Contact us if you have any questions about these specific problems or about the documents you must send to contest the changes. (11) Be sure to send the last page of this letter when replying by mail. (12) If we determine that your return was correct as filed, we have credited your account.

11. Sentence 3: **These changes and its effect on your refund are outlined below.**

    Which correction should be made to sentence 3?

    A. insert a comma after changes
    B. replace its with their
    C. insert a comma after refund
    D. change are to is

12. Sentence 5: **If you wish to contest this change, please send photocopies of one's records.**

    Which correction should be made to sentence 5?

    A. change wish to wishes
    B. change send to to send
    C. replace one's with your
    D. change you to one

13. Sentence 7: **Please review our calculations, which is appended to this letter.**

    Which correction should be made to sentence 7?

    A. change review to reviewing
    B. replace our with are
    C. remove the comma
    D. change is to are

14. Sentence 8: **These changes having been made to your return, there is an increase in the amount of taxes you owe.**

    If you rewrote sentence 8 beginning with

    Because of these changes to your return, the amount of taxes you owe

    the next words should be

    A. has increased
    B. have increased
    C. is increasing
    D. are increasing

15. Sentence 12: **If we determine that your return was correct as filed, we have credited your account.**

    Which is the best way to write the underlined portion of the sentence?

    A. are crediting
    B. will credit
    C. will have credited
    D. had credited

**Questions 16 through 20 refer to the following paragraphs.**

**Disability Etiquette**

**(A)**

(1) Many of us doesn't know how to act when meeting someone who has a disability. (2) The main thing to remember is that people with disabilities has feelings just like everyone else. (3) They want to be treated with respect and dignity. (4) Beyond that, try the following tips.

**(B)**

(5) When you meet a person with a disability, speak and act with he or she as you would with anyone else. (6) Use your usual tone of voice. (7) A person who has trouble hearing you will let you know. (8) Don't talk down to the person or stare. (9) Refrain from using a term like handicap, which focuses on the disability rather than on the person. (10) Instead, use a term such as physically disabled or say, "He uses a wheelchair."

**(C)**

(11) Any assistive equipment, such as a wheelchair, cane, or communication board, are the person's property. (12) Unless you have the person's express permission, you should not touch it. (13) Also, distracting a blind person's guide dog could put the owner in danger, so do not pet it.

**(D)**

(14) Finally, if you have a child with you, don't prevent him or her from talking to the person or asking questions. (15) Children are often more accepting than adults.

16. Sentence 1: **Many of us doesn't know how to act when meeting someone who has a disability.**

    Which is the best way to write the underlined portion of the sentence?

    A. does not
    B. don't
    C. didn't
    D. never does

17. Sentence 2: **The main thing to remember is that people with disabilities has feelings just like everyone else.**

    Which correction should be made to sentence 2?

    A. add a comma after remember
    B. change is to are
    C. change has to have
    D. change people to them

18. Sentence 5: **When you meet a person with a disability, speak and act with he or she as you would with anyone else.**

    Which is the best way to write the underlined portion of the sentence?

    A. he or her
    B. him or her
    C. him or she
    D. them

19. Sentence 11: **Any assistive equipment, such as a wheelchair, cane, or communication board, are the person's property.**

    Which correction should be made to sentence 11?

    A. remove the comma after wheelchair
    B. change are to is
    C. change person's to persons
    D. insert a comma after assistive

20. Sentences 13: **Also, distracting a blind person's guide dog could put the owner in danger, so do not pet it.**

    If you rewrote sentence 13 beginning with

    Also, don't pet a blind person's guide dog because distracting

    the next word(s) should be

    A. a blind person's guide dog
    B. it
    C. her
    D. them

**Review your work using the explanations that start on page 680.**

LESSON 1

# Comma Use

As a general rule, **commas** indicate where readers would pause in a sentence if they were reading it aloud. Below are specific guidelines for using commas.

**KEY IDEAS**

- In a compound sentence, use a comma before the coordinating conjunction.
- Be careful not to use a comma when only two words or phrases are joined by *and*.
- Insert a comma after an introductory word, phrase, or clause.

## Commas in Compound Sentences

In a compound sentence, place a comma immediately before the coordinating conjunction.

**EXAMPLES**

Some people are insecure about hosting a party, but others are relaxed and confident.

Many hosts have years of practice, and they have some organizational tips.

Watch out, though, for sentences that appear to be compound but are not. Some sentences have one main clause but have a compound subject or a compound predicate. If a sentence does not have two independent clauses, a comma is not needed before the coordinating conjunction.

**Incorrect:** Planning, and list making are two key organizational techniques.
**Correct:** Planning and list making are two key organizational techniques.

**Incorrect:** Making a list reduces disorganization, and helps you feel in control.
**Correct:** Making a list reduces disorganization and helps you feel in control.

## Commas after Introductory Elements

In general, a comma should follow an introductory word, phrase, or clause to separate the introductory element from the main part of the sentence.

**TASC TEST TIP**

*Read a sentence out loud to see if you hear a pause. Before you insert a comma, be sure that you can base your decision on a comma rule.*

**EXAMPLES**

**Introductory words:**
Yes, listing your ideas can be very helpful.
However, making a list is only the first step.

**Introductory phrases:**
Giving it some thought, carefully draw up a guest list.
For a casual feel, have an open house.
On the day of the party, do as much as you can first thing in the morning.
By party time, you should be able to relax.

**Introductory clauses:**
Before you make a list, decide what kind of party you will have.
If you are a good cook, you might choose to have a dinner party.

Remember that only a subordinate clause at the beginning of a sentence requires a comma after it. A subordinate clause at the end of the sentence generally does not.

**No comma:** Decide what kind of party you will have before you make a list.

# PRACTICE 1.1

**A. Directions: Insert commas where needed in the sentences below. If no commas are required, write *NC*.**

_____ **1.** Train travel is more pleasant than riding a bus but it can be more expensive.

_____ **2.** When you're on a train you can stand up and stretch if you need to.

_____ **3.** Most trains have club cars where passengers can get snacks and sometimes even sit at tables.

_____ **4.** Unlike buses trains sometimes have seats that face each other.

_____ **5.** Traveling through a scenic area you may find that your train has a double-decker car that offers a better view.

_____ **6.** Lowered air fares and many people's unwillingness to spend long hours in a train have contributed to the declining popularity of rail travel.

**B. Questions 7 through 9 refer to the following paragraphs.**

**Low-Fat Cooking**

**(A)**

(1) To have a more healthful diet, try cooking with less fat. (2) It's not as hard as you think! (3) For starters use cooking methods that require little or no oil or butter, such as steaming, poaching, or baking. (4) When you do include oil in the preparation of your dish, use less of it. (5) Vinegar can be used without oil in salad dressing and the flavor can be enhanced with fresh herbs.

**(B)**

(6) Another tactic is to cut down on dairy fat. (7) Avoid regular milk, cream, and sour cream. (8) Add low-fat dairy products or another liquid to your dish instead. (9) Many dairy foods come in a low-fat version, and though, not all of them may be pleasing to the palate, some are.

**STUDY ADVICE**

When you write, don't just make guesses about where to place commas. Use the rules outlined on these pages. People frequently misuse commas in daily life, so what feels right to you may not actually be correct.

**7. Sentence 3:** For starters use cooking methods that require little or no oil or butter, such as steaming, poaching, or baking.

Which correction should be made to sentence 3?

A. insert a comma after starters
B. remove the comma after butter
C. remove the comma after steaming
D. insert a comma after little

**8. Sentence 5:** Vinegar can be used without oil in salad dressing and the flavor can be enhanced with fresh herbs.

Which is the best way to write the underlined portion of the sentence?

A. dressing, and
B. dressing and,
C. dressing, or
D. dressing, for example

**9. Sentence 9:** Many dairy foods come in a low-fat version, and though, not all of them may be pleasing to the palate, some are.

Which correction should be made to sentence 9?

A. remove the comma after version
B. insert a comma after pleasing
C. remove the comma after palate
D. remove the comma after though

**Review your work using the explanations that start on page 681.**

KEY IDEAS

- Separate the items in a series with commas.
- Put commas around an appositive only if it gives nonessential details about a noun.
- Don't put a comma between a subject and a verb.
- Don't use a comma between two items joined by *and* or *or*.

TASC TEST TIP

*When an option involves removing a comma, see if you can apply a specific rule for using a comma in that place. If you cannot, the comma should probably be removed.*

## Commas in a Series

When three or more items are listed in a series, place commas *between* the items:

**EXAMPLES**

Keith, Darnelle, Marisol, and Doug are ready to take the TASC Test.
They have taken a class, studied together, and prepared well.

The comma before the final *and* or *or* is optional (for example, *March 7, March 14, or March 21*), but using one there will help you place commas correctly in the series.

## Commas with Appositives

An **appositive** is a word or group of words that gives more information about a noun by renaming it.

**EXAMPLES**

Marisol, an experienced writer, feels confident about the essay.
Doug's only sister, Gina, was the first in the family to receive a high school equivalency degree.

To decide whether to set off an appositive with commas, mentally cross out the appositive. Then ask, *"Can I still identify the person, place, or thing described in the sentence?"* If you can, use commas around the appositive.

**EXAMPLES**

Mann College, a local community college, offers TASC courses.
Keith, who attended TASC classes for a year, has done well there.

Here you can identify the noun without the appositive. Each appositive adds more information, but it is not essential to your understanding. Usually when an appositive is renaming a proper noun, it is not essential.

On the other hand, if you cannot identify the person, place, or thing without the appositive, do not set off the appositive with commas.

**EXAMPLES**

Keith and his friend Antoine plan to work in construction.
Students who study faithfully usually do well on the test.

In these examples, you cannot identify the nouns without the appositives. You would ask, *"Which friend?"* and *"Which students?"* The appositives are essential to your understanding and should not be set off by commas.

## Comma Errors to Avoid

It is easy to overuse commas. Avoid this error by following these guidelines:

Do not use a comma between the subject and the verb.

**Incorrect:** Park College, is the school Doug hopes to attend.

Do not use a comma between two subjects, two verbs, or two other items joined by *and* or *or.*

**Incorrect:** Science, and math are hard subjects for Keith.
**Incorrect:** Darnell writes practice essays, and reads literature.
**Incorrect:** They will review his application, and transcript.

# PRACTICE 1.2

**A. Directions: Insert commas where needed in the sentences below. If no commas are required, write *NC*.**

_____ **1.** Kwanzaa is a week-long African American holiday that celebrates culture community and family.

_____ **2.** Kwanzaa a wintertime holiday is based on an ancient African harvest celebration.

_____ **3.** It was developed in modern times by scholar Maulana Karenga.

_____ **4.** Kwanzaa celebrations include rituals such as singing dancing drumming and poetry reading.

_____ **5.** The family lights one candle every day for each of seven principles: unity self-determination responsibility cooperative economics purpose creativity and faith.

_____ **6.** A day during which people consider their moral worthiness marks the end of Kwanzaa.

**B. Questions 7 through 9 refer to the following paragraphs.**

**Childproofing Your Home**

**(A)**

(1) If you have small children, you no doubt appreciate the need to make your home as safe as possible. (2) It is a fact that home accidents, are responsible for more children's injuries than all childhood diseases combined. (3) Taking a few simple measures might reduce the number of times you take your kids to the emergency room.

**(B)**

(4) Start by putting childproof locks on all cupboards in which medicines poisons, or fragile objects are stored. (5) To keep babies and toddlers from entering dangerous areas, put baby gates in doorways and install sleeves on doorknobs. (6) Install safety locks on doors and windows. (7) Make sure that older children, those ten and up can open them in an emergency. (8) To prevent burns in the bathtub, keep the water temperature below 120°F. (9) Cover unused outlets with outlet plugs.

**7. Sentence 2:** It is a fact that home accidents, are responsible for more children's injuries than all childhood diseases combined.

Which correction should be made to sentence 2?

A. remove the comma
B. change <u>are</u> to <u>is</u>
C. insert a comma after <u>injuries</u>
D. insert a comma after <u>diseases</u>

**8. Sentence 4:** Start by putting childproof locks on all cupboards in which medicines poisons, or fragile objects are stored.

Which correction should be made to sentence 4?

A. change <u>Start</u> to <u>Starting</u>
B. insert a comma after <u>medicines</u>
C. insert a comma after <u>objects</u>
D. change <u>are</u> to <u>is</u>

**9. Sentence 7:** Make sure that older <u>children, those ten and up</u> can open them in an emergency.

Which is the best way to write the underlined portion of this sentence?

A. children those ten and up
B. children, those ten, and up,
C. children, those ten and up,
D. children those ten and up,

**Review your work using the explanations that start on page 681.**

LESSON 2

# Capitalization

To recognize capitalization errors on the TASC Writing Test and to use capital letters correctly in your response, follow these guidelines.

Capitalize proper nouns. A **proper noun** is the name of a specific person, place, thing, or idea. If a proper noun has two or more words, capitalize each word.

**EXAMPLES**

Claude Normand is a major contributor to Portland Community Hospital.
The hospital is located on Camden Road in Portland, Maine.
The hospital and charities such as the American Cancer Society rely on contributions from citizens.
All major religions, from Islam to Christianity, support giving to charity.

Note that the key words in addresses are proper nouns and are capitalized. The key words include the names of streets, cities, states, and countries.

Do not capitalize common nouns, which do not refer to a specific person, place, or thing.

**EXAMPLE**

**Incorrect:** Many Doctors volunteer at Clinics in the City.
**Correct:** Many doctors volunteer at clinics in the city.

Capitalize the names of proper adjectives. A **proper adjective** is formed from a proper noun.

**EXAMPLE**

Mr. Normand has a French Canadian heritage.

Capitalize a title before a person's name. Do not capitalize a title when it appears without a person's name unless it is used in direct address.

**EXAMPLES**

**Title before name:** Mr. Normand met recently with Dr. Halverson and Mayor Maresky.
**Title without name:** The doctor and mayor were very receptive to his ideas.
**Direct address:** He said, "Thank you, Mayor, for listening to my proposal."

Capitalize names of holidays, days of the week, and months. Do not capitalize the names of seasons.

**EXAMPLES**

Memorial Day is always the last Monday in May and is a paid holiday.
The project will be completed by the end of spring.

Capitalize names of specific school courses and all languages.

**EXAMPLE**

I am taking Introduction to Computers 101, English, and math.

**KEY IDEAS**

- Capitalize proper nouns and adjectives.
- Capitalize days of the week, months, and names of holidays but not seasons.
- Capitalize titles if they come before a person's name or are used to address the person.

**TASC TEST TIP**

*Use the "proper noun" test to determine if a word should be capitalized. To capitalize, make sure the word or phrase is the name of a person, place or thing: "my uncle" is fine, and so is "Uncle Leo."*

# PRACTICE 2

**A. Directions: Correct the capitalization errors in the sentences below.**

**EXAMPLE:**

I am writing to thank the ~~S~~[s]taff of the Waterside Physical Therapy ~~c~~[C]enter.

**1.** Last Spring, I broke my arm in a car accident.

**2.** My internist, doctor claudia McNally, referred me to Waterside.

**3.** The center's Director, Ilana Harris, assigned me a physical therapist named Ellie Royce.

**4.** Ellie studied physical therapy in her native London and used british methods of treatment that relieved my pain quite effectively.

**5.** She also did therapy with me in the pool at Rainbow health club.

**6.** I finished my treatments just before labor day, and I feel 100 percent better, thanks to Ellie.

**B. Questions 7 through 9 refer to the following paragraphs.**

**An Unusual Breed**

**(A)**

(1) The Akita is a Japanese dog breed that dates to ancient times. (2) The breed has a special spiritual meaning for many. (3) For example, when a child is born, well-wishers give the family small statues of Akitas to express hopes for future happiness and health. (4) In the past, only Emperors and nobles were allowed to own this breed.

**(B)**

(5) Akitas are massive, powerful dogs, used for hunting game and guarding. (6) Starting in the 17th century, they were trained to hunt game and waterfowl in the Mountains of Japan. (7) In 1937, Akitas were brought to america by author Helen Keller.

**7. Sentence 4:** In the past, only Emperors and nobles were allowed to own this breed.

Which correction should be made to sentence 4?

A. remove the comma
B. change Emperors to emperors
C. change nobles to Nobles
D. change were to are

**8. Sentence 6:** Starting in the 17th century, they were trained to hunt game and waterfowl in the Mountains of Japan.

Which correction should be made to sentence 6?

A. change Starting to Started
B. remove the comma
C. change Mountains to mountains
D. insert a comma after game

**9. Sentence 7:** In 1937, Akitas were brought to america by author Helen Keller.

Which correction should be made to sentence 7?

A. remove the comma
B. change america to America
C. change author to Author
D. change Helen Keller to helen keller

**Review your work using the explanations that start on page 681.**

LESSON 3

# Possessives and Contractions

KEY IDEAS

- Use apostrophes with possessive nouns but not with possessive pronouns.
- Use an apostrophe to replace the missing letters in a contraction.
- To decide whether to use a possessive or contraction, test to see whether the full form of the contraction makes sense in the sentence.

TASC TEST TIP

*Contractions are acceptable in informal speech and writing. However, try to avoid them in more formal writing situations, such as the TASC essay.*

Some of the most common spelling errors involve possessives and contractions. Follow these guidelines when spelling these words:

A **possessive** shows ownership. Use apostrophes with possessive nouns. Do not use apostrophes with possessive pronouns.

**EXAMPLES**
**Possessive nouns:** friend's car Marta's map the dogs' leashes
**Possessive pronouns:** his, hers, ours, yours, theirs, its
**Correct:** The car's tires are new. The map is hers.

If a noun is singular or if it is plural but does not end in *s*, add an apostrophe + *s* to form the possessive.

**Singular possessive:** cat's boss's women's

If a noun is plural and ends in *s*, add an apostrophe after the final *s*.

**Plural possessive:** workers' ladies'

A singular possessive often sounds like a plural noun. Use an apostrophe only with the possessive.

**Correct:** My company's benefits (possessive) make it one of the best companies (plural) to work for.

A **contraction** shortens two words by combining the second word with the first and leaving out one or more letters. An apostrophe takes the place of the missing letters. Some contractions combine pronouns with verbs.

**EXAMPLES**
here is → here's there is → there's I am → I'm

Other contractions combine verbs with the word not.

**EXAMPLES**
have not → haven't do not → don't will not → won't

Be careful to use the apostrophe in place of the missing letter or letters. Notice that the correct position is not necessarily the point at which the two words come together.

**Incorrect:** You do'nt have to come with us tonight. (*do'nt* should be *don't*)

Some possessives and contractions sound the same (*your* and *you're, its* and *it's, their* and *they're*). To determine whether to use a possessive or a contraction, substitute the two words that make up the contraction. If the substitution makes sense, the contraction is correct. If not, use a possessive.

# PRACTICE 3

**A. Directions: Underline the correct word or words to complete each sentence.**

**EXAMPLE:** I'm (your, you're) downstairs neighbor, and (I've, Iv'e) been having trouble sleeping lately because of noise late at night.

1. (Theirs, There's) a noise that sounds like the thumping beat of rock music.
2. I (ca'nt, can't) be sure (who's, whose) responsible, but (its, it's) coming from your apartment.
3. My roommates and I have discussed this, and (were, we're) running out of patience.
4. You should talk to your children if the stereo is (theirs, there's).
5. Please be considerate of your neighbors just as we are considerate of (our's, ours).

**B. Questions 6 through 8 refer to the paragraphs that follow.**

**Sales Trainees Wanted**

**(A)**

(1) Do you have a warm smile? (2) Do people feel comfortable with you? (3) Do you have a friendly phone manner? (4) Do you have good organizational skills? (5) Are you good at solving problems? (6) If you've answered yes to these questions, we need you're skills at Macro Software.

**(B)**

(7) Macro Software is one of the industry leaders in software distribution. (8) In addition to our chain of stores, were proud to offer a mail order service that was the first of its kind. (9) We pride ourselves on our high-quality products, quick delivery times, and excellent customer service.

**(C)**

(10) We are currently hiring sales trainees for our Miami office. (11) Interested parties should send they're resumes to Jim Burns, Macro Software, 904 Ocean Drive, Miami, Florida.

6. **Sentence 6:** If you've answered yes to these questions, we need you're skills at Macro Software.

   Which correction should be made to sentence 6?

   A. insert a comma after yes
   B. remove the comma
   C. change need to needs
   D. replace you're with your

7. **Sentence 8:** In addition to our chain of stores, were proud to offer a mail order service that was the first of its kind.

   Which correction should be made to sentence 8?

   A. replace our with hour
   B. change were to we're
   C. insert a comma after service
   D. replace its with it's

8. **Sentence 11:** Interested parties should send they're resumes to Jim Burns, Macro Software, 904 Ocean Drive, Miami, Florida.

   Which correction should be made to sentence 11?

   A. replace parties with party's
   B. replace they're with their
   C. replace resumes with resume's
   D. replace Burns with Burn's

**Review your work using the explanations that start on page 682.**

LESSON 4

# Homonyms

**Homonyms** are words that sound alike but are spelled differently and have different meanings. The following chart lists homonyms and other commonly confused words that people often misspell.

| Word | Meaning | Word in Sentence |
|---|---|---|
| accept | to receive willingly | I accept responsibility for my actions. |
| except | excluding | Everyone went except Molly. |
| affect | to have an impact | Did the medicine affect you? |
| effect | a result | The effects will wear off soon. |
| board | a piece of wood | Nail that board to the other one. |
| bored | not interested | Rami was bored in wood shop class. |
| brake | to stop; something that stops | Put your foot on the brake! |
| break | to shatter in pieces | Be careful, or you'll break your arm. |
| close | to shut | Please close that bag. |
| clothes | something to wear | I'm going to return those clothes. |
| desert | to leave behind; arid land | Don't desert a friend in need. |
| dessert | sweet food served after dinner | They offer dessert to their guests. |
| fare | money paid by a passenger | The subway fare was just raised. |
| fair | just, right | A lot of people think it's not fair. |
| forth | forward | Let's go forth! |
| fourth | in the 4th position | It is our fourth trip in three days. |
| grate | to shred | We need to grate some potatoes. |
| great | fantastic; of large size | It's going to be a great casserole. |
| hole | opening | There's a hole in the sweater. |
| whole | entire | Soon the whole thing will fall apart. |
| know | to understand | I don't know what's wrong with him. |
| no | opposite of *yes* | He has no sense. |
| led | past of the verb *lead;* brought | He led the worker to the supply room. |
| lead | a material in pencils | They gave her some lead pencils. |
| lessen | to decrease | Will you lessen the sugar in the recipe? |
| lesson | something you learn; moral | That will teach him a lesson. |
| male | a boy or man | There are both females and males in the Army. |
| mail | to send a message through the post office; a message sent | Send the letter through the mail. |
| passed | went by | Have you passed the post office? |
| past | opposite of *future* | Yes, in the past. |
| peace | opposite of *war* | When will there be world peace? |
| piece | a part | That's only a piece of the problem. |
| principal | head of a school | The principal has called a meeting. |
| principle | a guiding rule; a moral | He has no principles. |
| than | compared with | I used to have more money than you. |
| then | after that; at that time | Then I spent most of mine. |
| there | at that place | The car is over there. |
| their | belonging to them | It is their car. |
| they're | they are | They're going to sell it. |
| to | indicates a direction | Go to the grocery store. |
| too | also, in addition | Sharmaine will go, too. |
| two | the number 2 | Buy me two loaves of bread. |

**KEY IDEAS**

Homonyms are words that sound the same but have different spellings and different meanings.

**TASC TEST TIP**

*Possessives, contractions, and homonyms are the kinds of spelling items that appear on the TASC Writing Test. Study the ones that give you problems.*

# PRACTICE 4

**A. Directions: Underline the correct word or words to complete each sentence.**

**EXAMPLE:** The chairman of the (board, bored) has called this meeting.

1. This is our (fourth, forth) meeting on the topic of funding.
2. We don't (no, know) any other sources of funding.
3. The director of the organization brought up this (whole, hole) issue.
4. Next (weak, week), we plan to submit a proposal.
5. We worry that a request for funding may (affect, effect) our nonprofit status.
6. In the (past, passed), we could rely on government funding.

**B. Questions 7 through 9 refer to the paragraphs that follow.**

**Equal Pay for Equal Work?**

**(A)**

(1) In 1963, women earned only 59 percent of the wages men earned. (2) In 1997, the figure was still just 74 percent. (3) Women have logged great achievements in the workforce, so why don't they receive fare pay?

**(B)**

(4) One explanation is that the statistics include older women. (5) In principal, the age gap could account for the wage gap because older women still work in jobs in which attitudes and conditions of the past prevail. (6) In contrast, women under the age of 25 earn about 92 percent of what men earn. (7) However, upon closer examination, this theory falls flat. (8) Women in entry-level jobs have always earned salaries similar to those of their male peers. (9) The problem is that women don't receive the same raises and promotions that men get. (10) The affect is that, as women get older, the gap between men's and women's salaries becomes greater.

**STUDY ADVICE**

Homonyms can be tricky. If you are unsure whether you are using the correct word during your practice, be sure to look it up in a dictionary afterward. If you are unsure when writing an essay on Test Day, try to pick a completely different word to avoid an error.

7. **Sentence 3:** Women have logged great achievements in the workforce, so why don't they receive fare pay?

   Which correction should be made to sentence 3?

   A. change have to has
   B. replace great with grate
   C. replace fare with fair
   D. replace Women with Woman

8. **Sentence 5:** In principal, the age gap could account for the wage gap because older women still work in jobs in which attitudes and conditions of the past prevail.

   Which correction should be made to sentence 5?

   A. change principal to principle
   B. change work to working
   C. replace past with passed
   D. replace for with four

9. **Sentence 10:** The affect is that, as women get older, the gap between men's and women's salaries becomes greater.

   Which correction should be made to sentence 10?

   A. replace affect with effect
   B. change becomes to become
   C. replace greater with grater
   D. remove the comma after that

**Review your work using the explanations that start on page 682.**

## USING WRITING MECHANICS PRACTICE QUESTIONS

**Questions 1 through 5 refer to the following paragraphs.**

**Single Parents and Relationships**

**(A)**

(1) Children of single parents don't exactly cheer their parents on at the start of a new relationship. (2) Instead, children may have tantrums erase phone messages, and generally try to ruin their parents' chances. (3) If you are a parent in this situation, you need to understand, and show your children that you love them. (4) However, also let your kids know, that you feel you're doing the right thing.

**(B)**

(5) Your children may become quickly attached to a new date, even within the course of an evening. (6) Alternatively, they may fear that you plan to marry each potential partner you bring home. (7) For these reasons, it makes sense not to introduce all your dates to your children. (8) Try to see your dates at times when your children are'nt at home.

**(C)**

(9) Once you become committed to a particular person, it's important to include your partner in family events gradually. (10) Don't be surprised if your children have a negative reaction to your new partner. (11) This time may be difficult for your kids. (12) They're not used to seeing you with a new partner, and they may be realizing that a reconciliation with your ex-spouse is impossible. (13) If communication breaks down consider family counseling. (14) Children may be more willing to share their worries and complaints in that setting.

1. Sentence 2: **Instead, children may have tantrums erase phone messages, and generally try to ruin their parents' chances.**

   Which correction should be made to sentence 2?

   A. remove the comma after Instead
   B. insert a comma after tantrums
   C. change their to they're
   D. change have to has

2. Sentence 3: **If you are a parent in this situation, you need to understand, and show your children that you love them.**

   Which is the best way to write the underlined portion of this sentence?

   A. understand, and showing
   B. understand. And show
   C. understand and show
   D. understand, and you show

3. Sentence 4: **However, also let your kids know, that you feel you're doing the right thing.**

   Which correction should be made to sentence 4?

   A. remove the comma after However
   B. replace your with you're
   C. replace you're with your
   D. remove the comma after know

4. Sentence 8: **Try to see your dates at times when your children are'nt at home.**

   Which correction should be made to sentence 8?

   A. replace your with you're
   B. insert a comma after times
   C. change are'nt to aren't
   D. change are'nt to isn't

5. Sentence 13: **If communication breaks down consider family counseling.**

   Which is the best way to write the underlined portion of this sentence?

   A. down will consider
   B. down, consider
   C. down. Consider
   D. down, and consider

Questions 6 through 10 refer to the following paragraphs.

### The History of Daylight Saving Time

**(A)**

(1) We set our clocks forward every spring and back every fall, but few of us stop to think about why we do this. (2) One of the main reasons for daylight saving time, is to save energy. (3) In the evening, we use lights, TVs, and electrical appliances. (4) Daylight saving time makes the period between sunset and bedtime one hour shorter, and therefore less electricity is used.

**(B)**

(5) With daylight saving time, each time zone changes it's standard time by an hour. (6) Time zones were introduced by the railroads to make schedules standard across the country. (7) In 1918, congress passed a law making the rail time zones official. (8) That same year, a second law put the country on daylight saving time for the rest of World War I. (9) The law was unpopular, however, and it was repealed seven months later. (10) Daylight saving time was also in force during most of World War II.

**(C)**

(11) From 1945 to 1966, each state and town could decide whether to observe daylight saving time. (12) The resulting inconsistencies created a great deal of confusion. (13) For example radio and TV stations had to put out new schedules every time a state started or ended daylight saving time. (14) Then came the Uniform Time Act of 1966, which established starting and ending dates for daylight saving time, in the spring and fall. (15) This law was amended in1986, when the starting date was moved almost a month earlier to save energy.

6. Sentence 2: **One of the main reasons for daylight saving time, is to save energy.**

   Which correction should be made to sentence 2?

   A. insert a comma after reasons
   B. remove the comma
   C. change is to are
   D. change main to mane

7. Sentence 5: **With daylight saving time, each time zone changes it's standard time by an hour.**

   Which correction should be made to sentence 5?

   A. remove the comma
   B. replace it's with its
   C. replace hour with our
   D. insert a comma after standard time

8. Sentence 7: **In 1918, congress passed a law making the rail time zones official.**

   Which correction should be made to sentence 7?

   A. remove the comma
   B. change congress to Congress
   C. replace passed with past
   D. change making to made

9. Sentence 13: **For example radio and TV stations had to put out new schedules every time a state started or ended daylight saving time.**

   Which correction should be made to sentence 13?

   A. insert a comma after example
   B. change had to have
   C. change schedules to schedule's
   D. insert a comma after schedules

10. Sentence 14: **Then came the Uniform Time Act of 1966, which established starting and ending dates for daylight saving time, in the spring and fall.**

    Which correction should be made to sentence 14?

    A. change Act to act
    B. replace dates with date's
    C. remove the comma after time
    D. change spring and fall to Spring and Fall

**Questions 11 through 15 refer to the following paragraphs.**

### Rules and Regulations

**(A)**

(1) Thank you for joining Spring Valley Community center. (2) Before using our facility, please read these rules and regulations carefully.

**(B)**

(3) Please have your membership card with you at all times when your in the building. (4) When you enter the pool or exercise room, a security guard will request to see your card and will deny you entrance without it.

**(C)**

(5) Guests are welcome to use the pool and exercise room, but only when accompanied by members. (6) The guest fee is $10 per day. (7) When bringing guests, please have them sign in at the desk in the lobby. (8) They will be given a guest card for the day.

**(D)**

(9) Pool safety is very important. (10) If you are a week swimmer, life jackets and other flotation devices are available for your use. (11) Do not hesitate to ask lifeguards for help. (12) Children under the age of 12 must swim in the children's pool, unless they're supervised by an adult. (13) Swimming classes are available to help both children and adults improve their skills.

**(E)**

(14) You must register, and pay for any class you wish to take. (15) Members receive a significant discount. (16) Registration may be limited to a certain number of participants.

11. Sentence 1: **Thank you for joining Spring Valley Community center.**

    Which correction should be made to sentence 1?

    A. insert a comma after you
    B. change Community to community
    C. change center to Center
    D. change you to You

12. Sentence 3: **Please have your membership card with you at all times when your in the building.**

    Which correction should be made to sentence 3?

    A. insert a comma after Please
    B. replace have your with have you're
    C. replace times with times'
    D. replace when your with when you're

13. Sentence 10: **If you are a week swimmer, life jackets and other flotation devices are available for your use.**

    Which correction should be made to sentence 10?

    A. replace week with weak
    B. remove the comma
    C. insert a comma after available
    D. change your to you're

14. Sentence 12: **Children under the age of 12 must swim in the children's pool, unless they're supervised by an adult.**

    Which correction should be made to sentence 12?

    A. insert commas after Children and 12
    B. change children's with childrens'
    C. replace they're to their
    D. remove the comma after pool

15. Sentence 14: **You must register, and pay for any class you wish to take.**

    Which is the best way to write the underlined portion of this sentence?

    A. register, pay
    B. register and pay
    C. register. And pay
    D. register. Pay

Questions 16 through 20 refer to the following paragraphs.

### Racial Profiling

**(A)**

(1) African American and Hispanic motorists are much more likely to be stopped by police then their white counterparts, often for no apparent reason. (2) What's their offense? (3) It may be that these individuals have been targeted because of their race.

**(B)**

(4) Blacks and Hispanics, who some police officers believe are more likely to commit crimes, have been systematically targeted by police. (5) Police statistics from 23 states show that this policy, called racial profiling occurs in every geographic location. (6) Motorists, pedestrians, and airline passengers have been searched. (7) The police do not make class distinctions for nonwhites of every station in life have been victims of this practice.

**(C)**

(8) The statistical evidence shows a clear pattern. (9) On one Maryland highway, 73 percent of those stopped by police were African American, even though blacks represented only 17 percent of all drivers. (10) Hispanics make up only 8 percent of the population in illinois, yet 30 percent of drivers stopped there are Hispanic. (11) However, police superintendents chiefs of police, and other law enforcement officials dispute the studies that document racial profiling. (12) They maintain that the problem has been confined to a small number of officers and can be remedied easily.

16. Sentence 1: **African American and Hispanic motorists are much more likely to be stopped by police then their white counterparts, often for no apparent reason.**

    Which correction should be made to sentence 1?

    A. change motorists to Motorists
    B. insert a comma after then
    C. replace then with than
    D. replace for with four

17. Sentence 5: **Police statistics from 23 states show that this policy, called racial profiling occurs in every geographic location.**

    Which correction should be made to sentence 5?

    A. change states to States
    B. insert a comma after states
    C. insert a comma after profiling
    D. remove the comma

18. Sentence 7: **The police do not make class distinctions for nonwhites of every station in life have been victims of this practice.**

    Which is the best way to write the underlined portion of this sentence?

    A. distinctions. For nonwhites
    B. distinctions, for nonwhites
    C. distinctions moreover nonwhites
    D. distinctions nonwhites

19. Sentence 10: **Hispanics make up only 8 percent of the population in illinois, yet 30 percent of drivers stopped there are Hispanic.**

    Which correction should be made to sentence 10?

    A. change make to makes
    B. change illinois to Illinois
    C. remove the comma
    D. replace yet with and

20. Sentence 11: **However, police superintendents chiefs of police, and other law enforcement officials dispute the studies that document racial profiling.**

    Which correction should be made to sentence 11?

    A. remove the comma after However
    B. insert a comma after superintendents
    C. insert a comma after officials
    D. change studies to studies'

**Review your work using the explanations that start on page 682.**

UNIT 3

ABOUT THE TEST

# Mathematics

The TASC Mathematics Test assesses your ability to reason with numbers. On the Mathematics Test, you will have 105 minutes to answer approximately 52 questions. You will spend 50 minutes answering questions with the aid of calculator and 55 minutes answering questions for which you may not use a calculator. Questions on this test will target skills such as:

- Performing number operations to solve problems
- Solving word problems
- Understanding proportions and percentages
- Interpreting graphic representations of data
- Finding averages
- Understanding and performing operations with algebraic expressions
- Solving linear and quadratic equations
- Solving problems using geometric formulas

On the 2014 TASC, most of those questions will be multiple choice. Some of the questions will ask you to bubble a numerical answer into the grid below:

| | | | | |
|---|---|---|---|---|
| | / | / | / | |
| . | . | . | . | . |
| 0 | 0 | 0 | 0 | 0 |
| 1 | 1 | 1 | 1 | 1 |
| 2 | 2 | 2 | 2 | 2 |
| 3 | 3 | 3 | 3 | 3 |
| 4 | 4 | 4 | 4 | 4 |
| 5 | 5 | 5 | 5 | 5 |
| 6 | 6 | 6 | 6 | 6 |
| 7 | 7 | 7 | 7 | 7 |
| 8 | 8 | 8 | 8 | 8 |
| 9 | 9 | 9 | 9 | 9 |

You will learn how to fill in this grid beginning on page 252 of this unit.

The Mathematics Test will have two parts, which will be timed separately, with a 15-minute break between them. On one part, you will not be allowed to use a calculator. On the other part, you may use a calculator. As of the time of this writing, TASC had not yet determined how many questions or how many minutes will be allotted to those two sections.

## Tools

On the TASC Mathematics Test, two tools will be available to you to help you answer questions.

***Calculator:*** Whether you take the paper or computer versions of the TASC, you will have access to a scientific calculator for part of the Mathematics Test. See the next page for more information. You will learn how to use the calculator starting on page 238 of this unit.

*Formula sheet:* You will also be provided with a two-page formula sheet that lists common mathematical formulas. Become familiar with this sheet, which is reproduced on pages 230–231. If a formula is discussed in this book but not listed on the formula sheet, you will need to memorize it.*

**TASC TEST TIP**

*You are encouraged to purchase a hand-held version of the calculator you will use on Test Day for practice as you work through this book. You can buy one at office or school supply stores or online.*

# About Calculators

If you take the computer version of the TASC, you will have access to an onscreen version of the Texas Instruments TI-30XS MultiView™ calculator. For more information on using the online calculator, see page 228.

If you are taking the paper version of the test, there are a variety of calculators that will be acceptable to use. Please check your state's guidelines before you purchase a calculator for your practice. While the test maker has decided that all of the following calculators are acceptable, each individual state has the right to limit this list and your state might have done so. Once you have determined which calculators are allowed in your state, choose which one will work best for you and start practicing with it right away. The calculator options are listed here.

## TI-30XS MultiView™

On this calculator, you use the white numeric keypad to enter numbers, the decimal point, and the negative sign (–) for a negative number such as –213. The operation keys, on the right, allow you to add, subtract, multiply, and divide. The four arrows at the top right of the calculator allow you to move the onscreen cursor up, down, left, or right as needed. The delete key to the left of the arrows allows you to correct mistakes as you work.

The following Casio® calculators have the same basic key functions as the TI-30XS MultiView™, but some of the keys are in different locations and/or have slightly different symbolic representation for various functions. For example, the Casio® calculators use an "equals" key, whereas the TI-30XS MultiView™ has a button that says "enter", which performs the same function.

- **Casio FX-115ES PLUS**
- **Casio FX-115MS PLUS**
- **Casio FX-300ES PLUS**

## TI-30Xa™

This calculator has the same basic key functions as the TI-30XS MultiView™ with some distinct differences. The screen does not show as much information and there are no arrows to move your cursor within the display and thus correct work you have previously entered. Additionally, while all basic key functions are present, some of them are in different locations and/or have slightly different symbolic representation on the keys. This calculator is battery powered.

The following calculator has the same basic key functions as the TI-30Xa™ but some of the keys are in different locations and/or have slightly different symbolic representations.

- **Casio FX-260 Solar**

* Note: The information given here was the latest information available as of January 2014. It is possible that timing restrictions or the content of the formula sheet may change between this printing and your test date. For updates, visit www.tasctest.com.

### HP 35s Scientific Calculator

This calculator defaults to Reverse Polish Notation, which is different from the algebraic notation you are likely used to entering when using a handheld calculator. However, the user does have the ability to switch to algebraic data entry. As with the other calculators in this section, the same basic key functions are present, but some of the keys are in different places and/or have slightly different symbols to represent various functions.

Because we know that the TI-30XS MultiView™ is the calculator used for the computer test, and because it is one of the calculators that you may use on the paper test, you will see practice tips for using this calculator throughout the Mathematics unit. (See, for example, pages 229–229.) Please practice using your chosen calculator to gain familiarity with what you will see on Test Day. Remember: You do not have to use the calculator to solve problems; only use it if it is relevant to the problem or if you believe it will be helpful.

# A Note about the Mathematics Reference Sheet

On the next two pages, you will find mathematical formulas that will be provided to you on Test Day. The test maker has developed this formula sheet with a view toward changes they plan to implement in 2015 and 2016. Thus, there are topics on the Mathematics Reference Sheet that will likely not be tested on the 2014 TASC.* One such topic is trigonometry (trigonometric formulas appear in the bottom-right section of the first page of the formula sheet). At the time of this printing, limited information was available regarding which other topics from the formula sheet will not be tested in 2014. Kaplan's book reflects our estimates regarding material you will be required to know if you are testing in 2014. For updates, visit www.tasctest.com.

***Do not*** attempt to absorb and memorize these formulas here and now. Skip to page 232 to begin your math studies. Periodically you will refer back to these pages as you work through practice problems.

*Note: The information provided here is based on the latest updates available from the test maker as of early January 2014. The makers of the TASC may have introduced changes since the time of this publication. Visit www.tasctest.com for updates.

# MATHEMATICS REFERENCE SHEET

**Volume**

Cylinder: $V = \pi r^2 h$

Pyramid: $V = \frac{1}{3}Bh$

Cone: $V = \frac{1}{3}\pi r^2 h$

Sphere: $V = \frac{4}{3}\pi r^3$

**Coordinate Geometry**

Midpoint formula:

$$\left(\frac{x_1 + x_2}{2}, \frac{y_1 + y_2}{2}\right)$$

Distance formula:

$$d = \sqrt{(x_2 - x_1)^2 + (y_2 - y_1)^2}$$

Slope: $m = \frac{y_2 - y_1}{x_2 - x_1}, x_2 \neq x_1$

**Special Factoring**

$a^2 - b^2 = (a - b)(a + b)$

$a^2 + 2ab + b^2 = (a + b)^2$

$a^2 - 2ab + b^2 = (a - b)^2$

$a^3 + b^3 = (a + b)(a^2 - ab + b^2)$

$a^3 - b^3 = (a - b)(a^2 + ab + b^2)$

**Quadratic Formula**

For $ax^2 + bx + c = 0$

$$x = \frac{-b \pm \sqrt{b^2 - 4ac}}{2a}$$

**Interest**

Simple interest Formula:
$I = prt$

Interest Formula (compounded $n$ times per year):

$$A = p\left(1 + \frac{r}{n}\right)^{nt}$$

$A$ = Amount after $t$ years.

$p$ = principal

$r$ = annual interest rate

$t$ = time in years

$I$ = Interest

**Trigonometric Identities**

Pythagorean Theorem: $a^2 + b^2 = c^2$

$$\sin\theta = \frac{opp}{hyp}$$

$$\cos\theta = \frac{adj}{hyp}$$

$$\tan\theta = \frac{opp}{adj}$$

$$\sin^2\theta + \cos^2\theta = 1$$

$$Density = \frac{Mass}{Volume}$$

**Central Angle**

$m\angle AOB = m\overset{\frown}{AB}$

**Inscribed Angle**

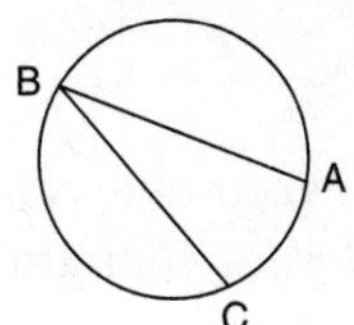


$m\angle ABC = \frac{1}{2} m\overset{\frown}{AC}$

**Intersecting Chords Theorem**

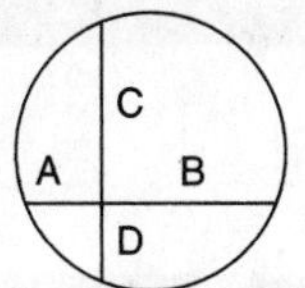


$A \cdot B = C \cdot D$

**Probability**

Permutations: ${}_nP_r = \frac{n!}{(n-r)!}$

Combinations: ${}_nC_r = \frac{n!}{(n-r)!r!}$

Multiplication rule (independent events): $P(A \text{ and } B) = P(A) \cdot P(B)$

Multiplication rule (general): $P(A \text{ and } B) = P(A) \cdot P(B)$

Addition rule: $P(A \text{ or } B) = P(A) + P(B) - P(A \text{ and } B)$

Conditional Probability: $P(B|A) = \frac{p(A \text{ and } B)}{p(A)}$

Arithmetic Sequence: $a_n = a_1 + (n-1)d$ where $a_n$ is the $n$th term, $a_1$ is the first term, and $d$ is the common difference.

Geometric Sequence: $a_n = a_1 r^{(n-1)}$ where $a_n$ is the $n$th term, $a_1$ is the first term, and $r$ is the common ratio.

# Number and Quantity Part I: Problem Solving

LESSON 1

## Compare and Order Numbers

KEY IDEAS

- When ordering numbers, compare the same place values between numbers.
- Round numbers to estimate answers or eliminate answer choices in multiple-choice questions.

TASC TEST TIP

*It's important to know the inequality symbols below.*
*< means "is less than"*
*≤ means "is less than or equal to"*
*> means "is greater than"*
*≥ means "is greater than or equal to"*

### Place Value

Numbers are part of your everyday life. Whether you're paying with cash, reading bus schedules, or changing television channels, you're using whole numbers.

The value of a number depends on the **place value** of its digits. On the place-value chart below, note that the value of a digit increases as you move to the left.

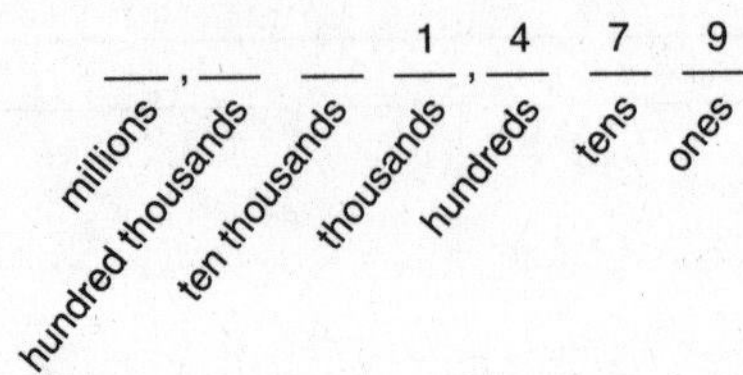


In the whole number shown on the chart, 1 has the greatest value. The number would be read as "one thousand four hundred seventy-nine."

### Comparing and Ordering Values

To **order** numbers, you need to compare the value of their digits. Align the place values of the numbers you are comparing. Start at the left and compare the value of the first digit of each number.

**Example 1:** Place the numbers 342, 98, and 317 in order from least to greatest.

1. Compare the first digit in each number. Since 98 is a two-digit number, and the other numbers are three-digit numbers, 98 has the smallest value.
2. Next, compare the first digit of the remaining numbers. Since both numbers have the same digit (3) in the hundreds place, compare the digits in the tens place. Since 1 is less than 4, 317 is less than 342.

hundreds tens ones

342
98
317

From least to greatest: **98, 317, 342**

### Rounding Numbers

Place value is also essential to **rounding** numbers.

**Example 2:** Round 2451 to the nearest hundred.

1. Locate the place value that you want to round to. Then look at the place value to the right. If the digit to the right is 5 or greater, round up. If the digit to the right is less than 5, then don't change the number in the hundreds place.
2. Round up the digit in the hundreds place. Then change the digits to the right of the hundreds place to zeros.

2451

The value to the right of the hundreds place is a 5. Round up.

2451 rounds up to **2500**

# PRACTICE 1

**A. Write the digit from the number below that corresponds to the listed place value. The first one is done for you.**

1,436,879

_4_ **1.** hundred thousands

____ **2.** hundreds

____ **3.** ones

____ **4.** millions

____ **5.** thousands

____ **6.** tens

____ **7.** ten thousands

**B. Round these numbers as directed.**

**8.** Round 544 to the nearest hundred.

**9.** Round 76 to the nearest ten.

**10.** Round 1058 to the nearest hundred.

**11.** Round 11,632 to the nearest thousand.

**12.** Round 1525 to the nearest thousand.

**13.** Round 84 to the nearest hundred.

**C. In each of the following pairs, which number is greater?**

**14.** 100 or 89

**15.** 339 or 341

**16.** 1099 or 1145

**17.** 125,391 or 119,450

**D. Write these numbers in order from least to greatest.**

**18.** 23 18 45 39

**19.** 111 89 109 91

**20.** 1087 932 909 1139

**21.** 1429 1420 1432 1425

**22.** 12,071 11,098 12,131

**23.** 15,356 15,309 15,298

**E. Choose the one best answer to each question.**

**24.** When stacking items, the heaviest items should be placed at the bottom. Starting at the bottom, in what order should items weighing 45 pounds, 40 pounds, 50 pounds, and 48 pounds be stacked?

A. 40, 45, 48, 50
B. 45, 50, 40, 48
C. 50, 48, 45, 40
D. 50, 40, 45, 48

**25.** Which of the following correctly shows 1,543,976 rounded to the nearest hundred thousand?

A. 2,000,000
B. 1,600,000
C. 1,500,000
D. 1,540,000

**Review your work using the explanations that start on page 683.**

**STUDY ADVICE**

Not a math person? Have no fear! The math concepts tested on the TASC Mathematics Test are covered in this book; you just need to plan your study schedule to include plenty of time to master these topics.

LESSON 2

# Whole Number Operations

## Addition and Subtraction

You use **addition** when you need to combine amounts. The answer in an addition problem is called the **sum,** or **total.** When you are adding, it's helpful to stack the numbers in a column. Be sure to line up the place-value columns and then work from right to left, starting with the ones column.

Sometimes the digits in a place-value column add up to 10 or more. When this happens, you will need to **regroup** to the next place value.

**Example 1:** Add 40 + 129 + 24.

1. Align the numbers you want to add on the ones column. Working from right to left, add the ones column first. Since the ones column totals 13, write the 3 in the ones column and regroup, or **carry**, the 1 ten to the tens column.

$$\begin{array}{r} {}^{1}\phantom{0} \\ 40 \\ 129 \\ +\ 24 \\ \hline 3 \end{array}$$

2. Add the tens column, including the regrouped 1.

$$\begin{array}{r} {}^{1}\phantom{0} \\ 40 \\ 129 \\ +\ 24 \\ \hline 93 \end{array}$$

3. Then add the hundreds column. Since there is only one value, write the 1 hundred in the answer.

$$\begin{array}{r} {}^{1}\phantom{0} \\ 40 \\ 129 \\ +\ 24 \\ \hline \mathbf{193} \end{array}$$

You **subtract** when you want to find the **difference** between amounts. Write the greater number on top, and align the amounts on the ones column. You may also need to regroup as you subtract.

**Example 2:** If Sue is 57 and Kathy is 38, how many years older is Sue?

1. Find the difference in their ages. Start with the ones column. Since 7 is less than the number being subtracted (8), regroup, or **borrow**, 1 ten from the tens column. Add the regrouped amount to the ones column. Now subtract $17 - 8$ in the ones column.

$$\begin{array}{r} {}^{4\,17} \\ \not{5}\not{7} \\ -\ 38 \\ \hline 9 \end{array}$$

2. Regrouping 1 ten from the tens column left 4 tens. Subtract $4 - 3$ and write the result in the tens column of your answer. Check: $19 + 38 = 57$.

$$\begin{array}{r} {}^{4\,17} \\ \not{5}\not{7} \\ -\ 38 \\ \hline \mathbf{19} \end{array}$$

Sue is **19 years older** than Kathy.

### KEY IDEAS

- Add when combining amounts and subtract when finding the difference.
- Align place-value columns when adding or subtracting.
- Always look to the next place-value column to regroup.

### TASC TEST TIP

*Another way to check answers is to round the numbers in a problem and find an approximate answer.*

# PRACTICE 2.1

**Example 3:** Find the difference between 205 and 67.

1. Subtract. Start with the ones column. Since 5 is less than the number being subtracted (7), regroup. Since there are 0 tens in the tens column, regroup 1 hundred from the hundreds column. From 10 tens, regroup 1 ten to the ones column. Now subtract 15 − 7 in the ones column.

$$\begin{array}{r} 9\phantom{\ 15} \\ 1\ \cancel{10}\ 15 \\ \cancel{2}\ \cancel{0}\ \cancel{5} \\ -\ 6\ 7 \\ \hline 8 \end{array}$$

2. Regrouping 1 ten from the tens column left 9 tens. Subtract 9 − 6, and write the result in the tens column of your answer.

$$\begin{array}{r} 9\phantom{\ 15} \\ 1\ \cancel{10}\ 15 \\ \cancel{2}\ \cancel{0}\ \cancel{5} \\ -\ 6\ 7 \\ \hline 3\ 8 \end{array}$$

3. Regrouping 1 hundred from the hundreds column left 1 hundred. Subtract the hundreds column: 1 − 0. Check: 138 + 67 = 205.

$$\begin{array}{r} 9\phantom{\ 15} \\ 1\ \cancel{10}\ 15 \\ \cancel{2}\ \cancel{0}\ \cancel{5} \\ -\ 6\ 7 \\ \hline \mathbf{1\ 3\ 8} \end{array}$$

---

**A. Solve.**

1. $\begin{array}{r} 54 \\ +23 \\ \hline \end{array}$

3. $\begin{array}{r} 73 \\ -21 \\ \hline \end{array}$

5. $\begin{array}{r} 105 \\ +85 \\ \hline \end{array}$

7. $\begin{array}{r} 100 \\ -57 \\ \hline \end{array}$

2. $\begin{array}{r} 46 \\ +54 \\ \hline \end{array}$

4. $\begin{array}{r} 55 \\ -19 \\ \hline \end{array}$

6. $\begin{array}{r} 2386 \\ +1692 \\ \hline \end{array}$

8. $\begin{array}{r} 2500 \\ -383 \\ \hline \end{array}$

**B. Rewrite the problems in columns before solving.**

9. 20 + 12 + 33 =
10. 245 − 131 =
11. 30 + 75 + 75 =
12. 378 − 85 =
13. 144 + 238 + 101 =
14. 545 − 89 =
15. 2095 + 324 =
16. 1250 − 350 =
17. 10,326 + 982 =
18. 15,890 − 705 =
19. 108,755 + 22,442 =
20. 44,789 − 13,890 =

**C. Choose the <u>one best answer</u> to each question.**

21. What is the total weight of the boxes below?

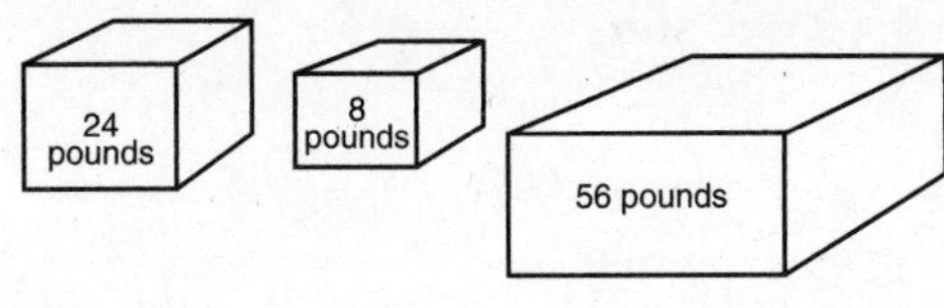


A. 78
B. 88
C. 150
D. 160

22. Celia's share for lunch is $7. If she pays with a $20 bill, how much change should she get?

A. $3
B. $7
C. $13
D. $27

**Review your work using the explanations that start on page 683.**

## Multiplication and Division

You **multiply** to combine the same amount multiple times. For example, instead of adding $24 + 24 + 24$, you could multiply 24 by 3. If a problem asks you to find the **product** of two or more numbers, you should multiply.

**Example 4:** Find the product of 24 and 63.

1. Align place values as you rewrite the problem in a column. Multiply the ones place of the top number by the ones place of the bottom number: $4 \times 3 = 12$. Write the 2 in the ones place in the first partial product. Regroup the 1 ten.

$$\begin{array}{r} ^{1} \\ 24 \\ \times 63 \\ \hline 2 \end{array}$$

2. Multiply the tens place in the top number by 3: $2 \times 3 = 6$. Then add the regrouped amount: $6 + 1 = 7$. Write the 7 in the tens place in the partial product.

$$\begin{array}{r} ^{1} \\ 24 \\ \times 63 \\ \hline 2 \end{array}$$

3. Now multiply by the tens place of 63. Write a **placeholder** 0 in the ones place in the second partial product, since you're really multiplying by 60. Then multiply the top number by 6: $4 \times 6 = 24$. Write 4 in the partial product and regroup the 2. Multiply $2 \times 6 = 12$. Add the regrouped 2: $12 + 2 = 14$.

$$\begin{array}{r} ^{2} \\ 24 \\ \times 63 \\ \hline 72 \\ 1440 \\ \hline \mathbf{1512} \end{array}$$

4. Add the partial products to find the total product: $72 + 1440 =$ **1512**.

To **divide** means to find how many equal parts an amount can be divided into. The amount being divided is called the **dividend.** The number you are dividing by is the **divisor,** and the answer to a division problem is the **quotient.**

**Example 5:** At a garage sale, 3 children sold their old toys for a total of \$54. If they share the money equally, how much money should each child receive?

1. Divide the total amount (\$54) by the number of ways the money is to be split (3). Work from left to right. How many times does 3 go into 5? Write the answer 1 directly above the 5 in the dividend. Since $3 \times 1 = 3$, subtract $5 - 3 = 2$.

$$\begin{array}{r} 1\phantom{4} \\ 3\overline{)\$54} \\ -3\phantom{4} \\ \hline 2\phantom{4} \end{array}$$

2. Continue dividing. Bring down the 4 from the ones place in the dividend. How many times does 3 go into 24? Write the answer 8 directly above the 4 in the dividend. Since $3 \times 8 = 24$, subtract $24 - 24 = 0$.

   Each child should receive **\$18.**

$$\begin{array}{r} 18 \\ 3\overline{)\$54} \\ -3\phantom{4} \\ \hline 24 \\ -24 \\ \hline 0 \end{array}$$

**Example 6:** Divide $1006 \div 4$.

1. Divide the total amount (1006) by 4. Work from left to right. Since 4 doesn't divide into 1, use the next place value in the dividend. How many times does 4 go into 10? Write the answer 2 directly above the first 0 in the dividend. Since $4 \times 2 = 8$, subtract $10 - 8 = \mathbf{2}$.

$$\begin{array}{r} 2\phantom{06} \\ 4\overline{)1006} \\ -8\phantom{06} \\ \hline 2\phantom{06} \end{array}$$

# PRACTICE 2.2

2. Continue dividing. Bring down the 0 from the tens place in the dividend. How many times does 4 go into 20? Write the answer 5 directly above the second 0 in the dividend. Since 4 × 5 = 20, subtract 20 − 20 = 0. Bring down the 6 from the ones place in the dividend. How many times does 4 go into 6? Write the answer 1 above the 6 in the dividend. Since 4 × 1 = 4, subtract 6 − 4 = 2. Write the **remainder** of 2 as part of the quotient.

```
   251 r2
4)1006
 -8
  20
 -20
   06
   -4
    2
```

By reviewing and memorizing multiplication tables, you can save yourself precious time on the TASC Mathematics Test.

---

**A. Solve.**

**1.** 121 × 4

**2.** 250 × 4

**3.** 342 × 8

**4.** $5\overline{)65}$

**5.** $7\overline{)735}$

**6.** $9\overline{)189}$

**7.** 45 × 30

**8.** 105 × 25

**9.** 211 × 16

**10.** $10\overline{)280}$

**11.** $15\overline{)225}$

**12.** $19\overline{)114}$

**B. Solve. If multiplying more than two numbers, find the product of two numbers before multiplying by the next number, and so on.**

**13.** 50 × 5 =

**14.** 179 ÷ 4 =

**15.** 5 × 6 × 10 =

**16.** 1004 ÷ 5 =

**17.** 25 × 3 × 2 =

**18.** 7452 × 9 =

**19.** 10,760 ÷ 20 =

**20.** 12 × 8 × 4 =

**21.** 144,140 ÷ 12 =

**C. Choose the one best answer to each question.**

**22.** A fruit juice container holds 16 servings. If the serving size is 6 ounces, how many ounces does the container hold in all?

A. 10
B. 22
C. 76
D. 96

**23.** A cashier has fifteen $5 bills. How much does he have in $5 bills?

A. $15
B. $25
C. $75
D. $150

**24.** How many 2-foot lengths can be cut from the string shown below?

12 ft

A. 2
B. 6
C. 12
D. 24

**Review your work using the explanations that start on page 683.**

# Number and Quantity Part I: Problem Solving

## LESSON 3

# TASC Test Calculator Skills

If you take the paper version of the TASC, you will be able to use a handheld scientific calculator. See page 228 for more information on the various calculator options for the paper-and-pencil test. If you take the computer version of the TASC, you will have access to an on-screen version of the Texas Instruments TI-30XS MultiView™. Whenever the word *Calculator* appears on the screen, you can click on that link to open the calculator. If necessary, use your mouse to move the calculator so that it does not cover the problem. When you are finished with a calculation, click on the *X* at the top of the window to close the calculator.

Some things to keep in mind when using the TI-30XS MultiView™:

- When you are finished with a calculation, use the enter button. (There is no "equals sign" button on this calculator.)
- Every time you begin a calculation, press the clear button above the operation keys to clear the calculator's memory.

Look at the reproduction of the calculator below and follow the examples that demonstrate how to use the calculator's **operation keys**.

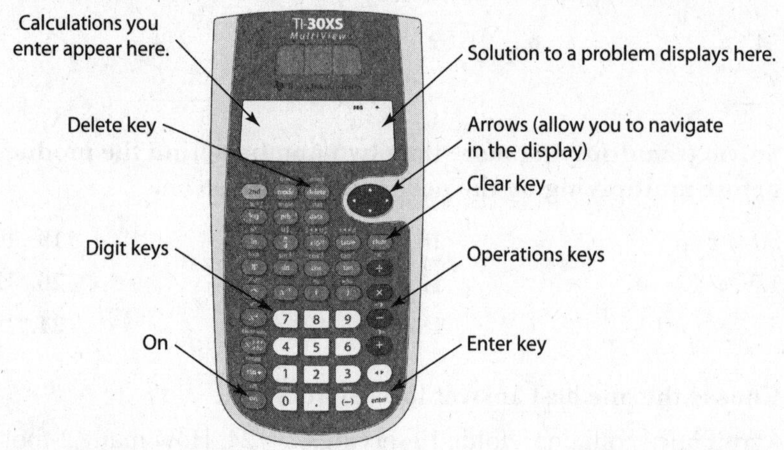


**Example 1:** Add 63 + 97 + 58 + 32 + 81.

1. Always clear a calculator before starting a new computation. On the TI-30XS MultiView™, use the *clear* key. — (clear)
2. Enter each number followed by the plus sign. As you type, the numbers and plus signs will appear on the calculator's screen. If you make a mistake, press *delete* to go back and reenter a number. — 63 (+) 97 (+) 58 (+) 32 (+) 81
3. Press *enter* to find the total. — (enter)

The total, **331**, will appear on the right-hand side of the display: — **331**

### KEY IDEAS

- Practice questions in this book with the calculator you will use on Test Day. This lesson discusses the calculator used on the computer version of the TASC.
- Use the calculator when you think it will save you time or improve your accuracy.
- Learn the placement of the keys and how to perform specific functions before you take the test.

### TASC TEST TIP

*You can buy a handheld TI-30XS MultiView™ calculator for practice as you work through this study guide. It may be available at online retailers, at office supply stores, or other places where calculators are sold.*

# PRACTICE 3.1

**Example 2:** Find the difference between 15,789 and 9,332.

1. Always clear a calculator before starting a new computation. — clear
2. Enter the greater number first, followed by the minus operator. NOTE: Use the minus key that is on the right side of the calculator with the other operation symbols. Don't use the (–) key at the bottom of the calculator; that key is used to enter a negative number. — 15789 (–)
3. Enter the number being subtracted. — 9332
4. Press the *enter* key to find the answer. — enter

The answer **6457** will appear on the right-hand side of the display. — **6457**

**Example 3:** Find the product of 309 and 68.

1. Always clear a calculator before starting a new computation. — clear
2. Enter the first number, followed by the multiplication operator. (The multiplication sign will appear in the display as an asterisk rather than an ×, but the *multiplication key* looks like an ×.) — 309 (×)
3. Enter the next number. — 68
4. Press the *enter* key to find the product. — enter

The answer **21012** will appear on the right-hand side of the display. — **21012**

**Example 4:** Divide 12,456 by 12.

1. Always clear a calculator before starting a new computation. — clear
2. Enter the number to be divided first, followed by the division operator. — 12456 (÷)
3. Enter the number you are dividing by. — 12
4. Press the *enter* key to find the quotient. — enter

The answer **1038** will appear on the right-hand side of the display. — **1038**

---

**A. Practice solving the following problems on your calculator.**

**1.** $19 + 26 + 85 + 23 =$

**2.** $2579 - 1392 =$

**3.** $4 \times 28 \times 7 =$

**4.** $2568 \div 107 =$

**5.** $12,356 + 14,728 =$

**6.** $107,899 - 93,457 =$

**7.** $209 \times 56 =$

**8.** $972 \div 18 =$

**9.** $20,540 \div 13 =$

**STUDY ADVICE**

Not all questions will require you to do lots of math, so don't just start plugging numbers into the calculator. First think about what the problem is asking for.

**B. Choose the one correct answer to each question.**

**10.** Dan bought a used car with 16,741 miles on it. If the car now has 42,920 miles on it, how many miles has Dan put on the car?

A. 16,741
B. 26,179
C. 42,920
D. 59,661

**11.** A shipment of 20 computers arrived at a warehouse. If each computer is valued at $995, what is the total value of the shipment?

A. $995
B. $1015
C. $1990
D. $19,900

**Review your work using the explanations that start on page 683.**

## Using the *2nd* Key for a Second Function

To access some of the functions on the TI-30XS MultiView™, you need to press the *2nd* key in the upper left corner of the keypad. This bright green key will activate the second function also shown in green above the corresponding key. To access the second function of a key, press the *2nd* key first—do not press it at the same time as the function key. Highlighted below are two commonly used second functions—square root and percent. Use the process shown here for all *2nd* function keys.

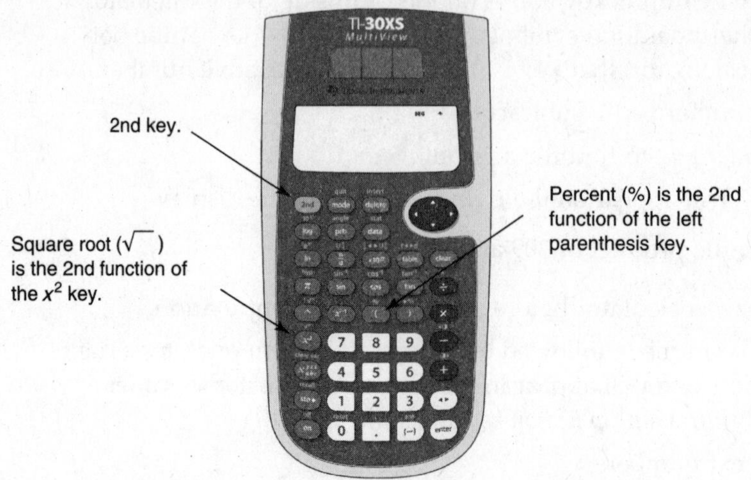


| **Example 5:** Find the square root of 169. | Keys to Press | On the Display |
|---|---|---|
| 1. Always clear a calculator before starting a new computation. | clear | |
| 2. Recognize that square root is a *2nd* function over the $x^2$ key. Press the *2nd* key. (Note that the term *2nd* now appears in the upper left corner of the display.) | 2nd | 2nd |
| 3. Next, press the $x^2$ key to activate the square root function in green over the key. You will see a blinking cursor under the square root. | $\sqrt{}$ $x^2$ | $\sqrt{\square}$ |
| 4. Now that you have the square root function, enter the number. The number will appear under the square root symbol in the display. | 169 | $\sqrt{169}$ ▶ |
| 5. Press the *enter* key to find the square root. The answer, **13**, will appear on the right-hand side of the display. | enter | $\sqrt{169}$ 13 |

For more information about square roots, see page 338.

**Remember:** For all *2nd functions*, (1) press the *2nd* key first to activate the *2nd* function, (2) press the key, and (3) enter the numbers.

# PRACTICE 3.2

**Example 6:** Find the part if you are given the percent and the whole. Find 10 percent of 500.

1. Always clear a calculator before starting a new computation. — clear
2. Enter the number you want to find the percent of. — 500
3. Press the multiplication sign. — ×
4. Enter the percent number. — 10
5. Press the *2nd* key and then press the open, or left, parenthesis key to activate the percent function. — 2nd % (
6. Press the *enter* key to find the answer. — enter

The answer, **50**, will appear on the right-hand side of the display. Ten percent of 500 is 50. — **50**

**Example 7:** Find the percent if you are given the whole and the part. What percent of 240 is 60?

1. Always clear a calculator before starting a new computation. — clear
2. Enter the part. — 60
3. Press the division sign. — ÷
4. Enter the whole. — 240
5. Press the *2nd* key and then press the close, or right, parenthesis symbol. This tells the calculator to translate the answer into a percent. — 2nd 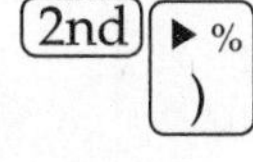
6. Press the *enter* key to find the answer. — enter

The answer, **25%**, will appear on the right-hand side of the display. Sixty is 25% of 240. — **25%**

For more information about percents, see pages 286–297.

---

**A. Practice solving the following problems on your calculator.**

**1.** $\sqrt{625}$

**2.** $\sqrt{324}$

**3.** $\sqrt{1225}$

**4.** Find 20% of 680.

**5.** Find 10% of 1250.

**6.** 15 is what percent of 300?

**7.** Find 5% of 40.

**8.** Find 30% of 450.

**9.** 20 is what percent of 400?

**B. Choose the <u>one best</u> answer to each question.**

**10.** Tanya paid 20% of $1680 as a down payment. How much was the down payment?

A. $20
B. $168
C. $336
D. $840

**11.** Aaron received a credit of $48 on a purchase of $960. What percent of $960 is $48?

A. 5%
B. 20%
C. 48%
D. 912%

**Review your work using the explanations that start on page 683.**

LESSON 4

# Word Problems

To pass the Mathematics Test, you will need to solve word problems. These questions are easier to manage if you use a **five-step problem-solving process**. Practice this process with word problems in this book.

**Step 1.** What is the **question** asking me to find?

*Read the problem carefully. State the question in your own words.*

**Step 2.** What **information** from the problem do I need?

*Select only the information you need to answer the question.*

**Step 3.** Which **operation** do I need to perform—addition, subtraction, multiplication, or division?

*Choose from one of the four operations above based on your understanding of the question.*

**Step 4.** What is my **solution**?

*Carry out the operation with the numbers you chose in step 2.*

**Step 5.** Does my answer **make sense**?

*Look back to make sure that you answered the question. Check that your answer makes sense.*

To help you decide which operation to use, keep the following ideas in mind.

| You... | in order to... |
|---|---|
| add | combine amounts of different sizes |
| subtract | find the difference between amounts |
| multiply | combine the same amount multiple times |
| divide | separate one amount into equal-sized groups |

**Example 1:** To cover a sofa, Sophia needs 12 yards of fabric that costs $14 per yard. How many yards does Sophia need for 3 sofas?

A. 4
B. 36
C. 42
D. 168

The correct answer is **B. 36 yards** of fabric. The question asked you to find the total number of yards of fabric Sophia needs for 3 sofas. Note that the cost of a yard of fabric is not needed to answer the question.

Since you were asked to find the amount of fabric for 3 sofas, you should multiply 12 yards × 3 sofas = 36 yards. Here are two common errors to avoid:

- If you had mistakenly divided, you would have gotten the incorrect answer of 4 yards of fabric for 3 sofas.
- If you had used the $14 price per yard and multiplied by either 3 sofas or 12 yards, you would have been tempted by wrong answers 42 or 168. However, the cost per yard is not needed.

### KEY IDEAS

- Successful math problem solvers use a five-step process.
- Read carefully to understand the question and select only the information needed to answer it.
- When you have found an answer, check that it makes sense.

### TASC TEST TIP

*Some questions on the Mathematics Test may include information that is not needed to answer the specific question. In multiple-choice questions, wrong answer choices may be based on mistakenly using this "extra" information, so read carefully.*

# PRACTICE 4.1

1. Peter wants to repaint his 700-square-foot apartment. He calculates that he has 3500 square feet of wall space to paint. (He will not paint the floor or the ceiling.) If each gallon of paint will cover 350 square feet of wall space, how many gallons will Peter need?

   A. 2
   B. 5
   C. 10
   D. 15

2. For a family get-together, Darryl wants to be sure that each child gets 2 party favors. The party favors cost $3 each, and there are 11 children coming. How many party favors will Darryl need?

   A. 9
   B. 11
   C. 18
   D. 22

3. Sarah and Kate live 18 miles apart, and they both work at the same office. If Sarah lives 25 miles from the office and Kate lives 30 miles from the office, how many miles farther from the office does Kate live than Sarah?

   A. 5
   B. 7
   C. 12
   D. 15

4. The Navarro family uses an average of 225 gallons of water per day, 5 gallons of which goes through the family's water filter. The Navarros' water filter can process 450 gallons before it needs to be replaced. After how many days of average water use will the family need to replace their filter?

   A. 9
   B. 45
   C. 90
   D. 225

**Questions 5 and 6 are based on the following information.**

Joyce owns a beauty salon, and she has posted the following information in her salon.

| Service | Minutes to complete | Price |
|---|---|---|
| Manicure | 30 | $15 |
| Pedicure | 30 | $25 |
| Manicure & Pedicure | 45 | $35 |
| Facial | 45 | $45 |
| Makeover | 60 | $60 |

5. How many minutes will it take Joyce to give 3 pedicures?

   A. 30
   B. 55
   C. 75
   D. 90

6. How much more does a customer pay for the makeover than for the manicure & pedicure combination?

   A. $15
   B. $20
   C. $25
   D. $35

---

7. Brandon is planning his part of the local community garden. He has calculated that he can plant 6 seedlings per row, and the garden allots 7 rows to each gardener. What is the maximum number of seedlings Brandon could plant?

   A. 7
   B. 13
   C. 24
   D. 42

**Review your work using the explanations that start on page 683.**

## Multi-Step Word Problems

The word problems on the previous two pages involved only one operation to solve. However, on the TASC Mathematics Test and other tests, you may need to do several math processes to solve a problem. These are called **multi-step problems.**

When you are working on multi-step problems, there are two important ideas to keep in mind. *What is the question asking me to find?* and *Did I answer the question?*

Review this example of a multi-step problem and the problem-solving process below.

**Example 1:** To win a prize, Sarah's daughter has to sell 75 boxes of cookies in 3 days. If she sold 16 boxes on day 1 and 34 boxes on day 2, how many boxes would she need to sell on day 3 to win the prize?

(1) 18
(2) 25
(3) 50

**Step 1.** What is the question asking me to find?

*The question asks me to find how many boxes Sarah's daughter needs to sell on the third day to make her goal of 75 boxes.*

**Step 2.** What information from the problem do I need?

*I know the total number of boxes she needs to sell (75 boxes).*

*I know how many boxes she sold on day 1 (16 boxes) and day 2 (34 boxes).*

**Step 3.** Do I need to do only one operation, or do I need to do more than one?

*I can add to find how many boxes Sarah's daughter has sold so far: 16 + 34 = 50.*

*However, that doesn't tell me <u>how many boxes she needs to sell on day 3</u>. I need one more step.*

**Step 4.** What is my solution?

*75 boxes total – 50 boxes sold = 25 boxes for day 3. The correct answer is (2)* ***25.***

**Step 5.** Does my answer make sense? Did I answer the question?

*By taking the additional step, I answered the question of how many boxes need to be sold on day 3.*

This sample multi-step problem involved only two operations: adding and subtracting. On the actual test, you may need to do three or more operations to answer a question, so read and think carefully about each problem.

As you think about the example, note the most common mistake people make with multi-step problems. Often they stop short of answering the question. Notice that choice (3) 50 is a **partial solution**, but it is not the answer to the question. Using the five-step problem-solving process will help you avoid that mistake.

# PRACTICE 4.2

**Questions 1–3 are based on the information below.**

Farhana's produce company distributes to several restaurants. The table below shows how many cases of different produce each restaurant ordered from Farhana's company in July.

| Produce Orders in July | | | | | |
|---|---|---|---|---|---|
| | Asparagus | Boston lettuce | Carrots | Romaine lettuce | Tomatoes |
| Restaurant A | 2 | 3 | 1 | 4 | 3 |
| Restaurant B | 4 | 4 | 2 | 2 | 1 |
| Restaurant C | 0 | 0 | 3 | 4 | 3 |
| Restaurant D | 1 | 2 | 2 | 3 | 4 |
| Restaurant E | 3 | 0 | 3 | 2 | 1 |

1. If Boston lettuce costs $17 per case and romaine lettuce costs $23 per case, how much did Restaurant D spend on lettuce ordered from Farhana in July?
   A. $85
   B. $93
   C. $103
   D. $143

2. Delivery costs $2 per case for the first 5 cases and $1 per case for each additional case of produce. What was Restaurant B's delivery charge in July?
   A. $13
   B. $18
   C. $20
   D. $26

3. If asparagus costs $22 per case and tomatoes cost $15 per case, which of the following restaurants spent the most on asparagus and tomatoes combined?
   A. Restaurant A
   B. Restaurant B
   C. Restaurant C
   D. Restaurant D

**STUDY ADVICE**

Word problems frequently involve rates, which you will read about next. Just remember: You frequently deal with rates in real life, e.g., miles per hour, miles per gallon. Your doctor may measure your heart rate in beats per minute. At your job, you may be paid in dollars per hour. TASC problems simply ask you to apply these real-life concepts, so don't let them throw you off.

4. At a certain store, loose-leaf paper comes only in packages of 400 sheets. If a student buys enough paper at this store to fill 3 binders with 150 sheets of paper each, how many sheets will be left over?
   A. 17
   B. 50
   C. 350
   D. 450

5. Three friends are baking cupcakes for a bake sale. Each batch of 24 cupcakes requires 2 cups of flour. The friends have a single 5-pound bag of flour that contains 19 cups of flour. How many whole batches of cupcakes can they bake?
   A. 9
   B. 38
   C. 216
   D. 228

6. A certain health insurance plan costs $3000 per year for a family of six. If each member of the family has $750 in medical expenses in a year, and the plan pays 100% of those expenses, how much will the family save by purchasing the plan?
   A. $1500
   B. $2000
   C. $2500
   D. $3000

**Review your work using the explanations that start on page 683.**

LESSON 5

# Distance and Cost

## Distance

On the Mathematics Test, you'll see questions that will require you to apply formulas. When a relationship is constant, use a formula to set up the information about how the different parts relate to each other. One of the most commonly tested formulas deals with distance, rate, and time. Distance is a product of the rate at which something travels and the amount of travel time:

$$\text{distance} = \text{rate} \times \text{time}, \quad \text{or} \quad d = rt$$

Notice that letters, or variables, can be used to represent the different parts of a formula. A formula allows you to substitute known values for certain variables and solve for the unknown variable.

**Example 1:** How many miles can you travel if you drive at an average speed of 55 miles per hour for 3 hours?

1. You know the rate (55 miles per hour) and the time (3 hours). Substitute the values in the distance formula. — distance $= 55 \times 3$

2. Multiply to find the distance. — $55 \times 3 =$ **165 miles**

## Cost

Another helpful formula is the cost formula. It expresses the relationship between cost, the number of units, and rate (price per unit). Note: The word *per* means for every one unit. The cost formula can be written as follows:

$$\text{total cost} = (\text{number of units}) \times (\text{price per unit}), \quad \text{or} \quad c = nr$$

**Example 2:** At a bakery, a package of frosted cookies is priced at $3 per package. If a teacher treats her class by buying 4 packages, how much would the cookies cost before tax?

1. You know the number of units (4 packages) and the price per unit ($3 per package). Substitute the values in the cost formula. — $c = nr$; total cost $= 4 \times \$3$

2. Multiply to find the total cost. — $4 \times \$3 =$ **$12**

If you know any two of the three variables in a formula, you can solve for the third variable.

**Example 3:** Max bought a set of 4 floor mats for $44. How much was the price per floor mat?

1. You know the total cost ($44) and the number of units (4 floor mats). Rewrite the formula to solve for the price per unit (*r*). — $c = nr$; $r = \frac{c}{n}$

2. Substitute the known values in the cost formula. Divide to find the price per unit. — $\frac{\$44}{4} = \mathbf{\$11}$

### KEY IDEAS

- The following all indicate multiplication:

  $n \times r \quad nr \quad n(r) \quad n \cdot r$

- The following indicate division:

  $c \div n \quad \frac{c}{n}$

- A formula can be rewritten to solve for each of its variables.

  $c = nr \quad \frac{c}{n} = r \quad \frac{c}{r} = n$

  $d = rt \quad \frac{d}{r} = t \quad \frac{d}{t} = r$

### TASC TEST TIP

*Substitute all of the values for variables back into a formula to check your answer.*

# PRACTICE 5

**A. Each problem below includes two of the three variables from either the distance formula or the cost formula. Write the missing variable you need to solve for. Then decide which of the following formula variations you would use in each situation. The first one is done for you.**

$d = rt$ $\quad \frac{d}{r} = t$ $\quad \frac{d}{t} = r$ $\quad c = nr$ $\quad \frac{c}{n} = r$ $\quad \frac{c}{r} = n$

1. Given: distance and time
   Solve for: rate
   Formula: $\frac{d}{t} = r$
2. Given: rate and time
   Solve for: ____________
   Formula: ____________
3. Given: distance and rate
   Solve for: ____________
   Formula: ____________
4. Given: cost and number of units
   Solve for: ____________
   Formula: ____________
5. Given: number of units and price per unit
   Solve for: ____________
   Formula: ____________
6. Given: cost and price per unit
   Solve for: ____________
   Formula: ____________

**B. Use the formulas provided in part A above to help you set up the problems. Solve for the unknown variable.**

7. Find the total cost of 4 flats of plants at $12 each.
8. Find the total cost of 12 boxes of cookies if each box costs $3.
9. If 4 tires cost $320, how much does a single tire cost?
10. How many tickets would you get for $25 if raffle tickets cost $5 apiece?
11. If you paid $20 for 10 bus transfer tickets, how much did you pay per ticket?
12. Find the distance traveled by a car averaging 60 miles per hour for 3 hours.
13. Find the distance traveled by a train averaging 50 miles per hour for 4 hours.
14. How long does it take for a bus to travel 25 miles at an average rate of 25 miles per hour?
15. If a train travels 270 miles in 3 hours, what is the train's average speed?
16. How long does it take to complete a delivery route of 75 miles at a rate of 25 miles per hour?

**C. Choose the one best answer to each question.**

17. A company sold a total of $640 in gift boxes. If the gift boxes cost $20 apiece, how many gift boxes did the company sell?
    A. 32
    B. 320
    C. 660
    D. 1280
18. A truck driver traveled 275 miles in 5 hours. What was his average speed in miles per hour?
    A. 1375
    B. 280
    C. 270
    D. 55

**Review your work using the explanations that start on page 683.**

LESSON 6

# Measurement

## The English System of Measurement

Measurements are used to describe an object's length, weight, or volume. We also use measurement to describe a quantity of time. Many people and institutions in the United States use the English system of measurement.

| Measurement Equivalencies | |
|---|---|
| **Length**<br>1 foot (ft) = 12 inches (in)<br>1 yard (yd) = 3 ft<br>1 mile (mi) = 5280 ft | **Weight**<br>1 pound (lb) = 16 ounces (oz)<br>1 ton (t) = 2000 lb |
| **Time**<br>1 minute (min) = 60 seconds (sec)<br>1 hour (hr) = 60 min<br>1 day = 24 hr<br>1 week = 7 days<br>1 year (yr) = 12 months (mo) | **Volume**<br>1 cup (c) = 8 fluid ounces (fl oz)<br>1 pint (pt) = 2 c<br>1 quart (qt) = 2 pt<br>1 gallon (gal) = 4 qt |

### KEY IDEAS

- Multiply to change from a larger unit of measure to a smaller one.
- Divide to change from a smaller unit of measure to a larger one.
- When dividing, the remainder is the same unit of measure as the number you are dividing by.

### TASC TEST TIP

*The measurement facts shown on this page and page 250 will not be given to you on the TASC Mathematics Test. You should memorize them to answer questions involving measurement.*

To solve problems, you will need to change from one unit of measure to another. If you need to *change a larger unit of measure to a smaller one*, you need to *multiply*. To change a *smaller unit of measure to a larger one*, you *divide*. Use the measurement equivalencies provided in the chart.

**Example 1:** A picture frame is 3 ft 8 in long. What is the length of the frame in inches?

1. Change 3 feet to inches using the fact that 1 foot = 12 inches. $3 \text{ ft} \times 12 = 36 \text{ in}$
2. Add the remaining 8 inches. $36 + 8 = 44 \text{ in}$

The picture frame is **44 inches** in length.

**Example 2:** A package weighs 84 ounces. What is the weight of the package in pounds?

$$\begin{array}{r} 5 \\ 16\overline{)84} \\ -80 \\ \hline 4 \end{array}$$

1. Change 84 ounces to pounds. Because 1 pound = 16 ounces, divide by 16.
2. The remainder is in ounces, the same unit you started with. Therefore, the package weighs **5 lb 4 oz**, or you can express the remainder as a fraction, $5\frac{4}{16} = \mathbf{5\frac{1}{4}}$ **lb.**

You may need to do a series of conversions.

**Example 3:** A container holds 1.5 gallons. How many cups does the container hold?

1. Change 1.5 gallons to quarts. (Use the fact that 1 gal = 4 qt.) $1.5 \text{ gal} \times 4 = 6 \text{ qt}$
2. Change 6 quarts to pints. (Use the fact that 1 qt = 2 pt.) $6 \text{ qt} \times 2 = 12 \text{ pt}$
3. Change 12 pints to cups. (Use the fact that 1 pt = 2 c.) $12 \text{ pt} \times 2 = 24 \text{ c}$

The container holds **24 cups.**

# PRACTICE 6

In a measurement problem, you may need to add, subtract, multiply, or divide measurements. You can only perform mathematical operations on measurements that use the same unit.

**Example 4:** A deck requires pieces of railing that are 5 ft 9 in, 15 ft 4 in, and 8 ft 6 in. What is the total length of railing needed?

1. Write the measurements in a column, aligning like units of measure.
2. Add like units.
3. Simplify the answer. (Change 19 in to 1 ft 7 in, and add to 28 ft.)

|  |  |
|---|---|
| 5 ft | 9 in |
| 15 ft | 4 in |
| 8 ft | 6 in |
| 28 ft | 19 in |

28 ft + 1 ft 7 in = 29 ft 7 in

The deck requires **29 ft 7 in** of railing.

To multiply a measurement by a whole number, multiply the units of measure separately. Then simplify the result.

**Example 5:** Tony has five lengths of plastic pipe, each measuring 6 ft 10 in. What is the combined length of the pipe?

1. Multiply each part of the measurement by 5.
2. Simplify using the fact that 1 ft = 12 in.

The combined length is **34 ft 2 in.**

$$\begin{array}{r} 6 \text{ ft } 10 \text{ in} \\ \times \quad 5 \\ \hline 30 \text{ ft } 50 \text{ in} \end{array} = 30 \text{ ft} + 4 \text{ ft } 2 \text{ in} = 34 \text{ ft } 2 \text{ in}$$

---

**A. Solve.**

**1.** How many inches are equal to 4 feet?

**2.** How many minutes are equal to 420 seconds?

**3.** How many hours are in 3 days?

**4.** Convert 40 fluid ounces to pints.

**5.** Five gallons are equal to how many quarts?

**6.** How many tons is 11,000 pounds?

**7.** Four yards equal how many inches?

**8.** How many hours are equal to 720 minutes?

**9.** How many cups are in two gallons?

**B. Choose the one best answer to each question. You MAY use a calculator.**

Questions 10 and 11 refer to the following information.

**Portable Air Cooler**
Duracool R612
3.75 gallon capacity
Runs 6 hours without refilling
width: 27 in; depth: 16 in
height: 13 3/4 in
shipping weight: 26 lb

**10.** Bob wants to buy an air cooler. He knows the capacity of several other models in quarts. Which of the following expressions could he use to find the capacity for this model in quarts?

A. 3.75 × 2
B. 3.75 ÷ 2
C. 3.75 × 4
D. 3.75 ÷ 4

**11.** Which of these measurements is equal to the width of the Duracool R612?

A. 2 ft 1 in
B. 2 ft 3 in
C. 213 ft
D. 2 ft 7 in

**12.** Max needs to ship six identical packages, each weighing 3 lb 12 oz. What is the total weight of the shipment?

A. 19 lb 2 oz
B. 22 lb 8 oz
C. 24 lb 12 oz
D. 25 lb 2 oz

**Review your work using the explanations that start on page 684.**

## The Metric System

The metric system is the measurement system used in most of the countries of the world. The main unit of length in the metric system is the **meter** (m). The **gram** (g) is the basic metric measure of mass (or weight). The basic unit of volume is called the **liter** (*l*). To form units of measure, add prefixes to the basic units described above.

| | |
|---|---|
| *milli-* (m) means one-thousandth<br>*centi-* (c) means one-hundredth<br>*deci-* (d) means one-tenth | *deka-* (da) means ten<br>*hecto-* (h) means one hundred<br>*kilo-* (k) means one thousand |

Therefore, a kilometer (km) equals 1,000 meters, a milligram (mg) equals one one-thousandth gram, and a centiliter (cl) equals one one-hundredth liter.

Memorize the following chart. As in our decimal place-value system, each column on the chart is 10 times the column to its right. To convert between metric units, count the spaces from the unit you are converting from to the unit you are converting to. Then move the decimal point that number of place values in the same direction.

| kilo- | hecto- | deka- | mewter | deci- | centi- | milli- |
|---|---|---|---|---|---|---|
| (km) | (hm) | (dam) | (m) | (dm) | (cm) | (mm) |
| 1000 m | 100 m | 10 m | 1 m | 0.1 m | 0.01 m | 0.001 m |

Although the chart uses the meter as the basic unit, the chart can also be used with liters (*l*) and grams (*g*).

**Example 1:** How many millimeters (mm) are equal to 3 centimeters (cm)?

1. Find *milli-* and *centi-* on the chart. The prefix *milli-* is one place to the right of the prefix *centi-*; therefore, you need to move the decimal point one place to the right to convert from centimeters to millimeters.
2. For example, 3 cm = 3.0 cm = **30 mm.**

**Example 2:** How many grams (g) are equal to 6,400 milligrams (mg)?

1. Start in the *milli-* column. The basic unit (or ones column) is three columns to the left. Move the decimal point three place-value columns to the left.
2. For example, 6,400 mg = 6,400. mg = **6.4 g.**

You may want to memorize the following common conversions:

| | |
|---|---|
| 1,000 meters = 1 kilometer | 1 meter = 1,000 millimeters |
| 1 meter = 100 centimeters | 1 centimeter = 10 millimeters |

## Solving Problems with Metric Measurement

Metric measurements are written as decimal numbers. Therefore, you can perform operations with metric measurements using the rules for adding, subtracting, multiplying, and dividing decimals.

**Example 3:** Three metal rods measure 1.5 meters, 1.85 meters, and 450 centimeters. What is the total length of the rods in meters?

1. Read the question carefully. You are asked to find the total length in *meters*.
2. The first two measures are written in meters. Convert the third measure to meters. 450 cm = 4.5 m
3. Add using the rules for adding decimals. The total is **7.85 m.**

# PRACTICE 6.2

**Example 4:** Alex is a buyer for a rug retail store. He plans to order 25 acrylic rugs to sell in the store. The shipping weight for each rug is 7.8 kilograms. What is the shipping weight in kilograms of the entire order?

1. Multiply the weight of one rug (7.8 kg) by 25.
2. The weight of 25 rugs is **195 kilograms.** Notice that the answer has the same unit of measure as the number you multiplied.

**Note:** A common mistake when solving metric problems is putting the decimal point in the wrong place. To avoid errors, estimate before you work the problem. Compare your answer to the estimate.

---

**A. Solve.**

**1.** How many meters equal 5 kilometers?

**2.** 600 centimeters equal how many meters?

**3.** How many milligrams equal 4 grams?

**4.** Eight kilograms equal how many grams?

**5.** How many centiliters is 40.5 liters equal to?

**6.** How many liters are equal to 1500 ml?

**7.** How many grams is 250 milligrams equal to?

**8.** How many meters are in 30 kilometers?

**9.** How many cl is 0.75 *l* equal to?

**10.** Fifty grams equal how many kilograms?

**11.** How many liters is 35,200 milliliters equal to?

**12.** How many centimeters are in 15 meters?

**B. Choose the one best answer to each question.**

**13.** A can of machine oil holds 118.3 ml. How many liters of machine oil does the can hold?

A. 0.01183
B. 0.1183
C. 1.183
D. 11.83

**14.** In a vitamin supplement, each capsule contains 500 milligrams of vitamins. How many grams of vitamins are found in each capsule?

A. 5,000
B. 50
C. 5
D. 0.5

**15.** A type of bonding gel comes in a small container that holds 4 g of the gel. How many of the small containers could be filled from 2.5 kg of the gel?

A. 6,250
B. 625
C. 62
D. 6

**16.** Sharon buys 4.8 meters of ribbon to use as trim on a set of kitchen curtains. She actually uses 350 centimeters. How many centimeters of the ribbon are left?

A. 13
B. 44.5
C. 130
D. 302

**Review your work using the explanations that start on page 684.**

LESSON 7

# Filling in the Answer Grid

Most of the questions on the TASC Mathematics Test are multiple choice. However, some questions will require you to indicate your answer by filling in an **answer grid.** Study the image to the right.

The answer grid can be used for answers that are in whole-number, decimal, or fraction form. For further information about using the answer grid with decimals or fractions, see page 276. Examples of using answer grids with whole-number answers follow.

**Example 1:** Mario drove 280 miles on Monday, 320 miles on Tuesday, and 75 miles on Wednesday. How many total miles did he drive for the 3 days?

1. Decide which operation to use. Since you need to find a total amount, add the three values.

   280 + 320 + 75 = **675**

2. Write your answer in the blank boxes provided at the top of the standard grid.
3. Darken in the matching circle in the column under each digit in your answer.

When filling in a standard grid, you can start your answer anywhere as long as the complete answer fits in the grid. (This is based on the information available as of January 2014. Check www.tasctest.com for updates about the TASC Mathematics Test.)

**Example 2:** Angela worked 40 hours every week for 51 weeks. How many hours did she work in all?

1. Decide which operation to use. Since you need to find the total of the same amount multiple times, multiply.
   40 × 51 = **2040**
2. Write your answer in the blank boxes provided at the top of the grid.
3. Darken in the matching circle in the column under each digit in your answer.

### KEY IDEAS

- Some questions on the TASC Mathematics Test require you to generate an answer and fill in a grid to indicate your answer.
- Always write your answer at the top of the grid before filling in the circles.
- Fill in only one circle per column. Columns that you do not need should be left blank.

### TASC TEST TIP

*When filling in your answers in a standard grid, fill in the appropriate circles carefully. If you change an answer, erase the first choice completely.*

# PRACTICE 7

**Directions: For each question, mark your answer in the circles in the appropriate grid.**

1. A veterinary clinic treated 435 cats over a 3-month period. At this rate, how many cats will the clinic treat in a 12-month period?
2. A quick oil change shop recommends changing a car's oil and filter every 3,500 miles. If a car is driven 35,000 miles, how many times should the oil and filter have been changed?
3. Attendance at a local play was 348 Friday night, 366 Saturday night, and 280 Sunday afternoon. What was the total attendance for the 3 days?
4. A restaurant sells cookies at the price of 3 for $1. How many cookies could you buy for $5?
5. How many sheets of paper would 4 copies of a 617-page document use, if the document is printed so that only one side of each sheet of paper is used?
6. How many months would it take to pay back $1,050 at $50 per month?

1.

2.

3.

4.

5.

6.

**Review your work using the explanations that start on page 684.**

# NUMBER AND QUANTITY PART I: PROBLEM SOLVING PRACTICE QUESTIONS

**Directions: You MAY use your calculator.**

1. A beverage container holds 12 servings. If the serving size is 8 ounces, how many ounces does the container hold in all?

   A. 20
   B. 32
   C. 48
   D. 96

2. Sales at 3 concession stands are $839, $527, and $726. What is the total amount in sales?

   A. $1581
   B. $2092
   C. $2178
   D. $2517

3. If you want to cut 24 two-foot braces, how many boards of the length shown below would you need?

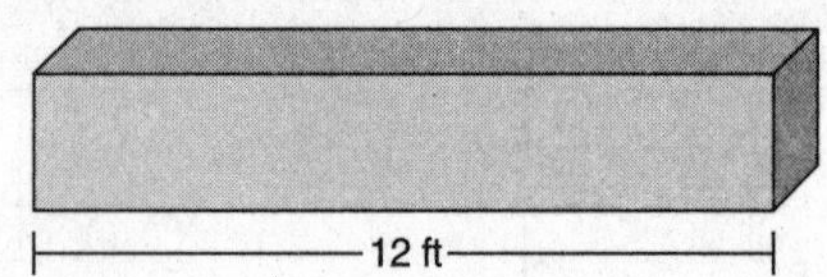


   A. 4
   B. 6
   C. 12
   D. 24

4. Using your calculator, find the value of $\sqrt{441}$.

   A. 11
   B. 21
   C. 221
   D. 441

5. Angelo bought a used car with 39,451 miles on it. If the car now has 70,040 miles on it, how many miles has Angelo driven the car?

   A. 30,589
   B. 39,459
   C. 70,040
   D. 109,491

6. Use your calculator to solve this problem. If Emory paid 20% of $3280 as a down payment, how much was the down payment?

   A. $164
   B. $328
   C. $656
   D. $6560

7. Inventory shows that a warehouse has 45 printers in stock. If each printer is valued at $125, what is the total value of the printer inventory?

   A. $5625
   B. $170
   C. $80
   D. $45

8. Linda can drive 180 miles in 3 hours. On Tuesday, she drove for 7 hours at that rate. How many miles did she drive on Tuesday?

   A. 60
   B. 420
   C. 600
   D. 1260

9. Janelle wants to drive from Danville to Brownsville. If she averages 60 miles per hour, how many hours will it take her to drive the distance?

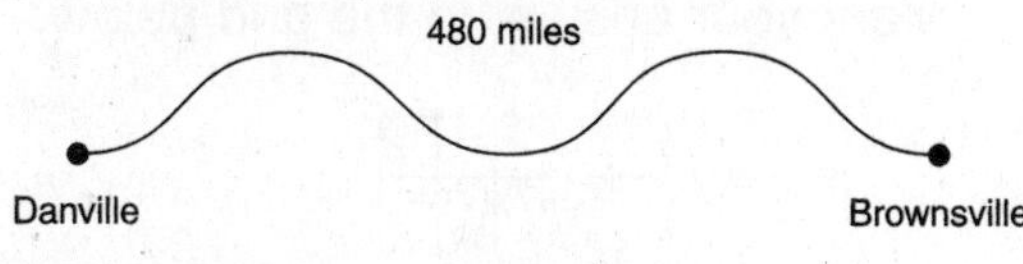


A. 6
B. 8
C. 60
D. 540

10. A company sold a total of $1440 in gift bears for Valentine's Day. If the gift bears cost $15 apiece, how many gift bears did it sell?

A. 15
B. 96
C. 144
D. 1440

11. In addition to interest charges, Richard's credit card company charges a $25 late fee for payments made after the payment due date. If he was charged a late fee for 8 different monthly bills, how much could he have saved by paying the bills on time?

A. $200
B. $80
C. $33
D. $25

12. A waiter has seven $5 bills and eighteen $1 bills from tips. In all, how much does he have in tips?

A. $18
B. $25
C. $35
D. $53

13. April has taken her car in for the recommended oil and filter change every 3,500 miles. If April bought her car brand-new, and the odometer now shows just over 17,500 miles, how many oil changes has her car received?

A. 5
B. 14
C. 123
D. 1236

14. A clinic treated 536 children over a 4-month period. At this rate, how many children did the clinic treat in 1 month?

A. 134
B. 536
C. 540
D. 2144

**For questions 15 and 16, mark your answers in the grids below.**

15. Attendance at a local play was 438 Friday night, 820 Saturday night, and 636 Sunday afternoon. How many more people attended the play on Sunday than on Friday?

16. Raquel has 4 payments left on her car. If each payment is $268, how much does she still owe on her car?

15.

16.

17. In what order should items weighing 51 pounds, 40 pounds, 48 pounds, and 44 pounds be stacked if you want them in order from heaviest to lightest?

A. 51, 44, 40, 48
B. 40, 44, 48, 51
C. 51, 48, 44, 40
D. 51, 40, 44, 48

18. Which of the following correctly shows 2,354,769 rounded to the nearest ten thousand?

A. 2,400,000
B. 2,355,000
C. 2,350,000
D. 2,000,000

19. What is the total weight in pounds of the packages below?

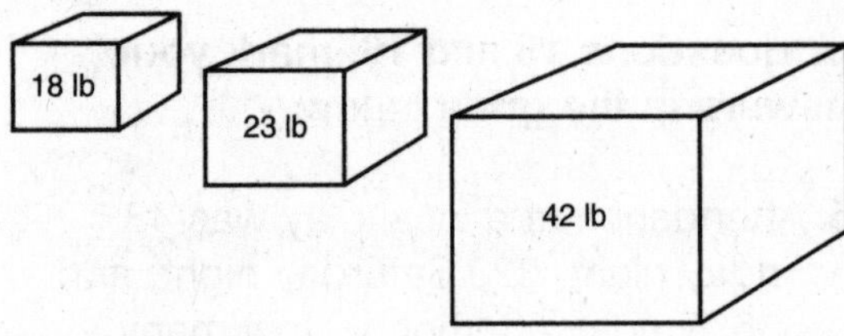


A. 83
B. 65
C. 60
D. 42

20. Jason paid a $14 dinner bill with a $20 bill. How much change should he receive?

A. $6
B. $7
C. $14
D. $34

21. Maria spent 8 minutes installing a new showerhead, 33 minutes rodding out a drain, and 18 minutes fixing a leaking faucet. About how many minutes did it take Maria to complete all three tasks?

A. 90
B. 60
C. 30
D. 20

22. Carla drove 248 miles in 4 hours. What was her average rate of speed, in miles per hour?

Mark your answer in the grid below.

23. A bulk bag of nuts contains 144 ounces of nuts. If the nuts are packaged in smaller 8-ounce bags, how many bags will there be?

A. 8
B. 12
C. 18
D. 136

24. If you drove 299 miles on 9 gallons of gasoline, about how many miles per gallon did the car get?

A. 10
B. 30
C. 270
D. 300

25. Nydia works in a photo lab. She uses 1 pt 6 fl oz of film developer from a full container. If the capacity of the container is 3 qt, how much developer is left in the container?

A. 2 qt 10 fl oz
B. 2 qt 6 fl oz
C. 2 qt 2 fl oz
D. 1 qt 10 fl oz

26. A shipment of 33 crates like the one shown below is delivered. <u>Approximately</u> how many pounds did workers unload?

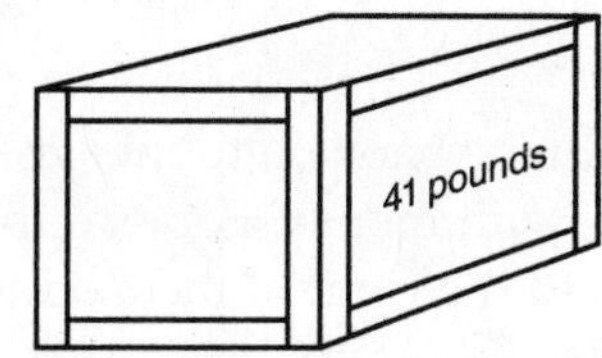


A. 40
B. 120
C. 1200
D. 2000

27. Four friends bought a birthday cake for $21 and balloons for $15. If they divided the cost equally, how much did each friend pay toward the birthday party?

A. $4
B. $5
C. $9
D. $36

28. David paid $20 toward a dinner bill of $128. If the remainder of the bill is divided equally among the remaining 9 people in the group, how much should each person other than David pay?

A. $12
B. $18
C. $20
D. $108

29. A driver traveled 4 hours at an average rate of 65 miles per hour. How many miles did the person drive?

A. 61
B. 69
C. 240
D. 260

30. Using the following information, how much would a large pizza with 3 toppings cost?

| Large 1-Topping Pizza for $14<br>$2 for Each Additional Topping |
|---|

A. $20
B. $18
C. $16
D. $14

31. Bagels are 2 for $1. What is the maximum number of bagels you could buy for $7?

A. 7
B. 10
C. 14
D. 15

**For questions 32 and 33, mark your answers in the grids below.**

32. How many months would it take to save $1800 at $75 per month?

33. How many 45-page documents would a binder hold if its maximum capacity is 630 sheets of paper?

32.

33.

**Review your work using the explanations that start on page 684**

**STUDY ADVICE**

How did these practice questions go? If you understood the concepts but made simple addition or subtraction mistakes, congratulate yourself and try to be more careful about small math errors. If this practice set did not go well, review the examples in this chapter.

# Number and Quantity Part II: Decimals and Fractions

### KEY IDEAS

- The decimal point separates the whole number from the decimal part.
- To round decimals, use the same rules as with rounding whole numbers.
- Adding zeros to the right of the last digit after the decimal does not change the number's value.

### TASC TEST TIP

*The Mathematics Test may show a zero written before the decimal point. The zero does not change the value of the number. Example: 0.75 = .75*

## LESSON 1

# Decimal Basics

## The Decimal System

**Decimals** are numbers that use place value to show amounts less than 1. You already use decimals when working with money. For example, in the amount $10.25, you know that the digits to the right of the **decimal point** represent cents, or hundredths of a dollar.

The first four decimal place values are labeled on the chart below.

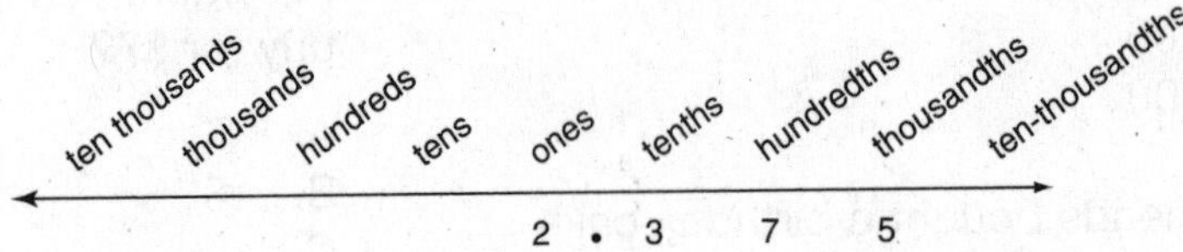


The number 2.375 is shown on the chart. Read *and* in place of the decimal point. After reading the decimal part, say the place value of the last decimal digit. This number would be read "two *and* three hundred seventy-five *thousandths.*"

## Rounding

Round decimals the same way you round whole numbers.

**Example 1:** A calculator display reads 3.62835. Round to the hundredths place.

1. Look at the digit to the right of the hundredths place. — 3.62[8]35
2. If the digit to the right is 5 or greater, round up. If the digit is less than 5, don't change the number. Then drop all digits to the right of the place you are rounding to. — Since 8 is greater than 5, round up. 3.62835 rounds to **3.63.**

## Comparing and Ordering

Comparing decimals is similar to comparing whole numbers.

**Example 2:** Matt ran the 400-meter race in 45.8 seconds. Alonzo ran the same race in 45.66 seconds. Which runner had the faster time?

1. Line up the decimal points. Add a zero at the **end** of 45.8 so that both times have the same number of digits after the decimal. — 45.80 / 45.66
2. Compare the decimal parts of the numbers as though they were whole numbers. **Alonzo's time was faster.** — 80 is greater than 66, so 45.8 is greater than 45.66.

# PRACTICE 1

When you compare more than two numbers, it is helpful to compare one place-value column at a time, working from left to right.

**Example 3:** Arrange the numbers 0.85, 1.8, 0.8, and 0.819 in order from greatest to least.

1. Write the numbers in a column, lining up the decimal points. Add zeros so that the numbers have the same number of decimal places.

   0.850
   1.800
   0.800
   0.819

2. Compare the digits, working from left to right. Only 1.8 has a whole number part, so it is greatest. The remaining numbers each have 8 in the tenths column. Looking at the hundredths column, 0.85 is next, followed by 0.819. The least number is 0.8.

   In order: **1.8**
   **0.85**
   **0.819**
   **0.8**

---

**A. Round these numbers as directed.**

**1.** Round 3.75 to the tenths place.

**2.** Round 5.908 to the ones place.

**3.** A calculator display reads 0.4285714. Round to the nearest hundredth.

**4.** Round 0.66667 to the nearest thousandth.

**5.** Round 8.125 to the nearest tenth.

**6.** A calculator display reads 2.7142857. Round to the nearest thousandth.

**B. In each of the following pairs, which number is greater?**

**7.** 0.45 or 0.449

**8.** 0.008 or 0.08

**9.** 4.68 or 4.086

**10.** 0.75 or 1.85

**11.** 1.0275 or 1.029

**12.** 0.14 or 0.104

**C. Write these numbers in order from least to greatest.**

**13.** 5.6 5.08 5.8 5.802

**14.** 0.1136 0.12 0.2 0.115

**15.** 14.005 4.52 4.8 4.667

**16.** 0.8023 0.8 0.803 0.823

**D. Choose the one best answer to each question.**

**17.** In a circuit board assembly, the weights of three parts are 0.572 grams, 0.0785 grams, and 0.6 grams. Which of the following lists the weights in order from greatest to least?

A. 0.0785 g, 0.572 g, 0.6 g
B. 0.6 g, 0.0785 g, 0.572 g
C. 0.6 g, 0.572 g, 0.0785 g
D. 0.572 g, 0.6 g, 0.0785 g

**18.** Which of the following correctly shows 1.3815 rounded to the nearest hundredth?

A. 1.4
B. 1.382
C. 1.381
D. 1.38

**Review your work using the explanations that start on page 685.**

Number and Quantity Part II: Decimals and Fractions

LESSON 2

# Decimal Operations

## Addition and Subtraction

Adding decimals is much like adding whole numbers. The trick is to make sure you have lined up the place-value columns correctly. You can do this by writing the numbers in a column and carefully lining up the decimal points.

**KEY IDEAS**

- Always add and subtract like place-value columns.
- Always line up the decimal points when you write a problem in columns.
- When adding or subtracting, place the decimal point in the answer directly below the decimal point in the problem.

**Example 1:** Add $0.37 + 13.5 + 2.638$.

1. Write the numbers in a column, lining up the decimal points.
2. You may add placeholder zeros so that the decimals have the same number of decimal places.
3. Add. Start on the right and add each column. Regroup, or carry, as you would with whole numbers.
4. Place the decimal point in the answer directly below the decimal points in the problem.

$$\begin{array}{r} 0.370 \\ 13.500 \\ +\,2.638 \\ \hline \end{array}$$

$$\begin{array}{r} {\scriptstyle 1\,1}\phantom{000} \\ 0.370 \\ 13.500 \\ +\,2.638 \\ \hline \mathbf{16.508} \end{array}$$

To subtract decimals, write the numbers in a column with the greater number on top. Make sure the decimal points are in a line.

**Example 2:** Find the difference between 14.512 and 8.7.

1. Write the numbers in a column, lining up the decimal points. Add placeholder zeros so that the numbers have the same number of decimal places.
2. Subtract. Regroup, or borrow, as needed. Place the decimal point in the answer directly in line with the decimal points in the problem.

$$\begin{array}{r} 14.512 \\ -\,8.700 \\ \hline \end{array}$$

$$\begin{array}{r} {\scriptstyle 13\;15}\phantom{12} \\ 14.512 \\ -\,8.700 \\ \hline \mathbf{5.812} \end{array}$$

**TASC TEST TIP**

*To make sure that your answer makes sense, mentally round the numbers to the nearest whole number and then add or subtract. The result should be close to your answer.*

The greater number may have fewer or no decimal places. In the next example, a decimal is subtracted from a whole number.

**Example 3:** What does 9 minus 3.604 equal?

1. Line up the place-value columns. Put a decimal point after the whole number 9 and add placeholder zeros.
2. Subtract, regrouping as needed. Place the decimal point in the answer.

$$\begin{array}{r} 9.000 \\ -3.604 \\ \hline \end{array}$$

$$\begin{array}{r} {\scriptstyle 8\;9\;9\;10} \\ 9.000 \\ -3.604 \\ \hline \mathbf{5.396} \end{array}$$

# PRACTICE 2.1

**A. Solve. You MAY NOT use a calculator.**

1. $\begin{array}{r} 4.025 \\ +\,3.971 \\ \hline \end{array}$

2. $\begin{array}{r} 6.5 \\ +\,4.008 \\ \hline \end{array}$

3. $\begin{array}{r} 2.8 \\ +\,9.46 \\ \hline \end{array}$

4. $\begin{array}{r} 8.04 \\ -\,2.19 \\ \hline \end{array}$

5. $\begin{array}{r} 8.5 \\ -\,1.074 \\ \hline \end{array}$

6. $\begin{array}{r} 10 \\ -\,7.89 \\ \hline \end{array}$

7. $\begin{array}{r} 17.294 \\ +\,0.8 \\ \hline \end{array}$

8. $\begin{array}{r} 4.07 \\ +\,1.047 \\ \hline \end{array}$

9. $\begin{array}{r} 17.52 \\ +\,3.8 \\ \hline \end{array}$

10. $\begin{array}{r} 3.8 \\ -\,2.905 \\ \hline \end{array}$

11. $\begin{array}{r} 14.64 \\ -\,10.8 \\ \hline \end{array}$

12. $\begin{array}{r} 100.5 \\ -\,98.15 \\ \hline \end{array}$

13. $0.236 + 2.4 + 2.87 =$

14. $38.06 - 16.9 =$

15. $0.006 + 0.09 + 0.549 =$

16. $8.5 - 6.074 =$

17. $1.02 - 0.87 =$

18. $0.45 + 1.8 + 0.07 + 2.56 =$

19. $12.5 - 0.7 =$

20. $25 - 10.984 =$

21. $0.01 + 2.052 + 0.96 + 1.5 =$

22. $12.9 - 10.54 =$

23. $0.68 + 12.3 + 4.9 =$

24. $32.9 - 15.675 =$

**B. Choose the one best answer to each question.**

**25.** James ran 3 miles. His times for the individual miles were 7.2 minutes, 6.8 minutes, and 8.25 minutes. How long did it take him, in minutes, to run the 3-mile distance?

A. 22.25
B. 22.7
C. 23.35
D. 96.5

**26.** Claudia earns overtime pay when she works more than 40 hours in one week. How many hours of overtime pay did she work for the week of March 4?

**Work Record for March 4–10**

| | |
|---|---|
| March 4 | 8.5 |
| March 5 | Off |
| March 6 | 9.25 |
| March 7 | 8.75 |
| March 8 | 10 |
| March 9 | Off |
| March 10 | 7.75 |

A. 44.25
B. 40.0
C. 4.25
D. 2.25

**27.** A plumber cut two lengths of pipe measuring 2.8 and 1.4 meters from a 6-meter length.

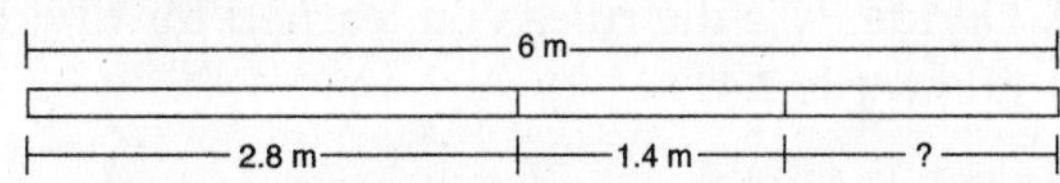


Assuming there was no waste when the cuts were made, what is the length in meters of the remaining piece?

A. 1.8
B. 3.2
C. 4.2
D. 7.4

**28.** Mona purchased the following art supplies: a storage box for \$16.98, a set of art markers for \$31.78, and a pad of paper for \$6.50. What was the cost of the three items?

A. \$48.76
B. \$53.26
C. \$55.26
D. \$61.76

**Review your work using the explanations that start on page 685.**

## Multiplication and Division

The rules you used to multiply whole numbers can be used to multiply decimals. You don't have to line up the decimal points. You will wait until you are finished multiplying before you place the decimal point in the answer. The number of decimal places in the answer equals the total number of decimal places in the numbers you are multiplying.

**Example 4:** Find the product of 2.6 and 0.45.

1. Set up the problem as though you were multiplying the whole numbers 26 and 45.
2. Ignore the decimal points while you multiply.
3. Now count the decimal places in the numbers you multiplied. The number 2.6 has one decimal place, and 0.45 has two decimal places, for a total of three.
4. Starting from the right, count three places to the left and insert the decimal point. Thus, the answer is **1.17**.

$$\begin{array}{r} 2.6 \\ \times .45 \\ \hline \end{array}$$

$$\begin{array}{r} 2.6 \\ \times .45 \\ \hline 130 \\ 1\,040 \\ \hline 1.170 \end{array}$$

When you divide decimals, you must figure out where the decimal point will go in the answer before you divide.

**Example 5:** Divide 14.4 by 6.

1. Set up the problem. Since the divisor (the number you are dividing by) is a whole number, place the decimal point in the answer directly above the decimal point in the dividend (the number you are dividing).
2. Divide. Use the rules you learned for dividing whole numbers. The answer is **2.4**.

$$\begin{array}{r} 2.4 \\ 6\overline{)14.4} \\ -12 \\ \hline 24 \\ -24 \\ \hline 0 \end{array}$$

If the divisor is a decimal, you must move the decimal points in both the divisor and the dividend before you divide.

**Example 6:** Divide 4.9 by 0.35.

1. Set up the problem. There are two decimal places in the divisor. Move the decimal point in *both* the divisor and the dividend two places to the right. Note that you need to add a zero in the dividend in order to move the decimal two places.
2. Place the decimal point in the quotient directly above the decimal point in the dividend.
3. Divide. The correct answer is **14**.

$$.35\overline{)4.90}$$

$$\begin{array}{r} 14. \\ 35\overline{)490.} \\ -35 \\ \hline 140 \\ -140 \\ \hline 0 \end{array}$$

**Note:** You may not need to finish dividing in order to choose the correct answer. You may be able to eliminate all but one of the answer choices after only one or two division steps.

# PRACTICE 2.2

**A. Solve. You MAY NOT use a calculator.**

1. $\begin{array}{r} 5.3 \\ \times 0.5 \\ \hline \end{array}$

2. $\begin{array}{r} 64 \\ \times 0.2 \\ \hline \end{array}$

3. $\begin{array}{r} 12.4 \\ \times 0.04 \\ \hline \end{array}$

4. $6\overline{)3.12}$

5. $8\overline{)28.8}$

6. $5\overline{)20.45}$

7. $\begin{array}{r} 6.25 \\ \times 1.4 \\ \hline \end{array}$

8. $\begin{array}{r} 13.5 \\ \times 0.25 \\ \hline \end{array}$

9. $\begin{array}{r} 9.62 \\ \times 1.005 \\ \hline \end{array}$

10. $1.25\overline{)30}$

11. $2.8\overline{)39.76}$

12. $0.003\overline{)47.4}$

13. $15.5 \times 2.2 =$

14. $0.944 \div 0.4 =$

15. $2.05 \times 0.32 =$

16. $1.32 \div 0.5 =$

17. $2.75 \times 0.6 =$

18. $12.825 \div 3 =$

19. $3.36 \times 1.1 =$

20. $15.03 \div 15 =$

21. $0.12 \times 0.06 =$

**B. Choose the one best answer to each question.**

22. One container of floor cleaner holds 3.79 liters. If Zachary bought 4 containers, how many liters of cleaner did he buy?
    A. 0.9475
    B. 7.79
    C. 12.83
    D. 15.16

23. Ribbon costs \$0.45 per foot. A sewing project calls for 20.5 feet of ribbon. To the nearest cent, what will be the cost of the ribbon for the project?
    A. \$0.92
    B. \$9.23
    C. \$9.90
    D. \$45.56

24. Armando drove 278.7 miles over a 3-day period. On average, how many miles did he drive each day?
    A. 9.3
    B. 90.3
    C. 92.9
    D. 836.1

**Questions 25 and 26 are based on the following information.**

| Cereal | Net Weight | Servings per Box |
|---|---|---|
| Toasted Oats | 22.8 oz | 19 |
| Crisp Rice | 16.9 oz | 13 |
| Honey Mix | 12.5 oz | 10 |

25. A box of Toasted Oats cereal is priced at \$4.94. What is the cost per serving? (*Hint:* Divide the price by the number of servings.)
    A. \$0.49
    B. \$0.29
    C. \$0.26
    D. \$0.22

26. Lee bought 4 boxes of Honey Mix cereal. How many ounces of cereal did she buy?
    A. 31.25
    B. 50.0
    C. 67.6
    D. 91.2

**Review your work using the explanations that start on page 685.**

**STUDY ADVICE**

You work with decimals in real life almost every day, because amounts of money are usually expressed in decimal form. *So don't be intimidated* by decimal problems: If you can understand prices, you can work with decimals!

# Number and Quantity Part II: Decimals and Fractions

**KEY IDEAS**

- The bottom number of a fraction tells how many parts the group or object has.
- The top number tells how many parts you are working with.
- When the top number is greater than the bottom number, the fraction is greater than 1.

**TASC TEST TIP**

*If you have trouble visualizing the fractions in a problem, draw a quick sketch of the information presented in the problem similar to the ones on this page.*

LESSON 3

## Fraction Basics

A **fraction** uses two numbers to represent part of a whole. The bottom number, called the **denominator,** tells how many equal parts are in the whole group or item. The top number, called the **numerator,** tells how many parts you are working with.

There are 4 equal parts in this rectangle. Since 3 are shaded, we say that $\frac{3}{4}$ of the rectangle is shaded.

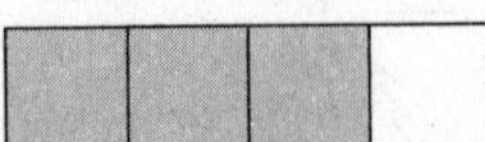

In a proper fraction, the numerator is less than the denominator. A **proper fraction** represents a quantity less than 1. An **improper fraction** is equal to or greater than 1.

There are 6 equal parts in the figure, and 6 are shaded; therefore, $\frac{6}{6}$ of the figure is shaded. $\frac{6}{6} = 1$

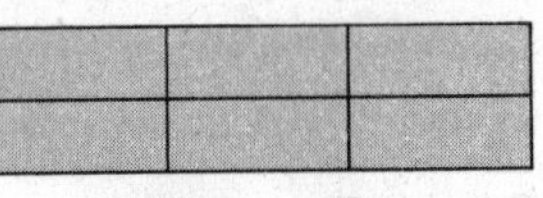

In this grouping, each figure is divided into 2 equal parts. A total of 3 parts are shaded, so $\frac{3}{2}$ are shaded.

A **mixed number** is another way to show an amount greater than 1. It consists of a whole number and a proper fraction. Another name for the shaded portion in the last figure is $1\frac{1}{2}$. The improper fraction $\frac{3}{2}$ equals $1\frac{1}{2}$.

You can also change an improper fraction to a whole or mixed number.

**Example 1:** Change $\frac{16}{5}$ to a mixed number.

1. Divide the numerator (16) by the denominator (5). Since 16 is not evenly divisible by 5, there is a remainder of 1. $16 \div 5 = 3 \text{ r } 1.$
2. The answer becomes the whole number, and the remainder becomes the numerator of the proper fraction. The denominator is the same as the one in the original fraction. $\frac{16}{5} = \mathbf{3\frac{1}{5}}$

You can also change a mixed number to an improper fraction.

**Example 2:** Change $7\frac{2}{3}$ to an improper fraction.

1. Multiply the whole number (7) by the denominator of the fraction (3), and add the numerator (2). $7 \times 3 = 21$ <br> $21 + 2 = 23$
2. Write the sum over the denominator of the original fraction. $7\frac{2}{3} = \mathbf{\frac{23}{3}}$

# PRACTICE 3

To perform operations with fractions, you need to be able to write equal fractions in higher or lower terms. The **terms** are the numerator and the denominator. A fraction is **reduced to lowest terms** when the two terms do not have any common factor except 1.

To **raise** a fraction, multiply both terms by the same number: $\frac{3}{4} = \frac{3 \times 3}{4 \times 3} = \frac{9}{12}$.

To **reduce** a fraction, divide both terms by the same number: $\frac{10}{15} = \frac{10 \div 5}{15 \div 5} = \frac{2}{3}$.

---

**A. Write a proper fraction for the shaded portion of each figure.**

**1.**

**2.** 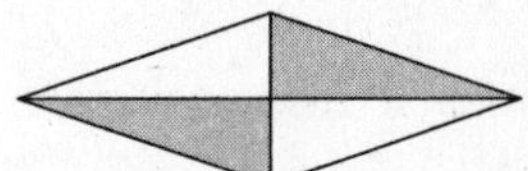

**3.** 

**B. Write an improper fraction and a mixed number for the shaded portion of each figure.**

**4.** 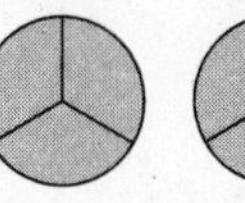 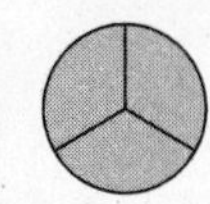 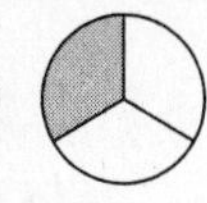

**5.** 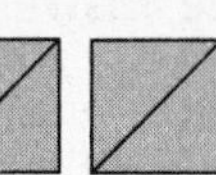 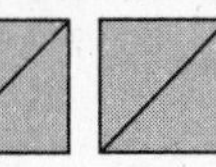 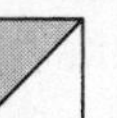

**6.** 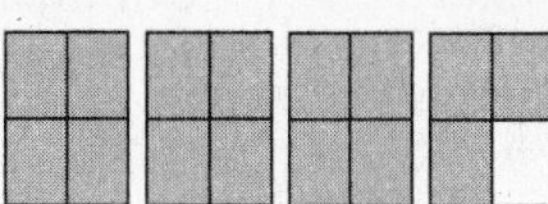

**C. Write improper fractions as mixed numbers and mixed numbers as improper fractions.**

**7.** $\frac{17}{3} =$ **9.** $\frac{24}{6} =$ **11.** $\frac{19}{4} =$ **13.** $\frac{43}{9} =$ **15.** $\frac{33}{4} =$

**8.** $3\frac{3}{5} =$ **10.** $5\frac{2}{9} =$ **12.** $2\frac{5}{12} =$ **14.** $1\frac{3}{4} =$ **16.** $5\frac{7}{10} =$

**D. Write an equal fraction with the given denominator.**

**17.** $\frac{3}{4} = \frac{}{16}$ **18.** $\frac{1}{3} = \frac{}{21}$ **19.** $\frac{4}{5} = \frac{}{60}$ **20.** $\frac{3}{8} = \frac{}{40}$ **21.** $\frac{6}{25} = \frac{}{100}$

(*Hint for question 17:* $4 \times ? = 16$)

**E. Reduce each fraction to lowest terms.**

**22.** $\frac{21}{28} =$ **23.** $\frac{4}{24} =$ **24.** $\frac{12}{20} =$ **25.** $\frac{26}{30} =$ **26.** $\frac{60}{90} =$

**F. Choose the one best answer to each question.**

**27.** Eighteen out of every 24 people surveyed say they went to at least one movie in December. What fraction of the people surveyed went to a movie in December?

A. $\frac{3}{4}$
B. $\frac{2}{3}$
C. $\frac{1}{3}$
D. $\frac{1}{4}$

**28.** Which of the following fractions equals $\frac{2}{5}$?

A. $\frac{15}{100}$
B. $\frac{30}{100}$
C. $\frac{40}{100}$
D. $\frac{80}{100}$

**Review your work using the explanations that start on page 685.**

Number and Quantity Part II: Decimals and Fractions

LESSON 4

# Fraction Operations

## Addition and Subtraction

You can add or subtract **like fractions.** Like fractions have a **common denominator.** In other words, their denominators are the same.

**Example 1:** Add $\frac{3}{10} + \frac{5}{10}$.

1. Since the denominators are the same, add the numerators. $\frac{3}{10} + \frac{5}{10} = \frac{8}{10}$

2. Reduce the answer to lowest terms. $\frac{8}{10} = \frac{8 \div 2}{10 \div 2} = \mathbf{\frac{4}{5}}$

**Example 2:** Subtract $\frac{2}{9}$ from $\frac{7}{9}$.
Subtract the numerators. The answer is already in lowest terms. $\frac{7}{9} - \frac{2}{9} = \mathbf{\frac{5}{9}}$

If the denominators are not the same, raise one or both fractions to higher terms so that they become like fractions.

**Example 3:** Add $\frac{5}{6} + \frac{1}{4}$.

1. One way to find a common denominator is to think of the multiples of both denominators. The lowest is 12.
   Multiples
   of 6: 6, [12], 18
   of 4: 4, 8, [12], 16

2. Raise each fraction to higher terms with a denominator of 12. $\frac{5 \times 2}{6 \times 2} = \frac{10}{12}, \frac{1 \times 3}{4 \times 3} = \frac{3}{12}$

3. Add the like fractions. Rewrite the sum as a mixed number. $\frac{10}{12} + \frac{3}{12} = \frac{13}{12} = \mathbf{1\frac{1}{12}}$

Use the same process to add or subtract mixed numbers. Example 4 shows how to regroup when subtracting mixed numbers.

**Example 4:** Subtract $4\frac{1}{16} - 1\frac{3}{8}$.

1. Raise the second fraction so that it also has a denominator of 16. $\frac{3 \times 2}{8 \times 2} = \frac{6}{16}$

2. Set up the problem. To subtract the fractions, you need to regroup 1 from the whole number column and add it to the top fraction. $4\frac{1}{16} = 3\frac{16}{16} + \frac{1}{16} = 3\frac{17}{16}$

3. Subtract the fractions and then the whole numbers. $3\frac{17}{16} - 1\frac{6}{16} = \mathbf{2\frac{11}{16}}$

### KEY IDEAS

- You can add or subtract fractions, but they must have the same denominator.
- If denominators are not the same, find a common denominator and raise one or both fractions.
- Always reduce answers to lowest terms and change improper fractions to mixed numbers.

### TASC TEST TIP

*If your solution to a fraction problem is not one of the given answer choices, make sure that you reduced your answer to lowest terms. On the Mathematics Test, answer choices are always written in lowest terms.*

# PRACTICE 4.1

**A. Solve. Reduce answers to lowest terms. Simplify improper fractions as mixed numbers.**

1. $\frac{3}{8} + \frac{1}{8}$

2. $\frac{1}{6} + \frac{5}{6}$

3. $\frac{8}{9} - \frac{5}{9}$

4. $\frac{7}{12} - \frac{5}{12}$

5. $\frac{1}{4} + \frac{2}{3}$

6. $\frac{1}{2} + \frac{5}{8}$

7. $\frac{9}{10} - \frac{3}{5}$

8. $\frac{7}{9} - \frac{1}{2}$

9. $2\frac{1}{5} + 1\frac{2}{3}$

10. $4\frac{1}{2} - 2\frac{3}{4}$

11. $5\frac{5}{6} + 2\frac{2}{3} =$
12. $6\frac{7}{8} + 4\frac{3}{4} =$
13. $12\frac{1}{10} + 9\frac{3}{5} =$
14. $2\frac{2}{9} + \frac{2}{3} + 4\frac{5}{6} =$
15. $3\frac{1}{3} + 5\frac{2}{3} + 3\frac{5}{6} =$
16. $\frac{3}{8} + \frac{7}{12} + 1\frac{2}{3} =$
17. $16\frac{2}{3} + 25\frac{3}{4} =$
18. $10\frac{1}{2} + 8\frac{4}{5} + 3\frac{1}{4} =$
19. $8\frac{1}{2} - 3\frac{4}{9} =$
20. $15 - 3\frac{7}{8} =$
21. $14\frac{1}{4} - 10\frac{3}{7} =$
22. $9\frac{11}{12} - 8\frac{5}{8} =$
23. $6 - 3\frac{4}{7} =$
24. $13\frac{1}{3} - 4\frac{4}{9} =$
25. $5\frac{5}{7} - 4\frac{4}{5} =$

**B. Choose the one best answer to each question.**

26. To make the top of a dining room table, Craig glues a piece of oak that is $\frac{5}{16}$ inch thick to a piece of pine that is $\frac{7}{8}$ inch thick. What is the total thickness, in inches, of the tabletop?

A. $\frac{9}{16}$
B. $1\frac{3}{16}$
C. $1\frac{1}{4}$
D. $1\frac{9}{16}$

27. Carol will use the two bolts shown below to assemble a book cart. How much longer, in inches, is bolt A than bolt B?

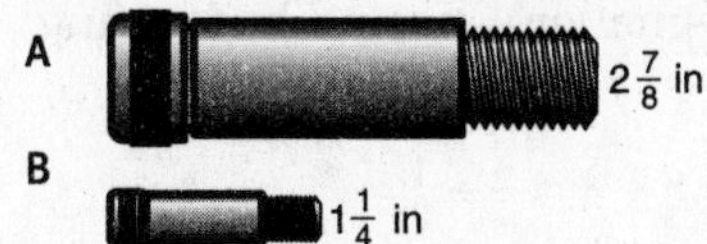


A. $\frac{5}{8}$
B. $1\frac{3}{8}$
C. $1\frac{5}{8}$
D. $1\frac{3}{4}$

28. At a fabric store, Melissa sold $8\frac{7}{8}$ yards of cloth to a customer. If the material was cut from a bolt of fabric containing $23\frac{1}{4}$ yards, how many yards are left on the bolt?

A. $14\frac{3}{8}$
B. $15\frac{3}{8}$
C. $15\frac{3}{4}$
D. $31\frac{7}{8}$

29. A batch of salad dressing requires $1\frac{2}{3}$ cups of olive oil, $\frac{1}{2}$ cup of vinegar, and $\frac{3}{4}$ cup of water. How many cups of salad dressing will this recipe produce?

A. $1\frac{2}{3}$
B. $2\frac{5}{6}$
C. $2\frac{11}{12}$
D. $3\frac{7}{12}$

**Review your work using the explanations that start on page 685.**

**STUDY ADVICE**

Remember that practice has three levels: Learn and Review, Practice and Review, Assess and Review. For each lesson, absorb the concepts on the left page. Then practice using the page on the right, and carefully review the explanations in the back of the book. Finally, use the question sets at the end of each chapter to assess your progress. Don't forget to review the explanations for those question sets, too.

## Multiplication and Division

It isn't necessary to find a common denominator to multiply and divide fractions. To multiply fractions, simply multiply the numerators and then the denominators. Reduce the answer, if necessary.

**Example 5:** What is the product of $\frac{7}{8}$ and $\frac{1}{2}$?

Multiply the numerators together, and then the denominators. The answer is in lowest terms. $\frac{7}{8} \times \frac{1}{2} = \frac{7 \times 1}{8 \times 2} = \mathbf{\frac{7}{16}}$

Before multiplying a mixed number, change it to an improper fraction.

**Example 6:** What is $\frac{1}{3}$ of $3\frac{3}{4}$?

1. Change $3\frac{3}{4}$ to an improper fraction. $3\frac{3}{4} = \frac{15}{4}$
2. Multiply the numerators and the denominators. $\frac{15}{4} \times \frac{1}{3} = \frac{15 \times 1}{4 \times 3} = \frac{15}{12}$
3. Change to a mixed number and reduce to lowest terms. $\frac{15}{12} = 1\frac{3}{12} = \mathbf{1\frac{1}{4}}$

You can use a shortcut called **canceling** to reduce the fractions as you work the problem. To cancel, divide both a numerator and a denominator by the same number. The numerator and the denominator can be in different fractions.

**Example 7:** Multiply $1\frac{1}{2}$ by $1\frac{1}{5}$.

1. Change to improper fractions. $1\frac{1}{2} = \frac{3}{2}$ and $1\frac{1}{5} = \frac{6}{5}$
2. Set up the multiplication problem. Both 6 (a numerator) and 2 (a denominator) are evenly divisible by 2. Divide them by 2. Then multiply using the new numerator and denominator. Finally, change the improper fraction to a mixed number. $\frac{3}{2} \times \frac{6}{5} = \frac{3}{\not{2}_{1}} \times \frac{\not{6}^{3}}{5} = \frac{9}{5} = \mathbf{1\frac{4}{5}}$

**The slash marks show that the numbers have been divided.**

You will need two additional steps to divide fractions. Before dividing, **invert** the divisor (the fraction you are dividing by). To invert the fraction, switch the numerator and the denominator. Finally, change the division symbol to a multiplication symbol and multiply.

**Example 8:** Jim has an 8-pound bag of nuts. He wants to fill smaller $\frac{1}{2}$-pound bags using the nuts. How many small bags can he make?

1. Divide 8 by $\frac{1}{2}$. Set up the division problem. Always write whole or mixed numbers as improper fractions. $8 \div \frac{1}{2} = \frac{8}{1} \div \frac{1}{2} =$
2. Invert the fraction you are dividing by. Then change the operation sign to multiplication. Multiply, following the rules for multiplying fractions. **Jim can make 16 small bags.** $\frac{8}{1} \times \frac{2}{1} = \frac{16}{1} = \mathbf{16}$

**Note:** When you multiply by a fraction less than 1, the answer is smaller than the number you started with because you are finding a "part of." When you divide by a fraction less than 1, the answer is greater than the number.

# PRACTICE 4.2

**A. Solve. Reduce answers to lowest terms. Simplify improper fractions as mixed numbers.**

1. $\frac{2}{3} \times \frac{1}{4} =$
2. $1\frac{5}{6} \times \frac{1}{2} =$
3. $\frac{2}{3} \times 21 =$
4. $50 \times \frac{3}{8} =$
5. $3\frac{1}{2} \times \frac{1}{4} =$
6. $\frac{3}{4} \times \frac{7}{8} =$
7. $2\frac{1}{3} \times 3\frac{2}{5} =$
8. $15 \times 2\frac{3}{4} =$
9. $\frac{5}{8} \times 3\frac{1}{4} =$
10. $\frac{7}{8} \div \frac{1}{16} =$
11. $\frac{4}{5} \div \frac{4}{9} =$
12. $12 \div \frac{1}{4} =$
13. $6 \div 2\frac{1}{2} =$
14. $3\frac{3}{4} \div 1\frac{2}{3} =$
15. $9 \div \frac{1}{3} =$
16. $26\frac{2}{3} \div 3\frac{1}{3} =$
17. $40\frac{3}{8} \div 4\frac{1}{4} =$
18. $3\frac{7}{8} \div 5\frac{1}{6} =$

**B. Choose the one best answer to each question.**

**19.** A city is considering raising taxes to build a football stadium. A survey of registered voters yielded the following results:

| Position | Fraction of Those Surveyed |
|---|---|
| Against Tax Hike | $\frac{7}{16}$ |
| For Tax Hike | $\frac{3}{16}$ |
| Undecided | $\frac{3}{8}$ |

If 400 people were surveyed, how many support the tax hike?

A. 48
B. 75
C. 150
D. 175

**20.** A tailor has 20 yards of shirt fabric. How many shirts can she complete if each shirt requires $2\frac{3}{4}$ yards of fabric?

A. 6
B. 7
C. 8
D. 10

**21.** An insurance agent estimates that it takes $\frac{2}{3}$ hour to process a customer's claim. If the agent spends 22 hours per week processing claims, about how many claims does he process in a week?

A. $14\frac{2}{3}$
B. 33
C. 44
D. 66

**22.** A fluorescent lighting panel is $12\frac{5}{8}$ inches wide. If three of the panels are installed as shown below, what will be the width in inches of the combined panels?

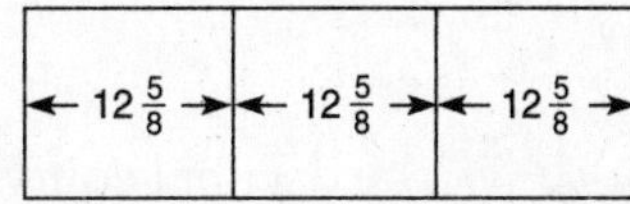


A. $13\frac{7}{8}$
B. $36\frac{5}{8}$
C. $37\frac{7}{8}$
D. $42\frac{7}{8}$

**Review your work using the explanations that start on page 685.**

Number and Quantity Part II: Decimals and Fractions

LESSON 5

# Fraction and Decimal Equivalencies

Fractions and decimals are two ways to show part of a whole. You can change fractions to decimals by dividing.

**Example 1:** Change $\frac{3}{8}$ to a decimal.

The fraction $\frac{3}{8}$ means $3 \div 8$. Use a calculator to divide. $3 \div 8 = \mathbf{0.375}$

You can also change a decimal to a fraction.

**Example 2:** Change 0.35 to a fraction.

Write the decimal number over the place value name of the last decimal digit on the right. The last digit, 5, is in the hundredths column. Reduce to lowest terms. $\frac{35}{100} = \frac{35 \div 5}{100 \div 5} = \mathbf{\frac{7}{20}}$

You will find it useful to memorize the most common fraction and decimal equivalents. These equivalents will also help you solve percent problems.

| Decimal | Fraction |
|---|---|
| 0.1 | $\frac{1}{10}$ |
| 0.125 | $\frac{1}{8}$ |
| 0.2 | $\frac{1}{5}$ |
| 0.25 | $\frac{1}{4}$ |
| 0.3 | $\frac{3}{10}$ |
| $0.33\overline{3}$ | $\frac{1}{3}$ |

| Decimal | Fraction |
|---|---|
| 0.375 | $\frac{3}{8}$ |
| 0.4 | $\frac{2}{5}$ |
| 0.5 | $\frac{1}{2}$ |
| 0.6 | $\frac{3}{5}$ |
| 0.625 | $\frac{5}{8}$ |
| $0.66\overline{6}$ | $\frac{2}{3}$ |

| Decimal | Fraction |
|---|---|
| 0.7 | $\frac{7}{10}$ |
| 0.75 | $\frac{3}{4}$ |
| 0.8 | $\frac{4}{5}$ |
| 0.875 | $\frac{7}{8}$ |
| 0.9 | $\frac{9}{10}$ |
| | |

The decimal equivalents for $\frac{1}{3}$ and $\frac{2}{3}$ are marked with a bar. The bar shows that the decimal repeats indefinitely.

You can use fraction and decimal equivalents to save time when solving math problems.

**Example 3:** Each dose of cough medicine contains 0.25 ounce of medication. How many ounces of medication are in 48 doses?

To solve the problem, you need to multiply 48 by 0.25, a time-consuming calculation. However, since $0.25 = \frac{1}{4}$ you can find $\frac{1}{4}$ of 48 to solve the problem. The answer is **12 ounces.** $48 \times \frac{1}{4} = \frac{48}{4} = \mathbf{12}$

## KEY IDEAS

- To change a fraction to a decimal, divide the numerator by the denominator.
- To change a decimal to a fraction, write the number without the decimal point over the place value of the last decimal digit. Reduce.
- Avoid time-consuming calculations by using fraction-decimal equivalents.

## TASC TEST TIP

*Look at the answer choices before you begin working a multiple-choice problem. Knowing whether you need an answer in fraction or decimal form may affect how you approach the problem.*

# PRACTICE 5

Knowing fraction-decimal equivalents can also help you interpret remainders when using a calculator.

**Example 4:** Ray inspects machine assemblies. He must inspect 12 assemblies during his 40-hour workweek. On average, how many hours can he spend on each inspection?

Using a calculator, divide 40 by 12: 40 [÷] 12 [enter]. The right side of the display reads 3.333333333.

Since you know that $0.33\overline{3} = \frac{1}{3}$, the answer is **$3\frac{1}{3}$ hours.**

---

**Solve. When possible, use fraction and decimal equivalents to make the work easier. You MAY use a calculator on questions 5 and 6.**

1. During a 25%-off sale, store clerks find the amount of the discounts by multiplying the regular price by 0.25. What is the discount on an item with a regular price of $80?

   A. $32.00
   B. $20.00
   C. $16.40
   D. $2.00

2. At Linton Products, $\frac{3}{10}$ of the workers are in the company's ride-share program. If there are 480 workers, which of the following expressions could be used to find the number in the ride-share program?

   A. $480 \times 0.7$
   B. $480 \div 0.7$
   C. $480 \times 0.3$
   D. $480 \div 0.3$

3. Sharon is using a calculator to find out how many hours she has spent on a certain job. She divides, and her display reads:

   [4.666666666]

   Assuming her calculations are correct, how many hours did she spend on the job?

   A. $4\frac{1}{6}$
   B. $4\frac{2}{3}$
   C. $4\frac{6}{7}$
   D. 46

4. A gourmet candy company charges the following prices per pound.

| Jelly Beans | $9.60 |
|---|---|
| Peanut Brittle | $12.00 |
| Almond Toffee | $28.50 |

   How much would a customer pay for 1.5 pounds of peanut brittle?

   A. $6.00
   B. $14.40
   C. $18.00
   D. $42.75

5. At 1 P.M., the amount of rain in a rain gauge is 1.125 inches. At 3 P.M., the gauge holds 1.875 inches. What fraction of an inch of rain fell between 1 P.M. and 3 P.M.?

   A. $\frac{7}{8}$
   B. $\frac{3}{4}$
   C. $\frac{7}{10}$
   D. $\frac{1}{8}$

6. A steel rod, 3 meters in length, is cut into 8 equal pieces. What is the length in meters of each piece?

   A. 0.125
   B. 0.333
   C. 0.375
   D. 2.333

**Review your work using the explanations that start on page 686.**

**STUDY ADVICE**

Memorizing some basic fraction-decimal equivalencies can save you time on the TASC Mathematics Test. Consider making flash cards to help you memorize them.

Number and Quantity Part II: Decimals and Fractions

LESSON 6

# Decimals and Fractions on the Number Line

On the TASC Mathematics Test you may need to recognize or locate fractions, mixed fractions, or decimals on a **number line**. A number line represents numbers in order from least to greatest. As you move to the left along a number line, numbers decrease in value. As you move to the right, numbers increase in value.

0 1 2 3 4 5

The arrows on the ends indicate that numbers continue forever in both directions. If you imagine zooming in on a portion of that number line, it might look like this:

0 0.25 0.5 0.75 1 1.25 1.5

Thus, a number line can include decimals and whole numbers. For example, the point represents 0.75, which is greater than 0.5 and less than 1.

A number line can also represent fractions and mixed fractions in order from least to greatest:

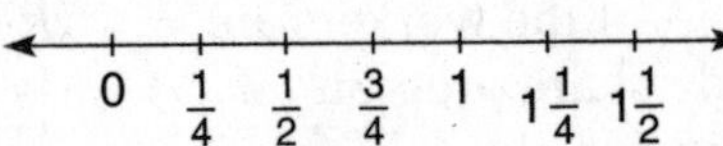


Use this question to practice working with number lines:

**Example 1:** John works five shifts per week. His boss asks him to spend exactly half of his time this week working on a specific project. How many work shifts will John devote to that project? Circle the answer on the number line below.

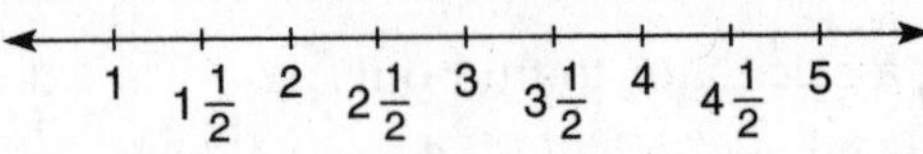


If you circled **$2\frac{1}{2}$**, you are correct. Multiply 5 by $\frac{1}{2}$ to determine that John will spend **$2\frac{1}{2}$** shifts on the project.

### KEY IDEAS

- A number line is a picture that helps you compare the sizes of numbers. Numbers on the left are smaller than numbers on the right.
- Number lines can also be used to represent and compare decimals.
- Fractions and mixed fractions can also be represented on a number line.

### TASC TEST TIP

*Questions on the Mathematics Test may ask you to recognize a fraction or a decimal on a number line, or they may ask you to place a dot on a line to represent a fraction or decimal value.*

# PRACTICE 6

**A. Choose the one best answer to each question.**

1. What is the value of the point on the number line below?

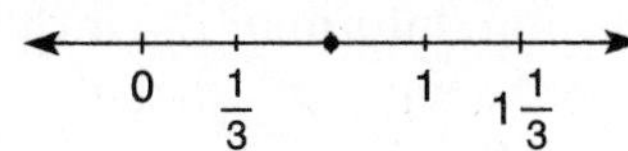


A. 0
B. $\frac{1}{2}$
C. $\frac{2}{3}$
D. $1\frac{1}{3}$

2. What is the value of the point on the number line below?

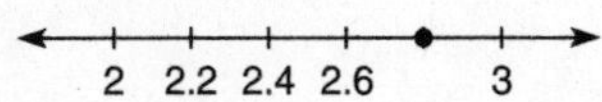


A. 2
B. 2.5
C. 2.7
D. 2.8

3. In the number line below, what is the value of *A* minus *B*?

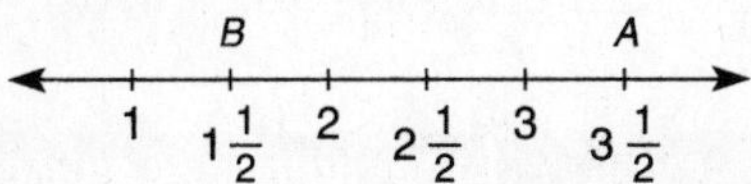


A. 1
B. $1\frac{1}{2}$
C. 2
D. $3\frac{1}{2}$

4. Angela baked 24 cookies and gave 16 of them to her neighbor. On the number line below, circle the fraction of Angela's cookies that she gave to her neighbor.

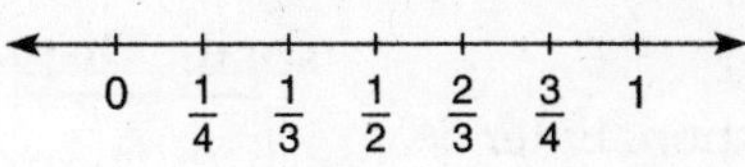


**B. Write the decimal values of the points on the number lines.**

For each of the number lines below, fill in the value of the point using decimals.

5.

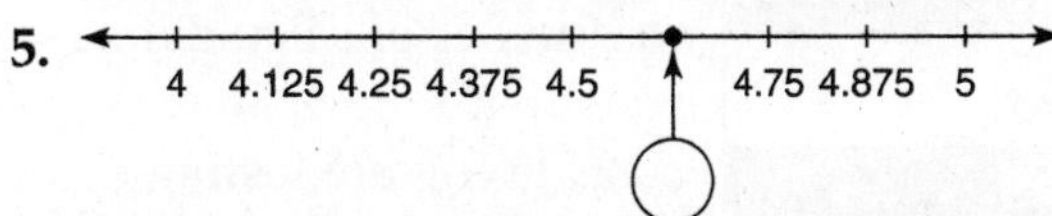


6.

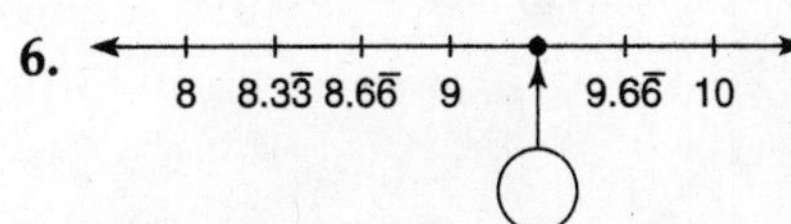


**C. Write the fraction values of the points on the number lines.**

For each of the number lines below, fill in the value of the point using mixed fractions.

7.

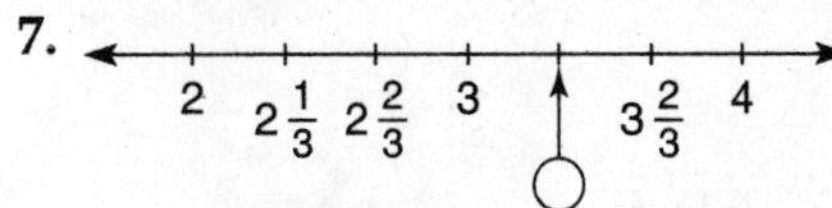


8.

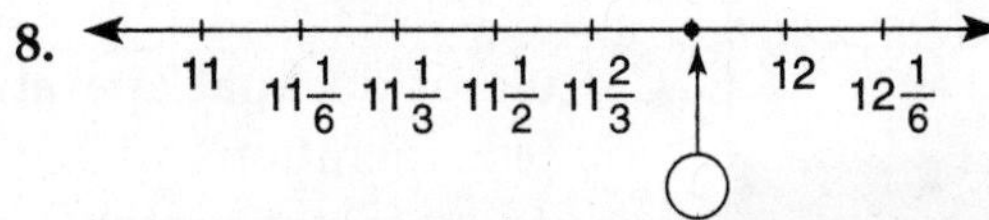


**Review your work using the explanations that start on page 686.**

# Number and Quantity Part II: Decimals and Fractions

## KEY IDEAS

- Fraction and decimal operations are entered in the same order as whole-number operations.
- On the TI-30XS MultiView™ calculator, use the decimal point key (.) for decimals and the fraction key, $\frac{n}{d}$, for fractions.
- To work with mixed fractions, use the 2nd function, U$\frac{n}{d}$, which is in green over the fraction key.

## TASC TEST TIP

*A fraction answer may appear in the form of an improper fraction. In order to change to an equivalent mixed number on the TI-30XS MultiView™, use the green 2nd function over this key:*

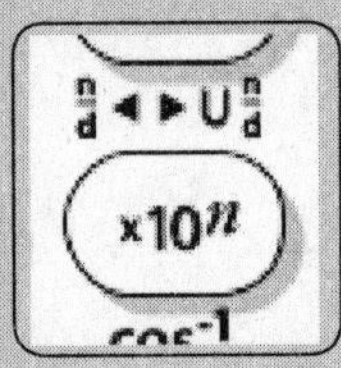

*All of the calculators permitted on the TASC paper exam have this capability. If you are not planning to use the TI-30XS MultiView™, be sure to find the appropriate keys on your calculator.*

LESSON 7

# Decimal and Fraction Calculator Skills

Several important calculator keys are used to work with decimals and fractions. Remember, if you are testing on paper, you might use any one of a number of calculators (see page 228 for more information), including the one that follows here. Your state may limit the types of calculators you can use. If you are testing on computer, you will use an on screen version of the calculator below.

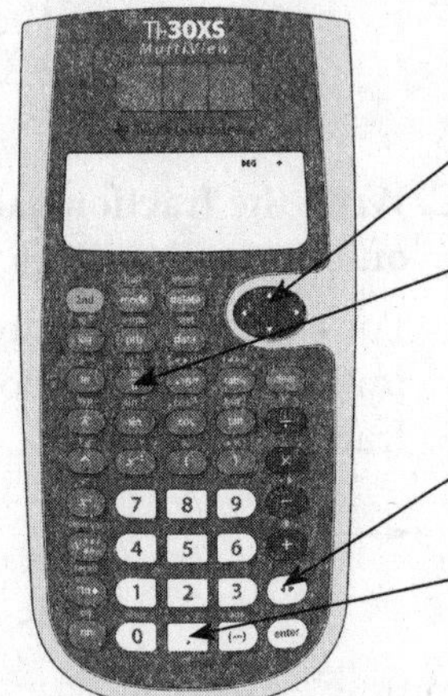


**Cursor keys** move the cursor on the screen up, down, left, and right.

The **fraction key** is used to enter fractions; the **mixed number 2nd function** is in green above it.

The **toggle key** changes between equivalent fraction and decimal forms of a number.

The **decimal point** key enters a decimal point.

Calculator **decimal operations** are performed in the same way that you use operations with whole numbers. You need to use the **decimal point key** (.) under the 2 in the white **numeric keypad**. Practice with these examples:

| To solve this problem... | Press these keys... | The right-hand side of the display reads... |
|---|---|---|
| 3.89 + 2.5 | 3.89(+)2.5(enter) | 6.39 |
| 5.2 − 0.78 | 5.2(−).78(enter) | 4.42 |
| 0.9 × 15 | .9(×)15(enter) | 13.5 |
| 1.7 ÷ 2 | 1.7(÷)2(enter) | 0.85 |

You will use several calculator functions to work with **fractions** and **mixed fraction operations**. First practice entering fractions and converting to decimals.

**Example 1:** Reduce $\frac{56}{448}$ to lowest terms and then convert to a decimal.

**On the Display**

1. Clear the calculator.
2. Press the $\frac{n}{d}$ button to enter a fraction. Enter 56 at the blinking cursor, in the numerator.

3. Use the down cursor key (▼) to enter 448 in the denominator.

4. Press (enter) to reduce the fraction to lowest terms, which appears on the right of your screen: $\frac{1}{8}$

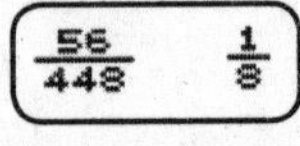

5. To express the fraction as a decimal, press the *toggle* button: (◄►). The decimal **0.125** appears on the right display.

$\frac{1}{8}$ ◂▸ 0.125

# PRACTICE 7

Now practice operations with **mixed fractions** using the *2nd function* key.

**Example 2:** A plastic pipe is to be cut into pieces measuring $1\frac{7}{8}$ feet. The original pipe was $20\frac{5}{8}$ feet long. How many pieces can be cut from the pipe?

| | Keys to Press | On the Display |
|---|---|---|
| 1. Clear the calculator. | (clear) | |
| 2. Recognize that a mixed fraction is a green *2nd* function: ($U\frac{n}{d}$) over the [n/d] key. Press the (2nd) key and the [n/d] key. Note both a whole number and a blinking fraction cursor on the display. | (2nd) [n/d] |  |
| 3. Enter the number being divided first–the whole pipe: $20\frac{5}{8}$. Enter 20, then follow the direction of the onscreen arrow and press the right arrow button to move to the fraction cursors. Enter 5 and then use the down arrow to enter the 8. Exit the fraction by pressing the right arrow again. | 20 ▶<br>5 ▼ 8 ▶ | 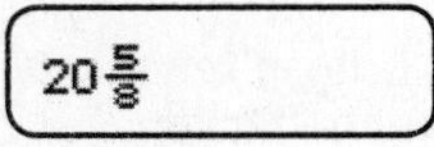 |
| 4. Press the division key. Then follow the same process with the second number: $1\frac{7}{8}$, starting with the 2nd function: ($U\frac{n}{d}$) | (÷) (2nd) [n/d]<br>1 ▶ 7 ▼ 8 ▶ | $20\frac{5}{8}\div1\frac{7}{8}$ |
| 5. Press the (enter) button for the solution. The answer 11 for **11 pieces** appears on the right side of the screen. | (enter) | $20\frac{5}{8}\div1\frac{7}{8}$ 11 |

---

**A. Solve the following problems using your calculator.**

**1.** $3.5 + 1.87 + 2.009$ **2.** $3\frac{2}{3} - 1\frac{5}{12}$ **3.** $\$25.35 \times 15$ **4.** $10\frac{1}{2} \div \frac{1}{4}$

**5.** Linda earns \$95 per day. If she works $\frac{8}{9}$ of a day, how much will she earn?

**6.** Aaron bought a refrigerator for \$956.88. The price includes tax and interest charges. If he makes 12 equal monthly payments, how much will he pay each month?

**7.** An insurance agent estimates the annual cost of insurance on a home by multiplying the sale price of the home by 0.0125. What will be the yearly cost of insurance on a home priced at \$118,000?

**8.** In a recipe, the total liquid added to a mixture is $1\frac{1}{2}$ cups of water and $2\frac{3}{4}$ cups of chicken broth. How many cups of liquid are used in the recipe?

**9.** A quilt costs \$84.99 and weighs 5.56 pounds. The shipping charge is \$1.20 per pound. To the nearest cent, what would be the shipping charge on the quilt?

A. \$5.56
B. \$6.67
C. \$8.26
D. \$10.20

**10.** A state park contains 64 acres. A wildlife preserve makes up $\frac{3}{8}$ of the park. How many acres are in the preserve?

A. 8
B. 21
C. 24
D. 27

**Review your work using the explanations that start on page 686.**

Number and Quantity Part II: Decimals and Fractions

### KEY IDEAS

- Write your answer in the top row of boxes. Then fill in the grid.
- Always write mixed numbers as improper fractions.
- For answers requiring decimals, the grid contains a decimal point bubble.

### TASC TEST TIP

*Double-check your work to make sure that you have filled in only one circle in each column. The fraction bar (slash) or decimal point cannot be marked in the same column as a number.*

## LESSON 8

# Filling in the Answer Grid Using Decimals or Fractions

On page 252, you learned how to fill in a numerical answer using a bubble grid. Some questions on the TASC Mathematics Test may require you to use this grid to answer questions involving decimals or fractions.

Study the following examples. Remember: You should write your answer in the top row of boxes, but this part of the grid will not be scored. You must correctly fill the circles in the grid to receive credit for your answer.

To enter a fraction on the answer grid, bubble in the slash mark to separate the numerator from the denominator.

**Example 1:** John needs $\frac{3}{4}$ cup of brown sugar for a recipe. If he wants to make only one-half the number of servings, how many cups of brown sugar will he need?

1. Multiply to find the answer. $\frac{3}{4} \times \frac{1}{2} = \frac{3}{8}$
2. Enter the fraction on the grid. Fill in a slash to represent the fraction bar.

You may not enter mixed numbers on the grid. If the answer to a problem is a mixed number, change the mixed number to an improper fraction.

**Example 2:** Elaine exercised for $1\frac{3}{4}$ hours on Monday and $1\frac{1}{2}$ hours on Tuesday. How many hours did she exercise in all?

1. Add. $1\frac{3}{4} + 1\frac{1}{2} = 1\frac{3}{4} + 1\frac{2}{4} = 2\frac{5}{4}$
2. Change the answer to an improper fraction. $2\frac{5}{4} = \frac{13}{4}$
3. Enter the answer on the grid.

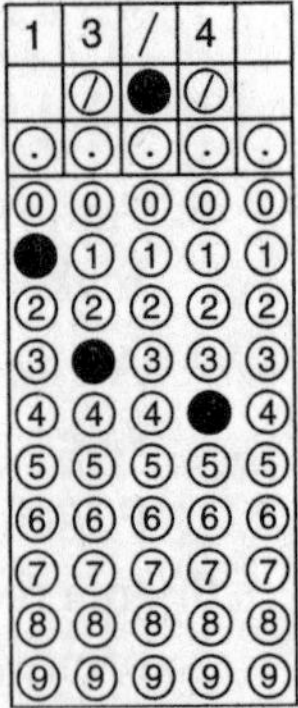

To enter a decimal, fill in a circle on the third row of the grid to show the location of the decimal point.

# PRACTICE 8

**Example 3:** A chemical compound weighs 12.8 kilograms. If the compound is divided equally into five portions, how many kilograms will each weigh?

1. Divide. $12.8 \div 5 = \mathbf{2.56}$

2. Write the answer in the blank boxes. Then fill in the appropriate circles in the grid. You can start your answer anywhere on the grid as long as the answer fits.

**Solve. Mark your answers in the grids on the right side of the page. You MAY use your calculator.**

1. On a business trip, Alex had to buy gasoline three times. He bought 12.6, 9.8, and 13.2 gallons of gasoline. How many gallons did he buy in all?
2. Aubrey withdraws $150 from her bank account and pays $100 to her day-care provider. What fraction of the withdrawal did she spend on day-care?
3. Colleen worked $9\frac{1}{2}$ hours on Monday and $7\frac{1}{2}$ hours on Tuesday. How many hours more did she work on Monday than on Tuesday?
4. A bottle holds 2.6 ounces of food coloring. How many bottles can be completely filled from 100 ounces of food coloring?
5. For a youth picnic, Leah bought 18 cases of soft drinks: 9 were root beer, 6 were lemon-lime, and 3 were cherry cola. Reduced to lowest terms, what fraction of the cases were cherry cola?
6. A sheet of foam board is 0.5 centimeter thick. How many sheets of the board can be stacked in a space that is 12.5 centimeters high?

## STUDY ADVICE

Are you sticking to your study schedule? If not, does it need to be adjusted to make way for other commitments, or can you cut out other activities to make more time to study? You *can* get your high school equivalency degree, but you've got to commit to your studies.

**Review your work using the explanations that start on page 686.**

# DECIMALS AND FRACTIONS PRACTICE QUESTIONS

**Directions: You MAY use your calculator.**

1. A wooden flooring strip is $20\frac{1}{2}$ inches long. If you cut off $4\frac{3}{4}$ inches from one end, what will be the new length of the strip in inches?

   A. $16\frac{3}{4}$
   B. $16\frac{1}{4}$
   C. $15\frac{3}{4}$
   D. $15\frac{1}{4}$

2. A box of cereal costs \$4.69. The package label says that the box contains 19 servings. What is the cost of 1 serving to the nearest cent?

   A. \$0.02
   B. \$0.25
   C. \$0.47
   D. \$2.46

3. How much would a computer system cost if it is priced as shown below?

   **Pay \$200 down and make 12 monthly payments of only \$98.85.**

   A. \$3586.20
   B. \$2400.00
   C. \$1386.20
   D. \$1186.20

4. Unleaded gasoline sells for \$2.869 per gallon. How much would $10\frac{1}{2}$ gallons cost? Round your answer to the nearest cent.

   A. \$13.40
   B. \$28.69
   C. \$30.12
   D. \$301.20

5. Three packages weigh $1\frac{1}{2}$ pounds, $4\frac{3}{4}$ pounds, and $2\frac{3}{10}$ pounds. What is the average weight, in pounds, of the packages? (*Hint:* Add the weights, then divide by the number of packages.)

   A. 2.14
   B. 2.85
   C. 4.75
   D. 8.55

6. Gina is paid \$8 an hour. If she earned \$258 in 1 week, how many hours did she work?

   A. $34\frac{1}{2}$
   B. $32\frac{1}{3}$
   C. $32\frac{1}{4}$
   D. $32\frac{1}{5}$

7. A developer plans to build homes on $20\frac{1}{2}$ acres. She estimates that $6\frac{1}{4}$ acres will be used for roads. The remaining land will be divided into $\frac{1}{4}$-acre lots. How many lots can the subdivision include?

   A. 7
   B. 57
   C. 81
   D. 107

8. A school buys 1000 white-board markers. Below is the price per marker for two brands. How much did the school save by buying Brand A instead of Brand B?

   Brand A: \$0.27 each
   Brand B: \$0.36 each

   A. \$0.09
   B. \$0.90
   C. \$9.00
   D. \$90.00

**Questions 9 and 10 refer to the following information.**

| Madison Small Animal Clinic Scheduling Guidelines | |
|---|---|
| New-Patient Appointment | $\frac{3}{4}$ hr |
| Immunizations | $\frac{1}{4}$ hr |
| Routine Physical | $\frac{1}{3}$ hr |
| Dental Scaling | $\frac{3}{4}$ hr |
| Sick Animal Visit | $\frac{1}{2}$ hr |
| Serious-Injury Visit (includes X-rays) | $1\frac{1}{4}$ hr |

9. Ray is a veterinarian at the small-animal clinic. He has four appointments scheduled for Monday morning: two new-patient appointments, a serious-injury visit, and a dental scaling. In hours, how much time should these appointments take?

   A. $2\frac{3}{4}$
   B. $3\frac{1}{2}$
   C. $3\frac{3}{4}$
   D. 4

10. Jennifer works $3\frac{1}{2}$ hours each morning at the clinic. How many routine physicals could she complete in one morning?

    A. 4
    B. 9
    C. 10
    D. 11

---

11. A minor-league baseball stadium has 6000 seats. On Beach Towel Night, the stadium sold 5500 of its available seats. What fraction of the seats were sold?

    A. $\frac{5}{6}$
    B. $\frac{8}{9}$
    C. $\frac{9}{10}$
    D. $\frac{11}{12}$

12. The City Center parking garage charges $3.50 for the first hour and $1.25 for each additional $\frac{1}{2}$ hour. How much would it cost to park at the garage for $2\frac{1}{2}$ hours?

    A. $4.75
    B. $6.25
    C. $7.25
    D. $9.75

**For questions 13 and 14, mark your answers in the grids below.**

13. Susan scheduled 84 appointments for patients at a hospital outreach clinic. Only 56 patients kept their appointments. What fraction of the scheduled appointments were kept?

14. This portion of a gas bill compares a household's natural gas usage for December of this year and last year.

| Gas Bill Comparison Average Daily Usage | | | |
|---|---|---|---|
| This Year | | Last Year | |
| Dec | 3.13 therms | Dec | 3.97 therms |

How many more therms of natural gas did the household use in December of last year than December of this year? Express your answer as a decimal.

13.

14.

15. Jim and Carl have until 1 P.M. to load 250 boxes. By 12:30 P.M., 175 of the boxes are loaded. What fraction of the boxes has not been loaded?

A. $\frac{1}{5}$
B. $\frac{3}{10}$
C. $\frac{3}{5}$
D. $\frac{7}{10}$

16. On the number line below, what is the value of *A* minus *B*?

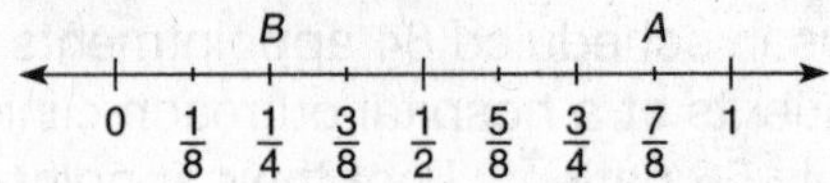


A. $\frac{1}{4}$
B. $\frac{5}{8}$
C. $\frac{7}{8}$
D. $1\frac{1}{8}$

17. Scott is driving about 380 miles from Los Angeles to San Francisco. He plans to cover $\frac{3}{4}$ of the distance before noon. How many miles does he plan to drive before noon?

A. 285
B. 254
C. 126
D. 95

18. A cookie recipe calls for $1\frac{2}{3}$ cups of sugar. If you wanted to make half the quantity shown in the recipe, how many cups of sugar would you use?

A. $\frac{2}{5}$
B. $\frac{2}{3}$
C. $\frac{5}{6}$
D. $1\frac{1}{6}$

19. How many miles would a map distance of $\frac{5}{8}$ inch represent if 1 in = 240 mi?

A. 40
B. 130
C. 150
D. 200

**Question 20 is based on the following information.**

| Carbide Steel Drill Bits | | |
|---|---|---|
| **Description** | **Size (inches)** | **Price** |
| Cutter | $\frac{9}{16}$ | $6.19 |
| Core Box | $\frac{5}{32}$ | $16.40 |
| Classic | $\frac{3}{8}$ | $17.85 |
| Bevel | $\frac{1}{2}$ | $10.50 |

20. Which of the following shows the drill bits arranged in order from least to greatest in size?

A. cutter, bevel, classic, core box
B. core box, bevel, classic, cutter
C. bevel, classic, cutter, core box
D. core box, classic, bevel, cutter

21. Joe is going to order a pizza. He will eat at least $\frac{1}{2}$ of it. If he's very hungry, he might eat as much as $\frac{7}{8}$ of it. Identify the two points on the number line below that represent the minimum fraction of the pizza Joe might have left over and the maximum fraction of the pizza Joe might have left over.

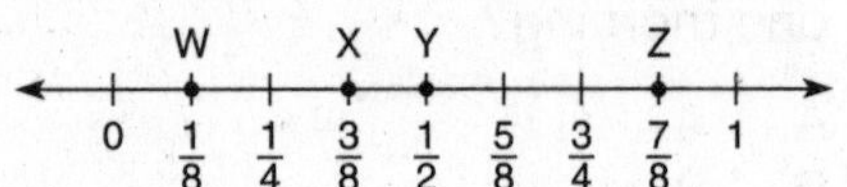


A. W and Z
B. W and Y
C. X and Z
D. Y and Z

22. A project should take no more than 60 hours. If John can spare 7.5 hours per day to work on the project, what is the maximum number of days it will take him to finish?

A. 6
B. 7
C. 8
D. 9

23. A survey shows that $\frac{2}{3}$ of all homeowners have a pet. Of those, $\frac{3}{4}$ have either a dog or cat. Of the homeowners surveyed, what fraction has either a dog or a cat?

A. $\frac{1}{2}$
B. $\frac{3}{4}$
C. $\frac{5}{7}$
D. $\frac{6}{7}$

24. At Wyman Shipping, 140 employees work during the day shift. At night, the crew is $\frac{2}{5}$ the size of the day shift. How many workers are scheduled to work the night shift?

A. 28
B. 56
C. 70
D. 94

**Question 25 refers to the following map.**

The map below shows the distance, in miles, between four stores.

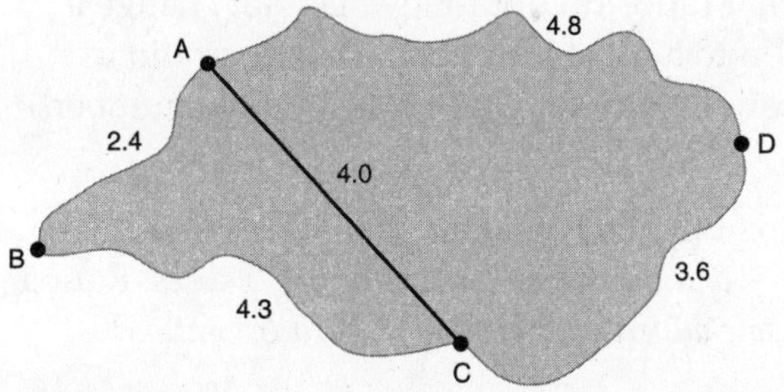


25. Maya drives a van that delivers supplies to each of the stores. On Friday, she traveled the following route.

Store A to Store B
Store B to Store C
Store C to Store D
Store D to Store C
Store C to Store A

How many miles did she drive in all?

A. 13.9
B. 15.1
C. 17.9
D. 19.1

26. From a wooden dowel $12\frac{1}{2}$ feet long, Jamie cut two pieces, each $3\frac{3}{4}$ feet long. How long, in feet, is the remaining piece?

A. $8\frac{3}{4}$
B. $7\frac{1}{2}$
C. $6\frac{1}{2}$
D. 5

27. Luis bought 20 shares of stock, priced at $26.38 per share. He also paid an $8 transaction fee. How much did he pay?

A. $687.60
B. $535.60
C. $527.60
D. $519.60

**For questions 28 and 29, mark your answers in the grids below.**

28. A mat board is 60 inches wide. How many strips measuring 0.75 inches wide can be cut from the board? (Assume no waste from the cuts.)

29. Of his take-home pay each month, Jerry spends $\frac{1}{6}$ on a car payment and $\frac{1}{4}$ on food. What fraction of his take-home pay is left after paying for these two items?

28.

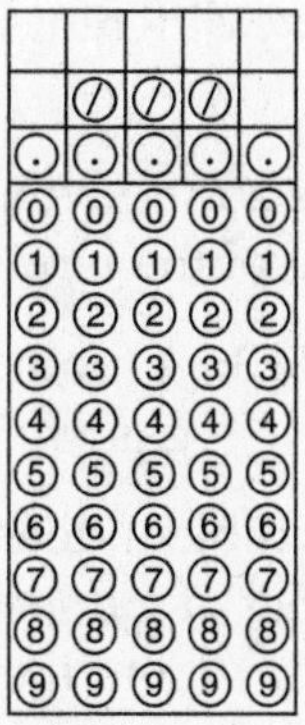

29.

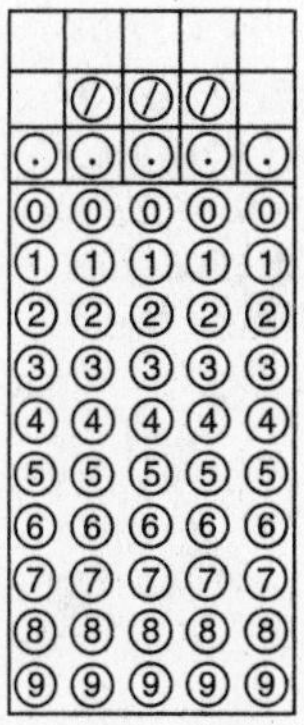

**Review your work using the explanations that start on page 686.**

# Number and Quantity Part III: Ratio, Proportion, and Percent

LESSON 1

# Ratio and Proportion

## Ratio

A **ratio** compares two numbers. You can write a ratio using the word *to,* using a colon (:), or using fraction form.

**Example 1:** A softball pitcher strikes out four batters for every one batter that she walks. What is the ratio of strikeouts to walks?

Always write the numbers in the ratio in the same order in which they appear in the question. **4 to 1** **4:1** $\frac{4}{1}$

Ratios are similar to fractions. They have two terms, and they can be simplified by reducing to lowest terms.

**Example 2:** Frank manages a small drugstore. During a two-hour period, he counts 25 cash sales and 15 credit card sales. What is the ratio of credit card to cash sales?

1. Write the ratio as a fraction with the terms in the correct order: credit card to cash sales. $\frac{\text{credit card sales}}{\text{cash sales}} = \frac{15}{25}$

2. Reduce to lowest terms. The ratio of credit card to cash sales is **3 to 5.** $\frac{15 \div 5}{25 \div 5} = \frac{3}{5}$

There are some fraction rules that ratios do not follow. Do not change a ratio that is an improper fraction to a mixed number. Also, if a ratio in fraction form has a denominator of 1, do not write it as a whole number. Leave it in fraction form.

Another important difference is in the use of labels. The terms in a fraction have the same unit labels: $\frac{5}{6}$ *of a pie means 5 slices out of 6 slices.* Ratios may have different labels: *The sale advertised 6 cans for $1, a 6:1 ratio.*

To write a ratio, you may need to perform one or more basic operations to find one of the terms.

**Example 3:** A football team won 12 games and lost 8. There were no tied games. What is the ratio of games won to games played?

1. The problem does not tell you the number of games played. Add the games won to the games lost to find the games played. 12 won + 8 lost = 20 played

2. Write the ratio in the correct order and simplify. **The team won 3 games for every 5 games it played, a 3:5 ratio.** $\frac{\text{games won}}{\text{games played}} = \frac{12}{20} = \frac{12 \div 4}{20 \div 4} = \frac{3}{5}$

### KEY IDEAS

- A ratio has two terms and can be written in words, with a colon, or as a fraction.
- Ratios are simplified by reducing to lowest terms.
- The terms in a ratio can have different labels.

### TASC TEST TIP

*The terms in a ratio must be written in the order given by the words of the question. Don't be fooled by an answer choice on a multiple-choice question that reverses the order of the numbers.*

# PRACTICE 1.1

**A. Write each ratio as a fraction in lowest terms.**

1. Stan made 24 sales in 6 hours. What is the ratio of sales to hours?
2. Carol's monthly take-home pay is $1500. She spends $250 a month on food. What is the ratio of food costs to take-home dollars?
3. A toy rocket travels 180 ft in 15 sec. What is the ratio of feet to seconds?
4. At Phil's work, there are 12 part-time workers and 18 full-time workers. What is the ratio of part-time workers to total workers?
5. Juanita drove 336 miles on 14 gallons of gasoline. What is the ratio of miles to gallons?
6. Lynn estimates that a roofing job will cost $1500. Bo estimates that the same job will cost $2400. What is the ratio of Lynn's estimate to Bo's estimate?
7. A basketball player attempted 32 free throws and made 20. What is the ratio of free throws made to free throws missed?
8. There are 10 men and 14 women in Kathleen's math class. What is the ratio of women to the total number of students in the class?
9. To paint his apartment, Alex bought 6 gallons of paint to cover 1440 square feet. What is the ratio of square feet to gallons of paint?

**B. Choose the one best answer to each question.**

**Questions 10 through 12 refer to the following information.**

Three candidates are running for mayor. Below are the results of a survey of 600 registered voters.

| Candidate | Number of Supporters |
|---|---|
| Stothard | 220 |
| Mesa | 180 |
| Newmark | 50 |
| Undecided | 150 |

10. What is the ratio of Mesa's supporters to Stothard's supporters?
    A. 9:11
    B. 11:9
    C. 11:20
    D. 20:11

11. What is the ratio of voters who prefer Mesa to the total number surveyed?
    A. 3 to 7
    B. 3 to 10
    C. 3 to 13
    D. 11 to 30

12. What is the ratio of undecided voters to voters who have made a decision?
    A. $\frac{1}{4}$
    B. $\frac{1}{3}$
    C. $\frac{3}{1}$
    D. $\frac{4}{1}$

13. Soan made a $400 down payment on a washer and dryer that cost a total of $1200. What is the ratio of the amount Soan has paid to the amount he still owes?
    A. 1 to 4
    B. 1 to 3
    C. 1 to 2
    D. 2 to 3

14. A team played 77 games and won 56 of them. There were no tied games. What is the ratio of wins to losses?
    A. 3:8
    B. 8:11
    C. 11:8
    D. 8:3

**Review your work using the explanations that start on page 687.**

## Proportion

A **proportion** is an equation that shows that two ratios are equal. The **cross products** in a true proportion are equal. In other words, when you multiply diagonally across the equals sign, the products are equal.

**Example 4:** The directions on a can of powdered drink mix say to add 3 cups of water to every 2 scoops of drink mix. Matt adds 12 cups of water to 8 scoops of drink mix. Did he make the drink correctly?

1. Write a proportion, making sure the terms of the ratios are in the same order. $\frac{\text{Cups}}{\text{scoops}}\ \frac{3}{2} \times \frac{12}{8}$

2. Cross multiply and compare the products. Since the products are the same, the ratios are equal. **Matt made the drink correctly.** $3 \times 8 = 24$ <br> $2 \times 12 = 24$

In most proportion problems, you are asked to solve for a missing term.

**Example 5:** A map scale says that 2 inches = 150 miles. What actual distance would a map distance of 5 inches represent?

1. Write a proportion with both ratios in the same form: inches to miles. The variable $x$ represents the unknown distance. $\frac{\text{inches}}{\text{miles}}\ \frac{2}{150} = \frac{5}{x}$
2. Locate the term in the first ratio that is diagonal from the known term in the second ratio. Cross multiply. $\frac{2}{150} = \frac{5}{x}$ <br> $150 \times 5 = 750$
3. Divide the result by the remaining known term to find the value of $x$. $750 \div 2 =$ **375 miles**

Some proportion problems ask you to find a **rate.** A rate compares a quantity to 1. When a rate is written in fraction form, its denominator is always 1. In word form, rates are often expressed using the word *per.*

**Example 6:** Connie drove 276 miles on 12 gallons of gasoline. How many miles per gallon did she get on the trip?

1. Gas mileage is one kind of rate. You need to find how many miles Connie drove on one gallon of gasoline. $\frac{\text{miles}}{\text{gallons}}\ \frac{276}{12} = \frac{x}{1}$

2. Solve. $276 \times 1 = 276$ <br> $276 \div 12 =$ **23 miles per gallon**

Using your calculator, you can solve proportion problems in one series of calculations.

**Example 7:** Find the value of $x$ in the proportion $\frac{6}{16} = \frac{21}{x}$.

You need to multiply 16 and 21, then divide by 6. On the TI-30XS MultiView™ calculator:

1. Press 16 [×] 21 [÷] 6.
2. Then press [enter]. The right side of the display will read 56.

The missing term is **56.**

**Note:** When working a problem, ask yourself if it can be solved using proportion. This may be possible when two quantities are compared or when three values are given and you are asked to find a fourth.

# PRACTICE 1.2

**A. Solve for the missing term in each proportion problem. You MAY use your calculator for questions 9 through 16. *Note*: Answers will not always be whole numbers.**

1. $\frac{2}{3} = \frac{x}{18}$
2. $\frac{3}{5} = \frac{27}{x}$
3. $\frac{6}{5} = \frac{3}{x}$
4. $\frac{15}{2} = \frac{x}{8}$
5. $\frac{4}{\$212} = \frac{7}{x}$
6. $\frac{25}{6} = \frac{400}{x}$
7. $\frac{7}{30} = \frac{x}{9}$
8. $\frac{0.5}{12} = \frac{3}{x}$
9. $\frac{20}{2.5} = \frac{100}{x}$
10. $\frac{\$5.96}{2} = \frac{x}{3}$
11. $\frac{12}{5} = \frac{3}{x}$
12. $\frac{4}{60} = \frac{2.5}{x}$
13. $\frac{3}{19} = \frac{x}{114}$
14. $\frac{9}{\$80.10} = \frac{x}{\$284.80}$
15. $\frac{\$26.00}{4} = \frac{x}{7}$
16. $\frac{24}{96} = \frac{7}{x}$

**B. Choose the one best answer to each question. You MAY use your calculator for questions 20 through 22.**

17. A store is advertising the following sale:

| Tomato Soup<br>4 cans for $0.98 |
|---|

To the nearest cent, how much would five cans of tomato soup cost?

A. $0.25
B. $1.23
C. $2.45
D. $4.90

18. The Bay City Cardinals have won 5 out of 8 games. At the same rate, how many games will they have to play to win 60 games?

A. 180
B. 120
C. 96
D. 12

19. Carla drove her truck 414 miles on 18 gallons of gasoline. How many miles did she drive per gallon?

A. 18
B. 23
C. 74
D. 95

20. The scale on a map reads, "2 cm = 150 km." How many kilometers would be represented by a distance of 4.6 centimeters?

A. 300
B. 345
C. 690
D. 1380

21. Two ingredients in a recipe are $2\frac{1}{2}$ cups of flour and $1\frac{1}{2}$ cups of sugar. If June keeps the proportion the same, how many cups of flour should she add to 4 cups of sugar?

A. $6\frac{2}{3}$
B. 6
C. 5
D. $3\frac{3}{4}$

22. Claudia drove 155 miles in 2.5 hours. Which of the following expressions could be used to find how many miles she can drive in 7 hours?

A. $155 \times 7 \div 2.5$
B. $2.5 \times 7 \div 155$
C. $155 \times 2.5 \div 4\ 7$
D. $7 \times 2.5 \times 155$

**Review your work using the explanations that start on page 687.**

## STUDY ADVICE

Proportions are useful in many ways. If you've ever doubled a recipe or thought about how much it would cost to fill up your car with gas, you've used proportions:

$$\frac{2\text{c flour}}{1\text{ batch}} = \frac{4\text{c flour}}{2\text{ batches}} \quad \text{or} \quad \frac{\$3.99}{1\text{ gallon}} = \frac{\$39.90}{10\text{ gallons}}$$

Proportions simply ask you to apply these real-world concepts.

# Number and Quantity Part III: Ratio, Proportion, and Percent

LESSON 2

## Percents

**Percent means** "per hundred" or "out of one hundred." For example, if you have \$100 and you spend \$25, you spent \$25 out of \$100, or 25% of your money.

Since percent is a way of showing part of a whole, it has much in common with fractions and decimals. To convert a percent to a fraction, write the percent over 100 and reduce. To convert percents to decimals, drop the percent symbol and move the decimal point two places to the left.

**Percent to Fraction**

$25\% = \frac{25}{100} = \frac{1}{4}$

**Percent to Decimal**

$25\% = .25 = 0.25$

In any percent problem, there are three elements: the base, the part, and the rate. The **base** is the whole quantity, or amount, that the problem is about. The **part** (also called a **percentage**) is a portion of the base. The **rate** is a number followed by the percent symbol (%).

**Example 1:** At a restaurant, Janice's bill is \$20. She gives the waiter a tip of \$3, which is 15% of her bill. Identify the base, part, and rate in this situation.

**The entire bill of \$20 is the base. The \$3 tip is part of the base, and the rate is 15%.**

One way to think of a percent problem is as a proportion. In Example 1, there are two ratios. The \$3 tip is part of the \$20 total bill, and 15% is the same as $\frac{15}{100}$. Since the two ratios are equal, they can be written as a proportion.

$$\frac{\text{part}}{\text{base}} \quad \frac{3}{20} = \frac{15}{100}$$

Cross multiply to prove the ratios are equal.

$$20 \times 15 = 300$$
$$3 \times 100 = 300$$

You can solve percent problems by setting up a proportion and solving for the missing elements. Just remember to express the percent as a number over 100.

**Example 2:** At a plant that manufactures lighting fixtures, it is expected that about 2% of the fixtures assembled each day will have some type of defect. If 900 fixtures are completed in one day, how many are expected to be defective?

1. Write a proportion. Remember that 2% means 2 out of 100. Use the variable $x$ to stand for the number of defective fixtures.

$$\frac{\text{part}}{\text{base}} = \frac{\text{rate}}{100}$$
$$\frac{x}{900} = \frac{2}{100}$$

2. Solve for $x$. Cross multiply and divide by the remaining number. **The company can expect about 18 defective fixtures.**

$$900 \times 2 = 1800$$
$$1800 \div 100 = \mathbf{18}$$

### KEY IDEAS

- The percent symbol (%) means "out of 100."
- The three elements of a percent problem are the base, the part, and the rate.
- Percent problems can be solved by writing a proportion that has a denominator of 100.

### TASC TEST TIP

*The word "of" often comes before the base in a percent problem. For example, if you are asked to find 75% of 250, you know that 250 is the base.*

# PRACTICE 2

**A. For each situation, identify and label the base, part, and rate.**

1. Victor owes his uncle $1000. Recently, he gave his uncle $200. The payment was 20% of the money he owes.
2. On a test with 80 problems, Sophie got 72 problems right. In other words, she answered 90% of the problems correctly.
3. The Kang family made a down payment of $2,740 on a new car. The down payment was 20% of the purchase price of $13,700.
4. Zoe's take-home pay each month is $2000. She spends $500 on rent each month, which is 25% of her take-home pay.
5. This year, Rafael has 60 regular customers, which is 150% of the 40 regular customers he had last year.
6. Kayla bought a dress for $38. She paid $3.23 in sales tax. The sales tax rate in her state is 8.5%.
7. Misako's employer withholds 15% of her salary each paycheck for taxes. Misako earns $900 each week, and her tax withholding is $135.
8. Harrison got a 10% raise. Before the raise, his hourly wage was $10.70. Now he earns an additional $1.07 per hour.
9. Kim Industries has 800 employees. Of those, 200 workers, or 25%, work part-time.
10. In an election, 5,000 of the 12,500 registered voters actually voted. Only 40% of the registered voters actually voted.

**B. Choose the one best answer to each question. Use the proportion $\frac{\text{part}}{\text{base}} = \frac{\text{rate}}{100}$ to solve each problem.**

**Questions 11 and 12 refer to the following information.**

A local newspaper printed the following high school basketball standings:

| Team | Wins | Losses |
|---|---|---|
| Fairfax | 9 | 3 |
| Hamilton | 8 | 4 |
| Bravo | 6 | 6 |
| Mountain View | 4 | 8 |
| Lincoln | 3 | 9 |

11. Which of the following expressions could be used to find what percent of its total games Fairfax has won?

A. $\frac{9 \times 100}{12}$

B. $\frac{3 \times 100}{12}$

C. $\frac{12 \times 100}{9}$

D. $\frac{6 \times 100}{12}$

12. What percent of its games did Bravo win?

A. 100%

B. 75%

C. 60%

D. 50%

13. A jacket with a price tag of $128 is on a rack with the following sign:

All Items:
25% off marked price
Discount taken at register

By how much will the price be reduced when the jacket is taken to the register?

A. $4

B. $25

C. $32

D. $96

**Review your work using the explanations that start on page 687**

# Number and Quantity Part III: Ratio, Proportion, and Percent

LESSON 3

## Using the Percent Formula

### Solving for Part

You have seen how to use proportion to solve percent problems. You can also solve percent problems using the formula ***Base × Rate = Part.***

Study the diagram at the right to learn how to use the formula. To use the diagram, cover the element you need to solve for: $B$ = Base, $R$ = Rate (percent), and $P$ = Part. Then perform the operation that connects the remaining elements.

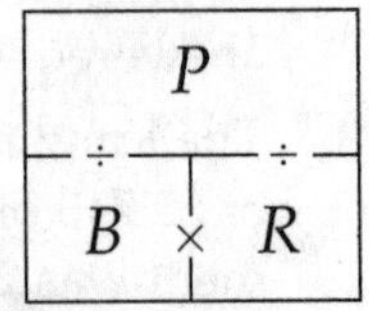


**Example 1:** A company offers its employees two health plans. In a recent newsletter, the personnel department stated that 70% of the employees chose Plan A. If the company has 320 workers, how many chose Plan A?

1. The rate is 70%, and the base is 320, the total number of workers. You need to solve for the part. Using the diagram, cover $P$ for part. You can see that you need to multiply to solve the problem.

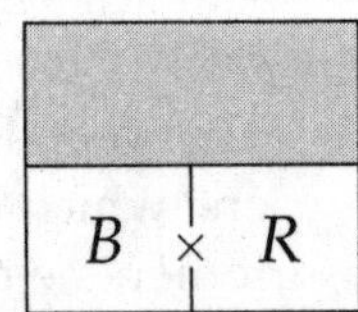


2. Change the percent to a decimal and multiply. **Out of 320 workers, 224 chose Plan A.**

$70\% = 0.7$

$320 \times 0.7 = \mathbf{224}$

### Solving for Rate

Rewrite the percent formula to solve for rate. Use the formula ***Part ÷ Base = Rate.*** You can use the diagram to help you remember the formula.

**Example 2:** A computer system is regularly priced at $1600. On Friday, the manager reduced the price by $640. By what percent did the manager discount the computer system?

1. The base is $1600, the regular price. The part is $640, the amount the price was reduced. You are asked to find the rate of the discount. Cover $R$ for rate (percent). You need to divide the part by the base to solve the problem.

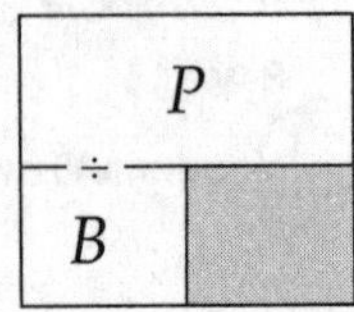


2. Divide 640 by 1600.

3. Convert the decimal answer to a percent by moving the decimal point two places to the right and adding the percent sign. The price reduction was a **40% discount.**

$$1600\overline{)640.0}\quad 0.4$$
$$640.0$$
$$0.4 = 40 = \mathbf{40\%}$$

Always ask yourself whether your answer seems reasonable. For example, you know that 40% is a little less than $\frac{1}{2}$, and $\frac{1}{2}$ of $1600 is $800. Since $640 is a little less than $800, it is a reasonable answer.

**KEY IDEAS**

- You can use a formula to solve percent problems: *Base × Rate = Part*.
- To change a percent to a decimal, drop the % sign and move the decimal point two places to the left.
- To change a decimal to a percent, move the decimal point two places to the right and add the % sign.

**TASC TEST TIP**

*When you take the Mathematics Test, make a quick sketch of the percent diagram on the scratch paper to help you analyze percent problems.*

# PRACTICE 3.1

**A. Solve. You MAY use a calculator for questions 9 through 16.**

1. What is 20% of $25?
2. Find 90% of 200.
3. What is 35% of 400?
4. What percent is 19 out of 20?
5. 42 is what percent of 168?
6. What percent is $18 out of $600?
7. Find $33\frac{1}{3}\%$ of 51. (*Hint:* $33\frac{1}{3}\% = \frac{1}{3}$)
8. What is 125% of $48?
9. 240 is what percent of 120?
10. What percent is 3 out of 60?
11. $52 is what percent of $650?
12. Find $8\frac{1}{2}\%$ of $46.
13. $0.65 is what percent of $10.00?
14. Find 28% of $1300.
15. What percent is 2.5 out of 4?
16. Find $66\frac{2}{3}\%$ of 108. (*Hint:* $66\frac{2}{3}\% = \frac{2}{3}$)

**B. Choose the one best answer to each question. You MAY use your calculator.**

17. Pat called 120 customers to offer a software upgrade. Of those he called, 72 purchased the upgrade. What percent agreed to the purchase?

A. 40%
B. 48%
C. 60%
D. $66\frac{2}{3}\%$

18. Douglas received a 6% raise. If his old monthly salary was $2,250, what is his monthly salary now? (*Hint:* Find the amount of the raise. Then add the raise to the previous monthly salary.)

A. $2,256
B. $2,385
C. $3,600
D. $13,500

19. At a restaurant, Levy's total bill is $46. If he wants to tip 15%, how much should he leave as a tip?

A. $690.00
B. $31.00
C. $15.00
D. $6.90

20. The following advertisement for sporting goods appeared in the newspaper. What percent of the original price is the sale price?

> Little League Package
> Magnum bat, tote bag, and youth cleats
> Only $45.50
> Originally $65

A. 20%
B. 31%
C. 44%
D. 70%

21. Lydia pays $3 sales tax on a $50 purchase. Which of the following expressions could be used to find the sales tax rate in her state?

A. $\frac{\$3 \times 100}{\$50}$
B. $\frac{\$3 \times \$50}{100}$
C. $\$3 \times \$50 \times 100$
D. $\$3 \div \$50$

**Review your work using the explanations that start on page 688**

**STUDY ADVICE**

Remember as you study to pay particular attention to words in bold and the Key Ideas on each page on the left. Also, study each worked example to see how to apply the concepts in your own practice.

## Solving for Base

Some problems on the TASC Mathematics Test may require you to solve for the base in a percent situation. Remember, the base represents the whole item or group. Read each situation carefully to figure out which element is missing. Then choose the correct method for solving the problem.

**Example 3:** In a math class, 75% of the students got at least a B grade on the final exam. If 18 students got at least a B, how many students are in the class?

1. Analyze the situation. The 18 students are part of the larger class. You know that the 18 students are 75% of the whole group, so 75% is the rate and the base is unknown.

   Use the diagram. Cover *B* for base. You need to divide the part by the rate to solve the problem.

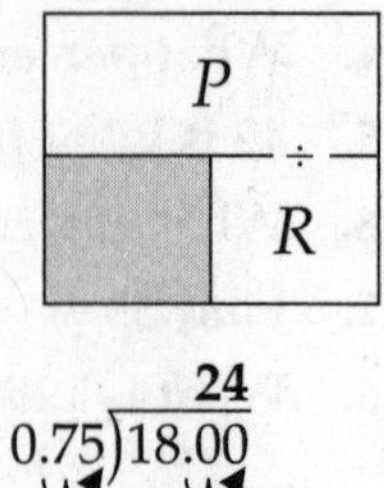


2. Convert the rate to a decimal (75% = 0.75) and divide. There are **24 students** in the class.

$$0.75\overline{)18.00} = \mathbf{24}$$

150
300
300

Most of the time, we work with percents that are less than 100%. When a percent is less than 100%, the part is less than the base. However, it is possible to have a situation in which the part is greater than the base. When this occurs, the percent will be greater than 100%.

**Example 4:** The workforce at Eastland Inc. is growing rapidly. The number of employees this year is 225% of the number last year. If there are 135 employees this year, how many employees did the company have last year?

1. The base is the number of employees the company had last year. This year's number is a percent of last year's number. Therefore, the rate is 225%, the part is 135, and the base is unknown.

P
÷
R

2. Convert 225% to a decimal. Drop the % sign and move the decimal point two places to the left.

$$225\% = 2.25 = 2.25$$

3. Divide the part (135) by the rate (2.25). Last year, there were only **60 employees.**

$$2.25\overline{)135.00} = \mathbf{60}$$

135.0

There is often more than one way to approach the solution to a problem. Both the percent formula presented in this lesson and the proportion method from Lesson 1 can be used to solve Example 4.

Formula method: $\frac{135}{2.25}$ Proportion method: $\frac{135 \times 100}{225}$

If you evaluate both methods using a calculator, both expressions equal 60, the correct solution.

**Note:** Don't begin calculations before you completely analyze a situation. Every percent problem has three elements. Make sure you know which one is missing before you multiply or divide.

# PRACTICE 3.2

**A. Find the missing element in each set. You MAY NOT use a calculator.**

1. \$35 is 20% of what amount?
2. 5% of what number is 14?
3. 3.2 is 50% of what number?
4. \$170 is 85% of what amount?
5. 24 is 80% of what number?
6. \$105 is 125% of what amount?
7. 190 is 95% of what number?
8. What number is 15% of 60?
9. 90% of \$15 is what number?
10. \$42 is what percent of \$168?
11. \$150 is 200% of what amount?
12. 15% of \$62 is what amount?
13. 9 is 1% of what number?
14. What percent is 126 of 140?
15. 65% of \$1200 is what amount?
16. 5% of an amount is \$156. What is the amount?
17. $2\frac{1}{2}\%$ of a number is 100. What is the number?
18. What percent is \$15.60 of \$156.00?

**B. Choose the <u>one best answer</u> to each question. You <u>MAY</u> use your calculator.**

19. Kevin's total payroll deductions are 30% of his earnings. If his deductions add up to \$369 for a two-week period, how much were his earnings for the period?

    A. \$110.70
    B. \$123.00
    C. \$1,230.00
    D. \$11,070.00

20. A city council established the following budget to improve public transportation.

| | Project Budget |
|---|---|
| Salaries | 50% |
| Office lease | 35% |
| Equipment | 6% |
| Supplies | 2% |
| Miscellaneous | 7% |

If \$72,000 is allotted for equipment, what is the total budget for the project?

A. \$432,000
B. \$940,000
C. \$1,200,000
D. \$120,000,000

21. Jack earns a 5% commission on each sale. If he is paid a \$160 commission, which of the following expressions could be used to find the amount of the sale?

    A. $\frac{5 \times 100}{160}$
    B. $\frac{160 \times 100}{5}$
    C. $\frac{5 \times 160}{100}$
    D. $5 \times 100 \times 1.60$

22. American Loan Company mailed 3600 customers an application for a new credit card. Only 20% of the customers returned the application. How many customers returned the application?

    A. 72
    B. 180
    C. 720
    D. 180,000

**Review your work using the explanations that start on page 688**

# Number and Quantity Part III: Ratio, Proportion, and Percent

## LESSON 4

# Percent Calculator Skills

By changing a percent to either a fraction or decimal, you can use a calculator to solve percent problems. The following examples are worked out using the keys on the TI-30XS MultiView™. Remember, your calculator may differ if you are taking the TASC on paper.

**Example 1:** What is 25% of 120? Try both decimals and fractions.

**On the Display**

Change 25% to the decimal (.25), multiply times 120, and press enter. **30** is on the right of the display.

.25*120 30

Change 25% to the fraction $\frac{25}{100}$ using the $\frac{n}{d}$ key, multiply times 120, and press enter. **30** is on the right of the display.

$\frac{25}{100}$*120 30

Using either decimals or fractions, you can find that **30** is 25% of 120.

When you use the *percent 2nd* function, you don't have to convert the percent to a fraction or decimal. Practice this function below to multiply to find the **part** when you are given the rate (percent).

**Example 2:** What is 65% of $360?

| | Keys to Press | On the Display |
|---|---|---|
| 1. Type the base, 360, and press the multiplication sign. | 360 × | 360* |
| 2. Type the rate (65). Press the 2nd function key and engage the percent 2nd function—over the ( key. Then press enter. | 65 2nd %( enter | 360*65% 234 |

The amount **$234** is 65% of $360.

You can use the percent function to divide to find the **base** when given the rate.

**Example 3:** Ned paid $150 for a stereo. The amount Ned paid was 20% of the original cost. What was the original cost of the stereo?

| | Keys to Press | On the Display |
|---|---|---|
| 1. Enter the base, 150, and press the division sign. | 150 ÷ | 150÷ |
| 2. Enter 20 and press the 2nd function key and the ( key. Then press *enter*. | 20 2nd %( enter | 150÷20% 750 |

The original cost of the stereo appears on the right of the display: **$750**.

### KEY IDEAS

- One way to solve percent problems on the calculator is to change the percent to a decimal or a fraction.
- On the TI-30XS MultiView™ calculator, you can use the percent 2nd function to find the part and the base.
- To create a percent, use the 2nd function, %, which is in green over the left parenthesis ( key.

### KEY IDEAS

*If you are using the TI-30XS MultiView™, practice using the* Delete *key when you make a mistake in a problem. That will erase your latest entry. The* Clear *key will erase the entire entry. If you are using a different calculator, find the appropriate keys for these two functions and practice using them.*

# PRACTICE 4

**A. Solve. You MAY use your calculator.**

1. Find 46% of $130.
2. 14% of what amount is $13.44?
3. What is 12% of $126?
4. What number is $62\frac{1}{2}$% of 64?
5. 12 is what percent of 400?
6. A number is 32% of 6500. What is the number?
7. 36 is what percent of 144?
8. 90% of what number is 63?
9. Find 7% of 360.
10. What number is $33\frac{1}{3}$% of 237?
11. 25 is what percent of 1000?
12. What is $12\frac{1}{2}$% of 384?
13. 390 is what percent of 500?
14. Find 2% of $800.
15. 32% of what number is 80?
16. What number is $87\frac{1}{2}$% of 16?
17. $112 is what percent of $1600?
18. A number is $66\frac{2}{3}$% of 414. What is the number?

**B. Choose the one best answer to each question. You MAY use your calculator.**

**Questions 19 and 20 refer to the following chart.**

| Shipping and Handling Information | |
|---|---|
| **For items costing:** | **% of order + handling:** |
| $20 or less | 3% + $1.50 |
| $20.01 to $50 | 4% + $2.50 |
| $50.01 to $100 | 5% + $4.00 |
| $100.01 or more | 8% |

19. Chanel placed an $84 order. How much shipping and handling will she be charged on her order?
   A. $4.20
   B. $4.40
   C. $8.20
   D. $8.36

20. Jason placed an order totaling $110. Zola placed a $90 order. How much more did Jason pay in shipping and handling than Zola?
   A. $0.30
   B. $4.30
   C. $4.50
   D. $20.00

21. In an election, 3190 out of 3625 registered voters voted against a tax increase. What percent of the registered voters voted against the increase?
   A. 43%
   B. 83%
   C. 88%
   D. 98%

22. A baseball player has the following statistics. To the nearest percent, what percent of the player's at bats were strikeouts?

| At Bats | Hits | Home Runs | Walks | Strikeouts |
|---|---|---|---|---|
| 410 | 108 | 2 | 70 | 63 |

   A. 90%
   B. 58%
   C. 26%
   D. 15%

**Review your work using the explanations that start on page 688**

**STUDY ADVICE**

Remember not to rely too much on the calculator during the TASC Mathematics Test. Not all questions will require you to do lots of math, so don't just start plugging numbers into the calculator. First think about what the problem is asking for.

LESSON 5

# Interest

**Interest** is a fee paid for the use of someone else's money. If you put money in a savings account, you receive interest from the bank. If you borrow money, you pay interest. In each case, the amount that you invest or borrow is called the **principal.**

**Simple interest** is a percent of the principal multiplied by the length of the loan. This is how simple interest is calculated:

**simple interest** Interest = principal × rate × time

Or, using abbreviations: $I = prt$

**Example 1:** Asher borrows $2500 from his uncle for three years at 6% simple interest. How much interest will he pay on the loan?

1. Write the rate as a decimal. $6\% = 0.06$
2. Substitute the known values in the formula. Multiply.

$$\begin{aligned} I &= prt \\ &= \$2500 \times 0.06 \times 3 \\ &= \mathbf{\$450} \end{aligned}$$

Asher will pay **$450** in interest.

Some problems ask you to find the **amount paid back.** This adds an additional step to an interest problem. In Example 1, Asher will owe $450 in interest at the end of three years. However, he will pay back the interest ($450) plus the principal ($2500): $2500 + $450 = $2950. When he has finished paying the loan, Asher will have paid his uncle $2950.

Most bank accounts, loans, and credit cards do not use simple interest. Instead, they use **compound interest,** which means that the interest is periodically added to the principal. That new total is then used to calculate the interest for that period. The formula for compound interest is as follows:

**compound interest** $A = p\left(1+\frac{r}{n}\right)^{nt}$

In the formula, $A$ is the amount that will be in the account or owed on the loan after $t$ years. Again, $p$ is the principal and $r$ is the annual interest rate expressed as a decimal. The letter $t$ stands for the number of years since the principal started earning interest. The letter $n$ represents the number of times per year the interest is **compounded**, or added to the principal.

That formula may look intimidating, but just remember: When you see a compound interest problem, simply figure out which pieces of information in the problem represent $p$, $r$, $n$, and $t$. Then plug those values into the formula. (Your calculator will be handy here. For more information about exponents, see pages 336–337.)

Notice that the simple interest formula at the top of this page allows you to calculate the interest. The compound interest formula allows you to calculate the total amount of the loan or investment after interest has been added. If a question asks you for just the interest on a loan or investment that has compound interest, use the compound interest formula and subtract the principle from the result.

### KEY IDEAS

- Simple interest is found by multiplying principal, rate, and time: $I = prt$.
- The time must be written in terms of years. Write months as a fraction of a year.
- To find the amount paid back, add the principal and the interest.

### TASC TEST TIP

*A formula sheet is provided when you take the Mathematics Test (see pages 230–231). Every time you see a formula in this book, check to see if it is on the formula sheet. If the formula is not there, you will need to memorize it.*

# PRACTICE 5

**Example 2:** Malik takes out a bank loan for \$2,000 for a period of two years. The bank will charge him 10% interest, compounded quarterly (that is, four times per year). How much will Malik have to pay the bank back two years from now? Round your answer to the nearest dollar.

Step 1: You are asked to solve for $A$. Identify the other values.

$p = 2{,}000 \quad r = 0.05$

$n = 4 \quad t = 2$

Step 2: Plug those values into the formula and solve.

$$A = 2{,}000\left(1 + \frac{.05}{4}\right)^{(4 \times 2)}$$

$$A = 2{,}000(1.0125)^8$$

$$A = 2{,}000(1.1045) = 2{,}208.97$$

Malik will pay the bank **\$2209** two years from now.

---

**A. Solve these problems using the interest formulas on the previous page. You MAY use your calculator. Round your answers to the nearest dollar.**

1. Leah borrows \$1500 for 2 years at a 12% *simple* interest rate. Find the interest on the loan.
2. Ricardo borrows \$1850 for 8 months at 12% *simple* interest. What is the amount he will pay back at the end of the loan period?
3. Dominica invested \$2000 for 3 years at an interest rate of 7%, compounded annually. How much interest did she earn on her money?
4. If you take out a loan of \$800 at 14% interest, compounded annually, for 2 years, how much will you have to pay back at the end of the 2 years?

**B. Choose the one best answer to each question. You MAY use your calculator.**

5. Jean borrowed \$1300 to buy tools for her job as an auto mechanic. The loan is for 1 year 6 months at 9% simple interest. Which of the following expressions could be used to find the amount she will pay back at the end of the loan period?
   A. $\$1300 \times 1.5 \times 0.09$
   B. $\$1300 \times 1.5 \times 9$
   C. $\$1300 + (\$1300 \times 9 \times 1.5)$
   D. $\$1300 + (\$1300 \times 0.09 \times 1.5)$

**Questions 6 refers to the following information.**

| Option | Length of Loan | Simple Interest Rate |
|---|---|---|
| A | $2\frac{1}{2}$ years | 12% |
| B | 3 years | 10% |
| C | 4 years | 9% |

6. Charlotte needs to borrow \$2400. She is considering the three loan options shown above. How much more interest would Charlotte pay if she takes loan option C instead of option A?
   A. \$108
   B. \$144
   C. \$720
   D. \$864

**Review your work using the explanations that start on page 688**

Number and Quantity Part III: Ratio, Proportion, and Percent

LESSON 6

# Percent of Change

Percent is often used to show change.

**Example 1:** Michelle recently started her own business. Last month, she earned \$1000. This month, she earned \$2000. How could she describe the increase in her earnings?

All of the following statements accurately describe the change.

- Michelle's earnings doubled from last month to this month.
- This month, her earnings increased by 100%.
- This month's earnings are 200% of last month's earnings.

**Percent of change** compares a new number, which shows an **increase** or a **decrease**, to the original number—the number before the change.

**Example 2:** Before her raise, Lisa earned \$10.50 per hour. Now she earns \$11.34 per hour. What percent raise did her boss give her?

1. Subtract to find the amount of change. $\$11.34 - \$10.50 = \$0.84$

2. Divide the amount of change by \$10.50, Lisa's wage before the change. Convert the decimal to a percent. Lisa's hourly wage **increased by 8%.** $\frac{\$0.84}{\$10.50} = 0.08 = \mathbf{8\%}$

Think carefully about a situation to decide which number is the original amount.

**Example 3:** A jacket is on sale for \$90. Three days ago, the jacket was on sale for \$120. By what percent was the price of the jacket reduced?

1. Subtract to find the amount of change. $\$120 - \$90 = \$30$

2. The price of the jacket was \$120 before it was \$90, so \$120 is the original price. Divide the amount of change by \$120. The new price is **25% less** than the price three days ago. $\frac{\$30}{\$120} = 0.25 = \mathbf{25\%}$

Percent of increase may be greater than 100%.

**Example 4:** Calvin started his business with 10 employees. Now he has 60 employees. By what percent has his workforce increased?

1. Subtract to find the amount of change. $60 - 10 = 50$

2. Divide by the original number. Convert the number to a percent. Calvin's workforce has **increased by 500%.** $\frac{50}{10} = 5.0 = \mathbf{500\%}$

**KEY IDEAS**

- The amount of change is the difference between the new number and the original number.
- Find the percent of change by dividing the amount of change by the original number.
- Percent of increase may be greater than 100%.

**TASC TEST TIP**

*You can work backward to check your answers. For example, if a price has decreased by 25%, the new price should be 75% of the original price, since 25% + 75% = 100%.*

# PRACTICE 6

**A. Solve as directed. If necessary, round your answer to the nearest percent. You MAY use your calculator for questions 7 through 10.**

1. Find the percent of increase from 2000 to 3000.
2. Find the percent of decrease from $2.00 to $1.25.
3. What is the percent of increase from 30 to 90?
4. Find the percent of decrease from 20 to 11.
5. Find the percent of increase from $25 to $30.
6. What is the percent of decrease from 500 to 340?
7. Find the percent of increase from $1.89 to $2.29.
8. What is the percent of decrease from 21 to 3?
9. Find the percent of increase from 65 to 338.
10. What is the percent of decrease from $1550 to $1025?

**B. Choose the one best answer to each question. You MAY use your calculator.**

11. Justin recently moved from a part-time to a full-time job. Because of the change, his weekly pay increased from $280 to $448. To the nearest percent, by what percent did his income increase?

A. 38%
B. 60%
C. 168%
D. 267%

12. David bought a computer game on sale for $36. The game was originally $48. What was the percent of decrease in the game's price?

A. 12%
B. 25%
C. $33\frac{1}{3}$%
D. 75%

13. The Utleys' rent increased from $600 to $636 per month. By what percent did the rent increase?

A. 4%
B. 5%
C. 6%
D. 7%

**Questions 14 and 15** refer to the following information.

Marc sells computer equipment. He buys printers at wholesale and sells them at retail price. Customers who join his discount club pay the member's price.

**Printer Pricing Chart**

| Model Number | Wholesale Price | Retail Price | Member's Price |
|---|---|---|---|
| L310 | $63.00 | $141.75 | $92.15 |
| L1430 | $86.00 | $150.50 | $105.35 |

14. What is the percent of increase from wholesale to retail price of the L310 model?

A. 56%
B. 78%
C. 125%
D. 225%

15. For the L1430 model, what is the percent of decrease from retail price to member's price?

A. 26%
B. 30%
C. 43%
D. 53%

**Review your work using the explanations that start on page 688.**

**STUDY ADVICE**

Here's a quick rule to remember: When determining percent of change—either increase or decrease—the denominator is always the original value. Study these examples to see percent of change in action.

# Ratio, Proportion, and Percent Practice Questions

**Directions: You MAY use your calculator.**

1. From a total yearly budget of \$360,000, the Kimball Foundation spends \$30,000 on leasing office space. What is the ratio of dollars spent on office space to dollars spent on other costs?

   A. 12:1
   B. 11:1
   C. 1:11
   D. 1:12

2. A worker can assemble 5 motors in 2 hours. Which of the expressions below could be used to find how long it would take the worker to assemble 50 motors?

   A. $2 \times \frac{50}{5}$
   B. $\frac{5 \times 50}{2}$
   C. $\frac{5}{2 \times 50}$
   D. $2 \times 5 \times 50$

3. Frank owns a discount music store. The table below shows how much Frank pays for certain merchandise items.

| Item | Wholesale Price |
|---|---|
| CDs | \$7.20 |
| Posters | \$5.60 |

   To find his selling price, Frank increases each price by 35%. What is the selling price of a poster?

   A. \$9.72
   B. \$7.56
   C. \$5.95
   D. \$1.96

4. Neva's car is now worth \$12,000. This is 60% of what she paid for it. How much did she pay for the car?

   A. \$7,200
   B. \$18,000
   C. \$19,200
   D. \$20,000

5. At a shop, the ratio of union to nonunion workers is 7 to 3. If there are 18 nonunion workers at the shop, how many union workers are there?

   A. 21
   B. 25
   C. 42
   D. 126

6. Camilla earned \$954 in commission on \$15,900 in sales. What is her rate of commission?

   A. 6%
   B. 9%
   C. $16\frac{2}{3}\%$
   D. 60%

7. John spent the following amounts of time building a workbench:

   drawing the plans: 2 hours
   cutting the wood: $1\frac{1}{2}$ hours
   assembling the workbench: 2 hours
   sanding and sealing: $3\frac{1}{2}$ hours

   What is the ratio of time spent cutting wood to total time spent on the project?

   A. 1:9
   B. 1:6
   C. 1:5
   D. 3:7

**Questions 8 and 9 refer to the following information.**

| Ford County Farmland Usage<br>Total Acreage: 40,000 | |
|---|---|
| **Usage** | **Number of Acres** |
| Dairy | 22,000 |
| Nursery/greenhouse | 3,600 |
| Vegetables/fruits | 5,200 |
| Grains | 9,200 |

8. What percent of Ford County farmland is used for the growing of grains, vegetables, or fruits?

A. 23%
B. 36%
C. 57%
D. 64%

9. One dairy farmer in Ford County is considering selling her farm to developers, who will convert it from a dairy farm to a resort. If this happens, the amount of farmland devoted to dairy in Ford County will decrease by 20%. How many acres of farmland will Ford County then have if the dairy farmer decides to sell?

A. 35,600
B. 32,000
C. 17,600
D. 4,400

10. A serving of peanut butter contains 3 grams of saturated fat and 13 grams of unsaturated fat. This amount of fat is 25% of the recommended amount of fat in a 2000-calorie diet. What is the ratio of grams of saturated fat to total fat in a serving of peanut butter?

A. $\frac{3}{16}$
B. $\frac{3}{13}$
C. $\frac{13}{16}$
D. $\frac{16}{3}$

11. A drawing of a company logo is 4 inches wide and 5 inches long. If the drawing is enlarged so that it is 12.5 inches long, and the original proportions remain unchanged, how many inches wide will the enlarged drawing be?

A. 7.5
B. 10
C. 15.625
D. 20

**For questions 12 and 13, mark your answers in the grids below.**

12. A local hospital currently has 184 male patients. If the ratio of male to female patients is 4:3, how many female patients are there in the hospital?

13. A newspaper advertisement contains the following information.

| Busy Body Fitness Center<br>Inventory Reduction Blowout!<br>All sale prices are 20% off original price! | |
|---|---|
| **Equipment** | **Sale Price** |
| Treadmill | \$1512 |
| Upright bike | \$720 |
| Home gym | \$3148 |

In dollars, what was the original price of the upright bike?

12.

13.

14. The Tigers' ratio of wins to losses is 5 to 4. If the team continues winning at the same rate, how many games will the Tigers win in a 72-game season?

A. 20
B. 40
C. 37
D. 52

15. A television station called 400 adults and asked the following question: "Do you approve of the governor's new education program?" The table below shows the results of the survey:

| Response | Percent |
|---|---|
| Undecided | 16% |
| Yes | 32% |
| No | 52% |

Of the people called, how many did not answer "no"?

A. 64
B. 128
C. 192
D. 208

16. The price of a carton of computer paper decreased from $25 to $20. What was the percent decrease in the price?

A. 80%
B. 50%
C. 20%
D. 5%

17. Six months ago, Sandra had 55 regular customers. Now, she has 220% as many regular customers as she had six months ago. How many regular customers does Sandra have now?

A. 121
B. 90
C. 66
D. 25

18. If 1 gram of fat equals 9 calories, what percent of the calories in a Munchies roast beef sandwich come from fat?

| Munchies Sandwich Facts | | |
|---|---|---|
| Sandwich | Fat (grams) | Calories |
| Roast Beef | 6 | 300 |
| Club Classic | 5 | 335 |

A. 2%
B. 3%
C. 6%
D. 18%

19. For every $8 in their budget, the Parks spend $3 on food. If their weekly budget is $704, how much do they spend on food each week?

A. $88
B. $192
C. $235
D. $264

20. Suddeth Travel estimates that 80% of its employees have more than 12 days of unused sick leave. If 140 employees have more than 12 days of unused sick leave, how many employees work at the agency?

A. 112
B. 164
C. 175
D. 700

21. The Gladstone Theater has 900 seats. At a recent show, the ratio of tickets sold to tickets unsold was 11 to 1. How many tickets were sold?
   A. 75
   B. 810
   C. 818
   D. 825

22. Matthew put $2200 in a savings account for one year and six months. If he earns simple interest at an annual rate of 8%, how much will he have in the account at the end of the time period?
   A. $2212
   B. $2376
   C. $2464
   D. $2640

23. A television set that is regularly priced at $410 is on sale for 20% off. What is the sale price of the television set?
   A. $82
   B. $328
   C. $390
   D. $492

24. On a county map shown below, the map scale reads, "0.5 in = 60 mi."
   What is the actual distance in miles between Lakeview and Riverside?

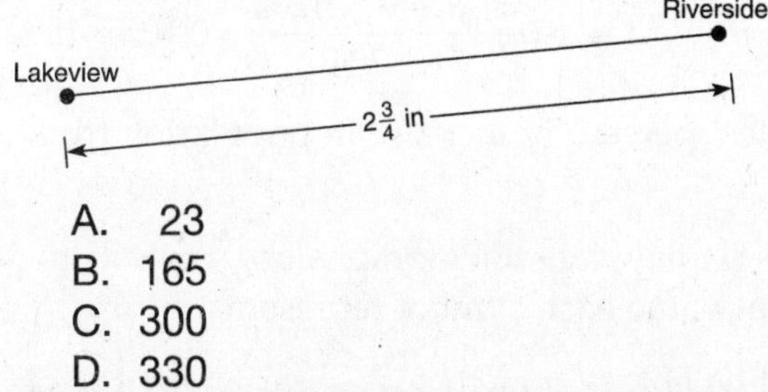


   A. 23
   B. 165
   C. 300
   D. 330

**STUDY ADVICE**

Congratulations! You've done a ton of work learning the "number and quantity" skills tested by the TASC. While 15% of the questions on the TASC Mathematics Test directly test number and quantity skills, you will also need these skills to work algebra, geometry, and statistics problems. Keep periodically reviewing the first three chapters of this unit as you work through the remaining chapters.

**Question 25 refers to the following information.**

Leo's Bookstore kept track of the number of customers who visited the store over a 3-day period and the number of those who made a purchase.

| Day | Number of Customers | Number of Customers Who Made a Purchase |
|---|---|---|
| Friday | 112 | 83 |
| Saturday | 138 | 45 |
| Sunday | 140 | 91 |

25. Which of the following could be used to find what percent of Sunday's customers did <u>not</u> make a purchase?
   A. $\frac{91}{140}$
   B. $\frac{91}{140} \times 100$
   C. $\frac{(140-91)}{140} \times 100$
   D. $\frac{(140-91)}{91} \times 100$

**For questions 26 and 27, mark your answers in the grids below.**

26. A school admits 9 out of every 14 who apply. At that rate, how many students will be admitted if 420 apply?

27. In a 40-hour workweek, Marcie spends 15 hours answering telephones. What is the ratio of hours spent answering telephones to hours doing other types of work? (Record your answer as a fraction.)

26.

27.

**Review your work using the explanations that start on page 688.**

# LESSON 1

## Tables and Pictographs

**Data** are facts and information. By analyzing data, we can make predictions, draw conclusions, and solve problems. To be useful, data must be organized in some way. A **table** organizes data in columns and rows. The labels on the table will help you understand what the data mean.

### KEY IDEAS

- Tables and graphs are often used to display data.
- Always read all labels to understand what data are presented in the table or graph.
- If symbols are used in a graph, a key will explain what each symbol represents.

**Example 1:** The table below shows population figures for selected counties in 2000 and 2010 and the land area in square miles for each county.

| County | 2000 Pop. | 2010 Pop. | Land Area in sq. mi. |
|---|---|---|---|
| Adams | 11,128 | 15,295 | 4,255 |
| Bell | 25,199 | 22,707 | 2,523 |
| Cook | 6,532 | 6,518 | 2,398 |
| Davis | 82,204 | 90,834 | 1,139 |
| Evans | 139,510 | 130,748 | 921 |

Which county showed the greatest percent of increase in population from 2000 to 2010?

1. **Read the labels.** The first column shows the county names. The second and third columns show population figures. The fourth column shows land area data. You don't need land area to answer this question.
2. **Analyze the data.** Only Adams and Davis counties show increases from 2000 to 2010.
3. **Use the data.** Find the percent of increase for Adams and Davis counties.

Adams: $\frac{15,295-11,128}{11,128} \approx 0.374 \approx 37\%$; Davis: $\frac{90,834-82,204}{82,204} \approx 0.105 \approx 10\%$

**Adams County** shows the greatest percent of increase in population from 2000 to 2010.

### TASC TEST TIP

*Tables provide a lot of information. When you are answering a question based on a table, use only the information that is needed to answer the question. As Example 1 shows, the question is about population, so you do not need to use information from the last column.*

A **pictograph** is another way to display data. Pictographs use symbols to compare data. A key shows what value each symbol represents.

**Example 2:** A city has three public library branches. A librarian kept track of the numbers of books checked out from each branch in a week. He used the data to create the pictograph below.

| Branches | Books checked out from March 4 to March 10 |
|---|---|
| North | 📖📖📖📖📖📖 and a half book |
| South | 📖📖📖📖 and a half book |
| West | 📖📖📖📖📖📖📖📖📖 |

Key: 📖 = 150 books

# PRACTICE 1

From March 4 to March 10, how many books were checked out from the South and West branches combined?

1. There are $4\frac{1}{2}$ symbols for the South Branch and 9 symbols for the West branch. Add: $4\frac{1}{2} + 9 = 13\frac{1}{2}$ symbols.

2. Find the value of the symbols. The key states that each symbol equals 150 books. Multiply by 150: $13\frac{1}{2} \times 150 =$ **2025 books.**

---

**A. Use the table on page 302 to answer questions 1 and 2. Use the pictograph on page 302 to answer questions 3 and 4. You MAY use a calculator.**

1. On average, how many people were there per square mile in Bell County in 2010?

2. To the nearest percent, what was the percent of decrease in Evans County's population from 2000 to 2010?

3. How many more books were checked out from North Branch than from South Branch during the week of March 4?

4. How many books were checked out from all three branches combined?

**B. Choose the one best answer to each question.**

**Questions 5 and 6 refer to the following table.**

**Percent of 3-year-old children with school-readiness skills for the years 2004 and 2010**

| | 2004 | 2010 |
|---|---|---|
| Recognizes all letters | 11% | 17% |
| Counts to 20 or higher | 37% | 47% |
| Writes own name | 22% | 34% |
| Reads or pretends to read | 66% | 67% |

5. If 100,000 children were surveyed in each year, which category showed the least percent of increase from 2004 to 2010?

A. Recognizes all letters
B. Counts to 20 or higher
C. Writes own name
D. Reads or pretends to read

6. A community had 350 three-year-old children in 2010. If the chart is representative of the community, how many were able to write their own name?

A. 34
B. 97
C. 119
D. 134

**Questions 7 and 8 refer to the following graph.**

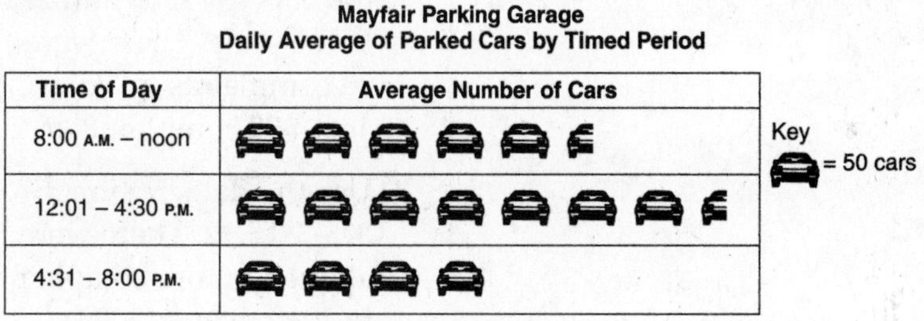

**Mayfair Parking Garage**
**Daily Average of Parked Cars by Timed Period**

| Time of Day | Average Number of Cars |
|---|---|
| 8:00 A.M. – noon | |
| 12:01 – 4:30 P.M. | |
| 4:31 – 8:00 P.M. | |

Key = 50 cars

7. How many cars are parked in the garage from 12:01 to 4:30 P.M.?

A. 275
B. 350
C. 375
D. 650

8. How many more cars are parked from 8 A.M. to noon than are parked after 4:30 P.M.?

A. 75
B. 100
C. 175
D. 200

**Review your work using the explanations that start on page 689.**

LESSON 2

# Bar and Line Graphs

## KEY IDEAS

- A bar graph uses bars to represent numbers.
- To find the value of a bar, compare its length to the scale shown on one of the axis lines. Estimate the value.
- A double-bar graph compares groups of data. Read the key to find the meaning of the bars.

## Working with Bar Graphs

A **bar graph** uses bars to represent values. Bar graphs have two axis lines. One line shows a number scale, and the other shows labels for the bars. By comparing the length of a bar to the scale, you can estimate what value the bar represents.

**Example 1:** A national corporation made a bar graph (shown below) to show the number of discrimination complaints made by employees during a six-year period. About how many more complaints were made in 2010 than in 2009?

1. **Read the labels.** Each bar represents the number of complaints made within a year. The years are shown beneath the bars.
2. **Analyze the data.** Compare the bars for 2009 and 2010 to the scale. There were 20 complaints in 2009 and about 32 complaints in 2010.
3. **Use the data.** Subtract: 32 – 20 = 12. There were **about 12 more** complaints in 2010 than in 2009.

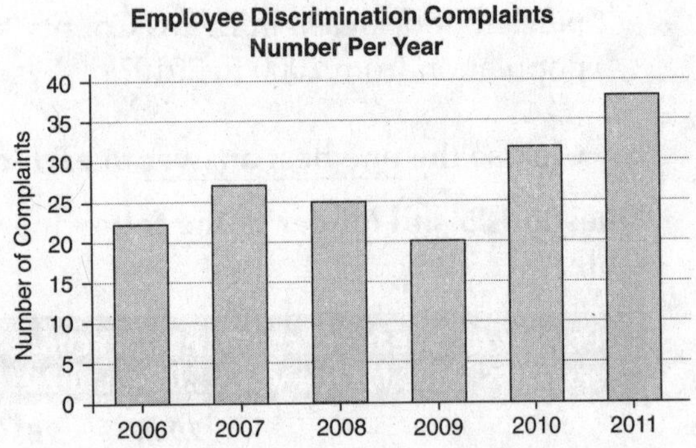


A **double-bar graph** compares more than one type of data.

## TASC TEST TIP

*You may not be able to find the exact value of a bar. If the bar falls about halfway between two numbers on the scale, use a whole number that lies in the middle.*

**Example 2:** A studio released four films in one year. The graph below compares the cost of making each movie to its box-office receipts, or ticket sales. Film B's cost is what percent of its box-office receipts?

1. **Read the labels.** Read the key to find the meaning of the bars. Notice that the scale represents millions of dollars.
2. **Analyze the data.** Film B's cost is about \$30 million. It brought in about \$65 million in receipts.
3. **Use the data.** Find what percent \$30 is of \$65.
$\frac{\$30}{\$65} \approx 0.462 \approx$ **46%**

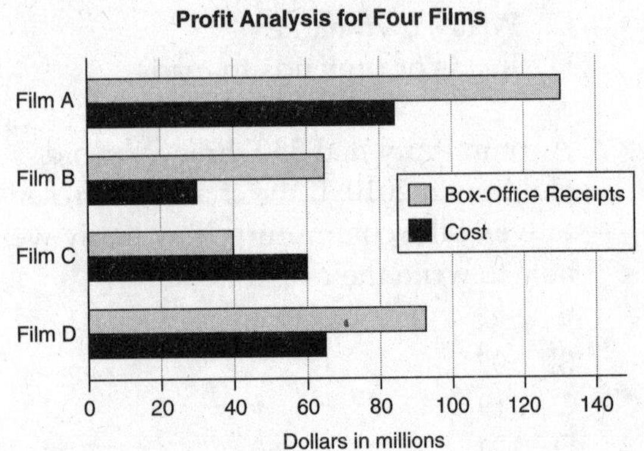

# PRACTICE 2.1

**A. For questions 1 through 3, use the bar graph entitled "Employee Discrimination Complaints" on page 304. For questions 4 through 6, use the bar graph entitled "Profit Analysis for Four Films" on page 304.**

1. To the nearest ten, how many employee discrimination complaints were there in 2006 and 2007?
2. To the nearest five, how many more complaints were there in 2011 than in 2006?
3. By what percent did the number of complaints decrease from 2008 to 2009?
4. About how much more did it cost to make Film A than Film D?
5. Which film made the greatest amount of profit? (*Hint:* profit = receipts − cost)
6. Film C's cost was what percent of its box-office receipts?

**B. Choose the <u>one best answer</u> to each question.**

**<u>Questions 7 and 8</u> refer to the following graph.**

Items Sold for the Week of Sept 20

Games
Toys
Books
Movies
T-shirts

0 20 40 60 80 100 120

Number sold

7. Approximately how many more T-shirts were sold than books and toys combined?

   A. 40
   B. 70
   C. 80
   D. 90

8. One-half of the games sold during the week of September 20 were on sale for \$16. The rest sold for the full price of \$24. Approximately how much money did the store take in for games sold during the week of September 20?

   A. \$400
   B. \$600
   C. \$800
   D. \$1000

**<u>Questions 9 and 10</u> refer to the following graph.**

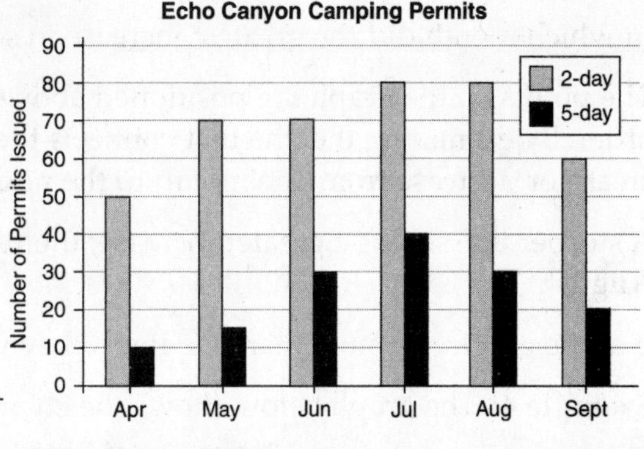


9. In May, what was the ratio of the number of 2-day permits to the number of 5-day permits?

   A. 2:5
   B. 3:17
   C. 14:3
   D. 14:17

10. In which month was there a <u>total</u> of 80 permits issued?

    A. June
    B. July
    C. August
    D. September

**Review your work using the explanations that start on page 689.**

## Working with Line Graphs

A **line graph** is useful for showing changes over time. By analyzing the rise and fall of the line, you can tell whether something is increasing, decreasing, or staying the same. Like a bar graph, a line graph has two axis lines. One is marked with a scale; the other is marked in regular time intervals.

**Example 3:** The graph below shows the number of patients who visited an emergency room for the treatment of scooter-related injuries.

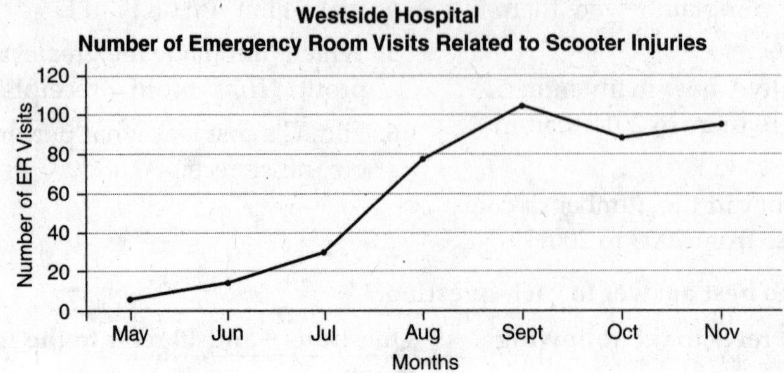


In which month did the greatest increase in scooter-related injuries occur?

The points on the graph are positioned above the months, which are arranged in calendar order. By examining the line that connects the points, you can tell whether there was an increase or decrease from one month to the next.

A steeper line shows a greater increase; therefore, the **greatest increase was from July to August**.

If a line graph has more than one line, a key will tell you what the lines represent.

**Example 4:** The graph below shows the changes in ticket prices for two amusement parks.

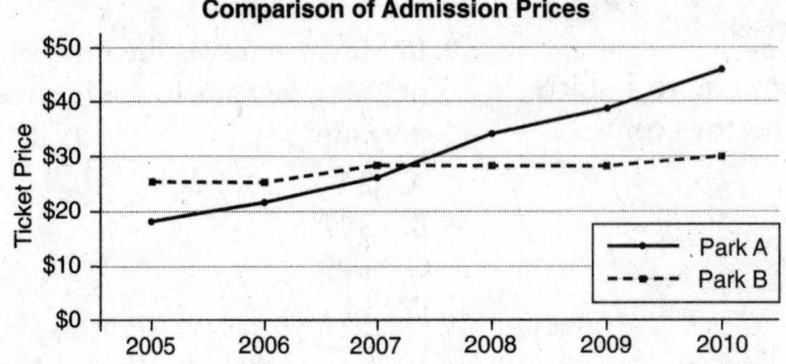


What was the last year in which the admission price to Park B was greater than the admission price to Park A?

The admission prices for Park A are represented by a solid line. Park B's prices are shown with a dotted line. The graph begins in 2005. In 2005, Park B's ticket price is greater than Park A's. Follow the two lines to the right. Between 2007 and 2008, the lines cross, and Park A's prices climb higher than Park B's. **The year 2007** was the last time that Park B charged more than Park A for a ticket.

**Note:** The steepest line shows the greatest increase or decrease, but it may not show the greatest percent of change. When the original value is small, a small change may result in a high percent of change.

# PRACTICE 2.2

**A. For questions 1 through 3, use the graph from Westside Hospital on page 306. For questions 4 through 6, use the graph "Comparison of Admission Prices" on page 306.**

1. In which month did the number of scooter-related injuries decrease?
2. To the nearest 10, how many emergency room visits were due to scooter injuries in August, September, and October combined?
3. Which of the following shows the greater percent of increase: the change in injuries from June to July or the change from August to September?
4. About how much more did it cost to buy a ticket to Park A than a ticket to Park B in 2009?
5. What was the percent of increase in the ticket prices at Park B from 2005 to 2010?
6. To the nearest 10, how much more did it cost to buy a ticket to Park A in 2010 than in 2005?

**B. Choose the <u>one best answer</u> to each question.**

**<u>Questions 7 and 8</u> refer to the graph below.**

**Inflation Facts**

*If a purchase cost $100 in the year 2000, what would its cost have been in the past?*

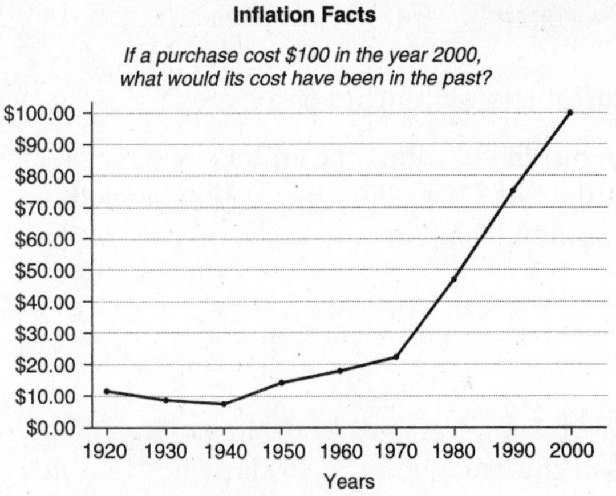

7. Over what period of time did the price of goods actually decrease?
   A. 1930 to 1940
   B. 1940 to 1950
   C. 1960 to 1970
   D. 1970 to 1980

8. Goods purchased in 1970 were about what fraction of their cost in the year 2000?
   A. $\frac{4}{5}$
   B. $\frac{1}{2}$
   C. $\frac{1}{3}$
   D. $\frac{1}{5}$

**<u>Questions 9 and 10</u> refer to the graph below.**

Lamp Depot has two stores. The graph shows the sales data from the two stores for an 8-week period.

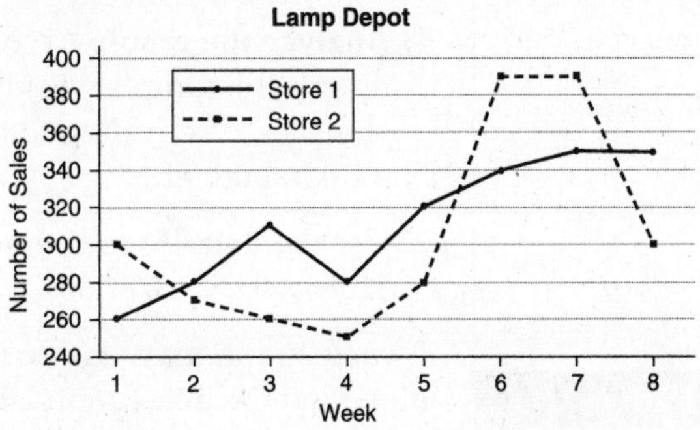

**Lamp Depot**

9. About how many more sales were there at Store 2 than at Store 1 in week 6?
   A. 110
   B. 50
   C. 40
   D. 25

10. During which week did Store 1 experience the greatest increase in sales from the week before?
    A. Week 2
    B. Week 3
    C. Week 4
    D. Week 5

**Review your work using the explanations that start on page 690.**

**STUDY ADVICE**

All of the graphics you're learning about in this chapter are simply ways of presenting numbers with pictures. Always begin by getting the big picture. Ask yourself what the graph represents and what you notice most about it. And don't overlook information such as the total represented by the graph.

LESSON 3

# Circle Graphs

## KEY IDEAS

- In a circle graph, the circle represents a whole amount, and the sections represent parts of the whole.
- Sections are usually labeled with percents, but they can show amounts.
- The size of each section of a circle graph is equal to the fraction or percent it represents.

A **circle graph** is used to show how a whole amount is broken into parts. The sections of a circle graph are often labeled with percents. The size of each section corresponds to the fraction it represents. For example, a section labeled 25% is $\frac{1}{4}$ of the circle.

**Example 1:** A graph below shows how a children's sports camp spends its weekly budget.

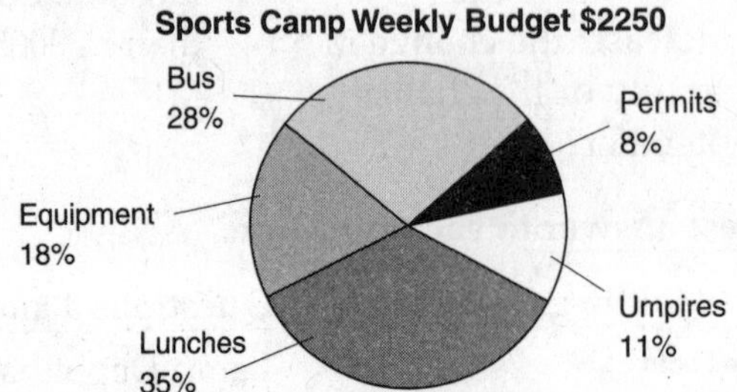


How much does the sports camp spend on lunches each week?

1. **Analyze the graph.** According to the heading, the entire circle represents the camp's weekly budget of $2250. Find the section labeled "lunches." According to the section label, lunches make up 35% of the weekly budget.
2. **Use the data.** To find the amount spent on lunches, find 35% of $2250: $\$2250 \times 0.35 =$ **$787.50.**

A circle graph may also be labeled using fractions or decimals. One common kind of circle graph labels each section in cents to show how a dollar is used.

## TASC TEST TIP

*Since a circle graph represents a whole, or 100%, amounts can easily be converted to percents. For example, $0.05 on a circle graph can also represent 5%.*

**Example 2:** According to the graph, what percent of the average energy bill is spent on drying clothes, lighting, and heating water?

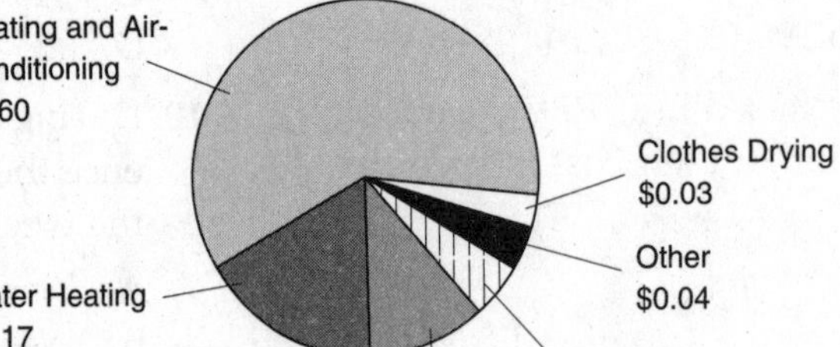


1. **Analyze the graph.** The entire circle represents $1. The amounts in the sections mentioned in the problem are $0.03, $0.05, and $0.17.
2. **Use the data.** Add the amounts: $\$0.03 + \$0.05 + \$0.17 = \$0.25$. Since $0.25 is 25% of a dollar, **25%** of an average bill is spent on these items.

# PRACTICE 3

**A. For questions 1 through 3, use the sports camp budget on page 308. For questions 4 through 6, use the circle graph on energy on page 308.**

1. What percent of the total sports camp budget is spent on equipment and umpires?
2. What fraction of the sports camp budget is spent on permits?
3. What amount does the camp spend each week on busing?
4. A family's energy bill is $180. Assuming the family's energy use is typical, how much did the family spend on water heating?
5. Which section is greater than 50% of an energy dollar?
6. Which energy cost is about $\frac{1}{10}$ of the energy dollar?

**B. Choose the one best answer to each question.**

**Questions 7 and 8 refer to the following graph.**

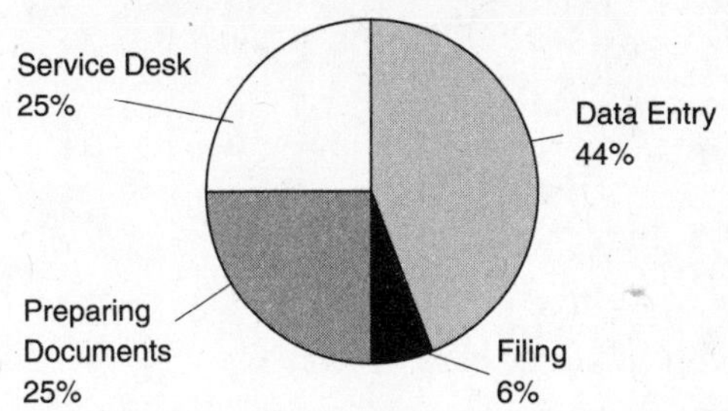


7. During a 40-hour workweek, how many hours does a records clerk spend preparing documents?

   A. 10
   B. 15
   C. 25
   D. 30

8. What percent of a records clerk's time is spent on tasks other than data entry?

   A. 25%
   B. 31%
   C. 44%
   D. 56%

**Questions 9 and 10 refer to the following graph.**

The employees of National Bank are given the following graph to explain how their retirement fund is invested.

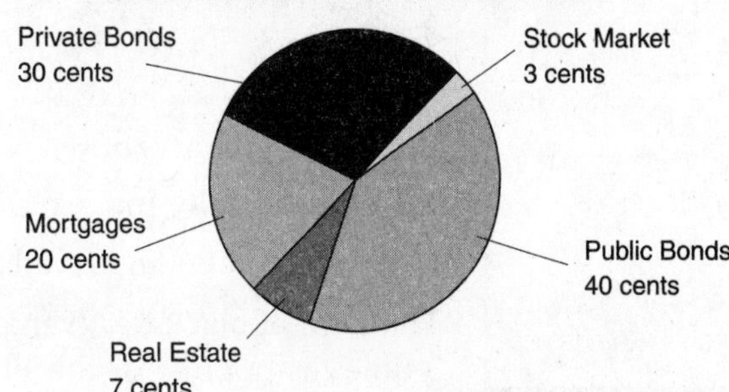


9. What percent of each retirement dollar is invested in real estate and the stock market?

   A. 4%
   B. 10%
   C. 40%
   D. 90%

10. Steve contributes $120 of each paycheck to his National Bank retirement fund. How much of each contribution is invested in public bonds?

    A. $36
    B. $40
    C. $48
    D. $84

**Review your work using the explanations that start on page 690.**

LESSON 4

# Measures of Central Tendency

## Using a Frequency Table

A **frequency table** shows how often an item appears in a data set. The data is in the form of tally marks next to a list of items.

**Example 1:** The sales manager at Montana Motors asked her sales staff to keep a record of the color of the cars that were chosen for test-drives in one month. Then she combined the data to make the frequency table shown below.

| Montana Motors—Car Color Preferences | |
|---|---|
| white | 𝍸 𝍸 𝍸 𝍸 𝍸 𝍸 |
| black | 𝍸 𝍸 𝍸 𝍸 𝍸 II |
| red | 𝍸 𝍸 𝍸 |
| green | 𝍸 𝍸 I |
| silver | 𝍸 IIII |
| other | 𝍸 𝍸 𝍸 I |

What was the ratio of black cars driven to silver cars driven?

1. Count the tally marks. There are 27 marks for black and 9 for silver.
2. Write the ratio and reduce to lowest terms. $\frac{27}{9} = \frac{3}{1}$

The ratio of black to silver is **3 to 1**. You can also say that the black cars are 3 times as popular as the silver cars.

Numerical data is often grouped in intervals. The table below shows data grouped in intervals of 18 to 24, 25 to 40, and so on. This way of presenting data is called a **grouped frequency table**.

**Example 2:** The table below shows the ages of the customers at Louise's Diner for a four-day period. What percent of the customers were from 25 to 40 years old?

| Louise's Diner<br>Customers by Age Group, February 19–22 | |
|---|---|
| under 18 | 𝍸 I |
| 18–24 | 𝍸 𝍸 𝍸 III |
| 25–40 | 𝍸 𝍸 𝍸 𝍸 𝍸 III |
| 41–55 | 𝍸 𝍸 |
| over 55 | 𝍸 III |

1. Find the data you need. There are 28 marks for the 25–40 age group. Add the tally marks for all age groups to find the total number of customers for the three-day period: $6 + 18 + 28 + 10 + 8 = 70$.
2. Find the percent. The base is 70, the total number of customers. The part is 28, the number of customers in the desired age group. Solve for the rate: $\frac{28}{70} = \frac{4}{10} = 0.4 =$ **40%**.

**KEY IDEAS**

- A frequency table is used to show how often data occurs.
- Tally marks are made next to a list to record the data.
- Numerical data is often grouped in intervals.

**TASC TEST TIP**

*If several problems refer to a frequency table, you may want to count the tally marks for each line and record the numbers on your scratch paper. Then use the numbers to solve all related problems.*

# PRACTICE 4.1

**A. For questions 1 through 3, use the frequency table from Montana Motors on page 310. For questions 4 through 6, use the frequency table from Louise's Diner on page 310.**

1. What was the total number of test drives of black and white cars combined?
2. How many more drivers chose red than silver cars?
3. What was the ratio of red cars to white cars chosen for test-drives?
4. What is the ratio of customers under 18 to those over 55?
5. What was the total number of customers from 18 to 40 years of age?
6. What percent of the total customers were from 41 to 55 years of age? (Round your answer to the nearest whole percent.)

**B. Choose the one best answer to each question.**

**Questions 7 and 8 refer to the following information.**

The frequency table shows the reasons customers gave for returning clothing merchandise to a store.

| Reason | Number |
|---|---|
| Wrong size | 𝍸 𝍸 𝍸 I |
| Unwanted gift | 𝍸 𝍸 𝍸 𝍸 |
| Found flaw after purchase | III |
| Changed mind | 𝍸 |

7. What is the ratio of customers saying the clothes were the wrong size to all the returns represented?
   A. $\frac{4}{15}$
   B. $\frac{4}{11}$
   C. $\frac{4}{7}$
   D. $\frac{4}{5}$

8. Approximately what percent of the customers who returned clothing said that the clothes were an unwanted gift?
   A. 20%
   B. 25%
   C. 45%
   D. 50%

**Questions 9 and 10 refer to the following information.**

A personnel office gives typing tests to people applying for a job. The test shows how many words per minute (wpm) a job applicant can enter correctly. After testing 90 applicants, the manager made the following table.

| Typing Speed | Number |
|---|---|
| Under 30 wpm | 𝍸 𝍸 𝍸 𝍸 𝍸 𝍸 𝍸 |
| 30–45 wpm | 𝍸 𝍸 𝍸 𝍸 𝍸 |
| 46–60 wpm | 𝍸 𝍸 𝍸 III |
| Over 60 wpm | 𝍸 𝍸 II |

9. What percent of the applicants had a speed of under 30 wpm?
   A. 14%
   B. 25%
   C. 28%
   D. 39%

10. What is the ratio of applicants who could type at a speed above 45 wpm to those who could type at a speed of 45 wpm or less?
   A. 1:3
   B. 1:2
   C. 2:3
   D. 6:5

**Review your work using the explanations that start on page 690.**

**STUDY ADVICE**

Remember that practice has three levels: Learn and Review, Practice and Review, Assess and Review. For each lesson, absorb the concepts on the left page. Then practice using the page on the right, and carefully review the explanations in the back of the book. Finally, use the question sets at the end of each chapter to assess your progress. Don't forget to review the explanations for those question sets, too.

## Mean, Median, and Mode

Suppose you were asked how much money you usually spend on groceries in a week. Some weeks, you may spend a great deal; other weeks, much less. You would probably choose an amount in the middle to represent what you typically spend. This middle value is called an **average**, or **measure of central tendency.**

The most common type of average is the **mean**, or the arithmetic average.

**Example 3:** In five football games, a team scored 14, 21, 3, 20, and 10 points. What is the mean, or average, score per game?

1. Add the values. $14 + 21 + 3 + 20 + 10 = 68$
2. Divide by the number of items in the data set. $68 \div 5 =$ **13.6 points per game**

Although it is impossible for a football team to score 13.6 points in a game, the number represents the center of the scores from the five games.

A calculator is useful for finding the mean. Do the calculations in two steps. Enter the addition operations. Then, if you are using the TI-30XS MultiView™, press *enter* to find the sum. Then key in the division operation. Try Example 1 above with a calculator.

Another measure of average is the median. The **median** is the middle value in a set of data.

**Example 4:** During a 7-hour period, a bookstore recorded the following numbers of sales. Find the median number of sales.

| Hour 1 | Hour 2 | Hour 3 | Hour 4 | Hour 5 | Hour 6 | Hour 7 |
|---|---|---|---|---|---|---|
| 43 | 28 | 24 | 36 | 32 | 37 | 48 |

1. Arrange the values by size. 24, 28, 32, 36, 37, 43, 48
2. Find the middle number. 24, 28, 32, **36**, 37, 43, 48

If there is an even number of values, the median is the mean of the two middle values.

**Example 5:** Robert has the following test scores in his math class: 90, 72, 88, 94, 91, and 80. What is the median score?

1. Arrange the values by size and find the middle. 72, 80, **88, 90,** 91, 94
2. Find the mean of the two middle values. The median score is **89**. Add: $88 + 90 = 178$ Divide by 2: $178 \div 2 =$ **89**

The **mode** is the value that occurs most often in a set of data. A set of data could have more than one mode if several items occur the same number of times. If each item of data occurs only once, there is no mode.

**Example 6:** Six weather stations recorded the following temperatures at 3:00 P.M.: 45°, 44°, 45°, 47°, 46°, and 45°. What is the mode of the data?

The temperature 45° occurs most often (3 times). The mode is **45°**.

# PRACTICE 4.2

**A. For each data set, find the mean, median, and mode. Round calculations to the nearest hundredth or cent. You MAY use a calculator.**

1. Golf scores for 7 rounds:
76, 82, 75, 87, 80, 82, and 79
2. Sales totals for 6 weeks:
$5,624; $10,380; $8,102; $6,494; $12,008; and $8,315
3. Cost of lunch for 8 days:
$4.50, $5.25, $4.50, $3.75, $4.50, $5.25, $6.10, and $4.25
4. Miles driven per day for 5 days:
330, 286, 342, 300, and 287
5. Grocery bills for 4 weeks:
$97.48, $106.13, $110.98, and $92.74
6. Scores on 7 quizzes:
90, 72, 86, 100, 88, 78, and 88
7. High temperatures for 10 days:
96°, 103°, 98°, 101°, 98°, 100°, 100°, 97°, 98°, and 100°
8. Inches of rainfall over 3-day period:
2.5, 1.8, and 1.4
9. Attendance figures at a play:
305, 294, 328, 296, 305, 315, and 292
10. Hours worked per week for 5 weeks:
36, 40, 38, 40, and 40

**B. Choose the one best answer to each question. You MAY use your calculator.**

**Questions 11 and 12 refer to the following information.**

**Homes Sold in Fairfield Heights in June**

| Home | Asking Price | Selling Price |
|---|---|---|
| #1 | $124,600 | $116,500 |
| #2 | $132,400 | $124,800 |
| #3 | $118,900 | $116,500 |
| #4 | $98,500 | $103,600 |
| #5 | $105,800 | $109,000 |
| #6 | $122,400 | $118,400 |

11. What was the mean asking price of the homes sold in Fairfield Heights in June?
A. $117,100
B. $116,500
C. $115,450
D. $114,800

12. What was the median selling price of the homes sold in Fairfield Heights in June?
A. $112,750
B. $114,800
C. $116,500
D. $117,450

13. The numbers of patients enrolled at four health clinics are 790, 1150, 662, and 805. Which expression could be used to find the mean number of patients per clinic?
A. $\frac{790 + 1150 + 662 + 805}{4}$
B. $790 + 1150 + 662 + 805$
C. $\frac{662 + 1150}{2}$
D. $(790 + 1150 + 662 + 805) \div 2$

14. What is the median value of $268, $1258, $654, $1258, $900, $1558, and $852?
A. $1258
B. $964
C. $900
D. $852

15. What is the mode of the following points scored: 14, 17, 14, 12, 13, 15, 22, and 11?
A. 13.5
B. 14
C. 14.75
D. 16.5

**Review your work using the explanations that start on page 690.**

# Line Plots

The same kind of information that can be expressed in a frequency table (see page 310) can also be expressed in a **line plot**. A line plot shows the frequency of data along a number line. Study the following example.

**KEY IDEAS**

- A line plot is a graph that shows the frequency of data along a number line.
- Based on frequency tables, line plots consist of a horizontal scale and points or x's placed over corresponding numbers.
- Line plots help us to interpret the distribution of data.

**Example 1:** The student health services department at a university surveyed several students and asked them how many times per week they visited the school's gym. The following frequency table shows the results for several students.

| Weekly Gym Visits | Number of Students |
|---|---|
| 0 | I |
| 1 | II |
| 2 | II |
| 3 | III |
| 4 | 0 |
| 5 | I |
| 6 | 0 |
| 7 | I |

Next, the health services department decided to create a line plot in order to see the distribution of gym visits. Each $x$ represents a student.

| 0 | 1 | 2 | 3 | 4 | 5 | 6 | 7 |
|---|---|---|---|---|---|---|---|
| x | x x | x x | x x x | | x | | x |

You can see from this line plot that there is an uneven **distribution**, or arrangement, of students across the numbers of possible gym visits. Three visits per week has the **highest frequency**, meaning that more students go to the gym three times per week than any other number of visits. You can also see that the data **range** extends from zero visits per week to seven visits per week—no student visits the gym more often than that. The data point showing the one student who visits the gym seven times per week is an **outlier**—that is, a data point that is distant from where most of the data is clustered.

The Mathematics Test may ask you to identify highest frequency, range, and outliers, or it may give you some data and ask you to place $x$'s or dots on a number line to create a line plot.

**TASC TEST TIP**

*One type of question may ask you to analyze data on a line plot. Another type of question could ask you to use a frequency table to place an element on a line plot.*

Use the following example to study these concepts further.

**Example 2:** Students in Ms. Jones's class took a math test. Their scores on the test are displayed on the line plot below. Each dot represents a student. Which grade displayed the highest frequency?

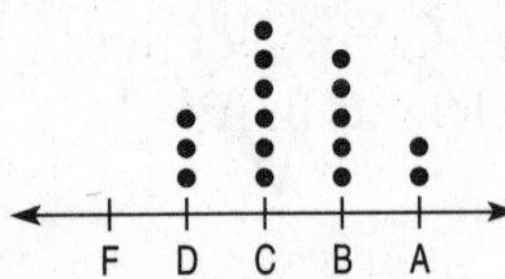


More students received a C than received any other grade. Therefore, grade **C** has the highest frequency of any grade on the line plot.

The range of grades on the math test was from D (the lowest grade received by any student) to A (the highest grade received by any student).

# PRACTICE 5

**For questions 1 and 2, <u>choose the line plot</u> that matches each frequency table. Use choices A–D below for <u>both questions</u>.**

1. Zoologists have counted the number of stripes on certain zebras in a zoo. The set of data from these observations is represented by the following frequency table:

| Number of stripes per side | Number of zebras with that many stripes |
|---|---|
| 24 | I |
| 25 | 0 |
| 26 | II |
| 27 | 0 |
| 28 | II |
| 29 | 0 |
| 30 | II |
| 31 | 0 |
| 32 | I |

Which line plot below represents this data?

2. At a certain elementary school, classes may have different numbers of students. The following frequency table represents how many students are in the classes this year:

| Number of students | Number of classes with that many students |
|---|---|
| 24 | 0 |
| 25 | 0 |
| 26 | 0 |
| 27 | I |
| 28 | I |
| 29 | III |
| 30 | 0 |
| 31 | I |
| 32 | II |

Which line plot below represents this data?

A.

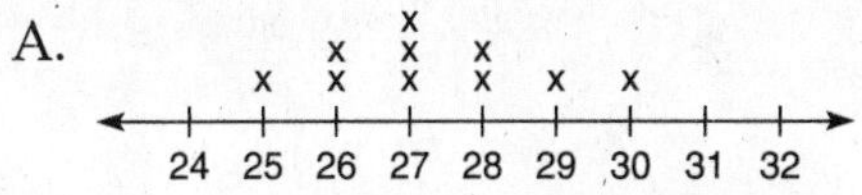


B.

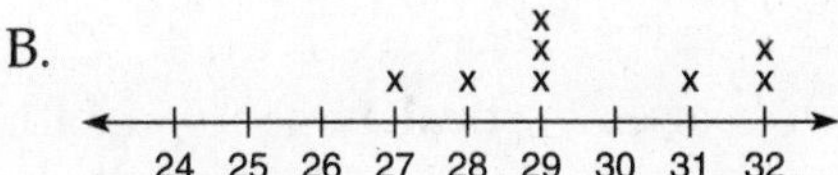


C.

24 25 26 27 28 29 30 31 32

D.

24 25 26 27 28 29 30 31 32

**<u>Questions 3 and 4</u> are based on the following information.**

Juana runs a community garden. She records how many different types of vegetables garden members are planting. The following line plot is based on Juana's data. Each point represents a member of the community garden. The values on the line plot represent the number of types of vegetables planted by each person.

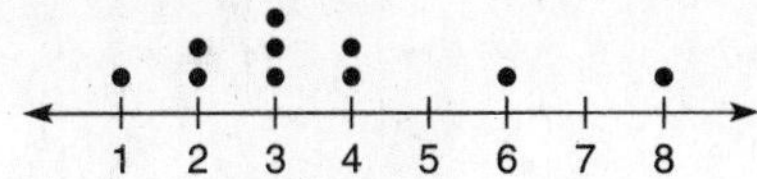


3. Which of the following can be described as (an) outlier(s)?
   A. the member who plants one type of vegetable
   B. the members who plant three types of vegetables
   C. the members who plant four types of vegetables
   D. the member who plants eight types of vegetables

4. Which value (number of types of vegetables) has the highest frequency in the data?
   A. 2
   B. 3
   C. 4
   D. 8

**Review your work using the explanations that start on page 691.**

# LESSON 6

# Histograms

**KEY IDEAS**

- A histogram is another form of data display based on utilizing groups and counts within a group.
- Groups are plotted on the horizontal axis, and frequencies are plotted on the vertical axis.

Like line plots, **histograms** display **frequencies**, but they do so in a very different way. Consider the following example:

**Example 1:** Graham is a veterinarian. Last year he decided to track client appointments for spring shots. The following table and histogram represent his results:

| Week of | Number of Appointments |
|---|---|
| March 1–7 | 2 |
| March 8–14 | 4 |
| March 15–21 | 8 |
| March 22–28 | 11 |
| March 29–April 4 | 14 |
| April 5–11 | 17 |
| April 12–18 | 13 |
| April 19–25 | 7 |
| April 26–May 2 | 5 |

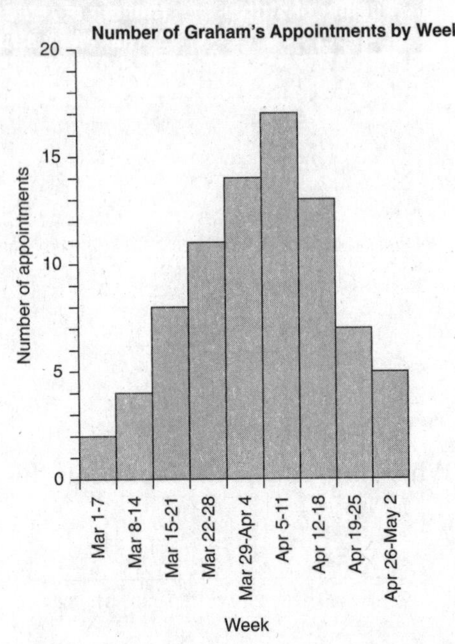


**TASC TEST TIP**

*Some multiple-choice questions may ask you to identify graphs that represent different types of data collection. You may be given some data and asked which graph represents that set of data.*

The **histogram** above on the right has two axes: a **vertical axis** (or $y$-axis) representing numbers of appointments and a **horizontal axis** (also called an $x$-axis) that has increments representing the weeks. The **area** of each bar represents the number of appointments for that week. Thus, you can see not only how many appointments were in any given week but also how the **frequency** of appointments changed over the weeks in the chart.

Finally, histograms can also be used to show percentages. If we alter the histogram about Graham's appointments so that each bar represents the *percent* of total appointments each week, it will look like the one on the right.

Because the percentages add up to 100%, the areas of all the bars add up to 100.

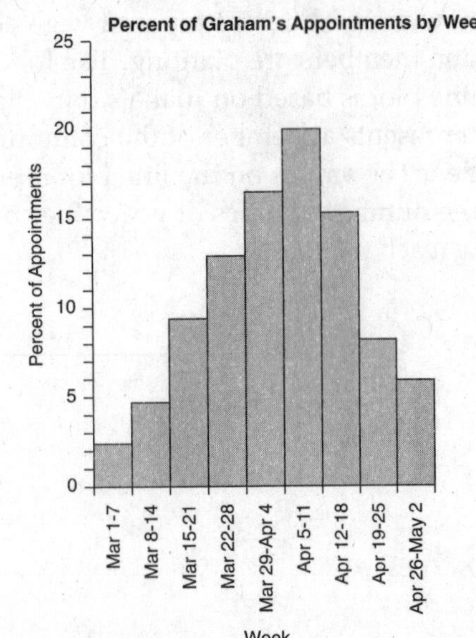

**Example 2:** What percent of appointments for spring shots occurred during the first two weeks of March?

You can figure this out by adding the percentages for those weeks (you can approximate based on the histogram): for March 1–7, about 2%; for March 8–14, about 5%. Approximately 7% of appointments for spring shots occurred during those two weeks.

---

**A. Choose the histogram that matches each frequency table. Use choices A–D below for both questions 1 and 2.**

1. Josefina runs a retail business. She posted a coupon to a social media site from 9:00 A.M. to 5:00 P.M. The table shows how many people downloaded or printed the coupon.

| Hour beginning with: | Number of people who downloaded or printed coupon: |
|---|---|
| 9:00 A.M. | 30 |
| 10:00 A.M. | 56 |
| 11:00 A.M. | 80 |
| 12:00 P.M. | 71 |
| 1:00 P.M. | 56 |
| 2:00 P.M. | 31 |
| 3:00 P.M. | 22 |
| 4:00 P.M. | 14 |

2. Mike administered a skills assessment to his employees. Possible scores on the skills assessment ranged from 200 to 1800. The following table shows how his employees performed on the assessment:

| Score range | Number of employees |
|---|---|
| 200–399 | 15 |
| 400–599 | 22 |
| 600–799 | 35 |
| 800–999 | 62 |
| 1000–1199 | 80 |
| 1200–1399 | 69 |
| 1400–1599 | 47 |
| 1600–1800 | 20 |

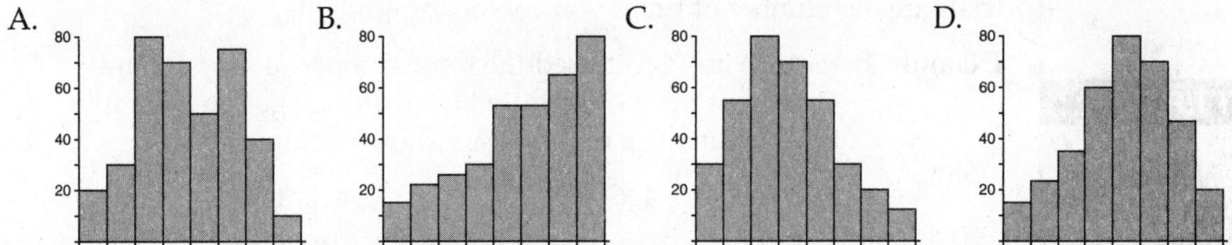


**B. Choose the one best answer to each question.**

**Question 3 refers to the following histogram and information.**

Influenza, or "flu," season in the United States tends to last from fall through spring.

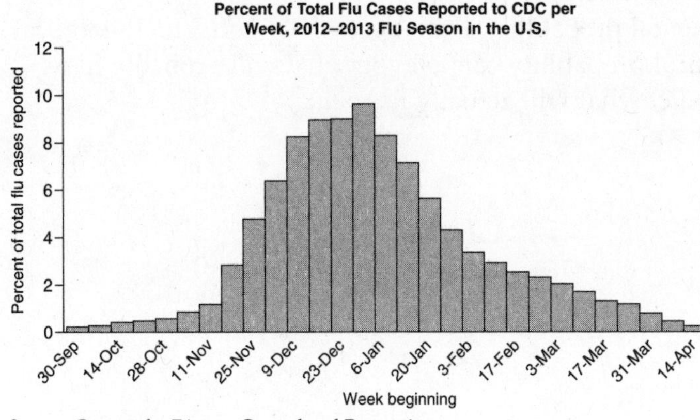

Source: Centers for Disease Control and Prevention

3. Approximately what percent of flu cases was reported to the CDC during the 2012–2013 season during the time period of December 9 to January 5?
   A. 7%
   B. 15%
   C. 36%
   D. 50%

**Review your work using the explanations that start on page 691.**

LESSON 7

# Probability

KEY IDEAS

- Probability is a ratio. It can be expressed as a ratio, fraction, decimal, or percent.
- Theoretical probability is the ratio of favorable outcomes to possible outcomes.
- Experimental probability is the ratio of favorable outcomes to the number of trials in an experiment.

## Simple Probability

Probability tells whether something is likely or unlikely to happen. The probability of any event can be expressed by a number from 0 to 1. If an event has 0 probability, the event is impossible. An event with a probability of 1 is certain to happen. Most events are somewhere in between.

To find the probability of a simple random event, we must identify favorable and possible outcomes. A **favorable outcome** is the event that we are interested in. The **possible outcomes** are all the possible events that could occur. **Theoretical probability** (sometimes called **simple probability**) is the ratio of favorable outcomes to possible outcomes.

**Example 1:** The spinner is divided into 8 equal sections. What is the probability of spinning a 4 on the spinner?

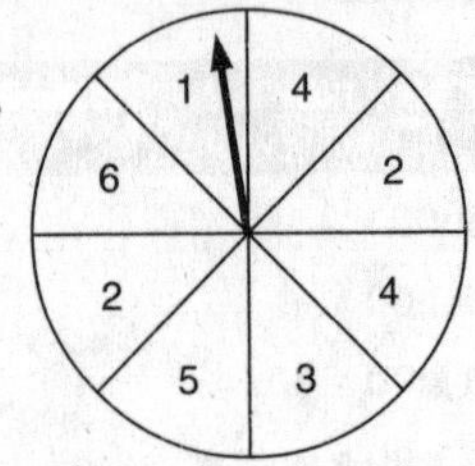


1. There are two sections labeled 4 on the spinner, and there are 8 sections in all.
2. Use the probability ratio: $\frac{\text{favorable outcomes}}{\text{possible outcomes}} = \frac{2}{8} = \frac{1}{4}$.

The probability of spinning a 4 on the spinner is **1 out of 4, $\frac{1}{4}$, 0.25, or 25%.**

In Example 1, probability was based on what we knew could happen. Another type of probability, called **experimental probability**, is based on what actually happens during the trials of an experiment. The number of trials are the number of times you try the experiment.

**Example 2:** Ricardo and Scott used the same spinner to play a game. They kept track of the numbers that they got on each spin for 20 spins. The numbers are shown below.

2, 4, 4, 6, 4, 3, 4, 6, 4, 3, 1, 6, 2, 2, 5, 2, 4, 2, 1, 2

Based on their results, what is the experimental probability of spinning a 4?

1. Ricardo and Scott spun a 4 six times out of twenty.
2. Use this ratio: $\frac{\text{favorable outcomes}}{\text{number of trials in experiment}} = \frac{6}{20} = \frac{3}{10}$, **0.3, or 30%.**

Notice that experimental probability is not necessarily equal to, theoretical probability. Theoretical probability can tell you what will probably happen, but it can't predict what will actually happen.

TASC TEST TIP

*In a multiple-choice probability problem, skim the answer choices to see if they are in fraction, percent, or ratio form. Knowing the answer form will help you decide how to do your calculation.*

# PRACTICE 7.1

**A. Express probability as a fraction, decimal, and percent for questions 1 through 5. Do not use a calculator.**

1. A game has 50 wooden tiles. Players draw tiles to spell words. If 20 of the tiles are marked with vowels, what is the probability of drawing a vowel from the tiles?

2. A spinner has five equal sections colored either red, white, or blue. After 40 spins, a player has the following results:

| Color | Frequency |
|---|---|
| red | 𝍸 |
| white | 𝍸 II |
| blue | 𝍸 𝍸 𝍸 𝍸 𝍸 III |

What is the experimental probability of not spinning blue on the spinner?

3. There are four red, four blue, and two green marbles in a bag. If one marble is chosen at random from the bag, what is the probability that the marble will be green?

4. A movie theater sells 180 adult tickets and 60 children's tickets to a movie. As part of a special promotion, one ticket will be chosen at random, and the winner will receive a prize. What is the probability that the winner will be a child?

5. A spinner has six equal sections numbered from 1 to 6. What is the probability of spinning either a 5 or 6?

**B. Choose the one best answer to each question. You MAY use your calculator.**

**Questions 6 and 7 refer to the following information.**

A deck of 12 cards is marked with the following symbols.

6. If a card is chosen at random, what is the probability of selecting a diamond (♦)?
   A. 6%
   B. 12%
   C. 50%
   D. 60%

7. If a card is chosen at random, what is the probability of selecting something other than a club (♣)?
   A. $\frac{3}{4}$
   B. $\frac{2}{3}$
   C. $\frac{1}{3}$
   D. $\frac{9}{100}$

**Questions 8 and 9 refer to the following information.**

Erin flipped a coin 40 times and made this table to show how many outcomes were "heads" and how many were "tails."

| | |
|---|---|
| heads | 𝍸 𝍸 𝍸 𝍸 IIII |
| tails | 𝍸 𝍸 𝍸 I |

8. Based on Erin's data, what is the experimental probability of getting tails on a coin flip?
   A. 3 out of 5
   B. 3 out of 4
   C. 2 out of 3
   D. 2 out of 5

9. Based on Erin's data, what is the experimental probability of getting heads on a coin flip?
   A. 3 out of 5
   B. 3 out of 4
   C. 2 out of 3
   D. 1 out of 2

**Review your work using the explanations that start on page 691.**

## Dependent and Independent Probability

You know how to find the probability of a single event. You can use this knowledge to find the probability of two or more events.

**Example 3:** Brad tosses two quarters into the air. What is the probability that both will land so that the heads' sides are showing?

One way to solve the problem is to list or diagram all the possible outcomes.

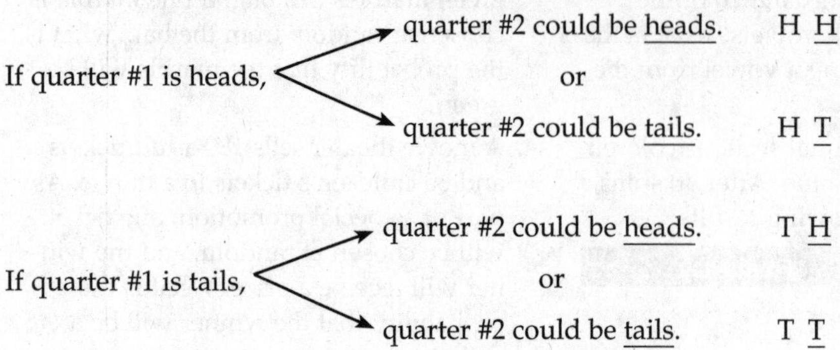


There are four possible outcomes, and only one is favorable (HH). Therefore, the probability of having both land with the heads side up is $\frac{1}{4}$, or **25%**.

You can also use multiplication to find the probability.

1. Find the probability of the individual events. The probability that one coin will be heads is $\frac{1}{2}$, and the probability that the other will be heads is $\frac{1}{2}$.
2. Multiply to find the probability of both events. $\frac{1}{2} \times \frac{1}{2} = \frac{1}{4}$.

The two coin tosses in Example 3 are **independent events**. When events are independent, one does not affect the probability of another. In Example 4 below, the events are **dependent**. Once the first event takes place, the probability of the second event is changed.

**Example 4:** A box contains four blue marbles and two red marbles. If you select two marbles, what is the probability that both will be blue?

(*Hint:* Even though the marbles in the box are taken out at the same time, think of one as the first marble and the other as the second marble.)

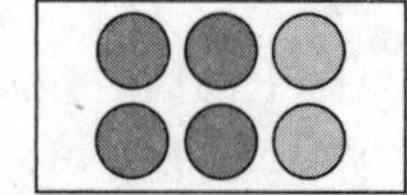

1. There are six marbles in the box, and four are blue. The probability that the first marble will be blue is $\frac{4}{6}$, which reduces to $\frac{2}{3}$.
2. Assume the first marble selected is blue. Now there are only five marbles in the box, and three are blue. The probability that the second marble will be blue is $\frac{3}{5}$.

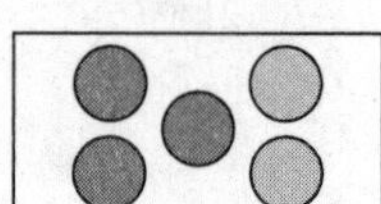

3. Multiply to find the probability of the two events. $\frac{2}{3} \times \frac{3}{5} = \frac{6}{15}$, or $\frac{2}{5}$.

The probability that both marbles will be blue is **2 out of 5**.

*Note:* The events in Example 4 would not be dependent if the first marble were replaced before the second marble was selected. Always think carefully about the situation to decide whether two events are dependent or independent.

# PRACTICE 7.2

**A. Solve as directed. Express answers as fractions.**

1. Kim rolls two standard six-sided dice. What is the chance that both will be 4s?
2. Ten cards are numbered from 1 to 10. Toni draws out a card, replaces it, and then draws another card. What is the probability that both cards will be numbers greater than 5?
3. A spinner has four equal sections. Two sections are red, one is green, and one is blue. If the spinner is spun three times, what is the probability that all three spins will be red?
4. Twenty marbles are placed in a bag. Ten are red, and ten are black. One marble is drawn from the bag and set aside. Another marble is drawn from the bag. What is the chance that both marbles will be red?
5. Allison tosses a coin four times. What is the chance that the coin will be heads all four times?
6. If you roll two standard dice, what is the probability that both will be an odd number?

**B. Choose the one best answer to each question. You MAY use your calculator.**

**Questions 7 and 8 refer to the following information.**

In a game a player rolls a die, numbered from 1 to 6, and spins a spinner. The spinner is shown below.

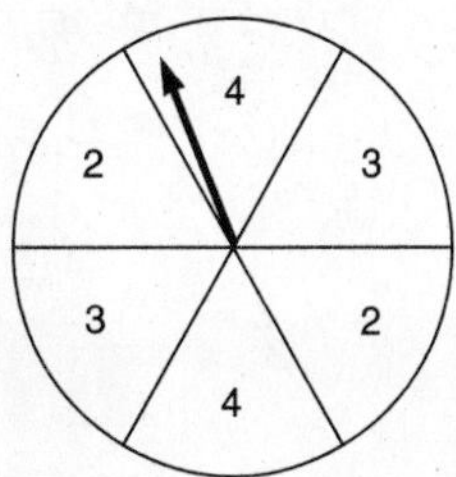


7. What is the probability of rolling a 5 and then spinning an even number?
   A. $\frac{1}{9}$
   B. $\frac{1}{6}$
   C. $\frac{2}{3}$
   D. $\frac{5}{6}$

8. What is the chance that a player will get the same number on both the die and the spinner?
   A. $\frac{5}{6}$
   B. $\frac{2}{3}$
   C. $\frac{1}{3}$
   D. $\frac{1}{6}$

Daniel uses the ten cards below in a magic trick.

9. Daniel shuffles the cards and asks an audience member to choose and hold two cards. If the cards are chosen randomly, what is the chance that both will be marked with a square?
   A. 8 out of 14
   B. 3 out of 5
   C. 1 out of 3
   D. 1 out of 5

10. There are 15 colored chips in a bag. Eight are green, and seven are white. Five white chips are removed. What is the probability that the next chip selected will be green?
    A. 100%
    B. 80%
    C. 75%
    D. 25%

**Review your work using the explanations that start on page 691.**

**STUDY ADVICE**

Consider making flash cards for some of the mathematical formulas presented in this unit. Then ask a friend to help you do drills using the flash cards.

LESSON 8

# Combinations

## Combinations with One Type of Item

**KEY IDEAS**

- Combinations are used to select several things out of a larger group when the order doesn't matter.
- If you are asked to find how many ways to combine items from one group, use an organized list or table.
- If you are asked to find how many ways to combine one item from each of a number of different types of items, use a tree diagram or the fundamental counting principle.

Sometimes the TASC Mathematics Test will ask you how many ways you can combine a set of items. Sometimes you may have only one type of item to combine, and sometimes you may have more than one type to combine. This difference will determine your problem-solving strategy.

Consider an example with *only one type of item:*

**Example 1:** Pablo is going shopping at a fruit stand that sells apples, bananas, grapes, and pears. Pablo will buy two different kinds of fruit. How many combinations of two kinds of fruit could Pablo buy?

The question is asking you to list possible groups of two out of the overall set of four. Notice that order doesn't matter—that is, *apples and bananas* is no different from *bananas and apples*. To solve this problem, you can make a list. Start with apples, and list all of the **combinations** that include apples: AB, AG, AP. Then make a list of groups that start with bananas and include the remaining fruits: BG, BP. Don't include BA because that's the same as AB. Then make a list of groups that start with grapes and include only the remaining fruits: GP. There are no remaining groups that start with P. You may find it easier to make this list in columns, as follows:

**AB**

**AG BG**

**AP BP GP**

There are **6** possible combinations.

**TASC TEST TIP**

*You can use your scratch paper to make a tree diagram or other diagrams to help you visualize problems.*

You can also draw a quick table like the following. Include a column for each of the fruits, and let each row represent a possible combination. Place two $x$'s in each row to represent a combination of two fruits.

| Apples | Bananas | Grapes | Pears |
|---|---|---|---|
| x | x | | |
| x | | x | |
| x | | | x |
| | x | x | |
| | x | | x |
| | | x | x |

Notice that you could not draw any more rows with two $x$'s without duplicating some of the existing rows. Count the rows: there are **6** possible combinations of two fruits.

# PRACTICE 8.1

If you are asked to find the number of possible combinations ($_nC_r$) in a problem that uses larger numbers, you can use this formula, which appears on the *Mathematics Reference Sheet:*

$$_nC_r = \frac{n!}{(n-r)!r!}$$

In the formula, $n$ is the number of items in the group. The letter $r$ represents the number of items you are asked to combine. The exclamation point indicates a **factorial,** which works like this: Multiply the number by all the smaller whole numbers greater than zero: $6! = 6 \times 5 \times 4 \times 3 \times 2 \times 1$.

**Example 2:** Maclellan will take 7 of her 9 friends for a fishing weekend. How many combinations of her 9 friends are possible?

Step 1: Plug in the values given in the problem.

$$C = \frac{9!}{(9-7)!7!}$$

Step 2: Either use your calculator, or write out the factorials and cancel.

$$C = \frac{9 \times 8 \times 7 \times 6 \times 5 \times 4 \times 3 \times 2 \times 1}{(2 \times 1)(7 \times 6 \times 5 \times 4 \times 3 \times 2 \times 1)}$$

$$C = \frac{9 \times 8 \times \cancel{7 \times 6 \times 5 \times 4 \times 3 \times 2 \times 1}}{(2 \times 1)(\cancel{7 \times 6 \times 5 \times 4 \times 3 \times 2 \times 1})}$$

$$C = \frac{(9 \times 8)}{2} = 36$$

---

**A. Solve.**

1. As a supervisor, Rob is choosing four of his employees to work on a special project. The employees are Angela, Barbara, Colin, David, and Elizabeth. Of those five employees, how many teams of four are possible?
2. Jessica wants to take three books on vacation with her. She has five books to choose from. How many possible combinations of three books could she take on vacation?
3. Grant is cooking a homemade pizza, and he has the following toppings available: anchovies, ham, mushrooms, and sausage. He will choose three of those toppings. How many ways could Grant combine those toppings?

**B. Choose the <u>one best answer</u> to each question about combinations.**

4. Celia is going to plant a small flower bed with four flowers. She can choose from begonias, fuchsias, hellebore, daisies, and salvia. How many combinations of four flowers are possible?

   A. 5
   B. 20
   C. 24
   D. 120

5. The Sarkesian brothers own a hardware store. There are five items the owners might display in the window. Joe Sarkesian thinks that the window should have two items, but his brother Rick thinks the window should have three items. Counting both Joe's ideas and Rick's ideas for the window, how many possible combinations of the five items are there?

   A. 10
   B. 20
   C. 30
   D. 120

**Review your work using the explanations that start on page 691.**

## Combinations with More Than One Type of Item

Sometimes you may be asked to count possible combinations with more than one type of item. Consider the following example:

**Example 3:** Sarah is deciding what to wear. She has three shirts, two pairs of pants, and two pairs of shoes. How many possible outfits does she have, if an outfit is one shirt, one pair of pants, and one pair of shoes?

This question differs from the question about Pablo on page 322. In that question, Pablo was choosing from one overall group of fruits. Here, Sarah is choosing one out of each of three groups—shirts, pants, and shoes. If you are given more than one type of item and must choose one of each type, you can use a tree diagram to figure out all the possible combinations. Study the following example:

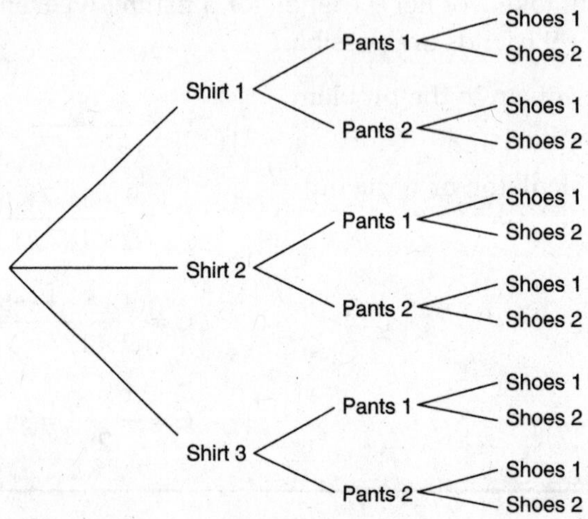


Each "branch" of the tree represents a possible combination. The number of branches on the right-hand side represents the possible number of combinations; in this case, there are **12** possible outfits.

However, you can solve the same type of problem (where you have more than one type of item and are choosing one of each type) using the **fundamental counting principle,** which works like this:

Start with shirts: for each shirt, Sarah has two pants options. That's $3 \times 2 = 6$. Additionally, for each of those six options, she has two options for shoes. That's $3 \times 2 \times 2 = \mathbf{12}$.

Use the fundamental counting principle to solve the following problem:

**Example 4:** Gordon is at a restaurant that serves a three-course meal: an appetizer, an entrée, and a dessert. There are three appetizers, six entrees, and four desserts to choose from. Gordon will order one of each. How many different meals could he order?

Multiply three appetizers by six entrees by four desserts: $3 \times 6 \times 4 = 72$. There are **72** possible ways Gordon could order his meal.

# PRACTICE 8.2

**A. Use a tree diagram or the fundamental counting principle to solve the following problems.**

1. Frank is making a sandwich. His sandwich will have one type of bread, one type of meat, and one condiment. He has four types of bread: white, wheat, rye, and a Kaiser roll. Meats he can choose from are chicken, turkey, and roast beef. For condiments, Frank can choose mayonnaise, mustard, vinaigrette, or horseradish. How many ways can Frank make his sandwich?
2. Van Ahn attended a trivia contest and won three rounds. For the first round she won, she could choose one of three restaurant gift certificates. The prize for another round was one of two T-shirts. Winning the third round allowed her to choose one of four souvenir hats. How many possible combinations of prizes were available to Van Ahn?
3. Henry is wrapping a gift for his daughter. He will use one type of wrapping paper, one type of ribbon, and one bow. He has three different types of wrapping paper, three different types of ribbon, and three different bows. How many ways can Henry wrap the gift?
4. Julio is looking forward to a three-day weekend. On Friday, he will either go to the beach or attend a street festival. On Saturday, he plans to visit a museum, but he is trying to decide among three different museums. On Sunday, he will try one of four new restaurants. How many ways could Julio combine these weekend activities?

**B. Choose the <u>one best answer</u> to each question about combinations. Determine whether you are being asked to find possible combinations from one type of item or from multiple types of items. You <u>MAY</u> use your calculator.**

5. The Nu Mu Beta fraternity is deciding what secret passphrase it should require its members to say before being admitted to meetings. The first and third words of the passphrase will be the names of Greek letters. There are 24 letters in the Greek alphabet. The second word will be a number from one to nine. How many possible passphrases are there?

   A. 24
   B. 57
   C. 576
   D. 5,184

6. A video game designer is creating a new superhero, who will have three of five potential superpowers. How many combinations of superpowers could the new superhero have?

   A. 10
   B. 15
   C. 100
   D. 125

7. A chef will make a soup with five ingredients: one of four meats, one of four vegetables, one of four kinds of noodles, one of four kinds of broth, and one of four spices. How many possible combinations of ingredients could the chef put into the soup?

   A. 20
   B. 256
   C. 1,024
   D. 3,125

8. A doctor is deciding how to treat a given disease. The doctor will prescribe one medication, one dietary change, and one type of vitamin supplement. There are five medications, five dietary changes, and five types of vitamins the doctor might prescribe. How many combinations are possible?

   A. 125
   B. 625
   C. 1,250
   D. 3,125

**Review your work using the explanations that start on page 692.**

LESSON 9

# Permutations

**KEY IDEAS**

- Permutations are used to find the number of possible outcomes when the order does matter.
- Use the total number of people or items and the number of possible outcomes to find the number of permutations that are possible.

**TASC TEST TIP**

*When you are reading a question that suggests that you may want to find a combination or a permutation, ask yourself, "Am I finding a number of groups (combinations), or am I finding the number of possible sequences (permutations)?"*

On the TASC Mathematics Test, you may be asked how many possible permutations, or sequences, are possible given a group of items. Consider the following example:

**Example 1:** Eliza is planning her day off. She wants to visit the art museum, try the new coffee shop, call her mom, and take a walk, but not necessarily in that order. How many possible sequences of those four activities are there?

This question asks you for all possible permutations, or ways to sequence the items. Thus, *coffee-art-mom-walk* and *art-coffee-mom-walk* are two different possible outcomes. Consider how this problem differs from the combinations problems on pages 322–325. In those cases, order did not matter; in a permutations problem, order does matter.

Start with how many things could go first: here, there are four possibilities for Eliza's first activity. Once she has done that first activity, three possibilities remain. After she has done a first and second activity, two possibilities remain, and then only one. So you simply multiply: $4 \times 3 \times 2 \times 1$. There are **24** possible permutations.

Some permutations questions may ask you to determine the possible orderings for only some of the items in a list. Consider this example:

**Example 2:** Ten runners are competing in a race. There are prizes for first, second, and third place. How many possible sequences of the top three prize winners are there?

Notice that you are not simply figuring out how many groups of three can be made out of the ten. Rather, you are figuring out how many sequences of three can be made out of the ten.

Now, multiplying $10 \times 9 \times 8 \times 7 \times 6 \times 5 \times 4 \times 3 \times 2 \times 1$ would give you all the possible permutations of all ten runners, so that approach will not work here. Instead, start with how many people could win first place: here, ten. Once someone has won first, there are nine possibilities for second place. Once someone has won first and someone else has won second, there are eight possibilities for third place. And then you stop multiplying: $10 \times 9 \times 8 = 720$. There are **720** possible ways that the runners could be arranged in the top three prize-winning slots. (Note that simply multiplying 10 by 3 will not work.)

The *Mathematics Reference Sheet* contains a formula that can be helpful if the question involves larger numbers. To find the number of possible permutations $\left({}_nP_r\right)$:

$${}_nP_r = \frac{n!}{(n-r)!}$$

In that formula, $n$ is the number of items in the group, and $r$ is the number of items you are asked to include in the permutations. To solve Example 2 using the formula, plug in the values and cancel out the values that appear in both the numerator and the denominator:

$$P = \frac{10!}{(10-3)!} = \frac{10 \times 9 \times 8 \times \cancel{7 \times 6 \times 5 \times 4 \times 3 \times 2 \times 1}}{\cancel{7 \times 6 \times 5 \times 4 \times 3 \times 2 \times 1}} = 10 \times 9 \times 8$$

# PRACTICE 9

**A. Read the problems and decide whether you are being asked to find combinations or permutations. Then solve.**

1. Noemi is trying to remember the password for her email. She knows that it has the following characters in it: M, Q, $, L, 7. But she can't remember the order they go in. How many possible sequences of those five characters are there?
2. Five students in a class have volunteered for a special project. Only three can actually help with the project. How many possible groupings of three out of the five are possible?
3. Tyrell is the curator at a gallery and is deciding how to arrange six paintings that will be displayed in a line along one wall. All six paintings will be included. How many possible sequences could Tyrell choose?

**B. Choose the <u>one best answer</u> to each question about combinations or permutations. You <u>MAY</u> use your calculator.**

4. Soraya has been given six tasks to do at work, but she has time to complete only four of them. She must decide in what order to do the tasks. How many possible orderings of four tasks are available to Soraya?

   A. 24
   B. 36
   C. 360
   D. 720

5. In a certain public garden, the gardener wanted to show the different visual effects that arranging flowers in different sequences can have. So he chose three kinds of flowers and planted flower beds showing each of the possible sequences of the three kinds. How many such flower beds did the gardener plant?

   A. 3
   B. 6
   C. 9
   D. 12

6. Ten people hope to become extras in a movie. The movie's casting director will choose four people to fill the following specific roles in the movie: Bystander #1, Bystander #2, Bystander #3, and Bystander #4. How many ways could those four roles be filled?

   A. 24
   B. 40
   C. 540
   D. 5,040

**<u>Questions 7 and 8</u> refer to the following information:**

Clark and his daughter are at the amusement park, and Clark is offering his daughter a choice. They don't have time to ride all six rides at the amusement park, but they can ride three of them.

7. How many combinations of three rides could Clark's daughter choose?

   A. 18
   B. 20
   C. 120
   D. 720

8. Clark's daughter can also choose the order in which she wants to enjoy the rides. How many possible orderings of three out of the six rides are possible?

   A. 18
   B. 20
   C. 120
   D. 720

**Review your work using the explanations that start on page 692.**

# STATISTICS AND PROBABILITY PRACTICE QUESTIONS

**Directions: You MAY use your calculator.**

**Questions 1 and 2 refer to the following graph.**

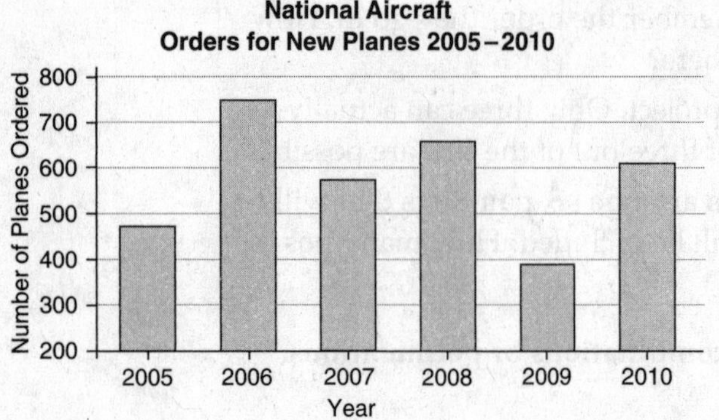


1. The mean number of aircraft orders for the six years shown on the graph is 573 planes. In which year was the number of orders closest to the mean?

   A. 2006
   B. 2007
   C. 2008
   D. 2009

2. By about what percent did orders at National Aircraft decrease from 2008 to 2009?

   A. 30%
   B. 40%
   C. 68%
   D. 75%

3. At a convention, Jim and his three friends each bought three raffle tickets. At the time of the drawing, 400 tickets had been sold. What is the probability that either Jim or one of his friends will win?

   A. $\frac{3}{100}$
   B. $\frac{1}{25}$
   C. $\frac{3}{50}$
   D. $\frac{9}{100}$

**Questions 4 through 6 are based on the following table.**

**Southland Weather March 9**

| Area | High Temp. | Low Temp. | Precipitation (in inches) |
|---|---|---|---|
| Downtown | 65° F | 53° F | 0.45 |
| Airport | 62° F | 50° F | 0.63 |
| Woodland Hills | 68° F | 50° F | 1.34 |
| East Village | 56° F | 48° F | 3.53 |
| Ventura | 62° F | 49° F | 2.57 |
| Highland Park | 64° F | 55° F | 0.84 |

4. Based on the data in the table, what was the median low temperature for March 9?

   A. 62.8°
   B. 51.5°
   C. 50.8°
   D. 50°

5. What was the mean amount of precipitation (in inches) on March 9 for the areas listed in the table?

   A. 0.65
   B. 1.09
   C. 1.56
   D. 1.99

6. For which area on the table was there the greatest range, or difference, between the high and low temperatures?

   A. Ventura
   B. East Village
   C. Woodland Hills
   D. Downtown

**STUDY ADVICE**

On the next few pages, you'll practice the statistics and probability skills you learned in this chapter. Remember, only about 10% of questions on the Mathematics Test will be about statistics and probability. So, definitely review these concepts if you need to, but also leave yourself time to study algebra, functions, and geometry (the next three chapters) in depth.

**Questions 7 and 8 refer to the graph.**

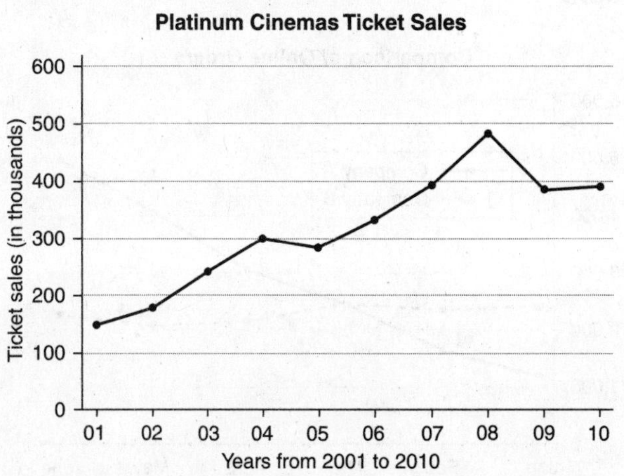


7. Platinum Cinemas opened its first theaters in 2001. The company's ticket sales increased steadily until what year, when there was a drop in sales?

A. 2004
B. 2005
C. 2008
D. 2009

8. Which year had the sharpest increase in ticket sales over the previous year?

A. 2002
B. 2006
C. 2008
D. 2009

---

9. At Nelson Stationers, the first 25 customers who visited the store on Monday morning received their choice of a gift. The table below shows how many customers chose each gift.

| | |
|---|---|
| pen and pencil set | 卌 |
| calculator | 卌 卌 II |
| mouse pad | 卌 III |

What percent of the customers chose a mouse pad?

A. 17%
B. 25%
C. 32%
D. $33\frac{1}{3}\%$

10. A standard deck of playing cards has 52 cards, with 13 cards each of hearts, diamonds, clubs, and spades. If a card is drawn randomly from the deck, what is the probability that it will be either hearts or diamonds?

A. 1 in 2
B. 1 in 4
C. 1 in 8
D. 1 in 16

**For questions 11 and 12, mark your answers in the grids below.**

11. Nita worked the following overtime hours over a six-week period.

Week 1: 5 hours

Week 2: $3\frac{1}{2}$ hours

Week 3: 4 hours

Week 4: 0 hours

Week 5: $1\frac{1}{2}$ hours

Week 6: 7 hours

What is the mean number of overtime hours Nita worked each week?

12. A spinner has five equal sections, and they are numbered from 1 to 5. What is the probability of spinning a number greater than 3? (Express the answer as a fraction.)

11.

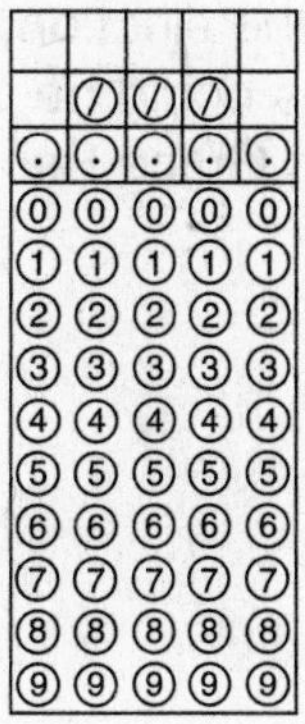

12.

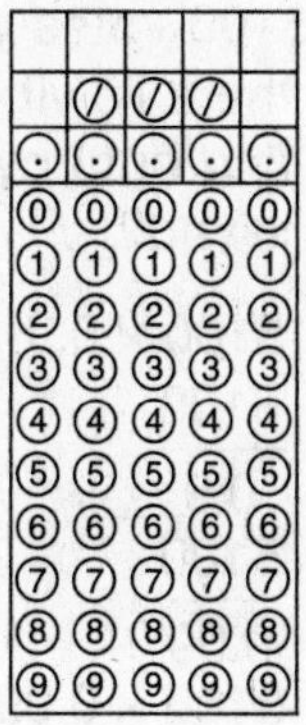

**Questions 13 through 15 refer to the following graph.**

In a recent election, five candidates ran for the city council seat from District 11. The results of the race are shown in the graph below.

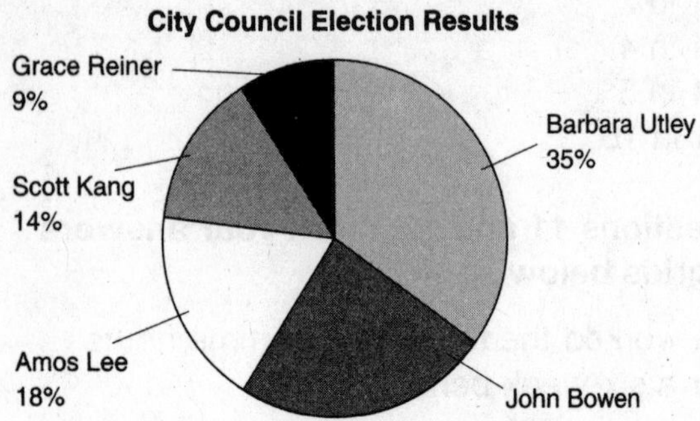


13. The three city council candidates who received the fewest votes received what percent of the total vote?

A. 23%
B. 41%
C. 56%
D. 77%

14. Which two candidates combined received about $\frac{3}{5}$ of the votes cast?

A. Grace and Utley
B. Kang and Utley
C. Bowen and Utley
D. Lee and Bowen

15. If 5100 votes were cast in the election, which of the following expressions could be used to find out how many votes Grace Reiner received?

A. $5100 \times 0.9$
B. $\frac{5100}{0.9}$
C. $\frac{5100}{0.09}$
D. $5100 \times 0.09$

**Questions 16 through 18 refer to the following graph.**

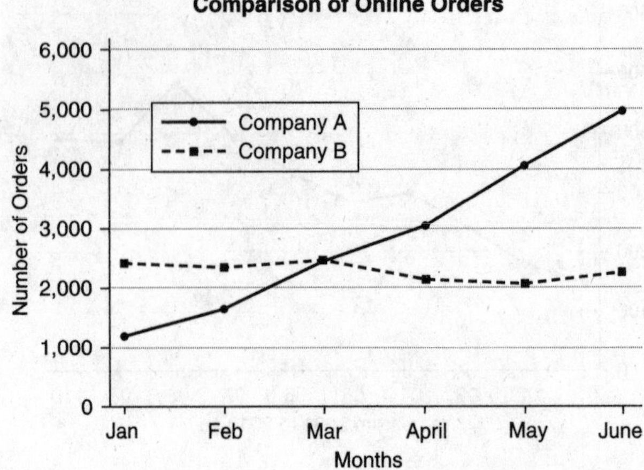


16. In which month did Company A and Company B receive about the same number of online orders?

A. February
B. March
C. April
D. May

17. Based on the trends shown by the data, what would be the best prediction for the number of online orders in July for Company A?

A. 7200
B. 5900
C. 5200
D. 4900

18. About 18% of the online orders in April at Company A are returned for credit or exchange. How many orders at Company A were returned for credit or exchange in the month of April?

A. 180
B. 360
C. 540
D. 600

**Questions 19 and 20 are based on the following information.**

A basketball player's statistics for an eight-game series are shown in the table below.

| Game | Shots Attempted | Shots Made |
|---|---|---|
| 1 | 25 | 10 |
| 2 | 23 | 12 |
| 3 | 26 | 10 |
| 4 | 24 | 13 |
| 5 | 29 | 15 |
| 6 | 18 | 7 |
| 7 | 24 | 12 |
| 8 | 27 | 10 |

19. What was the median number of shots attempted by this player in the series?

A. 24
B. 24.5
C. 25
D. 26.5

20. What is the mode of the shots made by this player during the series?

A. 12
B. 11
C. 10 and 12
D. 10

21. A bag contains 24 marbles. Eight are red, six are blue, and ten are white. A marble is drawn from the bag and replaced. A second marble is chosen at random from the bag. What is the probability that the first marble is red and the second is white?

A. $\frac{2}{5}$
B. $\frac{5}{36}$
C. $\frac{5}{48}$
D. $\frac{1}{48}$

22. A company has 36 employees. For three months, the owner has kept track of the number of sick days used by her employees per month.

| Month | Sick Days |
|---|---|
| Sept. | 34 |
| Oct. | 31 |
| Nov. | 42 |

Which expression could be used to find the average number of sick days taken each month?

A. $\frac{34+31+42}{36}$
B. $\frac{34+31+42}{3}$
C. $\frac{34+31+42+36}{4}$
D. $(34+31+42)\times 3$

**For questions 23 and 24, mark your answers in the grids below.**

23. Andy rolls two standard six-sided dice. What is the probability of rolling two 1s? Express your answer as a fraction.

24. Angelique, a teacher, is making a reading list for her students. She wants to include one historical novel, one work of science fiction, one book of poetry, and one graphic novel. She has five of each type of book to choose from. How many possible combinations of books could she include in her reading list?

23.

24.

25. A charity's board has ten members. One of the members will be elected president, then another will be elected treasurer, and then a third will be elected secretary. If no member can hold more than one position, how many ways can the members fill those positions?

A. 27
B. 30
C. 720
D. 5,040

**<u>Questions 26 and 27</u> are based on the following information.**

The frequency table below displays the reasons why patients visited a walk-in clinic during a certain week.

| Reason | Number of patients |
|---|---|
| Colds and flu | 𝍸 𝍸 𝍸 I |
| Cuts and scrapes | 𝍸 𝍸 III |
| Sprained muscles | 𝍸 𝍸 II |
| Tetanus shots | 𝍸 II |
| Severe headaches | 𝍸 𝍸 II |

26. What percent of the patients represented in the table visited the walk-in clinic because of sprained muscles?

A. 17%
B. 20%
C. 24%
D. 75%

27. In the week represented in the table, what was the ratio of the number of patients with colds or flu to the number of patients with severe headaches?

A. 4:15
B. 4:3
C. 3:4
D. 1:5

**<u>Questions 28 and 29</u> are based on the following information and graph.**

A hundred people are participating in a medical study. As a first step, the researchers collected information about participants' weight. The graph below represents how many people fell into each weight category.

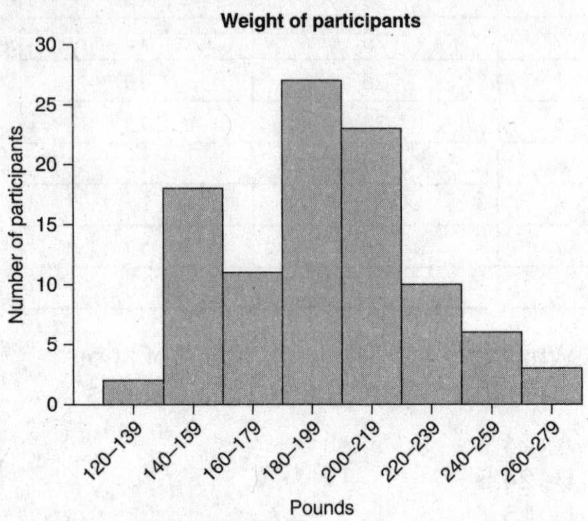


28. Which weight category displays the highest frequency?

A. 120–139 lbs
B. 180–199 lbs
C. 200–219 lbs
D. 260–279 lbs

29. Consider only the 100 individuals represented in the graph. Which one of the following groups contains the most people?

A. Participants weighing 200 lbs or more
B. Participants weighing less than 200 lbs
C. Participants weighing 180–199 lbs
D. Participants weighing less than 180 lbs

30. There are four children in Mr. Martin's class. Three of them will be selected to be hall monitors. How many combinations of hall monitors are possible?

A. 3
B. 4
C. 9
D. 12

**<u>Questions 31 through 33</u> refer to the following information and table.**

The owner of a taxi company measures the gas mileage of each of the cars in her fleet. The frequency table below shows her results.

| Average miles per gallon | Number of cars |
|---|---|
| 15 | II |
| 20 | 𝍸 II |
| 25 | 𝍸 |
| 30 | 𝍸 I |
| 35 | I |

31. Which of the values (average miles per gallon) displays the highest frequency?
    A. 15 miles per gallon
    B. 20 miles per gallon
    C. 30 miles per gallon
    D. 35 miles per gallon

32. What is the ratio of taxis that get 35 miles per gallon on average to the number of taxis that get 15 miles per gallon on average?

    A. $\frac{1}{2}$

    B. $\frac{3}{2}$

    C. $\frac{4}{5}$

    D. $\frac{1}{10}$

33. Choose the line plot that represents the information in the table.

A.

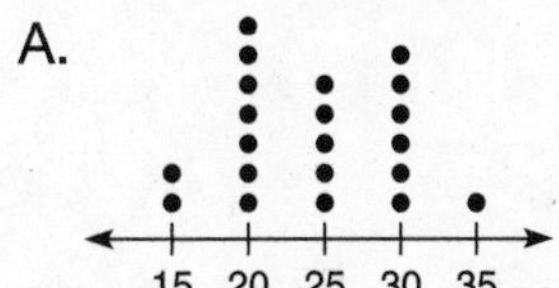


B.

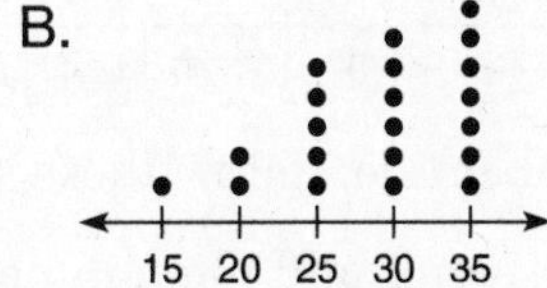


C.

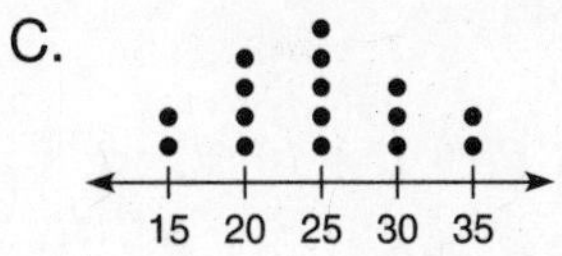


D.

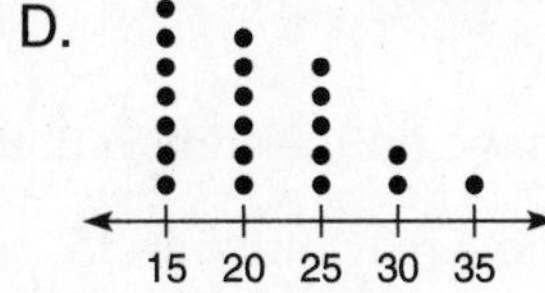


34. Ahmed works at the ticket window of a theater, and one night he decides to track when the patrons arrive for a 7:30 P.M. show. The table below represents his data.

| Time period | Percent of patrons who arrive |
|---|---|
| 5:30 to 5:59 pm | 2% |
| 6:00 to 6:29 pm | 14% |
| 6:30 to 6:59 pm | 25% |
| 7:00 to 7:29 pm | 48% |
| 7:30 to 8:00 pm | 11% |

Which one of the histograms below accurately represents Ahmed's data?

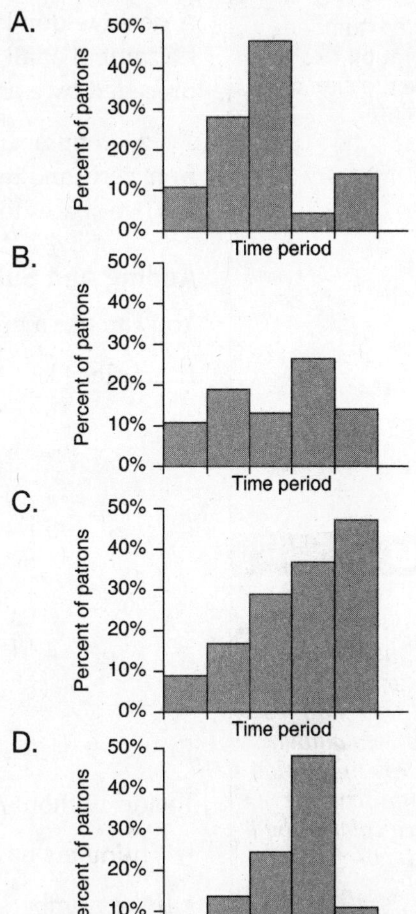


**Review your work using the explanations that start on page 692.**

LESSON 1

# The Number Line and Signed Numbers

## Understanding Signed Numbers

**Signed numbers** include zero, all positive numbers, and all negative numbers. Zero is neither positive nor negative. On a number line, the positive numbers are shown to the right of zero, and the negative numbers are shown to the left.

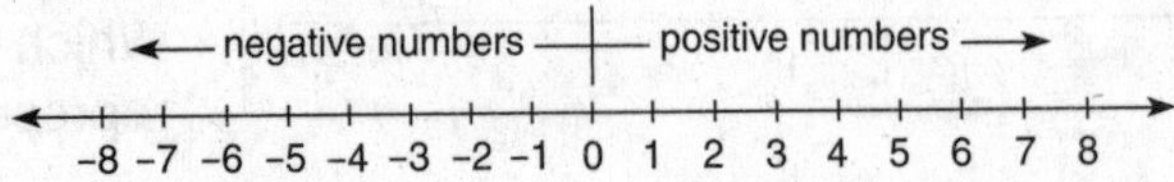


A positive number may be written with a plus (+) symbol. If a number has no symbol at all, we assume that it is positive. A negative number *must* be preceded by a minus (–) symbol.

A signed number provides two important facts. The sign tells the direction from zero, and the number tells you the distance from zero. For example, –5 lies five spaces to the left of zero, and +4 lies four spaces to the right of zero.

### KEY IDEAS

- If numbers have like signs, add and keep the same sign.
- If numbers have unlike signs, find the difference and use the sign from the larger number.
- To subtract signed numbers, change the operation to addition and change the sign of the number you are subtracting.

## Adding and Subtracting Signed Numbers

You can use a number line to model the addition of signed numbers.

**Examples:** $1 + (-4) = -3$ Begin at +1; move 4 in a negative direction (left).

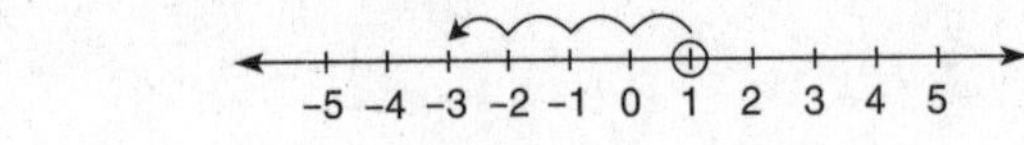


$-5 + 4 = -1$ Begin at –5; move 4 in a positive direction (right).

$-2 + (-3) = -5$ Begin at –2; move 3 in a negative direction (left).

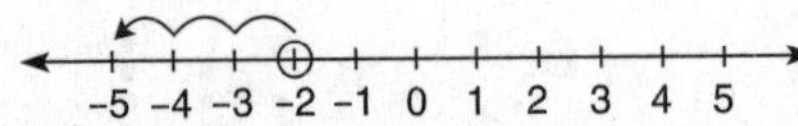


### TASC TEST TIP

*If you are testing on a computer, you can use the "change sign" key (–) at the bottom of the online calculator. This changes a positive to a negative number, and vice versa. If you are testing on paper, locate the "change sign" key on the calculator you'll be using on Test Day.*

To add without a number line, follow these steps:

- If numbers have like signs, add the numbers and keep the same sign.
- If the numbers have unlike signs, find the difference between the two numbers and use the sign of the larger number.

**Example 1:** Add $15 + (-25)$.

1. Since the numbers have unlike signs, subtract. $25 - 15 = 10$.

2. Use the sign from the larger number. $15 + (-25) = $ **–10.**

Subtraction is the opposite of addition. To rewrite a subtraction problem as an addition problem, change the operation symbol to addition and change the sign on the number you are subtracting. Then apply the rules for adding signed numbers.

# PRACTICE 1.1

**Example 2:** Subtract $3 - 8$.

1. Change the operation symbol and the sign of the number you are subtracting. $3 - 8$ becomes $3 + (-8)$.

2. Add. $3 + (-8) = -$ **5.**

You can use the same rules to combine several signed numbers.

**Example 3:** $(-5) + 6 - 4 - (-2) = ?$

1. Rewrite each subtraction as addition. $(-5) + 6 + (-4) + 2$.

2. Add the positive terms: $6 + 2 = 8$.

   Add the negative terms. $-5 + (-4) = -9$.

3. Combine the results. $8 + -9 =$ **−1.**

---

**A. Solve.**

1. $8 + (-3)$
2. $50 - 5$
3. $11 - (-2)$
4. $-1 + 2$
5. $-4 - (-5)$
6. $8 - (-2)$
7. $6 - 9$
8. $2 + 11$
9. $(-7) - (-3)$
10. $(-4) + 6$
11. $-15 + (-7)$
12. $36 - 4$
13. $-60 - (-10)$
14. $-5 - 6$
15. $12 + 13$
16. $-55 + 20$
17. $7 + (-3) + (-5) - 10$
18. $66 + (-22) - 33$
19. $-14 - (-6) + 18$
20. $80 - (-15) - 20$
21. $6 - (-3) + (-5) + 8$
22. $-23 + (-11) - (-15) + 21$
23. $3 + 9 - 5 + 12 - 9 - 11$
24. $-7 - 20 - (-14)$

**B. Choose the <u>one best answer</u> to each question.**

**<u>Question 25</u> refers to the following number line.**

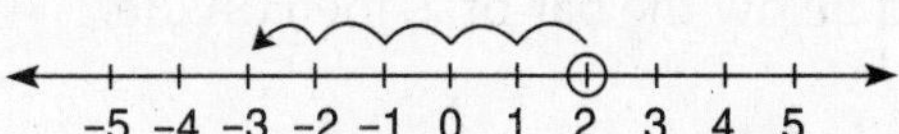


25. The number line above shows which of the following expressions?
    A. $2 + (-3)$
    B. $2 + (-5)$
    C. $-3 + 2$
    D. $-3 - (+2)$

26. At noon, the temperature in the high desert was 92°F. A scientist observed the following temperature changes over the course of the next two hours: +12°, −5°, +6°, −3°, and +13°. What was the temperature in degrees Fahrenheit at the end of the two-hour period?
    A. 95°
    B. 103°
    C. 115°
    D. 131°

**Review your work using the explanations that start on page 693.**

**STUDY ADVICE**

Number lines are very useful for understanding numerical information. They help you visualize the relationship between numbers and quantities. To review and learn about other uses for number lines, turn to pages 272 and 344.

## Multiplying and Dividing Signed Numbers

In algebra, multiplication is not shown using the times sign (×) because the symbol could be easily mistaken for the variable $x$. Instead, multiplication is shown using a dot or by placing two numbers next to each other. To avoid confusion, one or both of the numbers may be enclosed in parentheses. For example, the expressions $-5 \cdot 6$ and $-5(6)$ and $(-5)(6)$ all mean "–5 times 6."

In algebra, division can be written with the ÷ symbol, but it is usually shown with a line that means "divided by." The expression $\frac{20}{-5}$ means "20 divided by –5," as does 20/–5.

When multiplying or dividing signed numbers, use the following rules:

- If the signs are the same, the answer is positive.
- If the signs are different, the answer is negative.

**Example 4:** Multiply $4(-25)$.

1. Multiply the numbers only. $4 \times 25 = 100$.

2. Determine the sign. Since the signs on the numbers are different, the answer is negative: $4(-25) = \mathbf{-100}$.

**Example 5:** Divide $\frac{-160}{-8}$.

1. Divide the numbers only. $160 \div 8 = 20$.
2. Determine the sign. Since the signs on the numbers are the same, the answer is positive: $\frac{-160}{-8} = \mathbf{20}$.

A problem may contain more than two factors. Remember that each pair of negative factors will equal a positive product. Therefore, if there is an even number of negative terms, the product will be positive. If there is an odd number of negative terms, the product will be negative.

**Example 6:** $(-5)(6)(-1)(-2)(2) = ?$

1. Multiply. $5 \times 6 \times 1 \times 2 \times 2 = 120$.

2. There are three negative terms. Since 3 is an odd number, the product is negative: **–120.**

When a problem contains more than one operation, follow this **order of operations.** Do multiplication and division operations first, working from left to right. Do addition and subtraction operations last, also working from left to right. If a problem contains division presented with a division bar, do any operations above and below the bar first, then divide.

**Example 7:** $(-4)(6) - \frac{3+(-9)}{-2}$

1. Multiply. $-24 - \frac{3+(-9)}{-2}$.

2. Do the operation above the fraction bar. $-24 - \frac{-6}{-2}$.

3. Divide. $-24 - (+3)$.
4. Subtract. $-24 - (+3) = -24 + (-3) = \mathbf{-27}$.

**Note:** *Notice how parentheses clarify meaning:* 4 – 5 means "four minus five," but 4(–5) means "four times negative five."

# PRACTICE 1.2

**A. Solve. You MAY NOT use a calculator.**

1. $(5)(4)$
2. $(7)(-3)$
3. $(-8)(6)$
4. $(-2)(-9)$
5. $(-10)(1)$
6. $9 \div 3$
7. $12 \div (-4)$
8. $-25 \div 5$
9. $(-18) \div (-9)$
10. $\frac{40}{-8}$
11. $(14)(-2)$
12. $(-75) \div 25$
13. $13 \div (-13)$
14. $(-5)(15)$
15. $\frac{18}{3}$

**B. Solve. You MAY use a calculator.**

16. $\frac{25(4)}{-5}$
17. $(-3)(-5)(2)(-10)$
18. $20 \div (-5) \div (-2)$
19. $\frac{6(5)}{(-3)(2)}$
20. $(-11)(2)(-5)(6)$
21. $(12)(-2) \div (-2)$
22. $(-4)(-6)(-5)$
23. $50 \div (2)(-5)$
24. $(-1)(2)(-3)(2)(-1)$
25. $\frac{(3)(-4)(2)(5)}{-6}$
26. $\frac{4(-4)}{-8(-2)}$
27. $(-5)(-2)(0)(-1)$

**C. Choose the one best answer to each question.**

28. Janice is creating a computer spreadsheet. A portion of her work is shown below.

| | A | B | C |
|---|---|---|---|
| 1 | -3 | 4 | 7 |
| 2 | 2 | -5 | -8 |
| 3 | -1 | 3 | -2 |

Using the information from the spreadsheet, what is the value of the expression A1*C1*A3/(B3*A3)? (*Hint*: In a spreadsheet, the symbol * means multiplication.)

A. −21
B. −7
C. −1/7
D. 21

29. The product of 2 and 8 is divided by −8. Which of the following expressions could be used to find the value of the statement?

A. $\frac{\frac{2}{8}}{-8}$
B. $2(8)(-8)$
C. $\frac{2(8)}{(-8)}$
D. $\frac{2(-8)}{8}$

30. Which of the following is a true statement about the value of the expression $(52)(-103)(-45)(-8)(3)$?

A. The result is a fraction.
B. The result is greater than 1.
C. The result is a negative number.
D. The result is a positive number.

**Review your work using the explanations that start on page 693.**

**STUDY ADVICE**

Approximately 25% of questions on the Mathematics Test will target algebra skills. Therefore, even though this chapter is long, working your way through it will really pay off on Test Day. Concepts covered in the chapter will increase in difficulty as you go, but be sure to review previous lessons anytime you need to.

Algebraic Expressions

LESSON 2

# Powers and Roots

**Powers** are a special way to show repeated multiplication. For example, suppose you needed to multiply $5 \times 5 \times 5 \times 5$. This series of operations can be expressed as "five to the fourth power." In other words, the number 5 appears in the multiplication problem four times.

We can write the operations algebraically using **exponents**. In the expression $5 \times 5 \times 5 \times 5$ above, the number 5 is the base. The exponent, a small number written above and to the right of the **base**, tells how many times the base is repeated: $5 \times 5 \times 5 \times 5 = 5^4$.

To evaluate an expression, perform the multiplication indicated by the exponent.

**Example 1:** Find the value of $2^5$.

Write the base the number of times indicated by the exponent and then multiply:

$2^5 = 2 \times 2 \times 2 \times 2 \times 2 = \mathbf{32}$.

You may encounter some special uses of exponents on the TASC Mathematics Test. An exponent can be any positive number, or it can be 0, or a negative number. Memorize the situations described below.

1. A number raised to the first power equals itself: $8^1 = 8$.
2. A number other than zero raised to the power of zero equals 1: $6^0 = 1$.
3. A number raised to a negative exponent is equal to a fraction with a numerator of 1: $4^{-2} = \frac{1}{4^2} = \frac{1}{4 \times 4} = \frac{1}{16}$.

You can use a calculator to raise numbers to any power. Use the $x^2$ or ^ key. The following examples are worked out using the keys on the TI-30XS MultiView™. Remember, your calculator may differ if you are taking the TASC on paper.

**Example 2:** What is the value of $24^2$?

Press: 24 $x^2$ enter. The right side of the display reads 576.

The square of 24 is **576**.

**Example 3:** Find the value of $9^4$.

Enter the base, press ^, and enter the exponent. Then press enter.

Press 9 ^ 4 enter. The right side of the display reads 6561.

Nine raised to the fourth power is **6561**.

**Note:** To raise a negative number to a power using the TI-30XS MultiView™ calculator, you must enter that number in parentheses: ( (−) 4 ) $x^2$ enter.

To **square** a number, multiply the number by itself. For example, $6^2 = 6 \times 6 = 36$. In the expression $6 \times 6 = 36$, the number 36 is the **square**, and the number 6 is the **square root** of 36.

**KEY IDEAS**

- In the expression $2^3$, the base is 2 and the exponent is 3.
- To raise a number to a certain power, write the base the number of times shown by the exponent and then multiply.
- To find a square root, think, "What number times itself equals this number?"

**TASC TEST TIP**

*Make a list of common square roots by squaring the numbers from 1 to 15. Memorize them. You will need to know common square roots to solve geometry problems about area and right triangles.*

# PRACTICE 2

The symbol for square root is $\sqrt{\ }$. To find a square root, think, "What number multiplied by itself is equal to the number beneath the square root symbol?"

**Example 4:** Find the value of $\sqrt{144}$.

You know that $12 \times 12 = 144$, so the square root of 144 is **12**. Although $(-12) \times (-12)$ also equals 144, you will only be expected to find positive roots on the TASC Mathematics Test.

You may have to approximate the value of a square root.

**Example 5:** What is the square root of 90?

You know that $9 \times 9 = 81$ and $10 \times 10 = 100$. Therefore, the square root of 90 is **between 9 and 10.**

You can also use your calculator to find a square root. On the TI-30SX MultiView™, you must first press the (2nd) key to access the square root function. The $\sqrt{\ }$ function is directly above the ($x^2$) key. (Other calculators may not require the use of the (2nd) key.)

**Example 6:** Use your calculator to find $\sqrt{90}$ to the nearest tenth.

On the TI-30SX MultiView™, press (2nd) ($x^2$) 90 (enter). The right side of the display reads $3\sqrt{10}$.

Press the toggle key, (◀▶), to change the format of the answer into a decimal. The right side of the display now reads 9.486832981. Rounding to the tenths place, $\sqrt{90} \approx$ **9.5**.

---

**A. Solve each expression. You <u>MAY NOT</u> use a calculator.**

**1.** $3^2$

**2.** $4^1$

**3.** $\sqrt{9}$

**4.** $25^0$

**5.** $(-3)^2$

**6.** $\sqrt{49}$

**7.** $5^3$

**8.** $4^{-2}$

**B. Solve each expression below. You <u>MAY</u> use your calculator. Round your answer to the nearest tenth.**

**9.** $3^8$

**10.** $(-6)^4$

**11.** $\sqrt{150}$

**12.** $20^3$

**13.** $1^{15}$

**14.** $(-4)^{-2}$

**15.** $\sqrt{242}$

**16.** $(3.3)^2$

**17.** $\sqrt{57}$

**18.** $\sqrt{536}$

**19.** $112^0$

**20.** $(-2)^8$

**C. Choose the <u>one best answer</u> to each question.**

**21.** The cube shown below measures 6 inches on each side. You can find the volume of the cube by multiplying length × width × height. Which of the following expressions represents the volume of the cube?

A. $6^1$
B. $6^2$
C. $6^3$
D. $6^6$

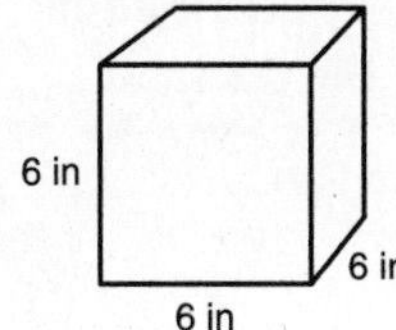


**22.** Which of the following expressions has the least value?

A. $3^{-3}$
B. $4^0$
C. $4^1$
D. $2^{-4}$

**Review your work using the explanations that start on page 693.**

# LESSON 3

## Scientific Notation

**Scientific notation** uses the powers of ten to express very small and very large numbers. In scientific notation, a decimal number (greater than or equal to 1 and less than 10) is multiplied by a power of ten.

### KEY IDEAS

- In scientific notation, a number equal to or greater than 1 and less than 10 is multiplied by a power of ten.
- Very small numbers are expressed by multiplying by a negative power of ten.
- In scientific notation, the number with the greatest power of ten has the greatest value.

Look for patterns as you review these powers of ten.

$10^1 = 10$ $10^2 = 100$ $10^3 = 1{,}000$ $10^4 = 10{,}000$ and so on.

$10^{-1} = 0.1$ $10^{-2} = 0.01$ $10^{-3} = 0.001$ $10^{-4} = 0.0001$ and so on.

Did you find the patterns? In the row with positive exponents, the exponent is the same as the number of zeros in the number written in standard form. In the row with negative exponents, the exponent is the same as the number of decimal places in the number.

You can use these patterns to change scientific notation to standard form.

**Example 1:** Write $6.2 \times 10^5$ in standard form. 6.20000

Move the decimal point five places to the *right* (the same number as the exponent). Add zeros as needed. **620,000**

**Example 2:** Write $3.82 \times 10^{-3}$ in standard form.

Move the decimal point three places to the *left* (the same number as the exponent). Add zeros as needed. **0.00382**

Work backward to write large and small numbers in scientific notation.

**Example 3:** To reach Mars, the Viking 2 spacecraft traveled 440,000,000 miles. What is the distance traveled in scientific notation?

1. Move the decimal point to the left until there is only a single digit in the ones place. 4.40000000
2. Multiply by 10 raised to a power equal to the number of places you moved the decimal point. $\mathbf{4.4 \times 10^8}$

### TASC TEST TIP

*Always try to save time. Suppose the multiple-choice answers are written in scientific notation. Instead of changing each choice to standard notation, change your answer to scientific notation.*

**Example 4:** Scientists find that a kind of bacteria moves at a rate of 0.00016 kilometers per hour. Write the measurement in scientific notation.

1. Move the decimal place to the right until there is a single digit in the ones place. 0001.6
2. Multiply by 10 raised to a negative exponent equal to the number of places you moved the decimal point. $\mathbf{1.6 \times 10^{-4}}$

# PRACTICE 3

You may be asked to compare numbers in scientific notation.

**Example 5:** Which is greater: $4.5 \times 10^3$ or $9.8 \times 10^4$?

You don't need to change the numbers to standard notation. Simply consider the powers of ten. Multiplying by $10^4$, or 10,000, must have a greater result than multiplying by $10^3$, which equals 1,000. In scientific notation, the number with the greater power of 10 has the greater value. Therefore, **$9.8 \times 10^4$ is greater than $4.5 \times 10^3$.**

---

**A. Write each number in scientific notation.**

1. 2300
2. 0.00042
3. 12,400,000
4. 14,320,000,000
5. 36,000,000
6. 0.0095
7. 0.00000058
8. 150,000,000,000
9. 0.000000009

**B. Convert from scientific notation to standard notation.**

10. $5.173 \times 10^{-4}$
11. $3.7 \times 10^6$
12. $4.8 \times 10^8$
13. $1.7 \times 10^{-5}$
14. $7.2 \times 10^{-3}$
15. $9.16 \times 10^5$
16. $8.591 \times 10^7$
17. $9.56 \times 10^{-6}$

**C. Answer the following questions.**

18. Many domestic satellites maintain an orbit approximately 23,500 miles above Earth. What is that distance in miles in scientific notation?

19. Modern technology measures very fast transactions in nanoseconds. One nanosecond equals $1.0 \times 10^{-9}$ of a second. How many seconds is a nanosecond, in standard notation?

20. The average distance of Neptune from Earth is $2.67 \times 10^9$ miles. Write the distance, in miles, in standard notation.

21. Light in the vacuum of space travels at a speed of nearly 300 million meters per second. Write the speed, in meters per second, in scientific notation.

**D. Choose the <u>one best answer</u> to each question.**

**<u>Questions 22 and 23</u> refer to the following table.**

| Unit | U.S. Equivalent | Metric Equivalent |
|---|---|---|
| 1 ton | 2,000 lb | 0.907 metric ton |
| 1 acre | 43,560 sq ft | 4,047 square m |

22. What is the number of square feet in an acre, written in scientific notation?
    A. $0.4356 \times 10^6$
    B. $4.356 \times 10^4$
    C. $4.356 \times 10^3$
    D. $43.56 \times 10^3$

23. A shipment of goods weighs 5 tons. Which of the following expressions could be used to express the weight in metric tons?
    A. $5 \times 0.907 \times 10^{-1}$
    B. $5 \times 9.07 \times 10^1$
    C. $5 \times 9.07 \times 10^{-2}$
    D. $5 \times 9.07 \times 10^{-1}$

**Review your work using the explanations that start on page 694.**

## LESSON 4

# Order of Operations

### KEY IDEAS

- To evaluate an expression correctly, you must follow the order of operations.
- If an expression uses more than one set of grouping symbols, start with the inside set and work to the outside.
- The division bar may be used as a grouping symbol.

### TASC TEST TIP

*You can use the parentheses keys on your online calculator to help you follow the order of operations.*

When a mathematical expression contains more than one operation, its value may depend upon the order in which the operations are performed. To avoid confusion, mathematicians have agreed to perform operations in a certain order.

**The Order of Operations**

1. Parentheses or any other grouping symbols that enclose operations
2. Exponents and roots
3. Multiplication and division, working from left to right
4. Addition and subtraction, working from left to right

Study the following example to see how to apply the order of operations. Notice that parentheses are used in two places in the expression; however, only the first set of parentheses encloses an operation.

**Example 1:** Evaluate the expression $\frac{(5+3)^2}{4}+3(-1)$.

1. Perform the addition operation in parentheses. $\frac{(8)^2}{4}+3(-1)$
2. Raise 8 to the second power. $\frac{64}{4}+3(-1)$
3. Divide, then multiply. $16+(-3)$
4. Add. 13

The value of the expression $\frac{(5+3)^2}{4}+3(-1)$ is **13**.

In more complicated expressions, one set of grouping symbols may be nested within another set. To avoid confusion, you can also use brackets [ ] or braces { } to group operations. To evaluate an expression with more than one set of grouping symbols, work from the inside to the outside.

**Example 2:** Evaluate the expression $4[5(-4+3)+2]$ .

1. Perform the operation in the inner set of grouping symbols: $(-4+3)$. $4[5(-4+3)+2]$ $4[5(-1)+2]$
2. Do the operations inside the brackets. Since multiplication comes before addition in the order of operations, multiply 5 and −1 and then add 2. $4[-5+2]$ $4[-3]$
3. Multiply 4 and −3. **−12**

The division bar is also a grouping symbol. Before you divide, perform any operations shown above and below the bar.

# PRACTICE 4

**Example 3:** Evaluate the expression $\frac{15+25}{2(5)}+6$.

1. Perform the operations above and below the fraction bar. $\frac{15+25}{2(5)}+6$

2. Divide, then add. $\frac{40}{10}+6$

$4+6=\mathbf{10}$

---

**A. Solve. You MAY NOT use a calculator.**

1. $4(3)-2+(6+4\cdot 2)$
2. $16\div(10-6)^2$
3. $5^2-(5-7)(2)$
4. $3(-3)+(7+4)$
5. $\frac{3^3}{5-2}-\frac{(4-2)^2}{2}$
6. $\frac{25}{(4+1)}\cdot 3+(6-1)$
7. $2^3+(8-5)^2-3$
8. $(4-12)(-6)+(10-3)$
9. $30\div 3(5-4)$
10. $15+(4)(3)-2^2$
11. $(4+2)^2+(7-2)^3$
12. $7^2\div(11-4)+(9+14)$
13. $2\left[(17-11)^2\cdot\frac{(15-5)}{2}\right]$
14. $(5^2+6-3)\div(16-3^2)$
15. $150-4\left[\frac{3+9}{4-1}\cdot(14-11)^2\right]$

**B. Choose the one best answer to each question.**

**Question 16 refers to the following information.**

Susan is in charge of planning Midvale Hospital's parent education classes. The table below shows the cost of each class to the hospital.

| Type of Workshop | Cost per Participant |
|---|---|
| Childbirth Classes | $35 per couple |
| Infant Care | $30 per person |
| Teaching Your Child to Read | $60 per person |

16. A local foundation has offered to pay 75% of the cost of infant care classes. The hospital will cover any remaining costs. There are 28 parents enrolled in the upcoming infant care class. Which of the following expressions could be used to find the amount the hospital will pay?

    A. $(75)(28)(30)$
    B. $(28)(30)-(0.75)(30)$
    C. $(1-0.75)(28)(30)$
    D. $(1-0.75)(30)+28$

17. In the expression

    $$5+2\left[7\left(\frac{10^2}{10}\right)+(6-2)(3)\right],$$

    what is the last operation you should perform to find the value of the expression?

    A. Subtract 2 from 6.
    B. Add 5.
    C. Multiply by 2.
    D. Find the square of 10.

18. Find the value of the expression $22+6[(14-5)\div 3(17-14)]$.

    A. 2.73
    B. 28
    C. 76
    D. 97

**Review your work using the explanations that start on page 694.**

**STUDY ADVICE**

An easy way to remember the order of operations is to memorize the phrase *"Please excuse my dear Aunt Sally. Love, Ron."* The first letters of that phrase correspond to the order of operations: Parentheses, Exponents, Multiply, Divide, Add, Subtract, and work Left to Right.

LESSON 5

# Absolute Value

The **absolute value** of a number is its distance from zero on the number line. For example, the absolute value of 5 is 5, since 5 is five spaces away from zero on the number line. But the absolute value of –5 is also 5, since –5 is also five spaces away from zero on the number line. Because **distance** is always **positive**, the absolute value of any positive or negative number is always positive.

Absolute value is written as two straight lines around a number, like this: **|–5|**.

–5 –4 –3 –2 –1 0 1 2 3 4 5

**|–5| = 5** **|5| = 5**

**Example 1:** Which of the following is equal to |–13|?

(1) 13

(2) –13

The correct answer is **(1)**. Absolute value is always positive.

Treat the absolute value sign as you would treat parentheses in the order of operations. If numbers inside the absolute value sign are being added, subtracted, multiplied, or divided, then do that operation before you do anything else.

**Example 2:** Which of the following is equal to $-20|17-34|$?

(1) 340

(2) –340

The correct answer is **(2)**. First perform the subtraction within the absolute value sign. Because you first found the absolute value, change –17 to 17. Then multiply by –20, like this:

$-20|17-34| = -20|-17| = -20(17) = \mathbf{-340}$.

We often think in terms of absolute value in real life, though we might not bother to call it that. For example, imagine that you have $314 in a checking account but you write a check for $400. You've overdrawn your account by $86. The bank will record your balance as –$86.00. But you'll think, "I'm $86 short." You'll just think of the absolute value, or **magnitude**, of the overdraft, without the negative sign.

### KEY IDEAS

- The magnitude of a number, without a sign, is called the absolute value.
- Absolute value is used to determine distance of a positive or negative number from zero.
- In the order of operations, absolute value is treated the same as a set of parentheses.

### TASC TEST TIP

*A signed number, positive or negative, is used to show its direction in relation to zero. However, when you see a number inside two straight lines, you are working with its distance from zero—which is always positive.*

# PRACTICE 5

**A. Find the absolute values.**

**1.** $|18|$
**2.** $|-107|$
**3.** $|423|$
**4.** $|95|$
**5.** $|-7026|$
**6.** $|-18|$
**7.** $|-5,708,432|$
**8.** $|-85.6|$
**9.** $|42|$
**10.** $|10.5|$
**11.** $|-163.24|$
**12.** $|-3.14|$

**B. Use absolute value to find the solutions.**

**13.** $5+|-6|$
**14.** $-3|52|$
**15.** $3|-52|$
**16.** $12 \div |-4|$
**17.** $-|110-201|$
**18.** $-14+|-28 \div 2|$
**19.** $706.2-|-86.4+0.2|$
**20.** $49 \div (-|-7|)$
**21.** $-5|-4|$
**22.** $|-6|-|-7|$
**23.** $|17| \div |-8|$
**24.** $|-5.5| \times (-2)$

**C. Choose the <u>one best answer</u> to each question.**

**25.** The temperature in Northville at 9:00 P.M. was –5°F. By 5:00 A.M. the following morning, the temperature was –15°F. By how many degrees did the temperature change?

A. –15 degrees
B. –5 degrees
C. 5 degrees
D. 10 degrees

**26.** Bob has errands to run. He walks 5 blocks east from his apartment to the barber shop, then walks 6 blocks west to the grocery store, then walks another 2 blocks west to the post office, and finally walks back home. Assuming that Bob's apartment, the barber shop, the grocery store, and the post office are all located on the same street, how many blocks did Bob walk in completing his errands?

A. 6
B. 11
C. 13
D. 16

**27.** Milania has a score of –65 points, and Chris has a score of 55 points. By how many points is Milania losing to Chris?

A. 55
B. 65
C. 120
D. 150

**28.** Absolute error is the absolute value of the difference between an actual value and its measurement. A deli scale gives a measurement of 25 ounces for a cut of meat that actually weighs only 23.5 ounces. What is the absolute error, in ounces, of the deli scale in this instance?

A. 1.5
B. 23.5
C. 25
D. 48.5

**Review your work using the explanations that start on page 694.**

# LESSON 6

## KEY IDEAS

- Algebraic expressions show mathematical relationships using numbers, symbols, and variables.
- Variables are letters that take the place of unknown numbers.

# Algebraic Expressions

## Writing Algebraic Expressions

An **algebraic expression** uses numbers, operations, and variables to show number relationships. **Variables** are letters (such as $x$ and $y$) that represent unknown numbers. Each time a letter is used within the same expression, it represents the same number.

To solve algebra problems, you will need to be able to translate number relationships described in words into algebraic expressions. Study the following examples.

| Algebraic expressions in words | In symbols |
|---|---|
| the product of 5 and a number | $5x$ |
| a number decreased by 12 | $x-12$ |
| the sum of 3 and the square of a number | $3+x^2$ |
| 6 less than the quotient of a number and 2 | $\frac{x}{2}-6$ |
| one-half a number increased by 15 | $\frac{1}{2}x+15$ |
| 4 times the difference of −3 and a number | $4(-3-x)$ |
| a number less another number | $x-y$ |
| 10 less the square root of a number plus 3 | $10-\sqrt{x+3}$ |

To do well on algebra questions on the TASC Mathematics Test, you must be able to translate a common life situation into mathematical symbols. You will use this skill to write equations and functions, to apply formulas, and to solve word problems.

## TASC TEST TIP

*To check whether the expression you have chosen is correct, substitute easy numbers into the expression and complete the operations. Then see if the result is reasonable for the situation.*

**Example 1:** Kyle processes sales for an online bookstore. The shipping and handling on an order is equal to 4% of the total cost of the order plus \$0.95 per book. If $c$ represents total cost and $n$ represents the number of books in an order, which of the following expressions could be used to find the shipping and handling for an order?

(1) $\frac{4}{100}nc+0.95$
(2) $(0.04+0.95)n+c$
(3) $0.04c+0.95n$

This kind of problem is called a **setup problem.** You need to recognize the correct way to find the shipping and handling based on the total cost and number of items. The relationship is described in the second sentence.

shipping and handling = 4% of total cost ($c$) plus \$0.95 per book ($n$)

$$= 0.04c + 0.95n$$

The correct answer is option **(3), $0.04c + 0.95n$.**

# PRACTICE 6.1

**A. Write an algebraic expression for each description. Use the variables *x* and *y*.**

1. a number decreased by 7
2. the product of 3 and the square of a number increased by that number
3. the product of 8 and a number less 10
4. the difference of −3 multiplied by a number and the product of 2 and another number
5. 5 less than the quotient of 10 and a number
6. the sum of −8 and the product of 7 and a number
7. the sum of 16 times a number and the number less another number times 3
8. a number squared plus the number raised to the fourth power
9. the sum of the square of a number and 4 divided by 7
10. 6 subtracted from the sum of 15 and the square root of a number
11. a number less the sum of another number and 13
12. the square of the sum of a number and 6
13. 17 less the sum of 2 times a number plus another number
14. a number increased by the quotient of 24 and the number
15. the difference of the product of 2 and a number and 15
16. 4 times the difference of two different numbers
17. 5 multiplied by the difference of a number squared and 3
18. the product of a number and the difference of 11 and the square root of 100

**B. Choose the <u>one best answer</u> to each question.**

19. A minor-league baseball team is giving a local charity the sum of \$1500 and \$0.50 for each ticket over 2000 sold for one game. Let $x$ represent the number of tickets sold. If the team sells more than 2000 tickets, which of the following expressions could be used to find the amount of the donation?

A. $\$1500 + \$0.50x$
B. $\$1500 + \$0.50(2000 - x)$
C. $\$1500 + \$0.50(x - 2000)$
D. $\$1500(2000 - x)(\$0.50)$

20. The sum of 3 times a number and 4 times another number is divided by the sum of 2 and a third number. Which of the following expressions represents this series of operations?

A. $(3x + 4y) \div (2 + z)$
B. $3x + 4y \div (2 + z)$
C. $3x + 4y \div 2 + z$
D. $(3x + 4y) \div 2z$

**<u>Question 21</u> refers to the following information.**

Appliance City employees earn an hourly wage plus commission. Wage options are shown below.

| Option | Hourly Wage | Commission on Sales |
|---|---|---|
| A | \$7.50 | 1% |
| B | \$6.00 | 3% |

21. Chandra is paid under Option B. If $h$ represents the number of hours worked and $s$ represents Chandra's total sales, which of the following expressions could be used to find her weekly pay?

A. $6 + h + 0.03s$
B. $6h + 0.03s$
C. $6s + 0.03h$
D. $0.03(h)(s)$

**Review your work using the explanations that start on page 694.**

## Simplifying and Evaluating Expressions

**Simplifying an expression** means to perform all the operations you can within an expression. When working with variables, you must remember an important rule: You can add or subtract like terms only.

A **term** is a number, a variable, or the product or quotient of numbers and variables. A term cannot include a sum or a difference.

**Examples:** $5x \quad 3y^2 \quad 13 \quad x^3 \quad \frac{x}{2}$

**Like terms** have the same variable raised to the same power. For example, $3x^2$ and $5x^2$ are like terms. $8y$ and $4y$ are also like terms. However, $6x$ and $2x^2$ are not like terms because the variables are not raised to the same power.

To simplify an expression, combine like terms.

**Example 2:** Simplify $2x - 5 + 4x^2 - 8 + 6x$.

Combine like terms. It is customary to write the term with the greatest exponent first and to continue in descending order.

$$\begin{aligned} &2x - 5 + 4x^2 - 8 + 6x \\ &= (2x + 6x) + (-5 + -8) + 4x^2 \\ &= 8x + (-13) + 4x^2 \\ &= \mathbf{4x^2 + 8x - 13} \end{aligned}$$

The **distributive property** allows you to remove grouping symbols to simplify expressions. We can state the distributive property using symbols.

$$a(b + c) = ab + ac \quad \text{and} \quad a(b - c) = ab - ac$$

In other words, each term inside the parentheses is multiplied by the term outside the parentheses, and the results are added or subtracted depending on the operation inside the parentheses. Example 3 applies the distributive property.

**Example 3:** Simplify $4x - 3(x + 9) + 15$.

1. Change subtracting to adding a negative number.
2. Use the distributive property. Multiply $-3$ by each term in the parentheses.
3. Combine like terms.
   (**Note:** $1x$ means $x$.)

$$\begin{aligned} &4x - 3(x + 9) + 15 \\ &= 4x + -3(x + 9) + 15 \\ &= 4x + (-3x) + (-3)(9) + 15 \\ &= 4x + (-3x) + (-27) + 15 \\ &= (4x + -3x) + (-27 + 15) \\ &= \mathbf{x - 12} \end{aligned}$$

**Evaluating** an expression means finding its value. To evaluate an expression, substitute a given number for each variable. Follow the order of operations.

**Example 3:** Find the value of the expression $\frac{3x + 2y}{4}$ when $x = 6$ and $y = 5$.

1. Replace the variables with the values given in the problem.

$$\frac{3x + 2y}{4} = \frac{3(6) + 2\,(5)}{4}$$

2. Perform the operations above the fraction bar. Then divide.

$$\frac{3(6) + 2(5)}{4} = \frac{18 + 10}{4} = \frac{28}{4} = \mathbf{7}$$

**Note:** To remove parentheses from an operation that follows a minus sign, imagine that the parentheses are preceded by 1. Then use the distributive property.

$$\begin{aligned} &-(2x + 3) \\ &= -1(2x + 3) \\ &= -1(2x) + (-1)(3) \\ &= \mathbf{-2x + (-3) \text{ or } -2x - 3} \end{aligned}$$

# PRACTICE 6.2

**A. Simplify.**

1. $5 + x^2 - 3 + 3x$
2. $2y + 5 + 17y + 8$
3. $3x - 6(x - 9)$
4. $6x^3 + 4 + 2x^2(15) + x^2$
5. $4(y + 8) + 3(y - 6)$
6. $5 - (x - 3) + 4x$
7. $16x + 6(x - 2)$
8. $5y^2 + 4 - 3y^2 + 5 + y$
9. $-3(x + 3) - 2(x + 4)$
10. $5x - (x + 4) - 3$

**B. Evaluate each expression as directed.**

11. Find the value of $6(x + 2) + 7$ when $x = 2$.
12. Find the value of $3x^2 + 3(x + 4)$ when $x = 3$.
13. Find the value of $\frac{(x + y)^2}{2} - 10$ when $x = 2$ and $y = 4$.
14. Find the value of $y^2 + 16 - (y - 5)^2$ when $y = 3$.
15. Find the value of $8x + 9y - (2x + y)$ when $x = 4$ and $y = 6$.
16. Find the value of $x^2 + 3y - 4 + 2(x - z)$ when $x = 7$, $y = 5$, and $z = -3$.
17. Find the value of $(14 - x)^2 + 20\sqrt{x}$ when $x = 9$.
18. Find the value of $\frac{3(2x - y)}{3} + 6(y - 5)$ when $x = -2$ and $y = 3$.
19. Find the value of $x^2 - (x^3 + 3)$ when $x = -2$.
20. Find the value of $30x + 2 + 2y^2 - 3(x - 2)^2$ when $x = 1$ and $y = 4$.

**C. Choose the <u>one best answer</u> to each question.**

21. Which of the following expressions is equal to $3x^2 + 3(x - 3) + x + 10$?
    A. $x^2 + 9x + 1$
    B. $3x^2 + 4x + 19$
    C. $3x^2 - 2x + 19$
    D. $3x^2 + 4x + 1$

22. Given the expression $4x^2 - 3(y + 6)$, which of the following values for $x$ and $y$ will result in a value of $-11$?
    A. $x = 2, y = 3$
    B. $x = -2, y = 4$
    C. $x = -1, y = 2$
    D. $x = 1, y = 0$

**<u>Question 23</u> refers to the following information.**

| Temperature Conversion Formulas | |
|---|---|
| To convert Fahrenheit ($F$) to Celsius ($C$) | $C = \frac{5}{9}(F - 32)$ |
| To convert Celsius ($C$) to Fahrenheit ($F$) | $F = \frac{9}{5}C + 32$ |

23. If the temperature is 68° Fahrenheit, what is the temperature in Celsius?
    A. 20°
    B. 36°
    C. 154.4°
    D. 180°

**Review your work using the explanations that start on page 694.**

**STUDY ADVICE**

Algebraic expressions are the foundation for much of the TASC Mathematics Test. In the next chapter, you'll take these skills one step further by working with expressions in word problems, equations, and functions. So, make sure you understand the material so far before moving on.

# Expressions and Calculator Skills

## KEY IDEAS

- On the Mathematics Test, you will use a scientific calculator that follows the order of operations.
- Use the *change sign* key to enter a negative number.
- Use the *grouping symbol* keys to change the order of operations.

## TASC TEST TIP

*To check your work when using a calculator, enter each calculation twice. If the results are the same, you probably pressed the keys that you intended.*

Sometimes a calculator may be helpful when you work algebra problems. The following examples are worked using the TI-30XS MultiView™, which you will use if you are taking the TASC on computer, and which you might use if you are taking the TASC on paper. Remember, your calculator may vary if you are testing on paper. Please see page 228 for more information about calculators. The TI-30XS MultiView™, like most scientific calculators, uses algebraic logic, which means that it follows the order of operations that you saw on page 342.

You need to practice using a scientific calculator with algebraic logic. You can find out whether your calculator uses algebraic logic by running this simple test.

Press: 4 [×] 3 [$x^2$] [enter]. (Your calculator may have an equal sign instead of an *enter* button.) If the display reads **36**, your calculator uses algebraic logic. If the display reads **144**, your calculator does not use algebraic logic. You should find another calculator to practice for the Mathematics Test.

You can use a calculator to evaluate an expression that contains several operations.

**Example 1:** Find the value of the expression $2x^2 + 3x - 5$ when $x = -4$.

When you come to the variable $x$, enter $-4$ by pressing [(−)] 4. The [(−)] key is called the **change sign key**.

Press: 2 [×] [(−)] 4 [$x^2$] [+] 3 [×] [(−)] 4 [−] 5 [enter].

The right side of the display reads **15.**

The value of the expression is 15.

Expressions sometimes contain grouping symbols to show a different order of operations. You can enter grouping symbols on a scientific calculator. On the TI-30XS MultiView™, the grouping symbols [(] and [)] are found above the [8] and [9], respectively. When you enter the left, or open, parenthesis, [(], the calculator waits until you enter the right, or closing, parenthesis, [)], before it calculates what is inside the symbols.

**Example 2:** Find the value of the expression $2(x + 4) + \frac{5x}{3}$ when $x = 6$.

Press: 2 [×] [(] 6 [+] 4 [)] [+] 5 [×] 6 [÷] 3 [enter].

The right side of the display reads **30.**

The value of the expression is **30.**

You can also use your calculator for only part of an expression.

**Example 3:** Find the value of the expression $\frac{3x + 6}{2} + \sqrt{225}$ when $x = 4$.

Substitute 4 for $x$ in the first part of the expression and calculate the results by hand or using your calculator: $\frac{3(4) + 6}{2} = \frac{12 + 6}{2} = \frac{18}{2} = 9$.

Now use your calculator to find the square root of 225.

Press: [2nd] [$x^2$] 225 [enter]. The right side of the display reads 15.

Add the results of the two steps: $9 + 15 = \mathbf{24}$.

# PRACTICE 7

**A. Use a calculator as needed to find the value of the expressions as directed.**

1. What is the value of $5x^2 - 3x + 5$ when $x = 2$?
2. Find the value of $\sqrt{7x} + 2x$ to the nearest tenth when $x = 5$.
3. If $x = -3$, what is the value of $7x^2 + 2x - 6$?
4. What is the value of $\frac{1}{2}x + 15$ when $x = 3$?
5. Find the value of $3(2x + 3 + y) - 14$ when $x = -2$ and $y = 9$.
6. If $y = -3$, what is the value of $4y^3 + 2(y^2 - 4)$?
7. What is the value of $2(x^2 + 6) + 3(x - 1)$ when $x = 5$?
8. If $x = 4$ and $y = -4$, what is the value of the expression $6x^2 + 3y^2 + 2$?
9. Find the value of $-2(x^3 + 3) + 16x + 2$ when $x = 2$.
10. If $x = 7$, what is the value of the expression $7 + 3(x - 2) - 2x^2$?
11. Find the value of $-(x + y) + 3(2z - y)$ if $x = -5$, $y = -7$, and $z = 4$.
12. What is the value of the expression $x^2 - 7(3 - y) + 4$ when $x = 5$ and $y = 4$?
13. If $x = -2$ and $y = 8$, what is the value of $x^2 + y - 6(y + 3)$?
14. What is the value of $\sqrt{760 - 4x^2}$ to the nearest tenth when $x = 6$?
15. If $x = 20$, what is the value of the expression $4(x + 7) - 3(x - 2)$?
16. Find the value of $\frac{x(25 + 2x - y)}{-z}$ when $x = -3$, $y = 4$, and $z = -1$.
17. What is the value of $5y^2 + 4x^2 - 6(x - y)$ when $x = 5$ and $y = -2$?
18. Find the value of $3x^2 \cdot \frac{2(x - 3y)}{6}$ when $x = 6$ and $y = 1$.
19. What is the value of the expression $(x^2 + 5)(x^2 - x + 2) - 3$ when $x = -4$?
20. Find the value of $(x + y)(x - y)(2x + y)$ when $x = 9$ and $y = 4$.

**B. Choose the <u>one best answer</u> to each question.**

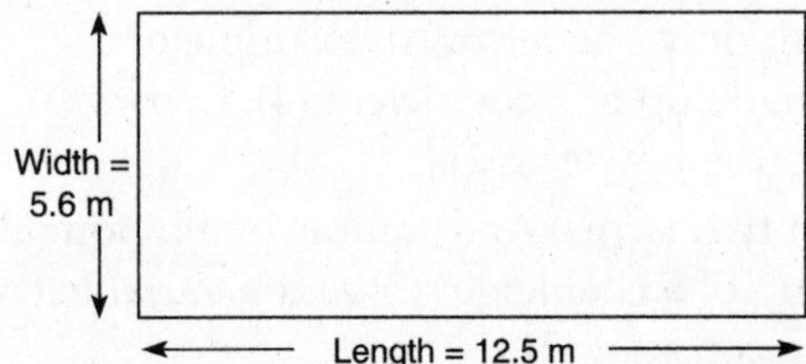


21. Jake has to buy enough fencing to enclose the rectangular garden shown above. The formula for finding the perimeter of (or distance around) a rectangle is $P = 2l + 2w$, where $P$ = perimeter, $l$ = length, and $w$ = width. Using the values from the drawing, what is the perimeter in meters of the garden?
    A. 18.1
    B. 36.2
    C. 70
    D. 140

22. If $x = -5$ and $y = 2$, which of the following expressions has the greatest value?
    A. $x + y$
    B. $-x + y$
    C. $xy$
    D. $-2xy$

23. What is the value of the expression $2 \div x^{-4}$ when $x = 2$?
    A. 32
    B. 16
    C. 8
    D. −16

**Review your work using the explanations that start on page 694.**

LESSON 8

# Understand Polynomials

The TASC Mathematics Test will expect you to understand polynomials. A **polynomial** is made up of terms, and since the prefix *poly-* means "many," a polynomial is a term in which many parts are being combined. Each term in a polynomial may be made up of a combination of coefficients, variables, exponents, and constants.

**Coefficients** include numbers such as 4, –25, or $\frac{1}{2}$ and will come before the variables. Coefficients can be negative, like –25. If there is no coefficient next to a variable, assume the coefficient is 1. In the expression $x + y + z$, the coefficient in front of each variable is equal to 1.

**Variables** are letters such as $x$ and $y$ in polynomial terms. In the polynomial $45a^2b$, the variables are $a$ and $b$.

**Exponents**, or powers, are a way of showing repeated multiplication. This is also known as raising a number or variable to a power. Polynomials must be raised to whole number exponents. There are no negative or fractional powers in polynomials. In the polynomial $6x^3y^4$, the exponents are 3 and 4. The **degree** of a polynomial with only one variable is the largest exponent of that variable. For example, in the expression $4x^3 + 3x^2 - 5$, the degree is 3 (the largest exponent of $x$.)

A **constant** is a number on its own that will always remain the same. It is not next to a variable. A constant can be either positive or negative, depending on whether it is being added or subtracted. In the expression $4x^3 + 3x^2 + 5$, the constant is 5. No matter what value you substitute for $x$, 5 will always be just 5.

Polynomials are built out of all of the components above, and there are different types of polynomials, including monomials, binomials, and trinomials. These are important to know.

- A **monomial** is a polynomial with only one term. An example of a monomial is $4xy^2$. This term is made up of a coefficient (4), two variables ($x$ and $y$), and an exponent (the power of 2).
- A **binomial** is a polynomial with two terms. An example of a binomial is $3x + 2$. The first term is made up of a coefficient (3) and a variable ($x$), and the second term consists of a constant (2).
- A **trinomial** is a polynomial with three terms. An example of a trinomial is $4x + 3y^2 - 4$. The first term is made up of a coefficient (4) and a variable ($x$). The second term is made up of a coefficient (3), a variable ($y$), and an exponent (the power of 2). The third term is made up of a constant, and this time it is a negative number (–4).

A few types of numbers are not categorized as polynomials and cannot be present in polynomial terms. These include the following:

- Division by a variable, such as $\frac{3}{x+3}$ or $\frac{1}{x}$
- Negative exponents, such as $4xy^{-2}$ (exponents can only be 0, 1, 2, etc.)
- Fractional exponents, such as $3a^{\frac{1}{2}}$
- Variables inside radicals, such as $\sqrt{x}$

In a polynomial term, however, you can divide by a constant or have numbers inside a radical. For example, $\frac{4x}{12}$ is allowed, as is $\sqrt{10}$.

**KEY IDEAS**

- A polynomial is an expression with more than one term—any combination of coefficients, variables, exponents, and constants.
- Specific types of polynomials include monomials, binomials, and trinomials.

**TASC TEST TIP**

*If there is no coefficient next to a variable, assume the coefficient is 1.*

# PRACTICE 8

**A. Identify whether each of the following is a monomial, binomial, or trinomial.**

1. $25a$
2. $2xy^2z$
3. $x - 4$
4. $x^3 + y - 1$
5. $7y - 1$
6. $2x^4 + 3x + 4$
7. $\frac{x}{3}$
8. $y^2$
9. $g^2h^2i^2j^2$
10. $x^2 + x^2$
11. $x^2 + 14x + 3$
12. $x^2y + x^2 + y$
13. $g + h$
14. $\sqrt{49}$
15. $3x^2 - 5$

**B. For each polynomial, identify the terms. Remember that a coefficient can be positive or negative.**

16. $3x^4 - 2x^2 + 3$
17. $12a^2bc$
18. $3g - 4h$
19. $x^2 + y$
20. $-4a - 3b^2 + c$
21. $25$
22. $4x^2 + 3x - 7$
23. $\frac{3x}{8}$
24. $\sqrt{25}$
25. $\frac{x^2}{9}$
26. $49x^2y^2z^2$
27. $18y^2 - 4y^2 + 8$
28. $3h - 4$
29. $x^2 - x + y^2 - 2$
30. $ab + ab^2 + b^2 - 4$

**C. Choose the <u>one best answer</u> to each question.**

31. What is the sum of the exponents in the expression $4x^3 + 3x^2 + 5$?
    A. 3
    B. 5
    C. 12
    D. 17

32. What is the sum of the coefficients in the expression $a - 3b - c + 2d$?
    A. −3
    B. −1
    C. 2
    D. 3

**Review your work using the explanations that start on page 695.**

**STUDY ADVICE**

If you're having trouble sticking to your study schedule, consider finding a study partner—someone else who is studying for anything (the TASC, the GED® test, or any other exam). The two of you can remind each other to stick to your study schedules, encourage each other, and even have study sessions together.

# Simplify Polynomials

## Combine Like Terms

When working with polynomials, you must work to combine like terms. **Like terms** have variables that are the same or are terms that have the same variable raised to the same power, or exponent. For example, $8x^3$ and $4x^3$ are like terms, and $5y$ and $3y$ are also like terms.

**Unlike terms** have variables that are different or have the same variable raised to different powers. For example, $3a$ and $5b$ are unlike terms. The terms $9x$ and $7x^2$ are also unlike terms because the variables are raised to different powers.

You can only combine like terms when simplifying polynomials. Unlike terms cannot be combined. For example, in the polynomial $7x^2 + 4x^3$, you cannot combine the terms because $x$ is raised to different powers in each term. However, in the polynomial $7x^2 + 4x^2$, you can combine terms that all have the same variable and the same exponent: $7x^2 + 4x^2 = 11x^2$.

**Example 1:** Combine like terms in the polynomial $4y^3 + 2x^3 - 7y^3$.

1. First, identify and group the like terms. $4y^3 - 7y^3 + 2x^3$

The two $y^3$ terms are alike; the $x^3$ term cannot be combined with them.

2. Combine the like terms. $\mathbf{-3y^3 + 2x^3}$

### KEY IDEAS

- Like terms can be combined; unlike terms cannot.
- Like terms are either numbers—positive or negative—or variables with the same degree of exponents.
- Polynomials with unlike terms cannot be simplified.

## Simplify Polynomials

Some polynomials may contain both like and unlike terms. The following example shows how like and unlike terms are handled when you have to simplify a polynomial. Start by combining like terms from the exponent with the largest number, or degree, and proceed to the exponent with the smallest number.

**Example 2:** Simplify the polynomial $7x^4 - 13x^2 + x^4 + 2x^2 + 5x + 3 + x$.

1. Combine like terms with the largest degree, which is 4. Add: $7x^4 + x^4 = 8x^4$.
2. You now have $8x^4 - 13x^2 + 2x^2 + 5x + 3 + x$. Combine like terms from the exponent with the next largest degree, which is 2. Add: $-13x^2 + 2x^2 = -11x^2$.
3. You now have $8x^4 - 11x^2 + 5x + 3 + x$. Finally, combine like terms with the next largest degree, which is 1. Add: $5x + x = 6x$.
4. You now have $\mathbf{8x^4 - 11x^2 + 6x + 3}$.

This is as much as you can simplify this polynomial by combining like terms. The simplified polynomial has no more like terms and must remain as is.

### TASC TEST TIP

*When working with polynomials, treat the minus sign before a coefficient or constant as an indicator of a negative number. This will help you to combine like terms using the rules of signed numbers that you learned on pages 334–335.*

# PRACTICE 9

**A. For each pair of terms, indicate if they are like terms or unlike terms.**

1. $4x^3, x^3$ __________ terms
2. $3x, x$ ________ terms
3. $b, b^2$ ________ terms
4. $-2x, 7y$ ________ terms
5. $-2x, 7x$ ________ terms
6. $4a, 4$ ________ terms
7. $g^2, g^2hi$ ________ terms
8. $2x^2y, 8x^2y$ ________ terms
9. $-5m, -5m^2$ ________ terms
10. $x^2y, xy^2$ ________ terms
11. $ab, 8ab$ ________ terms
12. $3y, 3y^2$ ________ terms
13. $14g, \frac{1}{3}g$ ________ terms
14. $12x^2, x^2$ ________ terms
15. $a, ab^2$ ________ terms
16. $15x^2, -x^2$ ________ terms
17. $10y, 11yz$ ________ terms
18. $x^2, \frac{x^2}{2}$ ________ terms
19. $g, -g^2$ ________ terms
20. $\frac{x}{8}, x^2$ ________ terms

**B. Simplify each expression by combining like terms.**

21. $3x^2y + 4x^2y$
22. $3b + b$
23. $a - 7a + 3$
24. $14ab + ab^2 + 2ab + 3$
25. $x^2 - 3x^2 + 7$
26. $ab + 2ab + ab$
27. $7g + 7gh + 7g + 7gh$
28. $g^2 + h^2 - 4g^2h^2 + g^2 + h^2 - 4$
29. $9y + y - y^2 - y$
30. $x^2 - 8x^2 + y - 3$
31. $11y + 11y - 7$
32. $9x^2y - 3x^2y + 4y^2 - 21 + y^2 - 2$
33. $8x^2 - 4x + 7 + 4x^3 - x^2 + 7x - 2$
34. $-3x^2 + 6x - 2x^2 - 10x + 5$
35. $9x^2 - 3x^3 + x - 2x^2$

**C. Choose the one best answer to each question.**

36. What is the simplified form of the expression $3a^2b + 4ab + 3a^2b + 5ab$?

    A. $6a^3b^2 + 8a^3b^2$
    B. $6a^2b + 9ab$
    C. $6a^2b + 8ab$
    D. $15a^6 + b^4$

37. When simplified, how many terms are in the polynomial $j^2 + k^3 - 2j^3 + 5k^3 - 2j^2$?

    A. 2
    B. 3
    C. 4
    D. 5

**Review your work using the explanations that start on page 695.**

LESSON 10

# Add and Subtract Polynomials

KEY IDEAS

- Monomials, binomials, or trinomials can be added or subtracted.
- In some cases, a polynomial needs to be simplified before it can be added or subtracted.
- When subtracting polynomials, distribute the minus sign across the second polynomial, changing the signs for coefficients, and then combine all the like terms.

## Add Polynomials with One Variable

On the Mathematics Test, you may be required to add polynomials that have one variable. You can add polynomials when they have like terms, including variables and exponents. When you see polynomials within parentheses linked by an addition sign, add them by combining the like terms across the polynomials.

**Example 1:** Add $(3x^2 + x + 4) + (2x^2 + 2x - 16)$.

1. To add these polynomials, simply combine like terms. Add: $3x^2 + 2x^2 = 5x^2$.
2. Add: $x + 2x = 3x$.
3. Add: $4 + (-16) = -12$.
4. Combine the results into one polynomial: $\mathbf{5x^2 + 3x - 12}$.

Sometimes, an expression needs to be simplified before you add and combine like terms.

**Example 2:** Add $(5x^2 + 8x - 4) + (2x^2 - 6x + 14x)$.

1. Simplify within the second parentheses. Add: $-6x + 14x = 8x$.
2. Combine like terms across the polynomials. Add: $5x^2 + 2x^2 = 7x^2$.
3. Use the simplified expression from step 1. Add: $8x + 8x = 16x$.
4. Combine the results into one polynomial: $\mathbf{7x^2 + 16x - 4}$.

## Subtract Polynomials with One Variable

The only difference between adding and subtracting polynomials is the minus sign between the parentheses. You must distribute the negative sign across the second polynomial. To distribute the negative sign across the second polynomial, simply reverse the signs of each term. Then drop the parentheses and combine like terms across both polynomials.

TASC TEST TIP

*When you subtract, you are simply reversing the signs within the second polynomial. Be careful to make all negative signs positive. Study Examples 3 and 4 carefully to avoid common errors.*

**Example 3:** Subtract $(3x^2 + x + 4) - (7x^2 + 2x - 16)$.

1. Distribute the negative sign to everything in the second set of parentheses by reversing the sign of each term: $-7x^2 - 2x + 16$.
2. Drop the parentheses from the entire expression and combine like terms:

   $3x^2 + x + 4 - 7x^2 - 2x + 16$
   $-4x^2 + x + 4 - 2x + 16$
   $-4x^2 - x + 4 + 16$
   $\mathbf{-4x^2 - x + 20}$

Note that subtracting a negative constant or coefficient is the same as adding a positive. In the next example, watch what happens to the negative coefficient inside the second set of parentheses when the sign is distributed.

# PRACTICE 10.1

**Example 4:** Subtract $(x^2 + 2x + 3) - (4x^2 - x + 6)$.

1. Distribute the negative sign to everything in the second set of parentheses by reversing the sign of each term: $-4x^2 + x - 6$

2. Drop the parentheses and combine like terms:
$x^2 + 2x + 3 - 4x^2 + x - 6$
$x^2 - 4x^2 + 2x + x + 3 - 6$
$-3x^2 + 3x - 3$

---

**A. Add the following polynomials.**

**1.** $(3x + 4) + (2x + 2)$
**2.** $(17y - y + 3) + (4y + 3y + 3)$
**3.** $(5x^2 - 3x - 4) + (3x^2 - 2x + 6)$
**4.** $(-a^2 + 2a) + (16a^2 + 6a)$
**5.** $(9x^2 - 3x - 2) + (2x^2 + 5x + 5)$
**6.** $(6a + 6) + (-5a - 5)$
**7.** $(-8g^2 + 7g + 6) + (8g^2 - 7g - 5)$
**8.** $(2x^2 + 5x) + (2x^2 + 4x + 7x - 9)$
**9.** $(13y + 4y + 4) + (7y - 7)$
**10.** $(-a^2 - a^2 - a - 4) + (-a^2 - a^2 - a - 5)$

**B. Subtract the following polynomials.**

**11.** $(3y - 4) - (2y - 2)$
**12.** $(x + 16) - (4x + 3)$
**13.** $(2a + 1) - (-a - 1)$
**14.** $(5x^2 + 2x + 4) - (2x^2 + x + 2)$
**15.** $(7y + 5y + 5) - (2y - 2)$
**16.** $(9x^2 + 4x + 5x + 4) - (7x^2 + 6x - 9)$
**17.** $(-g + g - 1) - (-g - g - 2)$
**18.** $(17a^2 - 4a - 4) - (16a^2 + 6a - 6)$
**19.** $(7b^2 + b - 8) - (7b^2 + b + 8)$
**20.** $(21x^2 + 3x^2 - 2x - 4 - 1) -$
$(3x^2 + x^2 + x + 2x - 5 - 1)$

**C. Choose the <u>one best answer</u> to each question.**

**21.** What is the sum of the polynomials $(2xy + 3xy^2 - 4x^2y) + (5x^2y - 3xy^2 + 2xy)$?
A. $x^2y + 4xy$
B. $4xy + 3x + y$
C. $7x - 2y$
D. $7x^2y - 2xy$

**22.** Which of the following equals $(5x^2 - 2x + 1) - (3x^2 - 3x - 2)$?
A. $x - 5x - 1$
B. $2x^2 - x + 3$
C. $2x^2 + x + 3$
D. $2x^2 - 5x + 3$

**Review your work using the explanations that start on page 695.**

**STUDY ADVICE**

Look back over your work. If you understood how to add or subtract polynomials, but you made small or careless errors in doing so, give yourself a pat on the back! You've learned the concept, and now you know to watch for small math errors.

## Simplifying Polynomials with More Than One Variable

Some polynomials contain terms with different variables—for example, the binomial $2x + 3y$ contains an $x$ term and a $y$ term. You add, subtract, and simplify polynomials with more than one variable just as you do polynomials with just a single variable. However, you have to be careful to add and subtract only like terms. Remember that in all polynomials, like terms have the *same variable* and the *same exponent*. For example, in the polynomial $x^2 + 2x + y^2 + 3x + 2y$, the only like terms are the two $x^1$ terms. You can combine the $2x$ and the $3x$, but you cannot combine $x^2$ with any other term, nor can you combine the $y^2$ or the $2y$ with any other term. The most simplified version of this polynomial is $x^2 + 5x + y^2 + 2y$.

A term that consists of two or more variables multiplied together cannot be combined with terms that contain only one of those variables. For example, you cannot combine $2xy + 7x$. However, you can combine $2xy + 7xy$ to get $9xy$.

**Example 5:** Simplify $6xy^4 - 20x^2 - 3 + xy^4 + 12x^2 - 30$.

Start by grouping the like terms together. Then add and subtract as appropriate.

$$6xy^4 - 20x^2 - 3 + xy^4 + 12x^2 - 30$$
$$= 6xy^4 + xy^4 - 20x^2 + 12x^2 - 3 - 30$$
$$= \mathbf{7xy^4 - 8x^2 - 33}$$

## Adding Polynomials with More Than One Variable

Adding polynomials that contain more than one variable requires the same process as adding polynomials that have only one variable. Just remove the parentheses and combine like terms across both polynomials. Remember that only like terms can be combined.

**Example 6:** Add $(3x^2 + 6x + 3xy) + (5x^2 - 6xy + 14y)$.

$$(3x^2 + 6x + 3xy) + (5x^2 - 6xy + 14y)$$
$$= 3x^2 + 5x^2 + 6x + 3xy - 6xy + 14y$$
$$= \mathbf{8x^2 + 6x - 3xy + 14y}$$

## Subtracting Polynomials with More Than One Variable

Subtracting polynomials that contain more than one variable is exactly the same as subtracting polynomials that contain only a single variable. Remember to distribute the minus sign across the second polynomial when you remove the parentheses. Also remember that only like terms can be combined.

**Example 7:** Subtract $(3xy^2 + x + 2xy + 4) - (7xy^2 + 2xy - 16)$.

$$(3xy^2 + x + 2xy + 4) - (7xy^2 + 2xy - 16)$$
$$= 3xy^2 + x + 2xy + 4 - 7xy^2 - 2xy + 16$$
$$= \mathbf{-4xy^2 + x + 20}$$

Notice that there is no $xy$ term in the final simplified expression because $2xy - 2xy = 0$.

# PRACTICE 10.2

1. $a^2 + 2a + b^2 + 3a + 3b^2$
2. $x + 3xy + y + 16 - 5x - 4xy$
3. $yz^2 - z^2 + 5 + 3yz - 3z^2 + 4yz$
4. $ab - b + c + 17 + 6ab - 34$
5. $a^4 + c^2 + 3ac - 5a^4 - 2c^2 + 5$
6. $19xyz + x - y + 3xyz + 6 + y$
7. $ef + ef^2 - 10 + 6ef + f$
8. $p + pq - q - p + 3pq - 3 - q + 7$

**B. Add the following polynomials.**

9. $(ab + b - c + 6) + (3ab - b + c - 6)$
10. $(x^2 + xy - y - 3) + (-x^2 - xy + y + 3)$
11. $(p^6 + p^5 + pq - p^2) + (2p^6 - p^5 + 3pq - q^2)$
12. $(x + xy + 7) + (y - xy + 8)$
13. $(9a + bc + c^2) + (-9a - b + bc - c^2)$
14. $(4xyz + 4x - 4y) + (6xyz - 4x - 4y + 16)$
15. $(5a + 5b + 4c - 6) + (a - b - 4c + d + 6)$
16. $(pq - q + 15) + (6pq - 15)$

**C. Subtract the following polynomials.**

17. $(ab + a + b + 6) - (8ab + a - b - 6)$
18. $(xy + x + y) - (xy + x + y)$
19. $(p^2 + q^2 + 14) - (3p^2 - 4q^2 + 7)$
20. $(x^4 + yz + z^4) - (yz + z^5)$
21. $(bc^2 + bc + c - 7) - (2bc - c - 7)$
22. $(xy + xz - xyz) - (4xy + xyz)$
23. $(c^3d^7 + c^2 - d + 35) - (2c^2 - 3d + 35)$
24. $(ef^2g - fg + 16) - (ef^2 + fg + 8)$

**D. Choose the <u>one best answer</u> to each question.**

25. Which of the following equals $(x + y + z) - (-2x + 2y + z)$?
    A. $-x + 3y + 2z$
    B. $-2x - y + 2z$
    C. $3x - 2y + 2z$
    D. $3x - y$

26. Which of the following equals $(2g^2 + 3h - 5k) + (g^2 + 2h + 3k)$?
    A. $g^2 + h - 8k$
    B. $3g^2 + 5h - 2k$
    C. $2g^2 + 6h^2 - 15k^2$
    D. $2g^4 + 5h - 2k$

**Review your work using the explanations that start on page 695.**

# Multiply Polynomials

## Multiply a Monomial by a Monomial

To multiply two monomials, multiply each component separately. Start by multiplying the coefficients (or numbers). If there is no coefficient given, assume that the coefficient is 1 (for example, $xy = 1xy$). Then, multiply each variable separately by adding the exponents of like variables. Remember that a variable with no exponent is a variable raised to the first power (for example, $x = x^1$). So $x\left(x^3\right) = x^1\left(x^3\right) = x^4$.

**Example 1:** Multiply $(2ab)(4b)$.

$$2 \times 4 \times a \times b^1 \times b^1 = \mathbf{8ab^2}$$

## Multiply a Monomial by a Binomial

To multiply a monomial by a binomial, multiply the monomial by the first term in the binomial, then multiply the monomial by the second term in the binomial. Finally, add the resulting terms.

**Example 2:** Multiply $-2z^2(z + 3yz)$.

1. Distribute the negative sign:
   $-2z^2(z + 3yz) = 2z^2(-z - 3yz)$.
2. Multiply the monomial by each term in the binomial:
   $2z^2(-z - 3yz) = [2 \times (-1) \times z^2 \times z^1] + [2 \times (-3) \times z^2 \times y^1 z^1]$.
3. Add: $-2z^3 + (-6yz^3) = \mathbf{-2z^3 - 6yz^3}$.

## Multiply Two Binomials

To multiply two binomials, multiply the first terms, then the outer terms, then the inner terms, and, finally, the last terms. Add the results and combine like terms. You can remember this process by the acronym **FOIL**, which stands for First, Outer, Inner, Last.

**Example 3:** Multiply $(2g^2 + 9)(3g^2 - 4)$.

1. Multiply using FOIL:
   $(2g^2 + 9)(3g^2 - 4) = \overbrace{(2g^2)(3g^2)} + \overbrace{(2g^2)(-4)} + \overbrace{(9)(3g^2)} + \overbrace{(9)(-4)}$.
2. Add: $6g^4 - 8g^2 + 27g^2 - 36$.
3. Combine like terms:
   $6g^4 - 8g^2 + 27g^2 - 36 = \mathbf{6g^4 + 19g^2 - 36}$.

### KEY IDEAS

- There are a number of ways to multiply polynomials.
- The basic concepts in all involve learning procedures for multiplying constants, variables, and exponents.
- A common method for multiplying binomials is called FOIL for short.

### TASC TEST TIP

*Always finish the FOIL method by combining like terms after you have multiplied.*

# PRACTICE 11

A. **Multiply the monomials.**

1. $(6x)(5x)$
2. $(2xy)(3y)$
3. $(7abc)(4bc)$
4. $(12y)(z)$
5. $(a)(9bc)$
6. $(5xyz)(2xy^2z^4)$
7. $(4ab)(bc^2)$
8. $(17f^2gh^3)(2fh^4)$

B. **Multiply the binomials by the monomials.**

9. $3z^2(6xy + 4z)$
10. $6x(7x - 6z)$
11. $-5ab(3b + 11c)$
12. $-3f^3(6h - 8fgh^2)$
13. $10z(7x^7 - 5z)$
14. $-z(-z - 6xy)$
15. $8b(9ab + 8a)$
16. $-9(-2x^4 + 3xy^2)$

C. **Multiply the binomials by using FOIL. Remember to complete by combining like terms wherever possible.**

17. $(x + 5)(x - 6)$
18. $(x + y)(x + y)$
19. $(z + 9)(z - 9)$
20. $(yz^2 + x)(yz^2 - 3x)$
21. $(3x + 3)(3x + 5)$
22. $(x + y)(x - y)$
23. $(y^2 - 6)(y^4 + 10)$
24. $(ab + 3)(ab - 4)$

D. **Choose the one best answer to each question.**

25. Which of the following expressions is equal to $(4a^3b^2)(3a^2c)$?

A. $12a^5b^2c$
B. $7a^5b^2c$
C. $12a^6bc$
D. $7a^6b^2c$

26. Martha has $2pc^2$ board games, and John has $6p^2c$ board games. Which of the following expressions represents the product of the number of board games that Martha and John have?

A. $8p^3c^3$
B. $8p^2c^2$
C. $12p^2c^2$
D. $12p^3c^3$

27. Which of the following expressions is equal to $(4ab + 2)(3ab - 7)$?

A. $7a^2b^2 + 22ab + 5$
B. $12a^2b^2 - 22ab - 14$
C. $12a^2b^2 + 22ab + 14$
D. $7a^2b^2 - 22ab - 5$

**Review your work using the explanations that start on page 696.**

**STUDY ADVICE**

How's your stress level? As you're working through difficult content, it's especially important to manage your stress. Stay on a regular sleep schedule, exercise, and eat right. Whenever you're stressing out, step away. Remember: You can do this. Just don't let stress get in your way.

# LESSON 12

## Divide Polynomials

### Divide Polynomials by a Number

The Mathematics Test will sometimes ask you to simplify a polynomial that is written as a fraction. To simplify, divide the numerator and denominator by a common term. A common term can be the following:

- A number
- A variable with a number as a coefficient
- A more complicated expression

You may need to factor the common term out of the numerator or denominator before you can do the division.

**Example 1:** Simplify $\frac{3x+6}{3}$.

$$\frac{3x+6}{3}=\frac{3(x+2)}{3}=\frac{\cancel{3}(x+2)}{\cancel{3}}=\mathbf{x+2}$$

### Divide Polynomials by an Expression

Dividing a polynomial by an expression is really no different from dividing by a number. You need a common term in the numerator and denominator, and you may have to factor out that common term (including any variables) before you can do the division.

**Example 2:** Simplify $\frac{25x^3-45x^2}{5x}$.

$$\frac{25x^3-45x^2}{5x}=\frac{5x(5x^2-9x)}{5x}=\frac{\cancel{5x}(5x^2-9x)}{\cancel{5x}}=\mathbf{5x^2-9x}$$

When the numerator has two added or subtracted expressions that both include the common term, it may be easier to split the polynomial into two separate fractions and simplify them separately. Doing it this way will help you keep straight exactly which terms you can cancel.

**Example 3:** Simplify $\frac{x(x+7)-3(x+7)}{x+7}$.

$$\frac{x(x+7)-3(x+7)}{x+7}=\frac{x(x+7)}{x+7}-\frac{3(x+7)}{x+7}$$

$$=\frac{x\cancel{(x+7)}}{\cancel{x+7}}-\frac{3\cancel{(x+7)}}{\cancel{x+7}}=\mathbf{x-3}$$

A fraction that has an algebraic expression in both its numerator and its denominator, as in the previous examples, is sometimes called a rational expression. Do not be confused if you see this term on the TASC: It simply means that you are being asked to simplify by dividing one expression by another.

**KEY IDEAS**

- You can divide a polynomial by numbers, expressions, or other polynomials.
- The key to dividing a polynomial is to isolate a common factor that divides into the numerator and denominator.
- Common factors can be numbers, variables, or a combination of the two such as addition, subtraction, or multiplication expressions.

**TASC TEST TIP**

*One algebraic expression divided by another is called a rational expression. If you are asked to simplify a rational expression on the TASC, you are simply dividing.*

# PRACTICE 12

**A. To simplify, divide each polynomial by a number. (You may need to factor the numerator and/or denominator to find the common term.)**

1. $\frac{2y+30}{2}$
2. $\frac{7x+21}{7}$
3. $\frac{4x+20}{4}$
4. $\frac{3a+3b}{3}$
5. $\frac{11x^2+22x}{11}$
6. $\frac{26x^2+39x+13}{13}$
7. $\frac{5x+10y}{5}$
8. $\frac{21a+14b}{7}$
9. $\frac{48x+32y}{32}$
10. $\frac{9a-15b}{12}$
11. $\frac{6b+24c}{18}$
12. $\frac{25a+5b+15c}{10}$

**B. Divide each polynomial. Decide whether it is easier for you to divide the original numerator by the common term (as in Example 2) or whether to split the numerator first (as in Example 3).**

13. $\frac{18x^2+6x}{3x}$
14. $\frac{10x^2+6x}{2x}$
15. $\frac{40y^2+10y}{5y}$
16. $\frac{42xy+49x}{7x}$
17. $\frac{38xy+38x}{19x}$
18. $\frac{3x+18}{x+6}$
19. $\frac{x(x+4)-6(x+4)}{x+4}$
20. $\frac{y(y+3)+7(y+3)}{y+3}$
21. $\frac{z(z+2)-5(z+2)}{z+2}$
22. $\frac{22x^2+66x}{11x}$
23. $\frac{x(y-2)-6(y-2)}{y-2}$
24. $\frac{a(b+3)+3(b+3)}{b+3}$

**C. Choose the <u>one best answer</u> to each question.**

25. Which of the following is equal to $\frac{21a+14b}{7}$?

A. $5a+5b$
B. $3a+14b$
C. $3a+2b$
D. $21a+2b$

26. James has $27x$ apples, Rachel has $51y$ oranges, and Glen has $60z$ peaches. Which of the following expressions represents the average number of pieces of fruit that James, Rachel, and Glen have in their baskets?

A. $9x+51y+60z$
B. $46x+46y+46z$
C. $9x+17y+60z$
D. $9x+17y+20z$

**Review your work using the explanations that start on page 696.**

# Algebraic Expressions Practice Questions

1. Which of the following expressions is equal to $6 - 4(x + 3)$?

   A. $4x + 3$
   B. $4x - 9$
   C. $-4x + 9$
   D. $-4x - 6$

2. If Kris makes $d$ dollars and Heidi makes 75 dollars less than 3 times Kris's wage, what does Heidi make in terms of $d$?

   A. $d + 75$
   B. $d - 225$
   C. $3d - 75$
   D. $3d - 225$

3. What is the product of 700 and 180,000 written in scientific notation?

   A. $12.6 \times 10^9$
   B. $1.26 \times 10^8$
   C. $1.26 \times 10^9$
   D. $1.26 \times 10^{10}$

4. If there are $4x$ identical schools in a region and each school has $3y$ classrooms each with $7x$ desks, how many desks are there in the region?

   A. $11x + 3y$
   B. $28x + 3y$
   C. $84xy^2$
   D. $84x^2y$

5. Which of the following is equivalent to $x^2 - 25$?

   A. $x(x - 25)$
   B. $(x - 5)^2$
   C. $(x + 5)(x - 5)$
   D. $(x - 25)^2$

6. If Tom has $9x$ baseball cards, Adam has 13 more than Tom, and Dave has $2y$ baseball cards, together they would have how many cards?

   A. $9x + 2y + 13$
   B. $18xy + 13$
   C. $18xy + 2y$
   D. $18x + 2y + 13$

**Questions 7 and 8 refer to the figure below.**

The figure below is a multiplication box. Each place represents the horizontal number multiplied by the vertical number; for example, the 9 in the lower right corner equals 3 multiplied by 3.

| | **5** | ***y*** | **3** |
|---|---|---|---|
| **1** | 5 | | 3 |
| ***c*** | 20 | *a* | |
| **3** | *b* | *d* | 9 |

7. Which of the following is equal to $ab$?

   A. $5y$
   B. $60y$
   C. $100y$
   D. $500y$

8. Which of the following is equal to $a - d$?

   A. $b$
   B. $c$
   C. $x$
   D. $y$

9. Multiply $7c^2(a^2 + 5b + 7c^2)$.

A. $7a^2c^2 + 35bc^2 + 49c^4$
B. $7(ac)^2 + 35(bc)^2 + 49c^4$
C. $7a^2 + 35b + 49c^4$
D. $a^2 + 5b + 14c^2$

10. A Little League pie sale fundraiser generated $900. If there were 6*x* pies sold, how much did each pie cost?

A. $10
B. $15
C. $\$\frac{x}{150}$
D. $\$\frac{150}{x}$

11. Simplify the expression $\frac{(a-4)^2\,(6b)}{2(3b)\,(a+4)\,(a-4)}$.

A. $\frac{a-4}{a+4}$
B. $\frac{a+4}{a-4}$
C. $\frac{a-2}{2}$
D. 1

12. Emilie buys *x* ounces of chicken for each of her guests at a dinner party. There are 8*y* people coming, and chicken is $*z* a pound. How much will the total amount of chicken cost in dollars? (*Hint*: There are 16 ounces in one pound.)

A. $8xyz$
B. $16xyz$
C. $\frac{xyz}{2}$
D. $\frac{xyz}{8}$

13. What is the value of the expression $6(x - y) - 8x$ when $x = -2$ and $y = 5$?

A. –58
B. –26
C. 2
D. 34

14. Which of the following would be equal to $x^2 + 6z$ multiplied by $2y - 4z$ if $x = 2$, $y = 4$, and $z = 3$?

A. –88
B. –72
C. 0
D. 104

15. What is the value of the following expression?

$$\frac{4^3 - [3(12 + 2^2)]}{6 + 5(4) - 15}$$

A. 0
B. $\frac{16}{41}$
C. $1\frac{5}{11}$
D. $3\frac{4}{11}$

16. If every member of a team is paid 5*p* dollars for his or her participation, and Team Alpha has 6*k* members, Team Beta has 4*p* members, and Team Delta has 9*h* members, which of the following represents the total amount paid to the members of all three teams?

A. $1080hkp$
B. $1080hkp^2$
C. $120p^2k + 45ph$
D. $30kp + 20p^2 + 45hp$

17. Which of the following is equal to $7x - [(5y)2x - 9y + 8x]$?

A. $x - 9y + 10xy$
B. $-3x - 4y$
C. $-x + 9y - 10xy$
D. $15x - 9y + 10xy$

18. If Stephanie has 5*c* CDs for every DVD Alyshia has, and Jeff has 4*d* DVDs, which is 15 more than Alyshia has, how many CDs does Stephanie have?

A. $20cd - 75c$
B. $20cd + 15$
C. $80cd - 15$
D. $80cd - 75c$

19. Divide $\dfrac{56x^4 + 49x^3y^3 - 84x^3 - 7x^2}{7x^2}$.

A. $8x^2 + 7xy^3 - 12x - 1$
B. $8x^4 + 7x^3y^3 - 12x^3 - x^2$
C. $8x^4 + 7y^3 - 5x^3 - 1$
D. $49x^2 + 42xy^3 - 77x$

20. A charity with a yearly budget of 80*d* gets all of its money from either its yearly ball or from private donations. If the charity raised 64*d* from the silent auction at the ball and 4*a* from ticket sales at the ball, what will need to be raised in private donations to meet the budget?

A. $16d$
B. $16d - 4a$
C. $16d + 4a$
D. $144d - 4a$

21. Divide $\dfrac{x^4 + 4x^2y^4 - 8x - y^2}{2y^2}$.

A. $\dfrac{x^4}{2y^2} + 2x^2y^2 - \dfrac{4x}{y^2} - \dfrac{1}{2}$

B. $\dfrac{x^2}{2y} + \dfrac{2x^2y^2 - 4x}{y^2 - \frac{1}{2}}$

C. $\dfrac{2x^4y^2 + 8x^2y^2 - 16x}{y^2 + 2y^4}$

D. $\dfrac{x^4 - 4x}{2y^2 + 2x^2y^2 - \frac{1}{2}}$

22. If 12*k* privates, 8*f* lieutenants, and 6*r* captains are divided into 2*r* equal squads, which of the following would express the number of members of one squad?

A. $6k + 4f + 3r$
B. $\dfrac{6k + 4f}{r} + 3$
C. $12k + 8f + 4r$
D. $12k + 8f + 3r$

23. If $q = 2$ and $r = 4$, which of the following would equal $\dfrac{r^2x^2 + q^3x}{(q^2x)}$?

A. $4x + 2$
B. $4x^2 + 2$
C. $16x^2 + 8x - 2$
D. $16x^2 + 2$

24. Simplify:

$$\frac{44x^6 + 55x^3y^4 + 88x^2 - 11y^2}{11x^2} - 6x^4 - 8$$

A. $4x^4 + 5xy^2 + 8x - 1$

B. $2x^4 + 5xy^3 - y^2 - 8$

C. $-2x^4 + 5xy^4 - \dfrac{y^2}{x^2}$

D. $10x^4 + 5y^4 - \dfrac{y^2}{x^2} - 8$

25. Simplify:

$(6x^2 + 5xy^2)(y) - (4xy - 9x)(4xy)$.

A. $5xy^3 - 16x^2y^2 + 42x^2y$
B. $5xy^3 - 16x^2y^2 - 30x^2y$
C. $6x^2y - 11x^2y^2 - 36xy^2$
D. $6x^2y + 5x^2y^2 - 36xy^2 + 16xy$

26. There are $4x$ workers, including managers, in an office. If the salaries of the 3 managers are not included, the average salary of each employee is $5x - 6$. What do the nonmanagerial employees earn in total?

A. $20x^2 - 24x$
B. $20x^2 - 24x - 3$
C. $20x^2 - 9x + 18$
D. $20x^2 - 39x + 18$

27. What is the value of $\frac{45xy + 63y^2}{9y}$ if $x = 6$ and $y = 3$?

A. 12
B. 51
C. 108
D. 153

28. Simplify

$$\frac{3x(x^2 + 3) - 2x(x^2 + 3) - (x^2 + 3)}{x^2 + 3}$$

A. $x^3 - 1$
B. $x^3 - 3x - 1$
C. $3x - 1$
D. $x - 1$

29. If the $3h$ people in one country and the $4k$ people in the neighboring country each consume $h - 17$ pounds of rice per year on average, how much rice would be consumed by both countries in one year?

A. $4h + 4k - 17$
B. $4h^2 + 4k - 68k$
C. $12hk + h - 17$
D. $3h^2 + 4hk - 51h - 68k$

30. Simplify:

$$\frac{4x^2(x + y) - 2(x + y)^2(x - y) - xy(x + y)}{x + y}$$

A. $2x^2 + 2y^2 - xy$
B. $4x^2 + xy - 2x - 2y$
C. $4x^2 - xy - 2x - 2y$
D. $3x^2 - 2xy^2 - xy$

**Questions 31 and 32 refer to the figure below.**

The figure below is a multiplication box. Each place represents the horizontal number multiplied by the vertical number; for example, the 20 in the lower right corner equals 5 multiplied by 4.

| | $a^2$ | $ab$ | 5 |
|---|---|---|---|
| $a$ | | | $ab$ |
| $c$ | $8b$ | | |
| 4 | | 40 | 20 |

31. Which of the following is equal to $a$?

A. 2
B. 4
C. 5
D. 10

32. Which of the following is equal to $a^2c$?

A. 13
B. 40
C. 42
D. 60

**Review your work using the explanations that start on page 696.**

# Equations

## Writing and Solving One-Step Equations

An **equation** is a mathematical statement that two expressions are equal.

**Examples:** $3+5=4\cdot 2$ $10-1=3^2$ $5(3+4)=35$

An equation can contain one or more variables. Solving an equation means finding a value for the variable that will make the equation true.

**Examples:** $4+x=11$ $3x=24$ $x-5=-2$

$\mathbf{x=7}$ $\mathbf{x=8}$ $\mathbf{x=3}$

The basic strategy in solving an equation is to isolate the variable on one side of the equation. You can do this by performing **inverse**, or opposite, operations. However, you must always follow one basic rule: whatever you do to one side of the equation, you must also do to the other side.

**KEY IDEAS**

- An equation states that two expressions are equal.
- To solve an equation, isolate the variable by applying inverse operations to both sides of the equation.
- Check your work by substituting your solution for the variable in the original equation and simplifying.

**Example 1:** Solve $x-23=45$.

On the left side of the equation, the number 23 is subtracted from $x$. The inverse of subtraction is addition. Add 23 to both sides of the equation.

$x-23=45$

$x-23+\mathbf{23}=45+\mathbf{23}$

$\mathbf{x=68}$

To check your work, replace the variable with your solution and simplify.
When $x=\mathbf{68}$, the equation is true.

Check: $x-23=45$

$68-23=45$

$45=45$

The following examples use the inverse operations of multiplication and division.

**Example 2:** Solve $\frac{x}{2}=17$.

The variable $x$ is divided by 2. Since multiplication is the inverse of division, you must multiply each side of the equation by 2.

$\frac{x}{2}=17$

$2\left(\frac{x}{2}\right)=2(17)$

$\mathbf{x=34}$

When $x=\mathbf{34}$, the equation is true.

Check: $\frac{34}{2}=17$

$17=17$

**TASC TEST TIP**

*If you are unsure about a multiple-choice algebra problem, substitute each of the answer choices for the variable in the equation. You may be able to do this quickly using your calculator.*

**Example 3:** Solve $5x=75$.

Since the variable $x$ is multiplied by 5, divide both sides of the equation by 5.

$5x=75$

$\frac{5x}{5}=\frac{75}{5}$

$\mathbf{x=15}$

When $x=\mathbf{15}$, the equation is true.

Check: $5(15)=75$

$75=75$

# PRACTICE 1.1

**A. Solve for the variable in each equation.**

1. $7x = 63$
2. $23 + m = 51$
3. $-13 = y - 12$
4. $\frac{x}{4} = -16$
5. $5a = 625$
6. $y - 17 = -30$
7. $x + 6 = 33$
8. $4c = 28$
9. $\frac{12}{x} = -3$
10. $26 = b + 33$
11. $93 = 3x$
12. $s + 16 = 8$
13. $36 = \frac{x}{3}$
14. $t + 14 = 53$
15. $\frac{x}{6} = 8$
16. $16y = -48$
17. $r - 35 = 75$
18. $24 = \frac{120}{x}$
19. $5y = -45$
20. $d + 45 = 20$
21. $16 = 4x$
22. $-4x = 24$
23. $19 = h - 7$
24. $\frac{x}{11} = 6$
25. $m + 24 = 14$
26. $5y = 45$
27. $14 - w = 42$
28. $18 = \frac{y}{4}$

**B. Choose the <u>one best answer</u> to each question.**

**<u>Questions 29 and 30</u> refer to the following table.**

**April Time Sheet Summary**
**Hours Worked per Week**

| Week | 1 | 2 | 3 | 4 |
|---|---|---|---|---|
| Kayla Sax | 36 | 40 | 40 | |
| Erin Grady | | 24 | 28 | 38 |

29. Kayla and Erin worked a total of 77 hours during Week 1. Let $x$ = Erin's hours for Week 1. Which of the following equations could be used to solve for Erin's hours during Week 1?

A. $x - 36 = 77$
B. $x + 77 = 36$
C. $x + 36 = 77$
D. $x - 77 = 36$

30. Erin worked twice as many hours as Kayla did during Week 4. Let $y$ = Kayla's hours for Week 4. Which of the following equations could be used to solve for Kayla's hours during Week 4?

A. $\frac{y}{2} = 38$
B. $38y = 2$
C. $2y = 38$
D. $\frac{1}{2y} = 38$

31. The quotient of a number divided by 4 is 32. What is the number?

A. 8
B. 28
C. 128
D. 512

32. The solution $x = -5$ makes which of the following equations true?

A. $14 - x = 9$
B. $\frac{x}{5} = 1$
C. $x + 3 = 8$
D. $12x = -60$

33. Mike had \$572.18 in his checking account. After writing a check, he had \$434.68. Which of the following equations could be used to find the amount of the check ($c$)?

A. $\$572.18 + c = \$434.68$
B. $\$572.18 - c = \$434.68$
C. $\$572.18c = \$434.68$
D. $\frac{\$572.18}{c} = \$434.68$

**Review your work using the explanations that start on page 697.**

## Solving Multi-Step Equations

Most equations require more than one operation in order to find a solution. Follow these basic steps:

- Simplify by combining like terms.
- Perform addition and subtraction steps.
- Perform multiplication and division steps.

**Example 4:** Solve $6x + 5 - 2x = 25$.

1. Combine like terms ($6x - 2x = 4x$).
2. Subtract 5 from both sides.
3. Divide both sides by 4.
4. Check by substituting the solution for $x$ in the original equation.

$$6x + 5 - 2x = 25$$
$$4x + 5 = 25$$
$$4x + 5 - 5 = 25 - 5$$
$$4x = 20$$
$$\frac{4x}{4} = \frac{20}{4}$$
$$\mathbf{x = 5}$$
$$6(5) + 5 - 2(5) = 25$$
$$30 + 5 - 10 = 25$$
$$25 = 25$$

In this example, the distributive property is used to simplify an expression. Notice that not every step is written out. As you gain experience, you can perform an operation on both sides of an equation mentally.

**Example 5:** Solve $-4(x - 6) = 2x$.

1. Use the distributive property to remove the grouping symbols.
2. Add $4x$ to each side.
3. Divide each side by 6.
4. Check.

$$-4(x - 6) = 2x$$
$$-4x + 24 = 2x$$
$$24 = 6x$$
$$\mathbf{4 = x}$$
$$-4(4 - 6) = 2(4)$$
$$-4(-2) = 8$$
$$8 = 8$$

Some of the time you will be expected to write an equation from information given in the problem. The problem will describe two expressions that are equal. Write each expression in symbols and connect the expressions with the equal sign (=). In many problems, the word *is* indicates the = symbol.

**Example 6:** The product of a number and 6 is 44 more than twice the number. What is the number?

1. Write an equation. The word *is* represents the equal sign.
2. Subtract $2x$ from both sides.
3. Divide both sides by 4.
4. Check.

$$6x = 44 + 2x$$
$$4x = 44$$
$$\mathbf{x = 11}$$
$$6(11) = 44 + 2(11)$$
$$66 = 44 + 22$$
$$66 = 66$$

The number described in the problem is **11**.

**Note:** Subtraction and division operations must be written in the order indicated by the words. "The difference between $x$ and $y$" must be written $x - y$, <u>not</u> $y - x$. "The quotient of $x$ and $y$" must be written $\frac{x}{y}$, <u>not</u> $\frac{y}{x}$.

# PRACTICE 1.2

**A. Solve for the variable in each equation.**

1. $3x - 20 = 130$
2. $2y - 8 = -3y - 18$
3. $6m = 14m - 16$
4. $2x + 5 + 6x = -27$
5. $5y + 3(y + 2) = 54$
6. $17 - 4z + 2z = 13$
7. $6m - 4 = m + 11$
8. $35 = x + 7 + 6x$
9. $5p - 2 = 6p - 9$
10. $50 = 3(s + 16) - 2(s - 2)$
11. $\frac{5(2x - 10)}{2} + 14 = 19$
12. $3(3 + r) = 2r + 4$
13. $5y = 2y + 22 + y$
14. $38 = 5(2b - 3) + 3b + 1$
15. $-5 - x = 2x - (4x + 6)$
16. $\frac{3h}{2} = 30$
17. $4(3 + 2x) + 8 = 92$
18. $-5(3 - z) = z + 1$
19. $10 - 3b + 3 = -1 + (b + 2)$
20. $5n + 8 - n = 6(n - 1)$

**B. Choose the <u>one best answer</u> to each question.**

21. Three times a number increased by 9 is 15 less than six times the number. Let $x$ = the unknown number. Which of the following equations could be used to find the value of $x$?

A. $3(9x) = 6(15x)$
B. $3x(9) = 6x - 15x$
C. $3x + 9 = 15 - 6x$
D. $3x + 9 = 6x - 15$

22. Dave has 500 baseball cards, which is as many as Eric and Travis have combined. Eric has three times as many cards as Travis has.

| Dave | Eric | Travis |
|---|---|---|
| 500 | $3x$ | $x$ |

From the information, you can write the equation $3x + x = 500$. How many cards does Eric have? (*Hint:* Solve for $x$. Then find how many cards Eric has.)

A. 150
B. 250
C. 350
D. 375

23. The difference of four times a number and 7 is 15 plus the quotient of the number and 3. Which of the following equations could be used to find the value of $x$?

A. $4x - 7 = \frac{x}{3} + 15$
B. $7 - 4x = \frac{x}{3} + 15$
C. $7 - 4x = \frac{3}{x} + 15$
D. $4x - 7 = \frac{3}{x} + 1$

24. Kim earned $x$ dollars at his part-time job on Friday. His wife earned \$12 more than twice Kim's pay $(2x + 12)$. Together, they earned \$174. How much did Kim earn on Friday? (*Hint:* Use the equation $x + (2x + 12) =$ \$174.)

A. \$54
B. \$87
C. \$108
D. \$120

**Review your work using the explanations that start on page 697.**

**STUDY ADVICE**

Remember to include rewards and breaks in your study schedule. Celebrate a job well done with a fun outing. Don't try to study seven days a week—this can lead to burnout. Plan a day off to rest, relax, and reward yourself for the focused studying you have done!

LESSON 2

# Equation Word Problems, Part I

Algebra problems describe how several numbers are related. One number is the unknown, which you will represent with a variable. Using the relationships described in the problem, you can write an equation and solve for the variable.

**KEY IDEAS**

- To solve a word problem, decide what quantity will be represented by $x$. Then write expressions for the other quantities in terms of $x$.
- Write and solve an equation. Answer the question asked in the problem.

**Example 1:** There are twice as many women as men in a class on auto repair. If there are 24 students in the class, how many are women?

1. Express the numbers in the problem in terms of the same variable. Let $x$ represent the number of men. Since there are twice as many women, let $2x$ represent the number of women.

2. Write and solve an equation. The total number of men and women is 24, so $x+2x=24$. Solve: $x+2x=24$
$$3x=24$$
$$x=8$$

Since $x=8, 2x=2(8)=16$. There are 8 men and **16 women** in the class.

**Consecutive numbers** are numbers that follow in counting order. For example, 1, 2, and 3 are consecutive numbers. The numbers 2, 4, and 6 are consecutive even numbers, and 1, 3, and 5 are consecutive odd numbers.

**Example 2:** The sum of three consecutive numbers is 105. What is the greatest of the three numbers?

1. Let $x$ represent the first number and $x+1$ and $x+2$ represent the other numbers.

2. Write an equation and solve:
$$x+(x+1)+(x+2)=105$$
$$3x+3=105$$
$$3x=102$$
$$x=34$$

3. Find the answer. The variable $x$ represents the first number in the sequence, so the three numbers are 34, 35, and 36. The problem asks for the greatest number, which is **36**.

**TASC TEST TIP**

*When you find x, you may not be finished solving a problem. Always reread the question. As shown in Example 2, you may need to use the value of x to calculate the solution in a multi-step problem.*

You may need to use the difference between numbers to write equations.

**Example 3:** The ticket prices for a play are \$12 for adults and \$8 for children. One evening, the box office sold 200 tickets. If the total box office receipts were \$2240, how many adult tickets were sold?

1. Let $x$ represent the number of adult tickets. Since 200 tickets were sold, the number of children's tickets sold can be written as $200-x$.

2. Multiply each term by the cost for that type of ticket. Set the total equal to \$2240, and solve for $x$.
$$12x+8(200-x)=2240$$
$$12x+1600-8x=2240$$
$$4x+1600=2240$$
$$4x=640$$
$$\mathbf{x=160}$$

3. There were **160 adult tickets** sold.

# PRACTICE 2

**A. Solve.**

1. Two houses are for sale on the same street. The second house has 1000 square feet less than twice the square feet of the first house. Together the houses have 4400 square feet. What is the square footage of the first house?
2. Julia has 24 coins in her pocket. The coins are either dimes or quarters. The total value of the coins is $4.50. How many coins are dimes? (*Hint:* The value of the dimes is $0.10x$, and the value of the quarters is $0.25(24-x)$.)
3. The Bulldogs won twice as many games as they lost. If they played a total of 36 games, how many did they win? (There were no tied games.)
4. The sum of four consecutive even numbers is 212. What is the third number? (*Hint:* Let $x =$ the first number, $x + 2 =$ the second number, $x + 4 =$ the third, and so on.)
5. A children's store is selling pants for $6 each and shirts for $4. Brenda bought 13 items and paid $62. How many shirts did she buy?
6. The sum of three consecutive numbers is 180. What is the least number in the series?
7. In a month Andrew spends twice as much on rent as he does on food for his family. Last month, he spent $1650 on rent and food. How much did he spend on rent?
8. George spends four times as much time helping customers as he does stocking shelves. Last week, he spent 35 hours on the two tasks. How many hours were spent helping customers?

**B. Choose the <u>one best answer</u> to each question.**

9. Sylvia scored 10 points better than Wiley on their science exam. Greg scored 6 points less than Wiley. Altogether, the students earned 226 points. How many points did Sylvia earn?

   A. 74
   B. 78
   C. 84
   D. 94

10. Two adults and four children paid $48 to get into the fair. A child's ticket is $6 less than an adult's ticket. What is the cost of an adult's ticket?

    A. $15
    B. $12
    C. $9
    D. $6

11. Jenny is four times as old as her niece Tina. In 12 years, Jenny will be only twice as old as Tina. The chart shows expressions for Tina and Jenny's ages now and in 12 years.

| | Jenny's Age | Tina's Age |
|---|---|---|
| Now | $4x$ | $x$ |
| In 12 Years | $4x + 12$ | $x + 12$ |

How old is Tina now?

A. 4
B. 6
C. 8
D. 12

**Review your work using the explanations that start on page 698.**

LESSON 3

# Inequalities

An **inequality** is a mathematical statement that connects two unequal expressions. The inequality symbols and their meanings are:

| | |
|---|---|
| $>$ greater than | $\geq$ greater than or equal to |
| $<$ less than | $\leq$ less than or equal to |

An inequality is solved much like an equation. Use inverse operations to isolate the variable.

**Example 1:** Solve for $x$ in the inequality $3x + 2 < 8$.

1. Subtract 2 from both sides. $3x + 2 < 8$
   $3x < 6$
2. Divide both sides by 3. $\mathbf{x < 2}$

The solution $x < 2$ states that any number less than 2 makes the inequality true. Check by substituting 1 (a number less than 2) for $x: 3(1) + 2 < 8$, which simplifies to $5 < 8$, a true statement.

There is one important difference between solving equalities and inequalities. Whenever you multiply or divide both sides of an inequality by a <u>negative</u> number, you must <u>reverse</u> the inequality symbol.

**Example 2:** Solve for $n$ in the inequality $-2n - 5 \geq 3$.

1. Add 5 to both sides to remove $-5$ from the left side of the equation. $-2n - 5 + 5 \geq 3 + 5$
   $-2n \geq 8$
2. Divide both sides by $-2$ and *reverse the inequality symbol.* $\frac{-2n}{-2} \geq \frac{8}{-2}$
   $\mathbf{n \leq -4}$

Check your work by substituting a number that is less than or equal to $-4$ into the <u>original</u> inequality. Here $-5$ is used for $n$. Since $5 \geq 3$ is a true statement, the answer is correct.

$$-2n - 5 \geq 3$$
$$-2(-5) - 5 \geq 3$$
$$5 \geq 3$$

When an inequality contains a variable, there is usually a range of numbers that make the inequality true. For that reason, we often graph the solution. In the examples below, a closed dot means that the number is included in the solution set. An open dot means the number is not included.

**Examples:** $x < 2$

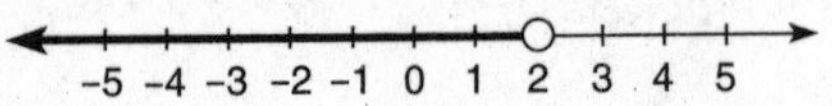


$x > -3$

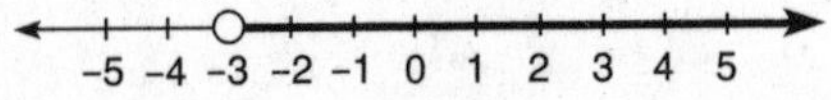


$x \leq 1$

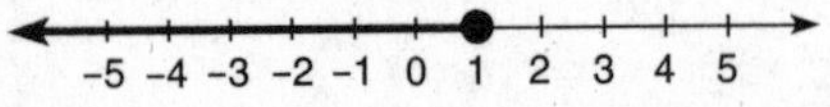


$x \geq -2$

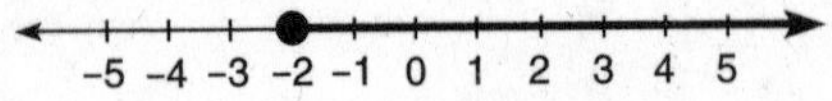


### KEY IDEAS

- Use $<$, $>$, $\leq$, and $\geq$ to show the relationship between two unequal expressions.
- The symbol always points to the smaller expression.
- Use inverse operations to solve inequalities. Reverse the inequality sign if you multiply or divide by a negative number.

### TASC TEST TIP

*Avoid the most common mistake with inequalities: reversing the symbol accidentally. Always check your work by substituting any number that fits the solution into the original inequality.*

# PRACTICE 3

A **compound inequality** combines two inequalities. To solve a compound inequality, separate the inequalities and solve both. Then combine the solutions.

**Example 3:** Solve $3x + 4 < 5x < 16 + x$.

| | | |
|---|---|---|
| 1. Write two inequalities and solve each separately. | $3x + 4 < 5x$ | $5x < 16 + x$ |
| 2. Write the result as a compound inequality. $\mathbf{2 < x < 4}$ | $4 < 2x$ | $4x < 16$ |
| | $2 < x$ | $x < 4$ |

In other words, any quantity that is greater than 2 *and* less than 4 will make the compound inequality true.

**A. Solve.**

1. $3x - 7 > 5$
2. $13 < 2x - 1$
3. $4 + 2x \le -2$
4. $\dfrac{4 + x}{5} \le 8$
5. $2(x + 3) < 4$
6. $3 + 9x \ge 4(x + 7)$
7. $-4(x + 2) < 24$
8. $-2x + 9 < 1$
9. $\dfrac{x - 2}{3} > 2x + 11$
10. $6x < 5x + 2$
11. $x + 6 \le 8x - 15$
12. $5x + 14 > 2 + 7x$
13. $13x - 7 \ge 25 - 3x$
14. $x - 6 < 2(x + 2)$
15. $-5 + 3x \ge 4(3x - 8)$
16. $36 > 4(x - 12)$
17. $6 \le 3(x + 3)$
18. $\dfrac{4x}{3} > 8x - 20$
19. $x - 2 < \dfrac{2x + 6}{4}$
20. $x \ge 4x - 9$
21. $30 \ge 5(x + 4) \ge 10$
22. $-7x > -2(x + 15) < 10$
23. $3 < 5x - 27 < 53$
24. $22 \le 6x - 2 \le 4x + 16$

**B. Choose the one best answer to each question.**

**25.** The perimeter of a square can be found using the formula $P = 4s$, where $s$ is one side of the square.

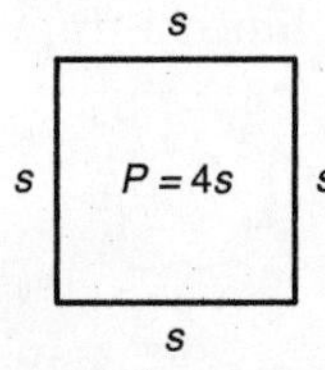


The perimeter of a square is less than or equal to 64 inches. Which of the following represents the possible measures of the side of the square in inches?

A. $s \le 16$
B. $s \ge 16$
C. $s \ge 8$
D. $s \le 64$

**26.** Three added to the product of –4 and a number ($x$) is less than 5 added to the product of –3 and the number. Which of the following is a graph of the solution set of $x$?

A. -5 -4 -3 -2 -1 0 1 2 3 4 5

B. -5 -4 -3 -2 -1 0 1 2 3 4 5

C. -5 -4 -3 -2 -1 0 1 2 3 4 5

D. -5 -4 -3 -2 -1 0 1 2 3 4 5

**Review your work using the explanations that start on page 698.**

**STUDY ADVICE**

Remember to take frequent breaks when studying, at least 10 minutes out of each hour. During your breaks, stand up and move around so you come back to studying refreshed.

LESSON 4

# Quadratic Equations

A **quadratic equation** contains a squared variable, for example, $x^2 - 3x = 4$. One way to solve quadratic equations is by factoring. This is the simplest method and the one you should use on the TASC Mathematics Test. When you factor an expression, you find the terms that divide evenly into the expression.

**KEY IDEAS**

- A quadratic equation can have two solutions.
- Set the quadratic equation equal to 0 and factor.
- Find the values for *x* that will make each factor equal 0.

**Example 1:** Factor the expression $15x^2 + 9x$.

1. Look for a term that divides evenly into both $15x^2$ and $9x$. Both terms can be divided by $3x$. — $15x^2 \div 3x = 5x$; $9x \div 3x = 3$
2. Factor out $3x$. Write the terms as factors. — $15x^2 + 9x = \mathbf{3x(5x+3)}$

Study Example 2 to learn how to multiply factors with more than one term.

**Example 2:** Multiply $\underbrace{\overset{\text{(factor)}}{(2x+3)}\,\overset{\text{(factor)}}{(x-4)}}_{\text{four terms}}$.

1. Multiply each term in the first factor by each term in the second factor.

$$2x \cdot x = 2x^2$$
$$2x \cdot -4 = -8x$$
$$3 \cdot x = 3x$$
$$3 \cdot -4 = -12$$

2. Combine the results.

$$2x^2 + (-8x) + 3x + (-12) =$$
$$\mathbf{2x^2 - 5x - 12}$$

This method of multiplying factors is called the FOIL method. The letters in FOIL stand for First, Outer, Inner, and Last. Use the word FOIL to make sure you have performed all the necessary operations.

You factor a quadratic equation to solve it. A quadratic equation may have two solutions. Find values that make the factors equal to 0. Since a number multiplied by 0 is 0, each of the values is a solution.

**TASC TEST TIP**

*The TASC* Mathematics Reference Sheet *(see pages 230–231) provides you with some shortcuts for factoring in special circumstances. See the left-hand side of page 230. If you see an equation in the form of one of the equations on that list, the Reference Sheet can help you find the factors.*

**Example 3:** Solve $x^2 - 3x = 4$.

1. Set the equation equal to 0 by subtracting 4 from both sides.

$$x^2 - 3x = 4$$
$$x^2 - 3x - 4 = 0$$

2. Factor by trial and error. Think: What factors of the last term, –4, when added, will equal –3, the number part of the middle term?
   $-4 \cdot 1 = -4$ and $-4 + 1 = -3$

$$(x\quad)(x\quad) = 0$$
$$(x+1)(x-4) = 0$$

3. If either one of the factors equals 0, then the product of the factors will be 0. Set each factor equal to 0 and solve for *x*.

$$x + 1 = 0$$
$$x = \mathbf{-1}$$
$$x - 4 = 0$$
$$x = \mathbf{4}$$

The solutions to the quadratic equation are **–1 and 4.**

# PRACTICE 4

**A. Multiply.**

1. $(x+4)(x+2)$
2. $(x-3)(x+5)$
3. $(x-1)(x+4)$
4. $(x-6)(x-3)$
5. $(x+8)(x-2)$
6. $(2x+1)(x-2)$
7. $(x-9)(x-5)$
8. $(x+1)(3x-2)$
9. $(x-2)(x+7)$
10. $(3x+8)(x+2)$
11. $(x-6)(x+5)$
12. $(x-10)(x-3)$
13. $(2x+1)(2x+2)$
14. $(x+9)(x-4)$
15. $(x-5)(x-5)$

**B. Factor each expression.**

16. $x^2+4x+3$
17. $x^2+4x-5$
18. $x^2+8x+12$
19. $x^2-x-6$
20. $x^2+5x-14$
21. $x^2-x-12$
22. $x^2+2x-35$
23. $x^2-12x+36$
24. $x^2-6x-7$
25. $x^2+4x-32$
26. $2x^2+5x-3$
27. $2x^2-8x-10$
28. $x^2+5x-50$
29. $4x^2+4x-3$
30. $x^2+x-56$

**C. Choose the one best answer to each question.**

31. What are two solutions for the equation $x^2-x=20$?

    A. −4 and 5
    B. 4 and −5
    C. −10 and 2
    D. −2 and 10

32. For which of the following equations is $x=-4$ a solution?

    A. $2x^2-8=0$
    B. $x^2-8x+64=0$
    C. $x^2-2x-15=0$
    D. $2x^2+2x-24=0$

33. What is the only positive solution for the equation $2x^2-7x-30=0$?

    A. 5
    B. 6
    C. 7
    D. 8

34. The area of a rectangle is found by multiplying the length by the width. In the rectangle below, the area of the rectangle is equal to the expression $2x^2-27x+70$.

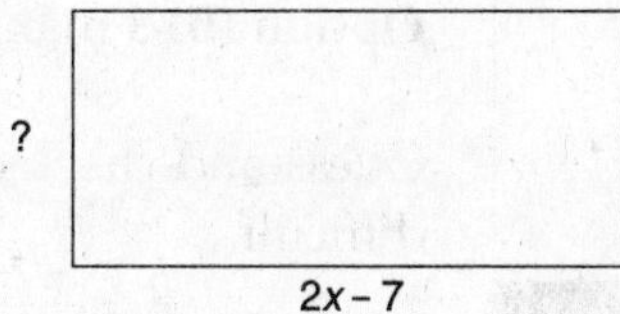


An expression equal to the length is shown on the diagram. Which of the following expressions is equal to the width of the rectangle?

    A. $x+10$
    B. $x-10$
    C. $2x+10$
    D. $2x-10$

**Review your work using the explanations that start on page 698.**

LESSON 5

# Algebra Problem Solving

One strategy that can help you save time on the more complicated algebra problems is **guess-and-check.** Guess-and-check means selecting one of the answer choices and trying that value in the problem. If you guess correctly, you can move on to the next question. If not, guess again. Guess-and-check is a good strategy for problems involving quadratic equations and expressions.

**KEY IDEAS**

- Guess-and-check is a strategy for answering complicated multiple-choice problems.
- Choose an answer from the options and try the value in the problem. If it works, you have found the correct answer.

**Example 1:** Which of the following is a solution for the equation $2x^2 - 12 = 2x$?

A. 4
B. 3
C. 0
D. −1

To solve the problem, you would have to rewrite the equation so that the quadratic expression equals zero, factor the expression, and solve.

Instead, substitute each answer choice into the equation.

Option (A):
$$2x^2 - 12 = 2x$$
$$2(4)^2 - 12 = 2(4)$$
$$20 \neq 8$$

Option (B):
$$2x^2 - 12 = 2x$$
$$2(3)^2 - 12 = 2(3)$$
$$6 = 6$$

**Option (B) 3** makes the equation true.

Guess-and-check can also save time when writing an equation seems difficult.

**TASC TEST TIP**

*Use your judgment. Do not use guess-and-check if you can quickly see how to solve the problem. Trying each answer choice may take longer than simply solving the problem.*

**Example 2:** Terry is ten years older than his brother Tomas. Twenty years ago, Terry was twice as old as Tomas. How old is Terry now?

A. 25
B. 30
C. 40
D. 45

Instead of writing an equation, try each age in the answer choices for Terry.

A. If Terry is 25 now, Tomas is 15. Twenty years ago, Tomas would not have been born.
B. If Terry is 30 now, Tomas is 20. Twenty years ago, Tomas would have been 0 years old, and Terry would have been 10.
C. If Terry is 40 now, Tomas is 30. Twenty years ago, Tomas would have been 10, and Terry would have been 20, which is twice as old as 10.

Therefore, **option (C) 40** is correct.

# PRACTICE 5

**A. Use guess-and-check to solve the following problems.**

**1.** A number divided by 2 is equal to 12 less than the original number. What is the number?

A. 12
B. 20
C. 24
D. 28

**2.** For a fund-raiser, Sandra raised three times as much money as Barbara, and Barbara raised $50 more than Matt. Together they raised $950. How much money did Barbara raise?

A. $150
B. $175
C. $200
D. $325

**3.** The three packages below weigh a total of 15 pounds.

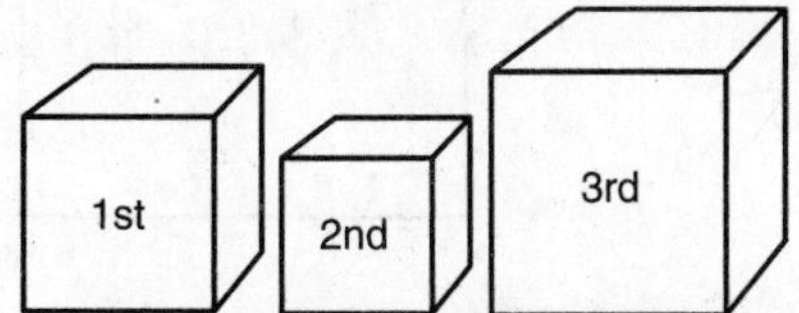


The first package weighs twice as much as the second package. The third package weighs three times as much as the second package. How many pounds does the first package weigh?

A. 2
B. 4
C. 5
D. $6\frac{1}{2}$

**4.** Hannah scored a total of 170 points on two math tests. The score of the first test was 6 points lower than the score of the second test. How many points did Hannah score on the first test?

A. 76
B. 82
C. 88
D. 90

**5.** Nelson is twice as old as Maria. Six years ago, Nelson was five times as old as Maria. How old was Nelson six years ago?

A. 5
B. 10
C. 15
D. 20

**6.** Which of the following is a solution for the quadratic equation $2x^2 + x - 15 = 0$?

A. $-3$
B. $-1$
C. 2
D. 3

**7.** An amusement park sells adults' and children's passes. An adult's pass is $25, and a child's pass is $15. A group spent $440 on 20 passes. How many children's passes did the group purchase?

A. 5
B. 6
C. 9
D. 14

**8.** The rectangular garden below is twice as long as it is wide. If the total distance around the garden is 120 feet, what is the width of the garden in feet?

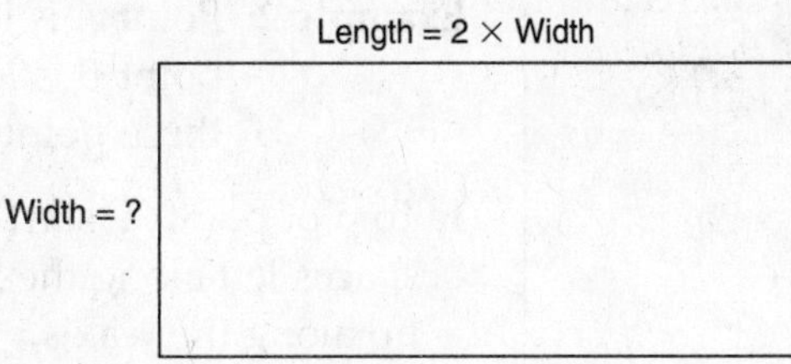


A. 15
B. 20
C. 30
D. 40

**Review your work using the explanations that start on page 699.**

# The Coordinate Plane

### KEY IDEAS

- A coordinate grid is formed by two intersecting axes, or number lines.
- The $x$-axis is horizontal, and the $y$-axis is vertical.
- The location of a point is shown by two numbers called an ordered pair: $(x, y)$.

A **coordinate grid** is a way to locate points that lie in a **plane,** or flat surface. The grid is formed by two intersecting lines, an $x$-axis and a $y$-axis. The $x$-axis is actually a horizontal number line, and the $y$-axis is a vertical number line. The point at which the two axes intersect is called the **origin.**

Each point on the grid can be named using two numbers called an **ordered pair.** The first number is the distance from the origin along the $x$-axis. The second number is the distance from the origin along the $y$-axis. The numbers are written in parentheses and are separated by a comma: $(x, y)$.

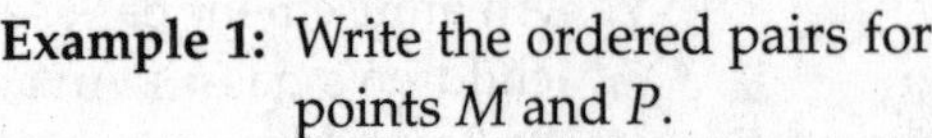

**Example 1:** Write the ordered pairs for points $M$ and $P$.

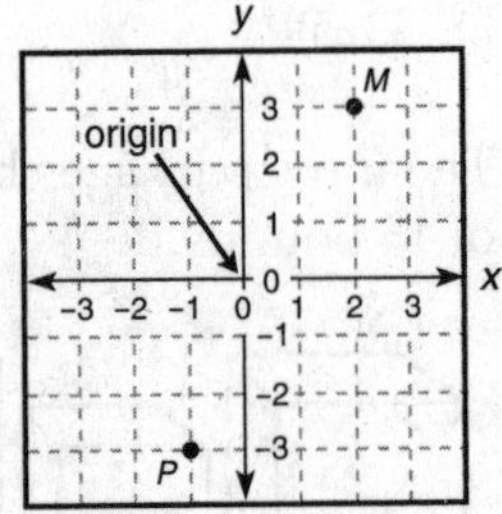


1. Point $M$ lies 2 spaces to the right of the origin along the $x$-axis and 3 spaces above the origin along the $y$-axis. The coordinates are **(2, 3).**

2. Point $P$ lies 1 space to the left along the $x$-axis and 3 spaces down along the $y$-axis. The coordinates are **(–1, – 3).**

### TASC TEST TIP

*If you are given a coordinate grid that is not labeled, remember that the origin is at (0,0). Starting at the origin, count either right or left first, then up or down.*

To plot points on the grid, use the number lines located at the axes. Remember that right and up are the directions for positive numbers and left and down are the directions for negative numbers.

**Example 2:** Point $A$ is located at $(-2, 1)$, and point $B$ is located at $(3, -2)$. Plot these points on a coordinate grid.

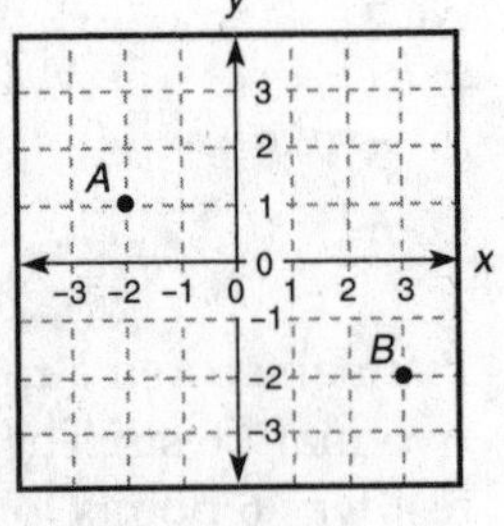


1. To plot point $A$, start at the origin. Count 2 spaces left along the $x$-axis. Count 1 space up along the $y$-axis.

2. To plot point $B$, start at the origin. Count 3 spaces right along the $x$-axis. Count 2 spaces down along the $y$-axis.

# PRACTICE 6

**A. Write the ordered pair for each point.**

1. Point *A*
2. Point *B*
3. Point *C*
4. Point *D*
5. Point *E*
6. Point *F*
7. Point *G*
8. Point *H*

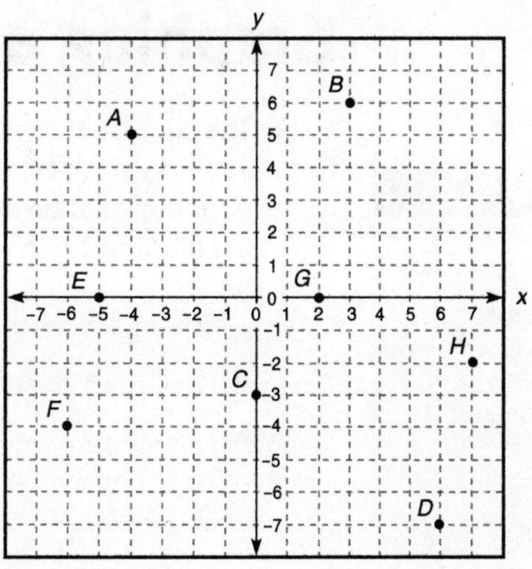

**B. Plot the points on the coordinate grid.**

9. Plot the following points:
   *J* at (–3, – 2)
   *K* at (4, 0)
   *L* at (1, – 3)
   *M* at (–4, 2)

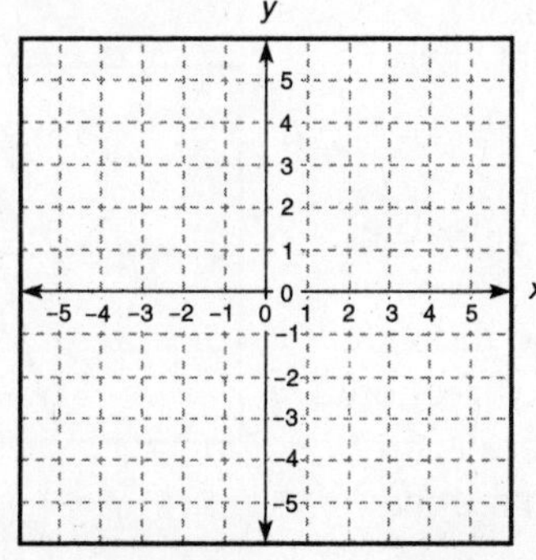

10. Plot the following points:
   *N* at (0, – 1)
   *O* at (–4, – 4)
   *P* at (3, 1)
   *Q* at (–3, 0)

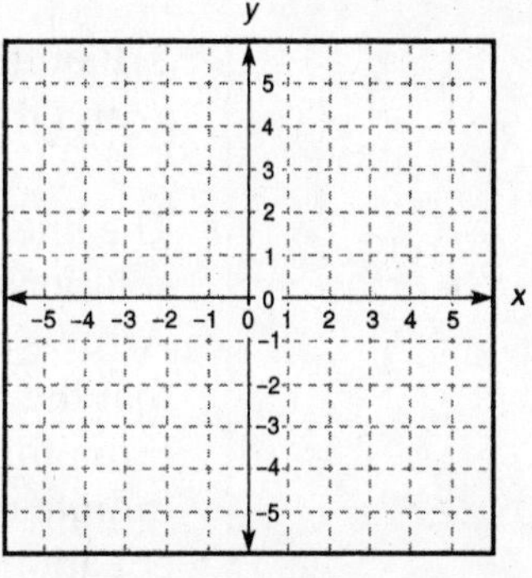

**C. Choose the <u>one best answer</u> to each question.**

11. On the coordinate grid below, a line passes through points *A* and *B*.

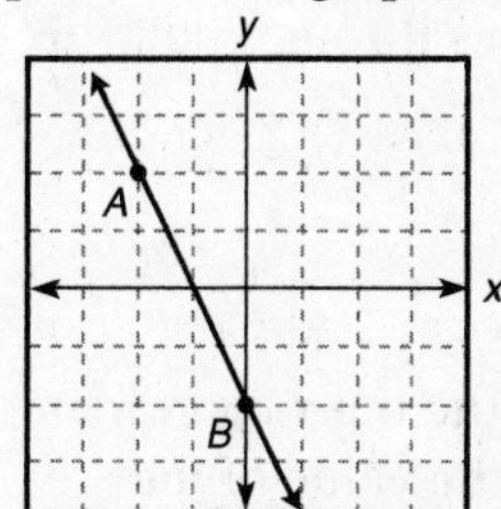

Which of the following ordered pairs also lies on the line?

A. (1, 0)
B. (1, – 1)
C. (0, – 1)
D. (–1, 0)

12. Two of the corners of a triangle are located at (3, – 3) and (2, 3). What is the location of the third corner as shown in the diagram below?

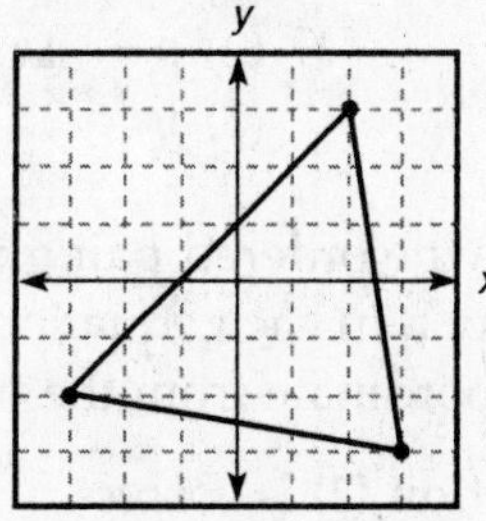

A. (–3, – 2)
B. (–3, 2)
C. (–2, – 3)
D. (3, – 2)

**Review your work using the explanations that start on page 699.**

LESSON 7

# Graphing a Line

**KEY IDEAS**

- A linear equation has two variables, *x* and *y*.
- When the solutions to a linear equation are graphed on a coordinate grid, the graph forms a line.
- To find a point on the line, substitute a value for *x* and solve for *y*.
- You must solve for at least two points in order to draw the line.

Using the coordinate system, we can graph equations. When an equation has only two variables, $x$ and $y$, and neither is raised to a power, the graph of the equation will be a line. When the graph of an equation is a straight line, the equation is a **linear equation.**

To graph an equation, you need to solve for two points on the line.

**Example 1:** Graph the equation $y = 3x - 4$.

1. Choose any value for $x$ and solve for $y$. Let $x = 1$.

   $y = 3(1) - 4$
   $y = 3 - 4$
   $y = -1$

   If $x = 1$, then $y = -1$. The ordered pair for the first point is $(1, -1)$.

2. Choose another value for $x$ and solve for $y$. Let $x = 2$.

   $y = 3(2) - 4$
   $y = 6 - 4$
   $y = 2$

   If $x = 2$, then $y = 2$. The ordered pair for the second point is $(2, 2)$.

3. Plot the points on a coordinate grid and draw a line through them.

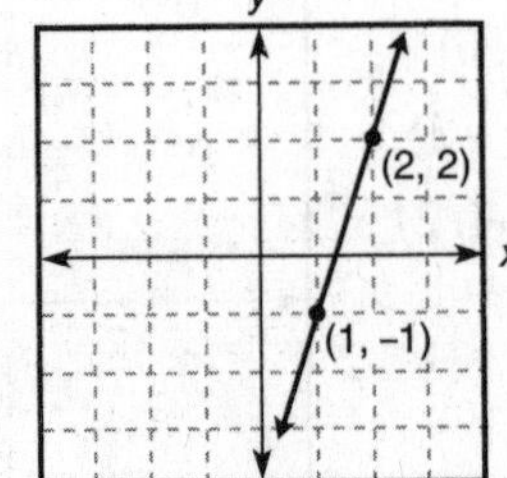


The line is the graph of all the possible solutions for the equation $y = 3x - 4$. Arrows at both ends of the line indicate that the line continues in both directions. From this, you can see that there is an infinite number of solutions to a linear equation.

**TASC TEST TIP**

*If a linear equation is not written with y on one side of the equation, use inverse operations to isolate y.*
*Example:* $2x + y = 15$.
*Subtract 2x from each side.*
$y = -2x + 15$.

Some linear equation problems don't require you to draw a graph.

**Example 2:** Point $A$ lies at $(5, -6)$ on a coordinate grid. The graph of which of the following equations passes through point $A$?

(1) $y = -5x + 18$
(2) $y = -4x + 14$
(3) $y = -2x - 13$

Use the ordered pair given in the problem. Substitute the $x$-coordinate, 5, for $x$ in each equation and solve for $y$. If $y = -6$, the value of the $y$-coordinate from the ordered pair, you have found the correct equation.

**Option (2)** is correct.

$y = -4x + 14$
$y = -4(5) + 14$
$y = -20 + 14 = -6$

# PRACTICE 7

**A. Fill in the $y$ column in each table and graph the equation.**

**1.** $y = \frac{1}{2}x + 3$

| If $x =$ | then $y =$ |
|---|---|
| –2 | |
| 0 | |
| 2 | |

**2.** $y + 3x = -1$

| If $x =$ | then $y =$ |
|---|---|
| –1 | |
| 0 | |
| 1 | |

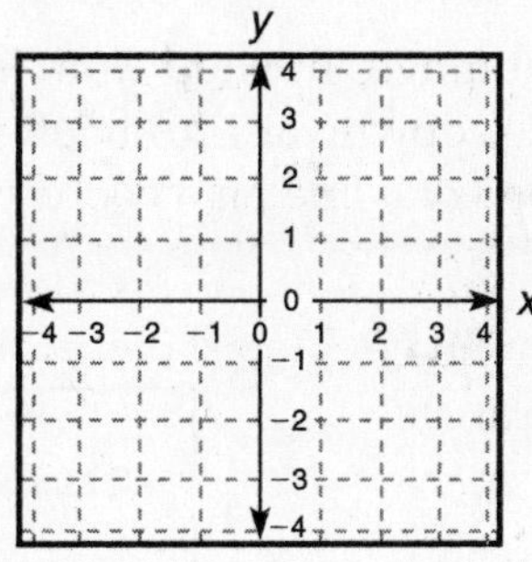


**3.** $-2 + y = -x$

| If $x =$ | then $y =$ |
|---|---|
| 1 | |
| 2 | |
| 3 | |

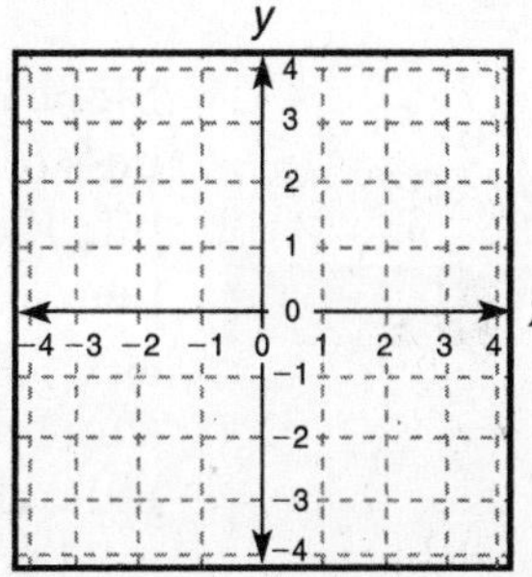


**4.** $y = 3 - 2x$

| If $x =$ | then $y =$ |
|---|---|
| 0 | |
| 1 | |
| 2 | |

**B. Choose the <u>one best answer</u> to each question.**

**<u>Questions 5 and 6</u> refer to the following coordinate grid.**

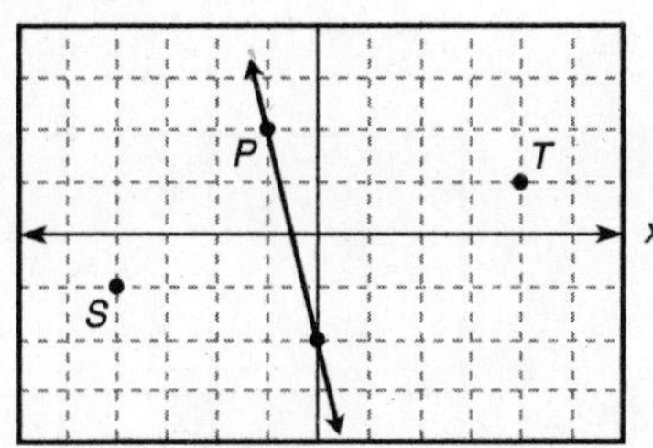


**5.** The graph of the equation $y = \frac{1}{4}x$ will pass through which of the following pairs of points?

A. point $S$ and (–1, 2)
B. point $S$ and (0, – 2)
C. point $T$ and (0, 0)
D. point $T$ and (0, – 2)

**6.** Line $P$ is the graph of which of the following equations?

A. $y = 4x + 1$
B. $y = -4x - 1$
C. $y = 4x + 2$
D. $y = -4x - 2$

**7.** Point C is located at (–3, 5). A graph of which of the following equations would pass through point C?

A. $3x + 2y = 5$
B. $2x + 3y = 9$
C. $4x - 2y = 8$
D. $3x - 3y = 6$

**Review your work using the explanations that start on page 699.**

**STUDY ADVICE**

Hang in there: You're more than halfway through the Mathematics unit! It may feel like a long haul until Test Day, but keep thinking about how good it will feel to have your high school equivalency degree in hand!

# Slope of a Line

**Slope** is the measurement of the steepness of a line. Imagine a road going up a hill. If the road must reach the top of the hill over a short distance, the road will be very steep. Slope measures the relationship between **rise** (how high the road must climb) and **run** (the distance the road goes forward).

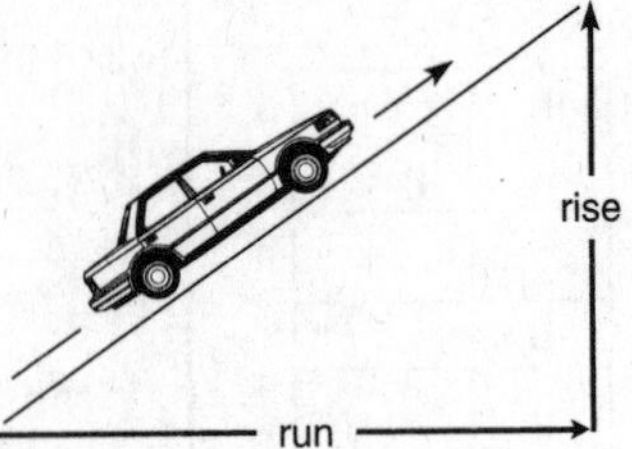


### KEY IDEAS

- Slope is the ratio of rise to run.
- Moving from left to right, a line that goes upward has a positive slope, and a line that moves downward has a negative slope.
- You can find slope by counting spaces and writing a ratio or by using the slope formula.

On a coordinate grid, a line that moves upward from left to right has a **positive slope.** A line that moves downward from left to right has a **negative slope.** You can find the slope of a line on a coordinate grid by writing the ratio of rise to run.

**Example 1:** What is the slope of line $P$ shown on the coordinate grid?

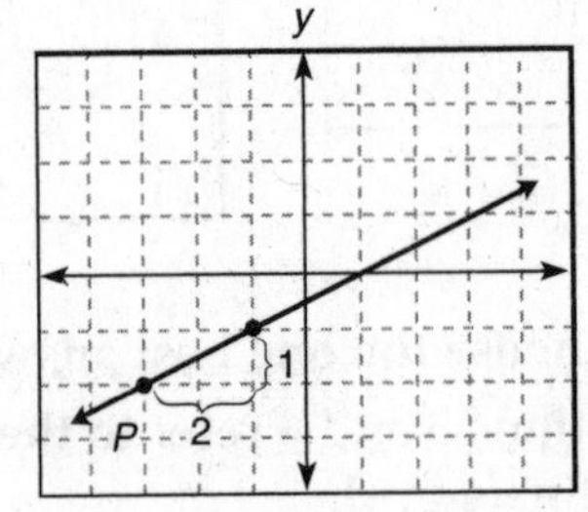


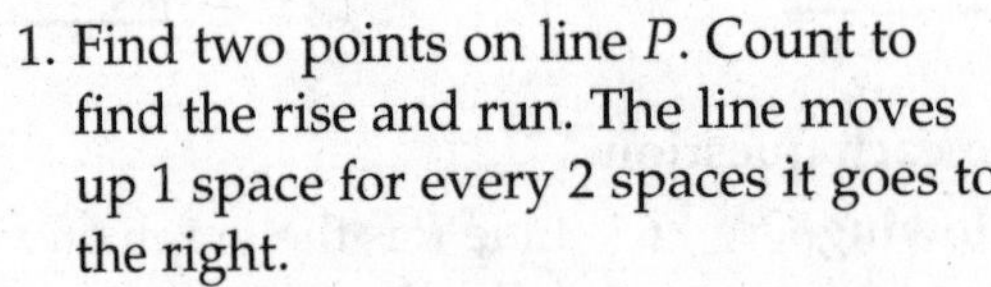
1. Find two points on line $P$. Count to find the rise and run. The line moves up 1 space for every 2 spaces it goes to the right.

2. Write the ratio: $\frac{\text{rise}}{\text{run}} = \frac{1}{2}$. The slope is $\frac{1}{2}$.

**Example 2:** What is the slope of line $S$ shown on the coordinate grid?

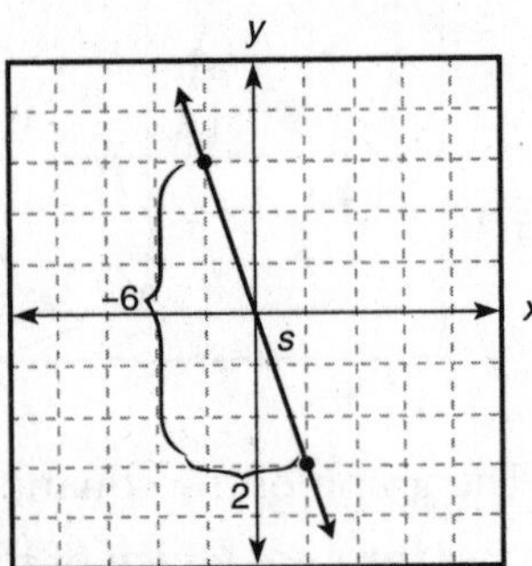


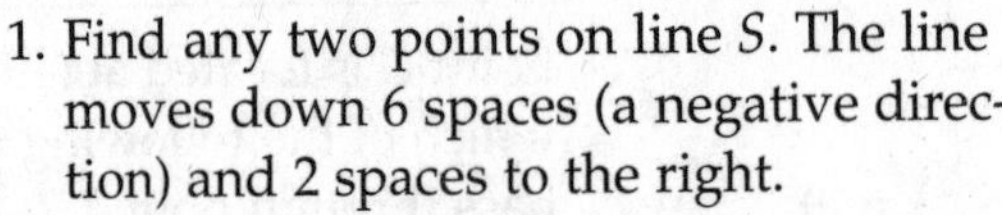
1. Find any two points on line $S$. The line moves down 6 spaces (a negative direction) and 2 spaces to the right.

2. Write the ratio: $\frac{\text{rise}}{\text{run}} = \frac{-6}{2} = -3$.

The slope of line $S$ is **–3.**

### TASC TEST TIP

*Think of the slope formula this way: write the difference of the y's over the difference of the x's. Just make sure that you always subtract the coordinates in the same order.*

You can also find slope using the slope formula:

slope of a line $= \frac{y_2 - y_1}{x_2 - x_1}$, where $(x_1, y_1)$ and $(x_2, y_2)$ are two points on a line.

**Example 3:** A line passes through points at coordinates (1, 4) and (–5, 2). What is the slope of the line?

1. Choose one point to be $(x_1, y_1)$. The other will be $(x_2, y_2)$. It doesn't matter which you choose. For this example, $(x_1, y_1) = (1, 4)$ and $(x_2, y_2) = (-5, 2)$.

2. Substitute the values into the slope formula and solve:

$\frac{y_2 - y_1}{x_2 - x_1}$ $\frac{2-4}{-5-1} = \frac{-2}{-6} = \frac{1}{3}$ The slope is $\frac{1}{3}$.

Since the slope is positive, you know that the line rises from left to right. You also know that it goes up 1 space for every 3 spaces it moves to the right.

In working with slope, there are a few special circumstances that you should memorize. A horizontal line, just like a flat stretch of roadway, has a **slope of 0**. The slope of a vertical line is **undefined**; in other words, our definition of slope will not work for a line that has no run at all.

**A. Find the slope of each line.**

**1.**

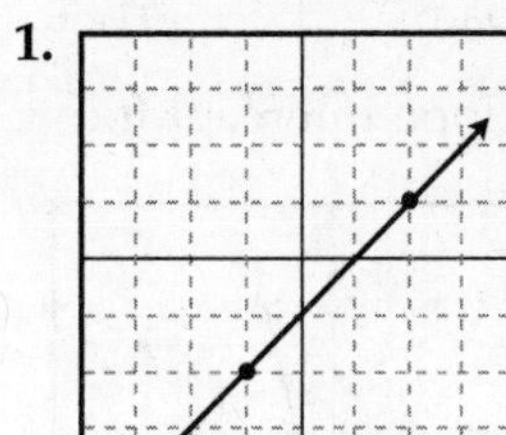

**2.**

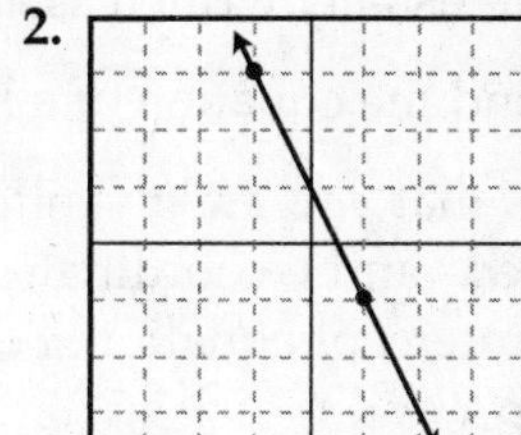

**3.**

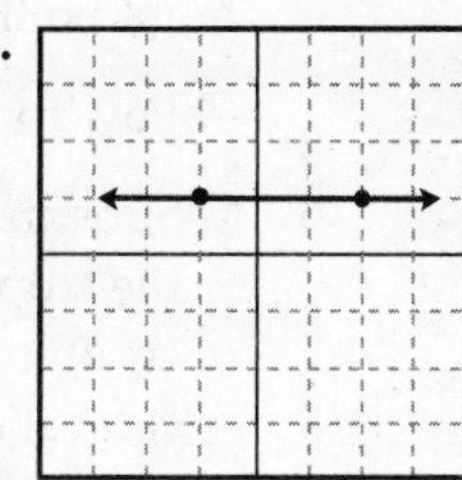

**B. Use the slope formula to find the slope of a line that passes through the following pairs of points.**

**4.** (3, 5) and (–1, 2)

**5.** (0, 2) and (4, 0)

**6.** (4, 2) and (2, 2)

**7.** (6, 1) and (0, 3)

**8.** (1, 4) and (–2, – 2)

**9.** (4, – 2) and (2, 4)

**C. Choose the one best answer for each question.**

**Question 10 refers to the following graph.**

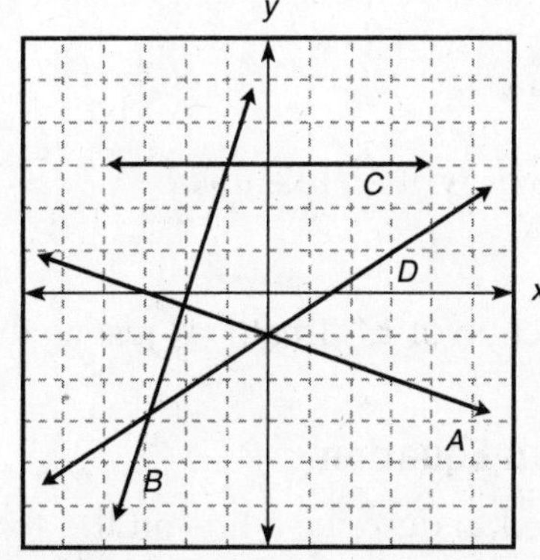


**10.** Which of the following lines shown on the graph has a slope of $-\frac{1}{3}$?

A. line *A*
B. line *B*
C. line *C*
D. line *D*

**11.** Line *N* passes through the following points: (0, 4), (1, 2), (2, 0), and (3, – 2). What is the slope of line *N*?

A. –4
B. –2
C. 2
D. 4

**12.** Line *L* passes through point (1, 0) and has a slope of 3. Which of the following points also lies on line *L*?

A. (0, 3)
B. (1, 3)
C. (2, 3)
D. (2, 5)

**Review your work using the explanations that start on page 700.**

# Slope and Equations

## Use the Slope-Intercept Form to Find an Equation

Lesson 8 showed how to find the slope of a line and graph it. The examples in this lesson show how you can use the slope and a point on the line to find the equation of a line in two different forms. (You might also need to find the equation of a line from two points. In this case, you would calculate the slope first, then use the slope and one of the points to find the equation.)

**KEY IDEAS**

- There are two ways to find an equation if you are given the slope of a line and a point.
- One method is the slope-intercept form.
- The other method is the point-slope form.

The first of these forms is the **slope-intercept form:** $y = mx + b$. In this form of the equation, the variable $m$ stands for the **slope** of the line. The variable $b$ stands for the **y-intercept,** which is the $y$-value at the point where the line crosses the $y$-axis. The variables $x$ and $y$ are the **x- and y-coordinates** of any point on the line and are usually written as an ordered pair.

Follow these steps to find the equation of a line in the slope-intercept form.

1. Substitute the values that you are given for the slope ($m$) and the $x$- and $y$-coordinates ($x$, $y$) into the slope-intercept equation. Be careful not to mix up $x$ and $y$.
2. Use inverse operations to isolate $b$.
3. Rewrite the equation in slope-intercept form, leaving $x$ and $y$ as variables and substituting values for $m$ and $b$.

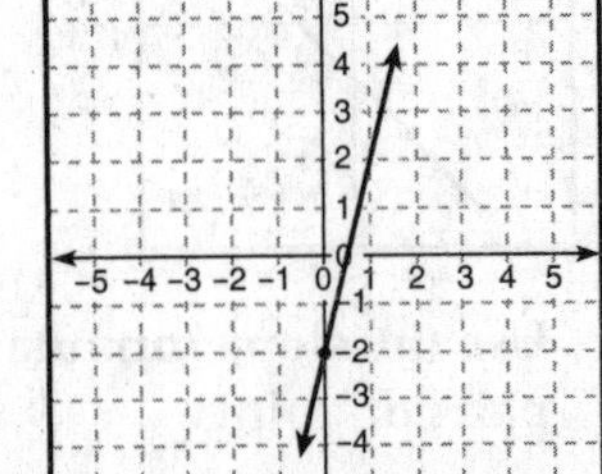


**Example 1:** Use the slope-intercept form to find the equation of a line that has the slope $m = 4$ and passes through the point (–1, – 6).

1. $-6 = (4) \times (-1) + b$
   $-6 = -4 + b$
2. $-2 = b$
3. $\mathbf{y = 4x - 2}$

**TASC TEST TIP**

*Memorize the formulas for the slope-intercept form and the point-slope form to save time on Test Day.*

Note that linear equations are sometimes written like this:

$f(x) = mx + b$

The symbol $f(x)$ simply means "a function of $x$." Treat f ($x$) just as though it were the variable $y$.

## Use the Point-Slope Form to Find an Equation

The second important form that is used to describe a line on the Mathematics Test is the **point-slope form:** $y - y_1 = m(x - x_1)$. In this form, $(x_1, y_1)$ is an ordered pair that corresponds to a point on the line. As in the slope-intercept form, $m$ stands for the slope. If you simplify an equation in point-slope form by solving for $y$, you will get the slope-intercept form of the equation.

Follow these steps to find the equation of a line in the point-slope form.

1. Call the point that you are given $(x_1, y_1)$.
2. Put the $x_1$ and $y_1$ values into the point-slope equation.
3. Put the slope value in the point-slope equation for $m$.

# PRACTICE 9

**Example 2:** Use the point-slope form to find the equation of the line that passes through the point (4, 3) and has a slope of 2.

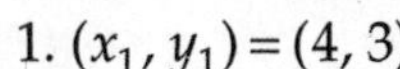

1. $(x_1, y_1) = (4, 3)$
2. $y - 3 = m(x - 4)$
3. $\mathbf{y - 3 = 2(x - 4)}$

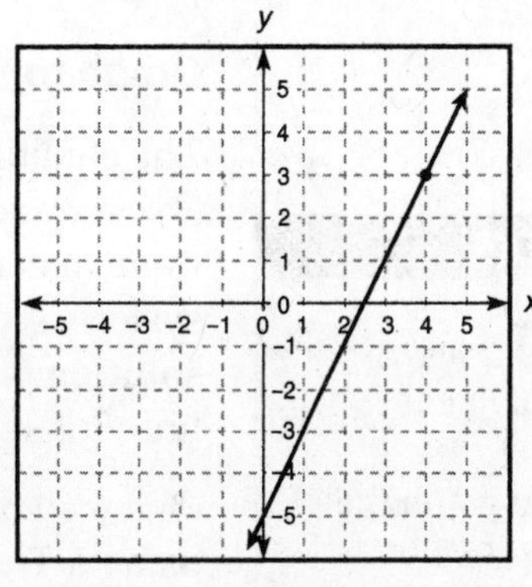


Notice that you can simplify the equation to find the slope-intercept form:

$$y - 3 = 2(x - 4)$$
$$y - 3 = 2x - 8$$
$$y = 2x - 5$$

---

**A. Use the slope-intercept form, $y = mx + b$, to find the equation of the line that passes through the given point and has the given slope.**

**1.** $(1, -2); m = -4$ **2.** $(-1, -4); m = 2$ **3.** $(-4, 2); m = -\frac{1}{3}$

**B. Use the point-slope form, $y - y_1 = m(x - x_1)$, to find the equation of the line that passes through the given point and has the given slope.**

**4.** $(2, 1); m = 3$ **5.** $(2, 0); m = -\frac{1}{3}$ **6.** $(1, -2); m = 1$

**C. Find the equation of the line that passes through the given points. Write your answer in slope-intercept form.**

**7.** $(-5, 3), (1, 1)$ **8.** $(-3, 0), (-2, 4)$ **9.** $(-3, -4), (7, 1)$

**D. Choose the <u>one best answer</u> for each question.**

**10.** Which of the following is an equation for the line that passes through $(-1, 0)$ and $(2, -3)$?

A. $y = 3x + 3$
B. $y = -3x + 9$
C. $y = -x - 1$
D. $y = x - 5$

**11.** Which of the following equations describes the same line as $y - 2 = \frac{1}{2}(x - 6)$?

A. $y = 3x + 2$
B. $y = \frac{1}{2}x - 4$
C. $y = -x + 12$
D. $y = \frac{1}{2}x - 1$

**<u>Question 12</u> refers to the following graph.**

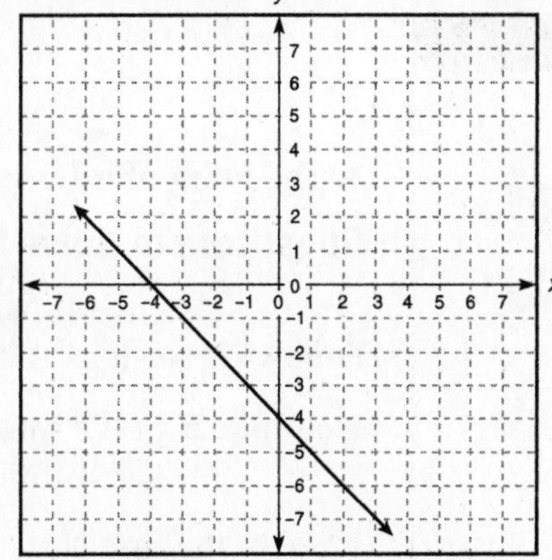


**12.** Which of the following equations correctly describes the line on the graph?

A. $y = x - 4$
B. $y = -x - 4$
C. $y = x + 4$
D. $y = -x + 4$

**Review your work using the explanations that start on page 700.**

# Systems of Linear Equations

## Graph to Solve the System of Equations

The equations in Lessons 7 and 9 are **linear equations:** they have two variables, $x$ and $y$, and represent straight lines in the coordinate plane. Two or more linear equations make up a **system of linear equations**. Solving a system of two equations means finding the values of both variables. The **solution** will give the $x$- and $y$-coordinates of the point at which the two lines intersect. You can express this solution as an ordered pair: $(x, y)$.

One way to solve a system of equations is by graphing each equation using a **T-chart**—like those that you filled in for the Lesson 7 practice. Graphing a system of linear equations provides a picture of the intersection. Follow these steps to solve a system of equations by graphing.

1. Set up an $x$ and $y$ T-chart for each equation. Find two ordered pairs for each equation: use $x = 0$ and find $y$ and then use $y = 0$ and find $x$.
2. Graph both lines, using the ordered pairs that you generated in step 1.
3. Find the point of intersection and express it in the form $(x, y)$.

**Example 1:** Graph the equations $6x + 3y = 12$ and $5x + y = 7$ to find the solution.

**1.** $6x + 3y = 12$

| X | Y |
|---|---|
| 0 | 4 |
| 2 | 0 |

$5x + y = 7$

| X | Y |
|---|---|
| 0 | 7 |
| $\frac{7}{5}$ | 0 |

**2.**

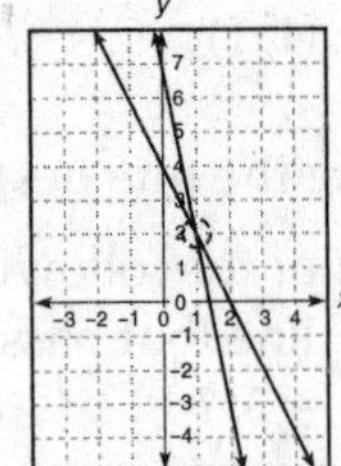

**3.** The point of intersection—that is, the solution—is **(1, 2)**.

## Substitute to Solve the System of Equations

You can also use **substitution** to solve a system of linear equations. Follow these steps to solve a system of linear equations by substitution.

**Example 2:** Solve the equations $6x + 3y = 12$ and $5x + y = 7$ by substitution.

1. Solve the first equation so that $y$ is expressed in terms of $x$.

$$6x + 3y = 12$$
$$3y = 12 - 6x$$
$$y = 4 - 2x$$

2. Substitute that value of $y$ into the second equation and solve for $x$.

$$5x + (4 - 2x) = 7$$
$$3x + 4 = 7$$
$$3x = 3$$
$$x = 1$$

3. Substitute that value of $x$ into the first equation and solve for $y$.

$$6(1) + 3y = 12$$
$$6 + 3y = 12$$
$$3y = 6$$
$$y = 2$$

The solution is **(1, 2)**.

### KEY IDEAS

- There are several ways to solve a system of linear equations.
- One method is to graph the equations to see the point of intersection.
- Another method is to find one value ($x$ or $y$) and substitute it into the other equation to find the solution.

### TASC TEST TIP

*You may be asked whether a point is a solution to a system of equations, and you can use either of the methods shown here to find the answer.*

# PRACTICE 10

**A. Find two pairs of coordinates for each equation by making a T-chart. Use the coordinates to graph the lines and find the solution.**

1. $y = 3x - 15$
   $x + y = 13$

2. $4x + 2y = 10$
   $y = -5x - 4$

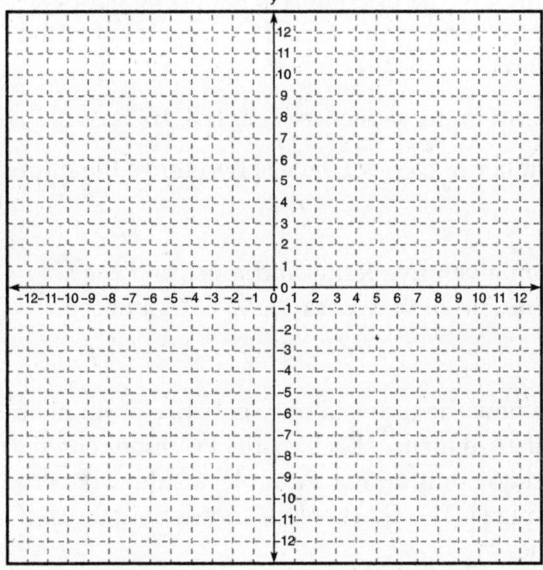

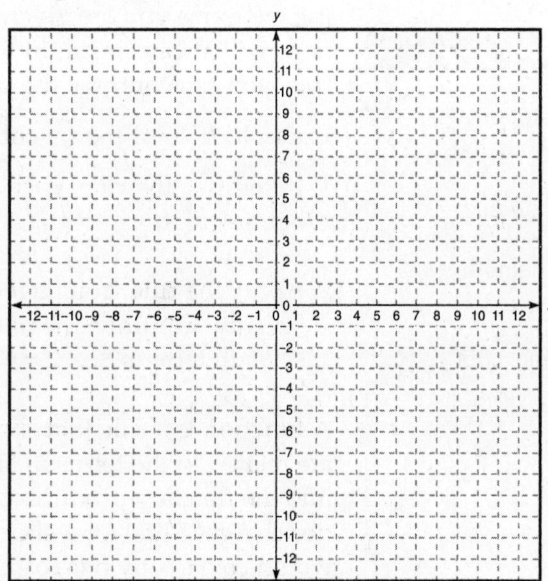

**B. Find the solution for the two equations by substitution. Express as an ordered pair in the form (*x*, *y*).**

3. $7x - y = 22$
   $4x + 2y = 10$

4. $x + y = 9$
   $2x - 3y = 8$

5. $y = 3x + 15$
   $5x - 2y = -26$

6. $10x - y = -1$
   $y = 12x$

**C. Choose the one best answer for each question.**

7. Where does the line with the equation $x - 2y = 4$ intersect with the line with the equation $6y + 5x = 4$?
   A. $(2, -1)$
   B. $(3, -2)$
   C. $(-2, 1)$
   D. $(-1, 2)$

8. Where does the line with the equation $y = x$ intersect with the line with the equation $y = -x$?
   A. $(1, -1)$
   B. $(-1, 1)$
   C. $(0, 0)$
   D. $(1, 0)$

9. Where does the line with the equation $y = -2$ intersect with the line with the equation $3y = 2x + 3$?
   A. $(-\frac{2}{9}, -2)$
   B. $(-\frac{1}{3}, -2)$
   C. $(-\frac{9}{2}, -2)$
   D. $(\frac{9}{2}, 2)$

10. Which of the following is the equation of a line that intersects $y = 4x + 2$?
   A. $2y = 8x + 2$
   B. $y = 4x - 2$
   C. $y = -4x + 2$
   D. $\frac{1}{2}y = 2x - 7$

**Review your work using the explanations that start on page 701.**

# Patterns and Functions

A **pattern** is a series of numbers or objects whose sequence is determined by a particular rule. You can figure out what rule has been used by studying the terms you are given. Think: What operation or sequence of operations will always result in the next term in the series? Once you know the rule, you can continue the pattern.

**KEY IDEAS**

- A pattern is a sequence of numbers determined by a mathematical rule.
- A function is a rule that shows how one set of numbers is related to another set of numbers.
- To use a function, substitute values for variables and solve.

**Example 1:** Find the seventh term in the sequence: 1, 2, 4, 8, 16, . . .

1. Determine the rule. Each number in the sequence is two times the number before it.

2. Apply the rule. You have been given five terms and must find the seventh. Continue the pattern. The sixth term is $16 \times 2 = 32$, and the seventh term is $32 \times 2 = \mathbf{64}$.

A **function** is a rule that shows how the terms in one sequence of numbers are related to the terms in another sequence. Each distinct number entered into the function produces a unique output. For example, a sidewalk vendor charges $1.50 for a slice of pizza. The chart below shows how much it would cost to buy one to six slices.

| Number of Pizza Slices | 1 | 2 | 3 | 4 | 5 | 6 |
|---|---|---|---|---|---|---|
| Cost | $1.50 | $3.00 | $4.50 | $6.00 | $7.50 | $9.00 |

Each number in the first row corresponds to a price in the second row. We could say that the amount a customer will pay is a function of (or depends upon) the number of slices the customer orders. This function could be written:

**TASC TEST TIP**

*To figure out what rule has been used to form a pattern, begin by finding the difference between each term and the term that follows it in the sequence.*

Cost = number of slices × $1.50, or $C = n(\$1.50)$.

If you know the function and a number in the first set of numbers, you can solve for its corresponding number in the second set.

**Example 2:** Using the function $y = 3x + 5$, what is the value of $y$ when $x = -3$?

1. Substitute the given value of $x$. $\quad y = 3(-3) + 5$
2. Solve for $y$. $\quad y = -9 + 5$

$y = \mathbf{-4}$

**Example 3:** Using the function $n = 100 - 4(3 + m)$, what is the value of $n$ when $m = 6$?

1. Substitute the given value of $m$. $\quad n = 100 - 4(3 + 6)$
2. Solve for $n$. $\quad n = 100 - 4(9)$

$n = 100 - 36$

$n = \mathbf{64}$

# PRACTICE 11

**A. Solve.**

**1.** Which number should come next in the following pattern?

$-12, -9, -6, -3,$ ________

**2.** What is the next number in the sequence?

21, 26, 31, 36, ________

**3.** In the function $y = 4x + 10$, if $x = -2$, what is the value of $y$?

**4.** In the function $y = 2x(4 + x) - 2$, if $x = 3$, what is the value of $y$?

**5.** Each term in the second row is determined by the function $y = 2x - 1$.

| $x$ | 1 | 2 | 3 | 4 | 5 | ... | 12 |
|---|---|---|---|---|---|---|---|
| $y$ | 1 | 3 | 5 | 7 | 9 | ... | |

What number belongs in the shaded box?

**6.** In the function $y = \frac{x+3}{6} - 8$, if $x = 21$, what is the value of $y$?

**7.** What is the next term in the pattern below?

1000, 500, 250, 125, 62.5, ________

**8.** What is the next number in the sequence?

3, –5, 7, –9, 11, ________

**9.** Each term in the second row is determined by the function $y = 3x + 5$.

| $x$ | –2 | –1 | 0 | 1 | 2 | ... | 9 |
|---|---|---|---|---|---|---|---|
| $y$ | –1 | 2 | 5 | 8 | 11 | ... | |

What number belongs in the shaded box?

**10.** In the function $y = (x - 7) + 12$, if $x = -10$, what is the value of $y$?

**B. Choose the one best answer to each question.**

**Question 11 refers to the following drawing.**

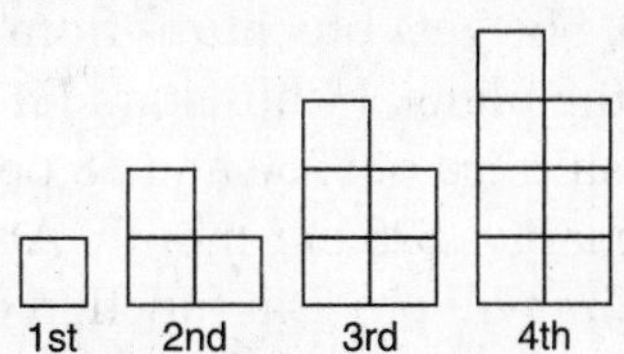


**11.** How many blocks would be needed to build the 25th construction in the sequence?

A. 47
B. 49
C. 51
D. 55

**12.** What is the sixth term in the sequence below?

$-14, -8, -2, 4, \ldots$

A. 10
B. 14
C. 16
D. 22

**13.** The price per scarf is a function of the number of scarves purchased. The table shows the price per scarf for purchases of up to four scarves.

| number ($n$) of scarves | 1 | 2 | 3 | 4 |
|---|---|---|---|---|
| cost ($c$) per scarf | \$5.00 | \$4.75 | \$4.50 | \$4.25 |

Which of the following functions was used to determine the prices shown in the table?

A. $c = n(\$5.00 - \$0.25)$
B. $c = \$5.00 - \$0.25(n - 1)$
C. $c = \$5.00 - \$0.25n$
D. $c = \$5.00n - \$0.25n$

**14.** Which of the following sequences of values of $y$ could be created using the function $y = 4x - 3$?

A. 1, 4, 7, 10, 13, . . .
B. 1, 5, 9, 13, 17, . . .
C. 1, 4, 8, 13, 19, . . .
D. 1, –1, –3, –5, –7, . . .

**Review your work using the explanations that start on page 701.**

LESSON 12

# Function Applications

Functions are used in many business applications. For instance, they can be used to calculate profit, cost, employee wages, and taxes. On the Mathematics Test, you will read about common work and life situations. The problems may contain or describe a function that you can use to solve the problem.

**Example 1:** Celino Advertising is finishing a series of print ads for a client. Finishing the project will cost \$2000 per day for the first seven days and \$3500 per day after seven days. The finishing costs can be found using the function $C = \$2000d + \$1500(d-7)$, where $C$ = the cost of finishing the project and $d$ = the number of days. If the project takes 12 days to complete, what will the project cost?

Use the function to solve the problem.

$$\begin{aligned} C &= \$2000d + \$1500(d-7) \\ &= \$2000(12) + \$1500(12-7) \\ &= \$24000 + \$1500(5) \\ &= \$24000 + \$7500 \\ &= \mathbf{\$31,500} \end{aligned}$$

You may be asked to use functions to make comparisons.

**Example 2:** Nita decides to join a health club. She gets brochures from two health clubs and compares the plans. Healthstars Fitness charges a one-time membership fee of \$250 and \$8 per month. Freedom Health Center charges \$25 per month. At both health clubs, the price ($P$) Nita will pay is a function of the number of months ($m$) she attends the club. The functions are:

Healthstars Fitness $P = \$250 + \$8m$

Freedom Health Center $P = \$25m$

Nita plans to move in 18 months. If she attends a health club until she moves, which one offers the better price?

1. Find the price at Healthstars Fitness:

$$\begin{aligned} P &= \$250 + \$8m \\ &= \$250 + \$8(18) \\ &= \$250 + \$144 \\ &= \$394 \end{aligned}$$

2. Find the price at Freedom Health Center:

$$\begin{aligned} P &= \$25m \\ &= \$25(18) \\ &= \$450 \end{aligned}$$

3. Compare the results. Even though Nita will have to pay a large amount up front, **Healthstars Fitness** offers the better price.

### KEY IDEAS

- Functions are used to make many common work calculations.
- Functions can be used to make comparisons.
- To use a function, you must know the meaning of the variables. This information should be given in the text of the problem.

### TASC TEST TIP

*There is often more than one way to work a problem, even when a function is given. Solve using the function. If you see another way to solve the problem, use it to check your answer.*

# PRACTICE 12

**A. Solve. You MAY use a calculator.**

1. The Chimney Sweep charges $25 for a chimney inspection. If the customer purchases additional services, $15 of the inspection fee is deducted. Let $s$ = the cost of any additional services. The total cost (C) of an inspection and services can be determined by the function $C = \$25 + (s - \$15)$ where $s$ is not 0.
   a. Jan has her chimney inspected and purchases a smoke guard for $89. How much will she be charged?
   b. After an inspection, Ahmed decides to have a new damper installed for $255. How much will he pay?

2. Ricardo does a great deal of driving for his work. He generally estimates his driving time in hours ($t$) using the function $t = \frac{m}{60}$, where $m$ = the number of miles.
   a. How many hours will it take Ricardo to drive 330 miles?
   b. How many hours will it take Ricardo to drive 255 miles?

3. A customer's phone charges are a function of the number of minutes of long-distance calls made. The graph shows a comparison of two plans available.

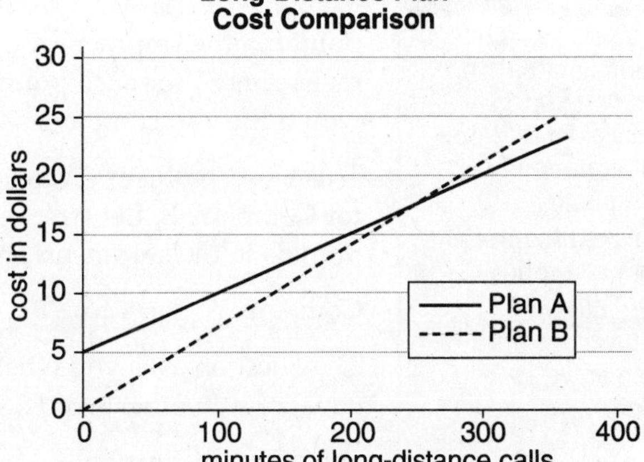


   a. Michelle looks at her previous phone bills and finds that she makes about 350 minutes of long-distance calls per month. Which plan is better for her?
   b. Craig usually makes about 150 minutes of long-distance calls per month. Which plan is better for him?

**B. Choose the one best answer to each question. You MAY use a calculator.**

**Questions 4 and 5 refer to the following information.**

Alicia is considering three job opportunities. At all three jobs, weekly pay ($P$) is a function of the number of hours ($h$) worked during the week. The functions are shown below:

| | |
|---|---|
| Job 1 | $P = \$9.75h$ |
| Job 2 | $P = \$70 + \$8.40h$ |
| Job 3 | $P = \$380 \times \frac{h}{38}$ |

4. If Alicia works 30 hours in a week, how much more will she earn at Job 2 than at Job 1?
   A. $5.33
   B. $29.50
   C. $40.50
   D. $59.00

5. If Alicia works 40 hours per week, which of the following is a true statement?
   A. Alicia will earn the least at Job 3.
   B. Job 1 will pay more than Job 3.
   C. Job 3 will pay more than Job 2.
   D. Alicia will earn the most at Job 2.

6. A company is awarded a $95,000 job that will cost $5,400 per day in expenses. Profits ($P$) can be calculated using $P = \$95,000 - \$5,400d$, where d = number of days. What is the company's profit if the job takes 14 days to complete?
   A. $10,800
   B. $19,400
   C. $66,100
   D. $75,600

**Review your work using the explanations that start on page 702.**

LESSON 13

# Equation Word Problems, Part II

Now that you have learned more about equations and systems of equations, you are ready to apply those skills to solve word problems.

**Example 1:** Two companies, A and B, charge for shipping by the pound. Company A charges a fixed fee of \$3 for any shipment plus \$1.50 for each pound in the shipment. Company B charges a fixed fee of \$6 for any shipment plus \$1 for each pound in the shipment. For what number of pounds would the two companies' shipping charges be the same?

This word problem gives you two equations: one for Company A and one for Company B. Let $y$ represent the shipping charge and $x$ represent pounds in the shipment, and write out the equations:

Company A: $y = 1.5x + 3$ Company B: $y = 1x + 6$

The question asks you what value of x will give the same value of y in both equations. In other words, what is the solution of the system of equations?

Solve by substitution:

$1x + 6 = 1.5x + 3$

$3 = 0.5x$

$\mathbf{6 = x}$

The companies would charge the same amount for shipping a **6-pound order.**

You may also be asked to infer an equation from a graphic. Study the following example.

**Example 2:** A charity was struggling to raise funds. In November of last year it raised only \$1500. It then decided to launch a social media campaign. The following graph shows how much money the charity raised for several months, starting with November of last year.

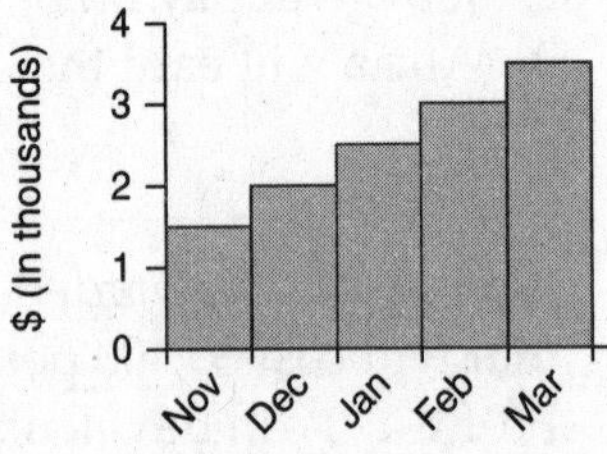


Which of the following equations could be used to find the money raised by the charity in the month $x$ months after November last year? Here, $y$ represents the money raised by the charity.

(1) $y = 1{,}500x + 500$

(2) $y = 500x + 1{,}500$

Choice **(2)** is correct: **\$1500** is the charity's starting place at the end of November. Each month after that it raises \$500 more. In February, which was three months after November, it raised \$3000: $500(3) + 1500 = 3000$.

## KEY IDEAS

- Some questions on the Mathematics Test may give you a word problem that portrays a linear equation or system of equations.
- You may be asked to infer an equation from a graphic.
- Carefully write out the equation(s) from the word problem, then solve as usual.

## TASC TEST TIP

*When working on word problems, use your scratch paper to write out the information given in the form of a mathematical equation.*

# PRACTICE 13

You may also be asked to solve word problems using quadratic equations. Study the following example.

**Example 3:** Xavier's age times Yelena's age is 120. Xavier is 2 years older than Yelena. How old are Xavier and Yelena?

Write two equations to represent the information given: $xy = 120$ $x - y = 2$

Solve using substitution.

1. Isolate a variable in the second equation: $x = 2 + y$
2. Substitute and simplify: $(2 + y)y = 120$

   $y^2 + 2y = 120$
3. Make the equation equal zero and solve by factoring: $y^2 + 2y - 120 = 0$

   $(y - 10)(y + 12) = 0$

   $y = 10 \text{ or } -12$

Now, it doesn't make sense for Yelena to have a negative age. So she must be **10 years old.** Substitute that value back into one of the original equations: $x - 10 = 2$

Therefore, Xavier is **12 years old.**

---

1. Marguerite, a salesperson, earns a base salary plus a commission based on how much she sells. The following graph represents how much Marguerite can make.

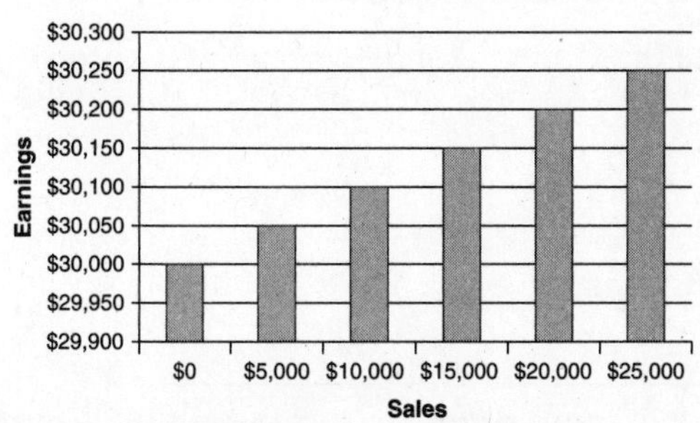


Which of the following equations accurately expresses Marguerite's earnings (e) in terms of her sales (s)?

A. $e = 30{,}000s$
B. $e = 0.3s + 5{,}000$
C. $e = 30{,}250 - 50s$
D. $e = 0.01s + 30{,}000$

2. A car dealership is offering a discount on used cars. For sedans, the discount is $1,000 plus $100 for each year of the vehicle's age. For minivans, the discount is $1,500 plus $50 for each year of the vehicle's age. At what age would a vehicle have the same discount whether it were a sedan or minivan?

A. 10
B. 12
C. 14
D. 16

3. A zoo has contacted two stroller manufacturers to replace its current strollers with upgraded versions. Company A will charge $2,000 initially and $40 per stroller. Company B will only charge $1,550 initially, but $55 per stroller. For what number of strollers will the two companies charge the same price?

A. 15
B. 20
C. 30
D. 35

**Review your work using the explanations that start on page 702.**

# FUNCTIONS PRACTICE QUESTIONS

**Directions: You MAY use your calculator.**

1. Which of the following expressions is equal to $6 - 4(x + 3)$?

   A. $4x + 3$
   B. $4x - 9$
   C. $-4x - 3$
   D. $-4x - 6$

2. Three increased by the product of 4 and a number is equal to the same number decreased by 6. What is the number?

   A. –3
   B. –1
   C. 1
   D. 3

3. What is the equation of a line with a slope of –4 that passes through the point (1, 2)?

   A. $y = -4x + 2$
   B. $y = -4x + 6$
   C. $y = 4x + 1$
   D. $y = 4x + 6$

4. The ordered pair (–2, – 1) is a solution to which of the following equations?

   A. $-4x - y = 7$
   B. $4x + y = -7$
   C. $4x - y = -7$
   D. $-4x + y = -7$

5. For a two-week period, Jan earned \$150 less than twice Tom's earnings. Together Jan and Tom earned \$1380. How much did Tom earn?

   A. \$720
   B. \$660
   C. \$510
   D. \$360

**Questions 6 and 7 refer to the following graph.**

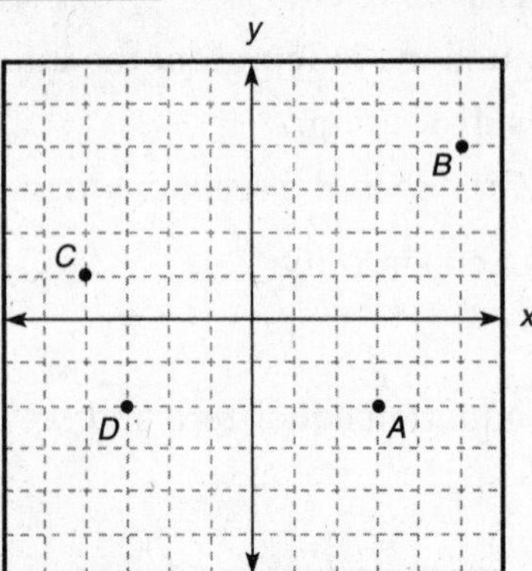


6. If the graph of the equation $y = -x - 5$ were drawn on the grid, which of the points would be on the line?

   A. *A*
   B. *B*
   C. *C*
   D. *D*

7. If a line were drawn through points *B* and *C*, what would be the slope of the line?

   A. –3
   B. $-\frac{1}{3}$
   C. $\frac{1}{3}$
   D. 3

---

8. Samuel is paid \$350 per month plus a 10% commission on his total sales for the month. If he needs to earn at least \$2100 per month, which of the following expressions represents the total sales (*s*) Samuel needs to achieve?

   A. $s \geq \$17,500$
   B. $s \leq \$17,500$
   C. $s \leq \$21,000$
   D. $s \geq \$21,000$

9. For its Checking Plus account, a bank charges \$3.95 per month plus \$0.10 for each check written after the first ten checks written that month. The function to find the total monthly fee ($F$) is $F = \$3.95 + \$0.10(n - 10)$, where $n$ = number of checks written.

   Greg writes 24 checks in March. How much will he pay in fees for the month?

   A. \$6.35
   B. \$5.35
   C. \$2.40
   D. \$1.40

10. The sum of four consecutive odd numbers is 104. What is the largest number?

    A. 23
    B. 25
    C. 27
    D. 29

11. Which value for $x$ makes the inequality $x > 400$ true?

    A. $7^3$
    B. $4^4$
    C. $3^6$
    D. $6^3$

12. Four less than the product of a number ($x$) and 5 is equal to 8 more than 2 added to 3 times the number. Which of these equations could be used to find the value of $x$?

    A. $4 - 5x = 8 + 2 + 3x$
    B. $5x - 4 = 8 + 2 + 3x$
    C. $5x = 4 - 8 + 2 + 3x$
    D. $5x - 4 = 8 + 2 + 3$

13. What is the slope of a line that passes through the points (2, 4) and (4, 6)?

    A. –2
    B. 1
    C. 2
    D. 4

14. What is the next number in the sequence?

    1, 7, 14, 22, ...

    A. 30
    B. 31
    C. 32
    D. 33

15. What is the $y$-intercept of the line with a slope of 2 that passes through the point (1, 2)?

    A. –2
    B. $-\frac{1}{2}$
    C. 0
    D. $\frac{1}{2}$

16. If the graphs of the equations $y = x + 3$ and $y = -2x - 3$ are drawn on a coordinate grid, at which point do the two lines intersect?

    A. (–3, 2)
    B. (–2, 1)
    C. (–2, –1)
    D. (2, 3)

17. A hotel is installing a swimming pool that gets deeper as you approach the center. The following graph shows the depth of the pool in relation to the distance from the edge.

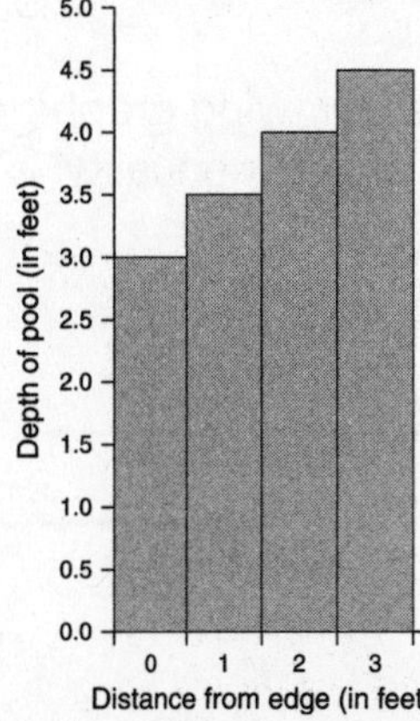


    Which equation properly represents this relationship if $x$ is the distance from the edge of the pool and $y$ is the depth of the pool?

    A. $y = 4.5 + 0.5x$
    B. $y = 4.5 + x$
    C. $y = 3 + x$
    D. $y = 3 + 0.5x$

18. Which of the following shows the product of –7 and $x$ decreased by the sum of 8 and $y$?

A. $-7x - (8 + y)$
B. $-7x - 8 + y$
C. $(8 + y) - 7x$
D. $(-7 + x) - (8 + y)$

19. What are the possible solutions for the quadratic equation $x^2 - 5x = 24$?

A. –8 and 3
B. –6 and 4
C. 8 and –3
D. 4 and –6

20. Cynthia is 6 times as old as Rebecca. In 6 years, Cynthia will be only 3 times as old as Rebecca. How old is Rebecca now?

A. 3
B. 4
C. 8
D. 12

21. The graph of which equation will pass through points (0, – 3) and (5, 7)?

A. $y = \frac{1}{2}x - 3$
B. $y = 2x - 3$
C. $y = 2x + 7$
D. $y = -2x + 3$

22. Which of the following graphs represents the solution set of the inequality $-2(x - 6) > 8$?

A. –5 –4 –3 –2 –1 0 1 2 3 4 5
B. –5 –4 –3 –2 –1 0 1 2 3 4 5
C. –5 –4 –3 –2 –1 0 1 2 3 4 5
D. –5 –4 –3 –2 –1 0 1 2 3 4 5

**Questions 23 and 24 refer to the following graph.**

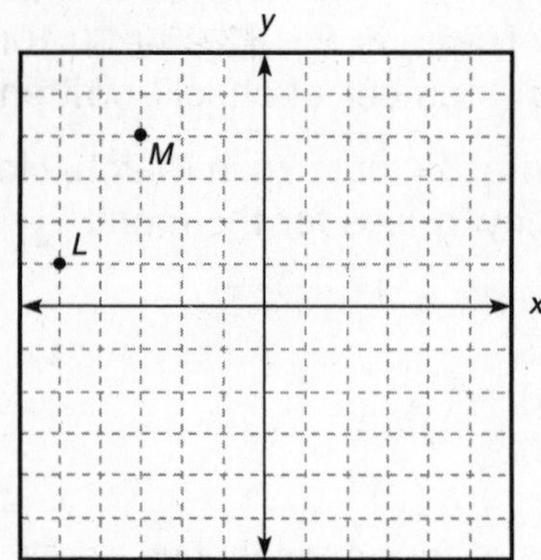


23. Which of the following ordered pairs shows the location of point $L$?

A. (–5, – 1)
B. (–5, 1)
C. (–1, 5)
D. (1, – 5)

24. What is the slope of the line that passes through points $L$ and $M$?

A. $\frac{-3}{2}$
B. $\frac{-2}{3}$
C. $\frac{2}{3}$
D. $\frac{3}{2}$

25. Bob, Celia, Sam, and Daniel contributed money to buy their boss a retirement gift. Sam and Daniel each gave the same amount of money. Celia gave \$12 more than Daniel. Bob gave half as much as Celia gave. If the four workers gave a total of \$81, how much did Sam give?

A. \$9
B. \$15
C. \$18
D. \$21

**STUDY ADVICE**

On Test Day, you will likely see several questions that give you a word problem, a table, or a graph, and ask you to apply an equation or infer an equation from the situation. Carefully review the last three lessons to master those skills.

26. What is the solution set of the inequality $-7x - 4 \geq x - 28$

A. $x \leq 3$
B. $x \geq 3$
C. $x \leq -3$
D. $x \geq -4$

27. A line goes through the points (0, 2) and (1, 3). What is the equation of the line?

A. $y = -\frac{1}{2}x + 3$
B. $y = \frac{1}{2}x + 2$
C. $y = x + 2$
D. $y = x + 3$

28. In a recent election, Perez got 5512 more votes than $\frac{1}{3}$ of the leading candidate's votes. Together the two candidates received 18,072 votes. How many people voted for Perez?

A. 6,024
B. 8,652
C. 9,420
D. 12,560

29. What is the value of $x$ in the equation $-4(x + 2) - 10 = 5x$ ?

A. $x = -18$
B. $x = -2$
C. $x = 2$
D. $x = 18$

30. Marcia counts the \$5 bills and \$10 bills in her cash register drawer. She counts a total of 35 bills with a total value of \$240. If $x$ = the number of \$5 bills in the drawer, which of the following equations could be used to find the number of \$5 bills in the drawer?

A. $\$5x + \$10x = 35$
B. $\$5x + \$10x + 35 = \$240$
C. $\$5(35 - x) + \$10x = \$240$
D. $\$5x + \$10(35 - x) = \$240$

**STUDY ADVICE**

Congratulations! You only have one more chapter to go in the Mathematics unit. If you've absorbed the concepts so far, you're almost ready to take the TASC Mathematics Test. Make sure to stick to your study schedule, and you'll soon be ready for Test Day.

**For questions 31 and 32, mark your answers in the grids below.**

31. The sum of five consecutive numbers is 370. What is the fourth number in the sequence?

32. A baseball pitcher's earned run average ($E$) is a function of the number of earned runs ($r$) given up and innings pitched ($i$). The function is written $E = \frac{9r}{i}$. What is the earned run average of a pitcher who gives up 8 runs in 18 innings?

31.

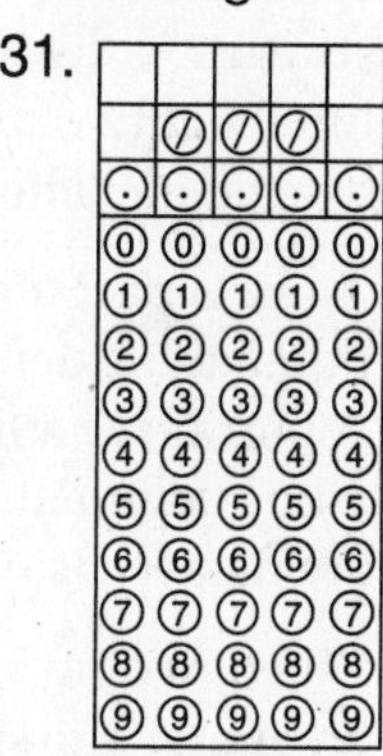

32.

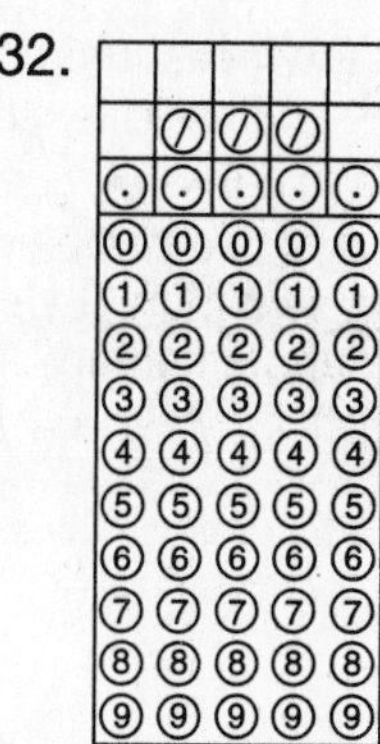

33. Tonya is selling boxes of cookies for charity. She will purchase five boxes of cookies herself and then try to sell more at her office. The following graph represents how many cookies she can sell as a function of how many of her coworkers are willing to purchase cookies.

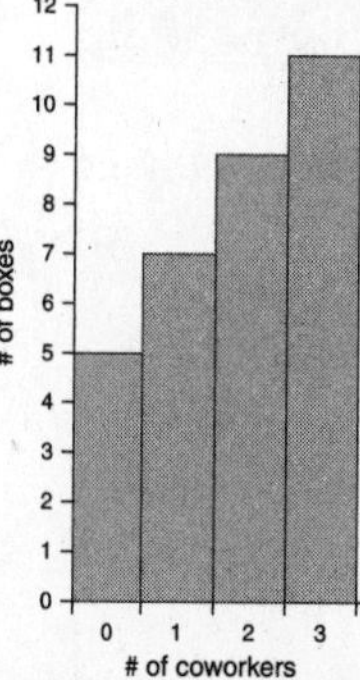


If $x$ is the number of Tonya's coworkers who are willing to buy cookies and $y$ is the number of boxes of cookies sold, which formula can be used to find the number of boxes of cookies Tonya will sell?

A. $y = 5 + x$
B. $y = 5 + 2x$
C. $y = 7 + x$
D. $y = 7 + 2x$

**Review your work using the explanations that start on page 702.**

LESSON 1

# Points, Lines, and Angles

### KEY IDEAS

- Most geometric figures are named by points that lie on the figure.
- Angles are measured in degrees and are classified by their measures.
- The sum of two complementary angles is 90°. The sum of two supplementary angles is 180°.

### TASC TEST TIP

*A geometric drawing may show several figures at once. As you read a problem, find each figure named in the problem.*

## Basic Definitions

A **point** is a single location in space. We assign a name to a point by writing a letter next to it. A **plane** is a collection of points that extends to form a flat surface. In the drawing, point *A* lies on plane *P*.

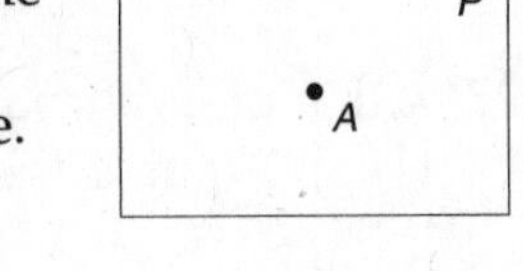


Much of your work in geometry will be concerned with lines and angles. A **line** is a straight pathway of points that extends indefinitely in two directions. A line may be named by a single letter or by two points on the line.

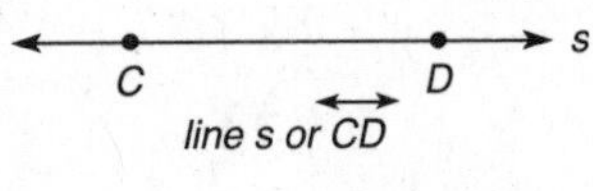


A **ray** is part of a line that begins at an endpoint and extends indefinitely in one direction. A portion of a line with two endpoints is called a **line segment.** Both rays and line segments are named using two points.

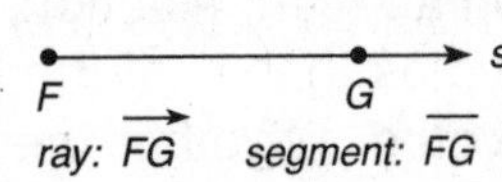


When two rays share an endpoint, they form an **angle.** The shared endpoint is the vertex of the angle. An angle can be named in different ways: by a number written in degrees inside the angle, by the vertex, or by the points on the angle. The symbol ∠ means angle.

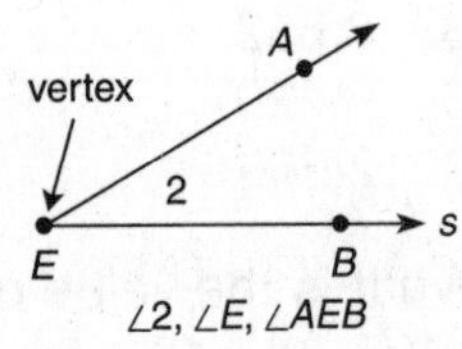


Angles are measured in degrees, indicated by a number and the symbol °. We classify angles by their measurement.

A **right angle** forms a square corner and measures 90°. A right angle is often identified by a small square drawn inside it, as shown here.

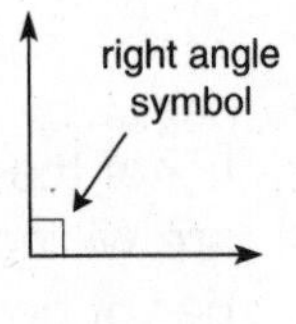


An **acute angle** is less than 90°.

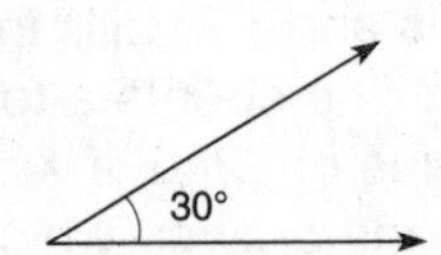


An **obtuse angle** is greater than 90° but less than 180°.

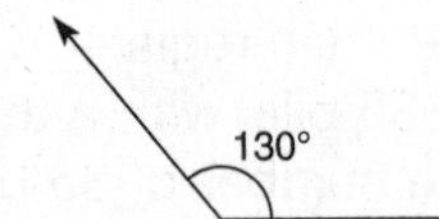


A **straight angle** measures 180°.

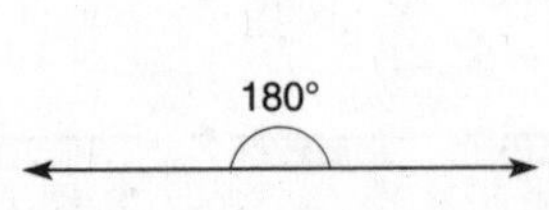


A **reflex angle** has a measure greater than 180° but less than 360°.

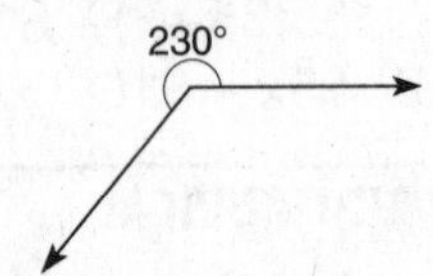


Some Mathematics Test problems are about angle relationships. When the sum of two angles is 90°, a right angle, the angles are **complementary.** When the sum of two angles is 180°, a line or straight angle, the angles are **supplementary.** You can use this information to solve for a missing angle measure.

# PRACTICE 1

**Example 1:** In the drawing, $\angle AOB$ and $\angle BOC$ are complementary. What is the measure of $\angle AOB$?

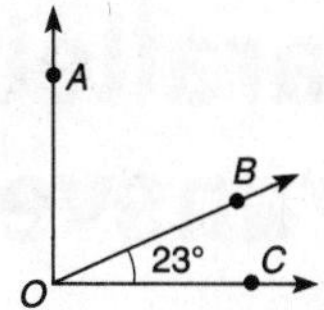


The measure of angle $BOC$ is given as 23°, or $m\angle BOC = 23°$. The sum of the angles is 90°. Therefore, $\angle AOB$ measures **67°**.

$$m\angle AOB + 23° = 90°$$
$$m\angle AOB = 90° - 23°$$
$$m\angle AOB = 67°$$

**Example 2:** In the drawing, $\angle 1$ and $\angle 2$ are supplementary. What is the measure of $\angle 1$?

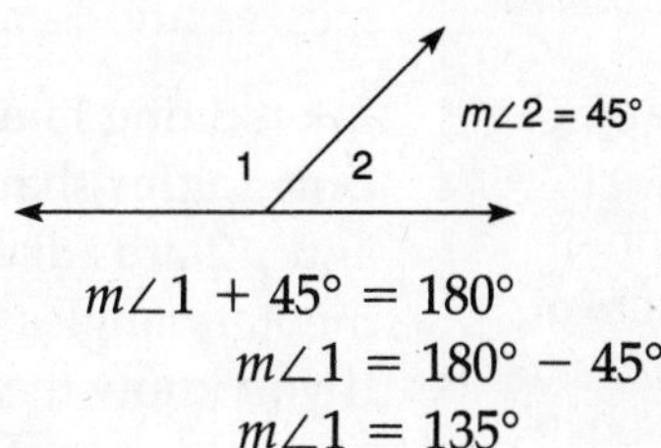


The measure of $\angle 2$ is 45°. The sum of the angles is 180°. $\angle 1$ measures **135°**.

$$m\angle 1 + 45° = 180°$$
$$m\angle 1 = 180° - 45°$$
$$m\angle 1 = 135°$$

---

**A. Classify each angle based on its angle measure.**

**1.** 55°
**2.** 95°
**3.** 180°
**4.** 18°
**5.** 270°
**6.** 90°
**7.** 30°
**8.** 110°

**B. Choose the <u>one best answer</u> to each question.**

**<u>Questions 9 and 10</u> refer to the drawing below.**

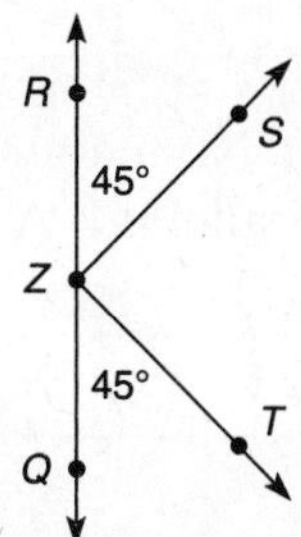


**9.** $\angle QZR$ is a straight angle. What is the measure of $\angle QZS$?

A. 135°
B. 125°
C. 90°
D. 60°

**10.** What kind of angle is $\angle SZT$?

A. acute
B. obtuse
C. right
D. straight

**<u>Questions 11 and 12</u> refer to the following drawing.**

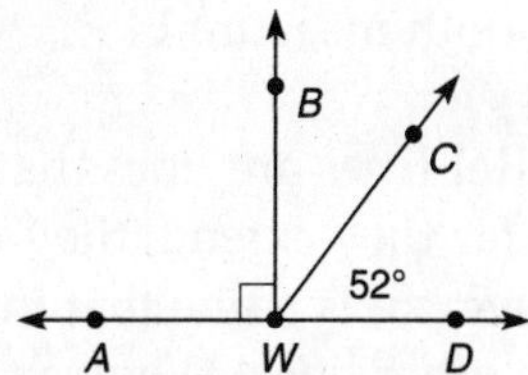


**11.** $\angle AWD$ is a straight angle. What is the measure of $\angle BWC$?

A. 38°
B. 52°
C. 128°
E. 142°

**12.** What type of angle is $\angle AWC$?

A. right
B. acute
C. obtuse
D. straight

**Review your work using the explanations that start on page 703.**

LESSON 2

# Parallel Lines and Transversals

## Working with Vertical Angles and Transversals

When two lines intersect, they form two pairs of vertical angles. **Vertical angles** have the same angle measure. In the drawing, $\angle 1$ and $\angle 3$ are vertical angles, as are $\angle 2$ and $\angle 4$.

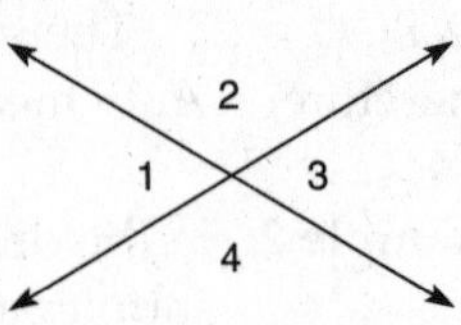


Intersecting lines also form adjacent angles. **Adjacent angles** share the same ray. For example, $\angle 1$ and $\angle 2$ are adjacent angles. The adjacent angles in this figure are supplementary angles because their sum is 180°, the measure of a straight angle. If you know the measure of one angle, you can find the measures of the other three angles.

**Example 1:** In the figure above, $m\angle 1 = 35°$. What are the measures of $\angle 2$, $\angle 3$, and $\angle 4$?

1. The measures of $\angle 1$ and $\angle 2$ are supplementary so their sum equals 180°. Solve for $\angle 2$.

   $m\angle + 35° = 180°$
   $m\angle 2 = 145°$

2. Angles 1 and 3 are vertical, so both measure 35°. Angles 2 and 4 are vertical, so both measure 145°.

   $\mathbf{m\angle 1 = 35°, m\angle 3 = 35°,}$
   $\mathbf{m\angle 2 = 145°, m\angle 4 = 145°}$

**Parallel lines** are lines that are exactly the same distance apart. No matter how far they extend, they will never touch. The symbol for parallel is $\|$. A **transversal** is a line that intersects two or more other lines. When a transversal intersects two parallel lines, special angle relationships are formed.

In the drawing, $M \| N$. The transversal, line $P$, forms eight angles.

Each angle matches another angle in the same position on the transversal. These angles, called **corresponding angles,** always have the same measure. The corresponding angles are $\angle 1$ and $\angle 5$, $\angle 2$ and $\angle 6$, $\angle 3$ and $\angle 7$, and $\angle 4$ and $\angle 8$.

**Alternate exterior angles,** which are also equal in measure, are on opposite sides of the transversal and are on the outside of the parallel lines. One pair of alternate exterior angles is $\angle 1$ and $\angle 7$. The other is $\angle 2$ and $\angle 8$.

**Alternate interior angles** are on opposite sides of the transversals and are inside the parallel lines. One pair of alternate interior angles is $\angle 3$ and $\angle 5$. The other is $\angle 4$ and $\angle 6$. Alternate interior angles are always equal in measure.

### KEY IDEAS

- Vertical angles, which are equal in measure, are formed when two lines intersect.
- When a transversal crosses two parallel lines, special angle relationships form.
- You can find the measure of any angle formed by the transversal if the measure of one angle is known.

### TASC TEST TIP

*You can often tell which angles are equal by looking at a figure. However, you must be able to prove two angles are equal to answer set-up questions and problems on logical reasoning.*

# PRACTICE 2

**Example 2:** In the figure, $C \parallel D$. If $m\angle 4 = 48°$, what is the measure of $\angle 5$?

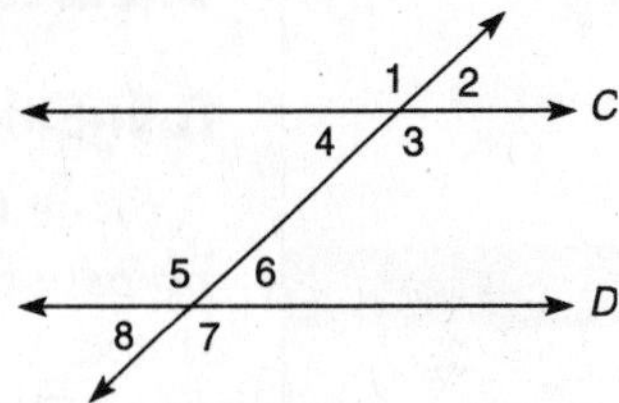


1. There are many ways to solve the problem. Here is one way: $\angle 4$ and $\angle 8$ are corresponding angles, so $m\angle 8 = 48°$.

2. $\angle 8$ and $\angle 5$ are supplementary angles, so $m\angle 5 + 48° = 180°$, and $m\angle 5 = 132°$.

**A. Using the figure shown at the right, solve as directed.**

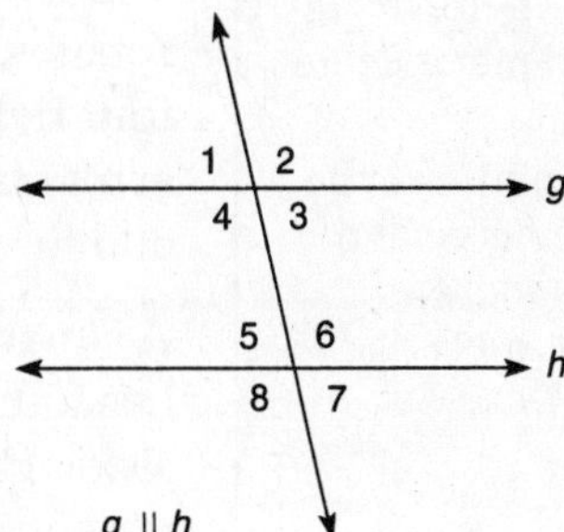


1. List one pair of alternate interior angles.
2. Which angle corresponds to $\angle 7$?
3. If $m\angle 3 = 80°$, what is $m\angle 8$?
4. List one pair of alternate exterior angles.
5. List one pair of vertical angles.
6. Which angle corresponds to $\angle 8$?

**B. Choose the <u>one best answer</u> to each question.**

**<u>Question 7</u> refers to the following figure.**

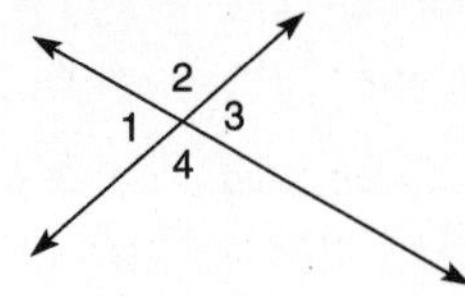


7. The measure of $\angle 3$ is 75°. What is the measure of $\angle 1$?
   A. 15°
   B. 75°
   C. 105°
   D. 115°

8. Which of the following is a true statement about corresponding angles?
   A. They are also supplementary angles.
   B. They are in the same position with respect to both parallel lines.
   C. They are also alternate interior angles.
   D. They are also alternate exterior angles.

**<u>Questions 9 and 10</u> refer to the following figure.**

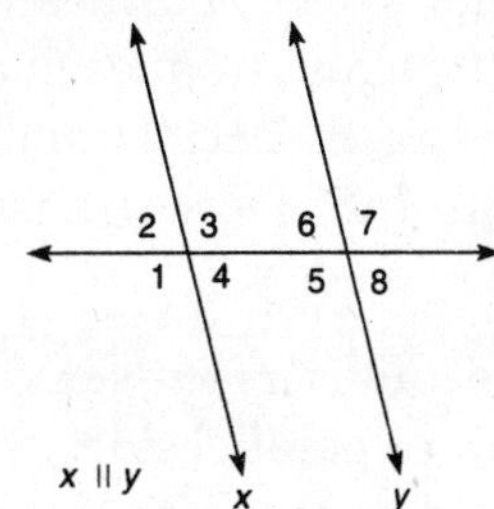


9. The measure of $\angle 7$ is 115°. What is the measure of $\angle 4$?
   A. 25°
   B. 65°
   C. 115°
   D. 245°

10. Which of the following angles is equal in measure to $\angle 2$?
   A. $\angle 1$
   B. $\angle 3$
   C. $\angle 5$
   D. $\angle 8$

**Review your work using the explanations that start on page 703.**

**STUDY ADVICE**

About a quarter of questions on the TASC Mathematics Test are about geometry. If these concepts seem new, take your time absorbing the basics. Geometry is challenging for a lot of people, but you can master these skills with practice.

# Plane Figures

## Four-Sided Plane Figures

A **plane figure** is a set of line segments, all lying on a single plane. To prepare for the TASC Mathematics Test, learn the properties of each shape. You will need to identify the characteristics of different types of four-sided plane figures and draw conclusions about their angles and sides.

**Sides with the same markings are equal.**

You are already familiar with rectangles and squares. A **rectangle** is a four-sided figure with four right angles. The opposite sides (sides across from each other) are the same length, and they are parallel.

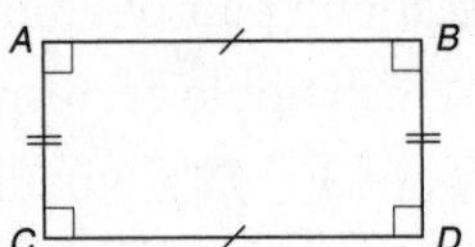


A **square** is actually a kind of rectangle. It, too, has four right angles with parallel opposite sides. However, a square has one additional property: its four sides are all the same length.

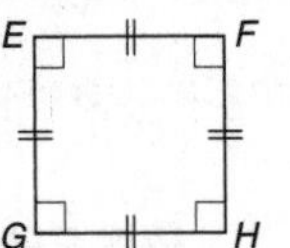


A **parallelogram** is a four-sided figure whose opposite sides are parallel and the same length. In addition, its opposite angles (the angles diagonally across from each other) are also equal in measure. A special parallelogram, called a **rhombus** (not shown), has four sides of equal length.

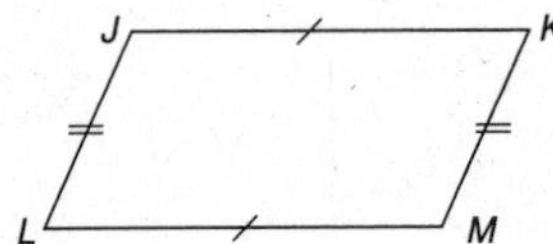


A **trapezoid** is a four-sided figure with exactly one pair of parallel sides. The definition of a trapezoid does not dictate the measure of the angles or the lengths of the sides.

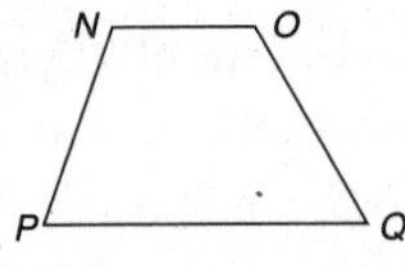


All four-sided plane figures have one important property in common. The sum of the measures of the interior angles is 360°. You can use this fact to find a missing angle measure.

**KEY IDEAS**

- Plane figures are classified by the properties of their sides and angles.
- The sum of the interior angles of any four-sided plane figure is 360°.
- By using the properties of any four-sided plane figure and algebraic reasoning, you can find missing angle measures.

**TASC TEST TIP**

*Don't rely on sight alone to identify a geometric figure. Read carefully to see which properties are given. Then identify the figure based on the properties.*

**Example 1:** In figure *ABCD*, the opposite sides are parallel. What is the measure of $\angle A$?

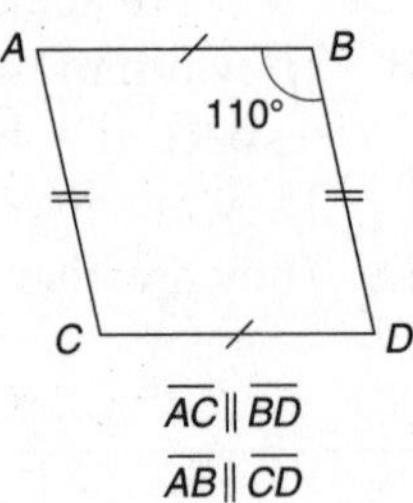


1. Identify the figure. The notation on the drawing tells you that the opposite sides are equal in measure. Since they are also parallel, the figure is a parallelogram.

2. Find the measure of $\angle C$. The opposite angles of a parallelogram are equal in measure; therefore, $m\angle C = m\angle B$. Both $\angle B$ and $\angle C$ measure 110°.

3. Find the measure of $\angle A$. You know the measures of $\angle A$ and $\angle D$ are equal and that the sum of all four angles equals 360°. Let $x = m\angle A$. Therefore, $2x =$ the sum of $m\angle A$ and $m\angle D$. Write an equation and solve.

$$2x + 110° + 110° = 360°$$
$$2x + 220° = 360°$$
$$2x = 140°$$
$$x = \mathbf{70°}$$

The measure of $\angle A$ is **70°**.

---

**A. List the names of four-sided plane figures introduced on page 404 that can exhibit the following properties. Write *None* if no four-sided plane figure has the given property.**

**1.** four right angles
**2.** opposite sides are equal in length
**3.** exactly one pair of parallel sides
**4.** all angles are equal in measure
**5.** only three right angles
**6.** opposite angles are equal in measure
**7.** all four sides are equal in length
**8.** sum of interior angles is 360°
**9.** sides are all of different lengths
**10.** four equal angles and four equal sides

**B. Choose the <u>one best answer</u> to each question.**

**<u>Questions 11 and 12</u> refer to the following figure.**

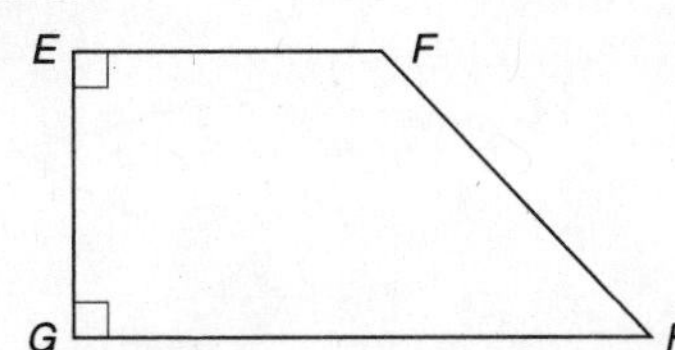


**11.** Angle $F$ is 20° more than three times the measure of $\angle H$. What is the measure of $\angle F$?

A. 40°
B. 120°
C. 140°
D. 180°

**12.** In order for figure $EFGH$ to be a trapezoid, which of the following must be a true statement?

A. $EF$ is the same length as $FH$.
B. $EF \parallel GH$.
C. $m\angle F = m\angle H$.
D. $m\angle G = m\angle F$.

**<u>Question 13</u> refers to the following figure.**

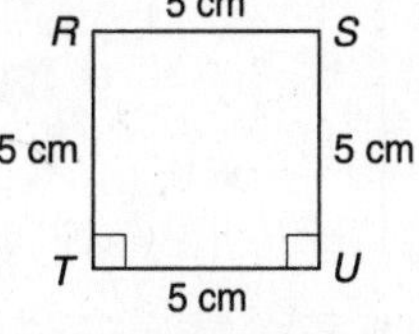


**13.** If the opposite sides in figure $RSUT$ are parallel, what is the measure of $\angle R$?

A. 5°
B. 20°
C. 90°
D. 270°

---

**14.** A four-sided plane figure has sides measuring 10, 15, 10, and 15. The opposite angles are equal, but there are no right angles. What is the figure?

A. rhombus
B. rectangle
C. parallelogram
D. trapezoid

**Review your work using the explanations that start on page 704.**

LESSON 4

# Triangles

## The Properties of Triangles

A **triangle** is a closed three-sided plane figure. From the definition, we can infer other properties. Since a triangle has three sides, it must also have three interior angles and three vertices.

A triangle is named by writing its vertices in any order. The triangle shown at right could be named $\Delta DEF$. Its sides are $DE$, $EF$, and $DF$.

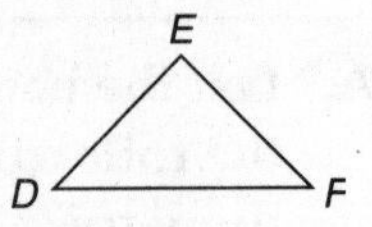


Triangles can be classified by the lengths of their sides and by the measures of their angles. In the figures below, sides with the same number of marks are equal.

**Classified by Side Lengths**

**equilateral triangle**
All sides are equal in length. Note that the angles also are equal.

**isosceles triangle**
Exactly two sides are equal in length. Note that the two angles opposite these sides are equal.

**scalene triangle**
No sides are equal in length, and no angles are equal.

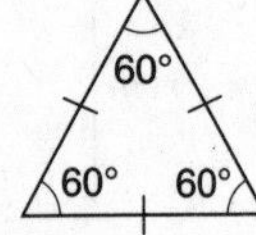


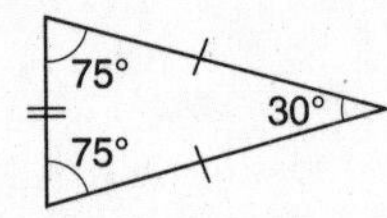


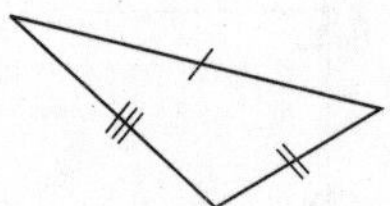

**Classified by Angle Measures**

**right triangle**
One angle measures 90°.

**acute triangle**
All angles measure less than 90°.

**obtuse triangle**
One angle is greater than 90°.

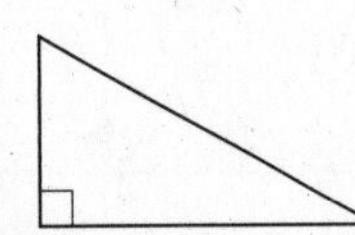

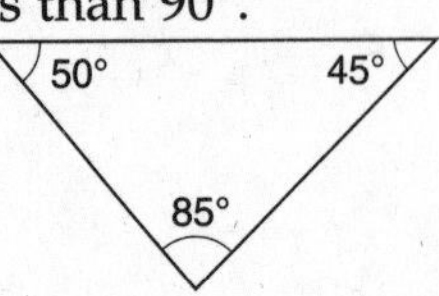

Each triangle can be classified in two ways.

**Example 1:** What kind of triangle is $\Delta PQR$?

1. Classify by its sides: Two sides have the same length, so $\Delta PQR$ is an isosceles triangle.
2. Classify by its angles: $\angle P$ is a right angle, so $\Delta PQR$ is a right triangle.

P
10 10
Q 14 R

$\Delta PQR$ is a **right isosceles triangle**.

### KEY IDEAS

- Triangles are named by their vertices.
- They are classified in two ways: by their side lengths and by their angle measures.
- The sum of the interior angles of any triangle is 180°.

### TASC TEST TIP

*Classify triangles by their properties, not by how they look. For example, the triangle in Example 1 may not immediately look like a right triangle because the right angle is at the top.*

# PRACTICE 4

The sum of the measures of the interior angles of any triangle is 180°. We can use this fact to solve for a missing angle.

**Example 2:** In $\Delta ABC$, $\angle A$ measures 55° and $\angle B$ measures 100°. What is the measure of $\angle C$?

Write an equation and solve.

$$55° + 100° + \angle C = 180°$$
$$155° + \angle C = 180°$$
$$\angle C = 25°$$

The measure of $\angle C$ is **25°**.

---

**A. Classify each triangle in two ways.**

1. 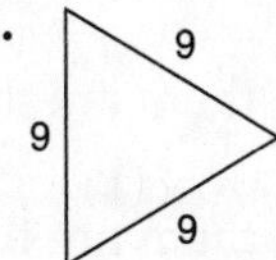


2. 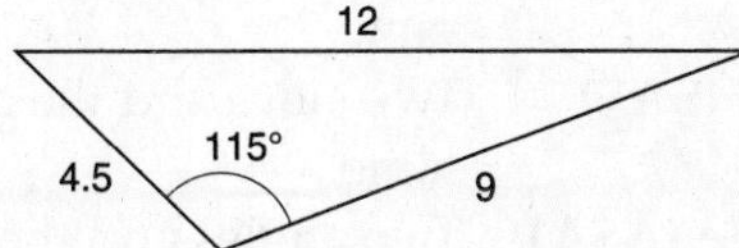


3. 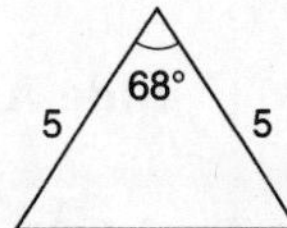


**B. Find the measure of the unknown angle in each triangle.**

4. 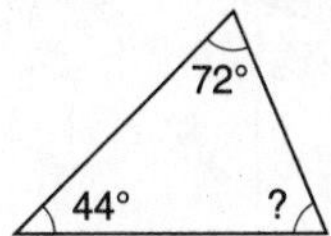


5. 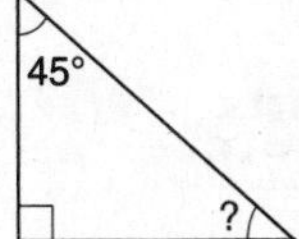


6. 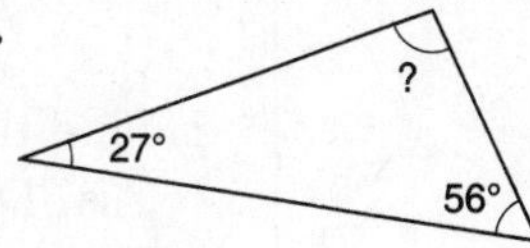


**C. Choose the <u>one best answer</u> to each question.**

**<u>Questions 7 and 8</u> refer to the following figure.**

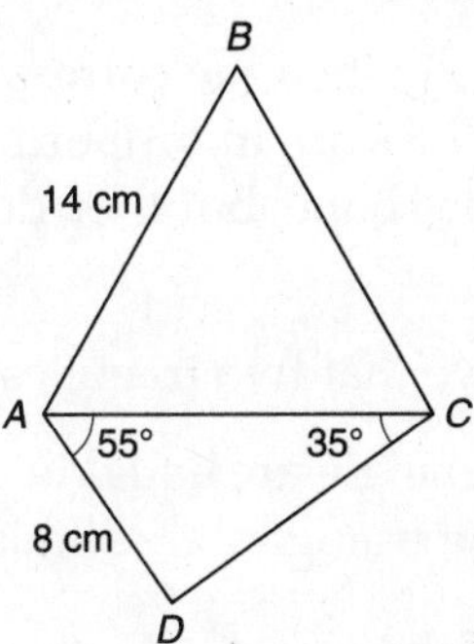


7. If $\angle DAB$ measures 115° and $\angle DCB$ measures 95°, what is the length of side $AC$ in centimeters? (*Hint*: Use the facts in the problem to find $m\angle BAC$ and $m\angle BCA$.)

   A. 6
   B. 8
   C. 14
   D. 22

8. What kind of triangle is $\Delta ACD$?

   A. isosceles
   B. acute
   C. right
   D. obtuse

---

9. One angle in a scalene triangle measures 38°, and another angle measures 56°. What is the measure of the third angle?

   A. 38°
   B. 56°
   C. 86°
   D. 124°

**Review your work using the explanations that start on page 704.**

LESSON 5

# Congruent and Similar Triangles

**KEY IDEAS**

- Congruent figures are the same size and shape. Similar figures are the same shape, but they do not have to be the same size.
- Prove triangles are congruent using the rules SSS, SAS, or ASA.
- Triangles are similar if two angles are congruent or if all corresponding sides are in proportion.

## Comparing Triangles

Figures are **congruent** (indicated by the symbol ≅) when they have exactly the same size and shape. In other words, two figures are congruent if their corresponding parts (the angles and sides) are congruent. You can often tell that two geometric shapes are congruent by looking. However, in geometry, you must be able to prove that figures are congruent.

Two triangles are congruent if the following corresponding parts are congruent:

**Side-Side-Side (SSS)** The side measures for both triangles are the same.

**Side-Angle-Side (SAS)** Two sides and the angle between them are the same.

**Angle-Side-Angle (ASA)** Two angles and the side between them are the same.

**Example 1:** Are triangles $ABD$ and $BCD$ congruent?

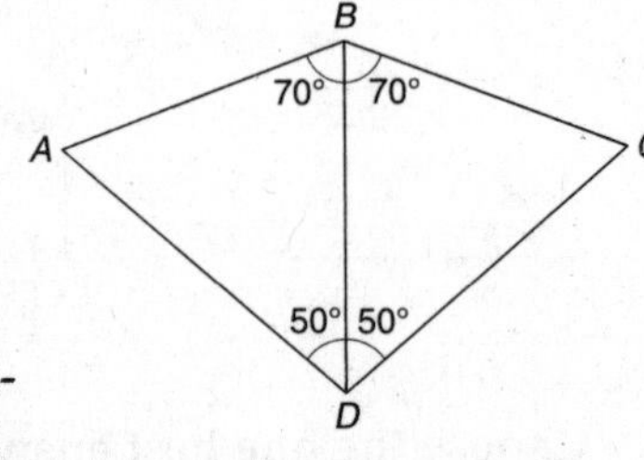


1. Find the known corresponding parts: $\angle ABD \cong \angle CBD$ and $\angle ADB \cong \angle CDB$. Both triangles share side $BD$.
2. Is this enough information to prove the triangles are congruent? Yes, two angles and the side between them are equal. Using the ASA rule, $\Delta ABD \cong \Delta BCD$.

## Understanding Similarity

Figures are **similar** (shown by the symbol ~) when the corresponding angles are congruent and the corresponding sides are in proportion. In other words, similar figures always have the same shape, but they do not have to be the same size.

There are two rules that you can use to prove that two triangles are similar:

**Rule 1:** If two angle measures in the first triangle are equal to two angle measures in the second triangle, the triangles are similar.

**Rule 2:** If all corresponding sides have the same ratio, the triangles are similar.

**Example 2:** Are triangles $JKL$ and $MNO$ similar?

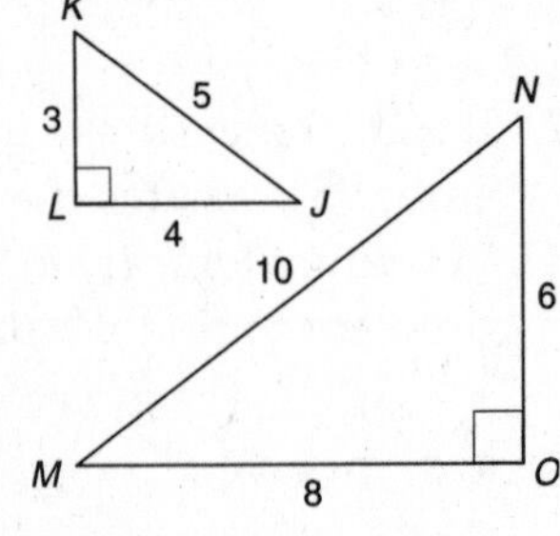


1. Compare corresponding angles. Since only one angle measure is given, you cannot use Rule 1 to prove the triangles are similar.
2. Write ratios comparing the sides in the first triangle to the corresponding sides in the second triangle. Each ratio is equal to $\frac{1}{2}$.

$$\frac{\Delta JKL}{\Delta MNO} \quad \frac{3}{6} = \frac{4}{8} = \frac{5}{10} = \frac{1}{2}$$

Because the ratios are equal, the triangles are similar: **ΔJKL ~ ΔMNO.**

**TASC TEST TIP**

*When a figure is flipped or turned, it may be difficult to identify corresponding parts. Try redrawing one of the figures so that it is turned to match the first figure. Always label your sketch carefully.*

# PRACTICE 5

If you know that two triangles are similar, you can use proportion to find an unknown measure.

**Example 3:** $\Delta XYZ \sim \Delta STU$. What is the measure of side $ST$?

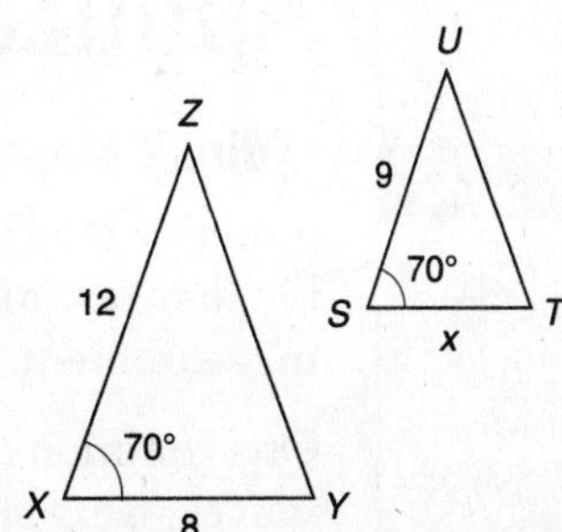


Side $SU$ corresponds to side $XZ$, and side $ST$ corresponds to side $XY$. Set up a proportion and solve.

$$\frac{SU}{XZ}=\frac{ST}{XY} \quad \frac{9}{12}=\frac{x}{8} \quad 12x=72 \quad x=6$$

Side $ST$ measures **6 units.**

---

**A. For these items, the figures are not drawn to scale. Decide whether the triangles are congruent. Write *Yes, No,* or *Not Enough Information.***

1.

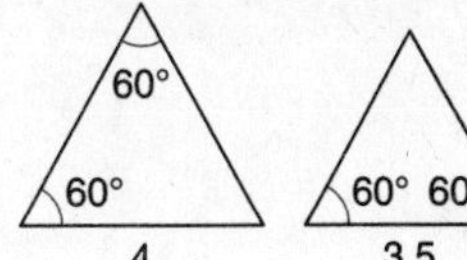


2.

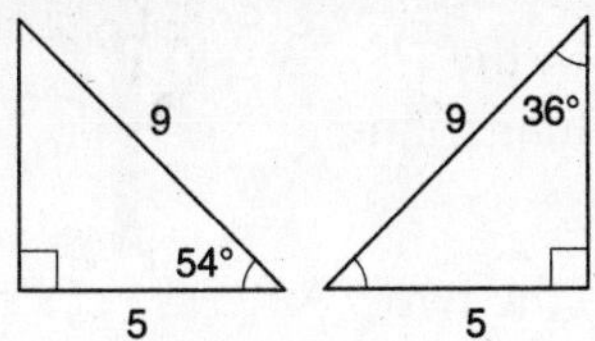


3.

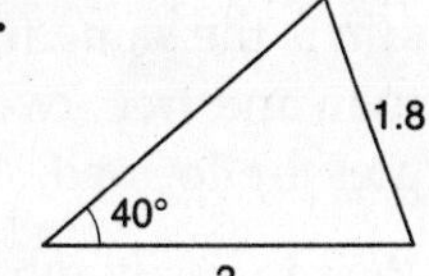


1.8
40°
3

**B. Choose the one best answer to each question.**

**Questions 4 and 5 refer to the following figure.**

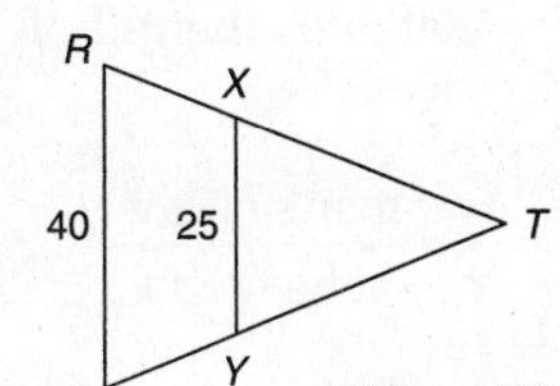


4. What is the measure of side $ST$ if side $YT$ measures 30 units?

   A. 40
   B. 45
   C. 48
   D. 55

5. If $m\angle S = 68°$ and $m\angle T = 48°$, what is the measure of $\angle TXY$?

   A. 48°
   B. 64°
   C. 68°
   D. 116°

**Question 6 refers to the following figure.**

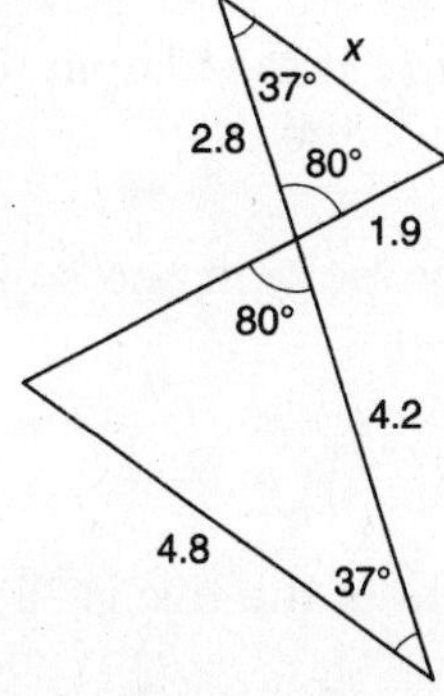


6. What is the measure of the side labeled $x$?

   A. 2.5
   B. 2.9
   C. 3.2
   D. 3.8

**Review your work using the explanations that start on page 704.**

LESSON 6

# Similar Triangle Applications

KEY IDEAS

- Use triangle relationships to indirectly measure distances.
- Objects and their shadows form similar triangles because the sun strikes both at the same angle.
- Use the corresponding angles and sides in similar triangles to measure the distance across a large object.

## Indirect Measurement

Similar triangles are often used to measure objects that would be impossible to measure using ordinary tools. This process is called **indirect measurement.**

One common application involves using shadows to find the height of a tall object. In the diagram, both a man and a tree cast shadows at the same time of day. Since the angle of the sun is the same for both the man and tree, two similar triangles are formed.

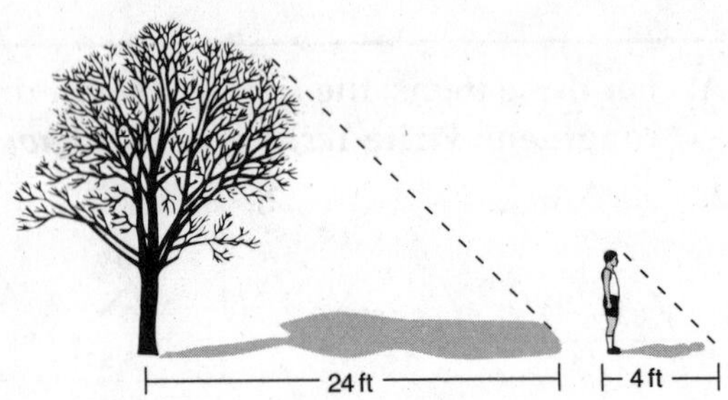


We can easily measure the two shadows using ordinary tools. We can also measure the man's height. Using these facts, we can solve for the height of the tree.

**Example 1:** If the man in the diagram is 6 feet tall, what is the height of the tree?

Write a proportion and solve. $\frac{\text{man's shadow}}{\text{tree's shadow}} \quad \frac{4}{24} = \frac{6}{x} = \frac{\text{man's height}}{\text{tree's height}}$

$$24(6) = 4x$$
$$144 = 4x$$
$$36 = x$$

The height of the tree is **36 feet.**

TASC TEST TIP

*Sometimes you can easily see the scale used in a problem. In Example 1, the tree's shadow is six times the man's shadow; therefore, the tree's height must be six times the man's height: 6 × 6 = 36 ft.*

We also use indirect measurement to measure distance across a large object.

**Example 2:** An engineer needs to know the width of a small lake. Using surveyor's tools, she marks off two similar triangles. She measures the distances shown on the diagram. Using her findings, what is the width of the lake?

The 10-ft side corresponds to the 25-ft side. The 24-ft side of the small triangle corresponds to the lake's width.

$\frac{10}{25} = \frac{24}{x}$

$$25(24) = 10x$$
$$600 = 10x$$
$$60 = x$$

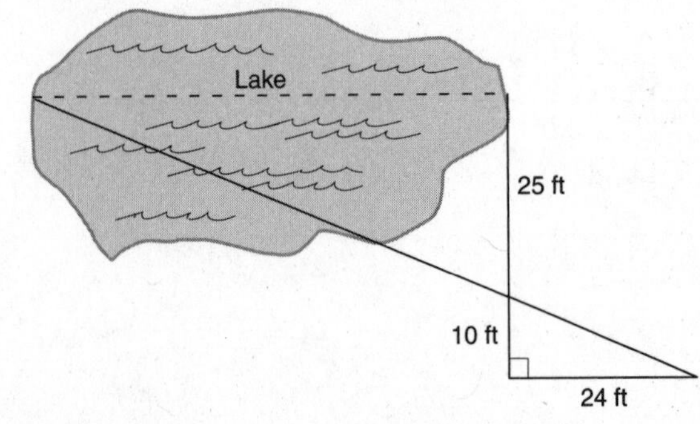


The lake is **60 feet wide.**

# PRACTICE 6

**Choose the one best answer to each question.**

1. An 8-foot-tall street sign casts a 6-foot shadow at the same time that a building casts a 48-foot shadow. How many feet tall is the building?

   A. 36
   B. 54
   C. 64
   D. 96

**Question 2 refers to the following diagram.**

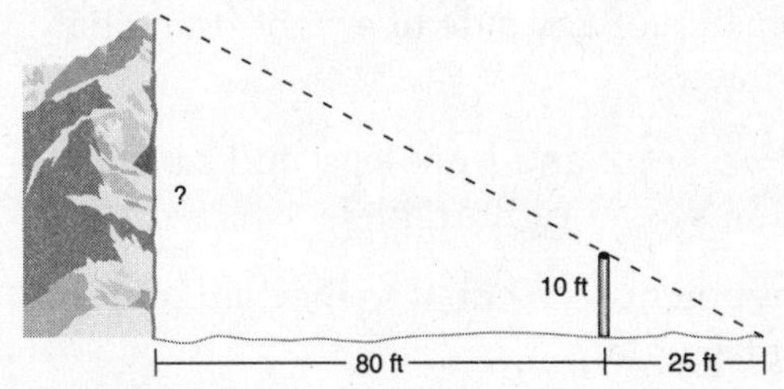


2. To find the height of a cliff, a surveyor puts a 10-foot pole in the ground, 80 feet from the base of the cliff. He then determines the point on the ground from which he can sight both the top of the pole and top of the cliff. Using the distances shown in the diagram, what is the height of the cliff?

   A. 32
   B. 42
   C. 105
   D. 200

3. A meter stick is placed in the ground near a flagpole. At the time that the meter stick casts a shadow 2.5 meters in length, the flagpole casts a shadow 22.5 meters long. Which of the following proportions can be used to find the height of the flagpole ($x$) in meters?

   A. $\frac{2.5}{22.5} = \frac{1}{x}$
   B. $\frac{22.5}{2.5} = \frac{1}{x}$
   C. $\frac{1}{2.5} = \frac{22.5}{x}$
   D. $\frac{22.5}{1} = \frac{x}{2.5}$

**Question 4 refers to the following diagram.**

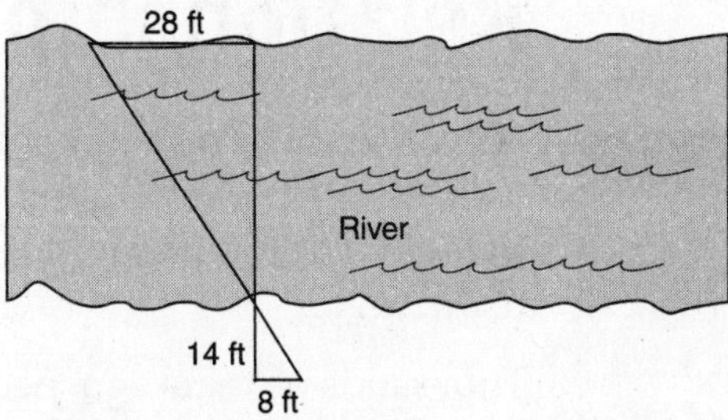


4. To find the distance across a river, a surveyor marks off two similar right triangles. Using the distances shown in the diagram, what is the distance, in feet, from one bank of the river to the other?

   A. 36
   B. 39
   C. 42
   D. 49

5. Phil is building a frame to hold a hammock. He wants to place a metal brace across the frame as shown in the drawing below. If he places the brace as shown in the diagram, what will be the length of the brace in feet?

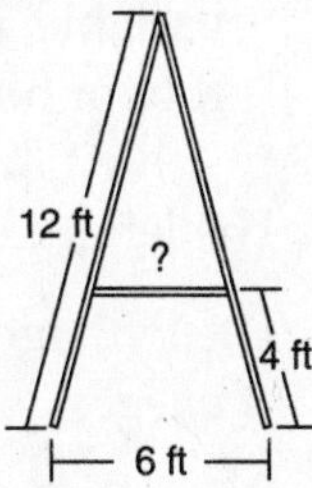


   A. 3
   B. 4
   C. 6
   D. 8

**Review your work using the explanations that start on page 704.**

## STUDY ADVICE

You will likely see a small number of questions about similar or congruent triangles on Test Day. However, you will see more questions that test area and volume (coming up in the next few lessons). So, review the concepts here but also leave yourself time to study area and volume in depth.

LESSON 7

# Pythagorean Relationship

KEY IDEAS

- The hypotenuse is the longest side of a right triangle. It is found opposite the right angle.
- The sum of the squares of the legs of a right triangle equals the square of the hypotenuse.

As you know, a right triangle has one right angle. The side directly across from the right angle, called the **hypotenuse**, is the longest side of the right triangle. The remaining sides, the rays of the right angle, are the **legs** of the triangle.

Thousands of years ago, people found a special relationship, called the **Pythagorean relationship**, among the sides of a right triangle. You can use this relationship to find the measure of any side of a right triangle if the other two side measures are known.

**Pythagorean relationship** $a^2 + b^2 = c^2$; $a$ and $b$ are legs, and $c$ is the hypotenuse of a right triangle

In other words, the square of the hypotenuse is equal to the sum of the squares of the two legs of the right triangle.

**Example 1:** What is the length of the hypotenuse of the right triangle shown in the diagram?

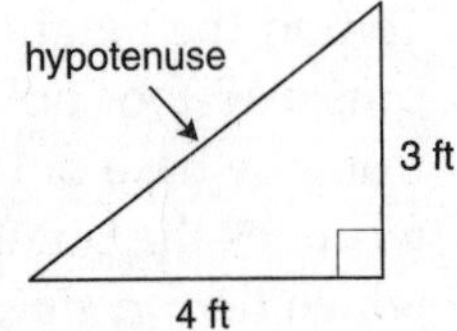


1. The lengths of the legs are 3 ft and 4 ft. Let one leg equal $a$ and the other equal $b$.
2. Solve for $c$. Substitute the values.
3. When one side of an equation equals a squared variable, isolate the variable by finding the square root of both sides.

$$a^2 + b^2 = c^2$$
$$3^2 + 4^2 = c^2$$
$$9 + 16 = c^2$$
$$25 = c^2$$
$$\sqrt{25} = c$$
$$5 = c$$

The length of the hypotenuse is **5 feet**.

TASC TEST TIP

*Watch for right triangles with sides in a 3-4-5 or 5-12-13 ratio. These triangles often appear on math tests because the measures of the sides are all whole numbers.*

The Pythagorean relationship can also be used to solve for the length of a leg.

**Example 2:** If John places a 13-foot ladder 3 feet from the base of a wall, how far up the wall will the ladder reach to the nearest tenth foot?

The wall, ground, and ladder form a right triangle. The hypotenuse is 13 ft in length. One leg is 3 ft. You need to find the length of the other leg.

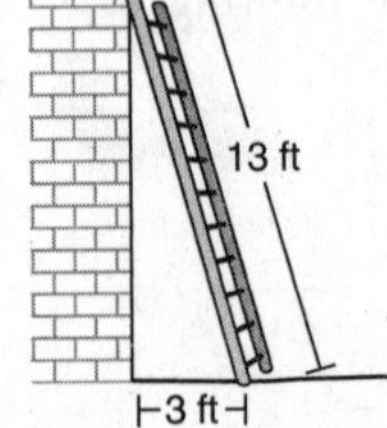


$$a^2 + b^2 = c^2$$
$$3^2 + b^2 = 13^2$$
$$9 + b^2 = 169$$
$$b^2 = 160$$
$$b = \sqrt{160}$$
$$b \approx 12.6$$

The ladder will extend **12.6 feet** up the wall.

**Note:** Most of the time, you will need to use your calculator for the final step when using the Pythagorean relationship. To find the square root of 160 on the TI-30XS MultiView™ calculator, press: [2nd] [$x^2$] 160 [enter] (use [◄►] to convert the result from a radical to a decimal format).

# PRACTICE 7

Some right triangles display special proportions, which are worth memorizing.
A right triangle whose angles are 45°, 45°, and 90° displays the following relationship:
leg : leg : hypotenuse = $x : x : x\sqrt{2}$.
A right triangle whose angles are 30°, 60°, and 90° displays the following relationship:
leg : leg : hypotenuse = $x : x\sqrt{3} : 2x$.

---

**A. The lengths of two sides of a right triangle are given. Find the length of the remaining side to the nearest tenth unit. You may use a calculator.**

**1.** leg $a$: 8 in
leg $b$: 8 in
hypotenuse $c$: ? in

**2.** leg $a$: 9 yd
leg $b$: 12 yd
hypotenuse $c$: ? yd

**3.** leg $a$: 1.5 cm
leg $b$: 2 cm
hypotenuse $c$: ? cm

**4.** leg $a$: ? m
leg $b$: 3 m
hypotenuse $c$: 6 m

**5.** leg $a$: 6 mm
leg $b$: ? mm
hypotenuse $c$: 10 mm

**6.** leg $a$: ? ft
leg $b$: 5 ft
hypotenuse $c$: 18 ft

**7.** leg $a$: 7 cm
leg $b$: 10 cm
hypotenuse $c$: ? cm

**8.** leg $a$: 15 in
leg $b$: ? in
hypotenuse $c$: 30 in

**9.** leg $a$: 4 km
leg $b$: 5 km
hypotenuse $c$: ? km

**B. Choose the one best answer to each question.**

**10.** On a coordinate plane, points $A$, $B$, and $C$ can be connected to form a right triangle.

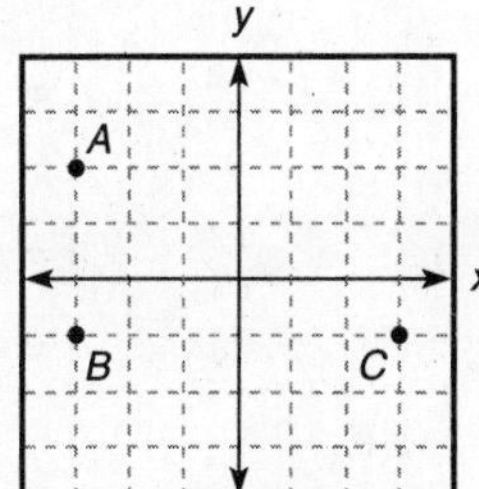


What is the distance from $A$ to $C$, to the nearest tenth unit? (*Hint:* Count units to find the lengths of the sides, and use the Pythagorean relationship to find the distance between the points.)

A. 5.2
B. 6.7
C. 8.4
D. 10.1

**11.** The two shorter sides of a right triangle measure 18 ft and 24 ft. What is the measure in feet of the third side?

A. 25
B. 28
C. 30
D. 42

**12.** Jan has built a rectangular frame out of wood to use for the bottom of a platform. He wants to add a diagonal brace as shown in the drawing below.

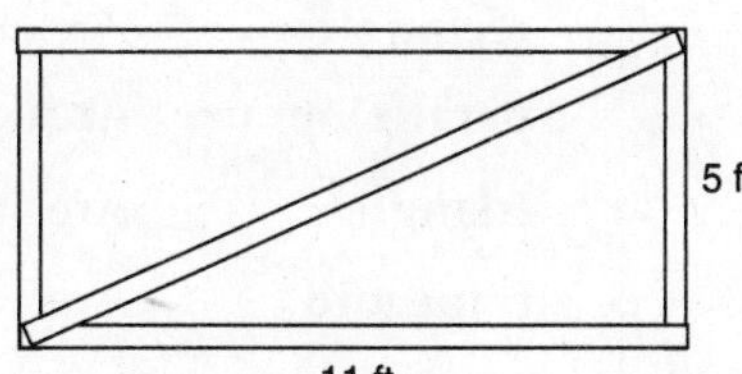


What will the length of the brace be, to the nearest tenth of a foot?

A. 16.0
B. 13.7
C. 12.8
D. 12.1

**13.** The hypotenuse of a right triangle measures 39 inches. If one leg measures 15 inches, what is the measure of the other leg, in inches?

A. 36
B. 24
C. 18
D. 12

**Review your work using the explanations that start on page 704.**

LESSON 8

# Perimeter and Area

## KEY IDEAS

- Perimeter is the distance around a figure.
- Area is the measure of the space inside a flat figure. It is measured in square units.
- You need to memorize the formulas on this page except those for area of a parallelogram and area of a trapezoid.

**Perimeter** is the distance around a figure. To find perimeter, simply add the lengths of the sides. For common figures, you can apply a formula to find the perimeter. You need to memorize these formulas.

| | | |
|---|---|---|
| **square** | Perimeter = 4 × side | $P = 4s$ |
| **rectangle** | Perimeter = 2 × length + 2 × width | $P = 2l + 2w$ |
| **triangle** | Perimeter = $\text{side}_1 + \text{side}_2 + \text{side}_3$ | $P = a + b + c$ |

**Example 1:** A rectangle is 16 inches long and 9 inches wide. What is the perimeter of the rectangle?

Use the formula: Perimeter = 2 × length + 2 × width
= 2 × 16 + 2 × 9
= 32 + 18
= **50 in**

**Area** is the measure of the space inside a flat figure. Area is measured in square units. For example, if the sides of a figure are measured in inches, its area will be measured in square inches. The formulas for finding area are shown below.

| | | |
|---|---|---|
| **square** | Area = $\text{side}^2$ | $A = s^2$ |
| **rectangle** | Area = length × width | $A = lw$ |
| **parallelogram** | Area = base × height | $A = bh$ |
| **triangle** | Area = $\frac{1}{2}$ × base × height | $A = \frac{1}{2}bh$ |
| **trapezoid** | Area = $\frac{1}{2}$ × height $(\text{base}_1 + \text{base}_2)$ | $A = \frac{1}{2}h(b_1 + b_2)$ |

## TASC TEST TIP

*No area formulas will appear on the formula sheet provided on the TASC. You will need to memorize the formulas on this page.*

Three of the formulas mention two new measures: base and height. The **base** is one side of the figure. The **height** is the length from the vertex to the base, forming a right angle to the base.

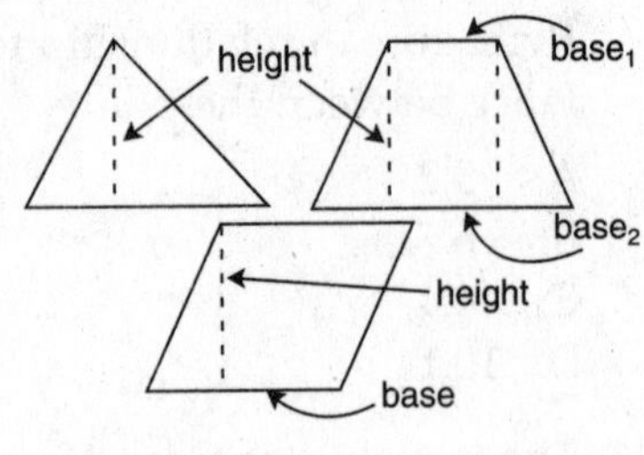


**Example 2:** Find the area of figure *ABCD*.

1. Identify the figure. *ABCD* is a parallelogram.
2. Find the facts you need. To use the formula for finding the area of a parallelogram, you need to know the height and the length of the base. Ignore the length of side *BD*.
3. Use the formula Area = base × height.

   Area = 12 × 7

   = **84 sq cm or 84 cm²**

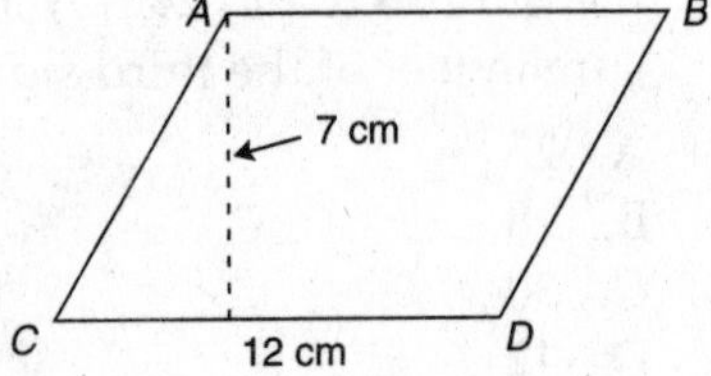

# PRACTICE 8

**A. Find the area and perimeter of each figure.**

**1.**

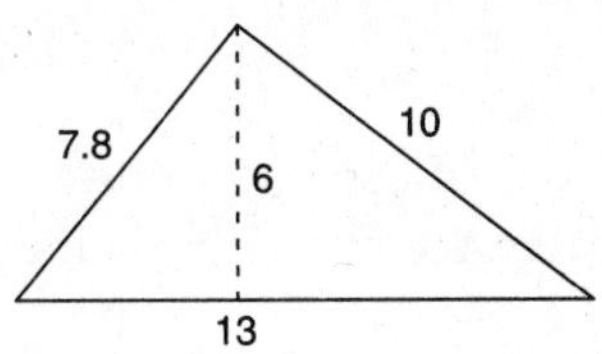


**2.**

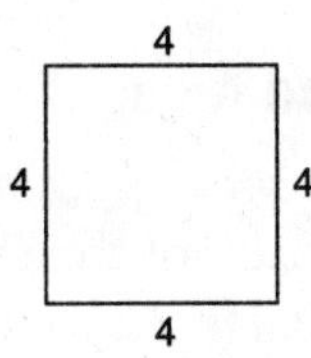


**3.**

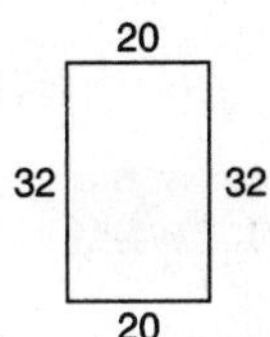


**4.**

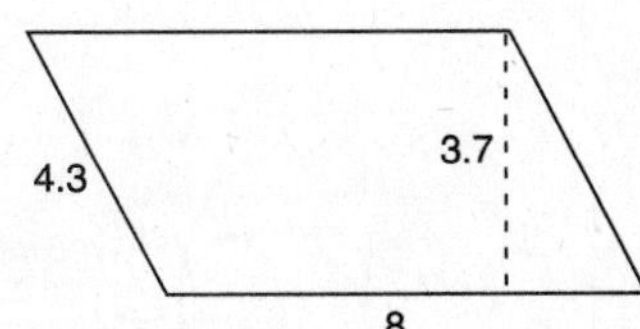


**5.**

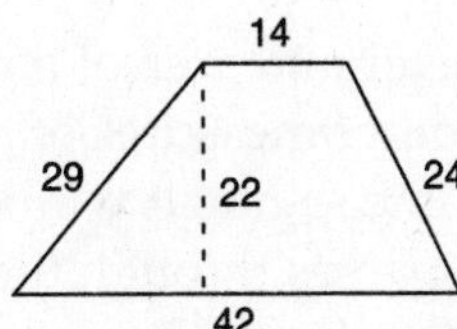


**6.**

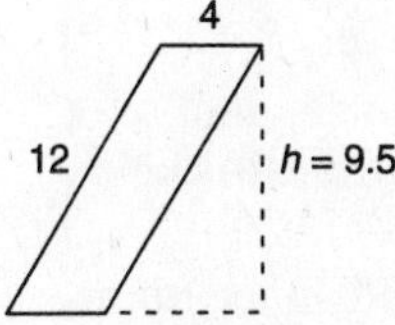


**B. Choose the one best answer to each question.**

**Question 7 refers to the following figure.**

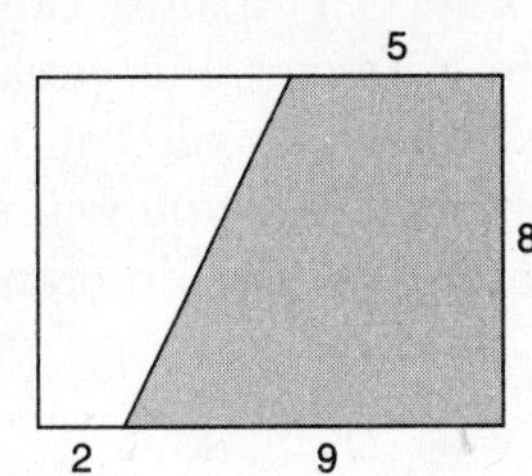


7. What is the area in square inches of the shaded portion of the rectangle?

   A. 38
   B. 40
   C. 56
   D. 88

8. The four sides of a rectangle measure 9 feet, 6 feet, 9 feet, and 6 feet. What is the area of the rectangle in square feet?

   A. 30
   B. 36
   C. 54
   D. 81

9. Martin is building a rectangular patio centered on one side of his yard. The rest of his yard, shown in the diagram, is planted in grass.

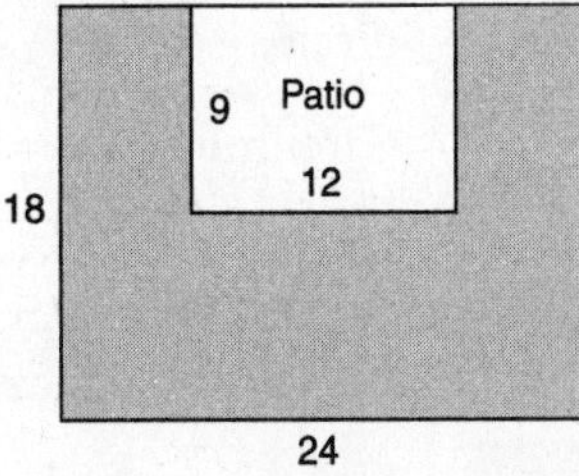


   If the measurements in the diagram are in feet, what is the square footage of the grass portion of Martin's yard?

   A. 108
   B. 162
   C. 324
   D. 432

10. A square measures 6 centimeters on one side. What is the perimeter of the square in centimeters?

    A. 12
    B. 24
    C. 36
    D. 216

**Review your work using the explanations that start on page 705.**

LESSON 9

# Circles

## Circumference and Area

A **circle** is a closed set of points that are all the same distance from a single point, the center of the circle. The **circumference** of a circle is its perimeter, or the distance around the circle. The **area** of a circle is the space inside the circle.

To find perimeter and area of a circle, you need to know two other measures of a circle. The **diameter** is a line segment with endpoints on the circle that passes through the center of the circle. The **radius** is a line segment that connects the center of the circle to any point on the circle. As you can see from the diagram, the radius is one-half the diameter.

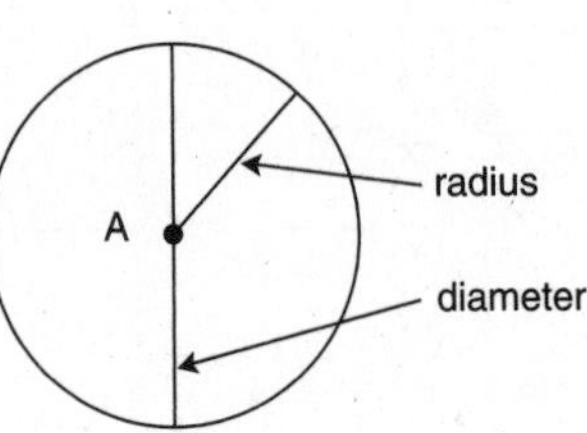


The formulas for circumference and area use a special quantity called **pi** ($\pi$). Pi is the ratio of the circumference to the diameter. It is equal to approximately 3.14. The digits for pi continue infinitely, so calculations with pi are always approximations. For the Mathematics Test, you will use 3.14 as the value of pi. Below is the formula for finding the circumference of a circle.

Circumference = $\pi \times$ diameter, or $C = \pi d$

**Example 1:** A china plate has a gold rim. If the plate's diameter is 10.5 inches, what is the distance around the rim to the nearest tenth of an inch?

Use the formula: $C = \pi d$

$= 3.14(10.5)$

$= 32.97$, which rounds to **33.0 inches**

Use this formula to find the area of a circle: Area = $\pi \times$ radius$^2$, or $A = \pi r^2$.

**Example 2:** The circular surface of a satellite component must be covered with heat-resistant tiles. If the radius of the component is 4 meters, what is the area in square meters?

Use the formula: $A = \pi r^2$

$= 3.14(4^2)$

$= 3.14(16)$

$=$ **50.24 square meters**

In some situations, you may need to solve for either the diameter or radius. Remember, the diameter is twice the radius ($d = 2r$), and the radius is one-half the diameter: $r = \frac{1}{2}d$.

**KEY IDEAS**

- Pi, expressed as 3.14, is the ratio of the circumference of a circle to its diameter.
- To find circumference, multiply pi by the diameter (distance across) the circle.
- The radius is the distance from the center to the edge of the circle. To find area, multiply pi by the square of the radius.

**TASC TEST TIP**

*Formulas for circumference and area do not appear on the TASC formula sheet. You will need to memorize these.*

# PRACTICE 9.1

**Example 3:** What is the circumference of circle $B$ to the nearest tenth of a centimeter?

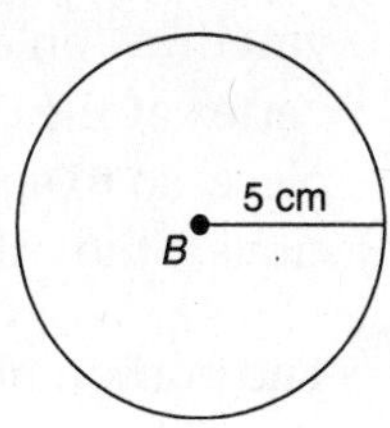


1. The radius of the circle is 5 cm. Therefore, the diameter is $2 \times 5$, or 10 cm.
2. Use the formula: $C = \pi d$
   $= 3.14(10)$
   $= \mathbf{31.4\ cm}$

---

**A. Find the circumference and area of each circle. Round answers to the nearest tenth.**

**1.**

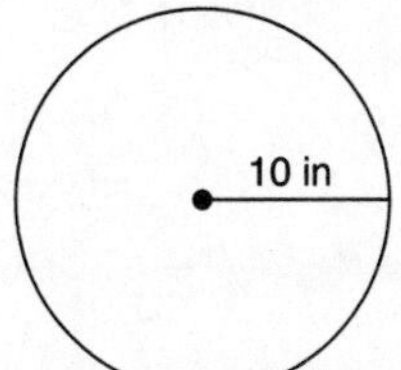


**2.**

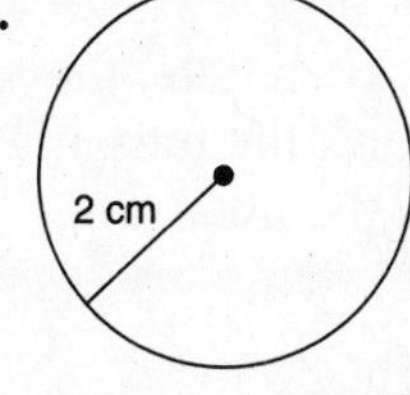


**3.**

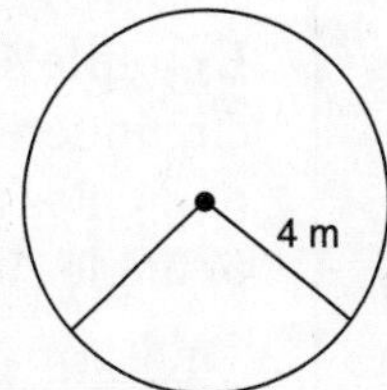


**B. Choose the one best answer to each question.**

**Questions 4 and 5 refer to the following drawing.**

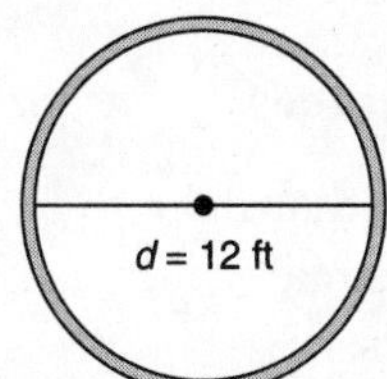


**4.** If workers lay a tile border around the edge of the fountain shown in the diagram, how many feet long will the border be to the nearest foot?

A. 19
B. 36
C. 38
D. 57

**5.** Which of the following expressions could be used to find the area of the bottom surface of the fountain?

A. $3.14 \times 6$
B. $3.14 \times 6^2$
C. $3.14 \times 12$
D. $3.14 \times 12^2$

**6.** The radius of a circle is 6.5 cm. What is the diameter of the circle in centimeters?

A. 3.25
B. 13.0
C. 33.16625
D. 132.665

**7.** On the target below, the 5- and 10-point bands are each 2 inches wide, and the inner circle has a diameter of 2 inches.

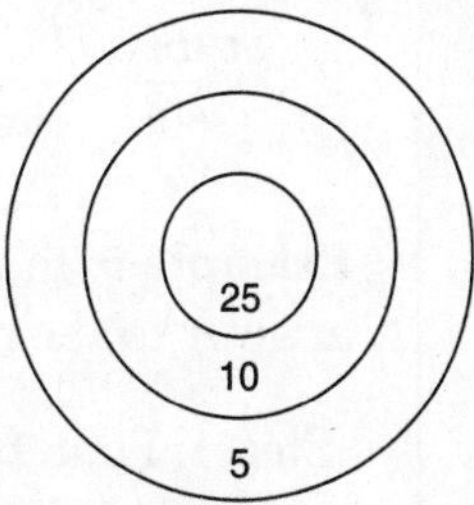


To the nearest inch, what is the outer circumference of the 10-point band?

A. 6
B. 13
C. 19
D. 113

**Review your work using the explanations that start on page 705.**

**STUDY ADVICE**

Here are two mnemonics (memory tricks) to help you learn the formulas in this lesson:

Circumference: Learn "Cherry pie's delicious" to remember $C = \pi d$.

Area: Learn "Apple pies are too" to remember $A = \pi r^2$.

## Interior Angles, Arcs, and Chords

**KEY IDEAS**

- A circle represents 360 degrees.
- An arc is a portion of the circumference of a circle. Its length can be calculated if you know the circumference of the circle and the degree measure of the angle that defines that arc.
- A chord is a straight line whose end points fall on the circumference of a circle.

You have learned that angles are measured in degrees. A circle represents 360 degrees. If you draw an angle of $x$ degrees with the vertex at the center of the circle, that pie piece, so to speak, will take up $\frac{x}{360}$ of the circle. Study the following diagram:

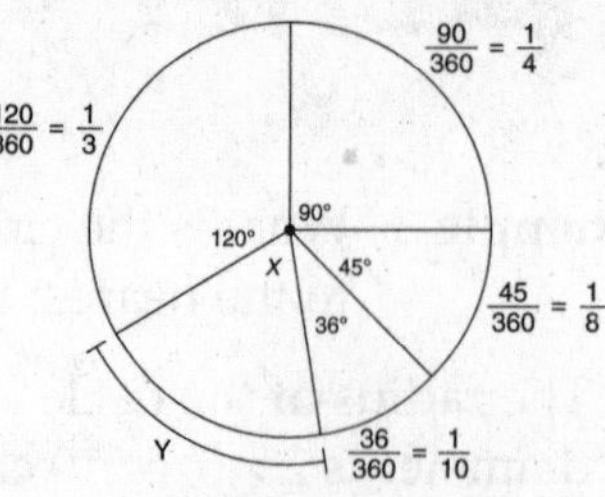


The portion of a circle's circumference that forms the outside of a "pie piece" is called an **arc.** The length of an arc has the same proportional relationship to the circumference that its angle does to 360. In the previous diagram:

$$\frac{\text{length of } Y}{\text{circumference}} = \frac{m\angle X}{360}$$

**Example 4:** In the circle shown here, the circumference is 400 feet and the measure of arc $S$ is 50 feet. What is the measure of angle $AOB$?

Step 1: Set up the proportion. $\frac{50}{400} = \frac{mAOB}{360}$

Step 2: Cross multiply and divide to solve the proportion. $400 \times m\text{AOB} = 50 \times 360$

The measure of angle AOB is **45 degrees.** $mAOB = \frac{18{,}000}{400} = 45$

**TASC TEST TIP**

*The TASC Mathematics Reference Sheet contains key formulas related to chords and arcs (see page 231), so you do not have to memorize these formulas.*

Now suppose you drew an angle so that its vertex was not on the center of the circle but on one side of the circle, like this:

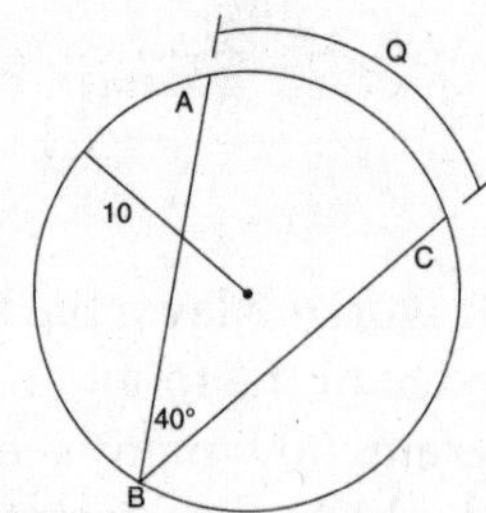


You could still use a proportion to find the length of arc Q. However, the proportion is different:

$$2\times\frac{mABC}{360} = \frac{\text{length of arc } Q}{\text{circumference of circle}}$$

**Example 5:** In the circle shown, what is the length of arc Q? Round your answer to the nearest tenth.

Step 1: First, find the circumference of the circle. The diagram shows that the radius is 10 units. $C = 20\pi \approx 62.8$

Step 2: Set up the proportion. Simplify.

$$2\times\frac{40}{360} = \frac{\textit{length of arc } Q}{62.8}$$

$$\frac{2}{9} = \frac{\textit{length of arc } Q}{62.8}$$

Step 3: Cross multiply to solve. $62.8 \times 2 \div 9 \approx \mathbf{14}$

Arc Q is **14 units** long.

## PRACTICE 9.2

A **chord** is a straight line that has its endpoints on the circumference of a circle. You can find the length of a chord if you know the circle's radius and how far the midpoint of the chord is from the center of the circle. That's because the radius forms the hypotenuse of a right triangle, as shown in the diagram.

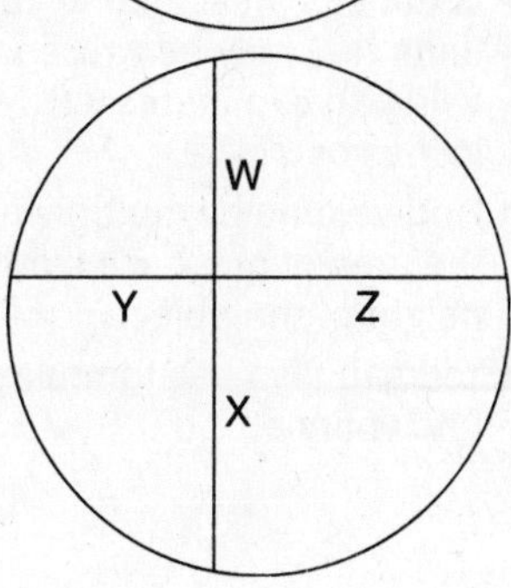


**Example 6:** In the circle shown, what is the length of chord *AB*?

| | |
|---|---|
| Step 1: One leg of the right triangle is 3, and the hypotenuse is 5. Set up an equation based on the Pythagorean relationship. | $(\text{length of } XB)^2 + 3^2 = 5^2$ |
| Step 2: Solve for the length of *XB*. | $(\text{length of } XB)^2 = 16$<br>$(\text{length of } XB) = 4$ |
| Step 3: Because *XB* is only half of chord *AB*, double the result to find the length of chord *AB*. Chord *AB* is **8 units** long. | $4 \times 2 = 8$ |

Two chords that intersect have the following relationship:

length of $W \times$ length of $X =$ length of $Y \times$ length of $Z$

---

**A. For each of the following circles, find either the measure of the angle marked *X* or the length of the chord marked *Y*. Use 3.14 for pi, and round your answer to the nearest unit.**

**1.**

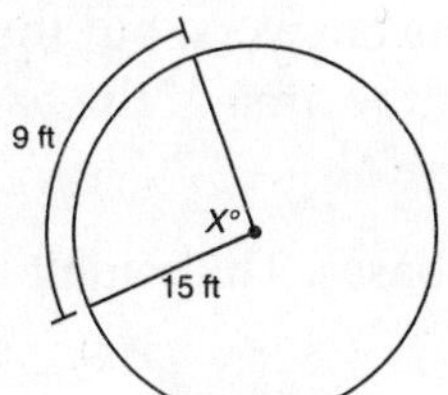


**2.**

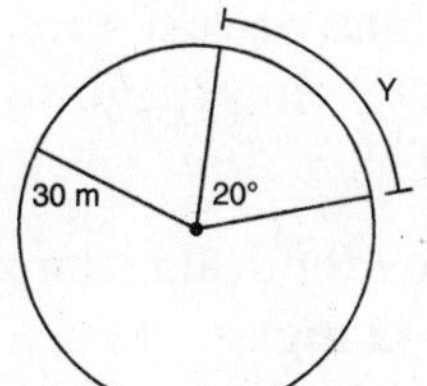


**3.**

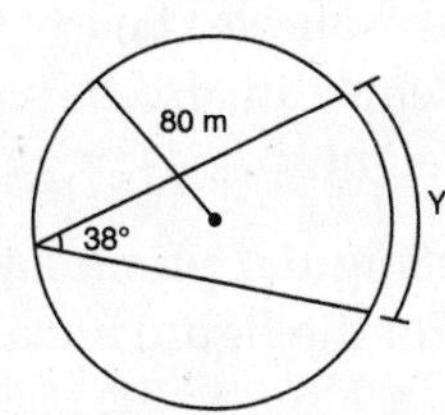


**B. Choose the <u>one best answer</u> to each question.**

**4.** In the following circle, what is the length of A in meters?

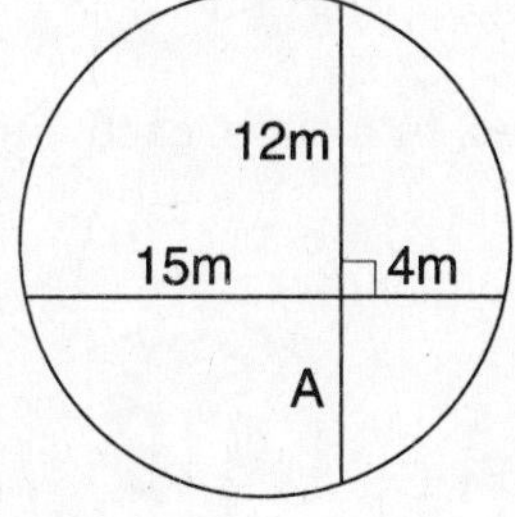


A. 4
B. 5
C. 6
D. 10

**5.** In the following circle, what is the length of chord *LM*?

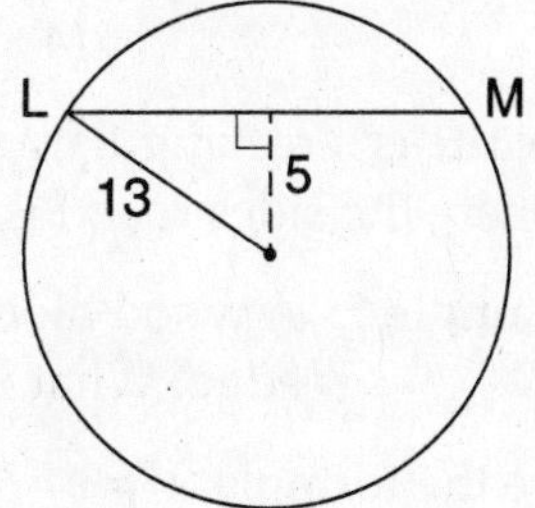


A. 12
B. 14
C. 24
D. 26

**Review your work using the explanations that start on page 705.**

Geometry

# LESSON 10

## Volume

### Rectangular Solids, Cubes, Cylinders, and Spheres

**Volume**, also called **capacity**, is the measure of space inside a three-dimensional object. You measure volume in cubic units. In other words, if the sides of an object are measured in inches, the volume is the number of cubes (one inch per side) you would need to fill the object.

Many common three-dimensional objects have at least two identical and parallel faces. Think of a cereal box or a soup can. Both objects have identical faces at the top and bottom of the container. Either of these faces can be called the base of the object. To find the volume of any container with identical bases, multiply the area of one base by the height of the object: Volume = area of base × height.

Another way to find the volume of an object is to use the formula that applies specifically to that object.

| | | |
|---|---|---|
| **rectangular prism** | Volume = base × height | $V = Bh$ |
| **cube** | Volume = edge$^3$ | $V = e^3$ |
| **cylinder** | Volume = pi × radius$^2$ × height | $V = \pi r^2 h$ |
| **sphere** | Volume = $\frac{4}{3}$ × pi × radius$^3$ | $V = \frac{4}{3}\pi r^3$ |

In the examples below, formulas are used to find the answers, but the problems can also be solved by simply multiplying the area of the base by the height.

A **rectangular prism** has two identical rectangular bases. The remaining sides of the figure are also rectangles.

**Example 1:** A cardboard box has the dimensions shown in the diagram. What is the volume of the box in cubic feet?

Use the formula: $V = Bh$, where $B$ is *length* × *width*
$= (4 \times 5)(3) =$ **60 cubic feet**

A **cube** is a rectangular prism with six identical faces. In a cube, each edge (where the sides meet) is the same length.

**Example 2:** A wood block measures 2 inches per edge. What is the volume of the block?

Use the formula: $V = e^3$
$= 2^3 =$ **8 cubic inches**

A **cylinder** has two circular bases. The bases are connected by a curved surface. Cans, barrels, and tanks are often in the shape of cylinders.

#### KEY IDEAS

- Volume is measured in cubic units that may be written using an exponent: 6 cubic inches or 6 in$^3$.
- Find volume by multiplying the area of one base by the height of the object.
- You can also use formulas to find volume.

#### TASC TEST TIP

*Learn which area formula goes with which shape. Once you know the area formulas for rectangular prisms, cubes, and cylinders, you can change them to volume by putting an h at the end. Compare:*

*Area of circle:* $\pi r^2$

*Volume of cylinder:* $\pi r^2 h$

# PRACTICE 10.1

**Example 3:** A storage tank has a radius of 1.5 meters and a height of 3 meters. What is the volume of the tank to the nearest cubic meter?

Use the formula: $V = \pi r^2 h$

$= 3.14(1.5^2)(3) = 21.195\ \text{m}^3$,

which rounds to **21 cubic meters**

---

**A. Find the volume of each object to the nearest whole unit.**

**1.**

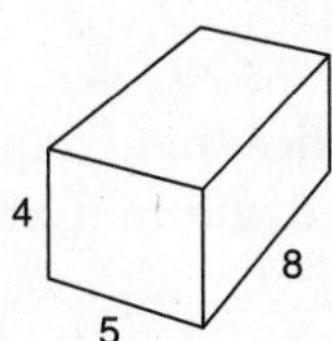


**3.**

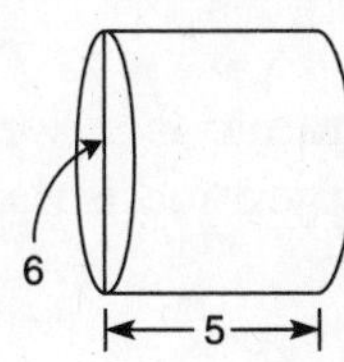


**5.**

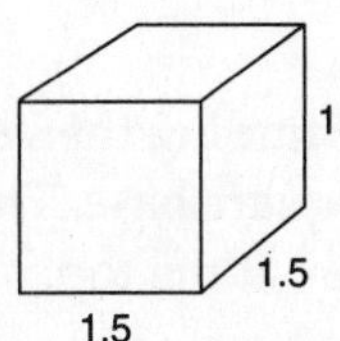


**2.**

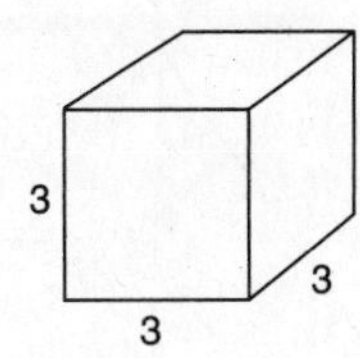


**4.**

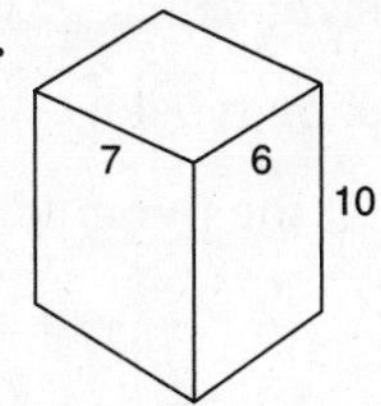


**6.**

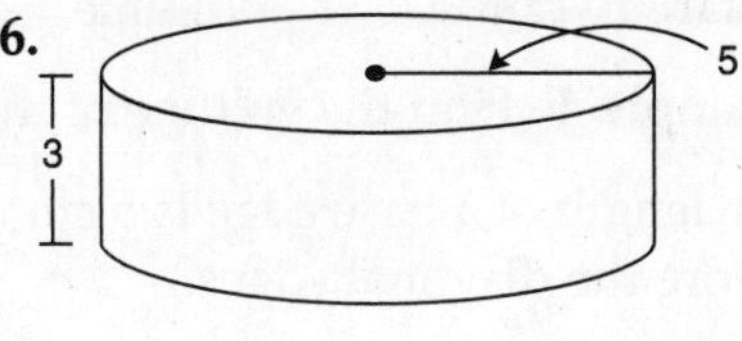


**B. Choose the one best answer to each question.**

Question 7 refers to the following drawing.

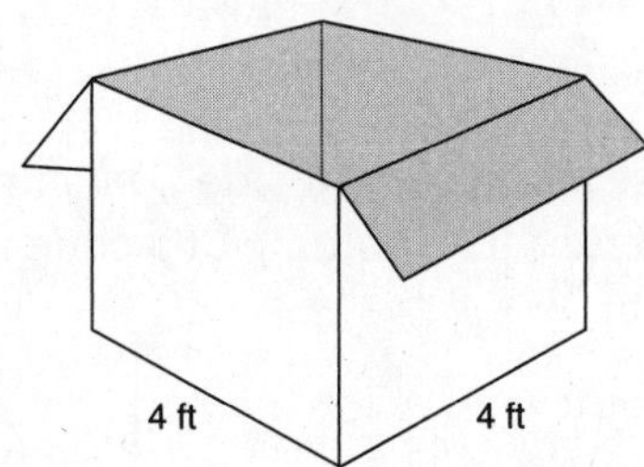


7. A rectangular box with a volume of 80 cubic feet has the length and width shown in the drawing. What is the height of the box?

   A. 5
   B. 10
   C. 16
   D. 20

8. A wooden crate measures 5 feet along each edge. What is the crate's volume in cubic feet?

   A. 15
   B. 25
   C. 125
   D. 150

Question 9 refers to the following drawing.

9. Linda adds a water stabilizer to her children's swimming pool once a week. The instructions tell her to add one scoop of the product for every 20 cubic feet of water. About how many scoops should she add per week?

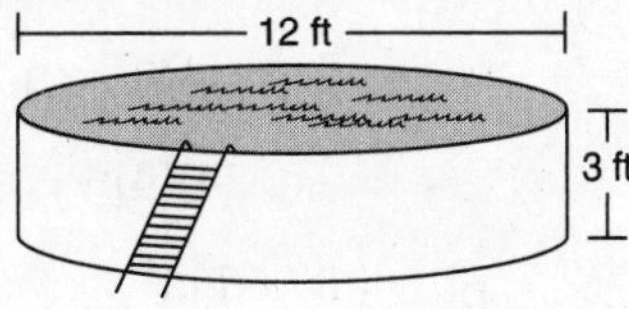


   A. 3
   B. 6
   C. 17
   D. 36

**Review your work using the explanations that start on page 705.**

## Volume of Pyramids and Cones

A **pyramid** is a three-dimensional object with four triangle faces that connect to the same vertex. The base of a pyramid can be any closed figure, but you will likely not see pyramids with complicated bases on the TASC. Here, we will focus on pyramids with square bases. But remember: If you can find the area of the base, you can find the volume of the pyramid.

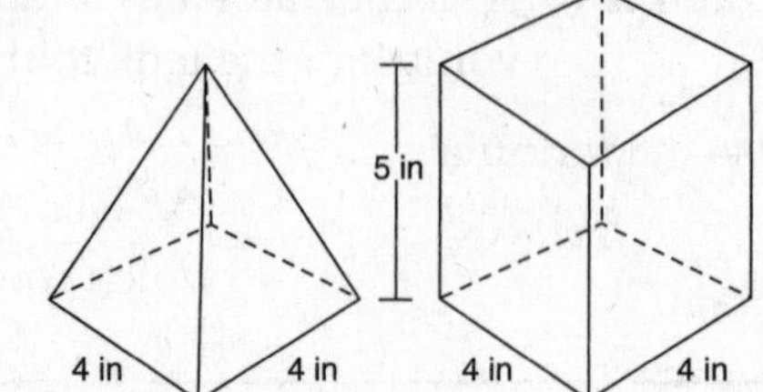


The rectangular prism and the pyramid shown here both have identical square bases and the same height. Compare the two figures. As you can see, the pyramid holds much less than the rectangular prism. In fact, it holds only one-third of the rectangular prism's volume.

The formula for finding the volume of a pyramid is as written below. Notice that $B$ equals the area of the square base. The height of a pyramid is the perpendicular distance from the base to the vertex at the top.

**square pyramid** Volume $= \frac{1}{3} \times \text{base} \times \text{height}$

**Example 4:** Find the volume of the pyramid shown below.

The length of a base edge is 5 cm. The height of the pyramid is 6 cm. Ignore the diagonal edges.

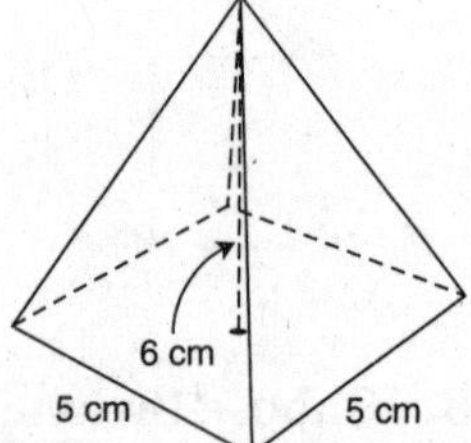


Apply the formula: $V = \frac{1}{3}Bh$

$= \frac{1}{3}(5^2)(6)$

$= \frac{1}{3}(25)(6)$

$= \mathbf{50\ cm^3}$

A **cone** is similar to a cylinder. Both have a circular base and a curved side. The curved side of a cone slants inward so that it meets at a point, or vertex. The volume of a cone is $\frac{1}{3}$ of the volume of a cylinder with the same size base and height.

Notice that the formula for the volume of a cone contains the formula for finding the area of a circle ($\pi r^2$).

**cone** Volume $= \frac{1}{3} \times \pi \times \text{radius}^2 \times \text{height}$

**Example 5:** Find the volume of the cone shown below.

The radius of the base is 2 inches, and the height is 9 inches.

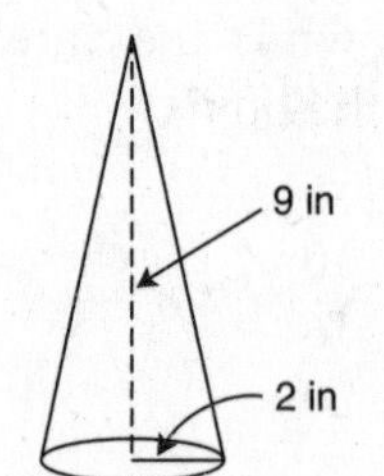


Apply the formula: $V = \frac{1}{3}\pi r^2 h$

$= \frac{1}{3}(3.14)(2^2)(9)$

$= \frac{1}{3}(3.14)(4)(9)$

$= \mathbf{37.68\ in^3}$

**Note:** In volume formulas for cones and square pyramids, the factor $\frac{1}{3}$ is shown first. However, do not begin with this factor. Multiply the other factors first and then divide by 3, unless one of the numbers is easily divided by 3.

# PRACTICE 10.2

A. **Find the volume of each object to the nearest unit.**

1.

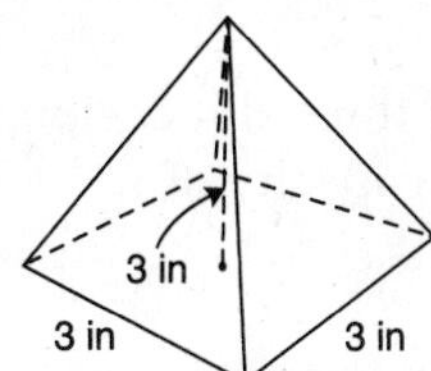


2.

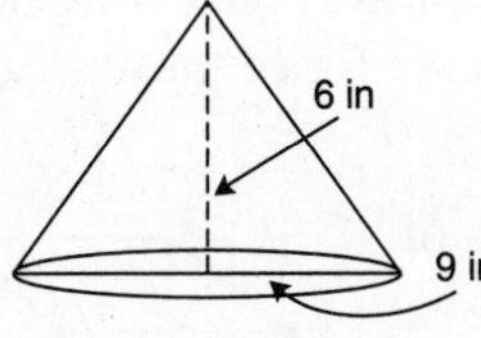


3.

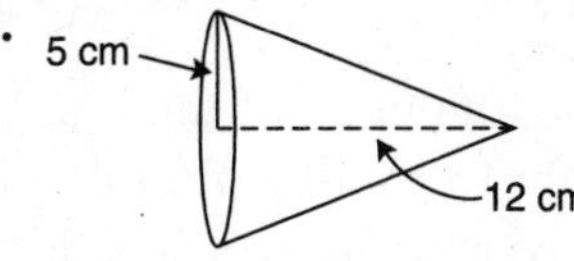


4.

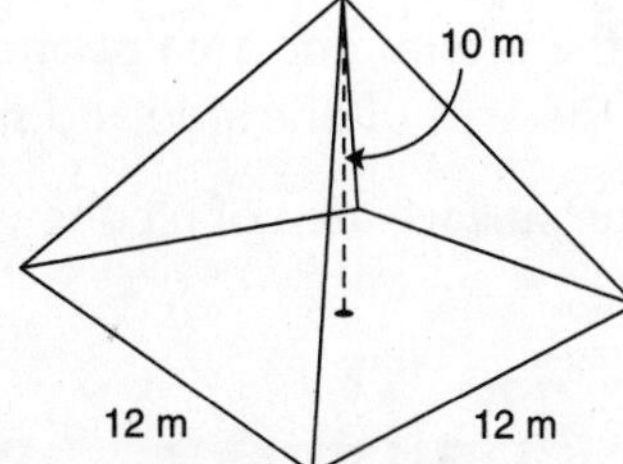


5.

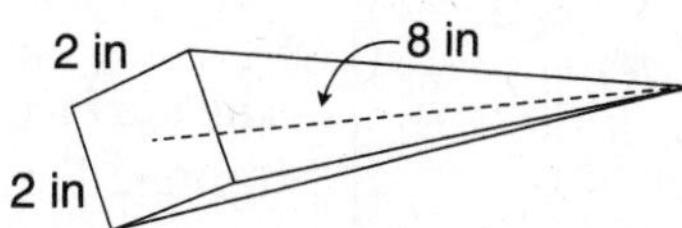


6.

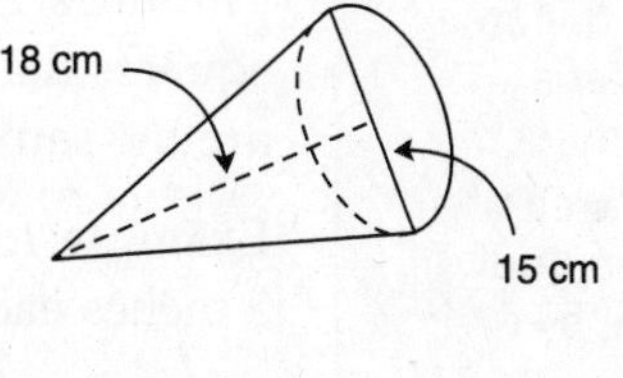


B. **Choose the one best answer to each question.**

7. Advertisers have designed this pyramid-shaped package to hold action figures.

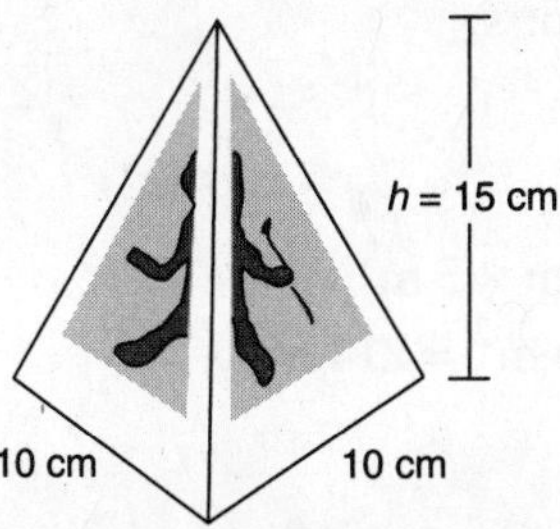


After testing the design, the manufacturer decides to increase both the length and width of the base by 4 cm. How many more cubic centimeters will the new package hold than the package shown above?

A. 480
B. 500
C. 980
D. 2940

8. The height of a cone is half the diameter of its base. If the cone's height is 4 inches, what is the cone's volume to the nearest cubic inch?

A. 21
B. 48
C. 67
D. 201

9. Which of the following is a true statement about the figures shown below?

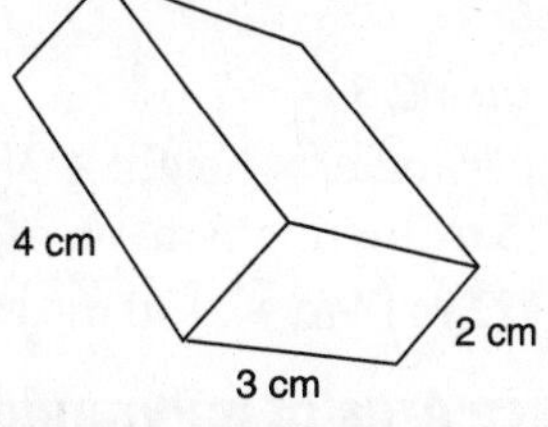

Figure A

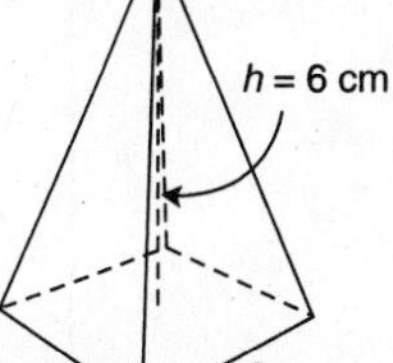

Figure B

A. The volume of *A* equals the volume of *B*.
B. The volume of *B* is greater than the volume of *A*.
C. Both *A* and *B* have a volume greater than 20 cubic centimeters.
D. The volume of *B* is less than the volume of *A*.

10. A cone's base is a circle with a radius of 8 inches. The cone's height is 15 inches. What is the cone's approximate volume in cubic inches?

A. 125
B. 250
C. 500
D. 1000

**Review your work using the explanations that start on page 705.**

# LESSON 11

## Surface Area

The **surface area** is the total area of the outside **faces** of three-dimensional figures. This is different from the **volume**, which is the capacity of what a figure can hold. Surface area is expressed in square units.

**KEY IDEAS**

- The surface area is the area of the total surface of a three-dimensional object.
- To find the surface area of a cube, you need to multiply the area of one side by 6.
- To find the surface area of a rectangular prism and a pyramid, you need to use formulas to find several dimensions and combine them.

### Surface Area of a Square Prism

The surface area of a **square prism (cube)** is the sum of the areas of the six squares that form the prism. The area of one square is $s^2$. Since these sides are the same, find the area of one side and multiply by 6.

**Example 1:** Find the surface area of a cube with sides of 3 inches each.

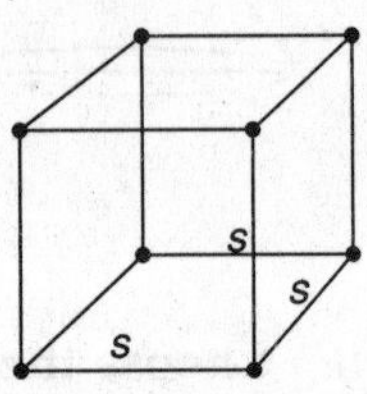


$SA = 6s^2$

$SA = 6(3\text{ in})^2 = 6\,(9\text{ in}^2) = \mathbf{54\text{ in}^2}$

### Surface Area of a Rectangular Prism

The surface area of a **rectangular prism** is the sum of the areas of the six rectangles that form the prism.

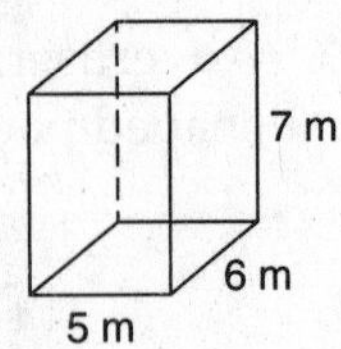


**Example 2:** Find the surface area of this box.

$SA = ph + 2B$

$SA = \text{perimeter} \times \text{height} + 2(\text{area of base})$

$SA = (5\text{ m} + 6\text{ m} + 5\text{ m} + 6\text{ m}) \times 7\text{ m} + 2(6\text{ m} \times 5\text{ m})$

$SA = (22\text{ m})7\text{ m} + 2\left(30\text{ m}^2\right) = 154\text{ m}^2 + 60\text{ m}^2 = \mathbf{214\text{ m}^2}$

### Surface Area of a Pyramid

The surface area of a **pyramid** is $\frac{1}{2}$ the perimeter of the base ($p$) times the **slant height** ($s$) plus the area of the base ($B$). The slant height is the length of a line segment from the **apex** (top) to the **base**.

**Example 3:** What is the surface area of a pyramid with a slant height of 5 feet, a base with a perimeter of 14 feet, and a base with an area of 12 feet?

slant height

$\text{SA} = \frac{1}{2}\,ps + B$

$\text{SA} = \frac{1}{2}\,\text{perimeter} \times \text{slant height} + \text{base area}$

$\text{SA} = \frac{1}{2}(14\text{ ft})\,(5\text{ ft}) + 12\text{ ft}^2$

$\text{SA} = \frac{1}{2}(70\text{ ft}^2) + 12\text{ ft}^2 = 35\text{ ft}^2 + 12\text{ ft}^2 = \mathbf{47\text{ ft}^2}$

**TASC TEST TIP**

*No surface area formulas will appear on the formula sheet provided on the TASC. You will need to memorize the formulas on this page.*

# PRACTICE 11.1

**A. Find the surface area of each object in square units. Use the formulas on page 424.**

1.

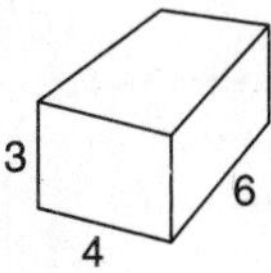


2.

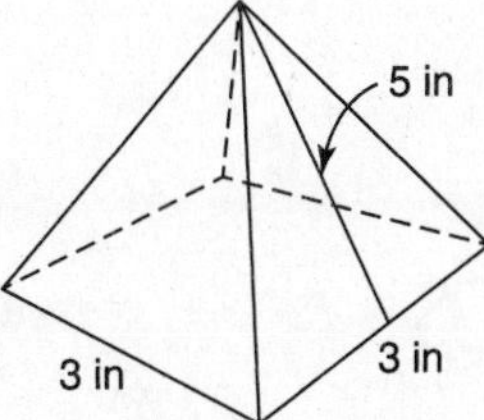


3.

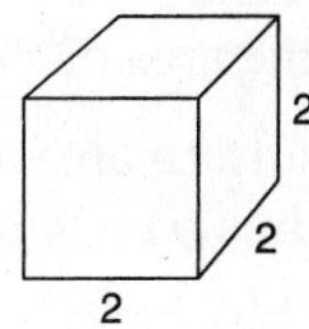


4.

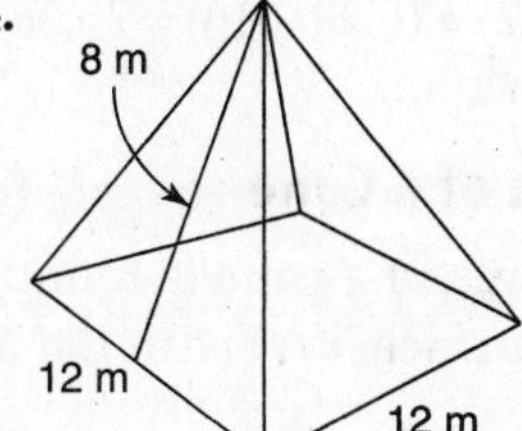


5.

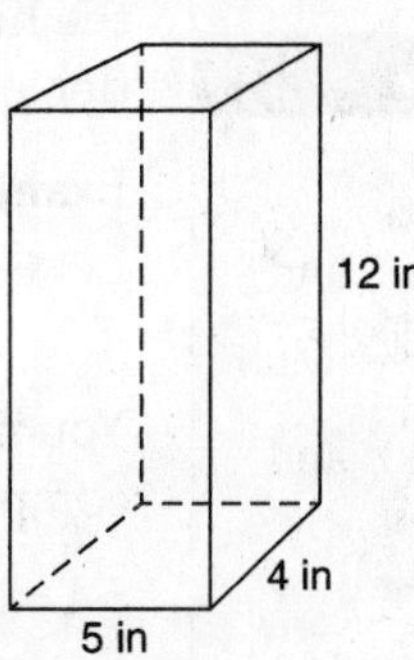


6.

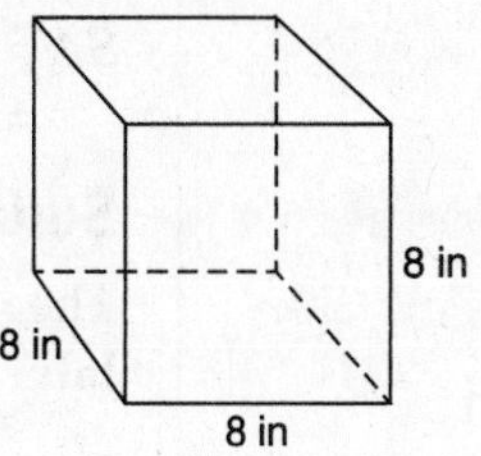


**B. Choose the one best answer to each question. Use the formulas on page 424.**

7. Which of the following is a true statement about the figures shown below? (Measurements indicated are all in the same units.)

5 5 5

Figure *A*

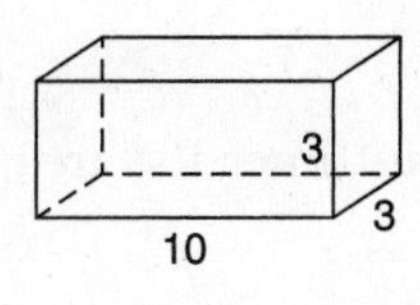


Figure *B*

A. The surface area of Figure *A* is equal to the surface area of Figure *B*.
B. The surface area of Figure *A* is half of the surface area of Figure *B*.
C. The surface area of Figure *A* is greater than the surface area of Figure *B*.
D. The sum of the surface areas of both Figure *A* and Figure *B* is greater than 300.

8. If the dimensions of the box below are doubled, by how many square centimeters does the surface area increase?

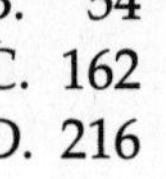

A. 8
B. 54
C. 162
D. 216

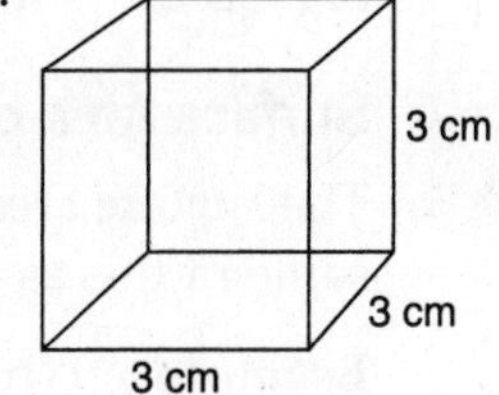


9. All the edges of a metal box are of equal length. If the surface area is 150 square inches, what is the length, in inches, of each edge of the box?

A. 5
B. 6
C. 25
D. 50

**Review your work using the explanations that start on page 705.**

**STUDY ADVICE**

Understanding surface area can be challenging. Be sure to allot ample study time to this important topic! You may see several questions about surface area on Test Day.

Finding the surface areas of cylinders, cones, and spheres involves using some dimensions of circles.

## Surface Area of a Cylinder

To find the surface area of a cylinder, multiply the circumference ($2\pi r$) by the **height** ($h$) and add the product to the area of the two ends of the cylinder, each of which is the area of a circle ($\pi r^2$).

**KEY IDEAS**

- The formulas for surface area of cylinders, cones, and spheres all use dimensions of a circle.
- All of the formulas use $\pi$ and the radius of a circle.

**Example 4:** Find the surface area of a cylinder with a radius ($r$) of 4 inches and a height ($h$) of 3 inches.

You may find the on-screen calculator helpful to complete these calculations effectively.

$SA = 2\pi rh + 2\pi r^2$
$SA = (2 \times 3.14 \times 4 \times 3) + (2 \times 3.14 \times 4^2)$
$SA = (6.28 \times 12) + (6.28 \times 16) = 75.36 \text{ in}^2 + 100.48 \text{ in}^2$
$= \mathbf{175.84 \text{ in}^2}$

## Surface Area of a Cone

The surface area of a **cone** is found by combining the **lateral side surface** ($\pi rs$) with the area of its **base** ($\pi r^2$).

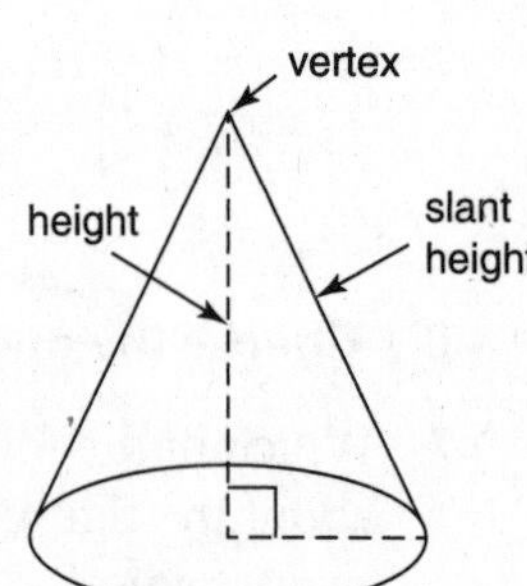


**Example 5:** Find the surface area of a cone with a radius of 2 feet and a slant height of 5 feet.

**TASC TEST TIP**

*Don't forget that you can use the TI-30XS MultiView™ calculator to perform calculations involving pi and exponents. It will come in handy on geometry problems such as the ones on this page.*

$SA = \pi rs + \pi r^2$
$SA =$ lateral side surface with slant height + area of base
$SA = \pi(2)(5) + \pi(2^2)$
$SA = 10\pi \text{ft}^2 + 4\pi \text{ft}^2 = 14\pi \text{ft}^2 = 14 \text{ ft}^2 \times 3.14 \cong \mathbf{43.96 \text{ ft}^2}$

## Surface Area of a Sphere

The surface area of a **sphere** is four times the area of a circle with the same radius as the sphere.

**Example 6:** What is the surface area of this sphere with a radius of 10 feet?

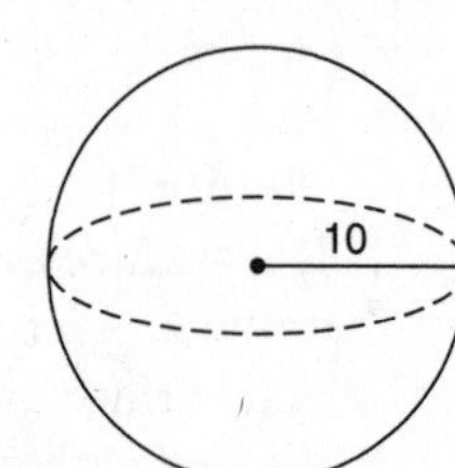


$SA = 4\pi r^2$
$SA \approx 4 \times 3.14 \times 10^2 \approx \mathbf{1256 \text{ ft}^2}$

# PRACTICE 11.2

**A. Find the surface area of each object in square units. Use the formulas on page 426.**

**1.**

**3.**

**5.**

**2.**

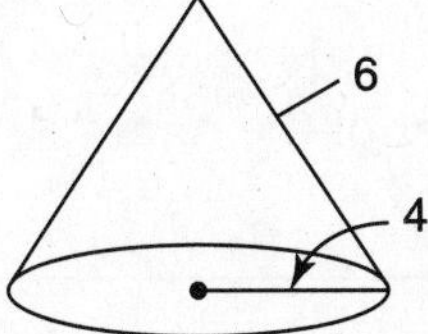


**4.**

**6.**

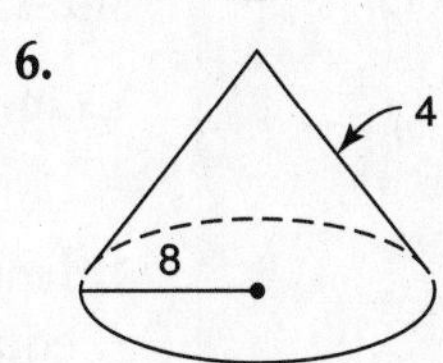


**B. Choose the <u>one best answer</u> to each question. Use the formulas on page 426.**

7. If the length of the diameter of a sphere is 8, how many square units is its surface area?
   A. $16\pi$
   B. $64\pi$
   C. $256\pi$
   D. $512\pi$

8. A cone, pictured below, has a slant height of 8 inches and a diameter of 8 inches. If the cone's slant height is doubled, and the diameter is halved, which of the following statements must be true?

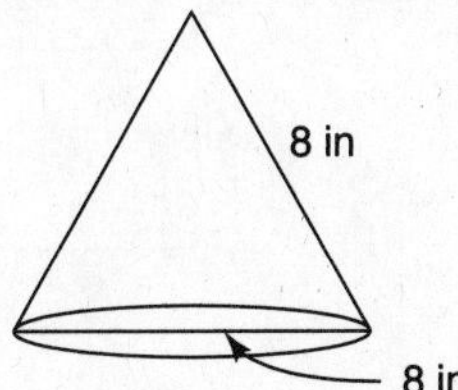
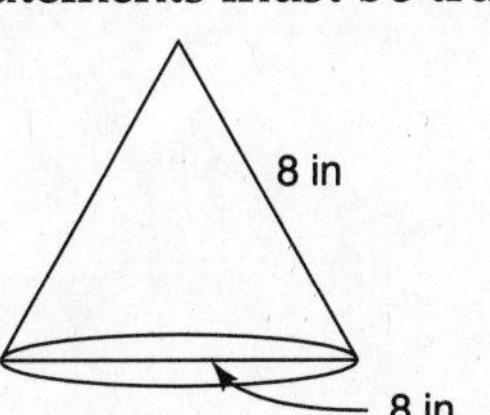


   A. The new cone will have the same surface area as the original cone.
   B. The new cone will have a surface area exactly half of the surface area of the original cone.
   C. The new cone will have a surface area exactly double that of the surface area of the new cone.
   D. The new cone will have a surface area less than the surface area of the original cone.

9. In the cylinder below, the diameter of the circular base is equal to the height of the cylinder. What is the surface area of the cylinder, to the nearest square inch?

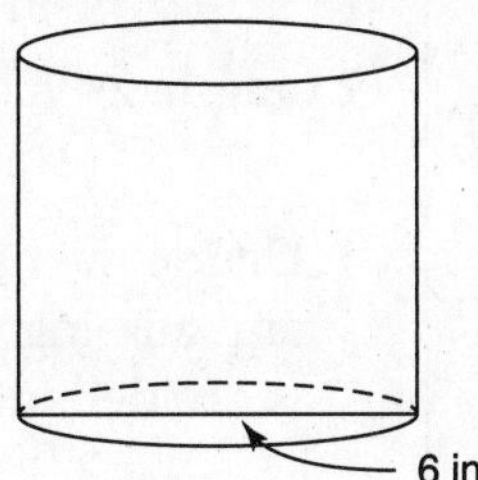


   A. 57
   B. 113
   C. 170
   D. 339

**Review your work using the explanations that start on page 706.**

# Combined Figures

**KEY IDEAS**

- Combined figures are made from two or more regular figures.
- To find the perimeter of a combined figure, add the lengths of all the sides.
- To find area or volume of a combined figure, break the figure into parts and find the area or volume of each part; then combine the results.

**TASC TEST TIP**

*There is usually more than one way to break down a combined figure. Solve the problem the way that seems easiest to you. The answer will be the same.*

## Breaking Combined Figures into Parts

A combined figure puts together geometric figures to form a new shape. To find the perimeter of a combined figure, simply add the lengths of the sides. You may need to solve for one or more missing lengths.

**Example 1:** A family room has the dimensions shown in the diagram. All measures are in feet. What is the perimeter of the room?

1. Find the missing measures. Measurement $x$ equals the combined lengths of the two opposite walls: $x = 8 + 4 = 12$ ft. You also know that $18 - 10 = y$, so $y = 8$ ft.

2. Add all distances to find the perimeter: $12 + 18 + 8 + 8 + 4 + 10 =$ **60 ft.**

To find the area or volume of a combined figure, break the figure into parts. Then apply the correct formula to each part.

**Example 2:** What is the area of the figure in square centimeters?

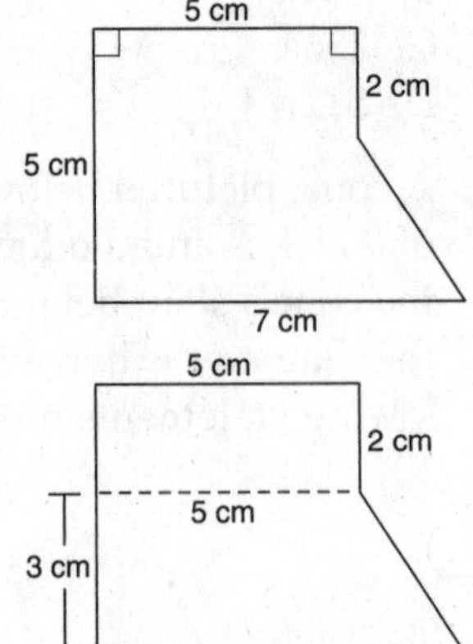


1. Divide the figure into two shapes, and find any missing measurements. Here the figure is divided into a trapezoid and a rectangle.

2. Calculate the area of each shape.
   Rectangle: $A = lw$
   $= 2(5) = 10 \text{ cm}^2$

   Trapezoid: $A = \frac{1}{2}h(b_1 + b_2)$
   $= \frac{1}{2}(3)(5 + 7) = 18 \text{ cm}^2$

3. Combine: $10 + 18 =$ **28 cm²**.

**Example 3:** Find the volume of the container shown below.

Break the figure into a cylinder and a cone and find the volume of each.

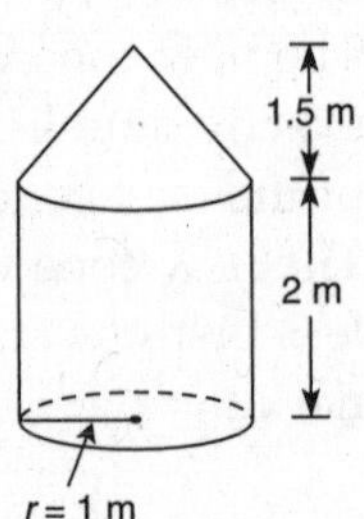


1. Cylinder: $V = \pi r^2 h$
   $= (3.14)(1^2)(2) = 6.28 \text{ m}^3$

2. Cone: $V = \frac{1}{3}\pi r^2 h$
   $= \frac{1}{3}(3.14)(1^2)(1.5) = 1.57 \text{ m}^3$

3. Combine: $6.28 + 1.57 =$ **7.85 m³** or **7.85 cu m.**

# PRACTICE 12

**A. Find the perimeter and area of each figure.**

**1.**

**2.**

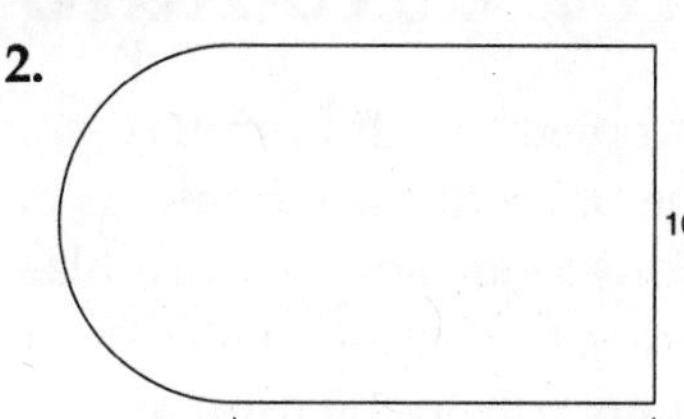


(*Hint:* Think of the figure as a rectangle and a half circle.)

**3.**

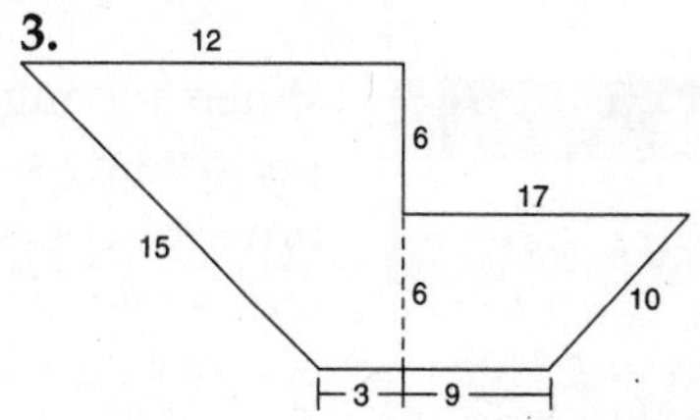


**B. Find the volume of each figure to the nearest cubic unit.**

**4.**

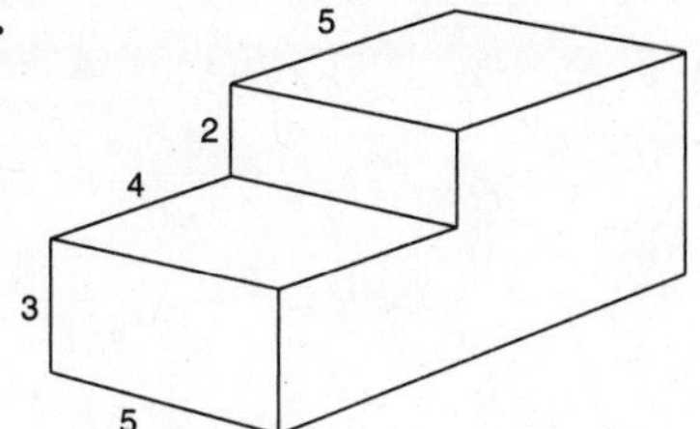


**5.**

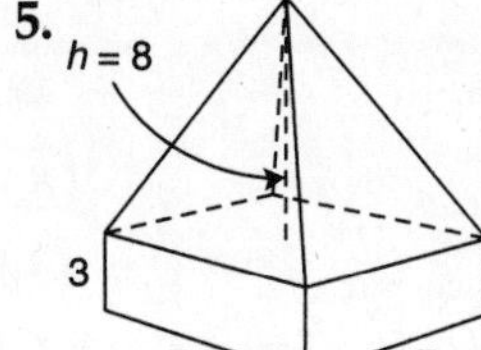


**6.**

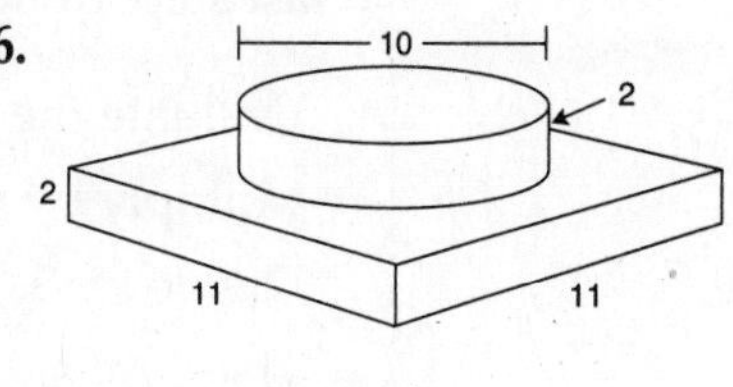


**C. Choose the one best answer to each question.**

7. A slab of concrete will have four concrete blocks in each corner as shown in the drawing below.

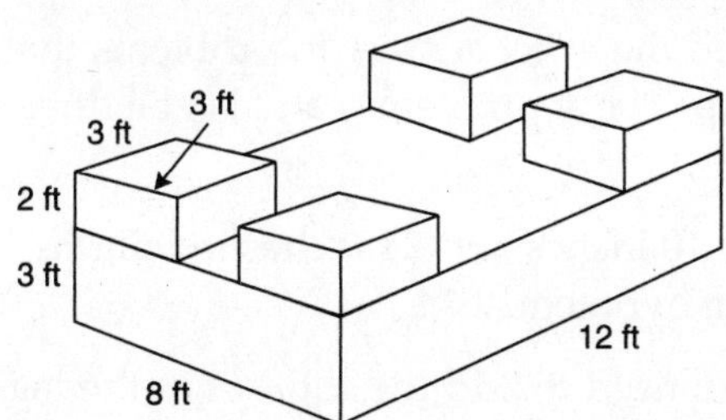


If each corner block has the same dimensions, what is the volume of the structure in cubic feet?

A. 72
B. 168
C. 288
D. 360

8. A candy package is in the shape of a cylinder with a cone on each end.

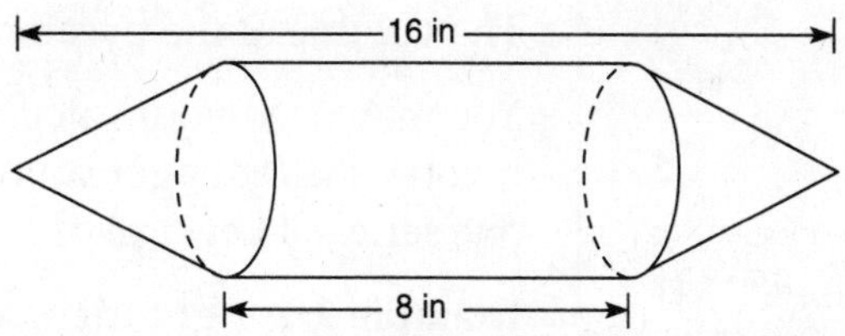


If the radius of the cylinder is 2 inches and the cones are identical, what is the capacity of the container to the nearest cubic inch?

A. 33
B. 100
C. 134
D. 201

**Review your work using the explanations that start on page 706.**

**STUDY ADVICE**

Any time you are feeling overwhelmed, step away and take a walk (or play basketball, or work on a hobby). Even though there is a great deal of information to absorb to do well on the TASC, you can do it if you maintain focus and be patient with yourself.

LESSON 13

# Geometry Calculator Skills

## KEY IDEAS

- When a problem involves many calculations, use the order of operations to decide which operation to do first.
- Check your work by estimating an answer or by quickly repeating the keystrokes to see if the result is the same.

When solving problems with formulas, you can generally save time by performing some or all of the operations on a calculator. Remember the order of operations when solving formulas and always check your work, either by reentering the key sequence or by estimating an answer and comparing your answer to the estimate.

**Example 1:** A pyramid has a height of 81 feet. The base is in the shape of a square with each side measuring 40 feet. What is the volume in cubic feet of the pyramid?

Use the formula for the volume of a pyramid: $\frac{1}{3}Bh$. Begin by calculating the area of the base: $40 \times 40$, or $40^2$. Multiply that by the height, 81. In the last step, dividing by 3 is the same as multiplying by $\frac{1}{3}$.

| | |
|---|---|
| Evaluate the exponent. | 40 [$x^2$] |
| Multiply by 81. | [×] 81 |
| Divide by 3. | [÷] 3 [enter] |
| The right side of the display shows the correct answer, **43,200**. | **43200** |

To enter this formula using a fraction using one series of keystrokes on the TI-30XS MultiView™ calculator, enter the following: [n/d] 1 [▼] 3 [×] 40 [$x^2$] [×] 81 [enter].

The right side of the display shows **43200**.

The volume of the pyramid is **43,200 square feet.**

You may need your calculator to find the exact answer to problems that involve the Pythagorean relationship. These problems can also be done in one series of keystrokes.

## TASC TEST TIP

*Watch the calculator display while you are entering all of these keystrokes. If you make a mistake, use the delete key to remove that mistake and then replace it with the correct number or function. Practice that with these examples.*

**Example 2:** A right triangle has legs 10 inches and 24 inches in length. What is the length of the hypotenuse?

Use the formula $a^2 + b^2 = c^2$. You will need to add the squares of the legs and then find the square root of the total.

Press: 10 [$x^2$] [+] 24 [$x^2$] [enter]. The display will read 676. Then press [2nd] [$x^2$] 676 [enter]. The right side of the display shows **26.**

The hypotenuse is **26 inches** in length.

If you need to include the quantity pi ($\pi$) in a calculation, the TI-30XS MultiView™ calculator includes a *pi* key, located three keys below the *2nd* key on the left-hand side of the keypad.

**Example 3:** What is the area of a circle with radius 2.4 cm? Round your answer to the nearest tenth.

Use the formula Area $= \pi r^2$. Press [$\pi$] [×] 2.4 [$x^2$] and then press [enter]. The right side of the display reads 18.09557368. Round that to find the answer: **18.1 cm²**.

# PRACTICE 13

**A. Use your calculator to evaluate each formula.**

1. Find the perimeter of a rectangle with a length of 16 inches and a width of 5 inches.
Perimeter = 2 × length + 2 × width

2. Find the area of a triangle with a base of 26 centimeters and a height of 15 centimeters. Area = $\frac{1}{2}$ × base × height

3. What is the volume of a cube if the edge measures 3.5 feet? Round to the nearest cubic foot. Volume = edge$^3$

4. What is the measure of the hypotenuse of a right triangle when the legs measure 13 cm and 9 cm? Round your answer to the nearest tenth.
Pythagorean relationship: $a^2 + b^2 = c^2$

5. Find the circumference of a circle with a diameter of 12 inches. Round to the nearest tenth.
Circumference = π × diameter

6. Find the volume of a cone with a radius of 12 cm and a height of 20 cm. Round to the nearest cm$^3$.
Volume = $\frac{1}{3}$ × π × radius$^2$ × height

**B. Choose the <u>one best answer</u> to each question. You <u>MAY</u> use your calculator.**

**<u>Question 7</u> refers to the following drawing.**

7. For a woodworking project, Paul cuts the shape shown above from plywood. What is the area in square inches of the piece? (*Hint:* Think of the shape as a triangle removed from a rectangle.)

A. 400
B. 480
C. 520
D. 640

8. To the nearest cubic meter, what is the volume of a cylinder with a radius of 1.5 meters and a height of 5 meters?

A. 25
B. 35
C. 45
D. 141

**<u>Questions 9 and 10</u> refer to the drawing.**

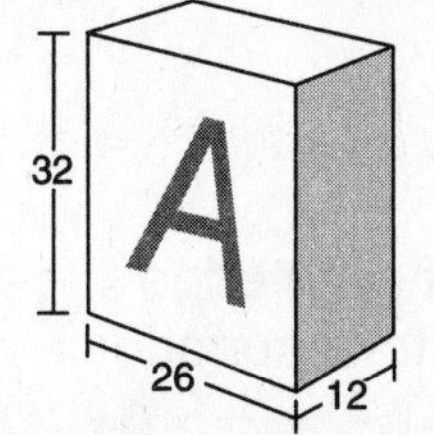


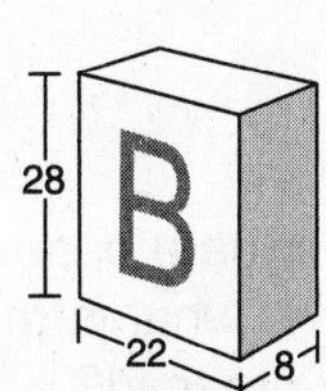


All measurements are in centimeters.

9. How many cubic centimeters greater is the volume of Box A than the volume of Box B?

A. 64
B. 1,448
C. 4,928
D. 5,056

10. An advertiser plans to print advertisements on one side panel of each of the boxes (the shaded faces in the drawing). What is the total area, in square centimeters, that the advertiser will cover?

A. 224
B. 384
C. 608
D. 1448

**Review your work using the explanations that start on page 706.**

# Geometry Practice Questions

1. What is the surface area, in square centimeters, of a cube with each edge length of 5 cm?

A. 15
B. 25
C. 125
D. 150

2. What is the surface area, in square centimeters, of a cylinder with a height of 10 cm and a radius of 6 cm?

A. $136\pi$
B. $160\pi$
C. $192\pi$
D. $256\pi$

3. What is the surface area, in square centimeters, of a cylinder that measures 8 cm tall with a diameter of 6 cm on its base?

A. $48\pi$
B. $57\pi$
C. $66\pi$
D. $132\pi$

4. A pyramid has a square base. If each edge of the pyramid is 4, what is the total surface area of the entire pyramid?

A. $8\sqrt{3}$
B. $8\sqrt{3}+16$
C. $16\sqrt{3}+16$
D. $64\sqrt{3}$

**Question 5 refers to the following figure.**

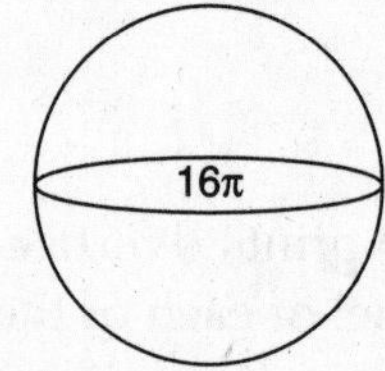


5. A toy factory paints all of its rubber balls with 2 coats of latex for durability. How many square centimeters of latex are needed to cover a rubber ball with a circumference of $16\pi$ cm?

A. $64\pi$
B. $128\pi$
C. $256\pi$
D. $512\pi$

6. The floor of a walk-in closet measures 7 feet by 4 feet. If the ceiling height is 8 feet, what is the volume in cubic feet of the closet?

A. 28
B. 56
C. 112
D. 224

**Question 7 refers to the following figure.**

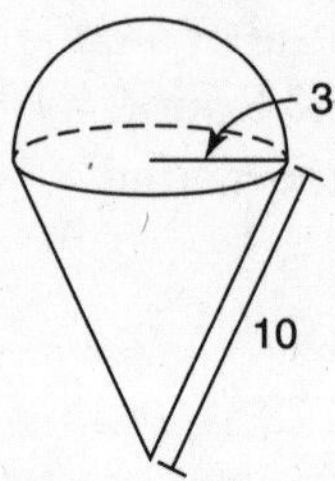


7. An ice cream cone has a spherical scoop of ice cream placed inside. Exactly one-half of the ice cream is visible above the rim of the cone. What is the surface area of the entire ice cream treat, in units squared?

A. $24\pi$
B. $30\pi$
C. $48\pi$
D. $60\pi$

8. The radius of Sphere A is 2, and the radius of Sphere B is 1. What is the ratio of the volume of Sphere A to that of Sphere B? (*Hint*: Use the formula for the volume of a sphere on page 420.)

A. 1:2
B. 4:1
C. 8:1
D. 8:3

**Question 9 refers to the following figure.**

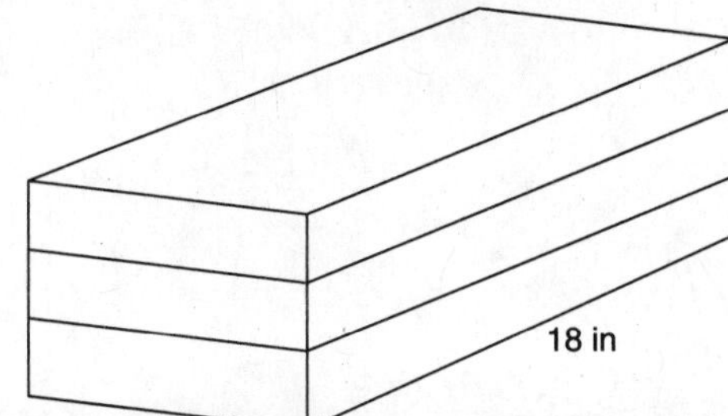


9. Three identical rectangular boxes are stacked one on top of another. The total height of all three boxes is the same as the width of one box. The length of the boxes is 18 in, and the width is half the length. What is the combined volume, in cubic inches, of all three boxes?

A. 1458
B. 1800
C. 2124
D. 3136

---

10. Using a compass, Max hikes 300 yards due north of his campsite. From that point, he hikes 400 yards due east. If he were to hike directly to his campsite from this point, how many yards would he have to hike?

A. 400
B. 500
C. 600
D. 700

11. The rectangular base of a container is 9 inches long and 7 inches wide. By how many cubic inches will the volume of the container increase if you increase the length of the base by 2 inches?

A. 84
B. 126
C. 168
D. 216

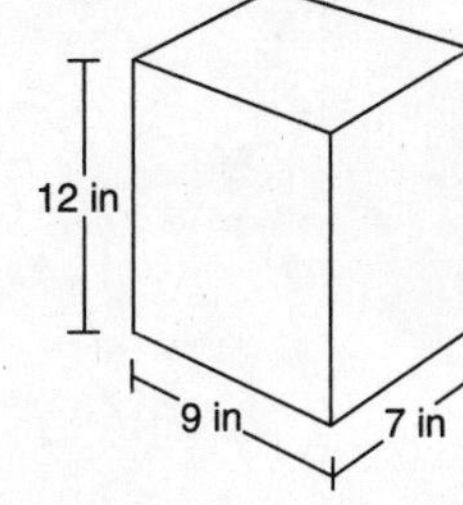


12. In a right triangle, the hypotenuse measures 15 inches. If one leg of the triangle measures 6 inches, which of the following equations could be used to find the length of the other leg ($x$) in inches?

A. $x = \sqrt{15 - 6}$
B. $x = 15 - 6$
C. $x^2 = 15^2 + 6^2$
D. $x^2 = 15^2 - 6^2$

13. The length of a rectangle is three times its width. If the perimeter of the rectangle is 96 inches, what is its length in inches?

A. 12
B. 24
C. 36
D. 48

**Question 14 refers to the following figure.**

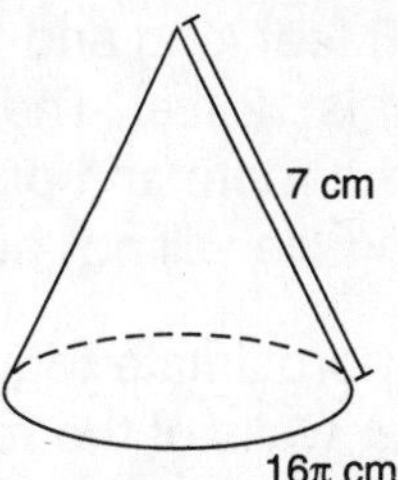


14. Sarah is making party hats for a birthday party. Each hat is in the shape of a cone and will have a circumference of $16\pi$ cm and a slant height of 7 cm. She will be making 20 hats. What is the total surface area, in square centimeters, of all 20 hats combined?

A. $32\pi$
B. $56\pi$
C. $112\pi$
D. $1120\pi$

**Question 15 refers to the following figure.**

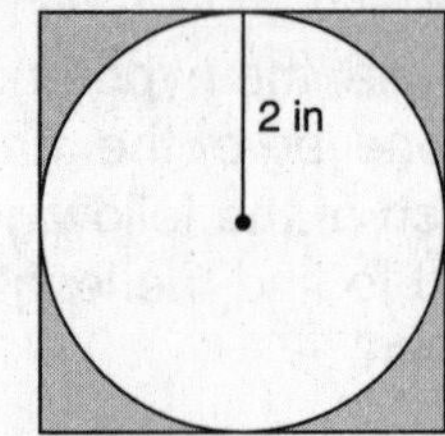


15. Use your calculator to make the following calculation. In the figure above, a square contains a circle such that each of the sides of the square is touching a point on the circle. What is the area, in square inches, of the shaded portion?

A. 3.43
B. 12.57
C. 16.00
D. 28.57

**Questions 16 and 17 refer to the following.**

A classroom is 40 feet long and 25 feet wide. The ceiling height is 12 feet. The school district plans to repaint the room and put in air-conditioning. The ceiling tile will not be painted.

16. What is the approximate total square footage of the four walls of the room? Ignore space taken up by windows and doors.

A. 1200
B. 1560
C. 1920
D. 4000

17. To choose an air-conditioning system, the school district must know the volume of the room. What is the volume in cubic feet?

A. 1000
B. 3120
C. 12000
D. 15625

**Question 18 refers to the following figures.**

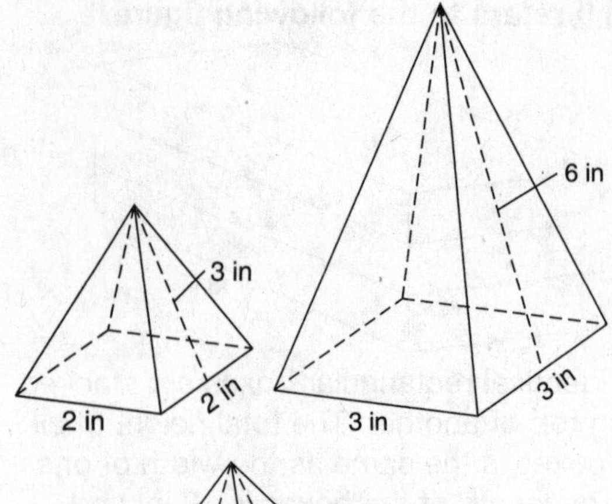


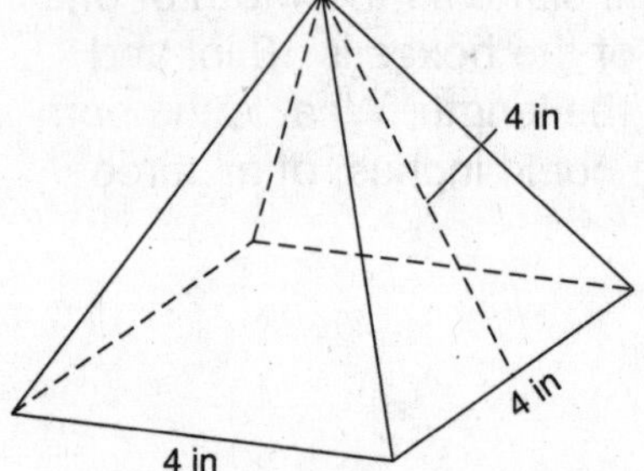


18. Laura is painting model pyramids for an art project. She needs one tube of paint for every 30 square inches of surface area. If Laura paints each pyramid and its base, approximately how many tubes of paint should she buy?

A. 4
B. 16
C. 48
D. 109

19. 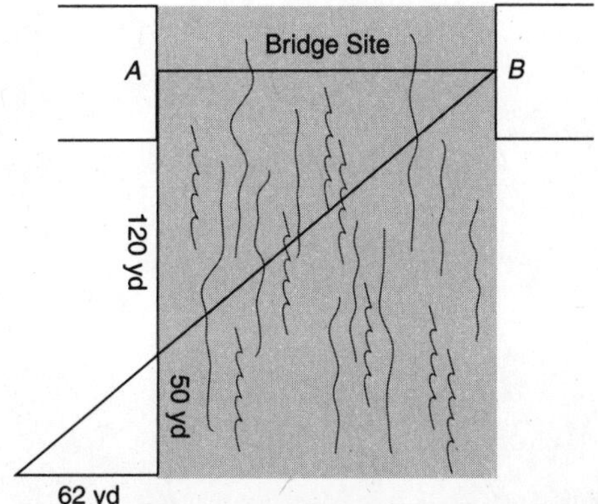


A city plans to build a bridge across a local river. To find the width the bridge will span, an engineer stakes out two similar triangles. What is the distance in yards from point *A* to point *B*?

A. 2.4
B. 25.8
C. 148.8
D. 170

**Questions 20 and 21 are based on the following figure.**

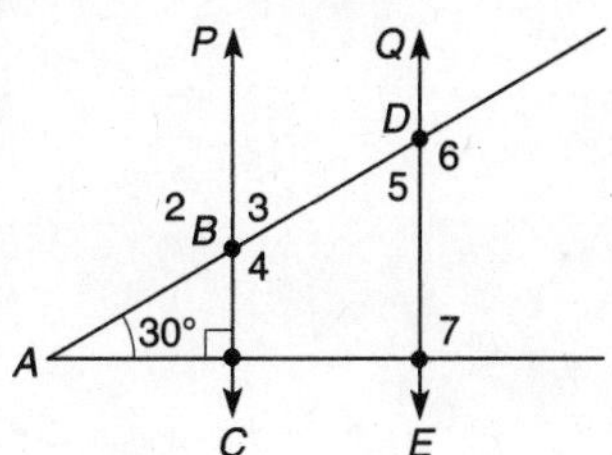


line $P \parallel$ line $Q$

20. Which of the following conclusions can you draw based on the information given in the drawing?

A. $m\angle 5 = 60°$
B. $\angle 7$ is an obtuse angle
C. $m\angle 3 = 30°$
D. $\angle 2$ must be a right angle

21. Which of the following is a true statement about the figure?

A. $m\angle 2 + m\angle 7 = 180°$
B. $m\angle 4 = m\angle 7$
C. $m\angle 3 + m\angle 4 = 90°$
D. $m\angle 3 + m\angle 6 = 180°$

**For questions 22 and 23, mark your answers in the grids below.**

22. The following diagram shows the length of the shadows of a man and a building at 4 P.M.

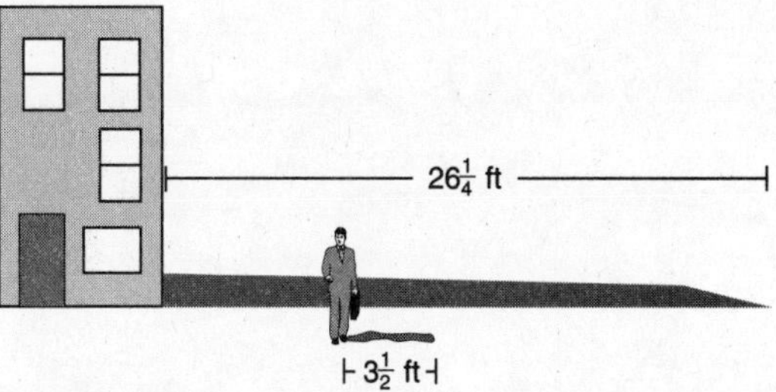


If the man in the drawing is 6 feet in height, what is the height of the building in feet?

23. A parallelogram has a base of 6 centimeters and a height of 10 centimeters. This parallelogram has the same area as a triangle with a height of 5 centimeters. What is the measure, in centimeters, of the base of the triangle?

22.

23.

**Review your work using the explanations that start on page 706.**

**STUDY ADVICE**

Congratulations! You've made it through the Mathematics unit. Reward yourself! And remember to review these concepts periodically as you continue to study, up until you take the TASC Mathematics Test.

ABOUT THE TEST

# Social Studies

The TASC Social Studies Test evaluates your ability to understand, interpret, and apply information. You will have 75 minutes* to answer approximately 47 items. On the 2014 TASC, all Social Studies items are in multiple-choice format.

## Content Areas

**Civics and Government (25%)** topics include modern and historic governments, constitutional government, levels and branches of the U.S. government, the electoral system, and the role of the citizen.

**U.S. History (25%)** topics stretch from colonialism and the American Revolution through the Civil War and Reconstruction into the modern era of industrialization, immigration, two world wars, the Cold War, and the movements for equal rights.

**Economics (20%)** topics include basic economics concepts and systems, the government and the economy, and labor and consumer economics issues.

**Geography (15%)** topics cover the relationship between resources, the environment, and societies.

**World History (15%)** topics cover major eras in world history.

## Social Studies Skills

In addition to testing your understanding of social studies passages and graphics, questions are based on your understanding of major skills, which introduce this unit on pages 438–455. After you study these skills, you will reinforce them as you work through the unit. They include:

- Determining **central ideas and making inferences**
- Analyzing **words, events,** and **ideas** in social studies contexts
- Analyzing authors' **purposes** and **points of view**
- Evaluate authors' **reasoning** and **evidence**
- Analyze **relationships within and between social studies materials**
- Interpret data and statistics in **graphs** and **charts**

(While you will be expected to interpret data, you will not have to perform extensive calculations during the TASC Social Studies Test. You will not have access to a calculator during the Social Studies Test.)

* Note: The information given here was the latest information available as of January 2014. It is possible that timing restrictions may change between this printing and your test date. For updates, visit www.tasctest.com.

LESSON 1

# Determine Central Idea and Draw Conclusions

The **central idea** of a passage or graphic is the main idea it is intended to convey. This is supported by **details** or **examples**.

At the outset of the Revolutionary War, the American colonies had a small navy of only 31 ships. To contest the far superior number of vessels in the British fleet, the colonies employed privateers, independent ships authorized to harass and capture enemy merchant and cargo ships. Armed with more than 14,000 guns, American privateers captured well over 2,000 enemy ships. These figures demonstrate how difficult it would have been, without the aid of privateers, for the colonies to win their independence against a larger, better equipped British Navy.

► What is the topic of this passage?

(1) the importance of colonial privateers to winning the Revolutionary War
(2) the fact that American privateers captured well over 2,000 enemy ships

Choice **(1)** is correct. The main point of the passage is that privateers were crucial to the colonies' success in their war for independence. The number of ships captured by privateers, referred to in choice (2), is used to support that point.

One skill needed to understand social studies information is the ability to **draw conclusions** from what you read or see. This skill requires you to go beyond what is directly stated and make an inference about what is meant or implied.

► Which of the following conclusions can be drawn based on this graph?

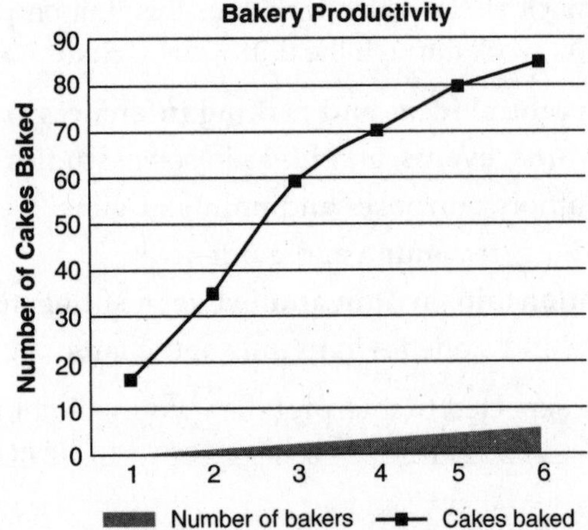


(1) The productivity of a bakery is based on a number of factors.
(2) The productivity of the bakery rises when more bakers are added.

You were correct if you selected choice **(2)**. As you look at the graph, the line—the number of cakes baked—rises steeply when more bakers are added. This associates the productivity of the bakery with the number of bakers. Choice (1) may well be true, but it is not a conclusion based on this graph.

## KEY IDEAS

- TASC Social Studies Test presentations consist of text, graphics, or a combination of the two.
- Comprehending social studies material requires understanding the central idea or point and its supporting details.
- Social Studies Test questions also require you to make inferences in order to draw conclusions.

## TASC TEST TIP

*To answer TASC questions based on a passage or graphic, ask yourself, "What is the main point? What evidence or details are used to support it? What conclusion can I draw?"*

# PRACTICE 1

**Questions 1 through 3 are based on the following passage.**

Theater was one of the most popular forms of art in ancient Greece, and one form of drama—tragedy—was central to Greek culture. Tragedies told familiar stories from Greek myths and epics, but actors portrayed the main roles, and a chorus narrated the background of the story and commented upon the action. These serious dramas centered on a main character who displayed exceptional attributes but also had a tragic flaw that caused his downfall. This flaw was often hubris, which is excessive pride or overconfidence.

1. Which of the following is the topic of the paragraph?

   A. the superiority of Greek theater
   B. the standard forms of Greek drama
   C. the characteristics of Greek tragedy
   D. the most popular Greek tragedies

2. Which of these details supports the central idea?

   A. Theater was one of the most popular Greek art forms.
   B. Tragedies were more important than comedies in ancient Greece.
   C. Greeks thought flaws other than hubris were not tragic.
   D. The main character in Greek drama has a tragic flaw that causes his downfall.

3. Which of these conclusions is supported by the paragraph?

   A. Ancient Greeks did not expect to see an original story each time they attended the theater.
   B. Playwrights in ancient Greece also wrote myths and epics.
   C. Tragedies in ancient Greece were judged on the basis of how serious their stories were.
   D. Only highly cultured people attended tragedies in ancient Greece.

**Questions 4 and 5 are based on this graphic.**

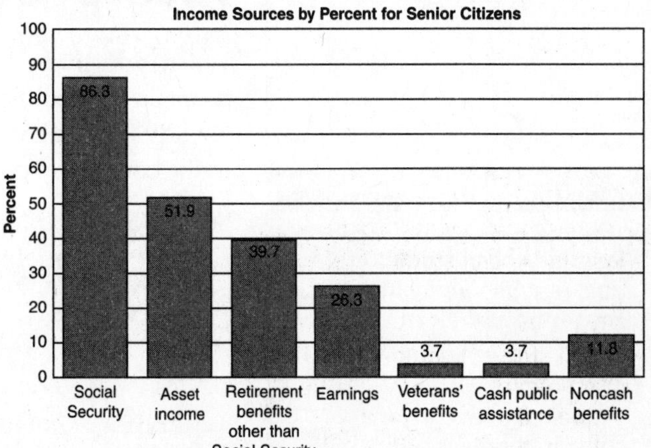


Source: Social Security Administration

4. The graph answers which of the following questions?

   A. What is the dollar value of the income for senior citizens?
   B. How much do senior citizens have in savings accounts?
   C. How many senior citizens are dependent upon veterans' benefits for their retirement income?
   D. Where do the incomes of senior citizens come from?

5. Which of the following conclusions can be drawn from this graph?

   A. More senior citizens need to continue to work in order to make ends meet now than in the past.
   B. Social Security benefits are the most widespread means of support for most senior citizens.
   C. Senior citizens who receive income from veterans' benefits also receive benefits from public assistance.
   D. Senior citizens who do not receive Social Security benefits get income from one or more other sources.

**Review your work using the explanations that start on page 708.**

## STUDY ADVICE

If you have trouble identifying the central idea of social studies passages, review the *Language Arts: Reading* lessons on pages 72–75. Identifying the main idea of a passage works the same way no matter what type of passage you are reading.

**LESSON 2**

# Interpret Words and Ideas

When you interpret social studies materials, you need to understand key **terms** in context. For instance, on page 472, the word *articles* is presented. You already know an everyday use of the word, such as "articles of clothing," but in the context on page 472, an *article* refers to a section of the U.S. Constitution.

Some social studies material is organized in **chronological** or time order. Look at the timeline below and answer a question about the sequence of events.

**Inventions in the 1870s**

| 1875 | 1876 | 1877 | 1879 |
|---|---|---|---|
| Blasting gel | Telephone | Cylinder phonograph<br>Carbon arc lightbulb | Cash register<br>Carbon filament lightbulb |

► Which of the following events preceded the invention of the carbon arc lightbulb?

(1) invention of the telephone
(2) invention of the carbon filament lightbulb

Timelines are read left to right from oldest to most recent, so choice **(1)** is correct. Choice (2) refers to the carbon filament lightbulb, invented in 1879, a year after the carbon arc lightbulb.

Another way that social studies material is organized is by **cause and effect**, which is another way of asking "What resulted from this action?" or "What made this event happen?" Read the following paragraph to practice this skill.

The prices of goods and services are determined by the relationship between supply and demand. When supply exceeds demand, sellers must lower prices to stimulate sales; on the other hand, when demand exceeds supply, consumers bid up prices as they compete to purchase items or services that they desire.

► Based on the theory of supply and demand, under which of the following scenarios would prices be most likely to rise?

(1) The demand for a product exceeds that product's supply.
(2) Producers and sellers advertise a product in order to stimulate demand for that product.

Choice **(1)** is correct. According to the law of supply and demand, prices rise when demand outpaces supply. Choice (2) describes a situation in which producers and sellers advertise to stimulate demand for their product, but without knowing whether the supply is limited, we cannot conclude that this would cause the price to increase.

Some questions may require you to understand that the fact that two events **correlate,** or happen at the same time, does not necessarily mean that one **caused** the other. Remember that causation can never be deduced from correlation alone.

**KEY IDEAS**

- Reading social studies materials requires understanding key terms in their context.
- Social studies material is often organized as a sequence of events or as steps in a process.
- Analyzing social studies materials often involves relating causes to effects.

**TASC TEST TIP**

*To learn key social studies terms, pay close attention to the meaning of the words in* ***bold type*** *throughout this unit.*

# PRACTICE 2

**Questions 1 through 3 are based on this passage.**

From 1820 to 1870, more than 7.5 million immigrants arrived on U.S. shores. That was more people than the entire U.S. population in 1810. Almost all of these immigrants came from Northern Europe, and a majority were Catholic. Historians have often focused on what pushed these emigrants out of Europe. During the 1840s, for example, Germany experienced a series of crop failures that, combined with social upheaval triggered by rapid industrialization in urban areas, produced riots, civil unrest, and open rebellion. During the same years, Ireland saw the infamous potato famine strike poor and working-class Irish families, killing an estimated 700,000 people.

While those crises spurred Europeans to emigrate, a variety of factors created a simultaneous pull to immigrate to the United States. Letters home from friends and family members who had immigrated earlier often described the United States as a "land of plenty" and related stories of successful employment and plentiful land. Steamship companies offering passage across the Atlantic advertised with posters that showed majestic scenes of American abundance.

1. According to the passage, which of the following was a cause of Northern European immigration to the United States in the 1840s and 1850s?

   A. Americans' desire to double the population of the United States
   B. efforts by Northern European governments to reduce the number of people living in poverty
   C. political and social instability in some Northern European countries
   D. efforts to spread Catholicism to the United States

2. Based on the passage, which one of the following was most likely to have been featured on a steamship company poster?

   A. a folk-art painting depicting the life of the rural poor in the United States
   B. a portrait of an American politician from the 1840s
   C. a poster advertising an American product
   D. a painting of pioneers settling and farming productive prairie land

3. Which of the following results of Northern European immigration to the United States in the mid-1800s can be inferred from the passage?

   A. a spread of poverty in the United States
   B. a decline in political upheaval in Northern Europe
   C. a growth in the population of the United States
   D. a number of Americans converting to the Catholic faith

**Questions 4 and 5 are based on this timeline.**

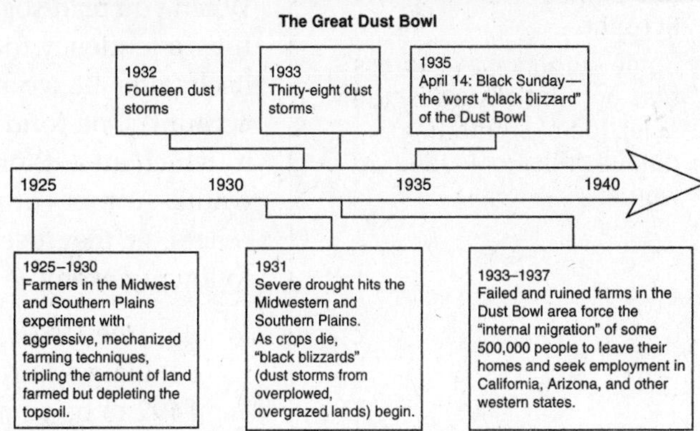


Source: www.pbs.org

4. Given the information in the timeline, which of the following would be a flawed inference?

   A. Mechanized farming contributed to dust storms.
   B. Internal migration led to overgrazing.
   C. Severe drought contributed to "black blizzards."
   D. Some farmers left the Dust Bowl before the worst dust storm hit the region.

5. Which of the following could have been a cause of the Great Dust Bowl?

   A. "black blizzards"
   B. internal migration
   C. depleted topsoil
   D. failed farms

**Review your work using the explanations that start on page 708.**

LESSON 3

# Analyze Author's Purpose and Point of View

Any author of social studies material has a viewpoint and a purpose. Social studies material can have many purposes, such as to inform or educate (for example, a textbook or magazine article). Other materials, such as newspaper editorials and online blogs, are used to convince people of a point of view.

An author's **point of view** is his or her way of looking at the world. Some social scientists follow a method of examining the facts and coming to a conclusion. In other cases, an author may start with a point of view and assemble facts or evidence to support it.

When you read social studies materials, determine whether an author has a **bias**, a tendency to see one point of view. A bias is not a bad thing in and of itself (after all, we all have biases), but you should take the author's bias into account. One kind of material that displays extreme bias is **propaganda**, in which an author tries to convince people to act and think as the author wants. Authors of propaganda selectively include certain facts and ignore others, or they use loaded words to trigger emotional responses. Use the following example to practice finding the author's point of view.

> Until the 1980s, most anthropologists mistakenly estimated the native population in North America at the time of Columbus's expedition in 1492 to be somewhere between 2 million and 7 million people. They based these estimates on the number of Native Americans alive at the time of their first contact with European explorers and settlers. However, the estimates ignored the impact of infectious diseases, such as smallpox, which traveled much faster than humans did and would have decimated the native population before Europeans made contact with native people.

► What is the author's point of view about the population of North America in 1492?

(1) that it was not exactly 2 million people or 7 million people but was somewhere in between those two numbers
(2) that it was probably much larger than 7 million people

Choice **(2)** is correct. The author points out a reason to think that anthropologists prior to the 1980s undercounted the native population. Answer (1) gives the estimate of most anthropologists prior to the 1980s.

► Which of the following words is a clue to the author's viewpoint?

(1) ignored
(2) estimated

The correct choice is **(1)**. The author believes that the anthropologists' estimates were flawed because they ignored relevant information about the impact of diseases on the native population. Answer (2) misses the author's point; he doesn't fault them for estimating, but rather for ignoring evidence when they made their estimates.

### KEY IDEAS

- Social studies material may be written to inform or to persuade.
- Thoughtful readers need to take an author's purpose and point of view into account.
- Some authors may express a bias or point of view by the selection of supporting details or use of loaded words.

### TASC TEST TIP

*You may be provided with a newspaper editorial, an online blog commentary, or a speech. Ask yourself, "What is the author's viewpoint? How are facts and evidence organized to be convincing? How are words chosen to have an impact?"*

# PRACTICE 3

**Questions 1 through 3 are based on the paragraph and poster below.**

During World War I, the U.S. National War Garden Commission began a campaign to encourage private citizens to grow their own food as a means of supporting the war effort. This practice became very popular. With increased private food production, the government could reserve much of the cheaper, mass-produced food for the troops. The money saved in feeding soldiers freed up resources for other military needs. In addition, planting war gardens, also known as victory gardens, gave American citizens a sense of empowerment.

Source: Library of Congress Poster by James Montgomery Flagg

1. Which of the following best describes the poster's use of the word *Victory*?

   A. ambiguous
   B. informative
   C. propagandistic
   D. impersonal

**STUDY ADVICE**

If you find it difficult to identify an author's point of view, review the *Language Arts: Reading* lesson on pages 88–89.

2. What is meant by the poster's caption "Every Garden a Munition Plant"?

   A. War gardens require a great deal of time to cultivate.
   B. Citizens who plant war gardens encourage a sense of community in their hometowns.
   C. Citizens who plant war gardens help supply the war effort with essential resources.
   D. War gardens provide an excellent opportunity to learn about gardening, canning, and food drying.

3. The author's primary purpose in writing the paragraph accompanying the poster is most likely to

   A. describe war gardens and explain their popularity in the United States
   B. encourage patriotism and continued support for a strong United States military
   C. distinguish the efforts of American citizens during World War I from those of citizens in other countries
   D. rebut the accusations of those who claimed that civilians did not do enough to support the U.S. war effort in World War I

**Question 4 is based on the following dialogue.**

Congresswoman Burns: The new organic food safety regulations are likely to increase the average cost of some food staples. The costs are justified, however, by the peace of mind that comes from knowing your food is safe and healthy.

Concerned Citizen: Rising prices are a cancer eating away at our families. High costs will drive people away from healthy foods and wind up harming our children's diets. Instead of buying wholesome, natural products, parents will feed their kids fast food.

4. Which of the following constitute "loaded" words the Concerned Citizen uses to support her point?

   A. high costs
   B. fast food
   C. a cancer
   D. our children's diets

**Review your work using the explanations that start on page 708.**

LESSON 4

# Evaluate Author's Reasoning and Evidence

Social studies authors in print and online publications use a variety of strategies to support their viewpoints. They may use the following:

- **Facts**—information that can be proven to be true
- **Opinions**—beliefs about a concept or situation
- **Judgments**—conclusions that are supported by reasons and evidence

On the TASC Social Studies Test, you need to read carefully to distinguish among these three concepts.

► Indicate whether each of the following statements is a fact (F), an opinion (O), or a judgment (J).

(1) ___ Because it raises the amount employers will pay in payroll taxes, the new tax bill may contribute to higher unemployment.

(2) ___ Last year, manufacturing output in our state rose by 4.6 percent over the previous year.

(3) ___ We should limit the role played by the federal government in formulating energy policy for our region of the country.

Statement (1) is a judgment; the author's conclusion (that the bill may increase unemployment) is based on evidence (that the bill raises payroll taxes). Statement (2) is a fact; the truth or falsity of the statement can be checked against empirical data. Statement (3) is an opinion; the author makes a recommendation (limit the role of the federal government) but offers no evidence or reasoning to support it.

To be credible, a author needs to support his or her claims with evidence. Part of your job on the Social Studies Test is to answer questions about whether or not an author's claims are supported.

Delaware was the first state to ratify the U.S. Constitution. Because of its history of favorable corporate tax policies, Delaware is today home to 63 percent of Fortune 500 corporations. There is no doubt then that Delaware's freedom-of-information act, requiring the state government to respond within 15 days of a request, should serve as a model for similar acts in other U.S. states.

► Does the author support the claim of the passage?

(1) Yes, because he believes and asserts that there is no doubt about the truth of the claim.

(2) No, because he asserts the truth of the claim without offering evidence relevant to the claim.

Choice **(2)** is correct. The author's claim is that Delaware's freedom-of-information act should serve as a model for similar acts in other states, but the other statements in the passage are irrelevant to that claim. Choice (1) is incorrect because stating a claim firmly ("no doubt") does not provide *support* for the claim.

### KEY IDEAS

- An author's point of view may be supported by facts, opinions, and reasoned judgment.
- While reading, analyze whether information is a fact, an opinion, or a conclusion based on reasoning or evidence.
- A careful reader evaluates whether an author supports his or her claims with evidence.

### TASC TEST TIP

*When you read social studies material, ask yourself, "What is the claim being made? Is evidence provided to support this claim? Is the evidence relevant to the claim and sufficient and credible enough to support it?"*

# PRACTICE 4

1. Consultant: Finding a reliable energy supply is vital to Cambodia, a country still recovering from decades of civil war and genocide in the late 1970s. Damming the Mekong River could solve Cambodia's energy supply problems. However, since the Mekong flows through China, Myanmar, Laos, and Thailand before it reaches Cambodia, regional cooperation will be necessary.

   Which of the following is an opinion, and not a fact, presented by the consultant?

   A. Damming the Mekong could solve Cambodia's energy problems.
   B. The Mekong River flows through several countries before reaching Cambodia.
   C. Cambodia experienced civil war.
   D. Many Cambodians were killed in the late 1970s.

**Question 2 is based on this cartoon referencing the labor movement of the early 20th century.**

Protected by George Matthew Adams.
SPITING HIMSELF.
—Morris for the George Matthew Adams Service.

Source: Literary Digest 9/6/19. Originally from the George Matthew Adams Service (Morris).

2. Which of the following represents the viewpoint of the cartoonist?

   A. Strikes can achieve better working conditions.
   B. Strikes have a detrimental impact on workers.
   C. Farmworkers are more likely to engage in strikes than are factory workers.
   D. Strikes should hamper production.

3. Historian: Ancient Greece was the greatest of the early civilizations. While the Babylonians may have had arithmetic and ancient Egypt built the pyramids, ancient Greece gave us our first taste of democracy.

   Which of the following is a fact that the historian uses to support her opinion?

   A. Ancient Greece was the greatest early civilization.
   B. Babylonians made use of arithmetic.
   C. The pyramids were built in ancient Egypt.
   D. Ancient Greece pioneered democracy.

**Question 4 is based on the following chart.**

The Articles of Confederation were the predecessor to the United States Constitution.

| | The Articles of Confederation | The Constitution |
|---|---|---|
| **Federal Court System** | No system of federal courts | Court system exists to deal with issues between citizens, states |
| **Regulating Trade** | No provision to regulate interstate trade | Congress has the right to regulate trade between states |
| **Executive Power** | No executive with power; president merely presided over Congress | Executive branch is headed by president who chooses Cabinet and has checks on power of judiciary and legislature |
| **Raising an Army** | Congress could not draft troops; depended on states to contribute forces | Congress can raise an army to deal with military situations |
| **Sovereignty** | Sovereignty resides in states | The Constitution is the supreme law of the land |
| **Taxes** | Congress could ask states to pay taxes | Congress has the right to levy taxes on individuals |

4. Which of the following is a conclusion supported by the table above, rather than a detail stated in the table?

   A. The Constitution allows Congress to enforce collection of taxes, whereas the Articles of Confederation did not.
   B. The Constitution grants more power to the federal government than did the Articles of Confederation.
   C. There were no national armed forces before the Constitution was drafted.
   D. Trade was not nationally regulated by the Articles of Confederation.

**Review your work using the explanations that start on page 708.**

LESSON 5

# Analyze Relationships Between Materials

KEY IDEAS

- Social studies materials may use graphics to illustrate key concepts.
- Circle, bar, and line graphs visually portray social studies information.
- Maps are drawings that show places and regions with keys, compasses, and scales.

TASC TEST TIP

*When you interpret a social studies graphic, carefully read the title and all labels and keys to make sure that you correctly understand the main idea and the type of information being displayed.*

## Content Presented in Graphic Format

Social studies content is often presented in graphic form. Two of the most useful displays are graphs and maps.

**Circle graphs** are used to show how a whole is divided into parts; they show fractions or percents.

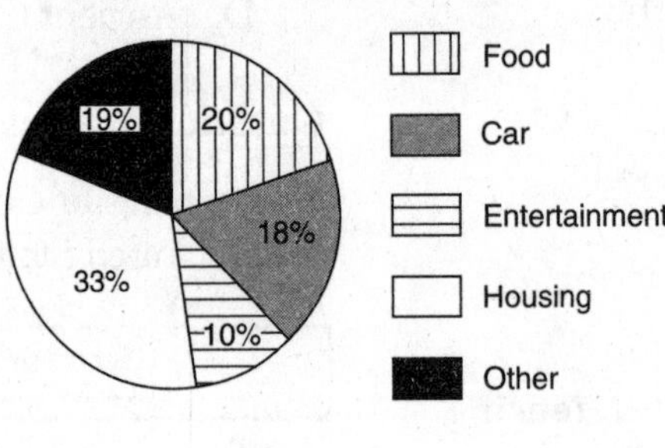


**Line graphs** and **bar graphs** organize material by using labels on the bottom axis and values on the side.

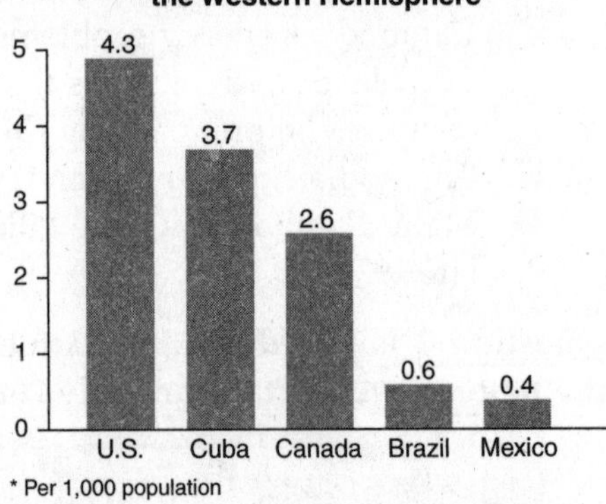


**Maps** use a **legend** (also called the **key**) to explain symbols, a **compass rose** to indicate directions, and **scales** to determine distances.

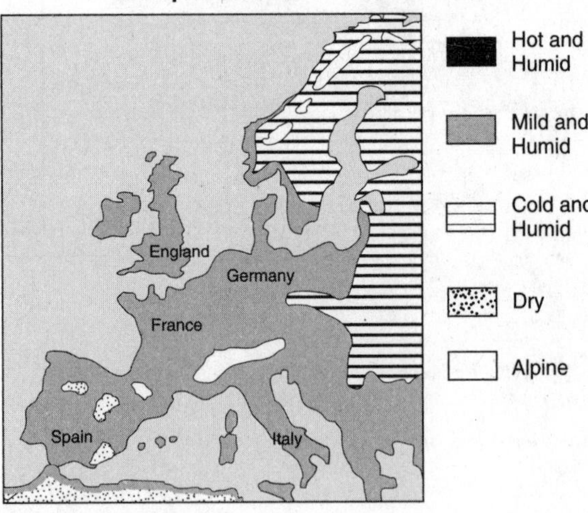


► According to the map, what is England's climate?

(1) mild and humid

(2) cold and humid

The correct answer here is choice **(1)**. To interpret information on a map, note any labels printed directly on the map—in this case, England appears just to the left and slightly above the center. Then check the legend to see whether the color, shading, or symbols shown give additional information. On this map, England is shown in gray, indicating that its climate is "mild and humid."

# PRACTICE 5.1

1. According to the circle graph on page 446, the greatest portion of the Sanchez family's budget is spent on which two items?

   A. housing and food
   B. housing and entertainment
   C. food and car
   D. entertainment and other

2. Which of the following statements is supported by the bar graph on page 446?

   A. Cuba has the highest divorce rate in the hemisphere.
   B. Mexico has the lowest divorce rate in the hemisphere.
   C. Mexico's divorce rate is decreasing.
   D. Brazil has a higher divorce rate than Mexico.

**Questions 3 and 4 refer to the following graph.**

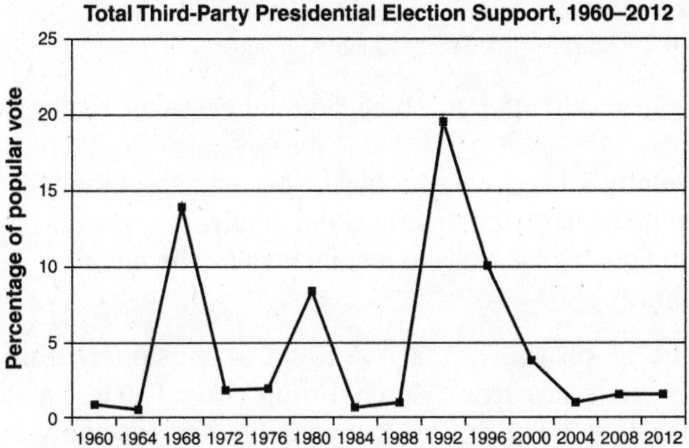


3. Based on the graph, you may validly infer that support for third-party candidates ________ during the 1980s and 1990s.

   A. steadily increased
   B. steadily decreased
   C. neither increased nor decreased
   D. fluctuated

4. The graph can be used to disprove which one of the following claims?

   A. Third-party candidates have not enjoyed significant support in the 21st century.
   B. The third-party candidate who garnered the most support since 1960 was Ross Perot in 1992.
   C. Third party candidates have never captured more than 10 percent of the popular vote in any presidential election.
   D. In most elections, all third-party candidates combined get less than 5 percent of the popular vote.

**Questions 5 and 6 are based on the following map.**

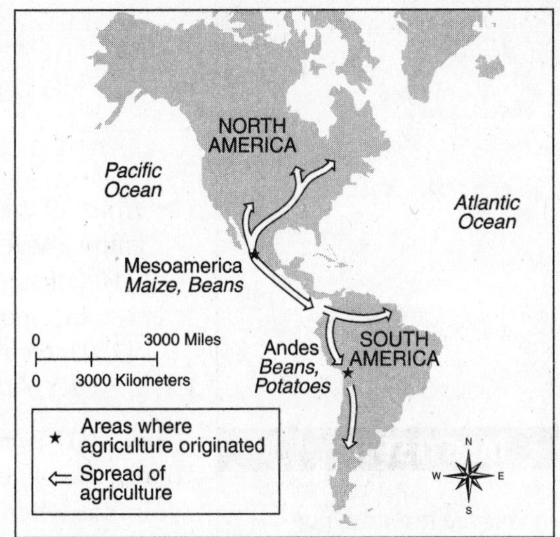


5. What does this map show?

   A. political boundaries in the ancient Americas
   B. physical features of the Americas
   C. how agriculture spread in the Americas
   D. all ancient civilizations of the Americas

6. Which of the following statements is supported by the information on the map?

   A. Both the Andes civilization and Mesoamerica domesticated maize.
   B. Both the Andes civilization and Mesoamerica domesticated beans.
   C. Agriculture developed in the Andes civilization before it did in Mesoamerica.
   D. Agriculture spread more rapidly northward than southward.

**Review your work using the explanations that start on page 708.**

## Integrating Text and Graphic Content

In reading social studies materials and the materials you encounter in daily life, you often have to combine text information with a graphic. For example, an online article about a conflict in Africa may have a map. A newspaper graph with information about new immigrants in your community may accompany a story about their contributions to local health care and manufacturing industries.

Practice combining information with the passage and graphic below.

> Consumer confidence is an economic indicator that reflects how optimistic consumers are about their personal finances, given the state of the economy. When consumer confidence shows a monthly trend of decline month after month, consumers are pessimistic about their chances of finding and keeping good jobs. When their confidence is low, consumers spend less—especially on nonessential items—and tend to save more of their money. On the other hand, when confidence is high, consumers will make more discretionary, or optional, purchases.

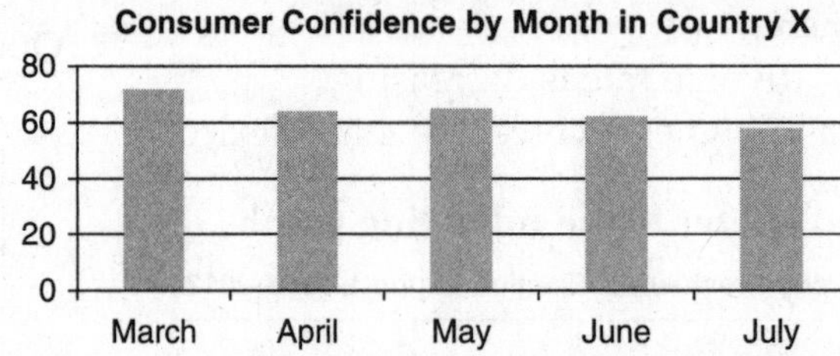


▶ Which of the following is a valid inference based on the passage and the graph above?

(1) Consumers in Country X likely spent a higher percentage of their income on luxury items in March than they did in July.

(2) Unemployment in Country X is likely to remain high for the remainder of the year shown.

Choice **(1)** is correct. The graph shows that the trend in consumer confidence has generally been in decline from March through July. The text tells you that when consumer confidence is lower, consumers are less likely to spend, especially on nonessential goods. These two statements combined support choice (1). Answer (2) cannot be inferred from the information in the passage or that in the graph. Neither of those sources provides a basis to make a prediction about future unemployment.

**KEY IDEAS**

- Some situations combine text information with a graphic.
- To better understand the main point or supporting evidence, you need to combine information from both sources.

**TASC TEST TIP**

*When you see text accompanied by a graphic, read the questions carefully. Some questions may ask about the text or the graphic individually. Others may ask you to combine information from both sources.*

# PRACTICE 5.2

**Questions 1 through 3 relate to the following passage and map.**

The sea otter (*Enhydra lutris*) is a marine mammal native to the coasts of the northern and eastern North Pacific Ocean. At one time, sea otters populated the entire coast of what is now the state of California and farther south along Mexico's Baja California coastline. Prior to 1741, the sea otter population worldwide is estimated to have been 150,000–300,000.

Between 1741 and 1911, however, sea otters were hunted extensively for their fur, and the world population fell to just 1,000–2,000 individuals. By 1911, the wild sea otter population in California was limited exclusively to a small area around Monterey Bay.

Fortunately, an international ban on hunting, conservation efforts, and programs to reintroduce the sea otter into previously populated areas have contributed to numbers rebounding, and the species now occupies about two-thirds of its former range. Despite these successes, sea otter populations in California have declined, and the sea otter remains classified as an endangered species.

**Current Range of the Sea Otter in California**

* Maps and ranges not to scale

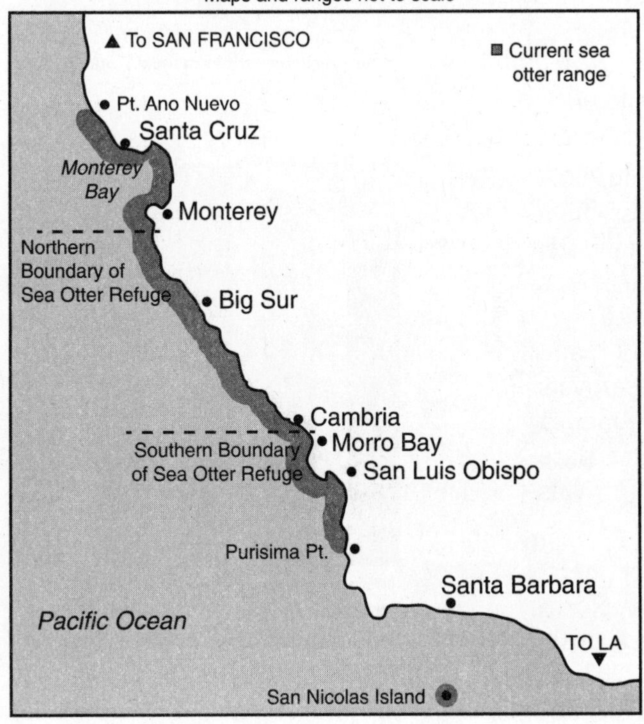


1. According to the passage, which one of the following statements about the sea otter is true?
   A. Sea otter conservation efforts have been more successful in areas outside of California than they have been within California.
   B. Sea otter populations were threatened by water pollution as well as by extensive hunting.
   C. The sea otter population is now about two-thirds of its pre-1741 number.
   D. Sea otters have been able to live in habitats from which they were once eliminated.

2. Which of the following conclusions can be drawn from the information in the passage and the map?
   A. Sea otters will soon have the same range they had prior to 1741.
   B. Sea otter habitat has been restored only within the boundaries of the Sea Otter Refuge.
   C. Sea otters are still hunted in the area north of Point Ano Nuevo.
   D. The current range of the sea otter in California is larger than it was in 1911.

3. The author of the passage would be most likely to agree with which of the following statements about the information in the map?
   A. The range of sea otters shown on the map indicates that sea otter conservation programs are no longer needed.
   B. The range of sea otters shown on the map is identical to the range of sea otters prior to 1741.
   C. Without conservation efforts and reintroduction programs, the range of sea otters in California would be smaller than what is shown on the map.
   D. Ten years from now, the range of sea otters in California will be larger than what is currently shown on the map.

**Review your work using the explanations that start on page 709.**

LESSON 6

# Interpret Data and Statistics

Social studies materials often involve data or statistics. The TASC Social Studies Test will not require you to perform extensive calculations, and you will not use a calculator during the Social Studies Test. However, you may be asked to interpret data to spot **trends,** make **comparisons** or **contrasts,** or make **inferences** from data.

### KEY IDEAS

- Tables and graphs are commonly used to present data in social studies materials.
- A measure of central tendency is used to summarize data with one number.
- Bar graphs are used to compare data, and line graphs are used to show trends.

**Franklin County Family Finances**

| Year | Median income (family of 4) | Average % to taxes | Average % to savings |
|---|---|---|---|
| 2009 | $40,800 | 27% | 5.2% |
| 2010 | $41,500 | 28% | 6.0% |
| 2011 | $42,300 | 29% | 5.5% |
| 2012 | $44,100 | 29% | 5.1% |

► Which of the following statements about Franklin County families is supported by the table?

(1) An increase in their median income over the last few years has caused those families to save less.

(2) An increase in their median income has not necessarily resulted in an increase in the percent of their income saved by those families.

Choice **(2)** is correct. As the median income has increased over the last few years, the rate of savings has not, on average increased. Choice (1) is not supported because the table contains no information about what causes Franklin County families to behave in any way.

Some questions may ask you to use graphs to make comparisons or to identify trends.

### TASC TEST TIP

*On the TASC Social Studies Test, you may be asked to interpret data in ways that do not involve calculations. Ask yourself, "What can I infer from this graph or table?" And also, "What can't I infer from it?"*

► What of the following trends is indicated by the data in the chart?

(1) Between 2003 and 2007, foreign arrivals from overseas grew at a faster pace than foreign arrivals from North America.

(2) Between 2003 and 2007, foreign arrivals from North America grew at a faster pace than foreign arrivals from overseas.

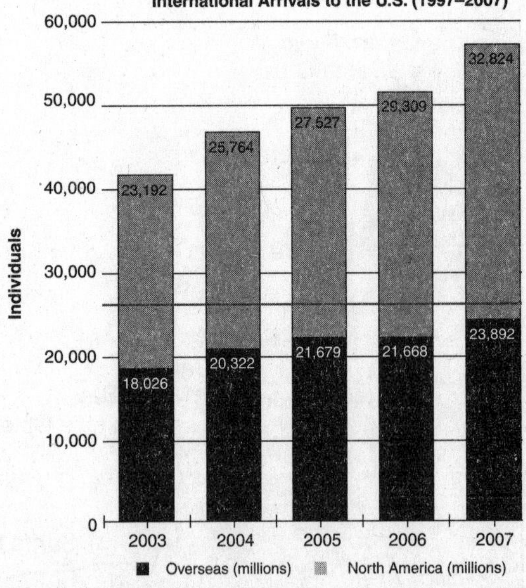

Source: U.S. Department of Commerce, Office of Travel and Tourism Industries

Choice **(2)** is correct here. Foreign arrivals from North America grew from a little over 23 million in 2003 to almost 33 million in 2007, an increase of around 41 percent. Meanwhile, overseas arrivals rose from roughly 18 million in 2003 to just under 24 million, a change of approximately 33 percent growth.

# PRACTICE 6

Question 1 is based on the following table.

| New Mexico: Population by Age, 2010 | |
|---|---|
| Under 18 | 518,672 |
| 18–19 | 61,169 |
| 20–24 | 142,370 |
| 25–34 | 267,245 |
| 35–49 | 393,362 |
| 50–64 | 404,106 |
| 65 & over | 272,255 |
| **Total** | **2,059,179** |

Adapted from U.S. Census Bureau

1. The table provides data that will allow you to answer which one of the following questions about New Mexico in 2010?

   A. What specific age was the median age?
   B. How many residents were teenagers?
   C. What percent of residents were 50 or older?
   D. Why were individuals over 65 such a small part of the population?

Question 2 is based on the following line graph.

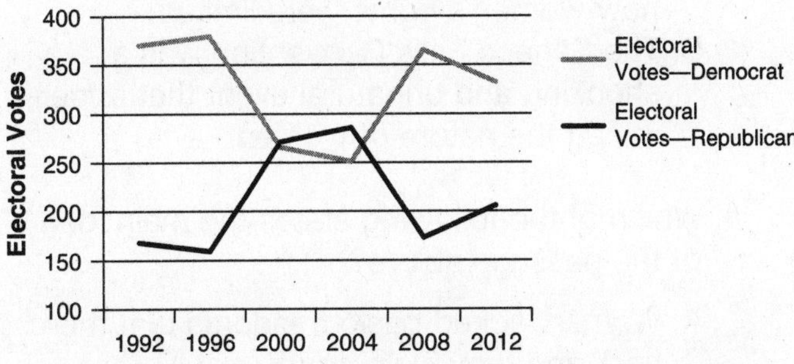


2. The information in the graph supports the conclusion that in the presidential elections from 1992 to 2012,

   A. Democrats and Republicans won the presidency an equal number of times.
   B. the average margin of victory was higher in years when a Democrat won than in years when a Republican won.
   C. the average margin of victory was higher in years when a Republican won than in years when a Democrat won.
   D. more electoral votes were cast in the 2008 presidential election than were cast in the 1996 presidential election.

Questions 3 and 4 are based on the following chart.

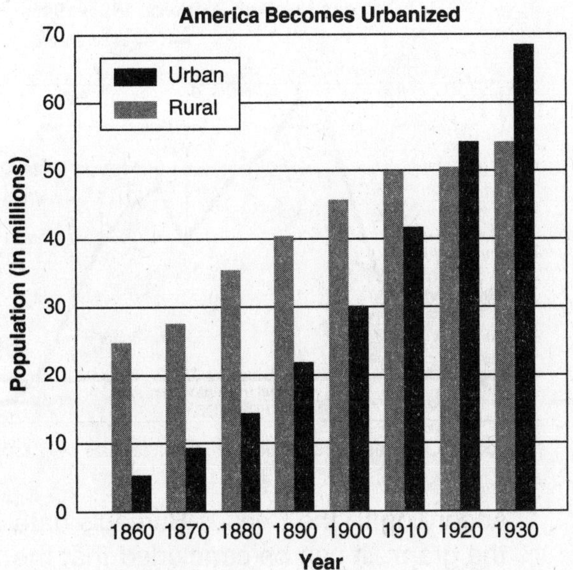


Source: U.S. Census (adapted)

3. According to the bar graph, in what year were there approximately as many Americans living in rural locations as there were in urban settings?

   A. 1860
   B. 1910
   C. 1920
   D. 1930

4. During the decades represented in the graph, the urban population of the United States grew at increasing rates, while the rural population

   A. continued to grow at a steady rate.
   B. grew and then shrank.
   C. continued to grow, but at decreasing rates.
   D. grew at first and then stopped growing.

**Review your work using the explanations that start on page 709.**

# SOCIAL STUDIES SKILLS PRACTICE QUESTIONS

**Questions 1 and 2 are based on the following line graph and timeline.**

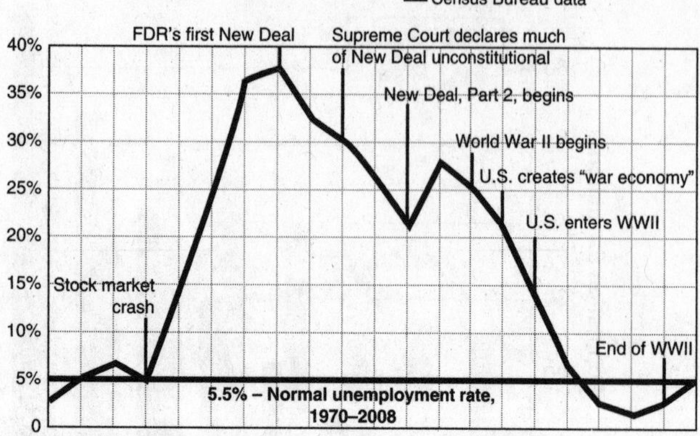


Source: U.S. Census Bureau, Bureau of Labor Statistics

1. According to the Census Bureau's data on the graph, it can be concluded that the onset of World War II contributed to which change in the U.S. unemployment rate?

   A. The unemployment rate stabilized at the beginning of World War II and remained stable until the war's end.
   B. The unemployment rate declined consistently until shortly before the war's end.
   C. The unemployment rate decreased during World War II but remained above the normal rate throughout the war.
   D. The unemployment rate increased gradually throughout the war.

2. According to the graph, the most significant and uninterrupted change in the U.S. unemployment rate between 1926 and 1946 occurred immediately after

   A. the stock market crash
   B. FDR's first New Deal
   C. New Deal, Part 2, began
   D. the U.S. entered World War II

**Questions 3 and 4 are based on the following passage.**

The women's rights movement in the United States gained strength with the 1848 Seneca Falls Convention. The defining document of this gathering was the Declaration of Sentiments, which was patterned after the Declaration of Independence but focused on the fact that women lacked basic freedoms that men enjoyed. The revolutionary nature of the Seneca Falls Convention was apparent in the public's response to the event. One newspaper described Seneca Falls as "the most shocking and unnatural event ever recorded in the history of womanity."

3. Which of the following statements based on the passage is an opinion, not a fact?

   A. The Seneca Falls Convention helped the women's rights movement gain strength.
   B. The Declaration of Sentiments was modeled on the Declaration of Independence.
   C. The Declaration of Sentiments described how women's rights were limited.
   D. The Seneca Falls Convention was a shocking and unnatural event that undermined the nature of women.

4. Which of the following states the main idea of the passage above?

   A. Women lacked basic freedoms that men had, and they were angry.
   B. The Seneca Falls Convention was open to both men and women.
   C. The women's rights movement was stronger in Seneca Falls than in the rest of the United States.
   D. The Seneca Falls Convention was important in the fight for women's rights.

**Questions 5 and 6 refer to the following map.**

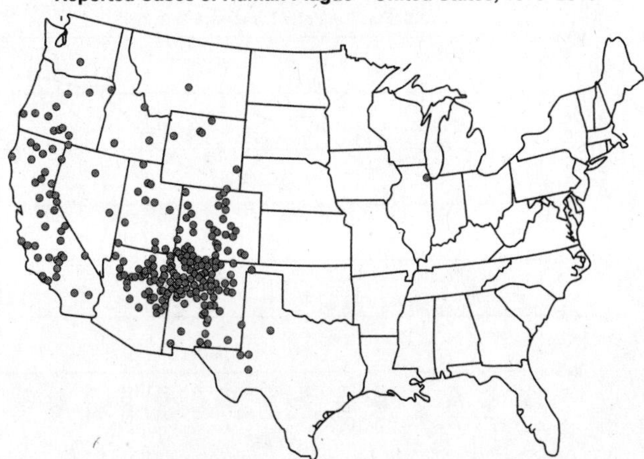


5. Which of the following conclusions is supported by this map?

   A. More than half of the reported cases of human plague in the United States between 1970 and 2010 were reported in four states.
   B. More than 99 percent of diphtheria-related deaths in the United States between 1970 and 2010 occurred in the western half of the United States.
   C. The majority of reported cases of plague in the American Southwest spread from one infected person.
   D. In the United States, human plague most frequently occurs within larger cities, where the risk of contagion is greatest.

6. The map above could be used to disprove which of the following claims?

   A. There were more cases of plague in the United States between 2000 and 2010 than there were between 1990 and 2000.
   B. Although many cases of plague have been reported in the United States since 1970, no deaths have been reported.
   C. Several cases of plague were reported on the East Coast of the United States between 1970 and 2010.
   D. Plague is less virulent in colder climates than it is in warmer climates.

**Question 7 is based on the following passage and chart.**

The invention of the cotton gin by Eli Whitney in 1784 revolutionized the cotton industry in the American South. The separation of the cotton seeds and fibers, once a painstaking task that slaves performed by hand, could now be done quickly by machine. This made cotton goods more affordable, thereby increasing international demand for these goods and, consequently, the profits of cotton farmers. Ironically, however, the cotton gin did not reduce the South's reliance on slavery. In fact, with the boom of the cotton industry, more slaves were used to pick the cotton at a faster rate to keep up with the increasing demand for cotton.

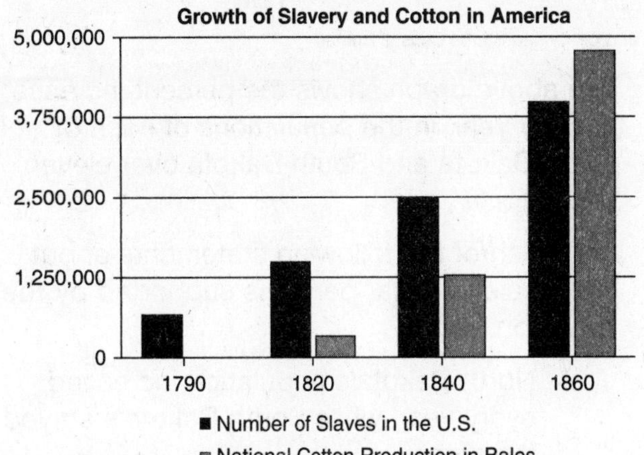


7. Which of the following conclusions is supported by the passage?

   A. Eli Whitney invented the cotton gin with the hope that it would reduce slavery.
   B. The cotton gin had little impact on the cotton industry in the South.
   C. After the invention of the cotton gin, many plantation owners found that they needed fewer slaves.
   D. The effects of the cotton gin on the cotton industry actually led to an increased demand for slaves in the South.

**Question 8 is based on the following graph.**

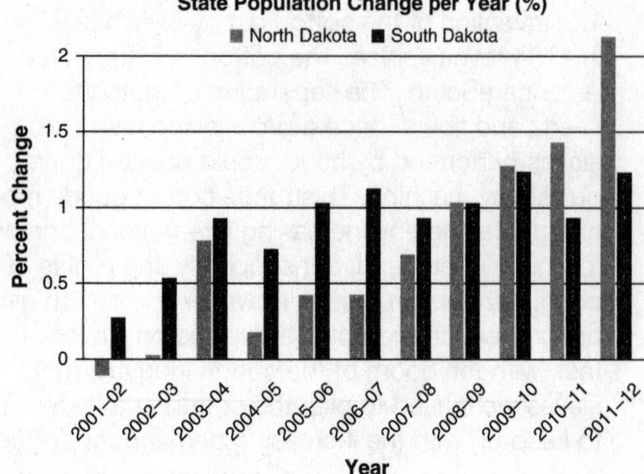


Source: United States Census Bureau

The above graph shows the percent increase, year by year, in the populations of each of North Dakota and South Dakota over eleven years.

8. Which of the following statements about the eleven-year period is supported by the graph above?

   A. North Dakota's population increased every year, while South Dakota's stayed the same.
   B. The population of South Dakota was originally greater than that of North Dakota, but in 2012, the population of North Dakota was greater than that of South Dakota.
   C. In most years, the percent population increase in South Dakota was greater than that in North Dakota.
   D. In most years, the percent population increase in North Dakota was greater than that in South Dakota.

**Questions 9 and 10 are is based on the following graphic.**

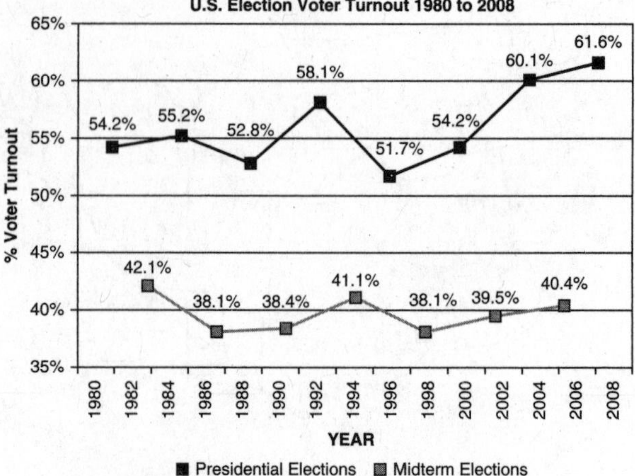


Source: weathertrends360.com

9. Which one of the following statements about elections in the years 1980–2008 is supported by the graph?

   A. Voter turnout for midterm elections displayed a greater range than voter turnout for presidential elections.
   B. The data for voter turnout for presidential elections displayed no mode.
   C. On average, half as many voters turned out for midterm elections as turned out for presidential elections.
   D. A smaller percentage of voters turned out for each midterm election than turned out for each presidential election.

10. The graph provides information that would allow you to answer which one of the following questions?

   A. Why did a greater percentage of voters turn out for the 1994 midterm election than for other midterm elections?
   B. The average voter turnout for midterm elections was approximately how much lower than that for presidential elections for the years 1980–2008?
   C. How does voter turnout for a presidential election affect voter turnout for the midterm election two years later?
   D. How did the presence of a high-profile third party candidate in the 1992 presidential election affect voter turnout?

**Questions 11 and 12 are based on the following excerpt from a speech.**

Today, 8 million adult Americans, more than the entire population of Michigan, have not finished five years of school. Nearly 20 million have not finished eight years of school. Nearly 54 million—more than one-quarter of all America—have not . . . finished high school.

Each year more than 100,000 high school graduates, with proved ability, do not enter college because they cannot afford it. And if we cannot educate today's youth, what will we do in 1970 when elementary enrollment will be 5 million greater than 1960? . . .

In many places, classrooms are overcrowded and curricula are outdated. Most of our qualified teachers are underpaid, and many of our paid teachers are unqualified. So we must give every child a place to sit and a teacher to learn from. Poverty must not be a bar to learning, and learning must offer an escape from poverty.

—President Lyndon Johnson, May 22, 1964
Great Society Speech, University of Michigan

11. Which of the following statements from the speech is an opinion rather than a fact?

 A. Each year more than 100,000 high school graduates do not enter college.
 B. 8 million adult Americans have not finished five years of school.
 C. Most of our qualified teachers are underpaid.
 D. More than one-quarter of Americans have not finished high school.

12. Which of the following would be the best title for this excerpt?

 A. "A History of Educational Problems"
 B. "Why Michigan Is Falling Behind"
 C. "Why College Is Unaffordable"
 D. "Our Duty Is to Educate Our Children"

**STUDY ADVICE**

Many questions on the TASC Social Studies Test will reward you for the skills you just learned. You may sometimes need to combine those skills with some basic knowledge of social studies content. The next five chapters will provide you with an overview of that content.

**Questions 13 and 14 are based on the following information and graph.**

From 1861 to 1865, the United States fought a devastating Civil War. The Union (the North) eventually defeated the Confederates (the South). The following chart gives facts about the population in both Union and Confederate states in 1860.

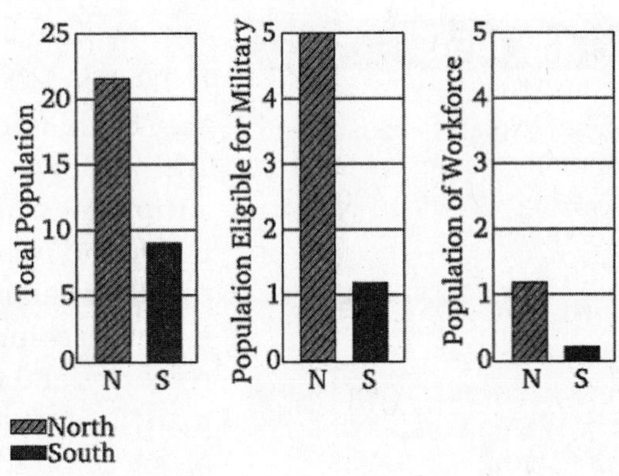


13. Which of the following statements is supported by the information and graph?

 A. The war was likely to end in a stalemate.
 B. Population differences would have no effect on the war's outcome.
 C. The Union states had significant population advantages in the war.
 D. The population in the Union states grew substantially during the war.

14. The graph provides information that allows you to answer which one of the following questions about the Civil War?

 A. What percentage of the total population in the United States fought in the military?
 B. What percentage of the total population of the United States was eligible for the military?
 C. Why was the population in the workforce much lower than the population eligible for the military?
 D. How did differences in skills held by people in the workforce affect the outcome of the Civil War?

**Review your work using the explanations that start on page 710.**

 LESSON 1

# Exploration, Colonialism, and the American Revolution

The first Americans traveled from Asia across the Bering Strait into North America and, over many generations, down to South America. Called **Native Americans**, they established extensive tribal cultures and several advanced civilizations.

### KEY IDEAS

- European explorers sought wealth and conquest in the New World from the 1400s to the 1600s.
- The Thirteen Colonies declared independence from England in 1776.
- America won its independence in 1783 and ratified the U.S. Constitution in 1788.

In the late 1400s, **explorers** from Europe searched for a sea route to Asia so they could trade for Asian gold and spices. They traveled around the tip of Africa. However, in 1492 Christopher Columbus convinced Spain to finance a trip west, across the Atlantic Ocean. When he reached land, he thought he had found India and called the inhabitants Indians. Later explorers realized that they had found a "New World," and many European nations set out to establish **colonies** there. The first explorers were searching for valuable resources and for the glory of conquest. This colonization led to tragedy for many Native Americans who died from diseases or were killed, enslaved, or forced off their lands.

In the 1500s and 1600s, European nations, including Spain, France, England, and the Netherlands, established settlements in North America. Settlements were established to gain power and wealth or to provide colonists a place for permanent residence. The first permanent English settlement was established in Jamestown, Virginia, in 1607. In 1620, the **Pilgrims** sailed to the Americas aboard the *Mayflower* and established a second English colony in Massachusetts. Beginning about 1675, colonists began importing a large number of slaves who had been forcibly taken from Africa. Many were put to work on the plantation system in the Southern colonies.

### TASC TEST TIP

*Reviewing key vocabulary can help you prepare for the TASC Test. As you review, look up any words that you do not understand. Pay special attention to the words in bold type.*

The colonies grew rapidly in the early 1700s. When England defeated France in the French and Indian War (1754–1763), England acquired many of France's American colonies. After the war, England sought to regain more control over the Thirteen Colonies. It also sought to recover economically from the debts caused by the costly war. New British taxes and policies troubled the colonists; however, it was not until 1775 that a war for independence seemed inevitable. After a series of skirmishes, the **Continental Congress** assigned George Washington to lead the Continental Army and ordered publication of the **Declaration of Independence** on July 4, 1776.

Despite the superiority of the well-trained British forces, the Americans had the advantage of defending their own land and eventually forged a fighting force with strong military leaders. The **American Revolution** lasted until the surrender of the British at Yorktown in 1781. In 1783, the final treaty to end the war resulted in the recognition of American independence. The new nation initially formed a weak national government through the **Articles of Confederation**. This first effort stressed a loose confederation of the states with strong local control. Over time, many colonial leaders recognized the need for a centralized government. The principles of this government were established in the **U.S. Constitution**, which was ratified in 1788. To counter fears of an overly powerful government, the first ten amendments to the Constitution, the **Bill of Rights**, promised many individual freedoms, such as freedom of speech and assembly.

# PRACTICE 1

<u>**Questions 1 and 2 refer to the following map.**</u>

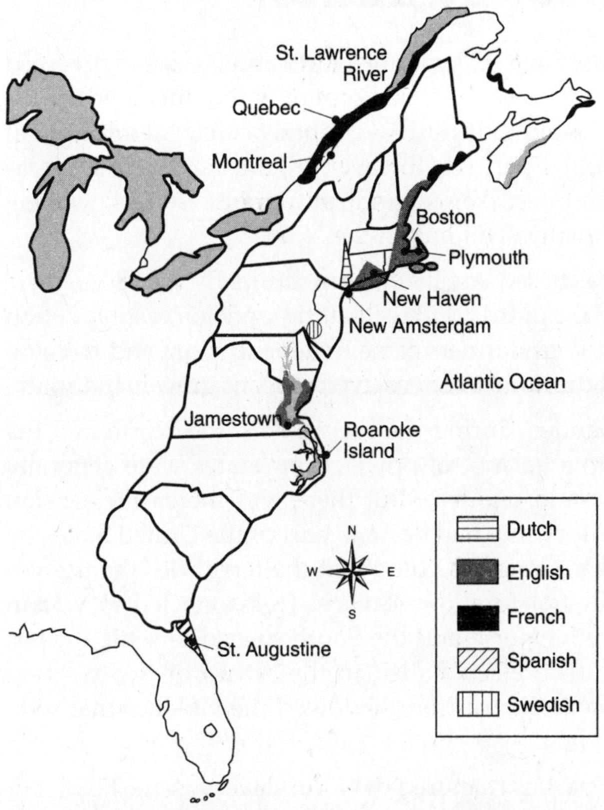


1. Choose the correct phrase that would fill in the blank.
   Based on the map, ______________ had the southernmost colony in 1650.

   A. the Dutch
   B. the English
   C. the Spanish
   D. the Swedish

2. Which of the following conclusions is supported by the map?

   A. By 1650, Spain had conquered most of North America.
   B. The English established several colonies in the New World.
   C. The Dutch established their colonies in the western part of North America.
   D. French colonies extended along the East Coast between Boston and Jamestown.

3. Some of the early colonists did not come to the New World to gain power and wealth. These groups came seeking freedom from persecution.

   Which immigrant group is most similar to those early colonists?

   A. African slaves who were involuntarily brought to work on plantations
   B. Mexican workers who came to the U.S. to earn better wages than they could at home
   C. British businessmen who visited the U.S. to invest in media companies
   D. Haitian refugees who fled to the U.S. to escape a dictatorship

4. Which of the following was a cause of the American Revolution?

   A. France's defeat in the French and Indian War
   B. increased British taxes and restrictions on the colonies
   C. Britain's acquisition of France's colonies in North America
   D. the publication of the Declaration of Independence

5. The first amendment to the U.S. Constitution states: "Congress shall make no law abridging the right of the people peaceably to assemble, and to petition the government for a redress of grievances."

   Based on the passage on page 456, what is the most likely reason the framers of the Constitution included these guarantees?

   A. They were planning to organize assemblies.
   B. They were concerned about the government becoming tyrannical.
   C. They were hoping to petition the government.
   D. They were attempting to prevent a redress of grievances.

**Review your work using the explanations that start on page 711.**

# Westward Expansion, the Civil War, and Reconstruction

### KEY IDEAS

- The economy of the South was based on slavery. The Northern economy was based on paid labor.
- Conflict over whether slavery should be allowed in the nation's new western territories led to the Civil War.
- The North won the war and ended slavery. During Reconstruction, the South was rebuilt.

### TASC TEST TIP

*As you study for the TASC Social Studies Test, focus on analyzing events to understand causes and effects, rather than memorizing names and dates.*

Early on in the history of the United States, the North and the South diverged economically. The North developed a varied economy that included industry and commerce as well as agriculture. Slavery had been legal throughout the North during the colonial period. However, by the early 1800s, it was **abolished** in all Northern states. Women and **immigrants**, as well as men, provided labor for the growing economy in the North.

The Southern economy was based largely on agriculture. By the 1800s, there was one major crop in the South: cotton. Planting and harvesting cotton required a lot of labor. Southern farmers came to depend more and more on slaves to do the work, and the number of enslaved persons grew in the South.

As the United States expanded during the early 1800s, the North and the South worked to maintain a balance of power. New states were generally added in pairs, one slave and one free. But there was increasing tension over the vast western territory that had become part of the United States by the mid-1800s. In the 1850s, Congress voted that the territories themselves should decide whether or not to allow slavery. This soon led to war in Kansas. People from both the North and the South rushed to settle the territory. Voter fraud in the 1855 elections led to the set up of two warring governments. The violence in Kansas foreshadowed the violence that soon tore up the nation.

In the late 1850s, political parties fractured over the slavery issue. Four candidates ran for president in 1860. Abraham Lincoln, who promised to halt the spread of slavery (although not abolish it where it already existed) won. Opposed to Lincoln's policies, most slave states **seceded** from the United States. They set up their own government, called the **Confederacy**. By April 1861, the United States (called the **Union**) and the Confederacy were at war.

At first it seemed as if the Confederacy might win. They had well-trained military leaders and soldiers who were willing to fight hard to hold onto their way of life, so the Confederacy won many early battles. However, by the summer of 1863, the Confederacy began to wear down. Ammunition, uniforms, and shoes were in short supply for Confederate soldiers, because the South lacked industry. There were food shortages for soldiers and civilians alike. The war was fought mostly in the South, and the destruction was terrible. After four long years, in 1865, Confederate general Robert E. Lee surrendered to Union general Ulysses S. Grant. The Civil War ended.

For the next 12 years, federal troops oversaw the rebuilding of the South. This period was called **Reconstruction**. Schools were established for former slaves, who were all freed when the war ended. However, the **sharecropping** system, which kept black farmers enslaved economically, soon came into being. Whites who came back to power as Reconstruction ended in the South in the 1870s prevented African Americans from exercising their right to vote. The Civil War ended slavery, but it did not end racism.

# PRACTICE 2

1. Which of the following disagreements was a main cause of the Civil War?
   A. whether cotton should be the main crop in the South
   B. whether slavery should continue to exist
   C. whether the United States should expand westward
   D. whether slavery should be permitted in territories in the West

2. In 1820, Missouri proposed to enter the Union as a slave state. Based on the passage, what do you think was the response of Northerners in Congress?
   A. They supported having another slave state join the Union.
   B. They lobbied against having Missouri join the Union at all.
   C. To balance the admission of Missouri, they agreed to a compromise in which Maine was admitted as a free state.
   D. They started a war to prevent Missouri from attaining statehood.

3. In the mid-1950s, the country of Vietnam was divided. There was a communist government in the North and a noncommunist government in the South. The two fought for control of Vietnam. In 1975, the communists won. Vietnam was united under this form of government. Because both wars __________, the Vietnam War and the U.S. Civil War can be said to share some similarities.
   A. involved racial conflict
   B. saw the addition of new territory upset the balance of power
   C. concluded with the formation of new nations
   D. concluded with the reunification of the nation

## STUDY ADVICE

If you find that Social Studies is your favorite subject so far, wonderful! You won't have trouble staying focused and motivated. However, if you find this material boring, do short study sessions with breaks in between. Four half-hour sessions can be more efficient than one two-hour session if you are having trouble concentrating on this material.

**Questions 4 and 5 refer to the following photographs of people who served in South Carolina's state government in 1868.**

Photography by Katherine Wetzel. Reprinted with the permission of The Museum of the Confederacy, Richmond, Virginia.

4. Which of the following is a fact confirmed by information in the photographs?
   A. Southern Democrats were treated very well during Reconstruction.
   B. It was unfair that former Confederate soldiers could vote during Reconstruction.
   C. In 1868, many African Americans served in the government of South Carolina.
   D. The most qualified leaders in South Carolina government in 1868 were African Americans.

5. Which of the following conclusions is supported by the photographs and the passage on page 458?
   A. Over the course of Reconstruction, African Americans in the South gained and then lost political power.
   B. Over the course of Reconstruction, African Americans in the South lost and then gained political power.
   C. Over the course of Reconstruction, whites in the South gained and then lost political power.
   D. In the early years of Reconstruction, African Americans served in government in each Southern state.

**Review your work using the explanations that start on page 711.**

LESSON 3

# Industrialization, Immigration, and the Progressive Era

In the mid-1800s, American industries, which had been growing steadily since the late 1700s, began a period of extremely fast growth. This rapid **industrialization** occurred for several interconnected reasons. With the addition of the vast western territories, the United States gained plentiful **natural resources**. Among these resources were materials, such as metals, needed to manufacture new products and machines, and fuels, such as coal, needed to run these machines. Another reason for rapid industrialization was the invention of many new machines and new industrial processes. With these new inventions and processes, manufactured goods could be produced more easily, more efficiently, and less expensively. A third reason for the rapid industrialization was the nation's booming population. The U.S. population more than doubled in the last 40 years of the 1800s. There were more people to buy more goods, spurring commerce and further industrial growth.

**KEY IDEAS**

- The U.S. underwent rapid industrialization starting in the mid-1800s.
- Immigrants came from many places to work in the expanding American industries.
- Rapid industrialization brought problems, which labor unions and reformers tried to solve, especially during the Progressive Era.

Rapid industrialization meant that many new factories were built in the mid- and late-1800s. Most were built in or near the nation's large cities, including New York, Boston, Chicago, Philadelphia, and Pittsburgh. These urban centers had large groups of people who could work in the factories and large groups of people who would buy the goods the factories produced.

U.S. factory jobs drew many **immigrants** to American cities. Although the United States has always been a "nation of immigrants," the late 1800s saw a sharp rise in the number of people moving here from foreign countries. The majority came from Europe, including Germany, Italy, Russia, and Eastern European countries. Many also came from Mexico and Central America. Asian immigration was declining because the government had passed laws barring Chinese from moving to the United States. However, thousands of Japanese came to this country, taking jobs in farm fields and mines.

**TASC TEST TIP**

*The TASC Social Studies Test examines your ability to interpret graphs, charts, maps, and other visual sources of information.*

America's factory workers, whether native- or foreign-born, worked very hard at grueling, dangerous work. Many received low pay for long hours on the job. Over time, workers began to unionize. By joining a **union**, workers pledged to work together for better and safer working conditions and higher wages. They called **strikes** when their employers cut their pay or refused to grant raises. Many of the laws we have today, including the eight-hour workday and the five-day workweek, came about through the bitter struggles for better working conditions that unions waged in the late 1800s and the early 1900s.

Unions weren't the only groups working to solve problems brought on by America's rapid industrialization. Some reformers worked to clean up slums, improve health care, and stop child labor. Others worked to preserve the nation's natural beauty by creating national parks. Still others worked to give more people a voice in government. For example, many women lobbied to gain the right to vote. In the early 1900s, groups were working toward so many sweeping social and political improvements that the time is called the **Progressive Era**.

# PRACTICE 3

1. Which of the following always occurs during a period of rapid industrialization?

   A. the annexation of new territory
   B. an increase in manufacturing
   C. an increase in population
   D. an increase in immigration

2. Which event directly contributed to the growth of American industries in the mid-1800s?

   A. the passage of the Chinese Exclusion Act, which banned Chinese immigration
   B. the passage of the Sherman Antitrust Act, which helped prevent businesses from forming monopolies
   C. the development of the Bessemer process, which made it easier to produce steel
   D. the development of settlement houses to aid impoverished immigrants and city dwellers

3. Based on the passage, which of the following would early union workers have valued the most?

   A. productivity in the workplace
   B. contact with people of all different backgrounds
   C. cooperation with others to improve worker safety
   D. the freedom to work whenever they pleased

4. What was a strong ideal held by people working toward reforms during the Progressive Era?

   A. efficiency
   B. wealth
   C. artistic beauty
   D. fairness

---

**Questions 5 and 6 refer to the following graphs.**

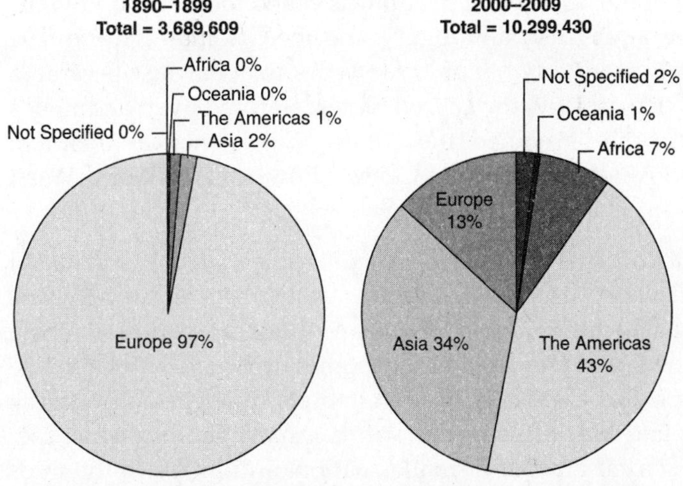


5. Which of the following best completes this statement? In the 1890s, the vast majority of persons gaining permanent legal residency came from Europe, whereas in the early 2000s, a majority of such persons came from _________.

   A. Europe and Asia
   B. Asia and the Americas
   C. Africa, Oceania, and Europe
   D. Africa and the Americas

6. A student looked at these graphs and said, "So I see that, in the years 1890–1899, roughly seven times as many people came to the United States from Europe than did in the years 2000–2009. After all, 97 is roughly seven times 13."

   Which of the following best describes the flaw in the student's reasoning?

   A. The student failed to differentiate between northern Europe and southern Europe.
   B. The student failed to consider the reasons why people immigrate to the United States.
   C. The student failed to consider the different totals represented by each pie chart.
   D. The student failed to explain what led to a decrease in immigration from Europe.

**Review your work using the explanations that start on page 712.**

LESSON 4

# The United States as an Emerging World Power

The expansion of U.S. industries in the mid-1800s had an effect not only on the nation's economy but also on its politics. Business and government leaders wanted access to more natural resources, which industries needed to continue growing. They also wanted to be able to sell more goods overseas. Regions in Africa, Asia, and Latin America had rich natural resources. People in these regions might buy what Americans wanted to sell. To promote industrial growth and increase its power, the United States became imperialistic. **Imperialism** is the policy by which a stronger nation extends economic, military, and/or political control over a weaker nation or region.

European nations had been engaging in imperialism for many centuries. In the late 1800s, the United States joined in. In 1898, the United States fought the Spanish-American War. Ostensibly, the United States declared war on Spain because of Spain's mistreatment of Cuba, which was a Spanish colony. Yet, after winning the war, the United States took over Spain's colonies of Cuba, Puerto Rico, the Philippines, and Guam. It granted independence to none of them.

The next war the United States was involved in was World War I, which began in Europe in 1913. It pitted two groups of nations against each other. One group was called the **Allies;** the leading Allied nations included Great Britain, Russia, and France. The other group was called the **Central Powers,** which included Germany, Austria-Hungary, and the Ottoman Empire. The Allies and Central Powers fought for three years in what fast became a deadly stalemate. Then, in 1917, the United States, alarmed over Germany's sinking of American ships, joined the Allies. With American help, in November 1918 the Allies defeated the Central Powers, and World War I ended.

Because the destruction was so terrible, some people called World War I "the war to end all wars." However, this was not to be. Within 12 years, by 1929, the world had fallen into a serious economic downturn, which Americans called the **Great Depression**. Economic problems aided the rise of **fascism** in Europe and elsewhere. Fascist nations squelched democracy and advocated the takeover of other nations. Germany, led by fascist dictator Adolf Hitler, started attacking smaller nations in Europe in the mid-1930s. Italy fought to take over Ethiopia, in Africa. Japan attacked China. Hitler built an alliance with Italy and Japan, which came to be called the **Axis**. By 1939, war again broke out between the Axis and the Allies.

The United States did not enter World War II until 1941, when the Japanese bombed the U.S. naval base at Pearl Harbor in Hawaii. This time, Americans fought not only in Europe but also in Africa and Asia as well. With its horrific battles, the fire-bombing of cities, the **Holocaust**, and the dropping of two atomic bombs on Japan, World War II led to massive destruction. The United States, which played a major part in the Allied victory in World War II in 1945, also played a major part in helping to rebuild war-scourged nations after the war was over.

### KEY IDEAS

- Industrialization spurred U.S. interest in gaining access to the raw materials and markets of other countries.
- The U.S. pursued imperialist policies in the late 1800s.
- The U.S. entered both WWI and WWII on the side of the Allies and contributed to their winning both wars.

### TASC TEST TIP

*When weighing answer choices, immediately eliminate ones that are directly contradicted by information in the passage or graphic.*

# PRACTICE 4

**Question 1 refers to the following chart.**

**Factors Related to the Growth of Imperialism**

| | |
|---|---|
| Economic | Desire for greater access to natural resources or new markets |
| Military | Desire for control of ports that could serve as refueling stations for long sea voyages or air flights |
| Political | Desire to spread the institutions of democracy or other political systems |
| Religious | Desire to spread Christianity or other faith |
| Cultural/Racial | Lack of respect for different cultures or races |

1. Cuba lies about 90 miles off the coast of Florida. After the United States freed Cuba from Spanish rule in 1898, the U.S. Navy built an important base there.

   Which of the following factors from the chart best explains the situation in Cuba after 1898?

   A. economic
   B. religious
   C. political
   D. military

2. What assumption do you need to make to fully understand the last sentence in paragraph 4 on page 462?

   A. In World War I, the Allies fought the Central Powers.
   B. In World War II, the Allies included England, France, and Russia.
   C. In World War II, the Allies included the Germans, Austrians, and Ottoman Turks.
   D. In World War II, the Axis included Germany, Italy, and Japan.

3. Franklin D. Roosevelt became president during the height of the Great Depression, in 1933. He soon instituted a set of federal programs called the New Deal to try to lower unemployment.

   Which conclusion about the effectiveness of New Deal programs does the text on page 462 and graph below support?

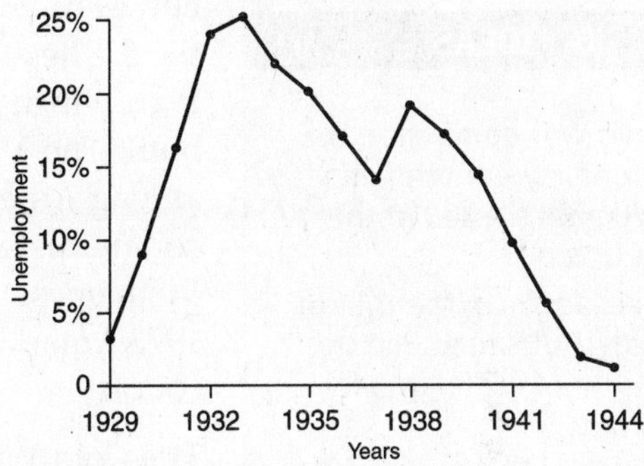


Source: *Historical Statistics of the United States*

   A. Within a year, the New Deal had raised unemployment to its pre-Depression level.
   B. Within a year, the New Deal had lowered unemployment to its pre-Depression level.
   C. Unemployment fell after the start of the New Deal and continued to fall sharply as the U.S. entered World War II.
   D. The New Deal lowered unemployment, but Allied victory in World War II lowered it further.

4. Which statement best summarizes the main idea of paragraph 5 on page 462?

   A. America entered World War II in 1941.
   B. Americans fought in Europe, Africa, and Asia.
   C. World War II involved more nations than any other war ever fought.
   D. America took a strong leadership role during and after World War II.

**Review your work using the explanations that start on page 712.**

**STUDY ADVICE**

If you feel like you have a good handle on U.S. History topics from the past 100 years, great! The TASC emphasizes these. If not, don't worry. Spend a little more of your time studying these lessons.

LESSON 5

# The Cold War and the Civil Rights Era

After World War II ended, the capitalist and communist nations soon began engaging in a power struggle called the **Cold War**. Leading the capitalist nations was the United States; leading the communist nations was the Soviet Union. The Cold War never led to direct fighting between these two superpowers, although there was a constant threat of nuclear war. Clashes between communism and capitalism did lead to numerous smaller conflicts. These included the Korean War of the early 1950s and the Vietnam War, which lasted from 1954 to 1975. The United States sent soldiers to both. The Vietnam War was long and difficult and caused deep division among Americans. The United States sent massive military aid to the non-communist South Vietnamese, but they kept losing to the communist North Vietnamese. Although a few Americans wanted to continue fighting, in 1973 America pulled out of Vietnam. In 1975, the communists took over the country.

The Cold War ended in 1991 with the breakup of the Soviet Union and the end of communism there. In the late 1980s, Soviet leader Mikhail Gorbachev had tried to reform the communist government. But the loosening of Soviet control had led to the collapse of many communist governments of Eastern Europe. The Berlin Wall, which had separated East and West Germany, was torn down. With communism no longer so threatening, world politics became less tense but also more unpredictable.

During the second half of the 20th century, the United States continued to face many challenges. In the 1950s, African American leaders launched the **civil rights movement** to try to end segregation and discrimination in the United States. Among their victories included the integration of public schools and other public facilities, the passage of laws protecting the voting rights of minorities, and the striking down of laws that permitted overt discrimination based on race or cultural background. However, minority groups and people of all backgrounds concerned about fair application of the law have continued to be vigilant in insisting that civil rights laws be upheld.

Another area of challenge in recent decades has been **technology**. Technology has led to many advances in science, medicine, and our personal lives. Computers, for instance, make many jobs easier and more productive. They allow almost instantaneous communication with co-workers, family, and friends. Furthermore, they allow people from around the world to share information quickly and easily, giving us the sense that we live in a "global village." However, our reliance on the use of technology has led us to pollute the air with exhaust from a growing number of cars. It has led us to pollute the water with acid rain, resulting from burning coal to generate increased electricity. It has led us to pollute our land with mountains of trash and tons of hazardous wastes.

### KEY IDEAS

- The Cold War dominated U.S. foreign policy from the end of WWII until the fall of the Soviet Union.
- Social changes in the U.S. in the mid-1900s included the expansion of civil rights for minorities.
- Technological advances have introduced benefits but also caused problems.

### ON THE TASC TEST

*The TASC Social Studies Test will include some questions that focus on the role of the United States in the world.*

# PRACTICE 5

1. The conflict during the second half of the 20th century between the United States and the Soviet Union was called the Cold War because it involved _________.

   A. communists and capitalists
   B. two countries at the far north of Earth
   C. the threat of nuclear war
   D. no direct combat

2. Which of the following best summarizes the message of the cartoon below?

   A. Nuclear bombs are extremely destructive.
   B. Expanding U.S. nuclear capabilities is a good idea.
   C. The buildup of nuclear arms increases fear and instability, not peace.
   D. The threat of nuclear war is lessened if both superpowers have equally powerful weapons.

3. Which of the following statements about the Vietnam War is a false generalization?

   A. Some Americans served in both Korea and Vietnam.
   B. The United States sent massive military aid to South Vietnam.
   C. Americans were in complete agreement about pulling out of Vietnam.
   D. The Vietnam War lasted much longer than the Korean War.

4. Which of the following goals would a civil rights activist be most likely to pursue?

   A. getting Congress to enact laws to restrict the sale of firearms
   B. petition for a city ordinance requiring those selling real estate to select a buyer without regard to race
   C. getting local companies to stop polluting the environment
   D. working with local clergy to publicize a worship service open to people of all religions

5. Which of the following is a conclusion about technology rather than a supporting detail?

   A. Reliance on technology has increased pollution.
   B. Cars cause air pollution.
   C. Coal-generating power plants cause acid-rain pollution.
   D. The ease of manufacturing disposable items has led to land pollution at landfill sites.

**Review your work using the explanations that start on page 712.**

# U.S. HISTORY PRACTICE QUESTIONS

**Questions 1 and 2 refer to the time line below.**

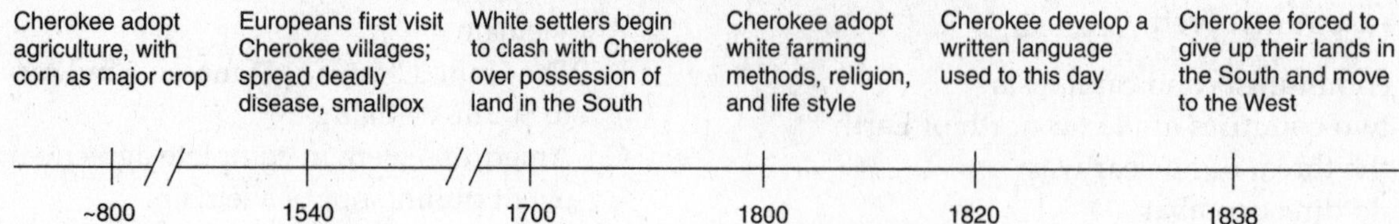


1. Which of the following is a conclusion based on multiple details in the time line?
   A. The Cherokee had begun farming around 800, before Europeans came to America.
   B. Although the Cherokee adopted many aspects of white culture, they were driven off their ancestral lands.
   C. The Cherokee traditionally considered land ownership to be a tribal matter rather than a right of individuals acting on their own.
   D. The Bible was one of the first books the Cherokee translated into their written language.

2. When President Andrew Jackson mandated that the Cherokee move west in 1830, he claimed that the U.S. government would be better able to protect the Cherokee from whites who might try to get their new land in the West. The Cherokee considered this to be illogical.

   Which of the following summarizes the logical fallacy?

   A. If the government can't protect us from white settlers here, now, how could it protect us from whites moving west in the future?
   B. If you ask us to move to the West now, how do we know you won't ask us to move back to the South in the future?
   C. If the land we have in the South is good, why wouldn't the land in the West be better?
   D. If the state governments are protecting us now, why can't the U.S. government help later?

---

3. In the late 1700s, Abigail Adams—wife of John Adams, who was our nation's second president—wrote the following in a letter to her sister:

   I will never consent to have our sex considered in an inferior point of light. Let each planet shine in their own orbit . . . if man is Lord, woman is *Lordess*—that is what I contend for.

   Based on this letter, which of the following principles was Abigail Adams advocating?

   A. the separation of church and state
   B. the abolition of slavery
   C. the promotion of scientific learning
   D. equal rights and opportunities for women

Questions 4 and 5 refer to the following map.

4. Which state permitted slavery but did not join the Confederacy?

A. West Virginia
B. Arkansas
C. Kansas
D. Tennessee

5. The loyalty of Maryland was of crucial importance to the Union. Based on the map, which statement best explains why this was so?

A. The nation's capital was located nearby.
B. The Confederate capital was located there.
C. It was close to Fort Sumter, where the Civil War began.
D. Important rail lines ran through Baltimore, Maryland.

6. In the Emancipation Proclamation, issued in 1863, President Lincoln freed all people enslaved in the states that had seceded from the Union. This proclamation was explicitly not to be put into effect in slave states that had remained in the Union. The proclamation went on to say:

I hereby enjoin upon the people so declared to be free to abstain from all violence . . . and make known that such persons of suitable condition will be received into the armed services of the United States to garrison forts, positions, stations, and other places, and to man vessels of all sorts.

Based on the information given about the Emancipation Proclamation and the text of the order itself, which of the following was a major reason Lincoln issued the proclamation?

A. to encourage states to secede from the Union
B. to punish slaveholders throughout the South
C. to weaken the North by enlisting former slaves in the Confederate army
D. to weaken the South by enlisting former slaves in the Union army

**Questions 7 through 9 refer to the following chart.**

**Civil Rights Amendment and Laws**

| | |
|---|---|
| 14th Amendment (1868) | Granted citizenship and equal protection of the law to all persons born in the United States (not applied to American Indians) |
| 15th Amendment (1870) | Granted voting rights to African Americans |
| Civil Rights Act of 1875 | Gave African Americans the right to serve on juries<br>Banned racial segregation in public places |
| Civil Rights Act of 1964 | Outlawed segregation by race in public places and racial discrimination in employment |
| Voting Rights Act of 1965 | Prohibited literacy tests for voting<br>Allowed the federal government to register voters |
| Civil Rights Act of 1968 | Outlawed discrimination in the sale or rental of homes |

7. An Asian American registers to vote and is given a reading test. Which of the following is the civil rights amendment or law relevant to this situation?

   A. Civil Rights Act of 1875
   B. Civil Rights Act of 1964
   C. Voting Rights Act of 1965
   D. Civil Rights Act of 1968

8. Which statement best summarizes what this chart shows about voting rights?

   A. African Americans were granted the vote five years after the Civil War ended.
   B. African Americans were granted the vote 100 years after the Civil War ended.
   C. African Americans were granted the vote soon after the Civil War, but laws enforcing these rights had to be passed a century later.
   D. African Americans were granted the vote in 1870 but American Indians were never granted these same rights.

9. How are the Civil Rights Act of 1875 and the Civil Rights Act of 1964 similar?

   A. They both guaranteed African Americans citizenship rights.
   B. They both prohibited the legal separation of people by race in public places.
   C. They both ensured that African Americans could serve on juries.
   D. They both make job discrimination illegal.

10. Alexander Graham Bell invented the telephone in the spring of 1876. In the fall, he exhibited it at an exposition in Philadelphia. When leading scientists saw Bell's invention, they said, "Here is the greatest marvel ever achieved in electrical science."

    Which of the following statements related to the passage is an opinion, not a fact?

    A. Bell invented the telephone in 1876.
    B. Bell exhibited the telephone at an exposition in Philadelphia.
    C. Scientists admired Bell's invention.
    D. The telephone was the greatest electrical invention ever.

**Questions 11 through 13 are based on the paragraph and the political cartoon below.**

In 1974, President Richard Nixon resigned from office. He had been involved in a scandal known as Watergate. The Watergate scandal implicated Nixon in covering up crimes committed by members of his reelection committee. These crimes ranged from illegally harassing political opponents to burglary and bribery. With Congress investigating him, he was sure to be impeached. This cartoon was published before Nixon resigned to avoid impeachment.

***Hey guys, do you really think we need that clause about impeachment in there?***

Cartoon by Robert Lawlor. Reprinted with permission of the *Philadelphia Daily News*.

11. In this cartoon, whom is Nixon addressing?

    A. the writers of the Declaration of Independence
    B. the framers of the U.S. Constitution
    C. the past presidents of the United States
    D. the present session of Congress

12. Which value was Congress furthering by investigating Nixon and Watergate?

    A. the pursuit of justice
    B. the duty of obedience
    C. loyalty to a friend
    D. love of mercy

## STUDY ADVICE

How did this practice set go? If you missed a few questions, go back and review those lessons. Remember as you study to pay particular attention to words in bold and the Key Ideas in each lesson.

13. About Watergate, one historian has written, "In a society in which distrust of leaders and institutions of authority was already widespread, the fall of Richard Nixon seemed to confirm the most cynical assumptions about the character of American public life."

    Which of the following was most likely a reason for Americans' growing distrust of their government in the years just prior to Watergate?

    A. mismanagement of the New Deal
    B. the beginning of rock music
    C. the escalation and failure of the Vietnam War
    D. the scandals of previous presidents, including John Kennedy and Bill Clinton

**Questions 14 and 15 refer to the graph below.**

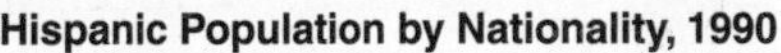

**Hispanic Population by Nationality, 1990**

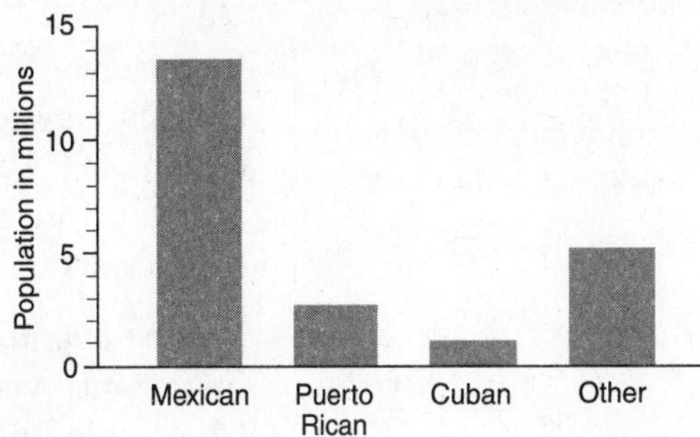


Source: U.S. Census Bureau

14. In 1990, approximately how many people of Cuban nationality lived in the United States?

    A. 100
    B. 100,000
    C. 1,000,000
    D. 5,000,000

15. A Hispanic family moved into an apartment next door to yours in 1990. Based solely on the bar graph, which place was the family most likely to be from?

    A. Cuba
    B. Mexico
    C. Puerto Rico
    D. Spain

**Review your work using the explanations that start on page 712.**

LESSON 1

# Historic Basis for U.S. System

The system of government in the United States is known as **representative democracy**. In this form of government, the citizens vote to elect representatives who make and execute laws. To understand this form of democracy, it is helpful to first distinguish democracy from other types of government. Then, you can trace the historical development of democracy and see how representative democracy differs from other types of democracy employed over time and around the globe.

**KEY IDEAS**

- The idea of democracy originated with the Ancient Greeks who spoke of the 'rule of the people.'
- The historic basis of the U.S. government came from the British system that limited the king's powers and protected individual rights.
- The U.S. system evolved from the British idea of a parliamentary democracy to a representative democracy.

The origins of **democracy** are ancient. The term *democracy,* which means "rule of the people" in Greek, arose in approximately 500 BCE in the Greek city-state of Athens. This distinguishes democracy from **monarchy**, the "rule of one person" (such as a king or queen); **aristocracy**, the "rule of an elite class" (lords or barons, for example); **theocracy**, the "rule of the church"; and **anarchy**, the "rule of the mob" (arguably not a form of government at all). Democracy is also distinct from forms of **authoritarian rule**, such as dictatorship, military rule, and fascism.

In ancient Athenian democracy, laws were voted upon by a council of all citizens, a system known as **direct democracy**. In ancient Athens, however, a "citizen" was defined as a free male landowner over the age of 20. Women, foreigners, slaves, non-landowners, and minors were excluded from the vote.

For the eventual development of democracy in the U.S., one of the most important events was the signing of the **Magna Carta** (Latin for Great Charter) in England in 1215. England was a monarchy, but some protested the king's absolute power. The result was the signing of the Magna Carta, a document limiting the king's rule and subjecting his decisions to review. This same period also saw the development of the legal doctrine of **habeas corpus**, which made it illegal for the government to hold or imprison individuals without granting them trials.

**TASC TEST TIP**

*While you will not need to memorize dates, it will be helpful to be familiar with key terms, such as the ones in **bold type**.*

Over time, the group allowed by the Magna Carta to review the king's decisions developed into a **parliament** of lawmakers appointed by title and/or elected by citizens. As the power of the parliament grew, England transformed into a **parliamentary democracy**. In this system, a government is formed by the party holding a majority of seats in the parliament. In most parliamentary democracies, the majority party appoints or authorizes the chief executive, such as the president.

Known as the Age of Enlightenment, the 17th and 18th centuries saw the spread of democracy to many other European countries. England, France, Holland, and other European powers also adopted **bills of rights** for individuals during this period. The philosophies dominant in this era emphasized reason and individual rights and encouraged government by the people. Enlightenment philosophers such as Adam Smith, John Locke, and Voltaire strongly influenced the founders of the United States.

# PRACTICE 1

1. Which of the following is a form of government in which laws are made and administered by lords who inherit their lands and titles?

   A. monarchy
   B. direct democracy
   C. representative democracy
   D. aristocracy

2. Which of following can be inferred about the Founding Fathers of the United States?

   A. They sought to establish the power of the king of England in the United States.
   B. They were concerned about protecting the rights of individuals.
   C. They argued that the United States should adopt a system of direct democracy.
   D. They thought representatives from the United States should sit in Parliament.

3. In the United States, laws are enacted by Congress, a group of representatives elected by the people. Which of the following was most likely the chief historical model for the U.S. Congress?

   A. Athenian council of citizens
   B. Magna Carta
   C. Parliament of England
   D. Declaration of the Rights of Man and the Citizen adopted in France in 1789

4. Some nations have been ruled by a form of government known as constitutional monarchy. While a king or queen is the single, sovereign ruler of the country, his or her power is limited by a constitution, a formal document outlining which of the monarch's decisions are subject to review or may be overruled by a court of law.

   Which of the following was most likely a constitutional monarchy?

   A. the ancient city-state of Athens
   B. any country ruled by fascism
   C. the United States at the time of its founding
   D. England during the Age of Enlightenment

5. If the United States were a parliamentary democracy, which of the following would be most likely to occur?

   A. The office of the president would decrease in power.
   B. The office of the president would increase in power.
   C. The president would be elected by a majority vote of all citizens.
   D. The president would be appointed by the majority party in the parliament.

**Review your work using the explanations that start on page 713.**

LESSON 2

# Constitutional Government

The Constitution of the United States is the foundation of our national government and legal system. The United States is a **republic**, a form of government in which citizens elect the people who will govern them. A republic is very different from a government system in which citizens do not choose their political leaders, such as a **monarchy** or **dictatorship**.

The people who wrote the Constitution set particular goals for the new nation, which they stated in the **preamble**, or introduction. They wanted to unite the states under one government, establish a nation where people could live peacefully and safely under the rule of law, and make prosperity and freedom possible for all citizens.

Following the preamble are the original seven **articles** of the U.S. Constitution. These articles provide for the three branches of government (see page 474), establish the rights of states, and set forth procedures for ratifying and amending the Constitution. Article 6 states that all government officials must uphold the Constitution as "the supreme law of the land" and that no other laws can contradict any part of the Constitution.

According to Article 5, a constitutional **amendment** can be proposed by Congress if it is supported by two-thirds majorities in both the House and Senate. The proposed amendment then must be ratified by three-fourths of the states. This process ensures that amendments have very broad national support.

The original Constitution did not specifically describe citizens' rights. Even as the Constitution was being written, some political leaders insisted that a bill of rights was needed to help develop citizens' trust in the new government. However, they agreed to wait to make amendments to the Constitution until after it was **ratified**. As a result of this compromise, the first ten amendments to the U.S. Constitution, passed in 1791, became the **Bill of Rights**. These rights are well known to many Americans. The First Amendment, for example, guarantees freedom of religion, freedom of speech, and freedom of the press. The Sixth and Seventh Amendments guarantee citizens' rights to trial by jury.

As Americans' ideas about citizenship and government have evolved, the amendment process has allowed the Constitution to evolve as well. The Thirteenth Amendment (1865) outlawed slavery; the Fifteenth Amendment (1870) established that the rights of citizens "shall not be denied or abridged … on account of race, color, or previous condition of servitude."

A number of constitutional amendments have extended voting rights to citizens. The Nineteenth Amendment (1920) gave women the right to vote. The Twenty-fourth Amendment (1964) banned poll taxes, which some states were using to prevent African Americans from voting. The Twenty-sixth Amendment (1971) lowered the voting age to 18.

### KEY IDEAS

- The U.S. Constitution is the basis for our government structure and legal system.
- The Bill of Rights—the first ten constitutional amendments—define the rights of citizens.
- Amendments to the Constitution require wide support, but many important amendments have gained enough support to be ratified.

### ON THE TASC TEST

*The TASC Social Studies Test may include an excerpt from or a reference to one of the following U.S. historical documents:*

- *Declaration of Independence*
- *U.S. Constitution, including the Bill of Rights and other amendments*
- *Landmark Supreme Court cases*

# PRACTICE 2

1. Which of the following is the main characteristic of a republic?

   A. voting rights extended to few adult citizens
   B. elected representatives exercising government power on behalf of citizens
   C. people governing themselves by voting directly on all issues
   D. power concentrated among a small group

2. The Constitution is a relatively brief document containing only about seven thousand words. It establishes the structure and powers of the U.S. government but does not give many specifics.

   What assumption were the drafters of the Constitution working under as they kept the document general and brief?

   A. There was not enough time to draft a long, detailed document before the states had to ratify it.
   B. Most of the power of the federal government would be reserved to the president, who could govern as he saw fit.
   C. The details of government would be worked out in the future, as the need arose, within the framework of the Constitution.
   D. Written constitutions were an untested basis for democratic government, so it was better to keep such a document brief.

3. Franklin Delano Roosevelt was elected to the presidency four times between 1933 and 1945. In reaction to this, the Twenty-second Amendment, ratified in 1951, allowed presidents a maximum of two terms in office.

   People who favored presidential term limits would most likely have valued which of the following?

   A. responsibility but no authority
   B. authority but no responsibility
   C. the power of an office, not an individual
   D. the power of an individual, not an office

4. The third paragraph of the passage on page 472 includes a summary of Article 6 of the Constitution, also called the supremacy clause.

   ____________ is an example of the supremacy clause in action.

   A. Congress voting to appropriate $2 billion for a federal highways program
   B. The Environmental Protection Agency issuing new regulations on a pollutant
   C. The U.S. Supreme Court refusing to hear a case
   D. The U.S. Supreme Court declaring an Illinois state law unconstitutional

**Question 5 refers to the following chart.**

**Methods of Amending the Constitution**

| Proposal | Ratification Method | When Used |
|---|---|---|
| Two-thirds vote in both houses of Congress to propose an amendment | By three-quarters of the state legislatures | For every amendment except one |
| | By special conventions in three-fourths of the states | Twenty-first Amendment (repealing Prohibition) |
| Two-thirds of states request Congress to call a constitutional convention to consider an amendment | By three-quarters of the state legislatures | Never used |
| | By special conventions in three-fourths of the states | Never used |

5. Which of the following would best explain why the third and fourth methods of amending the Constitution have never been used?

   A. State governments do not usually act together.
   B. Only Congress can propose amendments.
   C. State legislatures can vote on an amendment.
   D. Conventions meet more frequently than Congress and state legislatures do.

**Review your work using the explanations that start on page 713.**

## STUDY ADVICE

The TASC places high emphasis on the U.S. Constitution and the foundations of the American political system, so if you have a solid understanding of these topics, congratulations! If you still feel a bit shaky, review this chapter.

LESSON 3

# Levels and Branches of Government

The U.S. government works in layers with different responsibilities at the national, or **federal**, level; the state level; and local levels, including cities, villages, and counties. The federal government works across all 50 states, and its decisions and actions affect everyone. States have their own constitutions, similar to the U.S. Constitution. State governments also are quite powerful in shaping the lives of people in their states.

**KEY IDEAS**

- Under our Constitution, the federal government must share power with the states.
- The federal government has three major branches—executive, legislative, and judicial.
- The three branches of the government balance each other's power.

**Federalism**, which is a basic principle of the U.S. Constitution, means that power is shared between the national and state levels of government. Dividing power between federal and state government protects the rights of individual states, but also allows our national government to enforce certain rights of citizenship. The Constitution gives some powers only to the national government, some only to state government, and some to both. For example, only the federal government can declare war. States are given the power to establish schools. Both federal and state governments can levy taxes and set up court systems.

There are three branches of government at the federal level, each with different roles to play. The powers of each branch are described in the Constitution. The **executive branch** consists of the president and various advisors (including the president's cabinet) and government departments. The executive branch enforces the nation's laws and provides national leadership, setting goals and policies. The **legislative branch** consists of two houses of **Congress**: the **Senate** and the **House of Representatives**. Congress is responsible for making laws that all citizens, organizations, and businesses must follow. The **judicial branch**, made up of the federal court system including the Supreme Court, decides disputes related to laws, including the U.S. Constitution.

**ON THE TASC TEST**

*Editorial cartoons like the one on page 475 use pictures and humor to make a political point.*

U.S. citizens vote for the president and all members of Congress. As a result, these politicians have a responsibility to represent and serve their **constituents**—the people who elected them. The president may be elected to only two terms of four years each. Representatives are elected for two years and Senators for six years; these members of Congress may be reelected for any number of terms.

Federal judges, in contrast, are appointed by the president and **confirmed** by the Senate. They can serve in these positions for life. As citizens, we have a right to expect our federal judges to make **impartial** decisions based on the Constitution and the laws of the United States.

The people who wrote the U.S. Constitution were afraid to give any government body too much power. Therefore, the Constitution limits the power of each branch of the federal government. Each branch has separate powers. Each branch also has the power to act in ways that affect the other branches, in a system called **checks and balances**. For example, the president can **veto** laws made by Congress. Congress can override a presidential veto by repassing the law with a two-thirds majority. The Constitution is also now interpreted to mean that judges can review laws and declare them **unconstitutional**.

# PRACTICE 3

1. What is the key characteristic of federalism?

   A. division of power between national and state governments
   B. concentration of power in one government
   C. concentration of power at the local level
   D. a judicial system with trial, appellate, and supreme courts

2. Which of the following is an example of a government entity that is part of the executive branch?

   A. the Democratic National Committee
   B. Congress's House Rules Committee
   C. the U.S. Court of Appeals
   D. the State Department

3. Why do lifetime appointments help ensure that federal judges rule impartially on legal issues?

   A. Federal judges need not worry about pleasing their constituents in order to be reelected.
   B. Only people who demonstrate loyalty to the ruling political party are appointed.
   C. Lifetime appointments mean that federal judges acquire a great deal of experience.
   D. A federal judge must be impartial or he or she will not be reelected.

4. Senators serve ____________ year terms in Congress, and representatives serve ____________ year terms, with the option to be reelected for any number of terms.

   A. two; four
   B. six; two
   C. two; six
   D. four; two

**Question 5 refers to the following cartoon.**

**"Let's never forget that the constitution provides for three equally important branches of government: the legislative and the other two."**



5. Which of the following people is most likely depicted in the cartoon?

   A. the president
   B. a member of Congress
   C. the head of a government department
   D. a federal judge

---

6. Although the states have the power to make their own laws in many areas, in practice they cooperate with one another to a great extent. For example, when a person travels, his or her driver's license, which was issued by one state, will be honored in other states.

   On which of the following principles is this type of cooperation based?

   A. mutual respect and convenience
   B. centralization of authority
   C. common law
   D. division of power

**Review your work using the explanations that start on page 714.**

# The Electoral System

At the national level in particular, two **political parties** dominate the political arena in the United States: the **Democrats** and the **Republicans**. These parties represent different ideas about the role of government in our nation. In each election season, the parties and candidates work to promote their views, or **platforms**—their positions on issues like tax reform, Social Security, education spending, environmental protection, and so on.

The political parties have developed large organizations for raising money and getting their candidates elected. Each party runs its own **primary** election, in which candidates within the party compete with each other for the party's **nomination**. After the primary elections, the winners from each party's primary face off in the general election. In presidential elections, the primary season ends with a party **convention**, where delegates from each state gather to select the party's candidate. Citizens vote in a general election, and the results are tallied by state. Following the general election, electors from each state cast their state's votes in the **Electoral College**. The electors generally must cast their votes for the candidate who won the general election in their state. The candidate who wins the greatest number of electoral votes becomes president.

Although Democrats and Republicans are by far the largest political parties, there are small parties as well. At times, a "third-party candidate" like Ralph Nader or Ross Perot attracts enough support to influence the outcome of the national election. Even when small parties offer interesting new ideas or solutions to problems, they have great difficulty attracting money and public attention because the Democratic and Republican parties are so well established.

Although many voters consider themselves to be either Republicans or Democrats, many others are **independent**. Candidates and their political parties rely heavily on **opinion polls** to find out what voters think; they try to tailor their campaign messages to appeal to large numbers of voters. Groups of voters who might "swing" an election one way or another are particularly important targets for political campaigns. Sometimes opposing candidates participate in public **debates**.

Political campaigns can be very expensive, and the higher the office, the more expensive the campaign. To reach the public, candidates pay for mailings, TV ads, and events, including personal appearances. They need campaign staff and offices; they must pay for travel expenses. As a result, fund-raising has become a very important part of running for office.

In recent decades, Americans have become more and more concerned about the high cost of running for office. Many Americans believe that a candidate should not have to be wealthy to begin with, or be overly obligated to contributors, in order to gain political office. We now have laws that restrict the size of campaign contributions. We also have restrictions on how **political action committees** (PACs) operate. However, many people believe that more reforms are needed.

**KEY IDEAS**

- U.S. politics are dominated by the Democratic and Republican parties.
- Political parties hold primaries to select candidates for the general election.
- Political campaigns are very expensive, and many people believe that we must reform our campaign finance laws.

**TASC TEST TIP**

*When you are asked a question about a circle graph, remember that it represents a whole, or 100%.*

# PRACTICE 4

1. Which of the following is necessary for a candidate to win the presidency?

   A. earning a majority of primary wins
   B. receiving a majority of the popular vote
   C. receiving a majority in the Electoral College
   D. having no third-party opponent

2. An exit poll is one that surveys people as they leave a voting location. Instead of waiting for votes to be counted, the media often announce the winners of elections based on exit polls.

   Which of the following is an important drawback of using exit polls?

   A. Exit polls may be inaccurate if the people polled are not representative of the political unit as a whole or if the election is very close.
   B. Exit polls allow the media to present election results during prime time on election night instead of waiting until later in the evening.
   C. Exit polls have undue influence on the way politicians running for office conduct their campaigns.
   D. Exit polls are likely to be unreliable when there is a wide margin between the candidates.

3. Which of the following is an example of a primary election?

   A. A Democrat and a Republican oppose one another in a race for the U.S. Senate.
   B. A Republican and an independent candidate oppose one another in a race for the state senate.
   C. Once presidential candidates are chosen, they select their running mates.
   D. Two city council members are on a ballot to determine which one will run for mayor as a Democrat.

### STUDY ADVICE

If you've been working through this book in order, it might be time to review the Reading and Writing units. Don't forget to do periodic reviews of material you haven't seen in a while, so that those skills don't get rusty.

**Questions 4 and 5 refer to the following graphs.**

**2010 Election**

Senate Candidates' Funds $597,600,000

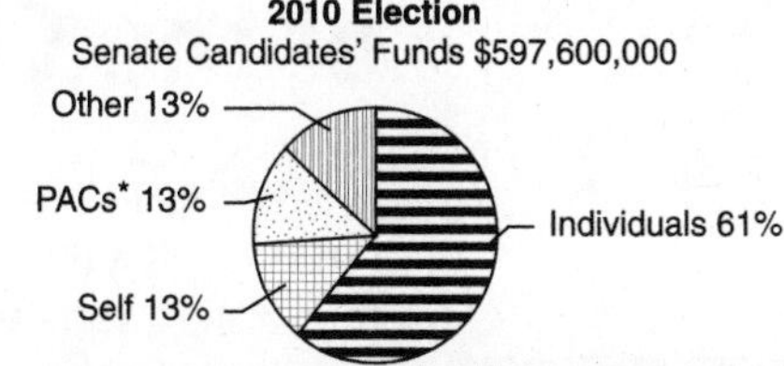


House Candidates' Funds $949,300,000

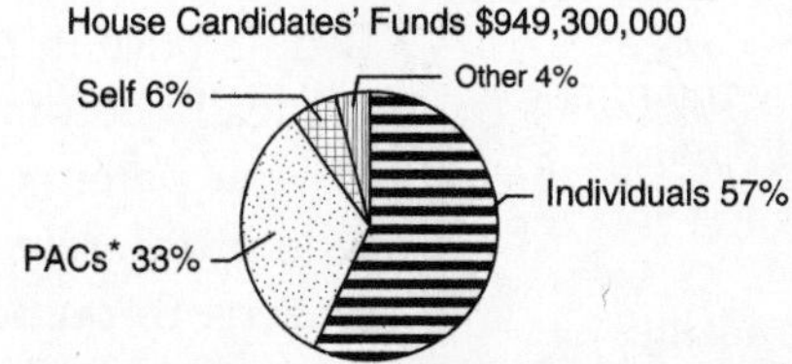


*PACs are Political Action Committees – groups that raise money for candidates.

Source: Federal Election Commission.

4. How do the campaign funding sources of Senate and House candidates compare?

   A. Individual donations provided a larger percentage of funds raised by House candidates than of those raised by Senate candidates.
   B. In total, individuals contributed a greater dollar amount to House candidates than they did to Senate candidates.
   C. Political parties provided a greater percentage of the funds raised by House candidates than they did of funds raised by Senate candidates.
   D. On average, Senate candidates received a greater percentage of their funds from PACs than did House candidates.

5. Which of the following statements is supported by the graphs?

   A. In 2010, self-funding was a larger source of funds for Senate candidates than it was for House candidates.
   B. In 2010, individual donations were the largest source of funds for Senate candidates but not for House candidates.
   C. In 2010, PACs were the largest source of funds for House candidates but not for Senate candidates.
   D. Fund-raising accounts for most of the work on a congressional campaign.

**Review your work using the explanations that start on page 714.**

LESSON 5

# The Role of the Citizen

**Citizenship** is a special relationship between a person and a nation: the nation owes the person certain rights and guarantees; the person has certain obligations to the nation. Thus citizens of the United States have both rights and responsibilities.

People born in the United States, no matter what the circumstances, automatically become U.S. citizens. Regardless of where you were born, if one of your parents was a U.S. citizen, then you are also a U.S. citizen. People who **immigrate** to the United States from other countries can become U.S. citizens through a legal process called **naturalization**; underage children are naturalized along with their parents.

Our rights of citizenship are established in the first ten amendments to the U.S. Constitution—the Bill of Rights (see page 472)—and in other sections of the Constitution. One of the most fundamental rights of U.S. citizens is our right to participate in our nation's political life. We are eligible to vote and to hold public office, and we elect representatives to govern us. In a famous phrase in the Gettysburg Address, Abraham Lincoln said that we have a government "of the people, by the people, and for the people."

As Lincoln's famous remark implies, a government "by the people" requires that citizens take responsibility. First and foremost, we must uphold the laws of our country. As citizens, we also make contributions to the national welfare. Our taxes pay for services that the government provides to benefit everyone. By voting, we not only choose our government representatives, but we also help to make the political process meaningful for everyone. Through national service—such as military service, holding public office, or participating in intensive volunteer programs like Teach for America—citizens may devote years of their lives to the responsibilities of citizenship.

Our **jury** system is an important example of the give-and-take of citizenship. Each of us is guaranteed the right to a fair and speedy trial, heard by "a jury of peers," if we are accused of a crime. However, we are also obligated to serve on juries or as **witnesses** when we are called by the court system. The fairness of our legal system depends on citizens participating in that system. Therefore, our employers are obligated to release us from work at the request of the courts.

In addition to the rights and responsibilities established by law, many citizens contribute their time and money in other ways that serve society as a whole. People volunteer to serve organizations in their communities or within their professions—serving meals in shelters, fund-raising for schools, offering free medical services, etc. People also give money to causes they think are important, from political campaigns to food pantries to environmental organizations. Many citizens also work hard to conduct their daily lives in ways that contribute to the general welfare: by recycling, cleaning up trash, and looking out for their neighbors and family members.

### KEY IDEAS

- U.S. citizens have the right to vote and to hold public office, as well as to enjoy many freedoms.
- Citizens are responsible for contributing to the general welfare of the nation.
- In our court system, citizens serve on juries in order to protect the rights of other citizens.

### ON THE TASC TEST

*The TASC Social Studies Test will ask you about the citizen's role in government. You may be asked to interpret materials about "civic life," such as election information or a voter registration document.*

# PRACTICE 5

1. _______________ outlines the rights of U.S. citizens.

   A. The Declaration of Independence
   B. The U.S. Constitution
   C. A U.S. passport
   D. A person's naturalization papers

**Questions 2 and 3 refer to the following information.**

Noncitizens can be classified into five groups:

**Resident alien** A foreigner who has established permanent residence in the United States.

**Nonresident alien** A foreigner who is staying in the United States for a brief, specified period.

**Enemy alien** A foreigner who is a citizen of a nation at war with the United States.

**Refugee** A foreigner fleeing his or her country to escape persecution or danger.

**Illegal alien** A foreigner who comes to the United States without legal documentation.

2. Louvina married an American and moved to the United States from Trinidad in 2010. Three years later, she filed a legal petition requesting U.S. citizenship. In what category of alien does Louvina belong?

   A. resident alien
   B. nonresident alien
   C. enemy alien
   D. refugee

3. What would happen to the legal status of noncitizens living in the United States if their country declares war on the United States?

   A. They would become nonresident aliens.
   B. They would become resident aliens.
   C. They would become enemy aliens.
   D. They would become refugees.

4. The United States must balance the right of society to protect itself against the rights of an accused criminal. One aspect of this tension is the Fourth Amendment guarantee of "the right of people to be secure in their persons, houses, papers, and effects, against unreasonable searches and seizures."

   Which of the following values is supported by the Fourth Amendment?

   A. free speech
   B. privacy
   C. civic duty
   D. volunteerism

**Question 5 refers to the following graph.**

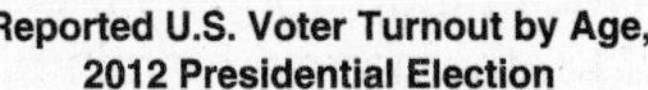


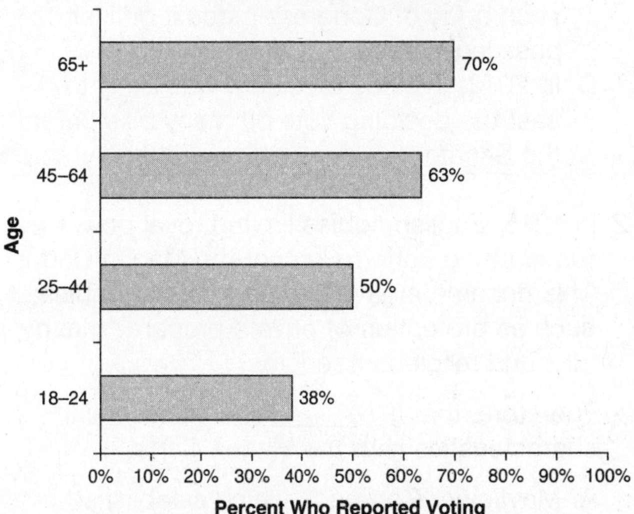


Source: United States Census Bureau

5. Which of the following is a conclusion based on the graph rather than a detail of the graph?

   A. About 63 percent of people aged 45 to 64 reported voting in the 2012 presidential election.
   B. Those aged 65+ reported the highest voter turnout in the 2012 presidential election, at 70 percent.
   C. If the 2012 presidential election is representative of elections generally in the United States, voter turnout increases with age.
   D. Only about 38 percent of young people reported voting in the 2012 presidential election.

**Review your work using the explanations that start on page 714.**

# Civics and Government Practice Questions

Question 1 refers to the following chart.

**Political Divisions in the 113th Congress, 2013**

| Party | House | Senate |
|---|---|---|
| Republicans | 234 | 45 |
| Democrats | 201 | 53 |
| Others | — | 2 (In case of a tie, Vice President Joe Biden (D) votes.) |
| Vacant | — | — |

1. Which of the following is the best summary of the chart above?

   A. Congress is made up of the House and the Senate.
   B. In 2013, a different major party controlled the House than controls the Senate.
   C. In 2013, the narrow margin of control in each body of Congress made it difficult to pass legislation.
   D. In 2013, the vice president was likely to cast the deciding vote on many bills before the Senate.

---

2. In 1215, English nobles limited royal power by forcing King John to accept the Magna Carta. This document gave certain rights to nobles, such as protection of private property, trial by jury, and religious freedoms.

   Therefore, the __________ shares essential characteristics with the Magna Carta.

   A. Mayflower Compact, which established a government for Plymouth colony,
   B. Bill of Rights of the U.S. Constitution, which guarantees citizens certain rights,
   C. Albany Plan of Union, which called for a colonial confederation,
   D. *Federalist Papers*, which encouraged ratification of the U.S. Constitution,

Questions 3 and 4 refer to the following passage.

In 1979, Congress passed legislation to allow political parties to raise unlimited amounts of general-purpose money not designated for particular candidates. In 1991, a lawsuit forced disclosure of such "soft money" contributions, and concern grew about the size of individual donations, the extent of total donations, and the ways in which the money was being spent. During the presidential elections of 1996 and 2000, campaign fund-raising, especially the raising and spending of soft money, was an issue, with the candidates promising reform. Finally, in 2001, after several years of hearings, the Senate passed the McCain-Feingold bill, which would eliminate the unregulated soft money contributions that make up a large proportion of the parties' budgets.

3. Which of the following is an example of a soft money contribution?

   A. a $250 ticket to a fund-raising dinner-dance to benefit a mayoral candidate
   B. a $3,000 donation to the campaign fund of an incumbent senator
   C. a $3,000 contribution to a party fund for TV ads on political issues
   D. a $1,000 gift to a senator's campaign fund in response to a direct mail solicitation

4. Which of the following is the most likely reason soft money was not a major issue in the 1980s?

   A. People were less aware of soft money because disclosure was not required at that time.
   B. Political campaigns were publicly financed, so soft money was not needed.
   C. Most candidates spent part of their campaign funds on television ads.
   D. McCain and Feingold had not submitted their campaign finance reform bill.

**Questions 5 and 6 refer to the following paragraph and graphs.**

In order to win a presidential election, a candidate must win a majority of the vote in the Electoral College. Each state has as many electors as it has senators and representatives in Congress. In most states, the winner of the popular vote gets all the electoral votes of the state. These graphs show the popular and Electoral College votes in the election of 2012.

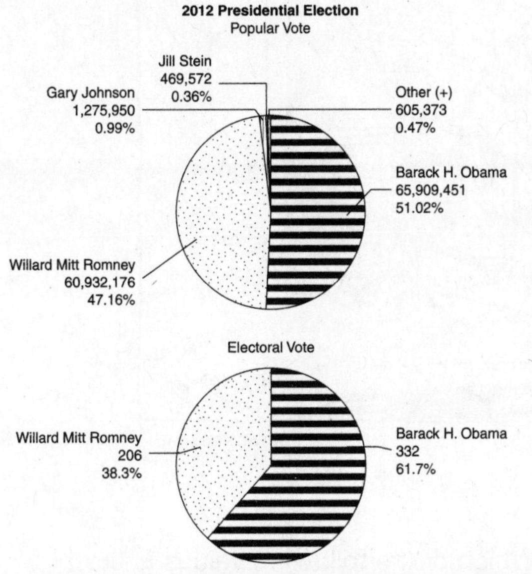


5. Which one of the following statements is supported by the information in the paragraph and the graphs?

   A. A presidential candidate will receive the same percentage of electoral votes as he or she received of the popular vote.
   B. Romney won a greater percentage of the electoral vote than of the popular vote in 2012.
   C. Jill Stein won a greater percentage of the popular vote than of the electoral vote in 2012.
   D. The total of popular votes cast for all candidates other than Barack Obama was greater than the total of those cast for Barack Obama.

6. Which of the following would be the best title for the paragraph and the graphs?

   A. 2012 Presidential Election: How Obama Defeated Romney
   B. 2012 Presidential Election: Third-Party Influence
   C. 2012 Presidential Election: Winning the Electoral College
   D. 2012 Presidential Election: Popular and Electoral Votes

**Question 7 refers to the following passage.**

**Where do I vote?** Your voting district is determined by your place of residence. Watch your local newspaper for an announcement indicating polling locations and times, or contact your local board of election to determine your voting location.

You may also obtain your polling place location by accessing the website of the Office of the Secretary of State at. You may also call the Office of the Secretary of State for assistance.

7. Which of the following is assumed but not stated outright in the voter guide above?

   A. The board of election is the county, city, or town office responsible for local voting.
   B. A voter's polling place is determined by his or her address.
   C. A voter can find his or her polling place on the Internet.
   D. A voter can call the Office of the Secretary of State to find out where to vote.

---

8. An interest group is an organization with specific goals that seeks to influence government policies. Which of the following entities constitutes an interest group?

   A. the Democratic Party, which nominates candidates and tries to win elections
   B. the National Association of Manufacturers, which lobbies for businesses
   C. the Federal Communications Commission, which regulates broadcasters
   D. the Cabinet, an advisory body for the president

**Questions 9 and 10 refer to the following cartoon.**

9. What is the main idea of this cartoon?

   A. Most voters are working people.
   B. Most registered voters don't vote.
   C. Voters should establish another political party.
   D. A non-voters' party would lose every election.

10. Which of the following values is the cartoonist appealing for?

   A. the work ethic
   B. majority rule
   C. civic duty
   D. national pride

11. An oligarchy is a system of government in which a small group of people holds power.

   Which of the following is an oligarchy?

   A. China, where the top leaders of the communist party control the government
   B. Iraq, when it had a dictator, Saddam Hussein
   C. Great Britain, with a monarch, a prime minister, and an elected parliament
   D. Greece, with a prime minister and an elected parliament

12. Three typical laws from the code of Hammurabi, written about 1700 B.C.E., are "If a son strike his father, his hands shall be hewn off. If a man put out the eye of another man, his eye shall be put out. If he break another man's bone, his bone shall be broken."

   What principle underlies these laws?

   A. retribution
   B. rehabilitation
   C. incarceration
   D. mediation

**Questions 13 and 14 refer to the following map and table.**

**The Death Penalty in the United States, 2013**

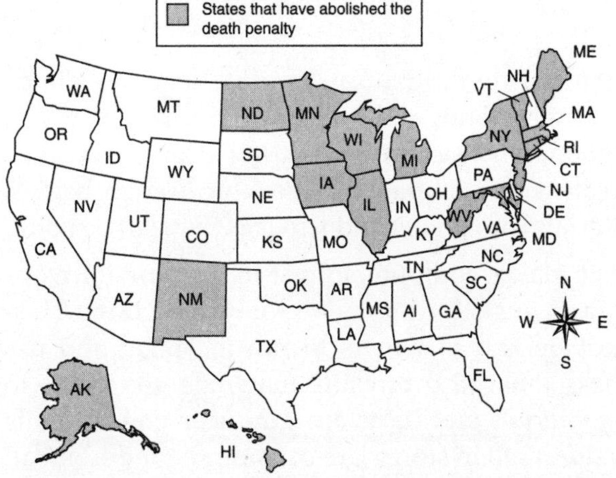


NOTE: Connecticut, Maryland, and New Mexico have abolished the death penalty prospectively. Anyone convicted of a capital offense that occurred prior to abolition of the death penalty in these states may be legally executed.

**Homicide Rate per 100,000 Population, 2010**

| Highest | Lowest |
|---|---|
| Louisiana, 11.9 | Vermont, 1.3 |
| Mississippi, 9.6 | New Hampshire, 1.4 |
| Alabama, 8.2 | Idaho, 1.5 |
| Maryland, 7.6 | Wyoming, 1.6 |
| New Mexico, 7.4 | Hawaii, 1.8 |

Source: National Center for Health Statistics and U.S. Bureau of the Census.

13. How many states have the death penalty?

A. 12
B. 18
C. 32
D. 40

14. People who favor capital punishment usually argue that it prevents serious crimes like homicide. Based on the map and chart, what is a logical flaw with this argument?

A. A life sentence without parole costs taxpayers more than executing an inmate.
B. Some executed inmates turn out to have been innocent based on newly discovered evidence.
C. Two of the five states with the highest per capita homicide rates have abolished the death penalty.
D. Two of the five states with the lowest per capita homicide rates have abolished the death penalty.

15. The U.S. Constitution gives the president the power to make treaties with foreign nations, and it gives the Senate the power to "advise and consent" on all treaties. Thus a two-thirds majority of the Senate must ratify any treaty presented by the president. In 1978, President Jimmy Carter persuaded the Senate to ratify treaties with Panama that transferred control of the Panama Canal from the United States to Panama. Many Americans were outraged and believed that U.S. interests had been given away.

Which of the following is an opinion rather than a statement of fact?

A. Presidents have the power to enter into treaties with foreign nations.
B. A two-thirds majority of the Senate is needed to ratify a treaty.
C. The 1978 Panama treaties sold out U.S. interests to Panama.
D. The 1978 Panama treaties gave control of the Panama Canal to Panama.

16. In the mayor-council form of city government, voters elect both a mayor and a city council. The mayor is the city's chief executive, operating the city on a day-to-day basis and also serving a ceremonial function. The city council is a legislative body, in charge of the city's finances and passing city laws. In the council-manager form of city government, voters elect a city council that makes city policies and laws. The council may elect a mayor who has a largely ceremonial function. It appoints a professionally trained city manager to oversee day-to-day operations.

What is the main similarity between the mayor's role in the mayor-council and in the council-manager forms of city government?

A. The mayor sets policy.
B. The mayor runs day-to-day operations.
C. The mayor is elected by voters.
D. The mayor has ceremonial duties.

**Review your work using the explanations that start on page 715.**

# Basic Economics Concepts

### KEY IDEAS

- Businesses utilize capital, labor, and materials to create goods and services to sell.
- Markets are systems that bring sellers' goods and services to buyers.
- The prices of goods and services are determined in part by supply and demand.

### ON THE TASC TEST

*Use the direction of lines on line graphs to spot trends and make predictions.*

In economics, *capital* is a term for things that can produce income. Money can be capital; so can equipment, land, and buildings. Businesses invest capital in order to create **goods** and **services** to sell for profit. However, capital by itself cannot create value. **Labor**, the work of human beings, transforms capital and materials into goods and services that can be sold.

For example, a business that makes computers must make capital investments to build a factory and install equipment for **production**. Then the business must hire workers and managers to run the plant and use the equipment. The business must also buy the materials and parts to build the computers. The materials and parts are **producer goods**, while the finished computers, ready to sell in stores, are **consumer goods**. Not all businesses make or build objects. Some businesses create value by selling intangible services to their customers—such as an employment agency that offers the service of matching people with jobs.

**Markets** are established routines and networks for selling and buying goods and services. There are producers' markets for producer goods; there are **retail** and **wholesale** markets for consumer goods; there are markets for **raw materials** such as minerals; there are financial markets for selling stocks and bonds. Some markets are more highly organized than others, and all markets are regulated by law to some extent. But markets, by definition, are not completely under the control of any government or agency.

Goods and services are **distributed** through markets so that they can be **consumed** where they are wanted. Through the market system, sellers and buyers negotiate prices and contracts; they **compete** for the best terms possible in that market. For example, a computer manufacturer might enter the consumer electronics market, competing with other manufacturers to sell its goods at a fair price to retailers. The retailers negotiate contracts specifying how many computers they are willing to buy and distribute to consumers through their stores or catalogs.

How are prices determined in the market system? In economics, price is related to **supply** and **demand**. Sellers need to earn money on the goods they have produced. Buyers want to spend as little as possible. When the supply of something is large, buyers shop around looking for the best price, and sellers lower their prices in order to move their **inventory**. On the other hand, if a product is **scarce**, buyers are less able to shop around, and sellers can raise their prices. When Florida has a hard freeze and fruit growers lose their citrus crops, the price of oranges goes up. That is because there are fewer oranges to buy and fewer sellers to buy them from, so those sellers can charge more.

Supply and demand most clearly influence price in a **free market economy**. The U.S. economy operates primarily, but not completely, as a free market. For example, governmental **price supports** ensure that farmers can sell certain agricultural products at prices that allow them to earn a profit.

# PRACTICE 1

1. What is the main role of labor in an economy?

   A. to provide capital to start new businesses
   B. to convert capital and raw materials into products and services
   C. to purchase all the goods and services that are produced
   D. to purchase raw materials in retail and wholesale markets

2. Which of the following is an example of a producer good rather than a consumer good?

   A. a pencil
   B. a can opener
   C. a cell phone
   D. a plastic material

3. When there are very few houses for sale in an area, the real estate market is said to be a seller's market.

   Why is this name appropriate?

   A. When the supply of houses is low and demand is high, sellers can raise their prices.
   B. When the supply of houses is low and demand is high, sellers will accept an offer lower than list price.
   C. Sellers are always at an advantage in the real estate market.
   D. Competition among sellers raises prices.

4. Why might the U.S. government offer price supports to farmers but not to toy manufacturers?

   A. Toy sales vary widely, depending on the appeal of a particular toy.
   B. Toys are not critical to a nation's economic and political well-being.
   C. Toys are sold to adults for use by children.
   D. Toys are distributed through conventional wholesale and retail channels.

**Questions 5 and 6 refer to the following graph.**

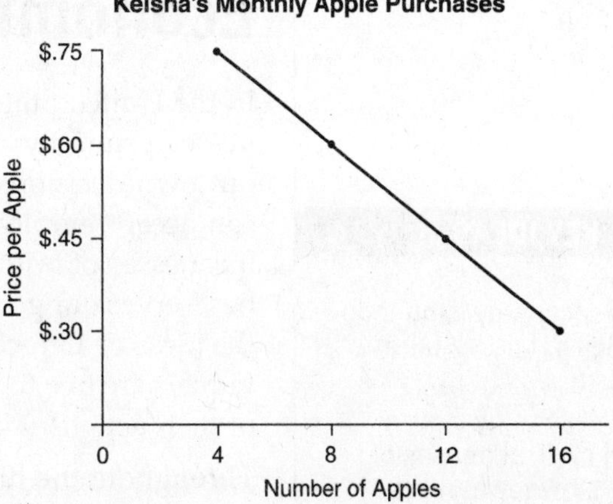


5. When apples cost 30 cents each, how many apples does Keisha buy each month?

   A. 4
   B. 8
   C. 12
   D. 16

6. Which of the following conclusions is supported by the data on the graph?

   A. As the supply of apples rises, Keisha buys fewer apples.
   B. As the supply of apples rises, the demand for apples falls.
   C. As the price of apples rises, Keisha buys fewer apples.
   D. As the price of apples falls, Keisha buys the same number of apples.

---

7. Which of the following is a service business?

   A. tool manufacturer
   B. paper mill
   C. microchip factory
   D. beauty salon

**Review your work using the explanations that start on page 715.**

## STUDY ADVICE

As you work your way through this chapter, pay attention to news stories about the economy. Think about how the concepts outlined in this chapter are at work in the news stories you hear. Doing so will sharpen your understanding of how the economy works.

LESSON 2

# The U.S. Economic System

In the United States, the economic activity of individual people and businesses primarily determines our economic health and growth. We make our own decisions about how to save and spend most of our income. We can accept employment as we choose, become **entrepreneurs** and build businesses of our own, and seek education and training to whatever level best serves our goals. These freedoms are based on **laissez-faire capitalism**, the ideas of 18th-century economist Adam Smith, who believed that if individuals are free to act in their own best interests economically, the sum total of their actions will be in the best interests of the society as a whole.

Throughout the history of the United States, **free enterprise** and **competition** have played important roles in the development of our economy. Businesses have incentives to grow larger—either by expanding their **capacity** or by integrating a broader set of functions into their **operations**—in order to make more **profit**. However, businesses are expected to compete with each other on the merits of their products and operations. Businesses are not allowed to form **monopolies**—single companies that control whole industries—and they also are not allowed to form **oligopolies**—tight-knit groups of companies that control whole industries.

Because the U.S. economy is not under government control, no one can predict or control exactly how the economy will behave. Our economy tends to move through a **business cycle** with identifiable phases, but the length and strength of a cycle and its phases vary greatly. The first phase of a cycle is the growth phase, in which businesses invest and expand optimistically. At some point, growth is slowed or stopped by one or more factors—limited resources, limited production capacity, tight employment, or market **saturation**—and the economy enters a slowdown phase. As businesses lay off workers, stop investing their capital, and cut back production, the economy enters a **recession** or **depression** phase. Unemployment rises, consumer spending slows down, and businesses act very conservatively, holding down wages and prices, avoiding risks, and managing cash flow tightly. Eventually, the economy moves into a recovery phase, perhaps initiated by a government action. Recovery may be slow or uneven across economic sectors, but eventually the economy moves into a new growth phase. **Inflation**, in which the combined price of goods and services grows faster than the purchasing power of the currency, is only partly related to these business cycle phases.

Banking and investment services, like most U.S. industries, are conducted on principles of free enterprise. A major role of **banks** and **savings and loan associations** is to create pools of savings in order to make money available as credit to businesses and consumers. **Stock exchanges** have a similar purpose; they allow investors to purchase shares of stock, which represent part ownership of a business. Both saving and investing make funds available for businesses to use to grow. When people invest in stock, they take risks because the value of the stock depends on the success of the business. However, the potential **return** is generally much higher than the **interest rate** on a savings account.

### KEY IDEAS

- The U.S. economy is built on principles of laissez-faire capitalism.
- The U.S. economy moves through cyclical phases of growth, slowdown, recession, and recovery.
- Saving and investing contribute to the economy by making money available for businesses to grow.

### ON THE TASC TEST

*A short reading passage may accompany a graphic, such as a map. Some questions may require you to use information from both the passage and the graphic.*

# PRACTICE 2

1. Why are monopolies not permitted in the United States?

   A. Monopolies are too efficient.
   B. Monopolies are part of laissez-faire capitalism.
   C. Monopolies result from free enterprise.
   D. Monopolies shut out competition.

2. According to the passage, _________ is one characteristic of a recession.

   A. increased job growth
   B. large investments of capital
   C. increased consumer spending
   D. rising unemployment

3. Private ownership of property (land or buildings) is a key characteristic of the free enterprise system. Owning property gives people a strong incentive to take care of it and use it productively.

   What is the basis for this incentive?

   A. Property owners have a stake in the future value of the property.
   B. Property owners work harder than tenants do.
   C. Property owners are given tax incentives by the federal government.
   D. Property owners must pay real estate taxes to local government.

4. Which of the following investments carries the most risk?

   A. opening a savings account at a local bank
   B. buying a certificate of deposit at a savings and loan institution
   C. buying stock in a new company, such as an Internet startup
   D. buying stock in an established company, such as Microsoft

**Question 5 refers to the following paragraph and graph.**

At different times during the business cycle, the gross domestic product—the total value of goods and services produced in a year—rises and falls.

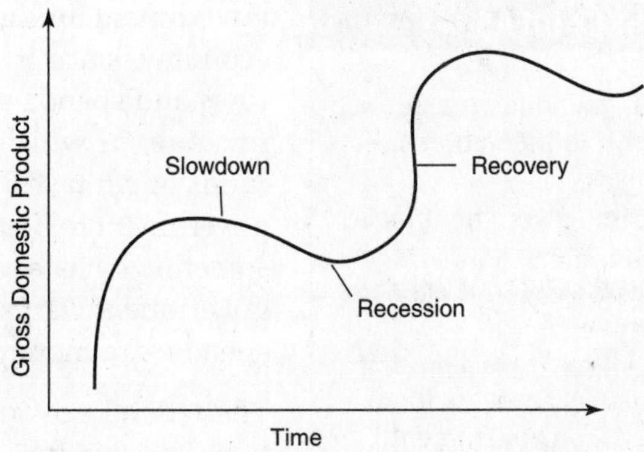


5. Which of the following conclusions is supported by the paragraph and the graph?

   A. High points in the business cycle are generally followed by recoveries.
   B. Low points in the business cycle are generally followed by slowdowns.
   C. During recessions, the rate of unemployment drops.
   D. Despite ups and downs, the gross domestic product generally increases over time.

6. What do saving and investing in stocks have in common?

   A. They provide capital for businesses to grow.
   B. They provide a sure rate of return.
   C. They pay a fixed rate of interest.
   D. They are without risk.

**Review your work using the explanations that start on page 716.**

# The Economy and the U.S. Government

Although the United States has primarily a free market economy, the U.S. government does have important economic functions. Both the executive and the legislative branches of government are involved in setting the U.S. government **budget**. The government has considerable impact on our economy, since it determines our taxes, employs many people, and borrows and spends much money. The federal budget may have a **surplus** of **revenue**, in which case elected leaders may either spend the additional funds or cut taxes; or the budget may have a revenue **deficit**, requiring the government to borrow money to cover its expenses. Government spending sometimes has a very direct impact on the economy. For example, if the government wants to boost the national economy out of a recession, it may spend extra money on projects that create new jobs.

The federal government is also responsible for maintaining good conditions for our free market system. The government must have laws and courts in place to maintain property rights. It must enforce fair legal standards for operating a business. The federal government provides a stable **currency** and operates the U.S. Mint, which makes coins and prints paper money. Our central banking system, the **Federal Reserve System**, manages the total amount of money available for lending and borrowing in the private banking system and partially controls interest rates. The **Federal Deposit Insurance Corporation** (FDIC) insures the money in individual bank accounts in case of bank fraud or failure.

One of the fundamental purposes of the federal government is to promote the general welfare of the nation. Therefore, the government takes over many functions that the free market system does not provide. For example, the free market does not distribute wealth according to what people need to live on, so the government collects taxes to redistribute some money to people who don't earn enough. The government also provides **infrastructure**, such as interstate highways, that indirectly supports economic activity.

Another role for government in the economy is protecting workers from health dangers and exploitation. The **Occupational Safety and Health Administration** (OSHA) is a special federal agency charged to protect workers on the job, particularly in hazardous industries. Many federal and state laws also protect the interests of workers. For example, all states regulate the hours and types of work that children may perform. A number of agencies are involved in enforcing safe and fair working conditions; they visit businesses, investigate reports of problems, identify violations, and initiate prosecution in some cases.

Another group of agencies protects consumers from fraudulent business practices and unsafe products. The **Food and Drug Administration** (FDA) is responsible for making sure that food products are safe, drugs are effective, and cosmetics and drugs are labeled properly. The **Federal Trade Commission** (FTC) ensures that product claims in advertising and on package labels are true and complete.

**KEY IDEAS**

- The U.S. government plays a major part in the nation's economy.
- The federal government facilitates the free market system while protecting workers and consumers.
- The free market system cannot effectively provide for all our needs, so government fills some gaps.

**TASC TEST TIP**

*Charts, such as the one on page 489, are used to summarize information. You may be asked to find specific information from the chart or to apply information from the chart to a specific situation.*

# PRACTICE 3

1. When the U.S. government __________, it is an indication that the government has a budget surplus.

   A. issues bonds through the U.S. Treasury
   B. attempts to boost the economy by cutting the discount rate
   C. registers expenditures that exceed its revenues
   D. registers revenues that exceed its expenditures

2. Which of the following legislative actions would lead to a direct increase in consumer spending?

   A. raising Social Security contributions
   B. decreasing spending on federal work projects
   C. cutting the federal income tax
   D. ratifying an international trade agreement

3. Which of the following is an example of infrastructure that supports economic activity?

   A. consumer demand
   B. the annual federal budget
   C. local sales taxes
   D. the air traffic control system

4. The federal government has two main ways to manipulate the economy. The first is fiscal policy, in which the government increases or decreases taxes and spending to influence the economy. The second is monetary policy, in which the government increases or decreases the supply of money in order to stimulate or slow the economy.

   What is the main similarity between fiscal and monetary policy?

   A. Both involve raising taxes.
   B. Both involve lowering taxes.
   C. Both are budgetary tools of state governments.
   D. Both affect the amount of money circulating in the economy.

**Questions 5 and 6 refer to the following paragraph and chart.**

Monetary policy affects the amount of money in circulation. When there is rapid economic growth and a risk of inflation, the Federal Reserve System (the "Fed") slows it down by tightening the money supply. This makes it more difficult for people and businesses to borrow and spend money. When the economy is sluggish, the Fed increases the money supply to stimulate borrowing and spending.

**The Fed's Monetary Policy Options**

| To Take Money out of Circulation | To Put Money into Circulation |
|---|---|
| Sell government securities (bonds and Treasury bills) to investors | Buy back government securities from bond holders |
| Raise the discount rate member banks are charged to borrow from the Fed | Lower the discount rate member banks are charged to borrow from the Fed |
| Raise the reserve requirement, the amount banks must keep on hand to cover deposits | Lower the reserve requirement |

5. Which of the following indicates a step the government might take to stimulate the economy?
   A. sell government securities (bonds and Treasury bills) to investors
   B. buy back government securities
   C. raise the discount rate member banks are charged to borrow from the Fed
   D. raise the reserve requirement, the amount banks must keep on hand to cover deposits

6. Since the Fed's monetary policy options have such specific effects, why does the Fed sometimes fail to head off recession or stimulate recovery?
   A. The Fed's board meets only four times a year.
   B. The people on the Fed's board lack experience.
   C. Our complex economy takes time to respond.
   D. Our economy can be controlled only by international economic forces.

**Review your work using the explanations that start on page 716.**

# Labor and Consumer Issues

KEY IDEAS

- Workers earn wages and some benefits and protections in exchange for their labor.
- The U.S. economy is now in a time of rapid change, and workers must prepare themselves to adapt.
- Consumers must protect themselves by being aware of risks and by spending their money wisely.

ON THE TASC TEST

*Some of the economics questions on the test will be based on everyday topics faced by workers and consumers.*

As workers, we earn **wages** and other **benefits** in exchange for our labor. People who are paid hourly wages are paid only for the number of hours they work. Their earnings may fluctuate depending on how much their labor is needed. People who earn salaries typically receive the same constant pay all the time, although the hours they work may fluctuate. Some people are paid for "piecework"—that is, for each piece of work they complete. Many workers receive benefits in addition to their wages, such as health insurance, vacation pay, and special savings plans. A worker's total **compensation** for a job is the combined value of wages and benefits.

Workers and their employers must pay taxes and buy insurance to cover work-related problems, including injury, disability, and **unemployment**. Workers who lose their jobs because they are fired or laid off usually can receive unemployment benefits for a time or until they find new jobs. Sometimes workers lose their jobs because of major economic changes. For example, rapid changes in the steel industry drove out much of the steel manufacturing in the United States. Plants closed, and workers who thought they would spend their lives making good wages in steel mills suddenly found their skills worthless. In most cases, these workers had to learn new skills. This kind of rapid change is common in our modern times. Because so many markets are international, and because transportation, communication, and shipping are possible even over very long distances, businesses can change strategies very quickly and change their workforce as a result. Workers need to anticipate changes in their industries and continually seek new training in order to be prepared for change.

Most workers have direct individual agreements with their employers. However, **labor unions** are common in certain industries and professions. Through **collective bargaining**, unions negotiate contracts for wages and working conditions on behalf of all union members. If these negotiations fail, the union can call a **strike**, in which workers refuse to work. When labor-management negotiations break down, federal **mediators** may be asked to intervene. The National Labor Relations Board helps companies and unions resolve disputes.

We all participate in the U.S. economy as **consumers**. The free market system offers U.S. consumers an amazing array of choices for the goods and services we want. As retailers and marketers woo our business relentlessly, we should all remember the maxim, "Let the buyer beware." Although government agencies must protect consumers, consumers must also protect themselves. For example, federal laws require that potentially hazardous products have special labeling and instructions. But these will not protect us as consumers unless we read them. Parents are required by law to strap their small children into automobile safety seats. But if the seats are incorrectly installed, the children are still at risk. Retailers who offer credit payment plans are required to disclose the interest rate, payment amount, and number of payments, but it's up to consumers to work out the total expense and compare the total with the purchase price of the item.

# PRACTICE 4

1. What is a worker's total compensation?

   A. wages only
   B. benefits only
   C. wages and benefits
   D. the amount received in unemployment benefits

2. Reread the second paragraph on page 490. Which of the following statements is a conclusion rather than a supporting detail related to the paragraph?

   A. Workers must learn skills throughout their lives to be prepared for changes in their industries.
   B. Most steel manufacturing moved out of the United States.
   C. Many steelworkers had to retrain themselves and learn new skills.
   D. Workers sometimes lose their jobs because of major economic restructuring.

3. A __________ is acting as a consumer.

   A. person working in a shopping mall
   B. professor teaching economics at a community college
   C. woman buying a computer
   D. teen starting a babysitting cooperative

4. Which of the following proverbs or slogans expresses the principle that underlies labor unions?

   A. All for one and one for all.
   B. Strike while the iron is hot.
   C. Work expands to fill the time available.
   D. Many hands make light work.

**Questions 5 and 6 refer to the following graph.**

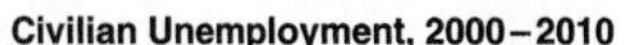


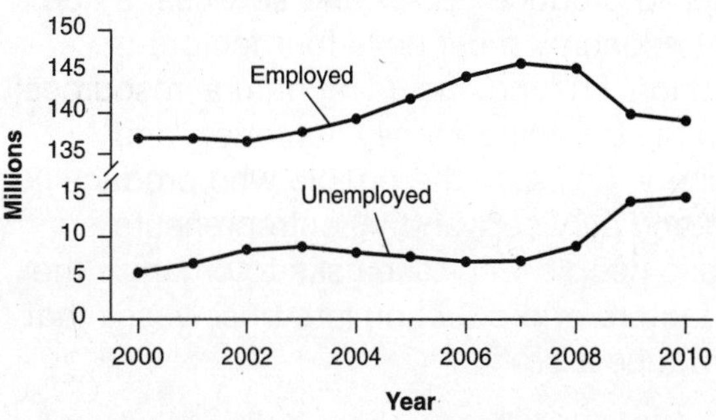


5. When was civilian unemployment at its lowest during the decade shown on the graph?

   A. in 2000
   B. in 2002
   C. in 2006
   D. in 2008

6. Which of the following statements is supported by the data in the graph?

   A. People who have stopped looking for work are not counted among the unemployed.
   B. As the number of employed civilians rose steadily from 2003 to 2006, the number of unemployed slowly declined.
   C. The rate of civilian unemployment during the 2000s exceeded the rate of civilian employment.
   D. Unemployed civilians made up about 25 percent of the total civilian workforce from 2000 to 2010.

**Review your work using the explanations that start on page 716.**

**STUDY ADVICE**

Economics questions on the TASC Social Studies Test will especially emphasize the relationship between the government and the economy. It will also emphasize the way individuals interact with the economy. As you review this chapter, pay particular attention to those two themes.

# Economics Practice Questions

**Questions 1 through 3 refer to the following passage.**

In order to produce goods and services, a free market economy must have four factors of production: (1) land, including natural resources; (2) capital, including money, factories, and machinery; (3) labor, the people who produce goods and services; and (4) entrepreneurs, business people who take risks to organize the other factors of production into businesses that will produce a profit.

1. Which of the following best defines the factors of production?

   A. the political organizations that support an economy
   B. the various types of resources needed for an economy to produce goods and services
   C. the way in which the work flow is organized in a factory or office
   D. all the transactions involved in producing goods and services

2. In a communist economy, a central government makes all of the economic decisions.

   Which factor of production is not part of a communist economy?

   A. land
   B. natural resources
   C. labor
   D. entrepreneurs

3. Which of the following is an example of capital?

   A. an office building
   B. a deposit of iron ore
   C. a skilled engineer
   D. the founder of a publishing business

4. Many fiscal conservatives believe that the U.S. budget should be balanced, with spending equal to income. They think it is wrong for the government to influence the economy by manipulating taxes or by borrowing. Instead, they feel that a balanced budget reassures business leaders that the economy is solid.

   Which of the following statements is a fact?

   A. In a balanced budget, revenues equal expenditures.
   B. The government should not use the budget to tinker with the economy.
   C. The government should not borrow money to balance the budget.
   D. A balanced government budget is the best indicator that the economy is healthy.

**Question 5 refers to the following graph.**

**U.S. Personal Income Sources, February 2013 (Billions of Dollars)**

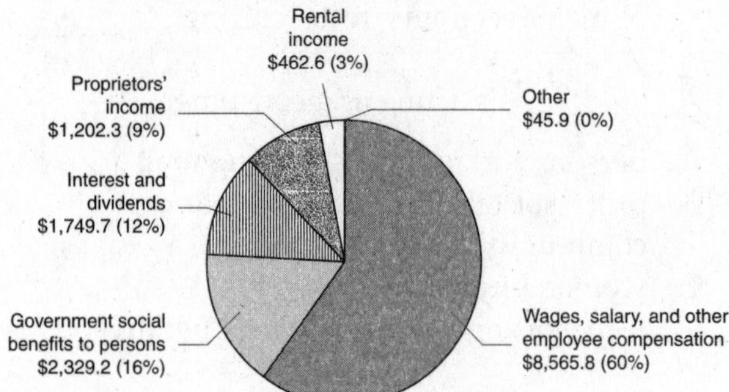


5. Which of the following statements is supported by the data on the graph?

   A. More than half of all personal income was earned through work in February 2013.
   B. Government social benefits accounted for more than one-quarter of personal income in February 2013.
   C. Interest and dividends accounted for one-third of personal income in February 2013.
   D. Per capita income was roughly $8,565 in February 2013.

**Questions 6 and 7 refer to the following cartoon.**

Reprinted with permission of the *Green Bay Press-Gazette,* Green Bay, Wisconsin.

6. Who does the man in the plaid shorts represent?

   A. a retiree
   B. an American taxpayer
   C. a corporate executive
   D. an investor

7. Why is the man in the plaid shorts calm about his ride on the roller coaster?

   A. He enjoys riding on roller coasters.
   B. He has made money buying bonds.
   C. He is accustomed to stock market ups and downs.
   D. All of his retirement savings are in stocks.

---

8. Employers withhold, or take out, federal income tax from their employees' paychecks. However, some people need to make estimated tax payments. According to the Internal Revenue Service, "Estimated tax is the method used to pay tax on income that is not subject to withholding (for example, earnings from self-employment, interest, dividends, rents, alimony, etc. ...)"

   A _________ is most likely to need to make estimated tax payments.

   A. factory worker
   B. student working part-time at the university
   C. person who runs a home day-care center
   D. gas station attendant

9. In a free market economy, people make their own decisions about working, buying goods and property, and starting businesses. Which of the following is most likely to be highly valued in nations with free market economies?

   A. cooperation
   B. individualism
   C. job security
   D. economic equality

**Questions 10 and 11 refer to the following graph.**

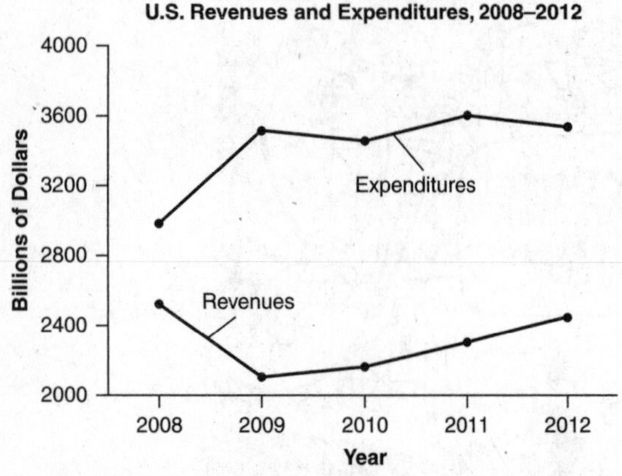


10. In which of the years represented in the chart did the United States run its largest budget deficit?

    A. 2009
    B. 2010
    C. 2011
    D. 2012

11. If a family wanted to make a graph of its economic situation similar to this graph of U.S. revenues and expenditures, what set of documents for the years 2008 to 2012 would be most useful?

    A. records showing all family members' sources of income
    B. income tax returns and expense records
    C. credit card bills and rent or mortgage statements
    D. records showing the value of the family's possessions

12. The Interstate Highway System, begun in 1956, consists of more than 45,000 miles of four- to eight-lane highways connecting most large U.S. cities. The federal government pays for almost 90 percent of the building and maintenance of interstate highways out of receipts from excise taxes on gasoline, tires, truck parts, and other related products.

    Which of the following best summarizes this information?

    A. In 1956, the federal government established the Interstate Highway System.
    B. The Interstate Highway System consists of thousands of miles of large highways.
    C. The federal government collects excise taxes on transportation-related items.
    D. The national network of interstate highways is paid for mostly by federal excise taxes.

13. In recent years, the United States has lowered protective tariffs (charges on goods imported from other countries), arguing that lower tariffs encourage free trade and benefit consumers by decreasing the cost of imported goods.

    From the perspective of a U.S. factory worker, what is the flaw in this argument?

    A. When cheaper imported goods force out U.S.-made goods, U.S. factory workers often lose their jobs.
    B. Free trade leads to cheaper imported goods because the cost of labor is less in many other nations.
    C. Factory workers cannot afford to buy imported consumer goods even if they are cheaper than U.S.-made goods.
    D. Lower protective tariffs actually raise the prices of all goods whether they are made in the United States or in foreign countries.

**Question 14 refers to the following chart.**

**U.S. Consumer Protection**

| Agency | Function |
|---|---|
| Food and Drug Administration | Protects public from poorly processed and improperly labeled foods and drugs |
| Federal Trade Commission | Protects consumers from misleading and/or fraudulent advertising |
| Consumer Product Safety Commission | Protects consumers from risk of injury or death from hazardous products |
| Securities and Exchange Commission | Protects investors from being misled about stocks and bonds |
| National Highway Traffic Safety Administration | Protects consumers by testing vehicle safety and monitoringn ationwide speed limits |

14. Which agency could be involved in a dispute over a commercial that implied something about a product that was not true?

A. Food and Drug Administration
B. Federal Trade Commission
C. Consumer Product Safety Commission
D. Securities and Exchange Commission

15. Equilibrium occurs when the supply of a product or service equals the demand for it. A product tends to be priced at the equilibrium point. When the price is greater than the equilibrium point, demand decreases and there is an oversupply of the product on the market.

______ is the result of the price falling below the equilibrium point.

A. A shortage of the product
B. A surplus of the product
C. The equilibrium point decreasing
D. The equilibrium point increasing

16. One approach to the study of economics is called macroeconomics. Macroeconomics deals with economies as a whole. For instance, a macroeconomist might study the causes of inflation or the factors that determine why some national economies grow quickly and others do not.

Which of the following is most likely to be studied by a macroeconomist?

A. how a firm prices its products or services
B. what causes high rates of unemployment
C. what determines consumer demand for a product
D. how a factory makes production decisions

**Question 17 refers to the following graph.**

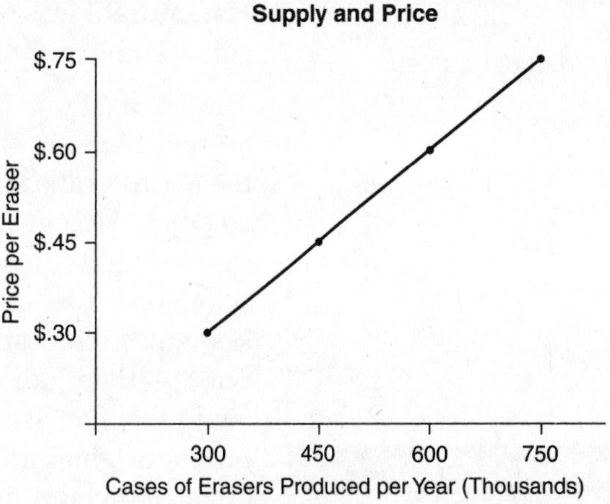


17. Which of the following conclusions is supported by the data on the graph?

A. As the price per eraser decreases, manufacturers supply more erasers.
B. As the price per eraser increases, manufacturers supply fewer erasers.
C. As the price per eraser increases, manufacturers supply more erasers.
D. As the supply of erasers increases, the demand for erasers decreases.

**Review your work using the explanations that start on page 717.**

**STUDY ADVICE**

As you study, remember to build in rewards and breaks. Celebrate a job well done with a fun outing. Don't try to study seven days a week—this can lead to burnout. Plan a day off to rest, relax, and reward yourself for the focused studying you have done!

LESSON 1

# Early Civilizations

**KEY IDEAS**

- Ancient civilizations developed where people could settle in one place with a secure food supply.
- The ancient republics of Greece and Rome were incubators for important ideas in modern government.
- Ancient civilizations also left legacies in art, architecture, science, and astronomy.

**ON THE TASC TEST**

*The world history questions require that you have familiarity with major topics in world history. You do not need to memorize names or dates.*

One of the earliest known **civilizations** is ancient Egypt. By 5000 B.C.E., people who lived along the **Nile River** had begun to take advantage of the fertile soil left behind by floods. The river and irrigation systems allowed the Egyptians to grow enough food to support a large population. Around 3000 B.C.E., Egyptian civilization grew under the rule of Egypt's kings, or **pharaohs**. Believing their pharaohs to be part god, Egyptians built the famous **pyramids** to house these rulers in their next lives. Many who built the pyramids and did the hard work to build this civilization were slaves.

Around the same time, in the **Fertile Crescent**—an area northeast of Egypt—**Sumerian** city-states were also developing irrigation and flood control methods. They also created a system of writing. In about 1800 B.C.E., the Sumerians were conquered by the Babylonians. One of the Babylonian kings, Hammurabi, is remembered for codifying laws. The **Code of Hammurabi** was written on a huge stone in a public place so all Babylonians could know and follow the law.

The civilization of **ancient Greece** did not develop around a river, but around the sea. The Greeks built an **empire**: they established colonies on the Mediterranean Sea and the Black Sea; then they imported food from the colonies. However, Greece itself was not politically unified. As its city-states fought for control of each other's land, Sparta, a particularly warlike state, took over a number of other city-states. Athens, another city-state, is known as the first political **democracy**. All Athenian citizens could vote—but less than half of Athenians were citizens. Women could not vote, nor could the many slaves. The Greek Empire lasted only a few hundred years, but its original ideas, such as democracy, and its stunning arts, including architecture and literature, remain influential even now.

Eventually, the Greek Empire fell to **Roman** conquerors. Rome began as a city on the Italian Peninsula, governed by its wealthy citizens through an elected Senate. Roman citizens were governed by a system of laws that is still influential in the United States. For example, the Romans believed that a person accused of a crime was innocent until proven guilty. The power of Rome grew, and the Romans took over many lands surrounding the Mediterranean Sea, pushing north as far as England and east into Asia by about 100 C.E. Roman leaders built systems and infrastructure to make their empire strong: schools, roads and bridges, hospitals, a tax system, and an army. The ancient Roman Empire lasted until 476 C.E.

Ancient Egypt, Greece, and Rome were only a few of the early civilizations in which people made important scientific discoveries and developed enduring ideas. In Central America, the **Maya**, whose culture was strongest from 300 to 900 C.E., invented a pictographic writing system in which they recorded remarkable discoveries in mathematics and astronomy. The **Inca Empire** in South America had a sophisticated system of government. The Incas built amazing roads and bridges in their rugged mountain lands. In Mexico, the **Aztecs** invented a written language and a calendar system and expanded their farmlands by dredging mud from lakes.

# PRACTICE 1

1. Which of the following Central American civilizations is particularly noted for achievements in both mathematics and astronomy?

   A. the Sumerians
   B. the Maya
   C. the Aztecs
   D. the Incas

2. According to the information on page 496, two ancient civilizations were particularly influential on the form of government adopted by the United States of America. Select the answer choice that correctly lists the two civilizations that had the greatest impact on America's systems of law and government.

   A. Sumer and Ancient Greece
   B. Ancient Greece and Ancient Rome
   C. Incas and Ancient Egypt
   D. Ancient Egypt and Ancient Rome

3. What did the ancient civilizations of Egypt and the Fertile Crescent have in common?

   A. Both developed flood control and irrigation technologies to boost food production.
   B. Both had a public code of law engraved on a huge stone.
   C. Both were centered on the shores of the Mediterranean Sea.
   D. Both developed systems of political democracy in which citizens could vote.

4. Once a society developed agriculture and domesticated animals, food surpluses and rising populations made possible which of the following developments?

   A. a nomadic lifestyle
   B. towns
   C. stone tools
   D. stone carvings

**STUDY ADVICE**

You won't be required to remember specific dates or lots of detailed facts for the TASC Social Studies Test. However, you should be familiar with the broad themes of world history. Pay particular attention to the Key Ideas and the terms in bold on each page on the left.

**Questions 5 and 6 refer to the following map.**

**Ancient China**

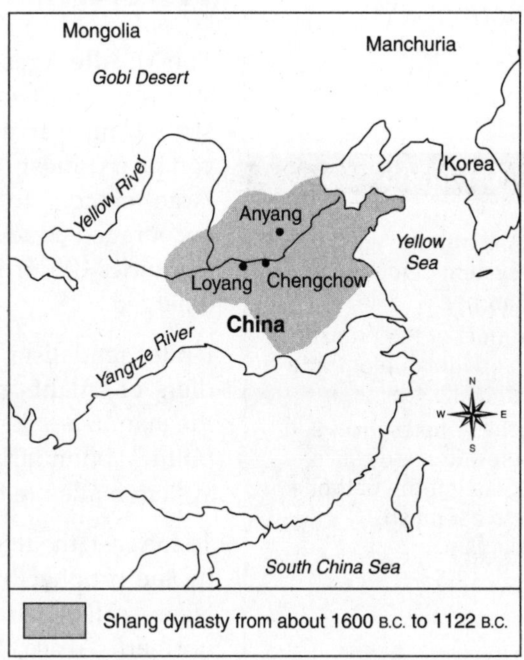


5. In the Yellow River valley, floods deposit a fertile yellow soil called loess that is easily worked by farmers.

   Which of the following civilizations arose under geographic conditions similar to those in ancient China?

   A. the Aztecs
   B. ancient Greece
   C. ancient Rome
   D. ancient Egypt

6. Which of the following statements is supported by the information in the map?

   A. The Yellow River is the only major river in China.
   B. The Shang dynasty, or ruling family, controlled China for almost a thousand years.
   C. The Yellow River was probably the main trade route between Loyang and Chengchow.
   D. The Shang civilization traded more with Korea than with Manchuria.

**Review your work using the explanations that start on page 717.**

LESSON 2

# Feudalism to Nation States

The **Middle Ages** in Europe lasted from about 500 to 1500 C.E. As the once strong government of Rome weakened, Europe became vulnerable to invasions from warring groups or tribes. A tribal ruler named **Charlemagne** conquered most of Europe by 800. Charlemagne was able to stabilize this large territory for a time. He established laws, spread Christianity, and encouraged education and commerce. When Charlemagne died in 814, the territories of Europe became unstable again, and the system of **feudalism** emerged.

**KEY IDEAS**

- During the Middle Ages, the feudal system helped to stabilize Europe.
- A by-product of the Crusades was the opening up of trade routes and city growth.
- During the Renaissance, education grew in importance, and people left the Catholic Church to establish Protestantism.

Under feudalism, kings granted control of land to nobles. A noble's soldiers, or knights, protected the noble's estate, or manor. **Peasants** farmed at the manor. Nobles paid taxes to kings; peasants paid taxes to nobles. As the political boundaries among the kings' lands became established, the feudal system made life in Europe more peaceful over several hundred years.

To the east, the religion of **Islam** was founded during the early Middle Ages by the prophet Muhammad, who was born in 570 C.E. The followers of Islam, called **Muslims**, conquered large territories in the Middle East, northern Africa, Spain, Persia, and India. They established a series of empires. Many people in these conquered lands converted to Islam while contributing their own knowledge and arts to the Muslim culture. Although the Islamic empires did not last, Islam and its culture have remained strong.

During the late Middle Ages, Christians and Muslim Turks fought over the holy city of Jerusalem in a series of wars called the **Crusades**. Christians gained control of Jerusalem from the Turks, but they ruled the city for less than 90 years. A more lasting effect of the Crusades was to open up trade between Europe and the Middle East and even China. As trade, money, and merchants grew in importance in Europe, feudalism declined. People left the manors and went to live and work in cities, where opportunities were greater. Cities gained political, economic, and cultural importance.

**TASC TEST TIP**

*To summarize a graph such as the one on page 499, ask yourself: What is the topic of the graph? What is the main point of the data? How could I say this in a sentence or two?*

During the Middle Ages, European nations began to form as **monarchs** combined territories of small rulers and took advantage of the wealth of cities. England's monarchy was established by 1100. France won the Hundred Years' War against England and emerged as a strong nation under its monarch. Spain united through the marriage of two rulers, Ferdinand and Isabella, who had each controlled smaller states.

The **Renaissance**, which spread from Italy across Europe between 1300 and 1600, brought growth in education, science, and the arts. The Renaissance also led to changes in the Catholic Church. During the **Reformation** in the 1500s, reformers criticized the church for abusing its power. Those who believed that people should read the Bible themselves rather than follow the pope split from the Catholic Church and formed the **Protestant** religion. King Henry VIII of England broke from the Catholic Church and formed the Church of England so he would not have to obey the pope.

# PRACTICE 2

1. What was the role of the knights in feudal Europe?

   A. to collect taxes for the king
   B. to take care of livestock
   C. to protect their noble's land from attack
   D. to administer justice

2. Given the information on page 498, in which of the following modern European nations are you most likely to find evidence of Muslim arts and culture?

   A. Spain
   B. France
   C. Germany
   D. Italy

3. During the late Middle Ages, the growth of trade spurred a migration of peasants from the manors to the towns. To which of the following events is this most similar?

   A. the migration of Puritans to the New World to escape religious persecution in the 1600s
   B. the migration of people from farms to industrial cities in the 1800s
   C. the migration of political refugees to the United States in the 1900s
   D. the migration of individuals with health problems from cold, damp regions to warm, dry regions

4. At the time of the Reformation, which of the following was one of the main differences between Roman Catholics and Protestants?

   A. Roman Catholics accepted the authority of the pope and Protestants did not.
   B. Roman Catholics lived on the manors and Protestants lived in the towns.
   C. Roman Catholics supported the monarchies in their nations and Protestants did not.
   D. Roman Catholics led the Church of England under Henry VIII and Protestants did not.

5. In England in the 1100s, any free man could bring a case before a royal court headed by a circuit judge, who formed juries of local people. The decisions of these courts were recorded and formed the basis for common law, which was applied to everyone in the kingdom. In contrast, justice in the manor courts, which were run by the nobles, could be fickle. There were few written laws, and the verdicts could be overturned by the lord.

   People usually preferred to be tried in royal courts rather than manor courts because the royal courts valued which of the following?

   A. accepted legal principles
   B. harsh punishment
   C. power for the local lord
   D. fines rather than imprisonment

**Question 6 refers to the following graph.**

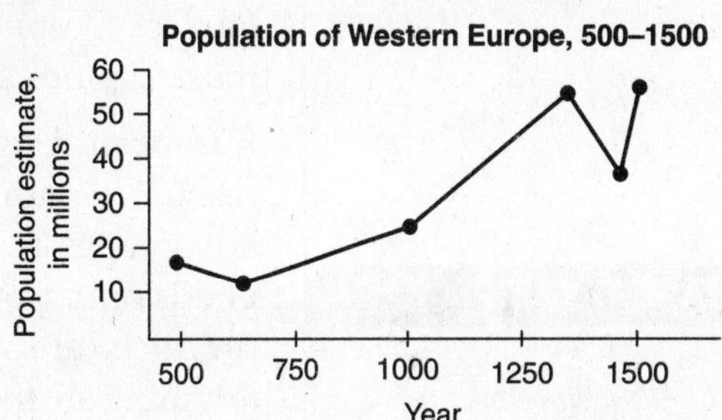


Source: Carlo M. Cippola, ed. *The Fontana Economic History of Europe: The Middle Ages* and Carlo M. Cippola *Before the Industrial Revolution: European Society and Economy, 1000–1700.*

6. Which of the following best summarizes the information shown on the graph?

   A. The population of western Europe showed the most growth between the years 750 and 1000.
   B. There were fewer than 50 million people living in western Europe at any given time.
   C. The population of western Europe showed almost constant growth with only brief periods of decline.
   D. The population of western Europe fell to its lowest around the year 1450.

**Review your work using the explanations that start on page 718.**

# Exploration and Colonialism

**KEY IDEAS**

- European explorers sought new sailing routes to make trading easier with India and Asia.
- European rulers set up colonies to extend their territories and gain new wealth.
- Native peoples and cultures were exploited by colonization.

About 500 years ago, explorers from European nations such as Spain and France sailed on risky voyages all over the world. Europeans had many reasons for leaving the shores of their own continent. Some were looking for trade routes and valuable goods, such as spices, to bring back. Others were missionaries bent on spreading the Christian religion. Still others were paid by their rulers to find new lands to conquer. No matter what the reasons for their journeys, they faced real dangers and uncertain rewards, and many left the lands they reached in ruins. Most Americans know the story of Christopher Columbus, who sailed west from Spain in 1492, expecting to reach Asia. Instead, he reached the **New World**—the Americas. In 1498, Vasco da Gama, a Portuguese explorer, sailed south around Africa to reach India. His journey took two years, but it was profitable: His four ships returned full of spices. In 1519, Ferdinand Magellan and his crew left Spain to sail around the southern tip of South America en route to India. Of Magellan's five ships, only one made it back to Spain; Magellan himself died in the Pacific. However, the ship that returned to Spain is believed to be the first ship to circumnavigate the globe. Not long after, French explorer Jacques Cartier tried and failed to find a river route through North America to the Pacific. Despite the sometimes negative consequences of their journeys, these explorers greatly expanded the Europeans' knowledge of geography.

European rulers turned to distant lands to expand their own power and resources, primarily for economic gain. **Colonies** offered a number of advantages to their ruling nations. Colonies could be required to **import** goods only from the ruling nation, and they could be forced to export their products and natural resources only to the ruling nation. Furthermore, anything in the colonized area was considered the property of the ruling nation. In the 1500s, Spain gained great wealth from its colonies in the New World by stealing valuable objects from the native civilizations and by mining and removing gold, silver, and other minerals from their lands. Colonialism could be utterly devastating to native cultures, economies, and populations, as colonizers brought not only weapons but also deadly diseases. Not only North America but also large parts of South America, Africa, and Asia suffered during the age of colonialism.

**TASC TEST TIP**

*Some questions will ask, "Which of the following statements is supported by the graph (or the map)?" Read the choices and carefully check each against the graphic.*

Historians distinguish among different types of colonies, depending on the relationship between the ruling nation and the colony. In colonies of **settlement,** people from the ruling nation migrated to the colony and established a government under the authority of the ruling nation. The English colonies in North America were colonies of settlement. Although Native Americans had long-established societies and territories of their own, the English settlers disregarded these. From the point of view of the British government, the lands belonged to England, and the Native Americans were subject to British law and had to obey the British colonial government.

Colonies of **exploitation** were common in tropical climates, where Europeans did not want to establish their own settlements. In these colonies, the ruling nation established a government to exploit the local labor force and natural resources. The native people were forced to produce goods and crops to benefit the ruling nation.

# PRACTICE 3

1. For what is Magellan best known?
   A. discovering a route north of North America to the Pacific Ocean
   B. discovering a route to India around the southern tip of Africa
   C. exploring North America's rivers
   D. leading the first expedition to result in an around-the-world voyage

2. According to the passage on page 500, what is the main reason European rulers explored the New World and established colonies?
   A. to convert people to Christianity
   B. to establish democratic governments
   C. to gain economic benefits
   D. to find a river route through North America

3. Which of the following is an example of a colony of exploitation?
   A. Pennsylvania, where Quakers and other religious minorities settled to escape religious persecution in Europe
   B. Malaya, where the British set up and ran rubber plantations worked by the native peoples
   C. the island of Manhattan and areas north along the Hudson River, where the Dutch established the settlement of New Netherlands
   D. Brazil, where the King of Portugal gave large parcels of land to loyal subjects, who enlisted others to settle on the land

4. Based on the passage, what was the main cause of population decline among native colonized peoples?
   A. emigration to other colonies
   B. slavery
   C. war and disease
   D. low birthrate.

**Question 5 refers to the following map.**

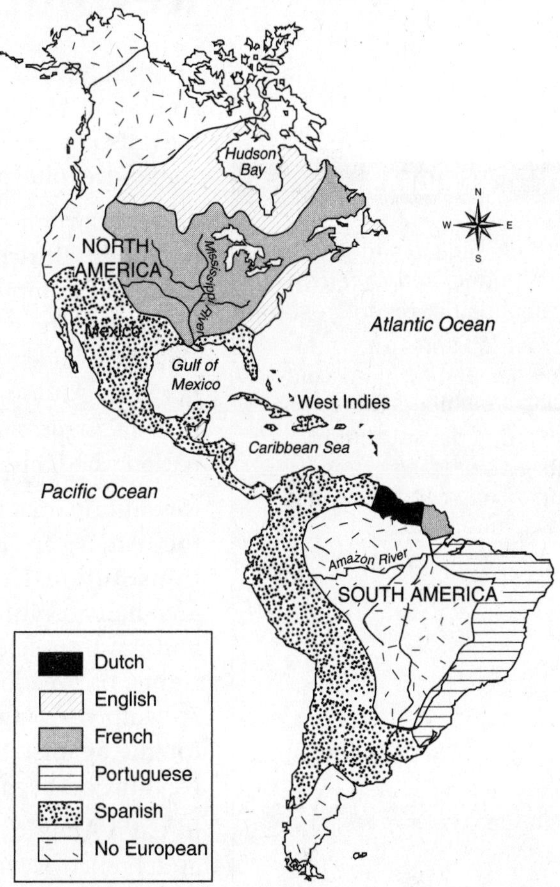


5. Which of the following statements is supported by information on the map?
   A. In 1700, most of the Amazon River valley was claimed by Portugal.
   B. The Dutch had the smallest claim in the Americas in 1700.
   C. By 1700, the English had claimed the west coast of North America.
   D. In 1700, Mexico was claimed by both the Portuguese and the Spanish.

**Review your work using the explanations that start on page 718.**

# The Age of Revolutions

Political revolutions often happen when people are unhappy about the conditions resulting from their system of government. Political revolutions may also be fueled by new ideas about who is best suited to govern. In the Age of Revolutions, many people wanted more political power.

### KEY IDEAS

- In the American and French Revolutions, people fought against unjust governments.
- Revolution spread to Latin America, ending many colonial governments there.
- The Industrial Revolution caused sweeping changes in work, living conditions, and social mobility.

One important cause of the **American Revolution** was British taxation. Although British citizens in England were represented in government through **Parliament**, the American colonists did not have representatives in that body. The colonists believed that they should not have to pay the special taxes levied on them, since they had had no voice in determining the tax laws. Although the colonists began by arguing for representation in the British government, by 1776 they had declared themselves a sovereign nation, the United States of America.

Revolutionaries in France were inspired by democratic ideas expressed in the American colonies' **Declaration of Independence** and the **U.S. Constitution**. Unlike England, France had no Parliament; the French monarch had absolute power. The nobility and the Church had many privileges and paid no taxes, while ordinary citizens paid heavy taxes and had few rights or freedoms. In 1789, the French people organized a National Assembly—a law-making body to represent them. When King Louis XVI fought against the establishment of the National Assembly, the **French Revolution** began. Its turmoil lasted for ten years.

In Latin America, many colonized people, inspired in part by the American and French Revolutions, began to shake off European rule. In Haiti, an island in the Caribbean Sea, slaves led by Toussaint L'Ouverture overturned French rule and established an independent nation in 1804. Mexican revolutionaries finally won their independence from Spain in 1821. In South America, revolutions rocked the continent until 1824, by which time most countries had gained their independence.

### TASC TEST TIP

*As part of the TASC Social Studies Test, you may be provided with basic historic information and asked to make comparisons—such as the similarities and differences between two revolutions.*

Important revolutions are not always political. The **Industrial Revolution** started in the late 1700s in the textile industry, when new equipment was invented for spinning thread and weaving cloth. Instead of workers using their own tools at home, factories could house many workers using machines to produce much greater quantities. This factory model for large-scale production spread along with **steam engines** and electricity. Workers moved into factory towns and cities to work for wages. The Industrial Revolution brought a mixture of benefits and problems—useful inventions, increasing wealth, and new **social mobility** were offset by dangerous factory jobs, **child labor**, crowded cities, and **pollution**.

The Industrial Revolution also brought sweeping social changes. The economic mainstay of the European **aristocracy** had been farmland. After the Industrial Revolution, manufacturing and trade became more important economically than agriculture. Thus, the merchant classes became more powerful. New ideas about political equality affected how people thought about social equality as well.

# PRACTICE 4

1. Which of the following had a great influence on the French Revolution?

    A. the Industrial Revolution
    B. the Mexican Revolution
    C. the U.S. Declaration of Independence
    D. the British monarchy

**Question 2 refers to the following paragraph and graph.**

Before the French Revolution, the French were divided into three groups by law, each with different privileges. In the First Estate were the higher clergy, who were nobles, and the parish priests, who were commoners. The Second Estate consisted of nobles who were not members of the clergy. The Third Estate was made up of commoners, including the middle class and peasants.

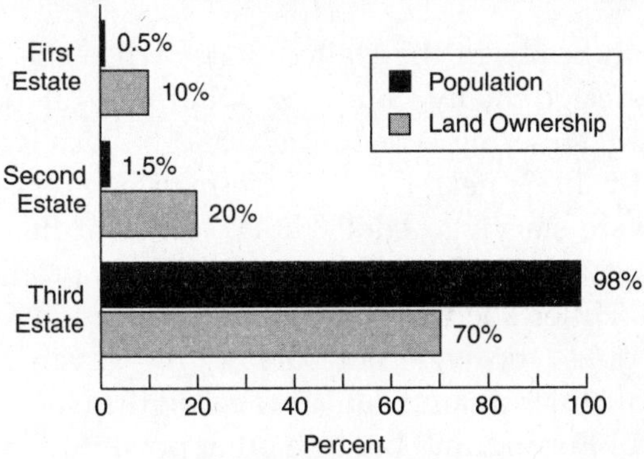


2. Which of the following statements is supported by the paragraph and the graph?

    A. All members of the nobility belonged to the First Estate.
    B. The members of the First Estate owned more property than members of the Second Estate.
    C. The distribution of wealth in prerevolutionary France favored the Third Estate.
    D. Members of the Third Estate owned the least amount of land per person.

**STUDY ADVICE**

How are you feeling about the TASC at this point? If you're feeling encouraged, that's fantastic. If you're feeling discouraged, don't give up. Most people have to work very hard to get their high school equivalency degree. Stick with it—you'll get there!

3. According to the information on page 502, what is the main difference between the English and French governments before 1789?

    A. England was a monarchy, while France was not a monarchy.
    B. England had a parliament, while France did not have a parliament.
    C. England was a democratic republic, while France was not a direct democracy.
    D. England was not a monarchy, while France was a monarchy.

4. On what was the economic power of the aristocracy based in 18th-century Europe?

    A. moral superiority
    B. attaining a high level of education
    C. possessing large landholdings
    D. belonging to the Church bureaucracy

5. Which of the following does the writer of the text on page 502 take for granted that you know, but does not state outright?

    A. The American colonists demanded representation in the British government before they declared independence.
    B. A sovereign nation is independent, having the power to govern itself.
    C. Many colonies were influenced by the American and French revolutions to seek independence.
    D. As manufacturing and trade became more important, the merchant classes gained power.

6. The Information Revolution of the late 20th century, spurred by the availability of personal computers and the Internet, is most similar to which of the following revolutions?

    A. the American Revolution
    B. the French Revolution
    C. the Mexican Revolution
    D. the Industrial Revolution

**Review your work using the explanations that start on page 718.**

LESSON 5

# The Twentieth Century

### KEY IDEAS

- Two devastating world wars occurred during the first half of the 20th century.
- The United States and Soviet Union emerged as superpowers after World War II.
- The superpowers faced off during the Cold War, which ended with the breakup of the Soviet Union in 1991.

### TASC TEST TIP

*You may be familiar with some of the world events covered on the TASC. However, answer questions based on the information provided on the test, even if it differs from what you remember.*

**World War I** resulted from **nationalism** and **imperialism**—the desire of nations to extend their empires. This desire for expansion led to military buildup. When war broke out in 1914 between Serbia and Austria-Hungary over the assassination of an Austrian leader visiting Serbia, a chain reaction started as other countries also declared war. Germany and Austria-Hungary were the mainstays of the **Central Powers**, who fought against the **Allies**—England, France, Russia, Serbia, and eventually the United States. When the Central Powers finally lost the war, millions of people had been killed. The war had devastated Europe, leaving many people jobless and homeless. In the 1918 **Treaty of Versailles**, Germany was blamed for the war and forced to pay **reparations** to the Allies.

Revolution in Russia began during World War I. The Russian **Czar** refused to pull out of the war, even though most Russians did not support involvement. In 1917, the Czar and his family were assassinated, and the **Russian Revolution** ended with Bolshevik leader Vladimir Lenin in power. The Bolsheviks founded the Soviet Union as a **communist** nation with one political party—the Communist Party.

The Great Depression, which began in the United States when the stock market crashed in 1929, affected many countries. One hard-hit nation was Germany, which was still suffering economically and politically from its defeat in World War I. By 1933, nearly half of German workers were unemployed, and people were starving. Adolf Hitler, leader of the Nazi Party, rose to power by appealing to German nationalism and promising to put people back to work. Hitler's terrible form of nationalism involved imprisoning and killing people who were not part of "the Aryan race." Jews were the main targets of Hitler's campaign, now called the **Holocaust**. Hitler wanted to take over all Europe, and because other powerful nations wanted to avoid war, they let him annex Austria, then Czechoslovakia. But when Hitler invaded Poland in 1939, England and France declared war on Germany, and **World War II** began. Many nations went to war, including the United States. Once again, Germany and the other **Axis Powers** (including Italy and Japan) were defeated by the Allies. The United States dropped the first **atomic bomb** on Hiroshima to end the war.

After World War II, the United States and the Soviet Union emerged as **superpowers**. Former allies, they each led opposing groups of countries, one group democratic, the other group communist. The two groups of nations so distrusted each other that the period following World War II was called the **Cold War**—a war fought through political and diplomatic contests instead of battles. To catch up with the United States, the Soviet Union started to build its own nuclear weapons, and the **arms race** began, soon followed by the "space race."

However, by 1990 the Soviet bloc was falling apart. The Soviet Union itself split into 15 countries in 1991. People who had lived under repressive governments for many years struggled to establish democracy—not only in the former Soviet bloc, but also in Africa, Latin America, and Asia.

# PRACTICE 5

1. As a result of the 1918 Treaty of Versailles, what did Germany have to do?

   A. pay the Allies money to repair war damages
   B. develop its military forces to protect Europe
   C. adopt a communist government
   D. promote nationalism among its people

2. What event was the immediate cause of England and France declaring war on Germany at the beginning of World War II?

   A. the annexation of Austria
   B. the annexation of Czechoslovakia
   C. the invasion of Poland
   D. the invasion of France

3. Before the atomic bomb was dropped on Hiroshima, the Allies warned Japan they would suffer "complete and utter destruction" unless they surrendered. Despite the fact that 80,000 people were killed and 40,000 wounded by the bombing of Hiroshima, Japan still refused to surrender. The United States then dropped a second atomic bomb on the city of Nagasaki, killing 40,000 more people. After the second bombing, the Japanese surrendered.

   Japan's refusal to surrender after the bombing of Hiroshima suggests that the Japanese placed a high value on which of the following?

   A. negotiation
   B. national pride
   C. the lives of military personnel
   D. a lasting peace

4. Which of the following is a similarity between World War I and World War II?

   A. Both were confined to Europe.
   B. Both occurred after the Russian Revolution.
   C. Both involved the use of atomic weapons.
   D. Both were won by the Allies.

**Questions 5 and 6 refer to the following chart.**

**Casualties in World War II**

| Nation | Military Dead | Military Wounded | Civilian Dead |
|---|---|---|---|
| Great Britain | 398,000 | 475,000 | 65,000 |
| Soviet Union | 7,500,000 | 14,102,000 | 15,000,000 |
| United States | 292,000 | 671,000 | very few |
| Germany | 2,850,000 | 7,250,000 | 5,000,000 |
| Japan | 1,576,000 | 500,000 | 300,000 |

Source: *The Second World War* by Henri Michel.

5. What was the main difference between the casualties sustained by the United States and those sustained by other nations in World War II?

   A. The United States had more military dead than wounded.
   B. The United States sustained only a few civilian casualties.
   C. The United States had the fewest wounded.
   D. The United States had more civilian than military casualties.

6. The main reason that the Soviet Union had so many casualties is that it was invaded by the German army, which got as far as the outskirts of Moscow and Leningrad. There the Germans halted in 1941. Severe winters, long supply lines back to Germany, and stiff resistance from the Soviets ultimately defeated the Germans.

   Which of the following events is most similar to the German invasion of the Soviet Union?

   A. the 1812 French invasion of Russia, which failed due to harsh weather and lack of supplies
   B. the occupation of Singapore by Japan in World War II, which gave Japan control of Malaya
   C. the 1941 Japanese attack on Pearl Harbor, which drew the United States into World War II
   D. the 1945 Allied invasion of Europe, which liberated Europe from German control

**Review your work using the explanations that start on page 718.**

# World History Practice Questions

1. The Germanic tribes that invaded the Roman Empire had relatively simple governments. There were few government officials and taxes. Rulers depended on the loyalty of their warriors rather than on a government bureaucracy. Germanic laws were based on custom and designed to prevent warfare between families.

   Which of the following is the best title for this passage?

   A. How Germanic Tribes Governed
   B. Germanic Tribes and the Roman Empire
   C. The Invasion of the Roman Empire
   D. Loyalty Among the Germanic Tribes

2. The mechanization of the textile industry, the invention of the steam engine, and the development of the coal and iron industries contributed to Great Britain's lead in the Industrial Revolution. However, after 1850, other nations began to challenge Great Britain's lead. Belgium, France, and Germany all industrialized quickly. By 1900, natural resources and railroad building helped make the United States the leading industrial nation.

   Which of the following is the best summary of this passage?

   A. The development of natural resources made Great Britain the leader in the Industrial Revolution.
   B. The Industrial Revolution started in Great Britain and spread throughout the world.
   C. The Industrial Revolution started in Great Britain and spread to Europe, but by 1900 the United States was the leading industrialized nation.
   D. Plentiful natural resources and a vast railroad system were the underpinnings of the Industrial Revolution in the United States.

**Questions 3 and 4 refer to the following map.**

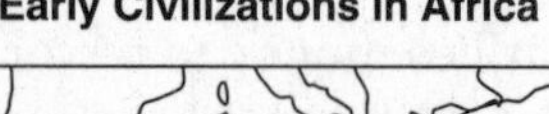


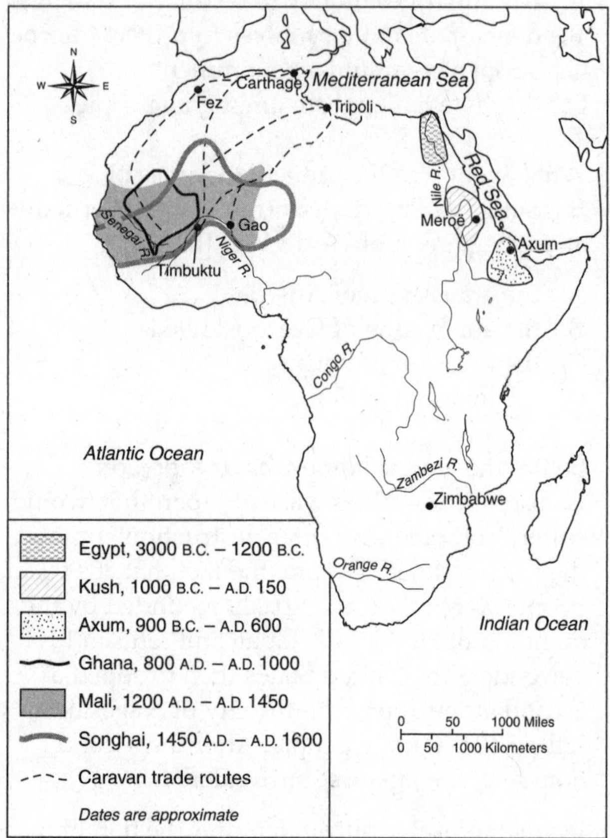


3. Which area on the map shows where the earliest civilizations in Africa developed?

   A. Egypt
   B. Kush
   C. Axum
   D. Mali

4. Which of the following statements is supported by information on the map?

   A. Over 800 years, several civilizations succeeded one another in western Africa.
   B. The Kingdom of Mali dominated western Africa for more than 500 years.
   C. Timbuktu was an important center of learning in Songhai.
   D. Gold and salt were transported along caravan trade routes in western Africa.

**Questions 5 through 8 refer to the following time line.**

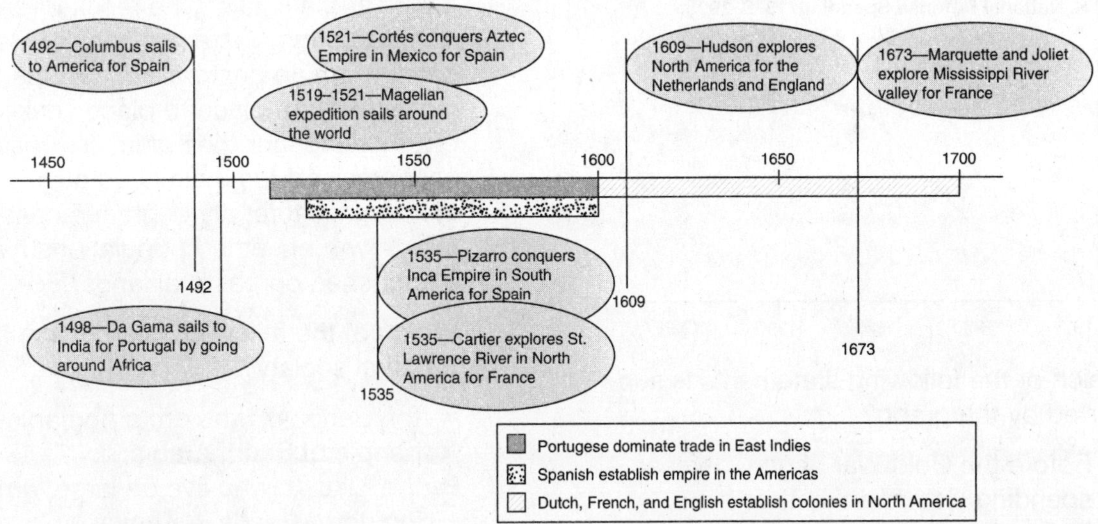


5. Portugal dominated trade in the East Indies for most of the 1500s. Which event from the time line most likely first triggered Portugal's superiority in the region?
   A. 1492—Columbus sails to America for Spain
   B. 1498—Da Gama sails to India for Portugal by going around Africa
   C. 1519–1521—Magellan expedition sails around the world
   D. 1535—Pizarro conquers the Inca Empire in South America for Spain

6. Which of the following statements is supported by information on the time line?
   A. Spanish and Portuguese domination of exploration gave way to that of the Dutch, French, and English.
   B. Henry Hudson discovered more places in North America than did Marquette and Joliet and Cartier.
   C. Both Cartier and Da Gama explored North America on behalf of France.
   D. French explorers cooperated with American Indians in establishing trade.

7. Instead of financing expeditions themselves, the rulers of Spain allowed conquistadors to establish outposts in the Americas. The conquistador financed his own expedition, but if he succeeded, he was allowed to keep four-fifths of any treasure he found. Cortés was a conquistador who became rich by conquering the Aztecs in Mexico.

   ________ was also a conquistador.

   A. da Gama
   B. Pizarro
   C. Cartier
   D. Hudson

8. Which of the following is the best title for this time line?
   A. The Spanish Explorers and Empire
   B. The Age of Exploration
   C. History of the 16th and 17th centuries
   D. European Colonies in the Americas

**Question 9 refers to the following graph.**

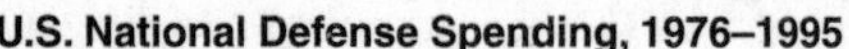


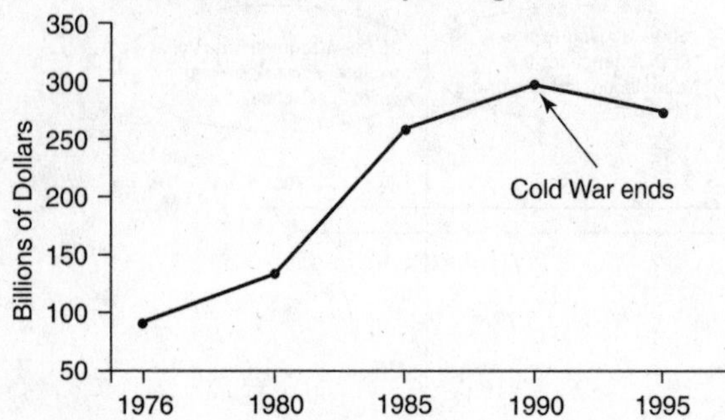


9. Which of the following statements is supported by the graph?
   A. Before the Cold War began, defense spending was at an all-time high.
   B. Defense spending remained steady throughout the Cold War.
   C. Defense spending declined steadily during the period 1976 to 1990.
   D. After the Cold War ended, defense spending began to fall.

---

10. When establishing colonies, European nations wanted their colonies to be economically self-sufficient. That meant that each colony paid for its government salaries and the cost of building and maintaining roads, railroads, and government buildings. To do this, European colonists or the colonial governments exported natural resources like gold or copper or grew cash crops like sugar or rubber.

    Which of the following statements is an opinion rather than a fact?

    A. European countries had similar goals in establishing their colonies.
    B. Colonies should be economically independent.
    C. European nations built railroads, roads, and government buildings in their colonies.
    D. Colonies provided natural resources that colonists could export.

11. During the Neolithic Age (about 8000 B.C.E. to 3500 B.C.E.), many societies domesticated plants and animals. One result of animal domestication was a new way of life called *pastoralism*. In pastoralism, groups of people move from place to place seeking new grazing lands for their animals. Pastoralism has remained the main alternative to settlement agriculture, although in recent times the growth of settled populations has encroached on pastoral lands.

    Which of the following is an example of a pastoral society?

    A. the Bedouin, who are a nomadic herding people of Saudi Arabia
    B. the Kikuyu, who live on large family farming homesteads in Kenya
    C. the Amish, who preserve traditional farming methods in the United States
    D. the Palestinian Arabs, many of whom live in refugee camps

12. During the Age of Imperialism (1870–1914), the nations of Europe and the United States dominated the political, economic, and cultural life of many countries in Africa, Asia, and Latin America.

    Which of the following is an example of imperialism?

    A. Communists under Mao Zedong won control of mainland China after World War II.
    B. Fifteen independent nations, of which Russia is the largest, were formed after the breakup of the Soviet Union.
    C. The United States gained influence over Panama through the building and running of the Panama Canal.
    D. After gaining independence from Great Britain, East Pakistan broke away from West Pakistan and formed the nation of Bangladesh.

**Questions 13 and 14 refer to the following map.**

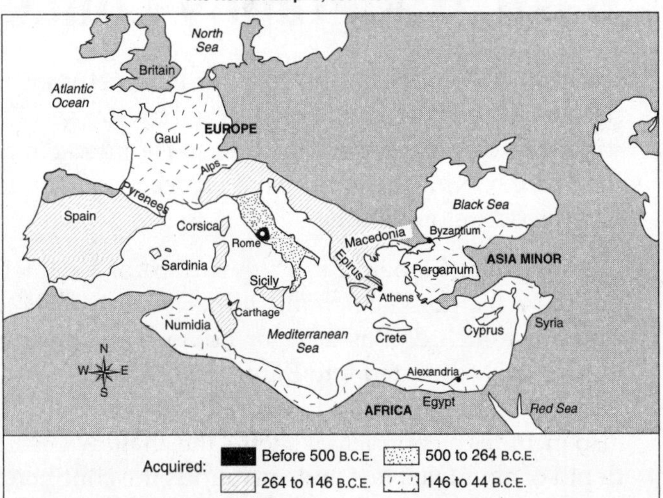


13. During which time period did the Roman Empire gain the most territory in Asia Minor?

    A. before 500 B.C.E.
    B. between 500 and 264 B.C.E.
    C. between 264 and 146 B.C.E.
    D. between 146 and 44 B.C.E.

14. Which of the following conclusions is supported by the information on the map?

    A. Before 264 B.C.E., Rome conquered through overland military campaigns; later conquests were made by navies as well.
    B. Numidia was added to the Roman Empire before the island of Sicily was.
    C. Corsica, Crete, and Cyprus were conquered by the Romans during the same military campaign.
    D. Hannibal marched from Carthage to Italy by way of Spain, crossing the Pyrenees into Gaul and the Alps into northern Italy.

**Questions 15 and 16 refer to the following passage.**

Society under Japanese feudalism had a class of warrior leaders, the *bushi*, at the top. Bushi possessed the responsibilities of enforcing laws, supervising the construction of public works, and collecting taxes. To assist them in the protection of their property, they built up their own armies of soldiers called *samurai*. The samurai lived by a code called *bushido*, which stressed absolute loyalty to one's lord. Bushido was followed by both men and women of the samurai class who, in addition to protecting their lord, were expected to protect the emperor. The code of bushido emphasized the preservation of family honor and willingness to face death rather than the acceptance of defeat or retreat. Because they were expected to provide the lord with military services, the samurai were released from agricultural responsibilities and were allowed a portion of the produce grown by peasants. The bushi and samurai depended on peasants to supply them with food while they devoted themselves to activities preparing them for war, such as archery and riding. Japanese peasants were placed in a subordinate position similar to that of serfs in medieval Europe. Unlike serfs, who were bound only to the land they worked, Japanese peasants were bound to both the land and their lord.

15. Aspects of the warrior's code of bushido resembles which of the following?

    A. the European ideal of chivalry
    B. the star player on a sports team
    C. neighborhood watch duty in a subdivision
    D. the death sentence

16. Agricultural responsibilities in feudal Japan fell to

    A. the bushi.
    B. the samurai.
    C. the peasants.
    D. the serfs.

**Review your work using the explanations that start on page 719.**

# Basic Geography Concepts

### KEY IDEAS

- Geographers study interactions between human life and Earth's natural features.
- The equator, the prime meridian, and other latitude and longitude lines allow us to locate places on Earth's surface.
- Geographic regions are defined by both natural and man-made characteristics.

### ON THE TASC TEST

*You will not have to memorize names and capitals of countries and states. Understanding the geography concepts in this section will help you to interpret the passages and graphics on the test.*

Geography focuses on the relationships between human culture and the natural features of Earth, including how those relationships vary among different regions of the world. Because interactions between people and Earth are complicated and have far-reaching implications, geography is a very broad field of study.

**Oceans** cover 71 percent of the surface of Earth. The three major oceans are the Atlantic, Pacific, and Indian Oceans. The Arctic Ocean is sometimes also included as a major ocean. The **continents,** including Eurasia (sometimes separated into Europe and Asia), Africa, North America, South America, Antarctica, and Australia, separate the oceans. Each continent also includes a continental shelf—the shallow ocean floor that extends to a depth of about 600 feet and surrounds the continent. Islands that sit on the continental shelf are considered part of the main continent. For example, England, Ireland, and Japan are all part of the Eurasian continent. New Zealand is part of the Australian continent, and Greenland is part of the North American continent.

Over the centuries, people have devised a system for locating places on Earth according to lines of **latitude** and **longitude**. Study these sets of horizontal and vertical lines on the following maps. Note that the longitude meridians run north and south. They are measured in relation to the prime meridian, which runs through Greenwich, England. Note that latitude parallels run east and west in circles around Earth. They are measured in relation to their distance from the equator, a circle marking the position halfway between the North and South poles. The area north of the **equator** is the Northern Hemisphere; south of the equator is the Southern Hemisphere. The exact position of any location on Earth can be identified according to its **degrees** of latitude and longitude.

Geographers identify **regions** based on both natural and man-made features. For example, the Great Plains of North America have a particular set of natural characteristics. They are flat or gently rolling, fairly dry, and covered mainly with grasses with only limited areas of forest. They also have a specific set of man-made characteristics, relating to how people use the land for farming and grazing livestock. Cultural and economic factors can be extremely important in defining a geographic region. For example, a geographer might distinguish an **agricultural** region from an **urban** region even though both are within the Great Plains.

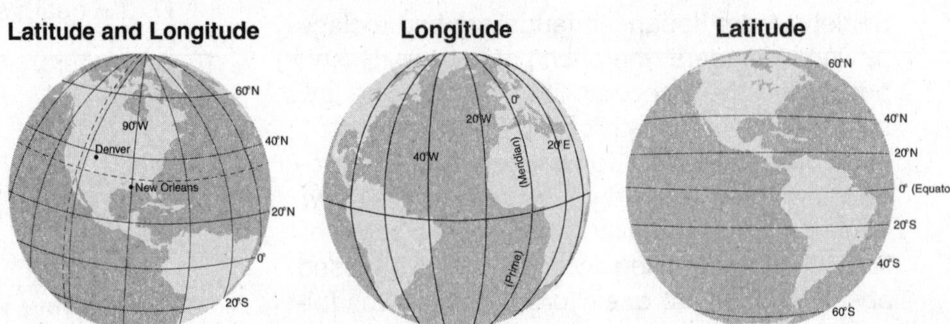

# PRACTICE 1

1. To what continent do England, Ireland, and Japan belong?

   A. a Europe
   B. Asia
   C. Eurasia
   D. Australia

2. What is the main difference between lines of latitude and longitude?

   A. Lines of latitude are measured in miles, and lines of longitude are measured in degrees.
   B. Lines of latitude are measured in degrees, and lines of longitude are measured in miles.
   C. Lines of latitude run north-south, and lines of longitude run east-west.
   D. Lines of latitude run east-west, and lines of longitude run north-south.

3. A branch of the military wants to pinpoint a target site for bombing practice.

   Which of the following describes the location of the target site most accurately?

   A. the distances from two nearby cities
   B. the distance from the nearest city
   C. the latitude and longitude
   D. the distance from the equator

4. How do geographers define a region?

   A. by its natural and man-made features
   B. by its average temperature
   C. by its distance from the nearest ocean
   D. by its distance from the North and South poles

**Questions 5 and 6 refer to the following paragraph.**

Some geographers argue that it makes more sense to divide the United States into cultural regions than into states. According to these geographers, many political state boundaries are meaningless. For example, North and South Dakota are part of a single cultural region with similar terrain and agriculture. In fact, before North and South Dakota became separate states, they formed the Dakota Territory. Many metropolitan regions provide examples of cultural regions that are more meaningful than local state boundaries. For example, a person who lives in northeastern New Jersey is actually part of the New York metropolitan region and probably has more in common with other people in the metro region than with people who live in the southern, rural part of New Jersey.

5. Which of the following statements is an opinion rather than a fact?

   A. North and South Dakota were formerly united in the Dakota Territory.
   B. The southern part of New Jersey is rural, and the northeastern part is urban.
   C. The United States should be divided into cultural regions rather than states.
   D. The New York metropolitan region encompasses areas from neighboring states.

6. Which of the following is an example of a cultural region rather than a political unit?

   A. the state of Pennsylvania in the United States
   B. the St. Louis metropolitan region, which includes portions of Missouri and Illinois
   C. the Sudan, a nation in Africa with a Muslim majority in the north and a Christian majority in the south
   D. the nation of Canada in North America

**Review your work using the explanations that start on page 720.**

LESSON 2

# Humans and the Environment

**KEY IDEAS**

- When populations grow, decline, or shift, changes in geographic regions occur.
- Populations change as a result of many different political and economic factors.
- Population growth and urbanization have a negative impact on the environment.

**TASC TEST TIP**

*Some questions give a definition and ask you to apply it. To answer an application question such as number 2 on page 513, check each of the answer options against the given definition.*

**Populations**—particularly the movement and growth of population groups—play a major role in defining and altering geographic regions. A population may be **native** to a geographic area, as the Taino, for example, were native to the Caribbean when Columbus arrived there. Sometimes population groups **migrate** over long distances, as did many Irish people who came to the United States during the Potato Famine in the mid-1800s. However, when people feel strong ties to a place, they may stay there even when conditions are unfavorable; they may even develop new economic and cultural strategies that strengthen their population. The **distribution** of population within a region depends on many factors, not all of which humans can control. People tend to move where there are resources, jobs, and other favorable conditions. But these conditions are ever changing, depending on politics, climate, economic development, and so on.

**Urban** and **rural** development have a strong impact on the distribution of a population. Industrialized regions generally see their populations shift away from rural areas into cities and towns. **Suburban** development very often follows urban growth. As cities become crowded, the urban population spreads into the countryside, often taking up agricultural lands for housing and commercial development. Agriculture also changes in most industrialized regions. Farming is done on a larger scale by fewer people using more mechanized tools. Industrialized regions usually can support a larger population at a higher standard of living than nonindustrialized regions. However, these regions also may lose some of their distinctive traditional cultures, arts, farming methods, and so on.

When political boundaries are in dispute, or ethnic groups declare war on each other, local population shifts may dramatically change the character of a region. For example, during World War II, Hitler depopulated Europe of millions of Jews through deportation and death camps. After World War II, the state of Israel was established in the Middle East, drawing many Jews to the region. Continuing conflicts within the Middle East have led to further population shifts of different Arab and Jewish groups there.

When human populations grow, they significantly affect the natural environment. **Manufacturing** and **urbanization** cause air and water **pollution**. Commercial agriculture tends to degrade both soil and water. Eventually food and water supplies become endangered. For example, these problems, along with a loss of farmland to urbanization, are very prominent in China today, where the government has been trying since the 1970s to reduce population growth.

Overall, government policies and international agreements have not been strong enough nor widely enforced when it comes to reducing the destructive impact of growing populations, large cities, and damaging agricultural methods in many parts of the world.

# PRACTICE 2

1. What is migration?

   A. a form of society in which people move on after they consume an area's resources
   B. temporary travel to another geographic region to scout for resources
   C. the move of an individual or population from one geographic area to settle in another
   D. the relative distribution of populations in urban and rural areas

2. Migration within a country's borders is called internal migration. Which of the following is an example of internal migration?

   A. the movement of the Irish to the United States during the Potato Famine in the 1800s
   B. the westward movement of the American population from the 1700s to the present
   C. the movement of Mexican workers into the southwest United States during the 1900s
   D. the movement of people from former British colonies to Great Britain

3. Urban areas _________ suburban areas.

   A. are more densely populated than
   B. have been more recently settled than
   C. contain more remnants of farms than
   D. have more agricultural workers than

4. Which of the following technologies was the most likely contributor to the rapid growth of suburbs in the United States?

   A. the telephone
   B. the telegraph
   C. the airplane
   D. the automobile

**STUDY ADVICE**

You can learn more about issues related to resources and the environment by keeping up with local, national, and world news.

**Questions 5 and 6 refer to the following graph.**

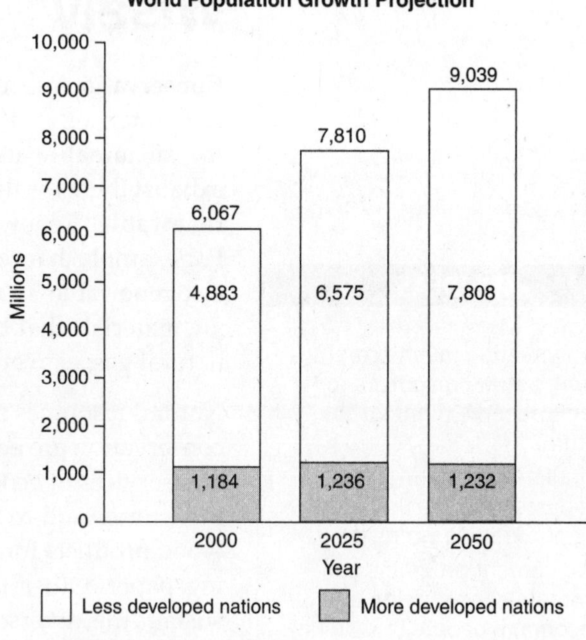


Source: Population Reference Bureau

5. What does the figure 9,039,000,000 represent?

   A. the projected population of less developed nations in 2025
   B. the projected population of less developed nations in 2050
   C. the projected population of more developed nations in 2050
   D. the projected total world population in 2050

6. Which of the following conclusions is supported by the data on the graph?

   A. The total world population will double in the 50 years from 2000 to 2050.
   B. About half the world's population lives in the more developed nations.
   C. Most of the population growth in the 50 years from 2000 to 2050 will occur in the less developed nations.
   D. Most of the population growth in the 50 years from 2000 to 2050 will occur in the more developed nations.

**Review your work using the explanations that start on page 720.**

# Using Resources Wisely

**Conservation** means using natural resources—such as soil, plant and animal life, water, air, and mineral reserves—carefully. Conservationists encourage the **sustainable use** of resources—using resources in ways that do not exhaust them for the future. Natural resources are either **renewable** or **non-renewable.** Renewable resources can be sustained through replacement. For example, harvested plants can be replanted. Solar and wind energy are also renewable, since their supply never runs out. Nonrenewable resources are materials that humans use but cannot replace—such as petroleum and natural gas, as well as minerals such as coal, copper, and iron.

### KEY IDEAS

- Conservation means carefully using natural resources to help preserve them for the future.
- Conflicts over natural resources require the balancing of different interests.
- Government programs can promote conservation and encourage people to develop alternative energy sources.

Natural resources need to be protected for many reasons. Some reasons for conservation are economic: natural resources are needed to produce goods and services of economic value. Petroleum provides fuel to run equipment in factories and to transport materials and goods. We also need wood and wood products for building structures, making furniture, and manufacturing paper. Other reasons for conserving resources relate to our need to sustain the diverse **ecosystems** of Earth to help keep the planet healthy. These diverse ecosystems help maintain the following resources: water; air; and plant, animal, and human life. Finally, natural resources inspire our sense of beauty and wonder; natural areas and materials play important roles in people's cultural and spiritual traditions.

When natural resources are **scarce** or become threatened, different people's interests can come into conflict. For example, water resources in a region might not be adequate to provide clean drinking water, irrigate local farms, sustain wildlife, and supply water for industrial development. If these interests are not balanced, some people will lose what they need. These problems become even more difficult when political boundaries are involved. Perhaps one nation's water supply comes from a river that flows through another nation; if the second nation builds a dam on the river, it could cut back the flow of water to the first nation. Such conflicts can be very difficult to negotiate. Industry, agriculture, natural ecosystems, clean air and water, and historical and cultural preservation—all these factors influence how people decide to allocate natural resources.

### ON THE TASC TEST

*Some questions are based on important current topics such as the development and conservation of resources. Reading the newspaper will help you become familiar with many of these issues.*

Many countries have laws that protect **endangered species** of plants and animals. Industrial and agricultural interests have to be balanced against **biodiversity**—the maintenance of many different species of organisms. New international agreements attempt to protect the **ozone layer** in the atmosphere, which is critical to maintaining Earth's climate patterns. In some nations—although not in the United States—high taxes on gasoline pay for clean air programs and encourage people to reduce their use of cars. **Fossil fuels** are relatively inexpensive and available, so industrialized regions are highly dependent on them. But they are nonrenewable and cause a great deal of pollution. Globally, we will have to develop more sustainable sources of energy on a large scale—such as **solar** and **wind energy**—to keep our planet healthy in the long run.

# PRACTICE 3

1. What are renewable resources?

   A. materials that will never run out or can be replaced if used
   B. materials that we do not use and so can use at a later date
   C. materials that we use but cannot replace
   D. an incentive to conserve materials

2. Which of the following is an example of the sustainable use of a resource?

   A. burning fossil fuels
   B. strip mining
   C. overgrazing livestock
   D. rotating crops

3. Since conflicts over scarce or polluted resources sometimes cross national boundaries, which of the following methods would be most likely to solve problems related to these resources?

   A. negotiating in an international forum
   B. taking unilateral action
   C. importing resources
   D. selling resources

4. In the United States, there is disagreement about how to reduce dependence on foreign oil. Some favor exploiting domestic sources of oil even if that means polluting the environment. Others prefer to concentrate on developing alternative, renewable sources of energy.

   Which of the following best characterizes the underlying difference in points of view between the pro-oil and pro-alternative energy factions?

   A. self-sufficiency versus interdependence
   B. competition versus cooperation
   C. short-term benefit versus long-term benefit
   D. patriotism versus internationalism

5. Which of the following actions could a family take to conserve nonrenewable resources?

   A. incinerate the trash
   B. carpool to work and school
   C. plant trees in the yard
   D. burn more firewood

**Questions 6 and 7 refer to the following chart.**

**Current Natural Gas Resources and Reserves (in trillion cubic feet)**

| Region | Current Production | Proved Reserves | Reserves to Production Ratio |
|---|---|---|---|
| N. America | 25.5 | 312.7 | 12/1 |
| S. America | 2.1 | 189.1 | 90/1 |
| Europe | 9.2 | 216.3 | 24/1 |
| Former U.S.S.R. | 25.7 | 2,057.5 | 80/1 |
| Africa | 2.6 | 341.6 | 131/1 |
| Middle East | 3.9 | 1,594.3 | 409/1 |
| Asia/Oceania | 6.5 | 350.6 | 54/1 |

Source: Congressional Research Service.

6. According to the chart, which world region currently produces the most natural gas?

   A. North America
   B. Former U.S.S.R.
   C. Africa and the Middle East
   D. Asia/Oceania

7. Natural gas is a nonrenewable resource. As gas is produced for consumption, reserves are depleted. Assume that each of the regions listed in the chart continues to produce natural gas at its current rate and does not discover any additional reserves. Which region will run out of natural gas first?

   A. North America
   B. Europe
   C. Former U.S.S.R.
   D. Africa

**Review your work using the explanations that start on page 720.**

# GEOGRAPHY PRACTICE QUESTIONS

1. According to experts in world agriculture, the poor nutrition and starvation of millions of people stems not from a global scarcity of resources, but from the uneven distribution of resources among nations. Experts claim the world has the resources to feed its population if the political will of the richer nations were brought to bear on this problem.

   Which of the following is an opinion rather than a fact?

   A. Millions of people worldwide are undernourished.
   B. The world has abundant natural resources.
   C. Natural resources are distributed unevenly among nations.
   D. The problem of feeding the world's population is a matter of political will rather than one of resources.

2. The 2000 Census showed that the United States has 281,421,906 people, an increase of 13.2 percent over the 1990 Census. Population growth and immigration accounted for this increase. The state population counts showed the largest relative gains in the South and West, with Nevada's population increase the highest at 66.3 percent. Because state population figures are used to allocate seats in the House of Representatives, every ten years a shift in political power occurs. In 2000, states in the Northeast and Midwest lost seats, and states in the West and South picked up seats.

   Which of the following is implied by the paragraph?

   A. Nevada had a 66.3 percent population increase.
   B. Nevada gained seats in the House.
   C. People moved away from the Northeast and Midwest.
   D. The U.S. population in 2000 was about 281 million people.

**Questions 3 and 4 refer to the following map.**

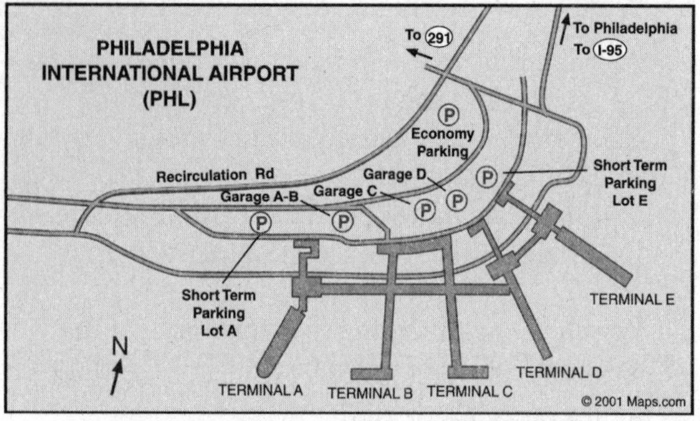


3. Which of the following people is most likely to use the map above?

   A. a geologist surveying land features in the Philadelphia area
   B. a visitor to Philadelphia
   C. an employee of the Federal Aviation Administration
   D. a commercial airline pilot

4. Which of the following statements is supported by the data on the map?

   A. More than 20 airlines have landing rights at Philadelphia International Airport.
   B. Route 95 borders the south side of Philadelphia International Airport.
   C. It is possible to get to Philadelphia International Airport by plane, car, or rail.
   D. Labels for terminals and parking areas are coordinated to provide convenient parking.

**Questions 5 and 6 refer to the following passage.**

Desertification, the spread of deserts, is usually caused in part by human activity. Agricultural practices, such as clearing trees and brush, depleting the soil through plowing and planting, overgrazing, and irrigation, contribute to the sterilization and erosion of the land. A period of drought is often enough to tip the balance toward a desert ecosystem.

For example, in the 1930s, excessive plowing, overgrazing, and well-digging left the American Great Plains vulnerable to desertification. A lengthy drought led to conditions so severe the topsoil was blown away, creating what is known as the Dust Bowl. Formerly valuable farmland became almost worthless in a period of years. The area was spared permanent desertification only because normal rainfall eventually resumed.

5. Which of the following was the most likely result of the Dust Bowl?

   A. the Great Depression of the 1930s, an economic downturn
   B. the migration of thousands of farm families to other regions
   C. the permanent cessation of agriculture in the Great Plains
   D. restoration of the Great Plains ecosystem as it was before agriculture

6. Which of the following is an example of desertification?

   A. the shrinking of the Greenland ice sheet
   B. the shifting sandbars along the coast of Lake Michigan
   C. the extension of grazing onto land that is part of the National Forest system
   D. the spread of the Sahara into the grazing land on its southern border

**Questions 7 and 8 are based on the following information and map.**

The earliest maps we have were etched on clay tiles and consisted primarily of land and property surveys in Mesopotamia. The following map, made in about 1300 B.C., shows the property boundaries of the king's estate.

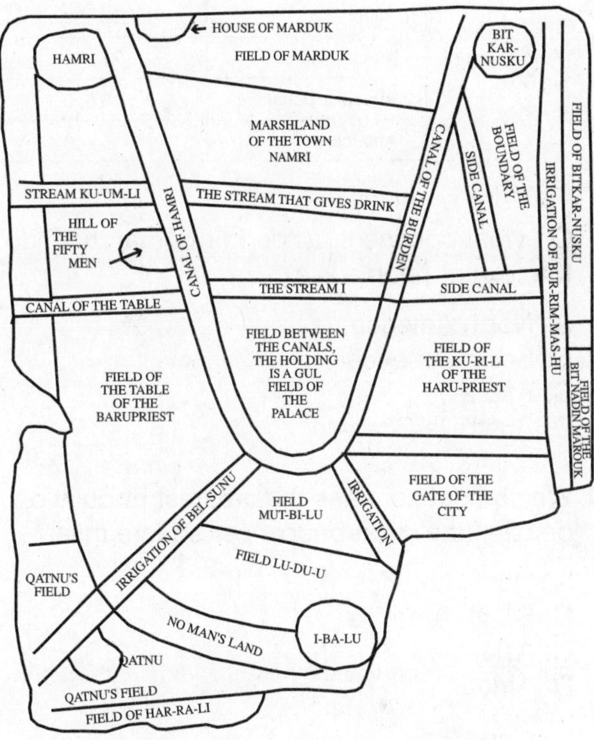


7. Which of the following formed many of the field boundaries shown on the map?

   A. oceans
   B. large rivers
   C. irrigation canals
   D. roads and paths

8. The king's property map is most similar to which of the following modern maps?

   A. a town tax assessor's tax map
   B. a U.S. Geological Survey topographic map
   C. a map showing tourist attractions
   D. an automobile club's road map of a city

**Questions 9 through 11 are based on the following table.**

**Area and Population of the Continents**

| Continent | Area (thousands of sq. mi.) | Percent of Earth's Area | Estimated Population, 1998 (thousands) | Percent of Total World Population |
|---|---|---|---|---|
| North America | 9,400 | 16.2 | 301,000 | 5.3 |
| South America | 6,900 | 11.9 | 508,000 | 9.0 |
| Europe | 3,800 | 6.6 | 508,000 | 9.0 |
| Asia | 17,400 | 30.1 | 3,528,000 | 62.6 |
| Africa | 11,700 | 20.2 | 761,000 | 13.5 |
| Australia/Oceania | 3,300 | 5.7 | 30,000 | 0.5 |
| Antarctica | 5,400 | 9.3 | — | — |

9. On what continent, aside from Antarctica, do the fewest people live?
   A. North America
   B. South America
   C. Africa
   D. Australia/Oceania

10. Which continent has the greatest population density (the most people per square mile)?
    A. North America
    B. South America
    C. Asia
    D. Africa

11. Which of the following statements is supported by the data in the chart?
    A. South America has about one-third more land area than North America.
    B. More than half of Africa's population lives south of the Sahara.
    C. Together, Asia and Europe account for more than one-third of Earth's land area.
    D. North America and Europe are about the same size.

12. The Nile River flows down from the mountains of East Africa, north through Egypt, to the Mediterranean Sea. A student looking at a map of Africa could not understand why the map showed the Nile River flowing up, rather than down, to the Mediterranean.

    What was wrong with this student's thinking?
    A. The compass direction north does not mean "up" in terms of elevation.
    B. The map of Africa was turned the wrong way, with south at the top.
    C. The Nile River really flows south to the Mediterranean.
    D. North and south have no real meaning on a topographic map.

## Questions 13 and 14 are based on the following map.

**Roads, Canals, and Railroads in 1849**

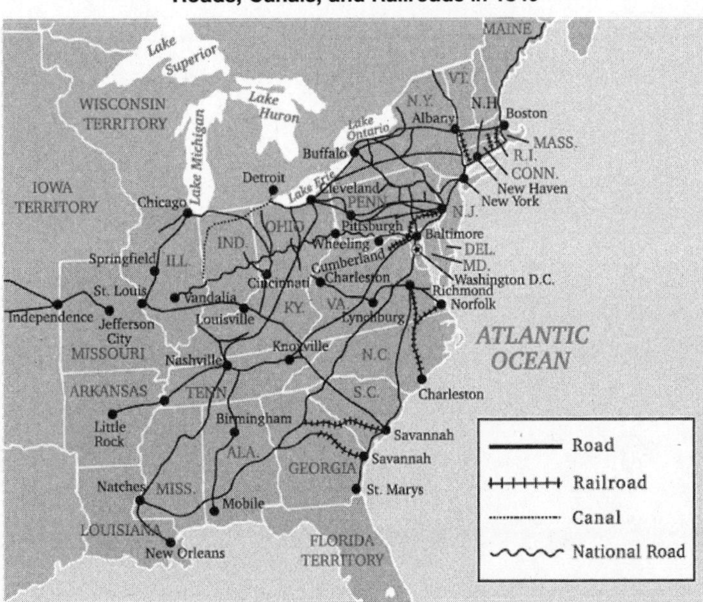


13. Which of the following is an accurate statement, based on the map?

    A. In 1849, railroads in the United States tended to be near the eastern coast, whereas major roads reached further inland.
    B. In 1849, major roads in the United States tended to be near the ocean, whereas railroads reached further inland.
    C. In 1849, canals were a major source of transit across state lines.
    D. In 1849, most Midwestern cities were connected by national roads.

14. Later in the 19th century, railroads were extended across the continent. Which one of the following was most likely a direct result of the building of railroads?

    A. the acquisition of the Territory of Florida
    B. the establishment of cities on the West Coast
    C. the Texas oil boom that began in 1901
    D. the establishment of the Coast Guard

15. Areas with average or above average rainfall have humid soils. Humid soils are usually fertile because they contain decaying plant matter. However, humid soils in northern coniferous regions of the United States are not fertile. Acid from the pine needles that cover the ground leaches into the soil, making it unsuitable for agriculture. In the humid, subtropical regions of the southeast, heavy rainfall washes large amounts of minerals from the soil. Growing crops there usually requires heavy use of fertilizers.

    Which of the following is a conclusion based on the paragraph rather than a detail?

    A. Humid soils have organic material in them.
    B. Except for soils in northern coniferous regions, humid soils can be used or modified for crops.
    C. The pine needle ground cover of coniferous regions makes the soil acidic.
    D. Rain leaches minerals from the soil in the southeastern United States.

**Review your work using the explanations that start on page 721.**

**STUDY ADVICE**

Congratulations! You've made it to the end of the Social Studies unit. Only one more unit to go. By the way, if you haven't reviewed the Mathematics unit lately, you might want to at this point. Remember not to let your skills get rusty!

UNIT 5

ABOUT THE TEST

# Science

The TASC Science Test assesses your ability to understand, interpret, and apply scientific information. You will have 85 minutes to answer approximately 47 multiple-choice questions. On the 2014 TASC, all science questions are in multiple-choice format.

Each question will assess both your familiarity with a content area and your ability to perform a skill related to understanding and interpreting scientific information.

## Science Content Areas

**Life Science (34%)** topics include cell structures and processes, human body systems, health and nutrition, heredity and reproduction, genetics and DNA, evolution and natural selection, and the organization of ecosystems.

**Earth and Space Science (33%)** topics include the structure of Earth, plate tectonics, geological cycles and processes, renewable and nonrenewable natural resources, weather and climate, the solar system, and the universe.

**Physical Science (33%)** topics include atoms and molecules, properties and states of matter, chemical reactions, energy and work, motion and forces, waves, electricity, and magnetism.

## Science Skills

In addition to testing your understanding of science passages and graphics, the TASC Science Test questions are based on your understanding of skills that are used in scientific study and investigation. These skills are introduced on pages 522–531. After you study these skills, you will reinforce them as you work through the unit. The science skills include:

- **Comprehending scientific presentations** to interpret passages and graphics
- **Using the scientific method** to design investigations, reason from data, and work with findings
- **Reasoning with scientific information** to evaluate conclusions with evidence
- **Applying concepts and formulas** to express scientific information and apply scientific theories
- **Using statistics and probability** in a science context

You will have to perform some calculations on the Science Test. For those questions, you will be able to use a scientific calculator just as you may on the Mathematics Test. See the Mathematics unit on pages 228–229 for more information about using a calculator on the TASC.

*Note: The information given here was the latest information available as of January 2014. It is possible that timing restrictions may change between this printing and your test date. For updates, visit www.tasctest.com.

LESSON 1

# Comprehend Scientific Presentations

The TASC Science Test consists of questions based on science passages and graphics. To comprehend science presentations, you need to understand main ideas and their supporting details.

The **main idea** of a science presentation or graphic is its topic or the writer's point. Use this science diagram to practice finding the main idea.

**KEY IDEAS**

- TASC Science Test presentations consist of text, graphics, or a combination of the two.
- Understanding science presentations on the Science Test requires understanding the main idea or point.
- Main ideas in science materials are supported by specific facts, details, or evidence.

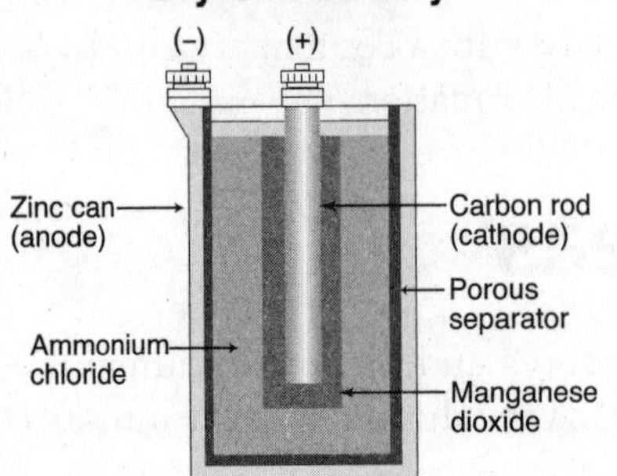


► What is the topic of this diagram?

(1) the components of a dry cell battery
(2) how a dry cell battery powers machinery

The correct answer is choice **(1)**. The diagram displays the different components (that is, the parts) of a dry cell battery. It does not show the process by which the battery actually operates or powers machinery, so (2) is incorrect.

Science writers support their main ideas with **details**, **facts**, and **evidence**.

Read the paragraph below and answer the question.

> Earthquakes can be classified as either surface earthquakes or deep-focus earthquakes. Scientists agree that surface earthquakes occur when rock in Earth's crust fractures to relieve stress. Deep-focus earthquakes originate from seismic activity more than 300 kilometers below Earth's surface. The causes of deep-focus earthquakes remain a subject of debate, but scientists believe they may be caused by the pressure of fluids trapped in Earth's tectonic plates.

**TASC TEST TIP**

*To answer TASC Science Test questions based on a passage or graphic, ask yourself, "What is the main point? What evidence or details are used to support it?"*

► Which of the following details supports the main point of this paragraph?

(1) The causes of deep-focus earthquakes remain a subject of debate among scientists.
(2) Surface earthquakes are caused by stress in Earth's crust, while deep-focus earthquakes may be caused by pressure.

The correct answer is choice **(2)**. The main point of the paragraph is that earthquakes can be classified into two types based on their causes, and **(2)** provides supporting details that illustrate the differences between the two types. While (1) is mentioned in the paragraph, it is not a fact that supports the main point about the classification of earthquakes.

# PRACTICE 1

**Questions 1 through 3 are based on the passage below.**

Despite the prevalence of type 2 diabetes, the causes of the disease remain somewhat uncertain. It is likely that some combination of genetics and lifestyle contributes to the development of type 2 diabetes. However, scientists have not fully determined the roles played by various lifestyle factors (such as diet and exercise).

For Americans, one contributing factor may be high sugar consumption. Sugar from food is broken down and absorbed into the bloodstream, and insulin is required for the body to be able to use that sugar. In a study of individuals 18–25 years old who consumed more than the recommended amount of sugar daily, it was shown that the majority had significantly elevated levels of glucose (that is, sugar) in their blood but normal levels of insulin. In other words, these subjects could not produce enough insulin to allow their bodies to use the amount of sugar they were consuming. Elevated blood glucose levels may put individuals consuming high amounts of sugar at higher risk of developing type 2 diabetes.

**1.** Which one of the following is the topic of the entire passage?

A. sources of sugar in Americans' diet
B. the role of insulin in metabolizing sugar from food
C. the causes of type 2 diabetes
D. how to prevent type 2 diabetes

**2.** Which of the following is the main idea of the first paragraph?

A. It is likely that sugar consumption contributes to the development of type 2 diabetes.
B. It is likely that genetics plays a role in the development of type 2 diabetes.
C. Researchers have discovered the causes of type 2 diabetes.
D. The causes of type 2 diabetes are not fully understood.

**3.** The main idea of the second paragraph is that high sugar consumption may put individuals at greater risk of developing type 2 diabetes. Which of the following details from the second paragraph supports that main idea?

A. Sugar from food is absorbed into the bloodstream.
B. A study of 18- to 25-year-olds showed that a majority did not produce enough insulin to offset the high amounts of sugar they were consuming.
C. A study of 18- to 25-year-olds showed that high sugar consumption interacted with genetic factors in a majority of those individuals in order to suppress insulin production.
D. It has not been proven that sugar is a contributing factor to the development of type 2 diabetes.

---

**Question 4 is based on this graphic.**

**How Topography Contributes to Precipitation**

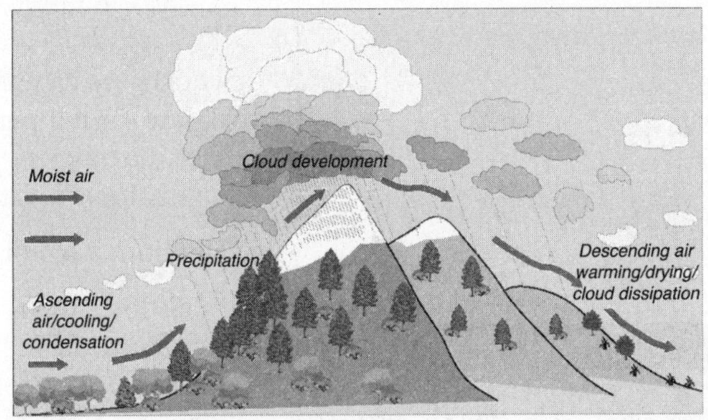


Source: U.S. Geological Survey

**4.** Which statement correctly describes the process depicted in the graphic above?

A. As moist, flowing air encounters rising elevations, it cools, which causes condensation, a stage that precedes precipitation and cloud development.
B. Once above the tree line, flowing air is likely to slow down and stop moving, and then collect in the form of snow.
C. Clouds dissipate before encountering mountain peaks.
D. Moist air flows from the west, while drier air usually flows from the east.

**Review your work using the explanations that start on page 722.**

LESSON 2

# Use the Scientific Method

The **scientific method** is a set of techniques that scientists use to investigate observable facts and occurrences and to acquire new knowledge. Here are the steps in the scientific method:

1. **Observe a phenomenon** and **formulate a question** about it. Formulate the question about something that you can observe and measure.
2. **Collect data** about the phenomenon you are studying. Scientific study is founded on **data**, or observable facts.
3. **Form a hypothesis**. A **hypothesis** is an educated guess about the answer to your question.
4. **Test the hypothesis through an experiment**. Your experiment should be a fair test of the hypothesis. You may need to adjust the experiment. You would do so by changing only one factor at a time while **controlling** other factors. You should also repeat the experiment to make sure the first results are valid.
5. **Draw a conclusion** about the hypothesis based on the experiment. When the experiment is complete, you may conclude that your hypothesis was supported by the data or that it was not, in which case you may formulate a new hypothesis.

### KEY IDEAS

- The scientific method is used to investigate events and to acquire knowledge.
- Scientists follow a series of procedures involving observing, collecting information, and forming a hypothesis.
- After the hypothesis has been tested in an experiment or study, scientists draw a conclusion.

Scientists are careful when drawing conclusions. The fact that two events **correlate**, or happen at the same time, does not necessarily mean that one **causes** the other. Remember that causation can never be deduced from correlation alone.

Read about a scientific observation and answer the question below.

> Scientists observed unusual plant and algae growth in a pond. They sampled the water and also discovered very high concentrations of bacteria. The pond was fairly close to neighboring farmland, and two streams carried water from the farm to the pond.

### TASC TEST TIP

*The TASC Science Test may present an experiment and ask you to answer multiple-choice questions interpreting it.*

► What could be a sound hypothesis about the growth in the pond?

(1) Runoff from the neighboring farm may be carrying excessive phosphates and nitrates from fertilizers into the pond.

(2) Proximity to farmland is the cause of plant and algae growth in ponds and other bodies of water.

Choice **(1)** is correct. That hypothesis is an educated guess about the reason for the unusual plant and algae growth in the pond. It could be tested by an experiment that compares samples from the pond water to samples from streams coming from neighboring fields. Choice (2) is an assertion that is very general and cannot be measured in this specific situation.

The phenomenon you are studying is called the **dependent variable**. A factor that you believe might be affecting that phenomenon is called the **independent variable**. In the example above, the unusual plant and algae growth would be the dependent variable. The runoff from the neighboring farm would be the independent variable.

# PRACTICE 2

Questions 1 through 3 are based on this passage.

A majority of teenagers develop acne, but scientists still struggle to explain its cause. It has long been thought that bacteria play a role, although until recently it was assumed that role was purely detrimental—contributing to acne. However, a team of researchers began to wonder whether different strains of bacteria might impact acne in different ways.

The research team studied 49 individuals with acne and 52 individuals without acne, and the researchers collected samples of bacteria from the nasal pores of all those individuals. The researchers found that some combinations of bacterial strains were highly likely to be found in clear-skinned individuals, while other combinations were highly likely to be found in individuals with acne.

After carefully analyzing their data, the scientists concluded that, while some bacterial combinations likely contribute to acne, other bacterial combinations may actually help to ward it off. The researchers suggested that, if further studies confirm these findings, we may want to treat acne by encouraging the growth of helpful bacteria.

**1.** What question is being investigated in this experiment?

A. What causes bacteria to collect in people's facial pores?
B. What are all the contributing factors to the development of acne?
C. What role do bacteria play in the development of acne?
D. What is the best way to treat acne?

**2.** What was the researchers' hypothesis?

A. Combinations of bacteria are a major cause of acne.
B. Different kinds of bacteria may impact acne differently.
C. We may want to change the way we treat acne, treating it by encouraging the growth of beneficial bacteria.
D. Some combinations of bacteria may actually help ward off acne.

**3.** What conclusion did the researchers reach based on their data?

A. Combinations of bacteria are a major cause of acne.
B. Acne sufferers have more types of bacterial strains in their facial pores than do non-sufferers.
C. The way we currently treat acne is misguided.
D. Some combinations of bacteria may actually help ward off acne.

---

**Questions 4 and 5 are based on the following information.**

Suppose that you notice your right knee hurts every time you play softball. You suspect that one of the movements involved in playing softball is causing your knee to hurt, but you are not sure which movement is the culprit. You decide to do a scientific investigation to find out more. That is, you form a hypothesis, design an experiment to test that hypothesis, perform your experiment and record your data, and draw a conclusion based on that data.

**4.** Which of the following steps in your investigation corresponds to forming your hypothesis?

A. You make a list of each of the movements involved in softball. In the off season (when you are not playing entire games), you plan to perform each movement several times without performing the others.
B. Based on the data you collected in your experiment, you think it is likely that stopping suddenly after running a short distance is indeed the cause of your knee pain.
C. Based on your experience, you make a guess about which of the movements involved in playing softball puts the greatest stress on the knees. You suspect that it may be stopping suddenly after running a short distance.
D. After performing each movement in isolation, you record how your knee feels, letting your knee recover between tests of each type of movement.

**5.** Which of the following is the dependent variable in your experiment?

A. playing softball
B. your knee pain
C. running and then stopping
D. your recorded data

**Review your work using the explanations that start on page 722.**

# Reason with Scientific Information

Some TASC Science questions require recognizing or citing specific evidence to support a conclusion. Another type of question may ask you to judge whether a **conclusion** or a **scientific theory**—a substantiated explanation of the natural world—is challenged by particular data or evidence.

Use the graph below to practice scientific reasoning.

**Rates of Infant Mortality, 1940–2009**

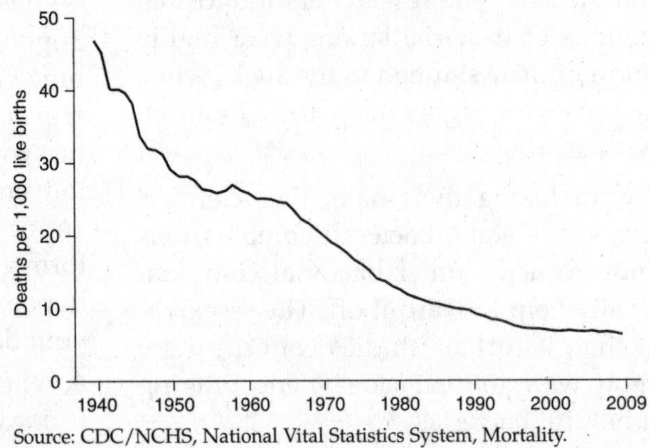


Source: CDC/NCHS, National Vital Statistics System, Mortality.

**KEY IDEAS**

- Reasoning with scientific information requires citing specific evidence to support a conclusion.
- In some cases, an existing theory can be challenged by new data or evidence.
- One of the ways scientists use information is in making predictions.

► Which conclusion is supported by the data on the graph?

(1) The rate of infant deaths in the United States experienced its sharpest decline between roughly 1940 and the late 1950s.

(2) In each year between 1940 and 2009, there were fewer infant deaths than in the year before.

The correct answer is **(1)**. The graph shows that the rate of infant mortality decreased most sharply between the years of 1940 and the late 1950s. After the late 1950s, it continued to decrease, but more gradually. Choice (2) is not a true statement based on the graph: around 1960, there was an uptick in the rate of infant deaths.

**TASC TEST TIP**

*When you interpret a line graph, carefully follow the direction of each line to see its trend. You can use trends to make predictions.*

Other questions will ask you to make a **prediction** based on evidence or data that the test provides to you. Based on the **trend** observed, scientists use data to predict, or forecast, what they think may happen in the future.

► Which of the following predictions is based on the graph above?

(1) Since there has not been an increase in infant deaths since 1960, there will likely be such an increase sometime soon.

(2) The rate of infant deaths is unlikely to experience sharp declines in the near future.

Choice **(2)** is correct: the line on the graph shows the trend in infant mortality has been one of very gradual decrease since the 1950s. A good prediction based on that pattern would be that the trend of gradual decline is likely to continue. The graph shows a downward trend, but gives no information to suggest a future increase, so choice (1) is incorrect.

# PRACTICE 3

1. Inertia causes an object to resist changes in its state of motion. In other words, inertia causes an object at rest to resist any attempt to set it in motion. Similarly, inertia causes an object in motion to resist any attempt to stop its motion. Objects with greater mass have greater inertia.

   These figures represent the mass of two objects:

   | | |
   |---|---|
   | Brick: | 100 grams |
   | Block of wood: | 70 grams |

   Which of the following is supported by the information above?

   A. It would require more effort to break the brick than to break the block of wood.
   B. If both objects were currently sitting still, it would require more effort to push the block of wood across the floor than it would to push the brick across the floor.
   C. If both objects were currently sitting still, it would require more effort to push the brick across the floor than it would to push the block of wood across the floor.
   D. The brick would absorb water more readily than would the block of wood.

2. In the last several decades, the spider population has exploded on the island of Guam: parts of the island have as many as 40 times more spiders than nearby islands do. One scientist has concluded that the explosion in the Guam spider population is due to an increase in the population of an invasive species of brown tree snake. The snake was introduced into Guam in the 1940s but was not introduced into the neighboring islands. The brown tree snake preys on birds.

   Which one of the following, if true, makes the scientist's conclusion more likely?

   A. The birds that the brown tree snake eats are the primary predators of spiders on Guam.
   B. The brown tree snake is typically introduced into islands via ships carrying tourists. Guam and the islands nearby have long been popular tourist spots.
   C. Brown tree snakes eat spiders as well as birds.
   D. In the rainy season, the island of Guam can have more than 40 times as many spiders as it did ten years ago.

**Questions 3 and 4 are based on the following passage:**

Melting ice sheets in Greenland and Antarctica have the potential to contribute significantly to rising sea levels in the next century. Some ice sheets melt more quickly than others, and scientists have wondered why. A team of researchers recently used data from both satellites and radar to study the composition of many of the ice sheets in Greenland and Antarctica. They found that some of the ice sheets formerly thought to sit on rock actually sit on water. This finding could be significant because it may be the case that ice sheets sitting on water tend to melt more quickly than those sitting on rock.

3. Which of the following is a prediction scientists might make based on the information above?

   A. If large areas of ice sheets sit on rock, the rising of sea levels may proceed more quickly than had previously been predicted.
   B. If large areas of ice sheets sit on water, the rising of sea levels may proceed more quickly than had previously been predicted.
   C. Ice sheets in Greenland will likely melt more quickly than ice sheets in Antarctica.
   D. All the ice sheets that are melting more quickly will be found to be sitting on water.

4. A scientist predicts that the ice sheets sitting on water will collectively discharge more water into the ocean than will those sitting on rock. Which of the following facts, if true, might weaken that prediction?

   A. Most of the ice sheets sitting on water are covering inland lakes with no access to the ocean.
   B. Water sitting under ice sheets flows directly into the ocean.
   C. Ice in a glass of water will melt even if the room is very cold.
   D. Radar used alone is an unreliable way to assess the composition of ice sheets.

**Review your work using the explanations that start on page 722.**

LESSON 4

# Express and Apply Scientific Information

KEY IDEAS

- Scientific information can be conveyed in multiple forms: in words, graphics, or formulas.
- Scientific formulas use numbers, letters, and symbols to represent a relationship or process.
- An important science reasoning concept is the ability to apply a scientific concept to a different situation.

ON THE TASC TEST

*When you are given a science concept and asked which one of the choices is the best example, carefully eliminate the three that do not have all the same characteristics.*

Scientific information can be expressed in different forms. On the TASC Test, you may be asked to find relationships among science passages, graphics, formulas, or equations.

Scientific equations for **chemical reactions** often use these symbols:

| Symbol | Meaning |
|---|---|
| + | Positive symbol separates two or more **reactants** or **products** from one another. |
| → | Yield symbol separates reactants from products and shows the reaction direction. |
| ⇆ | Reversible reaction symbol indicates that the reaction can proceed in both directions. |

For example, here is the general chemical formula for what happens when carbon (C) is burned:

$$C + O_2 \rightarrow CO_2$$

► Which statement describes the process in the formula?
(1) Carbon combines with oxygen to produce carbon dioxide.
(2) Carbon creates oxygen, which takes on another oxygen atom in order to produce carbon dioxide.

The correct answer is **(1)**. In this case, carbon and oxygen $(O_2)$ combine without losing any of their components. The result is carbon dioxide, a molecule made up of one carbon atom and two oxygen atoms. (The prefix *di-* means "two," so *carbon dioxide* means "a C and two Os.") The plus sign on the left-hand side of the formula indicates that carbon and oxygen are separate reactants, not that carbon creates oxygen. Thus, statement (2) is incorrect.

Other questions may ask you to understand a science concept and **relate** it to a specific situation.

> The term desertification describes a chain of events in which so much soil erodes from land that the land can no longer support plant or animal life. The lack of plant life allows for further soil erosion, making the land even more barren. It is very difficult to reverse desertification.

► Which of the following could be an example of the early stages of desertification?
(1) In a certain valley, overgrazing has nearly eliminated plant life. This lack of vegetation has led to rapid soil erosion.
(2) In a certain valley, the climate is arid, and soil erosion has occurred when the infrequent rains arrive. Farmers have devised an irrigation system to grow crops and thus reverse the rate of soil erosion.

Choice **(1)** is correct. Soil erosion is the cause of desertification, so the valley may be in the early stages of desertification. In choice (2), farmers have found a way to combat erosion, so this valley does not appear to be undergoing desertification.

# PRACTICE 4

**Questions 1 through 4 are based on the information below.**

Imagine a substance (such as salt or sugar) dissolved in a liquid (such as water or alcohol). The liquid in which the substance is dissolved is called the *solvent*. *Osmosis* is the diffusion (movement) of a solvent across a semipermeable membrane (a barrier that allows some substances to pass through it). The solvent moves from the side of the membrane with less dissolved material to the side of the membrane with more dissolved material. The result of osmosis is an equilibrium: that is, the rate the solvent flows across the membrane is the same in both directions.

Gillian conducted an experiment to see how quickly various liquids with a specific amount of sugar dissolved in them would undergo osmosis. She used vats of the same size with semipermeable membranes separating one side of the vat from the other, and she put equal quantities of various liquids in both sides:

**Container Used for Studying Osmosis**

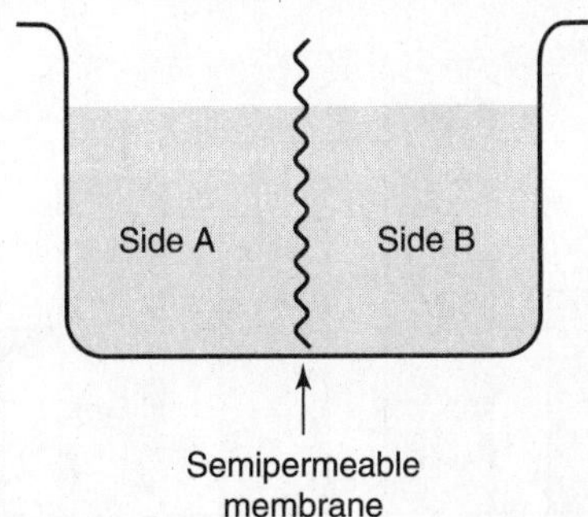


**1.** Gillian used one of the vats to test the rate of diffusion of liquid acetone in the process of osmosis. What did she most likely put on the two sides of the semipermeable membrane in that vat?

| | Side A | Side B |
|---|---|---|
| A. | Pure acetone | Sugar in a glass container, submerged in acetone |
| B. | A 50 percent solution of sugar in acetone | A 50 percent solution of sugar in acetone |
| C. | Pure acetone | A solution of sugar in acetone |
| D. | Pure acetone | Pure acetone |

Gillian's experiment yielded the following results.

| Solvent | Time Required to Reach Equilibrium |
|---|---|
| Water | 20 minutes |
| Acetone | 25 minutes |
| Acetic acid | 18 minutes |
| Formic acid | 15 minutes |

2. Based on the table above, which solvent had the highest rate of diffusion?

A. water
B. acetone
C. acetic acid
D. formic acid

3. Based on the table, what was the median time required for the solvents to reach equilibrium?

A. 15 minutes
B. 16 minutes
C. 18 minutes
D. 19 minutes

**4.** Osmosis is the reason why it is unhealthy and potentially dangerous to drink seawater. If you drink seawater, which contains a high concentration of salts and other dissolved material, some of the dissolved material will be absorbed into your bloodstream, causing your blood to have a higher-than-normal concentration of dissolved material. As that blood circulates through your body, water will move from your body's tissues into your blood vessels, causing your tissues to lose water and dry out.

Choose the choice that best completes the sentence: Based on the information given, your tissues would begin to lose water and dry out when your blood has a level of dissolved material __________ that of your body's tissues.

A. greater than
B. slightly less than
C. much less than
D. equivalent to

**Review your work using the explanations that start on page 723.**

LESSON 5

# Use Statistics and Probability

**KEY IDEAS**

- A measure of central tendency is used to summarize data.
- Probabilities are used to make predictions.
- Combinations and permutations are used to calculate numbers of ordered and unordered arrangements, respectively.

**ON THE TASC TEST**

*You will be permitted to use your calculator for some questions on the TASC Science Test. If you are taking the paper version of the TASC, be sure to have your handheld calculator available. If you are taking the computer version, the on-screen calculator icon will appear for these questions.*

Because scientists often need to perform calculations, you will do some math on the TASC Science Test. This math work will include the following:

- Central tendency: average (mean), median, mode, and range
- Independent and dependent probabilities
- Combinations and permutations

You may want to review these topics on pages 310–327 of the unit on Mathematics. For some of these questions, you may be able to use your calculator.

Scientists use **measures of central tendency** (mean, median, mode, and range) to summarize many pieces of data with one number.

Use the graph below to answer a question about central tendency.

**Annual Tornadoes, 2000–2006, Goodland (Kansas) 19-County Warning Area**

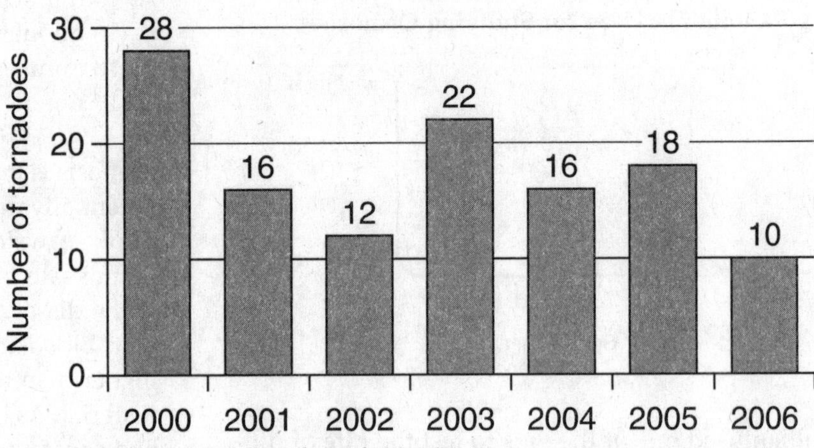


Source: National Oceanic and Atmospheric Administration

▶ Calculate the mean (arithmetic average) number of tornadoes that struck the Goodland area per year in the years 2002 through 2005. ________

To find the mean of a set of quantities, sum the quantities and divide by the number of items in the set. The list from 2002 to 2005 is 12, 22, 16, and 18. The sum of those numbers is 68. Divide by the number of items in the list (4), and the result is **17**.

Scientists frequently use data to investigate the **probability** that an event will happen. You may wish to review pages 318–321 to refresh your memory about working with probability.

# PRACTICE 5

**<u>Questions 1 through 4</u> are based on the following information.**

*Metabolism* is a set of chemical processes that occur in the tissues of living organisms. One example of a metabolic process in animals is the breaking down of carbohydrates from food into substances the body can store. Another example is the transformation of those same substances into energy that the animal can use. The *rate of metabolism* describes the speed at which these processes take place. Metabolic rate varies among different species. The graph below compares several animal species by both average metabolic rate and average body weight.

**Metabolic Rates of Seven Species**

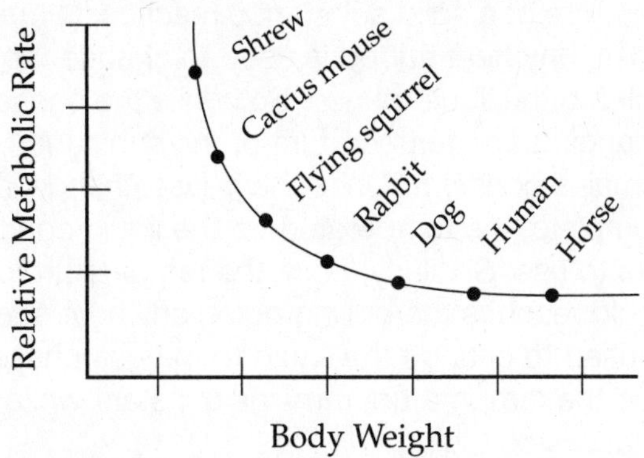


1. Of the species in this graph, which has the median body weight?

   A. shrew
   B. cactus mouse
   C. flying squirrel
   D. rabbit

2. Of the species in this graph, which has the median metabolic rate?

   A. rabbit
   B. dog
   C. human
   D. horse

**STUDY ADVICE**

When you see a figure, remember to ask:

What does the figure show?

What are the units of measurement?

When you see a figure with text, ask yourself how the text and the figure relate to one another.

3. Imagine that you could calculate the average (mean) of metabolic rates of all the animal species in this graph. Now imagine that the shrew were removed from the graph and that you recalculated the average of the remaining species. Without the shrew, the new average metabolic rate would be

   A. higher than the previous average.
   B. lower than the previous average.
   C. the same as the previous average.
   D. equal to the average of the metabolic rates of the horse and cactus mouse.

4. Adult elephants weigh more than adult horses. Based on the graph above, what would you predict would be true of elephants?

   A. Their metabolic rate would resemble that of cactus mice, which, like elephants, live in warm climates.
   B. Their metabolic rate would be equivalent to that of horses.
   C. Their metabolic rate would be slightly lower than that of horses.
   D. Their metabolic rate would be significantly higher than that of horses.

---

5. Growing the same crop on a field year after year can cause crop yields to decline as the soil becomes depleted and insect populations become firmly established. Crop rotation, or growing different crops in different years, is one way to avoid these problems. However, discovering the most effective rotation of a number of different crops is difficult, because there are so many possible orders in which to grow them and testing any given crop rotation takes several years.

   For example, imagine a proposed rotation of corn, peanuts, onions, beets, and carrots, with a different crop grown each year for five years. How many different orderings of these five crops are possible?

   A. 15
   B. 25
   C. 120
   D. 125

**Review your work using the explanations that start on page 723.**

# SCIENCE SKILLS PRACTICE QUESTIONS

**Questions 1 through 3 are based on the following passage.**

The 1543 publication of Nicolaus Copernicus's heliocentric, or sun-centered, theory of the universe marked an crucial moment in the history of science. Copernicus's theory that the planets revolve around the sun was controversial: at first, many refused to accept that Earth could be hurtling through space. However, we now know that Copernicus's theory was accurate in many ways.

Despite its importance as a breakthrough, Copernicus's theory contained a number of ideas that today seem primitive. For example, Copernicus maintained that the planets were embedded in crystalline spheres. Additionally, while Copernicus developed the novel, and later widely accepted, idea that Earth rotates on its axis, he also believed that the planets orbit around the sun in perfect circles. We now know that the planets move in elliptical orbits.

1. Which of the following is the main idea of the second paragraph?

   A. Primitive astronomers accepted Copernicus's theory when it was first published.
   B. While Copernicus's theory was an important development, it included elements that are outdated today.
   C. Copernicus believed that Earth moved around the sun, rather than the other way around.
   D. Earth does not hurtle through space.

2. Which of the following would be an appropriate title for this passage?

   A. "Important Landmarks in 16th-Century Science"
   B. "Copernicus: The Life of an Astronomer"
   C. "The Significance and Limitations of the Copernican Theory"
   D. "The Earth-Centered Universe"

3. Which of the following can be inferred from the passage?

   A. Astronomers now believe that the planets are not embedded in crystalline spheres.
   B. Astronomers now know that Earth does not move around the sun in an ellipse.
   C. All aspects of the Copernican theory have now been disproven.
   D. Copernicus took inspiration from the primitive astronomers who came before him.

---

4. Matter is generally found in one of three phases: solid, liquid, and gas. A substance can be converted from a solid to a liquid and then from a liquid to a gas by adding heat. Once the temperature of a solid substance reaches its melting point, any heat added is used to change the solid to the liquid phase. So, while the phase is changing, the temperature of the substance remains constant. Once the phase change is complete, the temperature of the liquid continues to rise. Similarly, once the temperature of a liquid reaches the boiling point, any heat added is used to change the liquid to the gas phase, and the temperature remains constant while the phase is changing.

**Temperature and Phase Changes of a Substance**

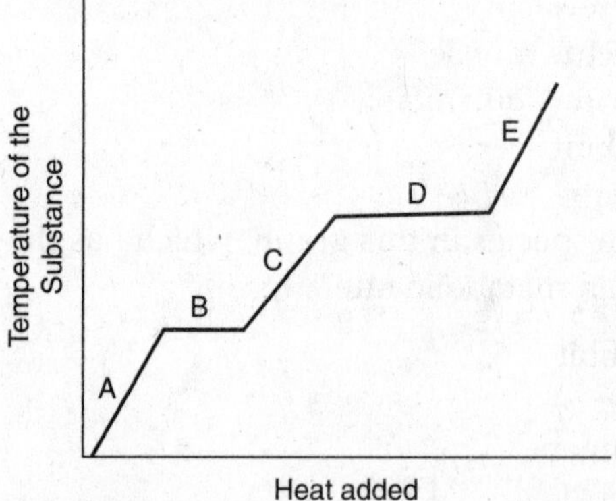


At which points are phase changes occurring in the graph above?

   A. A and E
   B. A, C, and E
   C. B and D
   D. C, D, and E

5. While all types of cancer share the common trait of uncontrolled cell growth, the causes of that uncontrolled growth are complex and varied. Nevertheless, a number of specific causes of several types of cancer are known. For example, long-term asbestos exposure can result in mesothelioma (a cancer that can affect multiple organs), while long-term regular inhalation of tobacco smoke can lead to lung cancer. In addition to such chemical causes, viruses are also responsible for a number of types of cancer: human papillomavirus precipitates cervical cancer, while the hepatitis B virus causes liver cancer.

   Given the previous information, which of the following medical procedures could potentially prevent a specific type of cancer from forming?

   A. surgery to remove a brain tumor
   B. chemotherapy to treat lung cancer
   C. annual mammography screenings for breast cancer
   D. a vaccine to prevent infection with the hepatitis B virus

6. The phalarope, a North American shorebird, feeds on tiny crustaceans. To catch them, the phalarope swims in rapid circles, creating a vortex that raises prey to the surface of shallow water. The bird then opens and shuts its long, narrow beak to draw water droplets containing its prey up to its mouth. Because drawing up the water droplets depends upon the surface tension of water, the phalarope is exceptionally vulnerable to oil spills; the phalarope cannot remove oil from its beak on its own, so once it is exposed to oil-covered water, it cannot feed.

   Which of the following must be true based on the passage?

   A. The phalarope prefers saltwater to brackish water or freshwater.
   B. At least some of the phalarope's prey is smaller than a water droplet.
   C. A phalarope whose beak becomes coated in oil will be able to feed if it can find clean water, not coated in oil, that contains tiny crustaceans.
   D. In addition to crustaceans, the phalarope feeds on small saltwater fish.

**Questions 7 through 9 are based on the following paragraph and graphic.**

Record high temperatures were recorded in numerous Australian cities in the summer of 2012. The chart below indicates current and former record temperatures for seven of those cities. For instance, Hobart's previous record was a little below 41°C, and its current record is a little above 41°C.

**Record High Temperatures in Australian Cities**

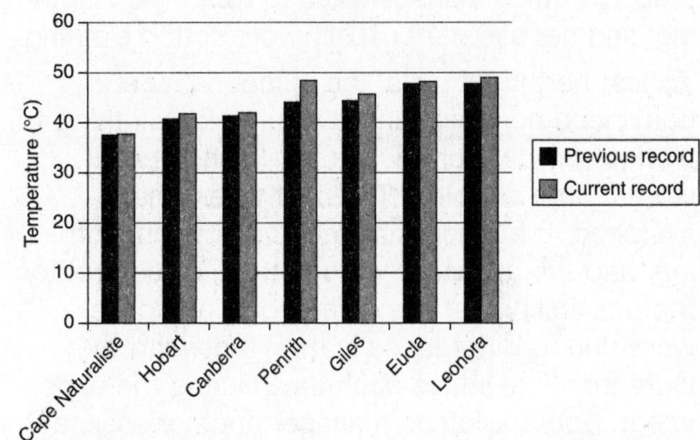


7. According to the chart, which city experienced the largest increase from its previous record to its current record?

   A. Hobart
   B. Penrith
   C. Eucla
   D. Leonora

8. Which of the following cities had a previous record equal to the median of all the cities' previous records?

   A. Cape Naturaliste
   B. Canberra
   C. Penrith
   D. Eucla

9. According to the chart, which of the following statements is true?

   A. Temperatures will likely continue to increase.
   B. Temperatures increased 5 degrees or less.
   C. Temperatures increased more than 5 degrees.
   D. Temperatures usually increase 2–5 degrees in the summer.

**Questions 10 through 13 are based on the following passage.**

An office manager noticed that each time she touched the metal filing cabinet next to her desk, she experienced an electrostatic shock (commonly known as "static"). Her assistant, however, only rarely experienced such shocks when touching the cabinet. The office manager wondered why this might be.

The office manager developed a hypothesis: perhaps differences in clothing could explain why she was experiencing more shocks than her assistant. The office manager liked to wear nylon clothing, and her assistant usually wore cotton clothing.

To test her hypothesis, the office manager convinced her assistant to wear nylon clothing to work every day for a week, while she herself wore cotton clothing. The next week, they switched: the office manager wore nylon clothing, and the assistant wore cotton. To control for the possibility that the differences in shocks were due to differences in their footwear, they wore identical shoes each day. During the experiment, both the office manager and her assistant recorded the number of times they touched the metal filing cabinet each day, and they also recorded the number of times they experienced electrostatic shocks when doing so.

At the end of the first week, they found that the assistant had experienced 73 electrostatic shocks, while the office manager had experienced 10. During the second week, the office manager experienced 68 shocks, and her assistant 12. The office manager concluded that these results supported her hypothesis, and as a result she decided to switch to wearing mostly cotton clothing.

10. Scientific investigations begin with a question. Which of the following is the question that formed the basis for the office manager's experiment?

 A. Is it better to wear cotton clothing or nylon clothing?
 B. Why does touching the metal filing cabinet produce more electrostatic shocks than touching other office furniture?
 C. Why, when I touch the metal filing cabinet, do I experience more electrostatic shocks than my assistant does when she touches it?
 D. Could my shoes be causing me to experience more electrostatic shocks than my assistant experiences?

11. Which of the following best summarizes how the office manager conducted her experiment?

 A. The office manager suspected that her nylon clothing was causing her to experience electrostatic shocks.
 B. The office manager switched to cotton clothing after seeing that her hypothesis was supported by her data.
 C. The office manager wore shoes of a different material than those of her assistant.
 D. The office manager wore one type of clothing, while her assistant wore another type of clothing, and they recorded the number of shocks they experienced.

12. Why did the office manager and her assistant wear the same type of shoes while conducting the experiment?

 A. They wanted to test the effect of their clothing on the number of shocks they experienced, and wearing different types of shoes might have confused their results.
 B. They wanted to test whether the office manager's shoes were causing the high number of electrostatic shocks she was experiencing.
 C. They believed that wearing cotton might cause the wearer to experience more electrostatic shocks.
 D. They wanted to protect themselves from the effects of electrostatic shock.

13. Imagine that the results of the office manager's experiment had demonstrated that her clothing was not in fact responsible for the large number of electrostatic shocks she was experiencing. After reviewing those findings, the office manager then wondered if her footwear might be responsible, and she decided to conduct a new experiment to test this idea. Before she conducted that experiment, the idea that her shoes might be responsible would be which of the following?

 A. a new conclusion based on findings
 B. a general principle from the study of physics
 C. a new hypothesis
 D. an experiment design

**You may use your calculator for questions 14 and 15.**

14. Common garden snails are hermaphroditic. That is, each individual snail produces both sperm and eggs. Mating between two garden snails involves the transfer of sperm from each partner to the other. A high school science teacher has created a large terrarium for his classroom that contains 6 adult garden snails. Assuming that all 6 snails are healthy, how many different mating pairs are possible?

    A. 2
    B. 12
    C. 15
    D. 36

15. The sun is a class G star, which is a type of main-sequence star. Approximately 90 percent of all stars in the Milky Way galaxy are main-sequence stars, and approximately 7 percent of all main-sequence stars are class G stars. What is the probability, expressed as a percentage, that any given star in the Milky Way galaxy is a class G star?

    A. 6.3%
    B. 9.7%
    C. 63%
    D. 97%

**Questions 16 and 17 refer to the information and table below.**

The table below contains data observed in a group of 58-year-old men. The study examined the relationship between tobacco use and formations called plaques that build up on the walls of arteries, which are blood vessels that carry blood from the heart to the body's tissues. The carotid and femoral arteries are two large and very important arteries.

**Average Characteristics of 58-Year-Old Men, by Smoking Status**

| | Never Smokers | Ex-Smokers | Current Smokers |
|---|---|---|---|
| Waist circumference (cm) | 93.8 | 99.1 | 95.4 |
| Carotid plaques (%) | | | |
| None | 62 | 55 | 53 |
| Small | 15 | 23 | 16 |
| Large | 23 | 22 | 31 |
| Femoral plaques (%) | | | |
| None | 80 | 54 | 45 |
| Small | 10 | 13 | 14 |
| Large | 10 | 33 | 41 |

16. In the study described, current smokers showed the highest percentage of which of the following kinds of plaques?

    A. small carotid plaques
    B. large carotid plaques
    C. small femoral plaques
    D. large femoral plaques

17. Why might the ex-smokers have the highest waist circumference of the groups listed in the chart?

    A. People who have never smoked tend to consume more high-calorie foods than do those who smoke currently.
    B. People who have never smoked tend to consume more high-calorie foods than do those who have smoked in the past.
    C. People who quit smoking tend to substitute snacking for smoking.
    D. Ex-smokers tend to exercise more than do current smokers.

**Review your work using the explanations that start on page 724.**

# 536Cell Structures and Functions

All living things are made of **cells**, the basic unit of life. Some organisms, like bacteria and protozoa, are **unicellular**—they consist of a single cell. Others, like plants and animals, are **multicellular**, consisting of many different types of specialized cells. For example, humans have skin cells, blood cells, and nerve cells, to name just a few. All cells carry out the basic life functions: movement, growth, cell maintenance, reproduction, and the manufacture of specialized substances.

Although cells differ widely in size and appearance, they all have basic structures in common. All cells have a **cell membrane**, a structure that keeps the cell's contents separate from its external environment. The cell membrane is selectively permeable, which means that it allows certain substances, such as water, nutrients, and wastes, to pass between the cell's interior and the surrounding environment. Inside the cell membrane is the **cytoplasm**, a watery, jellylike substance that can include other cell structures. Finally, all cells have **genetic material**, which contains coded instructions for carrying out the cell's activities. In bacteria, the genetic material consists of a single molecule suspended in the cytoplasm. Bacteria are called **prokaryotes**. In all other cells, the genetic material is contained within a **nucleus**. Such cells are called **eukaryotic cells**. All plant and animal cells are eukaryotic. A typical plant cell is shown below. Note that a plant cell has a **cell wall**, which gives the cell shape and rigidity, and an animal cell does not.

### KEY IDEAS

- The basic unit of all living things is the cell, which carries out the life functions, including movement, growth, and reproduction.
- All cells have a cell membrane, cytoplasm, and genetic material.
- Unlike an animal cell, a plant cell contains a cell wall—a structure that gives the cell rigidity and shape.

**A Plant Cell**

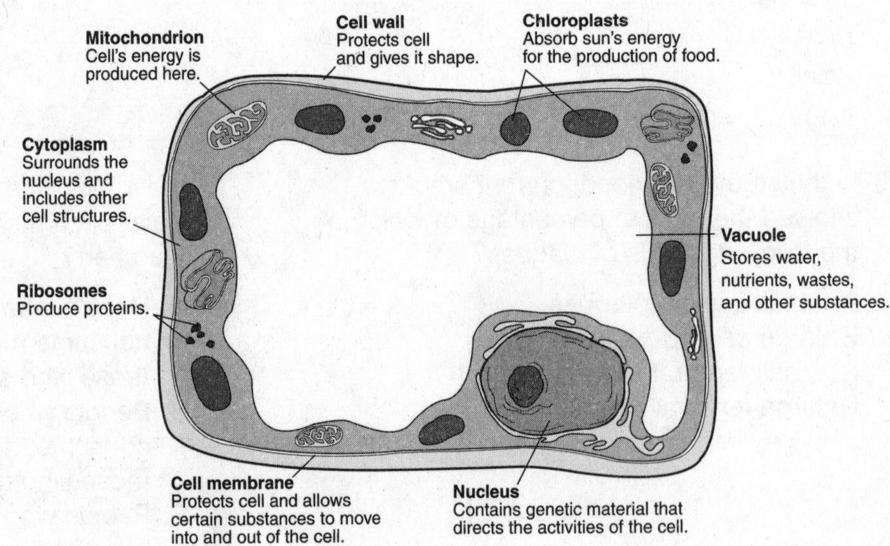


### TASC TEST TIP

*The title and labels of a diagram usually tell you the main idea of the diagram. Here, the main idea is that plant cells have cell structures with specialized functions.*

# PRACTICE 1

1. According to the diagram on page 536, the function of the _________ is to supply energy to the cell.

   A. nucleus
   B. ribosomes
   C. mitochondrion
   D. vacuole

2. In addition to the cell wall, the water stored in a plant cell's vacuole helps give the plant firmness and shape. When a plant is not taking in enough water from the soil through its roots, it uses up its stored water and its vacuoles shrink. When the vacuoles shrink, the plant wilts.

   Which of the following is a conclusion based on the paragraph above rather than a given fact?

   A. Cell walls help give a plant cell firmness and shape.
   B. Vacuoles help give a plant cell firmness and shape.
   C. Plants take in water from the soil through their roots.
   D. Cell walls cannot maintain a plant's shape and rigidity when the plant lacks water.

3. A student is examining a cell using a microscope. She is able to identify the cell membrane, cytoplasm, a small vacuole, and the nucleus, but she does not see a cell wall or any chloroplasts. She concludes that the cell is a eukaryotic cell.

   Which of the following is evidence that her conclusion is correct?

   A. the presence of a nucleus
   B. the presence of cytoplasm
   C. the absence of chloroplasts
   D. the absence of a cell wall

4. Cells were first seen during the 1600s, when English scientist Robert Hooke observed cork cell walls through a microscope that could magnify a specimen a couple of hundred times its original size. In the 1800s, the compound light microscope, which magnifies up to a thousand times, was developed. Electron microscopes, which can magnify up to a million times, were invented during the 1900s.

   Which of the following best explains why our knowledge of cells has grown with improvements in microscope technology?

   A. Each time the microscope is improved, scientists can see cell structures more clearly.
   B. With the first microscopes, all cell structures were clearly visible.
   C. Compound light microscopes can magnify cells up to a thousand times.
   D. Robert Hooke's microscope only allowed him to see the largest cell structures.

5. Diffusion is a process by which particles move from an area of higher concentration to an area of lower concentration. For example, oxygen diffuses through the cell membrane of a unicellular pond organism from the water, where there is lots of oxygen, into the cell, where there is less oxygen. Eventually, the concentration of oxygen inside and outside the unicellular organism is the same.

   What would happen if the concentration of oxygen were greater in the unicellular organism than in its watery environment?

   A. Water would diffuse from the unicellular organism into the pond water.
   B. Oxygen would diffuse from the unicellular organism into the pond water.
   C. Oxygen would diffuse from the pond water into the unicellular organism.
   D. Diffusion of oxygen between the organism and the pond water would stop entirely.

**Review your work using the explanations that start on page 725.**

## STUDY ADVICE

You don't have to know a lot of science vocabulary or facts in order to do well on TASC Science Test questions. You just need a basic familiarity with the science concepts discussed in this book. Remember to pay particular attention to the Key Ideas and the words in bold.

LESSON 2

# Cell Processes and Energy

All cells need energy to carry out the life functions, such as growth and reproduction. Green plants, some algae, and some bacteria use energy from sunlight to make food in a process called **photosynthesis**.

In photosynthesis, plants use sunlight to power chemical reactions that convert carbon dioxide gas and water into oxygen and the simple sugar **glucose**. In the first stage of photosynthesis, light energy is captured by chloroplasts inside plant cells. Chloroplasts contain **chlorophyll**, a pigment that gives plants their green color. Chlorophyll absorbs light energy for photosynthesis. In the second stage, water $(H_2O)$ that the plant gets from the soil and carbon dioxide $(CO_2)$ that the plant gets from the air undergo a complex series of chemical reactions inside the chloroplasts. The products of these reactions are oxygen $(O_2)$ and glucose $(C_6H_{12}O_6)$. Plant cells use the energy that is stored in glucose to power cell processes. Photosynthesis can be summarized in the chemical equation shown below:

$$6CO_2 + 6H_2O \xrightarrow{\text{light energy}} C_6H_{12}O_6 + 6O_2$$

In words, this means that carbon dioxide plus water, in the presence of light energy, yields glucose plus oxygen.

As a result of photosynthesis, energy is stored in sugars and other **carbohydrates** in the plant. To meet their energy needs, other organisms eat plants or eat organisms that eat plants. When energy is needed in a cell, carbohydrates are broken down to release the energy in a process called **cellular respiration**. In this process, oxygen from the air reacts with glucose from food to yield carbon dioxide, water, and energy. Cellular respiration can be summarized in the following chemical equation:

$$C_6H_{12}O_6 + 6O_2 \rightarrow 6CO_2 + 6H_2O + \text{energy}$$

In words, this means that glucose plus oxygen yields carbon dioxide, water, and energy.

If you examine the two equations, you will notice that the products of photosynthesis are the raw materials of cellular respiration, and the products of cellular respiration are the raw materials of photosynthesis. These two processes are part of a cycle. Plants release oxygen, a waste product of photosynthesis, into the atmosphere. Animals breathe in the oxygen and use it in cellular respiration. They breathe out carbon dioxide, a waste product of cellular respiration. The carbon dioxide is then used by plants in photosynthesis, and the cycle repeats. Between them, photosynthesis and cellular respiration help keep the amounts of oxygen and carbon dioxide in the atmosphere fairly constant.

## KEY IDEAS

- In photosynthesis, plants use light energy to form glucose from carbon dioxide and water. Oxygen is a by product.
- In cellular respiration, glucose is broken down in the presence of oxygen to release energy. Carbon dioxide is a by product.
- These two processes help maintain oxygen and carbon dioxide levels in the atmosphere.

## ON THE TASC TEST

*About 34% of the questions on the TASC Science Test are about life science topics.*

# PRACTICE 2

1. Which of the following are the products of cellular respiration?

   A. glucose and light energy
   B. carbon dioxide and oxygen
   C. glucose, oxygen, and energy
   D. carbon dioxide, water, and energy

2. A horticulturist wants to grow large, healthy plants by maximizing the rate of photosynthesis.

   Which of the following actions would be most likely to get the results she wants?

   A. increasing the amount of light the plants receive each day
   B. increasing the amount of oxygen the plants receive each day
   C. decreasing the amount of oxygen the plants receive each day
   D. decreasing the amount of carbon dioxide the plants receive each day

3. Carbon dioxide is one of the "greenhouse gases" that help keep Earth warm by trapping radiated heat in the atmosphere. Global warming is thought to be caused in part by increased amounts of carbon dioxide in the atmosphere.

   Which of the following would help reduce the level of carbon dioxide in the atmosphere and thus perhaps slow the global warming trend?

   A. increasing the population of domestic animals
   B. increasing the number of green plants
   C. increasing the harvest of trees
   D. increasing the amount of glucose in our food

**Questions 4 and 5 refer to the following information and diagram.**

In most plants, photosynthesis takes place primarily in the palisade cells of leaves.

**Cross Section of a Leaf**

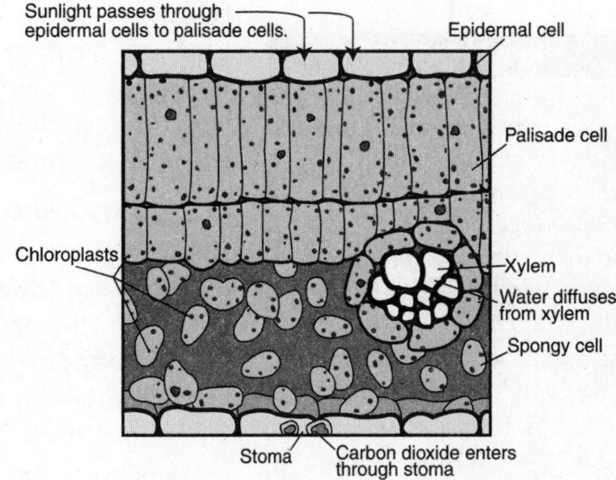


4. Which of the following is an opening in the lower surface of the leaf through which gases such as carbon dioxide can pass?

   A. palisade cell
   B. chloroplast
   C. xylem
   D. stoma

5. Chloroplasts are structures found within some of the cells in a leaf. They help in the process of photosynthesis. In the diagram, they are represented by small gray spots on the cells.

   Which of the following statements is supported by the information in the diagram?

   A. Palisade cells provide a means of transporting water through a plant.
   B. Most of a leaf's chloroplasts are found in its palisade cells.
   C. The spongy cells are soft, like a sponge.
   D. The epidermis blocks light from reaching the palisade cells.

**Review your work using the explanations that start on page 725.**

LESSON 3

# Human Body Systems

KEY IDEAS

- The circulatory system moves blood around the body, delivering and taking away substances.
- The respiratory system brings oxygen into the body and gets rid of carbon dioxide.
- The digestive system breaks down food into nutrients that cells can use.
- The nervous system controls body activities.

ON THE TASC TEST

*On the Science Test, you will have to answer questions that require you to use information from both text and a graphic, as in questions 4 and 5 on page 541.*

There are four levels of organization in the human body: (1) cells, the smallest unit of life; (2) **tissues**, groups of similar cells that perform a specific function, such as muscle tissue; (3) **organs**, groups of tissues that perform a function, such as the stomach; and (4) body systems, groups of organs working together to perform a function, such as digestion. Human body systems include the circulatory, respiratory, digestive, nervous, immune, endocrine, reproductive, urinary, skeletal, and muscular systems.

The **circulatory system**, sometimes called the cardiovascular system, consists of the heart and the blood vessels. Its main function is to move the blood, which transports substances like oxygen and nutrients, throughout the body. The major **organ** of the circulatory system is the **heart**, a muscle that contracts to pump blood. Blood moves through the blood vessels from large **arteries**, to smaller arteries, to **capillaries**, to small **veins**, to large veins, and back to the heart. Through the thin walls of the capillaries, oxygen, nutrients, and other substances pass from the blood into the body's cells, and carbon dioxide and other wastes pass from the cells into the blood.

The **respiratory system** consists of the nose, throat, **trachea** (windpipe), and **lungs**. Its function is to take oxygen from the air into the body when we inhale and to get rid of waste in the form of carbon dioxide when we exhale. The trachea branches into two tubes called the **bronchi**, one of which goes into each lung. The bronchi branch into smaller tubes called **bronchioles**, each of which ends in an **alveolus**, a tiny spherical sac. Inside the capillaries of the alveoli, oxygen diffuses into the blood and carbon dioxide diffuses out of the blood.

The **digestive system** consists of the mouth, **esophagus**, **stomach**, **small intestine**, and **large intestine**. Its function is to break down food into nutrients, which are used for cell processes including the production of energy, and to get rid of digestive wastes. Digestion begins in the mouth, where the teeth grind food into smaller pieces, and **saliva** begins to break it down chemically. Food is pushed by muscular action down through the esophagus into the stomach, where it is churned and further broken down by **enzymes** and stomach acids. From the stomach it travels to the small intestine, where most of the nutrients are absorbed into the blood through tiny capillaries in the **villi**. What remains goes to the large intestine, which removes water, leaving solid waste to be excreted through the **rectum**.

The **nervous system** consists of the **brain**, **spinal cord**, and **nerves**. Its function is to receive, process, and transmit information, controlling body activities. The brain has three main parts: the **cerebrum**, which controls functions such as thinking, seeing, and speaking; the **cerebellum**, which coordinates movement and position; and the **brainstem**, which controls breathing and heart rate. Information is transmitted to and from the brain through the nerves, which are bundled in the spinal cord and branch out from there into all parts of the body.

# PRACTICE 3

1. Which human body system interacts with each cell of the body?

   A. the circulatory system
   B. the digestive system
   C. the muscular system
   D. the skeletal system

2. How are the alveoli in the lungs and the villi in the small intestine similar?

   A. Both are structures located in the respiratory system.
   B. Both are structures located in the digestive system.
   C. Both are structures in which substances pass through capillary walls into the blood.
   D. Both are structures involved in coordination and movement.

3. In the 17th century, English physician William Harvey concluded that blood in the veins flows toward the heart.

   Which of the following facts helps support Harvey's conclusion?

   A. The heart pumps about 1,800 gallons of blood per day.
   B. The heart has four chambers: two atria and two ventricles.
   C. Large veins branch into smaller blood vessels called capillaries.
   D. Veins have valves that allow blood to flow in one direction only.

**Questions 4 and 5 refer to the following information and diagram.**

The kidneys of the urinary system remove cellular wastes and excess water from the blood. This material, called urine, is stored in the bladder until it is excreted from the body.

**The Urinary System**

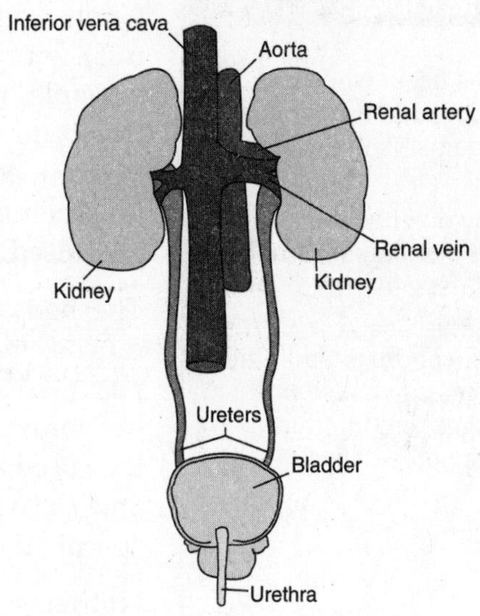


4. Which of the following is the name of the structure(s) through which urine passes from each kidney to the bladder?

   A. ureters
   B. urethra
   C. renal veins
   D. aorta

5. A urologist is a doctor who specializes in disorders of the urinary system.

   Which of the following patients is most likely to be treated by a urologist?

   A. a patient with low levels of iron in her blood
   B. a patient with a painful kidney stone
   C. a patient with swollen veins in the anus, called hemorrhoids
   D. a patient with chronic indigestion

**Review your work using the explanations that start on page 725.**

**STUDY ADVICE**

Speaking of health, how's your stress level? Remember that you have to manage your stress just as you manage any other aspect of your studies. Keep yourself on a regular sleep schedule, eat right, exercise, and find other healthy ways to manage your stress.

LESSON 4

# Health Issues

KEY IDEAS

- Infections occur when the body is invaded by germs—microorganisms that cause disease.
- A healthy diet has the right nutrients—proteins, carbohydrates, fats, vitamins, minerals, and water.
- The abuse of drugs and other substances can cause physical changes and interfere with a person's daily functioning.

ON THE TASC TEST

*All questions on the TASC Science Test are in multiple-choice format. For each question, you must pick the one correct answer from the four options that are given.*

Health can be affected by infections, nutrition, and substance abuse.

An **infection** is the invasion of the body by germs—microorganisms that cause disease. It is often characterized by fever and other symptoms. Germs can enter the body through breaks in the skin (for example, tetanus), with air (for example, influenza), in contaminated food and water (for example, food poisoning), by contact with contaminated blood or saliva (for example, rabies), or through sexual activity (gonorrhea). Infections can be grouped according to the type of microorganisms that cause them. The most common germs are **bacteria** and **viruses**, although infections can also be caused by fungi, protozoans, and worms.

The body has natural defenses against infection, such as the skin, the mucous membranes in the nose, tears, and acid in the stomach. If germs get past these defenses, the **immune system** produces **antibodies** that destroy the germs. In developed nations, infectious diseases are less common than they used to be because of better nutrition and living conditions, safer water and sewage systems, **immunization** (which provides protection against specific infectious diseases), and **antibiotics**, drugs that fight bacteria.

**Nutrients** are substances that are needed for growth, normal functioning, and maintenance of cells. The body does not produce nutrients; instead we get them from the food we eat. The nutrients that humans need for good health include **proteins**, **carbohydrates** (sugars and starches), **fats**, **vitamins**, **minerals**, and water. In a well-balanced diet, people get enough nutrients to provide energy as well as the right nutrients needed for all the body's functions. Too much or too little of a nutrient can cause problems. For example, a diet with too much fat can lead to obesity and contribute to heart disease. Too little vitamin C can cause scurvy, a painful disease.

**Drugs** are substances that affect the structure or function of the body. They are usually used to treat disease or relieve its symptoms, although some drugs, like nicotine in tobacco, have no medicinal purpose. The nonmedical use of a drug to the point that it interferes with a person's normal functioning is called **drug abuse**, or substance abuse. Drug abuse can lead to **addiction**, a severe form of dependence that causes physical changes in the body so that when the drug wears off or is stopped, withdrawal symptoms such as nausea and pain occur. Heroin, speed, alcohol, nicotine, and barbiturates are frequently abused addictive drugs. A milder form of dependence than addiction is **psychological dependence**, or **habituation**. In this type of dependence, the urge to take the drug is strong, even though there are no withdrawal symptoms. Examples of drugs that can cause habituation in humans are marijuana and hallucinogens. People also abuse substances that are not drugs, like glue, gasoline, and aerosols. Most of these substances are **inhalants**—they are sniffed for their effect on the nervous system. Inhalants generally depress, or slow, the functioning of the nervous system, sometimes causing their users to lose control or become unconscious.

# PRACTICE 4

1. Which of the following is among the body's first barriers against germs?

   A. the immune system
   B. antibiotics
   C. antibodies
   D. the skin

2. Each evening, Sara has a glass of wine. If there is no wine in the house, she feels a strong urge to get some, although she feels no ill effects if she does not.

   What is Sara's relationship to alcohol?

   A. addiction
   B. physical dependence
   C. habituation
   D. withdrawal

**Questions 3 and 4 are based on the following table.**

**Nutrients in the Diet**

| Nutrient | Description | Function | Source |
|---|---|---|---|
| Proteins | Complex molecules (amino acids) made of oxygen, carbon, nitrogen, hydrogen | Growth and maintenance of cells and metabolism | Meat, fish, eggs, dairy products, legumes, nuts, seeds |
| Carbohydrates | Molecules containing oxygen, carbon, and hydrogen | Body's main energy source, providing 4 calories of energy per gram; roughage for digestion | Bread, pasta, cereal, rice, fruits, potatoes |
| Fats | Fatty acids containing oxygen, carbon, and hydrogen | Concentrated source of energy, providing 9 calories of energy per gram; insulation; cell maintenance | Fish oils, vegetable oils, and animal fats |
| Vitamins | Substances used in very small quantities that are vital for body chemistry | Growth maintenance, repair of cells; protein synthesis; metabolism; and other functions | Various foods, daylight on skin (vitamin D), microorganisms in the bowel (vitamin K) |
| Minerals | Substances, such as iron and calcium, necessary for normal development | Many functions, including making red blood cells and building strong bones | Various foods |
| Water | A liquid made of oxygen and hydrogen atoms | Involved in almost all body processes | Beverages, soups, foods |

3. Which of the following statements is supported by the information in the table?

   A. Fats are a more concentrated source of energy than carbohydrates.
   B. Vitamins are more important in the diet than minerals.
   C. A good source of vitamin C is citrus fruits.
   D. Minerals provide a low-fat source of energy.

4. Which of the following is a fact, rather than an opinion, based on the table?

   A. Eating meat is the best way to get sufficient protein in your diet.
   B. Carbohydrates come from fruits as well as from bread and rice.
   C. Iron is the only mineral you need.
   D. Everyone should drink eight glasses of water each day.

**Review your work using the explanations that start on page 725.**

LESSON 5

# Reproduction and Heredity

KEY IDEAS

- In asexual reproduction, an offspring is identical to its parent; in sexual reproduction, an offspring is unique, inheriting traits from each parent.
- Gregor Mendel was the first to observe patterns of trait inheritance.
- Traits are controlled by genes, which come in forms called alleles. A dominant allele hides a recessive allele.

TASC TEST TIP

*As you take the test, pace yourself. If you are unsure of an answer, do your best and make a note to yourself to revisit that question. At the end of the test, you may have time to review those questions.*

All **species** of organisms reproduce in some way. There are two types of reproduction. In **asexual reproduction**, an individual organism produces offspring identical to the parent. For example, in a type of asexual reproduction called budding, a tiny freshwater animal called a hydra grows buds that develop into offspring. In **sexual reproduction**, two sex cells combine to form unique offspring with characteristics from both parent cells. In humans and many other species, those specialized sex cells are called **sperm** and **ova**.

Physical characteristics of organisms are called **traits**. The passing of traits from parents to offspring in sexual reproduction is called **heredity**. The first person to study heredity in a systematic way was an Austrian monk, **Gregor Mendel** (1822–1884). He bred plants and observed that sometimes offspring plants had the same traits as the parents and sometimes they did not. Mendel experimented with **purebred** pea plants—plants that always produced offspring with the same form of a trait as the parent. For example, purebred short plants always produced short offspring. First he crossed purebred short plants with purebred tall plants. In the first generation of offspring, all the plants were tall—the shortness trait had vanished. When the first-generation offspring reproduced, about three-quarters of the next generation of plants were tall, and one-quarter were short. The shortness trait had reappeared.

Mendel repeated his pea plant experiments with other traits over a ten-year period. Eventually he concluded that individual factors from each parent plant control the **inheritance** of specific traits. An offspring plant inherited one factor from the female parent and one from the male parent. Mendel concluded that one factor in a pair can hide the other factor. For example, the tallness factor hid the shortness factor in the first generation of offspring.

The factors that control traits are called **genes**. Different forms of a gene are called **alleles**. The gene that controls pea plant height, for example, has one allele for tallness and one allele for shortness. Each pea plant inherits one allele for the height gene from each parent. Therefore, any particular pea plant may have (1) two alleles for tallness, (2) two alleles for shortness, or (3) one allele for shortness and one for tallness. In the third case, the **dominant allele**, the tallness allele, controls the appearance of the trait. The **recessive allele**, the shortness allele, is hidden. For a recessive trait to appear in an individual, the individual must inherit two recessive alleles.

In Mendel's original experiment, the parent plants were purebred tall and purebred short. Thus, one parent had two dominant alleles for tallness, and the other parent had two recessive alleles for shortness. All the offspring in the first generation were **hybrid**—each had one allele for tallness and one for shortness. Because the tallness allele is dominant, all of the first generation plants were tall. In the next generation, some plants inherited two dominant alleles, some inherited two recessive alleles, and some inherited one dominant and one recessive allele, producing a mix of plants.

# PRACTICE 5

**Questions 1 through 3 refer to the following paragraph and diagram.**

The Punnett square below shows all the possible combinations of alleles for height in offspring pea plants when two tall hybrid pea plants are crossed. A capital *T* represents the dominant tallness allele, and a lowercase *t*, the recessive shortness allele. One parent's alleles are shown along the top of the square; the other's are shown on the left side. The **genotypes** of the offspring are shown in the boxes.

| | T | t |
|---|---|---|
| T | TT | Tt |
| t | Tt | tt |

1. Of the parent pea plants,

   A. both are tall.
   B. both are short.
   C. both are of medium height.
   D. one is tall and one is short.

2. What chance is there that an offspring will be short?

   A. 0 out of 4
   B. 1 out of 4
   C. 2 out of 4
   D. 3 out of 4

3. If you wanted to grow only tall pea plants in your garden over several growing seasons, which of the following genotypes would give you the best results?

   A. tt
   B. Tt
   C. tT
   D. TT

4. To show a recessive trait, an organism must inherit how many recessive alleles for that trait?

   A. none
   B. at least one
   C. at most one
   D. two

5. Why are organisms that reproduce sexually more genetically diverse than organisms that reproduce asexually?

   A. Organisms that reproduce sexually tend to produce more offspring than those that reproduce asexually.
   B. Organisms that reproduce sexually produce offspring that inherit diverse traits from only one parent.
   C. Organisms that reproduce sexually produce offspring with entirely new traits unlike those of either parent.
   D. Organisms that reproduce sexually produce offspring that have inherited a mix of traits from their parents.

6. A student is trying to repeat Mendel's experiments using the trait of fur color in rabbits. Black fur is dominant, and white fur is recessive. She starts with what she assumes is a purebred white female rabbit and a purebred black male rabbit. She crosses them and is surprised when one of the offspring has white fur.

   What probably was wrong with the student's experiment?

   A. The white female was actually a hybrid.
   B. The black male was actually a hybrid.
   C. Most of the offspring were hybrids.
   D. Most of the offspring were purebred.

**Review your work using the explanations that start on page 726.**

LESSON 6

# Modern Genetics

### KEY IDEAS

- Chromosomes are structures in a cell's nucleus that are composed mostly of genes, which are located on long molecules of DNA.
- DNA contains the genetic code for making proteins in the cell.
- Knowledge of genetics has led to advances in many fields but especially in medicine.

### ON THE TASC TEST

*Some questions on the TASC Science Test are based entirely on a graphic. Read the title of the diagram, chart, or graph to make sure you understand its main idea before you answer questions based on it.*

Years after Mendel died, scientists identified **chromosomes**, rod-shaped structures in the nucleus of each cell, as responsible for carrying genes from parent organisms to their offspring. Reproductive cells have half the number of chromosomes of an organism's other cells. When a sperm cell and an ovum unite, the resulting offspring has a full set of chromosomes. For example, human sex cells have 23 chromosomes and our other cells have 46.

One chromosome can contain thousands of genes on a single long molecule of **deoxyribonucleic acid (DNA)**. A DNA molecule is shaped like a spiral ladder. The sides of the ladder are made of deoxyribose—a sugar—and phosphate. Each rung of the ladder is made of a pair of nitrogen bases. There are four of these bases: adenine (A), guanine (G), thymine (T), and cytosine (C). The four bases pair up in a specific way: *A* always pairs with *T*, and *C* always pairs with *G*.

**DNA**

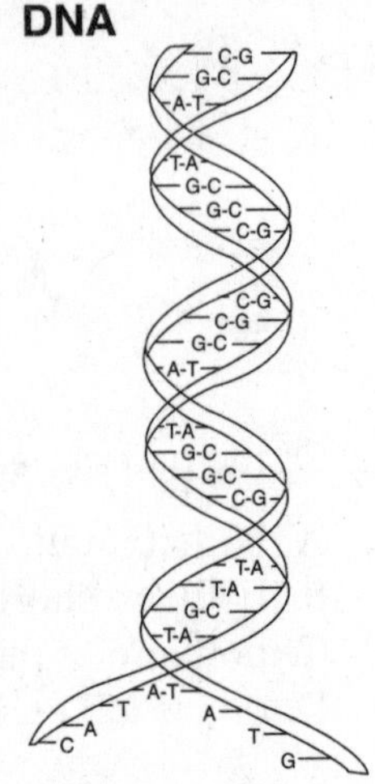


DNA controls the cell's production of proteins, which help determine all the characteristics and processes of the organism. During **protein synthesis**, the information from a gene in the cell's nucleus is used to produce a protein on ribosomes in the cytoplasm. Messenger **ribonucleic acid (RNA)**, transmits the code from the DNA. Each set of three base pairs on the messenger RNA, called a **codon**, contains instructions for creating an **amino acid**—a protein building block. The sequence of codons determines the sequence of amino acids in the protein and thus the specific protein to be made. So, the order of bases on the gene forms a **genetic code** for the synthesis of a particular protein.

There have been many recent advances in genetics, some controversial. Dolly the sheep and other animals have been cloned from single cells. Cloning bypasses sexual reproduction, raising the possibility that one day humans will be cloned—an idea that many find unethical. Through genetic engineering, the DNA of one organism can be introduced into the DNA of another organism, changing the second organism's traits. Genetic engineering has been used to produce medicines, such as insulin. It has been more controversial when used to improve foods. Finally, the entire **human genome**, or genetic code, has been decoded, making possible many advances in medicine. Scientists have identified genes involved in genetic disorders such as cystic fibrosis. They have also identified genes that predispose people to diseases such as breast cancer and Alzheimer's disease. Through genetic testing, people can find out whether they have any of these disease-related genes. In some cases, they can take steps to prevent the disease or to seek early treatment. In recent years, scientists have also succeeded in correcting certain genetic disorders through gene therapy.

# PRACTICE 6

1. Which of the following provides the code needed for a cell to make proteins?

   A. the number of chromosomes in the cell
   B. the amino acids in the cytoplasm
   C. the sequence of base pairs in a gene
   D. the pairing of adenine with thymine

2. A mutation is any change in the DNA of a gene. Which of the following is the most likely result of a mutation?

   A. the loss of one or more chromosomes
   B. an extra chromosome
   C. too much RNA in the cytoplasm
   D. a change in protein synthesis

3. Some animals have been genetically engineered to grow larger. Plants have been engineered to resist diseases or insects. Some fruits have been engineered to ripen more slowly. Genetic engineering of domesticated plants and animals is controversial. According to some people, these foods pose a risk because their effects on consumers and the environment are unknown. Others claim that genetically engineered foods are safe.

   Which of the following statements is an opinion about genetic engineering rather than a fact?

   A. Scientists have used genetic engineering to produce animals that grow larger.
   B. Disease-resistant plants have been produced by genetic engineering.
   C. Some genetically engineered fruit takes longer to ripen than its unaltered counterpart.
   D. Genetically engineered foods are safe for consumers and the environment.

4. When a cell reproduces through cell division, scientists call the reproducing cell the parent cell, and the two cells that result from the division are called daughter cells. The daughter cells are genetically identical to the parent cells. Before a parent cell starts to divide, the DNA in its nucleus replicates, or makes a complete copy of itself.

   Why is this process necessary?

   A. so that the parent cell will have an extra copy of DNA
   B. so that each daughter cell receives a complete set of DNA
   C. so that each daughter cell will not need to synthesize proteins
   D. so that each daughter cell will receive half its DNA from each parent cell

5. Which of the following statements is supported by the diagram and the passage on page 546?

   A. The DNA molecule unzips between the sugar and phosphate segments.
   B. The base guanine pairs only with the base cytosine.
   C. In a sequence of DNA bases, guanine always comes before adenine.
   D. About 10 percent of DNA contains genes; the remainder is "junk" DNA.

6. Proteins, which perform a variety of functions, are built from chains of __________.

   A. amino acids
   B. RNA
   C. codons
   D. enzymes

**Review your work using the explanations that start on page 726.**

## STUDY ADVICE

On Test Day, you will likely see some questions about inheritance and how traits can vary from one generation to the next. Be sure you've absorbed this lesson, and, as you read the next lesson, think about how heredity and evolution relate to each other.

LESSON 7

# Evolution and Natural Selection

In 1831, the British ship the *Beagle* set sail with naturalist Charles Darwin (1809–1882) aboard. Darwin's job was to observe living things he encountered. His observations during this five-year trip around the world led him to formulate an important scientific theory, the theory of **evolution**.

One of the *Beagle*'s stops was the Galápagos Islands, a group of islands in the Pacific Ocean off the South American coast. There Darwin saw great diversity of life forms. He noticed that many of the plants and animals resembled those he had seen on the South American mainland. However, there were also important differences between mainland and island organisms. For example, the iguanas on the mainland had small claws that allowed them to climb trees to eat leaves. On the Galápagos, iguanas had large claws that allowed them to grip wet, slippery rocks and eat seaweed. As Darwin traveled among the Galápagos Islands, he also observed that similar species of organisms sometimes differed from island to island. For example, small birds called ground finches had strong, wide beaks well-suited for breaking and eating seeds. However, different species of ground finches had different sized beaks, depending on which island they lived on. The sizes of the iguanas' claws and the birds' beaks are examples of **adaptations**, traits that help an organism survive in its environment. From these observations, Darwin concluded that organisms had originally come from the mainland and had changed, or evolved, over many generations to become better adapted to their new island environments.

Darwin explained that species evolve because of **natural selection**. By this process, individuals that are better adapted to their environments are more likely to survive and reproduce, passing their favorable adaptations to their offspring. Several factors are involved in natural selection:

1. Most species produce far more offspring than can survive.
2. These offspring compete with one another for scarce resources in their environment.
3. Members of a species have different traits, called **variations**. Some variations make individuals better adapted to survive in their environment.
4. Individuals with favorable variations are more likely to survive, reproduce, and pass the favorable traits to their offspring.
5. Over generations, helpful variations spread through a species, causing the species to change, or evolve.

Evolution through natural selection explains how species change over time. But how do new species evolve? Geographic isolation seems to play a big role in the evolution of new species. When a group of individuals remains separated from the rest of its species long enough, it may become a new species. This means that members of the new species will be unable to interbreed with members of the original species. For example, there are 13 species of finches on the various Galápagos Islands. They all probably evolved from a single ancestral species.

### KEY IDEAS

- Charles Darwin's observations in the Galápagos Islands led him to formulate the theory of evolution.
- Adaptations are traits that help an organism survive in its environment.
- Natural selection is the process by which individuals with favorable variations survive, reproduce, and pass the variations to their offspring.

### ON THE TASC TEST

*The TASC Science Test will likely not test memorized definitions of terms such as "adaptation" and "natural selection." However, you could be asked a question about the meaning of a term in the context of a science passage.*

# PRACTICE 7

**Questions 1 and 2 refer to the following paragraph and diagram.**

The forelimbs of humans, penguins, birds that fly, and alligators are similar. The similar pattern of the bones may be evidence that these animals evolved from a common ancestor. Similar structures that organisms may have inherited from a common ancestor are called homologous structures.

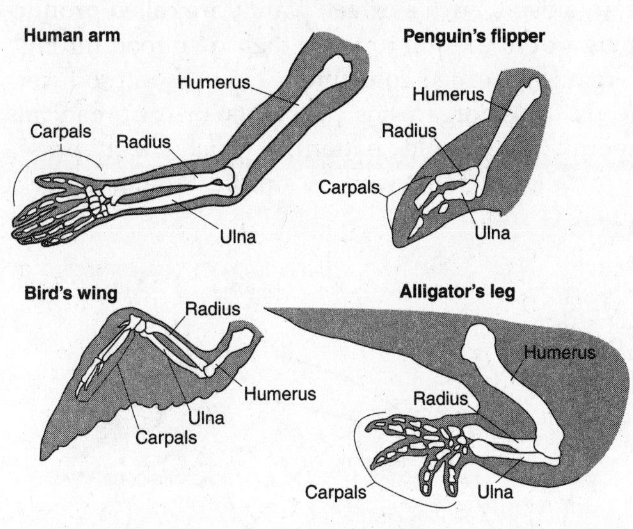


1. The forelimbs of frogs are homologous to those of human arms, penguins' flippers, birds' wings, and alligators' legs. Based on the diagram and paragraph, which of the following is likely to be true of frogs' forelimbs?

   A. Frogs use their forelimbs for swimming.
   B. Frogs' forelimbs contain carpal bones.
   C. Frogs' forelimbs resemble wings more than they resemble human arms.
   D. Frogs are more closely related to humans than they are to alligators.

2. Which of the following statements is supported by the paragraph and the diagram?

   A. The tip of a bird's wing is homologous to the upper arm of a human.
   B. Penguins are more closely related to humans than they are to birds.
   C. In penguins, flying birds, humans, and alligators, the forelimbs have similar structures despite performing different functions.
   D. Homologous structures have similar functions in modern organisms but had different functions in modern organisms' ancestors.

---

3. What are **adaptations**, according to the passage on page 548?

   A. traits that make an organism better able to survive in its environment
   B. traits that all members of a species possess
   C. traits that are learned and not inherited
   D. traits that appear only when two recessive alleles are inherited

4. The more similar the DNA of two species, the more closely related they are. Scientists have used modern DNA analysis to trace the evolutionary relationships among Darwin's 13 species of finches. DNA analysis revealed that the finch species all had very similar DNA. Thus, Darwin was correct when he proposed that they had evolved from a common ancestor.

   Which of the following best explains why DNA analysis provides better evidence to support the hypothesis that Darwin's finches evolved from a common ancestor than the scientific methods that Darwin used?

   A. DNA analysis takes less time than observation.
   B. DNA analysis is easier to do than observing birds in the wild.
   C. DNA analysis provides more objective data than observation does.
   D. Technological methods of obtaining evidence are inferior to observation.

**Review your work using the explanations that start on page 726.**

LESSON 8

# Organization of Ecosystems

An **ecosystem** is an area consisting of a community of organisms—plants, animals, fungi, bacteria—and the physical environment in which they live—soil, air, water, and climate. Earth as a whole is an enormous ecosystem called the **biosphere**. Smaller ecosystems include meadows, ponds, wetlands, and tidal zones. A healthy ecosystem contains a diversity of organisms. Some of the organisms, such as green plants, are called **producers** because they use energy from the sun to make their own food through photosynthesis. Other organisms, called **consumers**, depend on producers to meet their energy needs. These organisms eat plants, or eat organisms that eat plants, to get energy. The complex pattern in which energy passes through an ecosystem is called a **food web**. A simple food web for a wooded area is shown here.

KEY IDEAS

- An ecosystem is a community of organisms and their physical environment.
- Energy passes through an ecosystem from the sun, to producers (green plants), to consumers.
- Carbon, oxygen, nitrogen, and water cycle through the biosphere from the living to the nonliving components and back again.

ON THE TASC TEST

*On the TASC Science Test, you may see diagrams, like the one on this page, which contain arrows. Follow the directions of the arrows to understand the process.*

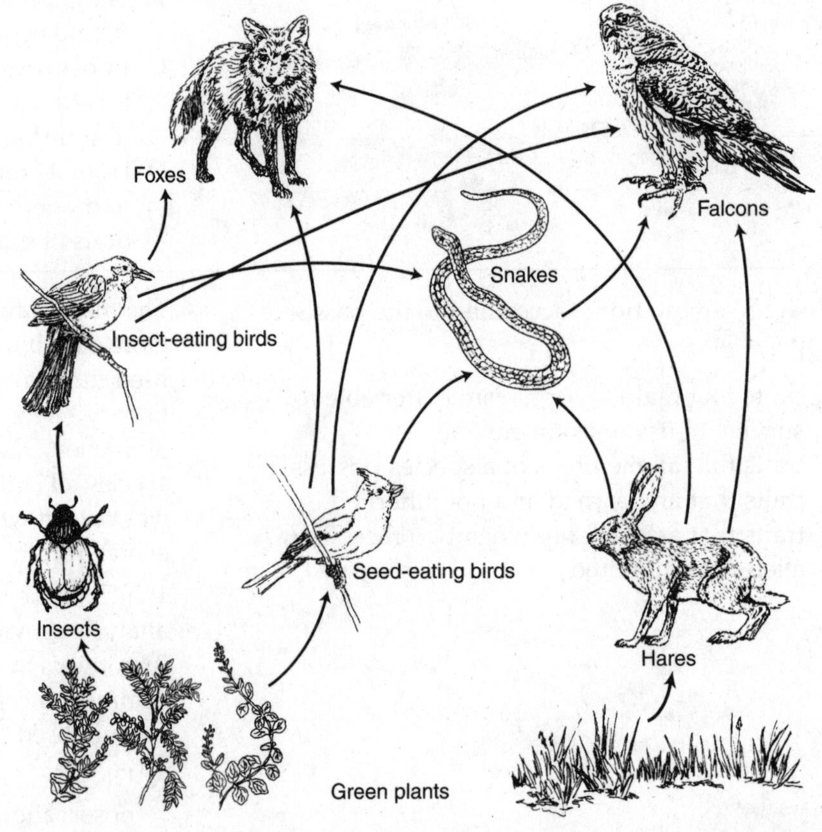


Carbon, oxygen, nitrogen, and water also cycle through ecosystems from the living to the nonliving components and back again. As discussed in Lesson 2, carbon and oxygen cycle through the biosphere as a result of photosynthesis and cellular respiration. Nitrogen cycles between the land, organisms, and the air through chemical processes. Water cycles between the oceans and other surface water, the air, land, and organisms through evaporation, condensation, precipitation, and transpiration from plants.

# PRACTICE 8

1. According to the passage, what is the ultimate source of energy for the food web on page 550?

   A. green plants
   B. mammals
   C. soil, air, and water
   D. the sun

2. Suppose most of the foxes in the woodland ecosystem on page 550 were hunted and killed. Which of the following is most likely to happen as a result?

   A. The amount of plant life in the woodland would increase.
   B. The populations of hares and seed-eating birds would increase.
   C. The populations of insects and insect-eating birds would decrease.
   D. The population of snakes would decrease.

3. Which of the following is most similar to a naturally occurring ecosystem?

   A. a diorama with dried vegetation and stuffed animals
   B. an aquarium with aquatic plants and herbivorous tropical fish
   C. a house with central air conditioning and heating
   D. a supermarket with a large section of fresh fruits and vegetables

4. In most cases, changes in one aspect of an ecosystem result in reactions in other parts of the ecosystem, restoring balance. In some cases, however, changes can be so great that the original ecosystem is replaced with another. When this occurs naturally, as when grasses are replaced by taller plants, shrubs, and eventually trees, it is called succession.

   Which of the following statements is supported by the information above?

   A. When changes are introduced into an ecosystem, its balance is permanently disrupted.
   B. Succession is usually caused by human destruction of an ecosystem.
   C. The intentional replacement of a wooded area by a field of cultivated wheat is an example of succession.
   D. The natural replacement of lichens by mosses and ferns, and then shrubs, is an example of succession.

5. Although more than three-quarters of the atmosphere is nitrogen, atmospheric nitrogen cannot be used directly by plants and animals. Instead, certain bacteria and blue-green algae take nitrogen from the air and, through a process called nitrogen fixation, turn it into compounds that plants can use. Nitrogen-fixing bacteria are found in the roots of some plants such as peas and beans. When these plants are present, the nitrate content of the soil is increased. Nitrates are absorbed by plants, which are eaten by consumers. Eventually the nitrogen returns to the soil in excrement and when organisms die.

   What is the role of nitrogen-fixing bacteria in the nitrogen cycle?

   A. to decompose dead plants and animals
   B. to add nitrogen to the atmosphere
   C. to turn atmospheric nitrogen into compounds plants and animals can use
   D. to take nitrogen from blue-green algae and turn it into compounds plants can use

**Review your work using the explanations that start on page 726.**

### STUDY ADVICE

Ecosystems are an area of emphasis on the TASC Science Test. Be sure to carefully review your work on this practice set to make sure you understand these concepts.

# LIFE SCIENCE PRACTICE QUESTIONS

1. Cell membranes are selectively permeable, allowing some substances to pass through and blocking others. The movement through the cell membrane takes place by means of passive or active transport. In passive transport, materials like water move through the cell's membrane without using any of the cell's energy. Active transport is the movement of materials in the cell from areas of low concentration to areas of high concentration. In active transport, the cell uses energy to move substances in and out. For example, transport proteins use energy when they carry molecules into and out of the cell.

   What is the main difference between passive transport and active transport?

   A. Active transport involves the passage of water, and passive transport does not.
   B. Active transport requires the cell to use energy, and passive transport does not.
   C. Active transport is used by animal cells, and passive transport is used by plant cells.
   D. Active transport takes substances out of the cell, and passive transport brings them in.

2. Ben set up an experiment to prove that ivy plants take in water through their roots. He took a jar, put an ivy plant in the open jar, and filled the jar with water to cover only the roots of the ivy. After a week, he checked the water level in the jar and found it had gone down. Ben concluded that the plant had absorbed water through its roots.

   Why does Ben have insufficient proof for his conclusion?

   A. Ben should have put more ivy plants in the open jar.
   B. Ben should have put several plants of different species in the open jar.
   C. The water level in the jar might have gone down because of evaporation.
   D. There should have been soil in the jar rather than water.

**Questions 3 and 4 refer to the following information and diagram.**

A pedigree shows the pattern of inheritance of a trait in a family. In a pedigree, circles represent females; squares represent males. A completely shaded shape indicates that the person has the trait. A half-shaded shape indicates the person carries the recessive form of the gene for the trait but does not have the trait. An unshaded shape indicates the person neither has nor carries the trait. In the following pedigree, Megan is a carrier of the genetic disorder cystic fibrosis, although she is healthy.

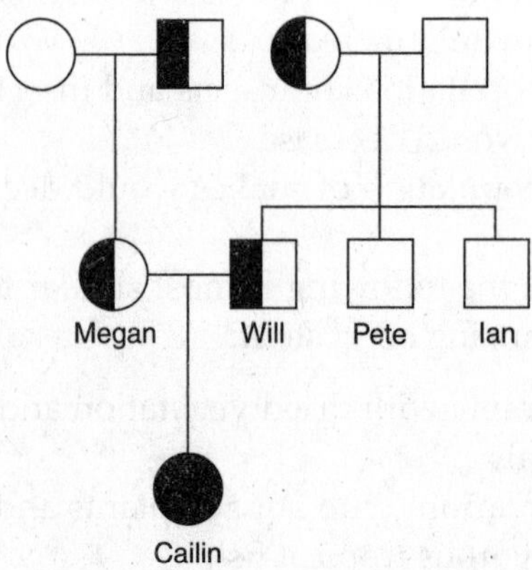


3. Which of the following people is a carrier of cystic fibrosis?

   A. Megan's mother
   B. Megan's father
   C. Will's father
   D. Pete

4. Which of the following best explains why Megan's and Will's families were surprised to learn Cailin had inherited cystic fibrosis?

   A. Megan and Will are carriers of cystic fibrosis.
   B. Some of Will's distant ancestors had cystic fibrosis.
   C. Megan's father and Will's mother are carriers of cystic fibrosis.
   D. No one in either Megan's or Will's immediate family has cystic fibrosis except Cailin.

**Questions 5 through 7 refer to the following paragraph and diagram.**

Mitosis is a type of cell division in which two daughter cells are formed that have the same genetic material as the parent cell. Before mitosis starts, each chromosome in the nucleus duplicates itself to produce two sections, called chromatids, which are linked. Those chromatids then split, so that each daughter cell has DNA identical to that of the parent cell and to that of the other daughter cell. The function of the spindle fiber in mitosis is to control the movement of chromatids during mitosis. During the metaphase, for example, the spindle fiber helps to align the chromatids in a line across the middle of the cell so that the chromatids can divide evenly. The spindle fibers then direct the movement of the chromatids after they split, ensuring that each daughter cell has a full set of identical chromatids.

**The Process of Mitosis**

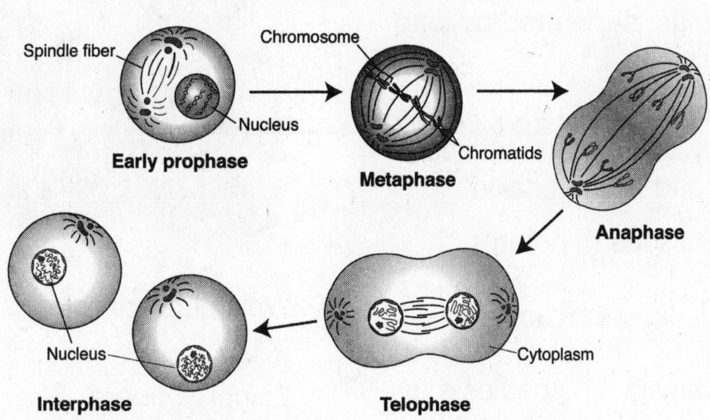


5. During which stage do the chromosomes line up across the middle of the cell?
   A. early prophase
   B. metaphase
   C. telophase
   D. interphase

6. Which of the following is true based on the paragraph and diagram?
   A. After mitosis, one of the resulting daughter cells is larger than the other one.
   B. After mitosis, the two daughter cells have their own nuclei.
   C. The first stage of mitosis is the division of the cell into two separate cells.
   D. The first stage of mitosis involves the formation of cytoplasm.

7. What is the function of the spindle during mitosis?
   A. to duplicate the chromosomes
   B. to control the movement of chromosomes
   C. to dissolve the nuclear membrane
   D. to help divide the cytoplasm for the two daughter cells

8. Charles Darwin thought that evolution took place gradually, with tiny changes eventually adding up to major change in a species. If this view is right, then there should be fossils, remains of long-dead organisms, that show the intermediate stages of evolution in a species. However, the fossil record often shows no intermediate forms for long periods of time. Instead, fossils of a species appear to suddenly become distinctly different. To account for this, some modern scientists have hypothesized that species evolve during short periods of rapid, major change, separated by long periods of relative stability.

   Which of the following hypotheses may also explain why evolutionary change sometimes seems to occur rapidly and dramatically?

   A. Organisms with soft tissues may form fossils.
   B. Fossils usually form in layers of sedimentary rock.
   C. The fossil record for any given species may be incomplete.
   D. Fossils do not provide evidence for evolution.

9. Blood consists of blood cells and proteins suspended in a yellowish liquid called plasma. Red blood cells carry oxygen to the body. White blood cells protect the body against infection. Plasma transports nutrients and hormones to the body's cells and removes waste.

   Which answer choice below describes some of the main functions of blood?

   A. energy production and movement
   B. movement and cell repair
   C. cell repair and respiration
   D. nutrient transport and immune defense

**Questions 10 and 11 refer to the following diagram.**

**Tooth Cross Section**

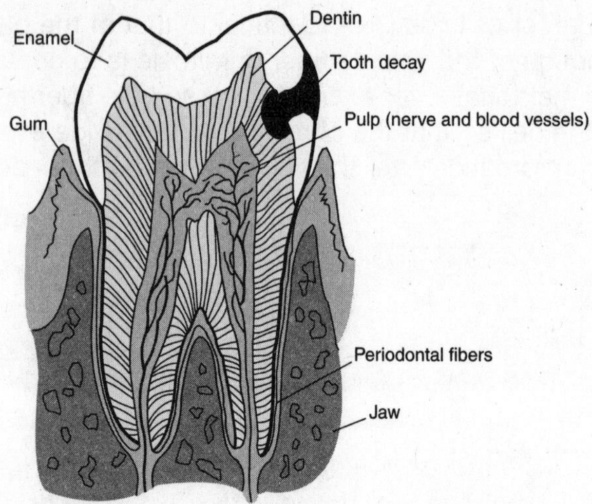


10. Which material covers the tooth's top surface?

   A. enamel
   B. nerve fibers
   C. blood vessels
   D. periodontal fibers

11. Tooth decay can eat away at the structure of a tooth. Tooth decay begins at the surface, but it must reach the pulp, which contains many nerve endings, before it will cause extreme pain. That suggests that the dentin contains __________.

   A. few or no nerve endings
   B. many nerve endings
   C. more minerals than the enamel
   D. fewer minerals than the enamel

---

12. The carrying capacity of an ecosystem is the maximum number of organisms it can support. If the carrying capacity is exceeded, there will not be enough resources, and one or more species will decline until a balance of organisms and resources is reached.

   Which of the following is an example of people overloading the carrying capacity of an ecosystem?

   A. using a park for recreation
   B. grazing too many cattle on grassland
   C. adding a room to a suburban house
   D. banning shellfishing in polluted waters

13. Classification is the grouping of organisms based on similarities in their traits and their evolutionary histories. In the past, scientists classified organisms based primarily on a visual analysis of their structures and on the fossil record. Today, DNA analysis of selected genes is overturning many traditional classifications. For example, it was thought that sperm whales and dolphins, both of which have teeth, were closely related. However, DNA analysis revealed that sperm whales are actually more closely related to baleen whales, which do not have teeth.

    What is the reason that DNA analysis has led to changes in the classification of organisms?

    A. DNA analysis provides more fundamental, accurate data than does a visual analysis of structures and fossils.
    B. Traditional classification was based on the erroneous assumption that organisms could be grouped by similarities.
    C. When organisms possess similar structures, it always means that they are closely related.
    D. When data from DNA analysis conflict with data from structural analysis, usually the structural data are correct.

14. *Homeothermy* refers to the maintenance of a constant body temperature in warm-blooded animals, such as dogs and human beings. Warm-blooded animals have specific body processes to help them gain or lose heat. For example, sweating helps cool the body through the evaporation of water, and shivering helps generate heat in cold environments.

    Which of the following is most likely an example of a homeothermic process in dogs?

    A. panting
    B. healing after a wound
    C. reproduction
    D. grooming

**Questions 15 through 17 refer to the following graph.**

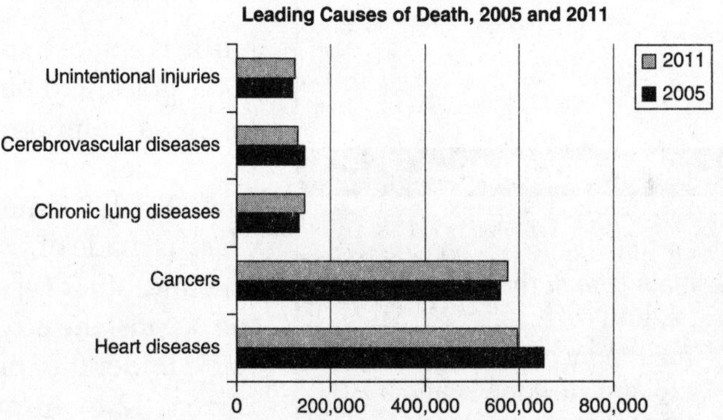


Source: National Center for Health Statistics

15. How many of the five causes of death depicted in the graph produced more deaths in 2011 than in 2005?

    A. 2
    B. 3
    C. 4
    D. 5

16. Compare the number of deaths from heart disease in 2005 to the number of deaths from heart disease in 2011. Of the causes of death depicted in the graph, that difference represents the

    A. biggest increase
    B. biggest decrease
    C. smallest increase
    D. smallest decrease

17. Which of the following approximately expresses the percentage change in deaths from heart diseases from 2005 to 2011? You MAY use your calculator.

    A. 8% increase
    B. 8% decrease
    C. 92% increase
    D. 92% decrease

**Review your work using the explanations that start on page 727.**

# Earth and Space Science

# LESSON 1

## KEY IDEAS

- Earth is made up of three main layers: the crust, mantle, and core.
- The theory of plate tectonics explains how the seafloor spreads, how major landforms are created, and how the continents move.
- At the margins between plates, plates move away from or toward each other, or they slide past each other.

## TASC TEST TIP

*When you read a multiple-choice question, try to answer it before you read the choices. If one of the choices is similar to your answer, it is probably correct.*

# Structure of Earth

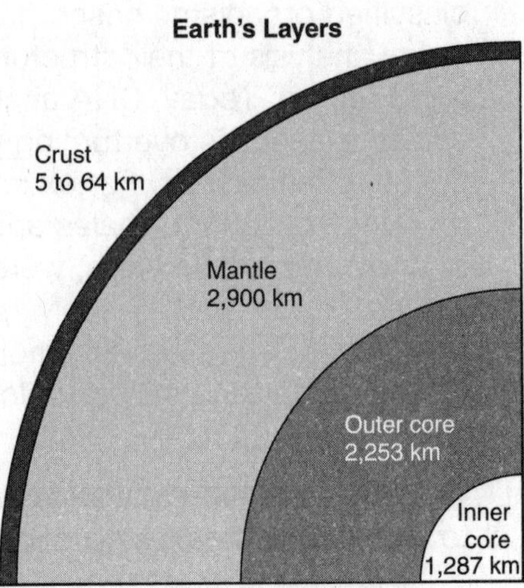


Earth is almost spherical, flattened at the poles, and bulging at the equator. It is composed of three main layers: the crust, the mantle, and the core. Earth's outer layer, its solid **crust**, is made of granite, basalt, gabbro, and other types of rock. Under the oceans, the crust is 3 to 6.8 miles thick; under the continents, the crust is from 12 to 40 miles thick. Below the crust is the molten **mantle**; it consists of silica and metal-rich minerals. The **core** has two layers: the outer core, which is mostly liquid iron, and the inner core, which is mostly solid iron. Extreme heat and pressure characterize the core.

The **theory of plate tectonics** explains phenomena of Earth's crust: seafloor spreading, the formation of major landforms, and the movement of continents. According to this theory, Earth's crust is made up of **tectonic plates** that fit together like a crude jigsaw puzzle. These plates move relative to one another at a rate of up to 15 centimeters (6 inches) a year. At the boundaries between plates, major landforms such as mountain ranges, volcanoes, ocean trenches, and mid-ocean ridges form, and earthquakes occur. There are three types of plate boundaries, or **margins**.

- At a **constructive margin**, two plates are moving apart and new crust is forming. Molten material from the mantle below wells up in the space between the plates, hardens, and forms new crust, usually at a mid-ocean ridge. For example, at the Mid-Atlantic Ridge, new crust is forming, causing the seafloor to spread and grow by about 5 centimeters (2 inches) a year.
- At a **destructive margin**, two plates are colliding and crust is being destroyed. When a continental plate collides with an oceanic plate, the denser oceanic crust may be forced under the other plate, forming a deep trench. When two plates consisting of continental crust collide, the crust crumples to form mountain ranges such as the Andes. When two plates with oceanic crust collide, a deep ocean trench is formed.
- At a **transform**, or **conservative**, **margin**, two plates are sliding by one another, and no crust is created or destroyed. For example, the San Andreas fault in California is the boundary between the North American plate and the Pacific plate, which is sliding northwest, causing many earthquakes.

As the plates move, they carry the continents with them. Scientists believe that a single large continent, **Pangaea**, existed about 250 million years ago. It gradually broke apart, and over millions of years the pieces (which are today's continents) drifted into the locations they are in today.

# PRACTICE 1

1. What does the theory of plate tectonics explain?

   A. changes in Earth's crust
   B. changes in Earth's mantle
   C. changes in the composition of Earth's layers
   D. why there is extreme heat and pressure in Earth's core

2. One similarity between Earth's inner and outer cores is that both

   A. consist primarily of iron
   B. consist primarily of granite
   C. are mostly liquid
   D. are mostly solid

3. The Japan Trench off the coast of Japan is part of the boundary between an oceanic plate called the Pacific plate and a continental plate called the Eurasian plate. At the trench, the Pacific plate is forced beneath the Eurasian plate, causing earthquakes in Japan.

   The Japan Trench is an example of which type of crustal feature?

   A. a tectonic plate
   B. a mid-ocean ridge
   C. a constructive margin
   D. a destructive margin

4. Which of the following provides evidence that the present-day continents were once one large continent that broke apart?

   A. Australia is a large, continent-sized island.
   B. Eurasia is the largest land mass on Earth today.
   C. Australia and Antarctica are located in the Southern Hemisphere.
   D. The west coast of Africa seems to fit into the east coast of the Americas.

5. Which of the following is implied by the fact that seafloor spreading at the Mid-Atlantic Ridge is causing the Atlantic Ocean to widen by about 5 centimeters a year?

   A. The Mid-Atlantic Ridge is thousands of miles long.
   B. The Mid-Atlantic Ridge is the largest underwater structure in the Atlantic Ocean.
   C. The continents of North America and Europe are moving apart.
   D. The continents of North America and Europe are growing larger at the Mid-Atlantic Ridge.

6. Which of the following is a theory rather than a fact?

   A. The San Andreas fault is the boundary between the North American and Pacific plates.
   B. A single large landmass called Pangaea existed about 250 million years ago.
   C. The Earth's crust is composed of rocks like granite, basalt, and gabbro.
   D. Earthquakes often occur along tectonic plate boundaries.

**Review your work using the explanations that start on page 728.**

**STUDY ADVICE**

If you have found yourself struggling to focus on science for long periods of time, feel free to mix in some of the other lessons in the book to lengthen your study session while maintaining concentration. For example, a study session might involve some science learning and some review of reading and writing skills from Units 1 and 2.

LESSON 2

# Earth's Resources

A **resource** is anything that is needed by humans to survive. Natural resources include air, water, soil, minerals, and energy. Air is involved in respiration, climate, and weather. Water is used for drinking, cooking, bathing, agriculture, and industrial processes. Less than 3 percent of the world's water is fresh water. **Soil** is the layer of loose disintegrated rock, organic matter, living organisms, air, and water in which rooted plants, including agricultural plants, grow. **Minerals** are the naturally forming inorganic substances with a crystalline structure of which rocks are made; they have many uses—from talcum powder to uranium fuel rods to diamond drill bits. **Energy resources** include fossil fuels, flowing water, wind, **solar energy**, and **geothermal energy**.

### KEY IDEAS

- Natural resources include air, water, soil, minerals, and energy.
- Resources are either renewable (having an endless supply) or nonrenewable (having a limited supply).
- Conservation efforts limit the consumption, overuse, and pollution of the natural environment.

Resources can be classified as nonrenewable or renewable. **Nonrenewable resources** are those that take millions of years to form naturally; when they are used up, there is no replacement for them. For example, fossil fuels, including peat, coal, natural gas, and oil, are nonrenewable resources because they form over millions of years from decaying plant remains. Fossil fuels are our main source of energy for heating, transportation, and the generation of electricity. Soil and minerals are also nonrenewable resources.

### ON THE TASC TEST

*Some Earth and space science questions may deal with the impact of humans on natural resources and the environment.*

**Renewable resources** are those whose supply will not run out, either because there is an unlimited supply, as is the case with **solar energy** (energy from the sun), or because the resource cycles through the environment, as is the case with water. In addition to solar energy, renewable energy resources include the water power of flowing rivers, tidal and wave power from the movement of ocean water, wind power from the movement of air, and geothermal power from the heat in the Earth's crust. All of these are used as alternative sources of energy to generate electricity.

People harm or destroy natural resources through consumption, overuse, and pollution. For example, some scientists estimate that we have already consumed between one-tenth and one-quarter of the world's supply of oil. Soil is subject to agricultural overuse and erosion. Air is polluted by fossil fuel emissions and its **ozone layer** is depleted by the release of compounds called chlorofluorocarbons (CFCs) into the atmosphere. Water is polluted by sewage, industrial waste, and agricultural and urban runoff.

**Conservation** is any action taken to preserve natural resources and protect the natural environment. Conservation involves a wide range of activities, including building more efficient combustion engines to reduce gasoline consumption; using catalytic converters to reduce the harmful emissions of burning fossil fuels; developing technologies to exploit renewable sources of energy; recycling glass, plastic, and metal wastes; using agricultural methods that protect the soil; building water treatment and sewage treatment plants; safely disposing of radioactive wastes; and cleaning up sites heavily polluted by industry.

# PRACTICE 2

**Questions 1 through 3 refer to the following graph.**

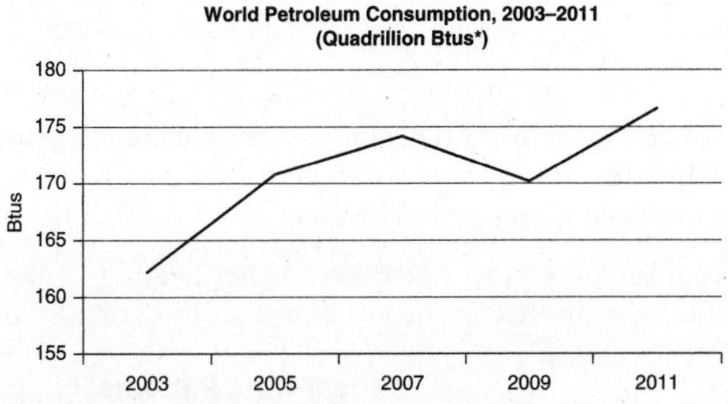


Source: US Energy Information Administration
*Btus = British thermal units, a measure of energy

1. Approximately how many quadrillion Btus of petroleum were consumed in 2011?

A. 160
B. 170
C. 174
D. 177

2. Between its low point in 2003 and its high point in 2011, the approximate range of the data regarding world petroleum consumption was ______ quadrillion Btus.

A. 10
B. 14
C. 162
D. 176

3. Which of the following sentences best summarizes the information in the graph?

A. World petroleum consumption increased by about 14 quadrillion Btus between 2003 and 2011.
B. World petroleum consumption fell by about 4 quadrillion Btus between 2005 and 2009.
C. World petroleum consumption increased by roughly 50 percent between 2003 and 2007.
D. World petroleum consumption fell by roughly 50 percent between 2007 and 2009.

4. Which of the following proverbs best expresses the views of a conservationist?

A. All that glitters is not gold.
B. Every cloud has a silver lining.
C. Oil and water don't mix.
D. Waste not, want not.

5. The overall demand for water in the developed nations is rising. But it is not rising as quickly as people had predicted it would. In fact, the rate of water consumption per person per year in developed nations has actually dropped. This means that even though population has increased and industrial output has grown, the rate at which people withdraw water from reservoirs, rivers, and aquifers has slowed.

Which of the following is a likely reason for the drop in per person consumption of water in developed countries?

A. Vast new supplies of water have been found in the developed nations.
B. Developed nations have started using water more efficiently than they did in the past.
C. Developed nations are sharing water resources with each other.
D. Some developed nations export fresh water to other nations that lack it.

6. Soil erosion occurs when soil is worn away by the natural action of wind, water, and ice or by deforestation and poor farming practices. If soil erosion continues for a long time, it can lead to the formation of deserts. Some scientists estimate that the world lost about 20 percent of its farm topsoil between 1950 and 1990. Contour plowing, planting trees to serve as windbreaks, and other techniques can all reduce soil erosion.

Which of the following statements is supported by the information above?

A. All deserts originally formed as a result of soil erosion.
B. Most soil erosion is caused by poor farming practices.
C. Improved farming techniques can completely halt soil erosion.
D. Soil erosion is caused by both natural forces and the actions of people.

**Review your work using the explanations that start on page 728.**

LESSON 3

# Weather and Climate

**KEY IDEAS**

- Weather is the day-to-day change in atmospheric conditions at a particular place. Climate is the average long-term weather conditions in a region.
- Weather and climate are influenced by global air patterns and ocean currents.
- Daily weather is caused by the movement of air masses and is predicted by meteorologists.

**ON THE TASC TEST**

*About 33% of the questions on the Science Test will cover Earth and space science topics.*

**Weather** is the day-to-day change in conditions in the **atmosphere** at a particular place on Earth. **Climate**, on the other hand, is the average weather conditions of a large region over a long period of time.

All weather and climate ultimately arise from the uneven heating of the Earth. The sun's rays fall more directly at the equator than they do at the North and South Poles. This resulting uneven heating causes global wind circulation patterns: the warm air at the equator rises, creating an area of low pressure, and moves toward the poles. Cold air at the poles sinks, creating an area of high pressure, and moves toward the equator. The result is a pattern of **prevailing winds** in both the Northern and Southern hemispheres.

**Global Wind Patterns**

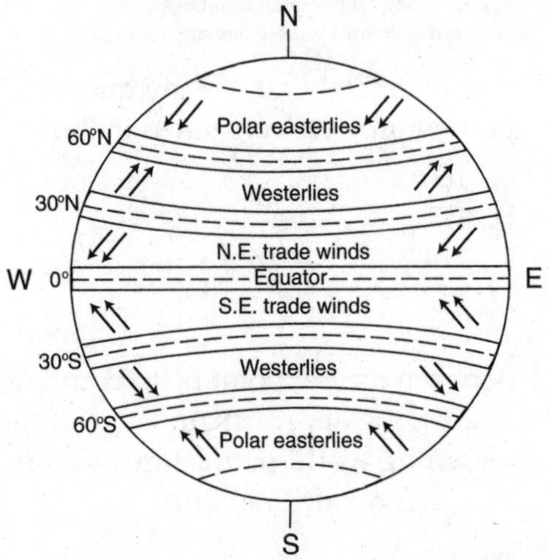

N
60°N
Polar easterlies
30°N
Westerlies
N.E. trade winds
W 0°
Equator
E
S.E. trade winds
30°S
Westerlies
60°S
Polar easterlies
S

Another major influence on weather and climate, also caused by the uneven heating of Earth, is the worldwide pattern of **ocean currents**. Ocean currents are caused by the wind and by variations in the density of water (warm water is less dense than cold water). Ocean currents help transfer heat from the equatorial regions to the poles.

Daily weather patterns are caused by the movements of **air masses**, large bodies of air with similar temperature, humidity, and pressure. The boundary between two air masses is called a **front**. A **cold front** occurs where a cold air mass overtakes and displaces a warm air mass. A **warm front** occurs where a warm air mass rises over a cold air mass. An **occluded front** occurs when a cold front catches up with a warm front and the two weather systems merge. Clouds and **precipitation** are characteristic of fronts.

**Meteorologists** study the short-term weather patterns and data of particular areas. At meteorological stations around the world, temperature, humidity, cloud cover, wind, and other weather data are collected. Satellites and radar are also used to collect weather data. Weather predictions are based on comparing present weather conditions to computer models of previous weather conditions and storm systems in an area. When hurricanes, tornadoes, blizzards, or floods are forecast, meteorologists issue storm watches and warnings. For example, if a hurricane might reach an area in 24 to 36 hours, a hurricane watch is issued. If a hurricane is expected in an area in less than 24 hours, a hurricane warning is issued, and people are urged to take precautionary measures against the storm.

# PRACTICE 3

1. The diagram of global wind patterns on page 560 suggests that weather systems between 30°N and 60°N generally move in which direction?

   A. northeast to southwest
   B. northwest to southeast
   C. southeast to northwest
   D. southwest to northeast

2. Based on the diagram on page 560, how do the prevailing winds in the Northern Hemisphere compare to the prevailing winds in the Southern Hemisphere?

   A. The winds in the Northern Hemisphere blow faster than those in the Southern Hemisphere.
   B. The winds in the Northern Hemisphere are a mirror image of those in the Southern Hemisphere.
   C. The winds in the Northern Hemisphere blow east and those in the Southern Hemisphere blow west.
   D. The winds in the Northern Hemisphere blow west and those in the Southern Hemisphere blow east.

3. Hurricanes are violent storms with high winds and rain that form over the ocean. They cover an area 300 to 600 miles across and move relatively slowly—between 5 and 15 miles per hour. Meteorologists can now predict their paths with a great deal of accuracy.

   Which of the following technologies best accounts for accurate hurricane tracking?

   A. anemometers, which measure wind speed
   B. thermometers, which measure air temperature
   C. the Beaufort wind scale, a method of estimating wind speed
   D. satellites, which transmit cloud photos and weather data

4. Which of the following help even out the unbalanced heating of Earth as a whole?

   A. precipitation associated with fronts
   B. local air masses
   C. tornadoes, blizzards, and floods
   D. global wind and ocean current patterns

**Questions 5 and 6 refer to the following chart.**

**Layers of the Atmosphere**

| Layer | Altitude | Temperature |
|---|---|---|
| Troposphere | 0 to 6 miles | Average 59°F |
| Stratosphere | 6 to 31 miles | –76°F to 32°F |
| Mesosphere and ionosphere | 31 to 50 miles | 32°F to –212°F |
| Thermosphere | 50 to 435 miles | Up to thousands of degrees |

5. For which of the following statements does the chart provide evidence?

   A. The higher you go in the atmosphere, the colder it gets.
   B. The higher you go in the atmosphere, the less oxygen there is to breathe.
   C. The highest layer of the atmosphere is the stratosphere.
   D. The highest temperatures in the atmosphere are in the thermosphere.

6. In which atmospheric layer does most human activity take place?

   A. troposphere
   B. stratosphere
   C. mesosphere
   D. thermosphere

**Review your work using the explanations that start on page 728.**

## STUDY ADVICE

Earth's systems (such as winds and weather) and Earth's place in the universe (which you will learn about in the next lesson) are areas of high emphasis on the TASC Science Test. Be sure to absorb these lessons.

LESSON 4

# Earth in the Solar System

The **solar system** consists of the sun, a star; the **planets**; their **satellites**, or moons; the **asteroids**, sometimes called the minor planets; and the comets. The sun contains more than 99 percent of the **mass** (amount of matter) in the solar system, and all the other celestial bodies revolve around it, held by the force of **gravity**.

The eight planets of the solar system include (in order from the sun) Mercury, Venus, Earth, Mars, Jupiter, Saturn, Uranus, and Neptune. Mercury, Venus, Earth, and Mars are called the **inner planets** because they are relatively close to the sun. They are all small, rocky planets. Jupiter, Saturn, Uranus, and Neptune are called the **outer planets** because of their great distance from the sun. The outer planets are gas giants. Some facts about the planets are presented in the following chart.

**The Planets of Our Solar System**

| Planet | Distance from sun | Diameter | Number of moons | Rotation period (day) | Revolution period (year) |
|---|---|---|---|---|---|
| Mercury | 36 million mi | 3,030 mi | None | 59 Earth days | 88 Earth days |
| Venus | 67 million mi | 7,500 mi | None | 243 Earth days | 225 Earth days |
| Earth | 93 million mi | 7,923 mi | 1 | 23 hr 56 min 4.1 sec | 365 days 5 hr 48 min 46 sec |
| Mars | 142 million mi | 4,210 mi | 2 | 24 hr 37 min | 687 Earth days |
| Jupiter | 484 million mi | 88,700 mi | 50 | 9 hr 51 min | 11.86 Earth years |
| Saturn | 0.9 billion mi | 75,000 mi | 53 | 10 hr 14 min | 29.46 Earth years |
| Uranus | 1.8 billion mi | 31,600 mi | 27 | 17 hr 12 min | 84 Earth years |
| Neptune | 2.8 billion mi | 30,200 mi | 13 | 16 hr 7 min | 164.8 Earth years |

Earth is unusual among the planets in that about 70 percent of its surface is covered by water. It is the only celestial body in the solar system on which life is known to exist. Earth's rocky satellite, the moon, is the fifth largest satellite in the solar system. It has no atmosphere, but it does have some surface ice, which was discovered in 1998. The moon revolves around Earth once every 27 days. During the lunar month, the moon appears to go through a series of **phases**—changes in the proportion of its surface that is in shadow. The cycle of phases takes approximately 29 days. U.S. astronauts landed on the moon in several missions from 1969 to 1972, making it the only celestial body visited by crewed spacecraft.

## KEY IDEAS

- The solar system consists of the sun; the planets; their satellites, or moons; the asteroids; and the comets.
- There are eight planets: Mercury, Venus, Earth, Mars, Jupiter, Saturn, Uranus, and Neptune.
- The moon revolves around Earth every 27 days and appears to go through phases.

## TASC TEST TIP

*Some Science Test questions are based on detailed charts similar to the one on this page. Read the question carefully and select only the specific information needed to answer the question.*

# PRACTICE 4

1. According to the chart on page 562, which of the planets takes the shortest time to revolve, or complete its orbit, around the sun?

   A. Mars
   B. Saturn
   C. Neptune
   D. Mercury

2. According to the chart, which of the following planets is most similar to Earth?

   A. Mercury
   B. Venus
   C. Jupiter
   D. Neptune

3. Before 1781, the only planets that were known were the ones visible to the naked eye: Mercury, Venus, Mars, Jupiter, and Saturn. In 1781, William Herschel, an astronomer who made his own superb and powerful telescopes, discovered a strange "star" that appeared as a greenish disk rather than a point of light. A few nights later, he observed that this "star" had moved relative to the background of the other stars. Herschel realized he had discovered another planet. It was named Uranus, after the Greek sky god. Later it was found that Uranus had actually been observed at least 20 times before, as far back as 1690, but each time it had been identified as a star.

   Which of the following is an unstated assumption that could help account for the fact that Uranus was misidentified as a star prior to 1781?

   A. Uranus takes 84 earth years to revolve around the sun.
   B. The length of a day on Uranus is about 17 hours.
   C. Uranus was not clearly visible with the telescopes generally in use at the time.
   D. Uranus was not visible when it was on the other side of the sun.

4. According to the chart on page 562, which of the following planets has the most moons?

   A. Jupiter
   B. Saturn
   C. Uranus
   D. Neptune

5. According to some estimates, it would cost about ten times more to send a crewed mission to Mars to collect geologic samples and look for life than it would cost to send a robotic mission. Some people think that a human mission would yield much more relevant data, justifying the additional cost. Others think there is no scientific reason to send crewed missions, which are costly and risky, when robotic missions will do.

   Which of the following values is most likely to provide the motivation to send a crewed mission to Mars despite the risk and the additional cost?

   A. a desire to provide equal opportunities for astronauts of all nationalities
   B. a desire for economic development
   C. a desire to demonstrate the superiority of computers over humans
   D. faith in human judgment and decision-making skills

6. The structure of the solar system, with the massive sun at the center and many objects revolving around it, is most similar to the structure of which of the following?

   A. a DNA molecule, with its twisted spiral shape
   B. an atom, with a dense nucleus and electrons orbiting the nucleus
   C. the electromagnetic spectrum, with waves of different lengths and frequencies
   D. the planet Earth, with its layers of crust, mantle, and core

**Review your work using the explanations that start on page 729.**

LESSON 5

# The Expanding Universe

KEY IDEAS

- Stars are globes of hydrogen and helium that produce their own heat and light through nuclear reactions.
- The sun is one star in the Milky Way galaxy, a large group of stars.
- The Big Bang theory helps explain the origin of the universe. According to this theory, the universe began as a compact spot of matter that exploded.

ON THE TASC TEST

*Some questions on the Science Test require that you understand cause-and-effect relationships.*

Our sun is a medium-sized yellow **star**, a globe of helium and hydrogen gas that produces its own heat and light through nuclear reactions. Stars like our sun generally have a 10-billion-year life cycle. They begin as **protostars**, which form from clouds of condensing gases and dust called **nebulae**. As a protostar reaches a certain density and temperature, nuclear reactions begin, releasing huge amounts of energy. At this point, the star is known as a **main-sequence star**, the longest stage in the stellar life cycle. After billions of years, the star begins to run out of hydrogen fuel. It may become a **red giant**. In time, the red giant becomes unstable and collapses, either exploding as a **supernova** and leaving behind a **neutron star** or losing mass slowly to become a **white dwarf**. A neutron star can be very dense, and gravity sometimes causes it to collapse in on itself, producing a **black hole**. Black holes are so called because their gravity is so great that light cannot escape from them.

The sun is just one star in a huge group of stars called the **Milky Way** galaxy. **Galaxies** consist of between one million and one trillion stars, along with clouds of gas and dust, which are held together by the force of gravity. Galaxies are classified according to their shape: spiral, barred-spiral, elliptical, and irregular. The Milky Way is a spiral galaxy. A spiral galaxy has a dense circular center with arms spiraling out from the core. Our solar system is located in one of the arms, called the Orion arm, of the Milky Way galaxy.

The Milky Way galaxy is part of a group of galaxies called the **Local Group**. There are 27 known galaxies in the Local Group, of which the Milky Way and the Andromeda galaxy are the largest.

The **universe** consists mostly of empty space with galaxies scattered throughout. Besides galaxies with stars at every stage of the life cycle, the universe has other bodies: **brown dwarfs** are objects that are less massive than a star but more massive than a planet; **pulsars** are thought to be rotating neutron stars that emit pulses of energy at regular intervals; and **quasars** are distant starlike objects that emit more energy than a hundred galaxies.

**Cosmologists** study the origin, properties, and evolution of the universe. One theory about the beginning of the universe is called the **Big Bang**. According to this theory, the universe began in a hot, superdense state smaller than an atom. The Big Bang caused all this compacted material to be flung outward, accounting for the still-expanding universe. There is evidence to support the Big Bang theory. First, galaxies appear to be moving away from one another in every direction, as if they had originated at a common point. Second, scientists have detected cosmic background radiation left over from the Big Bang. Cosmologists do not know what caused the Big Bang, but from the current rate of expansion of the universe, they estimate its age to be between 10 and 20 billion years.

# PRACTICE 5

**Questions 1 through 3 refer to the following paragraph and chart.**

In astronomy, magnitude is an indication of the brightness of a celestial body. Magnitudes are measured along a scale from positive to zero to negative, with brightness increasing as magnitude decreases. Apparent magnitude is the brightness as seen from Earth, either by the naked eye or photographically. Absolute magnitude is a measure of the actual brightness of an object. It is defined as the apparent magnitude of the object as seen from 32.6 light-years from the object.

**The Five Brightest Stars**

| Star | Distance from Earth (light-years) | Apparent magnitude | Absolute magnitude |
|---|---|---|---|
| Sirius | 8.7 | – 1.47 | + 1.41 |
| Canopus | 180 | – 0.71 | – 4.7 |
| Alpha Centauri | 4.3 | – 0.1 | + 4.3 |
| Arcturus | 36 | – 0.06 | – 0.2 |
| Vega | 26 | + 0.03 | + 0.5 |

**1.** If all the stars listed in the chart were viewed from 32.6 light-years away, then which of them would be the brightest?

A. Sirius
B. Canopus
C. Alpha Centauri
D. Vega

**2.** Which of the following would be true of a star with a position 32.6 light-years from Earth?

A. The star's absolute magnitude would be less than that of Alpha Centauri.
B. The star's apparent magnitude would be greater than its absolute magnitude.
C. The star's apparent magnitude would be equal to its absolute magnitude.
D. The star's apparent magnitude would be greater than that of Arcturus.

**3.** A magazine article makes the following statement about stars: A star's apparent magnitude and its absolute magnitude must always be close in value.

Which of the following explains why the magazine's statement is incorrect?

A. Stars form from huge masses of dust and gas.
B. The absolute magnitude of a star indicates how bright the star looks to viewers on Earth.
C. The apparent magnitude of a star is a measure of the amount of light the star puts out.
D. Not all stars are located approximately 32.6 light-years from Earth.

---

**4.** The sun is about 4.7 billion years old. Based on the information on page 564, at which stage of its life cycle is the sun?

A. It is a protostar.
B. It is a main-sequence star.
C. It is a neutron star.
D. It is a white dwarf.

**5.** Pluto has a diameter of just 1,438 miles. It is made mostly of ice and frozen rock. It is very small and has an irregular orbit. It was originally classified as the ninth planet from the Sun, but it has been recategorized as a dwarf planet within the Kuiper belt.

Which of the following is not a factual detail about Pluto?

A. Pluto has a diameter of 1,438 miles.
B. Pluto is made mostly of ice and frozen rock.
C. Pluto has an irregular orbit.
D. Pluto should be classified as a dwarf planet.

**Review your work using the explanations that start on page 729.**

# EARTH AND SPACE SCIENCE PRACTICE QUESTIONS

1. Tides are the twice-daily rise and fall of water along the shores of the oceans. Tides are caused mainly by the gravitational pull of the moon, and secondarily by the gravitational pull of the sun. The highest tides, called spring tides, occur when the sun, moon, and Earth are in line. Other high tides, called neap tides, occur when the sun and moon are at right angles with respect to Earth.

   Which of the following statements is supported by the information above?

   A. The moon and the sun exert the greatest pull on Earth's oceans when these bodies are all in a line.
   B. When the moon is at right angles to the sun with respect to Earth, tides do not occur along the ocean shore.
   C. Spring tides occur only in the spring, and neap tides occur only in the fall.
   D. Neap tides are generally higher than spring tides.

2. Geothermal energy is energy extracted from naturally occurring steam, hot water, or hot rocks in Earth's crust. It is used to heat buildings and generate electricity in areas where hot magma (melted rock) is close to the surface.

   In which of the following places is geothermal energy most likely to be used?

   A. Arizona, a state where abundant sunshine provides solar energy
   B. Cape Cod, a peninsula formed from glacial deposits of sand
   C. Iceland, an island nation in the Atlantic with active volcanoes
   D. Saudi Arabia, a Middle Eastern nation with ample oil and gas reserves

**Questions 3 and 4 refer to the following paragraph and graph.**

Scientists think there may be more matter and energy in the universe than has been directly observed because of some gravitational effects that cannot be explained otherwise. Dark matter and dark energy, so-called because they do not interact with light, may account for most of the stuff of the universe. In fact, ordinary matter, made of the chemical elements, may form only 4 percent of the universe.

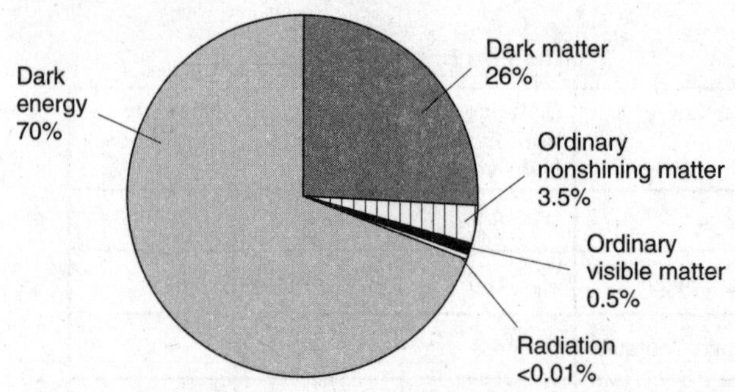


Source: Ostriker, Jeremiah and Paul Steinhardt, "The Quintessential Universe" *Scientific American,* January, 2001

3. According to the graph, about what percentage of the universe may consist of matter that does not interact with light?

   A. less than 0.01 percent
   B. 0.5 percent
   C. 4 percent
   D. 26 percent

4. Which of the following statements is a fact rather than a hypothesis about the makeup of the universe?

   A. Dark energy may account for 70 percent of the universe.
   B. Dark matter may account for 26 percent of the universe.
   C. Dark energy may cause gravitational effects.
   D. Ordinary matter is made of the chemical elements.

## Questions 5 through 8 refer to the following map.

**World Climate Zones**

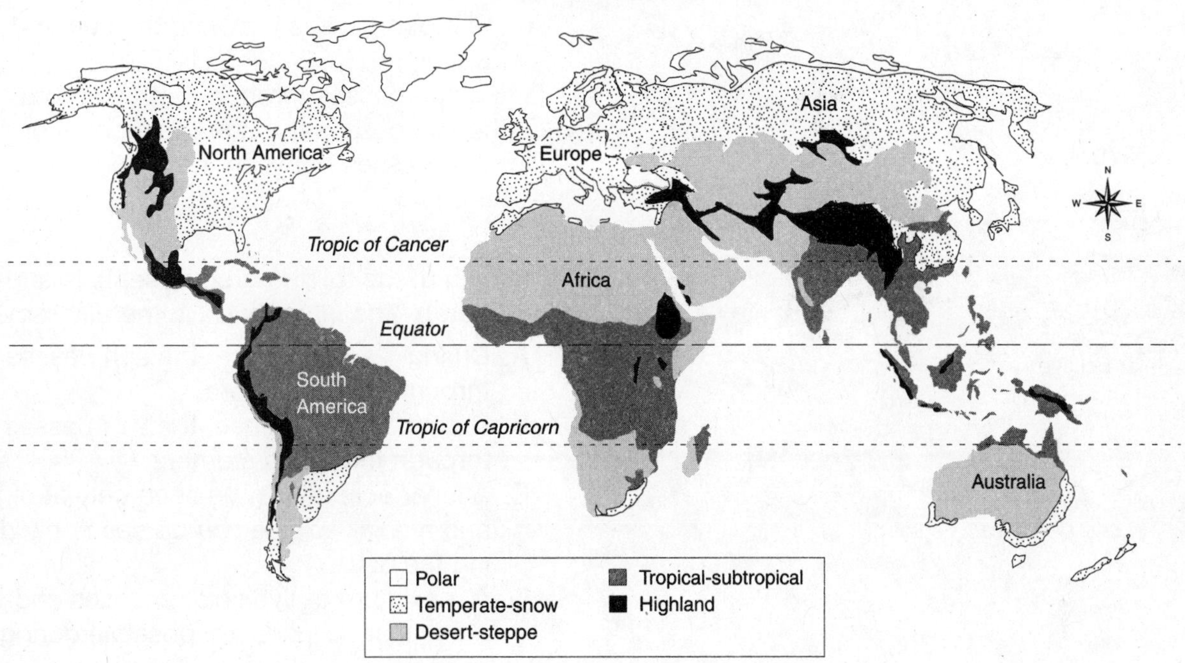


5. Which type of climate is characteristic of areas along the equator?
   A. polar
   B. temperate-snow
   C. desert-steppe
   D. tropical-subtropical

6. Which of the following statements is supported by information on the map?
   A. The continent with the least area of desert-steppe climate is Europe.
   B. Australia's climate is entirely tropical-subtropical.
   C. Africa and South America do not have areas with highland climate.
   D. Only North America has a large temperate-snow climate zone.

7. Temperate-snow climate zones hold only one-third of the world's people yet have historically produced about two-thirds of the world's wealth. This discrepancy between population and productivity could be best explained by the fact that temperate-snow climate zones, relative to other climate zones, have more
   A. farm output.
   B. seasons.
   C. tropical rain forests.
   D. mountains.

8. The continents shown have, on average, how many different climate zones? (Consider Europe and Asia as the single continent of Eurasia, and consider the island of New Guinea to be part of the Australian continent.)
   A. 3.2
   B. 4.6
   C. 5.6
   D. 6.4

**<u>Questions 9 and 10</u> are based on the following diagrams.**

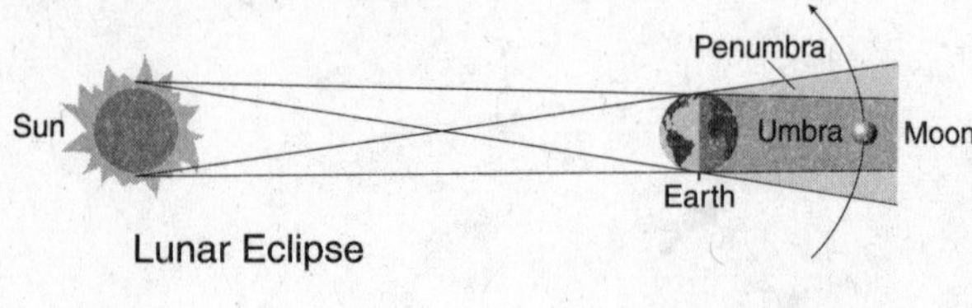


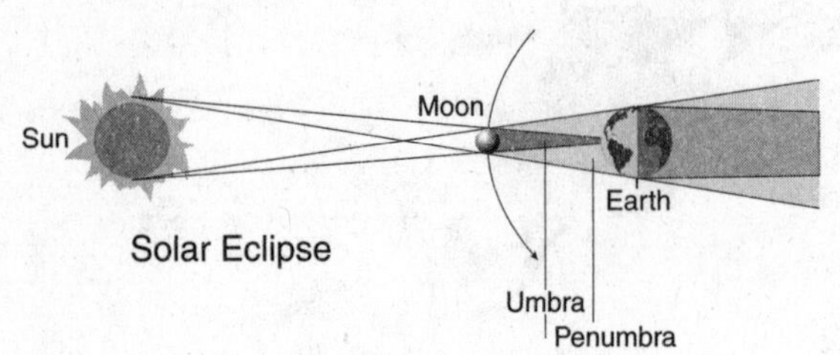


9. Based on the diagram, a lunar eclipse occurs when
   A. the moon passes between the sun and Earth.
   B. the sun passes through Earth's umbra.
   C. the sun passes through the moon's umbra.
   D. Earth passes between the moon and the sun.

10. Which of the following statements is supported by the information in the diagram?
    A. During a solar eclipse, the sun passes through Earth's umbra.
    B. During a lunar eclipse, the sun passes through the moon's umbra.
    C. A lunar eclipse can be seen only at night and a solar eclipse can be seen only during the day.
    D. A maximum of five solar eclipses and thirteen lunar eclipses are possible during each year.

**<u>Questions 11 and 12</u> are based on the passage below.**

Acid rain is a form of precipitation caused by the release of sulfur dioxide and nitrogen oxide into the atmosphere. Acid rain is comprised of a mixture of wet and dry deposition. If the acidic chemicals in the air blow into places with wet weather, the acids fall to the ground in the form of rain or fog, affecting plant and animal life. In drier climates, the acidic chemicals mix into dust or smoke, which will then fall to the ground or on trees or buildings. These deposits are later washed off by rainstorms. The addition of water to these chemicals makes the resulting mixture more acidic.

The acidic chemicals themselves form as a byproduct of burning fossil fuels, such as coal, oil, diesel, and gasoline. Acid rain alters the chemical balance of lakes, affecting aquatic life. It also alters the chemical balance of soil, harming plant life. In addition, it damages buildings and statues.

11. Which of the following technologies can help reduce acid rain?
    A. a diesel locomotive, which burns diesel fuel to produce energy that is used to turn the wheels
    B. an electric power plant that burns coal to heat water and produce steam to drive turbines, which power the generator
    C. a refinery, which purifies metals, petroleum, and other substances into a more useful form
    D. a catalytic converter, a device in the exhaust system of a vehicle that reduces harmful emissions from the engine

12. Which of the following would reduce the amount of ecological damage caused by acid rain?
    A. replacing a coal-burning power plant with a solar farm
    B. coating metal and stone statues in silicone
    C. constructing buildings from materials resistant to erosion
    D. using diesel fuel instead of gasoline in automobiles

**Questions 13 through 15 refer to the following diagram.**

**The Rock Cycle**

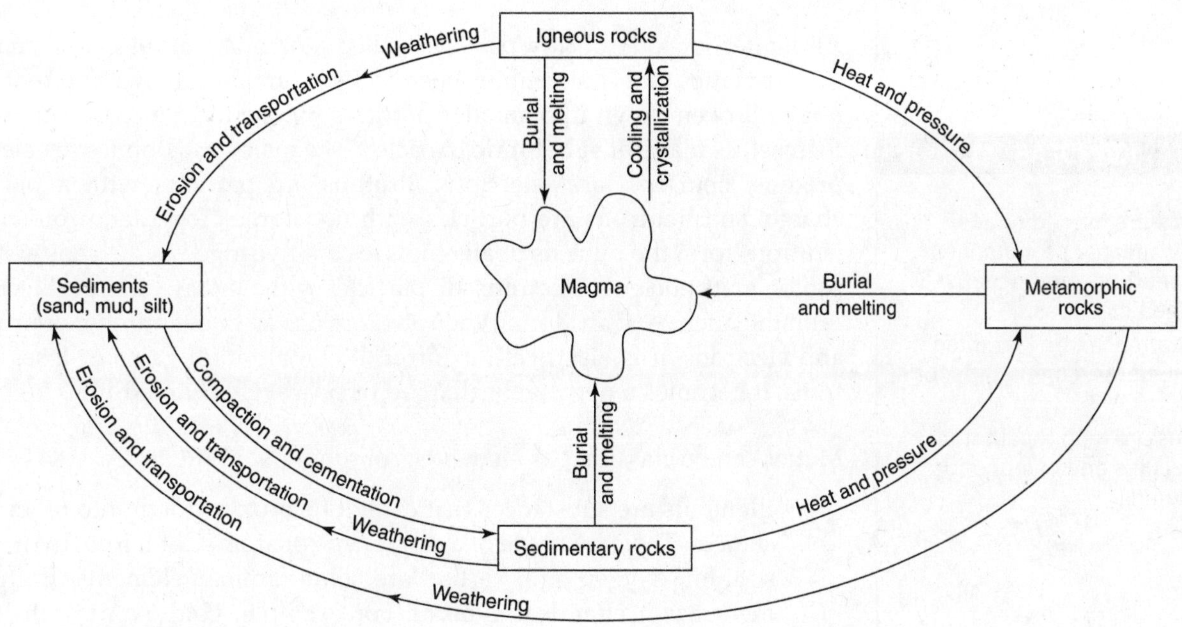


13. Which of the following statements is supported by the information in the diagram?
    A. The rock cycle is a continuous process of rock formation, destruction, and reformation.
    B. Sedimentary rocks form under conditions of heat and pressure.
    C. Metamorphic rocks form under conditions of compaction and cementation.
    D. Sediments form only from sedimentary rocks.

14. Fossils can form when plant or animal remains are buried under sand, mud, or silt. These materials can be compacted to form rock. A hiker knew she had found a(n) __________ because it contained the fossilized imprint of a fish.
    A. igneous rock
    B. sedimentary rock
    C. destructive margin
    D. rock formed from magma

15. What is magma?
    A. melted rock
    B. crystallized rock
    C. cooled rock
    D. eroded rock

16. In open-pit mining, surface layers of soil and rock are stripped to obtain coal, ores, or minerals. It is cheaper than shaft mining because there is no underground work.

    Which of the following is the most likely reason that some countries restrict open-pit mining?
    A. There are no underground deposits.
    B. Open-pit mining is more dangerous than shaft mining.
    C. Open-pit mining destroys valuable land.
    D. Open-pit mining yields low-grade coal, ores, and minerals.

**Review your work using the explanations that start on page 729.**

LESSON 1

# Atoms and Molecules

All matter is made of tiny particles called atoms. An **atom** is the smallest unit of matter that can combine chemically with other matter and that cannot be broken down into smaller particles by chemical means. Atoms are themselves made of **subatomic particles**. The major subatomic particles are protons, neutrons, and electrons. **Protons** are particles with a positive charge, and **neutrons** are particles with no charge. Together, protons and neutrons form the nucleus of all atoms except hydrogen, which has just one proton in its nucleus. **Electrons** are particles with negative charge. Electrons orbit the nucleus of an atom. When an atom has an equal number of protons and electrons, it is electrically neutral. When an atom gains or loses electrons, it becomes a negatively charged or positively charged **ion**.

### KEY IDEAS

- Atoms are formed of positively charged protons, neutral neutrons, and negatively charged electrons.
- All matter can be classified as elements, compounds, or mixtures.
- Atoms are held together in molecules and compounds by bonds.

Matter can be classified as elements, compounds, or mixtures.

- **Elements** are substances that cannot be broken down into other substances. They are made of a single type of atom. Gold, iron, hydrogen, sodium, oxygen, and carbon are some familiar elements. Each element has a **chemical symbol**. For example, gold is Au, iron is Fe, hydrogen is H, sodium is Na, oxygen is O, and carbon is C.
- **Compounds** are substances formed of two or more elements chemically combined in a definite proportion. Compounds have properties that differ from the properties of the elements that they contain. For example, at room temperature, water is a liquid compound made of the elements hydrogen and oxygen, which, uncombined, are both gases. Compounds are represented by **chemical formulas**. The chemical formula for water is $H_2O$, indicating that a water molecule is made of two atoms of hydrogen and one atom of oxygen.
- **Mixtures** are physical combinations of two or more substances that keep their own properties. For example, salt water is a mixture.

### TASC TEST TIP

*If you are having trouble choosing the correct answer to a multiple-choice question, eliminate the options that are clearly wrong. Of the remaining options, choose the one that makes the most sense.*

When elements combine to form **molecules** or ionic compounds, their constituents are held together by **bonds**. There are two main types of bonds: covalent and ionic. In a **covalent bond**, atoms share a pair of electrons, each atom contributing one electron. For example, the compound water is held together by covalent bonds. In an **ionic bond**, atoms gain or lose electrons to become ions, and the attraction between positively (+) and negatively (–) charged ions holds the compound together. For example, sodium chloride (NaCl), commonly called table salt, is an ionic compound.

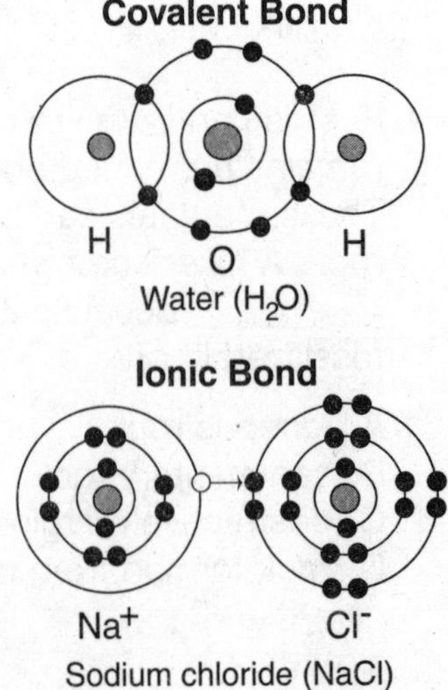

# PRACTICE 1

1. Sodium is represented by the chemical symbol Na and chlorine is represented by the chemical symbol Cl. According to the text and the diagram on page "Atoms and Molecules" on page 570, what happens when sodium chloride forms?

   A. The sodium atom loses an electron, becoming positively charged, and the chlorine atom gains an electron, becoming negatively charged.
   B. The sodium atom gains an electron, becoming negatively charged, and the chlorine atom loses an electron, becoming positively charged.
   C. The sodium atom gains an electron, becoming positively charged, and the chlorine atom loses an electron, becoming negatively charged.
   D. The sodium and chlorine atoms share a pair of electrons, becoming ions and forming a covalent bond.

2. Water is composed of two atoms of hydrogen and one atom of oxygen and has the formula $H_2O$. Glucose, a simple sugar, consists of 6 atoms of carbon, 12 atoms of hydrogen, and 6 atoms of oxygen.

   Which of the following is the chemical formula for glucose?

   A. CHO
   B. ${}_6C_{12}H_6O$
   C. $C^6H^{12}O^6$
   D. $C_6H_{12}O_6$

3. Based on the information on page 570, ions are

   A. electrically neutral atoms.
   B. atoms that have gained electrons to become positively charged.
   C. atoms that have lost electrons to become negatively charged.
   D. atoms that have either gained electrons to become negatively charged or lost electrons to become positively charged.

4. In 1911, British scientist Ernest Rutherford performed experiments that increased our knowledge of atomic structure. He bombarded an extremely thin sheet of gold foil with helium nuclei. (Helium nuclei, also called alpha particles, consist of two protons and two neutrons). He found that most of the helium nuclei passed right through the foil. Only a few were deflected back toward the source. On the basis of this experiment, Rutherford concluded that an atom has a dense nucleus with electrons orbiting it, but consists mostly of empty space.

   Which of the following is evidence that atoms consist mostly of empty space?

   A. Helium nuclei consist of two protons and two neutrons.
   B. Most of the alpha particles passed right through the gold foil.
   C. A few alpha particles were deflected off the gold foil and bounced back toward the source.
   D. Electrons orbit a dense nucleus consisting of protons and neutrons.

5. The number of protons in the nucleus of an atom is called the atomic number. Each element has a unique number of protons in its nucleus and therefore a unique atomic number.

   The atomic number of the element sodium is 11. How many electrons does a non-ionic sodium atom have?

   A. 10
   B. 11
   C. 12
   D. 22

**Review your work using the explanations that start on page 730.**

LESSON 2

# Properties and States of Matter

**KEY IDEAS**

- Matter has mass and occupies space.
- The three states of matter include solid, liquid, and gas. A substance's state of matter can be changed by adding or removing heat.
- Solutions are a type of mixture. The solute is the dissolved substance. The solvent is what the solute is dissolved in. Solvents and solutes can be any of the states of matter.

**ON THE TASC TEST**

*Approximately 33% of the questions on the TASC Science Test are about physical science topics.*

**Matter** is anything that has mass and takes up space. The **mass** of an object is the amount of matter that it contains, and its **weight** is a measure of the gravitational force exerted on it. The mass of an object like a shovel never changes, but its weight can change. For example, a shovel weighs less on the moon than it does on Earth because the gravitational pull of the moon is less than that of Earth.

Under most conditions, there are three **states of matter**, as described below:

- **Solids** have a definite shape and volume because the molecules of which they are made occupy fixed positions and do not move freely. In some solids, such as minerals, the molecules form an orderly pattern called a **crystal**.
- **Liquids** have a definite volume but no definite shape because the molecules in a liquid are loosely bound and move freely. For this reason, a liquid conforms to the shape of its container.
- **Gases** have no definite shape or volume. The attraction between the molecules of a gas is very weak. In consequence, the molecules of a gas are far apart and are always in motion, colliding with one another and with the sides of the container.

The states of matter can be changed by adding or removing heat energy. When heat is applied to a solid, it melts. This happens because the motion of the solid's molecules increases until the bonds between them are loosened, allowing them to flow freely. The temperature at which a solid becomes a liquid is its **melting point**. When heat is applied to a liquid, it boils and evaporates, turning into a gas as the motion of its molecules increases. The temperature at which a liquid becomes a gas is called its **boiling point**. When heat is removed from a gas, the motion of its molecules decreases and it turns into a liquid. The temperature at which a gas becomes a liquid is its **condensation point**. When heat is removed from a liquid, the motion of its molecules slows until it solidifies. The temperature at which a liquid becomes a solid is its **freezing point**. The temperatures at which a substance changes state are unique properties of that substance. For example, water boils at 100°C (212°F) and freezes at 0°C (32°F). Water is also the only substance that is found naturally in all three states on Earth.

As you learned in Lesson 1, mixtures are physical combinations of two or more substances that keep their original properties. A **solution** is a mixture (such as salt water) that is uniform throughout and that contains ions, atoms, or molecules of two or more substances. The substance in a solution that is dissolved is called the **solute**. The substance in which the solute is dissolved is the **solvent**. In salt water, for example, salt is the solute and water is the solvent. Water is called the universal solvent because so many substances dissolve in it. However, solutions are not always liquids. They can be solids, as when two or more metals are combined in an **alloy**, or they can be gases, as when oxygen and nitrogen are combined in the air.

# PRACTICE 2

1. Which of the following physical changes involve adding heat to a substance?

   A. melting and boiling
   B. boiling and condensing
   C. condensing and freezing
   D. evaporating and condensing

2. Density is the amount of mass in a particular volume of a substance. It can be expressed in grams per cubic centimeter. The chart shows the densities of some common substances.

**Densities of Substances**

| Substance | Density (g/cm³) |
|---|---|
| *Solids* | |
| Lead | 11.35 |
| Iron | 7.87 |
| Aluminum | 2.70 |
| *Liquids* | |
| Chloroform | 1.49 |
| Water | 1.00 |
| Ethyl alcohol | 0.79 |
| *Gases* | |
| Oxygen | 0.0013 |
| Nitrogen | 0.0012 |
| Helium | 0.0002 |

   Which of the following statements is supported by the information provided?

   A. Water is the least dense liquid on Earth.
   B. Solids are usually denser than liquids and gases.
   C. Density increases as the volume of a substance increases.
   D. Density decreases as the force of gravity decreases.

3. It is well known that the boiling point of water is 100° Celsius. More viscous, or thicker, substances often have higher boiling points. Glycerin, for example, boils at 290° Celsius, while olive oil boils at 300° Celsius.

   By what percentage is the boiling point of glycerin greater than that of water?

   A. 150%
   B. 190%
   C. 200%
   D. 290%

4. Water is different from most other substances. It changes from gas to liquid to solid at temperatures that are common on Earth. When it freezes, its molecules form a crystal lattice, so that its solid form is less dense than its liquid form. It is the most common solvent.

   Which of the following is a conclusion about water rather than a supporting statement?

   A. Water is a unique substance on Earth.
   B. Water changes state at temperatures typical on Earth.
   C. Frozen water is less dense than liquid water.
   D. Water is Earth's most common solvent.

5. When a solute is dissolved in a liquid solvent, the freezing point of the solution is lower than the freezing point of the pure liquid.

   In which of the following situations is this property of liquid solutions applied?

   A. Sugar dissolves in water more quickly if the solution is heated.
   B. Antifreeze added to water in a car's radiator lowers the freezing point below 0°C.
   C. The oil and vinegar in salad dressing is mixed more thoroughly by shaking.
   D. Spherical ice "cubes" freeze more quickly than regular ice cubes do.

6. A suspension is a mixture in which the distributed particles are larger than those of the solvent and in which the particles, in time, will settle out.

   Which of the following is a suspension?

   A. pure gold
   B. pure oxygen
   C. salt water
   D. dusty air

**Review your work using the explanations that start on page 730.**

# Chemical Reactions

**KEY IDEAS**

- In a chemical reaction, the atoms or ions of one or more reactants are rearranged, yielding one or more products. Mass is conserved during chemical reactions.
- Chemical reactions can be represented by chemical formulas.
- Chemical reactions are either endothermic or exothermic.

**ON THE TASC TEST**

*There is no penalty for getting a wrong answer on the test. If you are not sure of your answer, make your best guess, flag the question, and come back to it if you complete the test before time is up.*

In a **chemical reaction,** the atoms or ions of one or more substances, called the **reactants,** are rearranged, resulting in one or more different substances, called the **products.** For example, iron, water, and oxygen react to form hydrated iron oxide, or rust. Matter is neither created nor destroyed during a chemical reaction, so the mass of the products always equals the mass of the reactants. This principle is known as the **law of conservation of mass.**

Chemical reactions can be represented by **chemical equations**. Chemical equations show the reactants on the left side and the products on the right side. They also show the proportions of the reacting substances—how many units of each reactant and each product are involved. Because of the law of conservation of mass, a chemical equation must balance. That is, the total number of atoms of an element on the left side must be equal to the total number of atoms of the element on the right side. Here is the chemical equation that represents the burning of hydrogen and oxygen to yield water.

$$2H_2 + O_2 \rightarrow 2H_2O$$

Restated in words: two molecules of hydrogen ($H_2$) combine with one molecule of oxygen ($O_2$) to form two molecules of water ($H_2O$). The equation balances because there are four hydrogen atoms on the left side and four on the right; there are two oxygen atoms on the left side and two on the right. To balance a chemical equation, you can change the coefficients—the number of units of any reactant or product. However, you *cannot* change the subscripts of any reactant or product.

Energy is involved in all chemical reactions. A reaction in which the reactants absorb energy from their surroundings is an **endothermic reaction**. For example, when you scramble an egg, you add heat energy and the egg solidifies. A reaction in which energy is given off with the products, usually in the form of heat or light, is an **exothermic reaction**. When you burn wood in a fireplace, for example, heat and light energy are given off. **Activation energy** is the amount of energy needed to get a reaction going. These energy relationships can be shown in graphs like those below.

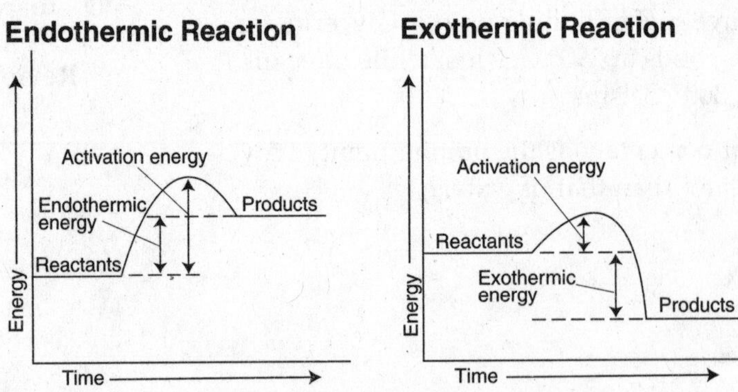

1. Which of the following chemical formulas represents the reaction in which copper (Cu) and oxygen gas ($O_2$) combine to form copper oxide (CuO)?

A. $2CuO \rightarrow 2Cu + O_2$
B. $Cu + O_2 \rightarrow 2CuO$
C. $2Cu + O_2 \rightarrow 2CuO$
D. $Cu + 2O_2 \rightarrow 2CuO$

2. Which of the following procedures would provide evidence for the law of conservation of mass?

A. Weigh the reactants, conduct the reaction in an open container, and weigh the products.
B. Weigh the reactants, conduct the reaction in a sealed container, and weigh the products.
C. Measure the volume of the reactants, conduct the reaction in a sealed container, and measure the volume of the products.
D. Write the chemical formula for the reaction and balance it.

3. Juanita would like to cook a scrambled egg on her gas stove. When she first turns on the stove's burner, the electronic ignition produces a spark that sets the gas burning. As the gas burns, it heats the frying pan. As the egg cooks, it absorbs the heat energy from the pan and solidifies.

Which form of energy is needed for each step of Juanita's cooking process?

A. Igniting the gas requires endothermic energy, the gas burning releases activation energy, and the egg solidifying requires exothermic energy.
B. Igniting the gas requires activation energy, the gas burning releases endothermic energy, and the egg solidifying requires exothermic energy.
C. Igniting the gas requires activation energy, the gas burning releases exothermic energy, and the egg solidifying requires endothermic energy.
D. Igniting the gas requires endothermic energy, the gas burning releases exothermic energy, and the egg solidifying requires activation energy.

4. In the graphs on page 574, what does the horizontal axis represent?

A. the instant the reaction starts
B. the instant the reaction stops
C. the time during which the reaction occurs
D. the energy level in the reaction

5. Organic compounds are those containing linked carbon atoms that form bonds with other atoms, usually hydrogen, oxygen, nitrogen, and/or sulfur. Organic compounds consist of chains, branching chains, rings, and other complex arrangements of carbon atoms with which other atoms bond. One type of organic compound is a polymer, a large long-chain or branching structure made up of many repeated simple units, called monomers. Natural polymers include cellulose. Synthetic polymers include polyethylene and other types of plastics.

Which of the following is taken for granted and not stated by the writer of the paragraph above?

A. Compounds are substances consisting of two or more elements chemically combined in a definite proportion.
B. Organic compounds have linked carbon atoms forming bonds with other atoms, usually hydrogen, oxygen, nitrogen, and/or sulfur.
C. Chains are among the arrangements carbon atoms in an organic compound can take.
D. Plastics are synthetic polymers and cellulose is a natural polymer.

6. An acid is a compound that releases hydrogen ions ($H^+$), or protons, in the presence of water. Strong acids, like battery acid and stomach acid, are corrosive. Most dilute acids, like lemon juice, have a sour taste.

A base is a compound that accepts hydrogen ions, or protons. Household cleaners like ammonia, lye, and bleach are bases. When an acid reacts with a base, the product is a salt and water. This reaction is called neutralization.

Which of the following is the best title for this passage?

A. Corrosive Substances
B. Acids and Bases
C. Acids and Bases in the Lab
D. Neutralization Reactions

**Review your work using the explanations that start on page 731.**

Physical Science

## LESSON 4

# The Nature of Energy

**Energy** is defined as the capacity to do work. **Work** is done whenever a force is applied to an object to set it in motion. Thus, anything that can force matter to move, change direction, or change speed has energy.

**KEY IDEAS**

- Anything that can force matter to move, change direction, or change speed has energy.
- Energy comes in many forms and can be converted from one form to another.
- The law of conservation of energy states that energy can neither be created nor destroyed, only changed in form.

**ON THE TASC TEST**

*Since many TASC Science Test questions are based on diagrams and graphs, it is important to carefully read the titles and all of the other information on all graphics. Make sure you understand a graphic before answering questions based on it.*

Energy comes in many forms. **Heat energy** can change a solid to a liquid and a liquid to a gas. It is also involved in most chemical reactions. **Light energy** can create an image by causing the chemicals on a piece of film to react. It provides the energy needed for the process of photosynthesis in green plants. **Electrical energy** can turn a motor, plate a set of flatware with a layer of silver, or store data on a hard drive. **Chemical energy** in food provides the energy humans need for life functions. It heats our buildings when we burn oil, gas, coal, or wood. Chemical energy in batteries provides electricity when the batteries are connected in a circuit. **Nuclear energy** from breaking apart the nuclei of atoms provides energy to produce electricity or power a submarine. **Mechanical energy** turns the axles of a car or the blades of a fan.

Energy can be converted from one form to another. Consider the production and use of electricity. In most electric plants, a fossil fuel (chemical energy) is burned, producing heat energy that turns water to steam. The energy in the steam turns the blades of a turbine, producing mechanical energy. The turbine powers the generator, which produces electrical energy. Electrical energy is used in homes to provide heat energy (in stoves and toasters), light energy (in light bulbs), sound energy (in the stereo), and mechanical energy (in a blender). Even though energy undergoes changes in form, the amount of energy in a closed system remains the same. This principle is known as the **law of conservation of energy**.

Two basic types of energy are **potential energy** and **kinetic energy**. An object has potential energy because of its position; it has kinetic energy when it moves. For example, when you raise a hammer, at the top of your upswing the hammer has potential energy. When you lower the hammer to hit a nail, the hammer has kinetic energy, the energy of motion. When the hammer hits the nail, it transfers energy to the nail. The energy transferred is equal to the work done by the hammer on the nail, and it can be measured in **joules**. The rate of doing work or consuming energy is called **power**, and it can be measured in horsepower (in the English system) or **watts** (joules per second in the metric system).

Physicist Albert Einstein discovered the relationship between energy and mass and expressed it in the equation $E = mc^2$, in which $E$ represents energy, $m$ represents mass, and $c$ represents the speed of light. Since the speed of light is a very large number, the equation indicates there is a great deal of energy in even the tiniest bit of matter. So, for example, in nuclear bombs and nuclear power plants, mass is changed to energy when large atoms are split into two or more smaller atoms with less mass than the original large atom.

# PRACTICE 4

1. Which of the following states the law of conservation of energy?

   A. Potential energy is the energy of position; kinetic energy is the energy of motion.
   B. Energy can be created and destroyed as well as changed in form.
   C. Energy cannot be created or destroyed, but can only change in form.
   D. Energy cannot be created, destroyed, or changed in form.

2. During a power outage, George relied upon his flashlight to move around his home. The flashlight is constructed with wires and a lightbulb enclosed in a plastic casing. It requires batteries to operate.

   Which one of the following types of energy powers George's flashlight?

   A. nuclear
   B. light
   C. mechanical
   D. chemical

3. An oak tree may grow very tall very slowly. It may take the tree a hundred years to absorb light energy and store it as chemical energy, yet only a single winter to be turned into heat energy in someone's wood stove. Which concept does this fact best relate to?

   A. work
   B. power
   C. force
   D. kinetic energy

4. What does Einstein's equation $E = mc^2$ express?

   A. the relationship between electricity and magnetism
   B. the relationship between energy and mass
   C. the speed of light in a vacuum
   D. the relationship between electrical energy and nuclear energy

**Question 5 refers to the following diagram.**

**A Pendulum's Energy**

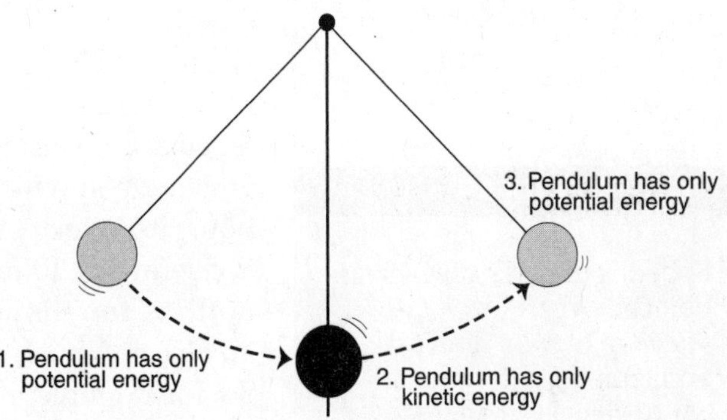


5. Which of the following statements is supported by the information in the diagram?

   A. At the high point of its swing, a pendulum has kinetic energy.
   B. At the high point of its swing, a pendulum has potential energy.
   C. As a pendulum swings through one arc, it loses all its energy.
   D. A pendulum can swing forever because of kinetic energy.

---

6. Heat energy is present in all matter in the form of the kinetic energy of its atoms and molecules. Heat energy can pass from one place to another through conduction: the transfer of kinetic energy from molecules in greater motion (hot areas) to molecules of lesser motion (cold areas). Solid metals like silver and copper are good conductors of heat energy; gases like air are poor conductors.

   What is the reason that air is a poor conductor of heat?

   A. The molecules in air are far apart.
   B. The molecules in air are very large.
   C. The molecules in air do not move.
   D. The molecules in air are very small.

**Review your work using the explanations that start on page 731.**

LESSON 5

# Motion and Forces

Everything in the universe is in motion. Even objects that seem to be at rest, like a building, are moving with Earth's rotation. **Speed** is the rate at which an object moves; **velocity** is its speed in a particular direction. **Acceleration** is the rate at which velocity changes. So a car's speed may be 40 miles per hour; its velocity may be 40 miles per hour toward the north; and it may accelerate by 10 feet per second until its velocity is 50 miles per hour to the north. A **force** is anything that tends to change the state of rest or motion of an object. A push or a pull on an object is a force, as are gravity and friction. So, for example, if you allow a car to coast on a level road, the force of friction will eventually bring it to a stop.

Sir Isaac Newton (1642–1727), an English physicist and mathematician, set down three laws by which the planets and all other objects move when acted upon by a force. These are called the **laws of motion**.

Newton's first law of motion, the **law of inertia**, states that an object at rest will stay at rest until a force acts upon it, and an object in motion will stay in motion at a constant speed in a straight line until a force acts upon it. Objects moving on Earth eventually slow down and stop because of the forces of friction and gravity. A bullet, for example, would continue its forward motion in a straight line, but friction from the air slows it down and the force of gravity pulls it toward the ground.

The second law of motion, sometimes called the **law of motion** or **acceleration**, states that the acceleration of an object depends on its mass and the force acting upon it. The greater the force, the greater the acceleration. The more massive the object, the more force it takes to accelerate it. Additionally, if a constant force acts upon an object, the object will move with constant acceleration in the direction of the force. This is why truck engines are more powerful than car engines: it takes more force to accelerate an object with more mass (a truck) than an object with less mass (a car).

Newton's third law of motion states that for every action, there is an equal and opposite reaction. This law was used to derive the law of conservation of momentum. **Momentum** is related to the amount of energy that a moving object has, and it depends on the mass of the object and its velocity. In fact, momentum is defined as an object's mass multiplied by its velocity. Newton's third law states that when an object is given a certain amount of momentum in a particular direction, some other object must receive an equal momentum in the opposite direction. Another way to state this is to say that all forces exist in pairs, and that all forces are interactions between objects. So, for example, when a bullet is fired out of a gun, the bullet's forward momentum causes the gun to recoil, or move backward.

### KEY IDEAS

- Speed is the rate at which an object moves; velocity is speed in a given direction; acceleration is the rate at which velocity changes.
- A force is anything that changes the state of rest or motion of an object.
- Newton stated three laws of motion that explain the inertia, acceleration, and momentum of objects.

### TASC TEST TIP

*If you are asked to apply a general law or principle of science to a particular situation, ask yourself: "What is similar about this situation and the general principle?"*

# PRACTICE 5

**1.** What is a force?

A. the rate at which an object moves in a particular direction
B. any change in an object's acceleration or deceleration
C. the inertia and momentum of an object at rest
D. anything that changes the rest or motion of an object

**2.** What is inertia?

A. the speed at which an object is moving
B. changes in an object's speed or direction
C. the force needed to move an object a certain distance
D. the tendency of an object to remain at rest or in motion

**3.** The force that is needed to keep an object moving in a circular path is called centripetal force.

Which of the following is an example of motion that requires centripetal force?

A. the tides occurring as a result of the moon's gravitational pull
B. the International Space Station orbiting Earth
C. a parachute slowing as it falls to the ground
D. a gun recoiling as a bullet is fired

**4.** A car is traveling at a velocity of 30 miles per hour across a narrow bridge when it is approached on a collision course by another car traveling at 30 miles per hour. The momentum of each car is propelling it forward, and there is no way to completely avoid an impact. Each driver should attempt to decrease his car's speed to lessen the severity of impact because

A. the momentum of the car decreases when its velocity decreases.
B. the momentum of the car increases when its velocity increases.
C. the momentum of the car decreases when its velocity increases.
D. the momentum of the car remains the same whether its velocity increases or decreases.

**Question 5 refers to the following graph, the paragraph below, and the information on page 578.**

Graphs are often used to convey information about motion. One type of motion graph shows distance and time. Distance is measured from a particular starting point. If the distance graph has a straight, horizontal line, the distance is unchanging and the object is not moving. If the distance graph has a straight line with an upward slope, the distance is changing at a constant rate; this means that the object is moving at a constant speed. If the distance graph is a curve, the object is accelerating or decelerating, depending on the shape of the curve.

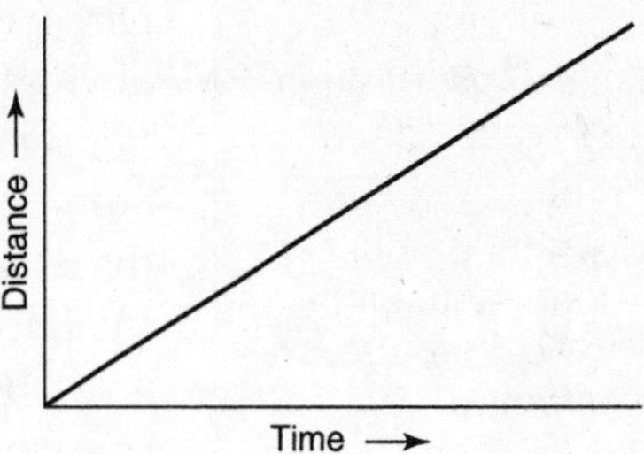


**5.** What does the graph above show?

A. an object that is not moving
B. an object that has a constant speed
C. an object that is accelerating
D. an object that is decelerating

---

**6.** A machine is a device that transmits a force, changing the direction or size of the force and doing work. The force applied to a machine is the effort force; the force it overcomes is the load. Types of simple machines include the inclined plane, wedge, lever, pulley, and wheel-and-axle.

Which of the following statements is supported by the information given?

A. The force a machine overcomes is called the effort force.
B. Work can be done only with machines.
C. Some machines simply change the direction of a force.
D. All machines change both the direction and size of a force.

**Review your work using the explanations that start on page 731.**

LESSON 6

# Electricity and Magnetism

As you recall from your study of atoms, electrons have a negative charge (–), and protons have a positive charge (+). This **electric charge** causes them to exert forces on one another. Particles with like charges repel one another, and particles with unlike charges attract one another. Sometimes electrons are temporarily pulled away from atoms, creating stationary areas of positive and negative charge. This can happen when two objects, like a balloon and a rug, are rubbed together, creating **static electricity**.

### KEY IDEAS

- Particles with like electric charges repel one another, and particles with unlike electric charges attract one another.
- The flow of electrons through a substance is called an electric current.
- An electric current produces a magnetic field, and a moving magnetic field produces an electric current.

The movement of charged particles, usually electrons, is an **electric current**. Direct current flows in one direction only, and it is used in battery-operated devices. Alternating current flows back and forth rapidly, and it is used in household wiring. A material that allows electrons to move freely from atom to atom is called a **conductor**. Metals are good conductors. A material that does not allow electrons to move freely from atom to atom is called an **insulator**. Rubber and plastic are examples of insulators. **Semiconductors** are substances whose ability to conduct electricity is midway between that of a conductor and an insulator. Semiconductors like silicon are used in electronic devices.

An electric current produces a **magnetic field** that affects magnetic substances such as iron in the same way a permanent magnet does. Magnetic fields are produced by moving charged particles. In an **electromagnet**, the charged particles move along a coil of wire connected to a battery or other power source. In a **permanent magnet**, the spinning of electrons creates a magnetic field. Every magnet has two ends, called the north and south poles. The north pole of one magnet attracts the south pole of another magnet; like poles repel one another.

**Magnetic Fields**

Bar magnet

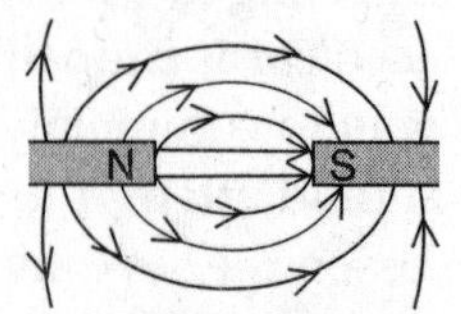

Unlike poles

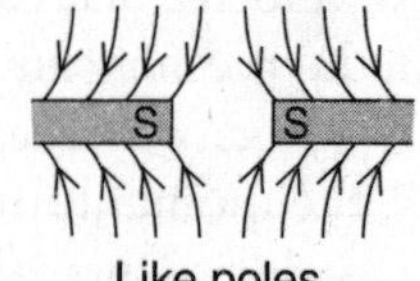

Like poles

### TASC TEST TIP

*You can use your knowledge of everyday things like electricity and motors to help you answer questions on the TASC Science Test.*

Just as an electric current produces a magnetic field, a moving magnetic field produces an electric current. This principle underlies electric motors, generators, and transformers. In an **electric motor**, for example, magnetic fields are produced by electric currents. The magnetic fields push against one another, turning the shaft of the motor. In a **generator**, a moving magnetic field produces electric current. In a **transformer**, an incoming electric current in coiled wire produces fluctuating magnetic fields, which in turn produce an outgoing electric current of a different **voltage**. The difference in voltage is caused by the differing sizes of the wire coils.

# PRACTICE 6

1. Suppose a drawing of two magnets with their north poles facing one another were added to the diagram on page 580. What would the new drawing show?

   A. two poles attracting one another
   B. two poles repelling one another
   C. magnetic lines of force connecting the poles
   D. magnetic lines of force flowing southward

2. What is the reason copper and aluminum are used for electrical wiring?

   A. Copper and aluminum are conductors.
   B. Copper and aluminum are insulators.
   C. Copper and aluminum are semiconductors.
   D. Copper and aluminum are magnetic.

3. Based on the information on page 580, which of the following devices is most likely to use direct current?

   A. a washing machine
   B. a desktop computer
   C. a toaster
   D. a flashlight

4. In an electric power plant, generators may produce electric current at about 10,000 volts. The current may be stepped up and transmitted along high voltage lines at 230,000 volts, and then stepped down to about 2,300 volts for transmission in a city. Finally, before it enters houses, the current is stepped down to 110 volts.

   Based on the information above and that on page 580, which of the following devices steps current up and down for efficient transmission?

   A. a conductor
   B. an electromagnet
   C. an electric motor
   D. a transformer

**Questions 5 and 6 refer to the following paragraph and diagram.**

An electric circuit is a complete pathway for the flow of electric current. It consists of a source of electricity, such as a battery, wires along which the current travels, devices called resistors powered by the current, and often a switch to start and stop the flow of current.

**A Series Circuit**

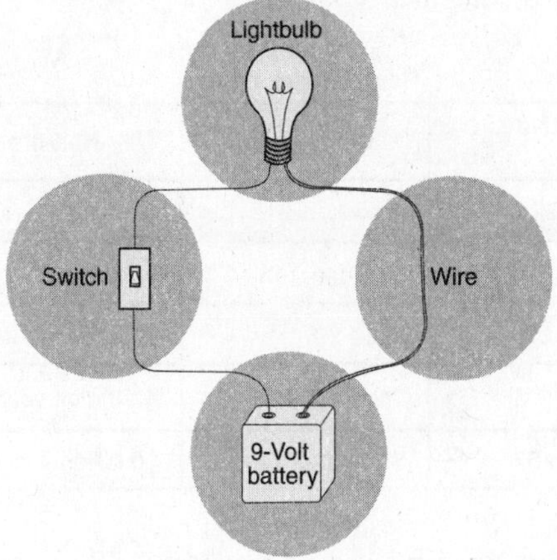


5. Which element in the diagram acts as a resistor in the circuit?

   A. the light bulb
   B. the switch
   C. the wire
   D. the 9-volt battery

6. A student was asked how the current in the circuit shown above could be stopped without using the switch. He answered that the only way to stop the current was to disconnect the battery.

   What was wrong with the student's response?

   A. Disconnecting the battery will not stop the current.
   B. Removing the fuse will also stop the current.
   C. Disconnecting the lightbulb will also stop the current.
   D. There is no way to stop the current without using the switch.

**Review your work using the explanations that start on page 732.**

**STUDY ADVICE**

Congratulations! Only one more practice set to go. If you've been working through the book in order, you've covered all of the concepts, and all that remains is to continue to review and practice them up until Test Day. Reward yourself for all your hard work!

# Physical Science Practice Questions

**Questions 1 and 2 refer to the following paragraph and chart.**

When the nuclei of unstable elements disintegrate, emitting radioactive radiation, the unstable elements change into other elements, becoming more stable. The amount of time it takes for half of a sample of a radioactive element to decay into its stable product is called the radioactive element's half-life.

**Radioactive Decay**

| Radioactive element | Decays into | Half-life |
|---|---|---|
| Radon-222 | Polonium-218 | 3.82 days |
| Carbon-14 | Nitrogen-14 | 5,730 years |
| Uranium-235 | Lead-207 | 713 million years |
| Uranium-235 | Lead-206 | 4.5 billion years |
| Rubidium-87 | Strontium-87 | 50 billion years |

1. What is the half-life of carbon-14?

   A. 3.82 days
   B. 5,730 years
   C. 713 million years
   D. 4.5 billion years

2. Uranium is used as fuel in nuclear power plants, resulting in radioactive waste, which is dangerous to living things.

   Which of the following arguments is likely to be used by opponents of nuclear power?

   A. Uranium is a plentiful source of fuel for generating electricity.
   B. Uranium is a renewable resource, and therefore its use is limitless.
   C. During the three days that radioactive waste is unstable, it may harm living things.
   D. Uranium produces radioactive waste that may harm living things for millions of years.

**Questions 3 and 4 refer to the following paragraph and diagram.**

An oscillation is a back-and-forth or up-and-down movement. When an oscillation travels through matter or space and transfers energy, it is called a wave.

**Longitudinal Wave**

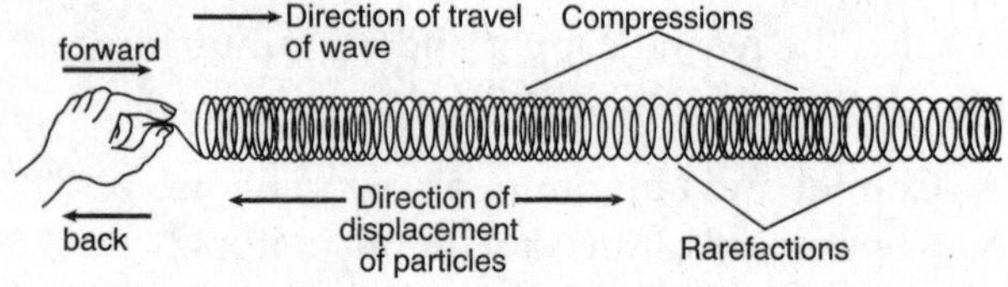


**Transverse Wave**

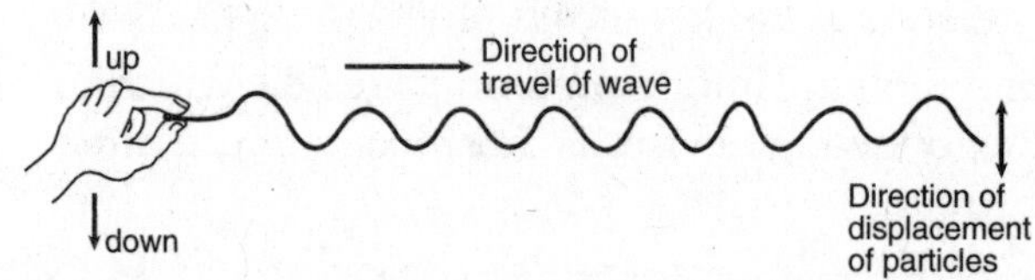


3. What is the main similarity between longitudinal and transverse waves?

   A. Both involve up-and-down displacement of particles.
   B. Both involve back-and-forth displacement of particles.
   C. Both involve compressions in which particles are pushed together.
   D. Both involve the transfer of energy through matter or space.

4. After a transverse wave passes through a substance, no particle ever ends up far from its original position.

   Which of the following illustrates this principle?

   A. A cork in water bobs up and down as waves pass.
   B. Sound waves travel through air.
   C. When two waves overlap, they interfere with one another.
   D. A stone dropped into a pond causes ripples to radiate outward.

5. According to the kinetic theory of matter, all matter is made up of molecules in a state of constant motion. The motion of molecules can be inferred by observing particles in a fluid (a liquid or a gas) as they are hit by molecules of the fluid. The random, zigzag movement of the particles is called Brownian motion.

   Which of the following is an example of Brownian motion?

   A. dust motes dancing in a shaft of sunlight
   B. the ground vibrating as a truck passes
   C. water evaporating from a puddle
   D. an inflatable raft floating on a lake

6. In a chemical reaction, the surface area of the reactants affects the rate at which the reaction occurs. The greater the surface area of the reactants, the faster the reaction rate will be.

   When dilute sulfuric acid reacts with marble, carbon dioxide gas is produced. Which of the following would increase the rate at which carbon dioxide gas is produced?

   A. increasing the size of the container in which the reaction is taking place
   B. decreasing the size of the container in which the reaction is taking place
   C. using larger chunks of marble
   D. using powdered marble

7. Boyle's law states that at a constant temperature, the volume of a fixed amount of gas varies inversely with the pressure exerted on the gas. Therefore, the volume of a gas __________ when the pressure on the gas increases.

   A. increases
   B. decreases
   C. increases initially but then decreases
   D. decreases initially but then increases

**Questions 8 and 9 refer to the following paragraph and chart.**

All of the elements are arranged in the periodic table according to atomic number—the number of protons in an atom of each element. The rows of the periodic table show elements according to the structure of their electron orbits. The columns, or groups, show elements with similar properties. A portion of the periodic table is shown below.

**Part of the Periodic Table**

| 13 | 14 | 15 | 16 | 17 | 18 |
|---|---|---|---|---|---|
| | | | | | He 2 |
| B 5 | C 6 | N 7 | O 8 | F 9 | Ne 10 |
| Al 13 | Si 14 | P 15 | S 16 | Cl 17 | Ar 18 |
| Ga 31 | Ge 32 | As 33 | Se 34 | Br 35 | Kr 36 |
| In 49 | Sn 50 | Sb 51 | Te 52 | I 53 | Xe 54 |
| Tl 81 | Pb 82 | Bi 83 | Po 84 | At 85 | Rn 86 |

8. Group 18 is also called the noble gases. Their electron orbits are completely filled, and they rarely react with other elements. Which of the following is a noble gas?

   A. nitrogen (N)
   B. chlorine (Cl)
   C. xenon (Xe)
   D. fluorine (F)

9. Which of the following statements is supported by the information given?

   A. Silicon (Si) is a very common element.
   B. Chlorine (Cl) and iodine (I) have similar properties.
   C. Arsenic (As) and antimony (Sb) have very different properties.
   D. Arsenic (As) has 85 protons in its nucleus.

**Questions 10 and 11 refer to the following paragraph and diagram.**

Electromagnetic radiation consists of electric and magnetic fields that oscillate back and forth. There is a wide range of types of electromagnetic radiation, which together form the electromagnetic spectrum.

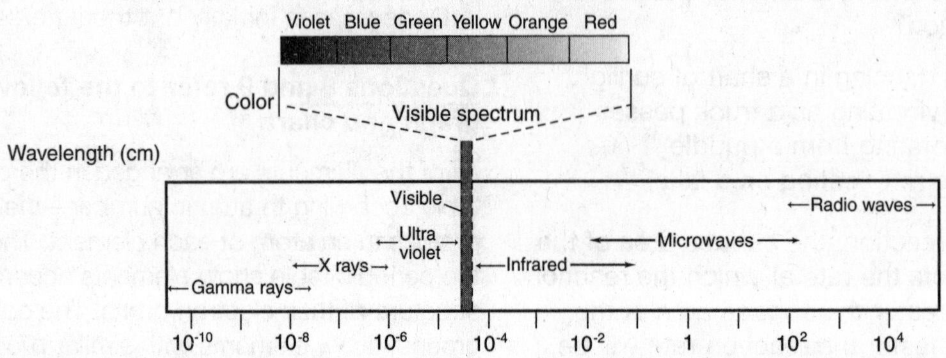


10. Which of the following types of electromagnetic radiation has a wavelength longer than those in the visible spectrum?

   A. microwaves
   B. ultraviolet light
   C. X-rays
   D. colored light

11. Which of the following generalizations is supported by the diagram?

   A. Unlike people, some insects can see ultraviolet light.
   B. Warm colors like yellow have a shorter wavelength than cool colors like blue.
   C. People can see only a small portion of the electromagnetic spectrum.
   D. In medicine, X rays are used to make images of bones.

12. Objects are attracted to one another by the force of gravity. Gravity is proportional to the mass—the amount of matter—objects have; gravity decreases as the distance between the objects increases. An object's weight is a measurement of the Earth's gravitational pull on the object.

   What happens to the mass and weight of a rocket as it travels beyond Earth's orbit?

   A. Its mass remains the same, and its weight increases.
   B. Its mass remains the same, and its weight decreases.
   C. Its mass decreases, and its weight decreases.
   D. Its mass increases, and its weight remains the same.

13. Heat energy can be transferred from one object to another. In summer, when you hold an ice-cold can of soda against your face, your face feels cooler. However, what is really happening is that the can is being warmed by heat from your body. You are actually losing a little body heat.

   Which of the following is an unstated assumption related to the paragraph?

   A. Heat can be transferred.
   B. Coldness cannot be transferred.
   C. A cool object can be warmed by your body.
   D. You can lose body heat.

**Questions 14 and 15 refer to the following table and paragraph. You MAY use your calculator.**

An aviation engineer tests five newly developed airplanes by measuring and recording the top speed of each plane. Unbeknownst to the engineer, the radar she used to measure the planes' speeds is faulty: it gives the speed of any object in motion as 3.7 km/hour faster than it really is. The following table shows the speeds that the engineer recorded using the faulty radar and the actual speed of each plane:

| Airplane | Recorded speed (km/hour) | Actual speed (km/hour) |
|---|---|---|
| 1 | 214.4 | 210.7 |
| 2 | 362.1 | 358.4 |
| 3 | 410.0 | 406.3 |
| 4 | 214.4 | 210.7 |
| 5 | 359.6 | 355.9 |

Using the speeds recorded from the faulty radar, the engineer then calculated the mean, median, mode, and range of the planes' speeds.

14. Which one of the engineer's calculations using the recorded speed is identical to what it would have been had the engineer made the same calculation using the actual speed of each plane?

A. the mean
B. the median
C. the mode
D. the range

15. After completing her measurements, the engineer selects at random two planes to demonstrate at an upcoming air show. What is the probability that the actual speeds of both planes selected are less than 360 km/hour?

A. $\frac{1}{5}$
B. $\frac{3}{10}$
C. $\frac{3}{5}$
D. $\frac{4}{5}$

16. Collisions can be elastic, inelastic, or totally inelastic depending on how much energy is transferred between objects. During elastic collisions, the objects bounce off of each other perfectly and there is no net change in momentum or energy. During inelastic collisions, there is a loss of energy. An experiment was conducted to verify these facts.

Consider the following data:

**Measurements of Momentums and Kinetic Energies**

| Trial | Initial Momentum (kg*m/s) | Initial Kinetic Energy (J) | Final Momentum (kg*m/s) | Final Kinetic Energy (J) |
|---|---|---|---|---|
| 1 | 10 | 50 | 10 | 50 |
| 2 | 15 | 75 | 15 | 50 |
| 3 | 20 | 100 | 20 | 75 |

From the information in the chart, you can see that the type of collision that occurred during Trial 1 was a(n) ______ collision.

A. elastic
B. inelastic
C. totally inelastic
D. plastic

17. The following graph illustrates the effect of temperature change on 1 gram of ice. Which point on the graph corresponds to the temperature at which the substance freezes?

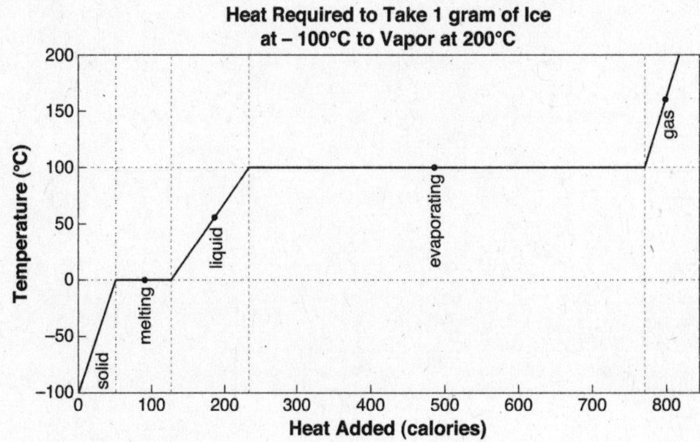


A. –100°
B. 0°
C. 100°
D. 200°

**Review your work using the explanations that start on page 732.**

# PRACTICE TESTS

**STEP 1:** To practice for the actual TASC test, you can take the following five practice tests. When you take the practice tests, follow the same time limits you will face on the actual tests.

**Language Arts: Reading**, 75 minutes, pages 588–601
50 multiple-choice questions

**Language Arts: Writing**, 105 minutes, pages 602–619
Part I: 50 multiple-choice questions, 55 minutes
Part II: 1 essay, 50 minutes

**Mathematics,** 105 minutes, pages 620–633
40 multiple-choice questions and 12 gridded-response questions

**Social Studies,** 75 minutes, pages 634–648
47 multiple-choice questions

**Science,** 85 minutes, pages 649–663
47 multiple-choice questions

For the multiple-choice questions, you can fill in the circles next to the correct answers in this book, or you can write your answers on a separate piece of paper.

You may use your calculator beginning on page 628 of the Mathematics Test and as needed during the Science Test. You may *not* use your calculator on the Social Studies Test.

**STEP 2:** Review your work using the Practice Test Answers and Explanations that begin on page 735, and fill in the Practice Test Evaluation Charts. These charts will allow you to see which study areas may still need work.

**STEP 3:** Confirm your readiness to take the actual TASC test.

# LANGUAGE ARTS: READING PRACTICE TEST

**Directions:** Use 75 minutes to answer the following 50 questions.

**Questions 1 through 7 refer to the following excerpt from an article.**

**Excerpted from "Sizing Up the Interviewer"**

1 It is intrinsic to human nature to take the measure of the people we meet. We do it all the time, automatically. We develop an instinctive way of reading others that is sometimes the saving of us and at other times can prove to be our undoing. It is this instinct that makes us form instant, lifelong relationships with some people or causes us to give a wide berth to others because we get a "funny" feeling about them. With some careful consideration and planning, though, these "feelings" can be honed into a useful tool for gauging the personality and character of interviewers and, by extension, their expectations of potential employees. Let's examine some clues.

2 **Their e-mail.** You can tell a lot about your interviewer by his or her e-mail messages. Some interviewers are very warm, writing in a conversational style, addressing you by your first name. Others are witty, mixing little jokes and humorous remarks in with job-related questions. Still others get right down to business—no chit-chat or informality. Before you ever meet the interviewer, you begin to form certain "pictures" of the person, based on his or her approach and style. But it still remains for you to check him or her out face-to-face.

3 **Their office.** Let's begin with the physical setting of interviewers' offices. Some put a desk the size of a 747 between themselves and you. This is a clear message to you to keep your distance. A straight-backed, rigid chair for the applicant says, "O.K. Let's get down to business, and then you leave so I can get back to mine." Here, you would be advised to adopt a crisp, businesslike style, with brief, professional answers. And, for heaven's sake, **don't touch that desk!**

4 Then, there is the homey, comfortable environment—kids' pictures on the desk, executive "toys" around, soft chairs, and a sofa. There may not even be a desk between the applicant and the interviewer, but rather two chairs grouped around a coffee table. This environment invites more intimacy. It says, "Be yourself. Tell me about who you are so I can get to know you." Here, your manner, though still professional, should be relaxed and open, more personable. It would be a mistake with this employer to sit ramrod straight and give cool, truncated responses to the questions.

by Fred Jandt and Mary Nemnich, Indianapolis: JIST Works.

1. The purpose of this article is to

- A. raise awareness about incompetent interviewers
- B. describe types of interviewers and how to approach them
- C. guarantee a perfect interview with an employer
- D. explain how to email an interviewer

2. Which of the following is a generalization made in paragraph 1 but NOT supported with evidence in the passage?

- A. Your "feelings" can be honed into a useful tool for gauging the personality and character of interviewers.
- B. An interviewer's office can tell you a great deal about that interviewer.
- C. Our ability to "read" others makes us form instant, lifelong relationships with some people.
- D. There is more than one type of clue you can use to gauge the personality of your interviewer.

3. Which of the following are contrasted in this passage?

- A. interviewers who welcome questions about themselves and those who do not
- B. interviewers who frequently use email and interviewers who do not
- C. interviewers who ask difficult questions and interviewers who ask very few questions
- D. interviewers with homey, comfortable offices and interviewers whose offices seem less welcoming

4. Which of the following best describes the structure of the passage?

- A. The author makes a generalization about how to read an interviewer and then gives specific suggestions about how to do so.
- B. The author lists a variety of approaches to email and makes inferences about each one.
- C. The author presents two sides of a debate about how to read an interviewer.
- D. The author summarizes other authors' approaches to reading an interviewer.

5. Which of the following is an assumption the author of this passage makes?

- A. Interviewers have some influence or control over their office arrangements.
- B. Because email can be impersonal, it is a poor way to communicate with a potential employer.
- C. Managers who enjoy chatting informally with employees never have large desks in the middle of their offices.
- D. In preparing for a job interview, it is more important to "read" your interviewer than to research the company where you have applied to work.

6. Which of the following best summarizes the author's main point?

- A. You should never respond to an interviewer who expects crisp answers with a rambling story about yourself.
- B. You should focus on details when attempting to understand your interviewer, since details are important.
- C. You should help your interviewer get to know you during the interview and beforehand.
- D. You should try to understand your interviewer's personality and tailor your responses to him or her accordingly.

7. What does "truncated" mean in the last sentence?

- A. short and tense
- B. angry and complaining
- C. helpful and informative
- D. friendly and conversational

**<u>Questions 8 through 14</u> refer to the following excerpt from a short story.**

### Excerpted from *The Living Is Easy*

1 He gave them each a copper, too, though he could hardly spare it, what with four of them to feed and Mama wanting yard goods and buttons and ribbons to keep herself feeling proud of the way she kept her children. Time was, he gave them kisses for toting his bucket. But the day Cleo brazenly said, I don't want a kiss, I want a copper, the rest of them shamefacedly said it after her. Most times Pa had a struggle to dig down so deep. Four coppers a day, six days a week, was half a day's pay gone up in smoke for candy.

2 Pa couldn't bring himself to tell Mama. She would have wrung out of him that Cleo had been the one started it. And Cleo was his eldest. A man who loved his wife couldn't help loving his first-born best, the child of his fiercest passion. When that first-born was a girl, she could trample on his heart, and he would swear on a stack of Bibles that it didn't hurt.

3 The sisters put their coppers in their pinafore pockets and skipped back through the woods. Midway Cleo stopped and pointed to a towering oak. "You all want to bet me a copper I can't swing by my feet from up in that tree?"

4 Lily clapped her hands to her eyes. "I doesn't want to bet you," she implored. "I ain't fixing to see you fall."

5 Serena said severely, "You bust your neck, you see if Mama don't bust it again."

6 Charity said tremulously, "Cleo, what would us do if our sister was dead?"

7 Cleo saw herself dressed up fine as Josie Beauchamp, stretched out in a coffin with her sisters sobbing beside it, and Pa with his Sunday handkerchief holding his tears, and Mama crying, I loved you best, Cleo. I never said it when you were alive. And I'm sorry, sorry, I waited to say it after you were gone.

8 "You hold my copper, Charity. And if I die, you can have it."

9 Lily opened two of her fingers and peeped through the crack. "Cleo, I'll give you mine if you don't make me see you hanging upside down." It was one thing to hear Cleo tell about herself. It was another thing to see her fixing to kill herself.

10 "Me, too," said Serena, with a little sob, more for the copper than for Cleo, whom she briefly hated for compelling unnecessary sacrifice.

8. Which of the following would Cleo probably enjoy?

- A. jumping from a roof before an audience
- B. sewing clothes with her mother
- C. reading a good book
- D. treating her sisters to candy

9. Whose point of view is explained by this quote from paragraph 2? "A man who loved his wife couldn't help loving his first-born best, the child of his fiercest passion."

- A. Cleo's
- B. Mama's
- C. the narrator's
- D. Pa's

10. Which one of the following happened before the day described in the excerpt?

- A. Cleo envisions her own funeral.
- B. Cleo's sisters offer her their coppers.
- C. Cleo says that she does not want a kiss but wants a copper instead.
- D. Cleo asks her sisters to bet on whether she can swing from her feet in an oak tree.

11. Why did Serena offer Cleo her own copper?

- A. Serena wanted Cleo to get in trouble for taking the others' money.
- B. Serena had placed a bet that Cleo could not swing from the oak tree.
- C. Serena felt that she had no choice but to give Cleo her copper to stop Cleo from doing something unsafe.
- D. Serena wanted to show how much she loved her sister.

12. What is meant by the following quote from paragraph 1? "Most times Pa had a struggle to dig down so deep."

- A. It was difficult for Pa to find it within himself to be generous.
- B. Pa had so few coins that they were usually far down in his pockets.
- C. Pa often searched for reasons not to give coppers to Cleo and her sisters.
- D. Pa could not really afford to give Cleo and her sisters money.

13. Which of the following statements best describes the theme of the passage?

- A. Cleo is wrong to take advantage of her sisters and her father.
- B. Cleo's boldness and her family's love for her sometimes make them feel powerless to resist her.
- C. Cleo's longing to be loved makes her vulnerable.
- D. Cleo and her sisters are becoming greedy as they learn how to extract money from each other and from their parents.

14. What is the "copper" that Pa gave each of the girls?

- A. a coin
- B. a piece of candy
- C. a kiss
- D. a piece of copper tubing

**Questions 15 through 21 refer to the following book excerpt.**

### Excerpt from *Small Business for Dummies*

1 The domestic automakers had a huge market share coming into the 1970s but, unfortunately, were upsetting customers left and right. The Detroit auto manufacturers were able to keep their costs low and profits high in part by producing sub-par cars. Sure, their cars looked nice on the auto dealer's lot, but after a short time in use, many of the U.S.-manufactured cars developed far more problems than their foreign equivalents. And, to add insult to injury, U.S. auto customers didn't get particularly good customer service when they brought their cars in for needed tune-ups and repairs.

2 The chief bean counters and the management of the major U.S. automakers weren't considering the bigger picture when they analyzed their companies' financial statements during the 1970s. These companies were too focused on their short-term profitability and weren't considering the after-sales service that was required as a result of their initially shoddy products.

3 Not surprisingly, the U.S. automakers lost tremendous market share at the expense of the best foreign automakers during the 1970s and 1980s. In fact, one of the big four U.S. automakers—Chrysler—nearly went bankrupt and was saved only because of a government bailout.

4 In the long run, the Detroit automakers learned the hard way that getting your product right the first time is less costly and more profitable than retrenching to play catch-up. Customers aren't stupid, and if you continually sell them shoddy merchandise (especially when better merchandise is available from other sources), they won't come back the next time they're in the market for the products and services you have to offer. What's more, they'll tell others of their lousy experience with your company.

5 Although the major U.S. automakers ultimately got their act together in the 1990s and have stopped the erosion of market share, they still feel the financial pain from the millions of customers they alienated and lost to foreign competitors in the two preceding decades.

From *Small Business for Dummies* by Eric Tyson and Jim Schell, Foster City, Calif.: IDG Books, 2000.

15. The passage states that in the 1970s and 1980s, the management of the major U.S. automakers was too focused on which of the following?
   - A. attractiveness of the cars they manufactured
   - B. after-sales service
   - C. manufacturing shoddy merchandise
   - D. short-term profitability

16. According to the passage, which of the following is a lesson learned by the Detroit automakers?
   - A. Getting your product right the first time is more profitable than fixing mistakes later.
   - B. Servicing your product is not profitable and therefore unimportant.
   - C. Bankruptcy is profitable for large companies due to government bailouts.
   - D. It is easy to win back customers a company has lost to a competitor.

17. What do the authors suggest was one of the goals of foreign automakers?

   Foreign automakers
   - A. studied and then improved on the design of U.S. cars
   - B. deliberately underpriced their cars to get a share of the U.S. market
   - C. wanted to build quality cars with few repair problems
   - D. put short-term profitability above all else

18. The author uses the phrase “chief bean counters” most probably in order to
   - A. underscore the fact that customers will not return once they have had a poor experience with a certain company
   - B. argue that foreign automakers provided better customer service than U.S. automakers
   - C. emphasize U.S. automakers’ preoccupation with keeping costs low and profits high in the short term, at the expense of their long-term outlook
   - D. indicate that domestic automakers enjoyed tremendous market share at the beginning of the 1970s

19. According to the passage, which one of the following was a cause of U.S. automakers losing business in the 1970s and 1980s?
   - A. Detroit automakers produced cars that looked nice on the dealer’s lot.
   - B. Chrysler was saved by a government bailout.
   - C. Detroit automakers ultimately learned a lesson the hard way.
   - D. Detroit automakers produced cars of low quality.

20. Which of the following best describes the authors’ tone toward U.S. automakers?
   - A. critical
   - B. proud
   - C. approving
   - D. arrogant

21. Later, the authors advise: “As a small-business owner, remember that if you don’t get your product right the first time, you may not have a second chance.”

   Based on this information and the excerpt, who did get a second chance?
   - A. U.S. automakers
   - B. foreign automakers
   - C. small-business owners
   - D. the government

**Questions 22 through 29 refer to the following passage from a short story.**

**Excerpted from "The Twins"**

1 After a while, there was a ring at the back door. The children scampered in from the garden, while Jennie answered the ring.

2 "Baker," said the man.

3 "Oh, yes," said Jennie: "wait, I'll get my purse."

4 I went on writing my letter, only half hearing the sound of Jennie's small-change as she, presumably, paid the baker's man.

5 In a moment, Marjie was by my side.

6 "Hallo," I said.

7 Marjie did not answer.

8 "Hallo, Marjie," I said. "Have you come to keep me company?"

9 "Listen," said little Marjie in a whisper, looking over her shoulder. "Listen."

10 "Yes," I said.

11 She looked over her shoulder again, as if afraid her mother might come in.

12 "Will you give me half-a-crown?" whispered Marjie, holding out her hand.

13 "Well," I said, "what do you want it for?"

14 "I want it," said Marjie, looking furtively behind her again.

15 "Would your mummy want you to have it?" I said.

16 "Give me half-a-crown," said Marjie.

17 "I'd rather not," I said. "But I'll tell you what, I'll buy you a—"

18 But Marjie had fled, out of the door, into the kitchen. "She'd rather not," I heard her say to someone.

19 Presently, Jennie came in, looking upset.

20 "Oh," she said, "I hope you didn't feel hurt. I only wanted to pay the baker, and I hadn't enough change. He hadn't any either; so just on the spur of the moment I sent Marjie for a loan of half-a-crown till tonight. But I shouldn't have done it. I never borrow anything as a rule."

21 "Well, of course!" I said. "Of course I'll lend you half-a-crown. I've got plenty of change. I didn't understand and I got the message all wrong; I thought she wanted it for herself and that you wouldn't like that."

22 Jennie looked doubtful. I funked explaining the whole of Marjie's act. It isn't easy to give evidence against a child of five.

23 "Oh, they never ask for money," said Jennie. "I would never allow them to ask for anything. They never do that."

24 "I'm sure they don't," I said, floundering a bit.

From "The Twins" by Muriel Spark, from the book *The Go-Away Bird and Other Stories*, J. B. Lippincott Company.

22. What does Marjie's looking over her shoulder suggest to the narrator?

The narrator thinks Marjie

- A. is imagining what she'll do with the money
- B. has forgotten something in the other room
- C. is shy and lacks confidence
- D. is hoping her mother won't hear her asking for money

23. Which of the following becomes evident during the discussion between Jennie and the narrator?

- A. Jennie knows the narrator wanted to lend her the money.
- B. Jennie can't believe that the narrator wouldn't lend her the money.
- C. Jennie is perplexed when the narrator blames Marjie.
- D. The narrator and Jennie eventually forget the misunderstanding.

24. If Jennie were criticized by her boss at work, what would she most likely do?

- A. resent it in silence
- B. discuss it defensively
- C. not take it seriously
- D. argue forcefully

25. The first person point of view allows the reader to know

- A. the narrator's thoughts
- B. the thoughts and actions of all characters
- C. only the actions of the narrator
- D. Marjie's opinions about the narrator

26. What kind of relationship do Jennie and the narrator have?

- A. They are cool and indifferent to each other.
- B. They frequently disagree on matters.
- C. They know each other but are not close.
- D. Jennie takes advantage of the narrator.

27. Which of the following best describes the situation presented in this excerpt?

- A. humorous
- B. sad
- C. uncomfortable
- D. sentimental

28. Which one of the following best describes Jennie?

- A. obedient
- B. untidy
- C. proud
- D. furtive

29. What does "funked" mean in paragraph 22?

- A. had a bad odor
- B. lied about
- C. shied away from
- D. agreed with

**Questions 30 through 36 refer to the following passage and graphic.**

## How Should We Measure the Rate of Poverty?

1 The rate of poverty appears to be increasing. Each year, the U.S. Census Bureau estimates the rate of poverty, or how many people in the U.S. are living in poverty. According to the Census Bureau, about 15.9 percent of the U.S. population was poor in 2011. That was a 15.3 percent increase over 2010. Moreover, the rate of poverty rose each year from 2007 to 2011.

2 It has been argued that the estimated rate of poverty is too low—that, in fact, more Americans are poor. To understand this, it is important first to understand how the Census Bureau determines who is poor. The Bureau surveys people about their income and then compares that income to the official "poverty threshold" (often called the "poverty line"). This poverty threshold varies depending on age, family size, and number of children. For example, in 2011 the poverty threshold for a single individual under 65 was $11,702. For a family of four, it was $23,021.

3 Some researchers have argued that these poverty thresholds do not account for taxes, living expenses, medical costs, or differences in cost of living. For example, in a major city, higher rents may leave individuals with less money for food. If the poverty thresholds were adjusted to account for these considerations, the estimated rate of poverty might be higher.

4 A panel of experts has proposed a different measure of poverty, which they call the Supplemental Poverty Measure, or SPM. The graph below shows what percentage of people are living in poverty as measured by the official poverty threshold and compares it to the percentage of people who would be considered poor by the SPM.

5 Why does it matter how many people are considered poor by the Census Bureau? One answer is that the Bureau's estimate of the rate of poverty is used by the federal government to allot resources to states and local communities. Local governments also use the estimate to figure out how many people are eligible for anti-poverty programs.

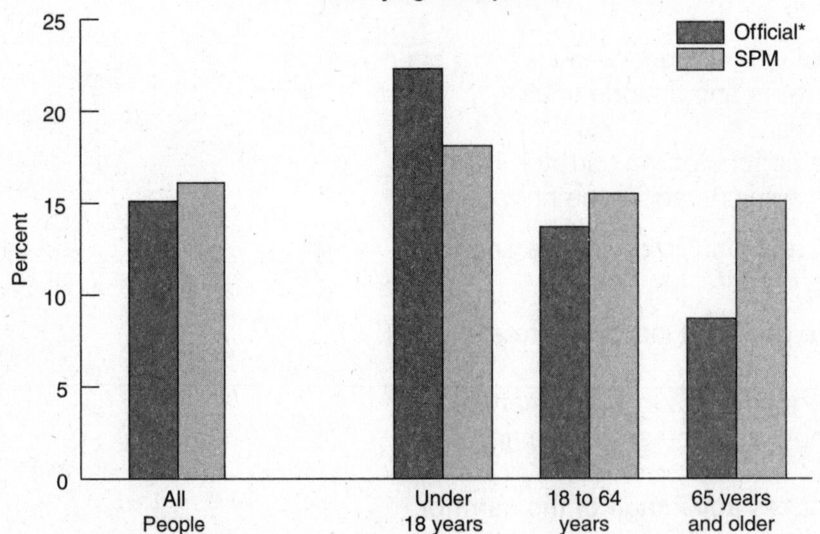


*Includes unrelated individuals under age 15.
Source: U.S. Census Bureau, Current Population Survey, 2012 Annual Social and Economic Supplement.

Adapted information from the U.S. Census Bureau

30. Which of the following best states the main idea of the passage and graph?

  - A. The Census Bureau uses a set of poverty thresholds to determine the rate of poverty.
  - B. If the Census Bureau adopted the SPM, the estimate of the rate of poverty among seniors would increase.
  - C. There may be more people in poverty than the Census Bureau's official estimate suggests.
  - D. It is important that the government take action to combat poverty.

31. Which of the following is a supporting detail, rather than a main idea, in paragraph 1?

  - A. The rate of poverty rose each year from 2007 to 2011.
  - B. The rate of poverty appears to be increasing.
  - C. The Census Bureau may underestimate the number of people living in poverty.
  - D. Differences in cost of living should be accounted for in how the government measures poverty.

32. How does the bar graph support the main idea of the passage?

  - A. The bar graph supports the claim that some people who do not think they are poor may actually be poor.
  - B. The bar graph supports the claim that the government should do more to combat poverty.
  - C. The bar graph supports the claim that a different way to measure poverty would produce a different estimate of the rate of poverty.
  - D. The bar graph supports the claim that 15.9% of people in the U.S. were poor in 2011.

33. Which of the following describes a cause and effect relationship mentioned in the passage?

  - A. The poverty thresholds cause individuals to have lower income.
  - B. The Census Bureau's estimated rate of poverty can cause government officials to care about poverty.
  - C. Higher rents can cause people to have less money for food.
  - D. The SPM would cause more money to be spent on programs for senior citizens.

34. If the SPM were adopted the official estimate of __________ living in poverty would be higher, and the official estimate of ________ living in poverty would be lower.

  - A. people over 65; people under 18
  - B. people under 18; people over 65
  - C. people under 18; all people
  - D. all people; people aged 18 to 64

35. A student reviewed this passage and graph and then said: "It's clear to me that if the Census Bureau adopted the SPM, then local governments would get significantly more federal money to spend on anti-poverty programs." Which of the following best describes the flaw in the student's reasoning?

  - A. The student has confused the causes of poverty with the effects of poverty.
  - B. The student has overlooked the fact that other factors might impact how much money local governments receive from the federal government.
  - C. The student has overlooked the possibility that not all local governments work to combat poverty.
  - D. The student has overlooked the fact that other countries have even higher rates of poverty.

36. This piece was most likely written by someone who _______________.

  - A. worries that the government spends too much money on anti-poverty programs
  - B. thinks poverty is too emotional a topic to be discussed publicly
  - C. wants governmental actions to be based on an accurate estimate of the rate of poverty
  - D. thinks that there is little that government can do about poverty

**Questions 37 through 43 refer to the following two passages.**

**Glenwood Community Improvement Council Member:**

As a member of the Glenwood Community Improvement Council, I fully support spending money to beautify our public parks. Over the last few years, several of our community parks have fallen into disrepair. Walking paths through the parks are not clearly marked, graffiti is visible on picnic shelters, and garden areas are overgrown with weeds. My neighbors tell me that they do not visit our parks because of the parks' condition. Some even said that they worry the parks are dangerous! We should spend money to ensure that our parks are good places to spend time with your family.

Improving and maintaining the parks would have a positive effect on crime and vandalism. If the parks are established as a source of pride for all of the community, vandals will be less likely to deface them. Well-maintained basketball and volleyball courts, picnic areas, and special events such as concerts in the parks would provide activities for the whole town and help neighbors spend time together.

Furthermore, beautiful public spaces are essential to community pride. Without community pride, Glenwood residents and others are unlikely to invest in creating and supporting small businesses. And small businesses are the heart of a thriving community. We must present Glenwood as a beautiful place to live in order to attract successful entrepreneurs from the surrounding area. If we do so, our investment in the parks will quickly pay for itself. Thus, we must improve our public parks.

**Concerned Local Business Owner:**

I think I speak for most of the business owners in Glenwood when I say that spending money to improve parks would be a complete waste of resources. The parks are not popular, and we do not know that they would become popular after being improved.

If we want a shining example of our town's successes to attract businesses, our growing business district is all we need! In the last four years, six new businesses have moved into vacant locations on Main Street. On top of that, several restaurants and shops downtown have survived the recent economic downturn and are now seeing more customers.

The city should do more to support these businesses. We should spend money to improve the infrastructure and appearance of the downtown business district. Improvements could be made to streetlights, signs, and building exteriors along our historic Main Street. We also currently are not able to plant public flower beds or clean and maintain the sidewalks. Investments in these areas would make downtown inviting to both customers and small business owners.

Beautifying our town is important if we want economic growth. But we should make sure that our beautification efforts are in the most important places. Clearly, beautifying downtown would help us build a healthy local economy. And once we have done so, then we can put money toward our parks.

37. The topic of both passages is

- A. the best way to enjoy public spaces
- B. what businesses should exist in Glenwood
- C. whether beautification projects create economic growth
- D. how best to spend public money

38. The writers of the passages disagree about which of the following claims about Glenwood Public Parks?

- A. They are in a state of disrepair.
- B. They are a current source of pride for the community.
- C. Improving them is a good use of funds right now.
- D. Park activities can lower the amount of crime.

39. What does "entrepreneurs" mean, in the last paragraph of the first passage?

- A. residents of the downtown area
- B. workers who maintain parks
- C. people who start businesses
- D. critics who write for newspapers

40. Which of the following is a detail used by the business owner to support her claim that the town's business district will attract new businesses?

- A. The city's parks are currently unpopular.
- B. Public flowerbeds have not been maintained.
- C. Money could be put toward the parks later.
- D. Several restaurants downtown have survived the bad economy.

41. How does the local business owner feel about projects that improve the appearance of the city?

- A. They are good when done in the best locations.
- B. They are always a waste of taxpayer money.
- C. The city parks are good enough the way they are.
- D. They have no impact on local business.

42. Which of the following would the two writers most likely agree on?

- A. Improving Glenwood Public Parks will have an immediate impact on local business.
- B. Investing in our community is important for the future of Glenwood.
- C. The parks would be used regularly if they were in better repair.
- D. Public activities are more important than encouraging new local business.

43. What can you infer happened before these passages were written?

- A. The council member and business owner argued publicly at a town meeting.
- B. Glenwood initially invested in building parks but then did not spend enough to maintain them.
- C. Glenwood had never invested any money in its parks and public spaces.
- D. The business owner conducted a survey of small business owners.

**<u>Questions 44 through 50</u> are based on the following passage.**

**Adapted from "Hazing"**

(The following information is adapted from a website for teens.)

1 Hazing is when a group—like a club or a sorority—requires that others who want to join do certain things. Sometimes these things are silly and are not harmful, such as wearing crazy clothes or a lot of makeup. Other times, the people in charge of the group make the newcomers do dangerous and even life-threatening things, such as drinking too much alcohol.

2 Bullying and hazing are similar to each other in some ways, but are different in others. Bullying can involve excluding someone from a group, whereas hazing is part of a process to join a group. Bullies usually act alone or in a small group, but hazing is usually done by an entire team or club. The victims of bullying do not choose to be bullied, but the victims of hazing have usually approached the team or club and asked to belong.

3 At the middle and high school levels, hazing often occurs in sports teams, with current team members "initiating" new members. Many people think of hazing as a harmless part of growing up, as something that everyone goes through at some point, but hazing can be harmful, both physically and emotionally. Physical wounds heal, but a victim of hazing can carry the emotional scars with them for life. People who conduct hazing may force their victims to go without sleep or personal hygiene. They may yell at, swear at, insult, or even beat their victims. Hazing victims may be forced to wear humiliating clothes in public, eat repulsive substances, undergo physical branding, engage in binge drinking, or even act out simulations of sex acts. At worst, hazing can involve sexual assault.

4 There are things you can do if you feel you are in danger. First, create a connection with your friends, and have a plan in case a dangerous situation comes up. Also, pick a trusted adult, and tell him or her what is happening. Remember—no one has a right to hurt you!

Adapted from www.girlshealth.gov

44. What is the main point of the passage?

- A. Hazing is conducted by girls more often than by boys.
- B. Hazing is more widespread than was previously thought.
- C. Hazing is frequently harmful.
- D. Hazing is different from bullying.

45. Which of the following is a pair of things between which the writer draws a contrast?

- A. hazing by girls and hazing by boys
- B. hazing and bullying
- C. hazing and entrance into a club or team
- D. hazing by friends and hazing by strangers

46. Which of the following details does the writer use to support his claim that hazing can be dangerous?

- A. Hazing can involve things like wearing too much makeup.
- B. Hazing can involve beatings.
- C. Hazing often occurs in sports teams.
- D. Hazing usually begins when someone wants to join a group.

47. Which of the following claims from the passage is not supported with evidence?

- A. Hazing can be harmful.
- B. There are things you can do if you are in danger.
- C. Bullying and hazing are different in some ways.
- D. A victim of hazing can carry emotional scars for life.

48. Which of the following people most likely wrote the passage?

- A. a teenager who is worried that she might be subjected to hazing
- B. a student club president who is deciding how to haze new members
- C. a high school guidance counselor who would like to stop hazing
- D. a parent who feels that hazing is a normal part of growing up

49. What does the word *repulsive* mean in the next-to-last sentence of the third paragraph?

- A. unusual
- B. varied
- C. delicious
- D. disgusting

50. Which of the following is true of bullying, according to the passage?

- A. Bullying is conducted by an entire team or club.
- B. Bullying is never acceptable.
- C. Bullying can involve binge drinking.
- D. Bullying is usually performed by an individual or small group.

**Review your work using the explanations that start on page 736.**

STOP. You have completed the *Language Arts: Reading Test.*

# Language Arts: Writing Practice Test
## Part I: Language Skills

**Directions:** Use 55 minutes to answer the following 50 questions.

**<u>Questions 1 through 6</u> refer to the following paragraphs.**

### Painting a Room

**(A)**

(1) Would you like to redecorate a room in your home? (2) Painting is a fast and inexpensive way to give that room a hole new look. (3) First, remove the furniture, or move it to the center of the room and cover it with drop cloths. (4) Prepare the room by stripping paint and extra layers of wallpaper, filling cracks, and add a coat of primer if necessary.

**(B)**

(5) Now you're ready to paint. (6) Use a brush to paint a clean line along all edges where paint stops, such as where the wall meets the door frame, and in places where the ceiling meet a wall of a different color. (7) This is called "cutting in."

**(C)**

(8) The next step was to paint the room in the following order: ceiling, walls, trim, doors, and windows. (9) Put no more than $\frac{3}{4}$ of an inch of paint, in the paint pan. (10) Run your roller through the paint, being careful not to overload the roller. (11) Apply paint to the ceiling and walls in a "W" or "Z" zigzag pattern.

**(D)**

(12) Spread the paint evenly by rolling either side to side or up and down, using gentle strokes so as not to leave roller marks. (13) After finishing an area, look for spots you missed, go over them with your relatively dry roller.

1. Sentence 2: **Painting is a fast and inexpensive way to give that room a hole new look.**

   Which correction should be made to sentence 2?

   - A. change <u>is</u> to <u>are</u>
   - B. insert a comma after <u>fast</u>
   - C. change <u>to give</u> to <u>giving</u>
   - D. replace <u>hole</u> with <u>whole</u>

2. Sentence 4: **Prepare the room by stripping paint and extra layers of wallpaper, filling cracks, and add a coat of primer if necessary.**

   Which correction should be made to sentence 4?

   - A. change <u>Prepare</u> to <u>Preparing</u>
   - B. insert a comma after <u>paint</u>
   - C. remove the comma after <u>wallpaper</u>
   - D. change <u>add</u> to <u>adding</u>

3. Sentence 6: **Use a brush to paint a clean line along all edges where paint stops, such as where the wall meets the door frame, and in places where the ceiling meet a wall of a different color.**

Which correction should be made to sentence 6?

- A. change ceiling meet to ceiling meets
- B. remove the comma after stops
- C. remove the comma after frame
- D. change ceiling meet to ceiling met

4. Sentence 8: **The next step was to paint the room in the following order: ceiling, walls, trim, doors, and windows.**

Which is the best way to write the underlined portion of this sentence?

- A. was
- B. being
- C. is
- D. had been

5. Sentence 9: **Put no more than $\frac{3}{4}$ of an inch of paint, in the paint pan.**

Which correction should be made to sentence 9?

- A. change pan to pans
- B. change no more to anymore
- C. remove the comma after paint
- D. insert a comma after Put

6. Sentence 13: **After finishing an area, look for spots you missed, go over them with your relatively dry roller.**

Which is the best way to write the underlined portion of this sentence?

- A. missed, and go
- B. missed, and going
- C. missed go
- D. missed, but go

**<u>Questions 7 through 12</u> refer to the following passage.**

### Starting a Community Garden

**(A)**

(1) In many cities, neighborhood groups are forming community gardens in vacant lots, in parks, or on rooftops. (2) These gardens is an ideal way for both children and adults to work with nature while making the neighborhood more beautiful. (3) If you would like to start a community garden first determine whether people are truly interested in the project. (4) If they are, organize a meeting of interested people, and choose someone to be the garden coordinator. (5) Form committees for tasks like finding money for the garden.

**(B)**

(6) Once your group is organized, approach a sponsor this could be a group or individual who can support your garden. (7) Keep in mind that contributions of seeds, tools, and land are just as important as money. (8) Schools, churches, citizen groups, and private businesses are all potential sponsors.

**(C)**

(9) Find out how the land has been used in the past to avoid places that may be contaminated. (10) Pick a site that gets at least six hours of direct sunlight a day, and make sure that water is available. (11) Contact the owner of the site try to get a lease that allows you to use the land for at least three years.

**(D)**

(12) After choosing a site, the group of gardeners needs to decide how to organize the garden. (13) What size should each plot be, and how will plots be assigned? (14) Finally, establish a procedure to follow to maintain tidiness and piece in the garden.

7. Sentence 2: **These gardens is an ideal way for both children and adults to work with nature while making the neighborhood more beautiful.**

   Which correction should be made to sentence 2?

   - A. change gardens to garden
   - B. change is to are
   - C. replace way with weigh
   - D. insert a comma after children

8. Sentence 3: **If you would like to start a community garden first determine whether people are truly interested in the project.**

   Which correction should be made to sentence 3?

   - A. change would to will
   - B. insert a comma after garden
   - C. replace whether with weather
   - D. change are to is

9. Sentence 6: **Once your group is organized, approach a sponsor this could be a group or individual who can support your garden.**

   Which correction should be made to sentence 6?

   - A. insert a comma after sponsor
   - B. insert a period after sponsor and capitalize this
   - C. remove the comma after organized
   - D. insert a comma after group

10. Which sentence would be most effective if inserted at the beginning of paragraph C?

    - A. Next, choose a site for the garden.
    - B. Land use is a very significant factor.
    - C. We all know that you are going to need land for your garden.
    - D. Learn about the history of your site.

11. Which of the following would improve the effectiveness of paragraph A?

    - A. Start a new paragraph before sentence 2.
    - B. Start a new paragraph before sentence 3.
    - C. Combine sentences 2 and 3 into a compound sentence.
    - D. Combine paragraphs A and B.

12. Sentence 14: **Finally, establish a procedure to follow to maintain tidiness and piece in the garden.**

    Which correction should be made to sentence 6?

    - A. change to follow to to be following
    - B. change piece to peace
    - C. change tidiness to tidyness
    - D. change establish to establishing

**Questions 13 through 18 refer to the following paragraphs.**

### Sick Building Syndrome

**(A)**

(1) Do you often feel sick when at you're workplace? (2) Do you experience symptoms such as coughing, sneezing, nausea, headaches and difficulty breathing? (3) Do these symptoms seem to disappear once you leave work magically? (4) If so, we may be working in a sick building.

**(B)**

(5) "Sick building syndrome" is a term that refers to working in a building that makes you sick. (6) The syndrome may be caused by improper building design. (7) Over the past 20 years, architects have designed office buildings with an eye to saving energy. (8) The buildings are tightly sealed so that little heat escapes, and the air inside the buildings is recirculated to avoid the cost of heating fresh air. (9) Although this design reduces energy costs, the lack of ventilation causes a buildup of toxins in the air. (10) On the other hand, an older isn't necessarily immune to the syndrome. (11) Even if they originally opened to let in fresh air, adding insulation, caulking, and weather stripping at a later date may have made the windows airtight.

**(C)**

(12) Toxins in the air come from a variety of sources. (13) Biological agents, including bacteria, viruses, fungi, and pollen, may be found in poorly maintained air circulation systems and dirty washrooms. (14) The deadly gas, carbon monoxide can seep into a building's air through an improperly ventilated garage or a leaky duct. (15) Formaldehyde is frequently found in furniture, paneling, draperies, glues, and upholstery.

**(D)**

(16) It is possible to "cure" a sick building. (17) Steps to take include eliminating tobacco smoke, providing good ventilation, keeping the ventilation system in good repair, and removing all sources of pollution.

13. Sentence 1: **Do you often feel sick when at you're workplace?**

    Which correction should be made to sentence 1?

    - A. insert a comma after sick
    - B. change sick to sickly
    - C. replace you're with your
    - D. change Do to Are

14. Sentence 3: **Do these symptoms seem to disappear once you leave work magically?**

    The most effective revision of sentence 3 would include which group of words?

    - A. disappear magically once you leave
    - B. once you disappear magically
    - C. upon leaving work magically
    - D. seem to disappear, once you leave

15. Sentence 4: **If so, we may be working in a sick building.**

    Which correction should be made to sentence 4?

    - A. replace a with the
    - B. insert a comma after working
    - C. replace we with you
    - D. replace may with are

16. Sentence 10: **On the other hand, an older isn't necessarily immune to the syndrome.**

    Which correction should be made to sentence 10?

    - A. change older to older building
    - B. change isn't to aren't
    - C. insert a comma after immune
    - D. replace to with too

17. Sentence 11: **Even if they originally opened to let in fresh air, adding insulation, caulking, and weather stripping at a later date may have made the windows airtight.**

    Which is the best way to write the underlined portion of this sentence?

    - A. them
    - B. it
    - C. the building
    - D. the windows

18. Sentence 14: **The deadly gas, carbon monoxide can seep into a building's air through an improperly ventilated garage or a leaky duct.**

    - A. delete the comma after gas
    - B. insert a comma after monoxide
    - C. replace can seep with is seeping
    - D. replace improperly with improper

**Questions 19 through 24 refer to the following flyer.**

**Save Compton Point!**

**(A)**

(1) Compton Point, home to many animal species that are threatened with extinction, now faces a threat of its own. (2) Developers are attempting to change the zoning in order to build a hotel, a tourist center, and an observation tower. (3) If they succeed in getting the rights to build, construction will begin next August.

**(B)**

(4) Sam Wanamaker, director of the Society for the Protection of Nature, warns that construction of the development is likely to drive out more than 30 animal species that live on the point. (5) Air pollution from tourist traffic will further reduce the animals' chances for survival, not to mention litter left behind by floods of tourists wandering through the area.

**(C)**

(6) The Compton Point area is zoned as natural parkland. (7) There are several other areas in the county that are zoned as natural parkland. (8) However, because this project is potentially so lucrative for the city, the zoning board seems to be bending to the will of the developer's.

**(D)**

(9) Developers argue that the new jobs resulting from their development would boost the region's sagging economy. (10) The influx of tourism would too. (11) Certainly, everyone in the community agrees that the economy around here could use a lift, but this is not the way to do it.

**(E)**

(12) Register your opposition to the development of Compton Point! (13) Come to a demonstration at 10 A.M. on Saturday, May 7, in front of the mayor's office, 34 Wilton road. (14) Bring signs with slogans that tell how you feel. (15) A strong turnout at this demonstration did send a message to developers.

19. Sentence 5: **Air pollution from tourist traffic will further reduce the animals' chances for survival, not to mention litter left behind by floods of tourists wandering through the area.**

The most effective revision of sentence 5 includes which group of words?

- A. Tourism increases both air pollution and litter, which will
- B. Litter, which tourists leave behind, and besides
- C. Animals will have less chance for survival when air pollution
- D. Air pollution and litter, having been caused by tourists,

20. Sentence 8: **However, because this project is potentially so lucrative for the city, the zoning board seems to be bending to the will of the developer's.**

Which correction should be made to sentence 8?

- A. remove the comma after <u>However</u>
- B. insert a comma after <u>will</u>
- C. change <u>seems</u> to <u>seem's</u>
- D. change <u>developer's</u> to <u>developers</u>

21. Which revision would improve the effectiveness of paragraph C?

- A. remove sentence 6
- B. move sentence 6 to follow sentence 7
- C. remove sentence 7
- D. move sentence 7 to follow sentence 8

22. Sentences 9 and 10: **Developers argue that the new jobs resulting from their development would boost the region's sagging economy. The influx of tourism would too.**

The most effective combination of sentences 9 and 10 would include which group of words?

- A. their development, with an influx of jobs,
- B. new jobs and the influx of tourism resulting
- C. an influx of new jobs, say the developers, plus an influx of tourism,
- D. The region, to have an influx,

23. Sentence 13: **Come to a demonstration at 10 A.M. on Saturday, May 7, in front of the mayor's office, 34 Wilton road.**

Which correction should be made to sentence 13?

- A. insert a comma after <u>demonstration</u>
- B. remove the comma after <u>Saturday</u>
- C. change <u>mayor's</u> to <u>mayors</u>
- D. change <u>road</u> to <u>Road</u>

24. Sentence 15: **A strong turnout at this demonstration did send a message to developers.**

Which correction should be made to sentence 15?

- A. change <u>did</u> to <u>will</u>
- B. change <u>did</u> to <u>have</u>
- C. change <u>did</u> to <u>has</u>
- D. no change necessary

**Questions 25 through 31 refer to the following paragraphs.**

### Kites and Science

**(A)**

(1) Who doesn't enjoy flying a kite? (2) When you seen people in your community flying kites on a windy day, you might think that kites are just for fun. (3) Kites have been flown in countries around the world and for centuries, by young and old alike. (4) However, kite flying, it may surprise you to know, have been responsible for a number of scientific discoveries.

**(B)**

(5) In 1752, Benjamin Franklin used a kite to prove the presence of electricity in storm clouds. (6) He did it by flying a kite during a thunderstorm with a brass key attached to the end. (7) The story goes that, when lightning struck the kite line and traveled down to the key, their was a spark of electricity.

**(C)**

(8) Kites also played a role in learning about the weather. (9) In 1749, Alexander Wilson of Scotland became the first scientist to send a thermometer aloft in a kite. (10) Starting in the 1890s, kites held meteorological instruments that also measured humidity and wind speed. (11) They measured barometric pressure too.

**(D)**

(12) Kites were an early form of aircraft. (13) The Wright Brothers, inventors of the first plane, experimented with kites. (14) Alexander Graham Bell, the physicist and inventor, used kites to learn about problems of airplane construction.

**(E)**

(15) So the next time you see some neighborhood children flying kites, just think. (16) You may be watching budding young scientists.

25. Sentence 2: **When you <u>seen</u> people flying kites in your community on a windy day, you might think that kites are just for fun.**

Which is the best way to write the underlined portion of the sentence?

- A. might see
- B. saw
- C. see
- D. have seen

26. Sentence 3: **Kites have been flown in countries around the world and for centuries, by young and old alike.**

Which revision should be made to the placement of sentence 3?

- A. move sentence 3 to the beginning of paragraph A
- B. move sentence 3 to follow sentence 1
- C. remove sentence 3
- D. no revision is necessary

27. Sentence 4: **However, kite flying, it may surprise you to know, <u>have been</u> responsible for a number of scientific discoveries.**

Which is the best way to write the underlined portion of the sentence?

- A. would be
- B. has been
- C. were
- D. are

28. Sentence 6: **He did it by flying a kite during a thunderstorm with a brass key attached to the end.**

The most effective revision of sentence 6 would begin with which group of words?

- A. By flying a kite with a brass key
- B. The kite was flown during a thunderstorm
- C. A brass key was attached to the end
- D. During a thunderstorm, he flew a kite with

29. Sentence 7: **The story goes that, when lightning struck the kite line and traveled down to the key, their was a spark of electricity.**

Which correction should be made to sentence 7?

- A. remove the comma after <u>key</u>
- B. replace <u>their</u> with <u>there</u>
- C. no correction is necessary
- D. insert a comma after <u>line</u>

30. Sentences 10 and 11: **Starting in the 1890s, kites held meteorological instruments that measured humidity and wind speed. They measured barometric pressure too.**

The most effective combination of sentences 10 and 11 would include which group of words?

- A. one of the purposes was measuring wind
- B. humidity, wind speed, and barometric pressure
- C. barometric pressure was measured along with
- D. the measurement of barometric pressure

31. Sentence 14: **Alexander Graham <u>Bell the physicist and inventor used</u> kites to learn about problems of airplane construction.**

Which is the best way to write the underlined portion of the sentence?

- A. Bell, the physicist and inventor, used
- B. Bell the physicist and inventor, used
- C. Bell, the physicist and inventor used
- D. Bell, the physicist and inventor, he used

**<u>Questions 32 through 38</u> are based on the following passage.**

### What Is a Hybrid Car?

**(A)**

(1) A hybrid vehicle uses at least two different sources of power, you have probably seen examples of hybrid vehicles without realizing it. (2) Some types of trucks or buses, and some trains use a combination of diesel fuel and electric power. (3) The most common hybrid cars in use today combine gasoline and electric power.

**(B)**

(4) There are two primary types of hybrid engine designs: the parallel hybrid and the series hybrid. (5) In both kinds electric motors and gasoline-powered engines. (6) In the parallel-hybrid design, the electric motor and the gasoline engine can power the car together or independently. (7) In the series-hybrid design, the gasoline engine does not power the car directly. (8) Instead, it run a machine called a generator that charges the batteries or powers the electric motor. (9) The electric motor actually powers the car. (10) However, the car cannot move unless the gasoline engine is on. (11) One of the benefits of hybrid cars is their fuel efficiency.

**(C)**

(12) In some hybrid models, the gasoline engine is used only when the car will move faster than 15 miles per hour. (13) That reduces fuel consumption in heavy traffic. (14) The designers who have created the hybrid car have tried to increase its efficiency in every way they can think of. (15) Hybrids are made from lightweight materials. (16) It is designed to drive smoothly, without being slowed down by things like wind, and even the tires on hybrid cars are designed to make the car run as efficiently as possible.

32. Sentence 1: **A hybrid vehicle uses at least two different sources of power, you have probably seen examples of hybrid vehicles without realizing it.**

    Which correction should be made to Sentence 1?

    - A. change uses to will use
    - B. change two different to two and different
    - C. change power, you to power. You
    - D. change realizing it to realizes it

33. Sentence 2: **Some types of trucks or buses, and some trains use a combination of diesel fuel and electric power.**

    What is the best way to revise the underlined portion of the sentence?

    - A. Some types of trucks, buses, some trains
    - B. Some types of trucks or buses or trains
    - C. Some types of trucks, buses, and trains
    - D. Some types of trucks, buses, or trains

34. Sentence 5: **In both kinds electric motors and gasoline-powered engines.**

    Which correction should be made to sentence 5?

    - A. change both kinds to both kinds of
    - B. change In both kinds to Both kinds have
    - C. change motors and to motors, and
    - D. change and to or

35. Sentence 8: **Instead, it run a machine called a generator that charges the batteries or powers the electric motor.**

    Which correction should be made to sentence 8?

    - A. remove the comma
    - B. change it to those
    - C. change run to runs
    - D. change run to is running

36. Sentence 12: **In some hybrid models, the gasoline engine is used only when the car will move faster than 15 miles per hour.**

    Which correction should be made to sentence 12?

    - A. remove the comma
    - B. change is used to is being used
    - C. change will move to moves
    - D. change faster to more

37. Sentence 16: **It is designed to drive smoothly, without being slowed down by things like wind, and even the tires on hybrid cars are designed to make the car run as efficiently as possible.**

    Which correction should be made to sentence 16?

    - A. change It is to They are
    - B. change designed to design
    - C. change wind, and to wind and
    - D. change as efficiently to more efficiently

38. Which of the following would improve the effectiveness of the passage?

    - A. delete sentence 4
    - B. start a new paragraph with sentence 8
    - C. move sentence 11 to the beginning of the next paragraph
    - D. delete sentence 16

**Questions 39 through 44 are based on the passage below.**

### Discounts for Student Skaters

To Whom It May Concern at Diego's Helmet Emporium:

**(A)**

(1) I am writing to you today to try and convince you to provide a discount for students wanting to buy one of your helmets. (2) A growing number of states across the country, including California and new Jersey, have passed laws that require people who use in-line skates and skateboards to wear a helmet. (3) Although some skaters are unhappy about these changes, these laws are based on common sense and logic. (4) I believe if the helmets could be purchased for less money, students would be more willing to buy them.

**(B)**

(5) Learning how to ride a skateboard or in-line skates are similar to learning how to ride a bicycle. (6) In the beginning, it can mean repeated stumbles and falls. (7) Knees and elbows are usually the first to get scraped up, they typically heal quickly. (8) Likewise, head injuries are more severe—they can even prove deadly. (9) Even a low-speed fall can do considerable damage, and the head has to be protected, and the right helmet—hopefully purchased from your store—can do just that if worn properly.

**(C)**

(10) Please consider providing a discount so that more students have the opportunity to be safe.

Best,
Kristin Zajchenko

39. Sentence 1: **I am writing to you today to <u>try and convince</u> you to provide a discount for students wanting to buy one of your helmets.**

What is the best revision of the underlined portion of sentence 1?

- A. try and hopefully convince
- B. try to convince
- C. trying to convince
- D. try, convince

40. Sentence 2: **A growing number of states across the country, including California and new Jersey, have passed laws that require people who use in-line skates and skateboards to wear a helmet.**

Which correction should be made to sentence 2?

- A. change <u>A growing number of states</u> to <u>A growing number, states</u>
- B. change <u>country, including</u> to <u>country including</u>
- C. change <u>California and new Jersey,</u> to <u>California and New Jersey,</u>
- D. change <u>people who use</u> to <u>people that use</u>

41. Sentence 5: **Learning how to ride a skateboard or in-line skates are similar to learning how to ride a bicycle.**

Which correction should be made to sentence 5?

- A. change <u>Learning how</u> to <u>To learn how</u>
- B. change <u>skateboard or</u> to <u>skateboard, or</u>
- C. change <u>are</u> to <u>is</u>
- D. change <u>similar to</u> to <u>a lot like</u>

42. Sentence 7: **Knees and elbows are usually the first to get scraped up, they typically heal quickly.**

An effective revision of sentence 7 would begin with which of the following phrases?

- A. Usually, knees
- B. Moreover, knees
- C. While knees
- D. Noting that knees

43. Sentence 8: **<u>Likewise, head injuries</u> are more severe—they can even prove deadly.**

What is the best way to revise the underlined portion of sentence 8?

- A. And additionally head injuries
- B. However, head injuries
- C. Similarly, head injuries
- D. Considering that head injuries

44. Sentence 9: **Even a low-speed fall can do considerable damage, and the head has to be protected, and the right helmet—hopefully purchased from your store—can do just that if worn properly.**

Which of the following would be the best way to revise Sentence 9?

- A. change the dashes to commas
- B. split it into two sentences
- C. change the commas to semicolons
- D. remove the first clause

**<u>Questions 45 through 50</u> are based on the following passage.**

**Letter to the Editor**

Dear Editor of *Western Weekly Digest*,

(1) In Major Cities all across the United States, a thick cloud of smoke hangs ominously on the horizon. (2) It's there in the morning when the sun rises and again at the end of the day. (3) The smog has become a normal part of our urban environments that weather forecasters all across the country issue daily reports about smog levels. (4) I am writing to urge you and all your readers to support Proposition 278, in favor of stricter pollution guidelines for our city. (5) Clean air proposals have been a part of the environmental movement for decades. (6) In many gas stations around the world, cleaner gas that you can get at gas stations has become a mainstay. (7) Vehicle emission tests are now a mandatory part of any car's life. (8) Over the course of all those years, some progress has been made. (9) And yet for every gain made, thousands of new cars enter our already crowded streets, bringing us one step forward and two steps back. (10) This cannot continue. (11) According to the California Air Resources' Board, cars and trucks are the single largest source of air pollution in California. (12) In fact, almost they emit five times as many pollutants as the next greatest source of air pollution. (13) We must pass Proposition 278 in order to curb the growing menace of smog.

Best regards,
Ciara Wilson

45. Sentence 1: **In Major Cities all across the United States, a thick cloud of smoke hangs ominously on the horizon.**

Which correction should be made to sentence 1?

- A. change Major Cities to major cities
- B. change Cities all across to Cities, all across
- C. remove the comma
- D. change hangs ominously to ominously hangs

46. Sentence 3: **The smog has become a normal part of our urban environments that weather forecasters all across the country issue daily reports about smog levels.**

What is the best way to revise the underlined portion of sentence 3?

- A. The smog, having become a normal part
- B. The smog will have become a normal part
- C. The smog has become such a normal part
- D. The smog has not become a normal part

47. Sentence 6: **In many gas stations around the world, cleaner gas that you can get at gas stations has become a mainstay.**

Which of the following is the best revision of sentence 6?

- A. Gas is available to be purchased at gas stations worldwide.
- B. Cleaner gas is around the world.
- C. Cleaner gas has become a mainstay in many gas stations around the world.
- D. In many gas stations around the world, a mainstay has now become cleaner gas.

48. Sentence 11: **According to the California Air Resources' Board, cars and trucks are the single largest source of air pollution in California.**

Which correction should be made to sentence 11?

- A. insert a comma after According to
- B. change Air Resources' Board to air resources' board
- C. change Air Resources' Board to Air Resources Board
- D. remove the comma

49. Sentence 12: **In fact, almost they emit five times as many pollutants as the next greatest source of air pollution.**

What is the best way to revise the underlined portion of sentence 12?

- A. they almost emit five times
- B. they emit almost five times
- C. they emit five times almost
- D. almost they will emit five times

50. Which of the following revisions would improve the effectiveness of the passage?

- A. move sentence 1 to follow sentence 12
- B. remove sentence 4
- C. move sentence 8 to follow sentence 5
- D. move sentence 13 to follow sentence 7

You have completed Part One of the Language Arts: Writing Test. You may take a 15-minute break before beginning Part Two.

## PART II: ESSAY

**Directions:** Based on both passages on pages 618 and 619, write a response to the prompt below. This task may take up to 50 minutes to complete.

The following two passages give the two sides of a debate about whether schools in a certain community should continue to require physical education. Read the two passages and weigh the claims on both sides. Then write an argumentative essay in which you argue for or against requiring students to complete physical education courses in order to graduate.

Before you begin planning your essay, read the two passages:

(1) Passage A: Why Physical Education Should No Longer Be a Requirement for Graduation
(2) Passage B: Physical Education Is an Important Requirement for Students

As you read the passages, think about what details you might use to support your argument. Take notes or highlight portions of the passages as you read. In your essay, be sure to:

- Introduce your thesis statement.
- Support your thesis statement with evidence from the passages and logical reasoning.
- Argue against the opposing claim.
- Organize your essay logically.
- Use connecting words and phrases to show the relationships between ideas.
- Use a businesslike style.
- Provide a concluding statement or paragraph that summarizes your argument.

**Passage A: Why Physical Education Should No Longer Be a Requirement for Graduation**

*This is the text of Councilwoman Juanita Sanchez's speech at last week's school board meeting.*

The job market is increasingly competitive. Because of this, we must ensure that our students' education fully prepares them to succeed in the future. A limited budget and limited time during the school day force us to make difficult decisions concerning what we teach. We must be willing to make these decisions with the best interests of our students at heart. With these goals in mind, I support the proposal to eliminate physical education as a core requirement for high school graduation in our district.

Time spent completing physical education requirements is time away from more productive educational pursuits. While our state's standardized test scores have continued to rise in past years, we are still seeing results that are below average in both mathematics and reading. Added instructional time is necessary to see our test scores meet the standards set for us. This additional time spent on core subjects will also better prepare students for a pursuit of higher education after high school graduation.

No one is suggesting that physical education and fitness classes be completely eliminated from our curriculum. Physical education is a worthwhile pursuit and should be provided for those students who are interested. But it should be an elective, or optional, course in the same way that music, art, and theater classes are offered as electives. Thus, this outdated requirement will no longer get in the way of more academically important pursuits.

### Passage B: Physical Education Is an Important Requirement for Students

*Letter from concerned parent published in the* City *Journal newspaper*

No one would disagree that preparing our students for a successful future is essential. Changes need to be made in order to help our children compete for college scholarships and career advancement. But as we make these changes, we have to be careful not to cause more harm than good. The current proposal places us in danger of damaging successful programs in our efforts to make improvements.

Having a healthy lifestyle is at least as important to a happy and successful future as mathematics and reading skills are. We currently are in the middle of an epidemic of health problems caused by lack of physical fitness among the children in our community. In our state, almost 20% of children between the ages of 12 and 18 are classified as obese. And obesity is linked to a number of life threatening health problems including diabetes and heart disease. Thus, this is a trend that we must make every effort to reverse.

Programs to offer healthier lunch choices for students have already been introduced. It would be ridiculous to now eliminate requirements that teach our children about other aspects of healthy living. What good is longer time spent in so-called core classes if students aren't healthy enough to fully participate?

I understand that the School Board members have students' best interests at heart. And I agree that it is important to find ways to improve the math and reading scores of our students. Unfortunately, the current plan to eliminate physical education will do much more harm than good. There is a reason P.E. has been a part of our school curriculum for so many years!

**STOP. You have completed the *Language Arts: Writing Test*.**

**Review your work using the explanations that start on page 740**

# Mathematics Practice Test

## Mathematics Reference Sheet

**The next two pages display formulas that you will be given when you take the TASC. You can refer to these pages as you work through the *Mathematics Test*.**

**Volume**

Cylinder: $V = \pi r^2 h$

Pyramid: $V = \frac{1}{3}Bh$

Cone: $V = \frac{1}{3}\pi r^2 h$

Sphere: $V = \frac{4}{3}\pi r^3$

**Coordinate Geometry**

Midpoint formula:

$$\left(\frac{x_1 + x_2}{2}, \frac{y_1 - y_2}{2}\right)$$

Distance formula:

$$d = \sqrt{(x_2 - x_1)^2 + (y_2 - y_1)^2}$$

Slope: $m = \frac{y_2 - y_1}{x_2 - x_1}, x_2 \neq x_1$

**Special Factoring**

$a^2 - b^2 = (a - b)(a + b)$

$a^2 + 2ab + b^2 = (a + b)^2$

$a^2 - 2ab + b^2 = (a - b)^2$

$a^3 + b^3 = (a + b)(a^2 - ab + b^2)$

$a^3 - b^3 = (a - b)(a^2 + ab + b^2)$

**Quadratic Formula**

For $ax^2 + bx + c = 0$

$$x = \frac{-b \pm \sqrt{b^2 - 4ac}}{2a}$$

**Interest**

Simple interest Formula:
$I = prt$

Interest Formula (compounded $n$ times per year):

$$A = p\left(1 + \frac{r}{n}\right)^{nt}$$

$A$ = Amount after $t$ years

$p$ = principal

$r$ = annual interest rate

$t$ = time in years

$i$ = Interest

**Trigonometric Identities**

Pythagorean Theorem: $a^2 + b^2 = c^2$

$$\sin\theta = \frac{opp}{hyp}$$

$$\cos\theta = \frac{adj}{hyp}$$

$$\tan\theta = \frac{opp}{adj}$$

$$\sin^2\theta + \cos^2\theta = 1$$

$$Density = \frac{Mass}{Volume}$$

**Central Angle**

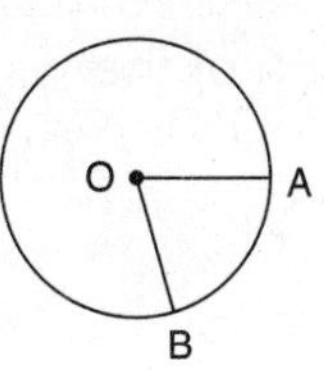


$m\angle AOB = m\widehat{AB}$

**Inscribed Angle**

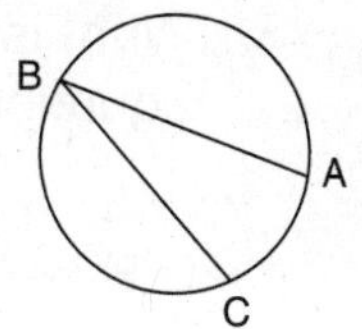


$m\angle ABC = \frac{1}{2} m\widehat{AC}$

**Intersecting Chords Theorem**

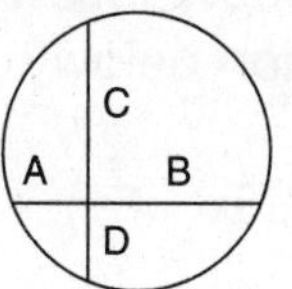


$A \bullet B = C \bullet D$

**Probability**

Permutations: ${}_nP_r = \frac{n!}{(n-r)!}$

Combinations: ${}_nC_r = \frac{n!}{(n-r)!r!}$

Multiplication rule (independent events): $P(A \text{ and } B) = P(A) \cdot P(B)$

Multiplication rule (general): $P(A \text{ and } B) = P(A) \cdot P(B|A)$

Addition rule: $P(A \text{ or } B) = P(A) + P(B) - P(A \text{ and } B)$

Conditional Probability: $P(B|A) = \frac{p(A \text{ and } B)}{p(A)}$

Arithmetic Sequence: $a_n = a_1 + (n-1)d$ where $a_n$ is the $n$th term, $a_1$ is the first term, and $d$ is the common difference.

Geometric Sequence: $a_n = a_1 r^{(n-1)}$ where $a_n$ is the $n$th term, $a_1$ is the first term, and $r$ is the common ratio.

# Part I: No Calculator Allowed

**Directions:** Use 55 or fewer minutes to answer the following 25 questions. Refer to the formula sheet on pages 620-621 as needed. YOU MAY NOT USE YOUR CALCULATOR ON THIS SECTION.

1. Which of the following is equal to the expression below?

   $(3x + 2y)(5x - 6y)$

   - A. $8x - 4y$
   - B. $15x^2 - 12y^2$
   - C. $15x^2 + 10xy - 12y^2$
   - D. $15x^2 - 8xy - 12y^2$

2. Find the area of the following triangle. Mark your answer in the grid.

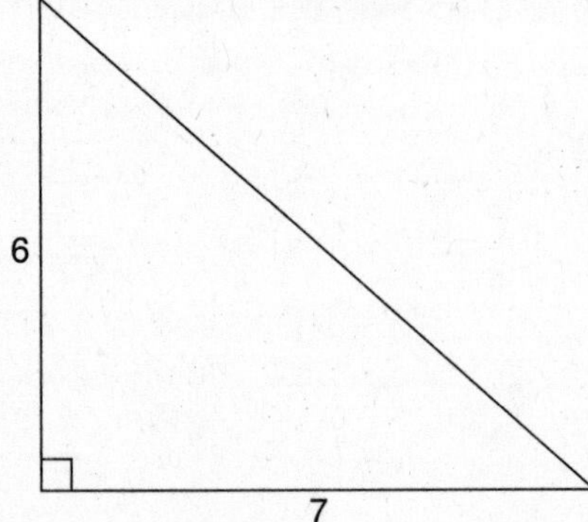


3. What is the only positive solution of the equation $x^2 - 4x - 21 = 0$?

   - A. −7
   - B. −3
   - C. 3
   - D. 7

4. What is the value of this expression?

   $$3 \times 5^2 + 2(4 - 18) + 3^3$$

   Mark your answer in the grid below.

5. Simplify the following expression: $2x^2 - 2xy + 4xy$

   - A. $x(x + y)$
   - B. $x(x - y)$
   - C. $2x(x - y)$
   - D. $2x(x + y)$

6. If all the measurements are in meters, what is the area of the following figure, in meters squared?

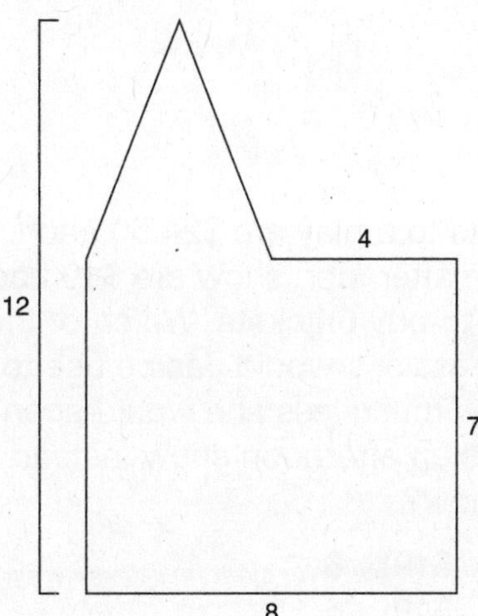


- A. 10
- B. 46
- C. 56
- D. 66

7. Simplify the following expression:
$x^2 + 2 + 7x + 3x^2 + 5x + 5$

- A. $3x^2 + 12x + 7$
- B. $4x^2 + 12x + 7$
- C. $4x^2 + 10x + 5$
- D. $3x^2 + 7x + 5$

8.

| | **A** | **B** | **C** |
|---|---|---|---|
| **1** | –2 | –4 | 1 |
| **2** | 8 | 4 | 3 |
| **3** | 5 | 2 | –1 |

In the computer spreadsheet above, $-[A1 - (C2 - A3) + C2 * B1]$ is equal to which of the following? (*Hint: on a spreadsheet,* * *means multiplication*)

- A. –22
- B. –12
- C. 12
- D. 22

9. Simplify the expression:
$(6x^4 + 7x + 5x^3) - (4x^4 - 2x^3 + 3x)$

- A. $10x^4 + 7x^3 + 18x$
- B. $2x^4 + 7x^3 + 4x$
- C. $2x^4 + 7x^3 + 18x$
- D. $10x^4 + 3x^3 + 12x$

10. The perimeter of the trapezoid below is 50. What is its area?

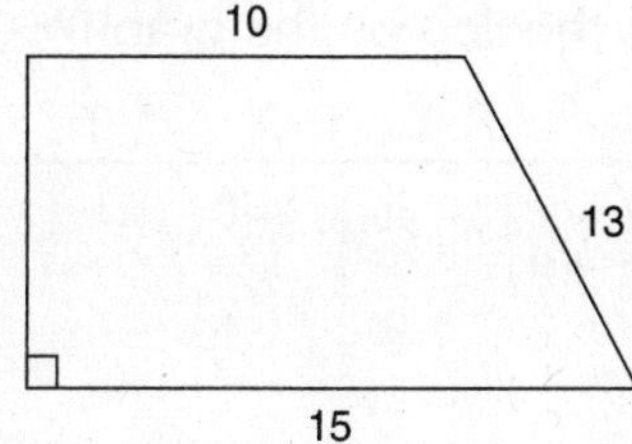


- A. 12
- B. 60
- C. 120
- D. 150

11. The graph of the equation $y = -\frac{3}{4}x + 1$ is a line that passes through points $C$ and $D$ on the coordinate plane. Which of the following points also lies on the graph of the equation?

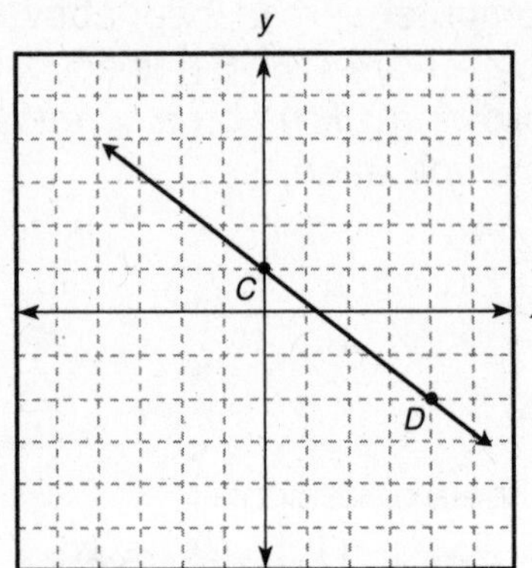


- A. (3, 1)
- B. (8, –5)
- C. (5, 3)
- D. (10, 6)

12. Which of the following equations correctly describes the line on the graph?

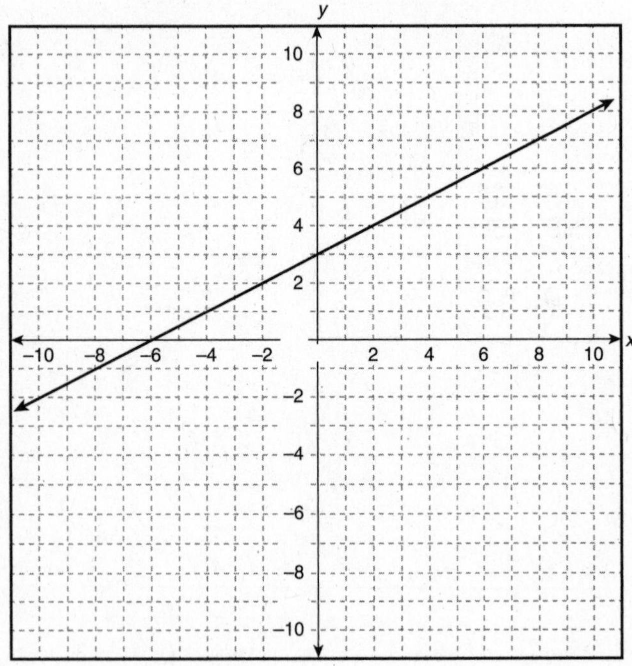


- A. $y = -\frac{1}{2}x - 6$
- B. $y = 2x + 3$
- C. $y = \frac{1}{2}x - 6$
- D. $y = \frac{1}{2}x + 3$

13. What is the 6th term in the sequence below?

1, 3, 7, 15, 31, __ , 127

- A. 62
- B. 63
- C. 68
- D. 77

14. Evening tickets to a play are \$24.50 each. Tickets for the afternoon show are \$19 each. Janice wants to buy 6 tickets. Which of the following expressions would Janice use to determine how much less she would spend if she chooses an afternoon show instead of an evening show?

- A. (\$24.50 – \$19) ÷ 6
- B. (\$24.50 – \$19) × 6
- C. (\$24.50 + \$19) × 6
- D. \$24.50 × 6

15. In a certain state, the legislature has 100 seats. In 2010, Party X held 54 seats. In the 2012 election, the party gained two seats. If, in the 2014 election, Party X loses 6 seats, but then gains 2 seats in the 2016 election, what will the absolute change in the number of seats held by Party X from 2010 to 2016 be?

Mark your answer in the grid below.

16. What is the surface area of the cylinder below?

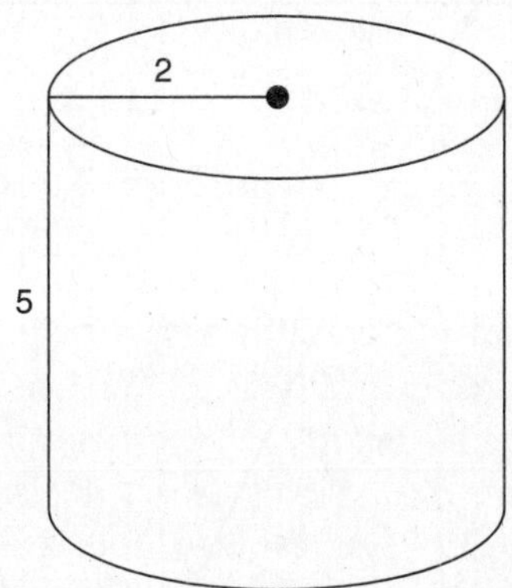


- A. $20\pi$
- B. $28\pi$
- C. $32\pi$
- D. $50\pi$

17. $\dfrac{2x^2 - 6x - 36}{2x - 12} =$

- A. $x - 6$
- B. $x - 3$
- C. $x + 3$
- D. $x^2 + 3x + 18$

18. Customers of Paul's Beauty Supply can make purchases online, from a catalog, or in the store.

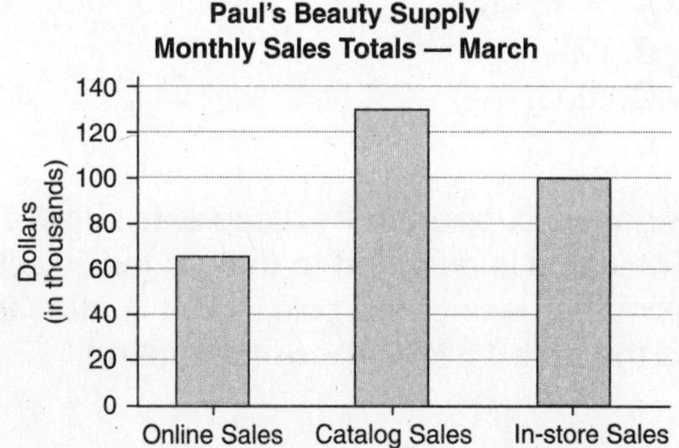


About how much more did the company make from catalog sales than from online sales in March?

- A. $35,000
- B. $65,000
- C. $130,000
- D. $195,000

19. Which of the following is a graph of the inequality $-2 \le x < 4$?

A.

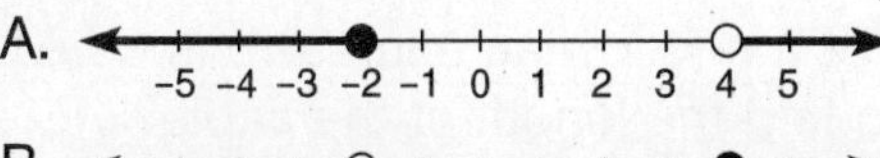


B. -5 -4 -3 -2 -1 0 1 2 3 4 5

C. -5 -4 -3 -2 -1 0 1 2 3 4 5

D. -5 -4 -3 -2 -1 0 1 2 3 4 5

20. At what point does the line with the equation $y = 2x + 3$ intersect with the line with the equation $y = -\frac{1}{2}x - 7$?

- A. $(-4, -5)$
- B. $(0, -7)$
- C. $(0, 3)$
- D. $(2, 7)$

21. A pole is supported by a cable as shown. The cable is attached to the ground 9 feet from the base of the pole, and it is attached to the pole 12 feet above the ground.

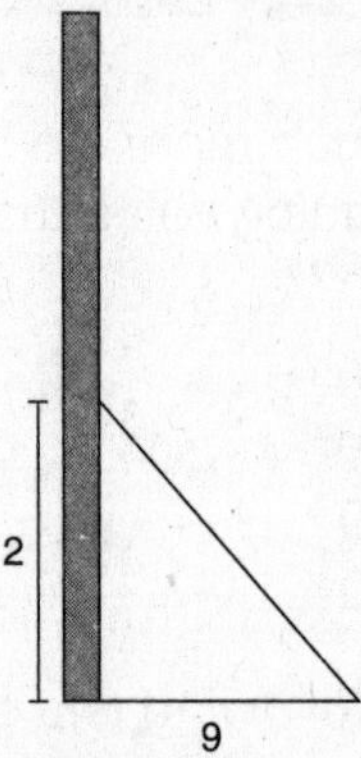


Which of the following expressions could be used to find the length of the cable?

- A. $9^2 + 12^2$
- B. $12^2 - 9^2$
- C. $\sqrt{9^2 + 12^2}$
- D. $\sqrt{12^2 - 9^2}$

22. What is the slope of the line shown below?

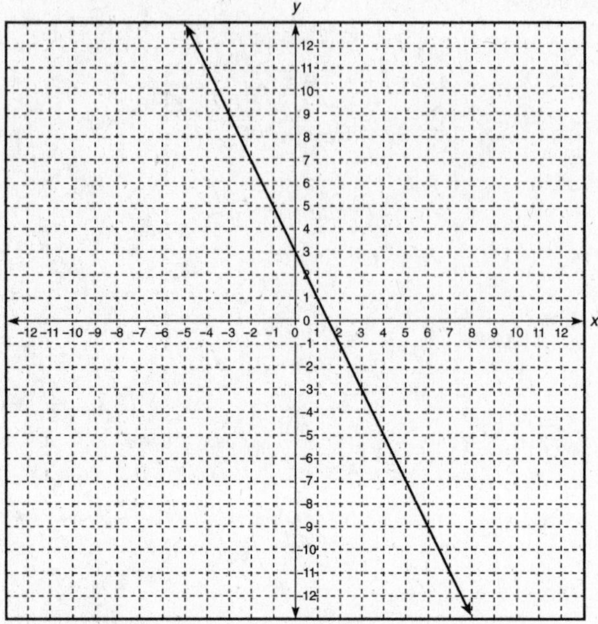


- A. $-2$
- B. $-\frac{1}{2}$
- C. $\frac{1}{2}$
- D. $2$

23. One number is 12 more than 3 times another number. The sum of the two numbers is $-20$. What are the numbers?

- A. 8 and 12
- B. 8 and $-12$
- C. $-2$ and $-18$
- D. $-8$ and $-12$

24. Which of the following pairs of numbers is a solution to the equation $3x^2 - 54 = -21x$?

- A. –6 and 3
- B. –2 and 9
- C. –3 and 6
- D. –9 and 2

25. Jonas is a salesperson. He earns a base salary plus commissions on his sales. The following graph represents Jonas's annual earnings as a function of how much he sells.

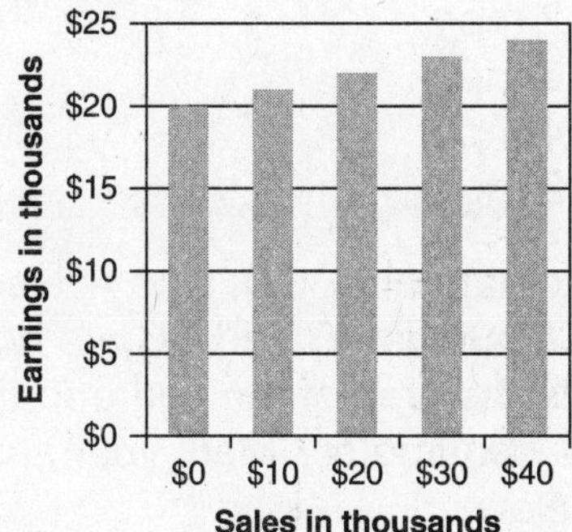


Which of the following equations represents Jonas's earnings, *e*, as a function of his sales, *s*?

- A. $e = 0.1s + 20{,}000$
- B. $e = 20{,}000s + 1{,}000$
- C. $e = 1{,}000s + 20{,}000$
- D. $e = 0.1s(1{,}000 + 20{,}000)$

STOP. You have completed Part I of the *Mathematics Test*. You may take a 15-minute break before proceeding.

## Part II: Calculator Allowed

**Directions:** Use a maximum of 50 minutes to answer 27 questions. Refer to the formula sheet on pages 620 and 621 as needed. YOU MAY USE YOUR CALCULATOR ON THIS SECTION.

26. A mountain resort charges for ski lessons as follows: each hour is \$22.50 plus an initial \$22.50 to reserve an instructor.

    Which equation best describes the relationship between the total cost, *c*, and the number of hours of lessons, *h*?

    - A. $c = 45h$
    - B. $c = 45h - 22.5$
    - C. $c = 22.5(h + 1)$
    - D. $c = 22.5h + 45$

27. Clarissa has cylindrical jars that she would like to fill with colored water to use as decorations at a party. If the cylinders are 10 inches tall, and the bases have a radius of 4 inches, how many cubic inches of colored water will she need for each jar? Use 3.14 for pi, and round your answer to the nearest tenth.

    - A. 50.2
    - B. 160.0
    - C. 502.4
    - D. 1,004.8

28. Brad's average golf score after six rounds was 81. For the first five rounds his scores were 78, 86, 82, 81, and 82. What was his score on the sixth round?

    Mark your answer in the grid below.

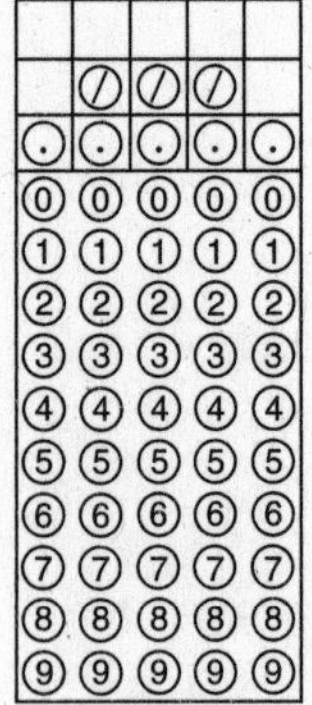

29. A kayaker spends 2 hours paddling up a stream from point A to point B, quickly turns her kayak around, and immediately heads back downstream. It takes her only 1 hour to float back down the stream from point B to point A. If points A and B are 6 miles apart, what was the kayaker's average rate of speed in miles per hour?

    - A. 12 mph
    - B. 6 mph
    - C. 4 mph
    - D. 2 mph

30. In quadrilateral *ABCD*, side *AB* is parallel to side *CD*. Sides *AD* and *BC* are not parallel. What is the area of the figure to the nearest square centimeter? Mark your answer in the grid below.

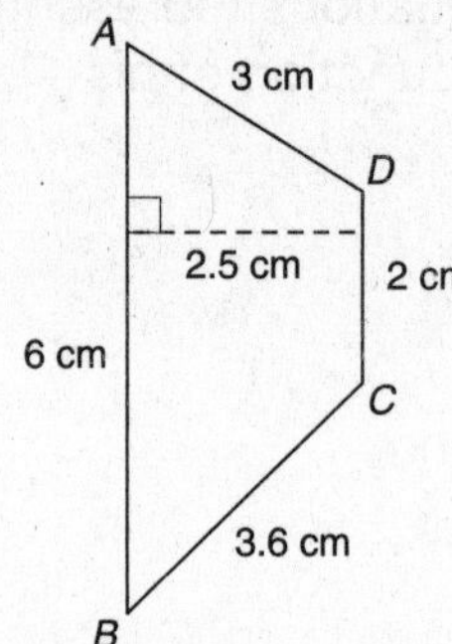


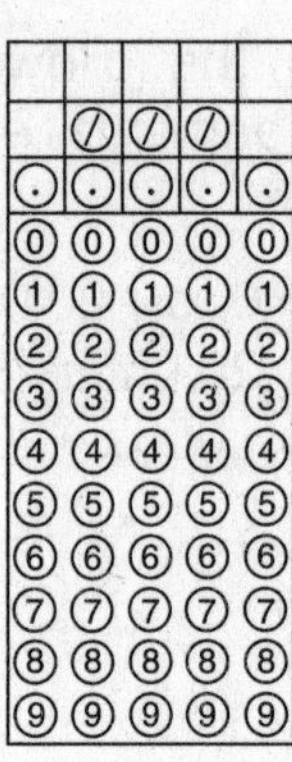

31. Risa wants to order business cards. A printing company determines the cost ($C$) to the customer using the following function, where $b$ = the number of boxes of cards and $n$ = the number of ink colors.

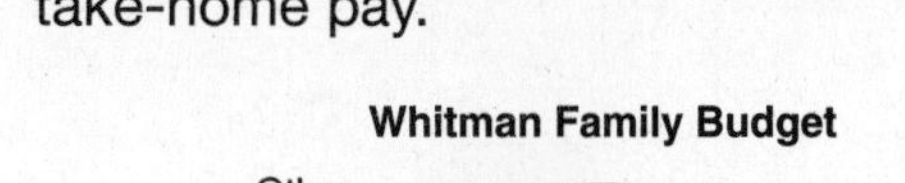

$$C = \$25.60b + \$14.00b(n - 1)$$

If Risa orders 4 boxes of cards printed in 3 colors, how much will the cards cost?

- A. $214.40
- B. $168.00
- C. $144.40
- D. $102.40

32. The Whitmans are trying to pay off their credit card debt, so they developed the following budget based on their monthly take-home pay.

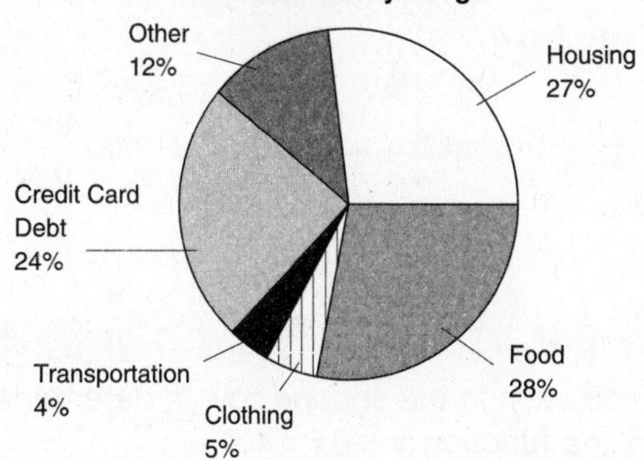


If the Whitmans' monthly take-home pay is $2500, about how much do they plan to pay each month on their credit card debt?

- A. $600
- B. $450
- C. $300
- D. $240

33. A market sells all varieties of pasta at a rate of 4 boxes for $5.00. Jennifer needs 3 boxes of ziti and 3 boxes of spaghetti. At this rate, how much will she spend for the pasta?

- A. $10.00
- B. $8.50
- C. $7.50
- D. $5.00

34. Mike borrowed $400 from his brother for six months. He agreed to pay simple interest at the annual rate of 5%. Including interest and principal, how much will Mike have paid his brother at the end of the six months?

- A. $10
- B. $120
- C. $410
- D. $500

35. Inge has been finding spiders in her apartment. In order to help her landlord understand the problem, she has kept track of how many spiders she found each week over an eight-week period. This is her record:

| Week | Number of spiders found |
|---|---|
| 1st | 3 |
| 2nd | 4 |
| 3rd | 6 |
| 4th | 5 |
| 5th | 4 |
| 6th | 4 |
| 7th | 7 |
| 8th | 2 |

Which of the following line plots accurately displays this data? Each dot represents a week, and the numbers on the line plots represent the number of spiders found.

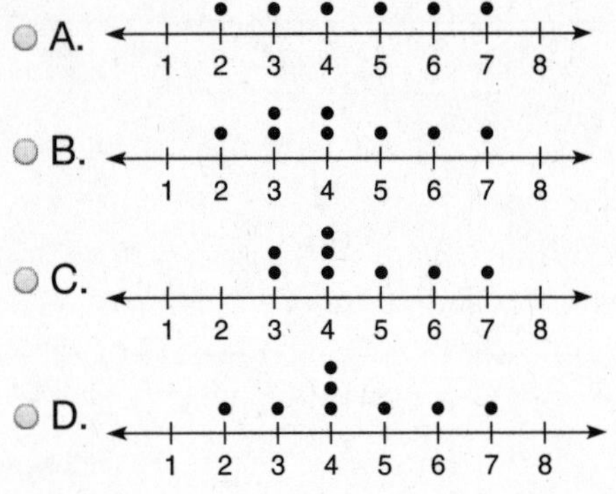


36. What is the value of the expression $3(2x - y) + (3 + x)^2$ when $x = 4$ and $y = 5$?

- A. 49
- B. 58
- C. 61
- D. 82

37. If the area of circle *O* is $36\pi$, what is its diameter?

- A. 6
- B. $6\pi$
- C. 12
- D. 18

38. In 2011, Karen's base salary was $52,500, and she earned an end-of-year bonus of $6,250. In 2012, her base salary was raised to $56,300 and her end-of-year bonus was $4,100. What was the percent increase or decrease in her overall earnings from 2011 to 2012?

Round your answer to the nearest tenth of a percent. Mark your answer in the grid below.

39. Each term in the second row is determined by the function $y = 5x + 4$.

| $x$ | 1 | 2 | 3 | 4 | ... | 15 |
|---|---|---|---|---|---|---|
| $y$ | 9 | 14 | 19 | 24 | ... | |

What number belongs in the shaded box? Mark your answer in the grid below.

40. Imtaez works as a server in a restaurant. On a certain night, he collected \$157 in tips and paid $y$ dollars to the food runner who helped him. The amount Imtaez had remaining after paying the runner was equal to (\$101 + $y$).

Which of the following equations could be used to find out how many dollars Imtaez paid to the food runner?

- A. $157 - y + 101 = y$
- B. $157 - y = 101 + y$
- C. $157 + 101 = 2y$
- D. $y = 157 + 101 - y$

41. If the following triangles are similar, what is the value of $x$? Mark your answer in the grid below.

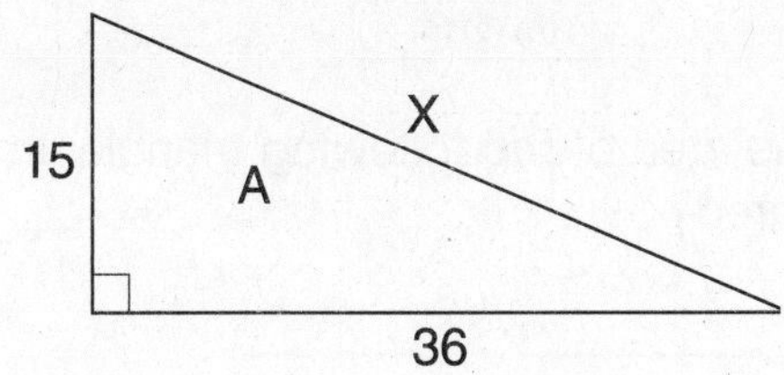


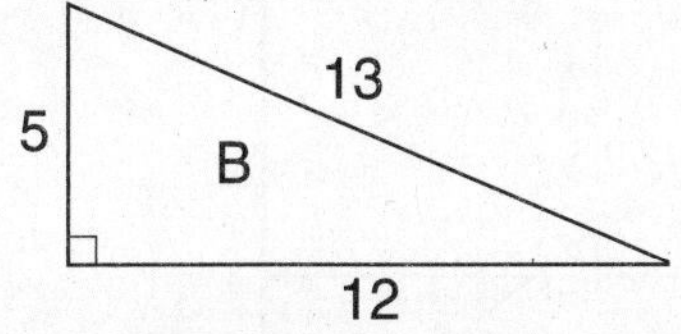


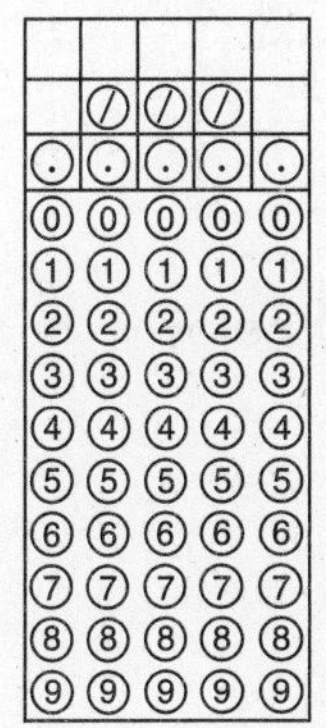

42. John needs to replace the boards on a 22-foot section of his fence. He plans to place the boards as shown below.

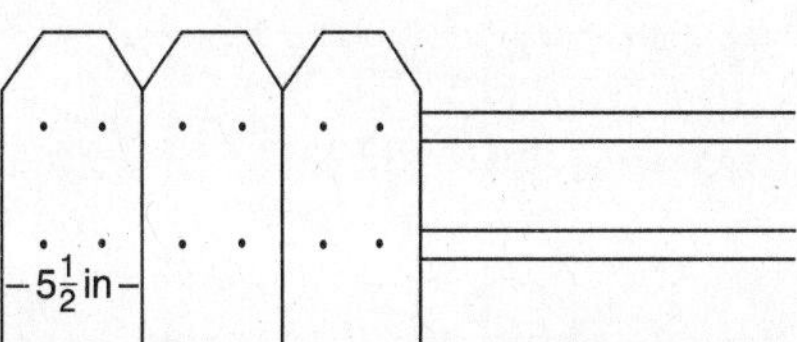


If the boards are $5\frac{1}{2}$ inches wide, how many boards should he buy to cover the distance?

- A. 4
- B. 12
- C. 48
- D. 121

43. Identify the solution to the following system of equations:

$y = x + 4$

$2y + 4x = 44$

- A. (6, 10)
- B. (10, 6)
- C. (6, 4)
- D. (4, 6)

44. A bag contains 12 red, 3 blue, 6 green, and 4 yellow marbles. If a marble is drawn from the bag at random, what is the probability that the marble will be either blue or yellow?

- A. 7%
- B. 12%
- C. 25%
- D. 28%

45. What is the volume of the following cylinder, in units squared? Round your answer to the nearest unit, and mark your answer in the grid below.

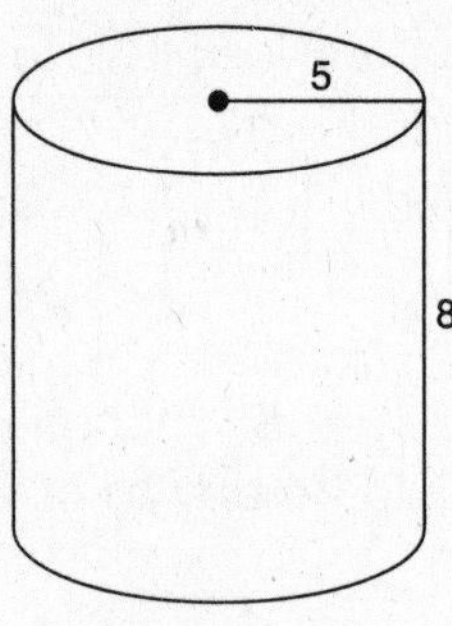


46. The right cone shown below has a base with a radius of 6.4 cm.

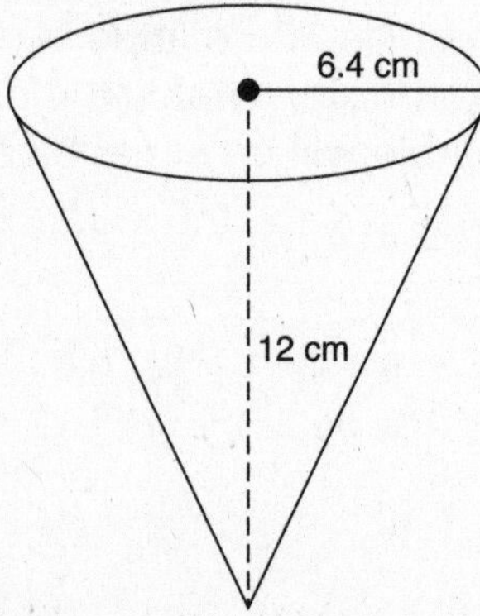


To the nearest cubic centimeter, what is the volume of the cone? Use 3.14 for pi.

- A. 40
- B. 81
- C. 129
- D. 514

47. Ten artists have entered an art show. There are three prizes to be awarded in the art show: first prize, second prize, and third prize. How many possible ways could those prizes be awarded among the ten artists?

Mark your answer in the grid below.

48. What is the area of the following triangle, in units squared?

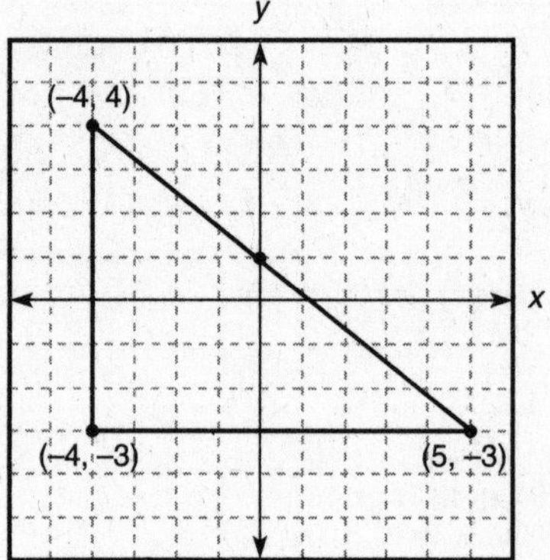


Mark your answer in the grid below.

49. At the end of baseball season, 5% of the children enrolled in a local youth baseball program will be chosen to play in the state tournament. If 12 children will be chosen to play in the tournament, how many children are enrolled in the program?

- A. 60
- B. 120
- C. 240
- D. 600

50. Fabio has his own computer repair business. He uses the following guidelines to estimate how long a project will take.

Install operating system: 1 hour
Replace motherboard: $1\frac{1}{2}$ hours
Reimage hard drive: 2 hours
Upgrade memory: 20 minutes
Install new hard drive: 45 minutes
Install sound card: 30 minutes
Install video card: 30 minutes

Fabio needs to install a new hard drive and an operating system for a customer. If Fabio charges $65 per hour, what will he charge the customer for his time?

- A. $94.25
- B. $105.00
- C. $113.75
- D. $146.25

51. There are approximately 1,335,000,000 cubic kilometers of water in Earth's oceans. Which of the following expresses that number in scientific notation?

- A. $1.335 \times 100 \times 100$
- B. $1.335 \times 10^3$
- C. $1.335 \times 10^6$
- D. $1.335 \times 10^9$

52. In the figure shown, opposite sides are parallel. What is the area of the following figure, in units squared?

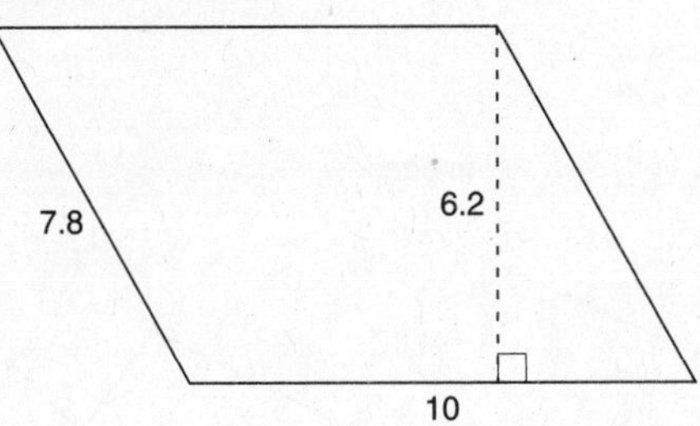


Mark your answer in the grid below.

STOP. You have completed the *Mathematics Practice Test.*

**Review your work using the explanations that start on page 743.**

# SOCIAL STUDIES PRACTICE TEST

**Directions:** Use 75 minutes to answer the following 47 questions.

**Questions 1 and 2 are based on the following paragraph and graph.**

When the value of exported goods—those sold abroad—is greater than the value of imported goods—those bought from foreign nations—there is a favorable balance of trade. On the other hand, when imports are greater than exports, there is an unfavorable balance of trade.

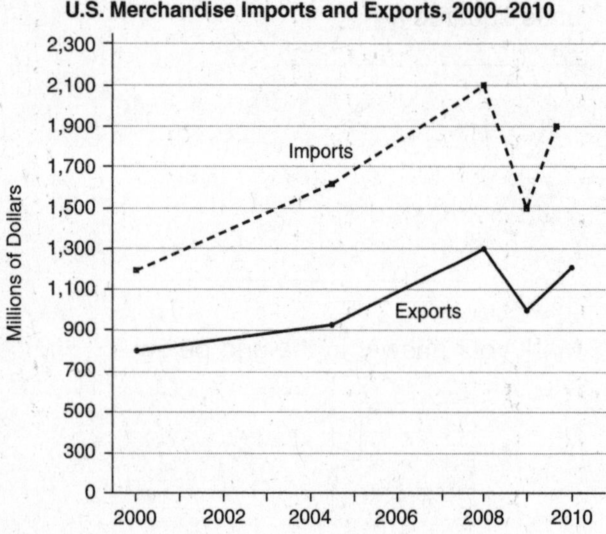


**Source:** *Statistical Abstract of the United States*

1. Which of the following statements is supported by the paragraph and the graph?
   - A. Exports equaled imports at the start of the 2000s.
   - B. Exports exceeded imports throughout the 2000s.
   - C. The United States had a favorable balance of trade in merchandise during the 2000s.
   - D. The United States had an unfavorable balance of trade in merchandise during the 2000s.

2. Which of the following statements about 2009 is supported by the graph?
   - A. In 2009, a recession caused a significant drop in the value of imports.
   - B. In 2009, the value of imports fell by a greater amount than the value of exports did.
   - C. In 2009, the value of exports fell by a greater amount than the value of imports did.
   - D. In 2009, a drop in the value of imports caused a drop in the value of exports.

**Question 3 is based on the following table.**

In an opinion poll, people were asked, "In politics, as of today, do you consider yourself a Republican, a Democrat, or an independent?" The chart below represents the results, by month, for the first six months of 2013.

| | Republicans % | Independents % | Democrats % |
|---|---|---|---|
| Jan 2013 | 27 | 38 | 33 |
| Feb 2013 | 28 | 38 | 32 |
| Mar 2013 | 27 | 36 | 35 |
| Apr 2013 | 26 | 40 | 33 |
| May 2013 | 28 | 39 | 32 |
| Jun 2013 | 26 | 41 | 31 |

**Source: Gallup**

3. Which of the following statements about the first six months of 2013 is supported by the table?
   - A. Independents outnumbered Republicans in the ratio of 2:1.
   - B. There were roughly 10 percent more independents than Republicans.
   - C. Two percent of Americans surveyed belonged to a third party such as the Green Party.
   - D. More people identified as independents than as Democrats, and more identified as Democrats than as Republicans.

**Questions 4 and 5 are based on the following information and graph.**

What standard of living do people in other countries enjoy? There are different ways to answer that question. Many economists hold that one good way is to calculate *gross domestic product* (GDP) *per capita*. GDP per capita is found by adding up the value of all the goods produced and services performed in a given country in a year and then dividing that total (the GDP) by the number of people living in that country.

The map below shows GDP per capita for each country in the world in 2008. Some, but not all, of the countries are labeled with the name of the country.

**Map of GDP Per Capita by Country**

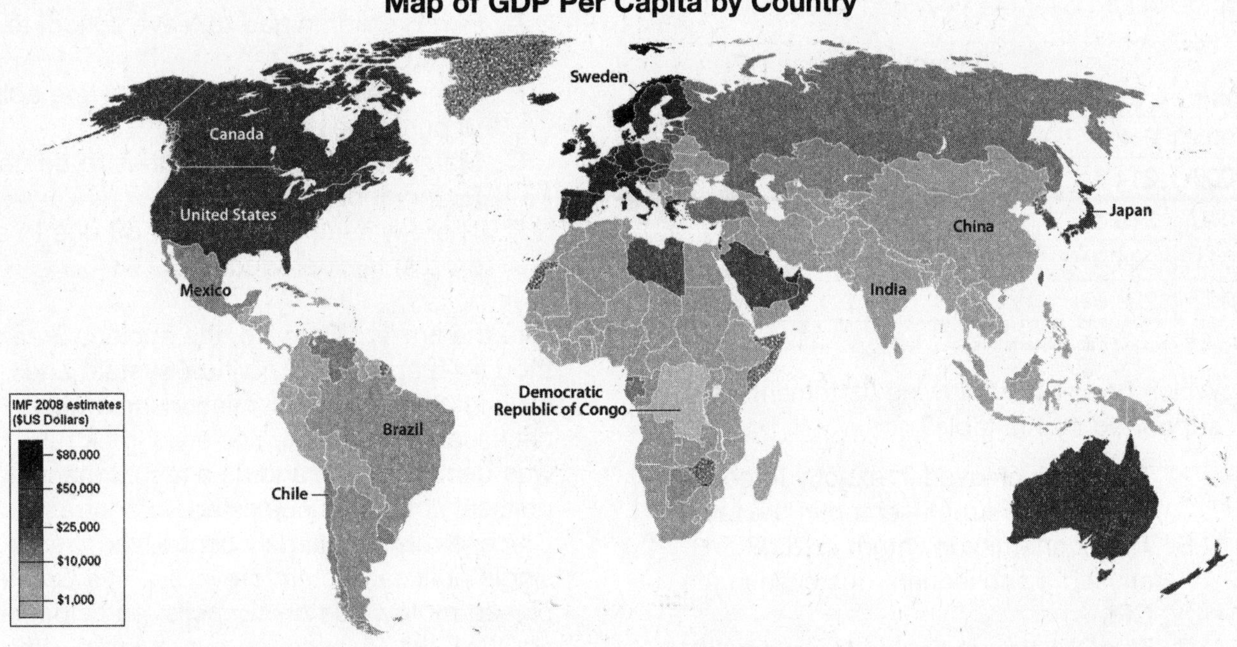


4. In 2008, which of the following continents had the highest percentage of countries with a GDP per capita of less than $10,000 per year?

   - A. Eurasia
   - B. North America
   - C. Africa
   - D. Australia

5. Which of the following statements about 2008 is supported by the map?

   - A. Differences in GDP per capita among African nations can be accounted for by oil and mineral deposits.
   - B. China had a higher GDP per capita than Japan because of its greater land area.
   - C. Having a long seacoast tended to have a positive effect on the GDP per capita of a nation.
   - D. European nations had, on average, higher GDP per capita than South American nations.

**Question 6 refers to the following information and chart.**

The Consumer Price Index (CPI) is a measure of the average prices paid by consumers for a typical assortment of goods and services, including housing, food, clothing, transportation, recreation, and medical care. A higher CPI indicates that prices have risen. The table below shows the CPI for several years, as well as the percent change in CPI over the previous year.

| Year | CPI | Percent change in CPI over previous year |
|---|---|---|
| 2008 | 215.3 | 3.8 |
| 2009 | 214.5 | –0.4 |
| 2010 | 218.1 | 1.7 |
| 2011 | 224.9 | 3.1 |
| 2012 | 229.6 | 2.1 |

**Source: Bureau of Labor Statistics**

6. Which one of the following statements is supported by the table?

   - A. The CPI increased in exactly three of the five years represented in the table.
   - B. The economic downturn in 2008 caused a subsequent decrease in the CPI.
   - C. The CPI almost doubled between 2010 and 2011.
   - D. The CPI grew in all but one of the years represented in the table.

7. The period from the mid-1700s to the mid-1800s, during which manufacturers adopted new technologies such as steam engines and electrically powered machines, is referred to as the "Industrial Revolution." During this time, many people who were previously farmers began to work in factories.

   Which of the following was most likely a result of the Industrial Revolution?

   - A. Fewer children had to leave school to work.
   - B. Many lower-class individuals were able to purchase machinery.
   - C. Many people moved to cities to be near factory jobs.
   - D. There were shortages of food due to a drop in farm production.

8. Like the ancient Chinese, the ancient Greeks thought that a sound political system and well-established social relationships were necessary for a stable society. Greek rule was decentralized, and as a result, many political structures coexisted. In contrast, Chinese rule was largely centralized, and a single political system prevailed. The Greeks placed more value on councils, participation, and law; the Chinese, on bureaucracy, hierarchy, and rules.

   Based on the paragraph, what did the ancient Greeks and the ancient Chinese have in common in regard to politics and government?

   - A. Both governed through a hierarchical bureaucracy.
   - B. Both valued a stable political framework for society.
   - C. Both had centralized councils.
   - D. Both had decentralized political systems.

**Question 9 refers to the following chart.**

**The Effect of World War II on Industry**

| Measure | 1939 | 1940 | 1941 |
|---|---|---|---|
| Index of manufacturing output (1939 = 100) | 100 | 116 | 154 |
| Corporate profits before taxes | $6.4 billion | $9.3 billion | $17 billion |
| Corporate profits after taxes | $5 billion | $6.5 billion | $9.4 billion |

Source: Fute, Gilbert C., and Reese, Jim E. *An Economic History of the United States*

9. Which of the following best explains why the war had the effect on industry indicated by the chart?

- A. Even before the United States entered the war, corporate profits had increased sharply.
- B. Manufacturing output increased by over 50 percent in two years.
- C. The war created a huge demand for military equipment and supplies.
- D. With men gone to serve as soldiers, more women were employed in factories.

10. The U.S. president has a great deal of influence over foreign policy. In part, this is because international relations often require quick and decisive action, which is best undertaken by an individual. In times of foreign crisis, the public usually rallies to the support of the president, at least at first.

Which of the following values probably underlies Americans' initial approval of a president's emergency foreign policy actions?

- A. patriotism
- B. imperialism
- C. self-expression
- D. self-sacrifice

11. To combat the anticompetitive nature of monopolies or "trusts" such as US Steel, Standard Oil, and the American Tobacco Company, the US Congress passed the Sherman Antitrust Act in 1890. That act made it illegal for an individual to monopolize or conspire to monopolize an industry or to act with others to restrain trade or commerce among the States or abroad. While the Sherman Antitrust Act was, and remains, very influential, it was not sufficient to solve all of the problems raised by monopolies. Because of its broad language and its focus on the intent to create monopolies, courts interpreted the Sherman Antitrust Act differently and inconsistently in the many cases to which it was applied. As a result, Congress passed the Clayton Antitrust Act in 1914, which targeted specific actions—such as favorable price discrimination and exclusive dealings contracts—that were used to create monopolies.

In the passage above, the writer's main point is that

- A. courts struck down the Sherman Antitrust Act because its broad language made it unconstitutional.
- B. problems with consistently enforcing the Sherman Antitrust Act led to further legislation to prevent monopolies.
- C. monopolies like US Steel, Standard Oil, and the American Tobacco Company successfully avoided prosecution under the Sherman Antitrust Act.
- D. the Sherman Antitrust Act ended monopolies like US Steel, Standard Oil, and the American Tobacco Company, but did not prevent new monopolies from arising.

**Questions 12 through 13 are based on the following passage.**

Environmental scientists have long been warning about the impact of unchecked carbon emissions into the atmosphere, a threat that many researchers conclude has already led to climate change. Of the many dangers of climate change, some of the most destructive involve lengthy droughts, diminishing fresh water supplies, and decreased world food production. Although some point to the potential benefits of the temperature changes, such as longer growing seasons and more temperate climates in some places, the hazards far outweigh any potential advantages. Since the United States has the second highest rate of carbon emissions per person, it must lead the way by dramatically cutting industrial emissions and finding alternate sources of fuel that do not release carbon dioxide as a byproduct. Positive efforts are underway, particularly through the Environmental Protection Agency, which has fostered several international partnerships to limit the production of carbon dioxide.

12. With which one of the following would the author agree?
   - A. The United States has failed to take any action against carbon emissions.
   - B. The dangers of climate change are more significant than the possible benefits.
   - C. Wind energy is preferable to solar energy.
   - D. Climate change will not impact the world food supply.

13. Which of the following does the author give as a reason why the United States must lead the way in combating climate change?
   - A. Environmental scientists have long been warning about the dangers of climate change.
   - B. Climate change can lead to lengthy droughts and decreased food production.
   - C. Climate change may result in longer growing seasons.
   - D. The United States has the second highest rate of carbon emissions per person.

**Questions 14 through 15 refer to the following map.**

**Forced Resettlement of American Indians, 1830s**

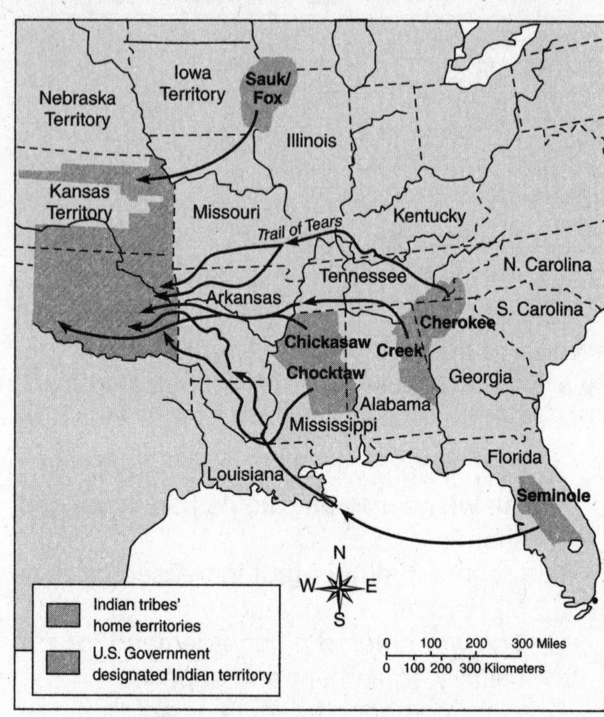


14. Which of the following is the most likely reason that American Indians were forcibly relocated in the 1830s?
   - A. Whites wanted lands in the Kansas and Nebraska territory for settlement.
   - B. Whites wanted to take over Indian lands in the eastern states.
   - C. Indians of different tribes wanted to settle in a single Indian territory.
   - D. Indians in the eastern states wanted to look for gold in the West.

15. Which American Indian tribe was moved the farthest from its tribal lands?
   - A. the Sauk/Fox
   - B. the Cherokee
   - C. the Chocktaw
   - D. the Seminole

**Question 16 refers to the following cartoon.**

16. With which of the following opinions would the cartoonist be most likely to agree?

- A. People shouldn't have to stand around waiting to see their elected representatives.
- B. Senators should pay attention to special interest groups as well as to voters.
- C. Special interest groups are treated better than voters by members of Congress.
- D. Senators are nicer to their constituents than are members of the House.

---

17. In the late 1800s, industrialization caused a large-scale migration from rural to urban areas in the United States. Parents who moved to cities with their children left behind the social support of their extended families. In addition, city families found that children, who were an asset on the farm because they could work at an early age, were more of an economic drawback in the city. As a consequence, the birthrate dropped during this period and average family size shrank.

Which of the following is the best summary of this passage?

- A. Industrialization led to increased urbanization in the late 1800s.
- B. City families lost the social support of their extended families back on the farm.
- C. Industrialization and urbanization caused many changes in family life in the late 1800s.
- D. In the late 1800s, average family size shrank due to the fall in the birthrate.

**Questions 18 and 19 refer to the following chart.**

**Acts of Parliament Directed at the American Colonies**

| Act | Description |
|---|---|
| Revenue Act of 1764 (Sugar Act) | Imposed duties (tariffs) on foreign sugar and luxuries to raise money for Great Britain |
| Quartering Act of 1765 | Required colonists to provide food and shelter for British soldiers |
| Stamp Act of 1765 | Required colonists to purchase revenue stamps for all important documents, including legal documents, newspapers, and ads |
| Declaratory Act of 1766 | Asserted the right of Parliament to make laws for the colonies |
| Townshend Acts of 1767 | Imposed new duties on the import of tea, glass, and paper |

18. How did the Declaratory Act differ from all the other acts of Parliament shown in the chart?

- A. It did not involve the quartering of British soldiers.
- B. It related only to the import of luxury goods.
- C. It did not impose direct economic costs on the colonists.
- D. It was enacted long after the other acts of Parliament.

19. The information in this chart would have been most useful for the writing of which of the following documents?

- A. The Declaration of Independence, which explained why the colonies broke away from Great Britain
- B. The Articles of Confederation, which established a central government consisting of a congress
- C. The U.S. Constitution, which established the structure of government for the newly independent nation
- D. Washington's Farewell Address, in which he warned the new nation of policies and practices he thought unwise

**Questions 20 and 21 are based on the following map.**

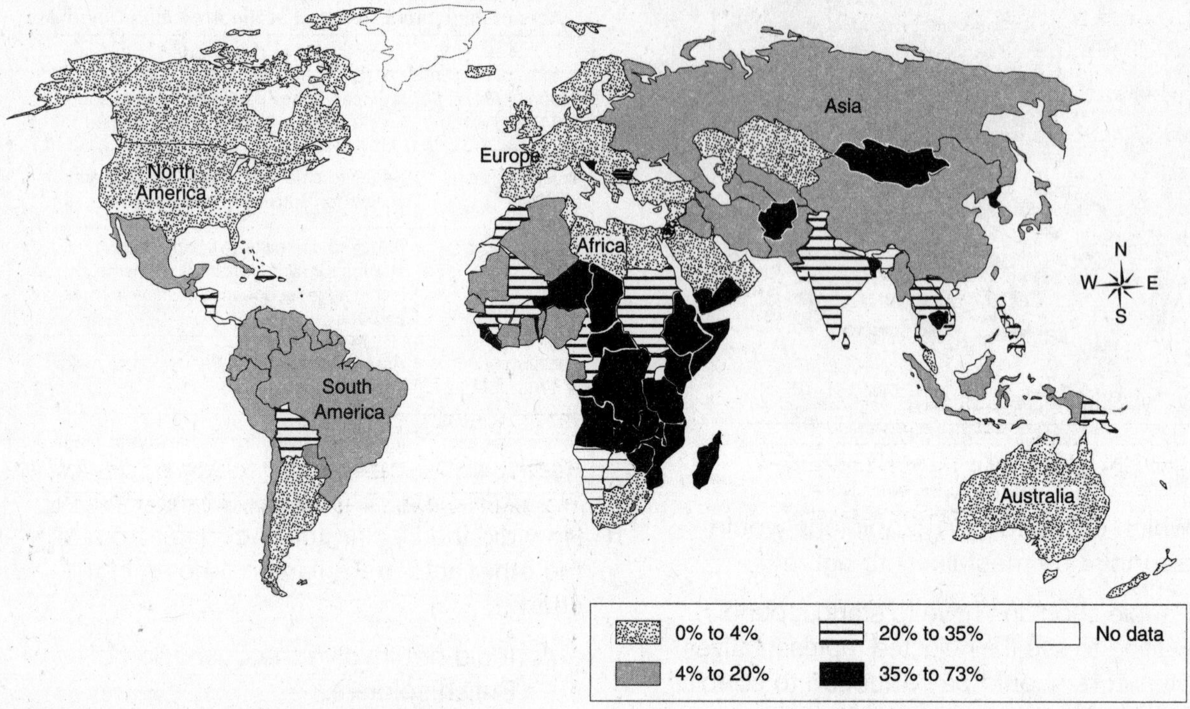


Source: The United Nations, World Food Program

20. According to the map, what is the percentage range of people in the United States who do not get enough food and nutrients?
   - A. 0% to 4%
   - B. 4% to 20%
   - C. 20% to 35%
   - D. 35% to 73%

21. Which of the following statements is supported by the information on the map?
   - A. All areas with more than 35% of the population undernourished are inland nations.
   - B. World hunger would disappear if food were distributed more fairly.
   - C. There are no areas of hunger in Europe or Australia.
   - D. Hunger is a major problem in many countries in Africa.

**Questions 22 and 23 refer to the following chart.**

**Important Political Documents Preceding the Declaration of Independence and the U.S. Constitution**

| Year | Document | Description |
|---|---|---|
| 1215 | Magna Carta | Limited the power of the English king and granted rights to the nobles |
| 1620 | Mayflower Compact | Set rules by which the Pilgrims would govern themselves in Plymouth colony |
| 1628 | Petition of Right | Limited the English king's powers further |
| 1636 | Great Fundamentals | Established the first basic system of laws in the English colonies, in Massachusetts Bay Colony |
| 1688 | English Bill of Rights | Declared that the king rules with the consent of the people's representatives in Parliament; granted ordinary people certain rights |

22. What do the Mayflower Compact and the Great Fundamentals have in common?

- A. Both limited the power of the king.
- B. Both granted rights to the nobles.
- C. Both established methods of self-government in English colonies.
- D. Both applied to the government in England.

23. One of the major grievances the American colonists had against the British was that the British taxed the colonists without granting them representation in the British Parliament. Part of the Declaration of Independence is a list of political and economic rights that American colonists complained that the British king had deprived them of.

By which of the following documents were the writers of the Declaration probably most influenced as they drafted their list?

- A. the Mayflower Compact
- B. the Petition of Right
- C. the Great Fundamentals
- D. the English Bill of Rights

24. The civil rights movement of the 1950s and 1960s inspired historians to reinterpret slavery's impact on U.S. society in general and on African Americans in particular. One interpretation that emerged was that slaves and owners were always in conflict and that slavery was destructive. The extent of slavery's destructiveness was debated. Some historians argued that slavery destroyed the culture and self-respect of the slaves and their descendants. Others thought that slaves overcame hardship by developing a unique African American culture that included, among many different things, strong religious and musical traditions.

Based on the paragraph, which of the following statements is an opinion rather than a fact?

- A. The civil rights movement took place during the middle of the twentieth century.
- B. The civil rights movement caused historians to take another look at slavery.
- C. Historians debated slavery's negative effects on slaves and their descendants.
- D. Slavery destroyed the culture of the slaves, diminishing their self-respect.

**Questions 25 and 26 refer to the following paragraph and graph.**

The market price of a product tends to change in a way that brings supply and demand into balance, a condition called equilibrium. This is illustrated in the graph below, which shows supply and demand for apples.

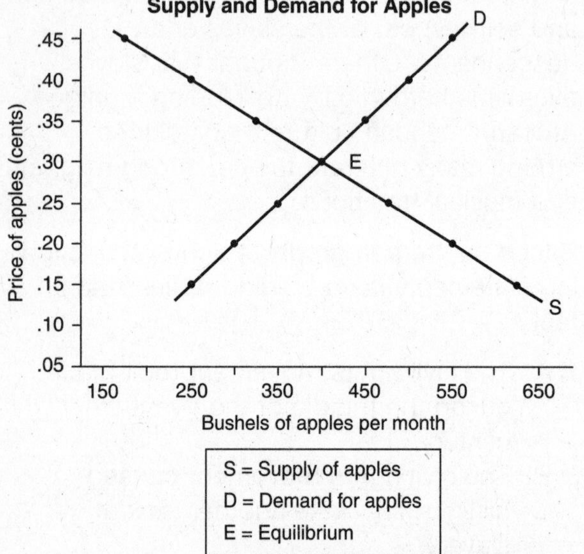


25. According to this graph, what is the market price of apples—also known as the price at equilibrium?

- A. 45 cents
- B. 30 cents
- C. 20 cents
- D. 15 cents

26. Which of the following would result if part of the apple crop were destroyed but demand remained the same?

- A. Supply would increase.
- B. The market price would remain the same.
- C. The market price would go down.
- D. The market price would go up.

**Question 27 refers to the following paragraph and map.**

The Battle of Fort Sumter was the first battle of the American Civil War. South Carolina had seceded from the Union and insisted that Union troops in South Carolina leave. A small band of Union soldiers was finally forced to evacuate Fort Sumter, on the South Carolina coast. After that, President Lincoln called for 75,000 volunteers to help put down the rebellion in the south. Following his call, four additional states seceded from the Union and joined the Confederacy. The progress of secession is shown here.

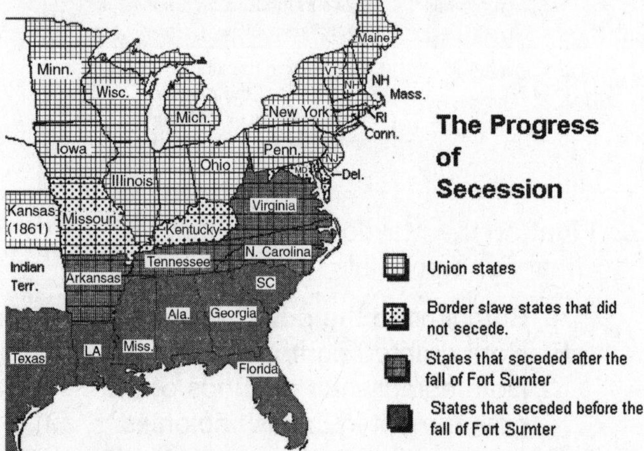


**Reprinted from "The South Secedes," U.S. History Online Textbook, ushistory.org.**

27. Which of the following states belonged to the Confederacy both before the battle of Fort Sumter and after the battle of Fort Sumter?

- A. Iowa
- B. North Carolina
- C. Delaware
- D. Alabama

**Questions 28 through 30 refer to the following paragraph and diagram.**

Most cases that arise under federal law are tried in the federal court system. The federal court system has several levels of courts and several routes by which cases may be appealed to a higher court.

**Routing Cases Through the Federal Court System**

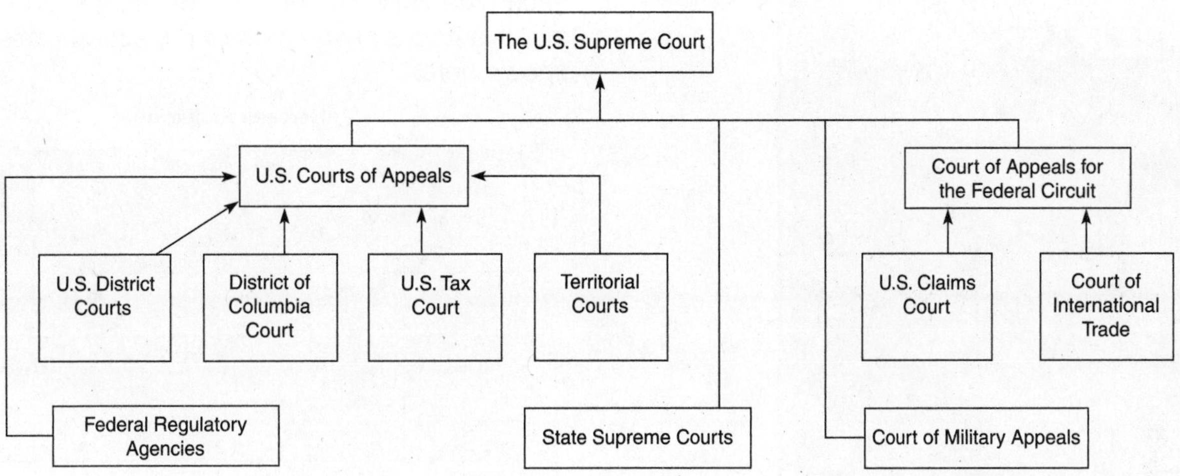


28. A U.S. import-export firm files a lawsuit against a foreign trading company. In which court is the suit most likely to be filed?
   - A. the United States Claims Court
   - B. the United States Court of Appeals
   - C. the Court of International Trade
   - D. the United States Tax Court

29. The U.S. Constitution established only the Supreme Court, but it gave Congress the power to create inferior (lower) federal courts.

   Which of the following is the most likely reason that Congress established other federal courts?
   - A. The justices of the U.S. Supreme Court were not well versed enough in the law to handle all federal cases.
   - B. The volume and variety of federal cases were too great for a single court to handle.
   - C. A system of inferior federal courts gave the United States prestige in the eyes of the rest of the world.
   - D. The Supreme Court's power to interpret the Constitution was established in *Marbury v. Madison.*

30. If cases are not resolved in any of the lower federal courts, to which court may they eventually, finally be appealed?
   - A. the Supreme Court of the United States
   - B. the United States Courts of Appeals
   - C. the Court of Appeals for the Federal Circuit
   - D. the Court of Military Appeals

## Question 31 refers to the following poster.

The poster below was published during World War I.

**Source: Library of Congress. Poster by James Montgomery Flagg**

31. Which of the following opinions is the artist attempting to propagate?
   - A. Americans are not yet part of civilization.
   - B. The war effort needs the help of everyone, including men, women and children.
   - C. Every man, woman and child should rest in preparation for the war effort.
   - D. Americans are part of a lazy civilization.

## Questions 32 and 33 refer to the following paragraph and maps.

Mapmakers have devised many solutions to the problem of projecting the curved surface of Earth onto a flat piece of paper. However, all map projections involve some distortion, and each type of projection has advantages and disadvantages. Two types of projections are shown here.

**Mercator Projection**

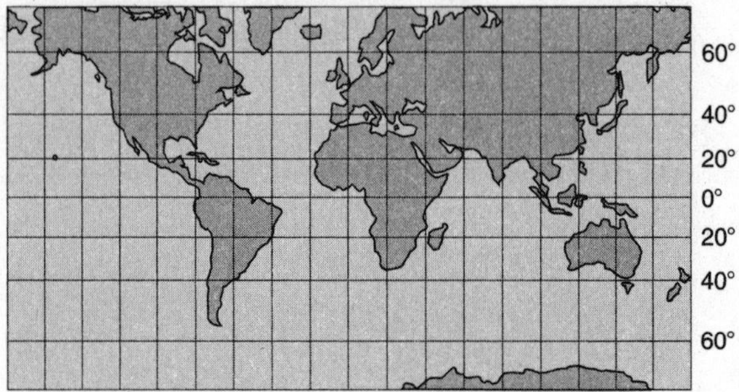


**Interrupted Projection**

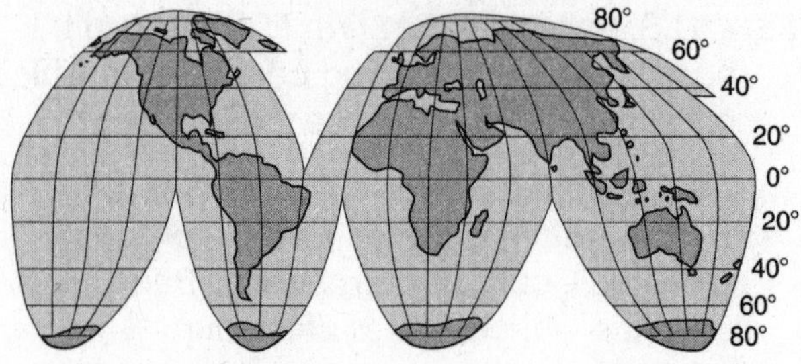


32. Approximately where is there the least distortion on these projections?
   - A. at 60° north and south latitude
   - B. at 40° north and south latitude
   - C. at 20° north and south latitude
   - D. at 0° latitude

33. A sailor who wanted to plan an around-the-world sailing trip decided to use the interrupted projection. What was wrong with his decision?
   - A. The interrupted projection distorts distances across the continents at midlatitudes.
   - B. The interrupted projection distorts distances across the oceans.
   - C. The interrupted projection distorts the shapes of mid-latitude land masses.
   - D. The interrupted projection shows only a few of the world's oceans.

**Question 34 refers to the following paragraph and map.**

After the Roman Empire had reached its greatest extent in the 2nd century C.E., emperors consolidated its borders in various ways: where the frontiers were over land, they were seen as vulnerable, and so the emperors often built heavy fortifications, such as forts or walls to defend the borders; where there was a natural barrier like a river or a desert, light fortifications, such as watchtowers, were viewed as adequate; and where there were major barriers, such as the ocean, the emperors concluded that no defense was needed.

**Northwestern Frontiers of the Roman Empire, 2nd Century CE**

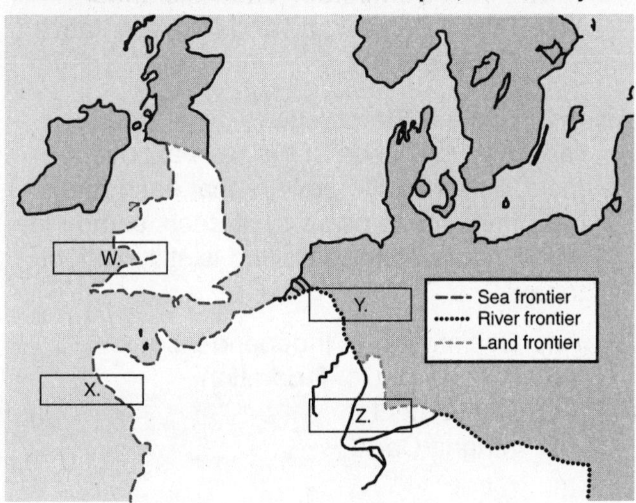


34. For which of the following frontiers would the Roman emperors have built no fortifications at all?

- A. W only
- B. W and X only
- C. W, X, and Y only
- D. W, Y, and Z only

35. Constitutional guarantees of fairness and equality under the law, our basic civil liberties, are called due process of law. The Fifth and Fourteenth Amendments state that government shall not deprive anyone of "life, liberty, or property, without due process of law." The Fifth Amendment protects people from actions of the federal government. The Fourteenth protects people specifically from actions of governments of the individual states.

What is a main difference between the Fifth and Fourteenth Amendments?

- A. The Fifth Amendment applies to adults, and the Fourteenth Amendment, to children.
- B. The Fifth Amendment applies to due process, and the Fourteenth Amendment, to freedom of speech.
- C. The Fifth Amendment applies to the federal government, and the Fourteenth Amendment, to state governments.
- D. The Fifth Amendment applies to life, and the Fourteenth Amendment, to liberty.

36. Haiti, which became a republic in 1804, is the second-oldest republic in the Western Hemisphere. Previously, it had been controlled by France and was important in the slave trade. Slaves in Haiti fought for independence for almost 10 years before finally breaking away from France. When the Republic of Haiti was established, it was the first independent nation in the Caribbean or Latin America. It would be several decades before another Caribbean nation would gain independence. Haiti was also the first democratic republic in the world to be led by African Americans. It is the only country in the Western Hemisphere where the dominant language is French.

Which of the following is the best summary of this passage?

- A. Several factors make Haiti unique among Caribbean nations.
- B. Haiti became a republic in 1804, long before any other Caribbean nation.
- C. Haiti has long been led by African Americans.
- D. Haiti is a French-speaking republic in the Caribbean.

37. For many centuries, a set of important international trade routes, called the "Silk Road," brought traders from Europe into Asia and vice versa. Silk from China was being sold in Europe and Africa by the first century B.C.E. (if not before), and gold and other valuables from Europe and Africa flowed into the Far East in exchange. Over time, not only silk but also spices, minerals, and many other types of goods were carried along the Silk Road. As a by-product of this trade, ideas, religions, and even diseases were also carried back and forth between East and West.

The city of Damascus was on one of the Silk Road routes. Which of the following was most likely true of Damascus?

- A. Even its poorer citizens possessed silk clothing.
- B. People in Damascus were aware of religions practiced elsewhere.
- C. Some of the gold flowing into China was mined in Damascus.
- D. People in Damascus never died from foreign diseases.

38. Review the table and answer the following question.

**Differences Between ___________**

| | |
|---|---|
| • Citizens vote on each issue or governmental action<br>• The system of ancient Athens | • Citizens elect representatives who vote on issues or actions<br>• The system of the United States national government |

Which of the following best completes the title of the table?

- A. Democracy and Aristocracy
- B. Democracy and Oligarchy
- C. Direct Democracy and Referendum
- D. Direct Democracy and Representative Democracy

39. In the United States, the _______ establishes the branches of the federal government, lists specific powers that each branch has, limits those powers, protects some individual rights of citizens, and is still in effect today.

- A. Declaration of Independence
- B. Articles of Confederation
- C. Constitution
- D. Magna Carta

**Questions 40 and 41 are based on the following passage.**

In 1096 C.E., peasants and soldiers from Europe invaded Jerusalem in the first of a long series of conflicts in the Middle East. The soldiers and their leaders were motivated by several factors. Some, who were influenced by the Pope at the time, wanted to regain control of Christian holy sites. Some wanted to unite the Eastern and Western branches of the Christian church. Some were likely motivated by religious prejudice against Islam or Judaism. It is probable that some wanted to rob Middle Eastern cities of gold and other resources. Some may have been adventurers hoping to achieve personal glory. Regardless of why they happened, the resulting wars killed hundreds of thousands over a period of two centuries.

40. What historical event does the preceding passage describe?

- A. the Crusades
- B. the Wars of the Roses
- C. the Palestinian Conflict
- D. World War I

41. A famous historian described these wars as "the most signal and most durable monument of human folly that has yet appeared in any age or nation." Based on the passage, what did the historian most likely mean by the phrase "monument of human folly?"

- A. a stone statue displaying the dates of the wars
- B. a signal conveying the location of a monument
- C. a reason to remember how foolish people can be
- D. a structure erected in honor of those who died in the wars

42. Read the list contained in the box and answer the question.

- Rising unemployment
- Slowdown in consumer spending
- Slowdown in business expansion
- Businesses and consumers avoiding risk

Which of the following does the preceding box describe?

- A. inflation
- B. recovery
- C. saturation
- D. recession

43. Which one of the following is most likely a consumer good rather than a producer good?

- A. 16-by-10 foot sheets of aluminum
- B. bricks of refined copper
- C. 5-ounce tubes of oil paint
- D. 1,000-foot bales of fiber-optic cable

44. James Madison, who helped draft the Constitution, wrote about it: "The powers delegated by the proposed Constitution to the federal government are few and defined. Those which are to remain in the State governments are numerous and indefinite. The former will be exercised principally on external objects, as war, peace, negotiation, and foreign commerce . . . The powers reserved to the several states will extend to all the objects which, in the ordinary course of affairs, concern the lives, liberties, and properties of the people, and the internal order, improvement and prosperity of the State."

What aspect of the United States' government's structure was Madison describing?

- A. democracy
- B. federalism
- C. the Commerce Clause
- D. representation

45. The first three Articles of the Constitution of the United States define the powers of the legislative, executive, and judicial branches of the government. The following table gives brief summaries of the duties of those three branches:

| Legislative | Executive | Judicial |
|---|---|---|
| • Makes laws<br>• Declares war and raises armies<br>• Establishes tariffs<br>• Regulates commerce between the states | • Executes the laws<br>• Establishes executive agencies to help execute laws | • Decides disputes between individuals or between branches of government and individuals |

Which of the following functions is NOT performed by the Supreme Court of the United States?

- A. deciding whether state laws violate the Constitution
- B. deciding whether federal laws violate the Constitution
- C. hearing the final appeal in criminal cases
- D. outlawing behavior such as drug use or robbery

46. Much of the money spent on political campaigns is spent by individuals or companies who are not officially part of the campaign. For example, XYZ Corporation might pay for an expensive television ad supporting Candidate Smith for election. Because some feel that this gives wealthy people or companies too much influence, the federal government restricted this type of spending in 2002. However, in 2010, the U.S. Supreme Court ruled that part of the 2002 law was unconstitutional because the law restricted the expression of political ideas.

Which of the following parts of the Constitution did the Supreme Court most likely base its decision on?

- A. the First Amendment, which protects the right of free speech
- B. the Commerce Clause, which gives Congress the power to regulate trade
- C. the Fifth Amendment, which prohibits government from taking property without legal process
- D. the Necessary and Proper Clause, which gives Congress the power to make laws

47. The National Labor Relations Act, passed by Congress in 1935, guarantees the right of workers to organize into unions, engage in collective bargaining, and strike if collective bargaining fails.

Which one of the following activities is most likely NOT protected by the National Labor Relations Act?

- A. George is offended by a joke made by a co-worker and complains to his manager about it.
- B. Lupe tells her co-worker that she thinks they should join a union and gives him a union pamphlet.
- C. Workers at the XYZ Company hold a vote about whether they want to be represented by a union.
- D. A union decides that negotiations with a company have failed and calls for a strike.

STOP. You have completed the *Social Studies Practice Test.*

**Review your work using the explanations that start on page 747.**

# Science Practice Test

**Directions: Use 85 minutes to answer the following 47 questions.**

Question 1 refers to the following paragraph and diagram.

Newton's third law of motion states that when one object exerts a force upon another object, the second object exerts an equal force on the first, in the opposite direction. An airplane in motion changes the speed and direction of the air, exerting a force on it. The opposing force of the air keeps the airplane aloft.

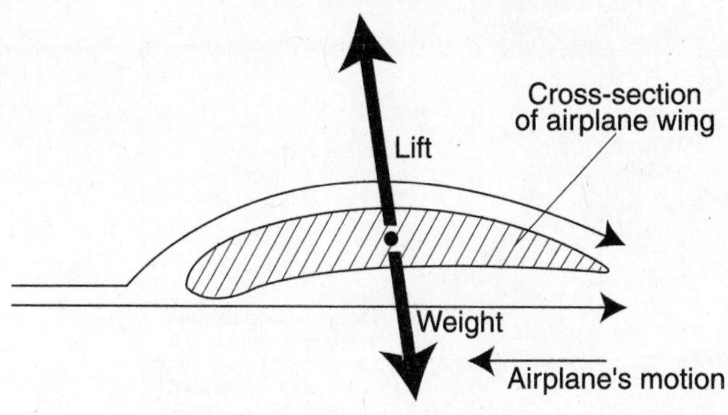


1. What vertical force holds the airplane up?

   A. lift
   B. Newton's Third Law
   C. weight
   D. air resistance

---

2. Sleep may have evolved in humans for several reasons. First, people were unable to hunt, gather food, or travel in the dark. Second, sleep provides an opportunity to repair our body's cells, especially those in the brain. Third, our body temperature is lower during sleep, which conserves energy. Fourth, during deep sleep the pituitary gland releases a growth hormone, so sleep may play a role in growth.

   Which of the following is the best title for this paragraph?

   A. "Sleep and Growth"
   B. "Our Brains During Sleep"
   C. "Why We Sleep"
   D. "The Role of Deep Sleep"

3. You MAY use your calculator on this question.

   A scientist shines a laser through six beakers, each containing a different liquid substance, and measures the laser beam's angle of refraction. The scientist records her measurements for liquids A–E in the table below; her measurement for liquid F is lost.

| Liquid | Angle of Refraction (degrees) |
|---|---|
| A | 15 |
| B | 32 |
| C | 12 |
| D | 47 |
| E | 15 |
| F | ? |

   However, the scientist recalls that the mean of all six angle measurements was 23 degrees. What must the laser beam's angle of refraction through liquid F have been?

   A. 15
   B. 17
   C. 23
   D. 32

**Questions 4 through 6 are based on the following information and graphic.**

The processes that circulate nitrogen between the atmosphere, land, and organisms are called the nitrogen cycle.

**The Nitrogen Cycle**

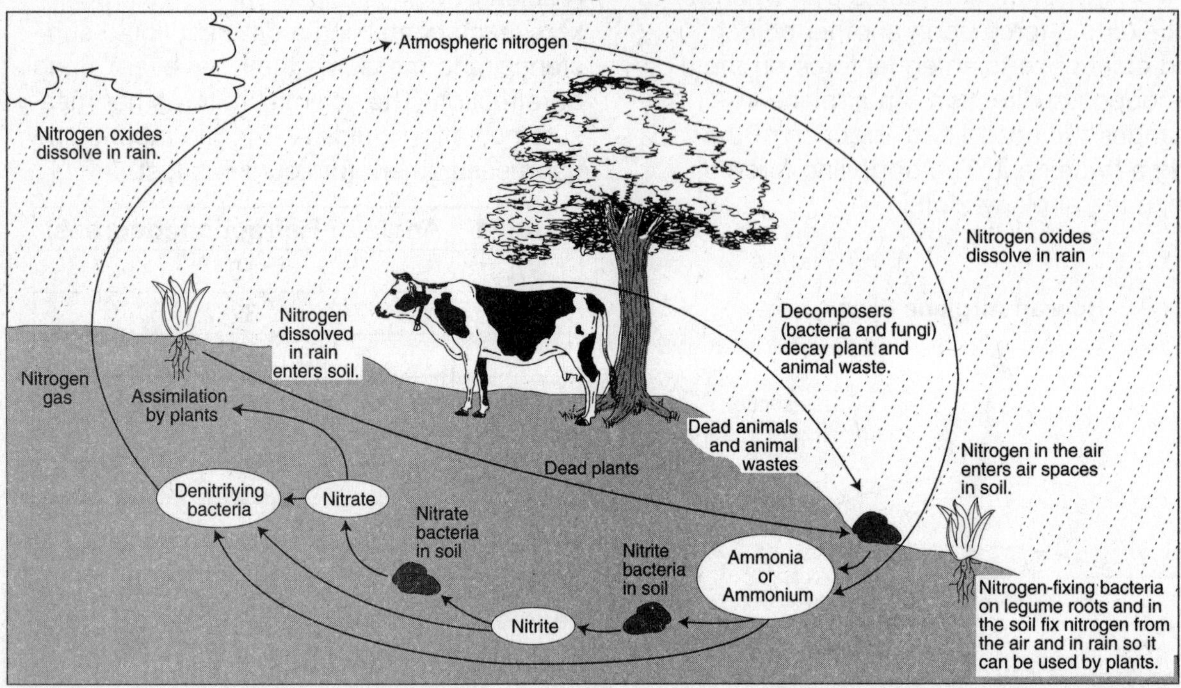


4. Nitrogen-fixing bacteria are found both in the soil and on the roots of legumes like peas and beans. From where do these bacteria get nitrogen?

   - A. ammonia and ammonium
   - B. the air and rainwater in the soil
   - C. animals and animal wastes
   - D. animal wastes and decaying plants

5. Which of the following statements is a conclusion about the nitrogen cycle rather than a detail in the diagram?

   - A. Nitrogen oxides dissolve in rainwater.
   - B. Nitrogen-fixing bacteria are found both in the soil and on the roots of legumes.
   - C. The recycling of nitrogen through the biosphere involves many complex processes.
   - D. Nitrite bacteria turn ammonia and ammonium into nitrites.

6. To increase the nitrogen content of the soil, many farmers spread synthetic fertilizers containing nitrogen compounds. What might an organic farmer, who does not use synthetic fertilizers, do to improve the fertility of the soil?

   - A. switch to crops requiring more potassium
   - B. compost with plant and animal wastes
   - C. plant more nonleguminous plants
   - D. switch to crops requiring more nitrogen

**Question 7 refers to the following graph.**

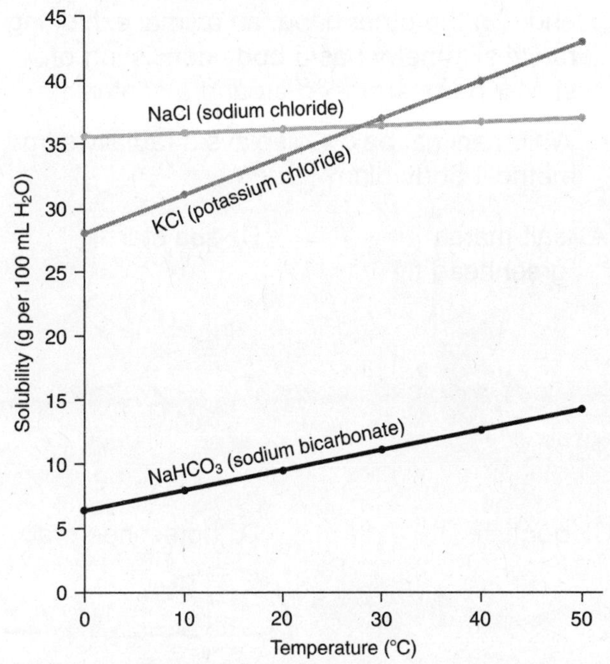


7. Which of the following statements is supported by the information in the graph?

   - A. About 15 grams of sodium bicarbonate will dissolve in 100 mL of water at 10°C.
   - B. About 30 grams of potassium chloride will dissolve in 100 mL of water at 30°C.
   - C. Sodium chloride shows the greatest increase in solubility with increase in temperature.
   - D. For the three compounds shown, solubility increases as temperature increases.

8. A certain scientist wondered whether water at different temperatures might affect houseplants differently. He guessed that slightly warm water might be better for plants than cool water. For six weeks, the scientist used water at 75 degrees to water plants in Group A and used water at 55 degrees to water plants in Group B. He recorded their growth during this period. At the end of six weeks, the plants in Group A were, on average, 2 inches taller than plants in Group B. The scientist interpreted this to mean that slightly warm water is better for plants than cool water.

   Which of the following statements from the passage describes the scientist's hypothesis?

   - A. He guessed that slightly warm water might be better for plants than cool water.
   - B. For six weeks, the scientist used water at 75 degrees to water plants in Group A and used water at 55 degrees to water plants in Group B.
   - C. He recorded their growth during this period.
   - D. The scientist interpreted this to mean that warm water is better for plants than cool water.

9. Atoms are composed of protons (positive charge), neutrons (no charge), and electrons (negative charge). Because an atom has an equal number of protons and electrons, it has a total charge of zero.

   What would happen if an atom lost an electron?

   - A. Its charge would become positive.
   - B. Its charge would become negative.
   - C. Its charge would remain neutral.
   - D. Its neutrons would gain a positive charge.

10. Weathering is the breaking down of rock by rain, frost, wind, and other elements. No transport is involved in weathering. The weathered rock remains in place. Weathering can be physical, involving abrasion—the wearing away of a surface—or changes in temperature; it can be chemical, involving chemical reactions; or it can be organic, involving the action of living things.

Which of the following is an example of physical weathering?

- A. the cracking of granite from the expansion of freezing water
- B. the breakdown of calcite by reaction with acids in fertilizer
- C. the transport of sand by the wind
- D. the breakdown of crumbling rock in the soil by burrowing worms

11. When removed from the body, large organs live only a few hours or days under cold conditions. Therefore, organ transplants must be performed quickly. Many organs go to waste because the organ cannot be transported to an appropriate patient in the short time available. Unfortunately, it is not yet possible to freeze large organs to preserve them for a longer period. That's because they contain many different types of cells, all of which react differently to freezing. Some cells are even destroyed by the ice crystals that form during freezing.

Which of the following studies is most likely to yield information that might help solve the specific problem of freezing whole organs for transplant?

- A. how the time it takes to locate patients who need organs can be decreased
- B. how the time it takes to transport organs to their destinations can be decreased
- C. how special fluids keep insects alive during subfreezing weather
- D. how radioactive isotopes can be used to diagnose the condition of donated organs

12. Most animals have bodies that exhibit either bilateral symmetry or radial symmetry. If you drew a straight line down the middle of an animal exhibiting bilateral symmetry, the two sides would be mirror images of one another. Such animals have a front end and a rear end. On the other hand, an animal exhibiting radial symmetry has a body consisting of similar parts arranged around a center.

Which animal below displays a radially symmetrical body plan?

A. salt marsh greenhead fly

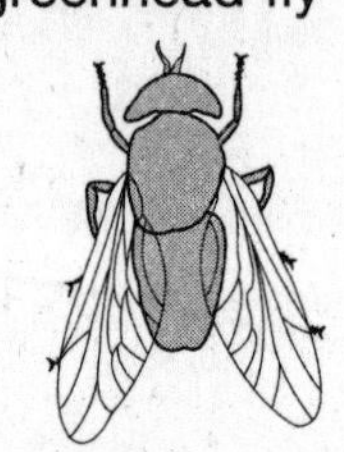

B. sea star

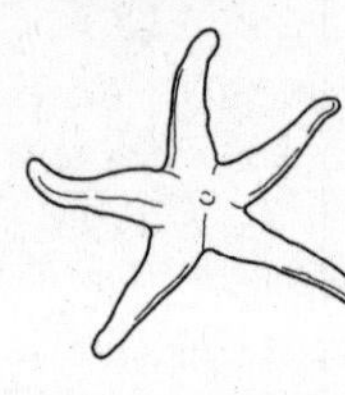

C. dogfish

D. horseshoe crab

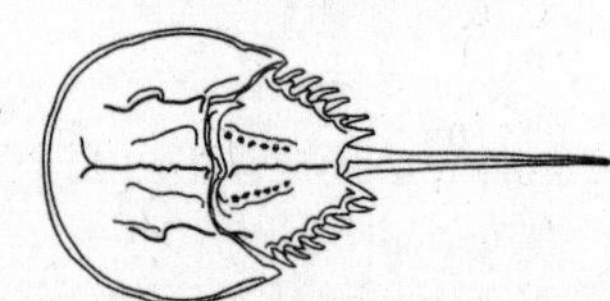

13. Hydrogen peroxide molecules are composed of two hydrogen atoms and two oxygen atoms. Water is also composed of hydrogen and oxygen, but water has one fewer oxygen atom than hydrogen peroxide does. Which of the following statements best describes the chemical reaction shown in the equation below?

$$2H_2O_2 \rightarrow 2H_2O + O_2$$

- A. Hydrogen peroxide is being made out of water and air.
- B. Hydrogen peroxide is decomposing into pure water.
- C. Hydrogen peroxide is decomposing into water and oxygen.
- D. Water and oxygen are combining to make hydrogen peroxide.

**Question 14 refers to the following chart.**

**Melting and Boiling Points**

| Element | Melting Point, °F | Boiling Point, °F |
|---|---|---|
| Mercury | −38 | 675 |
| Bromine | 19 | 138 |
| Iron | 2,795 | 5,184 |
| Carbon | 6,420 | 8,720 |
| Gold | 1,945 | 5,379 |

14. Which of the following statements is supported by the information in the chart?

- A. Mercury and bromine are liquids at room temperature.
- B. Iron has a higher melting point than carbon.
- C. Iron has a higher boiling point than gold.
- D. Mercury, bromine, iron, carbon, and gold are all metals.

---

15. In 1969, the U.S. Surgeon General announced that infectious bacterial diseases would soon become a thing of the past because antibiotic drugs had become so effective against them. However, since that time, strains of disease-causing bacteria that are resistant to antibiotics have evolved. Some types of pneumonia and gastrointestinal infections are now untreatable by antibiotics. About 17 million people worldwide still die annually from infectious diseases.

Which of the following best explains why the U.S. Surgeon General's prediction was wrong?

- A. Antibiotic drugs are not effective against most disease-causing bacteria.
- B. Infectious diseases are also caused by viruses and parasites.
- C. Infectious diseases have remained a problem outside the United States.
- D. Bacteria quickly evolved resistance to antibiotic drugs.

16. A student did an experiment to see how far a ball would roll on different surfaces. He made five different ramps, each with a different surface: a plain pine board, a painted board, a board covered with sandpaper, a board covered with artificial turf, and a board covered with shag carpet. He set up his experiment on a smooth, level floor. To make the ramps, he raised one end of each board with a book. He collected four copies of the science textbook his class was using and set up four of the ramps with these books. He couldn't find a fifth copy of the book, so he used a thinner science study guide to set up the fifth ramp. He rolled a tennis ball down each ramp and measured how far the ball traveled each time. Then he compiled his data and drew conclusions.

Why was the student's experiment flawed?

- A. The student should have used a ball with a smooth surface rather than a tennis ball.
- B. The student should have used books of the same height for all of the ramps.
- C. The student should not have used sandpaper as one of the surfaces.
- D. For a control, the student should have rolled the ball across a piece of wood that was level.

**Question 17 refers to the following paragraph and diagram.**

Herbivores are animals that eat only plants; carnivores are animals that eat animals. Typical herbivore and carnivore teeth patterns are shown below.

**Typical Teeth Patterns in Carnivores and Herbivores**

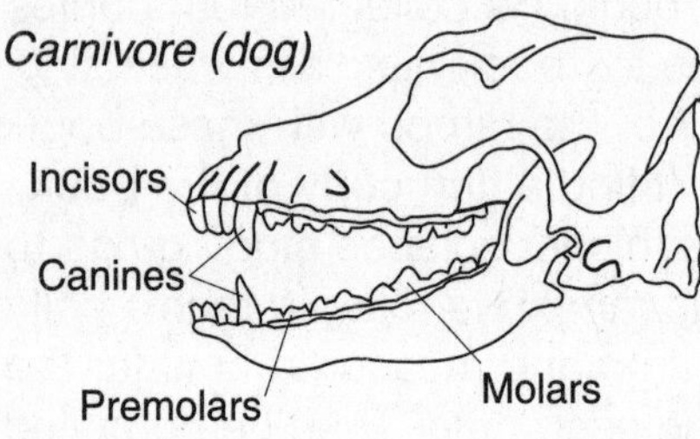


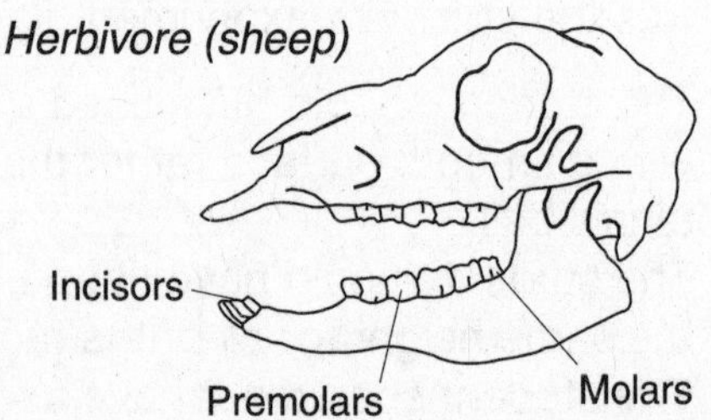


17. What is the most notable difference between the dog's teeth and the sheep's teeth?

- A. The dog has fewer teeth than the sheep does.
- B. The dog has molars and the sheep does not.
- C. The dog has incisors and the sheep does not.
- D. The dog has canines and the sheep does not.

**Question 18 refers to the following chart.**

**The Five Largest Asteroids**

| Name | Average distance from sun (Earth = 1) | Time to orbit sun |
|---|---|---|
| Ceres | 2.77 | 4.6 years |
| Pallas | 2.77 | 4.6 years |
| Vesta | 2.36 | 3.6 years |
| Hygeia | 3.13 | 5.5 years |
| Interamnia | 3.06 | 5.4 years |

18. Which of the following statements is supported by the information in the chart?

- A. Pallas is further away from the sun than Hygeia is.
- B. Of the five largest asteroids, Vesta has the longest orbital period.
- C. The five largest asteroids are all farther from the sun than Earth is.
- D. Of the five largest asteroids, only Interamnia takes more than five years to orbit the sun.

19. The American lobster, *Homerus americanus,* is typically bluish-green to brown in coloration. However, a rare genetic mutation, estimated to occur in 1 in 2 million lobsters, can result in a bright blue-colored shell. In 2011, 220 million pounds of lobsters, typically weighing 1–9 pounds each, were caught; two blue lobsters were reported in that time.

In 2011, the experimental probability of catching a blue lobster was ____________ the estimated probability of a lobster having the blue mutation.

- A. greater than
- B. approximately the same as
- C. less than
- D. dependent upon

**Question 20 is based on the following diagram.**

**Structure of a Volcano**

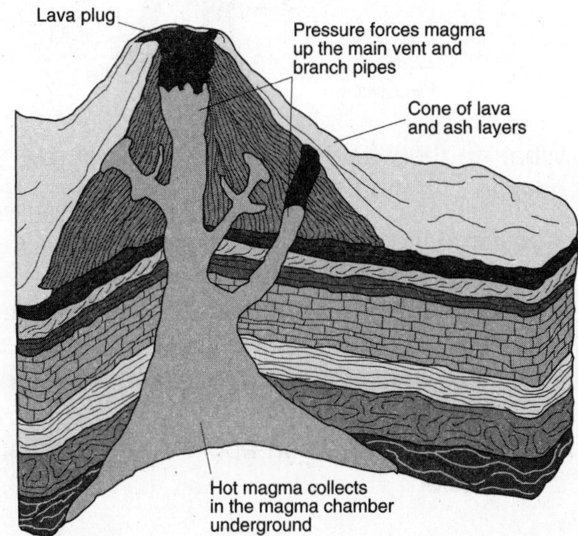


20. Based on the diagram, what causes a volcano to erupt?

- A. Pressure builds up inside the magma chamber and vent.
- B. Magma flows down toward the underground chamber.
- C. The lava plug at the top of the main vent wears away.
- D. The lava plug at the top of the main vent collapses inward.

21. In a chemical reaction, the atoms of the reactants are rearranged to form products with different chemical and physical properties. A catalyst is a substance that speeds the rate at which a chemical reaction takes place. The catalyst itself is unchanged at the end of the reaction. In which of the following reactions is a catalyst at work?

- A. when an acid is neutralized, as when hydrochloric acid is added to sodium hydroxide yielding sodium chloride and water
- B. when food is digested, as when an enzyme in saliva called ptyalin breaks down starch into sugars without itself changing
- C. when copper is oxidized by combining with nitric acid to yield copper nitrate, nitrogen dioxide, and water
- D. when baking soda is heated, causing the sodium bicarbonate to break down, yielding carbon dioxide gas as a byproduct

22. For five years, researchers at the University of Wisconsin Medical School ran an experiment in which they evaluated the hearing of 3,753 people between the ages of 48 and 92. Of the group, 46 percent were nonsmokers, 30.3 percent were former smokers, and 14.7 percent still smoked. The scientists found that smokers were nearly 1.7 times as likely as nonsmokers to suffer hearing loss. The study suggests that age-related hearing loss might be preventable.

Which of the following statements is most likely to have been the researchers' hypothesis?

- A. Smoking has been shown to harm health in many different ways.
- B. People can reduce their chances of developing age-related hearing loss by not smoking.
- C. The University of Wisconsin study group consisted of 3,753 people between the ages of 48 and 92.
- D. Smokers were nearly 1.7 times as likely as nonsmokers to suffer hearing loss.

**Question 23 refers to the following graphs.**

**Elements in Humans and Bacteria**

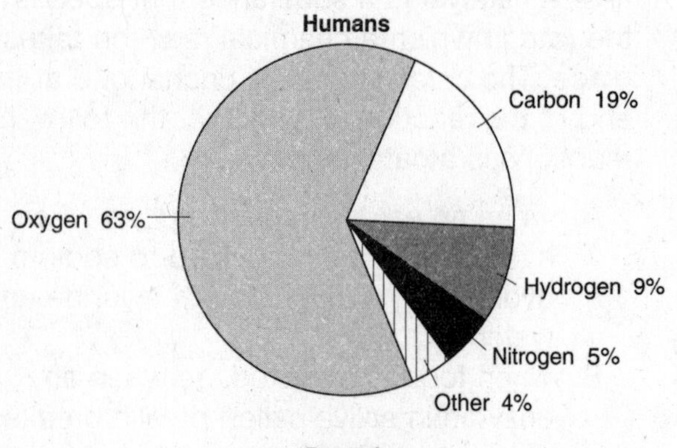


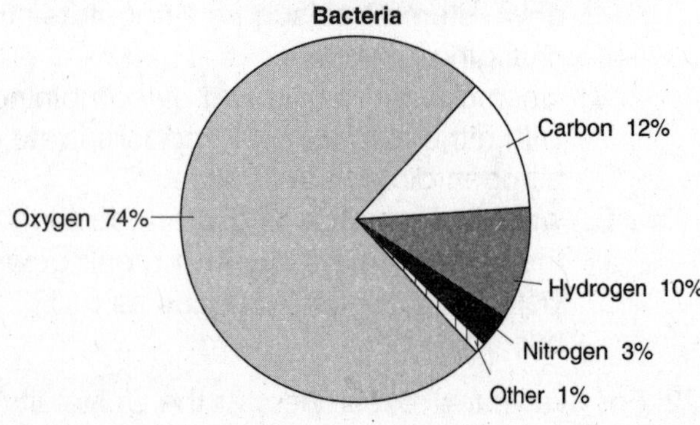


23. What is one of the main differences between the composition of humans and that of bacteria?

- A. Humans contain elements other than oxygen, carbon, nitrogen, and hydrogen and bacteria do not.
- B. Humans contain a higher percentage of oxygen than bacteria do.
- C. Humans contain a higher percentage of hydrogen than bacteria do.
- D. Humans contain a higher percentage of carbon than bacteria do.

**Question 24 refers to the following diagrams.**

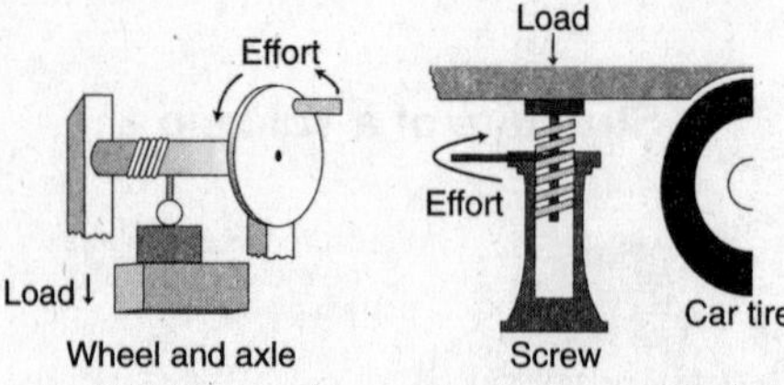


24. What do the wheel and axle and the screw have in common?

- A. Both increase the effort needed to move a load.
- B. Both involve effort applied with circular motion.
- C. Both involve effort applied with horizontal motion.
- D. Both involve effort applied with vertical motion.

---

25. During various periods in Earth's history, average global temperatures have dropped, resulting in ice ages. During an ice age, glaciers cover large regions of Earth. Scientists disagree about what causes ice ages. One hypothesis suggests that there have been long term changes in Earth's orbit, causing the planet to periodically move farther from the sun. Another view proposes that a periodic increase in volcanic activity increases the dust in the atmosphere, blocking the sun's rays. Still another hypothesis suggests that changes in Earth's own radiant energy cause ice ages. And finally, other scientists propose that changes in the direction of ocean currents cause ice ages.

Which of the following statements is a fact and NOT an opinion or hypothesis?

- A. During an ice age, temperatures drop and ice covers vast areas of Earth.
- B. Changes in Earth's orbit cause temperature fluctuations and ice ages.
- C. Large amounts of volcanic dust blocking the sun's energy cause ice ages.
- D. Changes in the Earth's own radiant energy cause ice ages.

**Question 26 refers to the following diagram.**

Ether ($C_2H_6O$)

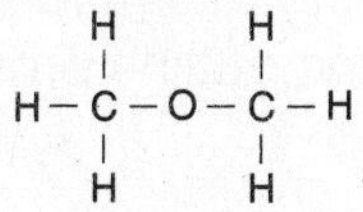

```
    H       H
    |       |
H - C - O - C - H
    |       |
    H       H
```

Ethanol ($C_2H_5OH$)

```
    H   H
    |   |
H - C - C - OH
    |   |
    H   H
```

Key

C = Carbon

H = Hydrogen

O = Oxygen

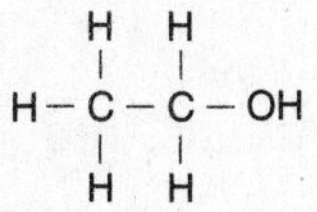

26. What is the main difference between the hydrocarbons ether and ethanol?

 A. Ether has carbon, hydrogen, and oxygen atoms, and ethanol has only carbon and hydrogen atoms.
 B. Ether has three carbon atoms and ethanol has two carbon atoms.
 C. Ether has one oxygen atom and ethanol has two oxygen atoms.
 D. The arrangement of the carbon, hydrogen, and oxygen atoms in the two hydrocarbons is different.

---

27. In 1861, Charles Darwin, a naturalist who formulated the theory of evolution, remarked that the science of geology had made much progress in his lifetime. He wrote, "About thirty years ago there was much talk that geologists ought only to observe and not theorize; and I well remember someone saying that at this rate a man might as well go into a gravel-pit and count the pebbles and describe the colors. How odd it is that anyone should not see that all observation must be for or against some view if it is to be of any service!"

Which of the following statements best summarizes Darwin's view of the role of observation in science?

 A. Observation is the best way to gather facts about any aspect of nature.
 B. Observation is useful as long as it is supported by statistics.
 C. Observation should be used only in the field of geology.
 D. Observation is useful as long as the results are used to support or disprove a hypothesis.

28. The four types of processes that create minerals in Earth's crust are called *magmatic*, *hydrothermal*, *metamorphic*, and *surficial*. Magmatic processes involve the heating and cooling of magma deep inside the Earth's mantle to form crystals. Hydrothermal processes are caused by the movement of water within Earth's crust. Metamorphic processes involve combinations of heat, pressure, time, water, and various solutions to change existing mineral deposits and form new ones. Surficial processes are physical processes that affect rock at Earth's surface or in the loose material—soil and dust—that covers Earth's crust.

Fill in the blanks. Wind eroding away the softer components of sandstone is an example of a _________ process, while the movement of seawater through fractured rock underground is an example of a _________ process.

 A. magmatic; surficial
 B. hydrothermal; metamorphic
 C. surficial; hydrothermal
 D. metamorphic; hydrothermal

**Question 29 refers to the following graph. You MAY use your calculator.**

**Rainfall in 5 Cities in California, 2008–2010**

| | 2008–2009 Rain (in.) | 2009–2010 Rain (in.) |
|---|---|---|
| **Crescent City** | 49.35 | 62.77 |
| **Eureka** | 29.75 | 44.51 |
| **Ukiah** | 22.68 | 40.52 |
| **Redding** | 23.71 | 30.45 |
| **Sacramento** | 16.33 | 20.74 |

**Source: Golden Gate Weather Services**

29. Which city had the median increase in rainfall between the two time periods displayed in the table?

- A. Crescent City
- B. Eureka
- C. Ukiah
- D. Redding

---

30. Earth's atmosphere has several distinct layers. The layer closest to Earth's surface, called the troposphere, is the densest. Most familiar weather phenomena, such as rain clouds and thunderstorms, occur exclusively in the troposphere. The layer above the troposphere is called the stratosphere. Blue jets, a type of upper-atmosphere lightning not typically seen from Earth's surface, occur in the stratosphere, generally several miles directly above a thunderstorm discharging ordinary lightning. However, phenomena occurring far above the stratosphere, such as meteor showers and auroras, may be visible from Earth's surface without a telescope.

Which of the following phenomena can occur in either the troposphere or the stratosphere?

- A. lightning
- B. meteor showers
- C. rain clouds
- D. blue jets

31. Brock's physics teacher has assigned everyone in his class the task of conducting an experiment. To write up their experiments, everyone must use the outline provided below.

**Experiment Outline**
Step 1. Formulate a question about a phenomenon.
Step 2. Form a hypothesis.
Step 3. Test the hypothesis through an experiment.
Step 4. Draw a conclusion.

The following choices represent the steps that Brock took, but they are not listed in order. Which one represents "Step 3: Test the hypothesis through an experiment"?

- A. Brock placed wooden cubes that weighed 1 cc, 10 cc, and 100 cc in water. He observed their buoyancy. Then he placed iron cubes of 1 cc, 10 cc, and 100 cc in water and observed their buoyancy.
- B. Brock said: "Since all the wooden cubes floated and all the iron cubes sank, it must be that size does not affect the buoyancy of an object in water."
- C. Brock asked, "Does size affect the buoyancy of an object in water?"
- D. Brock said: "For an object made of a given material, I predict that increasing the size of the object won't affect its buoyancy in water."

32. Like the Earth's surface, Mars's surface features include mountains, valleys, canyons, polar ice caps, and impact craters. Many of the rocks covering its surface also have similar compositions to those found on Earth.

Based on this information, which of the following compounds is definitely found on Mars?

- A. arginine
- B. methionine
- C. DNA
- D. water

33. In 1993, after years of fluctuating water levels in their reservoir, the residents of Weyland County built a dam at one end of the reservoir to regulate and stabilize the water levels. Which point on the graph below most likely represents 1993?

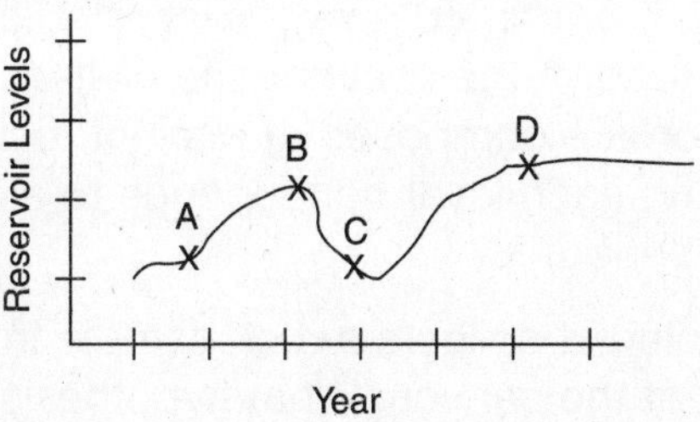


- A. A
- B. B
- C. C
- D. D

34. In the early 20th century, J. J. Thomson discovered the electron and proposed a theory of atomic structure that was dubbed the "plum pudding" model. At the time, plum pudding was a popular dessert and consisted of plum slices dispersed through creamy custard. Thomson suggested that the structure of an atom was similar to the structure of a plum pudding. That is, he believed that an atom was composed of individual electrons surrounded by a uniform cloud of positive charge. However, Ernest Rutherford later disproved this model. Rutherford proposed that atoms were composed of a dense, charged nucleus and electrons orbiting around this nucleus.

The subatomic particle that the plum in Thomson's model corresponds to is a(n)

- A. positron
- B. electron
- C. neutron
- D. proton

35. One property of a gas is that its molecules spread out to fill their container. Which of the following best illustrates this property of gases?

- A. A teacher's perfume can be detected at the back of the classroom.
- B. Rain puddles evaporate more quickly when the sun comes out.
- C. Water is produced when hydrogen gas is burned in oxygen gas.
- D. Liquid oxygen is denser than gaseous oxygen.

36. Photosynthesis is the process by which living plants take in carbon dioxide and water and turn those into nutrients and energy that the plant can use. The chemical equation for photosynthesis is:

$$6CO_2 + 6H_2O \rightarrow C_6H_{12}O_6 + 6O_2$$

Based on this equation, which of the following must be true?

- A. Plants do not need oxygen to survive.
- B. Oxygen is one of the products of photosynthesis.
- C. Plants produce oxygen out of pure energy.
- D. Photosynthesis destroys energy.

37. Air enters the human lungs through the left and right *bronchi*, which divide into smaller airways called *bronchioles*. The bronchioles end in sacs called *alveoli*, which are surrounded by tiny blood vessels called *capillaries*. Deoxygenated blood is pumped by the heart from the various parts of the body to the lungs. In the lungs, the blood takes on oxygen. This happens when oxygen moves from air in the alveoli to the blood in the surrounding capillaries. Oxygenated blood then leaves the lungs through the pulmonary veins and flows back to the various body parts.

    The movement of oxygen from the alveoli into the surrounding capillaries is called *diffusion*. Which two bodily systems are involved in diffusion?

    - A. urinary and respiratory
    - B. circulatory and endocrine
    - C. circulatory and respiratory
    - D. respiratory and nervous

38. Sixty-five million years ago, many plant and animal species died out all at once, but scientists are not sure what caused this mass extinction. One theory states that a gigantic asteroid struck the Earth, kicking up a tremendous dust cloud. The dust in the atmosphere prevented the sun's energy from reaching plants growing on Earth. The plants could not photosynthesize and died. The effect of the dying vegetation was devastating all the way up the food chain, with the result that many plant and animal species went extinct.

    If the mass extinction 65 million years ago was caused by a dust cloud, but that dust cloud was not in fact caused by an asteroid, which of the following events might have led to the mass extinction?

    - A. a solar eclipse
    - B. a series of massive volcanic eruptions lasting many years
    - C. a massive flood
    - D. a solar flare

39. The Grand Canyon is one of the largest geological phenomena in the world. It is approximately 280 miles long and has a maximum depth of 6,000 feet. It was formed over the course of millions of years by the Colorado River. The movement of the river's water eroded, or carried away, layer after layer of rock to form the canyon. The walls of the canyon are composed of distinct rock layers and each layer corresponds to a different time period.

    A geologist collects a rock sample from each layer of the canyon. What hypothesis could best be tested using the rock samples?

    - A. Rock samples obtained from the bottom are older than rock samples obtained from the top.
    - B. Flooding of the Colorado River is frequently due to heavy rainstorms.
    - C. Rock layers tend to erode at the same rate no matter where in the world they are located.
    - D. Winds have less force at the bottom of the Grand Canyon than at the top.

40. Hurricanes are circular storms with high wind speeds. These storms tend to form near the equator. The *Coriolis effect* causes hurricanes to rotate counterclockwise in the northern hemisphere and clockwise in the southern hemisphere. Initially, east-to-west trade winds tend to blow hurricanes westward. The Coriolis effect also causes hurricanes to move north or south toward one of the poles. When a hurricane moving toward one of the poles encounters the mid-latitude westerly winds, a hurricane turns eastward.

**Global Wind Patterns**

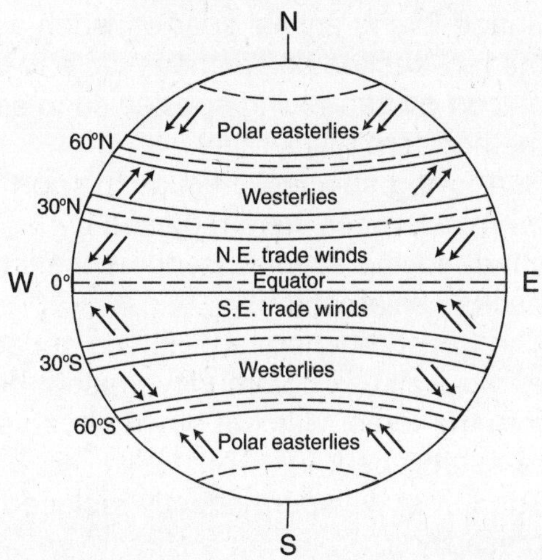


Which of the following most accurately describes the probable rotation and path of a hurricane in the northern hemisphere?

- A. It would rotate counterclockwise and move westward, then southward, and finally eastward.
- B. It would rotate clockwise and move eastward, then northward, and finally westward.
- C. It would rotate counterclockwise and move eastward, then northward, and finally westward.
- D. It would rotate counterclockwise and move westward, then northward, and finally eastward.

41. Newton's Law of Gravitation states that the force (represented by *F*) of gravitation (or attraction) between two objects is represented by the following equation.

$$F_g = \frac{Gm_1m_2}{r^2}$$

The equation shows that the force of gravitation is directly proportional to the product of the objects' masses (where each mass is represented by *m*) but inversely proportional to the square of the distance between them (where the distance between them is represented by *r*).

Consider two objects that both have the same mass. If the distance between these objects is increased, what will happen to the force of gravitation between them?

- A. The force will be increased.
- B. The force will be reduced.
- C. The force will not change.
- D. The force will change, but in a way that cannot be predicted.

42. Frogs living in temperate climates reproduce in the spring and summer months, when food is plentiful. They are often exposed to freezing temperatures during the winter. Frogs are amphibians—that is, creatures that live part of their lives on land and part of their lives in water.

Given this information, which of the following must be true?

- A. Frogs maintain a stable body temperature year-round, even in the winter.
- B. Frogs exposed to freezing temperatures during the winter invariably die.
- C. Frogs' bodies have a way to prevent their cells from freezing in cold temperatures.
- D. Frogs can find sufficient food in the winter to reproduce even in freezing temperatures.

43. In a healthy person, blood sugar levels in the bloodstream do not exceed a tightly controlled range. This metabolic control is called *homeostasis*. In a person with diabetes mellitus, homeostasis is interrupted, and blood sugar levels are higher than in a healthy individual. Diabetes mellitus can have a number of different causes. However, the most direct reason for high blood sugar is either the inability of the pancreas to produce sufficient insulin, or the inability of cells in the body tissues to respond to whatever insulin is produced.

Which of the following might be an appropriate treatment for a person with diabetes mellitus?

- A. bed rest
- B. blood transfusions
- C. insulin injections
- D. medication to restore calcium homeostasis

44. The human liver performs a number of functions including protein synthesis and storage, turning carbohydrates into energy, and removing toxins from the body. The liver rids itself of toxins by producing bile, whose yellow color comes from a substance called *bilirubin*.

Based on this information, which of the following symptoms is a primary indication of liver disease?

- A. pain in the extremities due to neurological problems
- B. hearing loss due to atherosclerosis
- C. loss of night vision caused by vitamin A deficiency
- D. jaundice, a yellow discoloration of the skin due to a systemic buildup of bilirubin

45. An old growth forest is a climax community and tends to be a fairly stable ecosystem. When the trees in an old growth forest burn or are cut down, they are replaced by a succession of other species, and the food web changes dramatically. Eventually, the forest returns to its climax state, but this process can take hundreds of years.

Imagine a mature Adirondack hemlock forest in New York State shortly after all the trees were cut down sometime in the 19th century. Which of the following changes probably took place?

- A. Shade-loving animal species, such as the red-backed salamander, were replaced by sun-loving species such as the northern black racer.
- B. Sun-loving species, such as the northern black racer, were replaced by shade-loving species, such as the red-backed salamander.
- C. The forest regenerated within a decade, and the climax community present before the forest was cut down became re-established.
- D. The forest was permanently replaced by grasslands.

46. The life cycle of many plants, including spore-producing plants such as ferns, takes place in two generations that alternate: the *gametophyte* generation and the *sporophyte* generation. In ferns, the gametophyte is a very small, heart-shaped structure. During the gametophyte generation, sex cells are produced, two of which fuse to produce a zygote. The zygote grows into the sporophyte. In ferns, the sporophyte is the familiar green plant with leaves, stems, and roots. During the sporophyte generation, gametes, which grow into the gametophyte, are produced.

Which of the following conclusions is supported by this information?

- A. Ferns are the only plants that have different forms in alternating generations.
- B. Most people would not recognize the gametophyte generation of a fern.
- C. Some animal life cycles consist of alternating generations with different forms.
- D. All plants that reproduce sexually have leaves, stems, roots, and flowers.

47. Light waves travel in a straight line, but when they strike most surfaces, they bounce off; this is known as reflection. When light is reflected off a smooth surface like a mirror, the incoming rays, called the incident rays, hit the surface at the same angle as the reflected rays bounce off it.

**The Reflection of Light**

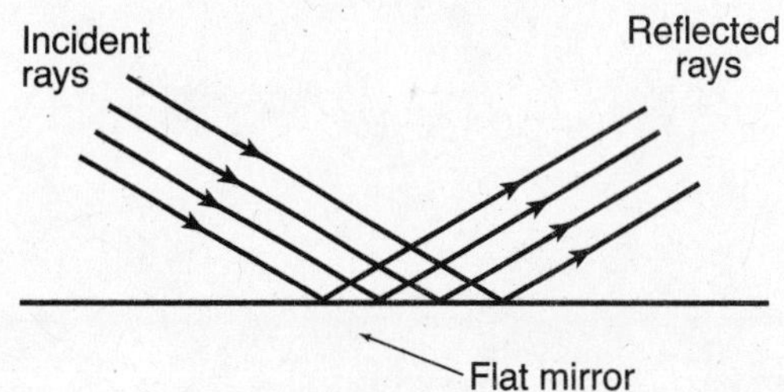


In the preceding diagram, all of the reflected light rays are parallel. Under which of the following circumstances would the reflected light rays travel in many different directions?

- A. if the source of light were distant
- B. if the surface were irregular or rough
- C. if the surface were perfectly flat
- D. if the incident rays were parallel

STOP. You have completed the *Science Test.*

**Review your work using the explanations that start on page 751.**

# TASC Unit Answers and Explanations

# Language Arts: Reading Answers and Explanations

## Interpreting Informational Text

### Lesson 1: Main Ideas and Details

**Practice 1, page 73**

1. **A. searching for a place to call home** The author states this feeling directly in the first two lines and in the last paragraph.
2. **D. the gods** The second sentence in the second paragraph says, "It was ordained by the deities."
3. **D. It was simply part of their beliefs to follow the pole** The meaning of the pole is explained beginning with the fourth sentence of the second paragraph. The last sentence explains that the Chickasaws lacked sorrow because they trusted the pole's command.
4. **C. understands that her tendency to search is part of her Chickasaw heritage** The details about the author's search for a home, combined with the information that "the search for a homeland is part of the Chickasaw migration legend," helps you understand this main idea.
5. **D. accepts that she is Chickasaw** You can see that the writer is saying that her Chickasaw heritage is an inescapable part of who she is.

### Lesson 2: Rephrasing and Summary

**Practice 2, page 75**

1. **C. lack of proper paperwork** As the writer discusses the problems, he states that he wants an "itemized list" and "a proper bill of sale." He does mention the premium price, choice (D), but that price is the reason he expects proper paperwork and is not a complaint in and of itself.
2. **B. the car to be repaired free of charge if the cause of the problem is discovered** This expectation is stated in the fifth paragraph of the letter.
3. **C. The service and warranty on the customer's car have been unacceptable.** The letter is a detailed list of the customer's complaints. They can be summed up by saying that both the service and the warranty have not been as promised.

### Lesson 3: Application of Ideas

**Practice 3, page 77**

1. **A. overcoming a bad habit** The writer advises those trying to break free of credit card debt: "Stick with it until you're free again."
2. **B. never use the credit cards** The last paragraph implies that the author approves of using credit cards only once you have already gotten out of debt, and then only for convenience. Thus, if you are in debt, you should stop using your credit cards.
3. **C. losing weight by avoiding all-you-can-eat buffets** Basically, the advice is that you gradually lose your debt by not adding anything to it. This is similar to helping yourself lose weight by not adding to it with portions of food you don't need.
4. **C. "Live within your means."** This statement can be inferred from the advice "Don't borrow any more," and "What I'm against is buying more on your credit cards than you can pay for at the end of the month."

### Lesson 4: Cause and Effect

**Practice 4, page 79**

1. **C. It affected nearly everyone.** This answer summarizes the meaning of the first two sentences of the passage.
2. **A. Many people lost the mortgages on their homes.** This answer is stated in the first paragraph: "men and women who saw their mortgages foreclosed." Choices (B) and (D) are both mentioned as causes, not effects, of the depression.
3. **B. low worker incomes** The second paragraph states, "but the actual cause of the collapse was an unhealthy economy. . . . Most laborers . . . could not afford to buy the automobiles . . . because their incomes were too low."
4. **B. They had little effect.** The writer tells what Herbert Hoover did as president to curb the depression ("loans to businesses and banks") but then states that "his efforts proved to be too little and too late."
5. **D. The depression left people emotionally scarred.** The first paragraph states, "No one who lived through those years . . . could ever completely forget." The statement about eating mustard that is provided in the question addresses this emotional effect rather than issues related to farmers, workers, the economy, or the number of individuals affected.

### Lesson 5: Comparison and Contrast

**Practice 5, page 81**

1. **D. leave some of his possessions behind** This answer is found in the seventh and eighth lines of paragraph 1.
2. **C. They provided milk and pulled wagons.** The selection states that "cows . . . gave milk all the way to the sink of the Humboldt where they died, having acted as draught animals for several weeks after the oxen had perished."
3. **A. the provisions of each group of travelers** Each paragraph talks about a different group and what it had to offer the wagon train. For example, "Much in contrast to these men were four batchelors . . . , who had a wagon drawn by four oxen . . . cows following behind."
4. **A. be happy to have people who could cook and sew** The writer was interested in assessing how self-sufficient the group could be and what each group could offer the entire wagon train. For example, she writes, "but as he was a wagon maker and his companion a blacksmith by trade and both were accommodating there were always ready hands to 'pry the wheel out of mire.'"

5. **A. They must cooperate and work together.** Throughout the excerpt, there is evidence that all the travelers depended on each other for animals, food, and physical help, such as pulling wagons out of the mud.

## Lesson 6: Conclusions and Generalizations

### Practice 6.1, page 83

1. **A. It is rewarding and one of life's joys.** The passage states that "my teacher's genius, . . . made the first years of my education so beautiful." She also delights in observing and learning from the tadpole.
2. **D. insightful and grateful** The writer has insight about the connection between herself and the tadpole: "Thus I learned from life itself. At the beginning I was only a little mass of possibilities." The writer is also grateful to her teacher: "nor has she ceased trying . . . to make my life sweet and useful."
3. **C. show Helen how addition is used in everyday life** You can apply what you learn in the diary entry: "Thus I learned from life itself. . . . She has never since let pass an opportunity to point out the beauty that is in everything. . . ." The teacher would therefore probably use everyday life situations to teach.
4. **D. as an anecdote followed by a generalization based on the anecdote** The writer tells the story of the tadpoles (an anecdote) and relates it to her attitude toward life and learning.
5. **D. Their development is not entirely smooth.** The writer describes the tadpole having difficulty after leaping out of the bowl. This is similar to the quotation about "the stony course" of a child's education.

### Practice 6.2, page 85

1. **C. On the whole, temperatures are not rising.** The writer states that rising temperatures are "quite simply not what is happening," based on the cold temperatures of the day before.
2. **A. Shady Hollow was hit with a record cold temperature yesterday.** This one piece of information is the example the author uses to support the generalization that temperatures, generally speaking, are not rising.
3. **D. worldwide data tables of temperatures from the 1980s through today** The author's generalization suffers from being based on one temperature reading. His generalization would be more likely to be valid if informed by many temperature readings over time.

## Lesson 7: Word Choice

### Practice 7, page 87

1. **D. the CoolForter blanket** The first sentence of paragraph 2 tells you two things about the CoolForter blanket: that "it works like an electric blanket" and that "it feels like a dream."
2. **B. to show that the blanket is a pleasant indulgence** To "coddle" is to treat gently or take care of a person. Choice (B) describes this idea.
3. **A. fluid** Many people associate the word *chemical* with toxicity or harm. A more neutral word to describe the cooling substance without inaccurate specificity is *fluid.*
4. **C. bland** The word *bland* indicates a lack of interesting features. Unlike the word *neutral,* which also indicates a lack of characteristic features, the word *bland* can carry a negative connotation.
5. **D. It allows the consumer to compare the CoolForter's energy usage to that of a familiar item.** The author's choice of a light bulb, an item with which most readers are probably familiar, emphasizes that the CoolForter blanket will not use excessive amounts of energy.

## Lesson 8: Writer's Tone and Point of View

### Practice 8, page 89

1. **C. the Internet writers** The writer mentions "Internet sass" and then goes on to say that "you gotta love it" because it keeps writers "off the street and out of trouble."
2. **A. The Internet reviews were much more interesting than the TV show.** The review states, "They [Internet writers] were taking hours and hours of primetime dross and turning it into decadent, amoral, sharp, electronic gold."
3. **A. The show was boring.** The reviewer's main opinion of the show is that it was bad and boring ("non-goings-on of the non-people in the non-house"). Someone yawning supports the idea of boredom.
4. **C. informal and hip** Phrases such as "the dude" and "you gotta love it" contribute to an informal and modern, or hip, tone.
5. **C. someone knowledgeable about the media** The reviewer talks knowledgeably about both television and the Internet.

## Lesson 9: Text Structure

### Practice 9, page 91

1. **B. exposure to the cowpox disease** As seen in the text, James's recovery from cowpox followed his exposure to it. Note that choice (D) refers to Jenner exposing James to smallpox, not cowpox.
2. **C. "After being exposed to the disease"** The transition word *After* tells the reader that James's exposure came before his catching cowpox and recovery from it. Thus, it gives the reader explicit information about the order of the steps in the process.
3. **B. A number of factors can damage a garden.** As discussed in the passage, factors such as weather, pests, and diseases can affect plants and cause damage, undoing the time and work that have been invested.

## Interpreting Informational Text Practice Questions, pages 92–95

1. **D. hit a boy in the arm to get his attention** The writer talks about breaking a ruler over the head of a boy she likes; you can therefore conclude that she

would hit a boy in the arm to get his attention. She responds physically and without much thought to consequences.

2. **B. She was just pretending she didn't want to go to the principal's office.** The circumstances of Brer Rabbit pretending he was afraid to go into the briar patch where he was born and raised are similar to the speaker pretending to be afraid to go to the principal's office.
3. **C. unusual** From the different examples of how Frank Doleman behaved (allowing a young girl to play chess in his office and not punishing boys sent to his office), you can conclude that he was an unusual principal.
4. **A. confident** The additional information you get from the new quotation and the examples of her behavior, plus the overall tone of the excerpt, suggest a confident young girl.
5. **C. concerned but hopeful.** The author is worried about the health impact of soda consumption on teenagers. But she is also hopeful; in the last sentence, she states that more "can" be done to reduce the consumption of sugary beverages.
6. **D. Young people will choose healthier beverages if they are better educated about the dangers of regular soda consumption.** The last paragraph supports this choice. Choice (A) is unsupported by the passage: even though the author does not condemn the legal measures mentioned in paragraph 2, you do not know whether she would support an overall ban. Choice (B) is unsupported also; the author never mentions diet soda.
7. **C. Young people who drink these beverages regularly will eventually suffer from the same ailments as those who drink soda regularly.** The author points out that, even though juice and energy drinks have somewhat less sugar than soda, regular consumption of those products "is likely to be just as damaging in the long term."
8. **B. effective to some extent.** After describing the measures, the author begins paragraph 3 by stating, "These efforts appear to be paying off" but goes on to explain why they may not fully solve the problem of sugar consumption among teenagers.
9. **C. Reducing excessive consumption of soda.** The author is referring to the efforts described in paragraph 2, all of which attempted to reduce soda consumption.
10. **C. The cost of mandated coverage will lessen the ability of NATS to hire and supply temporary workers.** This question is basically answered in paragraph 2: "the cost of mandates could weaken the ability of the temporary help industry to act as a 'jobs bridge.'"
11. **A. Many workers are losing their jobs and need temporary jobs until they find permanent work again.** The third paragraph explains this reason.
12. **D. to raise awareness of one side of an issue** The whole passage—plus knowledge of who Edward A. Lenz is—helps you see that its purpose is to explain the position of the NATS.
13. **B. Women will not resort to wearing pants or other restrictive men's clothing.** This statement and the lines that follow it help you see that Stanton is saying men can wear their restrictive clothing; women want no part of it.
14. **D. a cloth worn around the neck** By looking at the context clues—or words around the word *stock*—you can see that it is something worn around the neck.
15. **B. speak up about current events** This very direct speech of Stanton's indicates her straight-to-the-point personality. She is not interested in criticism for its own sake but rather speaks up about issues she strongly believes in.
16. **A. Women are fighting for the right to vote.** The phrase "over the horns of bigotry" helps you see that women are fighting for something. The last paragraph of the excerpt helps you see that they are fighting for the right to vote.

## Analyzing Informational Text

### Lesson 1: Purpose of Text

#### Practice 1, page 97

1. **B. tell how creative engineers saved astronauts** This passage is a narrative about the process of saving the lives of the Apollo 13 astronauts, including in particular the role of engineers. Choices (A), (C), and (D) are all far too broad.
2. **B. supports the writer's main recommendation** The writer recommends that the state cut sales taxes on new vehicles. Preventing deaths with the modern safety features on new cars is one of the reasons for this recommendation.
3. **D. inform about the historical importance of silk** The passage begins by discussing the "historical importance" of silk, and continues throughout to introduce new points about this topic.
4. **C. It provides examples of silk's historical importance in trade and culture.** Nomads traveling to China for silk and the creation of the "Silk Road" are examples of silk's importance.

### Lesson 2: Effectiveness of Argument

#### Practice 2, page 99

1. **B. The federal government should automatically raise the minimum wage to match price increases.** The author states that "[s]everal states have taken the sensible step of automatically raising their minimum wage to adjust for inflation and consumer price increases." Later she also states that "the federal government should follow the lead of the states." Thus, the author is recommending that the federal government should adjust the minimum wage for price increases. The rest of the passage serves to support this recommendation.

2. **D. Those states have systems superior to the federal system of manual increases.** The author's main point is that the federal government should adopt automatic minimum wage increases, as some states currently have done. Thus, she believes that the states' systems are better than the current federal system.
3. **C. Over the past 40 years, the federal minimum wage has not kept pace with inflation.** Choice (C) is a historical fact provided in the second paragraph as evidence to support the writer's argument.
4. **B. Ensuring sustainable incomes for hardworking citizens is a responsibility of lawmakers.** The author states that lawmakers must ensure stability for workers but does not justify why they must do so. She assumes that this is part of the job lawmakers should do.

## Lesson 3: Validity of Arguments

### Practice 3, page 101

1. **C. DRE systems offer more security and accuracy than other voting systems.** The writer introduces DRE voting, describes several voting systems, and concludes by suggesting that DRE prevents the problems associated with these systems and is therefore better.
2. **B. DRE voting avoids problems associated with other voting systems.** The writer supports the assertion that DRE voting is the most accurate and secure voting system by listing problems that might be encountered with other voting systems and then stating that DRE voting avoids such problems.
3. **A. Each voter's choices are recorded in the DRE voting system.** This is one of the facts that the writer cites in support of the assertion that DRE is secure and accurate. The other three answer choices cite facts that are included in the passage, but those facts are all background information and do not give direct support to the writer's main point.
4. **C. The writer fails to consider that even if DRE voting addresses all the flaws of previous systems, it may introduce unique flaws of its own.** The writer's conclusion is based solely on the fact that DRE voting avoids problems that have been associated with the other systems mentioned in the passage. Because no information is given about possible flaws of DRE voting, the reader has no way to verify the writer's claim that DRE voting is the most accurate and secure system.

## Lesson 4: Text Related by Theme or Topic

### Practice 4, page 103

1. **C. online piracy of music files** Both passages are focused on reasons why online piracy is harmful and the need to take further action.
2. **B. additional action to combat online piracy is warranted because piracy causes financial loses to the music industry.** The first passage concludes that more must be done to prevent online piracy. The main factual information the writer uses to support this thesis is information about the financial damage that piracy causes.
3. **A. Fear of piracy makes it difficult for new, experimental acts to get signed.** Both passages reach the same conclusion: more must be done to prevent piracy of music files. Choice (A) is the only answer choice that provides direct support for the conclusion of Passage 2, and, therefore, also for that of Passage 1.
4. **A. Online piracy of digital files has a harmful effect on the music industry.** Both authors provide different reasons as to why piracy is potentially harmful, but both agree that it has a negative effect on the industry.

## Lesson 5: Text with Opposing Arguments

### Practice 5, page 105

1. **C. the MPAA movie rating system** Each writer is making an argument about the relevance and trustworthiness of the MPAA rating system.
2. **B. The MPAA rating system is a useful tool for parents.** The writer of the Argument (Passage 1) uses information about the MPAA rating system to support her argument that the system helps parents to make sound decisions.
3. **D. The MPAA rating system should not be trusted.** In the second sentence, the writer indicates that the MPAA rating system is not a useful guide, and concludes by recommending that parents use a different source of advice.
4. **A. She largely approves of the MPAA rating system as a guideline for parents.** The passage provides no information about the writer's own childrearing decisions, choice (B), or about her opinion of the effect of the Hays Code on the movie industry, choice (D). Also, her statements about the rating system are uniformly positive, making choice (C) incorrect.

## Lesson 6: Texts with Related Graphic Information

### Practice 6, page 107

1. **D. Governing parties can use their power to shape electoral districts to their advantage.** The passage and the figures focus on demonstrating how gerrymandering works. Choices (A) and (B) are not supported at all by the passage, and choice (C) is far too extreme.
2. **B. Through gerrymandering, a governing party can be elected to a greater number of seats than its voter support might otherwise allow.** The second paragraph describes how the second grid figure shows one party winning 75 percent of the seats from 60 percent of the vote,

rather than the 50 percent of seats shown in the first grid figure.

3. **A. They illustrate the advantages a party can obtain through gerrymandering.** As discussed in the passage's second paragraph, the figures show how a party can benefit from the process. While choices (C) and (D) may or may not be true statements, they do not describe how the figures support the passage.

### Analyzing Informational Text Practice Questions, pages 108–111

1. **D. to discuss whether communication technology helps or hurts relationships** This answer choice reflects the scope of the article introduced at the end of the first paragraph.
2. **B. how technology affects interpersonal connections** The question at the end of paragraph 1 introduces this topic. Paragraph 2 discusses positive effects of communication technology while paragraph 3 discusses a negative effect.
3. **D. The caption reveals that the woman's friends will use their phones during their visit.** The caption is similar to a scenario described in the first paragraph of the passage. In both cases, people are choosing to use technology rather than to enjoy the company of those with whom they have an established relationship.
4. **B. New communication technologies may adversely impact important human relationships.** The author's concluding paragraph discusses how communication technology can connect us with so many people that we have less time and energy to spend on relationships with friends and family, and the caption of the image reveals that the visiting friends plan to spend time on their phones rather than in conversing with one another.
5. **B. the giant squid is the world's longest cephalopod** The author's introduction and conclusion both raise this point, and the evidence in the paragraph supports this thesis.
6. **D. The giant squid is longer than the colossal squid.** The author provides scientific evidence about the colossal squid to support the passage's main idea about the giant squid.
7. **C. The length of the longest known colossal squid specimen is ten meters.** This factual evidence supports the author's main idea.
8. **A. The longest known colossal squid is ten meters long, so there is no colossal squid longer than the longest giant squid.** According to paragraph 2, there are very few samples of colossal squid, and all of them have been juveniles. It is improper to draw a conclusion about the entire colossal squid species on the basis of such limited evidence.
9. **B. mercury dental amalgam** Though the authors have somewhat different opinions on the subject, both passages are centrally about mercury dental amalgam.
10. **C. Mercury amalgam fillings should be banned because they are unhealthy and bad for the environment.** The first sentence of Passage 1 states that mercury amalgam should be banned for use in dental fillings. The first paragraph cites health reasons for this opinion. The second paragraph cites environmental reasons. Choice (D) is mentioned in Passage 1, but it serves as support for the author's main point.
11. **D. It is a convincing statistic from a reliable source.** The statement that 40–50 percent of mercury in wastewater is from an easily preventable source is a convincing statistic. The EPA is a large non-political government agency and so is likely to provide reliable information.
12. **A. Consumers have no other reason, such as cost or durability, to prefer mercury amalgam to composite fillings.** The author of Passage 1 states that "banning mercury amalgam would draw no consumer backlash" because resin composite fillings are better for cosmetic reasons. The author assumes that there is no other reason to prefer mercury amalgam.
13. **B. Resin composite fillings look better than mercury amalgam fillings when each is used on visible tooth surfaces.** The author of Passage 2 states that amalgam is preferable to resin composite whenever there is no cosmetic need for a tooth-colored filling. Thus, you can infer that he believes that resin composite fillings look more like natural teeth than mercury amalgam.
14. **A. Passage 1, because it cites no sources for the study or the statistic it cites** The author of passage 1 says that "it has been estimated" that 4 percent of the mercury in Lake Superior comes from dental amalgam, but the author cites no source. The author also gives no source for the 2001 study that is cited in the first paragraph.
15. **D. Mercury that accumulates in body tissues causes a variety of health problems.** The study cited in the first paragraph of passage 1 found a correlation between mercury amalgam fillings and a number of health conditions. A correlation does not prove causation, but the author of passage 1 states that "this accumulated mercury causes a variety of health problems."

## Reading Literature

### Lesson 1: Plot Elements

#### Practice 1, page 113

1. **B. swearing that he was telling the truth** The following statement in the excerpt gives the context and meaning: "It is nevertheless God's own truth, the sacred truth. I repeat it on my soul and my salvation."
2. **D. confronted him and then asked to be searched** According to the excerpt, when the harness-maker comes in and repeats his story, the two "abused each other for an hour. At his own request, Maître Hauchecorne was searched."

3. **C. A peasant is accused of taking a pocket-book.** As you read the excerpt, you understand that a harness-maker has accused a peasant of taking a pocket-book, and the mayor of the town believes the harness-maker.
4. **C. The harness-maker is higher in social status than the peasant.** The harness-maker is characterized as "a man we can believe." The countryman is referred to as a "peasant." You can infer that the difference in the two men's social status affects the way their statements are viewed.

## Lesson 2: Inferences

### Practice 2, page 115

1. **A. had always loved her** In the first paragraph, Josephine recalls her husband's face: "the face that had never looked save with love upon her." The term *save* means "except."
2. **C. spread her arms out in welcome** The first paragraph explains that although Josephine knew she would cry at the sight of her dead husband, "that bitter moment" would soon give way to years of freedom, which she welcomed.
3. **A. she was overcome and thrilled to see her husband** The doctors assumed that Josephine was so glad to learn her husband had not died in an accident that she was shocked and overjoyed to see him walk in the door.
4. **B. She was shocked that she would not be free.** Much of the excerpt is about Josephine looking forward to the freedom of being without her husband. When she learns that her husband is alive, she also learns that she will not be free.

## Lesson 3: Character

### Practice 3, page 117

1. **B. He is frightened about seeing the ghost of his wife.** The witch, supposedly speaking as Yaji's wife, says that she lies in her grave longing for Yaji to die and join her. She then asks, "Shall I come to meet you?" Throughout the passage, Yaji seems uncomfortable. At this moment you can infer that he is scared.
2. **C. untrustworthy** The witch is tricking Yaji. The witch has her own interests at heart when she pretends it is the wife requesting, "Give this witch plenty of money."
3. **D. neglectful** The information we are given about Yaji suggests that he treated his wife poorly when she was alive and now does not tend her grave.

## Lesson 4: Theme

### Practice 4, page 119

1. **B. finds a new explanation** After his father tells the boy he is dreaming, the boy states, "I decided that it was a magic horse and man that I'd seen."
2. **B. imaginative** The detailed description of the dream and the boy's insistence on believing in it are signs of his imaginative powers.
3. **A. He wants to reconcile what he saw with what his father told him.** Initially the boy seems to think that he saw a real, ordinary horse, but his father explains why this is unlikely. However, the boy does not accept the explanation that he was merely dreaming. Thus, he thinks of a new explanation.
4. **B. having enough money to pay some bills** The father is a practical man, a realist—"where were poor people like us going to find big gray stallions?" Because of the family's poverty, the father would probably enjoy having money to pay bills.
5. **D. Morning and youth are full of possibility.** The end of the excerpt states, "I believed that magic hides in the early morning. . . . you might find something so beautiful . . . nothing else in life could ever be better."

## Lesson 5: Style and Point of View

### Practice 5, page 121

1. **B. He takes things in stride.** When Coach chides Bobby for having three malts, Bobby jokes with him and then pretends to hide them. Bobby is not angry or defensive in a way that could justify choice (D).
2. **C. the actions and speech of the characters** The narrator reports only what can be seen or heard by any observer. As a reader, you don't learn anyone's thoughts or feelings. You must infer them from their actions and speech.
3. **A. informal** Throughout the excerpt, people speak and act quite informally: Daphne washes up in a drinking fountain, Coach speaks with a spoon in his mouth, Bobby jokes with Coach, and so on.
4. **D. not entirely honest about his feelings** In his discussion with Daphne, Coach tries to explain his wife's need for an apartment of her own. Yet he sounds hostile and cuts his wife off when she speaks of her apartment. You can conclude he was hiding his real feelings from Daphne.

## Lesson 6: Figurative Language

### Practice 6, page 123

1. **B. rain clouds approaching** Lines 8–9 state,"patch of cloud spreads, darkening/Like a water-stain on silk." The following line mentions the coming rain: "*. . . quickly, before the rain!*"
2. **C. The rain caused their makeup to run.** The previous two lines mention "soaked by the shower" and "drenched." Immediately preceding the mention of "ruined faced" is a description of "streaked mascara." The girls' makeup is streaked because of the rain.
3. **B. the wind is so strong that it is blowing spray from the river into the boat** The figurative language helps you "see" the effects of the strong wind by painting a picture of curtains embroidered with white foamy water blown from the river.
4. **A. quick and easy** A knife cuts through a melon quickly and easily, and that is how cold, wet autumn weather has cut through the warm summer day.

5. **C. wry and observant** Throughout the poem the speaker observes and comments on what is going on around him with a dryly humorous, or wry, attitude.

### Reading Literature Practice Questions, pages 124–127

1. **C. self-concerned** Leroy's condition inspires Norma Jean to care for herself. She discusses herself and her body, and the passage gives no indication that any of the other answers fit her character.
2. **C. won't be driving his truck for a while** The passage tells us Leroy is injured and probably won't drive, so describing the truck as roosting, or sleeping, implies it will not be used.
3. **D. doesn't want to face what to do next** The passage says that Leroy is "not sure what to do next" and is making his crafts "in the meantime."
4. **A. It took some courage.** The fourth paragraph says the boy's "heart was in his mouth" and the sixth paragraph explains the boy was "scared as he looked down."
5. **B. alone** The boy has come to believe that you cannot rely on anyone but yourself. He is alone on the deck and sees the bird alone atop the mast. Even though it needs help, he is not going to help it at first.
6. **D. loneliness and sense of belonging** The sailor-boy begins the excerpt believing that everyone must look after himself. The final sentence of the excerpt states that his adventure leaves him with the belief that "the sky, the ship, the bird and himself were all one."
7. **D. triumphant** The mood of the piece rises as the boy climbs the mast to save the bird. At the top, he feels proud of what he has chosen to do and succeeded at doing and feels at one with everything.
8. **C. start singing again** A clue is given in the phrase "but his parched tongue clove to the roof of his mouth, he could not utter a stave." His mouth, dry from fear, could not utter a note of the song.
9. **A. panic** Reading those words both alone and in context gives you a sense of Ichabod's panic-stricken haste to get away.
10. **C. suspenseful** There is mystery and tension over whether the headless horseman will catch up with Ichabod and, if so, what he will do. The events that are happening and the way they are told create suspense.
11. **B. too scared to think rationally** When you realize that Ichabod mistakenly thought he saw a head when it was in reality a pumpkin, you can see that he was letting his fear get the better of his judgment.
12. **A. John Wright** Although Mrs. Peters insists they don't know who killed the bird, Mrs. Hale states, "Wright wouldn't like the bird—a thing that sang. She used to sing. He killed that, too. . . . I knew John Wright."
13. **B. someone who smothers all the joy in another person** Mrs. Hale says: "No, Wright wouldn't like the bird—a thing that sang. She used to sing. He killed that, too." From these comments, you can conclude that John Wright was capable of discouraging a person from singing, something that would have made that person happy.
14. **D. They understand how someone could be driven to murder.** The two women seem nervous and are evasive about the bird's death. But they are not protecting themselves. You can tell they suspect who might have murdered Wright and what might have driven the person to murder. References to "she," someone who liked to sing but stopped because of Wright ("He killed that, too"), someone who lived in loneliness and had only the bird as pleasure until the bird was killed, indicate that the women suspect that Mrs. Wright killed her husband.

# Language Arts: Writing Answers and Explanations

## Writing Effective Sentences

### Lesson 1: Simple Sentences

#### Practice 1, page 131

A. The revisions are samples. Your rewrites may differ.
1. F It drives his girlfriend crazy.
2. F As soon as he comes home from work, he starts talking on the telephone.
3. C
4. F Dave's sister and his best friend like to talk on the telephone, too.

B. 5. **C. call from** Choice (C) joins a sentence fragment to a complete sentence. "A calling conference" in choice (D) is badly worded.
6. **C. insert you before can** Choice (C) adds a subject to a sentence fragment, thus creating a complete sentence.
7. **C. service can** Choice (C) joins a sentence fragment to a complete sentence and makes sense.

### Lesson 2: Compound and Complex Sentences

#### Practice 2.1, page 133

A. 1. It was late, and I was walking home from work.
2. My co-worker, Judy, had offered to drive me, but I had refused.
3. It was a warm night, so I decided to get some fresh air.
4. It was really my choice. I could have taken a cab, or I could have walked.
5. I heard a loud noise, so I ran the last block to my house. Later, I learned that it was only a car backfiring.

B. 6. **B. remove the comma** A comma is required when two independent clauses are joined but not when two verbs are joined (*carries . . . gets*).
7. **A. airlines, but** *But* is the most logical coordinating conjunction here. Most travelers on major airlines can check baggage. Because there are two clauses (*couriers . . . fly, . . . they can't check*), a comma is needed.
8. **B. insert a comma after advance** A comma precedes a coordinating conjunction joining two independent clauses.

#### Practice 2.2, page 135

A. 1. Most fatal fires occur when a family is asleep.
2. Because a smoke alarm wakes you up, it can allow you to escape.
3. Try to replace the smoke detector's battery before it goes dead.
4. Although smoke detectors cost money, the expense is worth it.

B. 5. **B. insert a after making** An indefinite article is needed.
6. **A. replace Whenever with After** *Whenever* is used inappropriately; it does not convey the intended meaning.
7. **D. up, thank** Choice (D) correctly combines a sentence fragment and an independent clause to form a complex sentence.

### Lesson 3: Run-Ons and Comma Splices

#### Practice 3, page 137

A. There are several possible correct answers. There may be other correct answers in addition to those listed.
1. Jeff just got his driver's license, and he's very excited. OR Jeff just got his driver's license. He's very excited.
2. He bought a car that has a lot of miles on it, so it wasn't very expensive. OR Because he bought a car that has a lot of miles on it, it wasn't very expensive.
3. He doesn't have a lot of free time, but he'd like to take a car trip. OR Although he doesn't have a lot of free time, he'd like to take a car trip.
4. He needs to find out about car insurance, get a good map, and join an auto club.

B. 5. **A. pictures if you just** Choice (A) turns a run-on sentence into a complex sentence by adding a subordinating conjunction. The comma in choice (C) is unnecessary because the subordinate clause is the second half of the sentence.
6. **B. insert and after the comma** Choice (B) turns a comma splice into a compound sentence by adding a coordinating conjunction. Don't be misled by the apparent lack of a subject; both clauses are commands, meaning the subject, *you*, is implied but unstated.
7. **C. insert because after the comma** Choice (C) turns a run-on sentence into a compound sentence with a subordinating conjunction and a comma.

### Lesson 4: Subordinate Ideas

#### Practice 4, page 139

A. There are several possible answers for each question. Sample answers:
1. Tornadoes and earthquakes can cause a lot of damage.
2. Earthquakes are somewhat common in California, but many Californians do not seem to mind.
3. On May 20, 2013, a tornado in Oklahoma killed twenty-three people and injured almost 400.
4. Tornadoes can occur anywhere in the United States and at any time of year.

B. 5. **D. repaired up** Choice (D) combines two short, choppy sentences into one smooth sentence. The other choices are run-ons, excessively wordy, or both.
6. **A. brought or mailed to** Choice (A) forms a compound predicate and combines two short, choppy sentences into one smooth, effective sentence.
7. **D. accidents, mishandling, or faulty installation** Choice (D) combines two wordy, repetitive sentences into one smooth, detailed sentence by forming a compound predicate.

### Lesson 5: Modify Ideas

#### Practice 5, page 141

A. There are several possible answers for each question. Sample answers:
1. Trent's sister, who is a health professional, encouraged him to become a nurse.
2. When he wakes up the patients to take their blood pressure, they get rather annoyed.
3. He carefully writes their temperature and blood pressure on their charts.

4. It is hard to make visitors who are talking with patients leave at 9:00 p.m.

B. 5. **B. a person who is not the birth child** *not the birth child* is a misplaced modifier in the original sentence; choice (B) moves the modifier so it modifies the correct noun.

6. **C. An agency requires a "home study"** In the original sentence, it is not clear who is going through an agency.

7. **D. move <u>frequently</u> to follow <u>Lawyers</u>** Choice (D) moves the modifier to show that it is the lawyers who frequently handle adoptions, not the parents who frequently ask about them.

### Lesson 6: Parallel Structure

### Practice 6, page 143

A. There are multiple ways to revise these sentences. An example of each is listed below.

1. Jenna has worked in a factory, in a store, and as a waitress.
2. She would like to put her kids in a better school and to get a better job.
3. She thinks the kids' father is irresponsible, lazy, and uncaring.
4. He doesn't have the time, the energy, or the money to give them what they deserve.

B. 5. **C. insert <u>more</u> before <u>pleasant</u>** Choice (C) correctly makes all the adjectives into comparatives (*safer, more comfortable,* and *more pleasant*).

6. **D. computers, and** The original sentence combined single words and clauses in the same series. Choice (D) corrects the error by turning the last item in the list from a clause to a noun phrase (*lights, computers, and coffee makers*).

7. **C. change <u>be leaving</u> to <u>leave</u>** Choice (C) makes all the verbs in the sentence (*punch, press,* and *leave*) parallel.

### Writing Effective Sentences Practice Questions, pages 144–147

1. **B. remove the comma** When an independent clause comes before a subordinate clause in a complex sentence, there is no need to use a comma.
2. **B. during the day and 62°F** Choice (B) combines two short, choppy sentences into one smooth sentence.
3. **D. sunlight, keep** Choice (D) combines a subordinate clause sentence fragment and an independent clause to form a complex sentence.
4. **D. home. Do change** Choice (D) corrects the comma splice by adding a period, and is consistent with the theme of the paragraph as being a list of recommendations.
5. **A. Your home will not cool down any faster.** *Any faster* should be placed next to the phrase it modifies, *cool down.*
6. **B. insert a comma after <u>home</u> In this sentence,** *When* begins a subordinate clause. A comma should be placed after a subordinate clause that begins a complex sentence.
7. **A. replace <u>Returning</u> with <u>I returned</u>** Choice (A) adds a subject to a sentence fragment and corrects the verb form to make a complete sentence.
8. **A. He claimed that because** There is no clear subject for the verb phrase at the beginning of the sentence to modify. By adding the subject *He,* choice (A) makes it clear who was claiming that the TV had been used.
9. **A. angry and frustrated about the** Choice (A) makes a smooth complex predicate out of a choppy run-on sentence.
10. **C. refund or get** Choice (C) puts both verbs in the same form. Choice (A) is grammatically correct but illogically suggests that Jeffrey will return *and* repair the TV.
11. **A. work productively if you** This choice moves the idea of being productive closer to the word it modifies, *work.* It also reduces wordiness by using the adverb form *productively.*
12. **C. remove the comma** A comma is not required before a coordinating conjunction that joins two verbs.
13. **B. remove the comma** A comma is not required in a complex sentence when the subordinate clause follows the independent clause.
14. **A. work or talk** Both verbs in the sentence should be in the same form. There is no need for a comma when a coordinating conjunction joins two verbs.
15. **B. insert a comma after <u>hard</u>** A comma is required before the coordinating conjunction that joins the two independent clauses in a compound sentence.
16. **D. hoaxes designed** This choice joins a sentence fragment to an independent clause.
17. **B. To check a claim like this, contact** Choice (B) combines two choppy sentences into one smooth, effective sentence.
18. **C. know. This** Choice (C) splits a comma splice into two independent, correct sentences.
19. **D. remove the comma after <u>safe</u>** A comma is not needed in a compound predicate.

## Connecting Ideas

### Lesson 1: Organize Ideas into Paragraphs

### Practice 1.1, page 149

A. 1. The pharmacist at the local drugstore is very helpful.

2. No MI
3. Every vote counts, so let your voice be heard and vote!
4. When you are traveling, it's a good idea to mark your luggage clearly.
5. Listening to music can benefit you in many ways.

B. 6. **C. sentence 4** Sentences 1–3 explain who gets colds and how frequently. Sentences 4–6 are about the causes and prevention of colds.

7. **D. join paragraphs B and C** Sentence 10 in paragraph C is related to the main idea of paragraph B, the prevention of colds.

### Practice 1.2, page 151

A. Your topic sentences should be similar to these:

1. Satellites have many different functions in today's world.
2. All signs show that the economy is headed for a slump.
3. The library has adopted a new dress code for employees.

B. 4. **D. Repetitive strain injury is a painful condition resulting from repeated use of the hands.** The original topic sentence is too general. The other options don't tell the central point: what repetitive strain injury is.

5. **B. A number of factors contribute to repetitive strain injury.** This sentence covers the three causes of repetitive strain injury mentioned in the paragraph.

### Lesson 2: Use Logical Order and Relevant Ideas

**Practice 2, page 153**

A. 1. Irrelevant detail: Getting very ill is one bad thing that could happen.

2. Irrelevant detail: Adult students can also use school supplies.

3. Irrelevant detail: This job will be extremely expensive!

B. 4. **D. remove sentence 3** This sentence adds no new information to what was given in the previous sentences.

5. **D. remove sentence 6** The information about the secretarial job is not relevant to getting a job in carpentry.

6. **D. move sentence 10 to follow sentence 8** It would be more logical to place sentence 9 at the end of the letter.

### Lesson 3: Relate Sentences and Paragraphs

**Practice 3, page 155**

A. Your transitions should be similar to these:

1. Our marketing efforts need to be enhanced. Therefore, we will soon begin another marketing initiative.
2. Sales representatives say that their jobs are extremely demanding. However, the salary is attractive.
3. The marketing director has instructed sales representatives to try some new ideas. For example, sales representatives can give away free samples.
4. A new ad campaign will be launched in just a few weeks. As a result, we expect sales to increase.

B. 5. **B. insert <u>however,</u> after the comma** This position is the most logical for the transition. Also, because it is in the middle of a sentence, it should be set off by commas.

6. **B. restaurant. For example,** Sentence 6 offers an example of the broad menu described in sentence 5.

7. **A. In addition, having a cafe** This option inserts a helpful transition to move the reader smoothly from paragraph B to paragraph C.

### Connecting Ideas Practice Questions, pages 156–159

1. **C. sentence 5** Sentences 1–4 are about the general problem of sleep disruption, whereas sentences 5–8 are about reasons why people don't get enough sleep.
2. **B. High-achieving students get more sleep.** Both studies relate to the impact of lack of sleep on learning.
3. **A. grades. Similarly,** The ideas in the two sentences are similar, so they can be connected this way.
4. **D. remove sentence 13** The paragraph is about sleep, not losing weight.
5. **D. join paragraphs (C) and (D)** Both paragraphs contain tips for getting more sleep.
6. **B. sentence 4** Sentences 1–3 introduce the purpose of the passage. Sentences 4–7 contain general rules for stain removal.
7. **B. Choose the right water temperature for cleaning each stain.** This sentence is appropriate since the paragraph discusses hot, cold, and room-temperature water.
8. **D. juice, for example, removes** When a transition is placed in the middle of a sentence, commas should both precede and follow it.
9. **D. remove sentence 15** Sentence 15 explains a minor detail and moves away from the main idea of the paragraph.
10. **C. move sentence 19 to the beginning of paragraph D** Putting sentence 19 at the beginning of the paragraph lets readers know in advance what point the paragraph will make.
11. **C. remove sentence 5** Sentence 5 is a general statement about HMOs. It is not relevant to the explanation of which insurance carriers are being made available.
12. **A. insert a comma after <u>However</u>** A comma should follow when a transition begins a sentence.
13. **C. sentence 9** Until sentence 9, paragraph B is about the differences between the two insurance plans. Sentence 9 introduces the idea of the informational sessions.
14. **A. move sentence 14 to the end of paragraph C** Sentence 14 refers to the card that was mentioned in paragraph C and so continues that idea.
15. **A. move sentence 2 to follow sentence 3** The description of removing the wheel should start with the initial step.
16. **C. move sentence 11 to follow sentence 12** Sentence 11 tells what to do with the spot where there is a leak, so it should follow the information on finding that spot.
17. **C. The next step is to put the tire and tube back onto the rim.** Paragraph C describes the process of putting the tire and tube back on the rim.
18. **A. The final step is to reinstall the wheel.** Paragraph D describes the final step in the process; putting the wheel back on the bike.
19. **A. replace <u>Moreover,</u> with <u>Then</u>** *Then* is a more appropriate transition for describing steps in a process.

## Writing the Essay

### Lesson 1: Unpack the Writing Prompt

**Practice 1, page 161**

1. The writing assignment is about different types of calendars and how they developed.
2. Based on the prompt, I will be given one passage containing the history of the development of various types of calendars.
3. Explain the development of different types of calendars.
4. I am being asked to explain something.

5. I am being asked to include specifics and details from the passage.

### Lesson 2: Read the Passage(s) with the Prompt in Mind

**Practice 2, page 163**

Your answers should be similar to this, but your wording may vary.

1. Mandatory military service.
2. The writer remains neutral in this essay.
3. The author's purpose was to explain two differing viewpoints on the topic of mandatory military service.
4. Violence in video games
5. The writer has an opinion.
6. The writer supports his opinion in numerous ways. He cites studies linking violence to video games and he gives an example of the public making a change in the video game marketplace.

### Lesson 3: Develop a Thesis Statement

**Practice 3, page 165**

These answers are samples; your answers may vary.

1. The author makes an argument.
2. Prescription drug advertising on TV is harmful because it can lead patients to request or refuse medication for reasons that are not medically sound.
3. Advertising prescription drugs on TV is not in the public's best interest. The advertising can cause consumers to make poorly informed decisions regarding their healthcare.
4. The writer is neutral.
5. The author explains the various theories for how the moon was formed.
6. The various theories of how the moon was formed differ in their viewpoint on where the material initially came from and how the material was initially grouped together.

### Lesson 4: Collect Supporting Evidence

**Practice 4, page 167**

These answers are samples; your answers may vary.

1. The passage states that alcohol is particularly harmful to parts of the brain that grow later in life. Another fact from the passage is that alcohol causes long-term damage to the heart and liver. In support of this position, the text further says that the United Kingdom allows younger individuals to drink and also has high rates of alcohol-related death.
2. Choose either agree or disagree.
3. You might have written something like this:
   (Agree) One personal piece of evidence I would use to support my position is that teenagers are already at higher risk of accidents when driving, and alcohol would only exacerbate this fact.
   (Disagree) One personal piece of evidence I would use to support my position is that 18-year-olds can enter combat in the military and can vote for the president. Claiming they are not responsible enough for alcohol is inconsistent with the responsibilities and privileges we otherwise give 18-year-olds.

### Lesson 5: Plan Your Response

**Practice 5, page 171**

The following is a sample response. There is no objectively correct answer to the writing prompt. You may write your essay either for or against the author's position. Thus, answers to the following questions may vary.

1. **Sample thesis statement:**
   I think that the writer's position on owning a family pet is correct because the inconvenience and expenses cited outweigh the benefits, and because as someone allergic to cats, I agree with the writer's point that having pets can make it difficult for friends who visit.
2. **Sample outline:**
   I. The writer is correct that pets have more downsides than benefits and that families should not have pets.
   II. Monetary expenses; food, pet sitters, veterinary care, cleaning.
   III. Chores and time involved; kids may promise to help, but likely would not.
   IV. Friend can't visit; allergies, difficult with overnight guests.
   V. Pets are good friends and can be a calming influence when people are stressed.
      A Some people think this justifies any expense and difficulty in keeping animals.
         i. But, pets can keep away real friends and introduce stress as well, countering benefits.

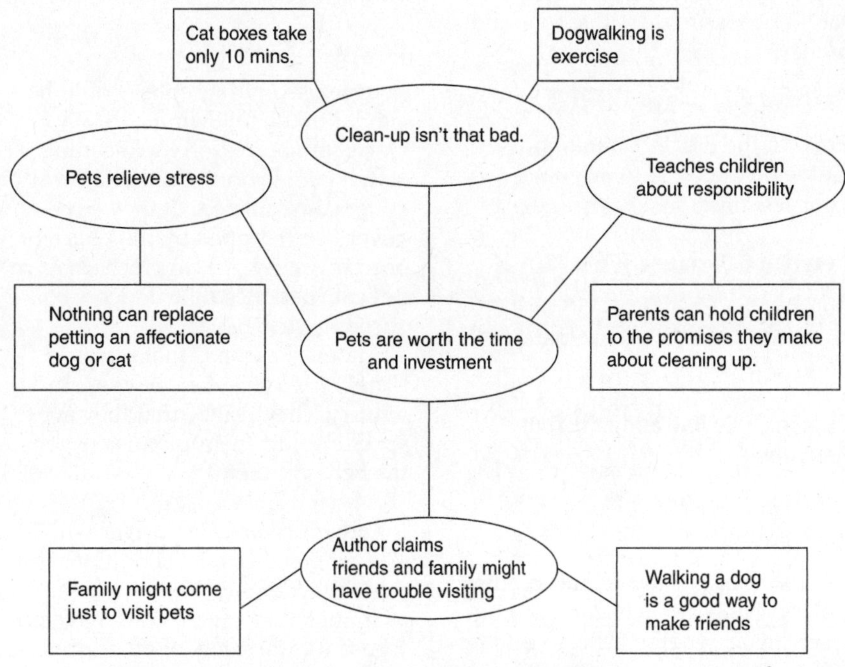

ii. Instead of petting a cat to relieve stress over money, it would be better to save the money you would spend on the cat's food and vet bills.

**3. Sample idea map:**
*The idea map below demonstrates how you might organize your thoughts to argue for pet ownership. Your idea map may vary.*

### Lesson 6: Draft Your Response

**Practice 6.1, page 173**

Your answers may vary.

**A. Sample topic sentences:**
Pet ownership is a major burden, and the time and money people invest in pets could be better spent elsewhere.

The author of the passage says that keeping a pet is not worth the trouble, but he fails to consider all of the many benefits of pet ownership.

Your supporting statements may vary quite a bit, so no samples are given here. Check to make sure that your supports are relevant to your topic statement.

**B. Sample concluding statements:**
And so, when all is taken into consideration, the conclusion is clear: the cost of a pet far outweighs the benefit.

Don't let the long list of difficulties listed by the author scare you away, because a pet can be a friend to you and your children, one whose value can't be measured against time and money.

**Practice 6.2, pages 174–175**

Refer to the Essay Evaluation Guide on page 758 to evaluate your response.

**Practice 6.3, pages 176–177**

Refer to the Essay Evaluation Guide on page 757 to evaluate your response.

### Lesson 7: Revise and Edit Your Response

**Practice 7.1, page 179**

**A, page 179**

Most of us are aware that speeding has consequences, which range from receiving a speeding ticket to getting into an accident. Nonetheless, a quick survey of any highway will show that many drivers exceed the speed limit. This raises the question: why do people speed?

One common reason is that people do not think they will suffer any consequences. If they have never been stopped by the police or ~~crashed their car,~~ been involved in a car crash, they don't see any reason to worry.

Another reason is that people simply need to get somewhere in a hurry. They realize that they are speeding but ~~they have such a need to arrive on time that they don't care~~ their impatience gets the better of them. ~~They've got ants in their pants.~~

¶A final reason is lack of respect for other drivers~~, one~~. One driver who is speeding makes road conditions less safe for everyone. Drivers who act as though they are in the Indy 500 they have no regard for the safety of others.

We know that people speed because ~~of impatience and they don't fear the consequences.~~ they're impatient and don't fear the consequences. ~~Another reason is no respect.~~ They also don't respect other drivers. Let's figure out what will make them stop speeding.

**B, page 179**

Refer to the Essay Evaluation Guide for Informative/Explanatory Essays on page 758 to evaluate your response.

**Practice 7.2, page 181**

Your revised paragraphs should be similar to the following.
One common reason for speeding is that people don't think they will suffer consequences. If they have never been stopped by the police or been involved in a car crash, they've never experienced the dangers of speeding first-hand.

Another reason is that people simply need to get somewhere in a hurry. They realize that they are speeding, but their impatience gets the better of them.

A final reason is lack of respect for other drivers. One driver who is speeding makes road conditions less safe for everyone. Drivers who act as though they are in a race have no regard for the safety of other drivers.

### Writing the Essay Practice, pages 182–185

**A.** Refer to the Essay Evaluation Guide on page 757 to evaluate your response.

**B.** Refer to the Essay Evaluation Guide on page 757 to evaluate your response.

## Polishing Your Writing

### Lesson 1: Strengthen Sentences

**Practice 1, page 187**

**A.** Your revised sentences should be similar to the following. The underlined parts show where your revision marks should be:

1. First, write down what you know about your family. Then interview relatives. (Run-on sentence)
2. Videotaping or recording the interviews is a good idea. (Structure not parallel)
3. Ask relatives to provide exact names, dates, and other details. (Structure not parallel)
4. Make copies of documents such as birth certificates and marriage licenses. (Sentence fragment)
5. When older family members are interviewed, they'll often tell you stories you never heard. (Dangling modifier)
6. Carefully record all the information you get and put it in a three-ring binder. (Misplaced modifier)
7. Some people use their computers to do genealogy searches, and they get very good results. (Comma splice; coordinating conjunction needed)
8. However, one must have the time, the patience, and the know-how to use the Internet. (Structure not parallel)
9. If you do decide to learn more about your roots, don't be surprised to find yourself at a huge family reunion. (Comma needed after subordinate clause)
10. The whole process of putting together a family tree and contacting long-lost family members is rewarding. (Sentence fragment)

**B. Sample revisions:**
It was a beautiful day, and the blue ocean sparkled in the sunlight. It was a perfect day for going to the beach. As Renelle looked across the sand, she saw two little girls building a sandcastle and making a moat next to it. Renelle spread out her towel, anchored it with her shoes and beach bag, and began to read a magazine. Suddenly she heard a voice say, "Are you going to get in the water, or are you just going to lie there?" Renelle looked up and saw her friend Terry. She laughed softly and got up to greet Terry. Putting on her sandals, she walked with Terry across the burning sand to the water's edge.

Renelle loved going to the beach. It relaxed her and helped her forget about her problems. It didn't cost money like most other forms of entertainment. Most of Renelle's friends also spent a lot of time at the beach, so that was another incentive.

## Lesson 2: Improve Organization

### Practice 2, page 189

A. Your revised paragraphs should be similar to the following (starting after the first revision made for you):

Why do people continue to litter? One reason people litter is that they just don't care about others. It doesn't bother them to leave their trash in front of someone else's apartment building, forcing another person to deal with the problem. This inconsiderate attitude is also reflected in the refusal to recycle plastic, glass, and newspapers. People figure that they won't be around in the future when the landfills are used up, so who cares?

¶Another possible reason for littering is low self-esteem. If people don't feel good about themselves, they won't be motivated to keep their environment looking attractive. ~~Low self-esteem can cause many other problems, including depression and lack of self-confidence.~~ People who have high self-esteem believe that it's important to keep their home, the planet Earth, clean and beautiful.

B. Ask a friend or family member to evaluate your work.

## Lesson 3: Word Choice

### Practice 3, page 191

**Sample answers:**

A. 1. nonprofit organization
2. thousands of
3. substandard
4. dollars
5. as soon as possible

B. If you ever order merchandise from a catalog, you should be aware of your rights. All companies, regardless of the state in which they are located, are required to ship your order within 30 days unless they have advertised a different shipping time. If a company is unable to meet the shipping deadline, it must send you an "Option Notice." You can choose to wait longer or get a refund.

Some consumers have complained about receiving merchandise that they did not order. Companies that engage in this practice are breaking the law. If you receive a product you haven't ordered, it is yours to keep.

If you receive a package that has been damaged, don't open it. Write "REFUSED" on the package, and return it to the seller. There's no need to add new postage as long as the package came by regular mail.

C. Have a friend or family member evaluate your work.

## Polishing Your Writing Practice Questions, pages 192–195

1. **C. gardener, it's important that** Sentence 2 is a subordinate clause, not a complete sentence. Use a comma to combine it with the independent clause in sentence 3, creating a complex sentence.
2. **A. replace not good with too extreme** The phrase *not good* is vague, since it provides no information about how a climate might be unsuitable. *Too extreme* allows the reader to anticipate the temperature and moisture requirements discussed in paragraph D.
3. **B. move sentence 8 to follow sentence 9** Sentence 9 is the topic sentence—it gives the main idea—for paragraph C. As such, it should be the first sentence of the paragraph.
4. **D. move sentence 11 to the beginning of paragraph D** The topic of paragraph C is choosing a garden spot, whereas the topic of paragraph D is choosing plants. Therefore, sentence 11, which is about choosing plants, should appear in paragraph D.
5. **C. plants to** Sentence 12 contains a comma splice joining two independent clauses. These clauses should instead be joined with a word or phrase that expresses the relationship between them.
6. **A. change which had come to and had come** The phrase *which had come* implies that Wales had come to the United States, not the boy. Replace *which* with *and* to clarify.
7. **D. ocean; it** A semicolon is required to separate two independent clauses, correcting the run-on sentence.
8. **C. replace really big with vast** Describing the ocean as *vast* conveys the sense of size more precisely.
9. **B. kidding me** The adverb *totally* is used informally here, and *pulling my leg* is slang that should be avoided.
10. **B. remove the sentence** Sentence 12 is unnecessary and should be removed.
11. **D. place a period after morality and begin a new sentence with She** Doing so corrects the run-on sentence.
12. **B. Many consider this her most shocking story.** Replacing "reckon" with "consider" replaces slang with more formal language.
13. **C. change lupus. The to lupus, the** As written, sentence 8 is not a sentence at all. It should serve as an appositive describing *lupus* in the previous sentence.
14. **A. Flannery maintained many fulfilling correspondences that gave her the insight into human behavior that is evident in her writing.** This construction eliminates wordiness while maintaining the original meaning of the sentence.

15. **A. remove always** The adverb *always* is unnecessary when paired with the verb *continue*.
16. **B. remove next** The adverbs *then* and *next* are redundant when used together.
17. **C. times. You** Insert a period and remove *and* between the two independent clauses.
18. **D. insert a comma after However** Unless *However* is followed by a comma, it seems that it is being used to modify the adjustment. Insert a comma to clarify that *However* introduces the sentence.
19. **B. replace repairs. Please with repairs, please** Sentence 9 is a fragment and must be joined to sentence 10 with a comma to present a complete thought.

## Using Grammar Correctly

### Lesson 1: Noun and Pronoun Agreement

#### Practice 1.1, page 197

A. 1. They
2. him
3. it
4. Her
5. she

B. 6. **A. replace me with I** *Bonetta and I* is a compound subject, so a subject pronoun is required.
7. **D. change getting to gets** The simple present tense is appropriate here.
8. **B. Walter or me** The phrase *Walter or me* is an object, so an object pronoun is required.

#### Practice 1.2, page 199

A. 1. Sally is moving to a small town. Her mother is concerned about the health care options it offers.
2. Sally tried to reassure her mother, but it was hard for her mother to believe Sally.
3. Sally asked a friend who lives in the town for information about its health care facilities. OR the town's health care facilities.
4. The town has a freestanding clinic where a person can go when he or she is sick. OR where people can go when they are sick.
5. There is also a nearby hospital, and it has a very good reputation.
6. If one is concerned about health care, one should sign up for a good insurance plan. OR If you are concerned about health care, you should sign up for a good insurance plan.

B. 7. **D. replace one's with their** The word *children* earlier in the sentence is the antecedent to the pronoun; *their* agrees correctly with that antecedent, while the singular *one's* does not.
8. **D. parents** Only choice (D) correctly identifies who should be clear about their expectations.
9. **C. replace them with the group** The term *play group* is a collective noun, so the plural *them* should not be used to refer to it. In this case, repeating the word *group* is the best way to make the meaning clear.

### Lesson 2: Verb Forms and Tenses

#### Practice 2.1, page 201

A. 1. had ceased
2. closed
3. functions
4. have visited
5. will open
6. looks
7. are thinking

B. 8. **B. is offering** The action is taking place right now, so the present progressive is the correct tense.
9. **D. change are signing to sign** The present-tense verb *sign* in the subordinate clause is appropriate, given the the future-tense verb *will receive* in the main clause.
10. **D. change will be amazing to will amaze** The verb *will amaze* is in the simple future tense. The future progressive tense in *will be amazing you* is incorrect and overcomplicated.

#### Practice 2.2, page 203

A. 1. came
2. showed
3. had spoken
4. took
5. seen

B. 6. **D. change begun to began** The action takes place in the past tense, so the verb should be in its past form, *began*. *Begun* is the past participle.
7. **C. was broken** *Broken* is the correct past participle.
8. **B. change given to give** The clue word *now* tells you that the action is still true, so the present-tense form of *give* is correct.

### Lesson 3: Subject-Verb Agreement

#### Practice 3.1, page 205

A. 1. is
2. become
3. is
4. have
5. seems
6. is

B. 7. **B. have heard** In this sentence, the indefinite pronoun *most* is plural ("most of us"). The verb *have heard* agrees with the plural subject.
8. **C. change start to starts** The verb *starts* agrees with the singular subject *plane*.
9. **B. change conducts to conduct** The verb *conduct* agrees with the plural subject *materials*.

#### Practice 3.2, page 207

A. 1. ~~on the market~~ carry
2. ~~carrying the seal~~ are
3. ~~an important ingredient in many toothpastes~~ strengthens, attacks
4. are
5. offer
6. ~~with fluoride and good flavor~~ is

B. 7. **C. change have to has** The verb *has* agrees with the singular subject *state*.
8. **A. determine** The verb *determine* agrees with the compound subject *Wage level and the length of employment*.
9. **C. change reports to report** The verb *report* agrees with the plural subject *workers*.

### Using Grammar Correctly Practice Questions, pages 208–211

1. **C. change doesn't to didn't** The past tense is required because the second clause in the sentence is discussing what happened in the past.

2. **A. they** The antecedent of the underlined pronoun is *girls,* so it should be plural. *They* is clear; repeating *the girls* (as in Choice (B)) is unecessary. Choice (D) *them* is incorrect because the pronouns is the subject of the dependent clause *while they practiced.*
3. **B. earned** The past tense is correct here because the action happened in the past over the course of a few years.
4. **D. change <u>is</u> to <u>are</u>** The verb *are* agrees with the plural subject *sisters.*
5. **D. change <u>been</u> to <u>is</u>** The main clause needs the present tense verb *is* because the introductory subordinate clause has a present-tense verb, *face. Been* is an incomplete verb form.
6. **B. change <u>will receive</u> to <u>have received</u>** The present perfect is correct here because the point is to find out about other people's past experiences with auto shops, not their predictions about them.
7. **A. change <u>have picked</u> to <u>pick</u>** Because this sentence is a command, the simple present tense is necessary.
8. **D. change <u>comes</u> to <u>come</u>** The verb *come* agrees with the plural subject *specials.* The agreement error could also be fixed with *came,* choice (C), but doing so would introduce a tense error in its place.
9. **D. replace <u>it</u> with <u>the repair job</u>** The pronoun *it* had no clear antecedent, so replacing it with a noun corrects the sentence.
10. **C. there are** The verb *are* agrees with the plural subject *limits.* The present tense is correct and should not be changed.
11. **B. replace <u>its</u> with <u>their</u>** The antecedent *changes* is plural, so the plural possessive *their* should be used.
12. **C. replace <u>one's</u> with <u>your</u>** *Your* is used in the rest of the paragraph, so it is appropriate here.
13. **D. change <u>is</u> to <u>are</u>** The word *which* is the subject of a subordinate clause. It refers to the plural noun *calculations.* Therefore, the verb *are,* not *is,* is required.
14. **A. has increased** The interrupting phrase *of taxes* does not change the fact that the subject of the new independent clause is *amount,* which is singular. The verb *has increased* therefore agrees with it.
15. **B. will credit** The future tense indicates an action that will take place at a later time, which is appropriate in this sentence.
16. **B. don't** The plural indefinite pronoun *many* is the subject of the sentence; the verb *don't* (don't=do+not) agrees with it. Changing to the past tense, choice (C), would be incorrect.
17. **C. change <u>has</u> to <u>have</u>** The verb *have* agrees with the plural subject *people.*
18. **B. him or her** The pronouns are objects of the preposition *with,* so the objective forms *him* and *her* are needed. The antecedent is *a person,* so the plural *them* in choice (D) cannot be used.
19. **B. change <u>are</u> to <u>is</u>** The verb *is* agrees with the singular subject *equipment,* and the interrupting phrase listing examples of assistive equipment is properly punctuated.
20. **B. it** *It* is the proper pronoun to use to refer to a dog.

## Using Writing Mechanics

### Lesson 1: Comma Use

#### Practice 1.1, page 213

A. 1. Train travel is more pleasant than riding a bus, but it can be more expensive.
2. When you're on a train, you can stand up and stretch if you need to.
3. NC
4. Unlike buses, trains sometimes have seats that face each other.
5. Traveling through a scenic area, you may find that your train has a double-decker car that offers a better view.
6. NC

B. 7. **A. insert a comma after <u>starters</u>** A comma is required after an introductory phrase.
8. **A. dressing, and** A comma should come before a coordinating conjunction in a compound sentence.
9. **D. remove the comma after <u>though</u>** The words *though not all of them may be pleasing to the palate* form a subordinate clause, and no commas are necessary in that clause.

#### Practice 1.2, page 215

A. 1. Kwanzaa is a week-long African American holiday that celebrates culture, community, and family.
2. Kwanzaa, a wintertime holiday, is based on an ancient African harvest celebration.
3. NC
4. Kwanzaa celebrations include rituals such as singing, dancing, drumming, and poetry reading.
5. The family lights one candle every day for each of seven principles: unity, self-determination, responsibility, cooperative economics, purpose, creativity, and faith.
6. NC

B. 7. **A. remove the comma** The subject and verb of a sentence should not be separated by a comma.
8. **B. insert a comma after <u>medicines</u>** Commas should be placed between items in a series.
9. **C. children, those ten and up,** You can mentally omit the phrase *those ten and up* and still understand the meaning of *older children.* Therefore, the appositive *those ten and up* should be set off by commas.

### Lesson 2: Capitalization

#### Practice 2, page 217

A. 1. Last <u>spring</u>, I broke my arm in a car accident.
2. My internist, <u>Doctor Claudia</u> McNally, referred me to Waterside.
3. The center's <u>director</u>, Ilana Harris, assigned me a physical therapist named Ellie Royce.
4. Ellie studied physical therapy in her native London and used <u>British</u> methods of treatment that relieved my pain quite effectively.
5. She also did therapy with me in the pool at Rainbow <u>Health Club</u>.

6. I finished my treatments just before Labor Day, and I feel 100 percent better, thanks to Ellie.

B. 7. **B. change Emperors to emperors** A title should be capitalized only when it comes directly before a person's name or is used in direct address.

8. **C. change Mountains to mountains** A geographic feature is capitalized only when it is part of the name of a specific place, like *Rocky Mountains.*

9. **B. change america to America** Proper nouns should be capitalized.

### Lesson 3: Possessives and Contractions

**Practice, page 219**

A. 1. There's
2. can't, who's, it's
3. we're
4. theirs
5. ours

B. 6. **D. replace you're with your** In this sentence, the pronoun in question is showing ownership, so *your* is correct.

7. **B. change were to we're** *Were* is a verb and is incorrect in this sentence. Rather, an apostrophe should be inserted to create the contraction *we're*, the combined form of *we are.*

8. **B. replace they're with their** In this sentence, the pronoun is possessive, so *their* is correct.

### Lesson 4: Homonyms

**Practice 4, page 221**

A. 1. fourth
2. know
3. whole
4. week
5. affect
6. past

B. 7. **C. replace fare with fair** A *fare* is what you pay to get on the subway; *fair* means *just.*

8. **A. change principal to principle** A *principal* is the head of a school; *principle* means *a guiding rule.*

9. **A. replace affect with effect** *Affect* is a verb meaning *to influence; effect*, which means *result*, is required here.

### Using Writing Mechanics Practice Questions, pages 222–225

1. **B. insert a comma after tantrums** The phrase *have tantrums* is the first item in series, so it should be followed by a comma.
2. **C. understand and show** A comma should not be used between two verbs, and removing the comma is simpler and cleaner than adding a new subject as in incorrect choice (D).
3. **D. remove the comma after know** All the possessives, contractions, and homonyms in the sentence are spelled correctly. The comma following the introductory transition *However* cannot be removed, but the comma after *know* is incorrect.
4. **C. change are'nt to aren't** The apostrophe in a contraction must be placed in the spot where a letter has been removed.
5. **B. down, consider** An introductory subordinate clause should be followed by a comma.
6. **B. remove the comma** The subject (*One*) and its verb (*is*) should not be separated by a comma.
7. **B. replace it's with its** The sentence is about ownership: each time zone has its own standard time. The possessive form *its* is correct.
8. **B. change congress to Congress** The name *Congress* refers to a specific body of lawmakers and should therefore be capitalized.
9. **A. insert a comma after example** An introductory phrase must be followed by a comma.
10. **C. remove the comma after time** There is no need to separate the final phrase from the rest of the sentence with a comma.
11. **C. change center to Center** When a proper name consists of more than one word, all the words should be capitalized.
12. **D. replace when your with when you're** The sentence is saying, "when you are in the building," so the contraction *you're* is needed.
13. **A. replace week with weak** A *week* is seven days. *Weak*, meaning *not strong*, is appropriate for this sentence.
14. **D. remove the comma after pool** The clause beginning with *unless* does not need to be set off with commas.
15. **B. register and pay** Two items joined by *and* do not require a comma unless both are independent clauses.
16. **C. replace then with than** The word needed in the sentence is *than*, meaning *compared with. Then* means *after that* or *at that time.*
17. **C. insert a comma after profiling** The phrase *called racial profiling* is an appositive but is not essential to understanding the sentence. It needs a comma before (which is already given) and after it.
18. **B. distinctions, for nonwhites** The conjunction *for* is connecting two independent clauses in a compound sentence, so it must be preceded by a comma.
19. **B. change illinois to Illinois** Names of states should be capitalized.
20. **B. insert a comma after superintendents** Three items are listed in the series: *police superintendents, chiefs of police, and other law enforcement officials.* There should be commas separating them.

# MATHEMATICS ANSWERS AND EXPLANATIONS

## Number and Quantity I: Problem Solving

### Lesson 1: Compare and Order Numbers

**Practice 1, page 223**

1. 4
2. 8
3. 9
4. 1
5. 6
6. 7
7. 3
8. 500
9. 80
10. 1100
11. 12,000
12. 2000
13. 100
14. 100
15. 341
16. 1145
17. 125,391
18. 18, 23, 39, 45
19. 89, 91, 109, 111
20. 909, 932, 1087, 1139
21. 1420, 1425, 1429, 1432
22. 11,098, 12,071, 12,131
23. 15,298, 15,309, 15,356
24. **C. 50, 48, 45, 40** Arrange weights from heaviest to lightest.
25. **C. 1,500,000** The digit in the ten thousands column is less than 5, so round down.

### Lesson 2: Whole Number Operations

**Practice 2.1, page 235**

1. 77
2. 100
3. 52
4. 36
5. 190
6. 4078
7. 43
8. 2117
9. 65
10. 114
11. 180
12. 293
13. 483
14. 456
15. 2419
16. 900
17. 11,308
18. 15,185
19. 131,197
20. 30,899
21. **B. 88** Calculate: 24 + 8 + 56 = 88
22. **C. $13** Calculate: $20 – $7 = $13

**Practice 2.2, page 237**

1. 484
2. 1000
3. 2736
4. 13
5. 105
6. 21
7. 1350
8. 2625
9. 3376
10. 28
11. 15
12. 6
13. 250
14. 44 r3
15. 300
16. 200 r4
17. 150
18. 67,068
19. 538
20. 384
21. 12,011 r8
22. **D. 96** Calculate: 16 × 6 = 96
23. **C. $75** Calculate: 15 × 5 = 75
24. **B. 6** Calculate: 12 ÷ 2 = 6

### Lesson 3: TASC Test Calculator Skills

**Practice 3.1, page 239**

1. 153
2. 1187
3. 784
4. 24
5. 27,084
6. 14,442
7. 11,704
8. 54
9. 1580
10. **B. 26,179** Press (clear) 42920 (−) 16741 (enter).
11. **D. $19,900** Press (clear) 995 (×) 20 (enter).

**Practice 3.2, page 241**

1. 25
2. 18
3. 35
4. 136
5. 125
6. 5%
7. 2
8. 135
9. 5%
10. **C. $336** Press (clear) 1680 (×) 20 (2nd) ( ( ) (enter).
11. **A. 5%** Press (clear) 48 (÷) 960 (2nd) ( ) ) (enter). The right side of the screen will display 5%.

### Lesson 4: Word Problems

**Practice 4.1, page 243**

1. **C. 10** No paint is needed for the floor, so ignore the 700 square feet. 3500 square feet of wall space ÷ 350 square feet per gallon = 10 gallons.
2. **D. 22** 11 children × 2 party favors per child = 22.
3. **A. 5** Calculate: 30 – 25 = 5. The information that Sarah and Kate live 18 miles apart is not needed.
4. **C. 90** Calculate: 450 gallons ÷ 5 gallons of *filtered* water use per day = 90 days.
5. **D. 90** The table states that it takes Joyce 30 minutes to give a pedicure. 3 × 30 = 90
6. **C. $25** Subtract the cost of the manicure & pedicure combination ($35) from the cost of a makeover ($60). $60 – $35 = $25
7. **D. 42** Calculate: 7 × 6 = 42

**Practice 4.2, page 245**

1. **C. $103** Restaurant D ordered 2 cases of Boston lettuce and 3 cases of romaine lettuce in July. (2 × $17) + (3 × $23) = $103.
2. **B. $18** Calculate: 4 + 4 + 2 + 2 + 1 = 13 total cases, and delivery for the first 5 cases costs $2 each. 13 – 5 = 8 cases remained after the first 5, so delivery for those 8 cases costs $1 each. (5 × $2) + (8 × $1) = $18.
3. **B. Restaurant B** Calculate the totals for each restaurant:

| Rest. | Asparagus | Tomatoes | Asparagus + Tomatoes |
|---|---|---|---|
| A | 2 × $22 | 3 × $15 | $44 + $45 = $89 |
| B | 4 × $22 | 1 × $15 | $88 + $15 = $103 |
| C | 0 × $22 | 3 × $15 | $0 + $45 = $45 |
| D | 1 × $22 | 4 × $15 | $22 + $60 = $82 |

4. **C. 350** Calculate: 3 × 150 = 450 sheets will be used. Since the paper sells in packages of 400 sheets, 2 packages are needed, and 2 × 400 = 800. 800 – 450 = 350 sheets left over.
5. **A. 9** Calculate: 19 ÷ 2 = 9 r1, so the friends can make 9 whole batches using 2 cups of flour for each batch (and 1 cup will be left over).
6. **A. $1500** Calculate: (6 × $750) – $3000 = $1500.

### Lesson 5: Distance and Cost

**Practice 5, page 247**

1. rate; $\frac{d}{t} = r$
2. distance; $d = rt$
3. time; $\frac{d}{r} = t$
4. price per unit; $\frac{c}{n} = r$
5. cost; $c = nr$
6. number of units; $\frac{c}{r} = n$
7. **$48** $c = nr$
   $4 \times \$12 = \$48$
8. **$36** $c = nr$
   $12 \times \$3 = \$36$
9. **$80** $\frac{c}{n} = r$
   $\frac{\$320}{4} = \$80$
10. **5** $\frac{c}{r} = n$
   $\frac{\$25}{\$5} = 5$
11. **$2** $\frac{c}{n} = r$
   $\frac{\$20}{10} = \$2$
12. **180 miles** $d = rt$
   $60 \times 3 = 180$
13. **200 miles** $d = rt$
   $50 \times 4 = 200$
14. **1 hour** $\frac{d}{r} = t$
   $\frac{25}{25} = 1$
15. **90 miles per hour** $\frac{d}{t} = r$
   $\frac{270}{3} = 90$

16. **3 hours** $\frac{d}{r} = t$
$\frac{75}{25} = 3$
17. **A. 32** $\frac{c}{r} = n$
$\frac{\$640}{\$20} = 32$
18. **D. 55** $\frac{d}{t} = r$
$\frac{275}{5} = 55$

## Lesson 6: Measurement

### Practice 6.1, page 249

1. 48 in
2. 7 min
3. 72 hr
4. $2\frac{1}{2}$ pt
5. 20 qt
6. $5\frac{1}{2}$ tons
7. 144 in
8. 12 hr
9. 32 c
10. **C. 3.75 × 4** 4 qt = 1 gal, so multiply the number of gallons by 4 to find the number of quarts.
11. **B. 2 ft 3 in** 12 in = 1 ft Divide. 27 ÷ 12 = 2 r3, or 2 ft 3 in
12. **B. 22 lb 8 oz** Multiply. 3 lb 12 oz × 6 = 18 lb 72 oz To simplify, divide. Use the fact that 1 lb = 16 oz. 72 ÷ 16 = 4 r8. 18 lb + 4 lb 8 oz = 22 lb 8 oz

### Practice 6.2, page 251

1. 5,000 m
2. 6 m
3. 4,000 mg
4. 8,000 g
5. 4,050 cl
6. 1.5 l
7. 0.25 g
8. 30,000 m
9. 75 cl
10. 0.05 kg
11. 35.2 l
12. 1500 cm
13. **B. 0.1183** There are 1,000 milliliters in 1 liter. 118.3 ml ÷ 1,000 = 0.1183 l
14. **D. 0.5** There are 1000 milligrams in 1 gram. 500 ÷ 1,000 = 0.5 g
15. **B. 625** Convert 2.5 kg to grams. 2.5 ÷ 1,000 = 2500 g Divide. 2,500 g ÷ 4 g = 625 containers
16. **C. 130** Convert 4.8 meters to centimeters. 4.8 × 100 = 480 cm Subtract. 480 − 350 = 130 cm

## Lesson 7: Filling in the Answer Grid

### Practice 7, page 253

1. **1740** There are four 3-month periods in a 12-month period, so multiply the number of cats treated in one 3-month period by 4: 435 × 4 = 1,740
2. **10** Divide: 35,000 ÷ 3,500 = 10
3. **994** Add the attendance for each day: 348 + 366 + 280 = 994
4. **15** Multiply the number of cookies you buy with $1 by the number of dollars: 3 × 5 = 15
5. **2468** Multiply: 4 × 617 = 2,468
6. **$21** Divide the amount owed by the amount paid per month: $1,050 ÷ $50 = $21

### Problem Solving Practice Questions, pages 254–257

1. **D. 96** Multiply: 12 servings × 8 ounces = 96
2. **B. $2092** Add to find the total: $839 + $527 + 726 = $2092
3. **A. 4** Divide the length of the sample board by the length of the brace you want: 12 foot board ÷ 2 feet per brace = 6 braces per board. Since you can get 6 braces from each board, divide the total number of braces you want by 6: 24 ÷ 6 = 4 boards.
4. **B. 21** Use the square root function on your calculator or multiply each answer option by itself to find the square root of 441.
5. **A. 30,589** Subtract to find the difference in mileage: 70,040 − 39,451 = 30,589
6. **C. $656** You can use your calculator. Multiply: $3280 × 20% = $656
7. **A. $5625** Multiply: $125 × 45 = $5625
8. **B. 420** Divide distance by time to find Lydia's speed per hour: 180 ÷ 3 = 60. Then multiply by the number of hours she drove on Tuesday: 60 × 7 = 420
9. **B. 8** Divide the distance by the speed to find the time: 480 ÷ 60 = 8 hours.
10. **B. 96** Divide the total cost by price per item to find the number of items: $1440 ÷ 15 = $96
11. **A. $200** Multiply the late fee by the number of times Richard has paid his bill late: $25 × 8 = $200
12. **D. $53** Multiply: 7 × $5 = $35 and 18 × $1 = $18. Add the two amounts: $35 + $18 = $53
13. **A. 5** Divide. 17,500 total miles ÷ 3,500 miles between oil changes = 5 oil changes.
14. **A. 134** Divide: 536 total children ÷ 4 months = 134 children per month
15. **198** Subtract to find the difference: 636 − 438 = 198
16. **$1072** Multiply: $268 per payment × 4 payments left = $1072
17. **C. 51, 48, 44, 40**
18. **C. 2,350,000** Since the digit to the right of the ten thousands place is less than 5, the digit in the ten thousands place remains the same.
19. **A. 83** Add: 18 + 23 + 42 = 83
20. **A. $6** Subtract: $20 − $14 = $6
21. **B. 60** Since the question says "about," you can use approximate, or rounded, figures. Round the amounts and add: 8 + 33 + 18 ≈ 10 + 30 + 20 = 60
22. **62** Divide distance by time to find the rate of speed: 248 ÷ 4 = 62
23. **C. 18** Divide: 144 ÷ 8 = 18
24. **B. 30** Since the question says "about," you can use approximate figures. Round 299 to 300 and 9 to 10 and then divide: 300 ÷ 10 = 30
25. **A. 2 qt 10 fl oz** 3 qt = 2 qt 2 pt = 2 qt 1 pt 16 fl oz Subtract.

|   | 2 qt 1 pt 16 fl oz |
|---|---|
| − | 1 pt 6 fl oz |
|   | 2 qt 10 fl oz |

26. **C. 1200** Use rounded figures: 33 rounds to 30, and 41 pounds rounds to 40: 30 × 40 = 1200.
27. **C. $9** Find the total and divide by 4: $21 + $15 = $36, then $36 ÷ 4 = $9
28. **A. $12** Subtract the amount David paid from the total: $128 − $20 = $108. Then divide the remaining amount by the remaining number of people in the group: $108 ÷ 9 = $12.
29. **D. 260** 65 miles per hour × 4 hours = 260 miles.
30. **B. $18** Add the cost of a 1-topping pizza and $2 for each of the 2 additional toppings: $14 + $2 + $2 = $18
31. **C. 14** Multiply by 2 for each dollar: 2 × 7 = 14
32. **24** Divide: $1800 ÷ $75 per month = 24 months
33. **14** Divide the maximum capacity by the number of pages per document: 630 ÷ 45 = 14

# Number and Quantity II: Decimals and Fractions

## Lesson 1: Decimal Basics

### Practice 1, page 259

1. 3.8
2. 6
3. 0.43
4. 0.667
5. 8.1
6. 2.714
7. 0.45
8. 0.08
9. 4.68
10. 1.85
11. 1.029
12. 0.14
13. 5.08, 5.6, 5.8, 5.802
14. 0.1136, 0.115, 0.12, 0.2
15. 4.52, 4.667, 4.8, 14.005
16. 0.8, 0.8023, 0.803, 0.823
17. **C. 0.6 g, 0.572 g, 0.0785 g** The correct answer lists the weights from greatest to least. Since none of the weights has a whole number part, compare the tenths places.
18. **D. 1.38** This is the only choice that is rounded to the hundredths place. Since the number in the thousandths place of 1.3815 is less than 5, round down.

## Lesson 2: Decimal Operations

### Practice 2.1, page 261

1. 7.996
2. 10.508
3. 12.26
4. 5.85
5. 7.426
6. 2.11
7. 18.094
8. 5.117
9. 21.32
10. 0.895
11. 3.84
12. 2.35
13. 5.506
14. 21.16
15. 0.645
16. 2.426
17. 0.15
18. 4.88
19. 11.8
20. 14.016
21. 4.522
22. 2.36
23. 17.88
24. 17.225
25. **A. 22.25** Add the times: $7.2 + 6.8 + 8.25 = 22.25$ minutes. You do not need to use the 3-mile distance to solve the problem.
26. **C. 4.25** Add to find Claudia's total hours for the week: $8.5 + 9.25 + 8.75 + 10 + 7.75 = 44.25$. Then subtract 40 to find the number of overtime hours: $44.25 - 40 = 4.25$ hours.
27. **A. 1.8** Add the lengths cut from the pipe: $2.8 + 1.4 = 4.2$. Then subtract from 6: $6 - 4.2 = 1.8$ meters.
28. **C. \$55.26** Add the amounts: $\$16.98 + \$31.78 + \$6.50 = \$55.26$

### Practice 2.2, page 263

1. 2.65
2. 12.8
3. 0.496
4. 0.52
5. 3.6
6. 4.09
7. 8.75
8. 3.375
9. 9.6681
10. 24
11. 14.2
12. 15,800
13. 34.1
14. 2.36
15. 0.656
16. 2.64
17. 1.65
18. 4.275
19. 3.696
20. 1.002
21. 0.0072
22. **D. 15.16** Multiply 3.79 liters by 4: $3.79 \times 4 = 15.16$ liters.
23. **B. \$9.23** Multiply $\$0.45 \times 20.5$: $\$0.45 \times 20.5 = \$9.225$, which rounds to \$9.23.
24. **C. 92.9** Divide to find the average daily miles: $278.7 \div 3 = 92.9$ miles.
25. **C. \$0.26** There are 19 servings in a box of Toasted Oats. Divide: $\$4.94 \div 19 = \$0.26$.
26. **B. 50.0** Find the weight in the table and multiply: $12.5 \times 4 =$ 50 ounces.

## Lesson 3: Fraction Basics

### Practice 3, page 265

1. $\frac{3}{5}$
2. $\frac{2}{4}$; $\frac{1}{2}$
3. $\frac{2}{3}$
4. $\frac{7}{3}$; $2\frac{1}{3}$
5. $\frac{7}{2}$; $3\frac{1}{2}$
6. $\frac{15}{4}$; $3\frac{3}{4}$
7. $5\frac{2}{3}$
8. $\frac{18}{5}$
9. 4
10. $\frac{47}{9}$
11. $4\frac{3}{4}$
12. $\frac{29}{12}$
13. $4\frac{7}{9}$
14. $\frac{7}{4}$
15. $8\frac{1}{4}$
16. $\frac{57}{10}$
17. $\frac{12}{16}$
18. $\frac{7}{21}$
19. $\frac{48}{60}$
20. $\frac{15}{40}$
21. $\frac{24}{100}$
22. $\frac{3}{4}$
23. $\frac{1}{6}$
24. $\frac{3}{5}$
25. $\frac{13}{15}$
26. $\frac{2}{3}$
27. **A. $\frac{3}{4}$** Of those surveyed, $\frac{18}{24}$ went to at least one movie. Reduce the fraction to lowest terms: $\frac{18 \div 6}{24 \div 6} = \frac{3}{4}$.
28. **C. $\frac{40}{100}$** Raise $\frac{2}{5}$ to an equivalent fraction with a denominator of 100 by multiplying both numbers by 20: $\frac{2 \times 20}{5 \times 20} = \frac{40}{100}$.

## Lesson 4: Fraction Operations

### Practice 4.1, page 267

1. $\frac{1}{2}$
2. 1
3. $\frac{1}{3}$
4. $\frac{1}{6}$
5. $\frac{11}{12}$
6. $1\frac{1}{8}$
7. $\frac{3}{10}$
8. $\frac{5}{18}$
9. $3\frac{13}{15}$
10. $1\frac{3}{4}$
11. $8\frac{1}{2}$
12. $11\frac{5}{8}$
13. $21\frac{7}{10}$
14. $7\frac{13}{18}$
15. $12\frac{5}{6}$
16. $2\frac{5}{8}$
17. $42\frac{5}{12}$
18. $22\frac{11}{20}$
19. $5\frac{1}{18}$
20. $11\frac{1}{8}$
21. $3\frac{23}{28}$
22. $1\frac{7}{24}$
23. $2\frac{3}{7}$
24. $8\frac{8}{9}$
25. $\frac{32}{35}$
26. **B. $1\frac{3}{16}$** Add to find the total: $\frac{5}{16} + \frac{7}{8} = \frac{5}{16} + \frac{14}{16} = \frac{19}{16} = 1\frac{3}{16}$ inches.
27. **C. $1\frac{5}{8}$** Subtract to find the difference in the lengths: $2\frac{7}{8} - 1\frac{1}{4} = 2\frac{7}{8} - 1\frac{2}{8} = 1\frac{5}{8}$ inches.
28. **A. $14\frac{3}{8}$** Subtract the amount sold from the amount on the bolt: $23\frac{1}{4} - 8\frac{7}{8} = 23\frac{2}{8} - 8\frac{7}{8} = 22\frac{10}{8} - 8\frac{7}{8} = 14\frac{3}{8}$ yards.
29. **C. $2\frac{11}{12}$** Add the amounts: $1\frac{2}{3} + \frac{1}{2} + \frac{3}{4} = 1\frac{8}{12} + \frac{6}{12} + \frac{9}{12} = 1\frac{23}{12} = 2\frac{11}{12}$ cups.

### Practice 4.2, page 269

1. $\frac{1}{6}$
2. $\frac{11}{12}$
3. 14
4. $18\frac{3}{4}$
5. $\frac{7}{8}$
6. $\frac{21}{32}$
7. $7\frac{14}{15}$
8. $41\frac{1}{4}$
9. $2\frac{1}{32}$
10. 14
11. $1\frac{4}{5}$
12. 48

13. $2\frac{2}{5}$

14. $2\frac{1}{4}$

15. 27

16. 8

17. $9\frac{1}{2}$

18. $\frac{3}{4}$

19. **B. 75** Find $\frac{3}{16}$ of 400 by multiplying: $400 \times \frac{3}{16} = \frac{\overset{25}{\cancel{400}}}{1} \times \frac{3}{\underset{1}{\cancel{16}}} = \frac{75}{1} = 75$.

20. **B. 7** Divide: $20 \div 2\frac{3}{4} = \frac{20}{1} \div \frac{11}{4} = \frac{20}{1} \times \frac{4}{11} = \frac{80}{11} = 7\frac{3}{11}$. Ignore the remainder since the problem asks how many shirts can be completed.

21. **B. 33** You need to find how many $\frac{2}{3}$ hours there are in 22 hours. Divide: $22 \div \frac{2}{3} = \frac{22}{1} \div \frac{2}{3} = \frac{11}{1} \times \frac{3}{1} = \frac{33}{1}$.

22. **C. $37\frac{7}{8}$** Multiply $12\frac{5}{8}$ inches by 3, the number of panels: $12\frac{5}{8} \times 3 = \frac{101}{8} \times \frac{3}{1} = \frac{303}{8} = 37\frac{7}{8}$.

## Lesson 5: Fraction and Decimal Equivalencies

### Practice 5, page 271

1. **B. $20.00** Instead of multiplying $80 by 0.25, you can also find $\frac{1}{4}$ of $80.
2. **C. 480 × 0.3** Find $\frac{3}{10}$ of 480. "Of" in "of the workers" indicates multiplication, and the decimal equivalent of $\frac{3}{10}$ is 0.3.
3. **B. $4\frac{2}{3}$** The decimal part of the calculator display equals the fraction $\frac{2}{3}$.
4. **C. $18.00** Multiply 12 by 1.5. The decimal $1.5 = 1\frac{1}{2}$. Convert that fraction to an improper fraction: $\frac{3}{2}$ Now multiply: $12 \times \frac{3}{2} = \frac{36}{2} = 18$.
5. **B. $\frac{3}{4}$** Subtract: $1.875 - 1.125 = 0.75$, which equals $\frac{3}{4}$ inch.
6. **C. 0.375** Instead of dividing 3 by 8, think: $3 \div 8$ means $\frac{3}{8}$, which equals 0.375.

## Lesson 6: Decimals and Fractions on the Number Line

### Practice 6, page 273

1. **C. $\frac{2}{3}$** The number line is in increments of $\frac{1}{3}$, and the value you are asked to identify comes halfway between $\frac{1}{3}$ and 1.
2. **D. 2.8** The number line is in increments of 0.2, and the value you are asked to identify comes halfway between 2.6 and 3.
3. **C. 2** A minus B is $3\frac{1}{2} - 1\frac{1}{2} = 2$.
4. **$\frac{2}{3}$** Angela gave 16 of 24 cookies to her neighbor: $\frac{16}{24} = \frac{2}{3}$.
5. **4.625** Each increment on this number line is 0.125 greater than the previous increment.
6. **9.33** Each increment on the number line is $0.3\overline{3}$ greater than the previous increment.
7. **$3\frac{1}{3}$** Each increment on the number line is $\frac{1}{3}$ greater than the previous increment.
8. **$11\frac{5}{6}$** Each increment on the number line is $\frac{1}{6}$ greater than the previous increment.

## Lesson 7: Decimal and Fraction Calculator Skills

### Practice 7, page 275

1. **7.379**
2. **$2\frac{1}{4}$** To work with mixed fractions on the TI-30XS MultiView™, use the (2nd) function above the [n/d] key: (2nd) [n/d] 3 ▶ 2 ▼ 3 ▶ ⊖ (2nd) [n/d] 1 ▶ 5 ▼ 12 (enter). The number $\frac{9}{4}$ will appear on the right-hand side of the display.
3. **$380.25**
4. **42**
5. **$84.44** Multiply: $95 × $\frac{8}{9}$ = 84.44$\overline{4}$. Round to get $84.44.
6. **$79.74** Divide: $956.88 ÷ 12 = $79.
7. **$1,475** Multiply: $118,000 × 0.0125 = $1,475
8. **$4\frac{1}{4}$ cups** Add: $1\frac{1}{2} + 2\frac{3}{4} = 4\frac{1}{4}$
9. **B. $6.67** Multiply the weight of the quilt by $1.20: 5.56 × $1.20 = $6.672, which rounds to $6.67.
10. **C. 24** You need to find $\frac{3}{8}$ of 64. Multiply. $64 \times \frac{3}{8} = 24$ acres.

## Lesson 8: Filling in the Answer Grid Using Decimals or Fractions

### Practice 8, page 277

1. **35.6** Add: $12.6 + 9.8 + 13.2 = 35.6$ gallons of gasoline.
2. **$\frac{2}{3}$** Divide the amount spent by the total: $\frac{\$100}{\$150} = \frac{2}{3}$
3. **2** Subtract: $9\frac{1}{2} - 7\frac{1}{2} = \frac{19}{2} - \frac{15}{2} = \frac{4}{2} = 2$
4. **38** Divide: $100 \div 2.6 = 38.46$ so 38 bottles can be filled.
5. **$\frac{1}{6}$** State the number of cherry colas as a fraction: $\frac{3}{18}$ of the cases were cherry cola, which equals $\frac{1}{6}$.
6. **25** Divide: $12.5 \div 0.5 = 25$ sheets of foam board.

## Decimals and Fractions Practice Questions, pages 278–281

1. **C. $15\frac{3}{4}$** Subtract: $20\frac{1}{2} - 4\frac{3}{4} = 20\frac{2}{4} - 4\frac{3}{4} = 19\frac{6}{4} - 4\frac{3}{4} = 15\frac{3}{4}$
2. **B. $0.25** Divide the cost by the number of servings: $4.69 ÷ 19 ≈ 0.247, which rounds to $0.25.
3. **C. $1386.20** To find the amount the 12-month plan will cost a customer, multiply $98.85 by 12 and add $200: ($98.85 × 12) + $200 = $1386.20.
4. **C. $30.12** Multiply using your calculator. Use 10.5 for $10\frac{1}{2}$: $2.869 × 10.5 = $30.1245, which rounds to $30.12.
5. **B. 2.85** Since the answer choices are decimals, use your calculator. Use decimals instead of fractions: $1\frac{1}{2} = 1.5$, $4\frac{3}{4} = 4.75$, and $2\frac{3}{10} = 2.3$. To find the average, add the three weights and divide the total by 3: $\frac{1.5 + 4.75 + 2.3}{3} = \frac{8.55}{3} = 2.85$,
6. **C. $32\frac{1}{4}$** Divide: $258 ÷ $8 = 32.25, which equals $32\frac{1}{4}$.
7. **B. 57** Subtract $6\frac{1}{4}$ from $20\frac{1}{2}$ and divide the difference by $\frac{1}{4}$. To do the work quickly, use the fraction keys on your calculator or change the fractions to decimals: $20\frac{1}{2} - 6\frac{1}{4} = 14\frac{1}{4}$; $14\frac{1}{4} \div \frac{1}{4} = 57$.
8. **D. $90.00** Brand B costs $0.09 more than Brand A, so the school will save $0.09 on each marker. Multiply the savings by 1000: $0.09 × 1000 = $90.00.
9. **B. $3\frac{1}{2}$** Add the times for the appointments: $\frac{3}{4} + \frac{3}{4} + 1\frac{1}{4} + \frac{3}{4} = 1\frac{10}{4} = 3\frac{2}{4} = 3\frac{1}{2}$
10. **C. 10** Divide $3\frac{1}{2}$ hours by the amount of time needed for a routine physical: $3\frac{1}{2} \div \frac{1}{3} = \frac{7}{2} \div \frac{1}{3} = \frac{7}{2} \times \frac{3}{1} = \frac{21}{2} = 10\frac{1}{2}$. Therefore, Jennifer can complete 10 physicals. Ignore the fraction remainder.
11. **D. $\frac{11}{12}$** Write the fraction and reduce it to lowest terms. You can save time by using the fraction key on your calculator, which automatically reduces a fraction to lowest terms. Press 5500 [n/d] ▼ 6000 (enter). The right-hand side of the display will read $\frac{11}{12}$.

12. **C. $7.25** The first hour costs $3.50, and there are $1\frac{1}{2}$ hours left. There are 3 half hours, or $1\frac{1}{2}$ hours, so you will pay $3.50 + (3 × $1.25) = $7.25.
13. **$\frac{2}{3}$** Write a fraction and reduce: $\frac{56}{84} = \frac{56 \div 28}{84 \div 28} = \frac{2}{3}$
14. **0.84** Subtract to compare: $3.97 - 3.13 = 0.84$
15. **B. $\frac{3}{10}$** Subtract: $250-175=75$. Thus, 75 out of 250, or $\frac{75}{250}$, have not been loaded. Reduce: $\frac{75 \div 25}{250 \div 25} = \frac{3}{10}$.
16. **B. $\frac{5}{8}$** $A - B = \frac{7}{8} - \frac{1}{4}$. Find a common denominator and subtract: $\frac{7}{8} - \frac{2}{8} = \frac{5}{8}$.
17. **A. 285** To find $\frac{3}{4}$ of 380, multiply. Change $\frac{3}{4}$ to 0.75. Then $380 \times 0.75 = 285$.
18. **C. $\frac{5}{6}$** To find half of $1\frac{2}{3}$, either multiply by $\frac{1}{2}$ or divide by 2. Both results are the same: $1\frac{2}{3} \times \frac{1}{2} = \frac{5}{3} \times \frac{1}{2} = \frac{5}{6}$.
19. **C. 150** You need to find $\frac{5}{8}$ of 240. Multiply: $240 \times \frac{5}{8} = \frac{\overset{30}{\cancel{240}}}{1} \times \frac{5}{\underset{1}{\cancel{8}}} = \frac{150}{1} = 150$.
20. **D. core box, classic, bevel, cutter** You could change the fractions to decimals to solve the problem, but the quickest method is to rewrite the fractions with a common denominator of 32:
    cutter: $\frac{9}{16} = \frac{18}{32}$;
    core box: $\frac{5}{32}$;
    classic: $\frac{3}{8} = \frac{12}{32}$;
    bevel: $\frac{1}{2} = \frac{16}{32}$.
    Then arrange the like fractions from least to greatest by their numerators.
21. **B. W and Y.** The most Joe will eat will be $\frac{7}{8}$ of his pizza, so the minimum he'll have left over will be $\frac{1}{8}$ of it. The least Joe will eat will be $\frac{1}{2}$, so the maximum he'll have left over will be $\frac{1}{2}$ of the pizza.
22. **C. 8** Divide: $60 \div 7.5 = 8$ days.
23. **A. $\frac{1}{2}$** Multiply: $\frac{2}{3} \times \frac{3}{4} = \frac{\overset{1}{\cancel{2}}}{\underset{1}{\cancel{3}}} \times \frac{\overset{1}{\cancel{3}}}{\underset{2}{\cancel{4}}} = \frac{1}{2}$.
24. **B. 56** Multiply: $140 \times \frac{2}{5} = \frac{\overset{28}{\cancel{140}}}{1} \times \frac{2}{\cancel{5}} = \frac{56}{1} = 56$.
25. **C. 17.9** Maya travels five segments of the route. Add to find the total distance: $2.4 + 4.3 + 3.6 + 3.6 + 4.0 = 17.9$.
26. **D. 5** Add to find the total amount to be cut off: $3\frac{3}{4} + 3\frac{3}{4} = 6\frac{6}{4} = 7\frac{1}{2}$. Subtract from $12\frac{1}{2}$: $12\frac{1}{2} - 7\frac{1}{2} = 5$.
27. **B. $535.60** Multiply $26.38 by 20 and add $8 to the result: $26.38 × 20 = $527.60. Then: $527.60 + $8.00 = $535.60.
28. **80.** Divide: $60 \div 0.75 = 80$.
29. **$\frac{7}{12}$** Add the fractions and subtract the total from 1: $\frac{1}{6} + \frac{1}{4} = \frac{2}{12} + \frac{3}{12} = \frac{5}{12}$. Then: $1 - \frac{5}{12} = \frac{12}{12} - \frac{5}{12} = \frac{7}{12}$.

## Number and Quantity III: Ratio, Proportion, and Percent

### Lesson 1: Ratio and Proportion

**Practice 1.1, page 283**

1. $\frac{24}{6} = \frac{4}{1}$
2. $\frac{\$250}{\$1500} = \frac{1}{6}$
3. $\frac{180}{15} = \frac{12}{1}$
4. $\frac{12}{30} = \frac{2}{5}$ Add $12 + 18 = 30$ to find the total workers.
5. $\frac{336}{14} = \frac{24}{1}$
6. $\frac{\$1500}{\$2400} = \frac{5}{8}$
7. $\frac{20}{12} = \frac{5}{3}$ Subtract $32 - 20 = 12$ to find the free throws missed.
8. $\frac{14}{24} = \frac{7}{12}$ Add $10 + 14 = 24$ to find the total students.
9. $\frac{1440}{6} = \frac{240}{1}$
10. **A. 9:11** Write the ratio in fraction form and reduce: $\frac{180}{220} = \frac{9}{11}$.
11. **B. 3 to 10** Calculate: $\frac{180}{600} = \frac{3}{10}$.
12. **B. $\frac{1}{3}$** Subtract to find the voters who have made a decision: $600 - 150 = 450$. Write the ratio and reduce: $\frac{150}{450} = \frac{1}{3}$.
13. **C. 1 to 2** Subtract to find the amount owed: $1200 – $400 = $800. Write the ratio and reduce: 400 to 800 = 1 to 2.
14. **D. 8:3** Subtract to find the number of losses: $77 - 56 = 21$. Write the ratio and reduce: $\frac{56}{21} = \frac{8}{3}$.

**Practice 1.2, page 285**

1. 12
2. 45
3. 2.5 or $2\frac{1}{2}$
4. 60
5. $371
6. 96
7. 2.1 or $2\frac{1}{10}$
8. 72
9. 12.5 or $12\frac{1}{2}$
10. $8.94
11. 1.25 or $1\frac{1}{4}$
12. 37.5 or $37\frac{1}{2}$
13. 18
14. 32
15. $45.50
16. 28
17. **B. $1.23** Calculate: $\frac{4}{\$0.98} = \frac{5}{x}$ $\$0.98 \times 5 \div 4 = \$1.225$, which rounds to $1.23.
18. **C. 96** Calculate: $\frac{5}{8} = \frac{60}{x}$; $8 \times 60 \div 5 = 96$.
19. **B. 23** Calculate: $\frac{414}{18} = \frac{x}{1}$; $414 \times 1 \div 18 = 23$.
20. **B. 345** Calculate: $\frac{2\text{ cm}}{150\text{ km}} = \frac{4.6\text{ cm}}{x\text{ km}}$; $150 \times 4.6 \div 2 = 345$.
21. **A. $6\frac{2}{3}$** Write the proportions using fractions. The process is the same: $\frac{2\frac{1}{2}}{1\frac{1}{2}} = \frac{x}{4}$; $2\frac{1}{2} \times 4 \div 1\frac{1}{2} = 6\frac{2}{3}$.
22. **A. 155 × 7 ÷ 2.5** Set up the proportion and think about the order of operations you would need to solve for $x$: $\frac{155}{2.5} = \frac{x}{7}$; $155 \times 7 \div 2.5 = x$.

### Lesson 2: Percents

**Practice 2, page 287**

1. base = $1000
   part = $200
   rate = 20%
2. base = 80
   part = 72
   rate = 90%
3. base = $13,700
   part = $2,740
   rate = 20%
4. base = $2000
   part = $500
   rate = 25%
5. base = 40
   part = 60
   rate = 150%
   60 is 150% *of* 40. The word *of* indicates that 40 is the base.
6. base = $38
   part = $3.23
   rate = 8.5%
7. base = $900
   part = $135
   rate = 15%
8. base = $10.70
   part = $1.07
   rate = 10%
9. base = 800
   part = 200
   rate = 25%
10. base = 12,500
    part = 5,000
    rate = 40%
11. **A. $\frac{9 \times 100}{122}$** Add the wins and losses to find the total games played: $9 + 3 = 12$; then write the proportion: $\frac{9}{12} = \frac{x}{100}$. To solve the proportion, you need to find the expression that multiplies 9 and 100 and divides by 12. Only choice (A) does this.
12. **D. 50%** Bravo played 12 games ($6 + 6 = 12$). Then $\frac{6}{12} = \frac{x}{100}$ and $6 \times 100 \div 12 = 50$.

13. **C. $32** To find 25% of $128, solve the proportion: $\frac{x}{\$128} = \frac{25}{100}$; $128 × 25 ÷ 100 = $32. Since 25% = $\frac{1}{4}$, you can also find the answer by dividing $128 by 4.

## Lesson 3: Using the Percent Formula

### Practice 3.1, page 289

1. $5
2. 180
3. 140
4. 95%
5. 25%
6. 3%
7. 17
8. $60
9. 200%
10. 5%
11. 8%
12. $3.91
13. $6\frac{1}{2}$% or 6.5%
14. $364
15. 62.5% or $62\frac{1}{2}$%
16. 72
17. **C. 60%** Calculate: 72 ÷ 120 = 0.6 = 60%.
18. **B. $2,385** Calculate: $2,250 × 0.06 = $135, and $2,250 + $135 = $2,385.
19. **D. $6.90.** Calculate: $46 × 0.15 = $6.90.
20. **D. 70%** Find what percent $45.50 is of $65 by dividing: $45.50 ÷ $65 = 0.7, which equals 70%.
21. **A. $\frac{\$3 \times 100}{\$50}$** You need to divide the part ($3) by the whole ($50) to find the rate; however, choice (D) states $3 ÷ $50, which equals 0.06. You still need to change 0.06 to a percent, which you can do by multiplying by 100. If you write a proportion to solve the problem, you will see that choice (A) is correct.

### Practice 3.2, page 291

1. $175
2. 280
3. 6.4
4. $200
5. 30
6. $84
7. 200
8. 9
9. $13.50
10. 25%
11. $75
12. $9.30
13. 900
14. 90%
15. $780
16. $3120
17. 4000
18. 10%
19. **C. $1,230.00** Solve for the base. $\frac{\$369}{0.3}$ = $1,230.
20. **C. $1,200,000** Solve for the base. $\frac{\$72,000}{0.06}$ = $1,200,000.
21. **B. $\frac{160 \times 100}{5}$** Set up the problem as a proportion: $\frac{160}{x} = \frac{5}{100}$. To solve the proportion, you would multiply 160 × 100 and divide by 5. Only choice (B) carries out those operations.
22. **C. 720.** The base is 3600, the total number who received the application. The part is the unknown number who returned the application. Since 20% = 0.2, you can solve for the part by multiplying the base by the rate: 3600 × 0.2.

## Lesson 4: Percent Calculator Skills

### Practice 4, page 293

1. $59.80
2. $96
3. $15.12
4. 40
5. 3%
6. 2080
7. 25%
8. 70
9. 25.2
10. 79
11. 2.5% or $2\frac{1}{2}$%
12. 48
13. 78%
14. $16
15. 250
16. 14
17. 7%
18. 276
19. **C. $8.20** Chanel's order falls between $50.01 and $100. Find 5% of $84: press: 0.05 ⊗ 84 (enter). The right side of the display reads 4.2, or $4.20. Add $4: $4.20 + $4 = $8.20.
20. **A. $0.30** Find the shipping and handling for Jason's order: 8% of $110 = $8.80. Find the shipping and handling for Zola's order: 5% of $90 = $4.50, and $4.50 + $4.00 = $8.50. Then find the difference: $8.80 – $8.50 = $0.30.
21. **C. 88%** Press: 3190 ⊕ 3625 (2nd) ( ) ) (enter). The right side of the display reads 0.88. You could also simply divide: 3190 ÷ 3625 = .88. Then mentally translate .88 into 88%.
22. **D. 15%** Divide strikeouts (63) by at bats (410): press: 63 ⊕ 410 (enter). The right side of the display reads 0.153658537, which rounds to 15%.

## Lesson 5: Interest

### Practice 5, page 295

1. **$360**
2. **$1,998** Because 8 months is $\frac{2}{3}$ of a year, use $\frac{2}{3}$ for *t* in the formula.
3. **$450**
4. **$1,040**
5. **D. $1,300 + ($1,300 × 0.09 × 1.5)** Find the interest by multiplying the amount borrowed ($1300) by the interest expressed as a decimal (0.09) by the time period in years (1.5). To find the amount paid back, the amount borrowed must be added to the interest. Only choice (D) shows this series of operations.
6. **B. $144** Find the interest for each loan option: Option A: $2,400 × 0.12 × 2.5 = $720; Option C: $2,400 × 0.09 × 4 = $864. Subtract to find the difference: $864 – $720 = $144.

## Lesson 6: Percent of Change

### Practice 6, page 297

1. 50%
2. 38%
3. 200%
4. 45%
5. 20%
6. 32%
7. 21%
8. 86%
9. 420%
10. 34%
11. **B. 60%** Subtract: $448 – $280 = $168. Divide by the original weekly pay: $168 ÷ $280 = 0.6, which equals 60%.
12. **B. 25%** Subtract: $48 – $36 = $12. Divide by the original price: $12 ÷ $48 = 0.25, which equals 25%.
13. **C. 6%** Subtract: $636 – $600 = $36. Divide by the original rent: $36 ÷ $600 = 0.06, which equals 6%.
14. **C. 125%** The wholesale price of the model is $63, and the retail price is $141.75. Subtract: $141.75 – $63 = $78.75. Divide by the wholesale price: $78.75 ÷ $63 = 1.25, which equals 125%.
15. **B. 30%** The retail price of the model is $150.50, and the member's price is $105.35. Subtract: $150.50 – $105.35 = $45.15. Divide by the retail price: $45.15 ÷ 150.50 = 0.3, which equals 30%.

## Ratio, Proportion, and Percent Practice Questions, pages 298–301

1. **C. 1:11** Subtract to find the dollars spent on other costs: $360,000 – $30,000 = $330,000. Write a ratio and reduce: $\frac{\$30,000}{\$330,000} = \frac{1}{11}$.
2. **A. 2 × $\frac{50}{5}$** Write a proportion: $\frac{5}{2} = \frac{50}{x}$. To solve it, multiply 2 × 50 and divide by 5. Only choice (A) performs these operations.
3. **B. $7.56** Find 35% of $5.60: $5.60 × 0.35 = $1.96; add: $1.96 + $5.60 = $7.56. Another way to get the

answer is to find 135% of $5.60. $5.60 × 1.35 = $7.56.

4. **D. $20,000** The current worth of the car ($12,000) is part of the base. Solve for the base: $12,000 ÷ 0.6 = $20,000.
5. **C. 42** Solve the proportion: $\frac{7}{3} = \frac{x}{18}$; 7 × 18 ÷ 3 = 42.
6. **A. 6%** The commission is part of the base. Solve for the part: $954 ÷ $15,900 = 0.06 = 6%.
7. **B. 1:6** Add to find the total time spent on the project: $2 + 1\frac{1}{2} + 2 + 3\frac{1}{2} = 9$ hours. $1\frac{1}{2}$ hours = 1.5 hours. Write a ratio using decimals and reduce: $\frac{1.5}{9} = \frac{1}{6}$.
8. **B. 36%** Add to find the acres used for grains, vegetables, or fruits: 5,200 + 9,200 = 14,400. Solve for percent: 14,400 ÷ 40,400 = 0.36 = 36%.
9. **A. 35,600** Calculate the decrease in acres of dairy farmland: 22,000 × 20% = 4,400. Subtract that amount from the total acreage of farmland to determine how many acres of farmland will remain: 40,000 – 4,400 = 35,600.
10. **A. $\frac{3}{16}$** The total fat is 3 + 13 = 16 grams. Write the ratio of saturated fat (3 grams) to the total (16 grams). The ratio cannot be simplified.
11. **B. 10** Write a proportion and solve: $\frac{4}{5} = \frac{x}{12.5}$. Then 4 × 12.5 ÷ 5 = 10 inches.
12. **138** Write a proportion and solve: $\frac{4}{3} = \frac{184}{x}$. Then 3 × 184 ÷ 4 = 138 female patients.
13. **$900** If 20% is the amount of the discount, then the sale price must be 80% of the original price. The sale price is the part, and the original price is the base. Solve for the base: $720 ÷ 0.8 = $900.
14. **B. 40** If the ratio of wins to losses is 5:4, then the ratio of wins to games played is 5:9. Write a proportion and solve: $\frac{5}{9} = \frac{x}{72}$; 5 × 72 ÷ 9 = 40 games won.
15. **C. 192** Add to find the number that did not answer "no": 16% + 32% = 48%. Find 48% of 400: 400 × 0.48 = 192.
16. **C. 20%** To find the percent decrease, subtract the lower price from the higher price and divide the difference by the original price. In this case, the original price is $25, the higher price. To change the answer to a percent, you must move the decimal point two places to the right or multiply by 100.
17. **A. 121** When the rate is greater than 100%, the part will be greater than the base. Solve for the part: 55 × 2.2 = 121.
18. **D. 18%** There are 6 grams of fat in the roast beef sandwich, so there are 6 × 9 = 54 calories in the sandwich from fat. The total number of calories in the sandwich is 300. Find what percent 54 is of 300: 54 ÷ 300 = 0.18 = 18%.
19. **D. $264** Write a proportion and solve: $\frac{\$8}{\$3} = \frac{\$704}{x}$; $3 × $704 ÷ $8 = $264.
20. **C. 175** The 140 employees who have more than 12 days of sick leave are part of the whole workforce. You need to solve for the base: 140 ÷ 0.8 = 175.
21. **D. 825** If the ratio of sold to unsold tickets is 11 to 1, then the ratio of sold to total tickets is 11 to 12. Write a proportion and solve: $\frac{11}{12} = \frac{x}{900}$; 11 × 900 ÷ 12 = 825.
22. **C. $2464** Use the formula for finding simple interest: $i = prt$: $2200 × 0.08 × 1.5 = $264. To find the amount in the account at the end of the time, add the interest to the original investment: $2200 + $264 = $2464.
23. **B. $328** Once you find the discount by multiplying 0.2 by $410, you will need to subtract the discount from $410 to find the sale price.
24. **D. 330** After changing $2\frac{3}{4}$ to the decimal 2.75, write a proportion and solve: $\frac{0.5}{60} = \frac{2.75}{x}$; 60 × 2.75 ÷ 0.5 = 330.
25. **C. $\frac{(140 - 91)}{140} \times 100$** There were 140 customers on Sunday, and 91 made a purchase. Therefore, 140 – 91 did not make a purchase. To find the percent rate, divide the difference by 140, the total number of customers on Sunday (the base). Then move the decimal point two places to the right or multiply by 100 to change the answer to a percent. Only choice (C) shows this sequence of operations.
26. **270** Write a proportion and solve: $\frac{9}{14} = \frac{x}{420}$.
27. 3/5 If Marcie spends 15 hours answering telephones, she spends 40 – 15, or 25 hours doing other tasks. Write a ratio and reduce: $\frac{15}{25} = \frac{3}{5}$.

## Statistics and Probability

### Lesson 1: Tables and Pictographs

#### Practice 1, page 303

1. **9** Calculate: 22,707 ÷ 2523 = 9
2. **6%** Calculate: (139,510 – 130,748) ÷ 139,510 ≈ 0.06, or 6%.
3. **300** There are $6\frac{1}{2}$ symbols in the "North" row and $4\frac{1}{2}$ in the "South" row. Two more symbols translates to 300 more books.
4. **3000** Count the number of symbols, 20, and multiply by 150.
5. **D. Reads or pretends to read** If 100 children were surveyed in each year, then the number of children who recognized all letters increased from 11 to 17. To find the percent change, use the percent change formula: $\frac{\text{amount of change}}{\text{original value}} = \frac{17-11}{11} = \frac{6}{11}$, or a roughly 55% increase. Performing similar calculations for all categories will reveal that "reads or pretends to read" showed the least percent increase: $\frac{67-66}{66} = \frac{1}{66} \approx 2\%$. Note that simply subtracting 66 from 67 does not give you the percent of change.
6. **C. 119** In 2010, 34% of 3-year-old children could write their own names. Find 34% of 350: 350 × 0.34 = 119.
7. **C. 375** There are $7\frac{1}{2}$ car symbols. Each symbol represents 50 cars. Multiply: $7\frac{1}{2} \times 50 = 375$
8. **A. 75** Compare the symbols for the two rows. There are $1\frac{1}{2}$ more symbols for 8 A.M. to noon than there are after 4:30 P.M. Multiply: $1\frac{1}{2} \times 50 = 75$

### Lesson 2: Bar and Line Graphs

#### Practice 2.1, page 305

1. **50**
2. **about 15** Estimate 38 complaints in 2011 and 22 complaints in 2006. Subtract and round.

3. **20%** The number of complaints decreased by 5, from 25 to 20. This represents a $\frac{5}{25} = 20\%$ decrease.
4. **about $20 million** Estimate values from the graph and subtract. Be sure to use the black bars that represent cost.
5. **Film A** Film A has the biggest difference in size between the bar representing box-office receipts and the bar representing cost.
6. **150%** Calculate: $\frac{60}{40} = \frac{3}{2} = 150\%$
7. **A. 40** There are approximately 110 T-shirts, more than 40 books, and a little fewer than 30 toys sold. Combined, about 70 books and toys were sold. Subtract 70 from 110, and you have about 40.
8. **D. $1000** There were about 50 games sold, so 25 sold for $16 and 25 sold for $24. Calculate: $(25 \times 16) + (25 \times 24) = 1000$.
9. **C. 14:3** Write a ratio and simplify: $\frac{70}{15} = \frac{14}{3}$
10. **D. September** Add the 2-day and 5-day permits for each month. Only September's permits equal 80.

### Practice 2.2, page 307

1. **October** The point representing October is lower than the point representing the previous month, and the line leading to it slopes downward. This indicates a decrease.
2. **270** Estimate totals for the three months and add.
3. **from June to July** The number of visits increased more from August to September, but because the number in June was so low, the percentage increase from June to July is nearly 100%.
4. **$10** Estimate values and subtract.
5. **20%** The price increased from about $25 to about $30, an increase of $5. $\frac{5}{25} = 20\%$.
6. **$30** The price increased from about $18 to about $45. This increase is almost $30.
7. **A. 1930 to 1940** The price of goods decreased over two decades, 1920 to 1940. Note the downward movement of the line. Only the time period 1930 to 1940 is included among the answer options.
8. **D. $\frac{1}{5}$** The price of the same goods was about $20 in 1970 and $100 in 2000. Write a ratio and simplify: $\frac{\$20}{\$100} = \frac{1}{5}$ .
9. **B. 50** There were about 390 sales in Store 2 and 340 sales in Store 1 in the sixth week: $390 - 340 = 50$.
10. **D. Week 5** The steepest line segment leads from week 4 to week 5, indicating the largest increase in sales from the previous week.

## Lesson 3: Circle Graphs

### Practice 3, page 309

1. **29%** Find those two categories on the circle graph and add.
2. $\frac{2}{25}$ $8\% = \frac{8}{100} = \frac{2}{25}$
3. **$630** Use the total budget. $\$2250 \times 28\% = \$630$.
4. **$30.60** 17 cents of every dollar are spent on water heating: $\$180 \times 0.17 = \$30.60$.
5. **Heating and Air-Conditioning** The section labeled "Heating and Air-Conditioning" takes up more than half the circle.
6. **Cooking and Refrigeration** This section is 11 cents of every dollar, which is about 10%.
7. **A. 10** According to the graph, a records clerk spends 25%, or $\frac{1}{4}$, of his or her time preparing documents. Then 25% of 40 hours is 10 hours.
8. **D. 56%** If 44% of the time is spent on data entry, then $100\% - 44\% = 56\%$ spent on other tasks.
9. **B. 10%** Add: 3 cents plus 7 cents in 10 cents. Then 10 cents out of 100 cents is $\frac{10}{100}$, or 10%.
10. **C. $48** 40 cents out of every dollar, or 40%, is spent on public bonds. Then 40% of $120 is found by multiplying: $\$120 \times 0.4 = \$48$.

## Lesson 4: Measures of Central Tendency

### Practice 4.1, page 311

1. **57** Count the number of tally marks and add.
2. **6** Count the number of tally marks and subtract.
3. **1:2** Calculate: $\frac{15}{30} = \frac{1}{2}$
4. **3:4** Calculate: $\frac{6}{8} = \frac{3}{4}$
5. **46** Count the tally marks and add.
6. **14%** Count the total number of tally marks, then divide: $\frac{10}{70} \approx 0.14 = 14\%$.
7. **B. $\frac{4}{11}$** There are 16 tally marks next to the reason "wrong size." Add all the tally marks: $16 + 20 + 3 + 5 = 44$. Write a ratio and reduce. $\frac{16}{44} = \frac{4}{11}$.
8. **C. 45%** Adding all the tally marks, you find that there were 44 clothing returns in all. Since there are 20 tally marks by "unwanted gift," $\frac{20}{44}$ or $\approx 45\%$ of the total reasons given were "unwanted gift."
9. **D. 39%** Calculate: 35 applicants had a speed under 30 wpm, out of a total of 90 applicants, so $\frac{35}{90} \approx 39\%$.
10. **B. 1:2** To find those who could type above 45 wpm, add: $18 + 12 = 30$. The number typing below 45 wpm is found by adding $35 + 25 = 60$. Write a ratio and reduce: $\frac{30}{60} = \frac{1}{2}$.

### Practice 4.2, page 313

1. mean: 80.14
   median: 80
   mode: 82
2. mean: $8,487.17
   median: $8,208.50
   mode: none
3. mean: $4.76
   median: $4.50
   mode: $4.50
4. mean: 309 miles
   median: 300 miles
   mode: none
5. mean: $101.83
   median: $101.81
   mode: none
6. mean: 86
   median: 88
   mode: 88
7. mean: 99.1°
   median: 99°
   mode: 98° and 100°
8. mean: 1.9 inches
   median: 1.8 inches
   mode: none

9. mean: 305
   median: 305
   mode: 305
10. mean: 38.8 hours
    median: 40 hours
    mode: 40 hours
11. **A. $117,100** Add the amounts in the column labeled "Asking Price" and divide by 6, the number of prices listed.
12. **C. $116,500** Arrange the selling prices in order: $124,800; $118,400; $116,500; $116,500; $109,000; $103,600. Since the number of items is even, there are two in the middle: $116,500 and $116,500. Since these are the same amount, the average of the two is also $116,500.
13. **A.** $\frac{790 + 1150 + 662 + 805}{4}$ To find the mean, add the numbers and divide by the number of items in the set. In this case, there are 4 numbers.
14. **C. $900** The median is the middle amount. Arrange the amounts in order and find the middle amount.
15. **B. 14** The mode is the number that occurs most often. Only 14 occurs more than once in the data.

## Lesson 5: Line Plots

### Practice 5, page 315

1. **C.** Look for a line plot that reflects that two zebras have 26 stripes, two have 28, two have 30, etc.
2. **B.** Look for a line plot that reflects three classes with 29 students, two classes with 32, etc.
3. **D. the member who plants eight types of vegetables** Most of the data points are clustered around the quantities 1 through 4. The member who planted 8 types of vegetables is distant from that cluster of data and so is an outlier.
4. **B. 3** Three people grew three vegetables—that's more people than grew any other specific number of vegetables.

## Lesson 6: Histograms

### Practice 6, page 317

1. **C.** Look for the histogram that begins with 30 and that has a second bar at 56, a third bar at 80, etc.
2. **D.** Look for the histogram that begins with 15 and that has a second bar at 22, a third bar at 35, etc.
3. **C. 36%** Estimate the percentages represented by the four bars that cover the time period of December 9 through January 5: 8%, 9%, 9%, and 10%. Add those estimates to find the approximate percentage of cases reported during that entire time period, resulting in 35%.

## Lesson 7: Probability

### Practice 7.1, page 319

1. **$\frac{2}{5}$, 0.4, 40%** Calculate: $\frac{20}{50} = \frac{2}{5}$
2. **$\frac{3}{10}$, 0.3, 30%** There were 12 non-blue spins out of 40 total spins: $\frac{12}{40} = \frac{3}{10} = 30\%$.
3. **$\frac{1}{5}$, 0.2, 20%** Calculate: $\frac{2}{2+4+4} = \frac{2}{10} = \frac{1}{5} = 20\%$
4. **$\frac{1}{4}$, 0.25, 25%** Calculate: $\frac{60}{180+60} = \frac{60}{240} = \frac{1}{4} = 25\%$
5. **$\frac{1}{3}$, 0.33, $33\frac{1}{3}$%** Calculate: $\frac{2}{6} = \frac{1}{3}$
6. **C. 50%** There are 12 cards in the deck, and 6 are diamonds: $\frac{6}{12} = \frac{1}{2} = 50\%$
7. **A. $\frac{3}{4}$** There are 3 clubs, so 9 are not clubs: $\frac{9}{12} = \frac{3}{4}$.
8. **D. 2 out of 5** Sixteen out of 40 trials resulted in tails: $\frac{16}{40} = \frac{2}{5}$.
9. **A. 3 out of 5** Twenty-four out of 40 trials resulted in heads: $\frac{24}{40} = \frac{3}{5}$.

### Practice 7.2, page 321

1. **$\frac{1}{36}$** The events are independent, so multiply. $\frac{1}{6} \times \frac{1}{6} = \frac{1}{36}$
2. **$\frac{1}{4}$** Because the first card is replaced, the two choices are independent. The cards greater than 5 are 6, 7, 8, 9, 10. Multiply: $\frac{5}{10} \times \frac{5}{10} = \frac{1}{2} \times \frac{1}{2} = \frac{1}{4}$
3. **$\frac{1}{8}$** Half of the sections are red, so there is a $\frac{1}{2}$ chance that the result will be red. Each spin is independent. Multiply: $\frac{1}{2} \times \frac{1}{2} \times \frac{1}{2} = \frac{1}{8}$
4. **$\frac{9}{38}$** The marble is *not* replaced, so the probabilities are not the same. There is a $\frac{1}{2}$ chance the first marble is red. But once one red marble is removed, the odds of a second red become $\frac{9}{19}$. Multiply: $\frac{1}{2} \times \frac{9}{19} = \frac{9}{38}$.
5. **$\frac{1}{16}$** Each flip is independent and has a $\frac{1}{2}$ chance of coming up heads: $\frac{1}{2} \times \frac{1}{2} \times \frac{1}{2} \times \frac{1}{2} = \frac{1}{16}$.
6. **$\frac{1}{4}$** Half of the numbers on a standard die are odd: $\frac{1}{2} \times \frac{1}{2} = \frac{1}{4}$.
7. **A. $\frac{1}{9}$** The probability of rolling a 5 is $\frac{1}{6}$. Of the six equal sections on the spinner, four are even numbers, so there is a $\frac{4}{6}$, or $\frac{2}{3}$, chance of spinning an even number. Multiply the probability of each outcome: $\frac{1}{6} \times \frac{2}{3} \times \frac{2}{18} = \frac{1}{9}$.
8. **D. $\frac{1}{6}$** The only numbers that are on the spinner are 2, 3, and 4. There is only one 2 on the die, one 3 on the die, and one 4 on the die. So, no matter what number comes up on the spinner, there is a $\frac{1}{6}$ chance the die rolls that number.
9. **C. 1 out of 3** Of the 10 cards, 6 are marked with a square; therefore, there is a 6 in 10, or $\frac{3}{5}$, chance of getting a square on the first pick. Now there are only 9 cards left, and 5 are squares, so there is a a $\frac{5}{9}$ chance of getting a square on the second pick. Multiply: $\frac{3}{5} \times \frac{5}{9} = \frac{15}{45} = \frac{1}{3}$.
10. **B. 80%** After the five white chips are removed from the bag, the bag contains 10 chips, with 8 green and 2 white. The probability of getting green is $\frac{8}{10}$, which equals 80%.

## Lesson 8: Combinations

### Practice 8.1, page 323

1. **5** Since Rob is choosing 4 team members, each possible team leaves out exactly 1 employee. There are 5 possible employees Rob could leave out, so there are 5 possible teams.
2. **10** Either an organized list or a table will work. To solve this problem using a list organized

in columns, assign the books letters: A, B, C, D, and E. Count possible combinations:

| A and B combinations | A and C combinations | A and D combinations | B and C combinations | B and D combinations | C and D combinations |
|---|---|---|---|---|---|
| ABC | ACD | ADE | BCD | BDE | CDE |
| ABD | ACE | | BCE | | |
| ABE | | | | | |

3. **4** Use either a table or an organized list, as above.
4. **A. 5** Use a table, an organized list, or the formula.
5. **B. 20** This question asks you to add the number of possible groups of two out of five to the number of possible groups of 3 out of 5. Perform each of those tasks separately, or realize that they will have the same solution because choosing 3 to be in the group is the same as choosing 2 to be out of the group. Then, add the possible combinations together.

### Practice 8.2, page 325

1. **48** Use the fundamental counting principle:
   4 (types of bread) × 3 (types of meat) × 4 (condiments) = 48.
2. **24** Use the fundamental counting principle: 3 (restaurant certificates) × 2 (T-shirts) × 4 (hats) = 24.
3. **27** Use the fundamental counting principle: 3 × 3 × 3 = 27.
4. **24** On Friday, Julio has 2 choices. On Saturday, he has 3. On Sunday, he has 4 choices. Use the fundamental counting principle: 2 × 3 × 4 = 24
5. **D. 5,184** There are three words in the passphrase: 24 choices for the first, 9 for the second, 24 for the third. Use the fundamental counting principle: 24 × 9 × 24 = 5184.
6. **A. 10.** You are asked for combinations from one set of items. Use either a table or an organized list. You can assign the superpowers letters A–E to make it easier to see how to combine them.
7. **C. 1,024** Use the fundamental counting principle:
   4 (meats) × 4 (vegetables) × 4 (noodles) × 4 (broth) × 4 (spices) = 1024.
8. **A. 125** Use the fundamental counting principle:
   5 (medications) × 5 (dietary changes) × 5 (vitamins) = 125.

## Lesson 9: Permutations

### Practice 9, page 327

1. **120** This is a permutations problem, because order matters. The question asks how many sequences of five items are possible. 5 × 4 × 3 × 2 × 1 = 120.
2. **10** This is a combinations problem: you are being asked how many groups of three are possible, given five students. Order does not matter. Use a table or an organized list; you may name the students A–E if that is easier.
3. **720** This is a permutations problem, because order matters. 6 × 5 × 4 × 3 × 2 × 1 = 720.
4. **C. 360** This is a permutations problem, in which you are counting possible sequences of four out of six tasks. 6 × 5 × 4 × 3 = 360.
5. **B. 6** This is a permutations problem: the question asks you how many possible sequences of three types of flowers are possible. 3 × 2 × 1 = 6.
6. **D. 5,040** This is a permutations problem, because you are told that the role of Bystander #1 is different from the role of Bystander #4. (Notice the phrase "specific roles" in the question.) Thus, order matters. The question is asking how many sequences of four are possible given ten people. 10 × 9 × 8 × 7 = 5040.
7. **B. 20** This is a combinations problem asking how many groups of three out of six are possible. Use a table or an organized list.
8. **C. 120** This is a permutations problem asking how many sequences of three out of six are possible. 6 × 5 × 4 = 120.

### Statistics and Probability Practice Questions, pages 328–333

1. **B. 2007** Only the bar for 2007 falls between 500 and 600 on the scale.
2. **B. 40%** Estimate the values for 1998 and 1999. Then find the percent of decrease. Estimate roughly 650 and 390 for 1998 and 1999. Subtract. 650 − 390 = 260. Divide by the original number. 260 ÷ 650 = 0.4 = 40%
3. **A. $\frac{3}{100}$** Jim and his friends bought a total of 12 tickets (4 people × 3 tickets). Then 12 out of 400 = $\frac{12}{400} = \frac{3}{100}$
4. **D. 50°** Arrange the low temperatures in order: 55°, 53°, 50°, 50°, 49°, and 48°. Find the middle of the list. Since there are two temperatures in the middle and both are 50°, the mean of the two must be 50°.
5. **C. 1.56** Add the six amounts, and divide by 6: 0.45 + 0.63 + 1.34 + 3.53 + 2.57 + 0.84 = 9.36, and 9.36 ÷ 6 = 1.56 inches. It makes sense to use your calculator on this question.
6. **C. Woodland Hills** Mentally subtract the low temperature from the high temperature for each area. The greatest difference is in Woodland Hills. 68° − 50° = 18°.
7. **B. 2005** Ticket sales increased each year from 2001 through 2004. The first year in which they declined was 2005.
8. **C. 2008** The line graph shows the steepest increase (line rising from left to right) from 2007 to 2008.
9. **C. 32%** Eight customers chose a mouse pad. 8 ÷ 25 = 0.32 = 32%
10. **A. 1 in 2** Of the 52 cards, 26 are either hearts or diamonds. $\frac{26}{52} = \frac{1}{2}$
11. **3.5 or $\frac{7}{2}$** Add the hours, and divide by 6, the number of weeks: 5 + 3.5 + 4 + 0 + 1.5 + 7 = 21 hours, and 21 hours ÷ 6 = 3.5 hours.
12. **$\frac{2}{5}$** Only the numbers 4 and 5 are greater than 3. The probability is 2 out of 5, $\frac{2}{5}$, or 0.4.
13. **B. 41%** The three candidates who received the smallest percentages of the vote also received the smallest number of votes. Add. 9% + 14% + 18% = 41%
14. **C. Bowen and Utley** Since $\frac{3}{5}$ = 60%, look for two candidates whose combined percent is close to 60%. Since 24% + 35% = 59%, the correct answer is choice (C).
15. **D. 5100 × 0.09** Grace Reiner received 9%, which equals 0.09. You know the percent and the base. Multiply to find the part.

16. **B. March** The lines for both companies cross in March.
17. **B. 5900** Company A's orders continue to climb at about the same rate. Imagine extending the solid line to the next month. The line would reach to almost 6000. Choice (A) is too high an increase.
18. **C. 540** The graph indicates that about 3000 orders were placed in April. Multiply: $3000 \times 18\% = 540$.
19. **B. 24.5** Use only the Shots Attempted column. Put the numbers in order, and find the middle: 29, 27, 26, 25, 24, 24, 23, 18. The two in the middle are 25 and 24. Find the mean of those numbers: $25 + 24 = 49$, and $49 \div 2 = 24.5$.
20. **D. 10** Use the Shots Made column. The mode is the number that occurs most often. In this case the mode is 10, which occurs three times.
21. **B.** $\frac{5}{36}$ The probability that a marble is red is $\frac{8}{24}$, or $\frac{1}{3}$. The chance that a marble is white is $\frac{10}{24}$, or $\frac{5}{12}$. Because the first marble is replaced, the two events are independent. Multiply: $\frac{1}{3} \times \frac{5}{12} = \frac{5}{36}$.
22. **B.** $\frac{34+31+42}{3}$ To find the mean, add the three numbers and divide by 3, the number of months in the list. There are 36 employees, but you don't need this number to solve the problem.
23. $\frac{1}{36}$ The probability of rolling one "one" is $\frac{1}{6}$. Multiply to find the chance of rolling two ones: $\frac{1}{6} \times \frac{1}{6} = \frac{1}{36}$.
24. **625** Use the fundamental counting principle: $5 \times 5 \times 5 \times 5 = 625$.
25. **C. 720** This is a permutations question, because the board is not simply picking three members. Rather, those members will also be ordered in a specific way. Multiply:
10 options for president $\times$ 9 options for secretary $\times$ 8 options for treasurer = 720.
26. **B. 20%** First find the total number of patients: 16 (colds and flu) + 13 (cuts and scrapes) + 12 (sprained muscles) + 7 (tetanus shots) + 12 (severe headaches) = 60. Now find what percent of 60 is represented by 12: $\frac{12}{60} \times 100 = 20\%$
27. **B. 4:3** The ratio of patients with colds or flu to the number of patients with severe headaches is 16:12, which simplifies to 4:3.
28. **B. 180–199 lbs** The bar corresponding to this weight range is the tallest bar on the graph.
29. **B. Participants weighing less than 200 lbs** Choices (C) and (D) are both subsets of choice (B), and so cannot be correct. Add the totals of the columns in the graph to reveal that the total for choice (B) is greater than that of (A).
30. **B. 4** In each combination, one child is left out. There are 4 ways to leave out one child.
31. **B. 20 miles per gallon** Seven cars got 20 miles per gallon on average, more than in any other line of the table.
32. **A.** $\frac{1}{2}$ One car got 35 miles per gallon, and two got 15 miles per gallon.
33. **A.**

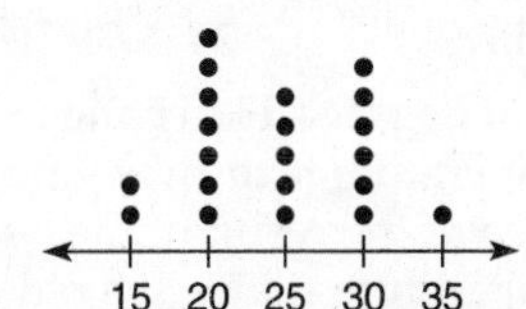


34. **D.**

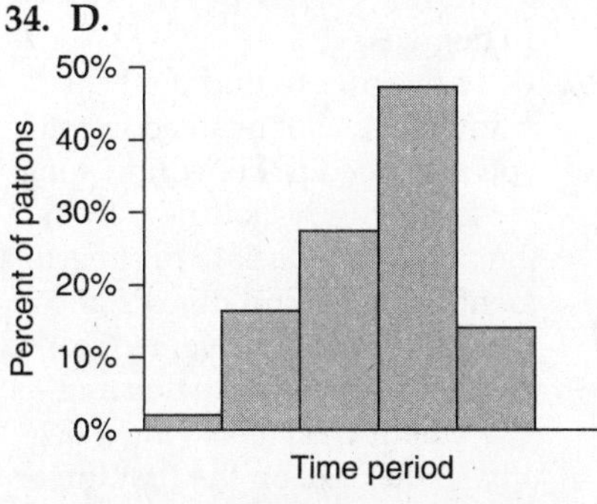


Only choice (D) reflects that 48% of visitors arrived during the fourth time period listed.

## Algebraic Expressions

### Lesson 1: The Number Line and Signed Numbers

**Practice 1.1, page 335**

1. 5
2. 45
3. 13
4. 1
5. 1
6. 10
7. −3
8. 13
9. −4
10. 2
11. −22
12. 32
13. −50
14. −11
15. 25
16. −35
17. −11
18. 11
19. 10
20. 75
21. 12
22. 2
23. −1
24. −13
25. **B. 2 + (−5)** The operation starts on + 2 and moves 5 units to the left (a negative direction).
26. **C. 115°** Begin with 92°. Then perform the following operations: $92° + 12° - 5° + 6° - 3° + 13° = 115°$

**Practice 1.2, page 337**

1. 20
2. −21
3. −48
4. 18
5. −10
6. 3
7. −3
8. − 5
9. 2
10. −5
11. −28
12. −3
13. −1
14. −75
15. 6
16. −20
17. −300
18. 2
19. −5
20. 660
21. 12
22. −120
23. −125
24. −12
25. 20
26. −1
27. 0
28. **B. −7** Substitute the numbers from the spreadsheet for the cells in the expression and solve. Note that A1 is column A, row 1; A3 is column A, row 3; and so on. $\frac{(-3)(7)(-1)}{(3)(-1)} = \frac{21}{-3} = -7$
29. **C.** $\frac{2(8)}{(-8)}$ To find the product of two numbers, multiply: 2(8). Then divide by −8, as directed in the problem.
30. **C. The result is a negative number.** Do not do any calculations. Instead, examine the factors. Since there is an odd number of negative factors, the answer will be negative. This is the only possible option.

### Lesson 2: Powers and Roots

**Practice 2, page 339**

1. 9
2. 4
3. 3
4. 1
5. 9
6. 7
7. 125
8. $\frac{1}{16}$
9. 6561
10. 1296
11. 12.2
12. 8000
13. 1
14. $\frac{1}{16}$
15. 15.6
16. 10.9
17. 7.5
18. 23.2
19. 1
20. 256

21. **C. $6^3$** To find the volume, you would need to solve $6 \times 6 \times 6$, which can be written as $6^3$.
22. **A. $3^{-3}$** Examine the choices. Choices (A) and (D) will result in a fraction, a value less than 1. Choices (B) and (C) will each have a value of 1 or greater.

    Choice (A): $3^{-3} = \frac{1}{3^3} = \frac{1}{27}$

    Choice (D): $2^{-4} = \frac{1}{2^4} = \frac{1}{16}$.

    Since $\frac{1}{27} < \frac{1}{16}$, choice (A) is correct.

## Lesson 3: Scientific Notation

### Practice 3, page 341

1. $2.3 \times 10^3$
2. $4.2 \times 10^{-4}$
3. $1.24 \times 10^7$
4. $1.432 \times 10^{10}$
5. $3.6 \times 10^7$
6. $9.5 \times 10^{-3}$
7. $5.8 \times 10^{-7}$
8. $1.5 \times 10^{11}$
9. $9 \times 10^{-9}$
10. 0.0005173
11. 3,700,000
12. 480,000,000
13. 0.000017
14. 0.0072
15. 916,000
16. 85,910,000
17. 0.00000956
18. $2.35 \times 10^4$
19. 0.000000001
20. 2,670,000,000
21. $3 \times 10^8$
22. **B. $4.356 \times 10^4$** In scientific notation, the whole-number portion must be a digit from 1 to 9. Choice (B) is correct because the decimal place must be moved 4 places.
23. **D. $5 \times 9.07 \times 10^{-1}$** In scientific notation, a ton = $9.07 \times 10^{-1}$ metric tons. Multiply this by 5 to find the equivalent weight of five tons.

## Lesson 4: Order of Operations

### Practice 4, page 343

1. 24
2. 1
3. 29
4. 2
5. 7
6. 20
7. 14
8. 55
9. 10
10. 23
11. 161
12. 30
13. 360
14. 4
15. 6
16. **C. (1 – 0.75)(28)(30).** The total cost of the class can be found by multiplying 28 members by \$30. Since the foundation pays 75%, or 0.75, the hospital will pay 100% – 75%, or (1 – 0.75). You must multiply the amount the class will cost by the percent that the hospital will pay. Only choice (C) performs these operations.
17. **B. Add 5.** The operations in the brackets must be performed first. Once these are completed, multiply by 2 and then add 5. Notice that it is not necessary to find the value of the expression to answer the question.
18. **C. 76**

    $22 + 6[(14 - 5) \div 3(17 - 14)]$
    $= 22 + 6[9 \div 3(3)]$
    $= 22 + 6[3 \times 3]$
    $= 22 + 6[9]$
    $= 22 + 54 = 76$

## Lesson 5: Absolute Value

### Practice 5, page 345

1. 18
2. 107
3. 423
4. 95
5. 7,026
6. 18
7. 5,708,432
8. 85.6
9. 42
10. 10.5
11. 163.24
12. 3.14
13. 11
14. –156
15. 156
16. 3
17. –91
18. 0
19. 620
20. –7
21. –20
22. –1
23. 2.125
24. –11
25. **D. 10 degrees** The change in temperature is the absolute value of the result of the new temperature minus the old temperature: $|(-5)-(-15)|=|10|$, or 10 degrees.
26. **D. 16** In order to find out how many blocks Bob walked in total, you also need to know how long the last leg of his journey (from the post office back to his apartment) was. To find this distance, you can think of movement east as having a positive value and movement west as having a negative value. So, on the first three legs of his journey Bob walked $5 + (-6) + (-2)$, leaving him 3 blocks from his house. The last leg of his journey is 3 blocks, and you can simply add the absolute values of each part of the trip: $|5|+|-6|+|-2|+|3|=16$
27. **C. 120** Add the absolute value of Milania's score to the absolute value of Chris's score: $|-65|+|55|=65+55=120$
28. **A. 1.5** The question defines absolute error as the absolute value of the difference between the actual and approximate values: $23.5 - 25 = -1.5$, and $|-1.5| = 1.5$.

## Lesson 6: Algebraic Expressions

### Practice 6.1, page 347

1. $x - 7$
2. $3x^2 + x$
3. $8x - 10$
4. $-3x - 2y$
5. $\frac{10}{x} - 5$
6. $-8 + 7x$
7. $16x + x - 3y$
8. $x^2 + x^4$
9. $x^2 + \frac{4}{7}$
10. $15 + \sqrt{x} - 6$
11. $x - (y + 13)$
12. $(x + 6)^2$
13. $17 - (2x + y)$
14. $x + \frac{24}{x}$
15. $2x - 15$
16. $4(x - y)$
17. $5(x^2 - 3)$
18. $x(11 - \sqrt{100})$
19. **C. \$1500 + \$0.50($x$ – 2000)** Let $x$ represent the number of tickets sold. The expression $x - 2000$ is the number of tickets over 2000 sold. Multiply this expression by \$0.50 to find the amount donated based on ticket sales. Then add \$1500. Only choice (C) shows this sequence of operations.
20. **A. $(3x + 4y) \div (2 + z)$** The sum of 3 times a number and 4 times another number is represented by the expression $3x + 4y$. The sum of 2 and a third number is represented by $2 + z$. The first expression is divided by the second. Parentheses are necessary to clarify the order of operations.
21. **B. $6h + 0.03s$** The correct sequence of operations shows the sum of 6 multiplied by the number of hours ($6h$) and 3% of the sales, or $0.03s$. Only choice (B) adds these two expressions.

### Practice 6.2, page 349

1. $x^2 + 3x + 2$
2. $19y + 13$
3. $-3x + 54$
4. $6x^3 + 31x^2 + 4$
5. $7y + 14$
6. $3x + 8$
7. $22x - 12$
8. $2y^2 + y + 9$
9. $-5x - 17$
10. $4x - 7$
11. 31
12. 48
13. 8
14. 21
15. 72
16. 80
17. 85
18. –19
19. 9
20. 61
21. **D. $3x^2 + 4x + 1$** Simplify the expression.

    $3x^2 + 3(x - 3) + x + 10$
    $= 3x^2 + 3x - 9 + x + 10$
    $= 3x^2 + 4x + 1$
22. **A. $x = 2, y = 3$** Substitute the values in the choices into the expression. Choice (A) equals –11.

    $4x^2 - 3(y + 6)$

$= 4(2^2) - 3(3 + 6)$
$= 4(4) - 3(9)$
$= 16 - 27$
$= -11$

23. **A. 20°** You need to convert a Fahrenheit temperature to Celsius.
$C = \frac{5}{9}(F - 32)$
$C = \frac{5}{9}(68 - 32) = 20$

## Lesson 7: Expressions and Calculator Skills

### Practice 7, page 351

1. 19
2. 15.9
3. 51
4. $16\frac{1}{2}$
5. 10
6. –98
7. 74
8. 146
9. 12
10. –76
11. 57
12. 36
13. –54
14. 24.8
15. 54
16. –45
17. 78
18. 108
19. 459
20. 1430
21. **B. 36.2** Use the formula stated in the problem.
$P = 2l + 2w$
$= 2(12.5) + 2(5.6)$
$= 25 + 11.2$
$= 36.2$
22. **D. $-2xy$** Try each expression: $x + y = -3$; $-x + y = 7$; $x - y = 3$; $xy = -10$; and $-2xy = 20$. The value of choice (D) is greatest.
23. **A. 32** If $x = 2$, then $2 \div x^{-4} = 2 \div \frac{1}{2^4} = 2 \div \frac{1}{16} = 32$.

## Lesson 8: Understand Polynomials

### Practice 8, page 353

1. Monomial
2. Monomial
3. Binomial
4. Trinomial
5. Binomial
6. Trinomial
7. Monomial
8. Monomial
9. Monomial
10. Binomial
11. Trinomial
12. Trinomial
13. Binomial
14. Monomial
15. Binomial
16. First term: $3x^4$, second term: $-2x^2$, third term: –3
17. First term: $12a^2bc$
18. First term: $3g$, second term: $-4h$
19. First term: $x^2$ second term: $y$
20. First term: $-4a$, second term: $-3b^2$, third term: $c$
21. First term: 25
22. First term: $4x^2$, second term: $3x$, third term: –7
23. First term: $\frac{3x}{8}$
24. First term: $\sqrt{25}$
25. First term: $\frac{x^2}{9}$
26. First term: $49x^2y^2z^2$
27. First term: $18y^2$, second term: $-4y^2$, third term: 8
28. First term: $3h$, second term: –4
29. First term: $x^2$, second term: $-x$ third term: $y^2$, fourth term: –2
30. First term: $ab$, second term: $ab^2$, third term: $b^2$, fourth term: –4
31. **B. 5** Two variables in the expression have exponents: $x^3$ and $x^2$. Add the values of the exponents: $3 + 2 = 5$
32. **B. –1** The coefficients in this expression are 1, –3, –1, and 2. Add those values: $1 + (-3) + (-1) + 2 = -1$

## Lesson 9: Simplify Polynomials

### Practice 9, page 355

1. Like
2. Like
3. Unlike
4. Unlike
5. Like
6. Unlike
7. Unlike
8. Like
9. Unlike
10. Unlike
11. Like
12. Unlike
13. Like
14. Like
15. Unlike
16. Like
17. Unlike
18. Like
19. Unlike
20. Unlike
21. $7x^2y$
22. $4b$
23. $-6a + 3$
24. $ab^2 + 16ab + 3$
25. $-2x^2 + 7$
26. $4ab$
27. $14g + 14gh$
28. $-4g^2h^2 + 2g^2 + 2h^2 - 4$
29. $-y^2 + 9y$
30. $-7x^2 + y - 3$
31. $22y - 7$
32. $6x^2y + 5y^2 - 23$
33. $4x^3 + 7x^2 + 3x + 5$
34. $-5x^2 - 4x + 5$
35. $-3x^3 + 7x^2 + x$
36. **B. $6a^2b + 9ab$** Identify and group like terms. Then combine:
$3a^2b + 4ab + 3a^2b + 5ab$
$= 3a^2b + 3a^2b + 4ab + 5ab$
$= 6a^2b + 9ab$
37. **B. 3** Identify and group like terms. Then combine:
$j^2 + k^3 - 2j^3 + 5k^3 - 2j^2$
$= j^2 - 2j^2 + k^3 + 5k^3 - 2j^3$
$= -j^2 + 6k^3 - 2j^3$
The expression has three terms.

## Lesson 10: Add and Subtract Polynomials

### Practice 10.1, page 357

1. $5x + 6$
2. $23y + 6$
3. $8x^2 - 5x + 2$
4. $15a^2 + 8a$
5. $11x^2 + 2x + 3$
6. $a + 1$
7. 1
8. $4x^2 + 16x - 9$
9. $24y - 3$
10. $-4a^2 - 2a - 9$
11. $y - 2$
12. $-3x + 13$
13. $3a + 2$
14. $3x^2 + x + 2$
15. $10y + 7$
16. $2x^2 + 3x + 13$
17. $2g + 1$
18. $a^2 - 10a + 2$
19. –16
20. $20x^2 - 5x + 1$
21. **A. $x^2y + 4xy$** Identify, group, and combine like terms:
$(2xy + 3xy^2 - 4x^2y) + (5x^2y - 3xy^2 + 2xy)$
$= 2xy + 2xy - 4x^2y + 5x^2y + 3xy^2 - 3xy^2$
$= 4xy + x^2y$
22. **C. $2x^2 + x + 3$** Distribute the negative sign to everything in the second polynomial. Then group and combine like terms:
$(5x^2 - 2x + 1) - (3x^2 - 3x - 2)$
$=5x^2 - 2x + 1 - 3x^2 + 3x + 2$
$=5x^2 - 3x^2 - 2x + 3x + 1 + 2$
$=2x^2 + x + 3$

### Practice 10.2, page 359

1. $a^2 + 5a + 4b^2$
2. $-4x - xy + y + 16$
3. $yz^2 - 4z^2 + 7yz + 5$
4. $7ab - b + c - 17$
5. $-4a^4 - c^2 + 3ac + 5$
6. $22xyz + x + 6$
7. $7ef + ef^2 + f - 10$
8. $4pq - 2q + 4$
9. $4ab$
10. 0
11. $3p^6 + 4pq - p^2 - q^2$
12. $x + y + 15$
13. $2bc - b$
14. $10xyz - 8y + 16$
15. $6a + 4b + d$
16. $7pq - q$
17. $-7ab + 2b + 12$

18. 0
19. $-2p^2 + 5q^2 + 7$
20. $x^4 + z^4 - z^5$
21. $bc^2 - bc + 2c$
22. $-3xy + xz - 2xyz$
23. $c^3d^7 - c^2 + 2d$
24. $ef^2g - ef^2 - 2fg + 8$
25. **D. $3x - y$** Distribute the negative sign. Then identify, group, and combine like terms:
$(x + y + z) - (-2x + 2y + z)$
$= x + y + z + 2x - 2y - z$
$= x + 2x + y - 2y + z - z$
$= 3x - y$
26. **B. $3g^2 + 5h - 2k$** Identify, group, and combine like terms:

$(2g^2 + 3h - 5k) + (g^2 + 2h + 3k)$
$= 2g^2 + g^2 + 3h + 2h - 5k + 3k$
$= 3g^2 + 5h - 2k$

## Lesson 11: Multiply Polynomials

### Practice 11, page 361

1. $30x^2$
2. $6xy^2$
3. $28ab^2c^2$
4. $12yz$
5. $9abc$
6. $10x^2y^3z^5$
7. $4ab^2c^2$
8. $34f^3gh^7$
9. $18xyz^2 + 12z^3$
10. $42x^2 - 36xz$
11. $-15ab^2 - 55abc$
12. $-18f^3h + 24f^4gh^2$
13. $70x^7z - 50z^2$
14. $z^2 + 6xyz$
15. $72ab^2 + 64ab$
16. $18x^4 - 27xy^2$
17. $x^2 - x - 30$
18. $x^2 + 2xy + y^2$
19. $z^2 - 81$
20. $y^2z^4 - 2xyz^2 - 3x^2$
21. $9x^2 + 24x + 15$
22. $x^2 - y^2$
23. $y^6 - 6y^4 + 10y^2 - 60$
24. $a^2b^2 - ab - 12$
25. **A. $12a^5b^2c$** The coefficients of each term are 4 and 3, so the coefficient of their product is 12. The product of $a^3$ and $a^2$ is $a^5$. Only choice A contains both of these elements.
26. **D. $12p^3c^3$** You need the product of $2pc^2$ and $6p^2c$, which can be calculated as $(2pc^2)(6p^2c)$. The product of the coefficients 2 and 6 is 12, the product of $p$ and $p^2$ is $p^3$, and the product of $c$ and $c^2$ is $c^3$. Only choice (D) has all three of these elements.
27. **B. $12a^2b^2 - 22ab - 14$** Use FOIL: $(4ab \times 3ab) + (4ab \times [-7]) + (2 \times 3ab) + (2 \times [-7])$
$= 12a^2b^2 - 28ab + 6ab - 14$
$= 12a^2b^2 - 22ab - 14$

## Lesson 12: Divide Polynomials

### Practice 12, page 363

1. $y + 15$
2. $x + 3$
3. $x + 5$
4. $a + b$
5. $x^2 + 2x$
6. $2x^2 + 3x + 1$
7. $x + 2y$
8. $3a + 2b$
9. $\frac{3x}{2} + y$
10. $\frac{3a}{4} + \frac{5b}{4}$
11. $\frac{b + 4c}{3}$
12. $\frac{5a + b + 3c}{2}$
13. $6x + 2$
14. $5x + 3$
15. $8y + 2$
16. $6y + 7$
17. $2y + 2$
18. 3
19. $x - 6$
20. $y + 7$
21. $z - 5$
22. $2x + 6$
23. $x - 6$
24. $a + 3$
25. **C. $3a + 2b$** Break the fraction up into two separate fractions:
$\frac{(21a + 14b)}{7} = \frac{21a}{7} + \frac{14b}{7}$
Then divide each numerator by 7 to get $3a + 2b$.
26. **D. $9x + 17y + 20z$** The average of a set of terms is equal to the sum of terms divided by the number of terms in the set. In this case, that can be represented by the expression
$\frac{(27x + 51y + 60z)}{3}$
Break this up into three separate fractions:
$\frac{27x}{3} + \frac{51y}{3} + \frac{60z}{3}$
Then divide each numerator by 3 to get $9x + 17y + 20z$.

## Algebraic Expressions, pages 364–367

1. **D.** $-4x - 6$
2. **C. $3d - 75$** Since Heidi makes 75 less than 3 times Kris's wage, multiply Kris's wage, $d$, by 3 and subtract 75 to get $3d - 75$.
3. **B. $1.26 \times 10^8$** Calculate: $700 \times 180{,}000 = 126{,}000{,}000$. Scientific notation reduces to a single digit in front of the decimal, and to do this requires moving up 8 digits, so it would be $1.26 \times 10^8$.
4. **D. $84x^2y$** Total desks = schools × rooms per school × desks per room. $4x \times 3y \times 7x = (4)(3)(7)(x)(x)(y) = 84x^2y$.
5. C. **$(x + 5)(x - 5)$** Multiply the monomials and polynomials in the answer choices until you find an answer choice that results in the expression in the question stem. For answer choice (C), use FOIL: $(x + 5)(x - 5) = x^2 - 5x + 5x - 25 = x^2 - 25$.
6. **D. $18x + 2y + 13$** Tom has $9x$, Adam $9x + 13$, and Dave $2y$: $9x + (9x + 13) + 2y = 18x + 2y + 13$.
7. **B. $60y$** The diagram shows multiplication problems done using a table, so the horizontal number times the vertical number will yield the value in the table. The table tells you that $a = yc$ and $b = 5 \times 3 = 15$. So $ab = 15yc$. Now look for a value for $c$. Since $20 = 5c$, $c$ must equal 4, and you have $ab = (15)(4)y = 60y$. There is not enough information to deduce the value of $y$, but since $y$ appears in all the answer choices, you do not need to try to find its value.
8. **D. $y$** The diagram shows multiplication problems done using a table, so the horizontal number times the vertical number will yield the value in the table. $d = 3y$ and $a = 4y$, so $a - d = 4y - 3y = y$.
9. **A. $7a^2c^2 + 35bc^2 + 49c^4$** Multiply each term by $7c^2$. $7c^2(a^2) + 7c^2(5b) + 7c^2(7c^2) = 7a^2c^2 + 35bc^2 + 49c^4$.
10. **D. $\$\frac{150}{x}$** To figure out the individual pie cost, divide \$900 by the number of pies, $6x$: $\frac{900}{6x} = \frac{150}{x}$.

11. **A.** $\frac{a-4}{a+4}$ Cancel out $6b$ in the numerator and $2(3b)$ (which equals $6b$) in the denominator. Then, one $(a-4)$ will cancel, leaving $\frac{a-4}{a+4}$.
12. **C.** $\frac{xyz}{2}$ To find the total cost, multiply ounces per guest by the number of guests by the cost per ounce. Since $\$z$ is the cost per pound, the result needs to be divided by 16. $\frac{(x)(8y)(z)}{16} = xyz\left(\frac{8}{16}\right) = \frac{xyz}{2}$.
13. **B. –26** Substituting –2 for $x$ and 5 for $y$ leads to $6(-2-5) - 8(-2) = 6(-7) - (-16) = -42 + 16 = -26$.
14. **A. –88** Substituting 2 for $x$, 4 for $y$, and 3 for $z$ leads to a product of $[2^2 + 6(3)] \times [2(4) - 4(3)] = (4 + 18) \times (8 - 12) = 22 \times -4 = -88$.
15. **C.** $1\frac{5}{11}$ Calculate: $\frac{4^3-[3(12+2^2)]}{6+5(4)-15} = \frac{64-[3(12+4)]}{6+5(4)-15} = \frac{64-[3(16)]}{6+20-15} = \frac{64-48}{6+20-15} = \frac{16}{11} = 1\frac{5}{11}$
16. **D.** $30kp + 20p^2 + 45hp$ Because $5p$ is paid to every member, each number of team members would be multiplied by $5p$, and the team totals would be added. $5p(6k) + 5p(4p) + 5p(9h) = 30kp + 20p^2 + 45hp$
17. **C.** $-x + 9y - 10xy$ Solve: $7x - [(5y)2x - 9y + 8x] = 7x - [10xy - 9y + 8x] = 7x - 10xy + 9y - 8x = -x - 10xy + 9y$.
18. **A.** $20cd - 75c$ Alyshia has $4d - 15$ DVDs. Multiply $5c$ by Alyshia's DVD total: $(4d - 15)$: $5c(4d - 15) = 5c(4d) - (5c)(15) = 20cd - 75c$
19. **A.** $8x^2 + 7xy^3 - 12x - 1$ Factor out $7x^2$: $\frac{56x^4+49x^3y^3-84x^3-7x^2}{7x^2}$
$= \frac{(7x^2)(8x^2+7xy^3-12x-1)}{7x^2}$
$= 8x^2 + 7xy^3 - 12x - 1$
20. **B.** $16d - 4a$ The amount $80d$ is needed. Anything earned at the ball will be subtracted, and $64d$ and $4a$ were both earned: $80d - 64d - 4a = 16d - 4a$ left to raise.
21. **A.** $\frac{x^4}{2y^2} + 2x^2y^2 - \frac{4x}{y^2} - \frac{1}{2}$ Split the fraction: $\frac{x^4+4x^2y^4-8x-y^2}{2y^2}$
$= \frac{x^4}{2y^2} + \frac{4x^2y^4}{2y^2} - \frac{8x}{2y^2} - \frac{y^2}{2y^2}$
$= \frac{x^4}{2y^2} + 2x^2y^2 - \frac{4x}{y^2} - \frac{1}{2}$.
22. **B.** $\frac{6k+4f}{r} + 3$ The total of the three groups $(12k + 8f + 6r)$ should be divided by the number of squads, $2r$:
$\frac{12k+8f+6r}{2r} = \frac{12k}{2r} + \frac{8f}{2r} + \frac{6r}{2r}$
$= \frac{6k}{r} + \frac{4f}{r} + 3$
$= \frac{6k+4f}{r} + 3$.
23. **A.** $4x + 2$ Substitute 2 for $q$ and 4 for $r$ in the expression: $\frac{4^2x^2+2^3x}{2^2x} = \frac{16x^2+8x}{4x} = 4x + 2$.
24. **C.** $-2x^4 + 5xy^4 - \frac{y^2}{x^2}$ Split the fractions and then simplify by factoring out $11x^2$:
$\frac{11x^2(4x^4+5xy^4+8)}{11x^2} - \frac{11y^2}{11x^2} - 6x^4 - 8$
$= 4x^4 + 5xy^4 + 8 - \frac{y^2}{x^2} - 6x^4 - 8$
$= -2x^4 + 5xy^4 - \frac{y^2}{x^2}$
25. **A.** $5xy^3 - 16x^2y^2 + 42x^2y$ Distribute:
$(6x^2 + 5xy^2)(y) - (4xy - 9x)(4xy)$
$= 6x^2(y) + 5xy^2(y) - (4xy(4xy) - 9x(4xy))$
$= 6x^2y + 5xy^3 - (16x^2y^2 - 36x^2y)$
$= 42x^2y + 5xy^3 - 16x^2y^2$
26. **D.** $20x^2 - 39x + 18$ The question states that the average salary of the non-managerial employees is $(5x - 6)$. That means that
$5x - 6 = \frac{\textit{Total of non-managers' salaries}}{\textit{Number of non-managers}}$
The question also states that the number of non-managers in the office is $4x - 3$. So,
$5x - 6 = \frac{\textit{Total of non-managers' salaries}}{4x-3}$
Then $(5x - 6)(4x - 3) = $ *total of non-managers' salaries* $= 20x^2 - 39x + 18$
27. **B. 51** Factor before substituting. $\frac{45xy+63y^2}{9y} = \frac{(9y)(5x+7y)}{9y} = (5x + 7y)$.
Substitute 6 for $x$ and 3 for $y$: $5(6) + 7(3) = 30 + 21 = 51$.
28. **D.** $x - 1$ Split the fraction: $\frac{3x(x^2+3)-2x(x^2+3)-(x^2+3)}{x^2+3}$
$= \frac{3x(x^2+3)}{x^2+3} - \frac{2x(x^2+3)}{x^2+3} - \frac{x^2+3}{x^2+3}$
$= 3x - 2x - 1 = x - 1$.
29. **D.** $3h^2 + 4hk - 51h - 68k$ Add the populations of both countries $(3h + 4k)$ and multiply by the rice consumption: $(h - 17)$:
$(3h + 4k)(h - 17)$
$= (3h)(h) + (3h)(-17) + (4k)(h) + (4k)(-17)$
$= 3h^2 - 51h + 4hk - 68k$.
30. **A.** $2x^2 + 2y^2 - xy$ Split the fraction:
$\frac{4x^2(x+y)}{(x+y)} - \frac{2(x+y)^2(x-y)}{(x+y)} - \frac{xy(x+y)}{(x+y)}$
$= 4x^2 - 2(x + y)(x - y) - xy$
$= 4x^2 - 2(x^2 - y^2) - xy$
$= 2x^2 + 2y^2 - xy$
31. **A. 2** The diagram shows multiplication problems done using a table, so the horizontal number times the vertical number will yield the value in the table. To figure out $a$, first look at the top right term. Since $5 \times a = ab$, $b = 5$. Another term with only $a$ and $b$ is the bottom middle, $4 \times ab = 40$. Substituting 5 for $b$ shows that $20a = 40$, so $a = 2$.
32. **B. 40** The table tells you that $a^2 \times c = 8b$. Use the table to find a value for $b$. Since the top right cell of the table shows that $5 \times a = ab$, $b$ must equal 5, and $8b = 40$.

# Functions

## Lesson 1: Equations

### Practice 1.1, page 369

| | |
|---|---|
| 1. $x = 9$ | 15. $x = 48$ |
| 2. $m = 28$ | 16. $y = -3$ |
| 3. $y = -1$ | 17. $r = 110$ |
| 4. $x = -64$ | 18. $x = 5$ |
| 5. $a = 125$ | 19. $y = -9$ |
| 6. $y = -13$ | 20. $d = -25$ |
| 7. $x = 27$ | 21. $x = 4$ |
| 8. $c = 7$ | 22. $x = -6$ |
| 9. $x = -4$ | 23. $h = 26$ |
| 10. $b = -7$ | 24. $x = 66$ |
| 11. $x = 31$ | 25. $m = -10$ |
| 12. $s = -8$ | 26. $y = 9$ |
| 13. $x = 108$ | 27. $w = -28$ |
| 14. $t = 39$ | 28. $y = 72$ |

29. **C.** $x + 36 = 77$ Erin's hours ($x$) plus Kayla's hours (36) = 77 hours.
30. **C.** $2y = 38$ Erin worked twice as many hours as Kayla ($2y$), and Erin worked 38 hours, so $2y = 38$.
31. **C. 128** A number ($x$) divided by 4 is 32. Solve for $x$: $\frac{x}{4} = 32$, $x = 128$.
32. **D.** $12x = -60$ Try –5 for $x$ in each equation. Only choice (D) is true when –5 is substituted for $x$.
$12x = -60$
$12(-5) = -60$
$-60 = -60$
33. **B. \$572.18 – *c* = \$434.68** When you subtract the check from the amount in the checking account, the result will be the current balance.

### Practice 1.2, page 371

| | |
|---|---|
| 1. $x = 50$ | 4. $x = -4$ |
| 2. $y = -2$ | 5. $y = 6$ |
| 3. $m = 2$ | 6. $z = 2$ |

7. $m = 3$
8. $x = 4$
9. $p = 7$
10. $s = -2$
11. $x = 6$
12. $r = -5$
13. $y = 11$
14. $b = 4$
15. $x = -1$
16. $h = 20$
17. $x = 9$
18. $z = 4$
19. $b = 3$
20. $n = 7$
21. **D. $3x + 9 = 6x - 15$** "Three times a number" is $3x$ and "increased by 9" means to add 9. "Six times the number" is $6x$, and "15 less" means to subtract 15. The word "is" shows that the two expressions should be connected by the = symbol.
22. **D. 375** Solve:
$$3x + x = 500$$
$$4x = 500$$
$$x = 125$$
The variable $x$ is the number of cards that Travis has. Eric has $3x$, or $3 \times 125$, which equals 375.
23. **A. $4x - 7 = \frac{x}{3} + 15$** Remember that differences and quotients must be written in the order stated in the problem. The difference of four times a number and 7 is $4x - 7$. The quotient of the number and 3 plus 15 is $\frac{x}{3} + 15$.
24. **A. \$54** Solve:
$$x + (2x + 12) = \$174$$
$$3x + 12 = \$174$$
$$3x = \$162$$
$$x = \$54$$

## Lesson 2: Equation Word Problems, Part I

### Practice 2, page 373

1. **1800 sq. ft.** Let the square footage of the first house be $h$, and the second house's square footage will then be $(2h - 1000)$. Then write an equation that combines both houses. The equation is $h + (2h - 1000) = 4400$. Solve for $h$.
2. **10 dimes** Let $x$ equal the number of dimes in Julia's pocket. The equation is $0.10x + 0.25(24 - x) = 4.50$.
3. **24 games** Let $w$ represent the number of wins, and then the number of losses will be half of $w$. Write an equation:
$$w + \tfrac{1}{2}w = 36$$
$$1\tfrac{1}{2}w = 36$$
$$\tfrac{3}{2}w = 36$$
$$3w = 72$$
$$w = 24$$
Alternatively, you could solve the equation by calculating the number of losses. Let $l$ = losses. Wins will be twice that much. Then the equation would read $l + 2l = 36$. Once you find $l$, remember to multiply it by two to find the number of wins.
4. **54** The equation is $x + (x + 2) + (x + 4) + (x + 6) = 4x + 12 = 212$. Solve for $x + 4$, the third number.
5. **8 shirts** Let $s$ represent the number of shirts Brenda bought, and then the number of pants she bought will be equal to $13 - s$. Then, write an equation using the dollar amount she spent: $\$6(13 - s) + \$4s = \$62$. Solve for $s$.
6. **59** Let $x$ equal the smallest of the three consecutive numbers. Then: $x + (x + 1) + (x + 2) = 180$. Solve for $x$.
7. **\$1100** Andrew spends twice as much on rent, which means he spends half as much as his rent on food. The equation is $r + \frac{1}{2}r = \$1650$. Solve for $r$.
8. **28 hours** Let $h$ represent the time he spends helping customers, and then stocking shelves will be one-fourth of $h$. Write an equation:
$$h + \tfrac{1}{4}h = 35$$
$$1\tfrac{1}{4}h = 35$$
$$\tfrac{5}{4}h = 35$$
$$5h = 140$$
$$h = 28$$
9. **C. 84** Let $w$ = Wiley's points, $w + 10$ = Sylvia's points, and $w - 6$ = Greg's points. Write and solve an equation:
$$w + w + 10 + w - 6 = 226$$
$$3w + 4 = 226$$
$$3w = 222$$
$$w = 74$$
Wiley scored 74 points, so Sylvia scored $74 + 10 = 84$ points.
10. **B. \$12** Let $a$ = the price of an adult's ticket and $a - \$6$ = the price of a child's ticket. The question states that the cost of 2 adults' tickets and 4 children's tickets is \$48. Write and solve an equation:
$$2a + 4(a - 6) = 48$$
$$2a + 4a - 24 = 48$$
$$6a - 24 = 48$$
$$6a = 72$$
$$a = 12$$
11. **B. 6** You know that in 12 years, Jenny will be twice as old as Tina. Therefore, if you multiply Tina's age in 12 years by 2, it will equal Jenny's age in 12 years. Write and solve an equation:
$$4x + 12 = 2(x + 12)$$
$$4x + 12 = 2x + 24$$
$$2x = 12$$
$$x = 6$$

## Lesson 3: Inequalities

### Practice 3, page 375

1. $x > 4$
2. $x > 7$
3. $x \leq -3$
4. $x \leq 36$
5. $x < -1$
6. $x \geq 5$
7. $x > -8$
8. $x > 4$
9. $x < -7$
10. $x < 2$
11. $x \geq 3$
12. $x < 6$
13. $x \geq 2$
14. $x > -10$
15. $x \leq 3$
16. $x < 21$
17. $x \geq -1$
18. $x < 3$
19. $x < 7$
20. $x \leq 3$
21. $-2 \leq x \leq 2$
22. $-20 < x < 6$
23. $6 < x < 16$
24. $4 \leq x \leq 9$
25. **A. $s \leq 16$** The perimeter must be less than or equal to 64, so solve the inequality: $4s \leq 64$, which leads to $s \leq 16$.
26. **D.**

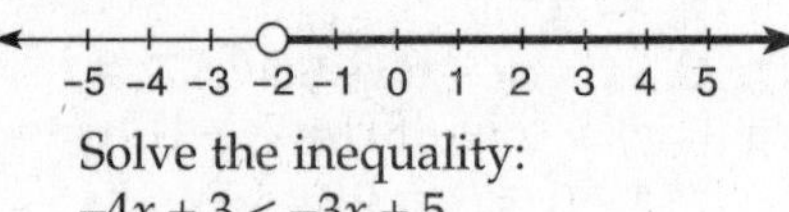


Solve the inequality:
$$-4x + 3 < -3x + 5$$
$$-x < 2$$
$$x > -2$$
To graph the solution $x > -2$, place an open circle at $-2$, because $-2$ is not included in the solution. Then, extend the line to the right to include all values greater than $-2$.

## Lesson 4: Quadratic Equations

### Practice 4, page 377

1. $x^2 + 6x + 8$
2. $x^2 + 2x - 15$
3. $x^2 + 3x - 4$
4. $x^2 - 9x + 18$
5. $x^2 + 6x - 16$
6. $2x^2 - 3x - 2$
7. $x^2 - 14x + 45$
8. $3x^2 + x - 2$
9. $x^2 + 5x - 14$
10. $3x^2 + 14x + 16$
11. $x^2 - x - 30$
12. $x^2 - 13x + 30$
13. $4x^2 + 6x + 2$
14. $x^2 + 5x - 36$
15. $x^2 - 10x + 25$

For questions 16–30, the order of the factors does not matter: $(2x - 1)(x + 3) = (x + 3)(2x - 1)$

16. $(x + 1)(x + 3)$
17. $(x - 1)(x + 5)$

18. $(x + 2)(x + 6)$
19. $(x - 3)(x + 2)$
20. $(x - 2)(x + 7)$
21. $(x - 4)(x + 3)$
22. $(x - 5)(x + 7)$
23. $(x - 6)(x - 6)$
24. $(x - 7)(x + 1)$
25. $(x - 4)(x + 8)$
26. $(2x - 1)(x + 3)$
27. $(2x - 10)(x + 1)$ or $(2x + 2)(x - 5)$ or $(2)(x - 5)(x + 1)$
28. $(x - 5)(x + 10)$
29. $(2x - 1)(2x + 3)$
30. $(x - 7)(x + 8)$
31. **A. –4 and 5** Get 0 on one side of the equation: $x^2 - x - 20 = 0$. Then, factor: $(x + 4)(x - 5) = 0$. Determine which values of $x$ will make each factor equal to 0. The solutions 5 and –4 will make the equation true.
32. **D. $2x^2 + 2x - 24 = 0$** Substitute –4 for $x$ in the answer choices. Only choice (D) works. $2(-4)^2 + 2(-4) - 24 = 2(16) + (-8) - 24 = 32 - 32 = 0$
33. **B. 6** Substitute the answer choices for $x$ in the equation. Only choice (B) makes the equation true: $2(6)^2 - 7(6) - 30 = 2(36) - 42 - 30 = 72 - 72 = 0$. You can also factor the original equation: $(x - 6)(2x + 5)$, so $x = 6$ or $x = -\frac{5}{2}$.
34. **B. $x - 10$** You know that length × width = area. You need to factor the expression $2x^2 - 27x + 70$, and you know that one of the factors is the length, $(2x - 7)$. So $2x^2 - 27x + 70 = (2x - 7)(x - 10)$. The width is $(x - 10)$.

## Lesson 5: Algebra Problem Solving

### Practice 5, page 379

1. **C. 24** Take each answer choice and divide it by 2. Then, check to see if the resulting number is 12 less than the answer choice. For example, choice (A) 12: $12 \div 2 = 6$. And 6 is not 12 less than 12. Thus, choice (A) is incorrect. Only choice (C) works: $24 \div 2 = 24 - 12$.
2. **C. $200** Try each number. Choice (A) says Brenda raised $150. If she did, Sandra would have raised $450, and Matt would have raised $100. Also, the three of them together would have raised $150 + $450 + $100 ≠ $950. Since those numbers don't total to $950, (A) must be incorrect. Only (C) works: $200 + $600 + $150 = $950.
3. **C. 5** The answer choices represent possible weights for the first package. Try (A): if the first package weighs 2, the second package would weigh 1, and the third package would weigh 3. Add them together to see if they total 15: $2 + 1 + 3 \neq 15$. So (A) is incorrect. Only (C) works: $5 + 2.5 + 7.5 = 15$.
4. **B. 82** The answer choices represent possible scores for the first test. If (A) 76 is Hannah's score on the first test, then her score on the second test would be 82, and $76 + 82 \neq 170$. Only choice (B) works: $82 + 88 = 170$.
5. **B. 10** The answer choices represent how old Nelson might have been six years ago. If (A) were correct, then Nelson would have been 5 six years ago, and he would be 11 now. Also, six years ago Maria would have been 1year old, and today she would be 7. Now, the question is, is Nelson's current age twice Maria's age? $11 \neq 2 \times 7$. So (A) is incorrect. Choice (B) does work: if Nelson was 10 six years ago, then Maria would have been 2. Today Nelson would be 16 and Maria would be 8, and 16 is two times 8.
6. **A. –3** To solve by guessing, plug each answer choice into the equation. Try (A):
$2(-3)^2 + (-3) - 15 = 0.$
$2(9) - 18 = 0.$
$18 - 18 = 0.$
7. **B. 6** If the group purchased 5 children's passes, as (A) suggests, then they would have purchased 15 adult's passes. Multiply each amount by the cost of that type of ticket, to see if the total equals $440: (5 × $15) + (15 × $25) = $450. Thus, (A) is incorrect. Choice (B) works: (6 × $15) + (14 × $25) = $440.
8. **B. 20** The answer choices represent possible values for the width. If (A) were correct, then the width would be 15 and the length would be 30. Add to find out whether choice (A) would give the value of 120 for the perimeter: $15 + 15 + 30 + 30 = 90$. Thus, (A) is incorrect. Choice (B) works: $20 + 20 + 40 + 40 = 120$.

## Lesson 6: The Coordinate Plane

### Practice 6, page 381

1. (–4, 5)
2. (3, 6)
3. (0, –3)
4. (6, –7)
5. (–5, 0)
6. (–6, –4)
7. (2, 0)
8. (7, –2)
9.

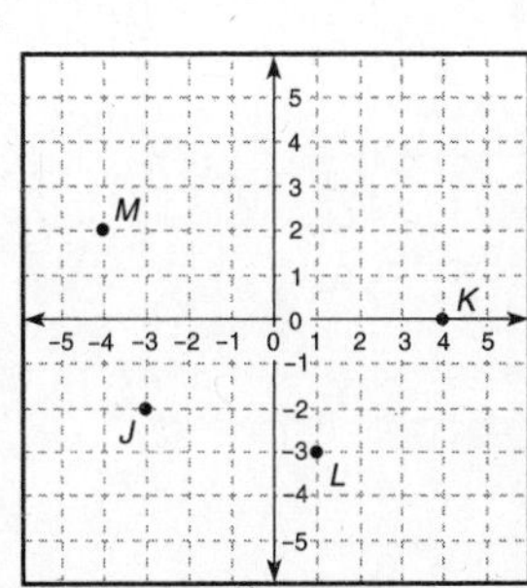


10.

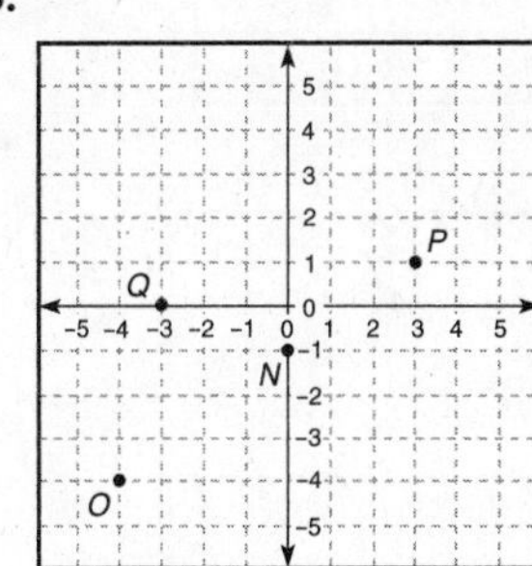


11. **D. (–1, 0)** Plot each point in the answer choices. Only choice (D) lies on the line that passes through points A and B.
12. **A. (–3, –2)** Find the two points discussed in the problem. Then locate the third corner of the triangle, and find the coordinates of the corner. The missing corner is 3 spaces to the left of the origin and 2 spaces down: (–3, –2).

## Lesson 7: Graphing a Line

### Practice 7, page 383

1.

| If $x =$ | Then $y =$ |
|---|---|
| –2 | 2 |
| 0 | 3 |
| 2 | 4 |

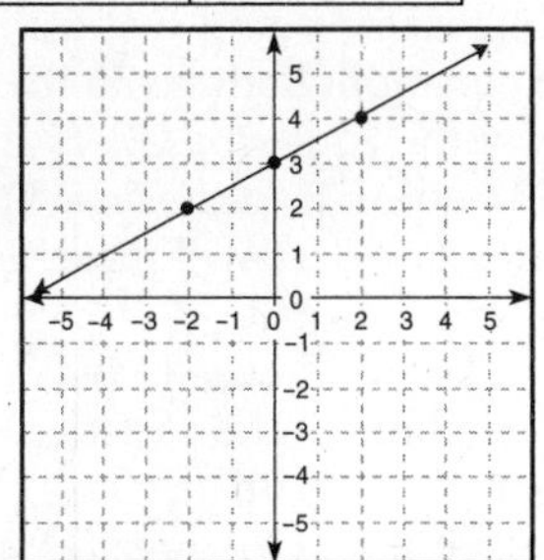

| If $x =$ | then $y =$ |
|---|---|
| –1 | **2** |
| 0 | **–1** |
| 1 | **–4** |

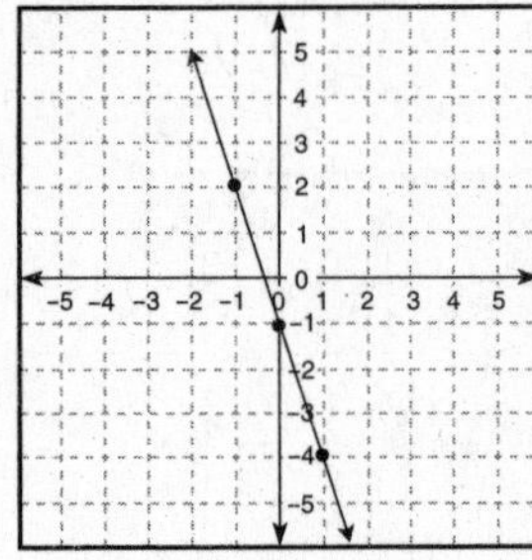

3.

| If $x =$ | then $y =$ |
|---|---|
| 1 | **1** |
| 2 | **0** |
| 3 | **–1** |

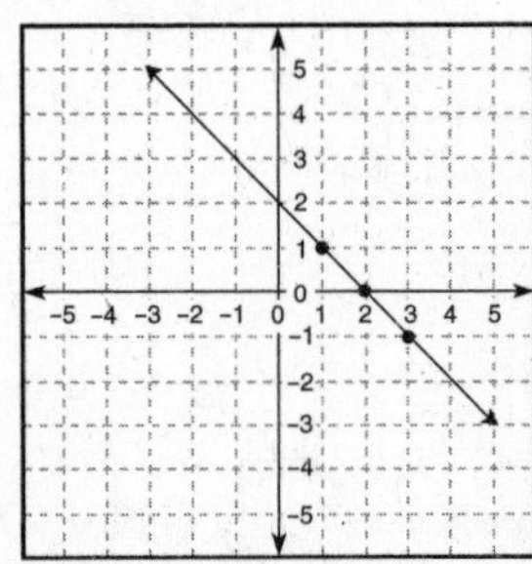

4.

| If $x =$ | then $y =$ |
|---|---|
| 0 | **3** |
| 1 | **1** |
| 2 | **–1** |

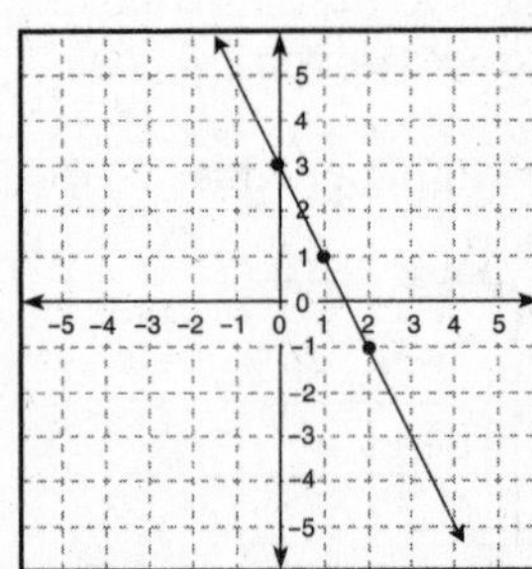

5. **C. point *T* and (0, 0)** Try the coordinates for points *S* and *T* in the equation. Both lie on the graph of the equation. Check the remaining points in the answer choices. Only (0,0) will make the equation $y = \frac{1}{4}x$ true.
6. **D. $y = -4x - 2$** Choose two points on line *P*. The easiest points to work with are the ones represented by dots: (–1,2) and (0,–2). Try one of those points in the equations. If the point works in the equation, try the other point as well. (You must try both because any number of lines may pass through a single point. To establish that the equation represents line *P*, it must fit both points.) Both points work only in choice (D): $y = -4x - 2$.
7. **B. $2x + 3y = 9$** Try the coordinates (–3, 5) in each equation. Only choice (B) is true.
$$2x + 3y = 9$$
$$2(-3) + 3(5) = 9$$
$$-6 + 15 = 9$$
$$9 = 9$$

## Lesson 8: Slope of a Line

### Practice 8, page 385

1. 1
2. –2
3. 0
4. $\frac{3}{4}$
5. $-\frac{1}{2}$
6. 0
7. $-\frac{1}{3}$
8. 2
9. –3
10. **A. line *A*** Of the answer choices, only line *A* has a negative slope, so it must be the correct answer. Line *A* moves down 1 space each time it goes 3 spaces to the right, a ratio of –1 to 3 or $-\frac{1}{3}$.
11. **B. –2** You have more information than you need. Choose any two points and use the slope formula to solve for the slope. For example, if you choose points (0, 4) and (1, 2), your calculations would be: $\frac{2-4}{1-0} = -\frac{2}{1} = -2$.
12. **C. (2, 3)** The best way to solve the problem is probably to make a quick sketch. Because the line has a slope of 3, start at point (1, 0) and count 3 spaces up and 1 space to the right. You are now at point (2, 3), which is choice (C). You can check your work using the slope formula.

## Lesson 9: Slope and Equations

### Practice 9, page 387

1. **$y = -4x + 2$**
$x = 1; y = -2; m = -4$
$-2 = -4(1) + b$
$b = 2$
2. **$y = 2x - 2$**
$x = -1; y = -4; m = 2$
$-4 = 2(-1) + b$
$b = -2$
3. **$y = -\frac{1}{3}x + \frac{2}{3}$**
$x = -4; y = 2; m = -\frac{1}{3}$
$2 = -\frac{1}{3}(-4) + b$
$b = \frac{2}{3}$
4. **$y - 1 = 3(x - 2)$**
$x_1 = 2; y_1 = 1; m = 3$
5. **$y = -\frac{1}{3}(x - 2)$**
$x_1 = 2; y_1 = 0; m = -\frac{1}{3}$
6. **$y + 2 = x - 1$**
$x_1 = 1; y_1 = -2; m = 1$
7. **$y = -\frac{1}{3}x + \frac{4}{3}$**
First, find the slope:
$m = \frac{3-1}{-5-1} = -\frac{1}{3}$.
Choose either ordered pair to substitute for $x$ and $y$:
$m = -\frac{1}{3}; x = 1; y = 1$
Follow the steps to find the equation of a line in the slope-intercept form.
$1 = -\frac{1}{3}(1) + b$
$b = \frac{4}{3}$
8. **$y = 4x + 12$**
$m = \frac{4-0}{-2-(-3)} = 4$
$0 = 4(-3) + b$
$b = 12$
9. **$y = \frac{1}{2}x - \frac{5}{2}$**
$m = \frac{1-(-4)}{7-(-3)} = \frac{1}{2}$
$1 = \frac{1}{2}(7) + b$
$b = -\frac{5}{2}$
10. **C. $y = -x - 1$** Plug both points into the slope formula. $m = \frac{-3-0}{2-(-1)} = -1$.
Then, use $m$ and one of the points to solve for $b$.
$0 = -1(-1) + b$
$b = -1$
11. **D. $y = \frac{1}{2}x - 1$** To answer this question, simplify the equation in the question to find an answer that matches:
$y - 2 = \frac{1}{2}(x - 6)$
$y - 2 = \frac{1}{2}x - 3$
$y = \frac{1}{2}x - 1$
12. **B. $y = -x - 4$** Because the line on the graph slopes down from left to right, its slope is negative, so you can eliminate choices (A) and (C) immediately. Then note that the line crosses the $y$-axis at (0, –4), so the $y$-intercept is –4. Therefore, the correct choice is (B).

## Lesson 10: Systems of Linear Equations

### Practice 10, page 389

1. **(7, 6)**

$y = 3x - 15$ $x + y = 13$

| $x$ | $y$ |
|---|---|
| 0 | –15 |
| 5 | 0 |

| $x$ | $y$ |
|---|---|
| 0 | 13 |
| 13 | 0 |

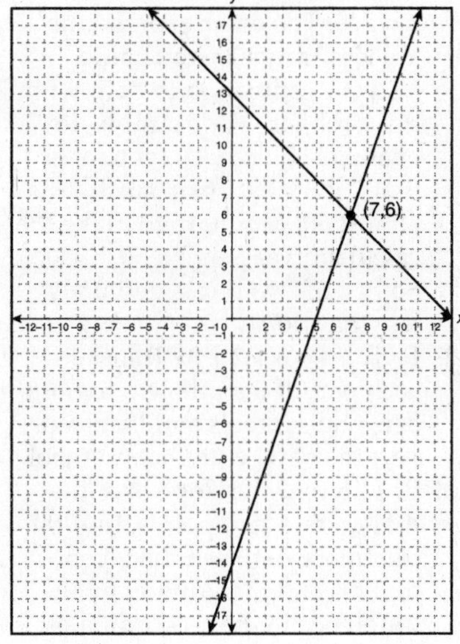


2. **(–3, 11)**

$4x + 2y = 10$ $y = -5x - 4$

| $x$ | $y$ |
|---|---|
| 0 | 5 |
| $\frac{5}{2}$ | 0 |

| $x$ | $y$ |
|---|---|
| 0 | –4 |
| $-\frac{4}{5}$ | 0 |

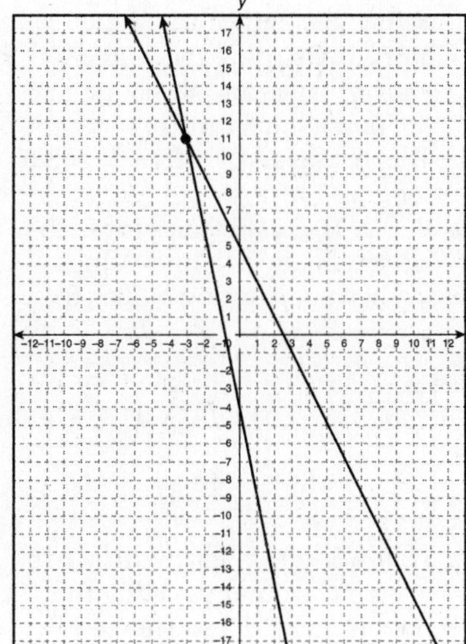

3. **(3, –1)**
Isolate $y$:
$-y = -7x + 22$
$y = 7x - 22$
Substitute:
$4x + 2(7x - 22) = 10$
$4x + 14x - 44 = 10$
$18x = 54$
$x = 3$
Substitute back:
$y = 7(3) - 22$
$y = -1$

4. **(7, 2)**
Isolate $y$:
$y = 9 - x$
Substitute:
$2x - 3(9 - x) = 8$
$2x - 27 + 3x = 8$
$5x = 35$
$x = 7$
Substitute back:
$y = 9 - 7$
$y = 2$

5. **(–4, 3)**
$y$ is already isolated.
$y = 3x + 15$
Substitute:
$5x - 2(3x + 15) = -26$
$5x - 6x - 30 = -26$
$-x = 4$
$x = -4$
Substitute back:
$y = 3(-4) + 15$
$y = 3$

6. **$(\frac{1}{2}, 6)$**
$y$ is already isolated.
$y = 12x$
Substitute:
$10x - (12x) = -1$
$-2x = -1$
$x = \frac{1}{2}$
Substitute back:
$y = 12\left(\frac{1}{2}\right)$
$y = 6$

7. **A. (2, –1)** Isolate $x$ in the first equation. $x = 2y + 4$. Then, substitute into the second equation to find a value for $y$.
$6y + 5(2y + 4) = 4$
$16y + 20 = 4$
$y = -1$
Finally, use that value of $y$ in the first equation to find a value for $x$. $x = 2(-1) + 4 = 2$

8. **C. (0,0)** The equation $y = x$ represents a line whose $x$-coordinate is always equal to the $y$-coordinate. The equation $y = -x$ represents a line whose $y$-coordinate is always equal to the negative of the $x$-coordinate. Neither line has a $b$ term in its equation, so both lines have a $y$-intercept of zero, meaning that they both cross the $y$-axis at (0,0).

9. **C. $\left(-\frac{9}{2}, -2\right)$** Since the only possible $y$-value for the line $y = -2$ is –2, simply substitute that value for $y$ in the equation $3y = 2x + 3$ to find the intersection:
$3(-2) = 2x + 3$
$-9 = 2x$
$x = -\frac{9}{2}$

10. **C. $y = -4x + 2$** Two different lines cannot intersect if they are parallel. Lines are parallel if they have the same slope. Only choice (C) does not have a slope of 4, so this is the correct choice.

## Lesson 11: Patterns and Functions

### Practice 11, page 391

1. 0
2. 41
3. 2
4. 40
5. 23
6. –4
7. 31.25
8. –13
9. 32
10. –5
11. **B. 49** To highlight the pattern, it might be useful to make a table or list:

| 1st | 2nd | 3rd | 4th |
|---|---|---|---|
| 1 block | 3 blocks | 5 blocks | 7 blocks |

The number of blocks in each construction equals $2n - 1$, where $n$ is the number in the sequence. The 25th construction would require $2(25) - 1 = 49$ blocks.

12. **C. 16** Each term is 6 greater than the term before it. The next (that is, the fifth) term in the sequence is 10, and the sixth term is 16.
13. **B. $c = \$5.00 - \$0.25\ (n - 1)$** The original price per scarf ($5) is reduced by 25 cents starting with the second scarf.
14. **B. 1, 5, 9, 13, 17, . . .** Try the numbers 1, 2, and 3 for $x$ in the function. This will result in the first three terms of the pattern: 1, 5, and 9. Only choice (B) contains these three terms.

## Lesson 12: Function Applications

### Practice 12, page 393

1. a. \$99
   b. \$265
2. a. 5.5 hours
   b. 4.25 hours
3. a. Plan A
   b. Plan B
4. **B. \$29.50** Use the functions for the two jobs, substituting 30 hours for $h$:
   Job 1: $P = \$9.75h = \$9.75(30) = \$292.50$
   Job 2: $P = \$70 + \$8.40h = \$70 + \$8.40(30) = \$70 + \$252 = \$322$
   Subtract: $\$322 - \$292.50 = \$29.50$
5. **D. Alicia will earn the most at Job 2.** Use the functions to find Alicia's wages at all three jobs based on 40 hours:
   Job 1: $P = \$9.75h = \$9.75(40) = \$390$
   Job 2: $P = \$70 + \$8.40h = \$70 + \$8.40(40) = \$70 + \$336 = \$406$
   Job 3: $\$380 \times \frac{h}{38} = \$380 \times \frac{40}{38} = \$10 \times 40 = \$400$
   Compare the three results. Alicia will earn the most at Job 2.
6. **B. \$19,400** Use the function to calculate the profit:
   $P = \$95{,}000 - \$5{,}400d$
   $P = \$95{,}000 - \$5{,}400(14)$
   $P = \$95{,}000 - \$75{,}600$
   $P = \$19{,}400$

## Lesson 13: Equation Word Problems, Part II

### Practice 13, page 395

1. **D. $e = 0.01s + 30{,}000$** Marguerite's base salary is \$30,000 and increases by 0.01 times the amount of her sales.
2. **A. \$10** Set up two equations using the given information: $\$1{,}000 + \$100x$ for sedans and $\$1{,}500 + \$50x$ for minivans, where $x$ represents the vehicle's age. Set the two equations equal to each other $\$1{,}000 + \$100x = \$1{,}500 + \$50x$. Then subtract $\$50x$ from both sides: $\$1{,}000 + \$50x = \$1{,}500$. Next, subtract \$1,000 from each side: $\$50x = \$500$. Divide both sides by \$50 to solve.
3. **C. \$30** Set up two equations using the given information. For company A, the cost is $\$2{,}000 + \$40x$ where $x$ represents the number of strollers. For company B, the cost is $\$1{,}550 + \$55x$. Set the two equations equal to each other $\$2{,}000 + \$40x = \$1{,}550 + \$55x$. Subtract $\$40x$ from both sides: $\$2{,}000 = \$1{,}550 + \$15x$. Next, subtract \$1,550 from each side: $\$450 = \$15x$. Divide both sides by \$15 to solve.

## Functions Practice Questions, pages 396–399

1. **D. $-4x - 6$** Use the order of operations: $6 - 4(x + 3) = 6 - 4x - 12 = -4x - 6$
2. **A. $-3$**
   $3 + 4x = x - 6$
   $3x = -9$
   $x = -3$
3. **B. $y = -4x + 6$** Choices (A) and (B) are the only two choices with the correct slope. Plug in $x = 1$ and $y = 2$ into both equations; only (B) works.
4. **C. $4x - y = -7$** Try $x = -2$ and $y = -1$ in each equation. Only choice (C) is true: $4(-2) - (-1) = -8 + 1 = -7$
5. **C. \$510** Let $t$ = Tom's earnings and $2t - \$150$ = Jan's earnings.
   $2t - \$150 + t = \$1380$
   $3t - \$150 = \$1380$
   $3t = \$1530$
   $t = \$510$
6. **D. *D*** The coordinates of *D* are $(-3, -2)$, which make the equation $y = -x - 5$ true.
   $y = -x - 5$
   $-2 = -(-3) - 5$
   $-2 = 3 - 5$
   $-2 = -2$
7. **C. $\frac{1}{3}$** Count the rise and run from *C* to *B*. The line moves up 3 spaces as it moves 9 to the right: $\frac{3}{9} = \frac{1}{3}$.
8. **A. $s \geq \$17{,}500$** Samuel's earnings can be represented by the expression $\$350 + 0.1s$, where $s$ represents total sales. Since Samuel needs to earn at least \$2,100, this expression must be greater than or equal to \$2,100. Solve:
   $\$350 + 0.1s \geq \$2{,}100$
   $0.1s \geq \$1{,}750$
   $s \geq \$17{,}500$
9. **B. \$5.35** Substitute 24 for $n$ and solve:
   $F = \$3.95 + \$0.10(24 - 10)$
   $F = \$3.95 + \$0.10(14)$
   $F = \$3.95 + \$1.40$
   $F = \$5.35$
10. **D. 29** Let $x$ = the first number. The remaining numbers are $x + 2$, $x + 4$, and $x + 6$. Solve:
    $x + (x + 2) + (x + 4) + (x + 6) = 104$
    $4x + 12 = 104$
    $4x = 92$
    $x = 23$
    The numbers are 23, 25, 27, and 29. The problem asks for the largest of these numbers.
11. **C. $3^6$** Calculate: $3 \times 3 \times 3 \times 3 \times 3 \times 3 = 729$. The other expressions are less than 400. You could also use estimation to help with this problem. For example, to evaluate choice (A), remember that $7 \times 7 = 49$. Then, since 49 is almost 50, round up to make the calculation easier: $7 \times 50 \doteq 350$. So $7^3 < 350$, and it is definitely less than 400.
12. **B. $5x - 4 = 8 + 2 + 3x$** Translate each part of the problem to numbers and symbols and then connect the parts with the = symbol.
13. **B. 1** To find the slope of a line that crosses two points, find the difference between the $y$-coordinates and then divide by the difference in the $x$-coordinates: $\frac{6-4}{4-2} = \frac{2}{2} = 1$.
14. **B. 31** From 1 to 7, there is a difference of 6. From 7 to 14, there is a difference of 7. From 14 to 22, there is a difference of 8. To find the next term, add 9 to 22: $22 + 9 = 31$.
15. **C. 0** To find the $y$-intercept of a line when given the slope and a point, plug the $x$- and $y$-coordinates and the slope into the point-slope form, $y = mx + b$. This results in $2 = 2(1) + b$. Solve for $b$.
16. **B. $(-2, 1)$** Create tables for each linear equation to find values of $y$ when substituting values for $x$:

    $y = x + 3$

    | $x$ | $y$ |
    |---|---|
    | 0 | 3 |
    | −3 | 0 |

    $y = -2x - 3$

    | $x$ | $y$ |
    |---|---|
    | 0 | −3 |
    | $-\frac{3}{2}$ | 0 |

17. **D. $y = 3 + 0.5x$** Start with what is given: around the edge the pool is 3 feet deep. Then add another 0.5 feet of depth for every foot you walk from the edge, which is represented by $0.5x$. Putting the two pieces of

information together yields the equation $y = 3 + 0.5x$

18. **A. $-7x - (8 + y)$** The word *product* indicates multiplication, and the word *sum* indicates addition. Choice (B) means that $y$ is added, rather than subtracted, from the product (due to order of operations), so it is incorrect.
19. **C. 8 and −3** Either solve by factoring or by trying each option in the equation. The correct factorization is as follows:
$x^2 - 5x - 24 = 0$
$(x - 8)(x + 3) = 0$
$x = 8$ or $x = -3$
20. **B. 4** Cynthia's age right now is six times Rebecca's, or $6r$. Thus, in six years, Cynthia will be $6r + 6$ years old, and Rebecca will be $r + 6$ years old. Write an equation and solve for $r$:
$6r + 6 = 3(r + 6)$.
21. **B. $y = 2x - 3$** Try the given points in the equations in the answer options. Only choice (B) works with both points.
22. **B.**
$-2(x - 6) > 8$
$-2x + 12 > 8$
$-2x > -4$
$x < 2$

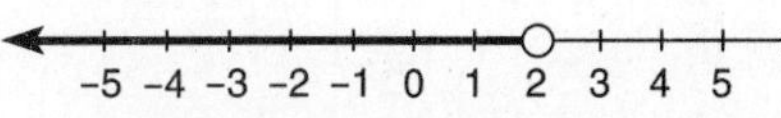


Remember to reverse the inequality symbol when you divide both sides by a negative number.
23. **B. (−5, 1)** Point $L$ is 5 spaces to the left of the origin along the $x$-axis and 1 space above the origin along the $y$-axis.
24. **D. $\frac{3}{2}$** The coordinates of point L are (−5, 1), and the coordinates of point M are (−3, 4). Find the slope by finding the difference of the $y$-coordinates, and divide by the difference of the $x$-coordinates: $\frac{1-4}{-5-(-3)} = \frac{-3}{-2} = \frac{3}{2}$.
25. **C. \$18** Let $s$ = Sam's gift. Then:
Daniel's gift = $s$.
Celia's gift $s + 12$ (since Sam and Daniel gave the same amount).
Bob's gift = $0.5(s + 12)$ (that is, one-half of Celia's gift).
Add those four quantities together and set the sum total to \$81:
$s + s + (s + 12) + .5(s + 12) = 81$
$3.5s + 18 = 81$
$3.5s = 63$
$s = 18$
26. **A. $x \le 3$** Remember to reverse the inequality sign when dividing by a negative number.
$-7x - 4 \ge x - 28$
$-8x \ge -24$
$x \le 3$
27. **C. $y = x + 2$** Start by finding the slope: $\frac{3-2}{1-0} = 1$. Now you know that the equation will be $y = x + b$, and you can eliminate choices (A) and (B). And in this case, no calculations are required to find the $y$-intercept, because one of the points given in the question is (0, 2)—the point where the line crosses the $y$-axis.
28. **B. 8,652** Let $x$ = votes for the leading candidate and $p$ = votes for Perez. Write an equation:
$p = \frac{1}{3}x + 5{,}512$.
Additionally, you can say that $p + x = 18{,}072$, or $p = 18{,}072 - x$
Substitute for $p$:
$18{,}072 - x = \frac{1}{3}x + 5{,}512$
$12{,}560 = \frac{4}{3}x$
$x = 9420$
That number represents the number of votes the opposing candidate received. Now, substitute that value back into the simpler of the two original equations:
$p + 9{,}420 = 18{,}072$
$p = 8{,}652$
29. **B. $x = -2$** Simplify:
$-4(x + 2) - 10 = 5x$
$-4x - 8 - 10 = 5x$
$-4x - 18 = 5x$
$-18 = 9x$
$-2 = x$
30. **D. \$5x + \$10(35 − x) = \$240**
The total value of the \$5 bills is \$5x. Since there are 35 bills, the number of \$10 bills must be $35 - x$. The value of the \$10 bills is \$10(35 − x). The sum of the value of the \$5 bills plus the value of the \$10 bills is \$240.
31. **C. 75** Let $x$ = the first number in the sequence. Then write an equation:
$x + (x + 1) + (x + 2) + (x + 3) + (x + 4) = 370$
$5x + 10 = 370$
$x = 72$
The first number in the sequence is 72. That means the fourth number (which equals $x + 3$) is 75.
32. **4** Substitute and solve: $E = \frac{9(8)}{18} = 4$.
33. **B. $y = 5 + 2x$** Because Tonya initially purchases five boxes of cookies, the equation will start out with 5. Each coworker can be counted on to purchase two boxes, written as $2x$. Thus, the amount of cookies sold can be represented with the function $y = 5 + 2x$.

## Geometry

### Lesson 1: Points, Lines, and Angles

### Practice 1, page 401

1. acute
2. obtuse
3. straight
4. acute
5. reflex
6. right
7. acute
8. obtuse
9. **A. 135°** $m\angle RZS + m\angle QZS = 180°$. Because $\angle RZS$ measures 45° $\angle QZS$ must measure 135°
10. **C. right** Because $m\angle RZQ = 180°$, subtract the two known angles to find the measure of $\angle SZT$. $180° - 45° - 45° = 90°$. Because $\angle SZT$ measures 90°, it is a right angle.
11. **A. 38°** $\angle AWB + \angle BWC + \angle CWD = \angle AWD$, a straight angle with a measure of 180°. You know that $m\angle AWB = 90°$ and $m\angle CWD = 52°$, so substitute those values in the first equation: $90° + m\angle BWC + 52° = 180°$, which results in $\angle BWC = 38°$.
12. **C. obtuse** $m\angle AWC$ is greater than the right angle $\angle AWB$ and less than the straight angle $\angle AWD$. $\angle AWC$ must be obtuse.

### Lesson 2: Parallel Lines and Transversals

### Practice 2, page 403

All possible answers are shown.

1. $\angle 4$ and $\angle 6$, $\angle 3$ and $\angle 5$
2. $\angle 3$
3. 100°
4. $\angle 1$ and $\angle 7$, $\angle 2$ and $\angle 8$
5. $\angle 1$ and $\angle 3$, $\angle 2$ and $\angle 4$, $\angle 5$ and $\angle 7$, $\angle 6$ and $\angle 8$
6. $\angle 4$
7. **B. 75°** $\angle 3$ and $\angle 1$ are vertical angles. Therefore, $m\angle 3 = m\angle 1$. $m\angle 3 = 75°$, so $m\angle 1 = 75°$.

8. **B. They are in the same position from one parallel line to the other.** The transversal and the parallel lines form eight angles. Corresponding angles lie on the same side of the transversal and have the same relationship to the nearest parallel line.
9. **B. 65°** Angle $\angle 7$ and $\angle 3$ are corresponding angles, so $m\angle 7 = m\angle 3$; therefore, $m\angle 3 = 115°$. Angle $\angle 3$ and $\angle 4$ are adjacent angles, which means $115° + m\angle 4 = 180°$ and $m\angle 4 = 65°$.
10. **D. $\angle 8$** Angle $\angle 2$ and $\angle 8$ are alternate exterior angles. Therefore, they are equal.

## Lesson 3: Plane Figures

### Practice 3, page 405

1. rectangle, square
2. parallelogram, rectangle, square, rhombus
3. trapezoid
4. rectangle, square
5. none
6. rectangle, square, parallelogram, rhombus
7. square, rhombus
8. rectangle, square, parallelogram, rhombus, trapezoid
9. trapezoid
10. square
11. **C. 140°** Let $h$ = the measure of $\angle H$. Then $3h + 20° = m\angle F$. The sum of the angles of a quadrilateral is 360°, so $3h + 20° + h + 90° + 90° = 360°$
    Solve the equation:
    $4h + 200° = 360°$, so $4h = 160°$, $h = 40°$, and $3h + 20° = 140°$.
12. **B. $EF \parallel GH$** In other words, line $EF$ is parallel to line $GH$. A trapezoid is a quadrilateral with exactly one pair of parallel sides.
13. **C. 90°** If the opposite sides of a figure are parallel and all four sides are equal, then the figure is either a square or rhombus. Since $\angle T$ is a right angle, the figure is square. Therefore, all the angles measure 90°.
14. **C. parallelogram** This quadrilateral has opposite sides that are equal and opposite angles that are equal. It has no right angles, and the two sets of sides are different lengths. The quadrilateral must be a parallelogram.

## Lesson 4: Triangles

### Practice 4, page 407

1. equilateral, acute
2. scalene, obtuse
3. isosceles, acute
4. 64°
5. 45°
6. 97°
7. **C. 14** Solve for $\angle BAC$: $m\angle BAC + 55° = 115°$, so $m\angle BAC = 60°$. Solve for $\angle BCA$: $\angle BCA + 35° = 95°$, so $\angle BCA = 60°$. If two of the angles of $\Delta ABC$ each measure 60°, the third angle also measures 60°. The triangle is equilateral, and all the sides of $ABC$ are equal to side $AB$.
8. **C. right** $55° + 35° + m\angle D = 180°$. Solve for the missing angle: $m\angle D = 90°$. Therefore, the triangle is a right triangle.
9. **C. 86°** The angles of a triangle add up to 180°. $38° + 56° = 94°$, so the third angle can be found by subtracting 94° from 180°: $180° - 94° = 86°$.

## Lesson 5: Congruent and Similar Triangles

### Practice 5, page 409

1. No
2. Yes
3. Not enough information
4. **C. 48** Because the triangles are similar, the sides must be proportional. Set up the ratio $\frac{25}{40} = \frac{30}{x}$ where $x$ equals the length of $ST$. Solve: $x = 48$
5. **B. 64°** Similar triangles have equal angle measures. If $m\angle S = 68°$, then $m\angle TYX = 68°$. $m\angle TYX + m\angle T + m\angle TXY = 180°$. Substitute and solve: $68° + 48° + m\angle TXY = 180°$ so $m\angle TXY = 64°$.
6. **C. 3.2** The two triangles are similar because two of the angle measures in one triangle are equal to two of the angle measures in the other triangle. The side labeled $x$ corresponds to the side with length 4.8. The side of length 2.8 corresponds to the side with length 4.2. Solve the ratio $\frac{x}{4.8} = \frac{2.8}{4.2}$: $x = 3.2$.

## Lesson 6: Similar Triangle Applications

### Practice 6, page 411

1. **C. 64** Set up a proportion comparing the sign's shadow to the building's shadow and the sign's height to the building's height. $\frac{6}{48} = \frac{8}{x}$: so $x = 64$.
2. **B. 42** The 10-ft pole is 25 ft from the vertex of the angle; the base of the cliff is 80 + 25, or 105 ft from the vertex of the angle. Set up a proportion. $\frac{105}{25} = \frac{x}{10}$: so $x = 42$.
3. **A. $\frac{2.5}{22.5} = \frac{1}{x}$** Set up a proportion comparing the meter stick's shadow to the flagpole's shadow and the meter stick's height to the flagpole's height.
4. **D. 49** Examine the two triangles to find corresponding sides. The 8-ft side of the smaller triangle corresponds to the 28-ft side of the larger triangle. Write a proportion and solve. $\frac{8}{28} = \frac{14}{x}$: so $x = 49$.
5. **B. 4** If you imagine a line drawn at the bottom of the frame, you will have two similar triangles. The base of the large triangle is 6 ft, and the base of the small triangle is unknown. The side of the large triangle is 12 ft and the side of the small one is 12 – 4= 8 ft. Write a proportion and solve: $\frac{8}{12} = \frac{x}{6}$, so $x = 4$.

## Lesson 7: Pythagorean Relationship

### Practice 7, page 413

1. $c = 11.3$ in
2. $c = 15$ yd
3. $c = 2.5$ cm
4. $a = 5.2$ m
5. $b = 8$ mm
6. $a = 17.3$ ft
7. $c = 12.2$ cm
8. $b = 26.0$ in
9. $c = 6.4$ km
10. **B. 6.7** The distance from $A$ to $C$ is 3 units, and the distance from $B$ to $C$ is 6 units.
    $c^2 = a^2 + b^2$
    $c^2 = 3^2 + 6^2$
    $c^2 = 9 + 36$
    $c^2 = 45$
    $c = \sqrt{45} \cong 6.7$
11. **C. 30** The shorter sides are the legs. Solve for the hypotenuse.
    $c^2 = a^2 + b^2$
    $c^2 = 18^2 + 24^2$
    $c^2 = 324 + 576$
    $c^2 = 900$
    $c = \sqrt{900} = 30$

12. **D. 12.1** The brace divides the rectangle into two right triangles with the brace as the hypotenuse of each. Solve for the hypotenuse of one of the triangles:
$c^2 = a^2 + b^2$
$c^2 = 5^2 + 11^2$
$c^2 = 25 + 121$
$c^2 = 146$
$c = \sqrt{146} \cong 12.08$, which rounds to 12.1.
13. **A. 36** Calculate:
$c^2 = a^2 + b^2$
$39^2 = 15^2 + b^2$
$1{,}521 = 225 + b^2$
$1{,}296 = b^2$
$b = \sqrt{1{,}296} = 36$

## Lesson 8: Perimeter and Area

### Practice 8, page 415

1. area: 39 sq units
perimeter: 30.8 units
2. area: 16 sq units
perimeter: 16 units
3. area: 640 sq units
perimeter: 104 units
4. area: 29.6 sq units
perimeter: 24.6 units
5. area: 616 sq units
perimeter: 109 units
6. area: 38 sq units
perimeter: 32 units
7. **C. 56** The shaded portion is a trapezoid: $\frac{1}{2} \times (5 + 9) \times 8 = 56$.
8. **C. 54** The area of a rectangle is its base times its height. $9 \times 6 = 54$.
9. **C. 324** Subtract the area of the patio from the area of the entire yard. Both are rectangles, so multiply length and width to find the area:
$(24 \times 18) - (12 \times 9) = 324$.
10. **B. 24** Add all four sides:
$6 + 6 + 6 + 6 = 24$ centimeters.

## Lesson 9: Circles

### Practice 9.1, page 417

1. $C = 62.8$ in; $A = 314.2$ in$^2$
2. $C = 12.6$ cm; $A = 12.6$ cm$^2$
3. $C = 25.1$ m; $A = 50.2$ m$^2$
4. **C. 38** Use the formula $C = \pi d$, where $d = 12$. $12 \times 3.14 = 37.7$
5. **B. 3.14 × 6²** The formula for the area of a circle is $A = \pi r^2$. The radius of a circle is half of the diameter. Half of 12 is 6. Substitute 6 for $r$ and 3.14 for $\pi$. $A = 3.14 \times 6^2$.
6. **B. 13.0** The diameter of a circle is twice the radius. $6.5 \times 2 = 13$.
7. **C. 19** Find the circumference of the 10-point band. First find the diameter, which passes through the 10-point band, the inner circle, and the 10-point band a second time on its way from one edge of the circle to the other. Add the width of the 10-point band twice and the diameter of the inner circle: $2 + 2 + 2 = 6$ inches. Now you can use the formula for circumference: $6 \times 3.14 = 18.84$, which rounds to 19 inches.

### Practice 9.2, page 419

1. **34.4°**
2. **10.5 m**
3. **106.1 m**
4. **B. 5** To solve for A, use the formula at the top of the practice page.
$12 \times A = 15 \times 4$
$A = \frac{60}{12} = 5$
5. **C. 24** Use the Pythagorean theorem to find half the length of $LM$:
(half of $LM)^2 + 5^2 = 13^2$
(half of $LM)^2 = 144$
half of $LM = 12$
$LM = 24$

## Lesson 10: Volume

### Practice 10.1, page 421

1. 160 cubic units
2. 27 cubic units
3. 141 cubic units
4. 420 cubic units
5. 3 cubic units
6. 236 cubic units
7. **A. 5.** $V = lwh$ You know that the length and width of the box both equal 4 and that the volume equals 80. Solve the equation:
$80 = 4 \times 4 \times h$
$80 = 16h$
$5 = h$
8. **C. 125** If each edge measures 5 feet, then the figure is a cube. $5^3 = 125$.
9. **C. 17** First, you must find the volume of the pool. The radius of the pool is 6 and the height is 3.
$V = \pi r^2 h$
$\approx 3.14 \times 6^2 \times 3$
$\approx 3.14 \times 36 \times 3$
$\approx 339.12$
Therefore, the volume is about 339. Solve the proportion $\frac{1}{20} = \frac{x}{339}$, where $x$ equals the number of scoops Linda must add: $20x = 339$; $x = 16.95$, about 17.

### Practice 10.2, page 423

1. 9 in$^3$
2. 127 in$^3$
3. 314 cm$^3$
4. 480 m$^3$
5. 11 in$^3$
6. 1060 cm$^3$
7. **A. 480** First, find the volume of the original package. Substitute the numbers given into the volume equation: $V = \frac{1}{3} \times 10^2 \times 15 = 500$. Then find the volume of the new package. Add 4 to the length and width of the base to get 14. Substitute into the volume equation again and solve: $V = \frac{1}{3} \times 14^2 \times 15 = 980$. Find the difference of the two volumes: $980 - 500 = 480$.
8. **C. 67** You know that the height of the cone is half of the diameter of the base. Since the radius of the base is also half of the diameter, the radius must equal the height. Therefore, the radius is 4. Now solve the equation: $V = \frac{1}{3} \times \pi \times 4^2 \times 4 \approx 67$.
9. **D. The volume of *B* is less than the volume of *A*.** First, find the volumes of the two figures. Figure $A$ is a rectangular solid. Use the formula $V = lwh = 4 \times 3 \times 2 = 24$. Figure $B$ is a pyramid. Use the formula $V = \frac{1}{3}Bh = \frac{1}{3} \times 3^2 \times 6 = 18$. Now compare the two volumes. Since $24 > 18$, choice (D) must be the answer.
10. **D. 1,000** Use the formula $V = \frac{1}{3}\pi r^2 h = \frac{1}{3} \times \pi \times 8^2 \times 15 \approx 1{,}005$, which is about 1,000.

## Lesson 11: Surface Area

### Practice 11.1, page 425

1. 108
2. 39
3. 24
4. 336
5. 256
6. 384
7. **C. The surface area of Figure *A* is greater than the surface area of Figure *B*.** Calculate both surface areas. Figure $A$: $25 \times 6 = 150$.

Figure $B$: $(30 \times 4) + (9 \times 2) =$ 138. Therefore, Figure $A$'s surface area is greater than Figure $B$'s.

8. **C. 162** The original box has a side length of 3 centimeters, so the surface area is 54 square centimeters. When the dimensions are doubled, the new box has a side length of 6 centimeters, so the surface area is 216 square centimeters. The difference in surface areas is 216 cm – 54 cm, which is 162 square centimeters.
9. **A. 5** If all the edges are the same length, then the box must be a cube, and each square face has the same area. There are 6 faces. Divide 150 by 6 to get an area of 25 for each face. Then $25 \div 5 = 5$, so each side has a length of 5 in.

## Practice 11.2, page 427

| | |
|---|---|
| **1.** $168\pi$ | **4.** $378\pi$ |
| **2.** $40\pi$ | **5.** $400\pi$ |
| **3.** $36\pi$ | **6.** $96\pi$ |

7. **B. $64\pi$** The formula for the surface area of a sphere uses the radius, and the radius is half the diameter, so $8 \div 2 = 4 = r$. Now use the formula for the surface area of a sphere: $SA = 4\pi r^2 = 4 \times \pi \times 4^2 = 64\pi$.
8. **D. The new cone will have a surface area less than the surface area of the original cone.** The original cone has a radius of 4, so its surface area is $\pi(4)(8) + \pi(4^2) = 32\pi + 16\pi = 48\pi$. The new cone will have a slant height of 16, a diameter of 4 and a radius of 2, so its surface area is: $\pi(2)(16) + \pi(2^2) = 32\pi + 4\pi = 36\pi$, which is less than $48\pi$.
9. **C. 170** The surface area of the cylinder is $\pi(6)(6) + 2\pi(3^2) = 36\pi + 18\pi = 54\pi = 54(3.14) \approx 170$ square inches.

## Lesson 12: Combined Figures

### Practice 12, page 429

1. $P = 150$ units
   $A = 1050$ sq units
2. $P = 49.7$ units
   $A = 159.3$ sq units
3. $P = 72$ units
   $A = 168$ sq units
4. $V = 185$ cubic units
5. $V = 278$ cubic units
6. $V = 399$ cubic units
7. **D. 360** Find the volume of the main rectangular slab: $V = lwh$, so $V = 3 \times 8 \times 12 = 288$ cubic feet. Find the volume of one of the blocks: $V = lwh$, so $V = 3 \times 3 \times 2 = 18$ cu ft. Multiply by 4, the number of blocks: $18 \times 4 = 72$ cu ft. Finally, add the main slab to the blocks: $288 + 72 = 360$ cu ft.
8. **C. 134** The radius of both the cones and the cylinder is 2. The height of one cone is 4 inches. Find the volume of one cone: $V = \frac{1}{3}\pi r^2 h = \frac{1}{3} \times 3.14 \times 2^2 \times 4 \approx 16.7$ cu in. Multiply by 2 to find the volume of both cones: $16.7 \times 2 = 33.4$ cu in. Find the volume of the cylinder: $V = \pi r^2 h \approx 3.14 \times 2^2 \times 8 \approx 100.48$ cu in. Add to find the total volume: $33.4 + 100.48 = 133.88$ cu in, which rounds to 134 cu in.

## Lesson 13: Geometry Calculator Skills

### Practice 13, page 431

| | |
|---|---|
| **1.** 42 in | **4.** 15.8 cm |
| **2.** 195 $cm^2$ | **5.** 37.7 in |
| **3.** 43 $ft^3$ | **6.** 3016 $cm^3$ |

7. **C. 520** Use the formulas for finding the area of a rectangle and the area of a triangle, and subtract the area of the cutout triangle from the area of the rectangle. On the TI-30XS MultiView™ calculator, enter the following: 32 ⊗ 20 ⊖ 20 ⊗ 12 ⊗ .5 (enter). The right side of the display will read **520.** You can enter the entire calculation in this fashion because the TI-30XS™ MultiView understands the algebraic order of operations. If you press enter after each of those operations, your answer will be incorrect.
8. **B. 35** Use the formula for finding the volume of a cylinder. Press: (π) ⊗ 1.5 ($x^2$) ⊗ 5 (enter). The right side of the display will read **35.34291735**, which rounds to 35 meters
9. **D. 5,056** Use the formula for finding the volume of a rectangular solid. Subtract the volume of Box B from the volume of Box A. Press: 26 ⊗ 12 ⊗ 32 ⊖ 22 ⊗ 8 ⊗ 28 (enter). The right side of the display will read **5056.**
10. **C. 608** Use the formula for finding the area of a rectangle. Combine the areas of the two faces. Press: 32 ⊗ 12 ⊕ 28 ⊗ 8 (enter). The right side of the display will read **608.**

## Geometry Practice Questions, pages 432–435

1. **D. 150** If the edge length is 5 cm, then each square surface has an area of 25 $cm^2$. There are 6 faces, so multiply by 6 to get 150 $cm^2$.
2. **C. $192\pi$** Substitute the values given in the question into the formula for the surface area of a cylinder:
   $SA = 2\pi rh + 2\pi r^2$
   $SA = 2\pi(6)(10) + 2\pi(6^2)$
   $SA = 120\pi + 72\pi = 192\pi$
3. **C. $66\pi$** The surface area of a cylinder is calculated with the formula $SA = 2\pi rh + 2\pi r^2 = (2 \times \pi \times 3 \times 8) + (2 \times \pi \times 9) = 48\pi + 18\pi = 66\pi$.
4. **C. $16\sqrt{3} + 16$** The surface area of a pyramid with a four-sided base is $SA = \frac{1}{2}ps + B$, where $p$ is the perimeter of the base, $s$ is the slant height of a face of the pyramid, and $B$ is the area of the base. The pyramid described in this problem has a square base with sides of length 4, so both the perimeter ($p$) and the area of its base ($B$) are 16. Each face of the pyramid is an equilateral triangle, the height of which represents the slant height ($s$) of the pyramid. Divide one of the equilateral triangles into two 30:60:90 triangles and use the side length ratio $x : x\sqrt{3} : 2x$ to determine the slant height of the pyramid. Since the base of one of these 30:60:90 triangles is 2 (half the length of a side of the pyramid's base) and the hypotenuse is 4 (the length of a side of the equilateral triangles making up the faces of the pyramid), the height of each 30:60:90 triangle (and, therefore, of each equilateral triangle face of the pyramid) is $2\sqrt{3}$. That is the slant height ($s$) of the pyramid as well. Now, plug in all of the relevant measures and solve: $\frac{1}{2}ps + B = \frac{1}{2} \times (16 \times 2\sqrt{3}) + 16 = 16\sqrt{3} + 16$.

5. **D. 512$\pi$** The circumference is $16\pi$ so the diameter is 16, and the radius is 8. The surface area is $4\pi r^2 = 256\pi$. The paint covers the ball twice, so multiply by 2 to get $512\pi$.
6. **D. 224** A closet is in the shape of a rectangular solid. To find the volume, multiply: $V = lwh = 7 \times 4 \times 8 = 224$ cubic feet.
7. **C. 48$\pi$** The cone has a surface area of $\pi rs = \pi \times 3 \times 10 = 30\pi$ (don't include the base of the cone). A sphere with radius 3 has a surface area of $4\pi r^2 = 4 \times \pi \times 3^2 = 36\pi$. The surface area of the ice cream is half of that, or $18\pi$. Add to get $30\pi + 18\pi = 48\pi$.
8. **C. 8:1** The formula for the volume of a sphere is $V = \frac{4}{3}\pi r^3$. Find the volumes of both spheres and simplify the ratio between those volumes. Or think about it this way: the ratio of the volume of Sphere A to that of Sphere B would be as follows.
$(\frac{4}{3}\pi \times 2^3)$ to $(\frac{4}{3}\pi \times 1^3)$
Find the value of the exponents:
$(\frac{4}{3}\pi \times 8)$ to $(\frac{4}{3}\pi \times 1)$
You know that you can simplify a ratio by dividing both sides of the ratio by a number. Here, divide both sides by $\frac{4}{3}\pi$ to get:
8 to 1.
9. **A. 1458** The height of all three boxes is 9 in, the length is 18 in, and the width is 9 in. The total volume is $18 \times 9 \times 9 = 1458$.
10. **B. 500** Since Max hikes directly east after hiking directly due north, he has made a 90° turn. The distances hiked therefore form a right triangle. The legs are 300 and 400 yards. To solve for the hypotenuse, use the Pythagorean relationship:
$$a^2 + b^2 = c^2$$
$$300^2 + 400^2 = c^2$$
$$90{,}000 + 160{,}000 = c^2$$
$$250{,}000 = c^2$$
$$500 = c$$
A quicker solution would be to notice that the distances form a large triangle with sides in the 3:4:5 ratio. Then it is easy to see that the hypotenuse of a triangle with legs of 300 and 400 yards is 500 yards.
11. **C. 168** The volume of the container as drawn in the diagram is $V = lwh = 9 \text{ in} \times 7 \text{ in} \times 12 \text{ in} = 756 \text{ in}^3$. If you increase the length by 2 inches, the volume is $11 \text{ in} \times 7 \text{ in} \times 12 \text{ in} = 924 \text{ in}^3$. Find the difference: $924 \text{ in}^3 - 756 \text{ in}^3 = 168 \text{ in}^3$. You can solve the problem more easily by multiplying the added length by the width and height: $2(7)(12) = 168$.
12. **D. $x^2 = 15^2 - 6^2$** Use the Pythagorean relationship. If $a^2 + b^2 = c^2$ and $c$ is the hypotenuse, then $b^2 = c^2 - a^2$, and $x^2 = 15^2 - 6^2$.
13. **C. 36** Use the formula for finding the perimeter of a rectangle. Let $3w$ = length.
$P = 2l + 2w$
$96 = 2(3w) + 2w$
$96 = 8w$
$w = 12$
So the width is 12 inches, and the length is $3 \times 12 = 36$ inches.
14. **D. 1120$\pi$** The circumference is $16\pi$, so $r = 8$ cm. A cone-shaped party hat does not have a base, so $SA = \pi rs = 56\pi$. Multiply by 20 to get $1120\pi$.
15. **A. 3.43** To find the area of the shaded region, subtract the area of the circle from the area of the square. One side of the square is equivalent to the diameter of the circle. The radius is 2, so the diameter—and each side of the square—is 4. So $A = 4^2 - \pi \times 2^2 \approx 3.43$.
16. **B. 1,560** You may find it helpful to draw a sketch of the room. Two walls measure 40 by 12 feet. Two measure 25 by 12 feet. Find the total area: $2 \times 40 \times 12 + 2 \times 25 \times 12 = 960 + 600 = 1{,}560$.
17. **C. 12,000** Use the formula $V = lwh$. Multiply: $40 \times 25 \times 12 = 12{,}000$.
18. **A. 4** Begin by finding the total surface area of all three pyramids. The formula for the surface area of a pyramid is $SA = \frac{1}{2}ps + B$. For each pyramid, plug in the values and calculate:
Top left pyramid:
$SA = \frac{1}{2}(2 + 2 + 2 + 2)(3) + (2 \times 2)$
$= 16$
Top right pyramid:
$SA = \frac{1}{2}(3 + 3 + 3 + 3)(6) + (3 \times 3)$
$= 45$
Bottom pyramid:
$SA = \frac{1}{2}(4 + 4 + 4 + 4)(4) + (4 \times 4)$
$= 48$
Thus, the total surface area for all three pyramids is:
$16 + 45 + 48 = 109$
The problem states that Laura needs one tube of paint for each 30 square inches. Thus, she needs $109 \div 30 \approx 3.6$. In order to finish her project, she should buy four tubes of paint.
19. **C. 148.8** Because the triangles are similar, the lengths of their legs are proportional. Set up a proportion: $\frac{50}{120} = \frac{62}{x}$, where $x$ is the length of the bridge. Then cross-multiply and solve:
$x = 120 \times 62 \div 50 = 148.8$.
20. **A. $m\angle 5 = 60°$** $m\angle ABC$ must equal 60° because the sum of the interior angles of a triangle is 180°, and you know that $\angle BAC$ measures 30° and $\angle ACB$ measures 90°. 180° = 30° + 90° + 60°. Since lines $P$ and $Q$ are parallel, triangles $ABC$ and $ADE$ are similar. Angle 5, or $\angle ADE$, corresponds to $\angle ABC$; therefore, $\angle 5$ measures 60°.
21. **D. $m\angle 3 + m\angle 6 = 180°$** Lines $P$ and $Q$ are parallel, so AD is a transversal. You know that $\angle 3$ and $\angle 4$ are adjacent supplementary angles, so their sum is 180°. $\angle 4$ and $\angle 6$ are corresponding angles, so they have equal measures. Since the sum of $m\angle 3$ and $m\angle 4$ is 180° and $m\angle 6 = m\angle 4$, the sum of $m\angle 3$ and $m\angle 6$ must be 180° as well.
22. **45** Imagine drawing a line from the top of the man to the end of his shadow and another line from the top of the building to the end of the shadow's building. Once you do so, you have two similar right triangles. Let $x$ equal the height of the building, and set up a proportion: $\frac{3.5}{26.25} = \frac{6}{x}$. Cross multiply and solve:
$26.25 \times 6 \div 3.5 = 45$.
23. **24** It may help to make a sketch. The area of the parallelogram is $6(10) = 60$ sq cm, so the area of the triangle is also 60 sq cm. To find the base of the triangle, use the formula for finding the area of a triangle and solve for base.
$60 = \frac{1}{2}b(5)$
$60 = 2.5b$
$24 = b$

# SOCIAL STUDIES ANSWERS AND EXPLANATIONS

## Social Studies Skills

### Lesson 1: Determine Central Idea and Draw Conclusions

#### Practice 1, page 439

1. **C. the characteristics of Greek tragedy** The passage describes tragedy as "central to Greek culture" and supports this point with details about the plots, staging, characters, and themes of Greek tragedy.
2. **D. The main character in Greek drama has a tragic flaw that causes his downfall.** Choice (D) cites one of the details the author uses to describe the characteristics of Greek tragedy. The other choices are all too broad (choice (A)) or misrepresent what the passage actually said (choices (B) and (C)).
3. **A. Ancient Greeks did not expect to see an original story each time they attended the theater.** Choice (A) is the only answer choice supported by information in the passage. The writer tells you that tragedies "told stories familiar from myths and epics," so it must have been the case that theatergoers knew the general story that would be acted out.
4. **D. Where do the incomes of senior citizens come from?** Choice (D) is correct because the graph tells you the sources of income for American senior citizens. The graph doesn't give any actual dollar amounts, nor does it state how many senior citizens there are in the U.S. You would need those numbers to answer the questions in choices (A), (B), and (C).
5. **B. Social Security benefits are the most widespread means of support for most senior citizens.** Each bar in the graph represents the percentage of all seniors who receive some of their income from that source. Since the Social Security bar is the tallest (representing more than 86% of all seniors), choice (B) must be true based on the graph.

### Lesson 2: Interpret Words and Ideas

#### Practice 2, page 441

1. **C. political and social instability in some Northern European countries** In the first paragraph of the passage, the author mentions "riots, civil unrest, and open rebellion" as some of the factors that pushed German citizens to migrate. Those events are examples of "political and social instability," so choice (C) is correct.
2. **D. a painting of pioneers settling and farming productive prairie land** In the passage, the author discusses "abundance" in the second paragraph, giving examples of the kinds of optimistic messages that attracted people to the U.S. The image of pioneers opening up productive farmland is symbolic of the economic opportunity promised to 19th century immigrants to the U.S., so choice (D) is correct.
3. **C. a growth in the population of the United States** In the first paragraph, the author tells you that the number of immigrants arriving in the U.S. between 1820 and 1870 was greater than the entire U.S. population just 10 years before that time period. You can conclude from the passage that the U.S. population grew.
4. **B. Internal migration led to overgrazing.** According to the timeline, aggressive agriculture occurred prior to 1930 and the "black blizzards," caused in part by overgrazing, began in 1931. Internal migration did not begin until around 1933. Inferring that internal migration (which began later) caused overgrazing (which had already occurred) would be illogical, so choice (B) is correct.
5. **C. depleted topsoil** The "aggressive, mechanized farming techniques" that depleted the topsoil in the American Midwest and Southern plains occurred prior to and contributed to the dust storms and "black blizzards" that characterize the Great Dust Bowl. Internal migration (choice (B)) and failed farms (choice (C)) were results, not causes, of the Dust Bowl.

### Lesson 3: Analyze Author's Purpose and Point of View

#### Practice 3, page 443

1. **C. propagandistic** Page 442 explains that propaganda uses emotional language to influence readers' behavior. Here, asking the readers to "have a part in Victory" is just such language.
2. **C. Citizens who plant war gardens help supply the war effort with essential resources.** As the passage explains, war gardens were encouraged so that, with citizens supplying more of their own food, the government could use its limited resources to feed and equip soldiers, sailors, and airmen. Choice (C) paraphrases this nicely.
3. **A. describe war gardens and explain their popularity in the United States** The author's tone is neutral and explanatory; he or she simply wants to explain what war gardens were and why they were popular during the two world wars. The author is not advocating a point of view (choice (B)), trying to compare or contrast the U.S. with any other country (choice (C)), or arguing against anyone else's position (choice (D)).
4. **C. a cancer** By using a frightening and often fatal disease such as "cancer" to describe the impact of the proposed regulations, the citizen is making an emotional comparison. The analogy is especially aggressive given that the issue addresses health and safety.

### Lesson 4: Evaluate Author's Reasoning and Evidence

#### Practice 4, page 445

1. **A. Damming the Mekong could solve Cambodia's energy problems.** The author argues for cooperation among Cambodia and its neighboring

countries, all of which share the Mekong river. The reason this is important, the author asserts, is because hydroelectric power from the Mekong would help solve Cambodia's energy problems. Nowhere in the argument, however, does the author support this contention.

2. **B. Strikes have a detrimental impact on workers.** The cartoon shows a laborer using a strike as a means of "cutting off" production, depicted as a tree branch. The joke is that the worker sits on the wrong side of the branch he's cutting. Once the worker is successful in cutting off production, the cartoonist implies, he will fall to the ground along with production. Choice (B) neatly sums up the cartoonist's point.
3. **D. Ancient Greece pioneered democracy.** The one reason the author gives for believing that Ancient Greece was the greatest of the early civilization is that it was the birthplace of democracy. Thus, choice (D) is correct. Choice (A) is the author's opinion, not a fact supporting that opinion. Choices (B) and (C) are both reasons that ancient Babylon and Egypt (and not the author's favorite, Greece) might be considered great.
4. **B. The Constitution grants more power to the federal government than did the Articles of Confederation.** In each category compared in the chart, the federal government has more power under the Constitution than it had under the Articles of Confederation, so choice (B) is a valid inference, though it is not explicitly stated anywhere on the chart. All three wrong answers cite specific facts stated in the chart.

## Lesson 5: Analyze Relationships Between Materials

### Practice 5.1, page 447

1. **A. housing and food** Study the circle graph (pie chart) to see that the two largest portions are labeled with white (33%) and vertical lines (20%). Checking the legend to the right shows that these "slices" correspond to housing and food, respectively.
2. **D. Brazil has a higher divorce rate than Mexico.** This bar chart directly supports choice (D): Brazil's divorce rate is 0.6 per thousand, while Mexico's is 0.4 per thousand. Choice (B) is incorrect because this chart shows five countries in the Western Hemisphere, not all of them. One of the countries not shown on the chart may have a divorce rate even lower than Mexico's. Choice (C) is incorrect because this chart conveys nothing about how divorce rates have changed over time.
3. **D. fluctuated** As you read the line graph left to right, showing the change over time, you see that percentage of votes for third-party presidential candidates went up and down multiple times, so "fluctuated" is accurate.
4. **C. Third party candidates have never captured more than 10 percent of the popular vote in any presidential election.** The statement in choice (C) is disproved by 1968 (14 percent) and 1992 (more than 19 percent).
5. **C. how agriculture spread in the Americas** The map shows two places at which agriculture originated independently (indicated by black stars) and where agriculture spread out from those two points (indicated by the white arrows). The map shows no political boundaries (choice (A)) or physical features (choice (B)) of the Americas, nor does it claim to name all of the ancient civilizations on the two continents (choice (D)).
6. **B. Both the Andes civilization and Mesoamerica domesticated beans.** Check right below the names of the two civilizations named on the map and you'll find the crops they learned to grow. "Beans" is the only crop listed for both the Andes and Mesoamerican groups.

### Practice 5.2, page 449

1. **D. Sea otters have been able to live in habitats from which they were once eliminated.** Choice (D) is directly supported by the third paragraph of the passage, which refers to successful "programs to reintroduce the sea otter into previously populated areas." Choice (C) is incorrect because, although the passage says that the sea otters in California have regained about two-thirds of their former habitat range, it does not indicate that they have reached two-thirds of their former population numbers. Choices (A) and (B) are not mentioned at all in the passage.
2. **D. The current range of the sea otter in California is larger than what it was in 1911.** According to the passage, the sea otter's range in 1911 "was limited . . . to a small area around Monterrey Bay." The map makes it clear that the sea otter's range now extends significantly to both the north and south of Monterrey Bay. Putting the information from the passage together with that from the map shows that choice (D) must be true.
3. **C. Without conservation efforts and reintroduction programs, the range of sea otters in California would be smaller than what is shown on the map.** In the third paragraph of the passage, the author states that conservation and reintroduction programs "have contributed to" the expansion of the sea otter's habitat range in California. This directly supports the statement in choice (C).

## Lesson 6: Interpret Data and Statistics

### Practice 6, page 451

1. **C. What percent of residents were 50 or over?** To calculate the percentage of New Mexico residents age 50 and over, you first find the number of residents 50 and over and divide that by the total number of residents. You can find the total number of residents who are at least age 50 by adding the categories for

50–64 and 65 & over. You are given the total number of residents so you can solve for this question. Because age brackets are grouped and exact ages aren't given, it is not possible to solve for choice (A). You cannot solve for choice (B) because the bracket "under 18" contains teenagers and nonteenagers with no distinction between the two. The chart gives no reasoning, only numerical information, so choice (D) is also incorrect.

2. **B. the average margin of victory was higher in years when a Democrat won than in years when a Republican won.** In both years in which a Republican won the presidential election (2000 and 2004) the final electoral vote count was very close. In each of the four years in which a Democrat won (1992, 1996, 2008, and 2012) the Democratic candidate captured a much larger portion of the electoral vote. Thus, choice (B) is supported by the graph.

3. **C. 1920** Of the years shown on the graph, 1920 is the point when the rural and urban populations are closest in number. Prior to 1920, the rural population was much larger than the urban population. After 1920, the urban population begins to be much larger than the rural population.

4. **C. continued to grow, but at decreasing rates** The rural population continued to increase during every decade shown in the graph. However, the increase in population growth was less in the later decades than in the earlier decades, as evidenced by the smaller differences between the heights of the bars in the later decades than the earlier ones.

## Social Studies Skills Practice Questions, pages 452–455

1. **B. The unemployment rate declined consistently until shortly before the war's end.** Checking the timeline, you can see that World War II began in 1939 and ended in 1945. Unemployment went down every year between 1939 and 1944, and rose just slightly in 1945. Thus, choice (B)'s description of the war's impact on unemployment is correct.

2. **A. the stock market crash** Immediately after the stock market crash in 1929, unemployment increases dramatically and directly until 1933. That makes choice (A) correct. After 1933, unemployment declines gradually until the end of the war, and the decline is interrupted by a small increase during 1937-1938.

3. **D. The Seneca Falls Convention was a shocking event that undermined the nature of women.** There is no objective way to prove that something is "shocking and unnatural." Those words reveal that the statement in choice (D) was the opinion of one newspaper's editors.

4. **D. The Seneca Falls Convention was important in the fight for women's rights.** The passage's primary purpose is to explain how the women's movement "gained strength" at the Seneca Falls Convention.

5. **A. More than half of the reported cases of human plague in the United States between 1970 and 2010 were reported in four states.** Even if you don't recognize the four states in question as Arizona, California, Colorado, and New Mexico, the map clearly shows the overwhelming concentration of reported plague cases as occurring there. Choice (A) is justified by the information in the map.

6. **C. Several cases of plague were reported on the East Coast of the United States between 1970 and 2010.** The statement in choice (C) is clearly false given the information in the map. No cases of plague were recorded east of Illinois during the time period depicted by the map.

7. **D. The effects of the cotton gin on the cotton industry actually led to an increased demand for slaves in the South.** The fact stated in choice (D) is directly supported by the end of the passage where the writer explains the effects of the cotton gin: "with the boom in the cotton industry, more slaves were used to pick cotton at a faster rate."

8. **C. In most years, the percent population increase in South Dakota was greater than that in North Dakota.** Choice (C) is correct. In seven of the eleven years shown (every year from 01-02 to 07-08 ) South Dakota's annual population increase was greater than that of North Dakota. The increases were approximately equal in 08-09, and North Dakota's increase was greater in the remaining three years. Choices (A) and (B) make statements about the populations of these states, but the graph only contains information about *percent increase,* or proportional increase, of the population.

9. **D. A smaller percentage of voters turned out for each midterm election than turned out for each presidential election.** The entire midterm election line graph falls below the line graph for the presidential elections, meaning that in each instance, the percentage of voters who turned out for the midterm election was smaller than the percentage that turned out for the presidential election.

10. **B. The average voter turnout for midterm elections was approximately how much lower than that for presidential elections for the years 1980–2008?** You can find the average voter turnout for each type of election by taking the average of each line graph. Dividing the average voter turnout for midterm elections by the average voter turnout for presidential elections and multiplying by 100 will answer the question in choice (B). The remaining answer choices all ask for the reasoning behind a given circumstance, and no rationale for the numbers can be determined using only the numbers themselves.

11. **C. "Most of our qualified teachers are underpaid"** Choice (C) is a value judgment. A fact is a statement that can be proven or disproven by direct experience or objective verification. An opinion is a statement of belief or judgment. President Johnson uses both facts and opinions to support his contention that there is a crisis in education, including statistical facts (choices (A), (B), and (D)) and the value judgment that teachers should be paid more.
12. **D. "Our Duty Is to Educate Our Children"** The excerpt is about the importance of educating every child in the country. It does not give a history of education, as stated in choice (A), nor does it mention the specifics of education in Michigan, as stated in choice (B). While the cost of college education is briefly mentioned in the second paragraph, it is simply a detail, not the main topic of the passage, so choice (C) is incorrect.
13. **C. The Union states had significant population advantages in the war.** It is clear that in all three graphs, the Confederate states were at a population disadvantage in comparison to the North at the start of the Civil War.
14. **B. What percentage of the total population of the United States was eligible for the military?** The percentage of the total population eligible for the military can be found by obtaining the total population and the total population eligible for the military. Both can be found by using the charts. There is no information given about the total number of people that actually fought in the military, so answer choice (A) cannot be determined. Choices (C) and (D) both ask for reasoning behind something, which cannot be determined from the numbers alone.

## U.S. History

### Lesson 1: Exploration, Colonialism, and the American Revolution

#### Practice 1, page 457

1. **C. the Spanish** According to the map and the key, Spain had the southernmost colony along the east coast of what would eventually become the United States.
2. **B. The English established several colonies in the New World.** The map shows several English colonies along the New England coast and in what is now Virginia and Maryland.
3. **D. Haitian refugees who fled to the U.S. to escape a dictatorship** Like the early colonists, the Haitian refugees of the mid- and late 1900s came to the United States seeking freedom from political persecution.
4. **B. increased British taxes and restrictions on the colonies** The fourth and fifth sentences of paragraph 4 link increased taxes and restrictions to the outbreak of the American Revolution.
5. **B. They were concerned about the government becoming tyrannical.** The first amendment guarantees citizens' rights to pressure their government. The passage explains that the framers of the U.S. Constitution did not want the government to become overly powerful. While choices (A) and (C) were both rights listed amongst the guarantees of the First Amendment, they do not explain *why* the Framers listed them. Choice (B) discusses their motivations and is correct.

### Lesson 2: Westward Expansion, the Civil War, and Reconstruction

#### Practice 2, page 459

1. **D. whether slavery should be permitted in territories in the West** This is implied in the third and fourth paragraphs of the passage. Choice (B) is incorrect because the fourth paragraph says that Abraham Lincoln promised to halt the spread of slavery, not to end it where it already existed.
2. **C. To balance the admission of Missouri, they agreed to a compromise in which Maine was admitted as a free state.** The third paragraph of the passage describes how the U.S. government tried to maintain a balance of power between the North and the South by adding states in pairs: one slave state and one free state. Since Missouri was a slave state, the most likely response of Northerners would be to propose the addition of a free state. (Indeed, Maine and Missouri were the 23rd and 24th states to join the United States.)
3. **D. concluded with the reunification of the nation** The information in the question indicates that North and South Vietnam were reunited under the Communists at the end of the Vietnam War. The passage implies that at the end of the U.S. Civil War, the North and the South again were united under the United States federal government.
4. **C. In 1868, many African Americans served in the government of South Carolina.** There are more than 20 African Americans included in this composite photograph of the South Carolina legislature. The other choices are opinions that cannot be confirmed by the photograph.
5. **A. Over the course of Reconstruction, African Americans in the South gained and then lost political power.** The number of African Americans in the composite photograph of the South Carolina state legislature of 1868 indicates that near the beginning of the Reconstruction period, African Americans had considerable political power. The last paragraph of the passage on page 458 states that by the 1870s, whites were preventing African Americans from exercising their newly won right to vote. This indicates that African Americans were losing political power as Reconstruction ended.

## Lesson 3: Industrialization, Immigration, and the Progressive Era

### Practice 3, page 461

1. **B. an increase in manufacturing** By definition, industrialization is related to increased manufacturing. This meaning is implied in the passage in paragraphs one and two.
2. **C. the development of the Bessemer process, which made it easier to produce steel** The first paragraph of the passage relates rapid industrialization to the invention of new industrial processes. The Bessemer process was one such process. It made steel more readily available for tools, railroads, construction, and other uses.
3. **C. cooperation with others to improve worker safety** The fourth paragraph indicates that union workers pledged to work together (cooperate) for better working conditions. The passage states that better working conditions include improved worker safety.
4. **D. fairness** The fifth paragraph discusses the Progressive Era. The fact that reformers were working to improve conditions for poor people and to give people a greater voice in government indicates that fairness was a strong ideal for them.
5. **B. Asia and the Americas** The second circle graph indicates that, in the years 2000–2009, 77 percent of persons obtaining legal resident status came from Asia and the Americas.
6. **C. The student failed to consider the different totals represented by each pie chart.** When comparing percentages that are based on two different totals, the percentages cannot be directly compared.

## Lesson 4: The United States as an Emerging World Power

### Practice 4, page 463

1. **D. Military** The building of a naval base indicates that the correct category is "military."
2. **B. In World War II, the Allies included England, France, and Russia.** The author assumes that you realize that the Allies of World War II included the same major powers as the Allies in World War I. If you do not recognize this unstated assumption, you will not understand who fought whom in World War II.
3. **C. Unemployment fell after the start of the New Deal and continued to fall as the U.S. entered World War II.** The graph shows a decline in the unemployment rate after the New Deal went into effect in 1934. It shows that unemployment went up in 1938 but then dropped after that and dropped considerably after the U.S. entry into World War II in 1941.
4. **D. America took a strong leadership role during and after World War II.** The paragraph focuses on the role the United States played during and after World War II. The other choices are details from the paragraph or they bring up information not included in the paragraph.

## Lesson 5: The Cold War and the Civil Rights Era

### Practice 5, page 465

1. **D. no direct combat** The first paragraph of the passage implies that the name "Cold War" was used because there was no direct fighting.
2. **C. The buildup of nuclear arms increases fear and instability, not peace.** The statement about peace and stability made by the man on the right in the bottom frame of the cartoon is supposed to be ironic. The cartoonist's mention of the man's trembling arms suggests that the situation is not stable, and that perhaps we should be afraid.
3. **C. Americans were in complete agreement about pulling out of Vietnam.** Paragraph one states that even when defeat for South Vietnam seemed fairly certain, a few Americans still wanted to continue contributing to the fighting. Therefore, it is an overstatement to say that Americans were in complete agreement that pulling out of Vietnam was the right thing to do.
4. **B. petitioning for a city ordinance requiring those selling real estate to select a buyer without regard to race** Paragraph three states that the aim of the civil rights movement was to end segregation and discrimination in the United States. Preventing the selective selling of real estate was one important way civil rights activists worked to end discrimination, making decreased segregation possible.
5. **A. Reliance on technology has increased pollution.** This is a conclusion—a general statement about a topic. The other choices are details—facts or examples—that support this conclusion.

## U.S. History Practice Questions, pages 466–469

1. **B. Although the Cherokee adopted many aspects of white culture, they were driven off their ancestral lands.** This statement is the only one with a large enough scope to be considered a conclusion. The other choices are details that are either included in, related to, or not based on the time line.
2. **A. If the government can't protect us from white settlers here, now, how could it protect us from whites moving west in the future?** This question shows the lack of logic in the government's claim that location was what made it difficult to protect Cherokee rights. Location had nothing to do with the government's lack of protection of Cherokee land in the South. The government did not have the political will to enforce laws protecting the Cherokee.
3. **D. equal rights and opportunities for women** Adams's statements that women are not inferior and her invention of the term *Lordess* both indicate that she advocated equality for women.
4. **A. West Virginia** The map shows that West Virginia was a slave state loyal to the Union.

5. **A. The nation's capital was located nearby.** If the nation's capital, located adjacent to the state of Maryland, had been surrounded by Confederate states, it would have been extremely difficult for the U.S. army to defend it. This would have given a great edge to the Confederacy during the Civil War. The other choices are untrue, irrelevant, or not verifiable by the map.
6. **D. to weaken the South by enlisting former slaves in the Union army** This was implied by the text of the Proclamation that is quoted. None of the other choices are supported by the text.
7. **C. Voting Rights Act of 1965.** The chart explains that this act prohibited literacy (reading) tests for voting.
8. **C. African Americans were granted the vote soon after the Civil War, but laws enforcing these rights had to be passed a century later.** This is implied by the passage of the 15th Amendment in 1870 and by the passage of the Voting Rights Act of 1965. Congress would not have passed the later law if the 15th Amendment were being upheld and enforced. Choice (A) is true, based on the chart, but is not a summary of the information in the chart.
9. **B. They both prohibited the legal separation of people by race in public places.** The chart shows that both the 1875 and the 1964 Civil Rights Acts banned racial segregation in public places.
10. **D. The telephone was the greatest electrical invention ever.** This statement is said to have been made by leading scientists of the time; this is not in the author's voice. It is the only opinion. Choices (A), (B), and (C) are all facts stated in the passage.
11. **B. the framers of the U.S. Constitution** The clothes of the men in the picture indicate that this cartoon is set in the late 1700s. Impeachment is discussed in the caption. Impeachment was a provision that the framers of the Constitution included in order to prevent the kind of abuse of presidential power carried out by Nixon. Impeachment of elected officials was not discussed in the Declaration of Independence, which laid out the reasons for the United States' independence from Great Britain, so choice (A) is incorrect.
12. **A. the pursuit of justice** By investigating the circumstances of Watergate, Congress was trying to make sure that the nation's laws were carried out.
13. **C. the escalation and failure of the Vietnam War** Of the choices listed, only (C) describes an event just prior to the Watergate scandal. The bloodshed and failure of the Vietnam War caused many people to question authority, including the government, and to question decisions made by the government.
14. **C. 1,000,000** The scale on the vertical axis of the bar graph shows that population is measured in millions. The bar for Cuba stands one unit high. This means that about 1,000,000 people of Cuban descent lived in the U.S. in 1990.
15. **B. Mexico** The bar graph shows that most people in the U.S. who are Hispanic originally came from Mexico. Therefore, Mexico is the most likely nation of origin of the unknown family.

## Civics and Government

### Lesson 1: Historic Basis for U.S. System

**Practice 1, page 471**

1. **D. aristocracy** In an aristocracy, the laws are made by members of the ruling class, who acquire their land, titles, and power through inheritance.
2. **B. They were concerned about protecting the rights of individuals.** According to the passage on the previous page, the Founding Fathers were influenced by the Enlightenment philosophers, who did place importance on the rights of the individual.
3. **C. Parliament of England** Similar to the United States Congress, the parliamentary system in England allows for citizens to elect representatives to a lawmaking body.
4. **D. England during the Age of Enlightenment** According to the passage on page 470, England adopted a bill of rights for the individual during the Enlightenment. This action limited the monarchy's power over the individual.
5. **D. The president would become the chief lawmaker.** In a parliamentary democracy, the majority party in the Parliament appoints the president. Since the Parliament is the lawmaking body of government, the President would become the chief lawmaker. Nothing in the text indicates whether this would make the office of the president more or less powerful than it currently is, so choices (A) and (B) are unsupported.

### Lesson 2: Constitutional Government

**Practice 2, page 473**

1. **B. elected representatives exercising government power on behalf of citizens** According to the first paragraph of the passage, the key characteristic of a republic is elected officials governing for the voters.
2. **C. The details of government would be worked out in the future, as the need arose, within the framework of the Constitution.** The leaders who drafted the Constitution were wise enough to realize that they could not anticipate every eventuality, so instead of trying to cover everything in the Constitution, they made it a general framework within which specific future decisions and laws could be made.
3. **C. the power of an office, not an individual** Roosevelt's long tenure worried many people as they saw his power growing with time. They pursued term

limits to prevent any individual from amassing too much power as president.

4. **D. The U.S. Supreme Court declaring an Illinois state law unconstitutional** The supremacy clause asserts the supremacy of federal law when it conflicts with state law. Therefore, the declaration that a state law is unconstitutional is an exercise of the supremacy clause.
5. **A. State governments do not usually act together.** The third and fourth methods of passing a constitutional amendment both require concerted action by state governments. Therefore, choice (A) would explain why those methods have never been used. Choice (B) and (D) are contradicted by information in the chart. Choice (C) repeats information in the chart, but does not provide a useful explanation.

## Lesson 3: Levels and Branches of Government

### Practice 3, page 475

1. **A. division of power between national and state governments** According to the second paragraph of the passage on page 474, a federalist form of government divides power between the national and state levels of government.
2. **D. the State Department** The State Department is part of the executive branch; its head is a member of the president's cabinet. The Democratic National Committee, choice (A), is not part of the government at all. Choice (B) is part of Congress, and therefore part of the legislative branch. Courts, choice (C), are in the judicial branch.
3. **A. Federal judges need not worry about pleasing their constituents in order to be reelected.** Because they do not need to please any constituents in order to be reelected, federal judges can preside without worrying about making unpopular decisions. This leaves them freer to be impartial judges of the law.
4. **B. six; two** A senator is a legislator who serves a six-year term. A representative is a legislator who serves a two-year term.
5. **B. a member of Congress** Although this person subscribes to the idea that the government is divided into three branches, he can only think of one of them—the one to which he belongs. Since he is probably in the legislative branch, he is likely to be a member of Congress. The way the desks are arranged and the way the man is standing to make his point are visual cues that the setting of the cartoon is Congress.
6. **A. mutual respect and convenience** Although in theory each state could insist on its own laws being followed even by residents of other states, in practice that would be too cumbersome. So on many matters, such as driver's licenses, states respect one another's laws because it is convenient to do so.

## Lesson 4: The Electoral System

### Practice 4, page 477

1. **C. receiving a majority in the Electoral College** According to the second paragraph of the passage on page 476 a president must have a majority in the Electoral College to be elected.
2. **A. Exit polls may be inaccurate if the people polled are not representative of the political unit as a whole or if the election is very close.** It is more likely that a poll will be wrong if an unrepresentative sample is used or if the election is very close. Under those circumstances it is hazardous to call an election based on exit poll results, as was shown in the 2000 presidential election, in which the media gave Florida's vote first to Gore, then to Bush, and only hours later declared the state too close to call.
3. **D. Two city council members are on a ballot to determine which one will run for mayor as a Democrat.** A primary is an election to choose among candidates of the same party. The winner of the primary then faces an opponent of another political party in the general election.
4. **B. In total, individuals contributed a greater dollar amount to House candidates than they did to Senate candidates.** Although Senatorial candidates received a higher percentage (greater by 4%) of their contributions from individual donors, the total dollar amount received by the House candidates was much higher (greater by approximately $350,000,000). Therefore, the total dollar amount of individual contributions received by the House candidates was ultimately greater than that received by the Senate candidates.
5. **A. In 2010, self-funding was a larger source of funds for Senate candidates than it was for House candidates.** The Senate candidates' own contributions accounted for 13% of the total Senate Candidates' Funds while the House Candidates' own contributions accounted for only 6% of the total House Candidates' Fund. In addition, calculations based on the total amount of funds reveal that Senate candidates spent more total dollars on self-funding than did House candidates.

## Lesson 5: The Role of the Citizen

### Practice 5, page 479

1. **B. The U.S. Constitution** According to the third paragraph of the passage, the Constitution sets forth the rights of citizens.
2. **A. resident alien** Because she moved here permanently as the wife of an American citizen, Louvina is a resident alien and will remain so until she qualifies for citizenship through naturalization.
3. **C. They would become enemy aliens.** If the country of aliens residing in the United States declares war on the United States, that nation becomes an enemy state, and the aliens become enemy aliens.
4. **B. privacy** The protection against unreasonable search and seizure is essentially a protection

of citizens' privacy rights. The government must demonstrate a good reason before it is allowed to search or seize property.

5. **C. If the 2012 presidential election is representative of elections generally in the United States, voter turnout increases with age.** This is the only statement general enough to be a conclusion. All the other options are details from the graph that support this conclusion.

### Civics and Government Practice Questions, pages 480–483

1. **B. In 2013, a different major party controlled the House than controlled the Senate.** According to the numbers of the 113th Congress, the Republicans had majority control in the House and the Democrats had majority control in the Senate. Choice (A) is too broad to be a summary of this chart which focuses on political divisions. The conclusions in choices (C) and (D) require more information than the chart provides.
2. **B. Bill of Rights of the U.S. Constitution, which guarantees citizens certain rights,** Like the Magna Carta, the Bill of Rights of the U.S. Constitution accords citizens certain rights and protections. Note that the scope of the Bill of Rights is broader in that it protects the rights of all citizens, not just a special group, as the Magna Carta did.
3. **C. a $3,000 contribution to a party fund for TV ads on political issues** Of all the choices, this is the only donation that is going to a political party fund rather than to a specific candidate, so it is a "soft money" contribution.
4. **A. People were less aware of soft money because disclosure was not required.** During the 1980s, political parties did not have to reveal the amount and sources of their soft money contributions, so the extent of this type of campaign financing was not generally known. Only when a law was passed requiring disclosure did people become aware of the scale of soft money donations and so began to raise their concerns about the issue.
5. **C. Jill Stein won a greater percentage of the popular vote than of the electoral vote in 2012.** Jill Stein won 0.36% of the popular vote, but she did not win any electoral votes in the 2012 election.
6. **D. 2012 Presidential Election: Popular and Electoral Votes** This is the only option that covers the topic of the paragraph as well as that of the graphs.
7. **A. The board of election is the county, city, or town office responsible for local voting.** Nowhere in this excerpt from the voter's guide is the board of election defined or explained; the writer assumes that the reader knows what it is.
8. **B. The National Association of Manufacturers, which lobbies for businesses** This is the only answer choice that contains a group with common interests and goals that working to influence government policies. The other choices are either political parties or part of the executive branch.
9. **B. Most registered voters don't vote.** Despite the fact that voting is one of the obligations of citizens, in most elections, less than half of the nation's registered voters actually vote.
10. **C. civic duty** The cartoonist is appealing to voters to take their civic duty to vote more seriously.
11. **A. China, where the top leaders of the Communist party control the government** Of the national governments described, only China is an oligarchy, a government with rule by a small group of people. The other options are not oligarchies; they are either democracies or autocracies.
12. **A. retribution** These laws all embody the urge to take revenge on wrongdoers, or to exact retribution. The other principles underlie the modern criminal justice system and other modern legal systems.
13. **C. 32** Look for the map key to determine the symbol for death penalty states. According to the map, 18 states do not have the death penalty, so 32 out of 50 states have the death penalty.
14. **D. Two of the five states with the lowest per capita homicide rates have abolished the death penalty.** If that argument were correct, then the states with the lowest homicide rates should all be death penalty states, but that is not the case. Two states—Vermont and Hawaii—that have homicide rates among the lowest in the nation do not have the death penalty.
15. **C. The 1978 Panama treaties sold out U.S. interests to Panama.** Choice (C) states an opinion about the Panama treaties, not a fact that can be tested or proved. The word in the passage that signals an opinion is "believed."
16. **D. The mayor has ceremonial duties.** In both the mayor-council and the council-manager forms of city government, at least part of the time, the mayor plays a ceremonial role.

## Economics

### Lesson 1: Basic Economics Concepts

**Practice 1, page 485**

1. **B. to convert capital and raw materials into products and services** According to the first paragraph of the passage, labor transforms capital and raw materials into goods and services that may be sold.
2. **D. a plastic material** A producer good is something used in the production of a finished good. Of all the choices, only plastic is a producer good. The remaining choices are consumer goods, in other words, finished products.
3. **A. When the supply of houses is low, demand is high and sellers can raise their prices.** Because of the law of supply and demand, when the supply of houses is lower than the demand, sellers have more control over the terms of sale. In that situation, they can raise the

asking price. Because there are many potential buyers, chances are high that a seller will get a good price.

4. **B. Toys are not critical to a nation's economic and political well-being.** The U.S. government prefers the free-market system and generally provides price supports only for industries that are extremely important to the nation's welfare, such as agriculture and transportation.
5. **D. 16** On the vertical axis, locate $.30, and then see where a horizontal line drawn through $.30 would meet the sloping demand line. The answer is 16 apples.
6. **C. As the price of apples rises, Keisha buys fewer apples.** The demand line on the graph shows that Keisha's apple purchases are related to the price of apples. As the price rises, her demand for apples falls, and she buys fewer apples. None of the other choices is supported by the data on the graph.
7. **D. a beauty salon** According to the passage, a service business does not produce or sell tangible goods but instead offers services. Of all the choices, a beauty salon sells services; the remaining choices are businesses that produce goods for sale.

## Lesson 2: The U.S. Economic System

### Practice 2, page 487

1. **D. Monopolies shut out competition.** When a company has a monopoly on a market, it has great power to squelch competing firms that try to enter the market. This is implied in the last two sentences of the second paragraph of the passage.
2. **D. rising unemployment** Of all the economic factors listed, only high unemployment is associated with recessions, according to the third paragraph of the passage.
3. **A. Property owners have a stake in the future value of the property.** Since property can increase or decrease in value, its owner is motivated to do things that will maintain or increase its value.
4. **C. buying stock in a new company, such as an Internet startup** In general, investing in stocks is riskier than choice (A), saving money in a bank, or choice (B) buying a certificate of deposit [or CD, as they're commonly called]. Choice (C), investing in a startup that has no track record of turning a profit, is also riskier than choice (D), investing in a big, well-established company like Microsoft.
5. **D. Despite ups and downs, the gross domestic product generally increases over time.** Even though the gross domestic product rises and falls with business cycles, the general trend shown by the graph is for the gross domestic product to rise over the long term.
6. **A. They provide capital for businesses to grow.** One of the similarities between saving and investing in stocks is the ultimate use of the money. In both cases, the money allows businesses to start or expand operations as banks loan money they hold in savings accounts and the purchase of stock directly funds the company issuing the stock.

## Lesson 3: The Economy and the U.S. Government

### Practice 3, page 489

1. **D. registers revenues that exceed its expenditures** As implied in the first paragraph of the passage on page 488, a budget surplus occurs when the government takes in more tax and other revenue than it spends.
2. **C. cutting the federal income tax** If Congress cut the federal income tax, consumers would have more money to spend. This strategy has been used to stimulate the economy. The other choices would decrease consumer spending or have no direct effect on consumer spending.
3. **D. the air traffic control system** Like the federal highway system, the air traffic control system facilitates transportation, which is critical for economic activity.
4. **D. Both affect the amount of money circulating in the economy.** Fiscal and monetary policies are two tools the government uses to control the money supply. Increasing the money supply by lowering taxes or lowering interest rates stimulates the economy, and decreasing the money supply slows the economy.
5. **B. Buy back government securities.** According to the passage, policies that increase the amount of money in circulation are used to stimulate the economy.
6. **C. Our complex economy takes time to respond.** Since the economy is made up of the actions of millions of people, any Fed action takes time to have an overall effect that is measurable.

## Lesson 4: Labor and Consumer Issues

### Practice 4, page 491

1. **C. wages and benefits** According to the first paragraph of the passage on page 490, the money a worker earns plus the value of his or her benefits equals total compensation.
2. **A. Workers must learn skills throughout their lives to be prepared for changes in their industries.** This is the conclusion that the writer comes to after describing the steelworkers who lost their jobs and had to retrain when much of their industry moved overseas.
3. **C. woman buying a computer** Of all the choices, this is the only one in which a person is buying a product, so that person is a consumer.
4. **A. All for one and one for all.** When workers unite in labor unions, all of them together have the power to benefit each of the individual members. Similarly, each member supports the goals of the union as a whole.
5. **A. in 2000** The lower line on the graph shows the number of unemployed civilians. That line is at its lowest point at the year 2000.

6. **B. As the number of employed civilians rose steadily from 2003 to 2006, the number of unemployed slowly declined.** The graph shows that the number of employed civilians rose from about 137 million to about 144 million from 2003 to 2006. At the same time, the number of unemployed civilians dropped slightly—by about 2 million.

### Economics Practice Questions, pages 492–495

1. **B. the various types of resources needed for an economy to produce goods and services** According to the passage, the factors of production include all the resources—natural, human, and man-made—needed to produce products and services.
2. **D. entrepreneurs** In a communist nation with centralized economic decision making, there is no place for individual entrepreneurs. The government decides what will be produced and how it will be produced.
3. **A. an office building** An office building is a capital resource. Choice (B) is a natural resource, choice (C) is labor, and choice (D) is an entrepreneur.
4. **A. In a balanced budget, revenues equal expenditures.** This explanation of a balanced budget is a fact. The remaining choices express opinions held by many fiscal conservatives.
5. **A. More than half of all personal income was earned through work in February 2013.** According to the chart, the primary source of personal income in 2013 (approximately 60%) was from wages, salary, and other forms of employee compensation.
6. **D. an investor** The man in the plaid shorts represents an investor who buys and sells stock on the stock market.
7. **C. He is accustomed to stock market ups and downs.** Like the roller coaster in the background, stocks gain and lose value, often precipitously. The investor is calm because he has experienced the ups and downs of the stock market, so a roller coaster ride feels familiar to him.
8. **C. person who runs a home daycare center** This is a person who is running a business out of his home and so is self-employed. Therefore, no federal income tax is withheld from his earnings, and he must pay estimated tax.
9. **B. individualism** Individualism is one of the core values of a society with a free enterprise economic system, because each person is free to make his or her own economic decisions.
10. **A. 2009.** A budget deficit occurs when the government is spending more money than it is collecting in revenue. The larger the gap between the revenues and the expenditures, the larger the country's deficit. In the five-year span depicted on the chart, the largest gap between the revenues and expenditures exists in the year 2009.
11. **B. income tax returns and expense records** The federal budget is similar to a family budget; it differs primarily in scale. For a family, income tax returns provide documentation of revenues (income), and expense records such as grocery receipts and credit card bills provide a record of expenditures. None of the other choices includes records of both income and expenditures.
12. **D. The national network of interstate highways is paid for mostly by federal excise taxes.** Of all the choices, (D) contains the main details of the paragraph. Choices (A), (B), and (C) each focus on only one supporting detail.
13. **A. When cheaper imported goods force out U.S.-made goods, U.S. factory workers often lose their jobs.** Free trade may benefit the economy as a whole in the long term, but as the economy adapts, some individuals (in this case, factory workers) lose in the short term.
14. **B. The Federal Trade Commission** According to the chart, the Federal Trade Commission exists to protect consumers from misleading and/or fraudulent advertising.
15. **A. A shortage of the product** When a product's price falls below the equilibrium point, demand for the product increases, and thus the supply decreases, causing a shortage of the product.
16. **B. what causes high rates of unemployment** The unemployment rate is a factor in the economy as a whole, so it is a subject of study to a macroeconomist. All of the other choices relate to the economic actions of individuals or companies, which are not the main interest of a macroeconomist.
17. **C. As the price per eraser increases, manufacturers supply more erasers.** According to the graph, as prices rise, manufacturers are willing to supply more erasers as they see an opportunity for more profit.

## World History

### Lesson 1: Early Civilizations

#### Practice 1, page 497

1. **B. the Maya** According to the passage, the Maya recorded their discoveries about mathematics and astronomy in a pictographic writing system.
2. **B. Ancient Greece and Ancient Rome** As stated in the passage, the Greek idea of democracy, in which citizens voted, and the representative government and laws of ancient Rome were great influences on the founders of the United States.
3. **A. Both developed flood control and irrigation technologies to boost food production.** Both ancient Egypt and the civilizations of the Fertile Crescent grew up along rivers. The passage points out that in both areas, people learned to control floods and irrigate fields in order to improve food production.
4. **B. towns** The food surpluses that result from agriculture mean that not everyone must grow or gather her own food. Therefore, some people are free to live in towns where they can pursue a craft or business in exchange for food from farmers.

The other options occur without the gathering together of people in settlements.

5. **D. ancient Egypt** Ancient China developed along a great river, the Yellow River. Of the civilizations listed, only ancient Egypt also grew up along a river, the Nile. In both ancient China and ancient Egypt, the river kept the soil rich and damp.
6. **C. The Yellow River was probably the main trade route between Loyang and Chengchow.** Not only were rivers the source of water for irrigation, they were major thoroughfares for the transport of goods. Since both cities are on the Yellow River, trade between them most likely took place by river at that time.

## Lesson 2: Feudalism to Nation States

### Practice 2, page 499

1. **C. to protect their noble's land from attack** According to the passage, the role of the knights in feudal society was to protect their noble's estate, or land.
2. **A. Spain** Of the lands mentioned in the passage that were conquered by the Muslims, only Spain is in Europe. Thus, of the European nations marked for selection in the map, Spain is the one in which you would most expect to find evidence of Muslim culture.
3. **B. the migration of people from farms to industrial cities in the 1800s** Like the migration to the cities in the 1800s, the migration from manors to towns in the late Middle Ages resulted from economic causes. In both migrations, people were seeking better economic opportunities than farming offered.
4. **A. Roman Catholics accepted the authority of the pope and Protestants did not.** According to the passage, this was one of the main differences between the two branches of Christianity.
5. **A. accepted legal principles** Since the manor court did not rely on a written body of legal rulings, its actions were unpredictable. Most people felt they would get a fairer ruling in the royal courts, which were bound by written common law that applied to everyone in the kingdom.
6. **C. The population of western Europe showed almost constant growth with only brief periods of decline.** This is the best summary because it contains the main idea (Europe's population rose from 500 to 1500) and important details (two brief periods of decline).

## Lesson 3: Exploration and Colonialism

### Practice 3, page 501

1. **D. leading the first expedition to result in an around-the-world voyage** The passage states that, although Magellan himself did not circumnavigate the globe, one of his ships did. The crew members of that ship are believed to be the first people to sail completely around the world.
2. **C. to gain economic benefits** According to the second paragraph of the passage, the main goal of European colonization was economic gain.
3. **B. Malaya, where the British set up and ran rubber plantations worked by the native peoples** Of all the options, only Malaya was a colony of economic exploitation rather than of settlement.
4. **C. war and disease** The second paragraph of the passage indicate that war and disease, more than economic exploitation, were primary causes of the population decline among native colonized peoples.
5. **B. The Dutch had the smallest claim in the Americas in 1700.** The map shows that by 1700, the Dutch had only a small claim on the northern coast of South America, and the other nations had much larger claims.

## Lesson 4: The Age of Revolutions

### Practice 4, page 503

1. **C. the U.S. Declaration of Independence** According to the passage, the American Revolution and its goals of democracy (as expressed in the Declaration of Independence and the Constitution) were big influences on the French.
2. **D. Members of the Third Estate owned the least amount of land per person.** With 98 percent of the population but only 70 percent of the land, the Third Estate owned the least land in proportion to its numbers. Members of the First and Second Estates owned more land in proportion to their percentage of the population.
3. **B. England had a Parliament; while France did not have a parliament** This contrast is stated in the third paragraph of the passage. It is one of the reasons French citizens were dissatisfied with their lack of representation in the monarchy of Louis XVI.
4. **C. possessing large landholdings** The last paragraph of the passage on page 502 states that farmland had been the economic mainstay of the aristocracy up until the time of the Industrial Revolution, which began late in the eighteenth century.
5. **B. A sovereign nation is independent, having the power to govern itself.** In the passage, the word *sovereign* is used but not explained; the author takes for granted you know what it means. The remaining options are all stated in the passage.
6. **D. the Industrial Revolution** Like the Industrial Revolution, the Information Revolution is an economic revolution that has brought about social change. The other revolutions are all political in nature.

## Lesson 5: The Twentieth Century

### Practice 5, page 505

1. **A. pay the Allies money to repair war damages** According to the passage, paying reparations was one of the provisions of the Treaty of Versailles.
2. **C. the invasion of Poland** The third paragraph of the passage indicates that to avoid going to war, the Allies permitted Germany to take over, or annex, Austria and Czechoslovakia. However, Germany's invasion

of Poland spurred England and France to declare war.

3. **B. national pride** The Japanese had a great deal of national pride, which they found difficult to put aside. Thus it took the destruction of two cities and thousands of deaths to overcome their reluctance to surrender.
4. **D. Both were won by the Allies.** Of the options listed, the fact that the Allies won both wars is the only similarity. Choices (B) and (C) are true only of World War II, and choice (A) is not true: both wars involved other parts of the world.
5. **B. The United States sustained only a few civilian casualties.** The chart indicates "very few" civilian dead in the United States; every other cell in the chart has a number in the thousands or millions.
6. **A. the 1812 French invasion of Russia, which failed due to harsh weather and lack of supplies** Both the French and German invasions failed due to weather and lack of supplies, making them similar. The campaigns and actions mentioned in the other answer choices failed for different or unspecified reasons.

## World History Practice Questions, pages 506–509

1. **A. How Germanic Tribes Governed** The focus of the passage is the minimal governmental structure of the Germanic tribes.
2. **C. The Industrial Revolution started in Great Britain and spread to Europe, but by 1900 the United States was the leading industrialized nation.** This summary statement has all the major details from the paragraph—the start of the Industrial Revolution in Great Britain, its spread to Europe, and the lead taken by the United States. The other choices either focus too narrowly on a couple of details or are too broad to be an effective summary.
3. **A. Egypt** The map key gives the dates of each civilization shown on the map. Egypt, Kush, and Axum were the earliest civilizations. They are all located along the Nile River in the northeast part of Africa.
4. **A. Over 800 years, several civilizations succeeded one another in western Africa.** The civilizations of Ghana, Mali, and Songhai developed one after the other in the same region of Africa. None of the other choices is supported by information on the map.
5. **B. 1498-Da Gama sails to India for Portugal by going around Africa.** Da Gama's voyage opened up new trading opportunities for the Portuguese. Note from the time line that the Portuguese dominated trade in the East Indies from about 1510 to 1600.
6. **A. Spanish and Portuguese domination of exploration gave way to that of the Dutch, French, and English.** According to the time line, most Spanish and Portuguese exploration and conquest took place during the 1500s. From the 1600s on, other nations such as England, France, and the Netherlands increased their activity considerably. The other choices are incorrect or cannot be determined from the information in the time line.
7. **B. Pizarro** Like Cortés, Pizarro explored on behalf of the Spanish rulers. He conquered the Inca Empire in South America.
8. **B. The Age of Exploration** This title describes the era and events shown. The other choices are too narrow, too broad, or simply incorrect.
9. **D. After the Cold War ended, defense spending began to fall.** The graph shows defense spending decreasing in the period 1990–1995, after the Cold War ended in 1990. None of the other choices is supported by data on the graph.
10. **B. Colonies should be economically independent.** Of all the choices, only this one is an opinion. The other choices are facts that are stated in the paragraph.
11. **A. the Bedouin, who are a nomadic herding people of Saudi Arabia** The Bedouin follow a pastoral lifestyle, moving their herds of animals and temporary settlements from place to place in search of good grazing.
12. **C. The United States gained influence over Panama through the building and running of the Panama Canal.** Among the choices, this is the only example of imperialism—the takeover of aspects of one nation by another. The other options involve either internal events or the independence of one nation from another.
13. **D. between 146 and 44 B.C.E.** First locate Asia Minor on the map and see how it is shaded or patterned. Then consult the map key to see when land in Asia Minor was acquired by the Roman Empire. The map shows that most of the land was acquired between 146 and 44 B.C.E.
14. **A. Before 264 B.C.E., Rome conquered through overland military campaigns; later conquests were made by navies as well.** The map shows that up to 264 B.C.E. all of Rome's conquests were located on the Italian peninsula, reachable by land-based military units. After that time, as Rome sought to expand beyond the peninsula, it built navies to help conquer overseas areas.
15. **A. the European ideal of chivalry** The ideals of loyalty, devotion, and service are similar in both bushido and chivalry.
16. **C. the peasants** The passage mentions that the bushi and samurai were released from agricultural responsibilities because they were preparing for war, and the peasants provided them with a supply of the food they grew.

## Geography

### Lesson 1: Basic Geography Concepts

Practice 1, page 510

1. **C. Eurasia** England and Ireland are part of Europe, and Japan is part of Asia. Europe and Asia are actually one large land mass or continent, Eurasia.
2. **D. Lines of latitude run east-west, and lines of longitude run north-south.** According to the passage and the maps on page 510, latitude runs east-west and longitude runs north-south.
3. **C. the latitude and longitude** Knowing the latitude and longitude of any place on Earth gives the most accurate description of its location because the place is located precisely at the intersection of the latitude and longitude.
4. **A. by its natural and man-made features** The natural characteristics of a region, such as rivers and terrain, and its man-made features, such as cities and roads, all factor into a definition of a geographic region.
5. **C. The United States should be divided into cultural regions rather than states.** According to the passage, this is a point of view held by some geographers. The other options are all facts that can be proved true.
6. **B. the St. Louis metropolitan region, which includes portions of Missouri and Illinois.** Like New York City, St. Louis is the hub of a large metropolitan region in which people are tied together by common geographic and cultural factors.

### Lesson 2: Humans and the Environment

### Practice 2, page 513

1. **C. the move of an individual or population from one geographic area to settle in another.** The first paragraph of the passage on page 512 implies that the key characteristics of migration are the movement of people and their settling in a new place.
2. **B. the westward movement of the American population from the 1700s to the present.** Because this migration took place within the U.S. borders, it is an internal migration. The other choices all involve people moving from one country to another.
3. **A. are more densely populated than** The passage describes suburban areas appearing as a consequence of urban areas becoming too crowded. Thus, the text implies that urban areas (cities) are more densely populated than suburbs (neighboring towns).
4. **D. the automobile** Automobiles make it possible for many people to live in the suburbs, where the distances between a home and retail stores and workplaces can be considerable and public transportation may be lacking.
5. **D. the projected total world population in 2050** To answer this question, first locate 9,039,000,000 on the graph. (Note that the figures are given in millions, so the number to locate is written as 9,039.) It represents a total world population figure. Then look at the bottom axis to see what year that bar represents.
6. **C. Most of the population growth in the 50 years from 2000 to 2050 will occur in the less developed nations.** The bar graph shows that the proportion of the world population living in the more developed nations (shown in gray) is relatively small, and shows that it is predicted to remain relatively small over the next 50 years. In contrast, the graph predicts that the population in the less developed nations (shown in white) will grow much more. The remaining choices are not supported by the data on the graph.

### Lesson 3: Using Resources Wisely

### Practice 3, page 515

1. **A. materials that will never run out or can be replaced if used** According to the first paragraph of the passage on page 514, a renewable resource can be replaced (for example, replanting a field that's been harvested) or is in endless supply (for example, wind and solar power).
2. **D. rotating crops** In crop rotation, a farmer plants different crops in succeeding growing seasons in order to conserve nutrients in the soil. The other choices are all examples of a nonsustainable use of a resource; eventually, each will cause the resource to be used up.
3. **A. negotiating in an international forum** An international forum provides a framework for nations to work to resolve conflicts over resource use before the problems escalate.
4. **C. short-term benefit versus long-term benefit** Finding and using new oil deposits is a short-term solution to U.S. energy problems because it doesn't solve the underlying problem in the long run. Developing alternative sources of energy requires more investment of time and capital with an uncertain outcome, but it has the potential to help meet long-term U.S. energy needs.
5. **B. carpool to work and school** Carpooling saves gas, a nonrenewable resource.
6. **B. former U.S.S.R.** The second column lists current production figures; the highest figure in the column is 25.7, that of the former U.S.S.R.
7. **A. North America** To answer this question, look at the column labeled "Reserves to Production Ratio." This column indicates the relationship between the amount produced annually and the total amount the region has. Regions with lower ratios will run out of natural gas before regions with higher ratios.

## Geography Practice Questions, pages 516–519

1. **D. The problem of feeding the world's population is a matter of political will rather than one of resources.** This is an opinion attributed to agriculture experts in the passage. The remaining choices are all facts stated in the passage.
2. **B. Nevada gained seats in the House.** The passage tells you that the population shifts were large enough that seats in the House were reallocated. Since Nevada had the largest population gain, it is likely that it also gained seats in the House. Choices (A) and (D) are stated outright rather than implied by the passage. Choice (C) does not have to be true based on the information in the passage. Because immigration may have also played a role in population changes, it does not have to be the case that people moved away from the Northeast and Midwest.
3. **B. a visitor to Philadelphia** This is a special-purpose map designed to help visitors find their way around the airport and locate transportation routes to and from the airport.
4. **D. Labels for terminals and parking areas are coordinated to provide convenient parking.** The map shows Terminal E by Lot E, Terminal D by Garage D, and so on.
5. **B. the migration of thousands of farm families to other regions** The Dust Bowl temporarily disrupted farming in the Great Plains, forcing farmers to migrate to find work. While the Dust Bowl contributed to the Great Depression, (see choice (A)), it was not the Great Depression's only or primary cause.
6. **D. the spread of the Sahara into the grazing land on its southern border** The Sahara, the desert that covers much of northern Africa, has been spreading steadily southward into the Sahel, a dry grasslands region that has been overused as grazing land.
7. **C. irrigation canals** Many of the fields that are indicated as belonging to different people are separated from one another by canals.
8. **A. a town tax assessor's tax map** Like the king's property map, a town's tax maps show property boundaries. Property ownership in Mesopotamia was a basis for taxation just as it is today in the United States.
9. **D. Australia/Oceania** The smallest population figure is 30,000,000, the population of Australia/Oceania. (Oceania refers to the islands of the Pacific.)
10. **C. Asia** Compare the percent of total world population to the percent of Earth for each continent. Europe and Asia are the only two continents that have a greater percent of world population than of Earth's area. Since Asia boasts a little more than a 2 to 1 ratio of total world population to percent of Earth, Asia has the greatest population density. (62.6 to 30.1 is approximately 60 to 30, or 2 to 1.)
11. **C. Together, Asia and Europe account for more than one third of Earth's land area.** Eurasia has about 36.7, or one-third, of the land area on Earth. None of the other options is supported by data in the chart.
12. **A. The compass direction north does not mean "up" in terms of elevation.** The student was confusing north and up on the map. The Nile does indeed flow "up" the map to the top of the page, but it is actually flowing north and down from the mountains of East Africa.
13. **A. In 1849, railroads in the United States tended to be near the eastern coast, whereas major roads reached further inland.** The railroads on the map are all clustered in the states that touch the Atlantic Ocean; they did not extend to the middle of the country in 1849. The major roads, on the other hand, extended throughout the eastern half of the United States.
14. **B. the establishment of cities on the West Coast.** After railroads that extended west were built, it became easier and more profitable for people to settle on the West Coast and establish cities. Neither Florida nor Texas would be affected by railroads extending throughout the country because they are in the eastern portion of the country, so choices (A) and (D) are incorrect. The Coast Guard deals with the water, not land, so it would not be impacted by railroads spreading across the country; choice (D) is incorrect.
15. **B. Except for soils in northern coniferous regions, humid soils can be used or modified for crops.** This is a general conclusion based on the details of the paragraph. The remaining options are all supporting details.

# Science Answers and Explanations

## Science Skills

### Lesson 1: Comprehend Scientific Presentations

**Practice 1, page 523**

1. **C. the causes of type 2 diabetes** The passage as a whole discusses the causes of type 2 diabetes. Choices (A) and (D) are not discussed in the passage. Choice (B) is mentioned in the second paragraph but is only a supporting detail.
2. **D. The causes of type 2 diabetes are not fully understood.** This question asks for the main point of just the first paragraph, which explains that scientists do not fully understand the role played by various factors in causing diabetes. Choices (A) and (B) both commit the same error: that is, they mention a specific detail from the first paragraph while missing the big picture. Choice (C) contradicts the paragraph.
3. **B. A study of 18- to 25-year-olds showed that a majority did not produce enough insulin to offset the high amounts of sugar they were consuming.** The question asks for a detail that serves to support the idea that high sugar consumption may contribute to the development of type 2 diabetes. Only choice (B) does so. Choice (A) is a detail that is indeed mentioned in the paragraph, but only as background information. It does not serve to support the author's point that sugar consumption may contribute to diabetes. Choice (C) brings in "genetic factors," which are not mentioned in paragraph two. Although choice (D) may be implied by the author's use of hesitant language, such as "one contributing factor *may* be high sugar consumption," this does not support the paragraph's main idea.
4. **A. As moist, flowing air encounters rising elevations, it cools, which causes condensation, a stage that precedes precipitation and cloud development.** In interpreting this diagram, follow the arrows. The diagram depicts air flowing toward hills or mountains. As it does so, the air cools and condensation happens. Based on the arrows, that stage happens before the stages of precipitation and cloud formation. Choice (B) suggests that the air becomes static at the highest elevations, which is not supported by the diagram. Choice (C) contradicts the diagram. Choice (D) is unsupported because the diagram does not have an east-west orientation: just because the air is depicted flowing from the left-hand side of the picture does not mean that it's flowing from the west.

### Lesson 2: Use the Scientific Method

**Practice 2, page 525**

1. **C. What role do bacteria play in the development of acne?** The researchers were studying the question of how different combinations of bacteria affect acne symptoms. Because the researchers thought acne symptoms might depend on differences in bacteria, acne was the researchers' dependent variable. Combinations of bacteria are not affected by acne symptoms, but the researchers thought bacteria might affect those acne symptoms. Therefore, combinations of bacteria were the researchers' independent variable.
2. **B. Different kinds of bacteria may impact acne differently.** The last sentence of the first paragraph provides this answer as well. The researchers "began to wonder whether different strains of bacteria might impact acne in different ways": that statement represents the idea they sought to test—that is, their hypothesis. Choice (A) describes an assumption that was widely held before the researchers began their study. Choice (C) is a suggestion the researchers made after concluding their study, and choice (D) is their conclusion—not their starting hypothesis.
3. **D. Some combinations of bacteria may actually help ward off acne.** This question asks for the researchers' conclusion—that is, the idea they embraced after concluding their study. That idea is described by choice (D). Choice (A) is an assumption many people held before the research began. Choice (B) is not supported by the passage. Choice (C) is not supported by the passage: after drawing their conclusions, the researchers suggested a way to treat acne in the future, but they did not suggest that current treatments are misguided.
4. **C. Based on your experience, you make a guess about which of the movements involved in playing softball puts the greatest stress on the knees. You suspect that it may be stopping suddenly after running a short distance.** Forming a hypothesis occurs before the actual experiment takes place. All of the other answer choices occur during the experiment itself or afterward.
5. **B. your knee pain.** A dependent variable depends on the various factors in the experiment. In this experiment, your knee pain is dependent on the actions taken.

### Lesson 3: Reason with Scientific Information

**Practice 3, page 527**

1. **C. If both objects were currently sitting still, it would require more effort to push the brick across the floor than it would to push the block of wood across the floor.** According to the passage, a heavier object has more inertia, and the brick is heavier than the block. Therefore, you can conclude that it would be harder to move the brick across the floor. Choice (A), breakage, and choice (D), absorbing water, are not mentioned and are irrelevant to this question. Choice (B) is the opposite of the correct answer.
2. **A. The birds that the brown tree snake eats are the primary predators of spiders on Guam.**

The scientist's conclusion is that the brown tree snake is the reason there are so many spiders on Guam. The question asks for a piece of information that makes that conclusion more likely—that is, a choice that makes the scientist's conclusion more reasonable or believable. Choice (A) explains why more brown tree snakes would lead to more spiders. Choices (B) and (D) don't link the spiders and snakes at all. Choice (C) describes a relationship between them, but it suggests that more brown tree snakes would lead to *fewer* spiders.

3. **B. If large areas of ice sheets sit on water, the rising of sea levels may proceed more quickly than had previously been predicted.** The main idea of the passage is that some ice sheets may be sitting on water and that those ice sheets may melt more quickly than ice sheets sitting on rock. The passage also states that melting ice sheets contribute to rising sea levels. Putting those two ideas together, a scientist could predict that ice sheets sitting on water might send more melted water into the oceans than would ice sheets on rock. Choice (A) expresses the opposite of that idea. Choice (C) introduces a comparison that is not supported by the passage. Choice (D) goes too far by insisting that *all* of the quickly melting ice sheets are sitting on water.
4. **A. Most of the ice sheets sitting on water are covering inland lakes with no access to the ocean.** Choice (A) would make the prediction less likely, because if most ice sheets sitting on water have no way to send water into the ocean, then the link between the ice sheets and rising sea levels would be undermined. Choices (B) and (C) actually make the scientist's prediction more likely. Choice (D) may seem to undermine the information in the passage—until you notice that choice (D) criticizes the use of "radar alone" to assess ice sheets. The passage indicates that researchers used both satellite and radar data, which makes choice (D) irrelevant to the prediction.

## Lesson 4: Express and Apply Scientific Information

### Practice 4, page 529

1. **C. pure acetone; a solution of sugar in acetone** The passage states that, during osmosis, a liquid moves from a place where there is a higher concentration of dissolved material to where there is a lower concentration of dissolved material. Thus, to test the rate of osmosis of a liquid, Gillian would want to put that same liquid on two sides of the vat, with more dissolved material on one side than on the other. Only choice (C) describes that arrangement.
2. **D. formic acid** The solvent with the highest rate of diffusion would be the solvent that took the least time to reach equilibrium. Here it took formic acid the least time to do so.
3. **B. 19** Put the numbers in order: 15, 18, 20, 25. The median is the middle number. Because there are an even number of values given, take the average of the two middle numbers by adding them together: 18+20=38 and dividing by 2: $\frac{38}{2}=19$.
4. **A. greater than** If your blood has more dissolved material than your tissues, water will move from the tissues into the blood, causing the tissues to dry out.

## Lesson 5: Use Statistics and Probability

### Practice 5, page 531

1. **D. rabbit** The median is the middle number of a set of numbers, and in this graph, the rabbit has a lower body weight than the dog, human, and horse and a higher body weight than the shrew, cactus mouse, and flying squirrel. It isn't necessary to know the animals' actual body weights to determine this.
2. **A. rabbit** Similarly, the graph shows that the rabbit has the middle metabolic rate of the seven species in the graph.
3. **B. lower than the previous average** To find an average, you add up all the numbers in a list and divide by the number of items in the list, like this:

   $$\frac{\textit{shrew} + \textit{c.mouse} + \textit{f.squirrel} + \textit{rabbit} + \textit{dog} + \textit{human} + \textit{horse}}{7}.$$

   Now, the shrew is the highest of those numbers: it has the highest metabolic rate. Therefore, if you removed it and recalculated the average, the new average would be lower than the previous average.
4. **C. Their metabolic rate would be slightly lower than that of horses.** The question states that elephants weigh more than horses. Thus, elephants would be to the right of horses on the line graph. Based on the curve of the line, you can guess that elephants would have a slightly lower metabolism than that of horses. Because the line continues to decrease slightly, choice (B) is unsupported.
5. **C. 120** The question asks how many different orderings, or sequences, of the five crops are possible. This is a permutations question, because order matters. Thus, multiply to find the number of permutations: $5 \times 4 \times 3 \times 2 \times 1 = 120$

## Science Skills Practice Questions, pages 532–535

1. **B. While Copernicus's theory was an important development, it included elements that are outdated today.** The first sentence of the second paragraph provides the main idea. The words "[f]or example" help to make clear that the second and third sentences are details supporting that main idea.
2. **C. "The Significance and Limitations of the Copernican Theory"** The title of a passage should reflect its topic or main idea. The topic of this passage is the importance, or significance, of Copernicus's theory, as well as the fact that Copernicus's

theory was not completely correct. Choices (A) and (D) are both too broad, while choice (B) is incorrect because the passage is not about Copernicus's life.

3. **A. Astronomers now believe that the planets are not embedded in crystalline spheres.** The question asks for something that can be inferred, or deduced, from the passage. Choice (A) is supported by the passage. Copernicus's idea that the planets are embedded in crystalline spheres is mentioned in the second paragraph as an example of an idea that is today considered "primitive." This implies that astronomers today no longer believe this to be true. Choices (B) and (C) are contradicted by the passage. Choice (D) is not supported by the passage: primitive astronomers who came before Copernicus are not discussed.
4. **C. B and D** The passage describes what happens when you add heat to a substance: the temperature of the substance increases, up to the point when the substance starts to change from a solid to a liquid or from a liquid to a gas. Then the temperature of the substance holds steady while the substance is undergoing that change. When more heat is added but the temperature of a substance remains constant, it must be undergoing a phase change. The places in the diagram where the temperature is flat—B and D—thus represent the two places where the substance is changing from solid to liquid or from liquid to gas.
5. **D. a vaccine to prevent infection with the hepatitis B virus** According to the passage, hepatitis B virus causes liver cancer. A vaccine that prevents infection with the hepatitis B virus would therefore also prevent liver cancer.
6. **B. At least some of the phalarope's prey is smaller than a water droplet.** If the phalarope feeds on prey that it draws into its beak via water droplets, the prey must be smaller than a water droplet.
7. **B. Penrith** The black bars on the graph represent each city's previous record, and the gray bars represent its current record. Find the city for which the gray bar is furthest above the black bar: Penrith.
8. **C. Penrith** The median number is the middle of a list of numbers. Here, because there are seven cities, the city with the "previous record equal to the median of all the cities' previous records" simply means the city with the middle value (among the previous record values). Fortunately, the cities are represented in the graph in such a way that their previous records are in ascending order, and the median previous record belongs to Penrith.
9. **B. Temperatures increased 5 degrees or less** The largest increase was in the city of Penrith and was approximately 5 degrees.
10. **C. Why, when I touch the metal filing cabinet, do I experience more electrostatic shocks than my assistant does when she touches it?** The first paragraph of the passage explains that the office manager "wondered why" she experienced more static shocks than her assistant. That's the question that prompted her experiment. While it is true that the office manager decided to switch to cotton clothing, she didn't begin by wondering whether it was better, so choice (A) is incorrect. Choice (B) distorts the office manager's thoughts. Choice (D) places too much emphasis on shoes, which were not the subject of the office manager's experiment.
11. **D. The office manager wore one type of clothing, while her assistant wore another type of clothing, and they recorded the number of shocks they experienced.** The office manager wanted to test her hypothesis that her nylon clothing was causing her to experience shocks when touching a metal filing cabinet. To do so, she conducted an experiment in which she wore cotton clothing for a week, while her assistant wore nylon clothing; both wore identical shoes. Then the manager and assistant recorded the number of shocks they each experienced during the course of a week. Choice (D) correctly describes this experiment. Choice (A) describes the office manager's hypothesis. Choice (B) describes the office manager's course of action after she had completed her experiment, while choice (C) is the opposite of what actually occurred during the experiment (both the manager and the assistant wore identical shoes).
12. **A. They wanted to test the effects of their clothing on the number of shocks they were experiencing, and wearing different types of shoes might have confused their results.** In an experiment, it is important to control factors other than the one thing the experimenter wants to study. In this case, the office manager wanted to study the effect of clothing on the number of static shocks she was receiving. Choice (B) wrongly suggests that shoes were the subject of the office manager's experiment. Choices (C) and (D) distort the passage: the two individuals had the opposite hypothesis about cotton clothes, and, during her experiment, the office manager was trying to study static shocks—not avoid them.
13. **C. a new hypothesis** Remember, a hypothesis is a guess that a researcher starts with and then tests through an experiment. If the office manager formed a new guess about what was causing the static shocks, and she intended to study that new guess through an experiment, that would be a new hypothesis. It would not, at that point, be (A), a new conclusion based on findings. While she might, as choice (D) suggests, design an experiment to test this idea, the idea itself is not an experiment design. And the idea is certainly not (B), a general principle from the study of physics; rather, the office manager is making a guess based on observation.
14. **C. 15** This is a combinations question: you are asked for all

possible groupings of two out of the six snails, and the order of snails within each group does not matter. Use a table or an organized list to find the number of possible groupings. Name the snails A–F if that makes it easier.

| AB | | | | |
|---|---|---|---|---|
| AC | BC | | | |
| AD | BD | CD | | |
| AE | BE | CE | DE | |
| AF | BF | CF | DF | EF |

Count the possible pairs: there are 15.

15. **A. 6.3%** The question asks for the probability that any given star is a class G star, and we have to combine two probabilities to find it. We know that there is a 90 percent chance, or a .9 probability, that a star will be a main sequence star. We also know that, if it is a main sequence star, there is a 7 percent chance, or a .07 probability, that it will be a class G star. Multiply those two probabilities to find the probability of *both* of them happening: $9 \times .07 = .063$ Express your answer as a percentage: 6.3%.
16. **D. large femoral plaques** Forty-one percent of current smokers had large femoral plaques. That is a higher percentage than is shown in the chart for any other type of plaque listed.
17. **C. People who quit smoking tend to substitute snacking for smoking.** This is a plausible reason why those who quit smoking tend to gain weight, and why they consequently have a higher waist circumference.

# Life Science

## Lesson 1: Cell Structures and Functions

### Practice 1, page 537

1. **C. mitochondrion** The diagram indicates that the mitochondria produce a cell's energy.
2. **D. Cell walls cannot maintain a plant's shape and rigidity when the plant lacks water.** Even though cell walls contribute to keeping a plant firm and rigid, they cannot do the job without water-filled vacuoles. This conclusion follows from the fact that a plant that lacks water will wilt.
3. **A. the presence of a nucleus** According to the passage, the presence of a cell nucleus defines a cell as eukaryotic.
4. **A. Each time the microscope is improved, scientists can see cell structures more clearly.** Since cell structures are tiny, the more a cell is magnified, the more detail can be seen.
5. **B. Oxygen would diffuse from the unicellular organism into the pond water.** Since diffusion is the movement of molecules toward areas of lower concentration, if the organism had more oxygen than the surrounding water did, oxygen would pass out of the organism into the water until the concentrations were equalized.

## Lesson 2: Cell Processes and Energy

### Practice 2, page 539

1. **D. carbon dioxide, water, and energy** According to the equation that summarizes cellular respiration, the products of this process are carbon dioxide, water, and energy.
2. **A. increasing the amount of light the plants receive each day** Because light is required for photosynthesis, increasing light is the best choice for increasing the rate of photosynthesis. The other options either would have no effect or would decrease the rate of photosynthesis.
3. **B. increasing the number of green plants** Because green plants use up carbon dioxide during photosynthesis, increasing the amount of greenery on Earth would help reduce the amount of carbon dioxide in the atmosphere.
4. **D. stoma** According to the diagram, carbon dioxide enters the leaf through the stomata (the plural form of *stoma*).
5. **B. Most of a leaf's chloroplasts are found in its palisade cells.** The diagram shows that most of the leaf's chloroplasts are in the palisade cells. Evidence to support the other choices cannot be found in the diagram.

## Lesson 3: Human Body Systems

### Practice 3, page 541

1. **A. the circulatory system** According to the passage on the page before this practice set, the circulatory system transports blood to all the cells of the body.
2. **C. Both are structures in which substances pass through capillary walls into the blood.** Both alveoli and villi are tiny structures containing capillaries in which substances pass to and/or from the blood. In the alveoli of the respiratory system, oxygen and carbon dioxide pass into and out of blood; in the villi of the digestive system, nutrients pass into the blood.
3. **D. Veins have valves that allow blood to flow in one direction only.** Of the four facts given, this is the only one that involves the direction of flow of the blood. Therefore, it helps to support Harvey's conclusion that blood in the veins flows toward the heart.
4. **A. ureters** The diagram shows that the ureters connect the kidneys to the bladder.
5. **B. a patient with a painful kidney stone** Because a kidney stone forms in the urinary system, the patient is most likely to be treated by an urologist.

## Lesson 4: Health Issues

### Practice 4, page 543

1. **D. the skin** As implied by the passage, the skin is one of the first defenses against germs, along with mucous membranes, tears, and stomach acid.
2. **C. habituation** Although Sara feels an urge to drink wine, she feels no ill effects if she does not; this indicates that she is habituated to alcohol. She has a psychological dependence rather than a physical dependence on alcohol. If her dependence were physical, she would feel the effects of skipping her daily drink.
3. **A. Fats are a more concentrated source of energy than carbohydrates.** According to the table,

carbohydrates provide 4 calories per gram while fats provide 9 calories per gram. None of the other statements is supported by the information in the table.

4. **B. Carbohydrates come from fruits as well as from bread and rice.** According to the table, bread and rice are not the only foods that provide carbohydrates; fruits and at least one type of vegetable (potatoes) also do. Choices (A) and (D) are opinions, not facts. Choice (C) is contradicted by the table.

## Lesson 5: Reproduction and Heredity

### Practice 5, page 545

1. **A. both are tall** Each parent pea plant has one dominant tallness allele and one recessive shortness allele. The dominant allele is the one that will be expressed, so both parent pea plants will be tall.
2. **B. 1 out of 4** According to the Punnett square, only one out of four possible combinations yields a short plant (one with two recessive alleles for height: tt).
3. **D. TT** If you want to grow only tall plants, then it is better to use purebred tall plants (TT). If you use hybrid tall plants—(Tt) or (tT)—then in the next generation, you will likely get some short plants in your garden.
4. **D. 2** The passage states that if even one dominant allele is present, the dominant trait will be expressed. For a recessive trait to be expressed, both alleles must be recessive.
5. **D. Organisms that reproduce sexually produce offspring that have inherited a mix of traits from their parents.** Because they are inheriting a mix of genes from two parents, the offspring of organisms that reproduce sexually are different from the parents and from each other, creating a more diverse population. When an organism reproduces asexually, the offspring are identical to the parent and to each other, which means less diversity in the population.
6. **B. The black male was actually a hybrid.** The only way a white rabbit and a black rabbit could produce a white offspring is if the black rabbit is carrying the recessive allele for white fur. That means the black rabbit was actually a hybrid, not purebred as the student had assumed.

## Lesson 6: Modern Genetics

### Practice 6, page 547

1. **C. the sequence of base pairs in a gene** According to the third paragraph of the passage on page 726, particular sequences of base pairs code for particular amino acids, which are the building blocks of proteins. Therefore, as the paragraph concludes, the order of bases on a gene forms a code for making a particular protein.
2. **D. a change in protein synthesis** Since DNA provides the blueprint for protein synthesis, any change in DNA may affect protein synthesis.
3. **D. Genetically engineered foods are safe for consumers and the environment.** This is an opinion; it is not a fact that can be proved true from the information in the text. All the other statements are facts, based on information given in the paragraph.
4. **B. so that each daughter cell receives a complete set of DNA** Cell division produces two daughter cells with genetic material, or DNA, that is identical to that of the parent cell. The DNA must be replicated in the parent cell first so that each daughter cell can receive an exact copy of it.
5. **B. The base guanine pairs only with the base cytosine.** According to both the diagram and the passage, in DNA sequences, the base guanine always pairs with the base cytosine. (Note that in the diagram, each base is represented by its initial.) The remaining statements are not supported by the passage or the diagram.
6. **A. amino acids** Proteins are composed of chains of amino acids.

## Lesson 7: Evolution and Natural Selection

### Practice 7, page 549

1. **B. Frogs' forelimbs contain carpal bones.** All four homologous structures in the diagram include the same layout of bones: humerus, radius, ulna, and carpal bones. Since frogs' limbs are homologous to those of the other animals, they will likely have the same bones. Choices (A), (C), and (D) may be true, but they are not supported by the diagram.
2. **C. In penguins, flying birds, humans, and alligators, the forelimbs have similar structures despite performing different functions.** Even though the forelimbs of these organisms look alike, they all perform different functions. The arm helps to lift and hold things, the penguin's flipper helps it to swim, the bird's wing helps it to fly, and the alligator's foreleg helps it to walk.
3. **A. traits that make an organism better able to survive in its environment** According to the passage on the page before this practice set, adaptations are traits that some individuals possess that enable them to compete successfully in their environment.
4. **C. DNA analysis provides more objective data than observation does.** DNA analysis is more objective than observation, because the person doing the observing must interpret what he or she sees.

## Lesson 8: Organization of Ecosystems

### Practice 8, page 551

1. **D. the sun** The ultimate source of energy for the food web on the previous page is the sun. This is implied by the first paragraph, which explains that the green plants at the bottom of the food web produce their own energy from the sun. The other species in the food web ultimately depend on those producers for food.
2. **B. The populations of hares and seed-eating birds would increase.** With fewer foxes to

hunt them, more hares and seed-eating birds would survive long enough to reproduce, increasing the populations of these organisms.

3. **B. an aquarium with aquatic plants and herbivorous tropical fish** An aquarium is a human-made ecosystem with living organisms in balance with one another and with their physical environment. It includes both producers (the aquatic plants) and consumers (the herbivorous, which means plant-eating, fish).
4. **D. The natural replacement of lichens by mosses and ferns, and then shrubs, is an example of succession.** According to the information, succession is a naturally occurring replacement of one ecosystem by another.
5. **C. to turn atmospheric nitrogen into compounds plants and animals can use** According to the information, nitrogen-fixing bacteria on the roots of plants like peas and beans take nitrogen and use it to form compounds that plants and animals can use.

## Life Science Practice Questions pages 552–555

1. **B. Active transport requires the cell to use energy, and passive transport does not.** According to the information given, the key difference between active and passive transport is the use of the cell's energy.
2. **C. The water level in the jar might have gone down because of evaporation.** Because the experiment did not control for evaporation, it does not prove that the water was absorbed by the ivy.
3.

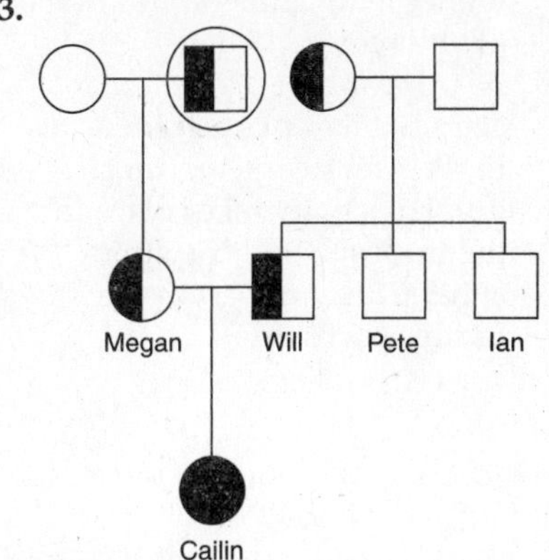


**B. Megan's father** The paragraph indicates that squares stand for males and half-shading represents genetic carriers. Of all the choices, only the square that represents Megan's father is half-shaded, indicating that Megan's father is a carrier of cystic fibrosis.

4. **D. No one in either Megan's or Will's immediate family has cystic fibrosis except Cailin.** Since everyone in the pedigree except for Cailin has only the recessive gene for cystic fibrosis, no one else suffers from the disease. Thus, Cailin's family members were probably unaware that some of them were carriers for cystic fibrosis.
5. **B. metaphase** According to the diagram, the chromosomes line up across the middle of the cell during metaphase.
6. **B. After mitosis, the two daughter cells have their own nuclei.** The two daughter cells in the interphase section of the diagram each have their own nuclei.
7. **B. to control the movement of chromosomes.** The spindle fibers help the chromatids move to different locations during mitosis.
8. **C. The fossil record for any given species may be incomplete.** Because fossils are found at random, scientists cannot be sure they have a complete fossil record for many species. An incomplete fossil record would also explain why evolution sometimes seems to take place in bursts rather than gradually.
9. **D. nutrient transport and immune defense** According to the information, plasma transports nutrients. White blood cells defend against infection.
10. **A. enamel** The diagram shows that the top surface of the tooth is made of enamel.
11. **A. few or no nerve endings** Pain is caused by nerves sending signals to the brain. If a decaying tooth does not become painful until the decay reaches the pulp, the outer parts of the tooth—the enamel and dentin—must not contain many nerve endings.
12. **B. grazing too many cattle on grassland** Overgrazing of domestic animals like cattle can destroy much plant life in grassland ecosystems. When that happens, the number of cattle the grassland can support decreases, as described in the paragraph.
13. **A. DNA analysis provides more fundamental, accurate data than does a visual analysis of structures and fossils.** Because DNA analysis involves genetic data at the molecular level, it is a better indicator of the relationships among organisms than visible similarities such as teeth. Thus, DNA analysis has changed the way scientists previously classified some organisms.
14. **A. panting** A dog's panting and a human being's sweating are both processes that cause loss of body heat through the evaporation of water. In other words, they are body processes that function to cool off an overheated animal.
15. **B. 3** According to the graph, unintentional injuries, chronic lung diseases, and cancers caused more deaths in 2011 than in 2005.
16. **B. biggest decrease** The number of deaths caused by heart disease decreased between 2005 and 2011. Of the remaining causes of death, only cerebrovascular disease caused fewer deaths in 2011 than in 2005, but this decrease is much smaller than that for heart disease.
17. **B. 8% decrease** To find the percent change, first subtract to find the amount of the change. The number of deaths from heart diseases in 2005 was roughly 650,000, and the number in 2011 was roughly 600,000. So the amount of change was 50,000. Now, divide that by the original value: $\frac{50,000}{650,000} \approx .08$. To convert that number to a percent, multiply by 100: 8%. Since the number of deaths from heart diseases in 2011 was lower than in 2005, there was an 8% decrease.

## Earth and Space Science

### Lesson 1: Structure of Earth

**Practice 1, page 557**

1. **A. changes in Earth's crust** According to the passage on the page before this practice set, the theory of plate tectonics explains how major landforms are created, the continents move, and the seafloor spreads, all of which are changes in Earth's crust.
2. **A. consist primarily of iron** The passage states that the outer core is mostly liquid iron, while the inner core is mostly solid iron.
3. **D. a destructive margin** According to the passage, destructive margins are places where one plate is being forced beneath another, and deep ocean trenches are characteristic of destructive margins between oceanic and continental plates.
4. **D. The west coast of Africa seems to fit into the east coast of the Americas.** Of the four choices, only this one provides evidence to support the idea that there used to be one continent made up of the pieces that are the continents we know today. The fact that two continents seem to fit together like the pieces of a jigsaw puzzle suggests that they were once part of one continent.
5. **C. The continents of North America and Europe are moving apart.** Since the Atlantic Ocean is getting wider, it follows that the continents on either side of the Atlantic are moving further apart.
6. **B. A single large landmass called Pangaea existed about 250 million years ago.** The existence of Pangaea is a theory based on evidence, not a fact. All the other choices are facts that can be proven true.

### Lesson 2: Earth's Resources

**Practice 2, page 559**

1. **D. 177** To find the consumption of petroleum in 2011, locate 2011 on the horizontal axis. Then imagine a straight vertical line from 2011 to the graph line. Imagine a straight horizontal line from that spot on the trend line to the vertical axis to find the approximate number of Btus.
2. **B. 14** The range of a data set is the difference between its highest value and its lowest value. In 2011, the world petroleum consumption was approximately 177 quadrillion Btus, and in 2003 it was approximately 163 quadrillion Btus. The difference between them is roughly 14 quadrillion Btus.
3. **A. World petroleum consumption increased by about 14 quadrillion Btus between 2003 and 2011.** This is the best summary of the graph because it includes the topic of the graph (world petroleum consumption) and the amount by which consumption changed during the period shown.
4. **D. Waste not, want not.** One of the basic approaches of conservationists is to reduce consumption of resources by decreasing waste ("waste not"). If that is done, in the future the resources will still be available ("want not").
5. **B. Developed nations have started using water more efficiently than they did in the past.** Since population and economic activity are increasing faster than water use in the developed nations, the most likely reason is that people have learned to conserve water, meaning they use water more efficiently now.
6. **D. Soil erosion is caused by both natural forces and the actions of people.** The first sentence mentions several causes of soil erosion. These include natural actions, such as wind, water, and ice, along with human actions, such as deforestation and poor farming practices.

### Lesson 3: Weather and Climate

**Practice 3, page 561**

1. **D. southwest to northeast** The label describes the winds as "westerlies," and the arrows indicate that the winds generally move from the southwest to the northeast. It follows that weather patterns move along with the winds, from southwest to northeast.
2. **B. The winds in the Northern Hemisphere are a mirror image of those in the Southern Hemisphere.** If you compare the two sets of winds, you will see that those in the Northern Hemisphere are a reflection of those in the Southern Hemisphere, just as an image is reflected in a mirror.
3. **D. satellites, which transmit cloud photos and weather data** Satellite photos of cloud patterns help meteorologists identify hurricanes and follow their paths; weather data help them follow changes in the intensity of the storm. Thus, the photos and data from satellites help meteorologists make predictions about the development and movement of hurricanes.
4. **D. global wind and ocean current patterns** According to the passage, both global wind patterns and ocean currents redistribute heat from the solar heating of Earth.
5. **D. The highest temperatures in the atmosphere are in the thermosphere.** According to the chart, the thermosphere has temperatures of up to several thousand degrees Fahrenheit—much higher than temperatures in the other layers.
6. **A. troposphere** Most human activity takes place at the Earth's surface. Thus, most human activity takes place in the troposphere—the atmospheric layer closest to the Earth's surface.

## Lesson 4: Earth in the Solar System

### Practice 4, page 563

1. **D. Mercury** A planet's revolution is its orbit around the sun. Locate the column that shows the planets' revolution periods. Then review the data in the column until you find the shortest revolution period. That would be 88 Earth days, which is the time it takes Mercury to travel once around the sun.
2. **B. Venus** Of all the planets, Venus is closest in size to Earth. Venus's year is also closest in length to Earth's year. These features make Earth and Venus the most similar of the choices given.
3. **C. Uranus was not clearly visible with the telescopes generally in use at the time.** According to the information given, Herschel made excellent, powerful telescopes, so he probably saw a much sharper image of Uranus than did previous astronomers and was therefore able to recognize its unique color and shape.
4. **B. Saturn** Saturn has 53 moons according to the chart. That is many more than Uranus and Neptune, and three more than Jupiter.
5. **D. faith in human judgment and decision-making skills** This is the only value that relates to the possible benefits of sending a crewed mission rather than a robotic mission.
6. **B. an atom, with a dense nucleus and electrons orbiting the nucleus** Of all these choices, the structure of the atom is most similar to the structure of the solar system, even though the atom is much tinier.

## Lesson 5: The Expanding Universe

### Practice 5, page 565

1. **B. Canopus** Absolute magnitude is the measure of brightness of a star as if it were 32.6 light-years away from Earth. Therefore, the star with the lowest absolute magnitude would be the brightest, if all were seen at 32.6 light-years' distance. Canopus has the lowest absolute magnitude, so it is the brightest of the stars.
2. **C. The star's apparent magnitude would be equal to its absolute magnitude.** Since the absolute magnitude of a star is defined as the brightness an object would have at 32.6 light-years from Earth and the apparent magnitude is its brightness as seen from Earth, then an object that was actually 32.6 light-years from Earth would have the same apparent and absolute magnitude.
3. **D. Not all stars are located about 32.6 light-years from Earth.** The apparent magnitude is a measure of how bright the star looks from Earth. (A small, close star might look very bright compared to a large, distant star.) However, the absolute magnitude is a measure of how bright a star would be if it were a set distance from Earth. These numbers are not necessarily similar, since the apparent magnitude does not take the star's distance into account while the absolute magnitude does.
4. **B. It is a main-sequence star.** According to the passage on the page before this practice set, stars like the sun have about a 10-billion-year life cycle. Since the main-sequence stage is the longest, a star that is about 4.7 billion years old would be a main-sequence star, in the middle of its life cycle.
5. **D. Pluto should be classified as a dwarf planet.** Choices (A), (B), and (C) are factual details about Pluto. Choice (D) is not a fact but rather a recommendation (that is, an opinion) of the scientists.

## Earth and Space Science Practice Questions, page 566–569

1. **A. The moon and the sun exert the greatest pull on Earth's oceans when these bodies are all in a line.** According to the paragraph, when the sun, moon, and Earth are in a line, the highest tides, called spring tides, occur. The paragraph also states that tides are caused by the gravitational pull of the moon and the sun on the oceans. Putting this information together, the paragraph supports the idea that the moon and the sun exert their greatest pull on the oceans when these bodies are all in a line, during spring tides. None of the other statements is supported by the paragraph.
2. **C. Iceland, an island nation in the Atlantic with active volcanoes** An area with active volcanoes has lots of magma near the surface, so it is ideal for geothermal energy, which is a renewable resource.
3. **D. 26 percent** According to the passage, dark matter is matter that does not interact with light, and according to the graph, dark matter may make up 26 percent of the universe.
4. **D. Ordinary matter is made of the chemical elements.** Of all the statements, only choice (D) is a fact that can be proved at this time. The other three choices are hypotheses, proposed explanations for things that have been observed but not proved.
5. **D. tropical-subtropical** First locate the equator on the map. Then consult the map key to identify the climate represented by the most common color that occurs near the equator.
6. **A. The continent with the least area of desert-steppe climate is Europe.** To find the answer to this question, you must check each statement against the map. If the map proves the statement is false, you can eliminate that statement. If the map doesn't show what the statement indicates, you can also eliminate that statement. Choice (A) is the only statement confirmed by the map.
7. **A. farm output** Temperate-snow climate zones do not have tropical rainforests (C) and do not necessarily have more mountains than other climate zones (D). Of the remaining

choices, only farm output is directly related to wealth.

8. **B. 4.6** Eurasia, North America, and South America all have five climate zones. Africa and Australia each have four climate zones. To find the average, add the number of climate zones for each continent and divide by 5 because there are five continents shown.
9. **D. the Earth passes between the moon and the sun.** According to the diagram, a lunar eclipse occurs when the Moon is in Earth's umbra, or shadow. This occurs when the Earth passes between the Moon and the sun.
10. **C. A lunar eclipse can be seen only at night, and a solar eclipse can be seen only during the day.** The lunar eclipse diagram indicates that a person on the daylight side of Earth would not be able to see the lunar eclipse; only a person on the nighttime side would see it. The solar eclipse diagram indicates that a person on the nighttime side of Earth would not be able to see the eclipse; only a person on the daytime side would see it.
11. **D. a catalytic converter, a device in the exhaust system of a vehicle that reduces harmful emissions from the engine** Of all the choices, only this one reduces the harmful pollutants of burning fossil fuel and so would reduce acid rain.
12. **A. replacing a coal-burning power plant with a solar farm** The passage states that coalfueled power plants produce acid rain. Replacing a coal-burning power plant with a power plant that uses solar panels would reduce emissions from burning coal and would, therefore, reduce the amount of acid rain that falls on vulnerable ecosystems.
13. **A. The rock cycle is a continuous process of rock formation, destruction, and reformation.** The diagram is a cycle diagram, which shows a process that occurs again and again; in this case, the process of the formation and destruction of rocks.
14. **B. sedimentary rock** Rock that forms from compacted sediment is called sedimentary rock.
15. **A. melted rock** According to the diagram, igneous, sedimentary, and metamorphic rocks all form magma by melting.
16. **C. Open-pit mining destroys valuable land.** An open-pit mine destroys a huge area, so it is restricted in many countries to prevent large-scale destruction of land. There is no reason to suspect, based on the information given, that (B) open-pit mining is more dangerous than shaft mining or that (D) it yields lower-grade minerals.

## Physical Science

### Lesson 1: Atoms and Molecules

#### Practice 1, page 571

1. **A. The sodium atom loses an electron, becoming positively charged, and the chlorine atom gains an electron, becoming negatively charged.** According to the diagram, the sodium atom gives up an electron to the chlorine atom. With one fewer electron than protons, the sodium becomes a positively charged ion. When the chlorine atom gains an electron, it has one more electron than protons, making it a negatively charged ion. The sodium and chloride ions are attracted to each other, forming an ionic bond.
2. **D. $C_6H_{12}O_6$** According to the passage on the previous page and the question text, a chemical formula represents the number of atoms of each element in a compound. Chemical symbols, which are letters, represent the elements, followed by subscripts, which represent the number of atoms.
3. **D. atoms that have either gained electrons to become negatively charged, or atoms that have lost electrons to become positively charged** An ion is defined as an atom that carries a charge. The only way for an atom's charge to change is for it to gain or lose electrons.
4. **B. Most of the alpha particles passed right through the gold foil.** Because most of the alpha particles passed right through the foil without being stopped or deflected, Rutherford concluded that atoms must consist mostly of empty space.
5. **B. 11** The atomic number of sodium refers to how many protons the atom has. An atom that is not an ion has the same number of protons as electrons. Therefore, a sodium atom has 11 electrons.

### Lesson 2: Properties and States of Matter

#### Practice 2, page 573

1. **A. melting and boiling** According to the passage on the previous page, adding heat to a solid melts the solid, and adding heat to a liquid causes it to boil, or change to a gas.
2. **B. Solids are usually denser than liquids and gases.** If you compare the densities of the solids, liquids, and gases in the chart, you will see that the solids are denser than the liquids and the gases.
3. **B. 190%** According to the paragraph, glycerin's boiling point is 190° greater than water's boiling point. To find the percentage by which glycerin's boiling point is greater than that of water, divide the difference between the two substances' boiling points by the boiling point of water and multiply the quotient by 100%. Thus, $\frac{190}{100} \times 100\% = 190\%$. Always read questions carefully. Glycerin's boiling point is 290% of water's boiling point, but this question asks for the percent by which glycerin's boiling point is *greater than* water's.
4. **A. Water is a unique substance on Earth.** This statement is a conclusion (a general statement) that is supported by the statements that give details about the properties of water.

5. **B. Antifreeze added to water in a car's radiator lowers the freezing point below 0°C.** Adding antifreeze (a solute) to water (a solvent) lowers the freezing point of the solution, the liquid in the radiator.
6. **D. dusty air** Dusty air is the only choice with large suspended particles. Gold and oxygen are elements, not mixtures. Salt water is a solution; it has small particles that do not settle out of the mixture.

## Lesson 3: Chemical Reactions

### Practice 3, page 575

1. **C. $2Cu + O_2 \rightarrow 2CuO$** You can eliminate choice (A) because the product (CuO) is on the left side of the equation rather than on the right side. To determine which of the remaining answer choices is correct, you must look for the equation that has two copper atoms and two oxygen atoms on the left side to balance the two copper atoms and two oxygen atoms on the right side.
2. **B. Weigh the reactants, conduct the reaction in a sealed container, and weigh the products.** This procedure should result in the weights of the reactants and products being equal, because none of the products would escape from the sealed container. The weight measurements would provide evidence for the law of the conservation of mass.
3. **C. Igniting the gas requires activation energy, the gas burning releases exothermic energy, and the egg solidifying requires endothermic energy.** Activation energy is the energy needed to start a chemical reaction. Exothermic energy is the energy given off by a chemical reaction, while endothermic energy is energy absorbed by a system.
4. **C. the time during which the reaction occurs** The horizontal axis is labeled "Time," so you can eliminate choice (D). The graph shows the progress of the reaction, which takes place over time, not just one instant of the reaction, so you can eliminate choices (A) and (B).
5. **A. Compounds are substances consisting of two or more elements chemically combined in a definite proportion.** The writer of the paragraph takes for granted that you know what a compound is and does not define the term *compound* in the paragraph. The other answer choices are stated explicitly in the paragraph.
6. **B. "Acids and Bases"** The passage gives an overview of acids and bases and describes what happens when they react with one another.

## Lesson 4: The Nature of Energy

### Practice 4, page 577

1. **C. Energy cannot be created or destroyed, but can only change in form.** According to the third paragraph on the previous page this is the law of conservation of energy.
2. **D. chemical** The potential energy stored in the batteries is chemical energy. This energy is used to power the flashlight.
3. **B. power** Power is the rate at which work is done or, in this case, the rate at which energy is consumed. The wood stove has greater power than the oak tree because it consumes the tree's energy in much less time than it takes the tree to consume the sun's energy.
4. **B. the relationship between energy and mass** According to the passage, Einstein's equation explains how energy can be converted to mass, and vice versa.
5. **B. At the high point of its swing, a pendulum has potential energy.** The diagram shows that at the high point of its swing, the pendulum has potential energy, the energy of position. The information in the diagram does not support any of the other statements.
6. **A. The molecules in air are far apart.** Because the molecules of a gas like air are far apart, they are in contact with one another less frequently than are the molecules of a liquid or solid, since liquids and solids are much denser. That is why gases have lower conductivity than liquids and solids do.

## Lesson 5: Motion and Forces

### Practice 5, page 579

1. **D. anything that changes the rest or motion of an object** According to the passage on the previous page this is the definition of a force.
2. **D. the tendency of an object to remain at rest or in motion** According to the third paragraph on the previous page inertia is described in Newton's first law of motion as the tendency of objects to remain at rest or keep moving until acted upon by a force.
3. **B. the International Space Station orbiting Earth** The key concept regarding centripetal force is circular motion, and the orbit of the space station is the only example of circular motion among the options given.
4. **A. the momentum of the car decreases when its velocity decreases.** Momentum is the product of mass and velocity. The mass of each car does not change, but each car's momentum will be directly proportional to its velocity.
5. **B. an object that has a constant speed** The graph shows a straight line that slopes upward. According to the paragraph, this type of graph shows an object that is moving at a constant speed.
6. **C. Some machines simply change the direction of a force.** According to the information given, a machine is a device that changes the direction *or* the size of a force, which means that some machines change only the direction of the force. An example is a simple pulley, which allows you to push down, rather than pull up, to lift a load.

## Lesson 6: Electricity and Magnetism

### Practice 6, page 581

1. **B. two poles repelling one another** According to the diagram, like poles repel, so a drawing of two north poles facing each other would look the same as the diagram of two south poles facing each other.
2. **A. Copper and aluminum are conductors.** Electrical wires need to be made of something that carries electricity easily, which is what conductors do.
3. **D. a flashlight** According to the passage, direct current is used in battery-powered devices. Choice (D) is correct because flashlights typically run on batteries.
4. **D. a transformer** According to the passage, transformers change the voltage of an incoming electric current.
5. **A. the light bulb** An incandescent light bulb is basically a thin tungsten filament through which current flows. This filament has resistance and thus functions as a resistor in a circuit.
6. **C. Disconnecting the light bulb will also stop the current.** To have current, you need to have a loop. Getting rid of any piece of the circuit—the battery, the switch, the lightbulb, or the wire—would break the loop and thus stop the current.

## Physical Science Practice Questions pages 582–585

1. **B. 5,730 years** This information is in the table, in the row for carbon-14 and the column for half-life.
2. **D. Uranium produces radioactive waste that may harm living things for millions of years.** Since the question asks what an *opponent* of nuclear power would say, the correct answer should be a negative fact about uranium. According to the table, uranium is unstable for millions or even billions of years, so choice (D) is both negative and true. Choice (C) is a negative claim about uranium, but it's a false one—uranium is unstable for much longer than three days.
3. **D. Both involve the transfer of energy through matter or space.** According to the paragraph, a wave is something that transfers energy through matter or space, so both types of waves would have that in common. Longitudinal waves have forward-and-back displacement, while transverse waves have up-and-down displacement, so choices (A) and (B) are incorrect. Choice (C) is incorrect because only longitudinal waves involve compressions.
4. **A. A cork in water bobs up and down as waves pass.** The question asks for an example in which something stays in roughly the same place after a wave passes through it. If a cork merely bobs up and down as waves pass, then the cork will be in its original position after the waves stop. Thus, choice (A) is the right example.
5. **A. dust motes dancing in a shaft of sunlight** Brownian motion is the random movement of particles in a liquid or a gas. Choice (A) is correct because dust motes move about randomly in the air, which is a gas. Choice (C) is wrong because it doesn't involve movement, choice (D) is wrong because the raft is *on* a lake (not *in* it), and choice (B) is wrong because the ground is a solid.
6. **D. Using powdered marble** The smaller the pieces of marble used, the greater their surface area will be and, therefore, the faster the reaction rate will be.
7. **B. decreases** "Varies inversely" means "is inversely proportional to." So as pressure increases, volume does the opposite—it decreases.
8. **C. xenon (Xe)** According to the chart, the noble gases are in column 18. Choice (C) xenon is the only choice in this column.
9. **B. Chlorine (Cl) and iodine (I) have similar properties.** According to the information given, elements in the same column have similar properties. Since chlorine and iodine are in the same column, choice (B) is correct. There is no mention in the paragraph or chart of common elements, so choice (A) is incorrect. Choice (C) is false because arsenic (As) and antimony (Sb) are in the same column and thus are similar, not different. Arsenic (As) is number 33, so there are 33 protons in its nucleus, not 85 as stated in choice (D).
10. **A. microwaves** According to the diagram, wavelengths increase as you go left to right. Since microwaves are to the right of the visible spectrum, choice (A) is correct.
11. **C. People can see only a small portion of the electromagnetic spectrum.** In the diagram, the visible spectrum—the section that people can see—is only a small piece of the entire electromagnetic spectrum.
12. **B. Its mass remains the same, and its weight decreases.** The mass of an object doesn't depend on anything; rather, mass is a property of the object. By contrast, the weight of an object gets smaller as the object gets farther from Earth. So, as a rocket travels away from Earth, its mass won't change, but its weight will get smaller.
13. **B. Coldness cannot be transferred.** The paragraph directly states that heat can be transferred, (A), a cold object can be warmed by your body (C), and that your body heat can be lost (D). What the passage assumes but doesn't say is that *only* heat can be transferred; coldness can't be. This is choice (B).
14. **D. the range** All of the engineer's recorded speeds are off by 3.7 km/hour, which skews the mean, mode, and median upward. However, the

range is unchanged, because the difference between the largest value and the smallest value is the same in both columns (195.6 km/hour).

15. **C. $\frac{3}{5}$** This question asks about the planes' actual speeds, so be sure to use the "actual speed" column. Four of the five planes have a speed less than 360 km/hour, and once one of those planes is chosen, three of the four remaining planes will have a speed less than 360 km/hour. Thus, the probability that both chosen planes have a speed less than 360 km/hour is $\frac{4}{5} \times \frac{3}{4} = \frac{3}{5}$.
16. **A. Elastic** In trial 1, both the final momentums and kinetic energies are equal to their initial values. Because momentum and kinetic energy are conserved, the collision that occurred in trial 1 must be elastic.
17. **B. 0°** The freezing point of water is 0°.

# Practice Tests
# Answers and Explanations

# LANGUAGE ARTS: READING
# PRACTICE TEST ANSWERS AND EXPLANATIONS

**Pages 588–601**

1. **B. describe types of interviewers and how to approach them** The author is chiefly concerned with explaining that different interviewers have different personalities and that you should approach those interviewers differently.
2. **C. Our ability to "read" others makes us form instant, lifelong relationships with some people.** The author makes this general claim in the first paragraph but does not support it with evidence. Choices (A) and (D) are stated or implied in the first paragraph and then supported with evidence in paragraphs 2–4. Choice (B) is a generalization made in paragraph 3, not paragraph 1.
3. **D. interviewers with homey, comfortable offices and interviewers whose offices seem less welcoming** The author contrasts these two types of interviewers in the third and fourth paragraphs of the passage.
4. **A. The author makes a generalization about how to read an interviewer and then gives specific suggestions about how to do so.** The author begins by introducing the idea that a job applicant can read an interviewer and then discusses the specifics of interpreting an interviewer's email and office arrangements.
5. **A. Interviewers have some influence or control over their office arrangements.** In paragraphs 3 and 4, the author explains that you can learn a great deal about an interviewer's personality from the type and arrangements of furniture in the interviewer's office. However, in order for this to make sense, the author must be assuming that interviewers have some say about their office arrangements. If an interviewer had no influence over her office, then the office would not provide reliable information about the interviewer's personality. The passage does not discuss the virtues of email (as in choice (B)) or the relative importance of different aspects of preparing for an interview (as in choice (D)). Choice (C) is out of scope. This passage is about prospective hires, not employees.
6. **D. You should try to understand your interviewer's personality and tailor your responses to him or her accordingly.** Only choice (D) summarizes the author's overall argument. The other choices are either details (such as choice (A)) or not mentioned in the passage (such as choice (C)).
7. **A. short and tense** You can infer the meaning of this word from the context. In this paragraph, you are told that in a homey, comfortable environment, your responses to interview questions should be friendly, open, and relaxed. It makes sense that "truncated" would mean the opposite of open and relaxed.
8. **A. jumping from a roof before an audience** Cleo loves attention. Her bet that she can swing upside down from an oak tree would have resulted in her either winning her sisters' money or gaining attention because she got hurt. Jumping from a rooftop would provide Cleo with attention whether it went well or poorly.
9. **D. Pa's** In this paragraph, the author describes Pa's love for Cleo and why she has so much influence over him.
10. **C. Cleo says that she does not want a kiss but wants a copper instead.** The first paragraph begins with Pa giving each of the girls a copper. It then explains that, at some point in the past, Cleo urged her father to give them coppers instead of kisses for doing chores.
11. **C. Serena felt that she had no choice but to give Cleo her copper to stop Cleo from doing something unsafe.** Serena does not want to give Cleo her copper; rather, Cleo is "compelling unnecessary sacrifice." Cleo does so by threatening to do something dangerous.
12. **D. Pa could not really afford to give Cleo and her sisters money.** The quote explains that Pa did not really have enough money to give some to Cleo and her sisters for doing chores. The phrase "dig deep" suggests that it was a sacrifice for him to do without that money, although he wanted to be generous. The language in the quote is figurative rather than literal, so choice (B) is incorrect.
13. **B. Cleo's boldness and her family's love for her sometimes make them feel powerless to resist her.** This passage is chiefly concerned with Cleo's character, which is bold and daring, and with the fact that her family members clearly love her. Both in the case of Pa giving the girls coppers and in the case of the sisters giving theirs to Cleo, Cleo's family members sometimes feel that they cannot refuse her.
14. **A. a coin** You can infer that a "copper" is money from this quote: "Four coppers a day, six days a week was half a day's pay."
15. **D. Short-term profitability** The last sentence of paragraph 2 states that "these companies were too focused on their short-term profitability."
16. **A. Getting your product right the first time is more profitable than fixing mistakes later.** The correct answer comes from the first sentence of paragraph 4: "In the long run, the Detroit automakers learned the hard way that getting your product right the first time is less costly and more profitable than retrenching to play catch-up."
17. **C. wanted to build quality cars with few repair problems** The U.S. automakers produced cars with "far more problems than their foreign equivalents." This suggests that quality was a priority for the foreign automakers but not for domestic automakers looking to "keep their costs low and profits high."

18. **C. emphasize U.S. automakers' preoccupation with keeping costs low and profits high in the short term, at the expense of their long-term outlook** "Bean counter" is a derogatory term for an accountant or manager who is excessively concerned with keeping expenses low. The author uses this term to underscore the idea that the U.S. automakers failed to consider the "bigger picture"—that is, failed to consider their long-term outlook.
19. **D. Detroit automakers produced cars of low quality.** According to the passage, the poor quality of cars produced by the United States in the 1970s caused many consumers to prefer foreign cars.
20. **A. critical** The authors speak negatively of the cars produced by U.S. automakers in the 1970s and 1980s and include comments such as "to add insult to injury" and "weren't considering the bigger picture."
21. **A. U.S. automakers** The last paragraph states that U.S. automakers eventually "got their act together in the 1990s and have stopped the erosion of market share."
22. **D. is hoping her mother won't hear her asking for money** The narrator misinterprets Marjie's actions. She thinks Marjie is asking for money for herself, not her mother. She therefore interprets Marjie's actions as trying to hide her request from her mother.
23. **C. Jennie is perplexed when the narrator blames Marjie.** When the narrator explains that she thought Marjie wanted the money for herself, "Jennie looked doubtful."
24. **B. discuss it defensively** Jennie meets with the narrator directly to try to explain what happened and express concern. However, she misunderstands the narrator's explanation, apologizes for trying to borrow money, and reacts defensively when it is suggested that her daughter would ask for money on her own. Jennie would likely have this same defensive reaction if criticized by a boss.
25. **A. the narrator's thoughts** The passage is written with a first person point of view from the narrator's perspective. This allows the reader access to the thoughts of the narrator as well as a description of the action that the narrator sees.
26. **C. They know each other but are not close.** The narrator is staying with Jennie and her family and obviously knows them, yet there is a formal tone to Jennie's explanation about borrowing money, and the narrator is unable to explain how she misunderstood Marjie and is left "floundering." Those aspects of their relationship help you infer they are not on close, intimate terms.
27. **C. uncomfortable** Jennie feels she has to explain why she was going to borrow money from the narrator, and the narrator not only misinterprets Marjie's actions but has a difficult time explaining to Jennie "the whole of Marjie's act." Jennie appears to doubt her and states her children would never ask for money, leaving the narrator "floundering a bit." The entire situation ends with the narrator (and perhaps even the reader) feeling uncomfortable over the situation.
28. **C. proud** Jennie's reaction in the last exchange with the narrator makes clear that she is proud and wants others to think well of her and her family.
29. **C. shied away from** The narrator decides not to explain why she thought Marjie wanted the money for herself. That's because, as she says, "It isn't easy to give evidence against a child of five." Tattling on Marjie was something she shied away from, or "funked."
30. **C. There may be more people in poverty than the Census Bureau's official estimate suggests.** Overall, the passage conveys this main point. Choices (A) and (B) are details rather than main ideas, and choice (D) is not supported by the passage.
31. **A. The rate of poverty rose during each year from 2007 to 2011.** The main idea of paragraph 1 is that the rate of poverty is increasing. This detail supports that main idea. Choice (B) is the main idea of paragraph 1. Choices (C) and (D) are suggested in later paragraphs.
32. **C. The bar graph supports the claim that a different way to measure poverty would produce a different estimate of the rate of poverty.** The bar graph shows that the SPM would produce different estimates of how many people are poor, a claim that the author makes in paragraph 4.
33. **C. Higher rents can cause people to have less money for food.** Paragraph 3 explains that "higher rents may leave individuals with less money for food." Higher rents are the cause, and less money for food is the effect. Choices (B) and (D) are too extreme. Choice (A) distorts the passage: the poverty thresholds measure who is poor—they don't cause people to be poor.
34. **A. people over 65; people under 18** Use the graph to answer this question. The lighter gray bars represent the estimates of poverty using the SPM. That bar is higher than the dark gray bar for people over 65 and lower than the dark gray bar for people under 18.
35. **B. The student has overlooked the fact that other factors might impact how much money local governments receive from the federal government.** The student has read in the passage that government spending on poverty is affected by the estimated rate of poverty. But even if the estimated rate of poverty were higher, that does not necessarily mean that government (at any level) would automatically spend more on poverty. After all, many factors go into governmental decision-making.
36. **C. wants governmental actions to be based on an accurate estimate of the rate of poverty** The author's chief concern is with the estimated rate of poverty

and whether or not it is accurate. Moreover, the author states in paragraph 5 that this matters because government spending is involved. None of the other choices here are supported by the passage.

37. **D. how best to spend public money** Both writers discuss their thoughts about the best way to use funds to improve Glenwood.

38. **C. Improving them is a good use of funds right now.** While both writers agree that the parks are not in good repair, they disagree over whether improving them is the best way to use resources at the present time.

39. **C. people who start businesses** The author's emphasis in the last paragraph of the first passage is on small businesses. He believes Glenwood needs more of them. Thus, you can infer that "entrepreneurs" are people who might start small businesses.

40. **D. Several restaurants downtown have survived the bad economy.** The business owner introduces her claim that the business district can attract new businesses in the second paragraph of the second passage. Choice (D) is one of the details used in that paragraph to support her claim.

41. **A. They are good when done in the best locations.** The local business owner doesn't feel that improving the public parks is the best use of funds right now, but she does feel that using those resources to improve the appearance of the business district would contribute to economic growth.

42. **B. Investing in our community is important for the future of Glenwood.** Both writers are arguing that public resources should be invested in improving the community to help ensure its prosperity in the long term.

43. **B. Glenwood initially invested in building parks but then did not spend enough to maintain them.** You know from the passage that Glenwood has more than one public park, with paths, picnic areas, and shelters. So it must be the case that, at some point, Glenwood invested money to build these spaces. You also know that these spaces are not well maintained, so Glenwood must not have invested in their upkeep.

44. **C. Hazing is frequently harmful.** The key idea the author wants to communicate is that hazing is harmful. Choices (A) and (B) are not supported by the passage, and choice (D) is a detail rather than the main idea.

45. **B. hazing and bullying** In the second paragraph, the author explains the differences between hazing and bullying.

46. **B. Hazing can involve beatings.** Of the four answer choices, only this detail supports the idea that hazing can be harmful.

47. **D. A victim of hazing can carry emotional scars for life.** The author makes this claim in the third paragraph but does not support it with evidence.

48. **C. a high school guidance counselor who would like to stop hazing** You can infer from the passage that it was written by someone who would like hazing to stop.

49. **D. disgusting** You can infer from the passage that "repulsive" has a very negative meaning. Only choice (D) fits.

50. **D. Bullying is usually performed by an individual or small group.** Only choice (D) is mentioned in the passage as being true of bullying. Choice (A) and (C) are used to describe hazing. Choice (B) might sound like a good principle, but it is not stated in the passage.

## Language Arts: Reading Practice Test Evaluation Chart

**Questions 1–50**

Circle the numbers of the questions that you got correct and then total them in the last column of each row.

| Content Area | Question Numbers | Number Correct/Total |
|---|---|---|
| **Interpreting Informational Text** Pages 71–95 | 3, 4, 6, 7, 15, 16, 17, 19, 20, 21, 30, 31, 33, 34, 36, 39, 41, 43, 44, 45, 48, 49, 50 | ____ out of 23 |
| **Analyzing Informational Text** Pages 96–111 | 1, 2, 5, 18, 32, 35, 37, 38, 40, 42, 46, 47 | ____ out of 12 |
| **Reading Literature** Pages 112–127 | 8, 9, 10, 11, 12, 13, 14, 22, 23, 24, 25, 26, 27, 28, 29 | ____ out of 15 |
| **TOTAL** | | ____ out of 50 |

If you do not have time to review the entire *Reading* unit, you may want to review the sections that need the most work.

As of the time of this printing, scoring information for the TASC Test was not available. To find out how the number of questions you got right on the Practice Test would translate into a final score, please visit your online center. See page viii for information about registering your Online Center.

# Language Arts: Writing Practice Test Answers and Explanations

**Pages 602–619**

**Part I: Language Skills**

1. **D. replace hole with whole** A hole is a place that is dug out of the ground; whole means "entire."
2. **D. change add to adding** The verb "add" should end with *-ing* to match "stripping" and "filling." All the verbs in a series should be in the same form.
3. **A. change ceiling meet to ceiling meets** "The ceiling" is a singular subject and requires a singular verb.
4. **C. is** The sentence should be in the present tense because the rest of the paragraph is in the present tense.
5. **C. remove the comma after paint** No comma is needed between the noun "paint" and the modifying phrase that follows it.
6. **A. missed, and go** Choice (A) corrects the comma splice with a logical conjunction.
7. **B. change is to are** The verb "are" agrees with the plural subject "gardens."
8. **B. insert a comma after garden** In a complex sentence, a comma should follow the dependent clause at the beginning of the sentence.
9. **B. insert a period after sponsor and capitalize this** Separating this sentence into two corrects the run-on.
10. **A. Next, choose a site for the garden.** Choice (A) is specific enough to be clear and general enough to cover all the details in the paragraph. It also includes a transition from the preceding paragraph.
11. **B. Start a new paragraph before sentence 3.** The first two sentences are about the benefits of community gardens. Sentence 3 begins a discussion of the steps involved in forming a community garden. Thus, a new paragraph is warranted.
12. **B. change piece to peace** A piece is a part of something; peace is a sense of calm and absence of conflict.
13. **C. replace you're with your** Because the workplace belongs to you, the possessive pronoun "your" is correct.
14. **A. disappear magically once you leave** What happens magically is that the symptoms disappear, not that you leave work. "Magically" should be placed closer to the part of the sentence that it modifies—symptoms disappearing.
15. **C. replace we with you** Because the rest of the passage uses the second-person pronoun you, this sentence should as well.
16. **A. change older to older building** A sentence needs both a subject and a verb. Here, the sentence was missing a noun to serve as its subject.
17. **D. the windows** The antecedent for the pronoun "they" was unclear; it did not appear until near the end of the sentence. Replacing "they" with "the windows" makes the meaning clear.
18. **A. delete the comma after gas** The phrase "deadly gas" modifies "carbon monoxide," so this comma is unnecessary.
19. **A. Tourism increases both air pollution and litter, which will** Choice (A) makes clear that tourists cause both pollution and litter.
20. **D. change developer's to developers** The word "developers" is plural—not possessive—so it should not have an apostrophe.
21. **C. remove sentence 7** The flyer focuses on the land on Compton Point. This sentence about other areas in the county is irrelevant and should be deleted.
22. **B. new jobs and the influx of tourism resulting** Choice |B| . smoothly combines the two sentences into a single sentence with a compound subject.
23. **D. change road to Road** All parts of a proper noun must be capitalized.
24. **A. change did to will** The demonstration is in the future, so the message will be sent to developers in the future.
25. **C. see** The verb form "see" is required with the subject "you." "Seen" requires the helping verb "have," but the present perfect tense "have seen" is not needed in the sentence, just the simple present.
26. **B. move sentence 3 to follow sentence 1** With sentence 1, sentence 3 catches the reader's attention and gives background information about the topic of the whole article. Sentences 2 and 4 introduce the main idea of the article.
27. **B. has been** The verb needs to agree with the subject "kite flying," which is singular.
28. **D. During a thunderstorm, he flew a kite with** In the original sentence, it sounds as if the thunderstorm had a key attached to it.
29. **B. replace their with there** The word "their" is a possessive meaning "belonging to them." Its homonym, "there," is needed in this sentence.
30. **B. humidity, wind speed, and barometric pressure** Choice (B) combines two sentences that have related details.
31. **A. Bell, the physicist and inventor, used** The phrase "the physicist and inventor" is an appositive describing Bell, so that phrase should be set off with commas.
32. **C. change power, you to power. You** The sentence as written contains a comma splice. Answer choice (C) corrects the comma splice.
33. **C. Some types of trucks, buses, and trains** In the original, there are three items in a series: trucks, buses, and some train engines. So the three things should be separated with commas. But the three things should also display parallel construction: the phrase "some types of" should apply to all three of them.

**34. B. change In both kinds to Both kinds have** The sentence as written is missing a subject. Choice (B) corrects this.

**35. C. change run to runs** The subject of the sentence is singular ("it") and requires a singular verb ("runs").

**36. C. change will move to moves** The clause containing the verb "will move" modifies the main clause, which is in the present tense ("is used"). Therefore, the modifying phrase should have the present tense as well.

**37. A. change It is to They are** The pronoun refers to "Hybrids" in the previous sentence and should be plural.

**38. C. move sentence 11 to the beginning of the next paragraph** Sentence 11 introduces a new idea which is discussed further in sentences 12 through 15. Thus, sentence 11 should be the topic sentence of the next paragraph.

**39. B. try to convince** "Try and convince" is not correct verb usage. "Try" should be followed by "to."

**40. C. change California and new Jersey to California and New Jersey** "New Jersey" is the name of a state and should be capitalized.

**41. C. change are to is** The subject of the sentence is "learning," which is singular and needs a singular verb.

**42. C. While knees** The sentence as written does not make clear the relationship between its first clause and its second. The writer is drawing a contrast between the frequency of injuries to knees and elbows and the low severity of those injuries.

**43. B. However, head injuries** The writer draws a contrast between head injuries, which can be severe, and the less serious knee and elbow injuries described in the previous sentence. Thus, a contrast word such as "However" is appropriate.

**44. B. split it into two sentences** As written, the sentence is overly long, with three independent clauses. Splitting it into two sentences would solve this problem.

**45. A. change Major Cities to major cities** The phrase "major cities" does not refer to any specific city and so should not be capitalized.

**46. C. The smog has become such a normal part** The phrase "that weather forecasters" later in the sentence refers back to this idea. Inserting the word "such" makes the phrase "that weather forecasters" follow logically.

**47. C. Cleaner gas has become a mainstay in many gas stations around the world.** The sentence as written is needlessly wordy. Choice (C) simplifies the original sentence without losing any of its meaning.

**48. C. change Air Resources' Board to Air Resources Board** The name of the board is the California Air Resources Board. In this case, "Resources" is a plural noun and not a possessive, so it does not take an apostrophe.

**49. B. they emit almost five times** The word "almost" should modify how much, so it should be placed before the phrase "five times."

**50. C. move sentence 8 to follow sentence 5** Sentence 8 introduces the idea that some progress has been made. Sentences 6 and 7 expand on that idea, so they should follow sentence 8.

**Part II: Essay**

Use the **Essay Evaluation Guide for Argument/Opinion Essays** on page 757 to evaluate your work.

## Language Arts: Writing Practice Test Evaluation Charts

### Questions 1–50

Circle the numbers of the questions that you got correct and then total them in the last column of each row.

| Content Area | Question Numbers | Number Correct/Total |
|---|---|---|
| **Writing Effective Sentences**<br>Pages 130–147 | 2, 6, 9, 14, 32, 33 | ____ out of 6 |
| **Connecting Ideas**<br>Pages 148–159 | 10, 11, 21, 22, 30, 38, 43, 50 | ____ out of 8 |
| **Polishing Your Writing**<br>Pages 186–195 | 15, 16, 17, 19, 24, 28, 34, 36, 37, 39, 42, 46, 47, 49 | ____ out of 14 |
| **Using Grammar Correctly**<br>Pages 196–211 | 3, 4, 7, 25, 26, 27, 35, 41 | ____ out of 8 |
| **Using Writing Mechanics**<br>Pages 215–225 | 1, 5, 8, 12, 13, 18, 20, 23, 29, 31, 40, 44, 45, 48 | ____ out of 14 |
| TOTAL | | ____ **out of 50** |

My essay score, based on the **Essay Evaluation Guide for Argument/Opinion Essays** on page 757, is _____.

If you do not have time to review the entire Writing unit, you may want to review the sections that need the most work.

As of the time of this printing, scoring information for the TASC was not available. To find out how the number of questions you got right on the Practice Test would translate into a final score, please visit your online center. See page viii for information about registering your Online Center.

# Mathematics Practice Test Answers and Explanations

**Part I: No Calculator Allowed, pages 620–633**

1. **D. $15x^2 - 8xy - 12y^2$** Use FOIL to distribute the terms in the expression: $(3x)(5x) + (3x)(-6y) + (2y)(5x) + (2y)(-6y) = 15x^2 - 18xy + 10xy - 12y^2 = 15x^2 - 8xy - 12y^2$
2. **21** The area of a triangle can be found using the formula $\frac{1}{2}bh$. In this triangle, the base is 7 and the height is 6. Plugging those values into the formula yields: $\frac{1}{2} \times 6 \times 7 = 21$.
3. **D. 7** First, factor to find the solutions to this quadratic equation: $x^2 - 4x - 21 = (x + 3)(x - 7)$. Then, set those factors equal to 0 to find the solutions to the quadratic equation: $x + 3 = 0$, $x = -3$ and $x - 7 = 0$, $x = 7$. The two solutions to the equation are –3 and 7. The question asks for the only positive solution, so the answer is 7.
4. **74** Following the order of operations, first simplify anything in parentheses:
$(4 - 18)$ becomes $-14$.
Next, simplify any terms with exponents:
$5^2 = 25$ and $3^3 = 27$
Now you have:
$3 \times 25 + 2(-14) + 27$.
Next, do multiplication and division in the order in which they appear:
$3 \times 25 = 75$ and $2(-14) = -28$.
Last, add and subtract in the order in which they appear:
$75 + (-28) + 27 = 74$
5. **D. $2x(x + y)$** To begin adding the polynomials together, factor out any like terms: $2x(x - y + 2y)$. Then combine any like terms together: $2x(x + y)$
6. **D. 66** To find the area of the figure, break it into two distinct shapes, a rectangle and a triangle. The rectangle has dimensions of 7 m and 8 m. Plugging these in to the area formula for a rectangle yields: $A = lw = 8\text{m} \times 7\text{m} = 56\text{m}^2$. The area for a triangle is $A = \frac{1}{2}bh$. In the triangle, the base is 8m – 4m = 4m and the height is 12m – 7m = 5m. Plugging these values in to the area formula for a triangle yields: $A = \frac{1}{2} \times b \times h = \frac{1}{2} \times 4\text{m} \times 5\text{m} = 10\text{m}^2$. Lastly, add both of the areas for the combined area of the figure: $56\text{m}^2 + 10\text{m}^2 = 66\text{m}^2$.
7. **B. $4x^2 + 12x + 7$** Combine like terms starting with the variable with the highest exponent, in this case: $x^2 + 3x^2 = 4x^2$. Next, combine the terms that contain a variable: $7x + 5x = 12x$. Lastly, combine the terms with no variables attached: $2 + 5 = 7$. Add these together: $4x^2 + 12x + 7$
8. **C. 12** Substitute appropriate values from the spreadsheet, then multiply, add, and subtract carefully, using order of operations.
$-[-2 - (3 - 5) + 3 \times (-4)] =$
$-[-2 - (-2) + (-12)] =$
$-[-2 + 2 - 12] =$
$-[-12] = 12$
9. **B. $2x^4 + 7x^3 + 4x$** Combine like terms from the exponent with the largest degree, which is 4: $6x^4 - 4x^4 = 2x^4$. Combine like terms from the exponent with the next largest degree, which is 3: $5x^3 + 2x^3 = 7x^3$. Finally, combine the terms from the exponent with the smallest degree: $7x - 3x = 4x$. The simplified polynomial is $2x^4 + 7x^3 + 4x$
10. **D. 150** The perimeter of the trapezoid is given as 50. Since the three sides shown add up to 38, the remaining side must be 12. The missing side is the height, so use the height and the two bases in the formula for the area of a trapezoid: $\frac{1}{2} \times 12(10 + 15) = 150$
11. **B. (8, –5)** Substitute the $x$ and $y$ values from each ordered pair into the equation. Only choice (B) makes the equation true.
$y = -\frac{3}{4}x + 1$
$-5 = -\frac{3}{4}(8) + 1$
$-5 = -6 + 1$
$-5 = -5$
12. **D. $y = \frac{1}{2}x + 3$** You can use the point-slope form to figure out the slope of the line first. Use (–6, 0) and (0, 3) as two points:
$0 - 3 = m(-6 - 0)$
$-3 = m(-6)$
$-3 = -6m$
$m = \frac{-3}{-6} = \frac{1}{2}$
Now you have the slope of the line, use either of the points to plug into the equation for a line, $y = mx + b$. Using (0, 3),
$3 = \frac{1}{2}(0) + b$
$3 = 0 + b$
$b = 3$
The equation of the line is
$y = \frac{1}{2}x + 3$
13. **B. 63** The pattern is that the next number is 1 more than double the previous number. To find the 6th term, use the 5th term, in this case 31: $31 \times 2 + 1 = 63$. To check your answer, confirm that 63 for the sixth term will yield 127 for the seventh term: $63 \times 2 + 1 = 127$.
14. **B. (\$24.50 – \$19) × 6** To determine how much Janice will save, she needs to determine the price difference between one evening and one afternoon ticket (\$24.50 – \$19) and then multiply that number by 6, the total number of tickets she intends to purchase. Thus, the equation that will supply her total savings is (\$24.50 – \$19) × 6.
15. **2** Absolute change refers to the difference, either positive or negative, between two numbers. Over the three elections listed, party $x$ gained 2 seats, lost 6 seats, and then regained 2 seats. That's a net loss of 2.
16. **B. $28\pi$** Use the radius of 2 and the height of 5 in the formula for the surface area of a cylinder: $2\pi(2 \times 5) + 2\pi(2^2) = 20\pi + 8\pi = 28\pi$
17. **C. $x + 3$** Every term in the expression is divisible by two, so begin by simplifying: $\frac{2x^2-6x-36}{2x-12} = \frac{x^2-3x-18}{x-6}$. Next, factor the numerator of the fraction and cancel:
$\frac{x^2-3x-18}{x-6} = \frac{(x-6)(x+3)}{x-6} = x + 3$
18. **B. \$65,000** About \$130,000 was made from catalog sales. About \$65,000 was made from online sales. Subtract \$65,000 from \$130,000 to get \$65,000.
19. **D.** The ≤ symbol indicates "greater than or equal to," which is indicated with a filled-in dot. The symbol < indicates "less

than" (but not equal to), which is indicated with an open dot.

**20. A. (–4, –5)** Solve by graphing or by substitution. The point of intersection will be where the lines cross each other. The lines intersect at the point (–4, –5).
To solve by substitution, use the first equation to substitute the value of $y$ in the second equation:
$2x + 3 = -\frac{1}{2}x - 7$
$2\frac{1}{2}x = -10$
$x = \frac{-10}{2\frac{1}{2}} = -4$
Now use that value of $x$ to find the value of y using the first equation:
$y = 2(-4) + 3 = -5$
The solution of the equation set is (–4, –5).

**21. C.** $\sqrt{9^2 + 12^2}$ The cable forms the hypotenuse of a triangle with side lengths of 9 feet and 12 feet. Use the Pythagorean theorem ($9^2 + 12^2 = c^2$) to determine the length of the hypotenuse $c: c = \sqrt{9^2 + 12^2}$.

**22. A. –2** To find slope, calculate $\frac{\text{rise}}{\text{run}}$. In this case, the line moves up two units for each unit it moves to the left. Thus, the slope is negative: $\frac{2}{-1} = -2$

**23. D. –8 and –12** To solve this system of linear equations, first write two equations with the information given. Call the numbers $x$ and $y$. The first sentence tells you that $x = 12 + 3y$, and the second sentence tells you that $x + y = -20$. Rewrite the second equation so that $x$ is isolated on one side of the equals sign: $x = -20 - y$. Now that each equation is written in terms of $x$, set the two expressions for $x$ equal to each other:
$12 + 3y = -20 - y$.
Simplify this equation: $4y = -32$, so $y = -8$. Substitute this value for $y$ back into the second equation: $x + -8 = -20$, so $x$ must equal –12.

**24. D. –9 and 2** To find the solutions to this quadratic equation, start by setting it equal to 0. The equation then becomes $3x^2 + 21x - 54 = 0$. Then, divide each term by 3 to make the equation $x^2 + 7x - 18 = 0$.
Now that the $x^2$ term has a coefficient of 1, factor the equation into two terms: $(x + 9)(x - 2)$.
So $x + 9 = 0$, and $x - 2 = 0$. $x = -9$ and $x = 2$. The correct answer is D.

**25. A. $e = 0.1s + 20{,}000$** If Jonas sells nothing, he earns \$20,000 per year. Then, the graph shows that he earns 10%, or 0.1, of whatever he sells. (This is a linear equation: 20,000 is the $y$-intercept and 0.1 is the slope.)

## Part II: Calculator Allowed, pages 628-633

**26. C.** $c = 22.5(h + 1)$ Because there is a charge of \$22.50 per hour, you need \$22.50$h$ within the equation. Then, add the initial \$22.50 and the equation becomes $c = 22.50h + 22.50$. To simplify, factor out the \$22.50 from the right side of the equation: $c = 22.50(h + 1)$.

**27. C. 502.4** This word problem is asking you for the volume of a cylinder. That formula is $V = \pi r^2 h$. Plug in the values you are given: $V = \pi \times 4^2 \times 10$. Substituting 3.14 for pi gives you $V = 3.14 \times 4^2 \times 10 = 502.4$

**28. 77** Brad's average golf score would be found like this:
$\frac{\textit{sum of scores}}{\textit{number of scores}} = \textit{average score}$
Plug the information you are given in the question into the formula and solve for the unknown:
$\frac{78 + 86 + 82 + 81 + 82 + x}{6} = 81$
$78 + 86 + 82 + 81 + 82 + x = 486$
$409 + x = 486$
$x = 77$

**29. C. 4 mph** The kayaker traveled for a total of 12 miles: 6 miles upstream and 6 miles downstream. This took her 3 hours (2 hours upstream + 1 hour downstream). Divide the distance by the time to find her average rate of speed per hour: $\frac{12 \text{ miles}}{3 \text{ hours}} = 4$ miles per hour.

**30. 10** Because sides AB and CD are parallel, the figure is a trapezoid. Use the formula for the area of a trapezoid: $A = \frac{1}{2}h(b_1 + b_2)$ and plug in the values given.
$A = \frac{1}{2}(2.5)(2 + 6)$
$A = \frac{1}{2}(2.5)(8)$
$A = 10$

**31. A. \$214.40** Substitute 4 for $b$ and 3 for $n$ into the function. Then solve the equation.
$C = \$25.60(4) + \$14(4)(3 - 1)$
$= \$102.40 + \$112.00$
$= \$214.40$

**32. A. \$600** Find 24% of \$2500. \$2500 × 0.24 = \$600. You could estimate this answer by thinking 24% is roughly $\frac{1}{4}$, and choice (A) is closest to one-fourth of the Whitman's budget.

**33. C. \$7.50** Six boxes of pasta will be purchased: 3 of ziti and 3 of spaghetti. Set up the proportion $\frac{4}{5} = \frac{6}{x}$ where $x$ is the price of 6 boxes of pasta.Cross-multiply and divide to solve for $x$: $5 \times 6 = 30$ and $30 \div 4 = 7.5$

**34. C. \$410** Use the formula Simple interest = principal × rate × time. Note that time is expressed in terms of a year, so 6 months = $\frac{1}{2}$ year: $I = \$400 \times 0.05 \times \frac{1}{2}$ which equals \$10. This is the interest, so Mike will pay back the interest plus the \$400 principal for a total of \$410.

**35. D.**

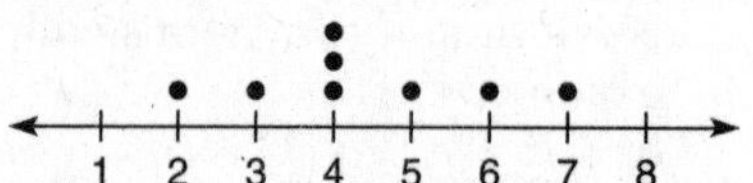


In three of the weeks, Inge found four spiders, which are represented by the three dots above the number 4. In the remaining weeks she found a different number of spiders each week ranging in number from 2 to 7. Thus, there should be one dot above the numbers 2, 3, 5, 6, and 7.

**36. B. 58** Plug in the values given for $x$ and $y$ and then follow the order of operations:
$3[2(4) - 5] + (3 + 4)^2 = 3(8 - 5) + 7^2 = 3(3) + 49 = 9 + 49 = 58$

**37. C. 12** The formula for the area of a circle is $A = \pi r^2$ where $r$ refers to the radius of the circle. The diameter of a circle (a straight line segment that goes from one edge of the circle to the other and passes through the center of the circle) is $2r$, or two times the length of the radius. The circle shown in this problem has an area of $36\pi$. Plug that into the area formula and find the length of the circle's radius:

$36\pi = \pi r^2$

$\frac{36\pi}{\pi} = \frac{\pi r^2}{\pi}$

$36 = r^2$

$\sqrt{36} = \sqrt{r^2}$

$6 = r$

Now that you know the radius has a length of 6, multiply that length by 2 to get the diameter: $6 \times 2 = 12$

**38.** **2.8%** To calculate the percent increase or decrease from Karen's 2011 earnings to her 2012 earnings, first find exactly how much she earned in each year. In 2011, she earned \$52,500 + \$6,250, which equals \$58,750. In 2012, she earned \$56,300 + \$4,100, which equals \$60,400.

To calculate the percent change from 2011 to 2012, use the percent change formula: $\frac{\textit{amount of change}}{\textit{original value}}$

In this case, that gives you $\frac{60{,}400 - 58{,}750}{58{,}750} = \frac{1{,}650}{58{,}750}$ which equals .028, or 2.8%.

**39.** **79** To get the answer, plug 15 into the equation for $x : y = 5(15) + 4 = 75 + 4 = 79$.

**40.** **B. 157 – $y$ = 101 + $y$** To begin with, Imtaez had \$157. He then paid \$y to the food runner, so he had (\$157 – $y$). According to the information given, that amount was equal to (\$101 + $y$).

**41.** **39** The two given legs of triangle A are 3 times the length of the two legs in triangle B. Because the triangles are similar, the hypotenuse of triangle A will be three times the length of the hypotenuse of triangle B: $3 \times 13 = 39$.

**42.** **C. 48** First, convert the length of the section of fence into inches: $22 \times 12\ in = 264$. That number represents how many inches John must cover with new boards. Divide that number by the width of each board to find out how many boards will be required: $\frac{264}{5.5} = 48$.

**43.** **A. (6, 10)** You can solve either by graphing the lines or by substitution. To solve by substitution, use the first equation to substitute the value of $y$ in the second equation:

$2(x + 4) + 4x = 44$

$2x + 8 + 4x = 44$

$6x + 8 = 44$

$6x = 36$

$x = 6$

Now use that value of $x$ to find the value of $y$ using the first equation:

$y = 6 + 4$

$y = 10$

**44.** **D. 28%** Probability is the ratio of the number of favorable outcomes to the number of possible outcomes. Add up the numbers of marbles to find out how many marbles are in the bag. 12 + 3 + 6 + 4 = 25. Therefore, 25 is the number of possible outcomes. 7 marbles are either blue or yellow. 7 is the number of favorable outcomes. $\frac{7}{25} \times \frac{4}{4} = \frac{28}{100}$, or 28%.

**45.** **628** To find the volume of a cylinder, use the formula $V = \pi r^2 h$. In this case, the radius is 5 and the height is 8. Plugging the equation into a calculator, yields $V = \pi \times 5^2 \times 8 \approx 628.3$. Round to the nearest unit. If you use 3.14 for pi, the answer to this problem will be the same: $3.14 \times 5^2 \times 8 = 628$.

**46.** **D. 514** To find the volume of a cone, use the formula from the formula sheet: $V = \frac{1}{3}\pi r^2 h$. Plug in values from the question stem and the approximate value of pi:

$V = \frac{1}{3}\pi(6.4)^2(12)$

$V = \frac{1}{3}(3.14)(40.96)(12) \approx 514.$

**47.** **720** This question asks how many orderings, or permutations, of three out of ten are possible. Multiply: $10 \times 9 \times 8 = 720$.

**48.** **31.5** To find the area of a right triangle, first find the base and the height. In this triangle, the base is the length along the $x$-axis: $5 - (-4) = 9$. The height is the length along the $y$-axis: $4 - (-3) = 7$. Plugging these into the area formula for a triangle is: $A = \frac{1}{2} \times b \times h = \frac{1}{2} \times 9 \times 7 = 31.5$.

**49.** **C. 240** Use the percent formula, $\% = \frac{\text{part}}{\text{whole}} \times 100\%$. You are given the part and the percent, and are solving for the whole.

$5\% = \frac{12}{x} \times 100\%$

$x = \frac{12 \times 100\%}{5\%}$

$x = 12 \times 20 = 240$

**50.** **C. \$113.75** It takes Fabio 45 minutes, or $\frac{3}{4}$ of an hour to install a hard drive. It takes him exactly one hour to install an operating system. It will take him $1\frac{3}{4}$ hours to complete the job. Since he charges \$65 per hour, multiply $1\frac{3}{4}$ by \$65 to find the total charge:

$1\frac{3}{4} \times \$65 = \$113.75$

**51.** **D. $1.335 \times 10^9$** You move the decimal point 9 places to the left to get 1.335. Multiply this by $10^9$ to get the scientific notation $1.335 \times 10^9$.

**52.** **62** The area of a parallelogram is the base times the height: $A = b \times h = 10 \times 6.2 = 62$.

## Mathematics Practice Test Evaluation Charts

Circle the numbers of the questions that you answered correctly and then total them in the last column of each row.

| Content Area | Question Numbers | Number Correct/Total |
|---|---|---|
| **Number and Quantity I: Problem Solving**<br>Pages 232–357 | 29 | ____/1 |
| **Number and Quantity II: Decimals and Fractions**<br>Pages 258–281 | 42, 50 | ____/2 |
| **Number and Quantity III: Ratio, Proportion, and Percent**<br>Pages 282–301 | 33, 34, 38, 49 | ____/4 |
| **Statistics and Probability**<br>Pages 302–333 | 18, 28, 32, 35, 44, 47 | ____/6 |
| **Algebraic Expressions**<br>Pages 334–367 | 1, 3, 4, 5, 7, 8, 9, 12, 14, 15, 17, 51 | ____/12 |
| **Functions**<br>Pages 368–399 | 11, 12, 13, 19, 20, 22, 23, 24, 25, 26, 31, 39, 40, 43 | ____/14 |
| **Geometry**<br>Pages 400–435 | 2, 6, 10, 16, 21, 27, 30, 37, 41, 45, 46, 48, 52 | ____/13 |
| TOTAL | | **____/52** |

If you do not have time to review the entire *Mathematics* unit, you may want to review the sections that need the most work.

As of the time of this printing, scoring information for the TASC Test was not available. To find out how the number of questions you got right on the Practice Test would translate into a final score, please visit your online center. See page viii for information about registering your Online Center.

# Social Studies Practice Test Answers and Explanations

**Pages 634–648**

1. **D. The United States had an unfavorable balance of trade in merchandise during the 2000s.** According to the passage, the balance of trade is the difference between exports and imports. When imports are greater than exports, the balance of trade is unfavorable. Since the graph shows that imports consistently exceeded exports during the 2000s, you can conclude that the balance of trade in merchandise was unfavorable during the decade.
2. **B. In 2009, the value of imports fell by a greater amount than the value of exports did.** In 2009, the value of imports was about $600 million less than the previous year. In 2009, the value of exports was about $300 million less than the previous year. Therefore, choice (C) is the opposite of what the graph represents. Choices (A) and (D) are not supported, because the graph includes no information about what may have caused a fall in the value of imports and exports.
3. **D. More people identified as independents than as Democrats, and more identified as Democrats than as Republicans.** This statement was true for all months represented in the chart. Choice (A) overstates the numerical gap between independents and Republicans. Choice (B) might have looked tempting if you misread "10 percent more" as "10 percentage points more." Choice (C) is unsupported as well. While it's true that the three columns total to 98 percent for most months, you cannot draw an inference about the remaining 2 percent.
4. **C. Africa** Look for the continent with the highest percentage of countries colored light gray.
5. **D. European nations had, on average, higher GDP per capita than South American nations.** The darker gray shading in many European countries indicates a higher GDP per capita than that in South American nations. None of the other answer choices are supported because each one suggests a cause for differences in GDP per capita. The map conveys no information about what might cause differences in GDP per capita.
6. **D. The CPI grew in all but one of the years represented in the table.** Look at the second column, which lists the actual CPI. In each year except for 2009, the CPI was higher than the year before. Choice (A) is unsupported because the CPI grew in four of the five years (not three of them). Choice (B) is incorrect because the table contains no information about what caused changes in the CPI. Choice (C) might have looked tempting if you were looking at the third column of the table, but that third column represents not the CPI itself but the percent of change over the previous year.
7. **C. Many people moved to cities to be near factory jobs.** The passage states that many people left farms to work in factories. You can infer that many of them moved from rural areas, where farms are located, to urban areas, where factories are often located. The other choices are not supported by the facts given.
8. **B. Both valued a stable political framework for society.** The paragraph indicates that this was one thing the ancient Chinese and the ancient Greeks had in common.
9. **C. The war created a huge demand for military equipment and supplies.** The chart shows that there was a substantial increase in manufacturing output between 1939 (when World War II began in Europe) and 1941. Even though the United States did not enter the war until late 1941, industry had already geared up to sell equipment and supplies to the Allies in Europe.
10. **A. patriotism** The tendency of the American public to support a president's emergency foreign policy actions is sometimes called the "rally 'round the flag" effect.
11. **B. problems with consistently enforcing the Sherman Antitrust Act led to further legislation to prevent monopolies** In the passage, the author explains the intention behind the Sherman Antitrust Act: to make monopolies illegal. He goes on to outline the limitations of the act, arguing that its broad language rendered it insufficient to solve the problems created by monopolies. He concludes the paragraph by telling how Congress responded to the problems in the Sherman Antitrust Act by passing additional laws to control monopolistic practices.
12. **B. The dangers of climate change are more significant than the possible benefits.** The author states that climate change may lead to benefits such as longer growing seasons but that "the hazards far outweigh any potential advantages." Choices (A) and (D) are contradicted by the passage. The author does not address choice (C).
13. **D. The United States has the second highest rate of carbon emissions per person.** All of the choices are mentioned in the passage, but only choice (D) is directly related to the author's claim that the United States must lead the way in combating climate change.
14. **B. Whites wanted to take over Indian lands in the eastern states.** The graphic shows the Indians being moved away from eastern states to Kansas and Oklahoma. The question asks about "forcible" relocation, so the correct answer can't be about what Indians wanted.
15. **D. the Seminole** The Seminole tribe's home territory was in Florida, which was farthest from the new, government-declared Indian Territory in the Midwest.
16. **C. Special interest groups are treated better than voters by members of Congress.** The cartoonist is using irony in the

caption to indicate that he thinks members of Congress treat voters badly, but treat people who represent special interest groups well.

17. **C. Industrialization and urbanization caused many changes in family life in the late 1800s.** This covers the main points of the passage, which discusses the impact of industrialization and urbanization on the American family. The other choices are all supporting details.

18. **C. It did not impose direct economic costs on the colonists.** All of the other acts of Parliament shown in the chart cost the colonists money, whether by having to pay import taxes, buy revenue stamps, or use their own resources to shelter British soldiers.

19. **A. The Declaration of Independence, which explained why the colonies broke away from Great Britain** The acts of Parliament listed in the chart were grievances used to justify declaring independence.

20. **A. 0% to 4%** First find the United States on the map and see what shade it is colored. Then consult the map key to see the percentage of undernourished people that shade represents. The map indicates that the percentage range is 0% to 4%.

21. **D. Hunger is a major problem in many countries in Africa.** More than 20 nations in Africa have a very high percentage of undernourished people. The remaining options are not supported by the data on the map.

22. **C. Both established methods of self-government in the English colonies.** Both documents set forth rules and laws for the self-government of specific English colonies.

23. **D. the English Bill of Rights** The English Bill of Rights tied the king's right to rule to the consent of the people's representatives, and the colonists' major grievance was taxation without representation. The colonists felt they should be granted the same representation and rights as other British citizens, which were listed in the English Bill of Rights.

24. **D. Slavery destroyed the culture of the slaves, diminishing their self-respect.** According to the paragraph, this is an opinion, or belief, held by some historians. The other choices are all facts stated in the paragraph.

25. **B. 30 cents** According to the passage, market price is reached under equilibrium conditions—when supply equals demand. According to the graph, supply and demand cross each other—and so are equal—at 30 cents.

26. **D. The market price would go up.** When the supply decreases and demand stays the same, the market price increases. The same number of people want to buy fewer apples, so the people will generally be willing to pay more for the apples.

27. **D. Alabama** Iowa and Delaware never seceded, so they never belonged to the Confederacy. Alabama seceded before the Battle of Fort Sumter, so it belonged to the Confederacy both before and after the Battle of Fort Sumter. North Carolina also belonged to the Confederacy, but it didn't secede until after the Battle of Fort Sumter.

28. **C. the Court of International Trade** "International trade" is commerce with foreign companies, so the case would most likely be filed in the Court of International Trade.

29. **B. The volume and variety of federal cases were too great for a single court to handle.** It would be impractical to have just one court handling all cases; the workload would be too great.

30. **A. the Supreme Court of the United States** According to the passage, cases are appealed to higher level courts; according to the diagram, the Supreme Court is the highest court of appeal.

31. **B. The war effort needs the help of everyone, including men, women and children.** The focus of the poster is to enlist the help of everyone in the country for the war effort. The sleeping woman represents an American population that needs to take action.

32. **D. at 0° latitude** On both of these projections the distortions are greatest near the north and south poles. Along the equator (0° latitude), the maps look most alike and most similar to a globe; the distortions increase as you go north or south toward the poles.

33. **B. The interrupted projection distorts distances across the oceans.** The interrupted projection was a poor choice because ocean areas are cut apart on the map, making it very difficult to measure distances on an around-the-world voyage.

34. **B. W and X only** The passage states that the Roman emperors built no fortifications along sea frontiers. The map indicates that W and X were sea coasts. Y is a river frontier and so would have taken light fortifications. Z is a land barrier and so would probably have been heavily fortified.

35. **C. The Fifth Amendment applies to the federal government, and the Fourteenth Amendment, to state governments.** According to the passage, this is one of the main differences between the two amendments.

36. **A. Several factors make Haiti unique among Caribbean nations.** Most of the facts cited in the passage explain how Haiti differs from other nations. Choice (A) summarizes these facts. The other choices are details and fail to summarize the gist of the passage.

37. **B. People in Damascus were aware of religions practiced elsewhere.** If Damascus was on the Silk Road, traders from Europe, Africa, China, and other parts of the world passed through Damascus, it is highly likely that the citizens of Damascus learned a little about those traders' cultures and religions. None of the

other choices are supported by the facts given.

38. **D. Direct Democracy and Representative Democracy** The table's left column describes direct democracy, and its right column describes representative democracy. Thus, choice (D) is the best title for the table.

39. **C. Constitution** The sentence describes the U.S. Constitution. The Declaration of Independence (A) claimed that the colonies were no longer under English rule but did not establish the structure of government. The Articles of Confederation (B) established an older system of government and are no longer in effect. The Magna Carta (D) is an English document.

40. **A. the Crusades** The Crusades were a series of Medieval conflicts in which Europeans invaded Middle Eastern cities.

41. **C. a reason to remember how foolish people can be** The historian is using figurative language and is not describing a physical monument. "Folly" means foolishness or error. The historian is saying that people can look back to the Crusades as a reminder of how human error can have terrible consequences.

42. **D. recession** A recession is a general slowdown in economic activity; the list in the box describes the various facets of a recession.

43. **C. 5-ounce tubes of oil paint** Producer goods are goods sold to companies that manufacture products or provide services. Aluminum sheets, copper bricks, and large quantities of fiber optic cable would most likely be sold to such companies. Five ounces of oil paint is a small quantity, so would most likely be sold to an individual who enjoys painting.

44. **B. federalism** Madison's quote describes a division of powers between the national (or federal) government and the state governments. That division of powers is federalism.

45. **D. outlawing behavior such as drug use or robbery** Legislatures (such as Congress or state legislatures) write laws. Courts, such as the Supreme Court, may sometimes pass judgment about whether or not those laws are Constitutional, but courts do not write laws.

46. **A. the First Amendment, which protects the right of free speech** The last sentence of the passage states that the Court decided that the law restricted the expression of political ideas—in other words, that it restricted speech.

47. **A. George is offended by a joke made by a co-worker and complains to his manager about it.** While many employers have policies prohibiting offensive jokes, the National Labor Relations Act does not cover that activity. It does cover employees discussing unions (B), joining unions (C), and striking (D).

## Social Studies Practice Test Evaluation Charts

**Questions 1–34**

Circle the numbers of the questions that you got correct and then total them in the last column of each row.

| Content Area | Question Numbers | Number Correct/Total |
|---|---|---|
| **U.S. History**<br>Pages 456–469 | 14, 15, 17, 18, 19, 22, 23, 24, 27, 31, 35 | ____ out of 11 |
| **Civics and Government**<br>Pages 470–483 | 3, 10, 16, 28, 29, 30, 38, 39, 44, 45, 46, 47 | ____ out of 12 |
| **Economics**<br>Pages 484–495 | 1, 2, 5, 6, 9, 11, 25, 26, 42, 43 | ____ out of 10 |
| **World History**<br>Pages 496–509 | 7, 8, 34, 36, 37, 40, 41 | ____ out of 7 |
| **Geography**<br>Pages 510–519 | 4, 12, 13, 20, 21, 32, 33 | ____ out of 7 |
| TOTAL | | ____ **out of 47** |

Most of the social studies questions in this practice test also test one of the Social Studies skills discussed on pages 438–455. For the sake of simplicity and readability, those skills have been omitted from this chart. However, if you missed several questions on the Social Studies Practice Test, be sure to review not only the relevant content area but also the chapter on Social Studies Skills.

If you do not have time to review the entire *Social Studies* unit, you may want to review the sections that need the most work.

As of the time of this printing, scoring information for the TASC Test was not available. To find out how the number of questions you got right on the Practice Test would translate into a final score, please visit your Online Center. See page vii for information about registering for your Online Center.

# SCIENCE PRACTICE TEST ANSWERS AND EXPLANATIONS

## Pages 649–663

1. **A. lift** As the diagram shows and the paragraph implies, the wing's weight and the opposing force of the air under it result in an upward force called *lift*.
2. **C. "Why We Sleep "** The topic of the paragraph is why sleep evolved in humans, and the paragraph cites several reasons for sleeping. The other options are too specific.
3. **B. 17** If the mean is 23 degrees, then the sum of all six angle measurements must be $23 \times 6 = 138$ degrees. Since the five given angles add up to 121 degrees, the sixth angle must make up the difference, or $138 - 121 = 17$ degrees.
4. **B. the air and rainwater in the soil** According to the diagram, nitrogen-fixing bacteria take nitrogen from both the air and rain found in soil.
5. **C. The recycling of nitrogen through the biosphere involves many complex processes.** This is a general statement, or conclusion, that is supported by the various details in the diagram. The other statements are details from the diagram.
6. **B. compost with plant and animal wastes** According to the diagram, plant and animal waste contains nitrogen compounds that decomposers, including nitrite bacteria and nitrate bacteria, break down. In this way, composting with plant and animal wastes results in the addition of usable forms of nitrogen to the soil. So composting with organic waste (plant and animal materials) would be an alternative to synthetic fertilizers.
7. **D. For the three compounds shown, solubility increases as temperature increases.** The graph shows all three substances having increased solubility as the temperature rises from 0°C to 50°C. None of the other statements is supported by information in the graph.
8. **A. He guessed that slightly warm water might be better for plants than cool water.** A hypothesis is a guess that a scientist intends to test through a study or experiment. The experiment itself (choice (B)) or the data it produces (choice (C)) are not the hypothesis. Choice (D) is the scientist's conclusion.
9. **A. Its charge would become positive.** If an atom loses an electron, it has more protons than electrons, and thus it has a net positive charge. (Such an atom is called a positive ion.)
10. **A. the cracking of granite from the expansion of freezing water** This is an example of physical weathering because it involves changes of temperature causing physical effects on rock. Choice (C) is not an example of weathering because transport is involved.
11. **C. how special fluids keep insects alive during subfreezing weather** Understanding how insects can survive freezing may be a key to finding a way to freeze organs without destroying them.
12. **B. sea star** Of the four animals shown, only the sea star has a center section from which similar parts radiate. All the other animals are bilaterally symmetrical.
13. **C. Hydrogen peroxide is decomposing into water and oxygen.** The chemical reaction begins on the left hand side of the equation, which represents two hydrogen peroxide molecules. Thus, it is incorrect to say that hydrogen peroxide is being made (as in choices (A) or (D)). Rather, hydrogen peroxide is decomposing, or breaking up, into two substances. What remains after the chemical reaction is written on the right hand side of the equation. The question stem explains that water is composed of two hydrogen atoms and an oxygen atom, so the results of the reaction are water and $O_2$, which you can infer represents oxygen. Choice (B) is incomplete and (C) is correct.
14. **A. Mercury and bromine are liquids at room temperature.** Room temperature is about 70°F. The chart indicates that both mercury and bromine are liquids at that temperature: each has a melting point—the temperature at which it becomes a liquid—well below room temperature. Also, each has a boiling point—the temperature at which it goes from liquid to gas—well above room temperature.
15. **D. Bacteria quickly evolved resistance to antibiotic drugs.** In 1969, the Surgeon General did not anticipate that bacteria would evolve to be resistant to the antibiotics that had been so effective until that time.
16. **B. The student should have used books of the same height for all of the ramps.** The height of the ramp affects how far the ball rolls. So the height of the ramp should be a controlled variable in this experiment. By using one ramp that is not as high as the others, the student is introducing a second variable into the experiment, which makes his data invalid for the ramp that is lower than the others.
17. **D. The dog has canines and the sheep does not.** If you compare the two diagrams, you will see that the sheep does not have any canines; instead the sheep has a large gap where the canines would be.
18. **C. The five largest asteroids are all farther from the sun than Earth is.** According to the chart, Earth's distance from the sun is set at 1, so any value greater than 1 indicates that the asteroid is farther from the sun than Earth is. All the asteroids have distance values of 2 or greater, so they are all farther from the sun than Earth is.
19. **C. less than** If all the lobsters weighed the maximum of 9 lbs, the 220 million pounds of lobster would still account for more than 20 million individual animals. Two blue lobsters out of 20 million lobsters is substantially less likely than the estimated 1 in 2 million occurrence of the blue mutation.

**20. A. Pressure builds up inside the magma chamber and vent.** If you examine the diagram, you will see that hot magma wells up into the volcano's cone. You need to infer that when the pressure builds up sufficiently, the volcano explodes, or erupts. None of the other events described would cause a violent explosion from the inside of the volcano.

**21. B. when food is digested, as when an enzyme in saliva called ptyalin breaks down starch into sugars without itself changing** The catalyst is the enzyme ptyalin; you can identify ptyalin as the catalyst, because it aids the chemical reaction of digestion but itself remains unchanged after the reaction. None of the other reactions include a substance that remains unchanged.

**22. B. People can reduce their chances of developing age-related hearing loss by not smoking.** Of all the options, this is the only one that is a hypothesis that the researchers could have been testing with their experiment. (A) is too general to be a hypothesis for this experiment and is stated more like a conclusion than a hypothesis. The other options are facts relating to the study.

**23. D. Humans contain a higher percentage of carbon than bacteria do.** To find the correct answer, you must check each statement against the graphs to see whether the information in the graphs supports the statement. The graphs show that humans have a higher percentage of carbon than bacteria have.

**24. B. Both involve effort applied with circular motion.** The diagrams show that the effort applied to each of these machines is circular.

**25. A. During an ice age, temperatures drop and ice covers vast areas of Earth.** According to the passage, scientists aren't sure what causes ice ages. Choices (B), (C), and (D) each offer a different hypothesis for what causes an ice age. By contrast, choice (A) is an objective fact.

**26. D. The arrangement of the carbon, hydrogen, and oxygen atoms in the two hydrocarbons is different.** Although ether and ethanol both have the same number of carbon, hydrogen, and oxygen atoms, the different arrangements of atoms in each compound results in two substances with different properties.

**27. D. Observation is useful as long as the results are used to support or disprove a hypothesis.** According to Darwin's remarks, it is a waste of time to observe phenomena if you do not use what you observe to evaluate your theories.

**28. C. surficial; hydrothermal** The passage explains that surficial processes happen at the Earth's surface, so the action of wind would be one such process. Hydrothermal processes involve the movement of water underground, so the movement of seawater underground would be an example of a hydrothermal process.

**29. A. Crescent City** Begin by finding each increase in rainfall:

| | |
|---|---|
| Crescent City | 13.42 |
| Eureka | 14.76 |
| Ukiah | 17.84 |
| Redding | 6.74 |
| Sacramento | 4.41 |

The median is the middle value in a group of numbers. Arrange the numbers above in order; the middle value belongs to Crescent City.

**30. A. lightning** The passage states that thunderstorms, which often generate lightning, occur in the troposphere, and that blue jets, a special kind of lightning, occur in the stratosphere.

**31. A. Brock placed wooden cubes that weighed 1 cc, 10 cc, and 100 cc in water. He observed their buoyancy. Then he placed iron cubes of 1 cc, 10 cc, and 100 cc in water and observed their buoyancy.** This choice describes the experiment Brock conducted in order to test his hypothesis. Choice (B) describes "Step 4: Draw a conclusion." Choice (C) corresponds to "Step 1: Formulate a question about a phenomenon." Choice (D) was Brock's "Step 2: Form a hypothesis."

**32. D. water** The passage states that Mars has polar ice caps. Those ice caps consist of frozen water. The passage provides no support for any of the other choices.

**33. D.**

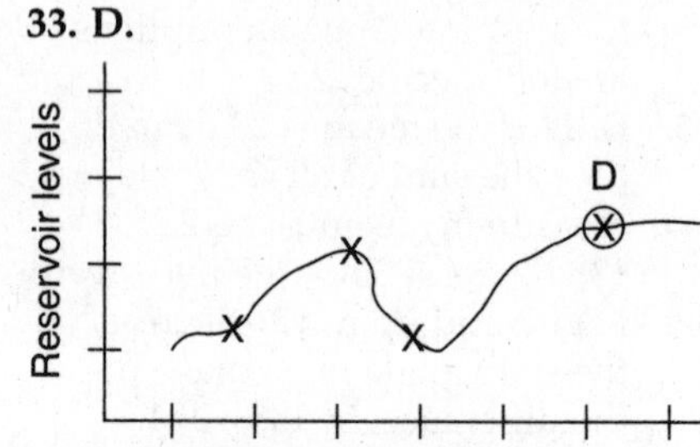


Since the dam was built to stop fluctuation, or change, in reservoir levels, 1993 must be the final year that reservoir levels changed.

**34. B. electron** In the model, the pudding is meant to represent the uniform cloud of positive charge and the plums are meant to represent the electrons.

**35. A. A teacher's perfume can be detected at the back of the classroom.** This is an example of diffusion, the spreading of gas molecules (perfume vapor) throughout a container (the classroom).

**36. B. Oxygen is one of the products of photosynthesis.** The products of the chemical reaction appear on the right hand side of the arrow. One of those products is six atoms of $O_2$, which is oxygen.

**37. C. circulatory and respiratory** The passage describes how the heart and blood vessels, which are part of the circulatory system, work with the lungs, which are part of the respiratory system, to infuse blood with oxygen and carry it throughout the body.

**38. B. A series of massive volcanic eruptions lasting many years** The dust from a series of major volcanic eruptions might block out sunlight, just as an asteroid impact could do.

**39. A. Rock samples obtained from the bottom are older than rock samples obtained from the top.** Multiple rock samples were obtained at corresponding depths and each depth corresponded to a different time period. The layers of rock samples could give the geologist information about when the layers were formed. They would be less likely to yield information about the causes of flooding or the speed of winds now. Choice (C) is incorrect because a geologist could not study rock layers worldwide using only samples from the Grand Canyon.

**40. D. It would rotate counterclockwise and move westward, then northward, and finally eastward.** The passage states that hurricanes tend to rotate counterclockwise in the Northern Hemisphere, and that hurricanes initially move westward, then toward the poles (which would be northward in the Northern Hemisphere), and finally eastward after encountering the mid-latitude westerly winds.

**41. B. The force will be reduced.** If the distance between the two objects were increased, the denominator of the fraction shown in the equation would become bigger. Increasing the denominator of a fraction makes the value of the fraction smaller. So the force would be reduced.

**42. C. Frogs' bodies have a way to prevent their cells from freezing in cold temperatures.** All amphibians, frogs included, are ectothermic, or cold-blooded. Given the fact that frogs reproduce in the spring, if all the frogs of a given species died in the winter, the species would go extinct. So it must be that frogs have some physiological mechanism that prevents their cells from freezing when a frog's body temperature drops during the winter.

**43. C. insulin injections** Some cases of diabetes mellitus are caused by the inability of the pancreas to produce insulin. Individuals with this form of the disease can keep their blood sugar levels stable only by regular use of insulin.

**44. D. jaundice, a yellow discoloration of the skin due to a systemic buildup of bilirubin** The liver metabolizes bilirubin, so a buildup of this substance in the skin is strongly suggestive of liver disease.

**45. A. Shade-loving animal species, such as the red-backed salamander, were replaced by sun-loving species such as the northern black racer.** The immediate impact of cutting down an old growth forest is that species that favor a shaded forest habitat will be replaced by species favoring sunny, open spaces.

**46. B. Most people would not recognize the gametophyte generation of a fern.** This conclusion is supported by the fact that the gametophyte is a small, heart-shaped structure and that the sporophyte generation of the fern is the familiar plant, with roots, stems, and leaves.

**47. B. if the surface were irregular or rough** If a surface is rough, each light ray will hit the surface at a different angle. Therefore, light rays reflecting off of a rough surface travel in all different directions.

## Science Practice Test Evaluation Charts

| | Life Science Pages 536–555 | Earth and Space Science Pages 556–569 | Physical Science Pages 570–589 | Number Correct Out of Total |
|---|---|---|---|---|
| **Science Skills** | | | | |
| **Comprehend Scientific Presentations** Pages 522–523 | 2, 4, 17, 23 | 20, 40 | 1, 24, 26, 36 | ___ out of 10 |
| **Use the Scientific Method** Pages 524–525 | 8, 11, 22 | 27, 28, 39 | 16, 31 | ___ out of 8 |
| **Reason with Scientific Information** Pages 526–527 | 5, 15, 37, 42, 46 | 18, 25, 30, 32 | 7, 9, 14, 34, 47 | ___ out of 14 |
| **Express and Apply Scientific Information** Pages 528–529 | 6, 12, 43, 44 | 10, 29, 38, 45 | 13, 21, 35, 41 | ___ out of 12 |
| **Use Statistics and Probability** Pages 530–531 | 19 | 33 | 3 | ___ out of 3 |
| **SUBTOTAL** | ___ out of 17 | ___ out of 14 | ___ out of 16 | ___ **out of 47** |

If you do not have time to review the entire *Science* unit, you may want to review the sections that need the most work.

As of the time of this printing, scoring information for the TASC Test was not available. To find out how the number of questions you got right on the Practice Test would translate into a final score, please visit your Online Center. See page viii for information about registering for your Online Center.

# TASC Resources

## Essay Evaluation Guide for Argument/Opinion Essays*

Assign your essay a score of 0–4 based on which of the following descriptions best fits your essay.

**4 My response is well developed. It effectively develops and supports an argument.**

- My thesis statement is stated in the first paragraph. It is clear and confident in tone.
- I supported my thesis statement with several pieces of logical reasoning and relevant evidence.
- My essay is organized into paragraphs, each of which introduces and supports one idea.
- The words I chose clearly convey my meaning while maintaining a businesslike tone.
- I frequently used connective phrases to show the relationships between ideas (*for example, such as, because, however, therefore*, etc.).
- I acknowledged and argued against the opposing view.
- I used grammar and writing mechanics correctly. Any grammatical errors do not interfere with my meaning.
- I concluded my essay by summarizing my argument.

**3 My response is a complete essay. It develops and supports an argument.**

- My thesis statement is clearly stated.
- I used reasons and evidence to support my thesis statement, but some of them could have been developed more effectively.
- My essay is organized into paragraphs, most of which develop one idea.
- My word choice does not interfere with my meaning, and I maintained a businesslike tone.
- I often used connective phrases to show the relationships between ideas (*for example, such as, because, however, therefore*, etc.).
- I tried to argue against the opposing view, but I could have done so more effectively.
- My essay has only a few errors in grammar and writing mechanics that interfere with my meaning.
- I concluded my essay by summarizing my argument.

**2 My response develops an argument, but it is not complete, or it is oversimplified.**

- My thesis statement is unclear or is buried in the middle of my essay.
- I used evidence and reasons to support my thesis statement, but some of those ideas seem incomplete or not as effective as they could be.
- My essay has paragraphs, but some paragraphs have more than one topic sentence or no topic sentence at all.
- My word choice could have been improved to make my meaning clear.
- I mentioned the opposing side, but I didn't argue against it effectively.
- My essay has some errors in grammar and writing mechanics, some of which make my meaning unclear.
- I included a concluding sentence or paragraph, but it doesn't effectively summarize my argument.

**1 My response was an attempt to develop an argument, but it was not effective or clear.**

- My thesis statement is missing, weakly stated, or only implied.
- I didn't include enough reasons or evidence to support my claim.
- My essay is very short, is not divided into paragraphs.
- I neglected to mention or argue against the opposing side.
- My word choice frequently interferes with my meaning.
- My essay has several errors in grammar or writing mechanics, and these interfere with my meaning.
- I did not include a concluding statement or paragraph.

**0 My response is completely irrelevant, only a sentence or two, or makes no sense.**

*NOTE: This evaluation rubric was adapted by Kaplan for student use. The rubric is based on criteria provided by CTB/McGraw-Hill. CTB/McGraw-Hill may have made changes to the TASC essay evaluation rubric since the time of this printing. Visit www.tasctest.com for more information.

## Essay Evaluation Guide for Informative/Explanatory Essays*

Assign your essay a score of 0–4 based on which of the following descriptions best fits your essay.

**4 My response thoroughly and clearly discusses or explains the topic and presents information relevant to that topic.**

- I clearly introduce the topic of my essay in the first couple of sentences.
- I explain the topic using several relevant and specific facts, details, and examples.
- My essay is organized into paragraphs, each of which develops one idea.
- The words I chose clearly convey my meaning while maintaining a businesslike tone.
- I frequently used connective phrases to show the relationships between ideas (*for example, such as, because, however, therefore,* etc.).
- I used grammar and writing mechanics correctly. Any grammatical errors do not interfere with my meaning.
- I concluded my essay by summarizing my explanation of the topic.

**3 My response discusses or explains the topic and gives relevant information but could have been more developed.**

- The topic of my essay is introduced in the first paragraph.
- I used relevant facts, details, and examples to explain my topic, but some of them could have been developed more effectively.
- My essay is organized into paragraphs, most of which develop one idea.
- My word choice does not interfere with my meaning, and I maintained a businesslike tone.
- I often used connective phrases to show the relationships between ideas (*for example, such as, because, however, therefore,* etc.).
- My essay has only a few errors in grammar and writing mechanics that interfere with my meaning.
- I concluded my essay by summarizing my explanation of the topic.

**2 My response discusses the topic, but it is not complete, or it is oversimplified.**

- My introduction of my topic is unclear or not included in the first paragraph.
- I used facts, details, and examples to explain my topic, but some of them are irrelevant or incomplete.
- My essay has paragraphs, but some paragraphs have more than one topic sentence or no topic sentence at all.
- My word choice could have been improved to make my meaning clear.
- My essay has some errors in grammar and writing mechanics, some of which make my meaning unclear.
- I included a concluding sentence or paragraph, but it doesn't effectively summarize my explanation of the topic.

**1 My response was an attempt to discuss the topic, but it was not effective or clear.**

- My introduction of my topic is missing, weakly stated, or only implied.
- I included very little information to develop my topic.
- My essay is very short, is not divided into paragraphs.
- My word choice frequently interferes with my meaning.
- My essay has several errors in grammar or writing mechanics, and these interfere with my meaning.
- I did not include a concluding statement or paragraph.

**0 My response is completely irrelevant, only a sentence or two, or makes no sense.**

*NOTE: This evaluation rubric was adapted by Kaplan for student use. The rubric is based on criteria provided by CTB/McGraw-Hill. CTB/McGraw-Hill may have made changes to the TASC essay evaluation rubric since the time of this printing. Visit www.tasctest.com for more information.

## Math Memory Aids

**You may tear this sheet out of your book if you like to serve as a portable study resource.**

| Concept | Memory Aid |
|---|---|
| **Order of operations:**<br>Parentheses, Exponents, Multiplication, Division, Addition, Subtraction, and work Left to Right | *Please excuse my dear Aunt Sally, Love Ron.* |
| **Circumference and area of a circle:**<br>$C = \pi d$<br>$A = \pi r^2$ | *Circumference: Cherry pie's delicious.*<br>*Area: Apple pies are, too.* |
| **Distance formula:**<br>$d = rt$ | Remember this formula by creating a "dirt graph" as follows. ("Dirt" is a word play on "d = rt.")<br>$d$<br>÷ ÷<br>$r \times t$<br>Cover the letter of the item you want to solve for, and what remains visible is the formula you need! |

| Concept | Memory Aid |
| --- | --- |
| **Percent, part, and whole:**<br>base x rate = part | **Use a similar box to remember how to figure the relationship between percent, part, and whole.**<br>$P$<br>$\div \quad \div$<br>$B \times R$<br>**Cover the letter of the item you want to solve for, and what remains visible is the formula you need.** |
| **Multiplying binomials:**<br>$(x + a)(x + b)$<br>$= x^2 + bx + ax + ab$ | FOIL: First, Inner, Outer, Last |

# MATHEMATICS REFERENCE SHEET

On the next two pages, you will find mathematical formulas that will be provided to you on Test Day. As you may remember reading in the Mathematics unit, there are topics on this sheet that will likely not be tested on the 2014 TASC. One such topic is trigonometry (trigonometric formulas appear in the bottom-right section of the first page of the formula sheet). At the time of this printing, limited information was available regarding which other topics from the formula sheet will not be tested in 2014. Kaplan's book reflects our best estimates regarding material you will be required to know if you are testing in 2014. For updates, visit www.tasctest.com

**Volume**

Cylinder: $V = \pi r^2 h$

Pyramid: $V = \frac{1}{3}Bh$

Cone: $V = \frac{1}{3}\pi r^2 h$

Sphere: $V = \frac{4}{3}\pi r^3$

**Coordinate Geometry**

Midpoint formula:

$$\left(\frac{x_1 + x_2}{2}, \frac{y_1 + y_2}{2}\right)$$

Distance formula:

$$d = \sqrt{(x_2 - x_1)^2 + (y_2 - y_1)^2}$$

Slope: $m = \frac{y_2 - y_1}{x_2 - x_1}, x_2 \neq x_1$

**Special Factoring**

$a^2 - b^2 = (a - b)(a + b)$

$a^2 + 2ab + b^2 = (a + b)^2$

$a^2 - 2ab + b^2 = (a - b)^2$

$a^3 + b^3 = (a + b)(a^2 - ab + b^2)$

$a^3 - b^3 = (a - b)(a^2 + ab + b^2)$

**Quadratic Formula**

For $ax^2 + bx + c = 0$

$$x = \frac{-b \pm \sqrt{b^2 - 4ac}}{2a}$$

**Interest**

Simple interest Formula:
$I = prt$

Interest Formula (compounded *n* times per year):

$$A = p\left(1 + \frac{r}{n}\right)^{nt}$$

$A$ = Amount after $t$ years.

$p$ = principal

$r$ = annual interest rate

$t$ = time in years

$I$ = Interest

**Trigonometric Identities**

Pythagorean Theorem: $a^2 + b^2 = c^2$

$$\sin\theta = \frac{opp}{hyp}$$

$$\cos\theta = \frac{adj}{hyp}$$

$$\tan\theta = \frac{opp}{adj}$$

$$\sin^2\theta + \cos^2\theta = 1$$

$$Density = \frac{Mass}{Volume}$$

**Central Angle**

O A

B

$m\angle AOB = m\overset{\frown}{AB}$

**Inscribed Angle**

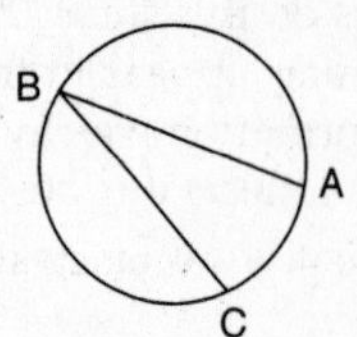


$m\angle ABC = \frac{1}{2} m\overset{\frown}{AC}$

**Intersecting Chords Theorem**

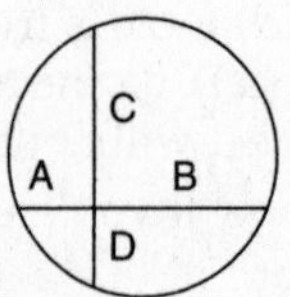


$A \cdot B = C \cdot D$

**Probability**

Permutations: $_{n}P_{r} = \frac{n!}{(n-r)!}$

Combinations: $_{n}C_{r} = \frac{n!}{(n-r)!r!}$

Multiplication rule (independent events): $P(A \text{ and } B) = P(A) \cdot P(B)$

Multiplication rule (general): $P(A \text{ and } B) = P(A) \cdot P(B|A)$

Addition rule: $P(A \text{ or } B) = P(A) + P(B) - P(A \text{ and } B)$

Conditional Probability: $P(B|A) = \frac{p(A \text{ and } B)}{p(A)}$

Arithmetic Sequence: $a_n = a_1 + (n-1)d$ where $a_n$ is the $n$th term, $a_1$ is the first term, and $d$ is the common difference.

Geometric Sequence: $a_n = a_1 r^{(n-1)}$ where $a_n$ is the $n$th term, $a_1$ is the first term, and $r$ is the common ratio.

# INDEX

## D

## N



## O



## P

## Q



## R

## S



## T

**U**



**V**



**W**



**X**



**Y**